FROM SLAVERY TO FREEDOM

A History of African Americans

NINTH EDITION

John Hope Franklin
(1915–2009)

Evelyn Brooks Higginbotham
Harvard University

Mc Graw Hill

Connect
Learn
Succeed™

The McGraw-Hill Companies

 Connect
Learn
Succeed™

FROM SLAVERY TO FREEDOM:
A History of African Americans, Ninth Edition

Published by McGraw-Hill, an imprint of The McGraw-Hill Companies, Inc., 1221 Avenue of the Americas, New York, NY 10020. Copyright © 2011 by The McGraw-Hill Companies, Inc. All rights reserved. No part of this publication may be reproduced or distributed in any form or by any means, or stored in a database or retrieval system, without the prior written consent of The McGraw-Hill Companies, Inc., including, but not limited to, in any network or other electronic storage or transmission, or broadcast for distance learning.

2 3 4 5 6 7 8 9 0 DOW/DOW 0

ISBN: 978-0-07-296378-6
MHID: 0-07-296378-6

Vice President, Editorial: *Michael J. Ryan*
Editorial Director: *William Glass*
Publisher: *Christopher Freitag*
Sponsoring Editor: *Matthew Busbridge*
Director of Development: *Nancy Crochiere*
Development Editors: *Jeannine Ciliotta, James Miller*
Editorial Coordinator: *Sarah Remington*
Editorial Intern: *Emily DiPietro*
Marketing Manager: *Pamela Cooper*
Senior Production Editor: *Mel Valentín*
Manuscript Editor: *Stacey Sawyer*
Interior Design and Cover: *BrainWorx Studio, Inc. (Jesi Lazar)*
Lead Photo Research Coordinator: *Nora Agbayani*
Photo Researcher: *Deborah Anderson*
Art Editor: *Sonia Brown*
Illustrator: *Patricia Isaacs/Parrot Graphics*
Media Project Manager: *Bethuel Jabez*
Senior Production Supervisor: *Tandra Jorgensen*
Composition: *10.5/13 Baskerville Regular by Laserwords*
Printing: *45# Pub Matte Plus, R. R. Donnelley & Sons*

Front Cover Photos: (slave family) A slave family in a Georgia cotton field, c.1860 (b/w photo) by American Photographer (19th century) Private Collection/Peter Newark American Pictures/The Bridgeman Art Library; (Barack Obama) Getty Images.

Back Cover Photo: Courtesy The Harvard Crimson.

Credits: The credits section for this book begins on page 677 and is considered an extension of the copyright page.

Library of Congress Cataloging-in-Publication Data

Franklin, John Hope, 1915–2009
Evelyn Brooks Higginbotham, 1945–
From Slavery to Freedom: a history of African Americans/John Hope Franklin,
Evelyn Brooks Higginbotham—9th ed.
Includes bibliographical refreces and index.
ISBN 0-07-229581-3
    1. Afro-American—History. 2. Slavery—United States—History.

A. 1943- . II. Title.99-047892
E. 185. F8266 2000973'.0496073—dc21

The Internet addresses listed in the text were accurate at the time of publication. The inclusion of a Web site does not indicate an endorsement by the authors or McGraw-Hill, and McGraw-Hill does not guarantee the accuracy of the information presented at these sites.

www.mhhe.com

Dedicated to the memory of John Hope Franklin

About the Authors

John Hope Franklin

John Hope Franklin was the James B. Duke Professor Emeritus of History, and for seven years was Professor of Legal History at Duke University Law School. A native of Oklahoma and a graduate of Fisk University (1935), he received the A.M. and Ph.D. degrees in history from Harvard University (1936 and 1941). He taught at a number of institutions, including Fisk, St. Augustine's College, and Howard University. In 1956 he went to Brooklyn College as Chair of the Department of History; and in 1964, he joined the faculty of the University of Chicago, serving as Chair of the Department of History from 1967 to 1970. At Chicago, he was the John Matthews Manly Distinguished Service Professor from 1969 to 1982, when he became Professor Emeritus.

Among his many published works are *The Free Negro in North Carolina* (1943), *Reconstruction after the Civil War* (1961), *A Southern Odyssey* (1971), and perhaps his best-known book, *From Slavery to Freedom: A History of African Americans*, now in its ninth edition. In 1990 a collection of essays covering a teaching and writing career of fifty years was published as *Race and History: Selected Essays, 1938–1988*. In 2005, he published his autobiography, *Mirror to America*.

During his long career, Professor Franklin was active in numerous professional and educational organizations. For many years he served on the editorial board of the *Journal of Negro History*. He also served as president of the following organizations: The Southern Historical Association, the United Chapters of Phi Beta Kappa, the Organization of American Historians, and the American Historical Association.

Dr. Franklin served on many national commissions and delegations, including the National Council on the Humanities, the President's Advisory Commission on Ambassadorial Appointments, and the United States delegation to the 21st General Conference of UNESCO. He was appointed by President Clinton to chair the President's Advisory Board for the One America initiative in June 1997.

He was the recipient of many honors. In 1978 *Who's Who in America* selected him as one of eight Americans who has made significant contributions to society. In 1995 he received the first W.E.B. DuBois Award from the Fisk University Alumni Association, the Organization of American Historians' Award for Outstanding Achievement, the NAACP's Spingarn medal, and the Presidential Medal of Freedom. In addition to his many awards, Dr. Franklin received honorary degrees from more than one hundred colleges and universities.

❚ Evelyn Brooks Higginbotham

Evelyn Brooks Higginbotham is the Victor S. Thomas Professor of History and of African and African American Studies at Harvard University. She is currently chair of the Department of African and African American Studies and has held this position since 2006. Professor Higginbotham earned a Ph.D. from the University of Rochester in American History, an M.A. from Howard University, and her B.A. from the University of Wisconsin-Milwaukee. Before coming to Harvard, she taught on the full-time faculties of Dartmouth, the University of Maryland, and the University of Pennsylvania. In addition, she was a Visiting Professor at Princeton University and New York University.

Professor Higginbotham's writings span diverse fields—African American religious history, women's history, civil rights, constructions of racial and gender identity, electoral politics, and the intersection of theory and history. She is the author of *Righteous Discontent: The Women's Movement in the Black Baptist Church, 1880–1920* (1993), which won numerous book prizes and was also included among *The New York Times* Book Review's Notable Books of the Year in 1993 and 1994. Professor Higginbotham is the editor-in-chief of *The Harvard Guide to African American History* (2001), and co-editor with Henry Louis Gates, Jr., of the *African American National Biography* (2008)—a multivolume-reference work that presents African American history through the lives of people.

Dr. Higginbotham has received numerous awards. The University of Rochester awarded her the Distinguished Rochester Scholar in 1994. In April 2003 she was chosen by Harvard University to be a Walter Channing Cabot Fellow in recognition of her achievements and scholarly eminence in the field of history. The Association for the Study of African American Life and History awarded her the Carter G. Woodson Scholars Medallion in October 2008, and the Urban League awarded her the Legend Award in August 2008.

Brief Table of Contents

Chapter 1   **Ancestral Africa** (circa 500 B.C.E to 1600)

Chapter 2   **Africans in the Atlantic World** (1492–1800)

Chapter 3   **Establishing North American Slavery** (1520s to 1720s)

Chapter 4   **Eighteenth-Century Slave Societies** (1700–1780s)

Chapter 5   **Give Me Liberty** (1763–1787)

Chapter 6   **Building Communities in the Early Republic** (1790–1830)

Chapter 7   **Southern Slavery** (1790–1860)

Chapter 8   **Antebellum Free Blacks** (1830–1860)

Chapter 9   **Abolitionism in Black and White** (1820–1860)

Chapter 10   **Civil War** (1861–1865)

Chapter 11   **Promises and Pitfalls of Reconstruction** (1863–1877)

Chapter 12   **The Color Line** (1877–1917)

Chapter 13   **The Era of Self-Help** (1880–1916)

Chapter 14   **In Pursuit of Democracy** (1914–1919)

Chapter 15   **Voices of Protest** (1910–1928)

Chapter 16   **The Arts at Home and Abroad** (1920s to early 1930s)

Chapter 17   **The New Deal Era** (1929–1941)

Chapter 18   **Double V for Victory** (1941–1945)

Chapter 19   **American Dilemmas** (1940–1955)

Chapter 20   **We Shall Overcome** (1947–1967)

Chapter 21   **Black Power** (1955–1980)

Chapter 22   **Progress and Poverty** (1980–2000)

Chapter 23   **Perspectives on the Present** (since 2000)

Contents

About the Authors iv
Preface xix

1 | Ancestral Africa (circa 500 BCE to1600) ... 1

An Ancient Land and People 2
  The Bantu Migration 4
  Iron Technology 4
  Nok Pottery and Sculpture 4
  Copper Technology 5

Early Commercial Networks 6
  West African Trade Routes 6
  Interregional Trade 7
  Internal Slave Trade 8

African Slavery 9
  Slavery in European Communities 9
  Slaves in Africa 10
  Slaves and Status 11
  Slaves in the Economy 11

The Great Empires 11
  Ghana's Trading Empire 12
  Mali's Rise 12
  Mansa Musa's Pilgrimage 13
  The Rise of Songhay 14
  Askia Muhammad's Reforms 15
  Dichotomy of Sovereignty 16

Other States 17
  The Mossi States 17
  The Hausa States 17
  The Kingdom of Benin 17
  The Christian Kongo 18
  Ndongo-Matamba 19
  Great Zimbabwe 20
  The Swahili Coast 20

2 | Africans in the Atlantic World (1492–1800) ... 22

Finding New Lands and Labor 23
  Africans and the Conquistadors 23
  Demand for Slave Labor 25
  From Indenture to Slavery 25

Trading in Slaves 27
  Acquiring Slaves 28

Africans in the Slave Trade 29
Slave Trade Challenges 30
The Trauma of Capture 32
African Resistance 33

The Middle Passage 33
  A Profitable Trade 35

Slavery in the Caribbean 35
  The Spanish Monopoly 35
  Loss of Spanish Control 36
  Living Conditions 37
  Slave Codes 37
  Punishment 38
  Slave Revolts 38
  Seasoned Slaves 40

Slavery in Mainland Latin America 40
  Mexico 41
  Central America 41
  South America 41
  The Viceroyalty of Peru 42
  Uruguay and Argentina 42
  Brazil 42
  Uprisings and Revolts 44

Slave Societies in the Americas 44
  The Catholic Church 45
  Intermarriage 45

3 | Establishing North American Slavery (1520s to 1720s) ... 47

Imperial Claims to North America 48
  Early Settlements 49
  Forms of North American Slavery 50

Before Permanent Bondage 51
  Early Virginia 51
  New Netherland 52
  Massachusetts Bay 53

The Legalization of Slavery 54
  Virginia Slave Codes 55
  New York Slave Codes 57
  New England's Laws 57
  The Carolinas 59
  Slave Courts 60
  Slave Laws in French Louisiana 60
  The Code Noir 61
  Spanish Louisiana 62

4 | **Eighteenth-Century Slave Societies** (1700–1780s) 64

New England 66
Slave Populations 66
Slave Occupations 66
Negro Election Day 67
Cotton Mather and Inoculation 67

The Mid-Atlantic Colonies 68
New York Colony 68
Expansion of Slavery 69
Pennsylvania Slavery 70

The Chesapeake Region 70
African Outsiders 71
Population Growth 71

The Lower South, Eastern Seaboard 72
The Slave Population 73
The Chesapeake and the Lowcountry 74
Rural and Urban Slave Life 75
People of Mixed Race 75
African Traditions 76
The Stono Rebellion 77
Menendez and Mose 78
The War of Jenkins' Ear 78
The End of Mose 80

The Lower Mississippi Valley 80
French Louisiana 80
Maroon Societies 82

5 | **Give Me Liberty** (1763–1787) 84

The Paradox of Slavery and Freedom 85
Freedom in a Slave Society 85
Birth of the Antislavery Movement 87
Crispus Attucks 87
Phillis Wheatley 88

Fighting for American Independence 89
Blacks against the British 90
The British Appeal 91
Washington's Response 92
The Revolution and Slavery 92
General Clinton's Proclamation 92
Individual State Policies 93
Black Military Distinction 93
Black Loyalists 95

The Movement to Free the Slaves 96
Antislavery Advocates 96
Antislavery Societies 98
Free North, Slave South 98

The Conservative Reaction 99
Shays's Rebellion 100
The Three-Fifths Compromise 100
The Slave Trade 101

Fugitive Slaves 101
The Language of the Constitution 101

6 | **Building Communities in the Early Republic** (1790–1830) 103

African Americans in Demographic Perspective 104
The Mid-Atlantic States and New England 105
Development of Black Communities 106
Black Migration to Boston 107
Blacks in Philadelphia 107
New York City's Black Community 108

Building Community Institutions 108
Independent Black Churches 109
The African Methodist Episcopal Church 110
Separate Black Institutions 110
White Philanthropy 111
Black and White Leadership Conflicts 111

Blacks and American Party Politics 112
Disfranchisement of Blacks 112
The Haitian Revolution 113

The Louisiana Purchase 114
Federalists and Free Blacks 114

Black Writing and Art in the New Nation 115
Pamphlet Literature 116
Appeals to Readers 117
The Jones and Allen Pamphlet 118
The Spiritual Autobiography 118
Banneker's Almanacs 119
The Painter Joshua Johnston 120

The War of 1812 121
Black Military Service 121
Gallant Service 122

Black Colonization 124
Colonization Efforts 125
Black Opposition 126

The Contagion of Liberty 126
Gabriel's Rebellion in Virginia 126
Plots and Rumors 127

7 | **Southern Slavery** (1790–1860) 129

The Domestic Slave Trade 130
King Cotton 131
The Interstate Slave Trade 132
A Capitalist Enterprise 134
Separation of Families by Sale 134
Market Prices 134

Persistence of the African Trade 136
Extent of the Illegal Trade 137
The Movement to Reopen the African Trade 137

The Slave Codes ... 137
  Enforcement ... 139
  The Patrol System ... 139
On the Plantation ... 140
  Field Hands ... 140
  Gender Division of Labor ... 142
  Overseers and Brutality ... 143
  The Slave Diet ... 143
Urban and Nonagricultural Slavery ... 144
  Black Artisans and Inventors ... 144
  Slave Hiring ... 145
Social and Cultural Life ... 147
  Religious Activity ... 148
  The Slave Church ... 148
  Slave Families ... 149
  Interracial Relationships ... 149
  Mulatto Slaves ... 150
Resistance ... 151
  Slave Market Gambits ... 151
  Sabotage and Suicide ... 153
  Running Away ... 153
  Violent Resistance ... 155
  Slave Revolts ... 155
  Denmark Vesey ... 155
  Nat Turner ... 157

8 | Antebellum Free Blacks (1830–1860) ... 159

Freedom's Boundaries ... 160
  Black Laws ... 161
  Migration West ... 161
  Disfranchisement ... 162
  Demographics ... 163
In a Culture of Racism ... 163
  Minstrel Shows ... 163
  Ethnology ... 164
  Bigotry and Prejudice ... 164
  Mob Violence ... 165
  South vs. North ... 166
Economic and Social Life ... 168
  Trades and Professions ... 168
  Property Ownership ... 169
  Urban Life in the North ... 169
  Boston ... 170
  New York ... 170
  Philadelphia ... 171
  Mutual Aid Organizations ... 172
  Cultural Contributions ... 172
Education ... 173
  Opportunities in the North ... 173
  Opportunities in the South ... 174

Higher Education ... 175
Black Convention Movement ... 176
  The Rochester Convention ... 176
  Fostering Group Consciousness ... 176
  Public Image and Behavior ... 176
  Biblical Imagery ... 177
Black Women ... 177
  Women Take Public Action ... 178
  Maria Stewart ... 178
  Sojourner Truth ... 179
The Debate on Emigration ... 179
  Efforts at Mass Colonization ... 180
  Opposition to the ACS ... 180
  The National Emigration Convention ... 182

9 | Abolitionism in Black and White (1820–1860) ... 184

Black Abolitionists ... 186
  Black Antislavery Societies ... 186
  Women Abolitionists ... 187
  Black Agents ... 188
  Newspapers ... 189
Antislavery Agendas ... 190
  The Abolitionist Argument ... 191
  The Crusade ... 191
  The American Anti-Slavery Society ... 192
  Black vs. White Abolitionists ... 193
  Black-White Cooperation ... 193
Proslavery Backlash ... 194
  The Proslavery Argument ... 194
  Defending the Institution ... 195
  Persecution and Violence ... 196
  Changing Attitudes ... 197
The Black Response ... 197
  Black Counterarguments ... 198
  Black Narratives ... 198
  Black Literature ... 198
The Underground Railroad ... 199
  Origins ... 199
  Railroad Operations ... 200
  Resources ... 201
  Black Conductors ... 202
  Harriet Tubman ... 202
  Jermain Loguen ... 203
The Path to Civil War ... 203
  The Compromise of 1850 ... 204
  The Christiana Riot ... 204
  The Sectional Truce Unravels ... 205
  The Dred Scott Decision ... 205
  The Appeal of Force ... 206
  John Brown's Raid ... 207

10 | **Civil War** (1861–1865)   208

Inconsistent Federal Policies   209
 Opposition to Lincoln's Policies   210
 The Confiscation Acts   211
 Lincoln's Plan   212
 Preliminary Proclamation   212
 The Emancipation Proclamation   213
 The Thirteenth Amendment   214

Aiding the Contrabands   215
 General Saxton's Plan   215
 Challenges to Effective Relief   215
 Private Relief   216
 Education   216

Black Troops   218
 Challenges to Black Recruitment   218
 A Change in Policy   219
 The First Black Soldiers   219
 The Success of Black Enlistment   220
 Black Officers   222
 Blacks as Spies and Scouts   222
 Women's Service   222
 Black Soldiers' Service   223
 Treatment of Black Prisoners   226
 Unequal Treatment   227

Slave Disruption   228
 Stronger Patrol Laws   228
 "Running the Negroes"   229
 Insubordination   229
 Fear of Uprisings   230

The Confederate Dilemma   231
 Impressment   231
 Enlisting and Arming Blacks   232

Victory   233

11 | **Promises and Pitfalls of Reconstruction** (1863–1877)   235

Presidential Reconstruction   236
 Lincoln's Ten Percent Plan   237
 Andrew Johnson's Policies   237
 Black Codes   238
 Congress Takes Charge   238
 The Black Conventions   240
 Black Mobilization   242

Radical Reconstruction   242
 New National Officials   243
 Blacks as State Legislators   245
 The Union League   246
 Black Women and the Black Community   247

The Social Consequences of the War   247
 The Freedmen's Bureau   248

 The Pivotal Role of Education   250
 Educators, Black and White   250
 Black Churches   251

Economic Adjustment   251
 The Desire for Land   252
 Women in the Labor Market   253
 Changing Conditions of Farm Labor   254
 Sharecropping   255
 The Freedmen's Bank   255

Reconstruction's End   256
 The Reign of Violence   256
 Corruption in Republican Governments   258
 Supreme Court Decisions   258
 The Campaign of 1876   259

12 | **The Color Line** (1877–1917)   260

The Path to Disfranchisement   261
 Preventing Black Voting Legally   261
 Black Reappearance in Politics   263
 The Radical Agrarian Movement   264
 Successful Coalitions   265
 Complete Disfranchisement   265
 The Black Response   267
 Effective Disfranchisement   268
 Back to Slavery   268

Legalizing Segregation   270
 Plessy v. Ferguson   270
 White Man's Country   271

Confronting the Urban
  Color Line   273
 Employment and Unions   273
 Housing   274
 Transportation   274

America's Empire of Color   275
 The United States Expands   275
 The Caribbean   276
 The Spanish American War   277
 Garrison Duty and Pacific Service   280
 The United States as a Great Power   280
 Puerto Rico   281
 The Virgin Islands   282
 Haiti   282
 Liberia   282

The Pattern of Violence   282
 Lynch Law   283
 Race Riots   283
 The Atlanta Riot   284
 Brownsville, Texas   285
 Violence in the North   285
 The Springfield Riot   286

13 | The Era of Self-Help (1880–1916)   287

Self-Help and Philanthropy   288
Supporting Education   289
Black Self-Determination   290
White Philanthropy   291
Educational Inequality in the South   293
Higher Education   293
The Talented Tenth   295

Divergent Paths to Racial Equality   295
Booker T. Washington   295
Opposition: T. Thomas Fortune   298
Ida B. Wells   299
William Monroe Trotter   300
W. E. B. Du Bois   300
Washington's Revenge   302
The Niagara Movement   303
Bookerites and Niagarites   304
Two Classes of Negroes   306

Economic and Social Striving   306
The Black Exodus   307
The New South   308
Innovation and Enterprise   308
Combating Old South Images   311
Black Women Entrepreneurs   312
Establishment of Black Banks   312
The Role of the Churches   313
The Social Gospel and Black Separatism   315
Mutual Benefit Societies   316

The Woman's Era   317
Gender-Specific Discrimination   317
The NACW   319
Urban Settlement Houses   320

Intellectual and Cultural Endeavors   322
Pan-Negroism   322
Scholarly and Literary Works   323
Sports Heroes   324

14 | In Pursuit of Democracy (1914–1919)   327

Answering the Call to Fight   329
The Selective Service Act   329
The NAACP   330
Emmett J. Scott   332

Jim Crow Military Camps   332
Locating Training Camps   332
Rampant Discrimination   333
African Americans Fight Back   333

Service Overseas   334
The 369th U.S. Infantry   335
Other African American Combat Units   337
German Propaganda   339

Slander Campaigns   339
Cultural Experiences   340
Coming Home   342
Wilson's Contradictory Positions   344

On the Home Front   344
African Americans Support the War   345
Curtailing Civil Liberties   345
Silencing Dissent   345
Black Exodus   347
New Opportunities   347
The National Urban League   348
Employment in Industry   349
Riots and Lynchings   349

15 | Voices of Protest (1910–1928)   351

Progressive Voices   352
The Work of the NAACP   353
The 1912 Election   354
Wilson Disappoints   354
African Americans Protest Racial Policies   357
The Amenia Conference   357

Violent Times   357
The Resurgent Ku Klux Klan   357
Race Riots   358
The Chicago Riot of 1919   359
More Riots   359
"Outside Agitation"   362

Civil Rights Vanguard   362
The Persistence of Lynching   363
NAACP Legal Efforts   364

Protesting with Their Feet   364
The Leaderless Migration   365
Migration from the Caribbean   366
Afro-Caribbeans in New York   366

New Negroes   368
Race and Class Politics: Civil Rights, Black Nationalism   368
Du Bois and "Close Ranks"   369
Marcus Garvey   370
Garvey's Decline   372
Father Divine   374

New Women   374
Black Feminism   375
Black Women Voters   377
Growing Political Involvement   377

16 | The Arts at Home and Abroad (1920s to early 1930s)   380

Recorded Music and Radio   381
Classic Blues   382
Black Swan Records   383
National and Live Broadcast Radio   385

Jazz Roots and Routes 387
The Evolution of Jazz: New Orleans to Chicago 388
Jazz in New York: Ragtime to Stride 389
The James Reese Europe Orchestra 389
Louis Armstrong Transforms Big Band Jazz 391
Duke Ellington and the Big Band Era 393
Motion Pictures 393
Black Talent in White Studios 395
Black Theater 395
Postwar Theater 396
Black Musicals 396
The Charleston 396
The Harlem Renaissance 398
The Tenderloin 398
The Marshall Hotel 398
Black Periodicals 399
Before the Civic Club 400
Countee Cullen 401
Langston Hughes 402
Harlem Renaissance Women 403
French Connections 405
Visual Artists 408
Photographers and Illustrators 408
Painters 409
Clashing Artistic Values 412
Art as Propaganda 412
Race Literature 413
Art and Social Change 414

17 | **The New Deal Era** (1929–1941) 417
In the Throes of Economic Depression 418
The Agricultural Crisis and Black Migration 419
African American Efforts at Relief 419
Political Resurgence 421
The Election of Oscar DePriest 422
The Shift to the Democrats 422
A Growing Sense of Political Efficacy 423
Success at the State and Local Levels 424
The Black Cabinet 425
African Americans in the National Government 426
Expanding Job Opportunities in the Federal Government 428
New Deal Programs 429
The Agricultural Programs 429
The Tuskegee Study 432
Organized Labor 433
The CIO 433
Organizing Activity in Agriculture 435
On the Left 436
The Appeal of Communism 436

Landmark Cases: Scottsboro and Herndon 437
The National Negro Congress and the Popular Front 437
The Southern Conference for Human Welfare 440
A Harvest of Artistic Expression 440
Augusta Savage 441
William Johnson 441
Blacks in Films 443
Paul Robeson and Lena Horne 443
Black Musicians and Composers 444
The Swing Era 445
Women Vocalists 447
Marian Anderson at the Lincoln Memorial 448

18 | **Double V for Victory** (1941–1945) 449
Reframing the Arsenal of Democracy 451
Blacks in the Armed Forces 451
The March on Washington 1941 454
Executive Order 8802 455
Hastie and Discrimination in the Armed Forces 456
In Military Service 456
Black Women in the Military 458
Tuskegee: Black Airmen 458
The Navy, the Marines, and Officer Training 460
Overseas Service—Europe 461
Service in the Pacific 462
Service in the Navy 463
Service in the Merchant Marine 463
Racism at Home 463
Racial Clashes 465
Recognition for Service 465
Keeping the Home Fires Burning 466
The Work of the FEPC 466
Support for the War Effort 468
Black-White Conflict at Home 469
The Problem of Low Morale 469

19 | **American Dilemmas** (1940–1955) 473
Intellectual Crosscurrents 474
An American Dilemma 475
The Emphasis on Assimilation and Culture 477
African Survivals 478
The Popularization of Black History 479
Abandoning the Culturalist Perspective 480
Literary and Dramatic Arts 481
Poets 482
Prose Writers 482
Richard Wright and Native Son 483
Ralph Ellison and Invisible Man 483
Frank Yerby 484

Writers in the Postwar Years   484
Theater   485

Black Internationalism   485
Ethiopia and Spain   486
The Rising Wind   487
The United Nations Charter   488
UNESCO's Work   489
The Trusteeship Council   490
The South Africa Resolution   490
The June 1946 Petition   490
The Appeal   491
Black Internationalism   491

Labor Civil Rights   492
Blacks in the CIO   492
The Early Civil Rights Struggle   493
R. J. Reynolds in Winston-Salem   494
Unionization in Detroit   495
Labor Civil Rights Activism in New York   497
Jackie Robinson   497
1947: Pivotal Year   497
The Failure of Operation Dixie   499
The Demise of Left-Labor Civil Rights   499

Truman and Civil Rights   500
To Secure These Rights   500
Freedom to Serve   501
The 1948 Election   501
The Howard University Address   502

Fighting for Civil Rights in the Courts   502
Charles Hamilton Houston   503
Battling Jim Crow in Higher Education   503
The Battle against Separate but Equal   506
The Brown Decision   507
Southern White Opposition   508

20 | We Shall Overcome (1947–1967)   510

Introducing Nonviolent Direct Action   511
CORE Activism   512
The Journey of Reconciliation   512

Anatomy of the Montgomery Movement   513
The Role of the Boycott   513
The Arrest of Rosa Parks   515
The Leadership of Martin Luther King, Jr.   516
Victory   518

Movement Milestones   518
New Leaders: James M. Lawson   518
The Lunch Counter Sit-In   519
The Albany Movement   521
Birmingham, 1963   522
Letter from Birmingham Jail   523
Victory   523
Freedom Summer 1964   524

Tragedy and Triumph   526
The Importance of Press Coverage   527

Movement Women   528
School Desegregation and Constance Baker Motley   529
Voting Rights Campaigns   530
Ella Baker and Fannie Lou Hamer   530
Septima Clark   531
Strength through Religious Faith   532

The Northern Side of the Movement   533
Electoral Power   533
Battling Discrimination   534
The Problem of Housing   535
In Cities: Substandard Housing and Poor Education   536

The Landmarks and Limitations of Government   536
Civil Rights in the 1950s   536
Court Victories   537
The Executive Branch   538
Congress Drags Its Feet   539
The Role of Civil Rights Advocates   539
The Civil Rights Acts of 1957 and 1960   541
The Kennedy Administration   541
The Freedom Rides, May 1961   542
Freedom to the Free, 1963   543
The Civil Rights Act of 1964   543
The Voting Rights Act of 1965   545
Political Revolution in the South   547

21 | Black Power (1955–1980)   549

Black Power's Antecedents   550
The Heritage of Appeals to Self-Reliance   550
Malcolm X   551
Activism in the South   552
Paramilitary Defense Units   553
Armed Revolution   553
Internationalizing the Struggle   554
Bandung 1955   554
Malcolm and the Dark World   555
The Assassination of Malcolm X   557

Proclaiming Black Power   557
Stokely Carmichael Makes History   557
The Black Panther Party   559
Revolutionary Nationalism versus Cultural Nationalism   562
Muhammad Ali   562

A Dissident Youth Culture   563
Campus Activism   564
The Afro   565

Black Artistic Power   566
Political Activists   566
The Cultural Side of Black Power   567
The Black Arts Movement   567
Blaxploitation Movies   568

Graphic Arts 569
Women Writers 571

Black Feminism 572
Reaction to the Moynihan Report 573
Women's Organizations 573

Social and Political Realities 577
Riots in the Cities: Watts 578
Newark and Detroit 578
The New Black Political Power 579

22 | **Progress and Poverty** (1980–2000) 583

Divergent Realities 584
Economic Differences 584
Rise of the Black Underclass 585
The Million Man March 587
New Opportunities 588
The Black Electorate 589
Jesse Jackson and the Rainbow Coalition 589
The Reagan-Bush Years 590
The 1992 Election: The Democrats Return to Office 592

In Conservative Times 593
Reagan's Efforts to Dismantle Civil Rights 593
George H. W. Bush and the Supreme Court 594
The Battle over the Clarence Thomas Nomination 595
Judicial Conservatism 596
Educational Disparities 596
Opposition to Affirmative Action 597
Racial Unrest 597
Racial Brutality: Abner Louima,
Amadou Diallo, James Byrd 598

Artistic Currents 598
Women Writers 599
Playwrights, Comedians, Filmmakers, Actors 599
Blacks on Television 600
Artists 601
Hip Hop Rising 602
Hip Hop Is Born 603
Hip Hop and the Culture Wars 603

Global Concerns 605
The End of Apartheid 606

African Americans on the International Stage 606
The Persian Gulf War 607

At Century's End 607

23 | **Perspectives on the Present** (since 2000) 612

Legal Challenges 614
The 2000 Presidential Election 614
Challenges to Affirmative Action 615
Demands for Reparations 616

Enduring Disparities: Health, Education,
and Incarceration 618
Socioeconomic Stressors 618
The AIDS Crisis 619
Incarceration and Education 620

Forgotten in Hurricane Katrina 622

Hip Hop's Global Generation 624
Hip Hop Abroad 624
Hip Hop Nation 626
Remaking American Hip Hop 626

New Great Migrations 627
Reverse Migration 628
Afro-Caribbean and African Migrants 631
Competing Interests and Ethnic Identities 633
In Search of Origins 633

The Politics of Change 634
A New Campaign Style 635
The Democratic Primaries 637
The Election 638

Bibliography 640

Credits 677

Index 683

Foreword

Remembering John Hope Franklin

▌ by Henry Louis Gates, Jr.
Harvard University

When I was twenty, I decided to hitchhike across the African continent, more or less following the line of the Equator, from the Indian Ocean to the Atlantic. I packed only one pair of sandals and one pair of jeans to make room for the three hefty books I had decided to read from cover to cover: *Don Quixote, Moby Dick,* and *From Slavery to Freedom,* the last of which I read while recovering from a severe bout of amebic dysentery sailing down the Congo River.

I first encountered John Hope Franklin through the pages of the paperback edition of his now classic textbook, *From Slavery to Freedom.* It proved so useful as a reference that I long kept a copy of that edition in the bookcase at my bedside.

Like just about everyone else black at Yale in 1969, I enrolled in the Introduction to Afro-American History survey course, taught quite ably by the Pulitzer Prize-winning historian, William McFeely, in spite of the fact that someone at the end of each class would find a way to bring up the fact that while our subject matter was black, McFeely was quite white, and hadn't he better find a way to remedy that fact? With the patience of Job, McFeely each week would graciously grant his accuser the point, add that he hoped to put himself out of a job just as soon as a black historian could be found to take his place, then remind us that the textbook around which our course was structured had been written by a black man, a black man who had been trained at Harvard.

John Hope Franklin was the last of the great generation of black historians trained at Harvard in the first half of the century. As quiet as it is kept, Harvard, more than any other single school, is directly responsible for the training of the first generation of black historians who institutionalized the study of African American History. The list is astonishingly impressive, actually: W.E.B. Du Bois in 1895; Carter G. Woodson (the father of Black History Month) in 1912; Charles Wesley in 1925; Rayford W. Logan in 1936, and the youngest and last of this group, Franklin himself, in 1941. Both because he was the youngest member of this academic royal family and because he was lean and elegant, poised and cosmopolitan, a younger generation would call him "The Prince." Franklin, by the way, was named after John Hope, a graduate of Brown who taught his parents at Roger Williams University in Nashville, before serving twenty-five years as the president of Morehouse College, then Atlanta University. His pedigree was a noble one.

Each of these Harvard-trained historians taught at historically black schools, and all but Du Bois taught in the history department at Howard. (Only one, John Hope Franklin, would ever be tenured at a white university.) In a very real sense, Harvard gave birth to a central component of the Howard History Department, which in many ways gave birth to the academic study of Black History. Howard would nurture and train the bulk of the great black historians until historically white universities in the seventies and eighties made Black History a standard part of their curriculum.

In 1947, Franklin published the work for which he is best known: his comprehensive synthesis of the African American past, a survey of black history that appealed to a general readership as well as to students. Although Franklin did not originally envision it as such, it became the first popular college textbook in the field. In that capacity, not only was *From Slavery to Freedom* the first of its genre, it was canon-forming. It gave to the black historical tradition a self-contained form through which it could be institutionalized—parsed, divided into fifteen weeks, packaged and taught—from Harlem to Harvard, and even or especially in those places where almost no black people actually lived. Every scholar of my generation studied Franklin's book in a survey course in African American history; in this sense, we are all his godchildren.

To take hold as an academic discipline, every field of study must, as it were, be marketable, must be delivered in a learned but easily digestible form, and that is what Franklin achieved in *From Slavery to Freedom*, which over the course of many editions has sold over 3 million copies. Every subsequent textbook in African American history is a revision of or reaction to Franklin's book.

As he put the matter squarely in his Preface to the first edition of his textbook, dated April 4, 1947, writing the history of the Negro in America in fact amounts to a re-writing of American history itself; the process "has involved a continuous recognition of the mainstream of American history and the relationship of the Negro to it. It has been necessary, therefore, to a considerable extent, to re-tell the story of the evolution of the people of the United States in order to place the Negro in his proper relationship and perspective," for the simple but undeniable reason that "historical forces are all pervasive and cut through the most rigid barriers of race and caste." Negroes have made America, but just as surely America has remade the Negro, Franklin maintains, pointing to the amount of attention he pays to "the interaction of the Negro and the American environment." If America is, to a large extent, "black," he implies, blacks are "as truly American as any member of other ethnic groups that make up the American population."

John Hope and I had met at Yale in the early eighties, over a small dinner attended by the great historians, David Brion Davis and John W. Blassingame, following his lecture. David Davis turned to me during dinner and asked if I had ever discovered how I had been selected in the first group of MacArthur Fellows. As I attempted to say no, John Hope from the far end of the table thundered out that he knew precisely how I had been selected, because he had done the selecting! It was a bit like winning the fellowship all over again, as I blinked back tears. I told him how influenced I had been by *From Slavery to Freedom*, and that I had carried my copy of the third edition, published in 1967, with me across the Continent, reading it from cover to cover.

My own tenure at Duke was regrettably brief. Still, it gave me time to get to know John Hope better, to listen to his stories about school and segregation, about the academic life before Brown and his role in and perceptions of the Civil Rights Movement. Best of all, I loved his anecdotes. His favorite story was about the day he met W.E.B. Du Bois. Franklin was a graduate student at Harvard, doing research in North Carolina for his thesis on the Free Negro in North Carolina before the Civil War. All black people had to find lodging in segregated boarding homes or guest houses, and take their meals in segregated restaurants, if such entities existed. John Hope, taking his evening meal in one of these, the Arcade Hotel in the spring of 1939, spotted the great Du Bois dining alone in a corner, his gaze was riveted on a book. John Hope loved describing what happened next:

"Seeing Dr. Du Bois dining alone and reading, I decided that this was an opportunity that I would not less pass. Crossing the dining room, I approached his table and spoke to him, giving him my full name. Surely he would recognize the fact that I was named for one of his closest friends and hearing it would embrace me. He did not even look up. Then I told him that I was a graduate of Fisk University, class of 1935. That, I assumed, would bring him to his feet singing

'Gold and Blue.' Again, he continued to read and eat, without looking up. Finally, as a last resort, I told him that I was a graduate student in history at Harvard and was in Raleigh doing research for my dissertation. Without looking up from his book or plate, he said, 'How do you do.' Dejected, I retreated, completed my dinner, and withdrew from the dining room."

John Hope loved to tell that story, always ending it with "Of course we became close friends later, when he and his wife, Shirley, lived in Brooklyn and I was teaching at the College." He also liked to tell the story as the cautionary tale explaining why he was so very generous with younger colleagues.

Two years before he died, Butler University invited us both to campus for a dialogue. I agreed, but only if I could play the role of interviewer, and if we could talk with no strict time limit attached. John Hope regaled a standing room only crowd in Clowes Memorial Auditorium for over two hours with stories about his family, his education, his political beliefs, his triumphs and his disappointments, and his mixed feelings about the state of black America. And then we dined together, sharing a bottle of Margaux, followed by a cognac.

I congratulated him on receiving the Presidential Medal of Freedom; he returned the compliment about my receipt of the National Medal of the Humanities. I congratulated him on Duke's creation of the John Hope Franklin Research Center, and the forthcoming edition of *From Slavery to Freedom*, being revised by my colleague Evelyn Brooks Higginbotham. I told him how much I valued the old third edition, the one with the black and white cover, and that I deeply regretted that it had gotten misplaced somehow. He told me he was proud of what we had created at Harvard. I shared with him the faculty's decision to co-name the library at the Du Bois Institute in his honor. He seemed touched by the gesture. He promised to visit, which he did following his speech "on behalf of the history profession" at Drew Faust's inauguration.

A few days later, a FedEx envelope arrived at my house in Cambridge. Inside was another package, carefully wrapped in brown paper, the way antiquarians in England wrap books that they mail. When I give books as Christmas presents, I wrap them the same way. There is something wonderful about that brown wrapping paper. It was a signed copy of *From Slavery to Freedom* ("With affectionate best wishes"), the black and white paperback edition, dated 1967, the same one that Professor McFeely had assigned us back at Yale. It sits in the bookshelf by my bedside.

We all know that John Hope loved the past; but any historian values the past as a way to confront and reflect the present and, in a sense, to restore the future, to affect its shape. We can see this clearly in his imaginative and thoughtful suggestion to ask Evelyn Brooks Higginbotham to rewrite the eighth edition of *From Slavery to Freedom* for a twenty-first century readership. Evelyn, the first African American to hold tenure in Harvard's History Department and the Chair of the Department of African and African American Studies, has transformed the eighth edition, creating a truly new survey of African American history that incorporates the latest scholarship in what is a still emerging field. This ninth edition is a comprehensive revision that includes the history of women, transnational movements, and cultural production in more detail than any other survey of the African American experience in this country. Evelyn brings to this new text—a marriage of minds between her and John Hope—her own historical insights and analytical perspectives, making this not so much an updating, but an exciting new text, which we can discern immediately in her organization of chapters and well as in the depth and discernment of the narrative she has written. John Hope Franklin could not have found a better person to carry on the legacy of his great book, and the ninth edition is a tribute to his vision and wisdom, and to the enormous talent of Evelyn Brooks Higginbotham.

Henry Louis Gates, Jr.

A Word from the Publisher

John Hope Franklin wrote *From Slavery to Freedom* in 1947, and in the years since its initial publication it became and has remained the preeminent history of Africa Americans. We at McGraw-Hill are honored to publish this classic work and thrilled that Dr. Evelyn Brooks Higginbotham of Harvard agreed to revise it for this ninth edition.

Certainly the task of revising a book that is considered the classic text in its field is a formidable one; however, Dr. Higginbotham not only accepted the torch that John Hope Franklin passed to her, but lifted it higher. Relying on the most recent scholarship, she has brought both the story of African American history and its telling into the 21st century. Among the most significant changes in the new edition are:

- New scholarship on ancestral Africa and Africa during the time of the slave trade, including internal trade across land and river systems and the role of Africans themselves in the Atlantic slave trade.
- Attention to the complexity of North American slave culture during the colonial period, treating not only the British Colonies, but also slave life in the Spanish, Dutch, and French colonies.
- Increased coverage of women and women's history.
- Consideration of the emergence of grassroots social movements in local communities across the U.S. in the mid-twentieth century.
- The important role of art and culture as a reflection of the events and ideas of their time periods, including discussion of individual writers, musicians, and artists. Images of representative works of art are woven into the text.
- "Windows in Time" features that expose the reader to actual voices from the past.

Of course, there is no book on African American history for which the election of Barak Obama as the first African American president of the United States provides a more fitting and hopeful ending. As Dr. Franklin said in an interview filmed by Duke University shortly after Obama's nomination, "It's an indication of the willingness as well as the ability of this country to turn a significant corridor toward full political equality. . . . I didn't think it would happen in my lifetime."

Since its publication, *From Slavery to Freedom* has sold over 3 million copies and been translated into many languages. To quote Harvard professor Henry Louis Gates, Jr., in his Foreword to this ninth edition, "Every scholar of my generation studied Franklin's book in a survey course in African American history; in this sense, we are all his godchildren."

We at McGraw-Hill are pleased that Dr. Higginbotham's re-envisioning of this classic work will continue its tradition as the definitive account of the African American experience in the United States.

Preface

The New *From Slavery to Freedom*

In 2004, when John Hope Franklin asked me to become his new co-author of *From Slavery to Freedom*, he passed the torch to me for the book's revision. Now in its ninth edition and more than sixty years old, *From Slavery to Freedom* is a new book. Its chapter titles are new, as are also many of the topics, historical actors, and scholarly findings throughout. Although John Hope Franklin did not live to see its publication, he read most of the chapters and over the past years heard me speak about the revisions at his dining room table, at conferences, and in other settings. He was pleased with the direction the revision was taking and, I believe, would have been proud of the final result.

I have viewed the process of revising *From Slavery to Freedom* as one of rejuvenation—of capturing what I call the "present in history." Indeed, as I wrote, the present in history took on several meanings for me.

The first meaning is obvious. The ninth edition carries the history of African Americans to 2009, and it also draws upon the latest historical scholarship. The new *From Slavery to Freedom* offers narrative, visual, and interpretive qualities that will appeal to today's readers. The most obvious indication of how the book treats the present in history is its discussion of the election of President Barack Hussein Obama, the first black president in American history.

The writing of African American history and of the various editions of *From Slavery to Freedom* in particular has always been a revisionist enterprise. In 1947 John Hope Franklin sought to insert the black experience squarely into American history—a narrative that had previously denied the black contribution or at best dismissed its importance. The ninth edition of *From Slavery to Freedom* comes to grips with the present moment in the writing of history, recognizing that black historical scholarship is not only different but far more complex than in 1947 or in 1967 or in 1988 or even in 2000—the dates of some of the earlier editions, including the eighth edition.

An ever growing mountain of scholarship on African Americans stands before us today. New disciplinary methodologies revise older interpretations. Several decades of archaeological excavation in Africa now refute many longstanding theories about "outside cultural influences" on ancient African civilizations, proving that Africans south of the Sahara were responsible for the development of metallurgy and stone monuments. Today, scholars know much more about Africa itself, about slavery in Africa, its internal trade across land and river systems, and the role of Africans themselves in the Atlantic slave trade. Based on new scholarship that utilizes digital technology in connection with social scientific research, the new *From Slavery to Freedom* provides a clearer picture as to the number of slaves carried across the Atlantic from Africa to the New World, thus bringing resolution to what seemed like an interminable debate on this subject. In the ninth edition, North American slave culture during the colonial period is rendered far more complex than the story of black life in the British colonies, capturing different slave experiences in Spanish, French, and Dutch colonies. Archaeological insight into unearthed burial grounds has also helped to give a sense of blacks' diet, disease, and living conditions in this early period.

The present in history calls attention to groups that have for too long been silenced or rendered invisible. New historical actors come to life in the ninth edition as never before. The extensive work in women's history makes possible a far greater incorporation of women than in earlier editions. Women appear throughout the book, but particularly in slavery, abolitionism, the Jim Crow era, and the civil rights/black power movement. The growing scholarship on local communities in the mid-twentieth century and its focus on the emergence of social movements in communities across the United States call attention to activism in the South and North in the 1940s through early 1960s. Such studies bring to light the lives and ideas of local people and grassroots mobilization, illuminating a richer, more textured story than the more familiar one of federal officials and national civil rights organizations. In addition, the ninth edition covers clashing viewpoints, since there has never been a consensus on political ideology, strategies for racial advancement, or artistic freedom, to name just a few issues of contention.

The role of culture and of cultural production figures significantly in the new *From Slavery to Freedom.* The ninth edition features representative African American musicians, literary, and visual artists in order to demonstrate the importance of the arts as a reflection of and influence on historical events and ideas. In addition, chapters showcase visual images of fine art that are discussed in some detail in the text. With today's large number of first-generation Americans of African descent (the children of African, Caribbean, and Hispanic immigrants) in the United States today, diversity within the black community has grown, and with it a growing interest in transnational black perspectives, specifically in the history of the black diaspora. Some global networks are artistic, and thus the ninth edition discusses the arts of the 1920s in a transnational way as well as global Hip Hop in the twenty-first century.

Another meaning of the present in history conveys the idea of history in the making. The new *From Slavery to Freedom* discusses the generation of scholar activists with PhDs who rose to prominence in the 1930s and 1940s (inclusive of a young John Hope Franklin), during a time that has come to be known as the initial phase of the "long civil rights movement" in America. The ninth edition frames this discussion in relation to the intellectual crosscurrents, internationalist perspectives, and political ideologies of some of the black and white scholar-activists who sought to better American race relations in those years.

A final meaning of the present in history focuses on the word "present" as meaning a "gift." In this regard, the present in history has been nothing short of John Hope Franklin's great willingness to share what he himself termed a "life of learning." His autobiography *Mirror to America,* published near the end of his long life, is one such gift to the historical record, to this nation, and to the world. However, the social milieu in which Franklin wrote his autobiography differed markedly from that in which he wrote the first edition of *From Slavery to Freedom.* While Franklin pursued his research at the Library of Congress in the 1940s, he could not take lunch breaks at nearby restaurants as his white colleagues were accustomed to doing. Nor could he freely go to public libraries in the South or sit in a reading room with white scholars in the state archives in Raleigh, North Carolina, or in Montgomery,

Alabama. Franklin's very appearance on the doorstep of those archives created a commotion—according to him a "panic and emergency." In the face of Jim Crow insults, he did not get discouraged, but instead recognized his good fortune. He was able to get direct access to his sources in a way impossible for earlier generations of black historians. Franklin found curators, who instead of completely denying him access, offered him Jim Crow accommodations in backroom facilities, removed from the company of white scholars. It was for the sake of scholarship that Franklin endured these indignities.

Surely, his fortitude alone was a gift, since he, more than any other scholar, brought the black presence squarely into the mainstream of American history. And despite his many publications, his mainstreaming of black history occurred primarily through the book *From Slavery to Freedom*, for which he is most remembered. With its centuries-sweeping coverage, Franklin brought black historical actors and their writings out of obscurity, onto the pages of history books, into the professional organizations, into the classroom, and into our consciousness. Before anyone else of color, Franklin served as the first black president of six historical professional organizations, and he worked to keep the door open for others of his race to follow. Because of him, the story of blacks' contributions to America—a record once denied, disregarded, and disrespected—no longer stands at the backdoor of scholarship. John Hope Franklin's great gift to all of us has been the transformative power of his life as a scholar, his intellectual vitality and generosity, and the quality and influence of his ideas in shaping the direction and the reception of African American History. I am truly honored to be his co-author and to dedicate this book, the ninth edition of *From Slavery to Freedom,* to his memory.

Evelyn Brooks Higginbotham
Harvard University

Acknowledgments

In the summer 2005, I recognized the need to rewrite in a comprehensive way this ninth edition, rather than simply to edit sentences and to add new information in certain places. This daunting task was made easier by a number of people. Some worked only for a few days, others for several weeks, but they played a variety of roles—researching, editing, proofreading, fact checking, and identifying illustrations and graphic arts. I am appreciative of the assistance of David Brighouse, Sara Byala, Josef Sorett, Erin Royston Battat, Mia Bagneris, Adam Ewing, Kelly Lee, Loren Brandt, D. Clinton Williams, Hilary Scurlock, Natalie Sherman, Cameron Leader-Picone, Miranda Pyne, Scott McDuffie, Yael Bat-Shimon, Debra Michaels, Sava Berhané, and Barbara Burg. The skills of cartographer Martin Gamache of Alpine Mapping Guild enhanced my understanding of West African river systems. I found conversations with my colleagues—linguists John Mugane and Marcyliena Morgan—illuminating. I want to thank my daughter Nia Higginbotham, who also assisted me, particularly in the crucial last weeks of completion. I am indebted to historians John Thornton, Paul Finkelman, and Linda E. Prince—scholars who read the manuscript at various stages and generously shared their expertise and perspectives. A sincere word of gratitude goes out to Mary Anne Adams for the many weekends that she devoted to this project from its beginning to its end. She typed, proofread, and baked scrumptious goodies to make the task a bit sweeter. I want to thank James Miller, who read every chapter. McGraw-Hill could not have found a better line editor than Jim. His extensive knowledge, questions to me, and corrections helped to make the final product better than it otherwise would have been. I also want to thank McGraw-Hill's Nancy Crochiere for her patience and support and Matthew Busbridge, the sponsoring editor. Finally, I want to acknowledge my beloved mother, who died in June 2009. She gave me tremendous support and encouragement throughout my life, and certainly throughout the years in which I worked on *From Slavery to Freedom*.

We would like to thank the following reviewers who read and commented on portions of the text.

Charles Pete Banner-Haley, *Colgate University*

Abel A. Bartley, *Clemson University*

Daina Ramey Berry, *Michigan State University*

Ernest Bridges, *Fullerton College*

Kristopher Burrell, *Hostos Community College*

Rachel Burstein, *CUNY Graduate Center*

Gerald R. Butters, Jr. *Aurora University*

Daryl A. Carter, *East Tennessee State University*

Anthony Cheeseboro, *Southern Illinois University–Edwardsville*

Pero G. Dagbovie, *Michigan State University*

Maceo Crenshaw Dailey, Jr., *University of Texas at El Paso*

Jay Driskell, *University of Arizona*

Eric D. Duke, *University of South Florida*

Lillie J. Edwards, *Drew University*

Yvonne Davis Frear, *Texas A&M University*

Paul Finkelman, *Albany Law School*

G. Jahwara Giddings, *Central State University*

Cheryll Hardison-Dayton, *Bethune-Cookman University*

Keith R. V. Heningburg, *Sacramento City College*

Angela Hornsby-Gutting, *University of Mississippi*

Eric R. Jackson, *Northern Kentucky University*

Selika Ducksworth Lawton, *University of Wisconsin—Eau Claire*

Cynthia Lehman, *Antelope Valley College*

Howard Lindsey, *DePaul University*

Marilyn Love-Hartman, *Pensacola Junior College*

Steven Millner, *San Jose State University*

Glenn Nance, *City College of San Francisco*

Susan O'Donovan, *Yale University*

Marilyn T. Peebles, *Miles College*

Tara Ross, *Onondaga Community College*

Dorothy Salem, *Cuyahoga Community College*

Tobin Miller Shearer, *University of Montana*

Bradley Skelcher, *Delaware State University*

Laurie Sprankle, *Penn State Altoona College*

Clarence Taylor, *Baruch College/City University of New York*

John K. Thornton, *Boston University*

Juliet E.K. Walker, *University of Texas at Austin*

Robert C. Watson, *Hampton University*

Christopher D. Jiminez y West, *Pasadena City College*

Donald West, *Trident Technical College*

Wyndham Whynot, *Livingstone College*

Regennia Williams, *Cleveland State University*

Supplements Available with the Text

Primary Source Investigator Online

McGraw-Hill's Primary Source Investigator (PSI), available online at www.mhhe.com/psi, is designed to support and enrich the text discussion in *From Slavery to Freedom*. PSI gives instructors and students access to more than 100 primary and secondary sources including documents, images, maps, and videos. Students can use these resources to formulate and defend their understanding of the topics discussed in each chapter. All assets are indexed alphabetically as well as by type, subject, place, and time period allowing students and instructors to locate resources quickly and easily.

Student Resources in PSI

Primary Source Documents: New in this edition of *From Slavery to Freedom*, this database includes items from a wide range of contemporary accounts. Each document is accompanied by a detailed description and a series of critical thinking questions that draw students into the content and engage them in thoughtful analysis. Sources include private papers, government documents, and a variety of publications.

Images: This extensive collection includes photographs of artifacts, and buildings as well as contemporary paintings, engravings, and drawings. Each image is also accompanied by a description and critical thinking question.

Interactive Maps: Each map's legend is interactive, allowing students to see historical change over time and compare various factors in the order of their choice.

Research and Writing Center: The PSI Research and Writing Center provides a wide range of resources to guide students in writing papers, conducting research, and organizing their efforts to achieve academic success. Divided into four sections, the Writing Center provides tips for success in college, tools for conducting research and formatting materials, avoiding plagiarism, and ultimately writing an effective paper.

Instructor Resources in PSI

Faculty Guide: The Faculty Guide provides easy reference to all learning assets, both in the text and on PSI. Each chapter is accompanied by a rich list of resources, including PowerPoint slides, image bank, outline maps, book maps, and test bank questions, all keyed to the chapter. In addition to learning assets, the Faculty Guide includes a chapter overview, list of themes, lecture strategies, discussion suggestions, suggestions for further reading, and chapter-specific film recommendations.

Additional Resources for Students

The Online Learning Center for students at www.mhhe.com/franklin9e serves as a robust study tool, providing a wide range of material to enhance learning and to simplify studying. Resources are keyed directly to this edition and include:

- **Student Quizzes** that allow students to check their understanding of the course material. The quizzes can be emailed directly to instructors.
- **Essay Quizzes** that can be emailed directly to instructors.
- **Map Exercises** keyed to series of questions that help students plot historical progress geographically.

Additional Resources for Instructors

This text offers a wealth of supplemental materials to aid both students and instructors. The Online Learning Center at www.mhhe.com/franklin9e is an Internet-based resource for students and faculty members. The Instructor's Resources are password-protected and offer:

- **Test Bank** that includes over 500 multiple choice, true-false, and matching questions.
- **Computerized Test Bank,** McGraw-Hill's EZ Test, is a flexible, easy-to-use electronic test-building program. It accommodates a wide range of question types and instructors may add their own questions. Any test can be exported for use with a course management system, and the program is compatible with Windows and Macintosh operating systems.
- **PowerPoint** slides enhanced by images from the text.

Split Volumes

In addition to a comprehensive version of the text, McGraw-Hill publishes two "split" volumes for those instructors teaching the African American history course over two semesters. The two volumes cover the following time periods:

From Slavery to Freedom, 9e, Volume I: ISBN 0-07-740751-2. Covers slavery's roots in ancestral Africa through Reconstruction (500 BCE to 1877);

From Slavery to Freedom, 9e, Volume II: ISBN 0-07-740752-0. Covers the Civil War to the present (1861–present).

FROM SLAVERY TO FREEDOM
A History of African Americans

CHAPTER 1

Ancestral Africa

An Ancient Land and People

Early Commercial Networks

African Slavery

The Great Empires

Other States

Timbuktu's Sankore mosque
Built in the 15th century, Timbuktu became a great international center of scholarly and cultural life in the 16th century.

I

In 1906 the black social scientist W. E. B. Du Bois, at the time a history professor at Atlanta University, marveled at the new scholarship on the African past that was introduced to him by the white anthropologist Franz Boas in an address to the Atlanta graduating class. Boas's recounting of the great African empires of Ghana, Mali, and Songhay between the tenth and fifteenth centuries left Du Bois quite literally speechless. This knowledge gave him a newly found pride in his African heritage. "All of this I had never heard," Du Bois later confessed in the preface to his 1939 book *Black Folk: Then and Now,* "and I came then and afterwards to realize how the silence and neglect of science can let truth utterly disappear or even be unconsciously distorted."

A century later, Africa is no longer known as the "Dark Continent," as it was commonly called in Du Bois's time. During the second half of the twentieth century, an array of scientific tools and methods contributed mightily to dispelling the myth and misinformation concerning Africa. With the 1974 discovery in Ethiopia of the fossil remains of "Lucy," one of the earliest known hominids, scientists now acknowledge that Africa is the continent from which humankind arose more than three million years ago.

Several decades of archaeological work have progressively refuted many longstanding theories about "outside cultural influences" on the ancient African civilizations that flourished several thousand years ago. Copper working, iron smelting, artistry, commerce, and early state formation—once attributed to non-African groups—are today recognized as emerging from groups and conditions indigenous to sub-Saharan Africa. Longstanding theories have been either refuted, such as the introduction of iron technology into Africa by non-African peoples, or seriously questioned, such as the theory of the Almoravid (Moroccan Berber) conquest of the Empire of Ghana in 1076. Other mysteries have been confronted as well. The digital technology of the 1990s in connection with social scientific research has provided a clearer picture of the number of slaves brought to the New World, thus bringing significant resolution to what seemed like an interminable debate on this subject—a debate to which Du Bois himself contributed in his first book, *The Suppression of the African Slave Trade* (1896). As new scholarship sheds greater light on the number and the ethnic pattern of slave shipments, it exposes not only European culpability but also the complicity of the African elite in the Atlantic slave trade. What Du Bois perhaps would find most gratifying is DNA sequencing by which today's descendants of this human commerce can locate their ancestral regions and identify their African ethnic heritage.

An Ancient Land and People

More than three times the size of the United States mainland, the African continent has historically encompassed a vast range of peoples and environmental conditions. Most of the continent lies within the tropics (in what environmentalists call the *intertropical convergence zone*), leaving only the northern and southern tips with a moderate, Mediterranean climate. In West Africa, from which the majority of slaves in the Atlantic slave trade came, various ecological zones are distinguishable, so that (moving from north to south) the Sahara produced salt; the Sahel, livestock; the Savannah, cereals; and the forest region, gold and kola. This ecological diversity affected social development in meaningful ways. For example, livestock can exist only in areas free of the tse tse fly—the insect that spreads trypanosomiasis (a fatal animal disease) itself has changed significantly over the centuries. Between 300 B.C.E. (Before the Common

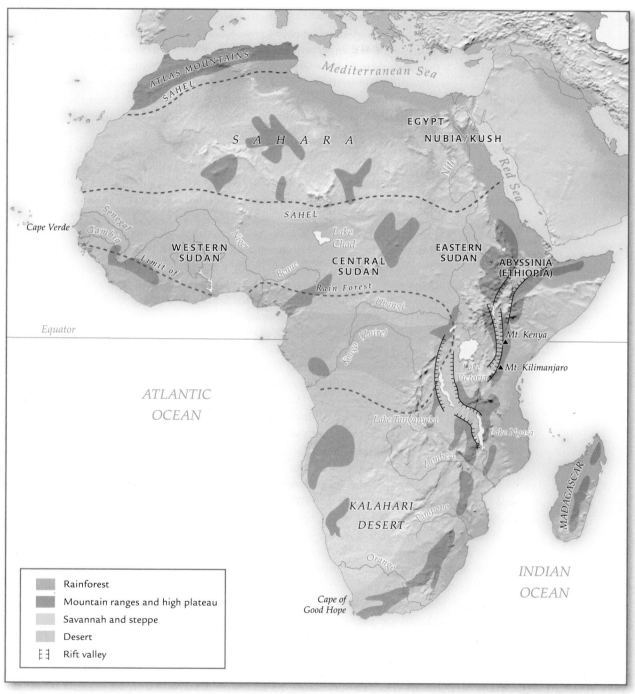

Legend:
- Rainforest
- Mountain ranges and high plateau
- Savannah and steppe
- Desert
- Rift valley

African climate and its impact on development

Era) and 1500 C.E. (Common Era), the Sahara region experienced progressively drier periods, a process known as *desiccation,* interrupted by occasional wet periods. Some scholars attribute early warfare and slavery to scarce resources.

The findings of historical linguistics have, in recent years, revealed ancient patterns of migration on the continent. Africa has about two thousand languages, which can be classified into four very different linguistic groups: Koisan in southern Africa; Afro-Asiatic in northern Africa; Nilo-Siharan in north-central Africa; and Niger-Congo in equatorial and southern Africa. The native languages of most African peoples belong to the Niger-Congo linguistic group, consisting of more than 1,400 different languages, the majority (more than five hundred) of which are Bantu. Scholars explain this linguistic dominance through the thesis of Bantu Migration.

The Bantu Migration

Briefly put, according to this thesis, Bantu speakers, who originally lived in what is today eastern Nigeria and southern Cameroon, cultivated yams and oil palms as they moved through the tropical rain forests and the adjoining savannas. Around 2000 B.C.E. they began to migrate in two waves—one to the south and the other to the east and southeast. The latter wave incorporated cereal cultivation in the Great Lakes region in eastern Africa—a vast area including modern Uganda, Rwanda, Burundi, and portions of Tanzania, Kenya, and the Democratic Republic of the Congo. Equipped with this agricultural knowledge, this group continued southward—in the course of their journey pushing aside, isolating, or absorbing other linguistic populations, most notably the Khoisan speakers in southern Africa. Eventually these Bantu-speaking peoples linked up with the wave of Bantu-speakers who earlier had migrated directly to the south. Linguists characterize this long, complex process of Bantu migration as a series of encounters and adaptations that caused the interconnectedness of various groups. Archaeologists' discovery of early iron-age pottery between the equator and the borders of South Africa also supports this interpretation of Bantu expansion. The pottery's rims, dimpled bases, and other decorative patterns reveal what one scholar has called "a general family relationship."

Not until the mid-twentieth century did archaeological methods of radio-carbon dating confirm the indigenous African origins of iron technology. Good-quality steel was produced by Africans as early as 600 B.C.E. in the Sahara desert fringe, an area today called the Jos Plateau of northern Nigeria. The iron findings, which included knife and ax blades, arrows, and fragments from an iron-smelting furnace wall, refute claims that iron smelting was introduced to Africa from an external, nonblack civilization. A preheating device, called a *tuyére,* which blasts hot air into a fiery furnace, has been shown to be indigenous to Africa and distinctively different from contemporaneous European techniques. In African societies, iron working was a highly skilled craft, one that conferred status and prestige and that was usually limited to members of a particular lineage or social group. Indeed, ironworkers were often thought to possess magical-religious powers. In the Yoruba culture, the deity Ogun was believed to be the god of iron.

Iron Technology

The ancient Nok people of the Jos Plateau have been identified by archeologists as an early iron-age society. Important excavation sites in this region at Taruga and Samun Dukiya suggest that, as early as 500 B.C.E, the Nok lived in organized, permanent settlements that were centers of both agriculture and iron work. Numerous stone axes and iron instruments used by the Nok have been excavated, as well as beautiful terracotta figures and pottery from this early period.

Nok terracotta figures, first unearthed in 1943 during tin mining operations on the Jos Plateau between the Niger and Benue rivers in Nigeria, are the most ancient extant examples of figurative African sculpture, as well as the oldest evidence of advanced, organized society in sub-Saharan Africa. Employing modern

Nok Pottery and Sculpture

technologies such as thermo-luminescence testing and radio-carbon dating, scientists date the Nok figures from 500 B.C.E. to 200 C.E. Fabricated from local clay, often mixed with gravel and fired in kilns, the terracotta Nok works are generally hollow human or animal figures of coil construction. Nok animal figurines are relatively realistic, whereas the portrait sculptures reveal a significant degree of stylization. Most surviving Nok pieces are heads that were once part of full-body figures. The heads appear disproportionately large, with facial features that include triangular-shaped eyes, flared nostrils, and full lips. Nok portrait heads are distinguished by meticulous renderings of elaborate hairstyles and jewelry, thus reflecting a culture that appreciated and emphasized bodily adornment.

Like most clay works, many of the Nok pieces were constructed by using an additive process. This technique produced a finished product by assembling parts together. Skillful Nok sculptors applied *slip* (a clay-water mixture) to the coil-constructed figures, producing a smooth, even surface. However, more than two millennia of erosion have made the once smooth exteriors of the figures appear grainy. The similarity of the Nok pieces to the brass and terracotta portrait-sculpture traditions of the later Ife Yoruba and Benin cultures suggests that the Nok culture may be their early ancestor.

Nok figure—Nok peoples, northern Nigeria, ca. 250 B.C.E.

Archaeological digs in the western-Sahara region also indicate that copper was smelted as far back as 570 to 400 B.C.E. For example, archaeologists have unearthed cylindrical copper-smelting furnaces, as well as copper bowls and spear points in present-day Mauritania. The use of copper and copper alloy was widespread in ancient Africa. Copper mines were indigenous to West Africa, and copper was a highly valued metal of commerce, exported and imported in the trans-Saharan trade in the form of bars, rings, and other artifacts. Copper was used extensively in West Africa and was important to the trans-Saharan trade. In 1353 C.E. the celebrated Arab geographer Ibn Battuta visited the copper mines of "Takedda," now identified with an ancient Hausa town in the Central Sudan that prior to the fifteenth century was famous for its copper mines and commercial vitality. In

Copper Technology

Benin, bronze and copper implements and art objects testified to the great skill of the smiths there, and many artisans, including those of the Yoruba lands and Mali, devoted considerable skill to making ornamental objects from silver and gold.

Dating from around 1400 C.E., Akan smiths in Ghana crafted innumerable copper pieces. African craftsmen used a variety of methods, including hammering, twisting, and casting, to transform imported copper into such forms as bars, rings, wires, bells, and a variety of accessories, sculptures, and plaques. These skilled artisans used the lost-wax method to create copper-alloy weights. In this technique, an object is first shaped in clay, which is then hardened and next covered with wax and an outer layer of clay; when fired, the wax melts and runs off, leaving a hollow mold into which molten metal can be poured, casting the final product. Called an *abrammuo,* the resulting weight was used to measure gold dust.

The weights had to conform to standard units of measure. Small enough to be easily portable, the weights were used to ensure fairness in gold transactions. Each party to a transaction would use his or her own *abrammuo* and a hand-held balance to verify the amount of the

Weight *(abrammuo)*—Akan peoples, Ghana, fifteenth–early eighteenth century

gold to be traded. Early examples of weights (1400–1700 C.E.), such as the one pictured here, tend to be geometric, whereas later weights (1700–1900) depict a variety of realistic figures, especially animals.

Early Commercial Networks

Ecological conditions in Africa shaped economic possibilities and made specialization and trade necessary. Certain villages, for example, specialized in fishing; others were known for metallurgy; still others for making weapons and utensils. Where such specialization was practiced, traders traveled from place to place to barter and purchase, returning laden with goods that they sold within their own communities. The trans-Saharan trade with the Muslim world, well underway by the ninth century C.E., brought West African peoples in contact with goods from as far north as the Mediterranean and as far east as Egypt. The merchants exchanged their wares—mostly luxury items—some having been procured from even more distant places by Muslim merchants, who in turn crossed the Sahara by caravan en route to the countries of the Sudan.

Evidence abounds of West Africans' trade with the outside world in the first millennium C.E.—in the appearance of new items such as glass beads, in traveler's reports, and in local records written in Arabic. These early documents also comment on the riches of Africa. Gold was Africa's most valuable trade item with both Arabs and Europeans before the discovery of the New World. Ninth-century Muslim travelers wrote of the gold-producing areas of Africa; the kingdom of Ghana was called the "land of the gold." In the eleventh century, at the height of Ghana's empire, the dominant source of gold was in Bambuk, where the Senegal and Faleme rivers meet. In the twelfth century, Bure on the Upper Niger had become prominent as a gold source, and around the fourteenth century gold also came from the Akan forest farther south.

West African Trade Routes

Specific West African groups came to dominate the long-distance trade. Known as *dyula* (or *djula*), these traders represented families, groups of families, and specific ethnic groups, such as the Mande-speaking traders who traveled from the Upper Niger area southward to the Lower Guinea coast. They utilized a complex system of weights and measures, as well as such forms of money as gold and cowry shells. They married across ethnic groups, establishing settlements as part of their commercial network, thus creating dispersed communities of self-identified traders. To facilitate commercial relations, the dyula developed their own pidgin—a contact language employing vocabulary and grammar borrowed from the differing languages of people who have to communicate with one another. They were among the earliest converts to Islam. Making use of language and law to guide their trading activities, they brought Islam to the African interior.

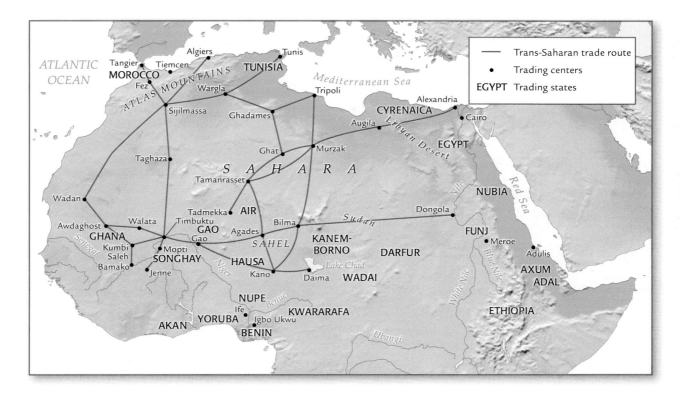

The pilgrimages of African kings and emperors who converted to Islam did much to create trade routes and stimulate commercial activity. Africa was therefore never a series of isolated, self-sufficient communities but an area of far-flung interests based on agriculture, industry, and commerce. The effects of such contacts were immeasurable. Trade routes became highways over which cultures as well as goods traveled. Africa gave much of its own culture to others and received much in return.

A thriving trade making use of numerous inland waterways linked African ethnic groups to one another in regional networks even before the trans-Saharan trade arose, and certainly before Europeans came into commercial contact with Africans. Archaeological and ecological evidence from Kintampo, in modern-day Ghana, reveals food production in the late Stone Age period from 1450 to 1300 B.C.E.

Interregional Trade

The terracotta utensils, polished stone axes, and pottery excavated at the site suggest early trade relations among the peoples of the upper woodland areas of the Volta basin and on the Accra plains. Archaeological findings also point to the role of first-millennium-C.E. regional trade along the Senegal and Niger rivers in the later rise of the Soninke empire of Ghana and in the growth of such cities as Jenne, which eventually became a famous intellectual center under the Mali and Sonhay empires. Archaeological evidence, too, suggests that African rice was cultivated by a wetland method at least 3,500 years ago in the flood plains of the upper Niger between Segu and Timbuktu in Mali and that this form of cultivation spread down the Gambia River to the Senegambia coast.

The great rivers of West Africa—the Niger, the Senegal, the Gambia, the Benue, and the Volta—made interregional trade possible. In his account of the twelfth-century Sudan,

Trans-Saharan trade routes

Ancient trade routes connected sub-Saharan West Africa to the Mediterranean coast. Among the commodities carried southward were silk, cotton, horses, and salt. Among those carried northward were gold, ivory, pepper, and slaves.

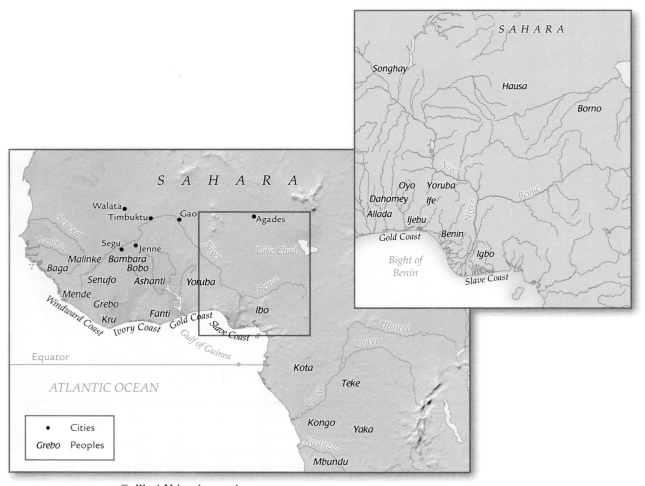

West Africa river system

the Muslim traveler Al-Idrisi describes "the strongly made boats" of the people of Ghana. Early Muslim writers erroneously called these rivers the "Nile [Nil] of the Blacks," thinking them extensions of the Nile in Egypt. Interlacing lakes, lagoons, and streams formed a riverine system that facilitated extensive trade between coastal areas and communities considerably farther inland. In West Central Africa, African traders sold their goods along the coastal waterways between the Zaire and Kwanzaa rivers.

African merchants used slaves, as well as draft animals, to carry their cargo along the overland trade routes that connected to rivers. For the trans-Saharan trade, West African gold and kola was transferred from boat to camel and then carried northward. West African merchants involved in the southern trade to the sub-Saharan regions conducted an extensive commerce from the Niger to the Senegal River and from the Senegal to the Gambia River. River systems figured significantly in the indigenous African slave trade, and their interlocking character would later facilitate the Atlantic trade along the West African coast.

A lagoon trade provided nearly unbroken communication for 400 miles from the westernmost kingdoms of Allada and Ouidah (Wydah) eastward to Lagos and to Benin farthest

Coronation of the King of Whydah

east. Muslim travelers and others wrote extensively of such rivers as the Senegal, the Gambia, the Niger, the Benue, the Volta, and the Kwanzaa. In 1508 a Portuguese traveler described the lagoon trade through the Lagos area of the Yoruba kingdom of Ijebu as a canoe-borne trade of cloth and slaves that moved along the coastal lagoons and streams spanning the area between the Volta River and the Niger **Internal Slave Trade** delta. Historian John Thornton thus argues: "Not only did the Niger-Senegal-Gambia complex unite a considerable portion of West Africa, but the Niger provided a corridor that ultimately added Hausaland, the Yoruba States, and the Nupe, Igala, and Benin kingdoms to a hydrographic system that was ultimately connected to the Atlantic."

A significant portion of slaves came from decentralized societies far in the interior. These stateless, or *acephalous,* societies formed small rural communities located in the region between the forest states and large savanna states and such middle-Niger cities as Jenne and the Hausa city-states. With less organization and fewer resources, the acephalous societies were weak, which made their people more vulnerable to capture. Once the Atlantic slave trade began, captives were carried via the waterways that had long brought commerce from the interior to the coast. Indeed, European traders would call the water routes the "slave rivers."

African Slavery

Slavery existed from the earliest known history of Africa. The ancient Egyptians enslaved various groups of people—Semitic, Mediterranean, and Nubian blacks. Slavery also existed throughout sub-Saharan Africa and comprised a range of statuses and experiences, some of which were similar to chattel slavery, some to serfdom, and some to dependent family membership. Moreover, slave status could and often did change within one's lifetime. In the four centuries leading up to European contact with Africa, slavery differed little from slavery in the Muslim world. Slavery figured prominently in Islamic societies, where slaves were viewed as inhabiting a temporary state of legal exclusion and as having the same spiritual value as a freeborn person. Muslim slaves were allowed to marry, to have a family and independent income, and to purchase their freedom. This was the general view in Islam from about the eighth century, when the religion began to penetrate sub-Saharan Africa.

However, unfree status was not unique to Africa or unique to other peoples of color. European communities embraced forms of coerced labor, even chattel slavery, prior to and during the early Middle Ages. Before the rise of feudalism, slaves were predominantly drawn from the Slavic heartland of Eastern Europe (hence the word *slave*, related to *Slav*). It was not until the fall of Constantinople in 1453, when Europe was severed from the Balkans, that it turned its attention to Africa for slaves, although some blacks had already trickled in through the Muslim trade. David Pelteret's exhaustive study of early medieval England reveals the prevalence of slaves of European descent. Investigating late Anglo-Saxon and early Norman England between 875 and 1125, Pelteret has shown that slave status was defined by law as resulting from birth, war captivity, and various forms of punishment. Slaves represented more than 10 percent of the English population in 1086, although slavery declined throughout the eleventh century and ended altogether in the later decades of the twelfth century. Nonetheless, in sixteenth-century England it was common for vagrants and the poor to be rounded up, imprisoned, and bound to forced labor.

Slavery in European Communities

Serfdom, another form of forced labor, has a long history in Eastern Europe. Unlike slaves, who were chattel (objects of property like animals and tools), serfs were considered persons with certain legal rights. They were bound to specific plots of land from which they supported themselves and paid tribute to the nobility, and to the state they owed taxes and military service. The treatment of serfs was coercive and harsh, however. The emancipation of Russian serfs occurred in 1861, just a few years before black slaves were freed in the United States.

In Africa, rulers and political elites used slaves as attendants, in positions of administrative trust, as soldiers and agricultural and household workers, and as laborers in mines. As noted earlier, African merchants purchased slaves for carrying goods on trade caravans. In some cases, enslaved persons represented members of the same ethnic group and came from the ranks of debtors, persons unable to pay court fines, and the poor, who for protection had placed themselves and their children in the service of a wealthy individual. Military and political dissidents within the same ethnic group could also end up in slavery. However, slaves more often came from a different ethnic group, usually a conquered political rival, and the warfare that fed the internal slave trade would escalate once trade relations were established with European nations.

Slaves in Africa

In the indigenous African trade, most slaves were women. Female slaves were purchased as wives, concubines, household servants, and agricultural laborers. Male slaves were used as miners, porters, craftsmen, herdsmen, brewers, soldiers, traders, and attendants. The internal trade, as well as the trans-Saharan trade, tended to favor women over men at a ratio of 2 to 1, the opposite gender ratio of the Atlantic slave trade, in which men far exceeded women. In contrast, slavery internal to Africa preferred women and children precisely because they could be more easily assimilated into local kinship groups. It is also interesting that women tended to perform the majority of agricultural labor in Africa. This, along with their natural reproductive capacity, resulted in the high valuation of women's labor.

The uniqueness of women in African labor systems, as compared to European, is best evidenced by comparing the marriage practice of African bridewealth and that of the European dowry. Bridewealth is given by the man's family to the woman's family, as compensation for the economic loss of a daughter's labor upon marriage. The dowry, in contrast, is brought by a woman to a man upon marriage, suggesting remuneration to the man for taking on a dependent. Historians and anthropologists have noted that bridewealth is found in parts of the world where women are more highly valued, both for their productive labor in cultivating the soil and for their reproductive labor in bearing children. These realities were reflected in the widespread African practice of polygamy, especially by powerful men, whose wealth was augmented by having several wives.

Slave ownership, or "wealth in persons," served to validate status and prosperity in Africa, which unlike Europe did not relate wealth to private ownership of land. In African societies, land ownership was collective rather than private. In no circumstance could a single African farmer sell or rent land to another, as in Europe, **Slaves and Status** although an African farmer could own and sell the products of the land. Land in Africa fell under the control of the state or the kinship group, which by tradition was identified as the descendants of the land's ancestral settler. Such descendants claimed hereditary use and trusteeship of the land. For some groups, a territorial deity was believed to have bequeathed the land to a particular lineage.

In African society slaves were often able to harness considerable control over their lives and even enjoy wealth and influence. Thus some scholars, instead of posing "personal freedom" as the opposite of slavery, speak of a "continuum" or varying levels of unfree status in traditional Africa, with slavery at one extreme and normal lineage relations at the other. Such arguments negate the utility of the word *freedom* in its western context, emphasizing that historically in Africa social relations have been based on the group rather than the individual. For example, Igor Kopytoff and Suzanne Miers note that in early Africa, where freedom was equated not with individual liberty but with belonging, holding a subservient but nonetheless protected position within a household unit could in certain instances be perceived more positively than in contexts that link freedom and liberty. Referring to ancient Near Eastern societies, especially Babylonia and Egypt, sociologist Orlando Patterson conveys similarly that in societies where slaves could become wealthy, freedom was not in and of itself a "valued state," since becoming free could entail "a loss of status and power."

However, slavery as a form of property in persons meant that slaves could be bought, sold, or given to someone else. The importance of slaves to the economies of different African states varied, from a domestic and thus marginal role to a more significant role. The rulers of the kingdoms of Kongo and Ndongo in West Central Africa used **Slaves in the Economy** military and other slaves in administrative posts to collect tribute from the dense slave populations living in villages near their respective capitals. A spectrum of statuses could be found in Wolof slavery, from the privileged status of military slaves to the low status of agricultural workers. Interestingly, in regard to Wolof agricultural production, slaves worked in a gang-labor format reminiscent of New World plantations. An eyewitness account of Wolof field slaves in 1685 described sixty slaves, weeding and working the soil, to the "sound and rhythm of the energetic music of six griots, who played drums and sang."

In Africa, the prevalence of slaves in many capacities, the presence of an internal slave trade as well as the centuries-old trans-Saharan slave trade with Muslim North Africa, and the existence of a slave-owning class of merchants and state officials all helped to set the stage for the commercial network that linked Europeans and complicit Africans in the capture and sale of other human beings.

The Great Empires

The first of the great West African states of which there is any record is Ghana, which lay about 500 miles northwest of its modern namesake. It was also known by its capital, Kumbi Saleh. Although its accurately recorded history does not antedate the seventh century C.E., there is evidence that Ghana's political and cultural history extends back perhaps into the first century C.E. Ghana first appears in history as a confederacy of settlements extending along the grasslands of the Senegal and the upper Niger rivers. Most public offices were hereditary, and its social order was stratified. The people of Ghana enjoyed some prosperity as farmers until continuous droughts turned their land into desert. As long as they were able to carry on their farming, gardens and date groves dotted the countryside, and there was an abundance of sheep and cattle in the outlying areas.

They were also a trading people, and the town of Kumbi Saleh was an important commercial center during the ninth century. By the beginning of the tenth century, Kumbi Saleh had a native and an Arab section, and the people were gradually adopting Islam. In the eleventh century, Ghana had a large army and a lucrative trade across **Ghana's Trading Empire** the Sahara desert. The Arab writer Al-Bakri, having gained his knowledge of the Sudan through written and oral travel narratives, noted at the time that "the king of Ghana, when he calls up his army, can put 200,000 men into the field, more than 40,000 of them archers." From the Muslim countries came salt, wheat, fruit, and sugar. Caravans laden with textiles, brass, pearls, and salt crossed the Sahara Desert to Ghana, where these imports were exchanged for ivory, slaves, and gold. Ghana's king, recognizing the value of the trade, taxed imports and exports and appointed a collector to look after his interests. At the height of its power, the Soninke empire of Ghana extended as far north as Tichit in present Mauritania and south to the gold mines of the valley of the Falémé River and the Bambuk Mountains in present-day Mali and Senegal. The yield from these mines supplied the coffers of the Soninke rulers, who also traded the gold for other luxury goods brought by caravan across the Sahara.

In faraway Cairo and Baghdad, Ghana was a subject of discussion among commercial and religious groups. In 1063 Tunka-Menin ascended to the throne of Ghana, having succeeded his maternal uncle. Tunka-Menin reigned over a vast empire, imposing taxes and tributes that were collected by provincial rulers. Al-Bakri described Tunka-Menin as a ruler who "led a praiseworthy life on account of his love of justice and friendship for the Muslims." The king, however, did not practice Islam. Tunka-Menin is described as living in a castle surrounded by round-shaped huts, the entire area fortified by a fenced wall. His palace displayed sculpture, pictures, and windows decorated by royal artists. The grounds also contained temples in which native gods were worshipped, a prison in which political enemies were incarcerated, and the tombs of preceding kings. In the late eleventh century, Ghana suffered economic decline, brought on by a series of droughts that dried up the important Wagadu and Bagana districts. Under such trying circumstances, Ghana was easy prey to waves of conquerors in the twelfth and thirteenth centuries. Oral tradition maintains that the Sosso people, once under the rule of Ghana, vanquished Ghana and extended their dominion over the area in the twelfth century.

Window in Time

Al-Bakri on the Royal Court of Tunka-Menin, King of Ghana, 1068

He sits in audience or to hear grievances against officials in a domed pavilion around which stand ten horses covered with gold-embroidered materials. Behind the king stand ten pages holding shields and swords of his country wearing splendid garments and their hair plaited with gold. The governor of the city sits on the ground before the king, and around him are ministers seated likewise. At the door of the pavilion are dogs of excellent pedigree who hardly ever leave the place where the king is, guarding him. Round their necks they wear collars of gold and silver studded with a number of balls of the same metals. The audience is announced by the beating of a drum [that] they call *dubá,* made from a long hollow log. When the people [who] profess the same religion as the king approach him, they fall on their knees and sprinkle dust on their heads, for this is their way of greeting him. As for the Muslims, they greet him only by clapping their hands.

From Al-Bakri, writing in 1068 in *Corpus of Early Arabic Sources for West African History,* translated by J. F. P. Hopkins and edited and annotated by N. Levtzion and J. F. P. Hopkins (Princeton, NJ: Markus Wiener Publishers, 2000), p. 80.

As Ghana declined, another kingdom—Mali, also called Melle—began to emerge as a power in 1235, although the nucleus of its political organization dates back to the beginning of the seventh century. Until the eleventh century, it was relatively insignificant, and its *mansas,* or kings, had little prestige or influence. The credit for consoli-

Mali's Rise

dating and strengthening the kingdom of Mali goes to the legendary Sundiata Keita. It was Sundiata who led the Malinke people, a subject group of the Sosso, in a successful revolt in the early thirteenth century, thereby freeing his people and extending Mali's rule over the land once dominated by ancient Ghana. The victory gave Mali control of the internal routes—part of the trans-Saharan trade—that carried gold north to its eventual destination.

In the fourteenth century, a descendant of Sundiata, Mansa Musa, carried Mali to even greater heights. From 1312 to 1337 this remarkable member of the Keita dynasty ruled an empire comprising much of what is now francophone Africa. The people of Mali were predominantly agricultural, but a substantial number were engaged in various crafts and mining. The fabulously rich mines of Bure were now at their disposal and served to increase the royal coffers.

Mansa Musa, an ardent and pious convert to Islam, made a famous and spectacular pilgrimage to Mecca in 1324. He first visited various parts of his

Mansa Musa's Pilgrimage

kingdom to show his subjects and vassals his tremendous wealth and to demonstrate his benevolence. He then proceeded to Tuat in the land of the Berbers and from there crossed the desert, visited Cairo, and finally went to the holy places of Mecca

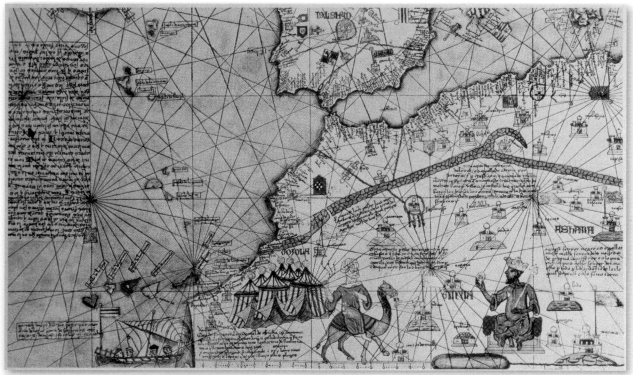

Mansa Musa portrait on fourteenth-century Catalan atlas

Mansa Musa, who ruled the West African Empire of Mali from 1312 to 1337, is portrayed at the bottom center of this portion of the fourteenth-century Catalan Atlas. Mansa Musa's crown, scepter, throne, and the huge gold nugget he displays symbolize his power and wealth.

and Medina, all along the way displaying his kingdom's wealth and power to the Muslim world. Cairo's El Omari described the historic pilgrimage as composed of an entourage of thousands of people, a large portion of which constituted a military escort. Gifts were lavished on the populace, and mosques were built where they were needed.

By the time his camels approached Mecca, their burden had become considerably lighter than it had been when they departed for the East. It was said that he gave away such large amounts of gold that he caused its devaluation in Egypt. He returned by way of Ghadames, in Tripoli, where he received many honors and from which point he was accompanied to his kingdom by El-Momar, a descendant of the founder of the dynasty of the Almohads. A more significant visitor to return with Mansa Musa was Abu-Ishak Ibrahim-es-Saheli, a distinguished Arab poet and architect from a Granada family, whom Mansa Musa engaged to supervise the building of elaborate mosques at Timbuktu, Jenne, Gao, and elsewhere.

Mansa Musa's fame spread from North Africa to Europe. At the time of his death in 1337, Mali could boast of a powerful and well-organized political state. Traveling in the area a few years later, the Arab geographer Ibn Battuta reported being greatly impressed by "the discipline of its officials and provincial governors, the excellent condition of public finance, and the luxury and the rigorous and complicated ceremonial of the royal receptions, and the respect accorded to the decisions of justice and to the authority of the sovereign."

In the middle of the fourteenth century, Europe was just beginning to feel the effects of its commercial revolution, and European states had not yet achieved anything resembling national unity; but Mali under Mansa Musa and his successor Suleiman enjoyed a flourishing economy with good international trade relations and a government that extended several hundred miles from the Atlantic to Lake Chad. With Suleiman's death, however, a civil war followed, and by the beginning of the fifteenth century, Mali began to lose most of its important provinces and showed signs of disintegration in the face of attacks from the Songhay and the Mossi states. Bereft of its former glory, Mali continued to exist for many years as a small, semi-independent state.

The kingdom of Songhay emerged triumphant after the decline of Mali. Its roots go back to the Sorko people (a proto-Songhay group) living in the Gao region in the Niger River bend in the late seventh century. The region itself, however, shows earlier pre-Sorko settlement patterns as early as the Late Stone Age. In 1993 an archaeological excavation, which unearthed pottery, copper, beads, hippopotamus tusks, and funerary objects dating from the ninth through the twelfth centuries, confirmed the existence of two towns that were first noted by Arab chroniclers al-Muhallabi (in the tenth century) and al-Bakri (in the eleventh century).

According to scholar Timothy Insoll, the archaeological find-**The Rise of Songhay** ings reveal that the entire Gao region was an important terminus of trade with both the surrounding hinterland and the trans-Sahara between the tenth and the thirteenth centuries. This region was composed of two settlements—the royal city of Old Gao, which was inhabited by the Sorko and thus indigenous Africans, and the commercial city of Gao-Saney, with its more diverse population of indigenous Africans, probably the Sorko, and Arabs. Funerary remains indicate that Islam was practiced at both sites in the early twelfth century, having been introduced through trade.

When Sonni Ali began his rule of the Songhay, most of West Africa was ripe for conquest. Mali was declining, and the lesser states, though ambitious, had neither the leadership nor the resources necessary to achieve dominance. The hour of the Songhay had arrived. Sonni Ali conceived of a plan to conquer the entire Niger region by building a river navy. In 1469 he conquered the important town of Timbuktu; in 1473 he captured Jenne, and afterward he moved on to other towns. Sonni Ali had used the riverine system to his advantage, deploying his military forces on the **View of the city of Timbuktu** Niger itself. They navigated the great river's waters in the conquest of the lands on both sides. Under Sonni Ali, Songhay had catapulted into a position of primacy in West Africa.

During the reign of Askia Muhammad, from 1493 to 1529, **Askia Muhammad's Reforms** the Songhay empire removed any doubt of its dominance in the Sahel. Askia Muhammad devoted his energies to solidifying his empire, making his people prosperous and encouraging learning. He built a professional army of slaves and prisoners of war and left his subjects to engage in farming and commerce. Local rulers, four vice-roys, and Askia's brother Omar, as chief lieutenant, maintained peace and administered the empire. In 1494 Omar and the army conquered all of Massina. In subsequent years, most of Mali, the Hausa, and many other West African kingdoms fell before the power of the Song-hay. Finally, the Songhay empire extended from the Atlantic to Bornu and from the Berber country in the north to the Mossi and Benin states in the south. It was by far the largest and most powerful state in the history of West Africa.

When Askia Muhammad, a Muslim, made his pilgrimage to Mecca in 1497, he doubtless believed that the journey would prove profitable in many ways. His retinue was composed pri-marily of scholars and officers of state, with a military escort numbering 1,500 men. He and his followers conversed with doctors, mathematicians, scientists, and scholars, and they learned much about how to improve the administration of the government, how to codify the laws of Songhay, how to foster industry and trade, and how to raise the intellectual level of the country. Even Askia Muhammad's investiture as caliph of the Sudan can be interpreted as a move to strengthen his country. Upon his return, Askia Muhammad instituted many reforms. He assigned carefully chosen governors, called *fari*, to rule over subdivisions of the empire. He reorganized the army and appointed chiefs, or *noi*, to administer provinces and large cities. Islamic law and the Koran served as the basis for administering justice. In the area of economic life, banking and credit were improved. A uniform system of weights and measures was established, and scales were inspected. The people of Songhay were encouraged to trade with other countries. Traders from Europe and Asia visited the markets of Gao, which was the political center of Songhay and home of its royal dynasty, and Timbuktu, which was an important place of learning.

It was in education that Askia Muhammad made his most significant reforms. Not only Timbuktu but also Gao, Walata, and Jenne became intellectual centers where the most learned scholars of West Africa concentrated. By the sixteenth and seventeenth centuries, a distinctly Sudanese literature was emerging. Timbuktu's University of Sankore offered stud-ies in grammar, geography, law, literature, and surgery. In 1512 Leo Africanus—a Muslim convert to Christianity whose travel accounts for a long time were Europeans' chief source of information about Africa and Islam—paid homage to this intellectual climate: "Here (in Timbuktu) there are great stores of doctors, judges, priests, and other learned men, bounti-fully maintained at the king's cost and charges. And hither are brought divers manuscripts or written books out of Barbary, which are sold for more money than any other merchandise."

The great power of Songhay was not to last. Askia Muhammad was dethroned by his oldest son, and civil wars, massacres, and unsuccessful military expeditions followed. Although there were brief periods of revival, the empire was definitely declining. The Moors viewed the Sudan covetously and began to push across the desert. With Spanish renegades as their allies, Moroccans overthrew the Songhay state and began their own brief rule in Timbuktu.

The rulers of empires often clashed with the leaders of the states under their control—with local authorities who resisted their mandates or acted on the basis of their own imperial ambitions. This division between central and local authority—a dichotomy of sovereignty—

Dichotomy of Sovereignty kept the great kings sensitive to the possibility of conflict within their realms. For example, during his pilgrimage to Mecca in 1324, Mansa Musa, the ruler of Mali, shared the story of his difficulty in enforcing Islamic beliefs and practices in the states under his dominion. Devout as he may have been, Mansa Musa extended greater tol-erance toward the local authorities of the gold-bearing regions, since gold production seemed to diminish whenever he attempted to impose his religion. In exchange for a more profitable gold trade, Mansa Musa agreed to respect indigenous religious customs. Few powerful kings of great empires and kingdoms ever achieved enough power to destroy completely the belief by local rulers that they themselves enjoyed a degree of sovereignty.

Other States

At the time of European exploration in the fifteenth and sixteenth centuries, village-states flourished throughout Africa. Such states, individually no larger than 1,500 square kilometers, together accounted for most of the land area and population in Atlantic Africa, especially that between the Gambia River and the Niger Delta. Small in territorial size, ministates closer to the coast were more densely populated than those inland. Some small states, however, did merge, voluntarily or by force, to form small kingdoms. These kingdoms, under favorable circumstances—for example, if they had able leadership, adequate resources, and strong military organization—could grow into federations or even empires.

In West Africa the densely populated Mossi states, founded in the eleventh century, were located south of the bend of the Niger River. For a time, five states constituted the loose Mossi confederation. The governors of the five states composed the council of state and served as the chief ministers in the imperial organization. The **The Mossi States** ministers oversaw such departments as the army and finance, and beneath them a hierarchy of officials extended down to local functionaries. Cohesion was greatest in time of emergency, and the Mossi managed to repel the attacks of Mali and Songhay and remain more or less independent until succumbing to European (in this case, French) colonial rule in Africa in the nineteenth century.

The strength of the Mossi states lay in their efficient political and military system. The emperor was absolute. His subordinates operated with carefully elaborated duties. Each morning the emperor received his ministers of state, who reported on the affairs of the realm. In the evening, the ruler dealt with matters concerning public order and criminal justice. The procedures of hearings and decisions bore a striking resemblance to trial by jury. There was no standing army, but the political and social system was so organized as to make it possible, on the briefest notice, to call up for military service every able-bodied man. The survival of the Mossi states in an area dominated by powerful empires such as Mali and Songhay testifies to their efficiency and wise leadership.

The Hausa city-states grew from trade relations with other African states and with North Africans across the Sahara. The best known of the Hausa city-states are Kano, Katsina, Kebbi, and Zaria, which grew also from their military conquest of agricultural villages to the south. Hausaland, expanding beyond its original towns and incor-**The Hausa States** porating farming areas that grew millet, rice, pepper, and livestock, attained prominence in the middle fifteenth century under Islamic rulers such as Muhammad Rumfa of Kano (c. 1463–1499) and the legendary Queen Amina of Zaria (late fifteenth century or sixteenth century). The Hausa occupied roughly the area of present-day northern Nigeria. Each city retained its identity, with Kano in the limelight for a while, then Katsina, and later others. Kano, a walled city at the end of the fourteenth century, engaged in the trans-Saharan trade and also traded with the Kororofa people of the Benue river valley to the southeast. Horses, which abounded in and around Kano, were traded for slaves. Kano also became a center of learning, famous for its studies in law and theology. Although Islamic influence was dominant at the state level, priest-chiefs and their indigenous religious beliefs continued to hold sway among the masses of the population. Not until the beginning of the nineteenth century did Islam make noticeable inroads into the larger Hausa population.

The kingdom of Benin extended westward, eventually gaining control of the Lagos area by deploying its fleet of war canoes on the inland lagoon routes. Known for its bronze and copper artistry, Benin wielded substantial military might, beginning in the sixteenth century, until in the eighteenth century its dominance was broken by the kingdoms of Dahomey and Oyo. During their heyday, Benin's kings controlled the use of copper in all forms, so that the metal was primarily employed to adorn the king's palace and to embellish royal regalia.

The Kingdom of Benin

Art played an important role in visually enhancing royal authority and power, often in the form of commemorative images cast from copper alloy. A guild of casters created images that memorialized a king's victory over a powerful opponent or the wealth and power of the royal court through its figurative representation of trade relations. For example, the copper alloy plaque shown here features a majestic warrior, possibly the *oba* (king) himself, accompanied by musicians, a page, and a number of smaller figures that represent the Portuguese trading partners with Benin at the time. Dutch observers in the early seventeenth century described plaques such as the one shown here—"cast copper . . . pictures of their war exploits and battles"—as lining the galleries of Benin's royal palace.

Plaque—Edo peoples, Benin kingdom, Nigeria, mid-sixteenth–mid-seventeenth century

Royal commemorative heads were included in ancestral altars in Benin. Art historian Suzanne Blier has described how the physical head itself was imbued with symbolism and perceived as the site of important qualities connected to royal authority, such as royal destiny, wisdom, intelligence, noble character, sound judgment, and strong leadership. These artistic renderings reveal Benin's veneration of both male and female authority. The office of queen mother, believed to have been established in the early sixteenth century by King Esigie in honor of his mother, Idia, was a highly esteemed position in the kingdom of Benin. In the sixteenth century, brass heads personifying queen mothers were placed on special altars and displayed both at the primary palace and the queen mother's own home.

Although in Benin the accession of a king had to be validated by two nobles whom he could summarily dismiss afterward, in other African states kings were elected by officials, even though the king's family or hereditary claims were also honored. Indeed, when Europeans first encountered African rulers in the sixteenth and seventeenth centuries, they noted existing practices of election in such states as Biguba (on the coast of modern Guinea-Bissau), in Sierra Leone, and in regions around Accra on the Gold Coast (modern Ghana). The right of "election," whether actual or merely ceremonial, as well as the power to check rulers, were granted to representatives of specific lineages, often those considered related to the original settlers of the land.

The kingdom of Kongo in West Central Africa was founded in the fourteenth century. It was unique for its voluntary conversion to Catholicism, which occurred after the **The Christian Kongo** Kongolese king Nzinga a Nkuwu asked Portuguese priests to baptize him in 1491. He adopted his baptismal name João I and established trade and religious relations with Portugal, allowing Portuguese merchants and priests into his kingdom. However, in Kongo, Africans and not the Portuguese controlled the church, and thus Catholic worship melded indigenous religious beliefs and practices with Christianity.

Christian beliefs, introduced by the Portuguese, complemented and reinforced local Kongo traditions, such as the cruciform (cross), which already existed as an indigenous symbol and powerful transitional space for communication between the earthly and the divine. Kongo leaders used Christian symbols like the crucifix as vehicles for communicating with deities and ancestors. Merging the secular and the spiritual, crucifixes were used to invoke divine favor in matters such as weather, hunting, and fertility, and played a significant role in legal proceedings and rainmaking rituals.

After King João's death in 1506, his son Afonso ruled from 1509 to 1543. He consolidated the power of the church in the kingdom of Kongo, beginning with the defeat of his brother—a non-Christian—who fought him for succession to the throne. Afonso's rule marked a rapid increase in the amount of trade with Portugal—trade that became increasingly involved in the export of slaves. Kongo reached its zenith in the mid-seventeenth century, and although it endured civil war and lost some of its centralization, it did not lose territory to the Portuguese.

Commemorative trophy head of the Queen Mother—Benin kingdom, Nigeria, late fifteenth, early sixteenth century

Another West Central African kingdom was Ndongo-Matamba, in what is now Angola. A decentralized state at the time of European contact in the 1560s, it (like many other African states during the Atlantic slave-trade era) became more centralized **Ndongo-Matamba** in the later decades of the sixteenth century. However, in the early years before the Portuguese initiated slave-trading relations, the king of Ndongo did not enjoy hereditary succession; instead, he was elected and held partially in check by the local authorities from Ndongo's constituent territories.

Crucifixion plaque—Kongo, Democratic Republic of Congo, collected 1874

The crucifixion plaque shown here, carved from ivory, represents a synthesis of Christian beliefs and values indigenous to the Kingdom of Kongo. The central Jesus figure is sculpted in the image of a Kongo man. The linear hair pattern was characteristic of Kongo traditions, and the beard connotes wisdom, status, and the authority of age in Kongo culture. The figures, kneeling in deference to Jesus and gripping his garment, suggest the Kongo tradition of kneeling when entering or leaving the home of a distinguished person.

The legitimacy of rulers appears to have become a more contentious issue once the Portuguese introduced the slave trade, and Portugal often allied with one African faction over another, exacerbating struggles over sovereignty. Such crises became particularly intense in the 1600s and, interestingly, involved an African woman ruler. Queen Njinga, born in 1582, was one of the first female rulers of Ndongo. She spent much of her reign, from 1624 until her death in 1663, justifying her claim to the throne and fighting off Portuguese encroachments on her land. Njinga, a convert to Catholicism, like the rulers of neighboring Kongo, seized power after her brother's death left only his 8-year-old son as heir to the kingship. Supported by royal or court slaves, Njinga countered military slaves initially under her rival Hari a Kiluanji, one of Ndongo's local territorial authorities. Leading her troops into battle, Njinga fought to retain her power over a more centralized state. Her alliance with the Portuguese collapsed when they supported her enemies, and in response Njinga abandoned Christianity and led her troops (which included a battalion of women) against the Portuguese during the late 1620s. The protracted struggle ended in a stalemate.

As early as 1000 C.E., East Africa was firmly incorporated into a larger international arena surrounding the Indian Ocean. The region had an abundance of coastal city-states along the Swahili Coast, stretching from modern Somalia to Mozambique, whose wealth and sophistication attested to their connections with both the continental interior and the outside world. The implications of this interaction can be seen far inland, with the emergence between 1100 and 1450 of the powerful state of Great Zimbabwe. Located in the South African Limpopo River basin, Great Zimbabwe benefited from its control of local gold resources, ivory, and cattle-raising. It is most famous for its large stone walls, stone towers, and an elliptical building whose architectural wonder was once attributed to the ancient Phoenicians rather than to indigenous African peoples. Yet archaeological excavations reveal Great Zimbabwe's African, and specifically proto-Shona and Shona, origins. Great Zimbabwe, as well as its precursor Mapungubwe (1000–1200 C.E.) and other smaller states between the thirteenth to the fifteenth century, have been linked to the Swahili coastal trade. The excavation of graves dating back to the fifteenth century has unearthed the remains of

Great Zimbabwe these societies' rulers and their adornments: gold jewelry, woven cloth of local African provenance, and imported glass beads, the last item indicating trade with the coastal areas along the Indian Ocean.

For centuries, the Swahili Coast was peopled by African, Arab, Persian, and Indian traders. As Islam spread through East Africa beginning in the eighth century and accelerating from

The Swahili Coast about the eleventh century onward, the Swahili Coast city-states blended African and Arab ways. The Swahili language is a Bantu language in terms of structure with some words borrowed from Arabic and other languages as dictated by commerce and religion. At its height from 1000–1500 C.E., the Swahili Coast had such flourishing seaside towns as Mogadishu, Malindi, and Kilwa. In 1498, Vasco De Gama explored East Africa, and more Portuguese explorers followed in the sixteenth century, leaving accounts of a sea-oriented trade already in place in Mombasa and Malindi. Historian Patrick Manning has shown that slavery in East Africa in the late eighteenth century, especially in Mozambique, led to the expansion of the slave trade, first to the Middle East and then to the Americas. Slaves were exported from Mozambique well into the nineteenth century because of the weak policing of the slave trade in the Indian Ocean, as opposed to efforts to suppress slave trading on the Atlantic.

The states described in this chapter represent only a sample of the many African political units. Some, like Egypt, Kush, and Carthage, flourished in ancient times, before the Common Era. Others came later. Some areas, such as present-day Zimbabwe and the savannah lands south of the Congo Basin, witnessed different civilizations rising on the sites of their predecessors. While Europeans were fighting in the Crusades, Muslim Swahili-speaking city-states along the Indian Ocean were trading with Arabia, India, and the East Indies (modern Indonesia). Ethiopians have a recorded history that goes back almost two thousand years. Other kingdoms are of more recent origin: the Zulu people of Southern Africa, for instance, did not form a powerful nation until the nineteenth century. To a greater or lesser degree, however, all had some connection with the African-descended peoples of the New World.

2 Africans in the Atlantic World

Finding New Lands and Labor

Trading in Slaves

The Middle Passage

Slavery in the Caribbean

Slavery in Mainland Latin America

Slave Societies in the Americas

Portuguese fort, Africa

The fortress of São Jorge de Mina on the African Gold Coast, built in 1482 as a trading post and supply base for the Portuguese navigators.

The Atlantic slave trade was forged in the crucible of Europe's Commercial Revolution. In Europe, a spreading knowledge of foreign lands and of maritime innovations undergirded a successful quest for ocean routes to the riches of Asia and the goldfields of Africa, and also (as some scholars posit) for alternative trade routes around the Muslim-dominated lands. In the fifteenth century, Portugal's maritime expertise increased, making it possible for that country's navigators to withstand the fierce winds and currents along the African coast. Before that the winds and currents had enabled ships to sail southward but prevented them from getting back home. Now, equipped with new skills and ships, Portuguese seamen pushed ever farther south along the western coast of Africa and claimed the islands of Cape Verde, São Tomé, and Principe. They sailed the waters of the Gulf of Guinea and established trade networks with African merchants on the mainland.

This commercial relationship brought European wares to Africans, who in turn supplied the Portuguese with gold, nuts, fruit, olive oil, pepper, ivory, and slaves. Eventually, human cargo would supplant gold as the most important and valuable African export. As the slave trade became an accepted and profitable part of European commerce in the late fifteenth century, Spanish vessels began sailing westward across the Atlantic to discover the riches of the uncharted "West" Indies. After Christopher Columbus reached the West Indian (now called the Caribbean) islands in 1492, Spain, and later other nations, dreamed of empires with colonies and slaves. They would use African slaves to help in the exploration, conquest, and settlement of the New World. Both Africans and Europeans stood on the threshold of a new global era. The number of slaves in the larger transatlantic migration surged, rising from one-fourth of the total in the years between 1492 and 1580 to more than three-fourths of the total between 1700 and 1780. The fate of millions of Africans and their descendants would henceforth be determined in the context of the Atlantic world.

Finding New Lands and Labor

From the onset of European exploration in the New World, Africans came as explorers, servants, and slaves. Even before the annual importation of thousands of Africans to work the New World's sugar, coffee, and tobacco plantations, African slaves and free blacks entered the New World alongside the early explorers. It is ironic that some slaves gained fame, if not also their freedom, for their participation in the conquest of the Americas, since they played a role in helping the Spanish conquistadors claim the land and lives of the Native American peoples.

Two hundred blacks traveled to Quito (the capital of present-day Ecuador) with the Spanish conquistador Pedro de Alvarado. They were with Hernando de Alarcón and Francisco Vásquez de Coronado in the Spanish conquest of New Mexico. Slaves served in Francisco Pizarro's Peruvian expedition and carried his body to the cathedral after his assassination. Blacks accompanied Pánfilo de Narváez on his expedition of **Africans and the Conquistadors** 1527 and Álvar Núñez Cabeza de Vaca in his exploration of the southwestern parts of the present United States. Thirty Africans, including Nuflo de Olano, were with Vasco Núñez de Balboa when he discovered the Pacific Ocean. Hernando Cortés carried blacks with him into Mexico, and one, Juan Garrido, planted and harvested the first wheat crop in the New World.

Little is known about most of these African-descended conquistadors, but sixteenth-century memoirs and records offer fascinating pictures of a few of them. Juan Garrido, for example, left a record of his life in a petition (*probansa*) that he sent to Spain's monarch, Charles V, in 1538.

23

Juan Garrido

Explorer Ponce de León was accompanied by African-born Juan Garrido.

He was born around 1480 on the West African coast and arrived in Lisbon as a free person during his teenage years. Some scholars speculate that he was the son of an African king or merchant with commercial ties to the Portuguese. In 1503 Garrido departed from Seville as part of a Spanish expedition to the Americas. Under the leadership of Juan Ponce de León, he participated in the Spanish settlement of Puerto Rico and Cuba and fought with the Spanish against the Carib Indians in an unsuccessful effort to conquer other surrounding islands.

Garrido also accompanied Ponce de León on his two expeditions to Florida in 1513 and 1521 and upon the latter's death served under Hernando Cortés in the army that destroyed the Aztec Empire in Mexico. Garrido received land for his military service and established himself in Mexico City (which the Aztecs called Tenochtitlán). For a time, he held the important position of caretaker of the city's aqueduct.

Another outstanding African explorer, who bore the Spanish name Estevan (also called Esteban), accompanied his master Andres Dorantes de Carranza on a Spanish expedition to Florida, led by the conquistador Pánfilo de Narváez in 1528. The group suffered tremendous loss of life; Estevan was one of only four survivors who made a tortuous trek across the continent back to Mexico City. In the journal kept by another member of this two-year trek, Cabeza de Vaca, it was recorded that Estevan proved especially valuable because of his superior ability to learn and interpret the languages of the Indian tribes among which the Spaniards traveled.

The story of this journey inspired another mission in the Southwest in search of cities of gold. Purchased as a slave by the leaders of this expedition because of his knowledge of the region and its inhabitants, Estevan helped to pave the new expedition's way by traveling ahead of the others. Estevan became known among Indians as the "Son of the Sun." The Zuni, however, killed him in 1539, perhaps thinking him the vanguard of a conquering force.

Africans were with the French explorers on the North American continent in the seventeenth century, traveling with the French Jesuit missionaries on their Canadian expeditions. When France took control of the Mississippi Valley in the late seventeenth century, Africans represented a substantial portion of the pioneers who settled there. And in the late eighteenth century, around 1790, Jean Baptiste Point du Sable, a French-speaking black, erected the first building in a place that later came to be known as Chicago. Although Africans did not accompany the English on their early explorations of North America, it is not without ironic significance that black people were extensively engaged in the task of opening the New World for European development.

When European countries began their exploration and conquest of the New World, they were interested primarily in exploiting the natural resources. **Demand for Slave Labor** Labor was obviously necessary, and the cheaper the better. Most of the key plantation crops, such as sugar, coffee, and cotton, were not indigenous to the New World. Rather, they were Old World tropical plants, imported along with African slaves.

In some cases, Africans were already familiar with the cultivation of these crops. For example, prior to the discovery of the New World the Portuguese had used Angolan slaves to grow sugar on the island of São Tomé, off the West African coast. Plantation crops such as sugar were labor-intensive, their great profitability deriving from the coerced, unpaid toil of those who actually produced them. However, in the New World slave labor initially came from the readily available native population. In coastal Brazil and many of the Caribbean islands, the European conquerors enslaved seminomadic Indians, working them excessively in mines and agricultural fields. In the indigenous states that the Spanish conquistadors seized—the Aztec empire in Mexico and the Inca empire in Peru—colonial rule was imposed over Indian social institutions, including preexisting forms of Indian slavery.

The great susceptibility of Indians to the diseases carried by Europeans, together with harsh labor conditions, nearly exterminated the native populations of the New World. In 1517 the Catholic friar Bartolomé de las Casas voiced his anguish over the plight of the Indians and suggested the greater use of Africans, who at the time were already being brought to the Americas. As early as 1501, the government in Madrid had authorized the introduction of Africans to make up for the deficiency in Indian labor. Black slaves had been shipped into Cuba in such large numbers by 1506 that the Spanish government, fearful of slave insurrections, tried to limit the rate of importation. For a decade, Africans trickled into Cuba, and the extensive use of Indians resumed. In 1516, however, Charles V licensed several Flemish traders to bring Africans to the colonies. It was in this context that Las Casas recommended black slavery, a position he later came to regret.

In this age of expansion and rivalry among European nations, finding acceptable workers in large quantities became the primary impetus for the growth of the Atlantic slave trade. Slaves from the Senegambia region of West Africa were brought to Portugal and then dispersed throughout the Iberian Peninsula. As early as the sixteenth **From Indenture to Slavery** century, the word *Ladino* came to be associated with these newly "Latinized Africans," many of whom were re-shipped from Lisbon to the Spanish colonies in the New World. Although Europe was undergoing drastic economic change in the fifteenth and sixteenth centuries, its new institutions did not make use of Africans on a large scale. To be sure, African slaves lived and worked in Lisbon, Seville, London, and many other European cities in the late fifteenth and early sixteenth centuries. A census of Lisbon

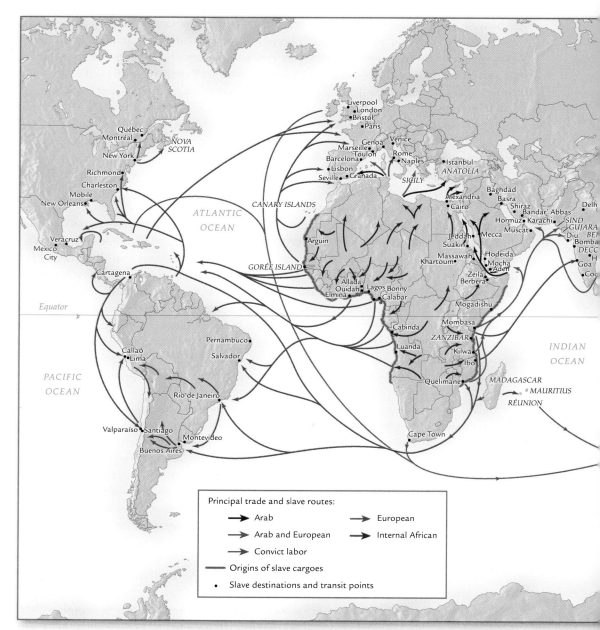

Routes of the slave trade

This map shows the general direction of the principal sea routes of Arab, European, and American trade in African slaves up to 1873.

Principal trade and slave routes:

→ Arab   → European

→ Arab and European   → Internal African

→ Convict labor

— Origins of slave cargoes

• Slave destinations and transit points

and its surrounding areas, for example, recorded 9,400 blacks. Yet the banking houses, ship-yards, mercantile establishments, and the homes of the newly rich could use only a limited number. There were many jobs to be performed, but much of the large white population, itself dispossessed of land by the enclosure movement in England and other parts of Europe, desperately sought employment. There appeared to be no future for slavery in Europe.

The land-to-man ratio in the New World, however, begged for laborers. European colonizers did not initially regard African slaves as the only solution to their labor needs in the Americas. England, more than the other nations, attempted to use white indentured labor,

but ultimately this proved unsatisfactory. Indentured servitude meant that a laborer agreed to serve a master for a term of years, after which he or she would gain freedom and, ideally, a grant of land. Terms of service became a constant irritant for all concerned. In the English colonies, not only did servants chafe at having to stay until their indenture expired, but many went so far as to sue masters and ship captains for illegal detention. Many servants also ran away and set up homesteads in unsettled lands, making their capture and return increasingly difficult, as well as expensive.

By the late seventeenth century, English masters in places such as Virginia began to ask themselves why they should worry about indentured servants when blacks presented so few of the difficulties that white laborers caused them. Because of their color, Africans could be easily recognized and apprehended. Furthermore, they could be purchased outright, thus stabilizing a master's labor supply. In the long run, Europeans argued, African slaves cost less, since the New World colonies, with their vast land area and their potential for mining and agriculture, provided the opportunity for amassing great wealth precisely because of an apparently inexhaustible supply of Africans that the slave trade made possible. In a period when economic considerations dominated colonial policy, this calculation made New World slavery a fixed institution.

Trading in Slaves

European countries large and small—Spain, Portugal, France, England, the Netherlands, Denmark-Norway, Sweden, and Brandenburg-Prussia—all pursued the wealth to be made from the Atlantic slave trade. After years of trial and error, European slave traders developed the techniques of slave trafficking. Along the African coast, the flags of the various European countries could be seen waving above their respective trading posts, also called "slave factories." The posts were actually forts, armed with cannons and garrisons for protection against European rivals, not Africans. For example, in 1621 the newly organized Dutch West India Company challenged Portugal's exclusive trading privileges on the African coast and in 1637 captured Elmina, the fortified outpost established by the Portuguese on the African mainland in the late fifteenth century. The fort's location on the Guinea Coast, in what is today Ghana, made it a valuable commercial hub. In 1682, Elmina had a population of 15,000 to 20,000, including Europeans, Africans, and a new generation of interracial people of primarily Portuguese and African descent. Such forts were indispensable bases of operation for the slave trade.

Ships laden with European goods provisioned the forts, so that trading could proceed. Cotton textiles of all descriptions, utensils of brass, pewter, beads of many sizes and shapes, guns and gunpowder, spirits—whiskey, brandy, and rum—and a variety of foodstuffs were some of the more important items that were exchanged for slaves. In the mid-eighteenth century, slave ships came in a variety of sizes. Bound for Africa from Liverpool, the 10-ton slaver *Hesketh* paled in comparison to the 566-ton *Parr,* another Liverpool ship. The *Parr,* which had a carrying

Christiansborg Castle, Gold Coast, ca. 1750

capacity of seven hundred slaves and a hundred crew, was described as "a very beautiful vessel and the largest employed out of this port in the African trade for which she was designed." The historian Marcus Rediker notes the *Parr's* shocking demise, when in 1798 it exploded off the coast of the Bight of Biafra after loading two hundred slaves. All aboard were killed.

A cargo's value varied with the size of the ship and the season of trading. According to the digital database, *The Trans-Atlantic Slave Trade*, the ship the *King Solomon* made four voyages between 1715 and 1758. In 1720 the *King Solomon* had an inventory of £4,250 worth of goods when it left London for Cape Coast Castle on Africa's west coast (in modern-day Ghana). At each trading post were stationed slave traders, called *factors*, who maintained friendly relations with Africans in order to procure slaves.

On arrival at a trading outpost in Africa, the European trader was ready to establish contact with African rulers or their representatives and with local African merchants who **Acquiring Slaves** assisted in securing the desired slaves. Slaves were mostly obtained through negotiation, although slave raids by Europeans did occur at times. The late sixteenth-century travel writer Richard Hakluyt wrote that the English slave trader John Hawkins "got his possession partly by the sworde and partly by other means to the number of 300 negroes." In the eighteenth century, the first lieutenant of the French vessel, the *Diligent*, complained in his journal about unlicensed slavers, calling them interlopers from Bordeaux, who captured African merchants and reduced them to slaves.

Slave factory in the Gulf of Guinea, in what is now called Nigeria

In the sixteenth century the Portuguese began a series of wars in West Central Africa that lasted several decades. Portuguese soldiers brought to Africa what historian John Thornton calls a "new art of war," combining African and European weaponry and strategies. The Portuguese more often attempted to forge military alliances with warring African factions, as in the Kingdom of Kongo and in Ndongo. Thus in the sixteenth century, Portugal was able to acquire slaves as a result of Kongo's expansionist policies toward its neighbors, and in the seventeenth century, it took advantage of Queen Njinga's struggle to succeed to the throne in the Angolan kingdom of Ndongo. In 1648 she ended hostilities with the Portuguese, returned to Catholicism, and established relations between her country and Portugal in the slave trade; thereafter she ruled Ndongo until she died in her eighties.

Europeans' sales of guns caused new levels of havoc and civil strife among Africans, thus ensuring that increasing numbers of slaves were captured for the transatlantic market. However, Europeans generally did not capture people for sale—overwhelmingly, that was done by Africans, because they wanted to thwart European attempts to move into the interior. Africans were both perpetrators and victims of the Atlantic slave trade. Well before the journey across the Atlantic in European ships, captive and shackled Africans experienced their first passage from freedom into slavery as they traveled from the interior over many miles on foot and by boat down the "slave rivers" to coastal areas. On the coast, the trading with Europeans began.

Africans in the Slave Trade

King Garcia II Nkanga a Lukeni of Kongo receiving a Dutch embassy in 1642

Contrary to stereotypes, Europeans did not convey attitudes of racial superiority or disrespect as they entered into trade negotiations with African rulers and traders. In fact, Europeans followed strict rules of protocol. The usual procedure was to pay a courtesy visit in order to secure permission to trade. After being properly persuaded with gifts, the African ruler then appointed various assistants who were at the disposal of the trader. Foremost among these was the *caboceer*, who assumed responsibility for collecting those to be sold at prices previously agreed on by the trader and the African ruler. The trading proceeded apace once the captives were brought before the trader for inspection. Some traders consulted physicians and other advisers about impending purchases, because frequently prospective slaves had been so cleanly shaven and soaked in palm oil that it was difficult to ascertain their age or physical condition. Prices varied greatly depending on the age and the condition of the slave, the period of the trading, and the location of the post. Many transactions were mere barter, but accounts also reveal that in the middle of the eighteenth century, £20 sterling was a typical price to pay for a healthy young man at Cape Coast Castle on the Gold Coast.

Trading in slaves proved to be more complicated than simply sailing into a port, loading up with slaves, and sailing away. In 1682, English traders at Cape Coast Castle followed **Slave Trade Challenges** attentively news of the warfare between the Abraer (Abrah) and Coromantee near Anomabo. Hoping to purchase the captives from the king of the victorious group, the English were disappointed by the outcome. In this case, the two groups shared a common affiliation. Both were members in the loose confederation of Fanti-speaking

Window in Time

Quobna Ottobah Cugoano on Eighteenth-Century Slave Trade

To give any just conception of the barbarous traffic carried on at those factories, it would be out of my power to describe the miserable situation of the poor exiled Africans, which by the craft of wicked men daily become their prey, though I have seen enough of their misery as well as read; no description can give an adequate idea of the horror of their feelings, and the dreadful calamities they undergo. The treacherous, perfidious and cruel methods made use of in procuring them, are horrible and shocking. Bringing them to the ships and factories, and subjecting them to brutal examinations stripped naked and markings, is barbarous and base. Stowing them in the holds of the ships like goods of burden, with closeness and stench, is deplorable; and, what makes addition to this deplorable situation, they are often treated in the most barbarous and inhuman manner by the unfeeling monsters of Captains. And when they arrive at the destined port in the colonies, they are again stripped naked for the brutal examination of their purchasers to view them, which, to many, must add shame and grief to their other woe, as may be evidently seen with sorrow, melancholy and despair marked upon their countenances. Here again another scene of grief and lamentation arises; friends and near relations must be parted never to meet again, nor knowing to whence they go. Here daughters are clinging to their mothers, and mothers to their daughters, bedewing each others naked breasts with tears; here fathers, mothers, and children, locked in each others arms, are begging never to be separated; here the husband will be pleading for his wife, and the wife praying for her children, and entreating, enough to melt the most obdurate heart, not to be torn from them, and taken away from her husband; and some will be still weeping for their native shore, and their dear relations and friends, and other endearing connections which they have left behind, and have been barbarously tore away from, and all be bemoaning themselves with grief and lamentation at the prospect of their wretched fate. And when sold and delivered up to their inhuman purchasers, a more heart-piercing scene cannot well take place. The last embrace of the beloved husband and wife may be seen, taking their dear offspring in their arms, and with the most parental fondness, bathing their cheeks with a final parting endearment.

Quobna Ottobah Cugoano, *Thoughts and Sentiments on the Evil and Wicked Traffic of the Slavery and Commerce of the Human Species* (London: n.p. 1787/New York: Penguin 1999).

polities. This affiliation, according to historian Stephanie Smallwood, did not rest on European understandings of an alliance, since the basis for confederation was defined not by territorially bounded "countries" or "states" but rather by the tradition of matrilineal-based kinship. Indeed, the political affiliation of the confederation's members was rooted in a common matrilineage, language, and culture. Although this shared lineage did not prevent war and violence

European trader offering imported goods to Africans

between member states, it did prohibit selling one another into the Atlantic slave trade.

Trading could also become complicated when Europeans ran into costly delays in disposing of the trade goods they had brought from Europe. Experience taught European traders what items to bring to African dealers and rulers in exchange for slaves, but at times they brought goods that were not particularly desired; in that case, they would have to return home with unwanted cargo. It was common for large ships not to find a sufficient number of slaves at a single trading post. In these situations, traders had to linger for two or three weeks before enough slaves could be rounded up to make the negotiations worthwhile. It was also not unusual for a ship to be compelled to call at four or five ports in order to purchase as many as five hundred slaves. Local inhabitants frequently scoured the interior and used much coercion to secure the desired quantity of slaves to meet the traders' demands.

At the trading post, Europeans obtained, in addition to slaves, such foodstuffs as corn, kidney beans, yams, fruits, coconuts, and plantains for the voyage across the Atlantic. Medicines were stocked for the ship's physician to administer to the slaves, who were almost certain to become ill en route. The last post at which the slaver could make such transactions was Gorée Island off the coast of Dakar in Senegal.

The Trauma of Capture For captured Africans, the initial encounter with whites was traumatic. In the best-known autobiography of an eighteenth-century slave, *The Interesting Narrative of the Life of Olaudah Equiano or Gustavus Vassa the African* (1789), Equiano described the terrifying moment of his first sight of white men on the slave ship where he was held captive:

> "I was now persuaded," he wrote, "that I was got into a world of bad spirits, and that they were going to kill me. Their complexions . . . differing so much from ours, their long hair, and the language they spoke, which was very different from any I had ever heard, united to confirm me in this belief. . . . When I looked round the ship, too, and saw a large furnace of copper boiling, and a multitude of black people of every description chained together, every one of their countenances expressing dejection and sorrow, I no longer doubted of my fate, and, quite overpowered with horror and anguish, I fell motionless on the deck and fainted. When I recovered a little, I found some black people about me, . . . I asked them if we were not to be eaten by those white men with horrible looks, red faces, and long hair?"

Recently, literary scholar Vincent Carretta has questioned Africa as Equiano's birthplace, having found the baptismal record in the church in England where Equiano was baptized as

Gustavas Vassa. The record gives "Carolina" as his birthplace. Scholars of African history, however, have challenged Carretta's interpretation, and the debate remains unresolved. The narrative's characterization of the Atlantic slave trade, even if not Equiano's personal experiences, represents a plausible account of how captured Africans must have felt.

Enslaved Africans offered stiff resistance to their capture, sale, and transport across the Atlantic. Fierce wars broke out between tribes when members of one group sought to capture members of another for slave-trading purposes. *Caboceers* and slave captains very early learned to keep their captives in chains, for without taking such precautions slaves would attempt to escape. One trader remarked that the "Negroes were so wilful and loth to leave their own country, that they have often leap'd out of the canoes, boat and ship, into the sea, and kept under water till they were drowned" to avoid being taken up by their captors. At the first opportunity, if it ever presented itself, many would leap off the ship into the mouths of hungry sharks to avoid enslavement in the New World.

African Resistance

European shipping records indicate that revolts occurred not only in the transatlantic passage but also earlier, on the African coastline. Numerous attacks against slave ships occurred while they anchored offshore and were being loaded. In some cases, mainland Africans attacked ships and longboats in an effort to rescue captives before they set sail, but more often the slaves themselves revolted on the ships. Historian David Richardson notes that in the trade south of the Upper Guinea, revolts were more likely to occur on ships with a larger number than usual of female captives. Men led the revolts, he argues, but women played crucial roles, since they were less likely to be shackled. Efforts to prevent revolts were costly. Crews on slave ships were usually 50 percent larger than crews on similar-sized ships that did not carry human cargoes. Netting placed around ships deterred slaves from jumping overboard, and surveillance, firearms, and whipping exacted fear and submission.

The Middle Passage

The voyage to the Americas, usually called the "middle passage," was a living nightmare. Overcrowding was normal; it became so common that the British Parliament felt compelled to specify that not more than five slaves could be carried for every three tons' worth of cargo on a two-hundred ton ship. This regulation, like so many others, was not enforced: ships as small as 90 tons sometimes carried 390 slaves, in addition to crew and provisions. More slaves meant more profits; hence few traders could resist the temptation to wedge in a few more. There was hardly enough standing, lying, or sitting room in the areas of the ship where slaves were kept. Shackled together hand and foot, slaves had no room to move about and no freedom to exercise. Such overcrowded conditions greatly increased the chance of sickness breaking out during the voyage.

One observer remarked that few slave ships escaped smallpox, which could reach epidemic proportions, killing slaves and crew alike. Perhaps even more frequent, and causing more slave fatalities, was "the flux," a vaguely defined malady typically including diarrhea from which whites on board the slave ships were less likely to suffer. Hunger strikes at times aggravated unfavorable health conditions and induced illnesses. The filth caused by the close, stinking quarters brought on more illness, and the mortality rate increased accordingly. Many of those who did not die of disease or commit suicide by jumping overboard were permanently disabled by the ravages of some dread disease or by maiming, which often resulted from struggling against the chains.

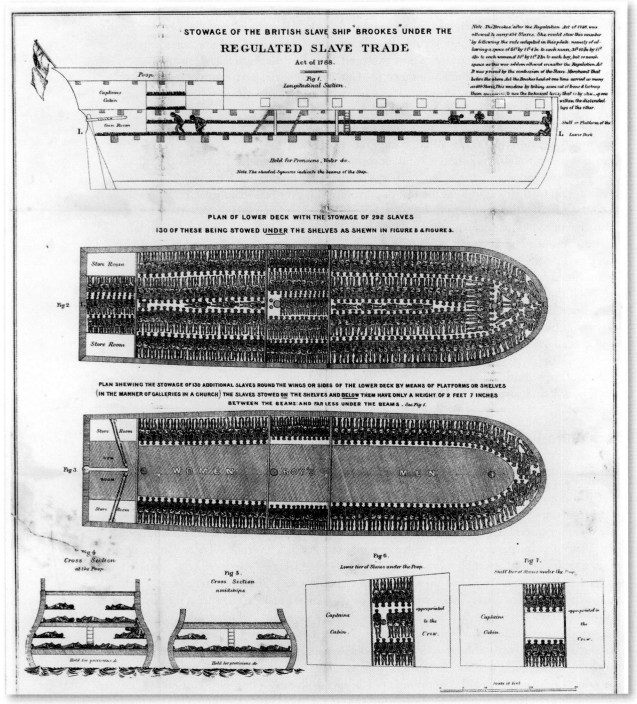

The plan of the *Brookes*

Fig. 1, lengthwise cross section; Fig. 2, lower deck without platforms; Fig. 3, lower deck with platforms; Figs. 4 and 5, breadthwise cross sections; Fig. 6, half-deck without platforms; Fig. 7, half-deck with platforms. The *Brookes,* a 320-ton vessel, was one of the eighteen slave-trading ships examined by a committee that was making recommendations to the English parliament for the regulation of such vessels in 1788. The abolitionists claimed that the *Brookes,* built to accommodate 451 persons, carried as many as 609 slaves on one of its voyages.

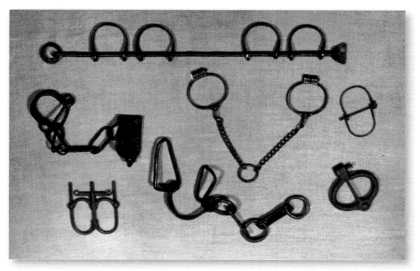

Three-person slave shackle on ship

Even including the great expenses attached to the trade and the extensive losses resulting from mortality of slaves in transit, the slave trade was one of the most important sources of European wealth in the seventeenth and eighteenth centuries. In the late eighteenth century, a ship captain could make a commission of £360 on the sale of 307 slaves and, on the same sale, a trader could earn £465. It was **A Profitable Trade** not unusual for a ship carrying 250 slaves to net as much as £7,000 on one voyage. A handsome profit of 100 percent was not uncommon for Liverpool merchants. In eleven years, from 1783 through 1793, Liverpool traders alone were responsible for the transport of 303,737 slaves; in the following eleven years, they were certainly responsible for as many more. Although the slave trade peaked in the closing years of the eighteenth century, the preceding two centuries had shown a steady increase.

Even into the nineteenth century, when international measures were being taken to suppress the slave trade, scholars estimate that 2 to 3 million Africans were brought to the Americas. Until the late 1860s, the trade to Cuba and Brazil continued. Considering the great many who were killed while resisting capture in Africa, those who died during the transatlantic passage, and the millions successfully brought to the Americas, the aggregate number of victims approaches staggering proportions. After decades of debate over the number of Africans carried to the New World as slaves during the era of the Atlantic slave trade, an extensive digital database, compiled under the leadership of historian David Eltis, concludes that approximately 12.5 million slaves were transported.

Slavery in the Caribbean

In the Caribbean, Europeans made their first serious effort to develop a lucrative economy in the New World. Thus it was to the Caribbean islands that the first large shipments of slaves were sent. Rivalries among European countries for control of these islands in the seventeenth century presaged their later intense rivalry on the North American mainland.

Spain's prior claim to the Caribbean islands, because of the explorations and to the pope's actions of 1493 (which divided between Spain and Portugal the newly discovered lands along a mid-Atlantic line), positioned it to channel its energies and capital into Cuba, Puerto Rico, Hispaniola, and Jamaica. Although the Spanish would lose some of these and other islands in various conflicts, they nevertheless made the most of their Caribbean holdings by producing staple crops, especially sugar, tobacco, and coffee, with slave labor.

The Spanish Monopoly

Early in the sixteenth century, large consignments of slaves went to the Spanish Caribbean, as in 1518, when the king of Spain granted a trader the right to ship four thousand Africans to the islands. By 1540, annual importation had reached approximately ten thousand. Moreover, an illicit trade of indeterminate size quickly developed, particularly because of English efforts to claim a share of the Caribbean trade—which, during the early years of Queen Elizabeth I's reign, already gave promise of being decidedly profitable.

England's attempt to break the Spanish monopoly was precipitated by the slave trader and privateer John Hawkins in 1562. Hawkins took slaves from the Guinea coast to Monte Christi, now in the Dominican Republic, believing the Spanish colonists' desire for them to be greater than their respect for the royal ban on unlicensed trade. The pattern set by Hawkins in selling slaves and other African goods was eagerly followed by other and less discreet English imitators who, if caught, were summarily arrested and punished by Spanish officials. Although for the moment Spain had checked the encroachment of foreign interlopers, it was only a matter of time before it would be forced to yield valuable ground in regard to its monopoly of the slave trade and New World territory.

In the seventeenth century, Spain lost all claim to exclusive control of the Caribbean. Denmark, the Dutch Republic, France, and England acquired their own respective islands. Dutch buccaneers were entrenched in Curaçao, St. Eustatius, and Tobago by 1640, and the Dutch West India Company, supported enthusiastically by the Dutch government, promoted the slave trade. At about the same time, the French Company of the Islands of America settled Guadeloupe, Martinique, and Marie Galante, and in the 1650s France acquired St. Lucia and Grenada. England secured control of St. Christopher in 1623, of Barbados in 1625, and of Nevis, Antigua, and Montserrat in the 1630s. In 1655 the English seized one of the great prizes of the Caribbean by driving the Spaniards out of Jamaica. In 1671 Denmark acquired St. Thomas in the Virgin Islands. The West Indies became a pawn in European diplomacy, as well as an important source of revenue. African slavery proved to be invaluable in building this revenue.

Loss of Spanish Control

Shipment upon shipment of slaves arrived for the sole purpose of producing sugar and other staple crops, making the West Indies the crown jewel of Europe's colonial possessions. As one writer of the day put it, the islands were "of immense importance to the grandeur and prosperity of England." If the importation of more slaves meant greater prosperity— and it seemed so to the island planters—they were imported with little regard for anything other than economic considerations. From the slaves' perspective, their humanity was of little value to their masters.

The increase in the islands' black population did not result from the predominance of births over deaths. Indeed, the death rate was extraordinarily high. In one year, 2,656 Africans were born on St. Vincent—and in the same year there were 4,205 deaths. On one plantation in Jamaica, more than half the children died in infancy, and miscarriages ran high. Scholars have attributed the Caribbean's high mortality rates to improper food and the ravages of disease, to the presence of far more male than female slaves, and to the intolerable working conditions of men and women of all ages. Doubtless these factors explain high mortality rates, but at their root was the masters' view that slaves could be obtained more easily through purchase than through natural reproduction.

Absentee landlordism was one important factor in the development of practices destructive of health and life among slaves. Some English landlords pleaded that the climate of the sugar colonies was "so inconvenient for an English constitution that no man will chuse to live there, much less will any man chuse to settle there, without the hopes of at least supporting his family in a more handsome man- **Living Conditions** ner, or saving more money than he can do by any business he can expect in England, or in our plantations upon the continent of America." Efforts were made in Europe and in the islands themselves to bring white settlers to the Caribbean. Some islands required planters to import proportionate numbers of whites for all the slaves they brought in, but many planters found it easier to pay the fines. The islands, then, were deemed to be not a place of residence but merely a source of wealth. A planter living in the Caribbean usually regarded his stay as a temporary sojourn. Soon he would return to his home country and, with the wealth he had amassed, buy an estate and live like a gentleman. Why, then, should he interest himself in schools, churches, and laws that would improve conditions of life for everyone?

Since slaves were constantly being brought to the islands from Africa, overseers found it necessary to develop a practice of "breaking in" the newcomers. In some places, the new arrivals were distributed among the "seasoned," or veteran, slaves, who taught them the ways of New World life. In other places, the newcomers were kept apart and supervised by a special staff of guardians and inspectors who were experienced in breaking in those who might resist adjusting to their new environment. The mortality rate among recent arrivals was exceptionally high—as much as 30 percent in a seasoning period of three or four years. Old and new diseases, change of climate and food, exposure incurred in running away, suicide, and excessive floggings were among the main causes of the high death toll.

In the Caribbean, slaves were sent at daybreak to the farms, where they toiled all day except for a thirty-minute period for breakfast and a two-hour period in the hottest portion of the day, which was frequently the time set aside for doing lighter chores. At harvest, the workday was much longer, sometimes eighteen hours. The driver or overseer did not distinguish between men and women in work requirements or in applying the lash. Investigations made by the British Parliament in 1790–1791 disclosed that pregnant women worked right up to childbirth and received, at most, a month for recovery afterward. Pregnant women were lashed severely when they were unable to keep pace with the other workers. Women who paused in the fields to care for their babies, who they carried on their backs, were lashed with cart whips for idling.

Food was, on the whole, insufficient for slaves. Planters did not often encourage any type of diversified agriculture that would have provided food for the workers. Where this was done at all, slaves were given small plots of land, sometimes far from their houses, which they could cultivate in spare moments. Even on Barbados, where planters had a reputation for providing better for their slaves than did the planters on other islands, slaves were generally ill fed. On one West Indian plantation, each adult slave received a daily allotment of a pint of grain and half a herring (not infrequently rotten). In the famous investigation of 1790–1791, no plantation was found in which a slave received more than nine pints of corn and one pound of salt meat per week. Fish of the least desirable grades was imported from the New England colonies, and a planter who distributed these fish among the slaves acquired a reputation for great benevolence.

On many islands the African population quickly came to outnumber the whites. In 1673 there were 10,000 blacks in Jamaica and 8,000 whites; little more than a century later, in 1775, at the height of the colony's profits from sugar, Jamaica's slave population stood at 200,000, whereas the white population had inched up to only 18,000. The growing preponderance of blacks over whites in the Caribbean promoted the enactment of slave codes of excessive severity. In 1667 the political influence of planters in England made it possible for Parliament to pass an "Act to regulate the Negroes on the British Plantations," in which Africans were referred to as "of wild, barbarous, and savage nature to be controlled only with strict severity." This act prohibited slaves from leaving the plantation without a pass or carrying any weapons. A slave who struck a Christian (a white person) was to be severely whipped, and for the second offense was to be branded on the face with a hot iron. Yet an owner who "accidentally" whipped a slave to death was not subject to fine or imprisonment.

Slave Codes

Other European countries had similar laws, but there seemed to have been considerable variation in enforcement. The French Code Noir, although relatively humane, constituted an agency of great brutality in the hands of some French colonists. When in 1790 the free mulatto Vincent Ogé and his associates were found guilty of conspiring to end discrimination against mulattoes in Saint Domingue (today Haiti), all were cruelly executed—"their arms, thighs, legs, and backbones were broken with clubs on a scaffold." After fastening the men to a wheel, face-up to the blinding sun, the judge ordered: "Here they are to remain for so long as it shall please God to preserve them alive," after which their heads were cut off and exposed on tall poles.

On the everyday level, the overseer's lash proved to be the most common punishment. Whipping functioned as an integral part of the seasoning process. A typical whip was made of plaited cowhide. In the hands of a stern overseer it could draw blood through the breeches of a slave. At times floggings inflicted wounds so deep that a finger could be inserted in them. Another favorite punishment was to suspend the slave from a tree by ropes and tie iron weights around his or her neck and waist. If these punishments would seem to shorten life and thus to reduce efficiency, one notes that Africans were being brought to the Caribbean at an increasing rate until the opening of the nineteenth century. There was consequently no great inclination to preserve life at the expense of "discipline."

Punishment

Planters believed that harsh, cruel treatment prevented uprisings and running away, but, in fact, such treatment had the opposite effect. Almost every island contains a record of some serious revolt against the plantation system, and everywhere there is evidence of constant slave flight. When the English took Jamaica in the middle of the seventeenth century, slave revolts during the 1670s and 1680s led to a large number of runaways, who formed their own separate communities in the mountainous interior of the island.

Slave Revolts

Fugitive slaves who attempted to create such communities were called *Maroons*. They continuously harassed planters by stealing, trading with slaves, and enticing them to escape. These Maroons, largely of Coromantee heritage (Akan-speaking slaves from the Gold Coast), mounted a war against the white planters over a fifteen-year period, from 1725 to 1740. Under the leadership of Colonel Cudjoe, the Maroons fought largely guerrilla-style against British regiments and seamen. They so terrorized whites that Britain had to sign treaties with the Maroons in 1739 and 1740, recognizing four Maroon towns, the largest of

Harsh treatment of slaves
Slaves lived under harsh conditions and were severely punished, as one can see in this picture of their lot on the Caribbean sugar plantations.

which was Trelawney Town, home to 276 ex-slaves, in St. James Parish. Revolt did not end, however, with the establishment and recognition of the Maroon towns.

In 1760 slaves on several plantations in St. Mary's Parish conspired to overthrow white rule and partition Jamaica into African-style principalities. With Britain at war with France and Spain in the Seven Years' War (1756–1763), slaves in Jamaica seized the opportunity to revolt. More than a thousand slaves under the leadership of a slave named Tacky fought for over a year for their freedom. The slaves drew courage from black religious leaders—obeah priests—who used charms, blood, rum, and grave dirt, all purported to ward off bullets. The rebels captured a fort, armed themselves, and killed about sixty whites. Tacky's Rebellion, however, was no match for the superior British forces. As a result, more than five hundred slaves were executed. Many others committed suicide or were deported to other islands. Tacky was decapitated, his head displayed on a pole along a well-traveled road. Indeed Tacky's fate reveals how slave beliefs could be manipulated by masters to deter insurrection.

In the seventeenth and eighteenth centuries, on the islands and the North American and South American mainland, the severed heads of slave insurrectionists were sometimes placed on poles for public display in order to thwart both slave revolts and suicide attempts. According to historian Vincent Brown, such spectacles of atrocity often reflected planters' knowledge and manipulation of African spiritual beliefs. In seventeenth-century Barbados, for example, one particularly cruel slave master, Colonel Walrond, made his slaves look at the lurid sight of the head of a slave who had committed suicide, as warning that suicide would make it impossible for them to return to Africa in the afterlife. Walrond is quoted by a contemporary as telling his slaves: "They were in a main errour, in thinking they went into their own Countreys, after they were dead; for, this man's head was here, as they all were witnesses of; and how was it possible, the body could go without a head."

Slaves in Saint Domingue also fled to freedom and formed their own communities as early as 1620, and the outlawed black community grew so large that the French colonial government recognized it in 1784. Maroons were largely responsible for the Saint Domingue uprisings of 1679, 1691, and 1704. In the middle of the eighteenth century, a native-born African named Macandal, who announced that he was the Black Messiah sent to drive the whites from the island, plotted a revolt to seize control of Saint Domingue. The plot was discovered, however, and the fear-stricken planters hunted down Macandal and executed him.

On the small Danish islands, slave resistance began to intensify in the 1720s, when lack of sufficient food drove many to steal and refuse to work. In 1726, officials executed seventeen of the leading offenders, but this did not quiet the slaves. The situation worsened, and in 1733 the governor of St. Thomas issued a drastic decree providing for severe punishment of slave offenders by burning, whipping, and hanging. The fruits of such seeds of cruelty were murder and bloodshed. Two months later, the blacks on the Danish island of St. John rose up against their masters in a desperate bid for freedom. Blacks carrying wood entered one of the forts of the Danish West India Company and stabbed the guard to death. Another group of slaves attacked six soldiers and killed five of them. Having captured the garrison, the slaves raised a flag and fired three cannon blasts, the signal for a general uprising on all the plantations on the island. With flintlocks, pistols, and cane knives the Africans commenced to kill all the whites they could find. Only after several days of terror was the militia able to bring the uprising under control.

It was the same everywhere—conspiracies, uprisings, revolts, and countless everyday acts of resistance, such as work slowdown, arson, poisoning, theft, and running away. Over time, Africans learned the plantation regimen and performed their duties, albeit reluctantly.

Seasoned Slaves Time also proved that they could adjust to the climate, disease, and food of the New World and create their own cultural meanings and patterns. Although their terms of service on the islands were by no means satisfactory, slaves were regarded as seasoned within three or four years and were shipped out again to the mainland or other islands. Although it is not possible to estimate the number of Africans transported to Cuba from the British islands, for instance, these islands were Cuba's most important source of slaves in the second half of the eighteenth century. Jamaica alone sent more than 10,000 to Cuba in 1756. Of the 90,331 Africans imported into the British West Indies between 1784 and 1787, some 19,964 were re-exported.

When Europeans' attention focused as well on the North American mainland, slaves were exported there from the West Indian islands. The demand for slaves in the mainland colonies steadily increased, since many planters in North America expressed a decided preference for "seasoned" slaves over the more rebellious "saltwater" blacks from Africa. Although the islands could not satisfy either the North or South American demand for slaves, they sent some of their surplus yearly, as the records amply testify. Indeed, re-exportation itself became a lucrative business. Historian Patrick Manning notes that slaves on the Dutch island of Curaçao and the British island of Jamaica were shipped to Cartagena and from there to present-day Colombia, Panama, and Peru. In the colonies, many firms did business directly with traders on the islands.

Slavery in Mainland Latin America

When Cortés launched his conquest of Mexico in 1519, Africans were in all the Spanish island colonies and were being rapidly introduced to the mainland. African slaves were brought to what are now Mexico, Panama, Colombia, Peru, and Argentina, all parts of Spain's vast New World empire, and from these points dispersed in all directions.

By these various routes of commerce more than sixty thousand Africans entered Mexico during the first century of conquest. In the following century, the number was even greater. Unlike the islands, with a more limited capacity to absorb slaves, the Mexican market was a veritable paradise for slave traders. Only the lines of supply directly **Mexico** from Africa or from the Caribbean entrepôts were officially recognized, but seventeenth-century smugglers and interlopers were not averse to bringing Africans from the English, French, or Dutch colonies or from other points when it was profitable to do so. The Jesuit Father Andrés de Rivas estimated that three or four thousand entered Mexico each year. Gonzalo Aguirre Beltrán, a Mexican historian, asserts that a conservative estimate for the seventeenth century would place the figure at 120,000 slaves. In the eighteenth and early nineteenth centuries, importation declined sharply, with no more than twenty thousand slaves entering the Viceroyalty of New Spain (Mexico) during that period. When Baron Alexander von Humboldt, one of the founders of modern geography and a renowned naturalist, visited the country in 1793, he said that there were only ten thousand blacks. Certainly two hundred thousand had entered the country by that time, but the majority had become so thoroughly mixed with the whites and the Indians that perhaps they were no longer recognizable as a distinct element in the population.

During the colonial period, Central America was largely a part of the Viceroyalty of New Spain, and no separate figures are available for the importation of slaves into that region. Africans in Central America formed a small but important segment of the population. They were imported into Guatemala as early as 1524, when **Central America** the Spaniards occupied the land. Although the number of slaves was never as large as ten thousand, they were a considerable source of trouble to the Spanish authorities. Runaways banded together in the woods of Sierra de las Minas in eastern Guatemala and with bows and arrows tormented the countryside for miles around. The entire military force of Guatemala City found it impossible to subdue them. Some slaves, however, became free and developed into substantial citizens. One such freedman became a large landowner and herdsman. Although he made a great profit from dairy products that he sold in Guatemala City, the authorities felt that perhaps some hidden treasure was the real source of his wealth. He periodically denied this, and until his death he exemplified what an African was able to accomplish in Central America.

Perhaps the largest concentration of blacks in continental Spanish America was in the Viceroyalty of New Granada (the modern states of Panama, **South America** Colombia, Venezuela, and Ecuador). New Granada's ports on the Caribbean coast early became entrepôts for black slaves, from which they were distributed to the interior. Panama, Caracas, and Cartagena were among the largest slave markets in the New World. By the time accurate census figures for the area became available, Africans were present in considerable numbers. In the Audiencia of Santa Fé (present-day Panama and Colombia), there were in 1810 approximately 210,000 Africans and mulattoes, slave and free, in a total population of 1.4 million. In the Captaincy General of Caracas (present-day Venezuela), Africans and mulattoes numbered 493,000 in 1810, out of a total population of 900,000. About the same time, the Presidency of Quito (modern Ecuador) had 50,000 Africans and mulattoes in a total population of 600,000.

One of the most striking features of the dispersion of Africans in Spanish America was the presence of large numbers on the Pacific coast in the colonial period. As Fernando Romero pointed out, "the slave trade in the Spanish South American colonies followed well-established lines from north to south and from south to north, the two currents converging on Peru." The Viceroyalty of Peru (roughly present-day Chile and Peru) was, thus, an area of concentration of Africans. Lima not only received a great share of slaves for its own exploitation but also served as a market from which Andean planters and herders purchased black workers, some arriving from Panama and Cartagena, while others came directly from Africa around Cape Horn. In 1622 the Viceroyalty of Peru was reported to have 30,000 Africans in his domain, of whom 2,000 were in Lima.

The Viceroyalty of Peru

When the first trustworthy census was taken in 1791, the population of Peru was approximately 1.25 million. Of that number, 40,000 were black and 135,000 white. The remainder were Indians, mestizos (people of Indian and white ancestry), mulattoes (of black and white parentage), and various combinations of races. Blacks constituted 25 percent of the population of Lima. At about the same time, the population of Chile was approximately 500,000, of whom 30,000 were blacks and mulattoes.

These figures do not tell the entire story of the African population in the Viceroyalty of Peru. Accurate statistics were always difficult to secure, because owners, fearing additional taxation, hid their slaves when census takers came around. The rapid absorption of Africans into the total population, moreover, made it difficult to measure their impact on the area into which they were sent.

The absence of considerable populations of blacks in modern Uruguay and Argentina does not mean that Spain neglected to furnish these colonies with African slaves. Instead, it is suggestive of the remarkable biological and cultural fusion that occurred after the end of the Spanish empire. During colonial times, Montevideo and Buenos Aires were major ports of entry for slave traders. Although no figures are available for the total African population in the Viceroyalty of La Plata, a large population of blacks lived in the estuary of Rio de la Plata, that is, Uruguay and the area around Buenos Aires. A contemporary estimated that in 1805 about 2,500 slaves were being imported annually. In 1803 Montevideo's black population was 1,040 out of a total of 4,726, and there is every indication that Buenos Aires also had a substantial black population. As late as 1827, there were seven African societies in the Argentine capital. The disappearance of Africans in the southern part of South America is a testimony to the absorption of black people by the tremendous migration of Europeans that occurred during the past century.

Uruguay and Argentina

The Portuguese, having been the first Europeans to sense the importance of African slave labor, made extensive use of Indian labor throughout the sixteenth century, although they brought Africans into Brazil as early as 1538, the year of Portugal's first shipment of slaves from the Guinea coast to Bahia. The introduction of sugar cultivation into the colony in 1540 stimulated the importation of Africans, and between 1580 and 1640 (decades

Brazil

during which Spain and Portugal were merged under the rule of the Spanish king), the slave trade to Brazil greatly accelerated. In 1585 there were 14,000 slaves in the colony, out of a total population of 57,000. Toward the end of the century, the Spanish brought in large numbers of slaves from Guinea, São Tomé, Mozambique, and other parts of Africa. Although the tendency was for the slaves to be concentrated in Pernambuco, Bahia, and Rio de Janeiro, they fanned out in various directions as sugar and coffee plantations were developed in fertile interior valleys.

There were five centers of distribution from which slaves were sent into the various parts of Brazil. From Bahia and Sergipe they were taken to plantations and to domestic service on the coast; from Rio de Janeiro and São Paulo they went to cane fields and coffee plantations or were kept to work in the capital; from Minas Gerais most slaves were dispatched to the province's great gold mines, such as those of Goyaz. Slaves from the distribution center at Pernambuco supplied the sugar-producing provinces of the northeast; and slaves from Maranhão and Pará were put to work on the cotton plantations of the north.

In the seventeenth century, it was estimated that more than 44,000 Africans arrived annually in Brazil, and the next century witnessed an average annual importation of no less than 55,000 blacks. In 1798 the first reliable estimate of the population listed 406,000 free blacks and 1,582,000 slaves in a total population of 3,250,000. By 1818 the total population rose to 3,817,000, in which there were 1,930,000 slaves and 585,000 freed blacks. Thus, in that twenty-year period Africans were largely responsible for the increase in the total population. The number of Africans imported into Brazil between 1538 and 1828 is estimated in excess of 4 million, giving Brazil

Slaves at work in Latin American gold mines
After indigenous populations had been depleted by disease and overwork, African slaves were imported to work the gold mines in Latin America. Here slaves mine and wash gold, drying it over a fire before turning it over to the Spanish overseer.

the largest percentage, ranging from 35 percent to 37 percent, of all slaves brought to the New World. Africans were imported in such large numbers that persons of African descent still constitute a considerable share of Brazil's population.

There were three distinct groups of slaves in colonial Brazil: urban slaves, mining slaves, and plantation slaves. Urban slaves worked as servants in the town homes of planters, in shops, at the docks, and in numerous other capacities. Some were skilled in arts and crafts and performed invaluable services that helped improve living conditions in urban areas. Others were kept in homes to render personal service. If there was insufficient work at home, owners sent their slaves out to find work. These freelancers, called *negros de ganho,* often stood on street corners ready to assist shoppers with their packages or went from house to house offering their services to people who did not have servants. Many were able to earn fairly good wages because of their special skills and their ability to read and write. With the opportunity to hire out their own services, some slaves not only made money for their masters but also eventually earned enough to purchase their freedom.

With the discovery of gold in the seventeenth century, large numbers of slaves were employed in Brazilian mines. The simultaneous decline in the sugar economy caused many planters either to sell or to hire out their slaves to prospectors and mine owners, thus moving blacks into the interior near Goyaz, Corumba, and the Mato Grosso plateau. Some were employed in the mines, but others demonstrated their aptitudes and abilities as iron workers, shoemakers, and even architects and sculptors.

The vast majority of Brazilian blacks—perhaps five-sixths—labored on great sugar, coffee, cotton, and cacao plantations. These farm workers fared the worst in Brazil. Their workday ran from sunrise to sunset, and they were supervised for the most part by stewards who, whip in hand, threatened, intimidated, and tortured them into performing their tasks. As in the Spanish colonies, Brazil had laws that sought to protect slaves from cruel masters and overseers, but because such statutes were extremely difficult to enforce, they did not provide much help. The invention of instruments of torture must have taxed the ingenuity of those in command. There was the *tronco*, constructed of wood or iron, by which the slave's ankles were fastened in one place for several days; the *libambo* did the same thing to the arms. *Novenas* and *trezenas* were devices by which a slave was tied, face down, and beaten for nine or thirteen consecutive nights.

There were some mitigating features of Brazilian slavery, however. No law forbade slaves to read and write. The law required that slaves be baptized within one year after arrival in the country, and afterward slaves were expected to attend Mass and confession regularly. The manumission of slaves occurred more frequently in Brazil than in the English colonies, and slaves' ability to earn their own money made it possible for them to purchase their freedom. As in other colonies, however, urban and female slaves were the most likely to be manumitted. Faithful nurses were often set free. Also facilitating manumission was the general custom that a slave mother was to be set free after she had given birth to ten children. Her children, however, continued to be slaves. The clergy urged pious Catholics to manumit their slaves at death if not sooner.

Slaves in South America were a source of profit, but they also made constant trouble. Living in small, crowded huts and subsisting on coarse fare, they frequently became restive

Uprisings and Revolts and sought to break the chains of bondage. In 1550, rioting slaves burned the city of Santa Marta in present-day Colombia. Five years later, an African there, calling himself king, led a violent insurrection that was subdued only with strenuous exertions by the authorities.

One of the most notable bids for freedom in the New World occurred in Brazil in the seventeenth century. Insurgent slaves established the Republic of Palmares in Alagoas (northeastern Brazil), where between 1630 and 1697 they created community institutions based on West Central African models. Fleeing the towns and plantations between Bahia and Pernambuco, runaway slaves penetrated the heavy forests and settled in communities in the Rio Mundahu valley. Despite sieges laid by the Portuguese and the Dutch, who in 1644 were attempting to occupy that part of Brazil, these Maroons held out until Portuguese soldiers entered the walled city of Palmares in 1697. Refusing to surrender, the leader and his principal assistants hurled themselves to certain death from the rocky promontory overlooking the city. No other insurrections, and no Maroon communities established elsewhere in Spanish and Portuguese America, ever equaled Palmares.

Slave Societies in the Americas

Several factors distinguished slave societies in the Americas. One was the relatively small number of Spanish and Portuguese settlers in the Latin colonies, as compared to Britons in the North American colonies. It was not at all unusual for slaves to outnumber by a large margin their Spanish and Portuguese owners and officials, who frequently had little or no family with them and who were, all too often, infrequent visitors to their New World domains. Large black-to-white ratios in Latin America and in the British and French Caribbean certainly aided the many more successful insurrections and Maroon communities there than in North America. Such a disproportionate number of blacks fostered a stronger cultural autonomy among slaves' religious practices, food, the arts, secret societies, and other shared experiences. For example, slave insurrections have been linked to, even emboldened by African-derived religious practices—Islamic influence in Bahia, Santería in Cuba, *myalism* and *obeah* in Jamaica, *vodun* in Haiti, and slaves' use of charms and African folk-beliefs in South Carolina.

Some scholars also argue for the pivotal role of the Catholic Church in shaping the slave experience in Latin America, thus distinguishing it from the slave experience in Protestant British America. Catholic priests often accompanied Spanish and Portuguese explorers and were usually present when settlers arrived, insisting that slaves be **The Catholic Church** baptized as Catholics and instructed in the Catholic faith. Catholic slaves were married in the church, and the banns were published regularly. No laws forbade them to learn to read the catechism, and thus the whole world of reading was opened to them. Moreover, owners were not permitted to work their slaves on Sundays and on the approximately thirty feast days during the year. If the Catholic Church in Latin America had some salutary influence, it clearly did not succeed in eliminating the cruel treatment and horrendous working conditions that led to a considerably higher black death rate than in the United States. Latin-American slave masters too often put profits above church laws.

When it came to marriage across racial lines, religion also played a role in distinguishing the Catholic Latin-American from the Protestant British colonies, although the far greater number of interracial marriages in the Latin countries may be more attributable to the relatively fewer white Spanish and Portuguese women in the New World. Choices for white men in the South American colonies **Intermarriage** were extremely limited. Even so, the stigma attached to whites' intermarrying with blacks in the British colonies was buttressed by strict legal prohibitions that were not countered by the sacred banns of the church. Intimate relationships between British Americans and blacks were generally clandestine and without benefit of clergy. In the British colonies, slaves could not enter into any kind of binding agreement; thus marriage in a legal sense was not an option. Permission of the owner was the only prerequisite for a slave man and woman to share the equivalent of a marital relationship. Although some slaveholders in the British colonies encouraged slaves to be religious and to attend church regularly, the Anglican Church encouraged but did not require owners to tend to the spiritual needs of their slaves, and such encouragement appears to have been rare before the beginning of the nineteenth century. Far from encouraging slaves to learn to read and write, the British colonies generally discouraged it, and some forbade it altogether.

Even aboard ships on the Middle Passage, and thus even before they arrived in the New World, black slaves began to fashion new words, trying to articulate new relationships among themselves and to give meaning to their condition. Once in the New World, they forged new traditions of belief and practice from their interactions among themselves—as African-born and as Creoles (persons born in the Americas)—and with the European and native populations they encountered. Black culture took root in the Atlantic world as a mosaic of cultures that continuously evolved through adaptation and transformation. African religious beliefs and social patterns responded and adapted to the demands of slave life and work.

At one end of the spectrum, African retentions remained strong enough to manipulate and reinterpret Christian symbols, saints, and rituals into identifiable African forms; this was especially true where large concentrations of African ethnic groups were brought as slaves to particular New World locations. At the other end of the spectrum, acculturation produced such a mixture of cultural beliefs that no patterns of African beliefs are clearly distinguishable from the similar and complementary beliefs in religious "signs and wonders" that early European settlers or Indians shared. Informed by individual memory and ethnic group history, along with African belief systems, slaves created cultures that differed from one another, as well as cultures that individually changed with time, with shifts in the ethnic make-up of the slave population, with changes in dominance of various rival European imperial powers, and with geographic region. Yet together these myriad slave cultures shaped the black diaspora.

Establishing North American Slavery

Imperial Claims to North America

Before Permanent Bondage

The Legalization of Slavery

New Amsterdam
This engraving on copper is probably the second oldest extant view of New Amsterdam; the figures in the foreground appear in several engravings depicting different parts of the New World.

Literally bound for the New World, chained and shackled Africans crossed the Atlantic as unwilling participants in what would be the largest intercontinental migration until the late nineteenth century. They traveled on slave ships, crowded together in densely packed configurations—the purchased items of the European nations whose flags flew proudly above their armed commercial fortresses along the African coast. The slaves differed by ethnic group, by religion, and by language when they set foot on the shores of North America. They were entering a strange land where the European powers had already staked their claims to colonies and were vying—through negotiation and war with one another and with the native populations—to increase their territorial control.

In the early seventeenth century, the economic and social system of racial slavery had yet to be firmly established in the New World. The North American mainland was too vast and its wilderness too great to achieve any certainty about how blacks might be defined in contrast to that of the white laborers who arrived under the indenture system. Blacks and whites toiled in similar capacities, often working together cutting trees, planting crops, and performing a variety of servant roles.

Throughout much of the sixteenth century and into the eighteenth, North American slavery evolved unevenly—by time, by region, and by European colonizer. African people endured a new but hardly monolithic black experience. They built houses, grew tobacco, rice, and sugar, and trapped fur-bearing animals. They worked in homes and on seaport docks. Slaves experienced religious conversions, but in many cases they also adapted their African religious beliefs to the Catholic, Anglican, Methodist, Baptist, and Dutch Reformed churches of which they became a part. Slaves eventually lost their African names, after being forced by their white masters to take on European names. In the mid-Atlantic colony of New Netherland in the 1650s, slave surnames included Schuyler and Van Wagener. Even earlier in Florida, slaves were called Estevan and Menendez. The Comingtee plantation in eighteenth-century South Carolina recorded the names Ebo Sylvia and Angola Ame, and in New Orleans a slave answered to the name Louis Congo. As these names themselves suggest, slaves spoke English, Dutch, Spanish, French, and a number of pidgin languages.

African acculturation to the ways of North American slavery occurred for slave communities and individual slaves in response to diverse external conditions. Many lived under conditions of harsh labor, disease, malnutrition, and violence that made it difficult, if not impossible, to endure and have children. In this formative period of slavery, however, newly imported Africans readily replenished the slave population. Above all, the evolution of slavery represented black resistance to customs and laws that defined black humanity as chattel property.

Imperial Claims to North America

Eight decades before the English founded the Virginia colony at Jamestown in 1607, people of African descent took part in the settlement of what would later become the United States of America. As early as the 1520s, blacks played an important role in Spain's efforts to gain a foothold in North America. This early black participation in America's colonization resulted from Spain's dominant role in the slave trade from Africa to the Western Hemisphere and also from the presence of individual slaves and free blacks in the parties of Spanish explorers, conquistadors, and settlers who laid claim to "La Florida"—the name that Spain gave to the massive area encompassing what we know today as Florida, South Carolina, and Georgia.

Slaves formed part of the mission led by Lucas Vasquez de Ayllón, who in 1526 brought 200 Spanish settlers from Santo Domingo, on the island of Hispaniola (today divided between Haiti and the Dominican Republic), to form a colony in North America. They established San Miguel de Gualdape, which is believed to have been located at what is now Sapelo Sound in Georgia. The colony **Early Settlements** was short-lived, however. After two months of hunger, disease, and slave rebellion, the surviving white population returned to the Caribbean—without their slaves. Historian Michael Gannon argues that those Africans who survived and stayed behind became "the first Old World settlers in what is now the United States."

In 1528, Africans were part of the expedition led by Pánfilo de Narváez to settle the area near present-day Tampa Bay, but this effort also failed tragically. The black slave Estevan (his name was also spelled Esteban) was one of only four survivors. Good fortune came finally to the Spanish in 1565, when they established St. Augustine, the oldest of the successful European settlements in North America. Blacks constituted part of St. Augustine's population, and they also provided much of the muscle needed to build the new outpost. Spain intended St. Augustine to be a strategic garrison, protecting its ships and its commercial and territorial interests from European rivals, who at first were principally the Dutch and the French and later also included the English.

North American slavery emerged at the height of the European powers' rivalries and struggles for colonies, trade, and key ports. Decisions made in the metropoles (mother countries) affected the nature of their respective slave systems, as well as the lived experiences of the many black peoples within the colonizing nations' particular spheres of authority. For example, in 1655 the Dutch successfully challenged Swedish control of the Delaware Valley, ending Sweden's imperial claim on the North American continent. The English and the Dutch waged war against each other in the 1650s and 1660s. These two Anglo-Dutch Wars coincided partly with the Restoration—the Stuart kings' return to the English throne in 1660. (Stuart rule had been interrupted by the English Revolution of 1640–1660, during which a short-lived republican government was in power.) Once back in power, the Stuart monarchy set out to realize a more systematic role for England's North American colonies in the European states' economic and military contests for empire.

The most immediate impact of the Restoration was the founding of four new colonies after 1660, as well as the seizure from the Dutch of New Netherland, which was renamed New York, in 1664. The new colonies of Carolina (chartered in 1663), New Jersey (1664), Pennsylvania (1681), and Delaware (1682, as the "Three Lower Counties"), were all products of colonizing decisions made by the English Crown. The advent of these settlements changed the map of early America. All these colonies became wedded to slavery, resulting in the importation of many thousands of African-descended people to mainland North America.

North American colonies, 1650

French
English
Dutch
Swedish
Spanish

Window in Time

A Spanish Explorer on the Slave Estevan's Role in the Settlement of North America

As long as we were with these [Indians] we traveled all day without eating until night, and we ate so little that they were astonished to see it. They never suspected us of being tired and to tell the truth we were so accustomed to hardship that we did not feel it either. Among them we had great authority and gravity and in order to preserve this [power] we talked to them few times. The black [was the one who] always spoke to them; he would inform himself about the trails we wanted to follow and the towns there were [ahead of us] and the things we wanted to know.

We passed through a great number and diversity of languages; among all of these [Indians] God our Lord favored us, because they always understood us and we understood them. And thus we asked and they would answer by means of signs if they would speak our tongue and we theirs, because although we knew six languages not everywhere could we take advantage of them because we found more than a thousand differences.

Krieger, Alex D., and Margery H., *We Came Naked and Barefoot: The Journey of Cabeza De Vaca across North America*, Texas Archaeology and Ethnohistory Series. Austin: University of Texas Press, 2002.

Most slaves brought to the North American colonies in the early years of settlement did not come on slave ships directly from Africa. Rather, ships brought African slaves first to the Caribbean islands or the larger Atlantic rim, where they were "seasoned"—broken into the harsh regime of slavery. Slaves bore Spanish and Portuguese names, and it was not uncommon for some to be multilingual, speaking African, European, and Native American languages. Over time, larger numbers of slaves would be labeled *Creoles*, which meant "born in the New World." However, the ability of the slave population to increase from natural reproduction, as opposed to increasing by importation alone, did not occur until the eighteenth century.

North American slavery assumed different forms, defined by the founding circumstances and by the laws of the different European metropoles, as well as by fluctuations in colonial jurisdictions during the era of New World conquest. In 1650, for example, slaves were brought to Spanish Florida, to Dutch New Netherland, to New Sweden, and to English colonies as different from one another as planter-led Virginia and clergy-led Massachusetts. A century later, in 1750, Great Britain controlled thirteen colonies, including New York (the former New Netherland) and New Jersey (once New Sweden), but several thousand blacks continued to live under French and Spanish rule in Louisiana and Florida, respectively.

Forms of North American Slavery

Although it is true that all the colonies in North America wrote laws and statutes that prescribed inferior status for blacks, for much of the seventeenth century, and especially before the consolidation of plantation agriculture, the character of servitude displayed a noticeable variation and flexibility.

Before Permanent Bondage

In 1619 twenty Africans were put ashore and sold in Jamestown by the captain of a Dutch frigate. Recent scholarship indicates that the captain acquired his human cargo on the high seas, as was common at the time, by seizing the captive Africans from a Portuguese slave ship. Upon entering Jamestown, the twenty blacks were not initially recognized as slaves in the legal sense of being held in perpetual, hereditary bondage. Neither England nor Virginia as yet had laws that defined slaves as chattel—as pieces of property that, like horses and cattle, could be sold, bartered, or bequeathed in a will. Blacks were listed as servants in the census counts of 1623 and 1624, and they found themselves in a society in which many whites were also "unfree."

Historians estimate that between 70 percent and 85 percent of the white colonists who arrived in the seventeenth-century Chesapeake colonies (Virginia and Maryland) came under "indentures," which meant that they owed several years of service to whoever bought their time in labor, in exchange for free passage to America. Indentured servants worked alongside African slaves and often received treatment that was just as harsh; many did not live long enough to receive their freedom. The majority of the white servants were men aged eighteen to twenty-two who expected, at the end of their indentures, to be given freedom and payment in the form of their own land to farm. As late as 1651, some blacks whose period of service had expired were assigned land in much the same way that it was granted to former white servants.

During its first half century, Virginia did not have strict criteria for distinguishing slaves from servants, and the records reveal a number of freed blacks, as well as slaves who functioned as though they were free. Some, such as Anthony Johnson and Francis Payne, had been slaves of the Portuguese in the Americas. At the time of John-son's arrival in Jamestown on a Dutch ship in 1621 and of Payne's **Early Virginia** arrival some years later, both were listed only by the names Antonio and Francisco. Both are assumed to have been of Angolan descent. Once in Virginia, they worked for white planters and eventually gained their freedom, becoming landowners and even slaveholders. Assimilating to English culture, they adopted Anglicized names. In 1655 Anthony Johnson sued his white neighbor for the return of a runaway slave and won his court case. By that time, he was the owner of several hundred acres on Virginia's Eastern Shore—which he named "Angola."

Francis Payne's story also illustrates the flexible terms of servitude in early Virginia. In 1637 he was purchased as a slave by Philip Taylor, and upon Taylor's death in 1646 Payne was valued at 2,400 pounds of tobacco. (Tobacco functioned as currency in the seventeenth-century Chesapeake colonies.) By 1648 Taylor's widow had remarried and moved with her new husband to Maryland, but she left Payne on the Virginia plantation in charge of tobacco production. She allowed him to keep a portion of the profit from the sale of the tobacco in order to buy his freedom. In exchange for his freedom, Payne was required to purchase for his mistress three male servants with six or seven years to serve. He immediately went to work to secure the necessary funds to obtain the servants, and he appears to have met the terms of the agreement in 1651.

It would take another five years, though, before Payne became legally free. In the interim years, he successfully sued a white Marylander for money owed him. In 1656 his owner, once again a widow, declared in a number of documents that Francis Payne had fully satisfied his part of their original bargain and that the "aforesaid Payne shall be discharged from all incumbrance of servitude (his child) or any person or persons that doth belong to the said Payne his estate." At the time of Francis Payne's death in 1673, he was a landholder married to an English woman. His will bequeathed his "worldly estate" to her. They had no children.

Despite these ambiguities, social distinctions in everyday practices and institutional form differentiated white servants from persons of African descent. For example, both Virginia and Maryland census records list no surname for black servants, as opposed to white ones. The courts tended to treat the two differently, as in a Virginia case in 1640, when three runaway servants, two white and one black, were captured. The court ordered the white servants to serve their master for one additional year. The black servant was ordered "to serve his said master or his assigns for the time of his natural life here or elsewhere." Even Anthony Johnson worked considerably longer than was typical of white indentured servants before gaining his freedom, since his servitude lasted about twenty years, compared to the normal seven-year period of white indentures.

There were certainly noteworthy exceptions, but by the 1640s racial distinctions were beginning to be codified, including a tax law in 1643 that appears to be Virginia's first statute calling for racial differentiation. It is interesting that this law was premised on the distinction between English and African women and thus, according to historian Kathleen Brown, provided a racial basis for "very different expectations for their future roles in the colony." The slave status of Africans and American-born blacks had yet to be fully elaborated and defined at this time, but the legal climate grew more severe with each passing decade.

In the Dutch colony of New Netherland, slavery developed in a different social and cultural milieu—one in which access to freedom was more available. In 1624 the Dutch West India Company founded the colony as a strategic imperial beachhead and commercial outpost. Two years later, in 1626, the company introduced slaves into its trading port, New Amsterdam (today, New York City), after failing to lure sufficient numbers of white indentured servants for agricultural and other labor. Slaves brought to New

New Netherland

Runaway slave advertisement

From the beginning to the end of slavery, people in bondage continued to seek freedom. This advertisement for Cyrus is typical of owners' efforts to recover their chattel.

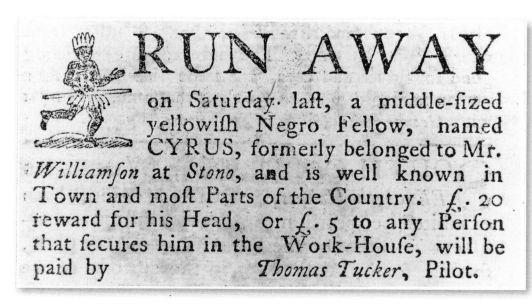

RUN AWAY on Saturday last, a middle-sized yellowish Negro Fellow, named CYRUS, formerly belonged to Mr. *Williamson* at *Stono*, and is well known in Town and most Parts of the Country. £. 20 reward for his Head, or £. 5 to any Person that secures him in the Work-House, will be paid by *Thomas Tucker*, Pilot.

Amsterdam came from the Caribbean, especially the Dutch colonies of Curaçao and St. Eustacia, but the Portuguese names of some suggest that many slaves were shipped directly from Portuguese-controlled slave-trading areas in Africa, such as Angola. In 1637 the Dutch captured key Portuguese ports in Africa, specifically Elmina in 1637 and Axim in 1641. The Dutch also held Angola between 1641 and 1649 and thus claimed critical African ports from which they shipped Africans to the New World.

In New Netherland, Dutch legal codes did not establish a permanently fixed status of racial slavery, although in practice increasing numbers of blacks experienced a lifetime of servitude. Throughout Dutch rule, blacks participated broadly in colonial society. They spoke Dutch, served in the militia, worshipped and baptized their children in the Dutch Reformed Church, and sought legal redress in the Dutch courts. Unlike English Virginia, Dutch New Netherland legally sanctioned slave marriage, and the wedding ceremonies of dozens of slave couples were held in the Dutch Reformed Church soon after slavery was introduced into the colony. Church records typically named the father, rather than the owner, of newly baptized slave children, suggesting the strength of family ties.

Baptism of slaves
Because Christian slaves were regarded as more obedient and adjusted, they were recruited into the church.

Manumission was not an uncommon reward for long or meritorious service, although it came with painful qualifications. The Dutch plan of "half-freedom" required the recently freed to pay annual dues to the Dutch West India Company, and it denied their children free status. As the Dutch settlement stepped up its agricultural production in the Hudson River valley, slave conditions worsened and manumissions decreased. At the same time, however, a free black community of farmers, merchants, and artisans took root in New Amsterdam. About 20 percent of New Amsterdam was black when the English seized the colony. Historian Ira Berlin notes that "by 1664, at the time of the English conquest, about one black person in five had achieved freedom in New Amsterdam, a proportion never equaled throughout the history of slavery in the American South."

Once under English rule, the colony's name was changed to New York in honor of the Duke of York, the younger brother of King Charles II. The status of slaves and free blacks would change significantly, but not immediately. As late as 1680, most blacks continued to speak Dutch and had Dutch surnames. They continued to exercise various legal rights—as free men, indentured servants, slaves, or partners with Dutch men or women in the system of "half freedom." The English would begin to curtail blacks' rights in the 1680s. At that time, options for manumission also began to disappear, with slaveholders discouraged from freeing their slaves by the heavy fines that the colony imposed.

Blacks in the Massachusetts Bay Colony encountered an English culture very different from that of Virginia. Founded in 1630, Massachusetts Bay was settled by Puritans who intended their "City upon a Hill" to serve as a conspicuous example of godliness in an ungodly world. With a Protestant ethic of piety and strong commercial interests, Massachusetts Bay stood poised to usurp from the Dutch the dominant mercantile role, including the slave trade, throughout colonial Atlantic waters. In 1638 the first black slaves arrived in the colony, when a slave ship under an enterprising captain named Pierce landed at Salem, Massachusetts. The Puritan colony of Massachusetts Bay was, in fact, the first of the English colonies to give legal sanction to slavery. A 1641 law recognized that human bondage was permissible for "lawful captives taken in just warres, and such strangers as willingly sell themselves or are sold to us." It is noteworthy that the 1641 statute was not racially or ethnically specific, and indeed Massachusetts Bay had already sentenced white men to slavery and had sold into Caribbean bondage Native Americans who were captured during the Pequot War in 1636 and 1637.

Massachusetts Bay

Unlike the migration of large numbers of single men and boys to early Virginia, the Puritans who crossed the Atlantic to Massachusetts Bay came in family groups, bringing with them religious beliefs and social relations that informed their understanding of domestic relations as well as servitude. The Puritan social structure included servants, who were incorporated into the families they served as dependents—not unlike wives, children, and apprentices, who were also considered the dependents of male heads of households. The master of the household supervised and instructed his servants in reading and understanding the Bible. After 1638 dependent servants also included blacks from Africa and the Caribbean. They were expected to adapt to the New England way, which also accorded certain rights. The same 1641 law that sanctioned slavery also spoke of "liberties and Christian usages" that affected enslaved persons.

The extent of these liberties is evident in the case of Angola and his wife Elizabeth. Angola, probably born in the 1630s, arrived in Massachusetts Bay via Bermuda. Angola's master, Robert Keayne, arranged for him to be married to Elizabeth, the African slave of Edward and Abigail Hutchinson. Their marriage in 1654 was the first recorded marriage of two Africans in Boston. After their marriage, Elizabeth continued to reside with her mistress. Upon Keayne's death, his will freed neither his African nor his Scottish servants. Angola was eventually permitted by Keayne's widow to purchase his freedom, after which he and Elizabeth started a family. However, Elizabeth appears to have remained enslaved. Interestingly, their children were not born slaves. They did not follow the condition of their mother, although in this case the children's freedom simply resulted from the benefit of timing. After 1670 in Massachusetts Bay slave status became hereditary.

The Legalization of Slavery

Beginning in the 1660s, and especially with England's growing power on the North American continent, slave codes and other racial restrictions hardened as colonial leaders began to fashion legal structures designed to lock blacks irrevocably into chattel slavery. Throughout the seventeenth century and well into the eighteenth, ever more comprehensive legal codes proscribed mobility, manumission, and interracial mixing.

The codification of slave laws justified the racial basis for slavery, thus removing initial religious reasons that had condoned the enslavement of "infidels" and "heathens." The laws protected slave masters' interests in the wake of blacks' growing conversion to Christianity, and they further protected the interests of slave masters by declaring that slave status

Window in Time

Slave Code in the Virginia Colony

[*A Virginia Law of 1669*]...if any slave resist his master (or other by his master's order correcting him) and by the extremity of coercion could chance to die, that his death shall not be accounted felony, but the master (or that other person &c.) be acquitted from molestation, since it cannot be presumed that prepensed malice (which alone makes murder a felony) should induce any man to destroy his own estate.

John Codman Hurd, *The Law of Freedom and Bondage.* New York: n.p. 1858, 232.

followed the status of the mother. The trend was steadily moving in the direction of a heredi-tary slave status for all blacks and free status for all whites. Colonial laws set the foundation for these markedly dissimilar social positions, although the English colonies themselves var-ied with regard to the ways and the degree that the two races would be dissimilar. Equally important were the commonalities, as well as the significant differences, in the slave laws of the English, French, and Spanish colonies.

In Virginia, the legalization of slavery occurred in response to growing perceptions of a labor shortage. The growing disinclination on the part of whites toward the enslavement of American Indians, falling English birth rates in the 1660s, a high death rate owing to diseases before 1640, and declining numbers of English men and women willing to inden-ture themselves as servants created tremendous labor needs, at a time **Virginia Slave Codes** when Virginia landowners needed more workers to clear forests and cultivate larger and better tobacco crops. As a result, Virginia began to structure a new legal code that sanctioned a per-petual slave condition and the inferior position of all people of African descent.

In 1662 a Virginia law held that the free or slave status of children born in the colony would depend on the condition of their mother—that is, a slave mother's children would be slaves. Protecting further the institution of slavery, a law in 1667 removed all opportunity for gaining freedom on religious grounds, asserting that "the conferring of baptisme doth not alter the condition of the person as to his bondage or freedome." Similarly, neighboring Maryland established slavery by law in 1663, but with a more drastic provision that sought to impose slave status on all blacks born in the colony regardless of the status of their mothers. In 1664 Maryland outlawed marriage between slaves and "freeborne English women." Not until 1681 did Maryland fall in line with the established practices of the other English colonies, declaring that black children born of white women and those born of free black women would be free.

An uprising in Virginia known as Bacon's Rebellion in 1676 precipitated a flurry of ever more stringent slave laws in the colony over the next twenty years. Nathaniel Bacon, a young English planter recently arrived in Virginia, organized and led the uprising, accusing colonial officials of failing to protect settlers from Indian raids. A group of black slaves, white inden-tured servants, and small farmers joined Bacon in rebelling against a treaty that Virginia's

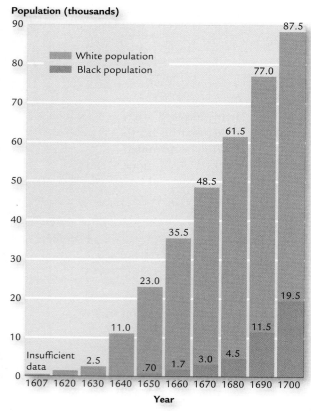

Population (thousands)

Legend:
- White population
- Black population

Values shown:
- 1607: Insufficient data
- 1620: 2.5
- 1630: 11.0 / .70
- 1640: 23.0 / 1.7
- 1650: 35.5 / 3.0
- 1660: 48.5 / 4.5
- 1670: 61.5
- 1680: 77.0 / 11.5
- 1690: 87.5 / 19.5
- 1700

Year

White and Black populations in the British Colonies, 1607–1700

royal governor, Sir William Berkeley, signed with various native peoples, principally the Doeg and the Susquehannocks. White and black rebels' desire for land served to ignite their initial violence against the Indians, as well as much of their frustration and hostility toward the colonial government. Blacks played a prominent role in the rebellion. Historian Philip Morgan notes that "one of the last groups to surrender was a mixed band of eighty blacks and twenty white servants." Black slaves and white servants had often run away together, and to Virginia's ruling authorities Bacon's Rebellion portended an even more troubling alliance of blacks and poor whites. The colonial government therefore moved to outlaw interracial contacts of all sorts.

In the last two decades of the seventeenth century, Virginia began to enact harsher statutes to reinforce slavery and the inferiority of blacks. Punitive measures were designed to break even the most rebellious blacks in the colony. For offenses such as robbing a house or a store, slaves were to be whipped with sixty lashes and locked in the pillory, where their ears were to be cut off. Acts of insolence or associating with whites and free blacks called for whipping, branding, or maiming. The sheriffs, the courts, and even nonslaveholding whites were all required by law to police the slave population.

The new laws coincided with the unprecedented growth in the number of slaves in Virginia. Black population growth outstripped that of whites. In 1650 the colony's 1,700 blacks represented 3 percent of the colony's population; in 1690 Virginia's 11,500 blacks had become 15 percent of the whole population. In addition, the slave population itself went through an important cultural shift. In 1679 slaves began to arrive directly from Africa in ever growing numbers, such that by 1710 African-born persons formed 73 percent of the total slave population. Although Virginians greatly appreciated the importance of slave labor in the development of the colony, they soon became apprehensive about the large numbers of blacks living among whites. Already whites and blacks were mixing, and a mulatto population was emerging. There were, moreover, persistent rumors of rebellious conspiracies, and many whites feared for their lives.

The first comprehensive laws were passed in 1680 and 1682 to discipline a slave population that white Virginians considered increasingly alien and resistant to slavery. The 1680 Virginia law borrowed heavily from English practices in the Caribbean and served as the model for other British colonies in North America. It forbade to slaves freedom of assembly, the right to carry weapons, and freedom of movement without a certificate from a master. Reflecting whites' fear that slaves were plotting insurrections, the 1682 act forbade any plantation owner from permitting a slave not owned by him to remain on his property for more than four hours. This law also required church wardens to read the 1680 and 1682 slave code twice a year during worship service, on pain of forfeiting 600 pounds of tobacco. (Clergy were paid in tobacco, not in money.) Successive laws reinforced the inferiority of blacks as a group. For example, the 1691 statute prohibited interracial marriage or sexual relationships, seeking to prevent "that abominable mixture and spurious issue…by Negroes, mulattoes and Indians intermarrying with English or other white women."

In this harsher social climate, the black population grew more restive. In 1687, while a funeral was taking place, a group of slaves in Virginia's Northern Neck region planned an uprising, but the plot was discovered before it could be carried out. Rumors continued, and various plots were uncovered—and where there were no plots there was general disobedience and lawlessness. By 1694 Virginia slaves had become so ungovernable that Governor Edmund Andros called for a more elaborate slave code. In addition, Virginia lawmakers began to limit the rights of free blacks, undermining their social status and branding them as racial inferiors. In 1723 the governor of Virginia left no doubt that such laws were to "make the free-Negroes sensible that a distinction ought to be made between their offspring and the Descendants of an Englishman, with whom they never were to be Accounted Equal."

In New York, the transition from Dutch to English practices at first moved rather slowly; not until 1702, almost forty years after the end of Dutch rule, did New York enact a comprehensive slave law, called the "Act for Regulateing [sic] of Slaves." In 1705 the New York colonial legislature enacted yet another law providing that slaves caught traveling forty miles north of Albany—that is, presumably trying to get to French-ruled Canada—were to be executed upon the oath of two credible witnesses. In 1706 the legislature gave further sanction to slavery by affirming that the baptism of a slave did not provide grounds for a claim to freedom and that the status of a child followed its mother. The law also affirmed that a slave could not be a competent witness in a case involving a white or a black freeman.

New York Slave Codes

In 1712 slave unrest in New York City flared into a fully organized insurrection, in which twenty-three slaves armed with guns and knives met in an orchard and set fire to a slaveholder's house. During the melee that followed, nine whites were killed and six were injured. In the ensuing trial of the accused blacks, twenty-one were found guilty and executed. Whites' hysteria after the riot resulted in a more comprehensive law, passed on December 10, 1712, that made arson punishable by death, restricted slave manumissions, and required that "no Negro, Indian or mulatto, that shall hereafter be made free, shall enjoy, hold or possess any houses, lands, tenements or Hereditaments within this colony."

A series of fires in 1741 set off the rumor that blacks and poor whites were conspiring to subvert law and order in New York City and seize control of the government. After the city offered generous rewards for the apprehension of the conspirators, a white indentured servant named Mary Burton implicated almost two hundred persons, black and white alike, in the plot. Her later accusations against leading white citizens and their slaves caused the justices to suspend the trials. Most whites at the time did not doubt her veracity as to the actual existence of a conspiracy, although historians today debate this point. Notwithstanding whether the plot was real or unreal, at least one hundred fifty blacks were accused, eighteen of whom were hanged, thirteen burned alive, and seventy banished from the city. Four whites, including two women, were hanged. No further serious outbursts took place during the colonial period.

In the late seventeenth century, New England began to pass laws that overturned some of the liberties that blacks had previously enjoyed. In 1670 Massachusetts enacted a law providing that the children of slaves could be sold into bondage, and ten years later it began to enact measures restricting the travel of blacks. In 1660 Connecticut barred blacks from military service, and in 1690 it restrained

New England's Laws

A LIST of White Persons taken into Custody on Account of the Conspiracy. 1741.

Names of Persons.	Occupations.	When committed.	Arraigned.	Convicted.	Confessed.	Executed.	Discharged.
Margaret Kerry, alias Salingburgh.		4 March.	2 & 4 June, for receiving stolen Goods.	4 June,		12 June.	
John Hughson,	Shoemaker and Alehouse keeper.	18 April:					
Sarah Hughson, Wife to John Hughson,		18 April.					
Sarah Hughson, the Daughter.		6 May.			8 July,		Pardoned.
5 John Romme,	Shoemaker, and Alehouse-keeper.	18 May.					Discharged on Security for his departing the Province.
Elizabeth Romme, his Wife.		8 May.					
Peter Connolly,	Soldier.	23 June.					31 August.
John Ury,	A Priest.	24 June.	15 & 22 July	29 July		29 August	
Edward Kelly,	Soldier.	25 June.					31 August.
10 William Kane,	Soldier.	4 July.			5 July,		December. Enlisted for (West-Indies.
John Coffin,	Pedlar.	6 July.					
Edward Murphey,	Soldier.	8 July.					
Andrew Ryan,	Soldier.	9 July.					31 August.
David Johnson,	Hat-maker.	9 July.					
15 John Corry,	Dancing-Master	13 July.					
Thomas Hughson,	Yeoman,						
Nathaniel, Walter, William, 20 Richard, } Thomas Hughson's Sons.	Yeomen,	12 and 13 June.					Pardoned, on Condition of departing the Province.
Corker, Fagan, Plummer, } mentioned in Kane's Evidence in Ury's Trial, and in his Examinations, never found.							

The 1741 New York City Conspiracy List

them from going beyond the limits of the town without a pass.

Black slaves in New England were allowed to marry in civil and religious ceremony after the late seventeenth century. However, their marriages were generally hampered, since in many instances husbands and wives were owned by different masters and thus lived apart. Such separate ownership had a decidedly negative impact on slave families, causing lower than average rates of natural increase. New England slave families also suffered because of the frequent refusal of masters, on economic grounds, to allow enslaved parents to keep their children. As a Boston observer explained to a correspondent in the late eighteenth century: "Negro children were reckoned an encumbrance in a family; and when weaned, were given away like puppies. They have been publickly advertised in the newspapers 'to be given away.'" More accurately, slave children were put up for sale, as is evident in the numerous slave advertisements in Massachusetts newspapers.

Because the number of slaves in New England remained small throughout the colonial period, there was less fear of insurrections than in other colonies. Nevertheless, many slaves resisted by running away. Others attacked their masters and even murdered them. Still others plotted to rebel. In 1658 some blacks and Indians in Hartford, Connecticut, decided to make a bid for their freedom by destroying several houses of their masters. An outbreak of arson in Boston in 1723 caused a panic and subsequently a proclamation from Lieutenant Governor William Dummer denouncing the acts of "villainous and desperate Negroes or other dissolute people." As a result, Boston's selectmen passed laws to regulate the movement of slaves, free blacks, Native Americans, and mulattoes. One of the laws specifically prohibited any member of these groups from being on the streets when fires broke out in the city. If caught outside his master's home on such an occasion, that person would be whipped and jailed for three days in the Boston House of Correction.

Overall, however, slaves in New England had more rights than slaves in the other British colonies. Slaves could testify in court, sue, and petition for their freedom. New England blacks also enjoyed greater freedom to associate with one another and with Indians and white servants. Thus the houses of some free blacks became meeting places for dancing, playing games, and telling stories. Such slaves as Lucy Terry of Deerfield, Massachusetts, and Senegambia of Narragansett, Rhode Island, had a seemingly limitless store of tales about Africa.

In the colony of Carolina (South Carolina and North Carolina were separated only in 1729), permanent servitude was etched in law even before actual settlement began. In 1663, King Charles II granted to a group of his most loyal courtiers the huge tract area of land that was to become Carolina colony. Not intending to colonize the American wilderness themselves, the proprietors encouraged the **The Carolinas** emigration of planters and their slaves from the overcrowded British plantation colony of Barbados, offering white settlers twenty acres for every black male slave and ten acres for every black female slave they brought into the colony in the first year. Land scarcity, crop failures, disease, and hurricanes were driving English settlers out of Barbados. Not until 1670, however, did settlers start arriving in Carolina, most of them white immigrants from Barbados and their slaves.

Well before settlement in 1670, the proprietors had hired John Locke to write the founding legal document for the colony. Drafted in 1663—thus after the English had begun the codification of the laws of slavery in Massachusetts and Virginia—Locke's *Fundamental Constitutions* decreed that Christian conversion would not affect slave status and further stated that "every freeman of Carolina shall have absolute power and authority over his negro slaves, of what opinion or religion soever." Although the document was never fully enacted as the governing law of the colony, this particular pronouncement with regard to slavery was observed.

In the early years of settlement, the Carolina colony's frontier conditions tended to mitigate white colonists' absolute power over their slaves. Slaves did an array of jobs, often working alongside their masters, indentured whites, and captive Indians. They cut down trees and cleared fields, collected pitch and turpentine for the trade in naval stores, and herded cattle. African knowledge of canoe construction and river navigation made slaves valuable to the colony's fishing and fur trade with the Indians. However, the Carolina colony did not go through a comparable period of legal ambiguity over the question of permanent and hereditary bondage. Clearly, black slaves were not the only form of unfree labor in the early colony, but in Carolina they were, from the very beginning, the only group deemed to be chattel and held for unlimited terms.

As in other North American colonies, in Carolina the growth of the black population led to the enactment of a series of laws aimed at controlling the activities of slaves. In the 1690s

Window in Time

The Desire for Slaves in Colonial South Carolina, 1682

But a rational man will certainly inquire, *when I have land, what shall I doe with it?* What comoditys shall I be able to produce that will yield me money in other countrys that I may be inabled to buy Negro slaves (without which a Planter can never do any great matter) and [[check]]puchase other things for my pleasure and convenience, that Carolina doth not produce.

Samuel Wilson, "An Account of the Province of Carolina" (1682), in Alexander S. Salley, ed., *Narratives of Early Carolina, 1650–1708*. New York: Charles Scribner's Sons, 1911, p. 174. Emphasis added.

the introduction of plantation agriculture, especially rice cultivation, led to a seemingly insatiable demand for slaves, which, in turn, quickly produced a majority-black population. Slave imports doubled, from three thousand in the decade 1700–1710 to six thousand between 1720 and 1730. An act in 1712 ominously directed that it "shall always be presumed that every Negro…is a slave" until proven otherwise. An act in 1722 authorized slave patrols to search blacks for guns, swords, and other weapons and to arrest them, if they were away from their home plantation and unable to produce a permit from their master less than one month old. Slave patrols (on which white citizens were required to serve) also had the authority to whip blacks deemed to be dangerous to the peace. Punishments for offenses by slaves were summary and severe. Carolinians had not established their controls too soon, for as early as 1711 rumors became widespread that blacks were growing unruly. In 1720 several slaves were burned alive and others were banished, because they were implicated in a revolt near Charleston. Subsequent years saw other revolts or rumors of revolts, the largest of which was the Stono Rebellion in 1739.

After the enactment of Carolina's first comprehensive slave code in 1696, law enforcement throughout the eighteenth century generally took place through a "slave court." This separate judicial system was not unique to South Carolina. In Pennsylvania between 1700 and 1780,

Slave Courts slaves and free blacks alike were tried for criminal acts in special courts composed of two justices of the peace and six of the colony's leading citizens. Similarly, whites in South Carolina perceived such court as reconciling slaveholders' and victims' interests. Presided over by justices of the peace, who were at the same time slaveholders, the slave courts dispensed local and swift judgment on slaves accused of crimes. South Carolina's separate court for slaves made it possible to resolve legal conflicts in the colony while at the same time preventing situations in which blacks could testify against whites. In the decades leading up to the Revolutionary War, South Carolina enacted one of the New World's most stringent set of laws governing slaves.

While ever more comprehensive and repressive laws were being enacted to accommodate the growth of plantation economies in the British colonies, slave laws were also emerging in the French and Spanish North American colonies. French Louisiana, although founded in 1699, was not firmly established until 1718, when France's regency government (under the Duke of Orleans, who ruled in the name of the boy king Louis XV) established the port town of New Orleans.

Slave Laws in French Louisiana

In 1719 the French brought rice seed directly from Africa to Louisiana, along with slaves familiar with growing the crop. Lower Louisiana was a brutal environment, plagued by disease, poverty, and danger from Native Americans and European rivals. The first Africans arrived in the colony during a period of war between French and Spanish militia over the claim of each country to Mobile and Pensacola. The Africans who arrived in Louisiana before 1724 found no hard and fast rules for racial subordination. In the early years of the colony, free and enslaved blacks encountered German-born indentured servants and outcasts from France—convict laborers and mistreated soldiers. A handful of wealthy French immigrants also brought their own free black servants.

Few in number during the early years, free blacks are identified in the documentary sources as bringing lawsuits in the New Orleans court. Raphael Bernard, for example, sued his employer for failing to pay his wages once he arrived in Louisiana. Free blacks were used to inflict public punishment on white criminals. A criminal case in 1720, in which a French soldier was convicted of robbery, reveals that a black man was used to give the soldier a public whipping over a three-day period. The Louisiana Superior Council, eager to meet the colony's need for a public executioner, went so far as to employ a slave, since the onerous nature and stigma of the job made it difficult to fill. The slave, Louis Congo, demanded certain terms before accepting the job—his own and his wife's freedom, as well as land to live on. The Council met all his conditions except his wife's manumission, although she was permitted to live with him. Employed in this despised job for over a decade, Louis Congo himself became a hated man, his life threatened on numerous occasions by other blacks and also Indians.

Slave codes arrived in French Louisiana on the heels of the importation of large numbers of Africans. The black population grew, not from natural increase but from the replenishing slave trade, and it soon outstripped the white population. Census data record 541 slaves in 1721 and 3,500 ten years later; between 1719 and 1731, more than 5,000 slaves arrived from such West African ports as Cabinda, Whydah, Cape Lahou, and Bissau. The slave trade to Louisiana would become negligible after 1731, reviving only after Spain took control of the colony in 1763. Yet blacks continued to outnumber whites.

Louisiana's *Code Noir* (Black Code) of 1724 echoed a 1685 French law that regulated slavery in the West Indies. The 1724 *Code* sought to reduce slave manumissions and to curb interracial mixing. However, the paucity of French women in the colony made for frequent common-law marriages between white men and slave women. At least two legal interracial marriages in the 1720s are documented: a white man married to a black woman and a white man married to a woman of mixed African-European parentage. In cases where bonds of love were shared, white fathers were known to manumit their children. The *Code* denied property rights to slaves, seeking to end the earlier practice in which slaves were able to work out arrangements with their masters for purchasing their freedom.

The Code Noir

The law decreed severe punishments for runaway slaves, including mutilation, branding, and in some cases death. Those harboring runaway slaves also faced legal sanctions: free blacks were fined, and if unable to pay could themselves be enslaved. Whites were also fined for such offenses, but less than the amount imposed on free blacks. The law was silent about the fate of whites who could not afford to pay the fine, thus reinforcing the inferior position of free blacks. All blacks, whether slave or free, were prohibited from selling their produce without permission, and freed slaves were commanded to show their former owners "profoundest respect."

However, in stipulating rules for the general governance of slaves the *Code Noir* required that masters provide religious instruction and adequate food and clothing. It also outlawed separating wives and husbands and taking children under age fourteen from their parents. The *Code* also provided certain avenues for the slaves to express grievances, especially over perceived mistreatment. Under the law, a slave had the right to bring a complaint to colonial officials. Still, it should be emphasized that the law was often broken to the detriment of the slave, with little consequence to the master who broke it. Masters often forced slaves to work on Sundays, in violation of the law. Additionally, though the law clearly stipulated religious instruction for slaves, masters seldom bothered to provide slaves with Catholic education. The prohibition on slaves testifying against whites in court probably only exacerbated the mistreatment of the enslaved. Finally, re-enslavement was always a possibility for the emancipated, whereas clearly this was not so for white Louisianans.

In the comprehensive code of 1751 the French reinforced the *Code Noir* of 1724 by attempting to punish more rigorously infractions that had previously been tolerated. According to one historian: "The language was not ambiguous. Any 'Negro' was to be whipped for being disrespectful to any white, attending church unsupervised by whites, or going out after curfew."

After 1763, Spanish law defined the conditions and terms of slavery in Louisiana. During the French and Indian War (1756–1763), France transferred the financially beleaguered colony to Spain, hoping to gain the Spanish as an ally against the British. Spanish rule had

Spanish Louisiana significant legal repercussions for slavery. Under the royal Black Code of 1777, slaves gained some rights that they had not before enjoyed, but they also lost vital protections. While the intent of French law had been to restrict the number of slave manumissions, Spanish law provided greater access to freedom. The Spanish law of *coartación* provided a process for slaves to purchase their freedom, superseding earlier French provisions that gave masters the right to reject any and all freedom agreements. This new legal right of the slave caused a notable increase in the free black population. In 1769, there were fewer than 200 free blacks in all of Louisiana, but by 1785 the number of blacks who had freed themselves by self-purchase had risen to 907 in New Orleans alone.

Access to freedom in Spanish Louisiana did not translate into full racial equality once freedom was attained. Although free men of color, for instance, received the right to form a militia, Spanish law continued many restrictive French policies: demanding obedience to sumptuary laws (which required the wearing of distinctively inferior apparel and fabric than that worn by whites); banning unskilled free blacks from New Orleans; demanding that free blacks carry freedom papers, gun permits, and horse registries; and permitting the summary execution of any free black who took part in a slave rebellion. Nor did those blacks who remained in slavery benefit from Spanish law. Slave families deteriorated under the Spanish, who abolished French laws forbidding the break-up of marriages and the sale of children under fourteen.

By 1800 Spain had come to realize that Louisiana was both too troublesome and too expensive to control, although the colony was not officially transferred back to France until nearly a month before the United States was scheduled to take it under the Louisiana Purchase in 1803—an international agreement negotiated between President Thomas Jefferson and Emperor Napoleon of France.

By the mid-eighteenth century, every North American colony had established racial slavery. Slaves were indispensable to labor and society in French Louisiana and Spanish Florida, even though the settlers of both colonies functioned under frontier conditions and neither as yet had established a profitable staple-crop export economy. In the twenty-year period between 1740 and 1760, black slaves poured into the cities and agricultural areas of the English colonies in unprecedented numbers.

Notwithstanding the early flexibility and ambiguity about slave status, in the eighteenth century the legalization of slavery caught up with colonial settlement. It was just a matter of time before slave laws would define the American social order in racial terms. In Quaker-influenced Pennsylvania and North Carolina, a few abolitionist voices could be heard, but they could not stop the expansion of slave laws. In the prohibitive codes of 1725–1726, Pennsylvania outlawed interracial marriage, restricted the movement of slaves, and punished free blacks with whipping and fines if they gave refuge to slaves or traded with them. Similarly, the authorities in North Carolina enacted comprehensive slave codes in 1715 and 1741.

Georgia, the only one of the Thirteen Colonies founded in the eighteenth century, provides perhaps the most telling example of the unstoppable rise of chattel slavery. Founded in 1733, Georgia was conceived as an experiment for reforming criminals and for raising orphans, who would come initially as indentured servants. Discharged British soldiers were also encouraged to settle there, to provide a military buffer against Spanish Florida. British lawmakers explicitly prohibited the colony from importing slaves in the belief that slavery would undermine the philanthropic ideal of ultimately producing virtuous white soldier-farmers.

The shortage of white immigrants and the lure of financial gain from rice cultivation, similar to neighboring South Carolina, heightened the pressure from planters to repeal the hated prohibition against slaves. In 1750, facing economic ruin and a drastic manpower shortage, Georgia legalized slave labor and opened the floodgates for importing slaves. From that point on, its black population grew rapidly, and slavery flourished. By 1760, Georgia held six thousand whites and three thousand blacks, and by the outbreak of the American Revolution the population was at least equally black (and slave) and white (and free). Georgia planters were described at the time as "stark Mad after Negroes."

4 Eighteenth-Century Slave Societies

New England

The Mid-Atlantic Colonies

The Chesapeake Region

The Lower South, Eastern Seaboard

The Lower Mississippi Valley

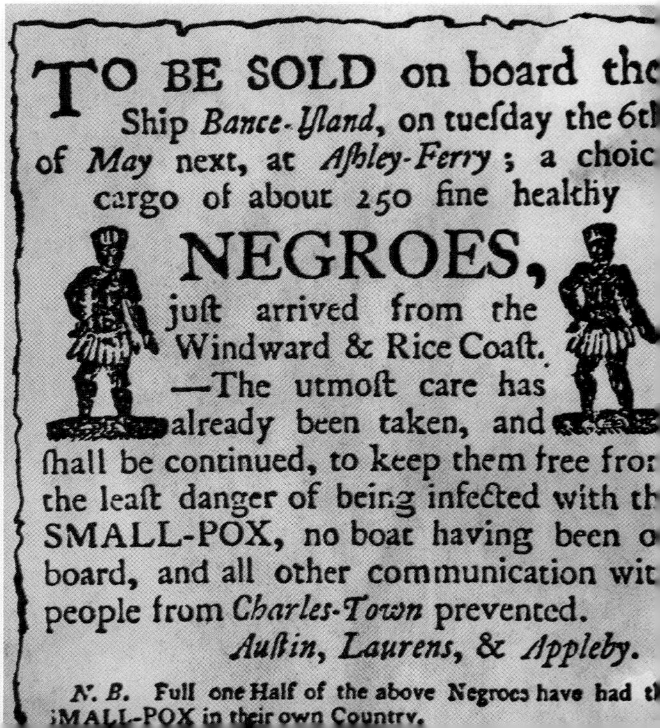

Shipment of African slaves to South Carolina, 1769.

TO BE SOLD on board the
Ship *Bance-Yland*, on tuesday the 6th
of *May* next, at *Ashley-Ferry*; a choic
cargo of about 250 fine healthy

NEGROES,
just arrived from the
Windward & Rice Coast.
—The utmost care has
already been taken, and
shall be continued, to keep them free from
the least danger of being infected with th
SMALL-POX, no boat having been o
board, and all other communication wit
people from *Charles-Town* prevented.
Austin, Laurens, & *Appleby.*

N. B. Full one Half of the above Negroes have had th
SMALL-POX in their own Country.

Distinct slave societies were consolidated in eighteenth-century North America in New England, the Mid-Atlantic, the Chesapeake, and two Lower South regions—one on the Eastern Seaboard and the other in the Lower Mississippi Valley. Variations within and among these five regions ensured that there was no single black slavery experience. Nor did a monolithic culture emerge from the combination of "saltwater" slaves brought directly from Africa, "seasoned" slaves brought from the Caribbean, and Creole slaves born in North America. It is more accurate to speak of diverse African American experiences and cultures, which were shaped by specific local conditions: the nationality of the colonizer; the geographical location of a colonial outpost; a colony's demographics; the varying modes of economic production; and the Atlantic world market in slaves, which affected the overall quantity, sex-ratio, and geographical source of the blacks themselves.

Two crucial demographic trends worked together to reconfigure North America's black population in the eighteenth century. First, the majority of slaves came directly from Africa, and they came in far greater numbers than the "seasoned" slaves from the West Indies of the seventeenth century. Men outnumbered women, and the Africans constituted a diversity of ethnic groups, differing by religious beliefs, languages, and cultural practices. Second, the American-born slave population began to grow through natural increase—that is, more births than deaths. This Creole population contained a growing number of multiracial persons, representing a mixture of African, European, and Indian ancestry. Creoles were usually acquainted with Protestant or Roman Catholic Christianity, although in some cases African-born slaves (specifically those from the Kingdom of Kongo) were already practicing Catholicism. Also, some African-born slaves, and to a lesser extent Creoles, adhered to the Muslim faith of their forebears. Islamic names appear on ships' bills of lading, in slaveowners' records, and in runaway slave advertisements.

The various black cultures of eighteenth-century North America differed in the degree and extent of cultural "syncretism," or the blending of African and European cultures to create a new form. The greater the syncretism that occurred, the more blacks had succeeded in incorporating and adapting material and spiritual elements from the African past into their new surroundings. Thus black acculturation represented a gradual and uneven negotiation between African retention and New World adaptation.

The process and pace of acculturation varied from one region to another. In the plantation districts of the Lower South, for example, African slaves had relatively little contact with whites and thus acquired greater cultural autonomy, which enabled them to retain more African values and practices. Farther north, however, blacks constituted a much smaller percentage of the population relative to whites, so that black-white interactions took place frequently and northern blacks became more assimilated into the dominant culture. Significant differences could also exist within a single region. This was especially true of the Lower South, where differences between the experiences of rural and urban slaves, between African-born and American-born slaves, between Indians and Europeans, and differences in the colonial policies of English South Carolina, Spanish Florida, and French Louisiana produced a complex mosaic of social distinctions among blacks themselves.

African-descended people drew upon different experiences and cultural patterns to escape bondage. Some slaves sought freedom by rebelling, running away, and forming Maroon communities. They often established networks of kinship and friendship with Native American groups. Blacks, both slave and free, drew on their knowledge of European cultures and rivalries to their own advantage. As European nations vied among themselves and against the native peoples of North America, some blacks merged completely into Native American groups, some aligned with Native Americans in wars against Europeans, and others sided with Europeans against the Native Americans. In addition, some slaves gained their freedom by fighting and serving in the armed forces of one European power in its conflict with another. By the end of the colonial era, a diversity of African-descended peoples had doubtless become African American, but this transformation differed by time, place, and freedom strategies.

New England

Fewer blacks lived in New England than in any other region in North America, yet slavery was important to the region's commercial life in the eighteenth century. New Englanders became the foremost shippers and carriers of goods for colonial America, sailing cargo vessels between the mainland North American colonies, the West Indies, the British Isles, and later Africa. Indeed, New England traders began to thrive after Great Britain secured the monopoly on the slave trade to the New World in 1713. In the first half of the eighteenth century, Boston, Salem, Providence, and New London bustled with commercial activity as rum, fish, and dairy products were loaded onto outgoing ships and as incoming ships brought slaves. Until the American War for Independence, the slave trade was a profitable segment of the New England economy.

New England's black population grew slowly at first, but then more quickly between 1720 and 1750, with an increase of slaves directly from Africa into New England, as well as into the American colonies in general. In 1700 Massachusetts had just 800 black inhabitants (less than 1 percent of the colony's population); in 1720 it had 2,150 blacks (2 percent of the total); and by 1750 the black population had nearly doubled, although it remained merely 2 percent of the whole. Connecticut's black population rose from 450 in 1700 to 3,010 in 1750, but with the percentage of blacks in the colony's overall population rising only from 2 percent to 3 percent. New Hampshire's black population also remained small, dropping during this period from 3 percent to 2 percent of the total.

Slave Populations

Ironically Rhode Island, founded in the early seventeenth century by the dissident Puritan Roger Williams as a haven for religious tolerance, was in the eighteenth century the only New England colony to see a significant growth of its slave population. Around Narragansett Bay, large slaveholding farms, reminiscent of southern plantations, provided foodstuffs that were exported to the Caribbean. The importance of slavery for these Rhode Island farms, geared to provisioning West Indies slave plantations, can be gauged by the increase in the colony's black population. In 1700 Rhode Island's 300 blacks accounted for 5 percent of the colony's people, but by 1750 the 3,347 blacks then living there accounted for 10 percent of the entire population.

Eighteenth-century slaves in the commercial port town of Boston worked in a variety of capacities. They were put to skilled trades as carpenters, shipwrights, weavers, seamen, blacksmiths, printers, painters, bakers, shoemakers, distillers, and tallow chandlers. Black men were also used increasingly in the eighteenth century as "body servants"—dressing wigs, shaving their masters, waiting tables, and driving carriages. Slave women worked primarily as domestic servants. Routinely tied to the households in which

Slave Occupations

they worked, they experienced far fewer opportunities than did slave men to move about the town. Interracial fellowship between black and white male servants at taverns and other public places was sufficiently commonplace to inspire laws aimed at curtailing street activities. Such male camaraderie would figure prominently in the Boston street protests against the British during the 1760s and 1770s.

Although blacks made up less than 2 percent of the eighteenth-century New England population, black cultural traditions emerged in the region. In the northern colonies, the most significant evidence of cultural syncretism is the festival tradition that developed. Every year, slaves in Massachusetts, Rhode Island, and Connecticut cel- **Negro Election Day** ebrated Negro Election Day—the public electing of black "kings" and "governors," a ceremony that adapted and inverted the region's white electoral celebrations. For slaves, the holiday helped to forge a sense of community, and for masters (who provided their slaves with costumes and other public support) it served as a way to secure obedience and loyalty.

Although eighteenth-century New England's black population was the smallest in North America, these small numbers were heavily concentrated in certain towns. In 1740 blacks made up 10 percent of Boston's population. In Rhode Island, they accounted for 17 percent of Newport County's population and for 15 percent of King's County's—the two counties that contained three-quarters of the colony's entire black population. In 1755 one-quarter of all Rhode Island blacks lived in Newport and formed 20 percent of its total population; concentrations were even more dramatic in the Rhode Island towns of South Kingston (30 percent) and Charlestown (40 percent). New Hampshire's black population of 633 in 1767 may have been numerically insignificant, yet one-third of these people lived in Portsmouth, constituting 4 percent of its population. Nearby Rockingham County contained half of all New Hampshire's black residents. In Connecticut, data available for 1774 reveals that half of the colony's blacks lived in the coastal towns of New London and Fairfield, which had black populations of 9 percent and 7 percent, respectively. It was this concentration of blacks in a few places that influenced the possibility and the quality of such black communal experiences as Negro Election Day.

For white New Englanders, exposure to African practices could have unusual and consequential effects. This was the case in Boston in 1721 to 1722, when the town suffered from a smallpox epidemic. Interestingly, the slave Onesimus, given to the illustrious clergyman Cotton Mather in 1706 by his parishioners at Boston's Second **Cotton Mather and Inoculation** Church, was responsible for introducing Mather to the process of inoculation (also called variolation). The grandson of the first settlers of the Massachusetts Bay Colony, Mather was the first North American elected to England's Royal Society, the country's most important learned society, which published the journal *Philosophical Transactions.* Thus it is all the more noteworthy that Mather wrote to Boston's and England's leading citizens with news that the idea of inoculation initially came to him from his slave Onesimus, a Coramantee born in Africa. Engaging the physician Zabdiel Boylston in his novel plan to inoculate the population, Mather tried to persuade the Boston public on the authority of African folk medicine.

The heated responses to his argument in favor of this "African solution" led to Mather's house being firebombed. But Mather and his African informants were proven correct, and for many Bostonians acceptance or rejection of African folk medical practice literally meant the difference between life and death. In 1722 Mather described Onesimus as a "pretty intelligent fellow" and discussed the African practice in the following way:

> He successively met with a Number of *Africans;* who all, in *their* plain Way, without any Combination, or Correspondence, agreed in *one Story, viz.* That in their country. . . it is now become a *common Thing* to cut a place or two in their skin, sometimes one place, and sometimes another, and put in a little of the matter of the *Small-Pox;* after which, they, in a few Days, grow a *little sick,* and a few *Small-Pox* break out, and by and by they dry away; and no Body ever dy'd of doing this; nor ever had *Small-Pox* after it.

Through Onesimus, Cotton Mather and Zabdiel Boylston introduced the life-saving medical technique of inoculation to America.

Although blacks in New England were not subjected to the harsh slave codes and brutal treatment meted out to their fellows in the southern colonies, it is nevertheless possible to exaggerate the humanitarian aspects of their treatment. Although New Englanders took their religion seriously, they did not permit it to interfere with the profits of slavery and the slave trade.

The Mid-Atlantic Colonies

Slaves encountered diverse European groups in the Mid-Atlantic colonies, unlike the English homogeneity of New England. In the bustling Middle Colonies of the eighteenth century—New York, New Jersey, Pennsylvania, and Delaware—black slaves came in contact with English, Dutch, German, and Swedish settlers, as well as the Scots-Irish, who arrived in growing numbers as the century progressed. The European settlers represented a great variety of religious groups, including at first Quakers, Huguenots (French Calvinists), Anglicans, Baptists, and several German Protestant sects, and later also Methodists. During the religious revivals of the Great Awakening of the 1740s, the number of Baptists and Methodists grew tremendously among whites and blacks alike.

The colony of New York had the largest number of slaves in the North throughout the eighteenth century. This population was derived from African slaves entering through the

New York Colony
port of New York City, from the domestic slave trade in the American colonies, and from the gradual natural increase of the slave and free black population. In 1698, the entire New York colony had only 2,170 blacks out of a total population of 18,067, not including Indians, and in 1723 the colony's census listed 6,171 blacks. In 1771 the black population had increased to 19,883 in a total population of 168,007.

The influence of the region's cultural diversity is evident in the black festival tradition of Pinkster. Celebrated in New York and New Jersey, the holiday blended African and Dutch cultures. Its roots were in the traditional Dutch Pentecost celebration, to which African and Creole slaves added their own traditions of dancing and the music of drums and banjos. According to an anonymous white onlooker, their "Guinea dance," as he termed it, assumed "wild" and writhing movements that appeared to transport the slaves, if only momentarily, "thousands of miles away in the heart of superstitious Africa." Like Negro Election Day in New England, Pinkster functioned as a cultural tool with which to build a distinctive black community identity.

Stevedores on the Chesapeake Bay Tobacco Wharves, ca. 1750

By the middle of the eighteenth century, the cities in the Middle Colonies had made a definite commitment to slave labor in various forms. By then, slaves worked in households, crafts, and the maritime industry. The colonies' expanding econo- **Expansion of Slavery** mies broadened opportunities for non-elite whites to buy slaves, while at the same time options for manumission began to disappear, since owners were discouraged from freeing their slaves by new legal requirements that they post heavy bonds before doing so. In fact, between 1698 and 1763, only 90 slaves were manumitted in Philadelphia, and in New York City the number was even lower.

This expansion and tightening of Middle-Colony slavery coincided with the planta-tion revolution in the southern colonies. Historian Graham Hodges argues that slavery in the Mid-Atlantic and southern colonies differed "in the character of the servitude, not the degree." Contradicting historians who have tended to paint differences between southern and northern colonies in broad strokes, Hodges concludes that "by 1700, slavery was a core legal, economic, and social system in New York and East Jersey." (East Jersey was one of the two parts into which the colony of New Jersey was temporarily divided.)

Slaves could be found in the cities and the countryside of the Mid-Atlantic colonies, and many had versatile work experiences, often shifting between country and city or between farm and urban shop, in response to specific labor demands. In the cities slaves moved from houses to artisan shops, working as personal servants, blacksmiths, tanners, and handy-men. They labored in tanneries, in copper mines, in Pennsylvania's ironworks. The region's increasing production of grain for export made it necessary for these colonies to rely more heavily on slave labor. By the middle of the eighteenth century, the expansion of slavery was particularly visible on the great estates of the Hudson Valley, where wealthy farmers amassed large slave holdings and exported foodstuffs to the West Indies. In the grain-pro-ducing regions of Pennsylvania, of northern New Jersey, and of New York's Hudson Valley and Long Island, slaves planted and harvested staple crops, manured land, chopped wood, pressed cider, repaired fences, cleared fields, and toiled as boatmen and wagoners in the carrying trade. With their access to horses and mules, slaves in the provisioning trades had greater opportunity for contact with slaves in other places or doing other kinds of work.

In 1721 Pennsylvania's black population stood at an estimated two thousand; thirty years later there were about three thousand black people in the colony. Between 1682 and

1760, slaves accounted for 20 percent to 30 percent of Philadelphia's workforce, with most of the city's slaveholders owning one or two slaves. Pennsylvania was relatively free from

Pennsylvania Slavery slave violence and white reprisal. Of all the British colonies, Pennsylvania had a religious constituency—the Society of Friends, or Quakers—whose members began to debate the morality of slavery. By mid-century, this attitude led to an early movement for manumission. Quakers also began to operate schools specifically intended to educate black children at this time.

Notwithstanding some ameliorative features, however, overall the conditions of life for slaves in the Middle Colonies were harsh. Death rates for Philadelphia's black population were almost 50 percent higher than for whites. One explanation is the difference in diet. Malnutrition appears to have been typical for many blacks in Pennsylvania and the other northern colonies. Indeed, the discovery in 1992 of an eighteenth-century slave cemetery in New York City revealed to archaeologists evidence of such health problems as rickets, stress from malnutrition, and serious dental problems resulting from chewing whole grains. Similarly, Philadelphia gravesites dating from the early nineteenth century show poor nutrition among black adults, most of whom would have lived as slaves in the preceding century. Slave housing also contributed to poor health conditions. Housed in stables, barns, attics, garrets, and cellars, slaves generally found themselves in unheated spaces without beds or mattresses, and their clothing did not provide suitable protection and warmth. Given this environment, northern blacks had especially high death rates during outbreaks of such diseases as measles, respiratory infections, and whooping cough.

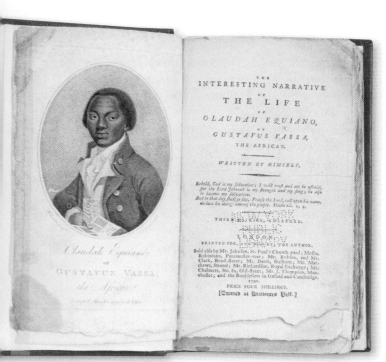

Frontispiece and title page, *The Interesting Narrative of the Life of Olaudah Equiano*

The Chesapeake Region

In the first four decades of the eighteenth century, the African-born population rose dramatically in Virginia. Between 1700 and 1740, the colony absorbed approximately 43,000 black slaves, 39,000 of them coming directly from Africa. Africans constituted 73 percent of all slaves brought to Virginia between 1710 and 1718, and 93 percent between 1727 and 1740. Specific ethnic groups dominated this human traffic. From 1712 through the 1720s, the majority of Virginia's African-born slaves were Igbos from the Bight of Biafra (present-day Nigeria). In the 1730s Angolans formed the largest group, representing 37 percent of all slaves identifiable by African origin.

Adjustment was difficult for the newly arrived slaves, since most of the Africans did not speak English. They could not understand or be understood by the Creole communities into which they were introduced. In his autobiography, Olaudah Equiano describes the painful experience of being an African outsider among English-speaking slaves in Virginia in the

Window in Time

1705 Virginia Statute

XXXIV. And if any slave resist his master, or owner, or other person, by his or her order, correcting such slave, and shall happen to be killed in such correction, it shall not be accounted felony; but the master, owner, and every such other person so giving correction, shall be free and acquit of all punishment and accusation for the same, as if such accident had never happened. And also, if any negro, mulatto, or Indian, bond or free, shall at any time, lift his or her hand, in opposition against any christian, not being negro, mulatto, or Indian, he or she so offending, shall, for every such offence, proved by the oath of the party, receive on his or her bare back, thirty lashes, well laid on; cognizable by a justice of the peace for that county wherein such offence shall be committed.

William Walter Hening, *Statutes at Large of Virginia*, Vol. III (October 1705), Chap XLIX, An act concerning Servants and Slaves, sec. 34, p. 459 (Philadelphia, 1823).

1750s: "I was now exceedingly miserable and thought myself worse off than any . . . of my companions; for they could talk to each other, but I had no person to speak to that I could understand." In contrast, slaves born in **African Outsiders** the Chesapeake faced the challenge of absorbing and readjusting to the influx of Africans into their communities. Some Creoles felt superior to the unassimilated "saltwater" slaves.

Death within the first year of residency in Virginia was the fate of about one-quarter of the African-born slaves. In a strange and hostile land, the newly arrived Africans attempted to escape the cruel fate of plantation slavery in a number of ways. Unlike the Creole slaves who tended to run away as individuals, Africans ran away in groups, including men and women. As Michael Gomez has shown in his study of Africans in North America, runaway notices called attention to their distinctiveness—filed teeth, African dialect, and the bodily scarification that slaveholders called their "country marks." Some sought refuge in the vast wetland called the Great Dismal Swamp in southeastern Virginia; others took to the mountains or wooded areas, hoping to build Maroon communities. Their efforts failed as white troops hunted them down and destroyed their fragile villages. Escape was often not realistic for men and women who sought, as best they could, to re-create the world from which they had been torn.

On Virginia tobacco plantations in the 1690s, slave owners preferred male to female slaves. The sex ratio of two men to one woman, along with long and hard workdays, discouraged stable family life and the natural increase of the black popula- **Population Growth** tion. In the 1720s, however, Virginians attempted to correct the imbalance by importing more women, and the slave population began to increase naturally. Indeed, as was later noted by Thomas Jefferson (who owned many slaves): "A woman who brings a child every two years [is] more profitable than the best man on the farm [for] what she produces is an addition to the capital, while his labor disappears in mere consumption."

Black Population Growth in Virginia, 1700–1800			
Period	Population Increase	Surviving New Immigrants	Annual Rate of Natural Increase (percent)
1700–1710	6,500	6,210	.2
1710–1720	7,500	5,680	.9
1720–1730	13,000	10,150	1.0
1730–1740	25,000	12,790	3.0
1740–1750	40,000	9,680	4.7
1750–1760	35,500	7,180	2.7
1760–1770	40,000	7,570	2.3
1770–1775	24,500	3,190	2.4
1770–1780	19,000	0	1.8
1780–1790	69,000	0	3.1
1790–1800	53,000	0	1.8

Source: Morgan, Philip D. *Slave Counterpoint: Black Culture in the Eighteenth-Century Chesapeake & Lowcountry* (Chapel Hill, 1998: University of North Carolina Press), p. 81.

Pewter slave passport

Inscribed: "Aunt Jemima Johnston, Born 1799, Nicholas Plantation, Warrenton, Virginia"

The large number of African slaves imported into Virginia in the first four decades of the eighteenth century combined with the naturally reproducing Creole population. In 1720 blacks constituted one-fourth of the colony's total population and by 1740, 40 percent. By the 1740s the number of Africans imported into the colony had declined, and it continued to drop precipitously in the decades to come.

After 1740, ethnic differences among slaves lessened, sex ratios became more balanced, health and longevity improved, and slave communities exhibited greater stability. Over the course of the eighteenth century, the offspring of Africans in the Chesapeake had become a new generation of African Americans and the first black population in the New World to grow by natural increase rather than by immigration.

The Lower South, Eastern Seaboard

The introduction of rice cultivation transformed black life in the South Carolina Lowcountry. It was Africans' knowledge of the crop and their labor that eventually turned swampland into a tidewater coastal plain of profitable rice fields. At the end of the seventeenth century, when the first generation of Carolina colonists were desperately looking for a profitable staple crop in an unpromising environment, African slaves taught their masters about growing rice. Africans in the Lowcountry employed the same planting techniques they had in West Africa, using their heels to make a depression in the ground for the rice seed and their feet to cover the seed with dirt. Rice had been grown in West Africa from the second millennium B.C.E., and, according to geographer Judith A. Carney, West Africans utilized a number of techniques to overcome periodic droughts. She notes that before the slave trade Africans had already come to depend on three ways to water rice crops: "the upland system—originally developed in the Guinea highlands—that relies solely on rainfall; inland swamps, which draw upon supplemental water from moisture-holding clay soils and groundwater reserves for cultivation; and tidal irrigation, which allows rice to be grown along flood plains and estuaries." Indeed many South Carolina planters expressed their preference for slaves from the rice-growing regions of the Gambia and the Windward Coast.

The increase in the number of African slaves in the colony paralleled the rising significance of rice as an export commodity. Before 1710, slave imports rarely exceeded three hundred per year. In 1720 rice had grown to more than half the value of all South Carolina exports, and by the 1730s slaves **The Slave Population** brought into the colony annually numbered more than two thousand. Despite drops in the 1740s and briefly during the Revolutionary War, by the end of the eighteenth century South Carolina returned to its pattern of extensive slave importation.

For most of the eighteenth century, the availability of Angolan slaves resulted in their preponderance among the total number of slaves imported by the British directly from Africa to South Carolina. The racial demographics of South Carolina looked more like that of the Caribbean colonies than of any English colony in mainland North America. In 1715

African Immigration to Virginia and South Carolina, 1700–1790		
	Number of African Immigrants	
Decade	**Virginia**	**South Carolina**
1700s	7,700	3,000
1710s	6,750	6,000
1720s	12,700	11,600
1730s	15,700	21,150
1740s	12,000	1,950
1750s	9,200	16,500
1760s	9,700	21,850
1770s	3,900	18,850
1780s	0	10,000
Total	77,650	110,900

Source: Morgan, Philip D. *Slave Counterpoint: Black Culture in the Eighteenth-Century Chesapeake & Lowcountry* (Chapel Hill: University of North Carolina Press, 1998), p. 59.

blacks outnumbered whites by 10,500 to 6,250. By 1750 South Carolina's 39,000 blacks represented 61 percent of the total population. This percentage was maintained in 1770, when the number of blacks rose to 75,178. As the black majority grew, so did the size of plantations; by mid-century, one-third of all Lowcountry slaves lived in groups of fifty or more and worked in large units. Two-thirds of the slaves imported into the colony were male, and in the malarial environment of the rice-cultivating areas, South Carolina slaves failed to reproduce naturally. Plantation owners continually imported Africans to replenish their workforce. Only in the 1760s, some four decades after the Chesapeake, did South Carolina achieve slave population growth through natural increase, with a greater number of births than deaths in its slave population.

However harsh, local conditions of plantation life and work had significant consequences in the form of a distinctive African American culture. South Carolina exhibited a far greater survival of African cultural elements than did the Chesapeake. Comparative research on the **The Chesapeake and the Lowcountry** South's two major slave systems, the Chesapeake and the South Carolina Lowcountry, points to different trends in slave work and culture. In the eighteenth-century Chesapeake, despite the rise of tobacco plantations and the gang labor associated with its production, most slaves had a varied work routine, growing grains, raising livestock, practicing crafts, and growing tobacco. Even with gang labor, slaves were divided into small units, surrounded and closely supervised by whites.

Interracial contact was daily and pervasive on Chesapeake farms and plantations, creating a reciprocal cultural influence in a world blacks and whites made together. Scholars note that in the seventeenth and early eighteenth century all American colonists believed in "signs," "wonders," magical explanations, and workers of magic. Whites occasionally sought black herbal remedies, such as antidotes to poison. Both in Africa and in Europe, certain rocks and stones were credited with curative powers, and thus black and white folk beliefs at times complemented each other.

Because black women were assigned the responsibility of taking care of their masters' young children, even serving as wet nurses for babies, their influence could become at times a target for criticism. They introduced speech patterns and black folklore into the white community. For this, in his tour of America in 1736, the British traveler Edward Kimber condemned white parents in Virginia: "One thing they are very faulty in, with regard to their Children, which is, that when young, they suffer them too much to prowl among the young Negroes, which insensibly causes them to imbibe their Manners and broken Speech."

By contrast, the great majority of South Carolina slaves lived on large plantations with few whites present, since Lowcountry slaveholders left the swampy, malaria-ridden rice areas for part of each year to reside in the healthier environment of Charleston (called Charles Town until the American Revolution). With masters rarely present in the summer months and even white overseers in short supply, it was commonplace for a trusted slave to serve in the role of "driver" or "overseer" and thus manage the other slaves. Slaves in the Lowcountry gained greater cultural autonomy than did those in the Chesapeake because of the more limited black-white contact and because of the nature of the labor regimen itself.

The Lowcountry task system allowed for less supervision, since it was based on the worker's output per day. After completing a defined task, slaves were allowed to spend the rest of their time cultivating their own gardens, supplementing their diets and providing a fragile ownership over their own products. They carried their produce to market on Sundays for sale. It was in the rural Lowcountry that large numbers of slaves lived together on

A view of Kamalia in Africa and a view of Mulberry Plantation in South Carolina

plantation units. Some historians describe the quarters as "village communities," with slaves often building their own housing in styles and materials reminiscent of Africa. In this setting, African survivals in religion, music, language, kinship patterns, and naming practices continued to inform African American life and culture.

Yet within the South Carolina slave system two very different types of black society coexisted: one rural and one urban. Urban slaves lived in close proximity to whites in small slaveholdings and in shared residences. As these slaves navigated **Rural and Urban Slave Life** through the urban white world, their dress and language skills bespoke far more Anglo-assimilation than was the case for slaves in the countryside. Slaves were crucial to the port city of Charleston. They were often hired out by their masters to work for others. They enjoyed greater mobility and more independent social lives.

In Charleston, male slaves included skilled laborers, such as carpenters, coopers, and shoemakers, and unskilled laborers such as servants, porters, and day workers. Female slaves were found in much larger numbers in the city as opposed to rural areas, working in their masters' homes and hired out as cooks and seamstresses. Slave women monopolized the public markets, selling their wares throughout the city; they sometimes manipulated the economic sphere and resisted their slave status through disorderly behavior. Some dressed so fashionably that the South Carolina legislature passed sumptuary laws to prohibit blacks from wearing such fabrics as silk or other fine apparel. These laws were continually broken, but their goal was to deny blacks the outward appearance of equality with whites.

In Charleston, slaves and free persons of mixed African and European descent formed a visible group with greater privileges and higher status than most blacks. South Carolina was different from most of the British colonies in that it did not pro- **People of Mixed Race** hibit interracial sexual contact. It was not illegal for white men and mulatto women to establish longstanding domestic relationships, or for white fathers to petition the court to serve as the guardian of a mulatto slave child, or to free their children born of these affectionate relationships.

As a group, mulattoes tended to be overrepresented among skilled laborers. Those of mixed parentage tended to be the most assimilated. For example, mulatto slaves were far more likely than other urban slaves to be baptized in the Anglican Church. Their religious

Window in Time

Establishing Black Inferiority in Law

WHEREAS, the plantations and estates of this Province cannot be well and sufficiently managed and brought into use, without the labor and service of Negroes and other slaves; and forasmuch as the said Negroes and other slaves brought unto the people of this Province for that purpose, are of barbarous, wild, savage natures, and such as renders them wholly unqualified to be governed by the laws, customs, and practices of this Province; but that it is absolutely necessary, that such other constitutions, laws and orders, should in this Province be made and enacted, for the good regulating and ordering of them, as may restrain the disorders, rapines and inhumanity, to which they are naturally prone and inclined; and may also tend to the safety and security of the people of this Province and their estates. . . .

"The Preamble to the *South Carolina Slave Code of 1712*," in *Statutes at Large of South Carolina*, vol. 7 (Columbia SC: A. H. Pemberton State Printer, 1840), p. 352.

assimilation stood in stark contrast with the retention of African beliefs by most rural slaves. The Society for the Propagation of the Gospel, an English-based organization promoting overseas missions, attempted to make Anglican inroads into the slave population in the early eighteenth century, but not until the 1770s, with the coming of the emotional worship style of the Baptists and Methodists, did large numbers of Africans convert to Christianity. Yet African spirituality persisted in combination with Christian beliefs and played an instrumental role with regard to escape, slave revolts, health, and relations among slaves themselves.

The West Central Africans whose numbers predominated on most plantations brought with them a belief in *minkisi*, or "sacred medicines," in which a person wore amulets or charms to control his or her own health and destiny or to affect favorably or

African Traditions
otherwise another's. Root "doctors," healers, and conjurers in the heavily populated slave quarters in the Lowcountry and Sea Islands, off the coast of South Carolina and Georgia, were New World practitioners of a belief system of blended African traditions.

Renowned in eighteenth-century South Carolina for his medicinal use of herbs and roots, the slave Caesar is noted in colonial records for his antidotes to poison. Caesar is believed to have been born in the 1680s, although historians are not sure whether he was born in Africa or in South Carolina. Nor is it known whether his knowledge was of African and/or Native American derivation. He became so well known for his remedies that on November 24, 1749, the proceedings of the Commons House of Assembly of South Carolina referred to the "Negro man named Caesar belonging to Mr. John Norman of Beach Hill, who had cured several of the Inhabitants of this Province who had been poisoned by Slaves."

Caesar offered to make known the ingredients of his antidote in exchange for his freedom. The South Carolina Assembly thus formed a committee, some of whose members were physicians, to verify the stories of his life-saving techniques and to assess his abilities.

Numerous witnesses testified to his knowledge, several of them prominent citizens who had experienced Caesar's skill first hand. The public treasurer was ordered to purchase his freedom from his master and also provide an annual sum of money to him for the rest of his life. At the time Caesar was sixty-seven years old. His cures were published in the *South Carolina Gazette* in May 1750, in the *Massachusetts Magazine* in 1792, and in William Buchan's *Domestic Medicine* in 1797.

Most slaves had little opportunity to gain freedom except through escape or rebellion. The slaves themselves were conscious of the tensions among the European powers, and they tried to exploit them for their own interests. Throughout the Lower South, the rival British, French, and Spanish colonies sought—with the **The Stono Rebellion** help of Indian allies—to contain, and indeed to conquer, one another. For slaves in South Carolina, the Spanish presence in Florida fomented flight and rebellion. Each year between 1687 and 1690, British-owned slaves escaped to St. Augustine, the largest town in Spanish Florida. In 1720 a foiled conspiracy in Charleston revealed slaves' plans to flee to St. Augustine. Four years later, Yamasee Indians helped escaping South Carolina slaves reach St. Augustine, and in 1726 fourteen slaves near Stono, South Carolina, successfully fled to the Spanish settlement. Historian Jane Landers argues that "the repeated crosscurrents of raids and migrations across the Southeast acquainted many blacks and Indians with the routes to St. Augustine."

Historians now point to the strategic importance of Florida and the Spanish to the Stono Rebellion, which occurred twenty miles west of Charleston. The Stono Rebellion broke out on September 9, 1739, when slaves killed two guards in a warehouse, secured arms, and launched a full-scale revolt against slavery. The Stono uprising was put down, but not for several days and not before thirty whites and forty-four blacks had lost their lives.

Plan of town and harbor of St. Augustine

Proclamations from the Spanish crown in 1693 and 1733, offering freedom to fugitive slaves who professed Roman Catholicism, lured many British-owned slaves to St. Augustine, particularly Portuguese-speaking Angolan slaves. This likely explains specific African patterns of conduct among the Stono rebels and in the African Catholicism of slaves from the Kongo-Angola region—an area with a long Catholic heritage. Thus freedom, along with the Catholic identity of Florida, inspired the slaves to rebel at Stono.

The second incentive for the Stono Rebellion was the free black town in Spanish Florida, Gracia Real de Santa Teresa de Mose. The first black town in North America, it was commonly known as Mose or Fort Mose and was established in 1738, one year before the Stono revolt, by male and female fugitives from South Carolina. Spanish sanction of this free black town was no doubt influenced by its strategic location, two miles north of St. Augustine. Mose was described as "a walled fort" with houses "resembling thatched Indian huts." The town offered St. Augustine a buffer against the encroaching British; for runaway slaves it offered freedom and self-determination. In 1738 and 1739 groups of fugitive slaves fled to Mose from South Carolina. Although Mose became the center of free black life in Florida, the Spanish continued to use slave labor. Slaves lived and worked in St. Augustine, and some of them were married to free blacks in Mose.

While Mose's population of one hundred men and women remained officially under Spanish rule, the town's leader in all practical regards was a free black man named Fran-

Menendez and Mose cisco Menendez. A former slave of the British, Menendez typified other slaves who sought freedom from bondage. Menendez is believed to have been African-born and was brought to North America sometime in the early eighteenth century. He lived as a slave in South Carolina, eventually fleeing slavery and then joining a black militia allied with the Yamasee Indians against the Carolina colonists.

During the Yamasee War (1715–1718), Menendez learned of Spain's offer to free slaves who fled the British colonies and converted to Roman Catholicism. In 1724 he succeeded, with the help of the Yamasees, in making his way from British-controlled territory to St. Augustine. Unfortunately, Menendez and his cohort of runaways arrived in the Spanish colony before the second freedom proclamation of 1733. At the time of Menendez's arrival, the governor of the colony refused to grant freedom to the runaways, arguing that they had arrived in Florida during a period of peace with England. Yet this was also a time when many officials in St. Augustine desired to own slaves. Whichever the explanation, Menendez and the other fugitives remained in slavery, once again the property of another.

Menendez continued to press for his freedom. In 1728 he led the colony's slave militia in the successful defense of St. Augustine against the British. Slaves were often manumitted because of their military service. In 1733 he presented his record of valor in a petition to the governor and to the bishop of Cuba. In 1737, with a newly appointed governor ruling the colony, Menendez finally obtained a sympathetic ear. Governor Manuel de Montiano accepted the testimony of a Yamasee Indian named Jorge, who recounted how Menendez and three others fought with him and his men against the British. In 1738, Montiano granted freedom to Menendez and the other slaves who petitioned him. Now free, they joined other freed slaves in building the town of Mose. In a community of their own, the free blacks established families. They adopted Spanish practices such as godparenthood (*compadrazgo*) and fostered a black Hispanic community linked to the slaves, Indians, free Africans, and whites of St. Augustine.

The Mose militia defended Spanish Florida during the so-called War of Jenkins' Ear (1739–1743)—an Anglo-Spanish conflict, marked by rising British nationalism in the

Window in Time

Spain's Founding of the First Black Town in North America, 1739

The Governor of Florida informs your majesty of having given freedom to several fugitive Negroes from the English colonies, placing them in a new settlement with a priest who teaches them and, during the interim until your majesty deigns to grant him an income, has designated for him the same that a missionary receives.

Sir:

With the motive of having presented themselves before me the black slaves who in different groups have come as fugitives from Saint George and other English settlements, begging me to grant them freedom by virtue of royal orders that for this purpose your majesty has issued; I found out and recognized several royal decrees in which your majesty piously favors all those who come to profess the Catholic religion, and having made "autos" in order to proceed with the proper justification, I freed them, publishing by one edict that those who in the future might come from the settlements mentioned with the same purpose will be, of course, granted freedom, the expressed words of which are from a royal decree of 29 October, 1733, of which I informed your majesty on 31 May of the most recently passed year, 1738, and I arranged for them to go to live in the territory called Mose, a half-league more or less to the north of this plaza, and that they form a settlement there.

The motive that obliged me to publish by edict the royal decision of your majesty was the immediacy with which we were preparing to go to expel the intrusive English in the territory of your majesty and to have favors and graces for your slaves so that they would join our forces and that, assured of their freedom, they would decide to come to enjoy the royal pardon, embrace the Catholic religion, and that they would join the town in which I am now settling them.

A. of I. 58-1-31, Document #73. Original. one sheet and cover (the Governor of Florida Don Manuel Montiano to His Majesty. Florida, 16 February, 1739).

colonies. The war in North America began with the aggression of James Oglethorpe, the governor and founder of Georgia, against the Spanish fortress at St. Augustine. Spain did not recognize the legitimacy of British Georgia, claiming that the new colony lay in Spanish territory. Warfare **The War of Jenkins' Ear** was inevitable as Spanish and British troops and their respective black and Indian allies patrolled the frontiers and borders over which the two colonizing powers clashed.

In 1739 in the larger context of imperial warfare, Oglethorpe led his Georgia troops, along with his Indian allies, the Creeks, and several hundred black slaves into Florida. The British captured and occupied Fort Mose, the townspeople having already been evacuated. However, in a surprise attack in June 1740, the joint forces of Menendez's black militia, Spanish troops, and their Indian allies recaptured Mose, thwarting the British capture of St. Augustine. The British continued to wage unsuccessful assaults on St. Augustine in 1742 and 1743. Francisco Menendez received much acclaim as a defender of the Spanish. His success in the recapture of Mose earned a commendation from the Spanish governor, who announced that Menendez had "distinguished himself in the establishment, and cultivation of Mose, to improve the settlement, doing all he could so that the rest of his subjects, following his example, would apply themselves to work and learn good customs."

The End of Mose The free blacks did not return to their war-ravaged fort. Menendez became a seaman and encountered more harrowing battles with the British before returning to Florida. In 1740 most of the Mose residents went to live in St. Augustine, but scarce resources, disease, poverty, and the continued influx of African fugitive slaves from the British colonies prompted the Spanish authorities to relocate the free blacks. In 1752 the free blacks reluctantly departed St. Augustine, having been ordered to settle and build a frontier village near their original site. Their new community, also named Mose, would be short-lived. Great Britain's victory in the French and Indian War in 1763 resulted in Spain being forced to give up Florida, the oldest North American colony. Concerned about the British colonies' harsher slave laws and discouraged by Mose's poverty and by the unsettled conditions produced by the war, Menendez and the other residents in 1763 evacuated Mose and resettled in Havana, Cuba. Eventually, after backing the American side in the War for Independence, Spain regained Florida. However, the black town of Mose was never re-established.

The Lower Mississippi Valley

Africans in French-controlled lower Louisiana formed part of a vast multi-ethnic region in the eighteenth century. Louisiana was home to numerous groups: persons of African descent, Indian nations, and a variety of Europeans—French and German settlers, later Acadians (French settlers expelled from Nova Scotia after Britain conquered that colony), English, Spanish, and settlers from Spain's Canary Islands. The slave-owning areas of lower Louisiana spanned the swamps, bayous, and deltas of the southernmost Mississippi Valley and stretched eastward along the Gulf Coast as far as present-day Mobile, Alabama. More than five thousand slaves arrived there between 1720 and 1731, when the slave trade was brought to a virtual halt by disease, revolts, and overall difficult conditions. One slave ship disembarked in Louisiana in 1743 and another in 1758, but after that there was no resumption of the trade until the Spanish acquired most of Louisiana, except for the Gulf Coast, from France in 1763. (The Gulf Coast became a small new British colony called West Florida in that year.)

French Louisiana As in South Carolina, in French-controlled lower Louisiana slaves managed to exercise significant cultural autonomy. However, Louisiana differed from South Carolina in that the earliest slave arrivals in 1719 were direct from Africa, not from the West Indies. During the next twelve years, large concentrations of African slaves, often of the same ethnic or linguistic groups, were held by a small number of white masters, members of the military and governing elite. Because of this concentration of the African population, lower Louisiana had what one historian called the "most Africanized slave culture," which continued to influence the culture of Creole generations.

Slaves practiced African religious beliefs and exhibited substantial knowledge of poisons and antidotes. Court records in the 1730s and records as late as the 1770s identified the slaves' use of charms or amulets to give themselves protection or to do harm to enemies, which were called *gris-gris* and *zinzin*. The words *gris-gris* and *zinzin* are similar in pronunciation and meaning to the words for charms used by the respective Bambara and Mande people of Africa. Court records also show that slaves in French Louisiana were more likely than the slaves of the other European colonies to retain their African names, which they used in addition to European names.

Like the slaves in South Carolina, African slaves, especially those from the region between the Gambia and Senegal rivers, came to Louisiana with prior knowledge of rice cultivation. Rice was the most important foodstuff consumed in the colony, although it did not become the great export staple that it was in South Carolina. Africans' knowledge of indigo cultivation and processing also proved useful, because indigo (a blue dye used on cloth) came from plants that grew wild in and around New Orleans. As slavery became firmly entrenched in the social and economic life of the colony in the 1720s, the French established plantations along the banks of the Mississippi and other waterways such as the Red and Yazoo rivers for cultivating locally consumed rice, as well as indigo and tobacco for export.

Yet slaves also actively engaged in the broader intraregional economy as traders, marketing the agricultural surpluses that they produced on their *concessions*, land allotted to them by their masters for subsistence. In what historian Daniel Usner terms a "frontier exchange economy," slaves, free blacks, European settlers (both French and German), and Indians all "brought grains, vegetables, fruits, and poultry to the multi-ethnic market at New Orleans," as well as in other towns and outposts along the various river systems in the colony, such as Natchitoches and Point Coupee, and in Natchez (in present-day Mississippi) and Mobile. In 1746 all five settlements had black majorities.

New Orleans, the capital of Louisiana, had the largest black population in the colony. In 1731 it had 905 white settlers, about 200 French troops, a few dozen Indian slaves and free blacks, and a little more than 3,000 African slaves, mostly from West Africa's Senegambia region. Slaves cleared and cultivated the land. They dug ditches and built levees and canals to drain swamp water and protect the settlement from Mississippi River floods. Slaves helped build fortifications, worked in skilled trades as carpenters, caulkers, and nurses, and performed a variety of service jobs. Although some African-born and Creole slaves in Louisiana gained their freedom because of military service on the French side in wars against Native Americans, others fought for their freedom by joining forces with Indian groups that opposed French seizure of their land.

The heavy importation of African slaves into the tobacco-growing Louisiana settlement at Natchez between 1726 and 1729 opened the way for a black–Indian alliance. With black support, the Natchez Indians rebelled in 1729, killing numerous white settlers. Blacks, too, played an important role in preventing the decimation of the Natchez forces during the successful counterattack by France and its Indian allies, the Choctaw. Once captured by the French, however, the black allies of the Natchez paid dearly: France turned the black captives over to the Choctaw, who killed the most active participants in the rebellion and enslaved the others. Not all black slaves chose to fight against the French, however. At least fifteen armed slaves stood with the French forces against the Natchez and as a result won their freedom.

Later, the colonial authorities of Louisiana explicitly adopted policies to prevent black slaves from making common cause with such Indian nations as the Natchez, the Chickasaw, the Illinois, the Arkansas, and a portion of the Miami. Offers of freedom were especially effective in deterring blacks from joining Indians in their attacks on white settlers in the 1730s.

Louisiana slaves also stole freedom by running away and forming Maroon societies, which in some cases lasted for several years. Indeed, runaway slaves in French Louisiana did **Maroon Societies** not appear to conform to patterns that distinguished Africans from Creoles in the British colonies. In the latter case, Africans tended to escape in groups, whereas Creoles ran away as individuals. In Louisiana during the last half of the eighteenth century, entire families of Creoles escaped to the swamps and the forests on the outskirts of

St. Malo Maroon communities, 1780s

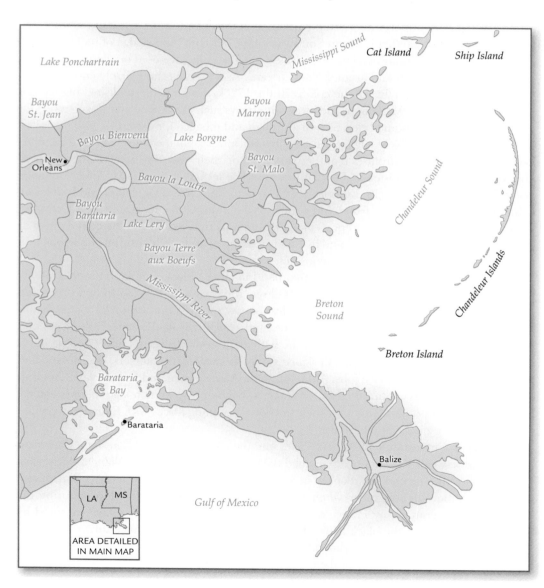

plantations and towns, setting up what they intended to be permanent settlements. These Creole Maroons built huts in which they housed guns and ammunition.

They grew vegetables, gathered berries, hunted, and fished. They also exhibited new patterns of Maroon behavior by engaging in trade, not simply raiding nearby plantations for cattle and food. They ventured in and out of New Orleans, where they marketed their own handiwork, such as woven basketry and homegrown corn and rice, before disappearing along secret paths to their villages.

Creole Maroon societies continued after the Spanish took control of Louisiana in 1763. During the early 1780s, and especially with the rise of the cypress lumbering industry, Maroons established villages in the cypress swamps of Bas du Fleuve, which lies between New Orleans and the mouth of the Mississippi River. They even worked out a labor relationship with local sawmill owners, who paid the Maroons for cutting and supplying cypress logs. According to historian Gwendolyn Midlo Hall, the most noted Maroon leader in Bas du Fleuve was Juan Maló, also known to the slaves as St. Maló. He and his followers controlled a number of Maroon villages, which they called Gaillardeland, located below New Orleans between the Mississippi River and Lake Borge.

Between 1782 and 1784, the Spanish governor of the colony undertook a mission to capture and destroy St. Maló's Maroon villages. Governor Miró often expressed his frustration in enlisting the aid of free blacks and mulattoes, since some of them feared repercussions and others shared bonds of blood and commercial relations with the Maroons. Using monetary incentives and punitive measures, the Spanish eventually succeeded in enlisting the support of black informants to hunt down the Maroons. In May and June 1784, the Spanish rounded up 103 Maroons. Among those captured and hanged were St. Maló and his wife Cecilia Canuet, who was charged with being his "inseparable companion in all his exploits."

From the arrival of the first Africans in St. Augustine in 1565 to the Revolutionary War more than two centuries later, black slaves gradually forged a new identity in mainland North America. Throughout the colonial period, the acculturation of Africans in the colonies was dominated by their role as laborers interacting with owners who viewed them primarily as tools to amass profits. Steadily, as historians such as Ira Berlin have made clear, the southern colonies moved from societies *with slaves,* in which black workers "were marginal to the central productive processes," to *slave* societies—places in which "slavery stood at the center of economic production, and the master-slave relationship provided the model for all social relations."

Throughout the North American colonies, blacks sought relentlessly to assert their humanity, while whites pursued every stratagem to make their slaves pliable tools in the labor system. As the eighteenth century drew to a close, some owners began to cloak their self-interest with arguments that slaves, as "members of extended plantation communities," were objects of "domestic affection" or even "family." Through escape, individual acts of noncompliance and hostility, the purchase of family members, court petitions, and even organized insurrections, the behavior of blacks told a different story—that of their quest for freedom.

CHAPTER

5 Give Me Liberty

The Paradox of Slavery and Freedom

Fighting for American Independence

The Movement to Free the Slaves

The Conservative Reaction

American foot
soldiers during
the Yorktown
campaign, 1781

t must have intrigued, if not perplexed, the slaves of Patrick Henry if they ever heard his stirring words: "Is life so dear or peace so sweet as to be purchased at the price of chains and slavery? Forbid it, almighty God. I know not what others may wish, but as for me, give me liberty or give me death." Armed with the love of liberty, so eloquently expressed by Henry and his revolutionary generation, thirteen of Great Britain's North American colonies fought to become a new nation and a new people. Blacks, too, contributed mightily to the story of American Independence. They fought as soldiers in the Revolutionary War. They believed in the independence of the individual and the consent of the governed. They valued in the most fundamental way what Thomas Jefferson and others would identify as the inalienable rights of life, liberty, and the pursuit of happiness. For African Americans, unlike Virginian Patrick Henry, the tyranny of slavery was not simply a metaphor for Anglo-American relations but a real and daily lived experience. Their wish for liberty broadened the ideology of the American Revolution to include black freedom.

The Paradox of Slavery and Freedom

The year 1763 proved to be a watershed for the American people. Great Britain brought to a triumphant conclusion its long war on the North American continent against France and her Native American allies. As loyal subjects, Americans fought in the French and Indian War for the British Crown, but the fruits of their victory were bittersweet. Great Britain's need to pay its massive wartime debts and to maintain a standing army in North America in order to hold and govern its newly acquired province, former French Canada, required additional revenue. Since King George III and Parliament tried to shift some of the cost of protecting and defending the colonies onto the colonists themselves, Americans came increasingly to view Britain's new policy as a threat to the economic and political freedoms they had enjoyed for generations. They resented the various taxation acts passed by Parliament, such as the Sugar Act of 1764 and the Stamp Act of 1765, and they decried the deployment of British troops in Boston in 1768 to maintain the peace and enforce the taxation.

When Parliament taxed the colonists without their explicit consent—after all, Americans did not sit in Parliament—colonial propagandists successfully distilled their objections into the rallying cry "no taxation without representation!" and brought thousands to the revolutionary movement. Colonial propagandists also adopted the emotionally charged language of race to register their complaints. **Freedom in a Slave Society** Using racial imagery, they demanded from Great Britain the traditional rights they were owed by the basic fact of their shared heritage. Thus John Adams, writing in the *Boston Gazette* under the pseudonym "Humphrey Ploughjogger," generated opposition to the Stamp Act by insisting: "We won't be their Negroes. Providence had never intended the American colonists for Negroes . . . and therefore never intended us for slaves. . . . I say we are as handsome as old English folks, and so should be as free." In a Pennsylvania newspaper, yet another colonist emphasized the shared English heritage by posing the questions: "Are you not of the same stock? Was the blood of your ancestors polluted by a change of soil? Were they freemen in *England* and did they become slaves by a six-weeks' voyage to *America*?"

In Virginia, the Revolution's rhetoric of freedom unified and rallied all classes of whites, while at the same time tightening slavery's grip on blacks. Virginia comprised, on the one hand, a white population of planters and small farmers who clung fiercely to the emergent republican notion of representative government and, on the other hand, a black population whose chattel status and coerced labor gave tangible meaning to the property-rights principles fundamental to republican government. By the second quarter of the eighteenth century, Virginia's white yeomen and former indentured servants increasingly were joining the ranks of small landowners and sharing with the wealthy planter class equality in racial identity and free status. Whites' veneration of the republican ideals of economic independence, freedom from tyranny, and civic virtue went hand in hand with the definition of a "freeman" as a property owner and, as such, a member of the polity.

These ideals, which also went hand in hand with the definition of black slaves as property (just as land was property), served to unite as a single propertied class both Virginia planters and the far more numerous yeomen farmers in the years leading up to the Revolutionary War. The Founding Fathers' devotion to freedom for all whites, which elevated them above all black slaves, led historian Edmund Morgan to label this perverse symbiosis of freedom and slavery the "American paradox."

It is telling, then, that large slaveholders such as Thomas Jefferson and Patrick Henry warned in their speeches and writings that, if Americans lost their political liberty, they would be transformed into slaves of a tyrannical British king and Parliament. In the Declaration of Independence, the words *slave* and *slavery* figure prominently, implicitly likening the colonists' condition under British tyranny to that of the blacks they themselves enslaved. The document expressed no sympathy for those men and women actually held in bondage, although the opportunity to do so had arisen. In his first draft of the Declaration of Independence, Jefferson had made explicit reference to blacks when he blamed George III for the slave trade—for waging "cruel war against human nature itself, violating its most sacred rights of life and liberty in the persons of a distant people who never offended him, capturing and carrying them into slavery in another hemisphere, or to incur miserable death in their transportation thither."

The Lower South delegations to the Continental Congress found Jefferson's words unacceptable. The passage, which the Massachusetts Patriot John Adams described as a "vehement philippic [polemic] against Negro slavery," was stricken from the final version of the document. It is not surprising, then, that the British found the colonists' protestations inconsistent, in their simultaneous outrage at having been made "slaves" by royal taxes on the one hand but with their continuing commitment to chattel slavery on the other. Memorably, the famous English writer Samuel Johnson snorted: "How is it that we hear the loudest *yelps* for liberty among the drivers of Negroes?"

Not all colonists accepted the slave order, however. In questioning their own inequality as Englishmen, some white Americans began to admit a marked contradiction in the identity of oppressed colonist *and* slaveholder. Already in the 1760s, John Woolman, an English-born New Jersey Quaker, and Anthony Benezet, a Philadelphia Quaker of French Huguenot parentage, began bringing slaveholding under public scrutiny in the Middle Colonies. When he was two years old, Benezet's parents had emigrated from France to London to escape religious persecution and then moved, when he was seventeen, to Philadelphia. There, Benezet joined the Society of Friends—the Quakers—and made his living as a schoolteacher. He authored nine antislavery pamphlets.

Others, such as the Philadelphia physician Benjamin Rush, also joined in the colonial agitation against slavery. In 1764 the Boston Patriot James Otis, Jr., perceived a danger in the agitation for freedom by slaveholders, proclaiming: "Those who everyday barter away other men's liberty will soon care little for their own." In *The Rights of the British Colonies Asserted and Proved*, Otis condemned slavery as "the most shocking violation of the law of nature." In 1767 Nathaniel Appleton of Cambridge, Massachusetts, defended his antislavery position on the basis of one's "natural right to be free." The Patriot propagandist Thomas Paine, whose 1776 pamphlet *Common Sense* most clearly stated the American colonists' case for their own freedom from Great Britain, published the year earlier another pamphlet entitled *African Slavery in America*, in which he associated slavery with "murder, robbery, lewdness and barbarity."

Such rhetoric, and the climate it created for openly questioning black slavery, was not lost on the slaves themselves. In Massachusetts, where Patriot protest had begun as early as the middle 1760s, slaves made their voices heard in a variety of ways. Boston slaves, with some assistance from sympathetic whites, were at the forefront of the black freedom petition movement during the Revolutionary era. In 1773 and 1774 blacks presented five petitions to the Massachusetts legislature and had them printed in newspapers and pamphlets. Drawing from the political ideology of the American revolutionary crisis, blacks made similar arguments in favor of their own natural rights. Slaves also brought freedom suits to court. Rev. Jeremy Belknap of Boston noted the rising number of freedom suits won by Massachusetts blacks during the 1770s. He described a 1770 case in which Boston blacks "collected money among themselves to carry on the suit, and it terminated favorable to them." In the two decades before 1783, thirty black men and women sued their masters for freedom in the Massachusetts courts, with only one unfavorable decision.

Birth of the Antislavery Movement

Northern blacks were not content with legal challenges alone; many took their protests to the streets. Economically depressed Boston frequently witnessed street demonstrations in which black men were active participants. In the eighteenth-century urban North, white servants and black slaves enjoyed a social camaraderie and shared social space. The elite, such as John Adams, spoke disparagingly of this union as socially problematic, referring to "a motley rabble of saucy boys, Negroes, and mulattos, Irish teagues and outlandish jack tars. . . ." Adams certainly characterized as such Crispus Attucks and the interracial mob that confronted British troops on the cold evening of March 5, 1770.

Attucks was a runaway slave and about forty-seven years old. Historians are unclear about the events of his life in the twenty years that followed his escape from his master, William Brown of Framingham, Massachusetts. At the time of Attucks's flight from slavery, Brown placed a runaway slave advertisement in the *Boston Gazette*, dated October 2, 1750, that offered a £10 reward for his return.

Crispus Attucks

The notice described Attucks as a "mulatto fellow about 27 years of age, named Crispus, 6 feet and 2 inches high, short curl'd hair, his knees nearer together than common; and had on a light coulor'd beaver skin coat, plain new buckskin breeches, blue yarn stockings and a checked woolen shirt." Brown concluded by saying that "all masters of vessels and others are hereby cautioned against concealing or carrying off said servant on penalty of law." Scholars think that Attucks may have spent time as a rope-maker on the docks and that he may also have sailed with a whaling crew out of Boston. If a seaman, he would have been aware of the restrictions that England's new navigation acts imposed. He likely applauded Sam Adams and his Sons of Liberty in 1765 when they incited the urban unrest that caused Parliament to repeal the Stamp Act the following year. On March 5, 1770, he was unquestionably front and center in what American Patriots quickly labeled the "Boston Massacre."

The Boston Massacre

This well-known engraving by Paul Revere is of the Boston Massacre, where Crispus Attucks lost his life.

Eyewitnesses later testified that the "stout mulatto" Attucks led the way by shouting to other men present: "The way to get rid of these soldiers is to attack the main guard!" The mob of men poured into King Street to protest the daily presence of the British redcoats. Theirs was a spontaneous explosion of anger in the wake of a rumor that soldiers had injured a young boy, but that anger had been steadily building throughout the two years that Boston had been occupied by the British army. The crowd converged at the Custom House on King Street, where a lone British sentinel stood. Insults flew at the sentinel, along with snowballs, clubs, and chunks of ice. British Captain Thomas Preston and additional soldiers came to the sentinel's aid. In the ensuing melee, Attucks met the full force of the soldiers' musket fire, becoming the first martyr for American freedom. The Boston Patriot Paul Revere listed Attucks along with the four other victims in his well-known engraving and broadside of the "Boston Massacre." Like the others, Crispus Attucks was buried with honors.

In the same year that Crispus Attucks was memorialized, a young black woman achieved her first significant acclaim as a poet. She was a slave in Boston, having been brought from Africa to America as a very young girl in 1761, on the ship *Phillis.* The six- or seven-year-old child was purchased by John and Susanna Wheatley and named Phillis Wheatley after the ship on which she had endured the Middle Passage. Susanna Wheatley recognized and nurtured her young slave's precocious intellectual and literary abilities and became Phillis's most dedicated supporter. It was Susanna who, in 1767, saw to the placement of one of Phillis's earliest poems in a Rhode Island newspaper. With publication of other poems in Boston, Phillis became a local celebrity and, as a black slave poet, a curiosity.

Phillis Wheatley

Phillis Wheatley rose to intercolonial and international fame in 1770, the year of the Boston Massacre, with her widely heralded and widely republished elegy for the evangelist George Whitefield, the personal chaplain to the powerful Countess of Huntingdon in England. The success of her Whitefield elegy led to the English publication of Phillis Wheatley's first book of poetry—*Poems on Various Subjects, Religious and Moral* (1773)—dedicated with permission to the Countess, who was also the patron of black autobiographical writers Olaudah Equiano and James Gronnishaw.

88

Wheatley, still a slave, traveled to England in 1773 to oversee the publication of her book and to meet her powerful patron along with other supporters, such as the well-known British abolitionist Granville Sharp.

Wheatley's poetry addressed subjects of religion, nature, revolutionary turmoil, and death. Given her slave status, initially the English, and indeed some Americans, doubted Phillis Wheatley's authorship. Thus her British publisher requested, and received in response, a written "attestation" from Boston worthies verifying Phillis Wheatley's authorship of her own poems. Her signatories came from the ranks of the town's slave owners and antislavery advocates alike. While she was in England, the British expressed surprise and discomfort with Wheatley's servitude. A London periodical in 1773 saw in Wheatley's slave status the opportunity to criticize the Americans' revolutionary fervor, remarking: "We are much concerned to find that this ingenious young woman is yet a slave. The people of Boston boast themselves chiefly on their principles of liberty. One such act as the purchase of her freedom, would, in our opinion, have done them more honour than hanging a thousand trees with ribbons and emblems." Wheatley herself later credited her manumission, granted by Mr. and Mrs. Wheatley on Phillis's return to Boston from London, to the efforts of her English supporters.

Wheatley did not miss the paradox of slavery and American freedom. Despite her reputation as a poet, Phillis Wheatley's most explicit remarks on the subject of slavery appear not in her poetry but in a letter to Samson

Phillis Wheatley
Born in Africa about 1753 and brought to America as a young girl, Wheatley received wide recognition during her lifetime for her essays and poetry as well as her mastery of Western manners and morals.

Occum, a Native American who moved in the same evangelical circles as Wheatley and her mistress Susanna. Although hers was a private letter dated February 11, 1774, someone (possibly Wheatley herself) saw to its eventual publication. In the letter, Wheatley called attention to the contradiction of slaveholders' cries for liberty, and she shared eloquently with Occum her belief in freedom as a God-given right: "In every human Breast, God has implanted a Principle, which we call Love of Freedom; it is impatient of Oppression, and pants for Deliverance; and by the Leave of our modern Egyptians I will assert, that the same principle lives in us. . . . How well the Cry for Liberty, and the reverse Disposition for the exercise of oppressive Power over others agree,—I humbly think it does not require the Penetration of a Philosopher to determine."

Fighting for American Independence

Beginning with the outbreak of hostilities in 1775, the question of arming blacks, slave and free, consistently plagued the Patriots. Official policy and practice in the colonies had never been uniform or consistent. In 1656 Massachusetts barred blacks from militia service, and in 1660 Connecticut followed suit. In actuality, however, blacks were frequently called on to fight in battles against other European groups and Indians, thus developing a tradition of African American military service that was alive at the time of the War for Independence. Men such as Briton Hammon, for example, fought in the Royal Navy as early as 1747, during King George's War, and continued in the navy during the French and Indian War. In 1760 Hammon published his exploits in what is considered to be the first African American narrative. Blacks served in militia companies in Georgia, North Carolina, Virginia, New York, Connecticut, Rhode Island, and Massachusetts. As historian Benjamin Quarles observed: "Despite the law, Negroes were enlisted for military service."

At Lexington and Concord in April 1775, the first battles of the war, blacks took up arms against the British, and they fought in subsequent battles in the spring and summer of that eventful year. Meanwhile, in May 1775 the Massachusetts Committee on Safety—commonly known as the Hancock and Warren Committee—took up the matter of black enlistment in the armed forces and decided that only freemen should serve, since using slaves would be "inconsistent with the principles that are to be supported." It is doubtful that this policy was adhered to very closely, because it is clear that slaves as well as free blacks fought in the Battle of Bunker Hill in June 1775. Indeed, some slaves were manumitted specifically to serve in the army. One of the outstanding heroes of the battle, Peter Salem, had previously been a slave in Framingham, Massachusetts.

Blacks against the British

Peter Salem was not the only black man to distinguish himself at Bunker Hill. Salem Poor, a soldier in a company and regiment composed largely of white men, won the praise of his superiors, who said that in the battle he "behaved like an experienced officer as well as an excellent soldier." In an official commendation presented to the General Court (legislature) of Massachusetts and signed by fourteen military leaders, the petition said: "We would only beg leave to say, in the person of this said negro centres a brave and gallant soldier. The reward due to so great and distinguished a character, we submit to the Congress."

While Peter Salem and Salem Poor stand out for their extraordinary feats of heroism, other blacks were integrated into the companies of whites and performed services for which they were later commended. The slave Prince Easterbrook is often mentioned as one who fought at the battles of Lexington and Concord. Other black soldiers whose names have been preserved include Caesar Brown of Westford, Massachusetts, who was killed in action; Barzillai Lew, a fifer and drummer; Titus Colburn and Alexander Ames of Andover; Prince Hall, later an abolitionist and Masonic leader; and many other Massachusetts blacks, including Cuff Hayes, Caesar Dickerson, Cato Tufts, Grant Cooper, and Sampson Talbert. Certainly not exhaustive, this list is indicative of the early use of blacks in crucial battles in Massachusetts.

Notwithstanding these initial battles, African Americans had by no means won the right to fight as soldiers in the War of Independence. A month after the formation of the Continental Army in June 1775, it was official policy to reject the services of black soldiers. In a meeting on July 9, 1775, a council of war convened under the army's commanding general George Washington, decided against the enlistment

Barzillai Lew
Revolutionary War fifer Lew was well known among his fellow Bostonians.

of "any deserter from the ministerial army, nor any stroller, negro, or vagabond, or person suspected of being an enemy to the liberty of America nor any under eighteen years of age." The ban on enlistment did not affect blacks already in the service. However, within a few months Edward Rutledge of South Carolina advocated the dismissal of all blacks, as "the military establishment which represented the thirteen colonies had to reflect the sentiments of all its components." Rutledge's motion failed despite support from many southern delegates, but it was only a matter of time before the issue was revisited.

In the fall of 1775 another council of war, consisting of Washington, major generals Artemus Ward, Charles Lee, and Israel Putnam, and several brigadier generals, addressed the question of whether to use black troops. On this occasion, the council agreed unanimously to reject all slaves and, by a large majority, to reject blacks altogether. Ten days later a group of civilians, among them Benjamin Franklin and Thomas Lynch, met with Washington and the deputy governors of Rhode Island and Connecticut to discuss plans for recruiting a new army. On November 12, 1775, General Washington issued an order instructing recruiters not to enlist free blacks, boys unable to bear arms, or old men unable to endure the fatigue of combat.

The British Appeal

Little did they know that a surprise move by the British a few days earlier would require a change in their policy toward black soldiers. On November 7, 1775, Lord Dunmore, the royal governor of Virginia, had issued a proclamation stating: "I do hereby declare all indentured servants, Negroes, or others (appertaining to rebels) free, that are able and willing to bear arms, they joining his Majesty's troops, as soon as may be, for the more speedily reducing this Colony to a proper dignity." Historian Woody Holton argues that Dunmore's strategy of soliciting black support was based on a growing rebelliousness among slaves, starting in the spring of 1775. In March of that year, whites began to comment with greater frequency on acts of slave resistance: in Georgia, several slaves rebelled and were burned alive, and the *Virginia Gazette* reported the foiling of a slave conspiracy in New York.

In April 1775 rumors spread about another slave conspiracy, this time in the Chesapeake around the James River. In the context of white apprehension about black unrest, Dunmore decided on April 21, 1775, to remove some barrels of gunpowder from Williamsburg, where Patriots could get their hands on them, to a British warship. Already aware of the fighting in Lexington and Concord and enraged over the ammunition relocation, the southern Patriots were further alarmed by Dunmore's threat to "declare Freedom to the Slaves, and reduce the city of Williamsburg to Ashes." In a reciprocal manner, black unrest and the revolutionary crisis in the southern colonies intensified. About a thousand slaves responded when, on November 7, 1775, Dunmore actually issued his official proclamation, summoning blacks to the Loyalist cause. They were enlisted as members of the "Ethiopian Regiment" and given uniforms. It is believed that the proclamation turned many white colonial neutrals into Patriots, because slaves of both Loyalists and Patriots escaped to freedom. Slave owners who might not have previously joined the rebels now opposed the British to prevent their own slaves from fleeing.

On November 23, 1775, an article appeared in a Williamsburg newspaper severely criticizing Dunmore's proclamation and pointing out to blacks that British motives were entirely selfish. On December 13 the committee of the Virginia Convention answered the Dunmore proclamation, not only denouncing the British for enticing slaves to rebel against their masters but also promising pardons to all slaves who returned to their masters within ten days. The alarm of the military high command and of the Virginians was fully justified. Patriot

Edmund Pendleton wrote Richard Henry Lee on November 27, 1775, that slaves were flocking to Dunmore in abundance.

During December, Washington grew increasingly worried at what the consequences of the wholesale enlistment of blacks in the British army might mean to Virginia. In a letter to Richard Henry Lee on the day after Christmas, Washington asserted that if Dunmore were

Washington's Response not crushed before spring, he would become the most formidable enemy to the cause of independence. His strength would increase "as a snowball, by rolling; and faster, if some expedient cannot be hit upon to convince the slaves and servants of the impotency of his design." Then, on December 31, Washington partially reversed his earlier policy against enlisting blacks in the Continental Army, announcing in a report to the president of the Continental Congress that he would permit free blacks to join the ranks. He noted that free blacks who had previously served in the army were very much dissatisfied at being discarded, and he feared that they would seek service in the British army. On January 16, 1776, the Continental Congress approved a policy permitting free blacks "who had served faithfully in the [Continental] army at Cambridge" to reenlist, but made it clear that no others were to be received.

The presence of British troops in America and the continuing revolutionary struggle itself had an unsettling effect on slavery. As large numbers of slaves of both Patriot and Loyalist masters escaped their bonds, the Revolutionary War became for African Americans a

The Revolution and Slavery struggle not simply between Great Britain and America, but also between master and slave. Slaves ran away even when they did not intend to reach British lines. Thomas Jefferson estimated that in 1778 alone more than 30,000 Virginia slaves ran away. In a letter to his brother in 1781, Richard Henry Lee wrote that two neighbors had lost "every slave they had in the world. . . . This has been the general case of all those who were near the enemy." Between 1775 and 1783, South Carolina lost 25,000 or more blacks, and during the war, Georgia lost perhaps 75 percent of its 15,000 slaves.

In 1779 in Phillipsburg, New York, British General Sir Henry Clinton issued his own proclamation regarding slavery. The proclamation, which served him during his command in New York and when he embarked on his military campaign in South Carolina, declared

General Clinton's Proclamation that slaves in the service of the Patriots were to be sold if captured, whereas slaves who deserted a rebel master and sought refuge with the British were to be protected. Eager to signal that the proclamation was a military strategy, not a program of general emancipation, Clinton and later General Charles Cornwallis, the commander of His Majesty's forces in the South, enlisted escaped slaves for service.

The British distinguished the slaves who fled to their lines for protection from those who were captured while serving the rebels. However, fugitive slaves often became the plunder of war for both sides. They were stolen, sold, and used for their captors' purposes. When the Americans finally defeated Cornwallis in the Lower South and he retreated to Virginia, in the summer of 1781, between four and five thousand runaway slaves trailed behind his army. With his provisions dissipating on his long march northward, Cornwallis drove off his black followers. A Hessian officer serving with the British, Johann Ewald, described that action as a breach of trust, explaining: "We had used them to good advantage and set them free, and now, with fear and trembling, they had to face the reward of their cruel masters." Some escaped and hid out as long as they could. According to historian Sylvia Frey, many of these runaway slaves had become infected with smallpox. As late as 1786 a corps of runaway blacks, trained by the British during the siege of Savannah, continued to call themselves the "king of England's soldiers" and raided Georgia plantations.

The British bid for black support, as well as the general course of the war, had a liberalizing effect on the American rebels' military policies. In addition to Washington's order for the enlistment of some free blacks after the Dunmore Proclamation, most states, either by specific legislation or merely by reversing their earlier policies, **Individual State Policies** began to enlist both slaves and free blacks for military service. In 1776 Virginia went so far as to permit free mulattoes to serve as drummers, fifers, and pioneers, and the following year, Virginia required that all black recruits simply have a justice of the peace give them a certificate of freedom. In 1778 Rhode Island and Massachusetts permitted slaves to serve as soldiers, demonstrating faith that sufficient black soldiers could be raised within their borders to form separate regiments. In the same year, North Carolina, while legislating against fugitive slaves, made it clear that the legal penalties did not apply to exslaves who were serving in the Patriot cause.

Indeed, it appeared as though states were now vying with one another in enlisting blacks. New Hampshire offered the same bounty to black soldiers that it was giving to whites, and masters received bounties as compensation for giving their slaves freedom. When it became increasingly difficult to recruit white soldiers in Connecticut, a vigorous effort to enlist blacks began. New York offered freedom to all slaves who would serve in the army for three years, with their owners given a land bounty for their slaves. Before the end of the war, most states, as well as the Continental Congress, were enlisting slaves with the understanding that they were to receive freedom at the end of their military service.

Only two states, Georgia and South Carolina, continued to oppose the enlistment of black soldiers. It was a source of considerable frustration to Colonel John Laurens, who repeatedly requested permission to raise several battalions of blacks in his native South Carolina. In 1779 the Continental Congress recommended that three thousand blacks be recruited in Georgia and South Carolina, which were facing a British invasion. The Congress promised to pay the owners not more than $1,000 for each slave recruited, and at the end of the war the slave was to be set free and given $50. Georgia and South Carolina took alarm over the plan and summarily rejected it. Despite continuing pleas from Laurens, neither state ever permitted such enlistment. By this time, Washington had so completely accepted the idea of blacks as soldiers that he could write of South Carolina and Georgia in a 1782 letter to Laurens: "That spirit of freedom which at the commencement of this contest would have gladly sacrificed everything to the attainment of its object, has long since subsided, and every selfish passion has taken its place." Even in these states, however, slaves were running away—to fight with the British and win their own freedom or to ally with the Patriots and win freedom for their country as well as themselves.

Of the more than 200,000 soldiers who served the cause of independence, approximately 5,000 were African Americans. The majority of black soldiers came from the North, even though the great bulk of the black population was in the **Black Military Distinction** South. Black soldiers served in every phase of the war and under every possible condition. There were, however, only a few separate black fighting units. In Massachusetts, a company was formed under Major Samuel Lawrence. His company was praised for its "courage, military discipline, and fidelity" when his men rescued him after he was completely surrounded by the enemy. Connecticut fielded a black company under the leadership of Captain David Humphreys, while Rhode Island's black company was commanded first by Colonel Jeremiah Olney and later by Colonel Christopher Greene. These units under white officers won admiration and respect.

At first, most white officers studiously avoided having to command all-black units, so there was some difficulty in securing a commander for Connecticut's black company. Finally, Captain Humphreys volunteered his services, and under his leadership the troops so distinguished themselves that thereafter officers were said to be as eager to obtain an appointment in that company as they had previously been of shunning it. In the Battle of Rhode Island, August 29, 1778, Colonel Greene's black regiment "distinguished itself by deeds of desperate valor." On three occasions, they repulsed Hessian soldiers who were charging down on them to gain a strategic position. In 1781 when Colonel Greene was surprised and killed near Points Bridge, New York, his black soldiers had fought valiantly to protect him. The enemy cut the black troops to pieces, trampling over their dead bodies to reach their leader. One white veteran described Greene's faithful men as "brave, hardy troops" who had "helped to gain our liberty and independence."

The vast majority of black soldiers served in integrated but primarily white units. So complete was the integration that one Hessian officer declared that "no regiment is to be seen in which there are not Negroes in abundance: and among them are able-bodied, strong, and brave fellows." Not only did blacks serve in the regiments of the New England and Middle Atlantic states, but they were also to be found fighting alongside white comrades in the southern states. Hardly a significant military action between 1775 and 1781 was without some black participants. They

John Singleton Copley, *The Death of Major Peirson*, January 8, 1781

were at Lexington, Concord, Ticonderoga, Bunker Hill, Long Island, White Plains, Trenton, Princeton, Bennington, Brandywine, Stillwater, Bemis Heights, Saratoga, Red Bank, Monmouth, Rhode Island, Savannah, Stony Point, Fort Griswold, Eutaw Springs, and Yorktown.

There were also many instances of blacks serving in the American naval forces during the War for Independence. Because they had piloted vessels in coastal waters before the war, their services were finally accepted during the dark days of the war, as able and ordinary seamen, pilots, boatswain's mates, and gunner's mates. They were among the crews of the coastal galleys that defended Georgia, North Carolina, South Carolina, and Virginia. Black sailors fought onboard the *Patriot, Liberty, Tempest, Dragon, Diligence,* and many other vessels. The Connecticut and Massachusetts navies (during the war some states also had their own naval forces) were manned by blacks, such as the three black seamen on Captain David Porter's *Aurora* and four of the crew of the privateer *General Putnam.* When he was but fourteen years old, James Forten, later a successful Philadelphia sail-maker and abolitionist, was a powder boy on Stephen Decatur's *Royal Louis* and participated in the victory over several British vessels. Later, when Forten was captured and offered a home in England, he refused, preferring to suffer as a prisoner of war rather than betray his country.

Most of the African Americans who served in the Revolutionary War will forever remain anonymous. Some, however, by virtue of their outstanding service won recognition from their contemporaries and a conspicuous place in Revolutionary War history. Tradition holds that two black men, Prince Whipple and Oliver Cromwell, were with General Washington when he made his dramatic and tactically brilliant crossing of the Delaware River on Christmas Day of 1776. Tack Sisson, by crashing open a door with his head, facilitated the capture of the British general Richard Prescott, at Newport, Rhode Island, on July 9, 1777. In that same year, Lemuel Haynes, who was later to become a distinguished minister to white congregations in New England, joined in the expedition to Ticonderoga to resist the invasion by Burgoyne's northern army. The victory of General "Mad Anthony" Wayne at Stony Point, New York, in 1779 was made possible by the espionage efforts of a black soldier named Pompey.

James Armistead Lafayette was a counterspy during the Revolutionary War. Known simply as "the slave James," he served under Gilbert du Motier (better known as the Marquis de Lafayette), who was on Washington's staff at the 1781 Battle of Yorktown, the climactic battle of the war. James's slave status enabled him to slip behind the battle lines into the British camp, where General Charles Cornwallis also employed his services, making James privy to secret information. James worked as a double agent, passing all the information he received to Lafayette for the remainder of the battle. After the war, James petitioned the Virginia House of Delegates for emancipation, which he received—following a second petition with a letter from Lafayette attached—in 1787. James, who adopted Lafayette as his last name, went on to become a property owner and collected a pension for his services in the nation's military.

In the fall of 1779, more than seven hundred Haitian free blacks were among the French forces that tried unsuccessfully to retake Savannah from the British forces, which had restored colonial rule a year earlier. Among the wounded soldiers was Henri Christophe, who would later play an important role in the liberation of St. Domingue (Haiti). When French Admiral Count D'Estaing recruited men in Saint Domingue to serve with the French forces that were scheduled to invade the American South, more than five hundred black and mulatto freemen volunteered, forming the French contingent known as the Fontages Legion. In addition to Christophe, future Haitian revolutionaries André Rigaud, Jean-Baptiste Villate, Jacques Beauvais, and Jean Savary gained military experience in the American Revolution as a by-product of the French alliance with the Americans. The black experience in the American Revolution had a direct effect on the revolution that would

New-York, 21st April 1783.

THIS is to certify to whomsoever it may concern, that the Bearer hereof *Cato Ramsay* a Negro, resorted to the British Lines, in consequence of the Proclamations of Sir William Howe, and Sir Henry Clinton, late Commanders in Chief in America; and that the said Negro has hereby his Excellency Sir Guy Carleton's Permission to go to Nova-Scotia, or wherever else *he* may think proper.

By Order of Brigadier General Birch,

Nova Scotian freedom certificate

bring into existence Haiti as the only black republic in the Western Hemisphere.

For blacks on the British side, the American victory caused a significant dispersal. Blacks were among the estimated 100,000 Loyalists evacuated from the British-occupied port cities of Savannah, Charleston, and New York in 1782 and from St. Augustine in 1783. However,

British-freed slaves and those still enslaved by Loyalist owners went in different directions. Slaves overwhelmingly were sent to the Caribbean, their large numbers reinvigorating and transforming plantation agriculture there. This was also true of the Bahamas, where **Black Loyalists** about 5,000 American slaves were relocated with their Loyalist masters. In Bermuda, former American slaves planted the first cotton crop in 1785–1786; by 1790 the island's cotton production stood second only to sugar in profitability. Some Loyalist-owned slaves were also used to supplement British troops in the Caribbean.

Freed blacks tended to go to Nova Scotia and to England. More than 1,300 freed blacks migrated to Nova Scotia in 1783; but, denied access to good land, many of them endured hardships as tenant farmers. Twelve hundred freed blacks went to London, where many suffered poverty and famine. In 1787 and in 1792, more than 1,000 blacks were transported from Nova Scotia and London and resettled under British abolitionist auspices in the African colony of Sierra Leone.

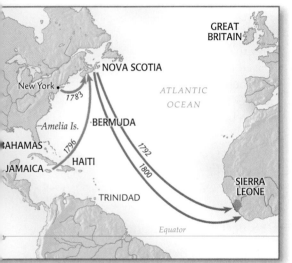

Loyalist black migration to Canada and Sierra Leone

British-freed blacks could be found in many locations after the Revolutionary War. For example, black religious leader George Liele and two former slaves were part of the evacuation in 1784 from Georgia to Jamaica. Having founded the First African Baptist Church in Savannah in 1777, Liele worked with the others in establishing Baptist missions in Jamaica.

Ultimately this diaspora of American blacks in the post-Revolutionary War era had important cultural and political implications. As historian Sylvia Frey argues: "By their very numbers, the movement of black Loyalists facilitated the transmission of culture, experience, and revolutionary sentiment to other parts of the world and ultimately tied the history of black people of the United States, the Caribbean islands, and West Africa together."

The Movement to Free the Slaves

By the end of the War for Independence, forces had been set in motion to effect a change in the status of American blacks. Even as the Battle of Lexington raged, North America's first antislavery society—the Pennsylvania Abolition Society—was just beginning to formulate its plans for action. Similar organizations soon arose in New York, New Jersey, Connecticut, and Rhode Island, attesting to the social implications of the Revolution's ideas of liberty and equality. So powerfully did those ideas act on American minds that almost every state in which slaves had been recruited for military service either freed them on enlistment or promised them manumission at the end of their service. The records of several states in the 1780s abound in deeds of manumission of black soldiers and their families.

Freedom for black soldiers did not go uncontested, however. At the end of the war, most masters sought to repossess slaves who had fought for freedom from Britain, and General **Antislavery Advocates** Washington found it necessary to authorize several courts of inquiry to establish the validity of such claims. Finally, some states resorted to the enactment of laws, such as one passed by the Virginia legislature in 1783, granting freedom to all slaves

British list of negro men and boys, 1783

"who served in the late war." A clear distinction was made between those slaves who served in the Patriot army and those who merely ran away from their owners or who escaped to the British lines. Even General Washington expressed alarm at the news that blacks were evacuating with British troops from various American ports, and he asked a friend in New York to help him retrieve some of his own runaways, whom he suspected of being in or around that city.

There was other evidence, beyond the manumission of blacks who had fought for the American Patriots, that the Revolutionary philosophy was taking effect. Numerous individuals of considerable stature, such as Alexander Hamilton, spoke out against the institution. Samuel Hopkins of Rhode Island, Ezra Stiles of Connecticut, and Jeremy Belknap of Massachusetts were outstanding among the group of theologians who expressed antislavery views. In Virginia, St. George Tucker's critical *Dissertation on Slavery* was studied by the author's students at the College of William and Mary, as well as by Virginia slave owners. Other antislavery educators were Jedidiah Morse, the father of American geography, and William Rogers of the College of Philadelphia (today, the University of Pennsylvania). Benjamin Franklin and Benjamin Rush spoke out against slavery, while the legal profession had outstanding antislavery spokesmen in Zepheniah Swift, Noah Webster, and Theodore Dwight.

Manumission and antislavery societies grew after the war. The Quakers organized the first one in 1775. In 1785, John Jay and Alexander Hamilton founded the New York Society for Promoting the Manumission of Slaves. In Delaware, a society was set up in 1788, and by 1792 there were antislavery societies in states from New England to the Upper South. Some sought to abolish the Atlantic slave trade. Others envisioned a scheme, however remote, that would completely abolish slavery in the new United States of America. Local societies collected information on slavery and published reports on the progress of emancipation. Others published orations and addresses designed to arouse public sentiment against slavery.

Doubtless the Revolutionary War had a direct effect on the expansion of the free black population. In the 1780s and 1790s, the legislatures of Delaware, Maryland, and Virginia revised their

Free North, Slave South

laws to make it easier for individual masters to free their slaves. In Virginia, the results were dramatic. In 1782 the percentage of free blacks in Virginia was less than 1 percent, that is, 1,800 free blacks out of the state's total black population of 220,592. By 1790 the number of free blacks had swelled to 12,766, or 4.2 percent of Virginia's black population.

In the Upper South, slaves were freed only by private acts of manumission. In the North, however, during the years following the Revolution slavery as an institution was by law put on the road to complete extinction—in the long run ensuring that in the post-Revolutionary period the United States would divide into a free North and a slave South. Two northern states could point to specific plans for abolition even before the war's end. The Vermont state

CONSIDERATIONS ON KEEPING NEGROES;

Recommended to the PROFESSORS of CHRISTIANITY, of every Denomination.

PART SECOND.

By JOHN WOOLMAN.

Ye shall not respect Persons in Judgment; but you shall bear the Small as well as the Great: You shall not be afraid of the Face of Man; for the Judgment is God's. Deut. i. 17.

PHILADELPHIA:
Printed by B. FRANKLIN, and D. HALL. 1762.

Considerations on Keeping Negroes
John Woolman wrote one of the earliest attacks on slavery, *Considerations on Keeping Negroes.* The title page is shown here.

Window in Time

Massachusetts Slaves' Petition, January 13, 1777

To the Honorable Counsel & House of Representatives for the State of Massachusetts Bay in General Court assembled, January 13, 1777:

> The petition of A Great Number of Blackes detained in a State of slavery in the bowels of a free & Christian County Humbly sheweth that your Petitioners apprehend that they have in Common with all other men a Natural and Unalienable Right to that freedom which the Great Parent of the Universe that Bestowed equally on all menkind and which they have Never forfeited by any Compact or agreement whatever but that were Unjustly Dragged by the hand cruel Power and their Dearest friends and sum of them Even torn from the Embraces of their tender Parents from A populous Pleasant and Plentiful country and in violation of Laws of Nature and of Nations and in Defiance of all the tender feelings of humanity Brought here Either to Be sold like Beast of burthen & Like them Condemned to Slavery for Life Among A People Professing the mild Religion of Jesus A people Not Insensible of the Secrets of Rational Being Nor without spirit to Resent the unjust endeavors of others to Reduce them to a state of Bondage and Subjugation your honouer Need not be informed that A Live of Slavery Like that of your petitioners Deprived of Every social privilege of Every thing Requisite and render Life Tolerable is far worse that Nonexistance.

Petition for freedom (manuscript copy) to the Massachusetts Council and the House of Representatives, 13 January, 1777. From the Jeremy Belknap papers, the collections of the Massachusetts Historical Society. Official copy submitted to the legislature, Massachusetts Archives.

constitution of 1777 outlawed slavery, and in 1783, the Massachusetts courts, buttressed by the state's constitution of 1780, weakened the institution of slavery beyond recovery.

Other northern states passed gradual emancipation laws: Pennsylvania in 1780, Connecticut and Rhode Island in 1784, New York in 1799, and New Jersey in 1804. Perhaps the highwater mark of the postwar antislavery movement came in 1787, when Congress added to the Northwest Ordinance a stipulation that neither slavery nor involuntary servitude should exist in the territory that would eventually form the states of Ohio, Illinois, Indiana, Michigan, and Wisconsin.

The Conservative Reaction

Despite their efforts, antislavery leaders failed to deal a nationwide deathblow to slavery after the War for Independence. Resistance to abolitionist schemes would harden in the Southern states, where so much capital was invested in slaves and where a new economic importance was already being attached to the institution. In the 1780s, moreover, there was the sobering fear that the social program that grew out of the struggle against Great Britain would get out of hand and uproot the very foundations of social and economic life in America. As small farmers and landless rural workers began to demand liberal and democratic land laws, moratoriums on their debts, and stronger guarantees of human rights, they challenged the authority by which the elite ruled the American states.

Some state leaders perceived the growing demand for democratization as a "horrid vision of disorder," in which they included abolitionist calls for the destruction of property in human beings and extension of liberty to all. What was to come of this dissen-

Shays's Rebellion

sion? In Massachusetts, Shays's Rebellion—the farmers' revolt for economic justice led by Daniel Shays during the fall and winter of 1786–1787—portended a disturbing answer to that question: another revolution, pure and simple.

African Americans participated in Shays's Rebellion, both as rebels and as volunteers in the Massachusetts militia that crushed it. Moses Sash of Worthington, a veteran of the Revolution, stood with the Shaysites; another Revolutionary veteran, Prince Hall of Boston, pledged seven hundred black men to Governor Bowdoin to fight against them. The governor refused Hall's offer; however, documents reveal that Boston's servant population, which included blacks, was drafted to help restore order. Shays's Rebellion only heightened the insistence by the new nation's leaders for a government stronger than the still functioning, but weak, wartime compact between the states known as the Articles of Confederation. In the summer of 1787 the Founding Fathers met in the Constitutional Convention in Philadelphia to stabilize and strengthen the national government. The result of their deliberation was a proposed new form of government: the United States Constitution, which was ratified in 1788.

At the Philadelphia Convention, slavery inevitably raised crucial questions. Slavery was central to two issues of long and critical concern to the framers of the new government: taxation and representation. How slaves should be counted for allocating taxes and seats in Congress caused heated debate. Most of the northern delegates could

The Three-Fifths Compromise

regard slaves in no light except as property and thus not entitled to any representation. However, delegates from Georgia and South Carolina—states where the majority of the people were slaves and the free white people a distinct minority—vigorously demanded that slaves be counted equally with whites when it came to apportioning congressional seats and electoral votes. Gouverneur Morris declared that the people of his state, Pennsylvania, would revolt against being placed on an equal footing with slaves, while Rufus King of Massachusetts flayed slavery in a fiery speech and condemned any proposal that would recognize it in the Constitution.

The three-fifths compromise finally written into the Constitution was perhaps satisfactory to no one, but it demonstrates clearly the strength of the proslavery interests at the convention. It was inserted in Article I, Section 2, and read:

> Representatives and direct Taxes shall be apportioned among the several States which may be included within this Union, according to their respective Numbers, which shall be determined by adding to the whole Number of free Persons, including those bound to Service for a Term of Years, and excluding Indians not taxed, three fifths of all other Persons.

Several states, including Massachusetts, Virginia, and Maryland, had already acted to prohibit the Atlantic slave trade within their own jurisdictions, although their motives differed. However, when the Constitutional Convention took on this issue, a fiery argument erupted. South Carolina's Charles Pinckney declared that his state could never accept a constitution that would prohibit the Atlantic **The Slave Trade** slave trade. Plantation owners in South Carolina and Georgia had suffered enormous losses of their human property during the war and were determined to rebuild their slave holdings by bringing even greater numbers of slaves from Africa. Significantly, Pinckney added: "If the States be all left at liberty on this subject, South Carolina may perhaps by degrees do of herself what is wished, as Virginia and Maryland have already done." His cousin, General Charles C. Pinckney, was more critical of Virginia and Maryland, asserting that the two states would profit from the cessation of the Atlantic slave trade because the price of their slaves would increase, thus ensuring their control of a domestic slave trade.

The fear of rupture at this critical moment led the states of the North and of the Upper South to reach a compromise that allowed the Lower South states to continue the Atlantic slave trade for at least twenty years. The provision finally adopted in Article I, Section 9, read:

> The Migration or Importation of such Persons as any of the States now existing shall think proper to admit, shall not be prohibited by the Congress prior to the Year one thousand eight hundred and eight, but a Tax or duty may be imposed on such Importation, not exceeding ten dollars for each Person.

By contrast, there was almost no opposition to the proposal that states be required to surrender fugitive slaves to their owners. The public obligation to return fugitive slaves, having already been provided for in several Indian treaties between 1781 and 1786, was established in the Northwest Territory in **Fugitive Slaves** 1787, at the same time that slavery was prohibited in that region. When the provision came before the Convention for consideration, it was late, August 28, and the delegates were impatient and eager to get home. The slave owners, having already won such sweeping constitutional recognition of slavery, found the question of fugitive slaves easily resolved. Without serious challenge, therefore, this provision was inserted in Article IV, Section 2:

> No Person held to Service or Labour in one State, under the Laws thereof, escaping into another, shall, in Consequence of any Law or Regulation therein, be discharged from such Service or Labour, but shall be delivered up on Claim of the Party to whom such Service or Labour may be due.

Given the heated debates over slavery during the drafting of the Constitution, it is ironic that the words *slavery* and *slave* never appear in the actual text, but rather the euphemisms *person, all other persons,* or *such persons.* Legal scholar A. Leon Higginbotham, Jr., argued that this "non-disclosure" on the part of the **The Language** **of the Constitution** drafters of the Constitution reveals their reluctance, at a time of growing antislavery sentiment, to debate the morality of human bondage or explicitly sanction it in this most important public document. For example, the word *slave* appeared in an early draft but not in the final version of the importation clause. In 1857 Supreme Court

Justice John McLean, in his dissenting opinion in the *Dred Scott* case, explained the omission of the words slave and slavery, stating: "We know as a historical fact, that James Madison, that great and good man, a leading member in the Federal Convention, was solicitous to guard the language of that instrument so as not to convey the idea that there could be property in man."

When the delegates to the Constitutional Convention returned home in September 1787, they could look back on three months of political maneuvering that effectively checked what the American elite had perceived as dangerous trends portending social upheaval. Clearly, the compromises around the slavery debates during the Constitutional Convention had stalled the nascent antislavery movement. Quakers and other antislavery groups could view the new document as lacking guarantees of human liberty, and zealous reformers regarded the Constitution as a victory for reaction. Nevertheless, the Constitution was ratified in 1788 and had gone into effect by the time George Washington was elected president in 1789. The drafters of the Constitution were dedicated to the sanctity of private property. For southerners, property meant slaves, just as surely as it meant land and livestock. In the protection of this property, the Constitution had given recognition to the institution of human slavery, and it would take seventy-five years to undo what was accomplished in Philadelphia in 1787.

The adoption of the federal Constitution marked the end of an era, not only in the political history of the American people but specifically in the history of African Americans. With British rule at an end and a stable national government in the making, Americans could no longer lay the onus for slavery at the door of the parent country. America's freedom had been the means of giving slavery itself a longer life than it was to have in the British Empire. Indeed, new factors on the horizon were about to usher in a new day for slavery as the old passed away.

CHAPTER 6

Building Communities in the Early Republic

African Americans in Demographic Perspective

Building Community Institutions

Blacks and American Party Politics

The Louisiana Purchase

Black Writing and Art in the New Nation

The War of 1812

Black Colonization

The Contagion of Liberty

Whaling captain Absalom F. Boston
Captain Boston sat for his portrait with gold hoop earrings and a white shirt under his formal coat. He sailed out of Nantucket in 1822 in the *Industry* with an all-black crew.

In the dawning years of the American republic, most blacks looked to the future with cautious optimism. The policies of the new federal government certainly inspired more caution than comfort. In 1790 Congress passed legislation that limited naturalization to white immigrants, and in 1792 the nation's lawmakers made militia service available to white men only. A federal law of 1793 mandated (as the Constitution had stipulated) interstate cooperation in the capture and return of fugitive slaves. Yet even the most casual observer could also see some changes for the better. In the years immediately after the Revolutionary War, an unprecedented number of slave manumissions occurred in the South. The northern states began to eradicate slavery altogether through various legislative, judicial, and constitutional procedures that in some cases meant immediate abolition but more often led to gradual emancipation.

Blacks drew inspiration from the global context of these times—the Age of Revolution. Not only had Americans fought for liberty, the French had done as well in 1789. Even more astonishing, slaves in St. Domingue (Haiti) rose up against their French oppressors in 1791. As word of the Haitian Revolution spread throughout communities in the North and the South, African Americans welcomed and celebrated the news of the first black victory over slavery.

In the early republic, urban blacks (slave as well as free) and rural free blacks all labored to build strong communities. They secured work and, in some cases, established their own businesses. Those who gained their freedom hastened to bring stability to their families, since under slavery husbands and wives often lived in different households. Black male property holders sought to participate as voters and members of the body politic in the face of rising black disfranchisement.

In the early years of the nation, blacks established their own churches, schools, fraternal lodges, and mutual-aid societies. Their belief in self-help and self-determination promoted a leadership of their own race, but wherever blacks could, they worked with white leaders and often benefited from what white abolitionist Dr. Benjamin Rush termed feelings of "virtuous and philanthropic joy." In the abolition-day celebrations held in their communities, blacks listened to their leaders' passionate and eloquent speeches in defense of freedom. In pamphlets and other printed media, they voiced their individual and collective concerns, their prayers, their protests, and their strivings. In so doing, the new nation's first black literary tradition was born.

Never a monolithic community, blacks debated their place and role in the United States. Some found emigration to Africa preferable to second-class citizenship in the land of their birth. Most, however, concluded that America belonged no less to them than to its white inhabitants. Some expressed patriotism in the efforts to safeguard the nation's welfare, as during the War of 1812. Others attempted to wage war against American slavery.

African Americans in Demographic Perspective

In 1790, the population of the United States stood at nearly 4 million, of whom 750,000 were persons of African descent. The vast majority of blacks, almost 89 percent, lived in the South Atlantic states. Most were slaves, bearing witness to the importance of the slave economy to the new nation. In sheer numbers, the South's free black population was larger than the North's, but in proportion to the slave population the number of free blacks in the South was miniscule—a mere 32,048, alongside 641,691 slaves. Virginia best exemplifies this pattern. In 1790 Virginia had, by far, the largest black population, slave or free, in the

Black Population Census of 1790		
State	Slaves	Free
Maine		536
New Hampshire	157	630
Vermont		269
Massachusetts		5,369
Rhode Island	958	3,484
Connecticut	2,648	2,771
New York	21,193	4,682
New Jersey	11,423	2,762
Pennsylvania	3,707	6,531
Delaware	8,887	3,899
Maryland	103,036	8,043
Virginia	292,627	12,866
North Carolina	100,783	5,041
South Carolina	107,094	1,801
Georgia	29,264	398
Kentucky	12,430	114
Tennessee	3,417	361
Total	697,624	59,557

Source: Negro Population in the United States 1790–1915. Arno Press and *The New York Times.* Copyright 1968 The New York Times Company. Reprinted by permission.

nation. No other state came close to approximating its nearly 13,000 free black inhabitants. Yet more than 96 percent of all black Virginians were slaves.

The Mid-Atlantic states of New York, New Jersey, and Pennsylvania had a combined black population of 50,000. Approximately half of this number lived in New York; New Jersey and Pennsylvania followed with slightly more than 14,000 and 10,000 blacks, respectively. Gradual abolition statutes explain the continuing presence of more than 3,000 slaves as late as 1830 in these states. New York passed a gradual abolition law in 1799, and slavery persisted there for another three decades. After 1830 most northern slaves, by now few in number, resided in New Jersey. By the eve of the Civil War, there were no slaves in the North, although New Jersey still had 18 elderly blacks who were considered lifetime "indentured servants," labeled as "slaves" in the 1860 census.

The Mid-Atlantic States and New England

Delaware was the only Mid-Atlantic state that failed to legislate in favor of emancipation, although the number of slaves there declined significantly relative to the number of free blacks. In 1790 Delaware had a black population of nearly 13,000, of which slaves more than doubled the free blacks. By 1810 the state's total population of African Americans stood at over 17,000, with more than three quarters of them free—most from private acts of manumission. Although Delaware's slave population declined over the next three decades, at least 13 percent (2,605) of the black population remained in slavery in 1840. Slavery would not end in Delaware until after the Civil War.

Flora, sold for 25 pounds sterling
In the eighteenth century, slaves were among the most valuable possessions of English people in the New World.

The demise of slavery in the Mid-Atlantic lagged behind what was happening in New England. There, in 1790 the census reported no slavery at all in Massachusetts and Vermont, although slaves could be found in New Hampshire, Rhode Island, and Connecticut. In 1790 slaves constituted one-fourth of New England's black population. Connecticut's 2,600 slaves accounted for the bulk of the 3,700 who remained in bondage in New England. But over the next two decades, slavery virtually vanished in every New England state.

Slavery was definitely not disappearing to the west of the southern Appalachians. Although Kentucky and Tennessee were not states in 1790, their rapid settlement made statehood imminent. African Americans came to those territories primarily as slaves, led across the Allegheny Mountains by slave owners and slave traders from Virginia and the Carolinas. In 1790 Kentucky had more than 12,000 slaves, and Tennessee had 3,400. Together they counted only 475 free blacks.

The timing and character of abolition were crucial to the process of building black communities. Community institutions developed most rapidly in cities, especially in the North, where the slave codes of the colonial era had either been abolished or were on the wane. But even where free status prevailed, blacks endured economic discrimination and social ostracism. Compared to whites, free blacks represented a significantly more urbanized group. They gravitated to the cities on the East Coast, which offered men greater opportunities in the maritime industry and women in domestic service. In

Development of Black Communities

1810, 22 percent of all blacks in Massachusetts lived in Boston, compared to only 7.1 percent of the state's white population; 32 percent of New York's free blacks lived in New York City versus 9.14 percent of the state's whites; and 41.7 percent of Pennsylvania's free blacks lived in Philadelphia as against a mere 10.6 percent of Pennsylvania's whites. Free blacks in the South were similarly overrepresented in such major cities as Richmond, Charleston, New Orleans, and Baltimore, the last having the nation's largest free-black population throughout the antebellum period. By 1820 free blacks in Baltimore outnumbered the slaves there.

African American population growth occurred during a period marked by increased opportunities in the maritime trades, new commercial and crafts opportunities, a building boom, and the emergence of new service industries. This was also a time of accelerating white migration. Boston, for instance, lost much of its original ethnic and cultural homogeneity owing to white migration from other states and from various parts of Europe. In her analysis of Boston tax assessment records, historian Jacqueline Barbara Carr shows that between 1780 and 1800 the majority of the city's blacks were servants and laborers but that some were identified as shop employees, barbers, seamen, cotton duck fabric mill employees, sawyers, coopers, and soap-makers. The data identify only one each as carpenter, rope-maker, chimney sweep, coachman, stable-hand, tailor, hatter, leather dresser, fiddler, lemon seller, baker, and painter—indicating that black Bostonians, compared to blacks in the large Mid-Atlantic cities, were slower to accumulate capital or to join the ranks of skilled laborers. Relative to Boston, Philadelphia had more affluent black businessmen, and New York had a greater number of black artisans. The occupational structure of black Boston was far more compressed into the lower economic ranks.

The early demise of slavery and the slave trade in Massachusetts spurred black migration to Boston. Between 1790 and 1800, the black population in Boston increased by more than 53 percent. Massachusetts leaders had already anticipated that their state would be perceived as a safe haven for escaped **Black Migration to Boston** slaves. In March 1788 the Massachusetts legislature passed a defensive measure to prevent black in-migration from other states: "No African or Negro, not a citizen of one of the United States," the law warned, "shall be suffered to tarry within this Commonwealth." The penalties included a whipping and deportation. In September 1800, no doubt anxious about the city's growing black population, Boston's chief of selectmen published a notice in local newspapers, identifying by name more than two hundred blacks, Indians, and mulattoes who were believed to have moved into Boston from Rhode Island, New York, Philadelphia, and the West Indies. They were warned to leave immediately. However, the law was rarely enforced, and soon it disappeared from the books.

In the state that boasted no presence of slaves, the black Revolutionary War veteran and leader Prince Hall advised his community to keep a positive attitude despite "the daily insults we meet on the streets of Boston," since "the darkest hour is just before the break of day." The black community would heed this advice. During the early national period, Boston's black leaders, like those in other cities, mobilized their community in laying the foundation of an institutional infrastructure. Black leaders also actively cultivated relationships with those whites they believed would support their community-building initiatives.

In Philadelphia, the early rise of the black community has been attributed to Pennsylvania being the first state to pass an emanci- **Blacks in Philadelphia** pation law, the Gradual Emancipation Act of 1780. Although the law's provisions did not liberate slaves born before 1780, and although those born after that date were required to serve a lengthy apprenticeship before becoming free, in Philadelphia the free black population grew quickly—from 1,805 in 1790 to 9,675 in 1810—while its slave population dropped from 273 to a mere 3. As slavery disappeared in Philadelphia, the living patterns of black families changed. In 1790 a little over half of all blacks lived in white households; by 1820 an important shift had occurred, with almost three-quarters of all blacks by then living in black households. Although the majority of African Americans in Philadelphia between 1800 and 1820 fell into the category of unskilled laborers and domestic or personal servants, some found skilled jobs in shipbuilding, the building trades, the leather trade, and metal crafts. A few became entrepreneurs. Most notable was James Forten, who worked with a white sail-maker for twelve years before taking over the venture upon his employer's retirement. Forten's sail-making business became very successful, employing an interracial workforce of about thirty men in 1807.

Philadelphia's black urban institutions spawned their own clergymen, teachers, and accountants, outstripping other cities. According to historian Gary Nash, Philadelphia had at least a dozen black clergymen and teachers. The first black teacher in Philadelphia was an African-born woman and former slave named Eleanor Harris, who at the time of her death was described as a "woman of character" and a "well-qualified tutoress of children."

New York City's Black Community Compared to Boston and Philadelphia, New York City's black community remained heavily enslaved, because slavery was legal in the state of New York until 1799. Only in that year did the state pass a gradual emancipation act, which provided freedom for the children of all slaves born in New York State and prohibited the importation of new slaves into it. In the decade before the passage of this law New York City's free population had grown larger. In 1790 the number of slaves in New York City was twice that of free blacks, and slaves constituted 66.5 percent of the city's total black population of 3,092. A decade later, the black population had risen to 5,865, with 43.2 percent in bondage. Yet the diminished proportion of slave to free in New York is misleading, since the city's actual number of slaves did not decrease; rather, it rose by 23 percent. These growing slave numbers were accompanied by a 33 percent increase in the number of slaveholders, some of them French plantation owners who came from Haiti with their slaves.

Outstripping the number of slaves, then, were the many free blacks who migrated into New York City from the surrounding countryside and the Upper South. Blacks were leaving those areas where they had been enslaved. The effects of gradual emancipation were not felt until 1810: census data for that year reveal a significant drop in New York City's slave population, whose actual number stood at 1,446, or 16.3 percent of the city's total number of blacks. Much of the labor available to blacks was unskilled, but representation in the artisan trades exceeded that in Philadelphia. New York City directories and census data list black carpenters, cabinetmakers, upholsterers, sail-makers, butchers, bakers, and other skilled workers.

Building Community Institutions

In the early years of the United States, blacks remained fairly well integrated in urban neighborhoods. The index of dissimilarity, which scholars use to assess segregation between two groups, reveals that some residential "clustering" had begun, but it did not conform to later patterns of residential density. Shared institutions, not shared neighborhoods, provided the initial cement for the building of cohesive free-black communities. The early institutions were the cornerstones around which black neighborhoods and communities were built.

The first such organization was the Free African Society of Newport, Rhode Island, founded in 1780. It was followed by Philadelphia's Free African Society in 1787, Boston's African Society in 1796, and the New York African Society for Mutual Relief in 1810. These nascent mutual-aid, quasireligious organizations also spawned black schools, burial grounds, and churches in their respective cities. For example, from Philadelphia's Free African Society emerged in 1794 both the African Church of Philadelphia (renamed St. Thomas's African Episcopal Church under the leadership of Rev. Absalom Jones) and the Bethel African Methodist Episcopal Church, called Mother Bethel, under Rev. Richard Allen.

Black institutions were founded not simply in response to white racism. They emerged because of blacks' desire to participate in shared cultural traditions. Nowhere is this more evident than in the movement to establish independent black churches.

Independent Black Churches

During the early years of the nation the first separate black churches formed. In the 1770s, blacks in Petersburg, Virginia, in Charleston, South Carolina, and in Savannah, Georgia, all began organizing separate churches, largely composed of the slave populations in those cities. Between 1773 and 1775, George Liele and David George founded a black Baptist church in Silver Bluff, South Carolina. However, the two men left the United States with the departing British troops at the end of the Revolutionary War. Andrew Bryan, on gaining his freedom in the 1790s, formed in Savannah the First African Baptist Church, which in 1803 spawned two additional churches.

Separate black churches would organize in black communities, North and South. From the 1790s through 1810, numerous separate black churches and denominations were organized: the African Methodist Episcopal Church in Philadelphia, New York, Baltimore, and other cities; the African Methodist Episcopal Zion Church in New York; and congregations of Baptists in Boston, New York, and Philadelphia, of Presbyterians in Philadelphia, and of Episcopalians in Philadelphia and New York. During the first decade of the nineteenth century, in Philadelphia alone ten churches of different denominations carried the word *African* in their names.

The religious revivals (known as the First Great Awakening) that began in the 1740s in New England and reached the South in the 1770s through the 1790s brought blacks increasingly into the evangelical fold of the Methodists and the Baptists, many of whom were anti-slavery advocates. At interracial revivals, blacks—as preachers and as converts—wept and shouted in ecstatic worship alongside whites. In the narrative of his life, black Methodist minister John Marrant recalled being "struck to the ground . . . speechless and senseless," when listening to the great English preacher George Whitefield in late 1769 or early 1770 in Charleston. As a result of his conversion experience, Marrant became a preacher who proselytized among both Native Americans and African Americans.

Likewise, slave-born Richard Allen was drawn into Methodism outside Dover, Pennsylvania, after hearing the charismatic and anti-slavery white preacher Freeborn Garretson. Indeed, Garretson persuaded Allen's owner of the sinfulness of slavery, making it possible

Richard Allen
Allen was the leading figure in events that produced the independent black church movement and led to the establishment of the African Methodist Episcopal Church. He served as the first bishop of the AME Church.

for Allen to buy his freedom. Allen's own preaching abilities drew him to the Methodist circuit, where he became known to the leading evangelical preachers of his day. Traveling to South Carolina, to New York, and to Indian lands in the Appalachians, Allen exhorted interracial audiences. After moving to Philadelphia in 1786, he continued to preach and to conduct prayer meetings specifically for black Philadelphians, while earning his living as a shoemaker. In 1787 Absalom Jones, a member of his black prayer group, joined Allen and other exslaves in forming the Free African Society.

The determination of Richard Allen and Absalom Jones to break away from the racially integrated St. George's Methodist Episcopal Church, of which they were members, stemmed from a racist incident during a Sunday service in 1792. Church officials pulled Allen and fellow worshippers Absalom Jones and William White from their knees during prayer and directed them to the balcony, ordering them to abide by a new segregated seating policy. When the prayer ended, Richard Allen recalled, "we all went out of the church in a body, and they were no more plagued by us in the church." However, the idea for a separate black church was not new to Allen and Jones. As leaders of the Philadelphia Free African Society, they had begun considerably earlier to network with sympathetic white donors such as Dr. Benjamin Rush, a well-known patriot and abolitionist, in a fundraising campaign for a black school and church. Thus on that fateful Sunday in 1792 neither Allen nor Jones felt the need to be submissive to the racism they encountered.

Even after the newly erected Mother Bethel opened its doors two years later, Allen continued to resist intrusive attempts by the white Methodist General Conference to control the church property, the licensing of preachers, church meetings, and his own authority over his parishioners. Resolution of the matter came only when the Supreme Court of Pennsylvania ruled in favor of the black church's independence. The court's decision in 1816 opened the way for founding the African Methodist Episcopal Church as the first black-led denomination. Representatives from black churches in other parts of Pennsylvania, in Baltimore, in Wilmington, Delaware, and in Salem, New Jersey, held a three-day meeting at Bethel to establish their own ecclesiastical structure and leadership. The conference chose Daniel Coker as its bishop, but after his resignation Allen was elected to fill the position.

The African Methodist Episcopal Church

Well before it achieved denominational status in 1816, the AME church had branches springing up in Baltimore, Wilmington, and various Pennsylvania and New Jersey towns, and Allen was able to enlist the aid of a number of able persons, such as Daniel Coker, Nicholson Gilliard, and Morris Brown. By 1820 Philadelphia alone had four thousand black Methodists, and in the Baltimore district there were almost two thousand. The denomination spread as far west as Pittsburgh and as far south as Charleston.

In the late eighteenth and early nineteen century, the building of separate black community associations and institutions—mutual-aid societies, fraternal lodges, schools, and churches—was creating a visible urban black leadership class. These pathbreaking organizations reflected a common set of values that included respectability and moral uplift, literacy and cultural achievement, and economic advancement and racial self-determination. For example, the first black fraternal organization was the African Masonic Lodge in America, founded in Boston under the leadership of Prince Hall. Hall was among fifteen free blacks initiated into Masonry by British soldiers during the occupation of Boston in 1775. After American Masons refused to grant a charter for his proposed African Masonic Lodge, Hall in 1784 applied to British Masons, who gave him the

Separate Black Institutions

recognition he needed to establish African Lodge Number 1. In 1787 this lodge was redesignated Lodge Number 459, with Prince Hall as Master. Over the next few years, Hall granted charters to African Lodges in other northern cities, including Philadelphia and Providence.

Boston's black leadership class sparked the petition for an African School in 1787. The Boston public schools (called "free schools") were not segregated by law, but in practice black children were denied access to them. Petitions from black parents led to the authorization of a school, but on condition that funds to support it were privately secured. In 1798 black Bostonians raised money to employ a teacher; several influential whites assisted in obtaining these funds, including William Emerson (father of the future philosopher Ralph Waldo Emerson) and William Thornton Kirkland (who would later become the president of Harvard College). Even so, it would take another eight years to secure an actual schoolhouse; in the meantime, the home of black Bostonian Primus Hall served this purpose. In 1812 the Boston School Committee—the city's school board—finally agreed to grant the African School an annual subsidy, but by doing so it assumed complete control of black education and thus gave Boston a racially segregated school system.

Black leaders' personal relationships with wealthy and benevolent whites enhanced institution building. For example, white philanthropy played an important role in the construction of the African Meeting House in Boston in 1806, thus making **White Philanthropy** it possible for blacks to move their school from a private home to a community edifice. Boston's black community also received significant contributions from the commonwealth's lieutenant governor and members of the local white ministry in constructing the African Meeting House. The building housed, as well, the first independent black church in Boston, the African Baptist Church, founded in 1805 and led by the black minister, Rev. Thomas Paul. Paul would also assist in organizing the Abyssinian Baptist Church in New York in 1809.

White philanthropists contributed to the construction of the Bethel AME Church in Philadelphia, as well as of a black Episcopal church, St. Phillip's, in New York. The New York Manumission Society, an antislavery group of prominent white citizens, in 1787 established the New York African Free School, which opened with forty students and never exceeded sixty in its first decade of existence. Withstanding initial opposition, the school attracted new interest in 1810, when the state required masters to teach all slave children to read the Scriptures. By 1820 the institution was accommodating more than five hundred black children. New Jersey began educating black children in 1777, and by 1801 schools, albeit short-lived, had been set up in Burlington, Salem, and Trenton. In addition, Quakers and other religious and humanitarian groups were teaching black children privately. As early as 1774, the Quakers of Philadelphia established a school for black children, and after the Revolutionary War the program was enlarged with funds provided by philanthropists such as the Quaker abolitionist Anthony Benezet. In 1787 a school was built, and ten years later there were no less than seven schools for blacks in Philadelphia. This interest in fostering black education continued into the nineteenth century.

However, black leaders did not always see eye to eye with white donors. In New York City, separate schools under black control appeared, which competed with the white New York Manumission Society's African Free School. This effort to establish separate schools produced the city's first significant black **Black and White Leadership Conflicts** leader, educator John Teasman, who became an important public spokesman for New York's growing free-black community. Teasman started his own school shortly after being fired from the Manumission Society's Free African School, attesting to conflicts between the black community and the white antislavery community. Historian John Rury identifies additional differences. When African American leaders proposed publicly celebrating the end of the Atlantic slave trade in 1808, the members of the New York Manumission Society opposed the idea, describing the celebration as "improper, in as much as it tended to injure themselves and cause reflections to be made on this society." The black leadership did not share this view. Instead, New York's black community joined Boston's and Philadelphia's in inaugurating an interstate celebration—the first annual holiday specifically for black people in the new United States.

Blacks and American Party Politics

Black Americans, like white Americans, understood the importance of electoral politics. At the dawning of the new nation, most adult Americans could not vote. Before 1830 property and tax-paying qualifications excluded many men, while gender proscriptions excluded all women, except in New Jersey, where some property-owning women could vote until 1807. The democratization of the franchise for males began during the first two decades of the nineteenth century, escalated in the late 1820s, and culminated in the 1830s. Ironically, this democratizing process, while swelling the white male electorate, yielded the opposite result for black voters. As state legislatures rescinded property restrictions, they concurrently enacted statutes that specifically disfranchised black men. Free-black property holders, who had once voted in most of the northern states and even in some southern states (Maryland, Tennessee, and North Carolina), now found it increasingly difficult, if not impossible, to do so.

In 1801, the Maryland General Assembly proposed legislation for the dual purpose of abolishing property restrictions and of ridding the state of black voters who were "histori-

Disfranchisement of Blacks

cally free" (that is, not born a slave). An earlier law had already excluded those freed from slavery from voting. The new statute, which was added to the Maryland State Constitution in 1802, stated explicitly "that every free white male citizen of this state, and no other . . . shall have a right of suffrage."

Black voters in New Jersey were disfranchised in 1807, along with property-owning women, whose suffrage had been guaranteed after the Revolutionary War. In Connecticut during the early years of the nineteenth century it is likely that some black property holders voted, as is suggested by an editorial in the *Connecticut Courant,* dated September 7, 1803, that mentioned "two citizens of colour" who were both Democratic-Republicans and free in Wallingford. However, in 1814 and 1818 the Connecticut legislature passed laws requiring that each voter meet the property and residence qualifications of the state—and that "he be a free white male person." When the Connecticut constitutional convention met in the latter year, delegates debated the wisdom of explicit racial wording, but the wording was accepted by a vote of 103 to 72.

In 1822 blacks in Rhode Island lost the right to vote. The state of New York democratized the right of suffrage for its white male citizens in the constitution of 1821 and in an amendment in 1826, but the law continued to grant the right to vote to black male citizens only if they owned property with the relatively high assessment of $250. Pennsylvania also disfranchised its black male voters, but later in 1842.

The black vote figured in the political partisanship that emerged in the 1790s with the onset of a party system. Historians have traditionally explained the rise of partisan strife to such issues as the nationalism of the Federalist Party versus the states-rights orientation of the Democratic-Republicans (who were not the predecessor of the modern Republican Party); the Federalists' pro-British attitudes, in this era of the French Revolution, versus the strong French sympathies of the Democratic-Republicans; and the elitism, xenophobia, and banking policies of such Federalists as John Adams and Alexander Hamilton versus the more popular orientation, egalitarian rhetoric, and rural interests of such Democratic-Republicans as Thomas Jefferson and James Madison. Yet to this list of early political divisions must be added the clashing positions of each party on questions involving slavery and black citizenship. The evidence reveals that the Federalists were more generally inclined to oppose slavery and to view more sympathetically the role of blacks as citizens.

The Haitian Revolution proved to be as important a touchstone as the French Revolution for delineating American partisan differences. After the French Revolution broke out in 1789, Democratic-Republicans took a far more optimistic view of what was happening in France than did the Federalists. However, the sympathies of the **The Haitian Revolution** two parties reversed when blacks in the French colonies looked to secure for themselves the same "liberty, equality, and fraternity" for which French people at home were fighting. One of these French colonies was St. Domingue, in the western part of the Caribbean island of Hispaniola. When the whites of St. Domingue demanded the abolition of property qualifications for voting, while at the same time opposing the right to vote

by property-owning free people of color [*gens de couleur*], the slaves joined the fray with their own demand for liberty and equality. In August 1791 they rose in rebellion. France sent troops to St. Domingue to quell the disturbance, but the rebels continued their armed resistance.

The intrepid leader of the black and mulatto rebel forces was the able and experienced soldier Toussaint Louverture, who by 1800 was at the height of his power. France's new ruler, Napoleon Bonaparte, however, regarded Toussaint as an obstacle to his plan to create a great French empire in the New World. With Louisiana in his hands and with St. Domingue as a key point in the Caribbean, Napoleon hoped to dominate the entire Western Hemisphere, or at least a substantial portion of it. He therefore dispatched a large army of 25,000 men under General LeClerc to subdue St. Domingue. Although the French succeeded, by a series of tricks, in capturing Toussaint and carrying him off to France, they could not subdue the colony. Yellow fever and the bitter determination of the followers of Toussaint to be free conspired to thwart Napoleon's aims. On January 1, 1804, after more than a decade of struggle, the Republic of Haiti became the world's first black republic and the second New World nation, after the United States, to win its independence.

Historian Donald R. Hickey persuasively argues that American party politics were divided over the revolution in St. Domingue. It was the Federalists, not the Democratic-

Toussaint Louverture

Toussaint Louverture
Leader of the Haitian Revolution against France

Republicans, who tended to support the Haitian Revolution, giving further evidence of their sympathy for African Americans. The Federalist administrations of presidents Washington and John Adams initially aided the embattled French planters but later reversed this policy as American discomfort grew over seeing French colonial power reestablished in the New World.

In 1798 the United States began an undeclared naval war with France, known as the Quasi-War, and in 1799 Secretary of State Timothy Pickering summed up the Federalists' position, writing letters noting: "Nothing is more clear than, if left to themselves, the Blacks of Saint Domingo will be incomparably less dangerous than if they remain the subjects of France. . . . France with an army of those black troops might conquer all the British Isles [in the Caribbean] and put in jeopardy our Southern States." In August 1799 President Adams supported establishing trade relations with the black rebel government. Subsequent congressional approval (called Toussaint's clause) authorized the president to reopen trade with "any island, port, or place" belonging to France if deemed in America's best interests. Toussaint Louverture, in turn, permitted armed American vessels to call at the island's ports, which, in turn, served the Americans as bases in the Quasi-War.

The Louisiana Purchase

The purchase of Louisiana was also connected with the trouble in the Caribbean. Democratic-Republican leader Thomas Jefferson gave voice to slaveholders' fears when he called the revolutionary slaves of Haiti "cannibals" and their "combustion" a threat to slavery in the United States. When Jefferson assumed the presidency in 1801, he broke all formal relations with the rebel government. France's reacquisition of Louisiana from Spain in 1800 had greatly disturbed him, since in 1795 the new republic had negotiated a satisfactory arrangement with Spain for navigation of the Mississippi River.

Representatives of the United States attempted to secure from France the promise that western farmers could continue to navigate the river. Instead, the French offered them the whole of Louisiana, which the United States purchased in 1803. Several reasons caused Napoleon to decide to sell Louisiana, but one important reason was his failure to hold Haiti and, as a result, the impossibility of his erecting a great empire in the New World with Louisiana and Haiti as crucial points. In an editorial in the *New York Evening Post* dated July 5, 1803, Federalist leader Alexander Hamilton responded to the Jefferson administration's purchase of Louisiana from Napoleon by praising not Jefferson's wisdom, but the "courage and obstinate resistance" of the Haitian revolutionaries. Hamilton contended that this revolution was a key ingredient to the fortuitous chain of events by which France lost its valuable New World colonies.

Free-black voters preferred the Federalists because of their prominence in the early republic's antislavery societies, especially in northern cities. Federalists John Jay (a future **Federalists and Free Blacks** justice of the Supreme Court) and Alexander Hamilton were among the founding members of the New York Manumission Society in 1785. In March of that year, Jay wrote to the Pennsylvania abolitionist Dr. Benjamin Rush: "I wish to see all unjust and all unnecessary discriminations everywhere abolished, and that the time may soon come when all our inhabitants of every colour and denomination shall be free and equal partakers of our political liberty." Based on such evidence, historian Paul Finkelman has argued that it was the Federalists who "helped lay the groundwork for what would become the abolitionist critique of American politics." Historians also point out that many of the leading abolitionists in the 1840s and 1850s were children of Federalists. Not all Federalists, though, were critical of slavery. The party's primary political base was New England, where antislavery sentiment ran strong, but southern Federalists defended the slave trade and the slave regime. Some even publicly condemned antislavery petitions.

Northern Federalists' commitment to the growth of cities, manufacturing, and the maritime trades helped open jobs for the increasingly urbanized free-black population. Federalists in New York and Boston courted black voters to counterbalance the votes of working-class Irish immigrants, who more often voted for the Democratic-Republicans. In Boston's heated election in 1800, for example, one observer attributed the increase in Federalist votes to "forty men of colour." Jefferson's victory in the presidential election that year ignited intense party rivalry in New York, where hitherto Federalists had maintained control. Democratic-Republican leaders condemned the Federalist-black alliance in race-baiting rhetoric that sought to win over white immigrant voters, and in the 1807 election Federalists spoke in equally pejorative language about the impact of "foreign born" voters in New York City.

New York elections were especially contentious during the first two decades of the nineteenth century, since the state was perceived as holding the balance of power between Federalist New England and the Democratic-Republican South. And black voters found themselves embroiled in New York's partisan battles. For example, in April 1808 black New Yorkers held their first state political caucus, known as the "General Meeting of the Electors of Colour," at which time they publicly endorsed the Federalist ticket in the upcoming state elections. In response, the Democratic-Republicans posted their own inspectors at polling places to intimidate black voters. They accused free-black voters of being slaves, turning them away from the polls if they came without proof of freedom.

In the northern states, African Americans voted for the Federalist Party and could be found among the participants in the party's annual parades and members of its Washington Benevolent Society. Some publicly defended the Federalists. In a speech delivered in 1809, a black New Yorker admonished members of his race to support their "Federalist friends," proclaiming it "the indispensable duty of bestowing our votes on those, and on those only, whose talents and whose political, moral and religious principles will most effectively promote the best interest of America."

The most outspoken black Federalist was Lemuel Haynes. Described as a mulatto, Haynes was a Revolutionary War veteran, a Congregationalist minister to churches in Connecticut and Vermont, and one of the earliest black contributors to the political pamphlet wars of the early republic. In his published orations and essays, which date back to 1776, Haynes attacked slavery and the hypocrisy of American rhetoric about equality. In a Fourth of July speech in Rutland, Vermont, in 1801, Haynes denounced the rhetoric of Democratic-Republican egalitarianism because of its collusion in slavery. Because of Haynes's staunch Federalist leanings, his Rutland church voted him out of the pastorate in 1818.

Black Writing and Art in the New Nation

In the early republic, blacks began to adopt various literary forms to define their own position in relation to the dominant white society—deferential pleading, defiant protest, pride of heritage, spiritual autobiography, and celebration. Phillis Wheatley's death in 1784 prevents her inclusion among the post-Revolutionary black writers, but significant among this group of writers were Absalom Jones, Richard Allen, James Forten, Prince Hall, Lemuel Haynes, John Marrant, Benjamin Banneker, Olaudah Equiano, Prince Saunders, Paul Cuffee, Daniel Coker, and Venture Smith. Their writings also linked African American communities with others of African descent in the Atlantic world, reflecting a racial consciousness that would be recognized today as a "diaspora" perspective, since the writers often intended their words to speak for dispersed blacks worldwide. For example, black pamphlet literature discussed such matters as the birth of the Haitian republic in 1804 after twelve years of fighting for independence and the abolition of the Atlantic slave trade to the United States on January 1, 1808. In commemorating these two events, black pamphleteers both reflected and promoted a sense of transnational identity as persons of African descent.

African Americans in Boston voiced their concerns and protest in the form of what today we would call op-ed articles in urban newspapers. For example, when Boston's *Independent Ledger* referred to the African Masonic Lodge as "St. Black's Lodge" and chided blacks for improperly using Masonic rituals, Prince Hall, the Lodge's Grand Master, retorted that "our title is not St. Black's Lodge; neither do we aspire after high titles." Negative images of African Americans were conspicuous in newspapers, but in these same papers free blacks also registered their protests. Not until 1827, with the appearance of the first black-edited newspaper *Freedom's Journal,* did blacks obtain a powerful alternative forum for publishing regular and frequent protests, debates, and community news.

Until the advent of black newspapers, pamphlet literature (usually published orations)

Pamphlet Literature arguably constituted the most prolific form of "black letters" available to counter racist depictions of blacks in the dominant society's print media. Just as Phillis Wheatley's volume of poems had done in the previous Revolutionary era, in the early republican period pamphlet literature testified to blacks' intellectual ability and writing skills.

Among the earliest extant black-authored pamphlets is the printed version of a public sermon by Methodist minister John Marrant, entitled *A Sermon Preached on the 24th Day of June 1789, Being the Festival of St. John the Baptist, at the Request of the Right Worshipful the Grand Master Prince Hall and the Rest of the Brethren of the African Lodge of the Honorable Society of Free and Accepted Masons in Boston by the Reverend Brother Marrant, Chaplain.* In this sermon, Marrant paid homage to the African Masonic Lodge, which is of particular importance, because local white Masons had ridiculed the group and questioned its legitimacy. In the course of his celebration of the "anciency of Masonry," Marrant located both its source and, indeed, human origins in "the principal part of African Ethiopia." Marrant demanded respect not only for the black lodge but also for Africa, which he identified as the cradle of civilization. The text of the sermon was printed and distributed by Prince Hall, who claimed to have had a hand in its writing.

In 1792 and again in 1797, Hall printed and distributed pamphlets under his own name. In *A CHARGE Delivered to the Brethren of the AFRICAN LODGE on the 25th of June, 1792, At the Hall of Brother William Smith, In CHARLESTOWN,* Hall acknowledged reports of violence in St. Domingue, but assured his white readers that the black Bostonians had "no hand in any plots or conspiracies or rebellion, or side or assist in them." Five years later, however, in the pamphlet *A Charge Delivered to the African Lodge, June 24, 1797, at Menotomy,* Hall adopted a more militant stance, remembering "our African brethren six years ago, in the French West-Indies." Evoking for his readers the "snap of the whip," the "hanging," and "tortures" of slavery, he declared the Haitian Revolution a providential event. "Thus doth Ethiopia begin to stretch forth her hand," Hall wrote, "from a sink of slavery to freedom and equality."

Even more influential for the growth of "black letters," and crucial to the black pamphlet tradition, was the series of printed orations commemorating the end of the Atlantic slave trade. In such communities as Boston, Philadelphia, and New York, blacks held annual celebrations, with parades and church services, and afterward published and disseminated abolition-day orations that denounced slavery and the domestic slave trade. Commemorations of the abolition of the slave trade were celebrated annually at least through the mid-1820s, when coordinated attacks by white ruffians contributed to their demise in northern cities. By then, the black parades had become politically charged events in the heightening racist environment of most cities with black populations.

Prince Hall

This eighteenth-century portrait of Prince Hall (1735–1807) dressed as a gentleman places him among Masonic symbols. A former slave, a skilled craftsman, an entrepeneur, an abolitionist, and an advocate of black education, Hall is best remembered as the founder of the African Lodge of North America, popularly known as the Prince Hall Masons.

Because the audience for the print media was potentially wide, the success of the pamphlet as a vehicle for social transformation depended on its appeal to white readers as well as to black. Sometimes black pamphleteers consciously sought to elicit sympathy from white readers. In 1808 a published oration by Philadelphia's black minister Absalom Jones portrayed "the anguish which has taken place when parents have been torn from their children, and children from their parents, and conveyed, with their hands and feet bound in fetters, **Appeals to Readers** on board of ships prepared to receive them." Similarly, in 1808, New York clergyman Peter Williams, Jr., asked his readers to imagine "the parting tear, rolling down their fallen cheeks: hear the parting sigh die on their quivering lips."

Black leaders also found themselves repeatedly issuing pamphlets that defended their claims for respect and their fitness for freedom and equal citizenship. In these defenses, Africa figured as a recurrent theme. Pamphleteers sought to recast the continent in a new and respected light, as the fountainhead of civilization and a proud black heritage. In a published oration in 1810, William Miller maintained that "ancient history, as well as holy writ, informs us of the national greatness of our progenitors. That the inhabitants of Africa are descended from the ancient inhabitants of Egypt, a people once famous for science of every description, is a truth verified by a number of writers." Just as such oration pamphlets burnished the image of Africa, so, too, by extension were the images of Africans and their descendants refurbished.

In 1794 Absalom Jones and Richard Allen became the first blacks to receive a copyright from the United Sates government for their pamphlet *A Narrative of the Proceedings of the Black People during the Late Awful Calamity in Philadelphia.* It was written in

The Jones and Allen Pamphlet

defense of the black community during the city's yellow fever epidemic of 1793. The pamphlet endeavored to combat the racist charges that had been leveled against black Philadelphians after they had responded to the mayor's request for help in removing and burying the dead. The mayor had even assured blacks that they were immune to the disease, although several of them died of it.

The initial public praise for their actions soon soured when a vicious pamphlet by Mathew Carey accused African Americans of using the opportunity for "plundering the distressed." Rebutting this racist accusation and adopting a deferential tone, Jones and Allen in their pamphlet presented white readers with a detailed account of blacks' benevolence to the "distressed, perishing, and neglected sick." Ostensibly a defense of black behavior during Philadelphia's yellow fever epidemic, the pamphlet spoke to the central challenge facing black leaders and their communities in the early national period. Not only these two authors, but other black leaders as well, walked a fine line between racial protest and racial self-critique. They strove to be effective spokesmen for their communities, replacing negative images of their race with group images of respectability.

Yet they also engaged in the internal policing of their communities to ensure that improper behavior did not reinforce the negative images and thereby undermine the positive ones. In their pamphlet, Jones and Allen argued that "we have many unprovoked enemies, who begrudge us the liberty we enjoy; and are glad to hear of any complaints against our colour, be it just or unjust; in consequence of which we are more earnestly endeavouring in all our power, to warn, rebuke, and exhort our African friends, to keep a conscience void of offence towards God and man."

As careful and deferential as such language was in printed northern discourse, it was even more careful in those few pamphlets of protest that appeared in the South. In 1810, for example, while teaching at the African School in Baltimore, Daniel Coker published his *Dialogue between a Virginian and an African Minister,* in which he very cautiously nudged his fictional Virginia slaveholder in an antislavery direction, using the device of a literate and very respectful black minister. Crucial to the slaveholder's conversion was his recognition of the minister's abilities in the context of a rational exchange of ideas. Thus Coker's fictional minister, by his dignified example, supported the argument for black freedom.

Another important form of black letters was the spiritual autobiography. One of the first

The Spiritual Autobiography

blacks to write of his search for intellectual and spiritual independence was Jupiter Hammon, a Long Island slave whose writings spanned from the colonial period to the first decade of the republic. Growing into manhood during the years when the Wesleyan religious revival movement was strong both in England and America, Hammon was greatly influenced by the writings of Charles Wesley and William Cowper. He published *An Evening Thought: Salvation by Christ, with Penitential Cries,* as a broadside in 1760, and the twenty-one stanza poem "To Miss Phillis Wheatley" in 1778. Other poems and prose pieces by him appeared during the next two decades. In *An Address to the Negroes of the State of New York,* published in 1787, Hammon confessed to feeling a personal Christian duty to bear slavery patiently, while at the same time acknowledging the evil of the institution and his hopes for the manumission of black youths.

During this period, the most widely reprinted book in English by a person of African descent was *The Interesting Narrative of the Life of Olaudah Equiano, or Gustavus Vassa*, first published in England in 1789. It was immediately successful, and within five years, eight editions had been issued in America and England. There can be no doubt about Equiano's resentment of slavery, for in his narrative he vigorously condemns Christians for their enslavement of blacks. Active in the British antislavery movement, Equiano presented a petition to Parliament in 1790 for the suppression of the slave trade. He lived as much in England, Montserrat, and Jamaica as in the United States. Equiano spoke for all black people held in bondage in his stirring condemnation of slavery:

> O, ye nominal Christians! might not an African ask you—Learned you
> this from your God, who says unto you, Do unto all men as you would
> men should do unto you? . . . Why are parents to lose their children,
> brothers their sisters, or husbands their wives? Surely, this is a new
> refinement in cruelty, which, while it has no advantage to atone for it,
> thus aggravates distress, and adds fresh horrors even to the wretchedness
> of slavery.

In the United States during the early national period, the most accomplished black man of letters was Benjamin Banneker. Born in 1731 in Maryland of thrifty and industrious parents, Banneker attended a private school open to whites and blacks near Baltimore and developed a keen interest in science and mathematics. While still a young man, he astounded his family and neighbors by construct-

Banneker's Almanacs

ing a clock from wooden materials. This display of mechanical genius attracted the attention of George Ellicott, a Quaker, who had moved into the neighborhood to establish a flour mill. Banneker frequently visited Ellicott's mills while they were being built, and his general knowledge of the mathematical and engineering problems drew the two men closer together. Soon Ellicott began to lend Banneker books on mathematics and astronomy. Within a few weeks, Banneker had not only mastered the material in the books but had even discovered several errors in the authors' calculations. By 1789 he had become so proficient in astronomy that he could predict a solar eclipse with considerable accuracy.

In 1791 Banneker began issuing his almanacs, an enterprise that he continued until 1802. Almanacs, which required elaborate and precise mathematical calculations, were essential for farmers and mariners, because they gave the times of high tide and low tide and the rising and setting of the sun. Among the prominent men attracted by this "black Poor Richard" was James McHenry, later President John Adams's secretary of war. Through McHenry, Banneker was able to establish a number of important connections with officials of the national government. McHenry said that Banneker's work "was begun and finished without the least information or assistance from any person, or from any other books" and that Banneker himself furnished "fresh proof that the powers of the mind are disconnected with the color of the skin, or, in other words, a striking contradiction of Mr. Hume's doctrine that 'the Negroes are naturally inferior to the whites and are unsusceptible of attainments in arts and sciences.'" Banneker sent a manuscript copy of his first almanac to Thomas Jefferson, in the

Window in Time

Benjamin Banneker to Thomas Jefferson, August 19, 1791

Sir, I freely and Cheerfully acknowledge, that I am of the African race, and in that color which is natural to them of the deepest dye (My Father was brought here a S[lav]e from Africa), and it is under a Sense of the most profound gratitude to the Supreme Ruler of the universe, that I now confess to you, that I am not under that State of tyrannical thralldom, and inhuman captivity, to which too many of my brethren are doomed; but that I have abundantly tasted of the fruition of those blessings which proceed from that free and unequalled liberty with which you are favored and which I hope you will willingly allow you have mercifully received from the immediate hand of that Being, from whom proceedeth every good and perfect gift.

. . . And now, Sir, altho my Sympathy and affection for my brethren hath caused my enlargement thus far, I ardently hope that your candor and generosity will plead with you in my behalf, when I make known to you, that it was not originally my design; but that having taken up my pen in order to direct to you as a present, a copy of an Almanack which I have calculated for the Succeeding year, I was unexpectedly and unavoidable led thereto.

Benjamin Banneker, Letter to Thomas Jefferson, August 19, 1791, in Milton Meltzer, ed., *In Their Own Words: A History of the American Negro, 1619–1865,* vol. 1. New York: Thomas Y. Crowell, 3 vols. 1964–1967.

accompanying letter making a strong appeal for a more liberal attitude toward blacks. He pointed to his own achievements as proof that the "train of absurd and false ideas and opinions which so generally prevails with respect to the Negro should now be eradicated."

The highest honor that Banneker received was appointment as a surveyor to define the boundary lines and lay out the streets of the District of Columbia. It was perhaps at the suggestion of his friend George Ellicott, himself a member of the commission, that Jefferson submitted Banneker's name for this position to President Washington. When he arrived in the district, accompanied by Ellicott and Major Pierre L'Enfant, who had prepared the plan of the future federal city, the Georgetown *Weekly Ledger* described Banneker as "an Ethiopian whose abilities as surveyor and astronomer already prove that Mr. Jefferson's concluding that that race of men were void of mental endowment was without foundation." After his work with the commission, Banneker returned to his home in Maryland, where he resumed work on his almanacs and continued his astronomical investigations.

In the late eighteenth and early nineteenth centuries, the first documented professional American painter of African descent was Joshua Johnston, who worked in and around

The Painter Joshua Johnston Baltimore. Johnston made his living as a portrait painter, advertising his skills in local newspapers such as the *Baltimore Intelligencer*. Of the more than eighty paintings signed by or attributed to Johnston, only two portraits of African

Americans have been identified, suggesting that Johnston served the members of his own community but that his primary patronage came from Baltimore's well-to-do white population, including merchants and slaveholders.

The War of 1812

For African Americans throughout the new nation, war played a role in mobilizing their communities in acts of patriotism. This was true of the War of 1812, the second conflict between the United States and Great Britain. Causes of the war include the impressment of American sailors on the high seas by the Royal Navy and British violations of Americans' neutral rights—in both cases, consequences of Britain's epic struggle with Napoleonic France. Another very important cause of the war was the expansionism of Americans moving (or hoping to move) west across the Appalachians. In Congress, so-called War Hawks clamored for a new war with the British to gain new territory in Canada, security against pro-British Indians in the Northwest, and, in the case of southerners, the expansion of slavery.

When war finally came in 1812, northern black communities pledged their allegiance to the American government. In 1814 New York passed an act for the recruitment of two regiments of men of color, each to consist of slightly more than a thousand men. They were

Joshua Johnston, *Portrait of a Gentleman*
Believed to be a portrait of the Reverend Daniel Coker

promised the same pay as white soldiers. The act also offered freedom to slaves who enlisted with the permission of their masters. The black response was positive. The *New York Evening Post* on August 20, 1814, featured an open letter to the black community under the title "A Test of Patriotism." Written by someone **Black Military Service** who identified himself simply as a "citizen of color," the article stressed the "duty of every colored man resident in this city to volunteer." Doubtless New York's black soldiers served faithfully; in 1854 at the New York State Convention of the Soldiers of 1812, a resolution was passed asking Congress to provide the officers, men, and their widows with a liberal annuity "and that such provisions should extend to and include both the Indian and African race . . . who enlisted or served in that war, and who joined with the white man in defending our rights and maintaining our independence."

When in 1814 British troops took and burned the city of Washington, Philadelphia and other eastern cities feared that they, too, would suffer the same fate. The Vigilance Committee of Philadelphia called on three leading black citizens, James Forten, Richard Allen, and Absalom Jones, requesting that they mobilize their community to help erect defenses for the city. More than 2,500 blacks responded. They met in the statehouse yard, went to Grays Ferry Bridge on the Schuylkill River, worked almost continuously for two days, and received the praise of a grateful city. Philadelphia organized a battalion of blacks, which was on the verge of marching to the front when, in early 1815, peace was announced.

A large number of blacks enlisted in the U.S. Navy, frequently without reference to race. Not all white officers desired to lead blacks, however. When Captain Oliver H. Perry expressed his reluctance to fight with the blacks sent to him, Commodore Isaac Chauncey admonished Perry to be proud of whomever he received. Chauncey believed the fifty blacks on his own ship among the best men he had. Later, after the Battle of Lake Erie, Perry would speak similarly of his black crew, declaring them "absolutely insensible to danger." Other naval officers spoke of the gallantry of black seamen.

Gallant Service

Black soldiers made their most lasting impression on the Plains of Chalmette, in the Battle of New Orleans, which in January 1815 brought the war to a triumphant end for the Americans. Back in the autumn of 1814, the war's most famous general, Andrew Jackson, faced with an urgent need to augment his forces defending New Orleans against an imminent British attack, called on the free men of color in Louisiana to come to the aid of their country. Jackson promised that all who enlisted would receive the same pay and bounty as white soldiers. He added, however, that their officers would be white, although they were allowed to choose noncommissioned officers from among themselves.

In the Battle of New Orleans, the soldiers of color occupied a position of strategic importance. They stood very near Jackson's main forces—on the left bank of the Mississippi River, just at the right of the advancing left British column. They erected the cotton-bag defenses for Jackson and contributed substantially to the American victory. As the British, under General Pakenham, attempted to take Jackson's position by storm, the soldiers of color joined with white soldiers, frontiersmen, and others in a counterattack that decimated the redcoats. An end to the fighting had already been negotiated in Europe, but word of that had not yet

The Battle of New Orleans

General Andrew Jackson was pleased to have blacks serve in the War of 1812. He is shown here commanding black troops at the Battle of New Orleans.

Window in Time

General Andrew Jackson
Describes the Battle of New Orleans

[In a letter addressed to Napoleon Bonaparte, Jackson gave this firsthand description of his famous victory at New Orleans.]

The battle commenced at a very little before 7 A.M., January 8, 1815, and as far as the infantry was concerned it was over by 9 A.M. I had portions of the Seventh and Forty-fourth regular infantry regiments, Kentucky and Tennessee riflemen, Creoles, United States marines and sailors, Baratarian men [Lafitte's pirates] . . . and two battalions of free Negroes. . . . The British strength was almost the same as mine, but vastly superior in drill and discipline. Of their force my riflemen killed and wounded 2117 in less than an hour, including two general officers (both died on the field, each a division commander), seven full colonels, with seventy-five line and staff officers. I lost 6 killed and 7 wounded. . . .

There was a very heavy fog on the river that morning, and the British had formed and were moving before I knew it. . . .

"God help us!" I muttered, watching the rapidly advancing line. Seventy, sixty, fifty, finally forty yards, were they from the silent kneeling riflemen. All of my men I could see was their long rifles rested on the logs before them . . . not a shot was fired until the redcoats were within forty yards. I heard Coffee's voice as he roared out: "Now, men, aim for the center of the crossbelts: Fire!" . . . in a few seconds after the first fire there came another sharp, ringing volley. . . . The British were falling back in a confused, disorderly mass, and the entire first ranks of their column were blown away. For two hundred yards in our front the ground was covered with a mass of writhing wounded, dead, and dying redcoats. By the time the rifles were wiped the British line was reformed, and on it came again. This time they were led by General Pakenham in person, gallantly mounted, and riding as though he was on parade. . . . I heard a single rifle-shot from a group of country carts we had been using, about one hundred and seventy-five yards distant, and a moment thereafter I saw Pakenham reel and pitch out of his saddle. I have always believed that he fell from the bullet of a free man of color, who was a famous rifle-shot, and came from the Atakappas region of Louisiana [probably Major Savory of the Santo Domingo battalion]. . . .

They sent a flag to me, asking leave to gather up their wounded and bury their dead, which, of course, I granted. I was told by a wounded officer that the rank and file absolutely refused to make a third charge. "We have no chance with such shooting as these Americans do," they said. . . .

William Hugh Robarts, "Napoleon's Interest in the Battle of New Orleans," *Century Magazine* 53 (January 1897): 360–361.

crossed the Atlantic, and a British triumph at New Orleans might well have annulled the yet-to-be ratified peace agreement. Thus Jackson's belated victory was enormously significant psychologically as well as strategically and politically.

After the battle, Jackson praised the gallantry of the soldiers of color, observing that they had surpassed his hopes. He promised to inform the president of their conduct, stating the "voice of the representatives of the American nation shall applaud your valor, as your general now praises your ardor."

However, blacks fought also on the British side during the War of 1812. In the Chesapeake region, slaves were more likely to assist the British as spies, guides, messengers, and laborers—and a smaller number, perhaps two hundred, served the British as soldiers. At Tangier Island, in the Chesapeake near the mouth of the Potomac River, Admiral Sir George Cockburn reported in May 1814 his ongoing efforts to recruit a "Corps of Colonial Marines from the People of Colour who escaped to us from the Enemy's shore in this Neighborhood to be formed, drilled, and brought forward for service." The British promised freedom to all fugitive slaves, just as they had done in the War for Independence. Between 1813 and 1815, slaves in Virginia and Maryland sought refuge on British ships, expecting to emigrate to free countries. The British carried them to Canada and the West Indies in 1813 and 1814, and at least two thousand slaves in 1815 sailed to Halifax, Nova Scotia, where they disembarked from British ships penniless and with no resources given to them by the British. Although some white Americans at the time claimed that the British sold escaped slaves to new masters in the West Indies, historians argue that there is no evidence for this claim.

Black Colonization

The idea of black settlement outside the United States appealed to various groups of black and white Americans, often for very different reasons. Slaves who escaped to the British lines during the Revolutionary War and the War of 1812 doubtless looked to Canada, the Caribbean, and Great Britain itself as places in which they could live in freedom. Some free blacks, who daily witnessed the abridgement of their citizenship rights, concluded that hopes for equality in America were hollow and thus looked outside America's borders to find self-respect and dignity. Some religious leaders in the black community, such as Daniel Coker of Maryland and Lott Carey of Virginia, sought to make a home in Africa for missionary purposes.

For various reasons, American whites also took an interest in colonization. Defenders of slavery often argued that, as the number of free blacks increased, they should be removed from the state—or even the nation—in order to make slavery more secure, for there could be no genuine discipline of slaves, they believed, as long as free blacks remained in their midst. In 1777 a Virginia legislative committee developed a plan for gradual emancipation and deportation.

Some abolitionists supported colonization plans, declaring it their responsibility to return blacks to the African homeland from which they had been torn. In many northern communities, antislavery whites felt that it was insufficient to grant emancipation and yet withhold equality, because the two races could not live together in harmony. For several organizations that supported manumission, such as the Connecticut Emancipation Society, the colonization of free blacks was the ultimate aim. Colonization thus fostered complicated and unseemly alliances, but at the heart of the matter was the issue of blacks' adjustment to American racial inequality.

The earliest organized campaign for colonization to Africa was led by William Thornton, a Quaker physician also known for being one of the architects of the United States Capitol. Although born to a slave-owning family on the Carib- **Colonization Efforts** bean island of Tortola, Thornton himself became an antislavery advocate. His growing pessimism about the possibility of amicable race relations in the United States led him to explore the idea of colonization. During the winter of 1786–1787 he found a receptive audience among blacks in Newport, Rhode Island, and in Boston. Indeed, the Free African Union Society in Newport had advocated colonization as early as 1783, antedating Thornton's plan. Not all black communities responded positively, however. One historian has noted that Thornton received a "chilly reception" in Philadelphia, when he presented his plan to the members of the city's Free African Society. Later, black Philadelphians would have several more opportunities to consider colonization.

The first such opportunity came in 1815, with the Massachusetts shipbuilder Paul Cuffee, a man of mixed African (Akan) and Indian (Wampanoag) descent. With the aid of James Forten, Cuffee brought his plan to Philadelphia. Both men were enterprising and exceptional achievers, and their friendship was no doubt enhanced by shared experiences in maritime work. At sixteen, in 1775, Cuffee had found work on a whaling vessel. The next year, on his second voyage, he was captured by the British and detained in New York for three months. In 1780 Cuffee began to build ships and to engage in commerce.

As his profits grew, he expanded his seagoing activities and built larger vessels. By 1806 he owned one large ship, two brigs, and several smaller vessels, besides considerable property in houses and land. After joining the Society of Friends, he became deeply interested, along with other Quakers, in the idea of colonization. On January 1, 1811, he sailed with his crew on his own vessel from Philadelphia to England, where he met prominent Quaker members of the African Institution, founded in England to take blacks to Sierra Leone. As early as 1787 the British had already established that colony, sending to it a number of blacks from England and black refugees from the American Revolution and settling them in the colony's capital, Freetown.

Cuffee proposed to establish an emigration and trade relationship with Sierra Leone and for this purpose organized the Friendly Society of Sierre Leone, with branches in black communities in the United States. Returning to America in 1812, Cuffee immediately took his idea on the road, traveling to black communities in Philadelphia, New York, and Baltimore. He solicited Forten's help in organizing a Philadelphia branch of the Friendly Society of Sierra Leone, which he hoped would have branches in other cities to promote emigration and religious missions to Africa.

In 1814, in the midst of the War of 1812, he petitioned Congress for permission to make the voyage, taking with him "a few sober and industrious families" to the British black settlement of Freetown in Sierra Leone. Because the United States was at war with Great Britain, Congress refused. But the next year, after the war had ended, Cuffee returned to his plan. James Forten,

Paul Cuffee
Leading political activist, sailor, and trader

as president of the African Institution of Philadelphia, wrote in 1815 that his organization "cordially unites with Paul Cuffee, in his disinterested and benevolent undertaking." Forten used his influence to solicit "persons of good moral character" for the settlement in Sierra Leone. In 1815 Cuffee sailed from Boston to Freetown with thirty-eight emigrants, at his own expense—approximately $4,000. Within two years of Cuffee's voyage, the white-led American Colonization Society (ACS) was organized. The ACS attracted a curious blend of slaveholders and abolitionists. Bushrod Washington (George Washington's nephew and a Supreme Court justice) was the society's first president, and among its other politically prominent members were Henry Clay and John Randolph of Roanoke—all slaveholders. Yet the ACS also included antislavery Quakers from North Carolina and Pennsylvania who supported it generously. Richard Rush, the son of abolitionist Dr. Benjamin Rush, was named an honorary vice president, and even young William Lloyd Garrison, later the country's most radical white abolitionist, briefly was a member. The ACS sought aid from the federal and state governments, and it sent its agents to meet with free blacks. As a result of these efforts, the colony of Liberia was formed, and its capital named Monrovia in honor of President James Monroe.

After the birth of the ACS, colonization evoked a very different response from Philadelphia blacks. To discuss the issue, on January 15, 1817, the city's black leaders called a general meeting at Richard Allen's Bethel Church. The meeting attracted three thousand black Philadelphians. Forten and leading black ministers—Absalom Jones, Richard Allen, and John Gloucester—spoke of colonization's potential advantages. The audience, however, disagreed with a resounding "no." Forten noted that the negative response was so vehement that it seemed "as it would bring down the walls of the building." Within ten years, black opposition rose to fever pitch at meetings in Baltimore, Boston, New York, Hartford, New Haven, Pittsburgh, and many other cities. New York blacks referred to the supporters of colonization as "men of mistaken views," and those of Lyme, Connecticut, described colonization as "one of the wildest projects ever patronized by enlightened men."

Black Opposition

Not all black communities, however, rejected colonization. The AME leader Daniel Coker left his city, Baltimore, for Sierra Leone in 1820, and the next year the black Baptist leaders Lott Carey and Colin Teague departed Richmond for Liberia. By 1830 the American Colonization Society had settled 1,420 blacks in Liberia. Whether to stay or to leave America would be an ongoing debate in black communities throughout the antebellum period and, indeed, into the twentieth century.

The Contagion of Liberty

The option of returning to Africa was not a reality for the great majority of African Americans. Some even attempted to stand and fight to the death for freedom. For many slaves and free blacks in the Richmond, Virginia, area in 1800, the chosen path was to rebel against slavery. Still remembering the American Revolution's ideology of liberty, and influenced even more directly by the egalitarian rhetoric of republicanism and by unfolding news from Haiti, African Americans in and around Richmond conspired to destroy slavery.

Gabriel's Rebellion in Virginia

Although it was rumored that two Frenchmen played a role in the conspiracy led by Gabriel, the slave blacksmith owned by Thomas Prosser ("Gabriel" was the slave's only name, though he was sometimes called "Gabriel Prosser," after his owner), all scholars agree that it was news of the Haitian Revolution that played a key factor in the planning of the revolt. Another factor was the arrival, starting in 1793, of French-speaking slave owners and their slaves, who in the wake of the revolt in Haiti poured into both northern and southern cities in the United States. Many of those refugees came to Norfolk and lesser numbers to Portsmouth, Virginia, and the lower Eastern Shore. French planters also took their slaves to Charleston, Baltimore, Philadelphia, and New York, as well as to other islands in the Caribbean.

Black sailors also carried news of the Haitian Revolution all over the Atlantic world. During the colonial period and the early years of the Republic, black mariners were influential in shaping the history and culture of America, as the research of W. Jeffrey Bolster has shown. They brought to isolated black communities information and stories about other parts of the world and alternative possibilities. By the early nineteenth century, Bolster estimates, one out of every five American seamen was black. On the eve of the Civil War, for instance, black mariners were banned from southern ports, because their very presence was regarded as a threat to slavery.

Throughout the 1790s, news of slave "Secret Keeper" conspiracies ran rampant through Virginia and South Carolina. In late July 1793, Virginia slave owner John Randolph of Roanoke made an official deposition of what he claimed to be a conspiratorial conversation, in which he overheard a slave talk about "how the blacks has kill'd the whites in the French Island . . . a little white ago." For months, Gabriel and his network of conspirators plotted the desperate move, gathering clubs, and turning scythes into swords for the appointed day.

The planter practice of hiring out skilled slaves, such as Thomas Prosser's Gabriel, to masters in urban areas enhanced black mobility and possibilities for holding secret meetings. Because Gabriel and other leaders were literate, they were able to forge passes, enabling conspirators to travel through the countryside. Black boatmen also carried local news. By all these channels, slaves and free blacks passed on information to other blacks in Norfolk, Petersburg, and Charlottesville. Their plan was to seize the arsenal at Richmond and, after securing arms and ammunition, to set fire to the city's commercial district and kill their adversaries. After capturing Richmond, so Gabriel and his followers plotted, they would then wait to hear that other cities had been taken or that slaves were escaping to Richmond. Their objective was to wreak so much havoc that Virginia's officials would have to negotiate an end to slavery.

On August 30, 1800, more than a thousand blacks met six miles outside Richmond and began to march on the city. But then bad weather unexpectedly undermined the insurgency: a violent storm washed out the roads and bridges. Already, two slaves had informed whites of what was afoot, and Governor James Monroe promptly called out more than six hundred troops and notified every militia commander in the state. In due time, scores of slaves were arrested, and 35 were executed. Gabriel was captured in Norfolk in late September, having been betrayed by a black crewman, and was hanged. Whites speculated extravagantly over the number of slaves involved. That Gabriel remained silent after his capture added to the stark terror of the whole situation.

The unrest among slaves continued into the following year, and plots were reported in Petersburg and Norfolk and in various places in North Carolina. That state became so alarmed that many slaves were lashed and branded, and at least 15 were hanged for alleged implication in conspiracies. During **Plots and Rumors** the years leading up to the War of 1812, there were reports of insurrection up and down the Atlantic seaboard. Conspiracy also crossed the mountains; in 1810 a plot was uncovered in

Lexington, Kentucky. The following year, more than 400 rebellious slaves in Louisiana had to be put down by federal and state troops. At least 75 slaves lost their lives in the encounter and in the trials that ensued. An uprising in New Orleans occurred in the following year.

There was no freedom to protest in slave communities, as there was in northern communities. There was no victory for slaves in the American South, as there had been for the slaves in Haiti. The "peculiar institution" had decades more to grow.

Southern Slavery

The Domestic Slave Trade

Persistence of the African Trade

The Slave Codes

On the Plantation

Urban and Nonagricultural Slavery

Social and Cultural Life

Resistance

Painting, *After the Sale: Slaves Going South from Richmond* [1852–1853]

They marched westward for hundreds of miles across the southern states—slave men and women, boys and girls, all shackled together. They were often paired, the women with a rope tied halter-like around their necks and the men with padlocked iron collars. They journeyed sometimes with their owners and more often with traders, who knew a profit when they saw one—the sale of slaves to a market hungry for labor. In addition to the overland trek, some slaves traveled the coastal waters by boat to meet their fate at the auction block in New Orleans, the major port of entry and the largest slave-trading center in the Lower South. Torn away from family networks and friends, slaves from the Chesapeake states and the Carolinas found themselves to be the coerced element of an unprecedented mass migration of the American people. In the mad westward scramble, slaves became a valuable investment for whites who were lured to the cotton fields of the South Central states, the Lower South, and the Gulf Coast region. Throughout the first half of the nineteenth century, the older southeastern seaboard states clung tenaciously to slave labor, although they were steadily losing their agricultural preeminence to states with more dynamic areas of economic activity—Louisiana, Mississippi, and Alabama. The demand for these states' cotton caused an explosion in the number of large-scale plantations and small farms that had come increasingly to depend on slave labor.

Standing at the center of the Southern economy's production of cash crops and other agricultural commodities, black people struggled daily to hold onto their families, their dignity, and their very humanity. As the Virginia slave (and later Boston minister) Peter Randolph wrote in his 1855 narrative, *Sketches of Slave Life: Or Illustrations of the "Peculiar Institution"*: "Slavery is *Slavery.* Dress it up as you may, in the city or on the plantation, the human being must feel that which binds him to another's will." Although this was surely true, slaves also expressed a will of their own. They defied the chattel principle, that they were mere property, on every occasion they could. In hidden, everyday forms of resistance to outright revolt, slaves fought for their personhood and dignity. Their religious worship spoke to their belief in a higher authority than their masters. Their religious songs rang out with messages of human equality, not racial subordination. Slaves developed a resilient culture, in the face of degrading circumstances—sale, whipping, rape, and death. They sought to keep families together, to find moments for pleasure, but most of all they sought to escape, even if only temporarily, the confines of their condition.

COTTON-GIN—GINNING COTTON.

The cotton gin

Eli Whitney is credited with the invention of the cotton gin, although some historians have argued that the idea originated with slaves. Regardless of where the credit belongs, slaves were used extensively in the operation of this new machinery.

The Domestic Slave Trade

In a peculiar twist of logic, it was technology that supported the expansion of slave labor in the United States. Eli Whitney's invention of the cotton gin, which he patented in 1794, revolutionized and streamlined the process of separating raw cotton from its seed, while the already burgeoning textile industry in the northeastern United Sates and its older counterpart in

Europe developed new processes for converting raw cotton into cloth. Even before the Revolutionary War, but particularly in the decades that followed it, white farmers began moving with their slaves to the West. There, after the beginning of the nineteenth century, cotton was fast becoming king.

Louisiana, having become a state in 1812, underwent a rapid population increase once the demand for cotton and sugarcane ushered in rising prices and profits. The same exponential growth was true for Mississippi and Alabama, which gained statehood in 1817 and 1819, respectively. According to the census (which did not count Indians), only about 40,000 people resided in the Alabama-Mississippi region in 1810, but by 1820 the population jumped to 200,000 inhabitants, and twenty years later it neared the 1 million mark. In 1832 the *Lynchburg Virginian* complained that "the constant emigration to the great West of our most substantial citizens, the bone and sinew of the country . . . is the daily subject of complaint among our mercantile men and of which our naked streets and untenanted houses are such emphatic evidence." Four years later, South Carolinian William Gilmore Simms wrote: "The spirit of emigration is still rife in our community. From this cause we have lost many, and we are destined, we fear, to lose more, of our worthiest citizens." However, the growing economic opportunities in the new states beckoned too strongly. Gone was the time when the southeastern states grew most of the cotton, as they had at the beginning of the century. By 1834 the new states along the Gulf Coast reigned as the land of King Cotton. Mississippi, Alabama, and Louisiana together produced more than

King Cotton

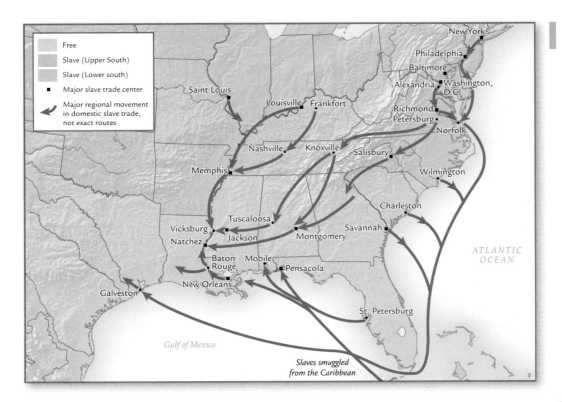

The domestic slave trade 1808–1865

50 percent of the nation's cotton, and in 1859 these states, along with Georgia, produced more than 79 percent.

As word of the growing prosperity in the new states got back to the eastern seaboard, the wave of migrants only grew—and so did the demand for slaves. The United States' acquisition of Florida from Spain in 1819, the settling of Missouri and its admission to the Union as a slave state in 1821, and the American annexation of Texas in 1845 and subsequent war with Mexico were direct results of the ascendant cotton kingdom. Nothing more clearly demonstrates the insatiable appetite of plantation slavery for new lands than the generation-long struggle for the acquisition of Texas. It was the high-water mark for the South's drive to absorb all the lands into which cotton production could be extended.

The domestic slave trade played a key role in augmenting this westward movement. Although many whites who resettled in the western cotton states took their slaves with them,

The Interstate Slave Trade

others looked to the Atlantic seaboard states to provide a continuous supply of new slaves. In Maryland, Virginia, and the Carolinas, slave trading took its place alongside diversified farming as a solution to the difficult problems of economic readjustment that plantation owners had to face. Especially after 1808, when American involvement in the Atlantic slave trade became illegal, the interstate trade grew increasingly profitable. The resulting rise in the value of slave property destroyed much of the antislavery sentiment in Maryland and Virginia, which had been considerable in the last years of the eighteenth century.

The domestic trade carried slaves overland through southwestern Virginia to Tennessee, then on to Alabama, Mississippi, and Louisiana. Slaves walked most of the way. When they reached the Ohio, Tennessee, and Mississippi rivers, they were placed on flatboats and shipped downstream like any other cargo. Whether by water or by land, they were usually transported in chains. Indeed, nonslaveholders' travel narratives of the time often express shock at the sight of migrating slaves, handcuffed, chained together, or both. Slaves remained under the watchful eye of the long-distance traders or their agents, who saw to it that none escaped, lest profits be proportionally reduced.

The machinery for handling this domestic trade developed rapidly, and before the very eyes of Americans a form of human commerce emerged as a substitute for the outlawed African trade. Many business firms that dealt in farm supplies and animals also carried a "line" of slaves. Auctioneers who disposed of real estate and personal property sold slaves along with other wares. Planters who had abandoned their holdings because of economic loss or some other necessary retrenchment passed news by word of mouth or advertised in the newspapers that they had slaves for sale. Benevolent organizations frequently sold slaves by lottery. Slave-trading firms such as Woolfolk, Saunders, and Overly in Maryland, Franklin and Armfield in Virginia, and Oakes in South Carolina greatly enriched the net worth of their owners. Newspapers were instrumental to the slave trade. Through advertisements and the posting of information, newspapers served a key middleman role between seller and purchaser.

Slave traders were ubiquitous. They could be found on plantations, in general stores and taverns, and at county fairs, turning up wherever they heard of the possibility of slaves being sold. When estates were to be probated or liquidated, slave traders sought out the individuals involved and pressed them for

CASH!

All persons that have SLAVES to dispose of, will do well by giving me a call, as I will give the

HIGHEST PRICE FOR

Men, Women, & CHILDREN.

Any person that wishes to sell, will call at Hill's tavern, or at Shannon Hill for me, and any information they want will be promptly attended to.

Thomas Griggs.

Charlestown, May 7, 1835.

PRINTED AT THE FREE PRESS OFFICE, CHARLESTOWN.

1835 advertisement for slaves

any available slaves. They could convincingly argue that a Virginian no longer needed his slaves, and then with equal firmness show a Mississippian that he needed at least ten new hands. Advertisements for the domestic slave trade reveal shrewd economic tactics. In 1834 Franklin and Armfield announced that the firm would pay cash for five hundred blacks and would offer higher prices than "any other purchaser who is now, or may hereafter come into the market." Such businesses moved thousands of slaves each year. At least thirty-two slave-trading firms advertised in the Charleston area in the 1850s, in addition to the many undocumented individuals who worked as part-time traders.

Speculation was integral to the slave-trading business. With loans from banks and private investors, traders promised cash payments to slave sellers. Fiercely competitive, traders made their bids to various slave owners in a rural district. The successful traders then collected their "purchases" bit by bit until satisfied with a sufficient number and carried their coffle of slaves to the closest trading center, which in the slave-exporting states were principally Baltimore, Washington, D.C., Richmond, Norfolk, and Charleston. In these cities, blacks were gathered into slave pens, such as the notorious Lumpkin Jail in Richmond, for direct shipment to New Orleans or for resale to other long-distance traders. An agent for the Oakes firm bought slaves in South Carolina's Sumter district and resold them in Charleston; from there, slaves were sent to Montgomery, Memphis, and New Orleans—the principal slave marts in the newer agricultural areas.

Practically every city in the South had pens, jails, and other necessary accoutrements for the effective handling of this human traffic. Although Washington, D.C., was never the largest slave market, it was one of the most notable until congressional action in 1850 ended the slave trade there. Interstate traders hitherto headquartered in the District of Columbia operated in both Maryland and Virginia. In June 1847, a trader wrote from the District to a Richmond auctioneer: "I have six agents out in the country buying so you may look for Negroes from me pretty often." Alexandria, which until 1846 was a part of the District of Columbia, afforded slave traders a good place from which to ship slaves by water or overland. The District was aptly called "the very seat and center of the slave trade." Foreign visitors to the city were shocked at the sight of slave auction blocks, slave jails, and slave pens. Northerners—and even a few southerners, such as the slaveholder John Randolph of Roanoke—roundly condemned the practice of selling human beings in the nation's capital.

In addressing numerous aspects of the domestic trade, scholars have debated whether the institution of slavery can accurately be characterized as a capitalistic enterprise. In the 1970s historian Eugene Genovese offered the influential interpretation that southern slavery, while operating in a global market, was itself "precapitalist" and that a "paternalist compromise"

Alexandria slave pen

governed master-slave relations. However, the debate has largely been decided in favor of seeing slavery as a capitalistic enterprise. Most recently, scholars such as Michael Tadman and

A Capitalist Enterprise Walter Johnson have portrayed the domestic trade as relentlessly financially
driven. They stress the ease with which owners separated families, selling wife
from husband and children from parents at the "moment of sale." Although slave family members were sometimes advertised as being for sale together, slaves usually brought higher prices
when sold separately. This is not to say that respect for the slave family was never manifested.
Few owners were so insensitive as to boast of dividing slave families by sale. However, the economic interests of slave owners and their heirs came first, not the family interests of the slaves.
More often than not, economic realities dictated the breakup of slave families at some point.

Such realities precipitated the escape of Harriet Tubman and launched her famous
career as a rescuer of slaves. Born around 1822 as Araminta Ross, Harriet Tubman's nuclear

Separation of Families by Sale family was owned by a couple on Maryland's Eastern Shore. The fate
of each family member significantly changed in 1824, when their mis-
tress died. Harriet's father Ben Ross remained with the slave owner Anthony Thompson,
but Harriet, her mother, and siblings formed part of the inheritance that passed to the son
of the deceased mistress. A skilled lumberman and a favorite slave of his master, Harriet's
father eventually gained his freedom in 1840, since Anthony Thompson had provided in his
will for the emancipation of all his slaves over a period of years.

Harriet, her mother, and her siblings were no longer Thompson's slave property and
thus had nothing to look forward to. Instead they remained locked in bondage to a less
financially stable or caring man. The quality and circumstances of their lives grew harsher
and more painful. To make ends meet, Harriet's owner sold three of her sisters into the
Lower South. He hired Harriet to several cruel masters for whom she worked in a variety of
jobs: taking care of children, trapping muskrats, and working on a timber gang. It was the
death of Harriet's master in 1849 that convinced her to escape. His debts had made inevitable the sale and separation of all her remaining family members, including her. Moreover,
Harriet was now married to a free black named John Tubman. She planned to escape with
her husband and brothers, but when the hour came only she had the courage to flee on foot
from Maryland to freedom in Pennsylvania.

Slave narratives, as well as planters' probate records, legal suits, and advertisements, all
confirm the persistent practice of family separation by sale. One firm, advertising for slaves in

Average Prices of Prime Field Hands (young slave men, able-bodied but unskilled)											
	1800	1808	1813	1818	1828	1837	1843	1848	1853	1856	1860
Washington, Richmond, and Norfolk	$350	$500	$400	$ 700		$ 900			$1,250	$1,300	
Charleston, SC	$500	$550	$450	$ 850	$450	$1,200	$500	$700	$ 900		$1,200
Louisville, KY	$400		$500	$ 800	$500	$1,200				$1,000	$1,400
Middle Georgia	$450	$650	$450	$1,000	$700	$1,300	$600	$900	$1,200		$1,800
Montgomery, AL				$ 800	$600	$1,200	$650	$800			$1,600
New Orleans, LA	$500	$600		$1,000	$700	$1,300	$800	$900	$1,250	$1,500	$1,800

Source: Ulrich Bonnell Phillips. *The Slave Economy of the Old South: Selected Essays in Economic and Social History,* ed. Eugene D. Genovese (Baton Rouge: Louisiana State University Press, 1968), p. 142.

Window in Time

William Wells Brown on the Domestic Slave Trade, 1847

In the course of eight or nine weeks Mr. Walker [slave trader] had his cargo of human flesh made up. There was in this lot a number of old men and women, some of them with gray locks. We left St. Louis in the steamboat Carlton, Captain Swann, bound for New Orleans. . . . I was ordered to have the old men's whiskers shaved off, and the gray hairs plucked out where they were not too numerous, in which case he had a preparation of blackening to color it, and with a blacking-brush we would put it on. This was new business to me, and was performed in a room where the passengers could not see us . . . and after going through the blacking process, they looked ten or fifteen years younger. . . .

The next day [after Natchez] we proceeded to New Orleans. . . . In a short time, the planters came flocking to the pen to purchase slaves. Before the slaves were exhibited for sale, they were dressed and driven into the yard. Some were set to dancing, some to jumping, some to singing, and some to playing cards. This was done to make them appear cheerful and happy. My business was to see that they were placed in those situations before the arrival of the purchasers, and I have often set them to dancing when their cheeks were wet with tears. As slaves were in good demand at that time, they were all soon disposed of.

William Wells Brown, *Narrative of William Wells Brown, a Fugitive Slave, Written by Himself,* in Gilbert Osofsky, ed., *Puttin' on Ole Massa* (New York, Harper & Row, 1969).

the age group between twelve and twenty-five, solicited in the newspaper: "Those having such property to sell, will find it in their interests to bring them to us, or drop a line to us and we will come and see them. One of us can always be found at home, prepared to pay the highest prices for such negroes as suit us, in cash." Nor was it unusual to see advertisements in which traders specifically sought young blacks from eight to twelve years of age. The large number of single slaves on the market testifies to the constant separation of families during the slavery period.

Market Prices The prices of slaves in the interstate trade also responded to market factors, contrary to interpretations of slavery as precapitalist. In the early nineteenth century, the price for "prime field hands" was modest, ranging from $350 in Virginia to about $500 in Louisiana. Later, as the demand for slaves increased in the Lower South, prices rose in both the Upper and Lower South, reaching a high point in 1836. In that year, Virginia alone reported no less than 120,000 slaves exported to the Lower South. In the following year, after the onset of the financial turmoil known as the Panic of 1837, there was a pronounced slump in both the price and the demand for slaves. The domestic slave trade succumbed, as did other commercial enterprises, to six years of a severe depression. By the 1850s, however, the slave trade rebounded with skyrocketing prices. In 1860 prime field hands sold for $1,000 in Virginia and $1,800 in New Orleans. To traders, slavery meant commissions and profits that ranged from 5 percent to 30 percent of the sale price of the slaves—no small return on a short-term investment.

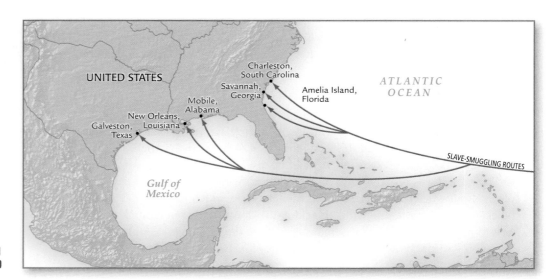

The illegal slave trade to the United States, 1808–1860

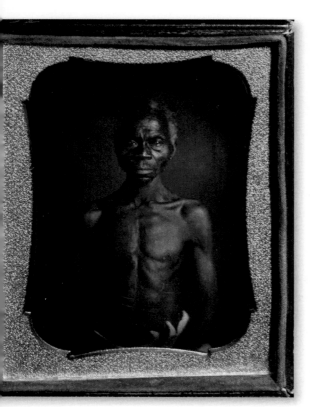

Renty

This daguerreotype produced in 1850 is believed to be of Renty, a field hand on the plantation of B. F. Taylor of Columbia, South Carolina. Although the slave trade was closed in 1808, many Africans such as Renty were imported after that time.

Persistence of the African Trade

As the demand for slaves increased, so, too, did the temptation to engage in the Atlantic slave trade with Africa. Although American participation in this trade had officially ended in 1808, the unguarded southern coast, the certainty of markets, and the prospect of huge profits were too much for some merchants to resist. After the War of 1812, it was generally admitted that American capital, American ships, and American sailors carried on an extensive slave trade between Africa and the New World. This laxity toward the illegal trade had caused some embarrassment on the part of Great Britain, which was now on friendlier terms with the United States. Committed to suppressing the slave trade, the British endeavored to bring to bear on the United States the pressure of world opinion.

Under such pressure, almost every year an American president or another public leader advocated the tougher enforcement of anti-slave-trading laws. In 1839 President Martin Van Buren declared it necessary to preserve the "integrity and honor of our flag" by amending and thereby strengthening the law against the illicit trade. In June 1841, President John Tyler (a Virginia slave owner) expressed dismay at hearing that the traffic was on the increase. Flagrant violations of the slave-trade ban did little to arouse American public opinion, at least not to the point of bringing action against those who profited from the traffic. Nor was this a profit that only the South enjoyed. New York merchants as well as those in New Orleans benefited from the illicit trade. In 1836 the United States consul at Havana reported that whole cargoes of slaves fresh from Africa were being shipped daily to Texas in American vessels and that more than a thousand had been sent within a few months. It was estimated that fifteen thousand Africans were annually being taken to Texas. The depot on Bay Island, in the Gulf of Mexico, held as many as sixteen thousand Africans for shipment to Florida, Texas, Louisiana, and other markets.

Extent of the Illegal Trade

The trade in Africans was linked directly to the politics of slavery's expansion. By 1854, slave traders had grown bold enough to advocate the official reopening of the Atlantic slave trade. Historian Manisha Sinha argues that the reopening of the African trade weighed heavily in the growing southern separatist ideology of the 1850s. South Carolina, most notable for its seces-

The Movement to Reopen the African Trade

sionist advocates, stood at the "storm-center" of the movement to reopen the trade. In 1856 at the height of demands for relegalizing the African slave trade, Robert Barnwell Rhett, who only a few years earlier had served as one of South Carolina's senators, noted: "If the attempt to open this trade should fail, it would give one more proof of how injurious our connection with the North was [sic] become to us, and would indicate one more signal advantage which a Southern Confederacy would have over the present heterogeneous association called the Union."

Between 1854 and 1860, every southern commercial convention considered proposals to reopen the trade. At the Montgomery convention of 1858, a furious debate erupted over the subject. With considerable logic, William L. Yancey, the Alabama "fire-eater" (strong southern-rights advocate), argued that "if it is right to buy slaves in Virginia and carry them to New Orleans, why is it not right to buy them in Cuba, Brazil, or Africa and carry them there?" The following year, at Vicksburg, Mississippi, the convention voted favorably on a resolution recommending that "all laws, State or Federal, prohibiting the African slave trade, ought to be repealed." Only the states of the Upper South, which reaped large profits from the domestic slave trade, opposed reopening the African trade.

The federal law of 1808 was so weak and the enforcement of it so lax that repeal was really unnecessary. When offenders were caught, they were placed under bond, which they promptly forfeited; they considered the loss a normal cost of doing business. Sometimes cases involving offenders never reached the courts. For all practical purposes, the Atlantic slave trade was open in the last decade before the Civil War, much to the distress of abolitionists. As the intersectional strife increased in intensity, importations from Africa into southern ports became increasingly bold. In some places, traders openly advertised newly arrived blacks for sale, and most southern cities had depots where they could be purchased if, for some reason, blacks from the Upper South were not desired. In doing everything possible to keep the African trade open, southerners sought to secure themselves against the future possibility of a declining domestic slave trade. There was the possibility, too, that an increase in the supply of slaves would lower their price.

The Slave Codes

New and more stringent laws accompanied the expansion of slavery into the Lower South and the Gulf Coast states in the late eighteenth and early nineteenth centuries. Generally called slave codes, these laws varied from state to state, but most of them expressed the same viewpoint: that slaves are not people but property and that laws should protect

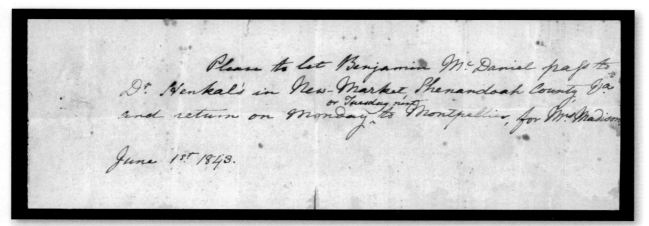

Slave pass

the ownership of such property and should also protect whites against any dangers that might arise from the presence of large numbers of slaves. These overtly repressive regulatory statutes merely reduced to legal phraseology the philosophy of the South toward the institution of slavery. A slave could not strike a white person, even in self-defense, but killing a slave, however maliciously, rarely constituted murder. The rape of a female slave by someone other than the master was a crime, but only because it involved trespassing on the master's property rights. Slaves had no standing in the courts: they could not be a party to a lawsuit; they could not offer testimony, except against another slave or a free black; and their legally defined "irresponsibility" meant that their oaths were not binding. Slaves could make no contracts. Ownership of property was generally forbidden them, though some states permitted slaves to have certain types of personal property.

Slaves could not leave their master's plantation without authorization, and any white person finding them outside without permission could capture them and turn them over to public officials. Slaves could not possess firearms, and in Mississippi they could not beat drums or blow horns. Masters feared that drums and horns could convey coded messages, especially on plantations with large slave populations of direct African origin or Creole slaves who exhibited greater cultural autonomy, as was the case on some of the larger plantations in South Carolina and Louisiana. Slaves could not hire themselves out without permission or in any other way conduct themselves as free people. They could not buy or sell goods. Slaves' relationships with whites and free blacks were to be kept at a minimum—for example, unless authorized otherwise, they could not visit the homes of whites or free blacks, nor could they entertain such individuals in their quarters. They were never to receive, possess, or transmit any incendiary literature calculated to incite insurrections. The many restrictions sought to ensure the slaves' subordination and to discipline them as workers, thus protecting the white population from revolt and safeguarding white economic interests.

Any insurrection, or rumors of one, usually led to the enactment of even more stringent laws to control slaves' activities and movement. For example, in Charleston, South Carolina, a scare stirred by the 1822 Denmark Vesey plot prompted the passage of a law requiring all black seamen to be imprisoned during the time that their ship was anchored in port. In the same panic, the city's African Methodist Episcopal Church was forced to close after rumors spread that implicated black Methodists in Vesey's plot. Realizing the futility of trying to carry on against such odds, the church's leader, Rev. Morris Brown, who later became a bishop, led his flock of free blacks to the North. The Nat Turner insurrection of 1831 in Virginia precipitated a barrage of repressive statutes not only in Virginia but in other parts of the South. By the 1840s, the slave codes in all the southern states had become so elaborate that there was hardly need for modification, even when threats arose to shake the foundations of the institution.

Ample machinery was set up to provide for effective enforcement and execution of the slave codes. In some states, slaves were tried in regular courts for infractions of the law. In other states, tribunals were specifically constituted for examining evidence and judging a slave's guilt or innocence. Some states required trials **Enforcement** by juries composed of slaveholders; others merely required the cognizance of one, two, or three justices of the peace. Most petty offenses were punishable by whipping, but more serious ones were punishable by branding, imprisonment, or death. Arson, rape of a white woman, and conspiracy to rebel were defined as capital crimes in all the slaveholding states.

There was considerable reluctance to imprison a slave for a long period or to inflict the death penalty, for the obvious reason that the slave represented an investment, and to deprive the owner of the slave's labor or life meant depriving the slave-owner of his property rights, as well as depriving the state of just that much taxable wealth. Slaveholders were therefore extremely cautious about judging a slave offender hastily because of the prospect of losing one of their own slaves through the same process at a later date. This is not to say that slaves enjoyed anything resembling due process of law or justice in any sense in which the term is applied to free persons. Since slaves were always regarded with suspicion, and since some crimes were viewed as threats to the social order, they were frequently punished for crimes they did not commit and were helpless before a panic-stricken group of slaveholders who saw in the rumor of an insurrection the slow but certain undermining of the entire system.

One of the devices set up to enforce the slave codes and thereby maintain the institution of slavery was the patrol, which has been aptly described as an adaptation of the militia. Counties were usually divided into "beats," or areas of patrol, and free white men were expected to serve for a stated period of time: one, three, or six **The Patrol System** months. Patrols apprehended slaves who appeared to be out of their proper place and returned them to their masters. They brought to jail escaping slaves or slaves accused of offenses; they entered slave quarters in search of weapons that might be used in an uprising; and they monitored assemblies of slaves where disorder might develop or conspiracy might be planned. The patrol system proved so inconvenient to some white citizens that they regularly paid the fines stipulated for dereliction of duty. Vigilance committees operated as part of the patrol system during emergencies, usually created by actual or rumored uprisings. At such times, it was not unusual for the committee to disregard all caution and kill any blacks whom they encountered in their search.

Despite the elaborate slave codes, both in the number of statutes and in the machinery of enforcement, innumerable infractions went altogether unpunished. In quiet times, the laws tended to be more easily disregarded and slaves given more freedom to conduct themselves in a manner that, during an emergency, would be regarded as highly offensive. All masters preferred, moreover, to take matters involving their own slaves into their own hands and to mete out justice in their own way. The strong individualism that was bred on the frontier plantation and in planters' images of themselves as the source of law and justice tended to discourage conformity to statutes even when they had been passed in the interest of the plantation system. Slaveholders usually maintained that they could handle their own slaves, if only something could be done about the slaves on the neighboring plantation. Such a point of view was not conducive to consistent enforcement of the slave codes.

On the Plantation

The work of slaves was primarily agricultural. It is estimated that in 1850 only 400,000 slaves lived in towns and cities, whereas approximately 2.8 million worked on farms and plantations. Nor does the large slave population mean that the majority of southern whites owned slaves. In 1860 there were only 384,884 slave owners, out of a total white population of 8 million. Fully three-fourths of the white people of the South had neither slaves nor an immediate economic interest in the maintenance of slavery or the plantation system. Most slaveholders in 1860 were small farmers with five slaves or less. Fully 338,000 owners, or 88 percent of all masters of slaves in 1860, held less than twenty slaves. However, most slaves tended to be on farm units with larger holdings. This concentration of wealth in slaves in the hands of a small percentage of white southerners meant that more than 50 percent of all slaves lived on plantations with holdings in excess of twenty slaves, and at least 25 percent of slaves lived on plantations with holdings in excess of fifty in 1860.

This concentration of slaves in the hands of the relatively few inevitably resulted in the bulk of staple crops being produced on the large plantations, the owners of which also dominated the political and economic thinking of the entire South. The tremendous labor productivity of the large plantations provided the slave-owning gentry with wealth and influence out of proportion to their number. In 1860 the southern states produced 5,387,000 bales of cotton. Of that total, more than 3.5 million bales were produced in just four states—Mississippi, Alabama, Louisiana, and Georgia. It is no accident that these same states were also at the top of the list in the number of large slaveholders. Of the states with individual holdings of more than twenty slaves, Mississippi led (just as it did in the productivity of cotton), followed by Alabama, Louisiana, and Georgia. The great majority of agricultural slaves grew cotton, while the remainder grew such staple crops as tobacco, rice, and sugarcane. The cotton farm or plantation was, therefore, the typical locale of the slave.

A large plantation always had at least two distinct groups of workers, house servants and field hands. The former cared for the house, the yards, and the gardens, cooked the meals,

Field Hands drove the carriages, and performed other tasks expected of personal servants. The favored ones frequently traveled with their owners and enjoyed other advantages in food, clothing, and education or experience. But most slaves toiled in the fields. On small farms, slaves served as both house servants and field hands. In such instances slaves found it necessary to do the chores in and around the master's house during hours that ordinarily would have been their own time on plantations with a division of field and house slaves. Owners of one or two slaves were often forced by economic necessity into the fields or to labor alongside their slaves in a variety of common tasks.

Whether on large or small slaveholdings, crop cultivation was a demanding undertaking. The work regimen was more intense for raising cotton than for tobacco. Slaves who migrated with their masters from Maryland and Virginia to the cotton states became quickly and painfully aware of the difference. They found little time to grow food in garden plots or to provide for their own subsistence as they had in the past. And Sundays held the promise of more chores. Charles Ball, sold out of Maryland to

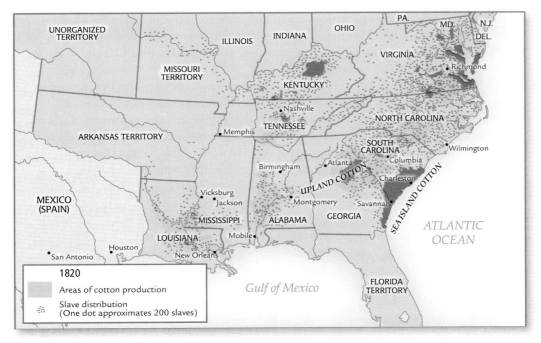

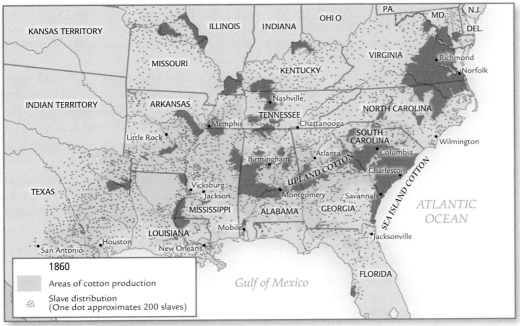

Cotton and
slaves, 1820
and 1860

upcountry Georgia around 1805, described cotton cultivation as "excessive" and "incessant throughout the year." However, during periods of economic depression, slaves on Georgia plantations found themselves burdened with even greater work. In these periods, owners demanded more pounds of cotton from their slaves, while simultaneously reducing their own costs by requiring the slaves to feed themselves. The task of raising

141

their own poultry and crops in individual subsistence gardens was difficult for those who worked in the fields from sunup to sundown. However, some slaves defiantly took this opportunity to market their extra produce, despite laws that forbade such slave autonomy.

The gang-labor system prevailed on most large plantations. Large groups of slaves were taken to the fields and put to work under the supervision of the owner or overseer. It was generally believed that one slave was required for every three acres of cotton raised. Planting, cultivation, and picking cotton required little skill but much time. Men, women, and children could be used, though the very young and the very old were of little value as field hands. Most slave children had the run of the plantation, and some played with the white children inside and outside the "big house," around the slave cabins, and through the yards. Much of this play came to an end, however, when black children reached the useful age for chores, which was very early. When they reached adolescence, interracial playing was over altogether, and blacks and whites alike were required to conform to the South's racial etiquette.

Aside from duties in connection with raising the crop, slaves cleared land, burned underbrush, rolled logs, split rails, carried water, mended fences, spread fertilizer, broke soil, and performed countless other tasks. Small wonder that many slaves worked not merely from sunrise to sunset but frequently long after dark. During harvest time the hours were longest, since the planter anxiously sought to harvest the crop before inclement weather could damage it. Under such circumstances, slaves were driven almost mercilessly. In 1830, for example, fourteen Mississippi slaves each picked an average of 323 pounds of cotton in one day (as a general rule, 150 pounds in one day was considered a satisfactory performance for an adult slave). On Louisiana sugarcane plantations it was not unusual for slaves to work eighteen to twenty hours each day during the harvest season.

Many slave women had work assignments equally as arduous as men, although most plantations maintained a gender division of labor. Certain jobs were clearly identified by

Gender Division of Labor
sex. Slave women watched the children, cleaned the interior of the big house, washed clothes, and sewed. Male house slaves served as butlers and coachmen. Women were more likely to be cooks, men to be blacksmiths. Women worked as chambermaids, wet nurses, and midwives. Slave women's skilled labor represented an integral part of the plantation economy. Their work with textiles, which included spinning, weaving, needlework, lace-making, sewing, and quilting, provided slaveholders with a reliable commodity, as well as personal clothing and items for use and display in the plantation household.

Historian Deborah Gray White and others have revealed that slave women esteemed and ranked each other's status within the slave community according to their creative abilities. This was evident in quilt-making. Before the Industrial Revolution, cloth was a costly and precious material item; therefore, piecework quilting was a particularly important skill, since it salvaged and used every remnant of old fabric as well as scraps of new fabric. Slave women prided themselves on transforming the material refuse of other products into inspired and useful works of art. Some slave women were even able to sell their work, and with the income they eventually purchased their own freedom.

The quilts of Harriet Powers are representative of slave women's skill and creativity. Born into slavery in Georgia in 1837, Harriet Powers most likely learned to quilt as a young girl, although it was not until after Emancipation that her reputation as a master quilter became known to the larger public. A white southerner and artist, Jennie Smith, discovered

Harriet Powers,
Bible Quilt, 1898

Powers' abilities, having seen and admired one of her Bible quilts at the 1886 Cotton Fair. Powers initially refused to sell the quilt, which she called "the offspring of my mind" to the white woman, but she eventually parted with it when her family fell on hard times. Although illiterate, Powers used her quilt work to interpret the biblical lessons she learned in church, revealing the quilt as a representation of her own particular religious testimony.

Women also worked under the hot sun in the fields along with men. Both men and women picked cotton. Although on some plantations women hoed and men plowed, the historical record reveals numerous cases of women who worked with plows. In the South Carolina Low Country, it was considered women's work to sow the rice seed. However, these Low Country slave women, like their men, labored in ditches and swamps, swinging axes and shovels. Travelers to the rice fields of South Carolina commented on seeing women engaged in clearing trees and building canals.

In the effort to get work out of slaves, overseers and masters used the lash on both men and women. Some planters went so far as to specify the size and type of whip to be used and the number of lashes to be given for certain offenses. Almost no master denied that whipping was an effective form of punishment, and the excessive use of the lash marked one of the most flagrant abuses of slavery. Many slaves fled because of brutal beatings by their owner or overseer.

It was on plantations with overseers that the greatest cruelty and brutality could be found. Overseers were employed on farms of more than twenty slaves or where the owner was an absentee landlord. Since overseers came from the non-slaveholding and frequently landless group, most had no personal **Overseers and Brutality** interest in the slaves' welfare. Too frequently they directed contempt toward slaves, because they blamed the slave system for their own unfortunate economic plight. Overseers managed the entire plantation in the absence of the slave owner or assumed a considerable portion of the responsibility of managing the slaves if he was present.

Overseers' authority over the slaves appeared almost unlimited. Slave owners demanded that the overseers get the maximum work out of the slaves while also producing a superior crop. With such a mandate, overseers could be ruthless in their treatment of slaves; and before a planter might reprimand the overseer for his brutality, irreparable damage had already been done. It must be noted, however, that unless an overseer's cruelty bordered on the sensational, many planters expressed no concern. Fights grew out of an overseer's attempts to punish slaves, however, and at times irate slaves were known to run a cruel overseer off the plantation. Some plantations also assigned the job of assisting the owner or overseer to a trusted slave, who in turn compelled work from his fellow slaves. Called the driver, a slave with such authority was viewed as a traitor and resented by the other slaves, especially if he took his duties seriously.

The Slave Diet The responsibility of masters to provide the necessities of life for their slaves determined the health of their slaves. The preoccupation with raising staple crops often resulted in the failure to grow sufficient food. Consequently, many plantations were compelled to purchase foodstuffs and other supplies not only for the family of the planter but for the slaves as well. Each slave household received a daily or weekly ration of meal and salt pork. For adults, the weekly ration was about a peck of meal and three to four pounds of meat. This allotment was at times supplemented with sweet potatoes, peas, rice, syrup, and fruit. In upcountry Georgia in the 1830s and in parts of South Carolina, some slaves gained permission to maintain small gardens and to hunt and fish. Some even successfully bargained with their masters for permission to market their produce. However, Georgia law made it illegal for slaves to market the products of their own gardens.

The break in the monotony of the unattractive fare of cornmeal and salt pork came on holidays such as Christmas, when the owner sometimes provided cheese, coffee, candy, or other items as a contribution to the festive spirit. In some instances the house servants, who usually ate the same food as the whites, whether permitted to do so or not, took food items from the owner and distributed it to family members and friends in the slave quarters, if the opportunity arose. These everyday acts of resistance could escalate into a larger conspiracy to deplete the owner's food supply. Historian Stephanie Camp and others note that slaves also stole away as best they could for moments of pleasure among themselves and sometimes in the company of free blacks in secretive gatherings. Not all such gatherings were for worship, indeed some were for dancing, singing, telling folktales, having barbecues, and playing sports. In such settings, slaves wrested their humanity from a society that deemed them to be property.

Haywood Dixon, slave carpenter
There were numerous black artisans, slave and free, before the Civil War. Shown here is Haywood Dixon, a slave carpenter in Greene County, North Carolina.

Urban and Nonagricultural Slavery

It was in nonagricultural pursuits that slaves displayed their diversity of talent and training. Many plantations had slave carpenters, masons, and mechanics, but such skilled slaves were more frequently found in towns. The majority of slaves in nonagricultural pursuits found work as domestic servants, porters, or common laborers in towns, but a large number of town slaves possessed some kind of skill. In the Charleston census of 1848, for example, there were more slave carpenters than free-black and white carpenters. The same was true of slave coopers. In addition, the Charleston census identified slave tailors, shoemakers, cabinetmakers, painters, plasterers, seamstresses, and other skilled slaves.

White artisans violently opposed, for the most part, the teaching of trades to blacks. However, most planters and proslavery leaders advocated training slaves in special skills, because having a skill increased their value. Only the most dema- **Black Artisans and Inventors** gogic of white racists claimed that it was impossible to train blacks as artisans. Too many examples belied such a contention. Advertisements frequently described a slave as a "first rate boot and shoe maker," an "experienced weaver and chair spinner," or an "excellent carpenter."

Many slaves labored in the prolific pottery mills of Edgefield, South Carolina, a district in the western part of the state where blacks outnumbered whites by a margin of four to one. Although dating back to at least 1815, Edgefield's mills reached their zenith between 1830 and 1860. One such skilled slave during this period was Dave the Potter. Unlike other enslaved potters who remain anonymous, Dave used his pottery as means of asserting his identity. He developed a signature style of thick roll-rimmed, wide-mouth storage jars of exceptionally large size, testifying to his own stature and strength. In addition, Dave emphasized his role as creator by signing and dating the vessels he made, boldly inscribing his full name "Dave" on the shoulder of the pots, rather than merely initialing the bottom, as was the contemporary convention.

Thus, Dave not only proclaimed his individual identity but also demonstrated his remarkable literacy during a time when teaching slaves to read and write was forbidden. Dave often inscribed his pots with trademark lines of clever verse, which provided an outlet for him to express, however briefly, his ideas about a range of topics. He inscribed on a jar used for meat preservation: "A very large jar which has four handles/pack it full of fresh meats—then light candles"; on another jar he referred to the separation of slave families: "I wonder where is all my relations/Friendship to all and every nation."

In Virginia slaves were used in mills, iron furnaces, and tobacco factories. The Saluda textile factory in South Carolina at one time employed 98 slave operatives. They were also in the textile mills of Florida, Alabama, Mississippi, and Georgia. In Kentucky they were employed in the salt-works of Clay County and in the iron and lead mines of Caldwell and Crittenden Counties. The southern railroads also employed a considerable number for construction work. It is reported that in 1838 a corporation purchased 140 slaves at a cost of $159,000 to work on the construction of a railroad between Jackson and Brandon, Mississippi. A slave served for ten years as an engineer on the West Feliciana Railroad, one of the oldest in the southern United States. Finally, slaves were frequently employed in river transportation and at docks. Slaves unloaded boats on the Mississippi River, and they worked on the docks at New Orleans, Savannah, Charleston, Norfolk, Baltimore, and other southern ports.

Slaves also proved their value as inventors. In 1835 and 1836, Henry Blair, designated in the records as a "colored man" of Maryland, received patents for two corn harvesters he had developed. By 1858, however, the attorney

Dave the Potter, *Great and Noble Jar*, May 13, 1859

general ruled that since a slave was not a citizen, the government could not enter into an agreement with him by granting him a patent nor could the slave assign the invention to his owner. Benjamin Montgomery, a slave owned by Jefferson Davis, invented a boat propeller toward the end of the slavery period. Davis made an attempt to have it patented, but failed. This experience perhaps accounts for a law passed by the Confederate Congress in 1861, providing that, if an owner took an oath that his or her slave had actually invented a device, the patent would be issued to the owner. It was not until after the Civil War that African Americans were able to secure patents for their inventions without any difficulty.

The practice of slave hiring was integral to the urban economy of the Old South. Some slaves were sent from plantations to cities specifically for hire, when owners sold their services to townspeople in the period between harvest and the new planting. In some cases, **Slave Hiring** urban slaves found their own employment, a practice known as self-hire. From the standpoint of a slave, the ability to hire out him- or herself was the next best thing to freedom. Urban slaves who hired out their own time tended to live in households independent of either their masters or hirers. In 1861 as much as 15 percent of Charleston's slaves were "living-out," the term at the time for a slave who lived independently. As letters to owners reveal, many self-hires were also literate. To self-hire was illegal under southern law, but slave owners were often complicit in the practice, because of its convenience (particularly in towns) and its opportunities for additional income.

On the most minimal level, slaves negotiated their own short-term employment, such as carrying luggage, doing laundry, and painting. However, some self-hires assumed full responsibility for procuring longer-term employment, as well as their food and lodging. A few were able to save a portion of the money they earned and buy their freedom, if the master permitted. Moses Grandy, for example, recounts in his slave narrative that his daughter peddled fruit on a Mississippi steamboat, regularly giving part of her income to her master and holding back part for her own upkeep. Over a period of years, she was able to amass $1,200, with which she purchased her freedom. Her father had not been as fortunate. After paying off the purchase price bit by bit, Moses Grandy's cruel master cheated him by refusing to manumit him and then selling him to a new owner.

Self-hire gave slaves the dual sense of both freedom and its limits. Frederick Douglass was permitted by his master Thomas Auld to find his own employment in Baltimore. Hired as a ship caulker, Douglass described in his narrative how he managed to collect his own wages, out of which he had to pay his master an agreed amount and use the leftover for his daily upkeep and the purchase of his tools. He clearly recognized the benefits of this arrangement, but he also recognized that at any time and for whatever reason his master had the prerogative to "put an end to my privilege," thus ever reminding Douglass of his slave status.

Slave men found a greater variety of hired jobs than did slave women. Whether employment was arranged by the master or by the slave himself, men labored not merely in unskilled work as porters, messengers, and factory workers but also in such artisan trades as caulkers, blacksmiths, coopers, and carpenters. Hired female slaves were concentrated in largely unskilled occupations, for example cleaning, washing, and peddling such marketable items as vegetables, fruit, fish, and oysters.

Since a slave could not legally contract his services, his master and the hiring employer drew up a legally binding agreement between them. Slaves often worked in factories in this way. However, in the case of self-hires it was common for the slave owner to operate on the basis of a verbal agreement made between the slave and his hirer. Such self-hired slaves constituted a relatively small proportion of all hired slaves. Historian Loren Schweninger's perusal of slaveholders' records notes at least 2,500 self-hired slaves in Virginia in 1860, or 10 percent of all hired slaves in the commonwealth.

Slaves were hired by the day, by the month, or by the year. When the contractual agreement was made directly between a slave owner and a hiring employer, the latter usually assumed responsibility for providing food, clothing, shelter, and medical care in addition to the stipulated wage. If the slave became ill or ran away, the wage continued to be paid to the owner. If the slave died, the wage ceased, but the party who had hired the slave was usually compelled to show that he or she was not in any way responsible for the slave's death. Annual contracts ran for fifty-one weeks and did not cover the period from Christmas to New Year's Day.

Hiring day was January 1 or some other day early in the year. Some communities set aside a hiring day and gave all interested persons an opportunity to transact their business with great ease, since the owners as well as the hirers would be able to find each other easily. On January 1, 1858, hiring day in Warrenton, Virginia, five hundred slaves were advertised as being for hire. Slave owners found a ready market in urban areas. Some whites desired slave labor but lacked the money to buy slaves outright; others merely had a temporary need for the services of a slave; still others found it more economical in the long run to purchase slave services without having the responsibility of providing for slaves in old age.

Slaves were hired for all kinds of rural labor as well. They were hired by small farmers who needed a few extra hands at harvest time, but they also worked in forests as woodcutters and turpentine hands. Hired slaves could be found in mines, on railroad construction jobs, and in canal digging. The rates of hire varied considerably, depending on the skill of the slave as well as on the supply. In 1800 a slave hand went for $100 per year in the Lower South. By 1860 the price had increased to $200 or more. Toward the end of the period, a young blacksmith in Mississippi was hired for $500, and several hands in Texas brought as much as $600.

Social and Cultural Life

Despite surveillance of their activities and long working hours with little free time for rest, slaves found sufficient "living space" within the confines of their bondage to forge a resilient culture of worship and song, love and courtship, family bonds and cultural creativity in many forms. Slaves stole moments for personal expression and recreation in a variety of ways, and by so doing they rejected the chattel principle that defined them as property. The rich expressive culture of the slaves, as evidenced in their spirituals, work songs, folktales, and religious worship, attests to their ability to hold fast to human creativity.

Holidays, fairs, militia musters, and election days provided occasions for relaxing the rules on the plantation, and at these times slaves gathered to sing, dance, and enjoy fellowship. There were two periods to which slaves could look forward as occasions for recreation and relaxation: the summer lay-by and Christmas. At the end of the cultivation period there was a considerable reduction of duties on some plantations, giving slaves an opportunity either to work for themselves or to engage in sports and other forms of recreation. The Christmas holiday brought a complete suspension of work, except for such bare essentials as cooking and washing. Weddings, anniversaries, and the like, whether of whites or blacks, could become opportunities for merrymaking.

Slave wedding in Virginia, 1838
'The Old Plantation,' 1800. Plantation slaves dancing in front of their wooden cabins accompanied by banjo and drum. From the collection of the Williamsburg Foundation, Williamsburg.

Masters often allowed some form of religious activity among their slaves. Under white supervision, worship services were held on larger plantations and in towns. White ministers preached to these slave congregations, but in some instances slaves and free blacks openly led. Richmond, Charleston, and Lexington, Kentucky, all had churches with large slave congregations. When news of slave conspiracies spread in southern communities and when the abolitionist movement grew louder in the North, planters became more cautious of their slaves' religious activities. More and more, slaves were required to attend the churches of their masters, with a white person presiding over their religious services. The goal was to keep a closer eye on slaves and to inculcate a religious message that reinforced slavery as divinely ordained. Slaves who attended the churches of planters usually sat in the gallery or in a special section designated for them. The earliest examples of racial segregation could be found in churches. In one instance, a white congregation constructed a partition several feet high to separate masters from slaves.

Religious Activity

Some masters even showed ambivalence toward these churches, fearing that it would be difficult if not impossible to control and monitor slaves' beliefs and practices. Such fears proved accurate, since many of the most pious Christian slaves had a keen understanding of the difference between the gospel as expounded by proslavery preachers and the biblical message of human equality before God. Unlike their masters, slaves did not view the church and the Bible as an affirmation of slavery. This was evident in their religious songs, which held multiple meanings as to otherworldly and this-worldly concerns. Slaves sang in the hope of being relieved of their burdens in the next world, but through their religious songs they also expressed what W. E. B. Du Bois called the "articulate message of the slaves to the world." This message conveyed sorrow, divine retribution, the perception of themselves as God's "chosen people," and even covert plans to flee slavery or to go off to the woods to worship together.

The spirituals critiqued the injustice of slavery and the surety of God's justice, with such diverse titles as "Dere's a Great Camp Meetin' in de Promised Land," "Steal Away," and "Heaven, Heaven, Everybody Talkin' 'Bout Heaven Ain't Goin' There." Slaves found inspiration in the Exodus story. Likening their plight in bondage to that of the ancient biblical story of the Hebrew slaves of Egypt, black slaves prophesied their deliverance in such verses as "Go down Moses, way down in Egyptland/Tell Old Pharoah, to let my people go." In their songs and folktales, slaves presented a collective identity that stood in stark contrast to images of black inferiority. In fact, the wording of black sacred and secular songs reveals that African Americans, slave and free, rejected the idea of slavery as God-ordained. Both southern and northern blacks adopted the Exodus story.

The sacred world of the slaves included a blending of Christianity and folk beliefs. Religious historian Albert Raboteau has traced some of the numerous ways in which slave religion produced a sustaining (and at times defiant) community through **The Slave Church** the slave church—the invisible institution in the antebellum South. The number of black preachers was always considerable, and few plantations were without at least one. When slaves gathered in the woods to worship in their own way and without the eyes of whites on them, it was the slave preacher who dominated. Conjurers also played an important leadership role.

Frederick Douglass identified the African-born slaves as the most powerful conjurers in the slave quarters, and Douglass himself spoke of the influence of the conjurer Sandy Jenkins. Clearly some of the slaves' religious views and practices had African origins. Folk beliefs were an integral part of the Christian beliefs of many slaves. For instance, when slaves gathered in the woods, they turned a large pot upside down in the middle of their circle of worshippers, believing that the pot could absorb the sound of their shouts, prayers, and songs so that whites would not hear them. This act emboldened slaves to practice their religion freely and to voice their beliefs with confidence. Folk beliefs, too, formed an integral part of overt slave resistance, since conjurers provided slaves with such protective charms as a claw or a tooth. Certainly the slaves, but even a few whites as well, solicited the aid of black conjurers. Court records identify slave conjurers whose white owners sought their predictions as to the outcome of business and personal matters.

The permanency of a slave marriage depended largely on the extent to which the couple had an opportunity to work and live together. There are numerous examples of loving and committed slave families, especially where children strengthened the bond and where the family was not divided through sale. Although the economic **Slave Families** interests of the masters were often inimical to the family life of the slaves, slave families proved remarkably resilient in many ways. Childbearing was often extremely hard for slave women. Lack of adequate medical care had a particularly negative effect during pregnancy, childbirth, and the period immediately thereafter. The breakup of families through sale often left children orphaned and wives and husbands forever separated. Division by sale was fiercely resisted. J. W. Loguen's mother, for example, had to be tied to a loom when her children were taken from her to be sold, and Josiah Henson wrote in his 1849 slave narrative that his mother looked on "in an agony of grief" as she saw her children sold one by one. When slave fathers were sold or when they lived on a different plantation, the slave mother took on the responsibility of stabilizing her family and keeping it together. "Fictive kin" networks, made up of more distant relatives and friends, served to ease the pain of separation by reproducing a sense of family for children sold away from their parents.

Although especially conspicuous in Charleston, Mobile, and New Orleans, children born of slave women and white men were visible throughout the rural and urban South.

Interracial Relationships The slave narratives of the antebellum period and the ex-slave interviews in the 1930s attest to the many instances when owners, overseers, and other white men forced slave women into sexual relations that led to pregnancy. Rape was not always the case, however. In New Orleans, the practice of young white men maintaining young mulatto women in long-term relationships, called *plaçage*, attracted the attention of travelers and local writers. Interracial relationships in antebellum Louisiana could take the form of concubinage, but some were recognized as a "marriage of conscience." In the latter, the wedding ceremony between a white person and a free person of African descent was performed by a Catholic priest—with the law of the church in defiance of Louisiana's civil law against miscegenation. More often, however, racial intermixture resulted from the physical coercion of a slave woman by a white man. A slave woman's resistance to rape could bring an even more violent reaction, and many slave women carried to their graves scars inflicted by their owners or other white men in such situations.

Sexual exploitation remained one of the most important distinctions between female and male slave experiences. In *Incidents in the Life of a Slave Girl*, Harriet Jacobs tells of her own efforts to resist the advances of her slave master. Writing under the pseudonym Linda Brent, Jacobs describes her tortured life in the household of her cruel, licentious master, Dr. Flint, and his jealous wife, who resents her husband's attraction to the fifteen-year-old Brent. In the narrative, Brent bemoans: "Soon she [the slave girl] will learn to tremble when she hears her master's footfall. She will be compelled to realize that she is no longer a child. If God has bestowed beauty upon her, it will prove her greatest curse."

The assumption that black women were by nature sexually promiscuous was widespread among whites. Such ideas would continue long after slavery, justifying the rape of black women with impunity in most southern states. In Mississippi in the late nineteenth century, it was not a criminal act to rape a black girl over the age of ten. In an ideological climate that attributed hypersexuality to black women, some slave women did not resist their master's advances, because they knew it would be futile to do so. Others sought the master's advances because of the prestige or material advantages that such a relationship might bring. The historical record also discloses cases of genuine affection between a master and his female slave.

Children born to interracial unions were nonetheless slaves, and the result of such extensive mixing was that by 1850 there were 246,000 mulatto slaves, out of a total slave population of 3.2 million. By 1860 there were 411,000 mulatto slaves and a total slave population of 3.9 million. The number may well have been greater, because census takers

Mulatto Slaves counted as mulattoes only those who appeared to have certain physical traits. The reactions of white fathers to their black progeny varied. Some had no feelings at all for their black children. Such children remained slaves, and the white masters who fathered them sold them away as easily as any other slave. Not infrequently, white fathers were encouraged to do so by their wives, who resented the presence of their husbands' slave children. However, historical records also reveal that some white fathers, although far less in number, developed a great fondness for their slave children, emancipating and providing for them. In most instances, such children were freed only after their white father's death. However, the decedent's wishes went often unrealized, and it was typical for white family members to sue successfully in court for ownership of these slave children.

The life of Amanda America Dickson, born in 1849, the daughter of the wealthy planter David Dickson of Hancock County, Georgia, reveals that in some cases older, repentant slave masters atoned for their rape of black women by affording their mixed-race children a lifestyle in no way typical of a slave's. David Dickson was forty years old when he fathered Amanda by his twelve-year old slave Julia Lewis. According to her biographer, Kent Anderson Leslie, Amanda was raised by Dickson's mother, in whose home she remained a slave but was treated as a loving granddaughter, being taught to read, write, and play the piano. After the war, Amanda married her white cousin Charles Eubanks, although their marriage proved short-lived. By 1870 she returned to her father's plantation with the two children from her marriage and officially adopted her father's surname, becoming Amanda America Dickson. She eventually attended a black college, Atlanta University, and on her father's death in 1885 became the beneficiary of his large and affluent estate. Although much of Amanda Dickson's exceptional story occurred after the demise of slavery, her position as a "privileged daughter," although a slave, accounted for much of her life that followed.

Resistance

Masters almost always sought to defend slavery by conveying the impression that their slaves were docile, tractable, and happy. Ironically, some antislavery advocates also portrayed similar images, contending that the system of slavery made blacks easily controlled and acquiescent. Both proslavery and antislavery advocates overstated the case to suit their respective purposes. If North American slaves had no revolutionary traditions, as Caribbean and South American slaves did, this did not mean the absence of slave protest or patterns of slave resistance. Even in the cases of slaves who did not overtly protest, revolt, or escape, there is no reason to conclude that bondage and exploitation permanently impaired their personalities or reduced them to complete docility—to the mindset of a childlike "Sambo"—as was argued by historian Stanley Elkins in the late 1950s. Slaves carried out countless everyday acts of resistance. By stealing food or clothing, feigning illness, or, in the case of women, pretending to be pregnant in order to escape an onerous job or punishment, and by simply attempting to "read" their masters' emotions and minds in order to get favored treatment, slaves adopted many strategies and tactics that resisted complete exploitation and hid their true feelings from their white oppressors.

Slaves in the New Orleans market, according to historian Walter Johnson, used every trick they could muster in order to gain control over their would-be purchasers. Some sought to be hired as house slaves rather than as field hands. Mothers tried their best to be bought together with their children. Slaves **Slave Market Gambits** sought to be sold to an owner who lived near the owner of other family members. Husbands and wives sorely grieved separation to places unknown. The location to which they would ultimately be sent after their sale figured significantly in the minds of slaves as they stood on the auction block. The slave Solomon Northrop overheard a potential purchaser identify himself as a resident of New Orleans, which appealed to Northrop. "I conceived," he recalled in his slave narrative years later, "that it would not be difficult to make my escape from New Orleans on some northern vessel."

Slaves attempted to exhibit behavior that would appeal to the master of their choosing. At the same time some slaves endeavored to undermine their sale to persons who had a reputation for being harsh or who may have exhibited undesirable gestures as they inspected the slaves on the auction block. Whatever the reason, slaves watched their would-be purchasers

Window in Time

Louisa Picquet Describes Her Experience on the Auction Block

Q: How did you say you came to be sold?

A: Well, you see, Mr. Cook [my master] made great parties, and go off to watering-places, and get in debt, and had to break up, and then he took us to Mobile, and hired the most of us, so the men he owe could not find us, and sell us for the debt. Then after a while, the sheriff came from Georgia after Mr. Cook's debts, and found us all, and took us to auction, and sold us. My mother and brother was sold to Texas, and I was sold to New Orleans.

Q: How old where you then?

A: Well, I don't know exactly, but the auctioneer said I wasn't quite fourteen. I didn't know myself.

Q: How old was your brother?

A: I suppose he was about two months old. He was a little bit of a baby.

Q: Where were you sold?

A: In the city of Mobile . . . They put all the men in one room, and all the women in another, and then whoever want to come and examine, and ask you whole lot of questions. They began to take the clothes off me, and a gentleman said they needn't do that, and told them to take me out. He said he knew I was a virtuous girl, and he'd buy me, anyhow. He didn't strip me, only just under my shoulders.

Q: Were there others there white like you?

A: Oh, yes, plenty of them. There was only Lucy of our lot, but others!

Continued

carefully in the attempt to manipulate the desired outcome. Slaves pretended to be stupid or physically weak. Some underplayed their skills of cooking or craft, contradicting what was advertised about them. By pretending to be sick or weak, or by displaying a bad attitude or other negative features, a slave might subvert his purchase by an undesirable master.

Being offered for sale meant that black men and women had their bodies put on public display, with potential buyers free to look at and touch the human merchandise to determine their market value. Thus slaves studied facial expressions and other gestures, attempting to discern the character of a potential owner. Slaves looked particularly for clues as to whether a buyer might be licentious, dishonest, cruel, or otherwise unsatisfactory. The slave Charles Ball wrote of having been on the auction block and encountering such a purchaser: "I never saw a human countenance that expressed more of the evil passions of the heart than did that of this man, and his conversation corresponded with his physiognomy."

Slaves engaged in an elaborate program of sabotage on both large plantations and small farms. They regularly broke farming tools, and they could be so ruthless in destroying fields that

Q: Were others stripped and examined?

A: Well, not quite naked, but just [the] same.

Q: You say the gentleman told them to "take you out." What did he mean by that?

A: Why, take me out of the room where the women and girls were kept; where they examine them—out where the auctioneer sold us . . . At the market, where the block is.

Q: What block?

A: My! Don't you know? The stand, where you have to get up.

Q: Did you get up on the stand?

A: Why, of course; we all have to get up to be seen.

Q: What else do you remember about it?

A: Well, they first begin at upward of six hundred for me, and then bid some fifty more, and some twenty-five more, and that way.

Q: Do you remember any thing the auctioneer said about you when he sold you?

A: Well, he said he could not recommend me for any thing else only that I was a good-lookin' girl, and a good nurse, and kind and affectionate to children; but I was never used to any hard work. He told them they could see that. My hair was quite short, and the auctioneer spoke about it, but said, "You see it good quality, and give a little time, it will grow out again." You see Mr. Cook had my hair cut off. My hair grew fast, and look so much better than Mr. Cook's daughter, and he fancy I had better hair than his daughter, and so he had it cut off to make a difference.

Hiram Mattison, *Louisa Picquet, the Octoroon: Or Inside Views of Southern Domestic Life* (Boston, 1861).

the most careful supervision was necessary to ensure the survival of crops until harvest time. Forests, barns, and homes were targets of arson. Indeed, the most far-fetched and inaccurate characterization of slaves is that they were satisfied, even happy, with their lot. If that were true, then it would be difficult to explain the elaborate machinery designed to keep them in bondage. The slave codes reveal the constant concern of owners not only to discipline their slaves but also to prevent them from absconding. Problems in management disclose the numerous ways in which slaves expressed their dissatisfaction.

Sabotage and Suicide

The magnitude of slaves' dissatisfaction also manifested itself in suicide and self-mutilation. It was not uncommon for slaves fresh from Africa to kill themselves in large numbers. In 1807 two boatloads of Africans newly arrived in Charleston starved themselves to death. Throughout the antebellum period, suicide was widespread. When his slave woman was found to have hanged herself in 1829, a Georgia planter expressed shock and dismay, asserting that he could see no reason why she should want to take her own life. And when two Louisiana slaves were returned to their owner after a thwarted escape in 1858, they drowned themselves in the bayou. One of the South's wealthiest planters, Charles Manigault, lost a slave by a similar act when the overseer threatened him with punishment. Sometimes slave mothers killed their own children to prevent them from having to grow up in slavery. Slaves also sought to resist bondage by desperate acts of self-mutilation. They cut off their own toes and hands and in other ways mutilated themselves so as to become ineffective as workers. One Kentucky slave carpenter, for example, cut off one of his hands and the fingers of the other when he learned that he was to be sold down the river. There were several instances of slaves shooting themselves in the hand or foot, especially when they were recaptured after trying to run away.

Running Away   The most common form of overt slave resistance was running away. When families were broken up through sale, slaves ran away to find children, parents, and spouses. In search of their loved ones, they fled to locations in the South. Slaves also escaped after learning of the death of a master, some fearing an imminent sale and others perceiving such a death as an opportune moment of weakness in the white household. On large plantations, a slave's absence might have been less noticeable, since a probate inventory could take from weeks to months. This was the case when slave owner Richard Benbury of North Carolina died; six months later, his estate notified newspapers to print a runaway slave advertisement. On occasion, slaves ran away to avoid punishment after an altercation or misunderstanding with the owner or overseer. Such escapes, especially prevalent among female slaves, were often temporary, as the slave tried to take leave and "lie out" a few miles away. Some temporary fugitives even dispatched demands to the owner or overseer for better treatment, time off, new clothes, and amnesty. Since lying out usually happened at planting or harvest times, the slaves were in a position to drive a hard bargain, which they were pleased to do. Running away occurred so often in Virginia that slave traders provided affidavits to prospective purchasers, asserting that the slave to be sold was in good health and was not a habitual runaway. Many slaves were, nevertheless, habitual runaways, and many of those who showed no signs of the lash and who could not claim abusive treatment persisted in running away.

$150 REWARD

RANAWAY from the subscriber, on the night of the 2d instant, a negro man, who calls himself *Henry May*, about **22** years old, 5 feet 6 or 8 inches high, ordinary color, rather chunky built, bushy head, and has it divided mostly on one side, and keeps it very nicely combed; has been raised in the house, and is a first rate dining-room servant, and was in a tavern in Louisville for 18 months. I expect he is now in Louisville trying to make his escape to a free state, (in all probability to Cincinnati, Ohio.) Perhaps he may try to get employment on a steamboat. He is a good cook, and is handy in any capacity as a house servant. Had on when he left, a dark cassinett coatee, and dark striped cassinett pantaloons, new—he had other clothing. I will give $50 reward if taken in Louisvill; 100 dollars if taken one hundred miles from Louisville in this State, and 150 dollars if taken out of this State, and delivered to me, or secured in any jail so that I can get him again.   WILLIAM BURKE.
Bardstown, Ky., September 3d, 1838.

Reward handbill for a runaway slave, 1837

Every southern community raised its annual crop of runaway slaves. Both federal and state legislation aided in their recovery, but many slaves escaped forever. Running away became so widespread that every state sought to strengthen its patrol and other safeguards, to little avail. Hardly a newspaper went to press without several advertisements listing runaways, and sometimes there were several columns of such advertisements. The following is typical:

Absconded from the Forest Plantation of the late William Dunbar, on Sunday the 7th instant, a very handsome Mulattress called Harriet, about 13 years old, with straight dark hair and dark eyes. This girl was lately in New Orleans, and is known to have seen there a man whom she claims as her father and who does now or did lately live on the Mississippi, a little above the mouth of the Caffa-laya. It is highly probable some plan has been concocted for the girl's escape.

Some slaves disguised themselves or armed themselves with free passes in their effort to escape. Others simply walked off the plantation, apparently hoping that fate would be kind and assist in their permanent escape. Some were inveterate runaways, such as the North Carolina woman who fled from her owner's plantation no less than sixteen times. Others were not as daring and gave up after one unsuccessful attempt. Although there is no way of even approximating the number of runaways, fleeing to freedom represented the most effective act of resistance against their masters. The slave narratives reveal the ingenious ways that slaves escaped to freedom in the North, especially through the Underground Railroad.

Much more disturbing to the whites of the South was the potential for violent resistance. Poisoning was always feared, and some planters even felt the need to maintain an official taster. As early as 1761 the *Charleston Gazette* remarked that the "Negroes have begun the hellish act of poisoning." Slaves used arsenic and other similar compounds. If such poisons were unavailable, slaves resorted to mixing ground glass in the **Violent Resistance** gravy for their owners' meals. Numerous slaves were convicted of murdering their owners and overseers, but some escaped. In 1797 a newly imported African slave killed his master, a planter in Screven County, Georgia. Another Georgia master died at the hands of his slave, who stabbed him sixteen times. The slave was later burned alive. William Pearce of Florida was killed by his slave with an axe when Pearce sought to punish him. Carolina Turner of Kentucky was choked to death by a slave whom she was flogging. Though local whites had long complained of the woman's merciless and brutal treatment of her slaves, the killer was summarily hanged. Southern newspapers reveal numerous instances when slaves murdered their overseers and owners in the fields or forests.

Rumors of insurrections struck terror in the hearts of slaveholders. In 1810 a plot was uncovered in Lexington, Kentucky. The following year, more than four hundred rebellious slaves in Louisiana had to be put down by federal and state troops. **Slave Revolts** At least seventy-five slaves lost their lives in the encounter and in the trials that ensued. Nevertheless, slaves revolted in New Orleans the following year. In the Upper South efforts to organize slave rebellions continued. In Virginia in 1815 a white man named George Boxley decided to attempt to free the slaves. He made elaborate plans, but a slave woman betrayed him and his conspirators. Although Boxley escaped, six slaves were hanged.

Nor were slaves oblivious to the Revolutionary era's pronouncements of liberty and equality in America, France, and Haiti in the late eighteenth and early nineteenth centuries and to the continuing rhetoric of "democracy" in American politics. In 1800 Gabriel's revolt in Virginia had been inspired by these ideals. In 1822 Denmark Vesey's elaborate conspiracy in Charleston drew on religious imagery, the Haitian Revolution, and knowledge of the congressional debates over the extension of slavery. Eugene Genovese notes that Vesey, a literate man, followed the coverage of the discussions that led to the Missouri Compromise. This is plausible, since in 1818, when Missouri sought admission to the Union as a slave state, the public became embroiled in a controversy over the extension of slavery in the western territories.

In 1819 and 1820, the press covered the heated debates between the proslavery and antislavery factions in the United States Congress. In 1820 an eventual compromise was reached, prohibiting slavery above the parallel 36°30'. In 1821 the territory of Missouri, although above this line, was allowed admission into the Union as a slave state. (Slaves had been there from the territory's early settlement.) To offset the imbalance between the number of slave and free states, Maine was admitted as a free state. Voices for and against slavery rang out loudly and passionately. Thomas Jefferson, in private correspondence, wrote despairingly of the ability of a "geographical line" to contain the "angry passions of men." He called the Missouri Compromise not a lasting effect but a "fire bell in the night." If for Jefferson, the controversy served as a harbinger of an inevitable, far greater disunion, for Denmark Vesey, the fight between slavery and freedom was felt even more immediately and closer to home.

Although born a slave, Vesey purchased his freedom in 1800 with money he had won from the Charleston lottery; and for a score of years he made a respectable living as a car-

Denmark Vesey penter in the city. As a sensitive, liberty-loving man, he was not satisfied with enjoying his own relatively comfortable existence. Over a period of several years, he carefully plotted a slave revolt and chose his assistants, most of whom were skilled slaves. One of his assistants was the African conjurer Gullah Jack (also known as Jack Pritchard). Invoking biblical verses and African charms, Vesey's conspirators made and collected their weapons: 250 pike heads and bayonets and 300 daggers. Vesey originally set the second Sunday in July 1822 for the day of the revolt, but when word of his plot leaked out, he moved it up one month; unfortunately, his assistants, who were scattered for miles around

Major American Slave Rebellions				
Year	Rebellion	Black participants	White deaths	End result for the rebels
1712	New York City conspiracy	30–40	9	21 executed, 6 estimated suicides, 6 pardoned
1739	Stono rebellion	75–80	25	Estimated 50 killed and executed in suppression
1800	Gabriel Prosser's conspiracy	40	0	35 executed, 4 escaped, 1 suicide
1811	Louisiana revolt	180–500	2	66 killed in battle, 16 executed, 17 escaped or dead
1822	Denmark Vesey's conspiracy	49	0	49 condemned: 12 pardoned, 37 hanged
1831	Nat Turner's rebellion	70	57	20 conspirators executed including Turner, 100 or more blacks killed in mass reprisals
1835–1838	Black Seminole rebellion, maroon & slave combined	935–1265	400	500 emigrated west with Indians, 90 or more caught and re-enslaved, hundreds more surrendered to slavery, casualties unknown
1835–1838	Black Seminole rebellion, plantation slave only	385–465	n/a	90 or more caught and re-enslaved, hundreds surrendered and returned to slavery, uncertain number emigrated west with Black Seminoles

Source: www.johnhorse.com/highlights/essays/largest.htm

Charleston, did not all hear of the change of plans. Meanwhile, whites—who were by now well aware of what was going on—began to round up suspects. At least 139 blacks were arrested, 47 of whom were condemned and executed, including Vesey. Four white men were fined and imprisoned for encouraging the revolt. Estimates of the number of blacks involved in the plot ran as high as 9,000.

In the late 1820s the entire South grew apprehensive about possible uprisings. Southern nerves were put on edge especially by the publication in 1829 of David Walker's *Appeal in Four Articles; Together with a Preamble, to the Coloured Citizens of the World, but in Particular and Very Expressly to Those of the United States of America.* Walker was born free in North Carolina, the son of a free mother and a slave father. Refusing to live in a state that allowed slavery, he traveled extensively before settling in Boston and opening a tailoring business. In the pamphlet, Walker wrote boldly to slaveholders, stating: "Compare your own language . . . , extracted from your Declaration of Independence, with your cruelties and murders inflicted by your cruel and unmerciful fathers and yourselves on our fathers and on us—men who have never given your fathers or you the least provocation!" With even bolder words, he stated that the "day of judgment was at hand" and called on the slaves to risk life itself and take up arms against their oppressors. Scholars today note that soon after its publication Walker's *Appeal* was secretly carried into black communities in Georgia, Virginia, North Carolina, and Louisiana. In August 1830, after the third and more militant edition appeared, Walker mysteriously died (it has been surmised from poisoning).

Although no direct correlation has been found between the pamphlet and a specific revolt, within a year or two of its publication, southern states faced a rash of slave uprisings and rumors of slave conspiracies. In 1829 several revolts were reported on Louisiana plantations, and in 1830 a number of North Carolina citizens asked their legislature for aid because their slaves had become "almost uncontrollable." Whites' fears rose to fever pitch in 1831, however, with the insurrection of Nat Turner.

Turner, a slave in Virginia's Southampton County, had early on defied slavery by running away but then decided to return to his owner. Regarded by other slaves as a prophet, exhorter, and even a messianic figure, Turner believed that he had been selected by divine power to deliver his people from slav- **Nat Turner** ery. When a solar eclipse occurred in February 1831, Turner interpreted it as a sign for him to lead his people out of bondage. He originally selected the Fourth of July as the day of reckoning, but when he became ill he postponed the revolt until he saw another sign. On August 13, when he thought that the sun turned a "peculiar greenish blue," he called the revolt for August 21. He and his followers began by killing Turner's master, Joseph Travis, and his family. In rapid succession other families fell under the blows of the blacks; within twenty-four hours, sixty whites had been killed. The revolt spread rapidly until the main group of the rebels was overpowered by state and federal troops. More than a hundred slaves were killed in the encounter, and thirteen slaves and three free blacks were immediately hanged. Turner was captured on October 30, and within less than two weeks he was tried and, on November 11, executed.

The Southampton uprising stunned the South—the stories of Turner's revolt becoming grossly exaggerated in many communities. In some reports it was falsely stated that whites had been murdered by the hundreds in Virginia. Several southern states felt it necessary to call special sessions of their legislatures to consider the emergency. Most states strengthened their slave codes, and white citizens literally lay awake at night waiting for slaves to

Nat Turner exhorting his followers

The 1831 revolt of Nat Turner and his followers in Virginia resulted in the deaths of his master and numerous other whites. Once the revolt was crushed, dazed whites strengthened slave codes and redoubled vigilance. The artist's depiction reflects whites' fears of the consequences of blacks meeting without the supervision of their owners.

make another break. Despite vigorous efforts on the part of the southern states to prevent slave uprisings, revolts continued after Nat Turner's death. In 1835 several slaves in Monroe County, Georgia, were hanged or whipped to death because of their alleged implication in a conspiracy. In the following decade, slave conspiracies or actual violence occurred in Alabama, Louisiana, and Mississippi. In 1853 a revolt in New Orleans involving 2,500 slaves was aborted by a free-black informant. In 1856 escaped slaves in North Carolina's Bladen and Robeson counties "went on the warpath" and terrorized the countryside.

Thus throughout the antebellum period the South lived in fear of the dreaded eventuality of a slave revolt. From the late 1820s through the 1850s, northern black abolitionists such as David Walker and Henry Highland Garnet and white radicals such as John Brown urged the slaves to strike for freedom in a group. The time and form of such a revolt were not as yet apparent to the many slaves, despite their desperate dreams of freedom. However, by 1862 this time had indeed come, and many thousands of slaves would flee their plantations, don the uniforms and shoulder the rifles of the Union army, and in the liberating battalions of the Civil War fight to end slavery forever.

..

Antebellum Free Blacks

Freedom's Boundaries

In a Culture of Racism

Economic and Social Life

Education

Black Convention Movement

Black Women

The Debate on Emigration

Eliza, Nellie, and Margaret Coplan, 1854—portrait by W. M. Prior

The Coplan family was one of the few African American families in antebellum America affluent enough to commission such a portrait.

F reedom from slavery did not mean equality of citizenship for those African Americans who were not in bondage in the decades prior to the Civil War. Nor did the escalating sectional debate about slavery from the 1820s through the 1850s preclude controversy over the mere presence of free blacks in both northern and southern states. The condition of free blacks became a frequent touchstone in debates over the morality or immorality of slavery, as proslavery southerners favorably compared the supposedly benevolent treatment of slaves to the harsh living conditions endured by free blacks in the North. Debating in 1830 with Massachusetts Senator Daniel Webster, South Carolina's Senator Robert Y. Hayne offered one of the most notorious public condemnations of free blacks' condition to come from a national political figure. "There does not exist on the face of the earth," insisted Hayne during a speech before the U.S. Senate in slavery's defense, "a population so poor, so wretched, so loathsome, so utterly destitute of all the comforts, conveniences, and decencies of life, as the unfortunate blacks of Philadelphia, New York, and Boston. Liberty has been to them the greatest of calamities, the heaviest of curses."

Unlike the defenders of slavery, antebellum free blacks saw their condition as far preferable to slavery, although they daily confronted the reality of racial discrimination and injustice. Refused the many rights and privileges that the law guaranteed to white Americans, they found no protection from the federal government and little from many state governments. Free blacks were denied suffrage, access to equal education, certain types of employment, and admission to state militias. They were troubled by nuisance regulations, insulting language, and racist caricatures in a variety of cultural forms. They were harassed in public, and their neighborhoods were attacked by rioting mobs. They lived under constant scrutiny, in a fishbowl of sorts, and therefore they believed that their actions had potentially momentous consequences, not only for themselves and their communities but also for the ultimate fate of their still enslaved brethren. The stakes of freedom were high. For antebellum free blacks, freedom was complex—a series of opportunities that they embraced and a set of challenges that they felt required to face and to conquer in order to counter white Americans' negative perceptions of blacks and of their "fitness for freedom." While they understood the obstacles placed in their path by whites in the North and South, antebellum free blacks were strengthened by their shared values of community self-determination and protest.

Freedom's Boundaries

In 1820 slavery was entrenched in the southern states and on its way to ultimate extinction in the North. Missouri's admission to the Union as a slave state had brought this duality into stark relief, crystallizing years of disputes over the westward expansion of slavery. However, slavery was not the only hotly debated issue. Missouri's state constitution, which included an addendum that forbade "free Negroes and mulattoes from coming to and settling in this state under any pretext whatsoever," ignited yet another fiery clash in Congress. A majority in the House of Representatives initially refused to accept Missouri as a state under these conditions. Some members cited the federal Constitution's guarantee that "the citizens of each state shall be entitled to all the privileges and immunities of the several states." The controversy ended in a nebulous formulation in March 1821, when Congress finally admitted Missouri to statehood without clarifying whether free blacks were citizens or not. Aside from functioning to "salve tender consciences," as New Hampshire Representative William Plumer, Jr., remarked at the time, Congress had not determined the actual rights of free blacks, nor had society generally acknowledged that blacks were members of the American body politic.

Although conducted at the national level, the Missouri debate formed part of a larger discussion within the individual states about the presence, character, and civil status of their own free black residents. Various southern states early on passed laws that barred the entrance of free blacks, presuming that any **Black Laws** substantial free black presence would threaten the permanency of slavery. Between 1800 and 1808, South Carolina, Maryland, and Kentucky enacted such laws in response to the significant numbers of manumissions inspired by the Revolutionary War's rhetoric of freedom, and other southern states followed suit in the years surrounding the Missouri Controversy and in the decades to follow: Georgia in 1818, Mississippi in 1819, Louisiana in 1830, Tennessee in 1831, and Alabama in 1832. Arkansas and Missouri added even more restrictions to black residency in 1843.

The South was not the only region that worried about the in-migration of free blacks. In 1821 the Massachusetts legislature charged a committee of its members with ascertaining whether the commonwealth needed to limit its growing black population. Although Massachusetts and other northeastern states ultimately rejected such a course of action, legal restrictions, called *black laws,* appeared throughout the Midwest—discouraging, if not completely eliminating, free black in-migration. In 1804 Ohio enacted a law that denied residency to any black or mulatto who was unable to produce a certificate of freedom from slavery. In 1807 the Ohio legislature passed a more stringent law, requiring African Americans in the state to post a bond of $500 as proof of freedom. The territorial legislatures of Michigan, Illinois, Indiana, and Iowa enacted black laws to deter free blacks from settling within their borders. Although Michigan repealed its black laws almost immediately after attaining statehood in 1837, and Ohio repealed them in 1849, Indiana and Illinois kept these laws on the books until after the Civil War. As legal historian Paul Finkelman has demonstrated, a few hundred blacks were held in bondage in Indiana until the early 1820s and in Illinois until the 1840s. Even in the far West, such territories as Oregon, New Mexico, and Utah passed statutes that banned black migrants. African Americans could be found in these places before and after statehood, however. California, the western state with the largest free black population, unsuccessfully attempted to enact black laws in the 1850s.

In his classic study of the early antebellum United States, *Democracy in America* (1835), French author Alexis de Tocqueville noted the paradox of extreme racial intolerance in those states where slavery had never existed. During an interview conducted for his book in 1831, Tocqueville's observations were **Migration West** confirmed when an Ohio attorney told him: "We try to discourage them [free blacks] in every possible way. Not only have we made laws allowing them to be expelled at will, but we hamper them in a thousand ways. A Negro has no political rights; he cannot be a juror; he cannot give evidence against whites." Nevertheless, despite the laws and the cultural hostility, free black populations in the Midwest grew dramatically, mostly from migration. By 1850 Ohio had the fourth largest free black population in the North.

Even in the face of such prejudice and discouragement, Ohio's free blacks founded at least two newspapers. One of them, the Columbus *Palladium of Liberty,* opined sarcastically that the racist presumptions embodied in Ohio's law to regulate persons of color would eventually lead to the regulation of everything, including time itself. In February 1844 the paper's editor, David Jenkins, wrote, "Since Ohio has been a free state, she regulates both clocks, watches, blacks and mulattoes, one a thing to behold, the other the image of God, the great I AM, the great Creator of all things, and the only regulator of mankind."

Seeking the same kind of economic opportunities that drew white pioneers by the thousands to the Old Northwest Territory, blacks continued to head west in the face of mounting restrictions. The 1830 census registered almost 15,000 free blacks in the three states of Ohio, Indiana, and Illinois; by 1840, that number had increased to more than 28,000, and by 1850 it exceeded 41,000. Some of these migrants were runaway slaves, but others were ex-slaves who sought greater opportunities. One such migrant was "Free Frank." Born in slavery in Kentucky, he eventually purchased his own and his wife's freedom and moved to Illinois, where he founded the town of New Philadelphia in Pike County and pursued a variety of commercial enterprises. Another successful black migrant to the Midwest, William Trail, ran away from his Maryland master in 1814 and finally won his freedom through court action; he became a prosperous landowning farmer in Union County, Indiana.

Despite these extraordinary individual achievements, free blacks witnessed the decline of their political rights. By 1830, most northern states had disfranchised black voters in the very constitutional conventions that had extended and democratized suffrage for white men. Some southern states followed suit. Tennessee disfranchised black voters in 1834, and in 1835 North Carolina did the same after considering—but rejecting—a proposal that the wealthiest black property owners could retain the suffrage. White North Carolinians concluded that allowing any free blacks to vote threatened slavery. One North Carolina delegate demanded the social and political subordination of free blacks, as he posed the rhetorical question: "If they are to be placed in the situation of free men, and to be our equals . . . why not admit our slaves to the same equality?"

Disfranchisement

Ambiguities in the Pennsylvania constitution of 1790 led to the infrequent exercise of the franchise by the commonwealth's blacks. In the case of wealthy sailmaker James Forten, personal influence substituted for wielding the ballot. Since Forten could not vote himself, he left his mark on the political process by encouraging his white employees to vote as he would. Black landowner William Fogg sought redress through legal channels, hoping to determine the political rights of black Pennsylvanians. In 1835 Fogg, described in the court record as a freeman and taxpaying citizen of the commonwealth of Pennsylvania, was denied the right to vote in his township of Greenfield.

His case, *Hobbs v. Fogg*, ultimately went to Pennsylvania's supreme court, which in 1837 held that even black taxpaying property holders were not eligible to vote because the founding fathers had never intended blacks to be part of the body politic. "It is finally urged," the court maintained, "that a free negro or mulatto is not a citizen within the meaning of the constitution and laws of the United States, and of the state of Pennsylvania, and, therefore, is not entitled to the right of suffrage." In 1838 Pennsylvania revised its 1790 constitution and explicitly disfranchised black voters, thus removing any ambiguity regarding black voting rights. This action drew a published protest titled *Appeal of Forty Thousand Citizens, Threatened with Disenfranchisement, to the People of Pennsylvania*, in which the free black leadership urged white citizens to reject the new constitution. Despite the combined efforts of the black

James Forten
This drawing of James Forten, by an unknown artist, is the only known image of the African American leader.

community and its white allies in the Pennsylvania Abolition Society, voters accepted the new constitution.

In the North, by the end of the antebellum period only the New England states granted black men the unrestricted right of suffrage. In 1843, Rhode Island adopted its first constitution that gave blacks equal suffrage rights; such rights were already assured in Massachusetts, Vermont, New Hampshire, and Maine, each of which had only small black populations. In New York, black men could vote only if they were property holders, whereas in Ohio and Michigan, black suffrage was limited to some school board elections and to voting on school bonds.

The legal restrictions that various northern states imposed on free blacks were increasing at the very time that the proportion of free blacks within the total U.S. population was declining. To be sure, in sheer numbers the black population was growing: in 1830 the nation's free black population totaled 319,599; in 1840 386,293; in 1850 434,495; and by 1860 488,070. But relative to the total **Demographics** United States population, the percentage of free blacks was declining: it stood at 2.5 percent in 1830 but at only 1.6 percent in 1860. In part, this decline resulted from increasingly rigid southern laws against manumission, but more significant were the increasing numbers of European immigrants pouring into the United States, particularly after 1840. The years from 1847 to 1854 witnessed unprecedented immigration, with an average of slightly more than 334,000 persons arriving from Europe annually. Roughly 45 percent of the immigrants came from Ireland, 32 percent from Germany, and 13 percent from Great Britain.

The large influx of white Europeans did not go unnoticed in black communities. In 1837 the New York-based *The Colored American,* one of the earliest black newspapers, bemoaned the treatment accorded to blacks in comparison with that given to recent immigrants: "Foreigners and aliens to the government of laws—strangers to our institutions—are permitted to flock to this land and in a few years are endowed with all the privileges of citizens; but we, native born Americans, the children of the soil, are most of us shut out."

In a Culture of Racism

Although notions of racial difference were hardly new in America, the antebellum years gave rise to mass-market cultural racism and to a new discourse of scientific racism. Woven into the fabric of everyday life, popular culture and scientific thought worked together to justify not only the institution of slavery but also the routine debasement of free blacks. Throughout the 1810s and 1820s, poems, lyrics, novels, and broadsides published by whites exaggerated black speech patterns. Indeed, popular literature and the media conveyed racist assumptions not only about blacks' inability to speak Standard English but also about their incapacity for freedom and equality. Visual images distorted black physical features, making black people appear both animalistic and ludicrous.

By the late 1830s, dialect speech and song and caricatured images were becoming popular through a form of entertainment called the minstrel show, in which white male performers in burnt-cork blackface makeup portrayed blacks in a series of **Minstrel Shows** loosely related songs, dances, and comedy sketches. In the early 1840s, the Virginia Minstrels (led by Daniel Emmett, a white man) became the first professional touring minstrel troupe. This blackface tradition and its imagery of physical caricature survived well into the twentieth century as a staple of the American entertainment industry; it satirized and promoted the stereotypical figures "Jim Crow"—the lazy and ignorant southern slave—and "Zip Coon"—the absurd northern free black fop. Both of these negative stereotypes undoubtedly fed antebellum racism. Historians of this racist genre argue that its appearance on stage and its dissemination in print, through the so-called penny press (cheap newspapers) and "dime novels," helped create a psychological sense of social and political solidarity among various white immigrant groups.

Minstrel images functioned as the antithesis of the image of the white American, thus dramatically reinforcing the perception. Regardless of minstrelsy's psychological meanings for antebellum white performers and audiences, antebellum blacks considered the genre deeply offensive. In 1848 the northern black leader Frederick Douglass railed in his newspaper *The North Star* against "the 'Virginia Minstrels,' the 'Christy's Minstrels,' [and] the 'Ethiopian Serenaders,'" calling them the "filthy scum of white society, who have stolen from us a complexion denied to them by nature, in which to make money, and pander to the corrupt taste of their white fellow-citizens."

In the first half of the nineteenth century, just as negative black stereotypes were being promoted in such popular cultural forms as minstrelsy and the penny press, the new racial science of ethnology emerged. Ethnology, which began to attain significant intellec-

Ethnology

tual credibility in the 1830s and 1840s, rejected eighteenth-century environmentalist explanations for races and professed instead methods and theories that stressed innate and immutable racial traits.

Integral to ethnology was craniology, the measurement of skull size to determine cranial capacity. Blacks, craniologists argued, exhibited a smaller brain size than whites did, thus proving blacks' lower intelligence. Such books as Samuel G. Morton's *Crania Americana* (1839), and *Crania Aegyptiaca* (1844) were seminal texts arguing for the biological basis of various racial groups, all of them ranked in a hierarchy with whites at the top and blacks at the bottom. The theory of polygenesis accompanied craniology. Polygenesis maintained that races emerged from different human origins and thus represented different human species.

The antebellum ethnological studies touted the inherent inferiority of blacks to justify their permanent enslavement or, in the case of free blacks, their permanent civic and social subordination. Morton's measurements of skulls, for instance, led him to conclude that the supposedly larger skulls of Caucasians gave them a "decided and unquestioned superiority over all the nations of the earth." His findings influenced both Harvard scientist Louis Agassiz and southern physician Josiah Nott. Writing in 1854, Nott asserted that "nations and races, like individuals, have an especial destiny: some are born to rule, and others to be ruled. . . . No two distinctly marked races can dwell together on equal terms."

During the 1830s the vicious word *nigger* also gained common currency among whites as a term of racial disparagement. Black essayist Hosea Easton became perhaps the first person

Bigotry and Prejudice

to write a public denunciation of this word in his *Treatise on the Intellectual Character, and the Civil and Political Condition of the Colored People in the United States and the Prejudice Exercised Toward Them* (1837). Easton decried this "opprobrious term, employed to impose contempt upon blacks as an inferior race." He further argued that the "term in itself would be perfectly harmless were it used only to distinguish one class of society from another; but it is not used with that intent . . . it flows from the fountain of purpose to injure."

In a cultural milieu that permitted and encouraged racial bigotry, prejudice manifested itself in numerous individual and collective acts of animosity directed at free blacks and their white sympathizers. In 1831 the people of New Haven, Connecticut, became alarmed over white abolitionist Simeon Jocelyn's proposal to establish a college for blacks and resolved to oppose it with all their resources. At about the same time, Prudence Crandall, a Quaker school teacher in Canterbury, Connecticut, provoked the town's wrath when she admitted a black female student to her popular private school for girls. When her white students withdrew, she opened the school to black girls, attracting students from free black families as far away as Philadelphia, Providence, New York, and Boston. Townspeople harassed the black girls on the streets and piled manure on the school property. The local doctor refused to treat the black students, and stores refused to do business with Crandall.

The Connecticut legislature went so far as to pass a law in May 1831 forbidding any school or academy to enroll out-of-state blacks. Convicted of disobeying this law, Crandall appealed to the Connecticut supreme court, which overturned the conviction on a technicality. A few years later, the legislature repealed what had become an embarrassing law. Although Crandall's experience reveals the racism of Connecticut in the early 1830s, it also demonstrates the power of the growing abolitionist movement to change the political culture and secure a repeal of the law.

The culture of racism also took more virulent turns. Economic shifts in the early nineteenth century created tensions that resulted in widespread violence by whites against blacks. As industrialization spread in northern urban centers, the economic autonomy of white artisans declined, and many became **Mob Violence** wage laborers with what they correctly perceived as diminished economic prospects. Caught in this downward spiral, they scapegoated free blacks as economic competitors who undercut white workers' wages.

The black elite also stirred resentments and provoked a backlash. Cartoons in white newspapers depicted affluent blacks in highly insulting ways, mocking their society balls, abolitionist activities, and other events. Whites harassed blacks in public spaces and perpetrated extreme acts of hostility, often targeting community institutions that contributed to black advancement.

Riots, murders, and the destruction of churches, schools, and orphanages occurred in the Midwest and the Northeast. For three days in 1829, bands of whites in Cincinnati took the law into their own hands, running out of the city those blacks who did not post the bonds that the state required of blacks to reside there. More than a thousand blacks found it advisable to leave, moving to Canada; but most of them soon returned to Cincinnati. In New York State, antiblack riots erupted in Utica, Palmyra, and New York City in 1834 and 1839. The most serious antiblack outbreaks, however, took place in Pennsylvania. On August 12, 1834, a white mob marched into the black section of Philadelphia and committed numerous acts of violence. The following day whites wrecked the African Presbyterian Church, burned homes, and mercilessly assaulted several blacks. The reign of terror entered its third day before the police put an end to it. According to historians Lois E. Horton and James Oliver Horton, the "official report laid the riot to whites' fears that blacks received favored treatment in hiring." Between 1834 and 1836, at least nine disturbances occurred in Philadelphia that can be labeled antiblack riots. Historian Patrick Rael identified the occurrence of similar race riots in Columbia, Pennsylvania (1834 and 1835); in Washington, D.C. (1835); in Cincinnati (again in 1841); and in Boston (1843). [Historian Patrick Rael identified race riots in Columbia, Pennsylvania (1834 and 1835); in Washington, D.C. (1835); in Cincinnati (again in1841); and in Boston (1843).]

The South enjoyed playing up northern hostility toward blacks. When an observer characterized African Americans in New York and Philadelphia as having an "aversion to labor and proneness to villainy," he was quoted extensively in the southern press. Southerners also recounted with pleasure the tale of how a black man returned to his home state of Georgia

Pl. 3.   LIFE IN PHILADELPHIA.

Eng.d by Cha.s Hunt.

"How you find yourself dis hot   "Pretty well I tank you M.r Cesar
Weader Miss Chloe?".   only I aspire too much!"

London, Pub. by Harrison Isaacs, Charles S.t Soho Sq.re

Cartoon caricature of middle-class African Americans
Cartoonist Edward Clay created many caricatures of Philadelphia's middle-class
African Americans, ridiculing what he termed their tendency to "aspire too much."

after attempting to live in Ohio and Canada for two years. Another story told of Louisiana
blacks who had suffered so much in New York City that they begged visiting southerners to
take them back with them. When a North Carolina free black remarked that he had been
kicked about and abused so much in Cincinnati that he would like to return to the South, a
Greensboro paper not only reported the incident but reprinted the article five years later as
though the event had just happened.

    As observers Fanny Kemble and Frederick L. Olmsted reported, many blacks were sorely
mistreated in the North and the West. Kemble said of northern blacks: "They are not slaves
indeed, but they are pariahs, debarred from every fellowship save with their own
despised race. . . . All hands are extended to thrust them out, all fingers point at

South vs. North

their dusky skin, all tongues . . . have learned to turn the very name of their race into an insult and a reproach." Olmsted seems to have believed the Louisiana black who told him that he could associate with whites more easily in the South than in the North and that he preferred to live in the South, because he was less likely to be insulted there. Such points of view delighted slaveholders who saw them as confirmation of their belief that slavery was better for blacks than freedom.

White southerners did not seem to recognize, however, one essential difference between the South and the North and West—outside the South, blacks could organize and agitate for their rights. Northern blacks also had the moral and material support of at least a few whites who defied mob law. However difficult conditions were for blacks in the North, they moved there in large numbers. More than half of Ohio's black population had come from the South, despite the state's black laws, which discriminated against them in a variety of ways. In the North, blacks could enter professions and hold jobs that were unavailable to them in the South. Most southern states prohibited blacks from being pharmacists, physicians, dentists, gunsmiths, lawyers, or even teachers—all professions that northern blacks had entered before 1860. Everywhere in the North, blacks could and did own land and other property.

In the southern states, free blacks experienced freedom in a far more tenuous and vulnerable way. One slip, or any ignorance of the law, could send them back into slavery. All slave states required free blacks to register with the authorities. Florida, Georgia, and several other states compelled free blacks to have white guardians. All southern states demanded that free blacks carry passes or wear badges, and any black person caught without verification of freedom was presumed to be a slave.

Year by year, the controls that southern states and communities exercised over free blacks mounted. In no southern state could they move about as they wished, lest they be thought fugitive slaves. North Carolina prohibited free blacks from traveling beyond the county adjoining the one where they resided. Penalties for violating these laws were severe. In Georgia, for example, the offender was fined $100, and failure to pay it—which could be expected—meant being sold into slavery. Laws also forbade free blacks from leaving the state for any length of time, usually sixty or ninety days. Numerous laws were designed to protect the white community against any perceived threats or dangers from free blacks. Virginia, Maryland, and North Carolina forbade free blacks from possessing or carrying arms without a license, and such permits were issued annually to only the few blacks whom whites deemed trustworthy.

All slave states prohibited the in-migration of free blacks, and every southern state with a seaport required that free black sailors from other states or countries be jailed while their ships were in port. If a ship's captain failed to pay the jailor for his free black sailors' room and board, they could be sold into bondage.

Slaveholding states also had a peculiar way of demonstrating their interest in the welfare of free blacks. Since their lives proved especially difficult, legislators passed laws to give free blacks the opportunity to choose their owners and become slaves. In 1857 Tennessee enacted a law to facilitate re-enslavement; the following year Texas enacted a similar law, and in 1859 and 1860, respectively, Louisiana and Maryland did so as well. Several other states, including North Carolina, seriously considered re-enslavement statutes but for various reasons failed to enact them. Arkansas went farthest along this path; in 1859 the legislature passed an act to remove free blacks and mulattoes from the state by compelling those who remained after one year to choose masters "who must give bond not to allow such negroes to act as free."

Economic and Social Life

Free blacks in both the North and the South faced many obstacles in their attempts to earn a living and build strong communities. Southern states had a number of racially discriminatory employment policies, although such laws were often breached. In 1805 Maryland prohibited blacks from selling corn, wheat, or tobacco without a license. In 1829 Georgia made it illegal for them to be employed as typesetters. Two years later, North Carolina required all black traders and peddlers to be licensed, while South Carolina forbade the employment of free blacks as clerks. A large number of states made it illegal for them either to buy or to sell alcoholic beverages. Georgia free blacks could not buy on credit without the permission of their white guardians.

Despite these restrictions, every state required free blacks to work and to have visible means of support. If unemployed, free adult blacks were hired or bound out, and their children were taken and placed in the care of white persons. Black children born out of wedlock to a parent who had violated the law or who had no means of support were apprenticed to be taught a trade and given moral instruction.

The majority of the South's free blacks worked as unskilled agricultural or common laborers. In some states, however, free black artisans achieved considerable economic independence and affluence before the Civil War. Despite the strong opposition of white workers, skilled and unskilled blacks often found work in areas experiencing labor shortages, especially in states hurt by white migration to the West. Free blacks worked in a range of occupations in spite of the restrictions placed on them in most southern states. They made clothing, grew and prepared foods, operated machines, piloted ships, and labored in the building trades. They were employed in more than seventy occupations in North Carolina, and those working in Baltimore in 1860 included several confectioners, druggists, and grocers.

Trades and Professions

Although free blacks worked in skilled occupations in both northern and southern cities, the South, and especially the Lower South, had the largest proportion of free black and skilled positions. In both North and South, the skilled trades fell primarily to whites, although certain trades in the Lower South, such as barber and blacksmith, were identified and stigmatized as black jobs. Still, free blacks in Baltimore, Charleston, and New Orleans could be found working in occupations that required a high degree of skill. A comparison of the cities of Boston and Charleston illustrates the contrasting opportunities afforded free blacks in the two regions. In 1860, 20 percent of all free black men in Boston engaged in skilled employment, whereas in Charleston more than 60 percent of free black men held such jobs. However, Boston's free black population included a number of professionals—lawyers, officeholders (including a justice of the peace), teachers, physicians, dentists, typesetters, and journalists—doing work from which South Carolina legally barred blacks. In addition, Boston's black ministers controlled their own churches and preached whatever

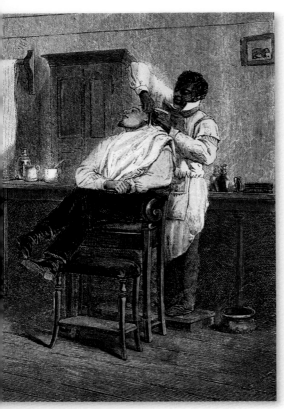

African American barber

Barbering was one of the skilled trades open to black men during the antebellum years. Several wealthy African Americans began their careers as barbers.

they wished, but in Charleston and other southern cities whites monitored church services.

Free people of color were among the widely celebrated cabinet-makers in New Orleans. Although they initially trained under white masters, by 1819 there were enough skilled craftsmen of color to permit new apprentices to train under artisans of their own race. Dutreuil Barjon received his training under the African American workshop system. In 1822 Barjon opened a shop on Royal Street, the elite center of furniture making in the city's French Quarter. By the 1830s he was recognized as a master artisan whose work equaled that of his white peers. The success of his shop allowed Barjon to open a furniture warehouse in 1834, in which he sold his own furniture as well as pieces imported from Europe.

New Orleans free black Julien Hudson was among the earliest recorded professional artists of African descent to work in the antebellum South. Hudson, the son of a free woman of color and a wealthy white ship chandler and ironmonger, grew up as part of New Orleans's Afro-Creole, French-speaking elite known as the *gens de couleur libre* (free persons of color). Hudson's self-portrait is the first extant self-portrait by an African American artist. The portrait reflects Hudson's perception of himself as cultured and elite, since he portrayed himself in a fashionable black frock coat, intricately patterned waistcoat, and black silk cravat in front of a conventional landscape background.

Julien Hudson—*Self-Portrait*, 1839

Regional differences in property ownership among free blacks are also illuminating. In the North, 11.7 percent of free blacks owned property in 1860, compared to 18.1 percent of whites. In the Upper South, 9.8 percent of free blacks owned property, while 19.4 percent of whites did so. In the Lower South, **Property Ownership** an astonishing 17.9 percent of free blacks held property; 18.8 percent of whites did so. These statistics may be misleading, however. Much of the "property" owned by southern free blacks included their own family members who remained slaves because their free black owners could not legally emancipate them. In North Carolina, free blacks owned $480,000 worth of real property and $564,000 worth of personal property (including slaves) in 1860. In Charleston, 352 blacks paid taxes on property valued in 1859 in excess of $778,000. Tennessee's free blacks owned about $750,000 worth of real and personal property in 1860.

The affluence of a large number of free blacks and creoles of color in New Orleans was well known; in 1860, they owned more than $15 million worth of property. Thomy Lafon, the free black tycoon of New Orleans, was worth $500,000 at his death. He had contributed so much to the development of the city that the state legislature ordered a bust of him carved and set up in a public institution in New Orleans. Small wonder that in the preceding year the city's leading white newspaper, *The Daily Picayune*, described New Orleans' free blacks as "a sober, industrious, and moral class, far advanced in education and civilization."

Antebellum free blacks in the North were more likely than whites to live in cities. In 1860, 63.5 percent of New England's **Urban Life in the North** free blacks lived in cities, and 49.7 percent of the free blacks in the Mid-Atlantic states were urban dwellers. The cities offered jobs and opportunities to build cohesive communities anchored by social, financial, and religious resources.

Boston

Of the three major northern seaport cities—Boston, New York, and Philadelphia—by far the smallest free black community was in Boston, numbering just under two thousand persons in 1850. In the early years of the nineteenth century, Boston's free-black population had been dispersed throughout the city, but by the 1840s and 1850s, following the pattern in other antebellum northern cities, residential segregation had produced a denser geographical concentration of the black community. Although economic factors limited the majority of free black men in Boston to low-skilled or unskilled jobs, the status and significance of such work held a different meaning in black and white communities. The job of "porter" held higher prestige in black Boston because, although low-skilled, "porters" worked as servants in wealthy whites' homes or as waiters in the city's prominent restaurants and hotels. Indeed, the servant Robert Roberts parlayed his expertise into a published book, *The House Servant's Directory: or, a Monitor for Private Families.* The 1860 census listed Roberts as a "gentleman." For black men such as Roberts, proximity to white centers of power probably increased their status in the black community. This was less true for black women who worked as domestics. Boston's black community included an upper class—lawyers, dentists, teachers, justices of the peace, and other middle-class professionals who, although slight in number, represented an activist group that was strong in the tradition of protest thought. Historians James and Lois Horton reveal that this activist group included not only professionals but also such persons as the caterer Joshua Smith, hairdresser John T. Hilton, and most notably David Walker, a tailor and dealer in second-hand clothes. Walker, a brilliant essayist, militant activist, and author of *David Walker's Appeal* (1829), was also a founding member in 1828 of the pioneering "Massachusetts General Colored Association," an organization devoted to local and national black rights. It was founded, as Walker articulated in his inaugural lecture, "to unite the colored population, so far, through the United States of America as may be practicable and expedient"—thus a forerunner of the black convention movement.

Free black women in Boston were concentrated in low-skilled or unskilled positions, primarily as domestics, yet there were notable exceptions. Harriet Hayden, wife of activist Lewis Hayden, ran a successful boardinghouse. George Ruffin's wife, Nancy, became an independent retailer who earned enough to buy her husband's family out of slavery in Virginia. Christiana Carteaux's success as a milliner and hairdresser proved helpful to securing clients for her artist-husband Edward Bannister. In the 1850s his portraits and landscape paintings enjoyed the support of such black abolitionists as John DeGrasse and William Cooper Nell. Bannister's art would gain national recognition after the Civil War, but his wife is noted for supplementing the income generated by his painting during this early period in his career.

New York

Black New Yorkers constituted a far more affluent community than did black Bostonians. In 1837 the free blacks of New York City reportedly owned $1.4 million worth of taxable real estate and had $600,000 on deposit in savings banks. But despite such evidence of economic success in portions of the antebellum black community, recent scholarship reveals clearly demarcated economic and cultural differences among blacks. In her analysis of free black life in antebellum New York City, historian Leslie Harris insists that class distinctions need to be reconsidered if that experience is to be recovered in its full complexity. For example, the editors of the city's pioneering black-owned newspapers *Freedom's Journal* and *The Colored American* spoke primarily for the black elite, often condemning the boisterous, "unrespectable" public behavior of lower-class blacks. Free black leaders Peter Williams, Jr., and Samuel Cornish frequently criticized less affluent free blacks for their rowdy celebrations, such as Emancipation Day, and lectured them on the values of frugality, decorum, and temperance.

The newspapers and the elite free black leadership of New York were particularly incensed, as were middle-class white reformers, by evidence of interracial mixing among the lower classes in the slums. Despite the contempt and violence that many working-class whites visited on free blacks, antebellum New York was rife with opportunities for interracial mixing. Indeed, economic factors created interracial enclaves of the poor, where cultural mixing was not only frequent but also increasingly subsidized by white travelers and voyeurs in search of cultural adventure.

One foreign observer was the English author Charles Dickens, who visited the notorious Five Points slum in 1842. In his journal *American Notes*, Dickens published a lengthy description of Almack's dance cellar, which was owned and operated by the free black entrepreneur Pete Williams. Dickens marveled at the throng of customers and their dancing, but he was particularly fascinated by one of the antebellum black culture's unsung heroes, who held center stage in the dance. Dickens described the man as "a lively young negro, who is the wit of the assembly, and the greatest dancer known." This was William Henry "Juba" Lane.

Philadelphia had the most studied antebellum northern free black population of the nineteenth century. To bolster free blacks' claims to civil rights, and also to undermine the negative stereotypes used by whites to deny those rights, both the Pennsylvania Abolition Society (PAS) in 1837 and the Society of Philadelphia Friends (Quakers) in 1847 sponsored fact-finding studies designed to demonstrate black progress in Philadelphia. The more comprehensive of the two, the 1847 *Statistical Inquiry into the Condition of the People of Colour of the City and Districts of Philadelphia*, was hailed by Frederick Douglass's *North Star* in 1849 as something to be "carefully read and pondered by colored men who are endeavoring to achieve their own elevation." In the report's preface, its authors suggested that their findings "should inspire hope and confidence in the future."

The report tabulated a Philadelphia free black population of 20,240. Of those enumerated, 6,896 (42.9 percent) were male and 9,146 (57.1 percent) were female. The investigators identified occupations for 3,358 men and 4,249 women, or roughly four-fifths of those they called "the able-bodied population." The majority of the men (1,581) were laborers, although there were significant numbers of mechanics (286), shopkeepers (166), waiters and cooks (557), and hairdressers (156). Male professionals included 33 musicians, 22 preachers, and 11 schoolteachers. Most women worked as washerwomen (1,970), although significant numbers fell into the categories of day laborers (786), needle-women (486), cooks (176), and traders (213). The female working population also included 33 keepers of boarding, eating, and oyster houses; 35 shopkeepers; and 13 school mistresses, including Sarah Ann Douglass, whom the report praised as running "an excellent school of many years standing."

Like New York, Philadelphia had distinct class divisions within the free black community. During the 1830s and 1840s, the poorest 50 percent of Philadelphia's free blacks owned only 5 percent of the city's black-owned wealth, while the top 10 percent held 70 percent, and the top 1 percent controlled 30 percent. In his *Sketches of Colored Society in Philadelphia*, the antebellum free black chronicler Joseph Willson portrayed a three-tiered class structure. There existed an upper class with "comfort and the enjoyment of all the sound blessings of this life," a class positioned in the "intermediate stages—sober, honest, industrious and respectable—having neither 'poverty nor riches,'" and at the bottom those "in the lowest depths of human degradation, misery, and want."

In addition to founding sixteen churches and numerous literary and benevolent societies, black Philadelphians were also active in the antebellum temperance crusade. A newspaper report from the *Philadelphia Daily Republic*, reprinted in *The North Star* in 1848, provides a glimpse of the fervor with which free black leaders embraced the crusade against alcohol. They associated temperance with respectability and racial progress. Thus the Phoenix and Garnet Unions of the Daughters of Temperance hosted an event at the Wesley Methodist Church with the fiery black abolitionist, Rev. Henry Highland Garnet, as the keynote speaker. Garnet was described as "the apostle of liberty and temperance, who for an hour and a half portrayed the terrible effects of alcohol and labored to allure the drunkard to the paths of soberness and peace."

Mutual Aid Organizations Free blacks also bound themselves together for social and cultural uplift, economic advancement, and mutual relief. In every city, mutual-aid organizations sprang up, some of which were secret societies. In Baltimore, thirty-five mutual aid organizations existed in 1835. The Friendship Benevolent Society for Social Relief, the Star in the East Association, and the Daughters of Jerusalem were among the more prominent groups with substantial savings in Baltimore banks. Associational life grew in other cities where mechanics, coachmen, caulkers, and other workers organized their own mutual-aid societies.

In the Deep South, such organizations were frowned on by most whites and outlawed altogether in most states. They persisted in some places, however. As late as 1860, benevolent associations were being organized in New Orleans, where the Band Society, with its motto Love, Union, Peace, had bylaws requiring members "to go about once in a while and see one another in love" and to wear the society's regalia on special occasions. In 1843, under the leadership of African-American sailor Peter Ogden, a group of free blacks in New York organized the Grand United Order of Odd Fellows, the charter for which was obtained from an English Grand Lodge, since the American Lodge refused to grant it. Like the Prince Hall Masons, who were also chartered in England, the Odd Fellows became a national African American fraternal organization.

Cultural Contributions Throughout the antebellum era, free black poets, playwrights, historians, newspaper editors, and artists contributed not only to the development of African American culture but also to the broader American culture. In North Carolina, for example, George Moses Horton, who was "virtually free," wrote poems that were widely read. In 1829 he published a volume entitled *The Hope of Liberty*, and for the next thirty years he wrote for students at the University of North Carolina and for various newspapers. Unfortunately, his interest in poetry diminished, perhaps as he realized that despite his exhaustive efforts to purchase his freedom, there was no hope of liberty.

Daniel Alexander Payne, who had a brilliant career as a bishop in the African Methodist Episcopal Church, published a small volume in 1850 entitled *Pleasures and Other Miscellaneous Poems*. Frances Ellen Watkins Harper, whose *Poems on Miscellaneous Subjects* appeared in 1854, would make her most significant literary contributions after the Civil War. Harriet E. Wilson of Massachusetts became the first black woman to publish a novel, *Our Nig; Or Sketches From the Life of a Free Black* (1859). Literary critic Henry Louis Gates, Jr., who discovered *Our Nig*, described it as "a 'missing link' . . . between the sustained and well developed tradition of black autobiography and the slow emergence of a distinctive black voice in fiction." The French-inspired cultural life of free persons of color in New Orleans is best represented by artists, furniture makers, and such literary figures as the seventeen poets who issued the volume *Les Cenelles* in 1845. The book's editor, Armand Lanusse, as well as several contributors, had lived or studied in France.

Cottage at Pass Opposite Ben Lomand, Robert S. Duncanson, 1866

The first African American to achieve a national and international reputation as a painter, Robert S. Duncanson spent most of his career in Cincinnati, a burgeoning arts center that called itself the "Athens of the West." In Cincinnati, Duncanson exhibited at the Western Art Union and was counted, along with noted white artists T. Worthington Whittredge and William L. Sonntag, as one of the city's most talented painters. Duncanson also traveled abroad, spending time and exhibiting his works to widespread acclaim in England, Scotland, Italy, and Canada. Recent scholarship by Joseph S. Ketner traces the artist's paternal origins to a successful landowning black family that had known two generations of freedom at the time of his birth in what is now Michigan. Like many free men of color in the nineteenth century, Duncanson's father was an artisan, and Duncanson was trained in the family businesses of house painting and carpentry, skills that inspired and helped prepare him for his chosen career in the fine arts.

Education

Free-black leaders in both the North and South insisted that education played a crucial role in securing their communities' progress.

In the antebellum North, by the eve of the Civil War opportunities for black education were widely available, although in most places public schools were racially segregated, and black children received an unequal share **Opportunities in the North** of school funds. Rhode Island and Connecticut maintained separate schools even though in the decade before the Civil War these states increased their funding for black education. In

1824 the New York City Common Council began to provide partial support for the privately run African Free Schools and took them over altogether in 1834. Although some communities in the state permitted black children to attend white schools, the legislature made it clear in 1841 that any district could establish separate schools. Still, in places such as Syracuse and Rochester blacks attended public schools with whites.

New Jersey and Pennsylvania maintained separate schools for black children, giving both public and private support to schools for blacks as they increased in number. Ohio excluded black children from public schools by law in 1829, although twenty years later the state provided funding for separate schools. Since the state never appropriated enough funds to set up creditable schooling for blacks, in a number of communities in northern Ohio, black children attended public schools with whites in the 1840s and 1850s. Citizens of Indiana and Illinois took no interest in meeting blacks' desires for education. Michigan and Wisconsin adopted more democratic policies, but most blacks in these states had to wait until after the Civil War before they could be educated in considerable numbers at public expense.

Massachusetts is particularly notable for shifting its African American educational policies away from exclusion and toward inclusion during the antebellum period. In 1798 free blacks and their white supporters founded a privately funded school for blacks in Boston, later called the Abiel Smith School. Not until 1820 did the city allocate any funds to the Smith school, however. In 1840 the black community under the leadership of author and printer William Cooper Nell joined white abolitionists William Lloyd Garrison and Wendell Philips in agitating for "equal school rights." Efforts to open all-white schools to black students occurred in Nantucket and Salem as well, and unlike Boston these towns achieved integrated schools in 1845.

In 1848 Benjamin Roberts sued the city of Boston in behalf of his five-year-old daughter Sarah after she was denied access to a number of nearby primary schools. He questioned the fairness of his daughter having to walk past white schools before reaching the segregated Abiel Smith School. Pleading his case were the abolitionist and future United States senator Charles Sumner and Robert Morris, the first black lawyer to pass the Massachusetts bar. Despite the arguments of Sumner and Morris and a boycott of Abiel Smith School by members of the black community, the commonwealth's highest court upheld the legality of racially separate schools in *Roberts v. City of Boston* (1850). Nell and others continued their protest until 1855, when the Massachusetts legislature prohibited segregated schools in the commonwealth.

Free blacks in the South experienced far greater difficulty obtaining an education. In contrast to the North, the region had no public schools, even for white children. Southern whites considered the responsibility for educating youth to be largely a private matter. Moreover, strong sentiment against educating free blacks prevailed in the South, where many whites believed that blacks would imbibe seditious and incendiary doctrines through reading. However, a surprisingly large number of them learned at least the fundamentals.

Opportunities in the South

In Baltimore, the Oblate Sisters of Providence, the first Catholic order for women of African descent, operated a school for black children throughout the 1830s and 1840s. In 1824 a black man, John Adams, began to teach children of his race in Washington, D.C. Thereafter, schools for blacks proliferated, and within a few years some of the best were located in the District, with students coming from Maryland and Virginia to study under teachers of their own race. Some free blacks in Virginia and North Carolina received private instruction from whites and other free blacks, but very little of their education took place in schools. In a notable exception to this rule, John Chavis of Raleigh, North Carolina, maintained a school where he taught whites during the day and free blacks at night for almost thirty years, but after 1831 Chavis confined his teaching to white children.

Charleston offered free blacks the best opportunities in the South for securing an education. As early as 1810, the city's blacks organized the Minor Society School for orphans. In Florida, some free blacks sent their children away to school, while others (in St. Augustine and Pensacola, for example) hired teachers to instruct them. Free blacks in New Orleans supported several schools, including the École des Orphelins Indigents, set up in 1840, and generously supported by wealthy creoles of color such as Thomy Lafon, Marie Couvent, and Aristide Mary. A few even went to France to be educated, such as Edward Dede, who studied music in Paris.

In spite of the efforts of southern free blacks to secure an education for themselves and their children, statistics support the general conclusion that they had far fewer opportunities than their northern counterparts to attend school. Of 2,038 free blacks in Boston in 1850, almost 1,500 were in school. In Baltimore, 1,400 free blacks attended school, as did a thousand in New Orleans. However, in 1860 only 155 children, out of a total of more than a thousand free black children of school age, were attending school in the entire state of Missouri. In the same year, only 275 of Louisiana's nearly 6,500 free black children were enrolled in schools. More strikingly, in Virginia only 41 out of 22,000 school-age free blacks attended school. In the South as a whole in 1860, about 4 percent of the school-age free black population received an education, as opposed to more than one third in the North.

Free blacks in the North also began to attend institutions of higher education during the antebellum years. In 1826 Edward Jones and John Russwurm graduated from Amherst and Bowdoin Colleges, respectively, and before the Civil War blacks were attending Oberlin, Franklin, and Rutland Colleges, Harvard **Higher Education** Medical School, and other institutions of higher learning. The doors of several institutions that were to become predominantly black colleges also opened during this period. In 1851 a young white woman from New York, Myrtilla Miner, established an academy for black females in Washington, D.C. So much opposition developed that the school was maintained only with difficulty. At the outbreak of the Civil War, it remained a small institution, but the idea had already been conceived that a teachers' college in Washington would bear her name. In 1839 plans were made for an Institute for Colored Youth in Philadelphia. The school was incorporated in 1842 and began to flourish ten years later under the leadership of Charles L. Reason of New York. A bequest of $300,000 by the Reverend Charles Avery led to the establishment in 1849 of a college for blacks in Allegheny City, Pennsylvania, that bore his name. With enough funds and an effective white and black faculty, the institution flourished.

Two denominational institutions founded during the antebellum period were Lincoln University in Pennsylvania and Wilberforce University in Ohio. Under Presbyterian sponsorship Lincoln University, which was originally called Ashmun Institute, was incorporated in 1854 and admitted its first students two years later. In 1855 the Cincinnati Conference of the Methodist Episcopal Church decided to raise money to establish a college for black youth that was incorporated in the following year as Wilberforce University, named for the great British abolitionist leader William Wilberforce. Its first students were mainly the mulatto children of southern planters. After a brief suspension of classes in 1862, at the beginning of the Civil War, Wilberforce reopened under the sponsorship of the African Methodist Episcopal Church in the following year and, like Lincoln University, remains in operation today.

Black Convention Movement

In 1830, when black delegates from New York, Pennsylvania, Maryland, Delaware, and Virginia met in Philadelphia to "devise ways and means for the bettering of our condition," the black convention movement was born. James Forten, John B. Vashon, Samuel Cornish, and other black leaders present at this meeting discussed raising funds to establish a college and debated the feasibility and desirability of black emigration. However, in 1833 the majority of the convention delegates rejected emigration as a sound solution to their problems; they focused instead on establishing a manual arts school and a college in New Haven, Connecticut. In their conventions and in newspapers, pamphlets, books, and public orations, black leaders promoted and debated their views.

The number of conventions reached a highpoint in the 1850s with free blacks gathering in Rochester, Cleveland, New York, Philadelphia, and several other cities. At one of the most **The Rochester Convention** important meetings, a three-day conference in Rochester in July 1853, over one hundred participants gathered to form the National Council of Colored People, which sought to advance equal rights for African Americans and fight for the end of slavery. The Rochester meeting produced a stirring memorial to the American people, which recited the various ways that free blacks had been mistreated and humiliated. Signed by Frederick Douglass among others, the memorial ended with the assertion that no other race could have made more progress "in the midst of such a universal and stringent disparagement."

In addition to general conventions, there were conventions of special groups. In 1848 **Fostering Group Consciousness** the Citizens Union of Pennsylvania was organized to fight for first-class citizenship for blacks. In 1850 the American League of Colored Laborers was formed in New York to better their pay and working conditions and to foster the education of young blacks in agriculture, the mechanical arts, and commerce.

The importance of national black convention meetings as formal mechanisms for fostering group consciousness and protest cannot be overstated. These gatherings marked the most visible and coordinated national endeavors by black Americans to promote collective discussion and action. Participants at conventions represented the black elite—literate, skilled or professional, and propertied. The leadership concerned itself with the burning issues of the day—abolitionism, colonization, women's rights, education, and the representation of African Americans as individuals and as a group.

The public image of the black community remained of crucial concern to its leaders. The very name that identified them as a people and as a race became a point of **Public Image and Behavior** contention. A series of debates over the appropriate group name occupied the leaders of the convention movement. After the American Revolution, for example, whites had begun to call free blacks "Africans," and free blacks referred to themselves by that term. By the 1830s, however, the preferred group appellations included "colored people," "people of color," or "Colored Americans." Black leaders maintained that the name of the race played an important role not only in self-representation but also in establishing their American citizenship and heritage in relation to white Americans.

Black leaders also emphasized group and individual behavior, stressing "correct and decorous deportment"—temperance, church attendance, and thrift. At the same time they opposed gambling, drinking, rude behavior, boisterous public celebrations, and outlandish modes of dress. Thus issues of educational training and literacy, employment, and behavioral decorum took center stage because leaders believed that they helped establish their race's respectability.

Antebellum black leaders often used religious imagery in addressing important issues of the day—emigration, abolition, education, economic progress, and women's rights. This intellectual tradition was not unique to black people. Religious **Biblical Imagery** rhetoric formed part and parcel of the speaking and writing patterns of most nineteenth-century Americans. For blacks, biblical images provided vivid allegorical and metaphorical meanings with which to demand justice and equality. Thus in his historic 1829 pamphlet, *Appeal,* David Walker invoked apocalyptic imagery as he warned of God's sure and coming judgment on slavery:

> Oh Americans! Let me tell you, in the name of the Lord, it will be good
> for you, if you listen to the voice of the Holy Ghost, but if you do not; you
> are ruined!!! Some of you are good men; but the will of God must be done.
> Those avaricious and ungodly tyrants among you, I am awfully afraid, will
> drag down the vengeance of God upon you. When God almighty commences his battle on the continent of America for the oppression of his people, tyrants will wish they were never born.

Like the slave community, the free black community drew repeatedly on the Old Testament story of Exodus, as scholars Albert Raboteau and Eddie Glaude have revealed, respectively, for plantation slavery and the free-black convention movement. As early as 1774, poet Phillis Wheatley had compared the experiences of blacks enslaved in America with those of the ancient Israelites enslaved by the Egyptians. In a letter discussing freedom, she pointed out the hypocrisy of slave-owning American Patriots, calling them "modern Egyptians."

The Exodus story held political, not merely religious, meaning for African Americans. The power of the free blacks' use of the Exodus story stemmed from a sense of a common oppression. Blacks perceived themselves as a nation within a nation, indeed even as a "chosen people." They used the Exodus story much as the larger white nation used this biblical story. During the first half of the nineteenth century, white Americans boldly proclaimed their belief in their "manifest destiny" to populate the North American continent from "sea to shining sea," portraying this idea as part of God's unfolding plan for the American nation. Against this backdrop, the free blacks' explication of Exodus retained a unique moral force precisely because of its appropriation of a familiar biblical story that allowed blacks to recast whites as enslaving Egyptians and themselves as the enslaved Hebrews. In so doing, African Americans forcefully reminded white Americans of God's justice, while presenting a providential counternarrative of freedom that afforded them a spiritual mooring and a political direction as they fought to end both slavery and racial discrimination.

Black Women

The antebellum black press gave full voice to the ideas debated in the conventions. Such Northern papers as *The Colored American, Freedom's Journal,* the *Aliened American,* the *Weekly Advocate,* and *The North Star* disseminated political and economic information throughout the black community. Not only did they feature current events, but they also prescribed the "proper" traits of black manhood and womanhood. For example, *The Colored American* proclaimed in 1839:

> Man is strong—Woman is beautiful
> Man is daring and confident—Woman is deferent and unassuming
> Man is great in action—Woman is suffering
> Man shines abroad—Woman at home

The black press, convention proceedings, and autobiographical narratives reveal that antebellum free black women embraced the belief that mothers were the guarantors of family, but they also felt the constraining effects of what historian James Horton calls "freedom's yoke." The pressure to conform to the gender roles of the larger white society—that is, emulating masculine privilege and authority over women—created difficulties for a people whose historical circumstances in labor and motherhood, both under slavery and in freedom, defied the nineteenth-century white ideal of a fragile and delicate womanhood.

In the struggle for racial advancement, some black women dared to question these gender conventions. In 1817 Jarena Lee, although a widow and a mother, felt herself called to

Women Take Public Action

preach. She gained the approval of an earlier-reluctant Richard Allen, the bishop of the African Methodist Episcopal Church, and won many converts in Pennsylvania. Upon Allen's death in 1831, however, Lee's strong support within the church eroded, and AME churchmen denied her access to the pulpit because of her gender. She related her experience of "being measurably debarred from my own Church as regards this privilege I had been so much use to" in her autobiographical narrative, *The Life and Religious Experiences of Jarena Lee* (1836).

Lee was not alone in bringing the issue of gender inequality prominently into the larger discussion of racial inequality. Because of the civic and social disabilities that all free blacks suffered, she and black women like her believed that they did not have the luxury of confining their moral suasion to the private sphere of the family home. Instead, they enlisted in public movements for black freedom. In August 1827 a young free black woman who signed as "Matilda" wrote a letter to the pioneering black newspaper *Freedom's Journal,* raising the issue of women's rights: "I don't know that in any of your papers, you have said sufficient upon the education of females. . . . 'Tis true, the time has been, when to darn a stocking, and cook a pudding well, was considered the end and aim of a woman's being. But those were days when ignorance blinded men's eyes. There are difficulties, and great difficulties in the way of our advancement; but that should only stir us to greater efforts. We possess not the advantages of those of our own sex, whose skins are not colored like our own; but we can improve what little we have, and make our one talent produce two-fold."

One of the earliest and most outspoken advocates of women's rights and abolition was Boston's Maria W. Stewart. She is noteworthy for being one of the earliest women to give

Maria Stewart

public lectures to mixed male-female audiences, thus determinedly stepping outside the antebellum domestic sphere. Born in 1803, she was orphaned at the age of five in Connecticut and worked as an indentured servant and later as a free domestic in Boston. She married James Stewart, the owner of a successful shipping company, and both became involved informally in distributing pamphlets that addressed racism in American politics. When James Stewart died in 1830, the court refused to accept his last will, thus stripping Maria of her comfortable middle-class lifestyle and leaving her penniless. In 1831 she professed renewed religious faith and published "Religion and the Pure Principles of Morality, the Sure Foundation on Which We Must Build," an essay that infused demands for gender and racial equality. She frequently quoted from the Bible in her lectures and writings. On one occasion she asked rhetorically: "What if I am a woman?" as she drew on the biblical precedents of a woman warrior, judge, and lawyer to demand gender equality. Maria Stewart is considered to be the first black feminist. As early as 1830, she explicitly spoke of women's rights before male and female audiences, as can be seen in her scathing question: "How long shall the fair daughters of Africa be compelled to bury their minds and talents beneath a load of iron pots and kettles?" Lecturing at the Franklin Hall in Boston in 1832, Stewart argued that African Americans should fight prejudice as well as raise their aspirations through moral and intellectual improvement. Influenced by the militant language of David Walker's *Appeal,* she explicitly and stridently criticized black men for insufficient perseverance and courage. Her outspoken stance on race and gender alienated several leaders in the black community.

Perhaps the best known black woman to participate in the women's rights and the abolitionist movements was Sojourner Truth, the name adopted by Isabella Van Wagenen. In *The Narrative of Sojourner Truth* (1853), she described traveling throughout the North speaking to audiences in support of women's rights and abolition. Around 1847, in response to Frederick Douglass's cynical remarks about the probability of a nonviolent end to slavery, she interrupted his lecture in Boston's Faneuil Hall by standing up and shouting with evangelical fervor: "Frederick, is God dead?" She was known to speak and act boldly. On the abolitionist lecture circuit in 1858, she bared her breast before an Indiana audience after a doubting listener questioned whether she actually was a woman. Perhaps more than any of her contemporaries, she is identified with exposing the socially constructed character of gender. The white suffragist Frances Dana Gage, in her account of a women's rights meeting in Akron, Ohio, in 1851, quoted Truth as asking "Ar'n't I a woman?" in a powerful speech that declared slave and free black women no less women. Although scholars now question whether the speech's

Portrait of Jarena Lee
This image of Jarena Lee was not included in the first edition of *The Life and Religious Experiences of Jarena Lee.* The several editions of her book made her one of the first women of the nineteenth century to reach a wide audience through print. In 1844 and 1852, women unsuccessfully petitioned the AME General Conference to allow ordination of black women.

Sojourner Truth

language as recounted by Gage is historically accurate and whether the speech should be attributed to Sojourner Truth at all, its message in defense of the women's movement conveyed the concerns of black women, and for this she has been immortalized.

The Debate on Emigration

By 1832 more than a dozen state legislatures had given official approval to the American Colonization Society (ACS). Northern states and the slaveholding states of Maryland, Virginia, Kentucky, North Carolina, and Mississippi all had local branches of the ACS. Thousands of dollars flowed into the society for purchasing and chartering ships to carry blacks to Africa. At first, only free blacks were transported, but after 1827 a few slaves were manumitted expressly for the purpose of colonization. By 1830 the society had settled 1,420 blacks in the colony of Liberia.

Despite various schemes to deport free blacks from the United States, no more than fifteen thousand migrated to new homes outside the United States—to Africa and also such

Efforts at Mass Colonization places as Haiti, Central America, and Canada. The ACS was responsible for transporting most of them—approximately twelve thousand—and the overwhelming majority went to Liberia. Yet mass colonization proved unworkable for a number of reasons. First, it was not economically feasible to send hundreds of thousands of blacks to Africa or anywhere else. Second, those who supported the ACS were such a heterogeneous lot that in the long run they could not agree on a single program. Some advocates of colonization hoped to see an end to slavery and a return of all blacks to their ancestral homeland. Others supported the schemes because of their conviction that blacks were incapable of adjusting to American society as free people and thus would never be allowed equal citizenship. Still others saw in colonization an opportunity to carry Christianity and civilization to Africa. Slaveholders hoped, of course, to drain off the free black population, thereby giving greater security to the institution of slavery. Motives as varied as these made a single colonization program or strategy impossible to achieve.

Opposition to the ACS grew steadily among black and white abolitionists. In the 1830s, such prominent white abolitionists as William Lloyd Garrison, Arthur Tappan, Gerrit Smith,

Opposition to the ACS and James G. Birney renounced their former support of colonization, having been persuaded to do so by the many free blacks who steadfastly refused to abandon those still enslaved. In 1832 Garrison published his blistering critique, *Thoughts on Colonization*, to which he appended statements by various local groups of free blacks denouncing colonization and claiming America as their own. From "Resolutions of the People of Color to the Citizens of New York, in Answer to the Colonization Society" came this unambiguous statement: "This is our home, and this is our country. Beneath its sod lie the bones of our fathers: for it some of them fought, bled, and died. Here we were born and here we will die."

Black leaders themselves divided over the issue of forsaking their homeland in the United States. The most noted leader to depart for Liberia in the 1820s was John Russwurm, a Bowdoin College graduate and the cofounder, with Samuel Cornish, of the newspaper *Freedom's Journal*. The two men began publication in 1827 to advocate for the downtrodden of their race. Within two years, Russwurm had become disillusioned, no longer believing in the possibility of racial equality in the United States, and in 1829 he relocated under the auspices of the ACS to Monrovia, Liberia.

Map of Monrovia, Liberia, ca 1830
This map shows the American Colonization Society's main Liberian settlement as it existed about ten years after its founding.

The proceedings of the National Negro Convention meetings from 1830 into the 1850s indicate recurring discussions of emigration, although its most vocal supporters (such as the black leaders H. Ford Douglas, James Theodore Holly, and Martin R. Delany) all tended to distance themselves from the American Colonization Society. In the early 1850s H. Ford Douglas, living in Cleveland, outspokenly championed both antislavery and emigration.

Window in Time

Debate on Colonization: Russwurm vs. Williams

John B. Russwurm, *Colonization Endorsed*

We feel proud in announcing . . . ourselves . . . ready to embrace the first convenient opportunity to embark for the shores of Africa. . . .

The subject of Colonization is certainly important, as having a great bearing on that of slavery: for it must be evident that the universal emancipation so ardently desired by us & by all our friends can never take place unless some door is opened whereby the emancipated may be removed, as fast as they drop their galling chains, to some other land beside the free states; for it is a fact, that prejudices now in our part of the country, are so high, that it is often the remark of liberal men from the south, that their free people are treated better than we are in the boasted free states of the north. If the free states have passed no law as yet forbidding the emigration of free persons of colour into their limits; it is no reason that they will not, as soon as they find themselves a little more burdened. We will suppose that a general law of emancipation should be promoted in the state of Virginia, under the existing statutes which require every emancipated slave to leave the state, would not the other states, in order to shield themselves from the evils of having so many thousands of ignorant beings thrown upon them be obliged in self-defense to pass prohibitory laws? . . . If no good whatever arose from the establishment of colonies, the fact that they remove all obstacles in the way of emancipation should gain for them the support and good wishes of every friend of humanity, & of every enlightened man of colour. It is true, that no such laws at present are in force to our knowledge, but who can foretell how soon before they may, without waiting of a period of general emancipation in any of the slaveholding states.

John B. Russwurm, "Colonization Endorsed," *Freedom's Journal* (New York), March 14, 1829.

Peter Williams, Jr., *Colonization Rejected*

The vast majority of free blacks rejected the African colonization movement. The views of Peter Williams, Jr. (ca. 1780–1840), a black Episcopal priest in New York City, were representative of their thoughts on the subject. Although Williams had encouraged Russwurm and others to go to Liberia, by 1830 he became an outspoken critic of colonization. He explains his reasons for that stance in the following document from that year, a Fourth of July sermon to his congregation. Williams spent his final decade toiling in the American antislavery movement.

Much has been said by the Colonizationists about improving the character and condition of the people of colour in this country by sending them to Africa. This is more inconsistent still. We are to be improved by being sent far from civilized society. This

Continued

Window in Time

is a novel mode of improvement. What is there in the burning sun, the arid plains, and barbarous customs of Africa, that is so peculiarly favourable to our improvement? What hinders our improving here, where schools and colleges abound, where the gospel is preached at every corner, and where all the arts and sciences are verging fast to perfection? Nothing, nothing but prejudice. It requires no large expenditures, no hazardous enterprises to raise the people of colour in the United States to as highly improved a state as any class in the community. All that is necessary is that those who profess to be anxious for it should lay aside their prejudices and act toward them as they do by others.

Peter Williams, Jr., "Colonization Rejected," *Emancipator* (Boston), April 22, 1834.

Having escaped from slavery in Virginia while a teenager, he settled in Ohio, where he became a barber, lecturer, and leader in the state's black convention movement.

Abolitionist Martin R. Delany became the most acclaimed advocate of emigration. Hostile to the ACS, Delany described the organization as "anti-Christian in its character and misanthropic in its pretended sympathies." To Delany, the ACS was "one of the Negro's worst enemies," and he denounced its leaders as "arrant hypocrites." Delany rejected the idea of Liberia as both a country independent of U.S. control and as a haven for black freedom, arguing that the main motive of the ACS was to safeguard slavery by ridding the United States of free blacks. James Theodore Holly had lived in Canada between 1851 and 1853 and associated with the abolitionist press there, but he returned to the United States to become an Episcopal priest, antislavery spokesman, and proponent of emigration to Haiti.

All three men were present at the National Emigration Convention that met in Cleveland in 1854 to promote a black-led movement. At the meeting, H. Ford Douglas argued that the migration of people in and out of nations was a common practice in history. Doug-

The National Emigration Convention

las had been influenced by Delany, who chaired the business committee on which Douglas sat and who authored the committee report on the "Political Destiny of the Colored Race." Delany's rousing speech drew the greatest attention, since it explicitly rebutted Frederick Douglass's speech of the previous year at the National Negro Convention in Rochester, in which Douglass had insisted that blacks should remain in the United States.

Delany's speech championed the idea of migration to Haiti and Central and South America. He also thought that Canada would be a satisfactory home as long as the area could not be annexed by the United States. For a brief period, from 1856 until the eve of the Civil War, Delany lived with his family in Chatham, Canada. H. Ford Douglas also moved to Canada, living there between 1856 and 1858 before returning disillusioned to Chicago. Facing growing factionalism in the emigration movement over whether Canada, Africa, or Haiti offered the most promising destination, Delany traveled to Africa, where he explored the Niger Valley and met with African rulers to discuss the idea of African

American immigration to what is now Nigeria. He published his pro-emigration views in his *Official Report of the Niger Valley Exploring Party* (1861).

The strongest female emigrationist voice was that of Mary Anne Shadd Cary. Reared in an abolitionist family in West Chester, Pennsylvania, she opposed the ACS. As a young woman in the 1840s, she taught black schoolchildren in Pennsylvania and New York. She soon found herself disgusted with the federal government's accommodation to slavery. The enactment of the Fugitive Slave Law of 1850, which demanded the return of all escaped slaves caught anywhere in the United States, caused her to forsake the land of her birth and establish residence in Windsor, Ontario. There she continued her role as a schoolteacher and joined Rev. Samuel Ringgold Ward in publishing the *Provincial Freeman,* through which she advocated emigration to Canada, abolition, and temperance. She brought the burning question of emigration to the national convention in Philadelphia in 1855. Her presence on the platform caused some controversy, since women were not generally accepted as public speakers at these meetings, but undeterred she criticized black leaders for failing to lend financial aid to Canadian communities. In 1856 she married Thomas Cary, a barber from Toronto, and continued to write, teach, and lecture.

On the eve of the Civil War, approximately a half-million African Americans were free, compared to the four million in slavery. The census for 1860 records a little more than half (258,346) of the total free-black population as living in the South. Whether in a free state or a slave state, they suffered the racist indignities that denied them the rights of American citizens. Although not economically or culturally monolithic, antebellum free blacks invested their energies overwhelmingly into building communities in the land of their birth. No matter how momentarily appealing the idea of a wholesale abandonment of the relentlessly hostile United States, free blacks, elite and non-elite alike, had roots in this nation and strenuously defended their role in its history. The majority of African Americans would heed Frederick Douglass's resounding words to the National Negro Convention in 1853—"We will fight it out here."

9 Abolitionism in Black and White

Black Abolitionists

Antislavery Agendas

Proslavery Backlash

The Black Response

The Underground Railroad

The Path to Civil War

Harriet Tubman and
John Brown

184

I n the three decades leading up to the Civil War, the fight against slavery was waged with militant words and radical actions. The gradualist arguments and strategies of antislavery societies in the early republic evolved into sweeping and uncompromising denunciations of human bondage by men and women who called themselves abolitionists. Abolitionists demanded slavery's immediate end. Through publications, lectures, and petitions, they also struggled to free slaves by purchasing their freedom, by attempting dangerous rescue missions, by hiding fugitives, and by unleashing actual slave revolts.

A cluster of three events heralded this age of militant abolitionism: the publication of David Walker's *Appeal* in 1829, the inaugural issue of William Lloyd Garrison's newspaper *The Liberator* in 1831, and the insurrection of Nat Turner that same year. In September 1829 the free black Bostonian David Walker startled the nation by urging the violent overthrow of slavery. His pamphlet *Walker's Appeal in Four Articles, Together with a Preamble to the Coloured Citizens of the World, But in Particular and very Expressly to those of the United States of America* represented one of the boldest verbal assaults on slavery ever printed in the United States. In unmistakable language, Walker invoked the Declaration of Independence in his call to blacks to rise up. He thundered:

> Are we men!! I ask you . . . are we MEN? Did our creator make us to be slaves to dust and ashes like ourselves? Are they not dying worms as well as we? . . . How we could be so submissive to a gang of men, whom we cannot tell whether they are as good as ourselves or not, I never conceive. . . .

On January 1, 1831, the first issue of Garrison's *The Liberator* appeared. Garrison had earlier served as assistant to the itinerant abolitionist Benjamin Lundy, the publisher of the newspaper *Genius of Universal Emancipation,* which advocated a complete program for the gradual emancipation and colonization of blacks. However, Garrison now rejected both gradualism and colonization. In *The Liberator's* first issue, Garrison, like Walker, cited the Declaration of Independence and demanded the immediate end of slavery, arguing that black people were as much entitled to "life, liberty and the pursuit of happiness" as white people. For Garrison, the swift and unconditional abolition of slavery was the only solution. He challenged slavery in dramatic words: "I will be as harsh as truth, and as uncompromising as justice. On this subject, I do not wish to think, to speak, or write, with moderation. . . . I am in earnest—I will not equivocate—I will not excuse—I will not retreat a single inch—AND I WILL BE HEARD." For an entire generation, Garrison and *The Liberator* expressed the country's best-known advocacy of nonviolent but militant abolition.

Nat Turner's revolt in Southampton, Virginia, in 1831 foreshadowed a different and even more radical abolitionist

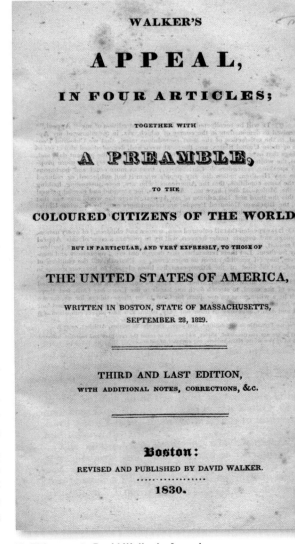

Title page to David Walker's *Appeal*

tactic—the physical assault on slavery. In a speech to the Convention of Colored Citizens at Buffalo in 1843, black abolitionist Henry Highland Garnet so vigorously praised Nat Turner and other slave insurrectionists that Frederick Douglass warned the audience against Garnet's incendiary tone. But after the passage of the Fugitive Slave Act of 1850, Douglass himself adopted the rhetoric of violence. In an editorial in 1852 titled "The True Remedy for the Fugitive Slave Bill," Douglass identified this remedy as a "good revolver, a steady hand, and a determination to shoot down any man attempting to kidnap." He then intoned: "We blush to our very soul when we are told that a negro is so mean and cowardly that he prefers to live under the slave driver's whip to the loss of life for liberty." As antislavery agitation heated up in the 1850s, the white abolitionist John Brown, his sons, and a handful of black and white freedom fighters would act on the belief that violence was inevitable, even desirable, for striking a death blow against slavery.

Black Abolitionists

Long before William Lloyd Garrison, African Americans openly advocated slavery's immediate end. Before the War for Independence, slaves in Massachusetts sued their masters for the freedom that they regarded as their inalienable right. During and after the Revolutionary War, blacks sought the abolition of slavery by petitioning the state and national governments to outlaw the slave trade and to embark on a program of general emancipation. Organizations such as the Free African Society of Philadelphia and commemorative committees for celebrating the Haitian Revolution passed resolutions calling for slavery's abolition.

In 1829 the voices of black abolitionists rang out with particular fervor and eloquent militancy. In addition to Walker's *Appeal,* a protest against slavery arose out of North Carolina, from the pen of the slave poet George Moses Horton:

> Bid Slavery hide her haggard face,
> And Barbarism fly:
> I scorn to see the sad disgrace
> In which enslaved I lie.

It was in 1829, too, that Robert A. Young of New York published his *Ethiopian Manifesto,* a defense of universal freedom. Like David Walker, Young prophesied that a black messiah-like figure would arise to liberate his people and "call together black people as a nation in themselves." Young did not create as much alarm as Walker, although he advocated measures fully as drastic to end slavery.

In the 1820s about fifty black-led antislavery societies operated in various cities. One of **Black Antislavery Societies** the strongest was located in New York and was named for the famous English antislavery leader Thomas Clarkson. Notable black abolitionist societies operated in New Haven, Boston, New York, and Philadelphia. The Massachusetts General Colored Association of Boston counted activist and pamphleteer David Walker as one of its founding members.

In 1830, blacks held their first national convention, and before the publication of Garrison's *The Liberator* they issued forceful denunciations of both colonization and slavery. With the appearance of *The Liberator,* black abolitionists eagerly aligned with Garrison. Of the 450 subscribers in the first year, 400 were blacks, and one enthusiastic affluent black abolitionist sent Garrison a gift of $50. Such contributions helped make possible Garrison's first trip to England as an international antislavery crusader.

Blacks also participated in the establishment of the interracial American Anti-Slavery Society in 1833. In 1838, one of its black members, the brilliant physician James McCune Smith, addressed the members at their annual convention on the subject of the Haitian Revolution—hardly an example of ending slavery through moral suasion, which was the nonviolent ideology professed by the Society. The racially integrated composition of the American Anti-Slavery Society was also evident in its committees. Three of the sixty-two members whose duty it was to draw up the society's Declaration of Sentiments were black, and five black leaders served on its first board of managers: Peter Williams, Robert Purvis, John B. Vashon, Abraham Shadd, and James McCrummell.

These black "founding fathers" of abolitionism were men of many interests and talents. Purvis, a Philadelphia abolitionist, was born in Charleston, the son of a well-to-do white father who generously provided for him. He was active in many causes. Purvis was the president of the Philadelphia Anti-Slavery Society. He raised funds for abolitionism, protested black disfranchisement in Pennsylvania and other northern states, campaigned for women's rights, and chaired the Philadelphia Vigilance Committee, which assisted fugitive slaves in the Underground Railroad. John B. Vashon owned a barbershop and bathhouse in Pittsburgh, and his financial success allowed him to give generously to the abolitionist cause. He introduced his son George B. Vashon to abolitionism at a young age, and George Vashon, who would later graduate from Oberlin College, became a renowned abolitionist as well.

Blacks gave their time, energy, and money to the work of local and regional antislavery organizations. They frequently held membership on vigilance committees, which raised funds to help slaves escape to freedom, and also served as officers in the white-dominated antislavery societies. In 1835 David Ruggles became secretary of the New York committee and remained active until his eyesight failed. In Philadelphia, Robert Purvis had charge of the first vigilance committee, which several years later was headed by William Still. Frederick Douglass was elected president of the New England Anti-Slavery Society in 1847.

Black women played significant roles in the antislavery cause, too. They formed their own antislavery organizations in such cities as New York, Rochester, Philadelphia, Boston, and Cincinnati. They gathered signatures for petitions to Con- **Women Abolitionists** gress and held fund-raising fairs where they sold toys, linens, foodstuffs, and decorative objects—products they often made themselves. Black women's organizations addressed not only abolition but also gender concerns. For example, the Afric-American Female Intelligence Society in Boston encouraged education for black women and confronted the reluctance on the part of male abolitionists to welcome women's voices in the public debate on slavery. Public speaking by women was not widely encouraged in early nineteenth-century America, and both black and white female lecturers faced verbal and physical attacks at times. In 1831 Maria Stewart's lecture on the moral duties of black men brought her jeers from the crowd, which pelted her with rotten tomatoes. The white abolitionist sisters Sarah and Angelina Grimké were ostracized in some abolitionist circles for their public pronouncements against slavery. Indeed, Sarah Grimké urged women to continue public agitation despite male opposition. In a metaphorical comparison of women and slaves, Grimké urged antislavery women to "rise from that degradation and bondage to which the faculties of our minds have been prevented from expanding to their full growth and are sometimes wholly crushed."

A number of black and white male abolitionists, with such notable exceptions as women's rights advocates Frederick Douglass and William Lloyd Garrison, opposed women officeholders in the prominent male-run societies such as the American Anti-Slavery Society. They disapproved of woman suffrage and deemed the women's rights movement a distraction from the abolitionist cause. Despite this opposition, numerous black women, such as newspaper publisher Mary Ann Shadd and writer Frances Ellen Watkins Harper, did not hesitate to make their voices heard. The most famous female black abolitionist and women's rights advocate was Sojourner Truth, a former slave from New York who traveled throughout New England and the upper Midwest, moving audiences by her eloquence, religious mysticism, and hatred of racial and gender inequality.

Blacks worked for the antislavery cause as agents and speakers for various societies, and several were hired by local or national bodies on a full-time basis. Among the better-known agents were Frederick Douglass, Theodore S. Wright, William Jones, Charles Lenox Remond and his sister Sarah Parker Remond, Frances E. W. Harper, Henry Foster, Lunsford Lane, Henry Highland Garnet, Charles Gardner, Andrew Harris, Abraham Shadd (the father of Mary Ann Shadd), David Nickens, James Bradley, and William Wells Brown.

Black Agents

Sell the Shadow to Support the Substance.
SOJOURNER TRUTH.

▌ Sojourner Truth

White abolitionists took great pride in introducing to doubting audiences black agents who presented eloquent and poignant first-hand accounts of slavery. Former slaves were among the best speakers. On one occasion, after Douglass had electrified an audience with his remarkable eloquence, Garrison rose to his feet and flung out the question: "Is this a man or a thing?" Black Presbyterian minister Henry Highland Garnet and author William Wells Brown were reputed to have made favorable impressions wherever they went. Several blacks, in addition to Douglass, Garnet, and Brown, carried the abolitionist message to Europe. Speakers such as James W. C. Pennington, Charles Lenox Remond, Nathaniel Paul, Ellen and William Craft, Samuel Ringgold Ward, Sarah Parker Remond, and Alexander Crummell helped to bring the American antislavery cause to England, Scotland, France, and Germany. They were received with enthusiasm almost everywhere and were instrumental in linking the humanitarian movement in Europe with various reform movements in the United States.

As a spokesman for antislavery, Frederick Douglass became an American hero. Called by Garrison "a representative black man," Douglass was in fact an extraordinary individual—a writer, speaker, thinker, and activist in black conventions, the Underground Railroad, and many other efforts to improve the conditions of his race. No antislavery leader did as much to carry the case of the slave to the people of the United States and Europe before the Civil War. A fugitive slave himself, Douglass was introduced to the movement when he attended an antislavery convention in Nantucket, Massachusetts, in 1841.

Frederick Douglass and Henry Highland Garnet

After speaking there he was employed by several societies and rapidly became one of the best-known orators in the United States, lecturing throughout the North and in England.

African American newspapers helped to disseminate the ideas and goals of the abolitionist movement throughout black communities. They played a crucial role in airing the debates and ideas of blacks themselves. One of the most outstanding black abolitionists was journalist Samuel Cornish who, with John Russwurm, in 1827 established *Freedom's Journal*, the first black newspaper. Cornish and Russwurm were also the first antislavery publishers to call for immediate abolition. In 1829, after Russwurm's departure to Liberia, Cornish published *Rights of All*, an extremely radical but short-lived paper. In 1836 he published the *Weekly Advocate*, and the following year, with the help of Charles B. Ray and Phillip A. Bell, he established the influential *Colored American*.

Other black abolitionist newspapers included the *National Watchman*, edited by William G. Allen and Henry Highland Garnet; the *Mirror of Liberty*, a quarterly issued by David Ruggles; and Mary Ann Shadd's *Provincial Freeman*, published from Canada. Most popular of all was *The North Star*, founded by Frederick Douglass and Martin Delany in 1847. Delany's growing attraction to emigration caused the men to part ways in 1850, and with Delany's departure and Douglass's conversion to political abolitionism, the paper's name changed to *Frederick Douglass's Paper*. Other short-lived periodicals were the *Mystery* (Pittsburgh, 1843), the *Colored Man's Journal* (New York, 1851), the *Mirror of the Times* (San Francisco, 1855), and the *Anglo-African* (New York, 1859).

Newspapers

Mary Ann Shadd Cary

Window in Time

Frederick Douglass on the Fourth of July, 1852

I am not included within the pale of this glorious anniversary! Your high independence only reveals the immeasurable distance between us. The blessings in which you, this day, rejoice, are not enjoyed in common. The rich inheritance of justice, liberty, prosperity and independence, bequeathed by your fathers, has brought stripes and death to me. This Fourth of July is yours, not mine. You may rejoice, I must mourn. To drag a man in fetters into the grand illuminated temple of liberty, and call upon him to join you in joyous anthems, were inhuman mockery and sacrilegious irony. Do you mean, citizens, to mock me, by asking me to speak to-day? If so, there is a parallel in your conduct. And let me warn you that it is dangerous to copy the example of a nation whose crimes, towering up to heaven, were thrown down by the breath of the Almighty, burying that nation in irrevocable ruin! I can to-day take up the plaintive lament of a peeled and woe-smitten people!

"By the rivers of Babylon, there we sat down. Yea! We wept when we remembered Zion. We hanged our harps upon the willows in the midst thereof. For there, they that carried us away captive, required of us a song; and they who wasted us required of us mirth, saying, Sing us one of the songs of Zion. How can we sing the Lord's song in a strange land? If I forget thee, O Jerusalem, let my right hand forget her cunning. If I do not remember thee, let my tongue cleave to the roof of my mouth."

Philip S. Foner, *The Life and Writings of Frederick Douglass*, II (New York, 1950), pp. 181–204.

Antislavery Agendas

Militant abolitionism formed part of a larger humanitarian movement that swept Europe and the northern United States. It articulated a growing spirit of reform and concern for the welfare of underprivileged persons. Abolitionism was also closely connected with religious revivalism during the years from 1800 through the 1830s and with humanitarian and perfectionist movements for peace, women's rights, temperance, and utopian communities. In the trans-Allegheny West, abolitionism was associated with the Second Great Awakening, the religious revival movement of the early nineteenth century. The Second Great Awakening's dominant figure, the lawyer-turned-preacher Charles Grandison Finney, emphasized the importance of being "useful," by which he meant releasing a powerful impulse toward social and moral reform.

Young converts joined Finney's Holy Band, eager to adopt his views on the evil of slavery. Finney and his followers insisted that slavery was contrary to the teachings of Christianity, since Jesus taught universal brotherhood. For them, one of the cardinal principles of Christianity was that all men were created in the image of God. The writings of white abolitionists, such as James G. Birney's *Letter to the Ministers and Elders* (1834) and Theodore Dwight

Weld's *The Bible against Slavery* (1837), carried biblical arguments to the logical conclusion that southern slavery must end.

Abolitionists commonly asserted that slavery was contrary to the fundamental principles of the American way of life, which valued freedom as an inalienable right of the individual. They drew upon the Declaration of Independence as they contrasted free- **The Abolitionist Argument** dom and slavery. Slaves, they contended, had no freedom to seek employment, no right to marriage or to family rights, no legal protection, and few opportunities to secure an education. Abolitionists argued that slavery was economically unsound because wageless workers could not be expected to be efficient or to conserve physical and human resources. The culture and civilization of the South suffered, moreover, because the master-slave relationship did not produce a gentility of spirit but instead emphasized the base aspects of the natures of both masters and slaves. Theodore Weld bluntly declared that the domination of one person by another was essentially uncivilized: "Arbitrary power is to the mind what alcohol is to the body; it intoxicates." Finally, abolitionist literature condemned slavery as a menace to the peace and safety of the country. The South was becoming an armed camp, abolitionists maintained, where whites lived in constant fear of a widespread uprising of slaves.

Although some white opponents of slavery had for years believed that colonization offered one way of ending slavery while solving the problem of what to do with former slaves, most supporters of colonization were not antislavery advocates. The colonization movement was strongest among slaveholders in the Upper South, like Virginia's Bushrod Washington, a Supreme Court justice, and Kentucky's Senator Henry Clay. Both men saw colonization as a way of getting rid of free blacks, not slaves. The rise of militant abolitionism presented the American Colonization Society (ACS) with a vocal and organized opponent.

In growing numbers, white abolitionists came to feel—as did the great majority of blacks—that colonization for the purpose of sending free blacks out of the country served only to buttress slavery. When Garrison organized the New England Anti-Slavery Society in 1832, it denounced the ACS. Garrison asserted that the group had "inflicted a great injury upon the free and slave population; first by strengthening the prejudices of the people; secondly, by discouraging the education of those who are free; thirdly, by inducing passage of severe legislative enactments; and, finally, by lulling the whole county into a deep sleep." Even more vigorous denunciations appeared in Garrison's *Thoughts on Colonization.* Published in 1832, it not only offered an extended argument against the logic and morality of colonization but also provided formal statements by various black urban organizations discrediting the ACS project.

Throughout the 1830s, the abolitionist cause grew—fast becoming a crusade that extended well beyond the borders of the Northeast. Many southerners with antislavery leanings had moved to Midwestern states like Indiana and Ohio. James **The Crusade** G. Birney, for example, left Alabama for Kentucky and from there went to Ohio. Levi Coffin abandoned North Carolina and carried on his abolitionist activities in Indiana and, after 1847, in Cincinnati. Later, these men were joined by others who found the atmosphere of their home communities in the South increasingly hostile to antislavery ideas. After the Massachusetts-born theologian Theodore Dwight Weld came to teach at Lane Theological Seminary in Cincinnati, he encouraged the students to discuss the problem of slavery and in 1834 began the free and open debates that won many people, including a few southerners, to the cause of abolition. The debates also led to his dismissal from Lane.

The students put their views into practice by going out into the community to organize groups to assist escaping slaves through the Underground Railroad. They also provided educational instruction to black youths. When the students withdrew from Lane rather than submit to a conservative administration, they went in large numbers to Ohio's Western Reserve in the northeastern corner of the state where they helped found Oberlin College. A theology department was established at Oberlin, in part with funds provided by the abolitionist businessmen and brothers Arthur and Lewis Tappan of New York. From its founding, Oberlin College became a hub of antislavery activism and the nation's first avowedly integrated school of higher learning. It was also the first coeducational American college to pay attention to questions of social reform.

In 1833 Weld, Arthur Tappan, and Garrison cofounded the American Anti-Slavery Society, which also had the support of such prominent white abolitionists as Lewis Tappan, James G. Birney, William Goodell, Joshua Leavitt, Elizur Wright, Samuel May, Beriah Green, as well as of a significant number of black supporters. All the founders of the society had been active in local antislavery societies, and Arthur Tappan was chosen to lead the new organization. The American Anti-Slavery Society published four periodicals—*Human Rights, Anti-Slavery Record, Emancipator,* and *Slave's Friend*—and distributed pamphlets throughout the North and, when possible, in the South. Through its many agents, the Society organized local units and raised money to further emancipation. In 1836 it sent seventy abolitionists out on the lecture circuit, drawn largely from the ministry, theological seminaries, and colleges.

The American Anti-Slavery Society

Differences between Garrison and the Tappan brothers and their respective supporters began to divide the Society. Garrison believed that the American Anti-Slavery Society did not press hard enough for abolition, and he sought to transform the group in a number of key ways. He criticized other leaders for their unwillingness to work for women's equality, to condemn the Constitution as a tool of slavery, and to denounce the churches for not taking an unequivocal antislavery stance. The Garrisonians succeeded in getting their views incorporated into the society's Declaration of Sentiments, and in 1839 they were elected to important offices in the society. Some of the newly elected Garrisonians were women, and the election to the executive committee of Lucretia Mott, Lydia Maria Child, and Maria Weston Chapman enraged those opposed to Garrison's "radicalism." "To put a woman on the committee with men," Lewis Tappan protested, "is contrary to the usages of civilized society."

The New York faction of the AASS, led by Tappan, broke away and formed the rival American Foreign Anti-Slavery Society, which took a stand friendly to churches and sought to use them to end slavery. The American Foreign Anti-Slavery Society focused solely on the slavery issue, rejecting altogether women's rights. Unlike Garrison's followers, Tappan's group was strong in the Border States and the Midwest, and it had advocates like Birney and Weld who believed in the power of political involvement to overcome constitutional and legal obstructions to emancipation. Garrison remained strong in New England, where his followers included noted figures such as John Greenleaf Whittier, the poet of abolition, and the orator Wendell Phillips, "abolition's golden trumpet," as well as women's rights activists. The movement splintered once again in 1840 with the creation of the Liberty Party, a third party that attempted to bring the issue of abolition into American electoral politics.

William Lloyd Garrison

Garrisonians were pacifist and antipolitical; they tended to condemn the political process itself as corrupt and immoral, and disdained political campaigning.

Although blacks were also split among the various antebellum abolitionist factions, several prominent blacks lambasted white abolitionists in general for not regarding them as equals. White abolitionists, blacks charged, were at best paternalistic and at worst openly discriminatory, explicitly denying free blacks their civil rights **Black vs. White Abolitionists** in northern communities. Supporting abolition did not necessarily mean supporting racial equality. Black abolitionists grew restive at the silence of their white compatriots on the issue of black disfranchisement and other forms of racial subordination in the North. And they grew incensed when some of the very persons who called for immediate abolition in the South appeared so patient with northern injustice. There had been instances, too, when white abolitionist women refused to let black women attend white antislavery fairs. Black abolitionist Samuel Cornish, although he sat on the executive board of the American Anti-Slavery Society, commented that if the white abolitionists did not "judge of us as they do of other men . . . they never can succeed."

White abolitionists' discomfort with the separate black convention movement also stirred debate within the black community. Although most black abolitionists supported the conventions, a few prominent black leaders, such as newspaper owner Samuel Cornish, businessman William Whipper, and physician James McCune Smith, objected to them. In 1840 McCune Smith hoped to discourage the idea of all-black meetings "because the Convention aims to do by separate action what can better be done by a movement based on principle, and carried on by all the influences, irrespective of complexion, that can be brought to bear." However, they seemed to become more accepting of separate black societies in the 1850s. This change in attitude may have reflected growing ideological differences with the Garrison-led movement. In 1855, for example, McCune Smith worked with a New York-based African American society that was devoted to abolishing slavery "by means of the Constitution; or otherwise." His use of the word *otherwise* alluded to the possible use of violence, and the Garrisonians unequivocally renounced violence.

Yet black and white abolitionists continued to work together in antislavery organizations and in other numerous ways. For example, white abolitionists played a critical role as the benefactors of nineteenth-century African American artists. The Cincinnati black **Black-White Cooperation** artist Robert Duncanson, whose work was inspired by the landscape style of paintings in the Hudson River School, benefited from the patronage of such white antislavery citizens in the Midwest as Robert Bishop, William Cary, Freeman Cary, Richard S. Rust, James Birney, and Nicholas Longworth. Duncanson's *Uncle Tom and Little Eva*, a painting commissioned in 1853 by James Francis Conover, is the only surviving record of his work that has an explicitly abolitionist subject. The general appeal of his landscapes, as opposed to more politically charged subject matter, probably accounts for his tremendous commercial success.

In some cases, black and white abolitionists shared powerful bonds of friendship. In New York, James McCune Smith, Frederick Douglass, and the white abolitionists Gerrit Smith and John Brown labored together as equals and friends, so much so that all four described themselves as having a similar spirit—what they termed, in respect to African American piety, "the black hearts of men." Gerrit Smith, more than anyone else, persuaded McCune Smith and Douglass to renounce the Garrisonian ideology of political noninvolvement; he also became a mentor and financial backer of Frederick Douglass's newspaper after 1850. In Massachusetts during the 1840s and 1850s, William C. Nell and other members of Boston's black community worked with such white abolitionists as Garrison, Phillips, and Charles Sumner to defeat segregated public education.

Proslavery Backlash

From the time that Thomas Jefferson published his *Notes on the State of Virginia* in the 1780s, southern leaders used his book to buttress the idea of black inferiority and thus to justify slavery. However, after 1830 the mounting abolitionist critique caused the ideological defense of slavery to take on new dimensions. Southerners refused to apologize for slavery or to refer, as some had done in the past, to slavery's unpalatable aspects as "necessary evils." Instead, southerners increasingly promoted and, with ferocious tenacity, clung to the idea that slavery was a "positive good." One by one, southern educators, scientists, politicians, literary figures, and ministers asserted that slavery was "good"—good for blacks, good for southern whites, and good for all Americans.

Proslavery theorists presented four main arguments. First, proslavery scientists and physicians argued that blacks constituted a biologically and mentally inferior race, even a different species of humanity. Physicians such as John H. Van Evrie, Josiah Clark Nott, and many others subscribed to an ethnological justification of slavery. They drew heavily on the cranial-measurement studies of the northern scholar Dr. Samuel Morton and quoted his conclusion that blacks were inferior to both Caucasians and Indians.

The Proslavery Argument

Claiming the sanction of science, southern physicians asserted that the anatomy of blacks differed from whites in ways that enabled blacks to withstand punishment without feeling as much pain as whites and to work harder than whites under the hot southern sun. Such claims enabled masters to justify, without any moral qualms, savagely whipping slaves, overworking them, and restricting their movements, because "science" justified their actions. One southern physician, Samuel Cartwright, published an article entitled "The Diseases of the Negro" in a well-respected medical journal, arguing that some slaves suffered from a disease, which he called "draeptomania," that made them suddenly run away. White people did not appear to be afflicted with this running-away disease.

The second proslavery argument maintained the necessity of slave labor as a basis for the rise of civilization and the economic development of the South. George Fitzhugh, Beverly Tucker, and others claimed that culture and civilization advanced only as societies became more unequal. James Henry Hammond, the governor of South Carolina from 1842 to 1844 and the state's U.S. Senator from 1857 to 1860, expressed similar views when he wrote: "In all social systems there must be a class to do the menial duties, to perform the drudgery of life. . . . Its requisites are vigor, docility, fidelity. Such a class you must have or you would not have that other class which leads progress, civilization, and refinement." He argued that like a house, every social system had a foundation—what he called a "mudsill"—and that blacks were the natural "mudsill" for American society. Southerners further argued that the products of slave labor—tobacco, sugar, and, most of all, cotton—were central to American prosperity. In a famous speech in Congress, Senator Hammond thundered: "You dare not make war on Cotton; Cotton is King."

The third proslavery argument held that history itself destined blacks to occupy a subordinate position in society. In *Southern Institutes,* George S. Sawyer maintained that "in no age or condition has the real negro shown a capacity to throw off the chains of barbarism and brutality that have long bound down the nations of that race; or to rise above the common cloud of darkness that still broods over them." Southern legal scholar Thomas R. R. Cobb asserted (with no historical evidence) that in ancient Rome the elite families had preferred black house servants, because they were so well suited to subordinate tasks. He even argued that, in nature, red ants enslaved black ants. The fourth and most important argument defended the southern system as divinely ordained, arguing that the Bible and the church sanctioned racially based slavery.

Southern ministers preached that "blackness" resulted from the "curse of Ham" as related in the Book of Genesis's story of Noah and that God had created blacks to make them slaves. White ministers also insisted that slavery offered a means of converting the heathen to Christian civilization. There was, of course, a contradiction between the theory that blacks were incapable of moral improvement and the assertion that they possessed the ability to become civilized and Christianized under slavery; but little attention was paid to this apparent discrepancy at the time, and each argument was used where it would do the most good. Rev. James Henley Thornwell, Bishop Stephen Elliott, and Dr. B. M. Palmer typified the many southern white religious leaders who in their sermons and writings promoted the idea that slavery functioned as a civilizing and Christianizing force. Many northern religious leaders rejected this view of slavery as a means of moral uplift, and entire denominations divided along regional lines: fifteen years before the Civil War, Baptists, Methodists, and Presbyterians all split into northern and southern branches.

In the South, the war of words between abolitionists and proslavery advocates became so bitter that free inquiry and free speech disappeared. Many people who expressed points of view at variance from the accepted proslavery creed were run out of the South. Southern men of letters such as William Gilmore **Defending the Institution** Simms and William J. Grayson wrote essays, poems, and songs extolling the virtues of slavery in general and black slavery in particular, and physician Josiah Nott published several proslavery books that offered economic, social, philosophical, and scientific defenses of slavery. Southern colleges became hotbeds of proslavery sentiment, and every agency in slaveholding communities was employed to defend the institution.

Southern leaders resolved to keep abolitionist ideas out of their communities by force if necessary. They worked up such popular resentment to the circulation of abolitionist literature in the South that citizens took matters into their own hands. In July 1835 a group of white rowdies broke into the Charleston post office, seized antislavery newspapers, and made a bonfire of them in the public square. Many other cities followed Charleston's example. When it appeared that the federal government would not punish them for their actions, southern postmasters began to ban abolitionist literature from the mails. It was not simply that the federal government refused to punish them; President Andrew Jackson actively supported the ban. Indeed his administration played a complicit role by demanding mail censorship in order to suppress the dissemination of antislavery publications.

The Old South perceived antislavery talk as causing irreparable damage to southern institutions. Thus in October 1831 the Georgia legislature offered a $4,000 reward for the arrest of Garrison. The reward posted for seizing Arthur Tappan was $12,000 in Macon and $20,000 in New Orleans. The vigilance committee of South Carolina offered $1,500 for the arrest of any person distributing *The Liberator* or *Walker's Appeal*. Most leaders of the abolitionist movement and the Underground Railroad could boast of bounties on their heads in the South.

Proslavery leaders even carried the fight into "enemy" territory. They not only went north in pursuit of runaway slaves but also sought to spread proslavery doctrine and to spy on abolitionists there. A Kentucky slaveholder dressed in Quaker garb traveled to Indiana seeking information about the Underground Railroad, though his unfamiliarity with Quaker speech and customs revealed him as an imposter. Another slaveholder went so far as to pose as an antislavery lecturer. Visiting several communities in Indiana and Ohio, he discovered where fugitives were hiding and notified their owners, who promptly came and reclaimed their property. These communities, however, were hostile to slavery, and the citizens insisted that the slaves be given a court hearing, which ultimately resulted in the slaves being set free.

The conflict between abolitionists and supporters of slavery did not remain a war of words, but escalated into acts of harassment, ostracism, and even violence against abolition-**Persecution and Violence** ists. People living in the South found it necessary to speak with extreme caution on the question of slavery. In Petersburg, Virginia, one white man was lashed and ordered to leave town for saying that "black men have, in the abstract, a right to their freedom." A Georgian who subscribed to *The Liberator* was dragged from his home by a mob, tarred and feathered, set afire, dunked in the river, and finally tied to a post and whipped. Amos Dresser, a former student at Lane Seminary, went to Tennessee to sell Bibles and was charged with spreading abolitionist doctrines. Even though the charges against him could not be proved in court, a mob lashed him in a public square at midnight with the hearty approval of several thousand onlookers. Whites who associated with blacks on any basis that suggested equality were severely dealt with. Several, for example, were murdered in Georgia and South Carolina for the "crime" of mixing with blacks in public.

Nor was all of the North a haven for abolitionist views. In the 1830s and early 1840s, most northerners condemned radical abolitionists, and many northern religious leaders denounced them as fanatics. For example, the Episcopal bishop of Vermont, John H. Hopkins, opposed the antislavery cause, claiming that blacks were better off as slaves than as free people. The mainstream press excoriated abolitionists. New York physician David M. Reese published a pamphlet in which he called the American Anti-Slavery Society the "purest of all humbugs" and accused it of encouraging interracial marriage and a mixed-raced population, which in this period was commonly called "amalgamation." (It was not until the early 1860s that the term *miscegenation* was coined.)

New York journalists sensationalized abolitionist activities, and their editorials warned of the threat that abolitionist "amalgamation" posed to the political and social order. Historian Leslie Harris reveals the violent consequences that the "rallying cry of amalgamation" produced in July 1834, when hundreds of white rioters attacked black and white abolitionists in New York. They destroyed the home of Arthur Tappan, the homes and churches of black and white abolitionist clergy, and the homes of black residents in New York City's impoverished Five Points neighborhood. Indeed, abolitionists frequently met with violence. White newspaper editor Elijah P. Lovejoy was run out of St. Louis for criticizing the leniency of a judge in the trial of whites accused of burning a black man alive. Later, in Alton, Illinois, Lovejoy was killed when a mob destroyed—for the fourth time—the press on which he printed the *Alton Observer*, an antislavery paper. In Cincinnati a mob destroyed James Birney's press in 1836, and he barely escaped with his life. Even Garrison was once dragged through the streets of Boston with a rope around his neck.

In these early years, antislavery lecturers often found it difficult to rent halls in which to speak. Even if they succeeded, they could not be certain that their programs would go as planned, since mobs broke up many a meeting. Black abolitionist speakers such as Frederick Douglass were especially vulnerable to attacks by infuriated whites. Women who supported the antislavery crusade risked public insults and other indignities. The federal government, headed in the 1830s and 1840s by the slaveholding presidents Andrew Jackson, John Tyler, James Polk, and Zachary Taylor, joined in the persecution of abolitionists. As petitions against slavery began pouring into the House of Representatives, Congress—where slave-holding southerners held leadership positions—adopted a rule in 1836 that required such petitions to be "tabled"—that is, to languish unaddressed. This "gag rule," as abolitionists dubbed it, was vigorously opposed by such congressmen as former president John Quincy Adams of Massachusetts and Joshua Giddings of Ohio, but it was not rescinded until 1845. As long as it stood, abolitionists complained that the constitutional right of petitioning the legislature for redress of grievances was being denied.

Violence against abolitionists and the "gag rule" ultimately backfired on the supporters of slavery. The killing of Lovejoy, for example, initially led to a meeting in Boston where conservative "men of property and standing" wanted to praise those who had killed him to preserve sectional harmony and the **Changing Attitudes** racial status quo. However, in his first act as an antislavery activist, the young lawyer Wendell Phillips gave a stirring speech in favor of freedom of the press and liberty. His speech completely altered the mood of those at the public meeting and signaled the coming change in how people would view antislavery. Similarly, abolitionists used the "gag rule" to drive home the point that slavery denied freedom not only to blacks but also to whites, by preventing them from exercising their First Amendment right to petition Congress.

By the late 1840s, most northern whites still thought abolitionists fanatics, but they also were beginning to see slavery as a deeply corrosive institution that threatened the liberty of all Americans. In the 1850s political opponents of slavery—many of whom also supported greater rights for African Americans—began to win elections and achieve legislative successes. In 1849, for example, members of the recently created Free Soil Party, which held the balance of power in the tightly divided Ohio state legislature, forced the normally negrophobic Democrats to support the repeal of most of the state's black laws. In the mid-1850s, antislavery Republicans, many of whom favored greater equality for blacks, won stunning victories in the North, campaigning on the slogan of "Free Soil, Free Labor, Free Speech, and Free Men." In those states where they could vote, blacks such as Frederick Douglass joined this new party, even though they understood that not all Republicans favored black equality and that, although opposed to slavery's territorial expansion, the party was not an abolitionist one.

The Black Response

From the 1830s until the eve of the Civil War, black abolitionists attacked proslavery claims on several levels. Black intellectuals responded forcefully to racist scholarship, questioning the use of "science" as a prop for racist social practices. As one writer noted in *The Colored American*, "we had hoped for much from science. . . . We had fondly dreamed that she would ever rear her head far above the buzz of popular applause, or the conflicting opinion of the moral world; it is therefore almost with the anguish that springs from a blasted hope that we view this first, however flimsy, attempt to demean her to the contemptible office of pandering to popular prejudices."

Historian Mia Bay argues that some black intellectuals similarly misused science for black audiences and sought to prove the superiority of African-descended people. One such black thinker was Robert Benjamin Lewis, who in 1836 published the imposing four-hundred-page *Light and Truth: Collected from the Bible and Ancient and Modern History, Containing the Universal History of the Colored and Indian Race, From the Creation of the World to the Present Time*. Lewis's treatise significantly ignores the existence of whites in history. African

American writers such as Lewis often sounded no less chauvinistic in their depictions of black superiority than did their white counterparts who promoted white superiority.

Some black writers sought to undermine racial chauvinism by showing the unity of humankind. In an address titled "The Claims of the Negro Ethnologically Considered,"

Black Counterarguments Frederick Douglass challenged proslavery theories of polygenesis, which argued that whites and blacks did not belong to the same human species. Douglass advocated instead the "oneness of man." The most erudite and prolific abolitionist to challenge ideas of innate black inferiority was James McCune Smith. His books, essays, and speeches directly addressed the various tenets of proslavery thought, and in the 1840s and 1850s his articles appeared both in African American newspapers and in the prestigious journals of white learned societies. In 1844 the *New York Journal of Medicine* published a statistical case study by Smith. In January 1859 the *Anglo-African Magazine* featured his article "Civilization: Its Dependence on Physical Circumstances," which laid out an environmental explanation for racial differences, arguing that geographical variations in climate had shaped human development across the ages. Indeed, Smith's scientific research earned him the distinction of being elected to the otherwise all-white American Geographical Society.

Blacks also refuted the notion that slaves were happy and contented with their lot. The largest and perhaps most influential group of black writers were ex-slaves, both fugitives and

Black Narratives freed. Their narratives offered first-hand accounts of the pain and suffering endured by slaves and represented a popular literary genre at a time when print culture was expanding in the United States. Frequently, white abolitionists, who desired to use these personal stories as powerful arguments against slavery, assisted ex-slaves in writing their narratives. In some cases, the whites wrote the narratives, based on stories told to them by former slaves. Some narratives, however, were produced by former slaves who had received the rudiments of an education. Among the best-known narratives published between 1840 and 1860 were those of William Wells Brown (1842), Lunsford Lane (1842), Moses Grandy (1844), Frederick Douglass (1845), Lewis Clarke (1846), Henry Bibb (1849), James W. C. Pennington (1850), Henry "Box" Brown (1851), Solomon Northup (1853), Austin Steward (1857), Jermain Wesley Loguen (1859), and Harriet Jacobs (1861).

Black abolitionists realized that the sheer quantity and quality of their literary contributions disproved charges of the innate inferiority of blacks. William Wells Brown described

Black Literature his foreign travels vividly in *Three Years in Europe* (1852), and he was the first black person to write both a play, *The Escape* (1858), and a novel, *Clotel; or the President's Daughter* (1853). Before publishing his narrative, James W. C. Pennington had written *Textbook of the Origin and History of the Colored People* (1841). A much more capable historian was William C. Nell, whose *Services of Colored Americans in the Wars of 1776 and 1812* first appeared in 1852. Three years later he substantially revised the book and issued the new edition under the title *The Colored Patriots of the American Revolution with Sketches of Several Distinguished Colored Persons to Which Is Added a Brief Survey of the Condition and Prospects of Colored Americans.* Martin Delany, physician and former co-editor with Frederick Douglass of *The North Star,* published *The Condition, Elevation, Emigration and Destiny of the Colored People of the United States,* and seven installments of a novel, *Blake; or the Huts of America,* that appeared in the *Anglo-African* magazine in 1859. The corpus of work by the abolitionist and physician James McCune Smith stands in a class by itself; Smith wrote over a hundred articles on historical, biographical, political, and scientific subjects.

The Underground Railroad

Perhaps nothing did more to intensify strife between North and South or better empha-sized the determination of abolitionists to destroy slavery than the Underground Railroad. Its origins date from the eighteenth century. By the end of the War for Independence, organized assistance to fugitive slaves was already evident. In 1786 George Washington complained about a slave "whom a society of Quakers, formed for such purposes, have attempted to lib-erate." The slave in question was able to escape from Alexandria, Virginia, to Philadelphia. In the following year, Quaker Isaac T. Hopper of Philadelphia, still in his teens, developed a plan for the systematic assistance of slaves escaping from the South. Within a few years, runaway slaves were being helped in a number of towns in Pennsylvania and New Jersey. Slowly these antislavery operations spread in various directions.

In 1804 General Thomas Boude, who had served in the Continental Army during the Revolution, purchased a slave, Stephen Smith (who would later purchase his own freedom for $100), and brought him home to Columbia, Pennsylvania. **Origins** Smith's mother, also a slave, fled her mistress and followed to find her son. The Boudes took her in. Within a few weeks the woman who owned Smith's mother arrived and demanded her property. Not only did the Boudes refuse to surrender her, but the town supported them. The people of Columbia resolved to champion the cause of fugitives,

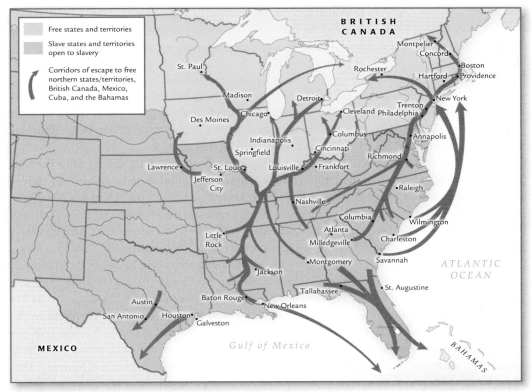

The Underground Railroad in the nineteenth century

Robert Duncanson, *View of Cincinnati, Ohio from Covington, Kentucky,* **ca. 1851**

and by 1815 this sentiment was being expressed in towns in Ohio. By 1819 underground methods were being used to spirit slaves out of North Carolina. Even before the period of militant abolitionism, the movement that came to be known as the Underground Railroad had grown into a widespread network of antislavery activists.

The name *Underground Railroad* was probably coined around 1831, shortly after the first steam railroads were built in the United States. There are several versions of how the movement got its name. One concerns a slave, Tice Davids, who escaped from his Kentucky owner in 1831 and got across the Ohio River. Although the owner followed in hot pursuit, he lost all trace of the slave after crossing the river and was so confounded that he declared the slave must have "gone off on an underground road." That was entirely possible, since by 1831 there were plenty of "underground" roads along the Ohio River, with "stations," "conductors," and "stationmasters," as the means of conveyance.

Robert Duncanson's painting *View of Cincinnati, Ohio from Covington, Kentucky* (ca. 1851) conveys an implicit abolitionist meaning about the Ohio River. One of the few paintings by Duncanson to include African American figures, presumably slaves given their home in Kentucky, Duncanson emphasizes their appearance as laborers in contrast to a more leisurely look. One holds a scythe, and the other hangs laundry, but visible across the river is "free-soil" Ohio. Indeed, art historian David Lubin argues that Duncanson's landscapes almost always feature bodies of water, suggesting the demarcation line between slavery and freedom (including the Ohio River) that so many fugitive slaves crossed in their quest for freedom.

The exact number of slaves who reached freedom via the Underground Railroad will forever remain a mystery. Governor John A. Quitman of Mississippi declared that between 1810 and 1850 the South lost 100,000 slaves, valued at more than $30 million. Although scholars are not in agreement as to the actual number of fugitives, historian Wilbur H. Siebert estimates that 40,000 fugitives passed through Ohio alone. The Underground Railroad intensified the resentment that slaveholding southerners felt toward the North. Ironically, the Railroad ran inside the South, and not only northerners but also white and black southerners were among its "engineers" and "conductors."

Until the outbreak of the Civil War, the Underground Railroad operated in flagrant violation of federal fugitive slave laws. It became the most eloquent statement of defiance against slaveholders that abolitionists could make. The majority of its opera-
Railroad Operations tions took place at night, the only time when fugitives and their helpers felt even somewhat secure. Slaves prepared to escape by taking supplies from their masters and, if necessary, by disguising themselves. Those of very light complexion frequently passed as white people and sometimes posed as their own masters. Darker-skinned fugitives pretended to be servants on their way to meet their owners. There are several cases on record of fugitives being provided with white babies at crucial moments in order to make believable their claims of being nurses. At times, men posed as women and women as men.

In its early days, most of the fugitives on the Underground Railroad were men, and they usually traveled on foot. Later, when traffic grew heavier and included more women and children, escorts and vehicles were provided. The conductors carried their human cargo in covered wagons, closed carriages, and farm wagons specially equipped with closed compartments. Blacks were occasionally put in boxes and shipped as freight by rail or boat; thus Henry "Box" Brown traveled from Richmond to Philadelphia via the Adams Express Company. When traveling at night, conductors and fugitives were guided by the North Star, by tributaries of the Ohio or other rivers, and by mountain chains. On dark, cloudy nights, fugitives resorted to feeling the moss on the north side of tree trunks to orient themselves.

Fugitives were pursued relentlessly by planters, slave traders, and local sheriffs, who resorted to the most desperate means to recover them. "Stations" where fugitives could eat, rest, and hide during the day were planned well ahead of the slaves' arrival. Slaves hid in barns, in attics, and in other out-of-the-way places while the word went out to succeeding stations via "the grapevine telegraph" that fugitives were on their way. One coded message sent by a conductor to the next stationmaster in 1859 gave much more information than a casual glance revealed: "By to-morrow evening's mail, you will receive two volumes of 'The Irrepressible Conflict' bound in black. After perusal, please forward and oblige."

All Underground Railroad lines led to the free states. They began on plantations in the South and, in the western slave states, ran up rivers and valleys and across mountains to the Ohio or upper Mississippi rivers; in the eastern slave states, they terminated at points in Pennsylvania and New Jersey. In the North, the route became clearer but was still dangerous, because slave catchers combed the free states for runaway slaves.

The Underground Railroad required substantial material resources to operate. Fugitives needed food and clothing and often incurred unexpected expenses,
Resources such as train fare in the North, to evade a pursuing owner, or money for clothing or other items that facilitated the display of affluence necessary to convey an impression of freedom. Abolitionists raised funds to carry on the work. The vigilance

committees of Philadelphia and New York solicited money, and philanthropists contributed, as did the conductors and others involved.

The Underground Railroad apparently did not suffer for want of operators. Historian Wilbur H. Siebert has catalogued more than 3,200 active workers, but many others will remain forever anonymous. Outstanding among the white workers was Levi Coffin, a Quaker who was the so-called president of the Underground Railroad. His strategic location in southern Indiana, as well as his zeal, enabled him to help more than three thousand slaves escape. Calvin Fairbanks, who had learned to hate slavery as a student at Oberlin College, began traveling south in 1837 to free slaves by transporting them from Kentucky to freedom. On one occasion, with the assistance of Delia Webster, a white teacher from Vermont, he facilitated the escape of three slaves who posed as her servants. It was said that not one of his fugitives was ever recaptured, although he spent many years in jail because of his work.

Perhaps the most daring white conductor on the Underground Railroad was John Fairfield. Son of a Virginia slaveholding family, Fairfield rejected slavery and chose to live in a free state. Before going north, he helped a slave who was his friend escape to Canada. News of this exploit spread, and other slaves sought his aid. He could not refuse them, and thus began his career as a conductor on the Underground Railroad. He delivered slaves "on order." Blacks in the North and in Canada gave him money and a description of their friends or relatives, and he would deliver them. At times he conveyed as many as fifteen fugitives on a single trip. To gain the confidence of slaveholders, he posed as a slaveholder, a slave trader, or a peddler of eggs and poultry in Louisiana, Alabama, Mississippi, Tennessee, and Kentucky. He proved so convincing in each role that he was seldom suspected of having helped slaves escape. In some cases, he delivered fugitives to Levi Coffin, who then arranged the rest of their journey. In perhaps his greatest triumph, Fairfield conveyed twenty-eight slaves to freedom by organizing them into a funeral procession. While doing his work, he suffered from privation, exposure, and on one occasion was shot, yet he continued until his death in 1860.

The Underground Railroad also relied on many black conductors. Jane Lewis of New Lebanon, Ohio, regularly rowed fugitives across the Ohio River. John Parker, who had purchased himself for $2,000, worked in league with John Rankin and other whites on the Railroad. Josiah Henson, born a slave, escaped with his wife and two children to Canada, learned to read and write, and returned south often to assist slaves in their escape. Once, after traveling to Kentucky by a circuitous route through New York, Pennsylvania, and Ohio to avoid suspicion, he took thirty fugitives out of Kentucky and led them to Toledo within a period of two weeks.

Black Conductors

Elijah Anderson has been called the general superintendent of the Underground Railroad in northwestern Ohio. From 1850 until his death seven years later in the Kentucky state prison, he worked arduously for fugitive slaves. By 1855 he had led more than 1,000 to freedom. John Mason, himself an escaped slave from Kentucky, was one of the most astute conductors. According to William Mitchell, a black missionary in Canada, Mason brought 265 slaves to Mitchell's home in the course of nineteen months. On one occasion Mason was captured and sold back into slavery, but again he made good his escape. In all he led about 1,300 slaves into free territory. William Still of Philadelphia, also a member of the American Anti-Slavery Society, often took fugitives into his home in the 1850s.

Harriet Tubman remains the most legendary conductor on the Underground Railroad. After her solo flight from enslavement as a field hand, she left the safety of the North and returned to Maryland fourteen times between 1849 and 1860 to bring

Harriet Tubman

out family members and other slaves. She worked as a domestic servant in the North in order to raise the money to accomplish this goal time and again. Although frail of body and suffering from recurrent spells of dizziness, she displayed remarkable ingenuity in managing her runaway caravans. She preferred to start the journey on Saturday night, so that she could be well on her way before owners had an opportunity on the following Monday to advertise the escape of their slaves. She also preferred to travel in the winter months, when daylight was shorter. She tolerated no cowardice and threatened to kill any slave who wished to turn back.

Tubman was well known in Philadelphia, New York, and Boston, cities where she frequently delivered escaped slaves. In Philadelphia, Tubman often stayed in the home of the black abolitionist William Still and also in the home of the white abolitionist and women's rights advocate Lucretia Mott. After Congress passed the Fugitive Slave Law in 1850, Tubman preferred to lead escaping slaves all the way to Canada, because, as she explained, she could not trust Uncle Sam with her people any longer. Tubman resided in Ontario, Canada, for periods in the 1850s. African Americans called Harriet Tubman the Moses of her people, and recent scholarly biographies credit her with liberating between seventy and eighty slaves. She is said to have never lost a "passenger."

Another heroic figure in the Underground Railroad was the African Methodist Episcopal minister Jermain W. Loguen. The son of a white master in Nashville, Tennessee, Loguen was sold to his father's brother in Alabama, a cruel and violent man. He fled to the North on horseback in the winter of 1834, crossing the icy Ohio River and ultimately reaching Windsor, Ontario. In 1841 he returned to the United States and settled in Syracuse, New York, where he became a minister and stationmaster on the Underground Railroad. Loguen openly denounced the Fugitive Slave Law of 1850, declaring: "I don't respect this law—I don't fear it—I won't obey it! It outlaws me, and I outlaw it, and the men who attempt to enforce it on me." Jermain Loguen's militant stand led the *Anglo-African Newspaper* to refer to him as the Underground Railroad King—fitting testimony to this outstanding and fearless abolitionist.

Harriet Tubman (1823-191 nurse, spy and scout

Harriet Tubman

Jermain Loguen

The Path to Civil War

Although abolitionism gained momentum in the 1850s, the problem of the expansion of slavery lay at the heart of the turmoil that ultimately led to the Civil War. The decade opened with a controversy over slavery in the newly acquired territory in the Southwest.

The discovery of gold in California in 1848 and the rapid settlement of the territory acquired as a result of the war with Mexico had only intensified the debate over expansion.

Some leaders held that the new territory should be divided into slave and free sections at the 36° 30' parallel, which had been established in 1820 by the Missouri Compromise. The abolitionists and many other northerners wanted slavery excluded altogether from the territories. Still others believed that the question should be decided by the people who lived in the new territories, an approach to the problem popularized by Illinois Democratic Senator Stephen A. Douglas. Finally, some insisted that slavery could not be legally excluded anywhere, a view vigorously advanced by South Carolina's John C. Calhoun, the leading defender of slavery and southern interests in the Senate until his death in 1850.

The issue of fugitive slaves also continued to be highly controversial. In 1842, in *Prigg v. Pennsylvania*, the Supreme Court upheld the fugitive slave law of 1793 and declared that the national government had an obligation to help return fugitive slaves, but it also ruled that local state officials could not be required to assist in the return of fugitives. That decision, although on the surface proslavery, nevertheless led many northern judges and other state officials to refuse to participate in the return of fugitive slaves. Without the help of local officials in the North, southerners claimed they could never recover slaves who had fled to that region.

In 1850, in an effort to diminish intersectional strife and diffuse controversy over the expansion of slavery into the territories, Congress passed the Compromise of 1850. It favored slaveholders' interests by including a stringent fugitive slave law, but it also

The Compromise of 1850

brought California into the Union as a free state. The Compromise's provisions also organized the other western territories without mention of slavery, bailed out Texas from the debts it had run up as an independent republic, settled the Texas-New Mexico border dispute largely but not wholly in favor of Texas (Texans did not win their demand for Santa Fe and Albuquerque), and ended the public sale of slaves in the nation's capital.

Southerners considered enforcement of the new fugitive slave act in 1850 essential for maintaining the Union. After the law was passed, owners of escaped slaves intensified their manhunts, determined to bring back into slavery even those runaways who had lived freely in the North for a long time. Escaped slaves who had once found safety in the North were now forced to look over their shoulders constantly. William Lloyd Garrison wrote in *The Liberator* that Boston had been, for over a week, "thrown into a state of intense excitement by the appearance of two prowling villains, named Hughes and Knight, from Macon, Georgia, for the purpose of seizing William and Ellen Craft, under the infernal Fugitive Slave bill, and carrying them back to the hell of Slavery." Although the Crafts remained free, in 1851 some sixty fugitives were returned, and by 1861 about four hundred had been captured and brought back to the South. But ten thousand or more fugitives still lived, albeit precariously, in the North.

The circumstances of the capture and return of fugitives to slavery served to inflame sectionalism in both the North and South. In February 1851 abolitionists rescued a slave, Shadrach, from a United States marshal in Boston who was preparing to

The Christiana Riot

return him to his owner. The black lawyer Robert Morris, who had served as Charles Sumner's co-counsel on the Boston school desegregation case (the *Roberts* case), was arrested but eventually acquitted of allegedly hindering federal marshals from returning Shadrach to the South. In September of that same year, efforts to thwart the capture of four runaway slaves in Pennsylvania gained widespread attention in what came to be called the Christiana Riot. The incident occurred when plantation owner Edward Gorsuch of Bel Air, Maryland, attempted to retrieve his slave property. Armed with a federal warrant secured in Philadelphia, Gorsuch and a posse of slave catchers descended on the home of former slave, William Parker, who was hiding the fugitives on his farm outside Christiana, near Lancaster County in southern Pennsylvania. African Americans in the area hurried to Parker's to protect the fugitives, and in the melee that followed, Gorsuch was killed. Parker then boldly rode a train to Rochester and met Frederick Douglass, who helped him escape to Canada.

On October 1, less than a month after Christiana, the "Jerry Rescue" ignited passions in Syracuse, New York. Federal officials seized Jerry McHenry, a fugitive slave living in the abolitionist stronghold of Syracuse, in an effort to prove that the law could be enforced in a city known for its abolitionist movement. But the attempt backfired. That night a mob led by abolitionists Jermain Lougen, Samuel J. May, and Gerrit Smith rescued McHenry. After some of the rescuers were later arrested for violating the Fugitive Slave Law of 1850, May, a white minister, defiantly wrote to Senator William Henry Seward (who would later serve as Secretary of State under Abraham Lincoln), stating "that if tried, we should acknowledge our participation in the rescue, and rely upon justifying ourselves to the Jury for resisting the execution of a Law so extremely wicked."

The Compromise of 1850 had hardly proved satisfactory in subduing the controversy over slavery. At the time of its passage, Georgia, Mississippi, Alabama, and South Carolina were seriously considering secession. The publication of *Uncle Tom's Cabin* in 1852 increased the strain on intersectional relations. Harriet Beecher Stowe's novel sold more than 300,000 copies in its first year and was soon dramatized in theaters throughout the North. Its story of blatant cruelty by masters and overseers, its description of slaves' suffering, and its complete condemnation of the South's slaveholding culture won thousands to the abolitionist cause and left southern leaders busy denying the truth of the novel.

The sectional truce unraveled further in 1854 when Congress passed (and President Franklin Pierce signed into law) the Kansas-Nebraska Act, repealing the Missouri Compromise and permitting legislatures in each of those territories to decide whether they would become free or slave states. The passage of the act precipitated a desperate struggle between North and South for the control of Kansas. In the ensuing years, abolitionist and proslavery factions fought and bled for Kansas in a precursor of the Civil War. The Kansas-Nebraska Act galvanized many antislavery leaders to political action to combat the relentless drive of proslavery forces. Northern Whigs, Free Soilers, and Democrats who opposed the act coalesced, and many of these disaffected northerners in the mid-1850s created the Republican Party. This new party, unalterably antislavery, created a platform broad enough to attract northern voters who were indifferent to slavery (but opposed its territorial expansion), as well as antislavery activists. Southerners meanwhile demanded the further extension of slavery into the territories and the reopening of the African slave trade.

The Sectional Truce Unravels

The significance of these trends had hardly become apparent when the Supreme Court in 1857 handed down its decision in *Dred Scott v. Sandford*. The case widened the breach between North and South. Scott, a Missouri slave, had accompanied his master, an army physician, to the free state of Illinois and subsequently to a federal military post in the northern part of the Louisiana Purchase (now Minnesota), from which the Missouri Compromise had excluded slavery. Scott lived in this free territory for four years, even marrying his wife there. Upon his return to Missouri, Scott sued for his freedom on grounds that his residence on free soil had liberated him.

The Dred Scott Decision

The majority of the Court held that Scott was not a citizen and therefore could not bring suit in the courts. Chief Justice Roger B. Taney, speaking for the Court majority, went further by declaring the Missouri Compromise itself unconstitutional: Congress, he ruled, could never ban slavery in the federal territories. Taney went on to declare that even free blacks could never be citizens of the United States and that blacks, whether free or slave, had "no rights that the white man was bound to respect." The decision reinforced the inequality of all blacks.

During these tumultuous times the idea that physical force could be used to defeat slavery became more attractive among some radical black and white abolitionists. It **The Appeal of Force** had certainly circulated in the free black community, with some debate, ever since David Walker's *Appeal* appeared in 1829. Abolitionist William Whipper, who had hidden fugitives in his home in Pennsylvania and financially supported the Underground Railroad, held tenaciously to the Garrisonian ideology of non-violent moral suasion. In a series of articles published in the *Colored American* in September 1837, Whipper insisted that "the practice of non-resistance to physical aggression is not only consistent with reason, but the surest method of obtaining a speedy triumph of the principles of universal peace." Samuel Cornish, the paper's editor, extolled the ideal of universal peace but countered Whipper's argument for moral suasion by noting its impracticability. "We honestly confess," Cornish posited, "that we have yet to learn what virtue there would be in using moral weapons, in defence against a kidnapper or a midnight incendiary with a lighted torch in his hand." In the 1840s, a more peaceful Frederick Douglass had debated the fiery Henry Highland Garnett on the merits of slave rebellion. But by the 1850s, the majority of the black community, including Douglass, had come to the conclusion that violence would be both necessary and inevitable if the fight against slavery was to be won.

Early on, some whites had also voiced support for slave insurrection. In 1841, when slaves aboard the *Creole* revolted on its voyage from Hampton Roads, Virginia, to New Orleans, where they were to be sold, Ohio congressman Joshua Giddings opposed treating them as common criminals and even praised them for seeking freedom. The House of Representatives, shocked by his open defiance of the law, censured Giddings. He immediately resigned, returned home to Ohio, and was soon returned to Congress by his antislavery constituency. The intrepid Giddings later praised other blacks and whites for seeking to abolish slavery and continued to use the floor of the House of Representatives to denounce slavery.

The *Dred Scott* case
Pictured are Dred Scott, his wife Harriett, and two daughters.

In the most radical abolitionist circles, blacks and whites actually attempted to deliver a violent deathblow to slavery. This was certainly the case for those involved in the plot that led to John Brown's raid on Harpers Ferry. White abolitionist John Brown had worked in the cause of freedom for many years. He was among those who resorted to violence during the antislavery battles in Kansas, and he had worked on the Underground Railroad in Missouri. In 1858 and 1859 Brown traveled throughout the North raising money and talking with white and black abolitionists. He enlisted the financial and moral support of Gerrit Smith and received advice as well as moral support from James McCune Smith, Frederick Douglass, and Harriet Tubman. He made plans to attack slaveholders and liberate their slaves, and on Sunday night, October 16, he took steps to realize this goal.

John Brown's Raid

With a small band of less than fifty men, Brown seized the federal arsenal at Harpers Ferry, Virginia (now West Virginia), hoping to secure sufficient ammunition to carry out a large-scale operation against slavery in the South. Immediately the countryside was alerted, and both federal and state troops were dispatched, quickly overwhelming Brown and his men. Among Brown's supporters were five blacks: Lewis Sheridan Leary, Dangerfield Newby, John Anthony Copeland, Shields Green, and Osborn Perry Anderson. Leary and Newby were killed, Copeland and Green were hanged, and Anderson escaped. Brown was captured and put on trial for treason against Virginia.

Brown's raid terrified the South, convincing slaveholders that abolitionists would stop at nothing to wipe out slavery. Rumors of slave insurrections abounded. The entire South moved toward military preparedness. Troops drilled regularly as far south as Georgia, and the militia commanders of most states increased their demand for arms and ammunition.

Brown was convicted and sentenced to death. But before he went to the gallows he told a reporter from the *New York Herald:* "I pity the poor in bondage that have none to help them; that is why I am here; not to gratify any personal animosity, revenge or vindictive spirit. It is my sympathy with the oppressed and wronged that are as good as you and as precious in the sight of God. . . . You may dispose of me easily, but this question is still to be settled—the negro question—the end of that is not yet."

John Brown was hanged on December 2, 1859. African Americans mourned his death and revered his memory. Most whites called him a madman, but a few of the nation's most illustrious white writers and thinkers eulogized him. Henry David Thoreau, Louisa May Alcott, and Ralph Waldo Emerson proclaimed Brown a martyr and hero at a memorial service they organized in Concord, Massachusetts, on the day of his execution. On that occasion, Thoreau described Brown as the embodiment of "transcendent moral greatness," while Emerson compared him to Christ. On another occasion, the champion of nonviolence, William Lloyd Garrison, commended Brown for the courage and moral dignity he displayed in his interview with a reporter after his capture. The American Anti-Slavery Society called for a show of sympathy for Brown by the tolling of bells for one hour in every northern town on the day of his execution.

A little more than a year after Brown's death, the fate of the nation and of slavery would be sealed in blood. The moral authority accorded Brown even by those who rejected his violent means is best illustrated by the statement of Governor John Andrew of Massachusetts, who declared that "John Brown himself was right." Among blacks Brown became a hero, and throughout the Civil War and era of Reconstruction blacks often kept a picture of him in their homes.

Inconsistent Federal Policies

Aiding the Contrabands

Black Troops

Slave Disruption

The Confederate Dilemma

Victory

Civil War 54th Regiment Recruiting Poster

When the government and armies came around to the idea of black men fighting in the war, they actively sought their recruitment with posters such as this, advertising the pay and other benefits.

On March 4, 1861, the day Abraham Lincoln took the oath of office as the sixteenth president of the United States, the nation was rapidly unraveling. He had run on the Republican Party ticket, campaigning against the extension of slavery into the western territories, and his victory had sent shock waves through the South. After Lincoln was elected but before he could be inaugurated, seven states—South Carolina, Mississippi, Florida, Alabama, Georgia, Louisiana, and Texas—had seceded from the Union and forged a new government, the Confederate States of America, with Jefferson Davis, formerly a U.S. senator from Mississippi, elected as its provisional president.

In an effort to prevent further disunion, Lincoln delivered his inaugural address with carefully crafted words, assuring the nation that he had "no purpose, directly or indirectly, to interfere with the institution of slavery in the States where it exists." Lincoln had one overarching goal—to preserve the Union. His caution could not maintain the fragile balance, however, and the moment of rupture came all too soon. In April 1861 the Confederates attacked a federal garrison at Fort Sumter in Charleston's harbor. Lincoln acted promptly to defend the fort and to assert the authority of the United States government in the South. This in turn precipitated the secession of four more slave states—Virginia, North Carolina, Tennessee, and Arkansas—and the nation plunged into civil war.

During the first year of the war the federal government provided no easy answers to questions about slavery and the role of blacks in the defense of the Union. What would be the government's position toward runaway slaves? Who would be responsible for their welfare and condition if they fled to Union lines? Would all slaves be freed, including those in the Border States that remained loyal to the Union: Delaware, Maryland, Kentucky, Missouri, and the western Virginia counties that would soon become West Virginia? Would the army enlist black soldiers? What did the war portend for the future status of black people? Could they become citizens?

African Americans wanted answers to those questions, but Lincoln and the United States government offered no clear or consistent script at the beginning of the war. African Americans themselves expressed little ambiguity as to the centrality of slavery to this sectional conflict and the importance of the Civil War to the abolition of slavery. Thus both slaves and free blacks strove mightily to secure a Union victory, believing the Civil War to be just as much their fight as that of white Americans. For blacks, the fight for the Union would determine not only the inviolable character of the United States but also the real crux of the matter—whether the true character of the nation would be slave or free.

Inconsistent Federal Policies

President Lincoln's initial constitutional, political, and military pronouncements, as well as his desire to maintain the loyalty of the Border States and the many thousands of northerners who opposed militant abolitionism, resulted in a vacillating federal policy toward African Americans. From the onset of the Civil War, a debate over emancipation raged not only in the loyal Border States but also throughout the North. A diverse set of actors opposed Lincoln's policies. Most northern Democrats rejected the idea of black freedom. In fact, most people in the North supported a war to restore the Union but not a military crusade to end slavery. In the southern parts of Ohio, Indiana, Illinois, and Iowa were many residents who had migrated from the South and held southern sympathies—or their forebears had done so. Newspapers in the North hostile to the Lincoln administration complained that it had led the country into a costly war to help undeserving blacks. The *Philadelphia Age* accused abolitionists of causing the war to fulfill "ebony ideals" that stood in stark contrast to the interests of millions of free white men.

Fear of a general exodus of former slaves to the northern cities and a growing competition for jobs heightened the already existing hostilities between white and black workers. In 1862 and 1863, antiblack riots broke out in Illinois, Michigan, Indiana, Ohio, Pennsylvania, and New York. In Brooklyn in August 1862, a group of black women and children who worked in a tobacco factory barely escaped death when white rioters set the factory on fire. Police intervention stopped the fire and saved their lives. The employment of black workers on the Camden and Amboy Railroad in New Jersey caused considerable agitation and threats of reprisals by whites. Longshoremen in Chicago, Detroit, Cleveland, Buffalo, New York, and Boston fought black workers whenever they were brought on the job.

Opposition to Lincoln's Policies

The implementation of a national military draft in 1863 precipitated a four-day riot in New York City. The Philadelphia-based *Christian Recorder*, news organ of the AME Church, covered the riot in detail. The white rioters, described for the most part as immigrants from Ireland, flew into a murderous rage on seeing their names posted on the public draft rolls. A few weeks earlier, black army volunteers had marched through the streets of New York in regiments bound for battlefields. According to one black eyewitness, the sight of blacks in uniform had inflamed the fury of the rioters, who linked the war to black freedom. The mob set ablaze the local draft office and then entered African American neighborhoods, killing individuals and destroying many homes and businesses, including the Colored Orphan Asylum. Northern associations organized to provide relief to the southern freed blacks found themselves having to aid black victims of the New York riot.

For very different reasons, militant abolitionists also opposed Lincoln's policies. They vociferously welcomed the coming of the war, perceiving it as a spiritual reckoning, an apocalyptic moment of social transformation. In her "Battle Hymn of the Republic," abolitionist Julia Ward Howe identified the war with God's purpose, justice, and "terrible swift sword." Yet abolitionists expressed considerable dismay at Lincoln's policies. Even before the onset of war, they criticized Lincoln and the Republican Party for failing to take an uncompromising stand on slavery. Initially supportive of Lincoln, the abolitionist stalwart Frederick Douglass ultimately backed the Radical Abolition party's candidate, Gerrit Smith.

In January 1860, during the presidential campaign, the black abolitionist physician and lawyer John Rock questioned Lincoln's focus only on the extension of slavery rather than on the entire institution of human bondage: "The idea of 'no more slave states' is good. . . . But they [Republicans] do not carry it far enough. I would have them say, 'No more slavery!'" In July of the same year, the Illinois black abolitionist H. Ford Douglas declared, in a lecture in Framingham, Massachusetts: "No party, it seems to me, is entitled to the sympathy of antislavery men, unless that party is willing to extend to the black man all the rights of a citizen. I care nothing about that slavery which wants to make the Territories free, while it is unwilling to extend to me, as a man, in the free States, all the rights of a man."

Abolitionists grew disgruntled in the war's first year because of the lack of a consistent policy toward slaves who escaped to Union lines. Each Union general seemed to use his own discretion. Some declared the fugitives free; others sought to return runaway slaves to their owners. When slaves fled to Fort Monroe, Virginia, in late May 1861, General Benjamin

Butler immediately declared them to be "contraband of war" and ordered that they not be returned to their owners. Aware of the Confederates' use of slaves in erecting military defenses, Butler put the fugitives to work for the Union army. For several months, however, he did not know whether the authorities in Washington endorsed his actions, since his requests to the War Department for policy clarification were met with evasive replies. Other military officers simply refused to accept fugitive slaves. Some, such as General Henry Halleck, who was stationed in the West, ordered slaves returned to their owners. Similarly, in July 1861 General Winfield Scott wrote to Brigadier General Irvin McDowell, in the name of President Lincoln, asking him to allow Virginia owners to cross the Potomac and recover runaways who had taken refuge behind Union lines.

In the summer of 1861 Congress tried to resolve the situation. In passing the first Confiscation Act on August 6, 1861, and the second Confiscation Act a year later, on July 17, 1862, the nation's lawmakers sanctioned the Union army's seizure of any rebel property, including slaves, since they could be used for the purpose of aiding or abetting insurrection against the United States. Such property **The Confiscation Acts** became the lawful subject of prize and capture wherever found. In short, slave "contrabands" were to become free. The "contraband" matter caused Lincoln grave concern. As commander in chief of the armed forces, he discouraged declarations of freedom in this early period of the war and at times restrained enthusiastic officers who emancipated slaves without his authorization. For example, after the First Confiscation Act was passed Lincoln did not endorse General John C. Frémont's sweeping proclamation of martial law and military emancipation for slaves of disloyal owners in Missouri. Instead, Lincoln ordered Frémont to modify the policy to include far more restrictions to freedom.

Group of contrabands at Foller's house, Cumberland, Virginia, 1862

Lincoln also countered the emancipation plans of the Union navy when it gained control of the islands off the South Carolina and Georgia coast in late 1861 and early 1862. Reports of the Union's conquest of these Sea Islands described the slaves as "wild" with joy and boldly carrying off clothing, furniture, and other portable items from the plantation houses. In May 1862 General David Hunter proclaimed slaves in Georgia, Florida, and South Carolina "forever free." Lincoln responded by nullifying Hunter's order. To Lincoln, Hunter's call for immediate and uncompensated emancipation risked losing the loyalty of the slave-owning Border States.

Contemplating a more uniform and decisive emancipation policy in the spring of 1862, Lincoln recommended that the United States government cooperate with any state plan for **Lincoln's Plan** gradually emancipating its slaves and compensating slave owners. He had advocated gradual emancipation for over a decade, and now with the nation at war he pleaded with the congressional delegations from the slaveholding Border States to support his policy. However, Lincoln's recommendation failed—denounced by both sides of the slavery debate. Lincoln's idea for compensated emancipation took hold only in the District of Columbia, when in April 1862 Congress passed a law that called for payment not to exceed $300 for each freed slave.

A significant feature of this early presidential emancipation plan was an appropriation of $100,000 to support the voluntary emigration of freedpeople to Haiti and Liberia. To Lincoln, colonization seemed almost as important as emancipation. In August 1862 he called a group of prominent free blacks to the White House to urge them to support colonization. "Your race suffer greatly, many of them, by living among us, while ours suffer from your presence," Lincoln told the free black leaders. "In a word we suffer on each side. If this is admitted, it affords a reason why we should be separated." Largely at Lincoln's suggestion, the State Department inquired of South American, Caribbean, and African governments about the possibility of colonizing black Americans. Only two replies were entirely satisfactory to Lincoln; they suggested that colonies of freedpeople could be established in Panama (which was then part of Colombia) and in the Caribbean. Until the very end of the war, Lincoln remained hopeful that colonization would remove at least a portion of the freed population from the United States.

As the war dragged on into the summer of 1862, Lincoln began to consider seriously the idea of an executive order of emancipation for all slaves in the rebel states. For two days, on **Preliminary Proclamation** July 21 and 22, the cabinet debated Lincoln's draft of an emancipation proclamation. The draft warned slave owners in the Confederate States of the penalties under the Confiscation Act and urged them to free their slaves forthwith, especially given the possibility of compensation. The proclamation reversed Lincoln's position on black troops and called for the enlistment of black soldiers. Most important, the proclamation stipulated a date for the government's emancipation of all slaves in the rebel states. Only two cabinet members, William Seward and Salmon Chase, agreed with Lincoln's proposed proclamation, and Seward strongly advised him not to issue it until the military situation became more favorable to the Union.

Rumor and speculation about the president's preliminary proclamation gave the date for emancipation sometime in August 1862. When this did not occur, advocates of emancipation were sorely disappointed. The journalist Horace Greeley, writing in the *New York Tribune,* urged Lincoln to proclaim emancipation. Several antislavery delegations called on him. Ironically, the president told one of them that he could not free slaves under the

Constitution, because the law could not be enforced in the rebel states. Any proclamation would be about as effective, from Lincoln's point of view, "as the Pope's bull [decree] against the comet." Lincoln would soon change his mind. The Union victory at Antietam on September 17, 1862, gave Lincoln the propitious moment that he awaited for revisiting and acting on the idea of emancipation. Five days after the victory, Lincoln issued his preliminary emancipation proclamation. In it, he revived the possibility of compensated emancipation and declared that he would continue to encourage the voluntary colonization of blacks "upon this continent or elsewhere." Convinced the time had come for more direct action, Lincoln ordered in the Emancipation Proclamation that on January 1, 1863, "all persons held as slaves within any State, or designated part of the State, the people whereof shall be in rebellion against the United States, shall be then, thenceforward, and forever free."

Emancipation Proclamation

The Proclamation was essentially a military directive and not a ringing declaration of liberation. Decorative copies such as this circulated for many decades after the Civil War.

The general reaction in the North to Lincoln's proclamation was unfavorable. Many whites felt that the war's original purpose of saving the Union had shifted to that of freeing the slaves. Some soldiers resigned rather than participate in such a struggle. The so-called Peace Democrats, who advocated making peace with the Confederacy, accused the administration of wasting the lives of white citizens in a costly abolitionist war. Abolitionists hesitated to condemn Lincoln's proposed proclamation, since it was certainly better than nothing, but to them it seemed too little compensation for all the struggles and sacrifices that they had made for more than a generation. Furthermore, they wondered, what would happen to slaves if the war ended early and there were no rebellious states on the first of January 1863? Such a prospect sent cold shivers down every ardent abolitionist's spine. The popular reaction was evident in the November 1862 elections. Republicans kept their majority in Congress, but Democrats won in many northern communities and gained substantially in both the House and Senate.

In the month approaching January 1, 1863, the suspense heightened as to the outcome of Lincoln's preliminary proclamation. On the night of December 31, 1862, blacks and whites gathered separately and together in churches in many parts of the country, holding watch meetings where they offered prayers of thanksgiving for the deliverance of the slaves. When the clock struck midnight at Tremont Temple **The Emancipation Proclamation** in Boston, Frederick Douglass, William Wells Brown, William Lloyd Garrison, Harriet Beecher Stowe, Charles B. Ray, and other fighters for freedom listened joyfully as the president's final Emancipation Proclamation was read, declaring freedom for more than three-fourths of the American slaves.

Although the Emancipation Proclamation instantly assumed significance as one of the great documents of history, the inescapable reality was that freedom did not come swiftly or comprehensively. President Lincoln declared slaves free only in the rebel states, not in the four loyal slave states. More than 800,000 African Americans remained enslaved in these Border States. Nor was the freeing of slaves in the seceded states a straightforward matter.

Rebel slave owners hardly felt duty-bound by Lincoln's decree, and they went to great lengths to keep information about the Emancipation Proclamation away from their slaves. Hundreds of thousands, if not millions, of slaves in the Confederacy did not learn about the president's proclamation until months after January 1, 1863. In areas isolated from the military front, like southwest Georgia and Texas, freedom came only at the war's end. Only then could officers from the Bureau of Refugees, Freedmen, and Abandoned Lands (better known as the Freedmen's Bureau), established by Congress in March 1865, declare and enforce black freedom. Finally, the proclamation did not free the slaves residing in those pockets within the Confederate States loyal to the Union from the beginning or those reconquered by the Union army: the forty-eight counties of Virginia that later in 1863 became the new state of West Virginia; thirteen parishes in Louisiana, including the city of New Orleans; and seven counties in eastern Virginia, including the cities of Norfolk and Portsmouth and the outskirts of Washington, D.C.

President Lincoln left little doubt that military expediency had been the primary justification for the Emancipation Proclamation. In its last paragraph he asserted that emancipation was "sincerely believed to be an act of justice, warranted by the Constitution upon military necessity." And the Proclamation's desired impact had surely been achieved by sowing confusion in the South and depriving the Confederacy of much of its valuable labor force. Union army officer Colonel Thomas Wentworth Higginson vividly portrayed the military impact of the Emancipation Proclamation in a February 1, 1863 report on the success of his raid along the Florida-Georgia border: "I was interested to observe that the news of the President's proclamation produced a marked effect upon them, and in one case it was of the greatest service to us in securing the hearty aid of a guide, who was timid and distrustful until he heard that he was legally free, after which he aided us glad and came away with us. . . ."

Although they recognized the limitations of the Emancipation Proclamation, African Americans understood its larger meaning and thus perceived January 1, 1863, to be a historic day of freedom. Many thought, as an editorial in the AME *Christian*

The Thirteenth Amendment

Recorder observed, that the proclamation sounded the death-knell for the institution of slavery and that all slaves would be eventually freed because of it. As a humanitarian document, it gave hope to millions of blacks that a better day lay ahead. As a diplomatic document, the Emancipation Proclamation succeeded in rallying to the northern cause many thousands of British and other European liberals and believers in democracy, as well as workers anxious to see laboring people throughout the world gain their freedom. For all such persons, Abraham Lincoln would forever after be the "Great Emancipator."

This image of Lincoln solidified as the war progressed, since he actively worked with members of Congress to push through legislation to abolish slavery once and for all. More than a year before the war's end, three Republican congressmen had proposed ending slavery by constitutional amendment. Although most Southern Democrats no longer sat in the United States Congress, the idea of such an amendment did not sail smoothly through both houses. The Senate passed the amendment in April 1864 by a vote of 38 to 6, but northern Democrats in the House of Representatives thwarted the required two-thirds majority for passage. It is Lincoln who is credited with playing the crucial role in mustering support for the amendment. In January 1865, as the Civil War continued, the proposed amendment passed by a vote of 119 to 56 compared to its earlier defeat by a 93 to 65 count. On February 1, 1865, President Lincoln signed a Joint Resolution, submitting the proposed Thirteenth Amendment to the states, but he would not live to see its ratification.

Aiding the Contrabands

The transition from slavery to freedom during the war years presented serious challenges both to the Union army and to the destitute blacks who poured over federal lines by the thousands. Trained to fight wars, most army officers were ill equipped to ensure the fair treatment of blacks, much less attend to the basic survival of fugitive slaves. The federal government appointed superintendents of "Negro affairs," whose duties included taking a census of the black population, contracting out black labor, protecting those who had hired themselves out to white employers, making sure that blacks had the necessities of life, and distributing among the ex-slaves land set aside by the government for their use. Some superintendents performed their duties conscientiously, but others did little to address black poverty and even facilitated exploitive and oppressive labor conditions.

In the months leading up to the Emancipation Proclamation, General Ulysses S. Grant appointed John Eaton to take charge of all fugitives in western Tennessee. In November 1862, Eaton set up a special camp for blacks at Grand Junction, Tennessee, where he supervised the hiring out of these ex-slaves, **General Saxton's Plan** leased abandoned plantations to whites who hired them, and saw to it that former slaves were paid for their work. In Louisiana, General Benjamin Butler leased blacks for $10 a month to loyal planters.

In December 1862, General Rufus Saxton, the head of the Department of the South, sought to reduce the confusion involving the employment and relief of fugitives by issuing an order for a general plan to be followed everywhere. Under this plan, abandoned lands (that is, plantations from which Confederate owners had fled when Union troops approached) were to be used for the benefit of former slaves. Black families received two acres for each working hand and were required to plant corn and potatoes for their own use with tools furnished by the federal government. Plowing was to be done by those assigned to that task, and all blacks were required to raise a certain amount of cotton for government use.

This federal policy initially led slaves to believe that the abandoned plantations might be made available to them as homesteaders. In January 1865, during the last few months of the war, General William Tecumseh Sherman's Special Order No. 15 distributed forty-acre parcels of land to slave families on the South Carolina Sea Islands, but the federal government eventually reclaimed the land and either returned it to the former owners or sold parcels to private investors.

Relief almost always proved difficult because of the small amount of land available for redistribution to blacks. In his report in 1864, Rev. Horace James, the Superintendent of Blacks for the Department in North Carolina, stated that "we control indeed a broad area of navigable waters, and command the **Challenges to Effective Relief** approaches from the sea, but have scarcely room enough on land to spread our tents upon." Although many of the freedpeople assumed that the plantations and other areas confiscated by the Union—the land on which they had labored as slaves without pay—would be eventually parceled out and distributed to them, few of them actually became landowners. The federal government had already sold to private parties much of the land that it was holding for nonpayment of taxes. Eastern capitalists and philanthropists bought most of the available land in South Carolina, and frequently these new owners had little interest in the plight of blacks.

Another difficulty in providing for blacks who lived behind Union lines arose because of the contest between the Treasury Department and the War Department over which of these executive agencies had primary authority to administer the affairs of black people. Although the secretary of war wanted the Treasury to control all confiscated property except that used by the military, officers in the field believed that they could best handle everything. While the controversy raged during 1863 and 1864, blacks suffered from the lack of any coordinated supervision. In 1864 a Union official admitted that mortality in black camps was "frightful" and that the "most competent judges place it at not less than twenty-five percent in the last two years."

The federal relief policy for former slaves developed so slowly that private citizens, both black and white, undertook to supplement it. Northern newspapers, religious groups, and **Private Relief** multiple organizations of blacks and whites alike told of the hunger and exposure of the "contrabands" and sought to provide relief to the newly freed black men, women, and children. African Americans organized their own contraband-aid societies in Boston, New York, Washington, D.C., Philadelphia, Baltimore, Cincinnati, Chicago, Cleveland, Detroit, and other northern cities. The National Convention of Colored Men, which met at Syracuse in October 1864, focused on the plight of southern blacks during the war, discussing the condition of freed slaves with respect to employment, enfranchisement, and effective relief efforts. White church-based organizations, such as the United States Christian Commission and the American Missionary Association, joined in providing relief for blacks. Collections were taken up, clothing and food solicited, and agents sent south to minister to the needs of ex-slaves.

In the sphere of education, private agencies made perhaps the greatest contribution to helping former slaves adjust to their new free status. Although the federal government had **Education** no educational policy toward former slaves, it was not averse to cooperating with philanthropic organizations. Private ventures in educating blacks began in 1861 when Lewis Tappan, the veteran white abolitionist and treasurer of the American Missionary Association (AMA), wrote General Butler to offer the services of his organization. Butler welcomed such aid, and Rev. Lewis C. Lockwood was sent to Hampton, Virginia, to develop a program for the hundreds of contrabands who had gathered in nearby Fort Monroe.

Blacks were already teachers to the contrabands in the summer of 1861—for example, escaped slave Peter Herbert and free black Mary S. Peake were each teaching forty to fifty students when the American Missionary Association representatives arrived in the Hampton area of Virginia. Historian Robert Engs notes that Mary Peake and her husband Thomas Peake were respected members of Hampton's black community before the war. Thomas Peake worked as a servant at the Hygeia Hotel and for the Union Army, while Mary Peake, a seamstress, started a school for slaves and free blacks as early as 1851—in violation of Virginia law at the time. The first black teacher hired by the American Missionary Association, Peake received payment beginning on September 17, 1861.

Mary Peake was the most revered of the teachers. While very ill in January 1862, Peake continued to teach, holding classes for 53 children from noon to midday and 20 adults in

Window in Time

Charlotte Forten on Thanksgiving Day, November 27, 1862

"This morning, a large number, superintendents, teachers, and many of the freed people, assembled in the Baptist Church. Gen. Saxton, and his brother, Captain Saxton, were present. The church was crowded, and there were many outside, at the doors and windows, who could not get in. It was a sight that I shall never soon forget—that crowd of eager, happy black faces, from which the shadow of slavery had passed forever. "FOREVER FREE! FOREVER FREE!" All the time those magical words were singing themselves in my soul, and never in my life before have I felt so deeply and sincerely grateful to God. It was a moment of exultation, such as comes but seldom in one's life, that in which I sat among the people assembled on this lovely day to thank God for the most blessed and glorious of all gifts."

Ray Allen Billington, "A Social Experiment: The Port Royal Journal of Charlotte L. Forten, 1862–1863." *The Journal of Negro History,* Vol. 35, No. 3 (Jul., 1950)

the evening. She taught reading, writing, spelling, arithmetic, and biblical precepts. She died of tuberculosis on February 22, 1862. Inspired by her life, Lewis Lockwood wrote the short biography *Mary S. Peake: The Colored Teacher at Fortress Monroe,* which was published in 1863.

The AMA continued to employ other African American teachers. For example, in November 1861 Lockwood wrote that he had established a "good school at the Fortress [Monroe] under the instruction of Mrs. Bailey, assisted by Miss Jennings," both African American. AMA schools for blacks operated in Hampton, Norfolk, Portsmouth, and Newport News, Virginia (all of which were controlled by Union forces), as well as on several plantations.

The Union occupation of Port Royal, South Carolina, in early 1862 ushered in a historic social experiment to educate freedpeople. In June of that year, General Rufus Saxton assumed command of the Port Royal area, including the Sea Islands. Under Saxton's direction, former slaves began to realize both the privileges and the duties of freedom. Laura Towne, a white abolitionist and physician from Philadelphia, answered the call for educated teachers among the freedpeople on St. Helena Island and established the Penn Normal, Industrial and Agricultural School. In October 1862, Charlotte Forten, the daughter of black Philadelphia sailmaker James Forten, joined Towne and another white teacher in the school. Forten's journal and letters to abolitionist friends in the Northeast bring to life the thrilling early moments of freedom, the recruitment of black soldiers, and the great passion of the ex-slaves to gain literacy.

Gradually education for blacks was extended to most areas occupied by Union troops. In 1863 General Banks established a system of public education under the Department of the Gulf, and a Board of Education for Freedmen supervised the schools. The enthusiasm of northern philanthropic associations for the education of blacks would continue to grow after the war. Southern blacks themselves also founded schools. In Natchez, Mississippi, for example, black women started three schools during the war. In Savannah, African Americans founded two large schools and their own board of education. Most schools for blacks had poor facilities, inadequate supplies, and too few teachers, but African Americans attended them in ever-growing numbers and would continue to do so after the war ended. The people responsible for establishing schools—northerners and southerners, whites and blacks—made a most significant contribution to the realization of freedom.

Black Troops

From the beginning of the war, large numbers of northern blacks rushed to offer their services to the Union army, but initially they found their patriotism rebuffed. White military officials offered a variety of reasons for refusing to enlist blacks. Some believed blacks to be a servile race and thus cowardly. Many held to the racist assumption that blacks were unfit to be soldiers and would easily surrender information and even weapons to the enemy. Army officers questioned whether black soldiers would undermine the morale of white soldiers. One Pennsylvania soldier predicted that "the southern people are rebels to the government but they are white and God never intended blacks to put white people down."

Some argued that black soldiers would return from war demanding rights of citizenship that would be difficult to deny. "If you make him the instrument by which your battles are fought, the means by which your victories are won," warned a congressman from Ohio, "you must treat him as a victor is entitled to be treated, with all decent and becoming respect." Initially the North was not willing to chance the possibility of enlisting African American soldiers who would claim the rights of citizens.

Challenges to Black Recruitment

Some whites feared the consequences of arming blacks. Failing to be accepted as enlisted recruits, blacks bided their time and did whatever they could to assist. In New York, they formed a military club and drilled regularly, until the police stopped them. Several Philadelphia blacks offered to go into the South and organize slave revolts, but this action was unthinkable to the federal government. In the nation's capital, blacks repeatedly requested that the War Department accept them into the army. At a meeting in Boston, African Americans passed a resolution urging the government to enlist them:

> Our feelings urge us to say to our countrymen that we are ready to stand by and defend our Government as the equals of its white defenders; to do so with "our lives, our fortunes, and our sacred honor," for the sake of freedom, and as good citizens; and we ask you to modify your laws, that we may enlist,—that full scope may be given to the patriotic feelings burning in the colored man's breast.

The government's early opposition to using black soldiers provoked criticism from abolitionists, who agitated

Company E, Fourth United States Colored Infantry
More than 186,000 blacks fought under the Union flag during the Civil War. Company E was one of the detachments, assigned to guard the nation's capitol.

for arming blacks. William Lloyd Garrison (despite being a pacifist) and Wendell Phillips declared that it was cruel to deprive blacks of the opportunity to fight for the freedom of their brothers and sisters. White northerners who were not abolitionists objected to fighting for the freedom of blacks when blacks themselves were not fighting. However, many citizens, including some soldiers, did not want blacks to wear the uniform of the Union, feeling that such a privilege should be reserved for those whose citizenship was unquestioned. Lincoln feared that the Border States would resist a policy of arming blacks and that most northern whites would be alienated. He therefore gave no serious consideration to arming them until the spring of 1862. But at that point the unfavorable course of the war dictated new policies.

Responding to considerable pressure from officers in the field, in October 1861, the secretary of war had authorized Brigadier General Thomas W. Sherman to "employ fugitive slaves in such services as they may be fitted for . . . with such organization as you may deem most beneficial to the service; this, however, not being a general arming of them for military service." Sherman adamantly refused to arm former slaves, preferring to use the contrabands in service roles such as cooking and laundering, digging ditches, and burying the dead.

A Change in Policy

In May 1862, however, San Francisco black abolitionist J. Madison Bell addressed the importance of arming escaped slaves rather than limiting their manpower. In his 1862 poem "What Shall We Do with the Contrabands," Bell wrote:

> Shall we arm them? Yes, arm them! Give to each man
> A rifle, a musket, a cutlass or sword;
> Then on to the charge! Let them war in the van
> Where each may confront with his merciless lord.
> And purge from their race, in the eyes of the brave,
> The stigma and scorn now attending the slave.

In May 1862, General David Hunter, who led Union troops occupying the southeastern coastal areas, issued a call for blacks to serve in the army, and within a few months he organized former slaves into the First South Carolina Volunteer Regiment. Almost immediately, Lincoln told Hunter to disband this unit, and the men were sent home unpaid and dissatisfied. However, Congress's Confiscation Act of 1862 had clarified not only the contraband problem but also the enlistment of black soldiers by empowering the president to "employ as many persons of African descent as he may deem necessary and proper for the suppression of this rebellion."

August 1862 marked a significant shift in Lincoln's policy toward black enlistment. Early in that month, Lincoln continued to reject black troops. On August 4, he refused to enlist two regiments of black soldiers from Indiana, stating that "to arm negroes would turn 50,000 bayonets from the loyal Border States against us. . . ." But as the Union army faced mounting deaths and desertions, as well as declining enlistments among whites that summer, Lincoln reconsidered his refusal to accept black troops. The Union's difficulties in battle and the Confederacy's use of slave and free black labor to construct its own defensive fortifications made increasingly clear the need for more Union recruits.

The First Black Soldiers

Bringing black troops into the military became a more viable solution to Lincoln as the month of August wore on, and on August 25 he authorized the War Department to reorganize Hunter's South Carolina regiment under General Rufus Saxton. By November, the regiment was fully mustered as the First South Carolina Volunteers under the leadership of the Massachusetts abolitionist Colonel Thomas Wentworth Higginson. "Their superiority," Higginson wrote of these troops, "lies simply in the fact that they know the country, which white troops do not. . . . Instead of leaving their homes and families to fight, they are fighting for their homes and families; and they show the resolution and sagacity which a personal purpose gives. It would have been madness to attempt with the bravest white troops what I have successfully accomplished with black ones."

In the autumn of 1862, black enlistments swelled in number. In Louisiana, free men of color, many of mixed French and African descent, appealed to Benjamin Butler to join the Union army. The men were already organized into the Louisiana Native Guards, a legally recognized unit of the state militia. Ironically, the Native Guards had been established in 1861 under the Confederacy, but their service had been limited to drills, parades, and flag ceremonies. Some of these creole-of-color soldiers, such as F. Ernest Dumas and André Cailloux, had even owned slaves. The tide turned, however, with Butler's conquest and occupation of New Orleans in the spring of 1862, and in late May officers of the Native Guards approached Butler with the request to join the Union forces. Butler noted their French speech and light skins, describing the darkest among them as similar in complexion to the late senator Daniel Webster.

The distrustful Butler at first refused their offer, but by August, especially after a Confederate attack on nearby Baton Rouge, he came to see the wisdom of enlisting the Native Guards and of making a broad-based public appeal for black troops. Large numbers of blacks responded to the call, and in September the first regiment of the Native Guards was fully mustered into service. By November 1862, three regiments of Native Guards, consisting of antebellum free men and newly freed slaves, had been organized, although Lincoln would not grant final sanction until after Butler's departure from New Orleans.

Machinery for the recruitment of black soldiers in the South gained momentum during the spring of 1863 with the assignment of Adjutant General Lorenzo Thomas to the Military Division in the Mississippi Valley for the "conduct of all matters referring to the organization of Negro troops." Eventually, blacks volunteered for military service in the Union army not only in federally occupied parts of the Confederate South but also in Missouri, Kansas, and Maryland.

In the North, black community leaders and newspapers championed the importance of the black soldier to the Union cause. At rallies in Boston, New York, and Philadelphia, speakers urged black enlistment, and the indomitable Frederick Douglass sent two of his sons to the war. From its beginning, Douglass had beseeched Lincoln to permit black troops, arguing that "this is no time to fight with one hand, when both are needed; that this is no time to fight only with your white hand, and allow your black hand to remain tied. . . ." In the fall of 1863, eight northern states had black regiments.

The enlistment of blacks proved to be a notable success. By the end of the war, more than 186,000 had enrolled in the Union army. More than 134,000 came from the slave states, and it

The Success of Black Enlistment

was the enlistment of black soldiers in the South that helped to fill the draft quotas of the northern states. The total figure of black soldiers who served may have been even larger than the official number, for some contemporaries insisted that many mulattoes served in white regiments without being designated as blacks.

Black troops, called United States Colored Troops to distinguish them from white units, were organized into regiments of light and heavy artillery, cavalry, infantry, and engineers.

Window in Time

Black Soldiers

In June 1863, the white commander of the Ninth Regiment of Louisiana Volunteers, Captain M. M. Miller, wrote to his aunt in Galena, Illinois, describing the conduct of his black soldiers during a bayonet attack by Confederate troops at Millikin's Bend, a Union stronghold on the Mississippi River near Vicksburg:

Dear Aunt: We were attacked here on June 7, about 3 o'clock in the morning, by a brigade of Texas troops about 2,500 in number. We had about 600 men to withstand them—500 of them Negroes. . . . Our regiment had about 300 men in the fight. We had about 50 men killed in the regiment and 80 wounded; so you can judge of what part of the fight my company sustained. I have never felt more grieved and sick at heart than when I saw how my brave soldiers had been slaughtered. . . . I never more wish to hear the expression, "the niggers won't fight." Come with me 100 yards from where I sit, and I can show you the wounds that cover the bodies of 16 as brave, loyal and patriotic soldiers as ever drew bead on a Rebel.

The enemy charged us so close that we fought with our bayonets, hand to hand. . . . It was a horrible fight, the worst I was ever engaged in—not even excepting Shiloh. The enemy cried "No quarter!" but some of them were very glad to take it when made prisoners. . . .

What few men I have left seem to think much of me because I stood up with them in the fight. I can say for them that I never saw a braver company of men in my life. Not one of them offered to leave his place until ordered to fall back; in fact very few ever did fall back. . . . So they fought and died defending the cause that we revere. They met death coolly, bravely—not rashly did they expose themselves, but all were steady and obedient to orders.

Source: McPherson, James M. *The Negro's Civil War: How American Negroes Felt and Acted During the War for the Union.* Urbana, IL: University of Illinois Press, 2003.

For the most part, white officers led them, joined by some black noncommissioned officers. Initially, securing white officers for black outfits proved difficult, because regular army men generally opposed having blacks in the service. West Pointers were especially averse to the idea of commanding black troops and ostracized fellow graduates who undertook the task. Other officers, however, enthusiastically assumed the responsibility and made such reputations for themselves and their men that it became easier to persuade white officers to command black units toward the close of the war. White officers who proved to be outstanding leaders included Colonel Thomas Wentworth Higginson of the First South Carolina Volunteers, Colonel Robert Gould Shaw of the Fifty-fourth Massachusetts Regiment, and General N. P. Banks, who for a time commanded the First and Third Louisiana Native Guards.

Some blacks held commissions in the Union army. Two regiments of General Butler's Corps d'Afrique were entirely staffed by black officers, including Major F. E. Dumas and **Black Officers** Captain P. B. S. Pinchback. Captain H. Ford Douglas and First Lieutenant W. D. Matthews led an independent battery at Lawrence, Kansas, and the 104th Regiment had two black officers, Major Martin R. Delany and Captain O. S. B. Wall. Among the black surgeons who received commissions were Alexander T. Augusta of the 7th Regiment and John V. DeGrasse of the 35th. Black soldiers Charles B. Purvis, Alpheus Tucker, John Rapier, William Ellis, Anderson Abbott, and William Powell served as hospital surgeons in Washington, D.C. Among the black chaplains with commissions were Henry McNeal Turner, William Hunter, James Underdue, Williams Waring, Samuel Harrison, William Jackson, and John R. Bowles.

In addition to serving as soldiers, ex-slaves aided the Union cause tremendously by sharing their knowledge of the southern terrain. Organized into raiding parties, they penetrated **Blacks as Spies and Scouts** Confederate lines to destroy fortifications and supplies. Since they knew the southern countryside better than most white soldiers and could pass themselves off as slaves, they were used extensively as spies and scouts. White officers relied on information secured by black spies.

One such spy was the veteran slave rescuer Harriet Tubman, who reconnoitered many points along the eastern seaboard. Tubman later recalled a unique situation in which she found herself handicapped by women's clothing during a raid on the Combahee River. The experience convinced her to ask a friend for bloomers, the billowy pantlike women's apparel that would become controversial as "unfeminine" attire after the war. Tubman's dictated letter brings an interesting perspective to the war experience:

> In our late expedition up the Combahee River, in coming on
> board the boat, I was carrying two pigs for a poor sick woman,
> who had a child to carry, and the order "double quick" was given,
> and I started to run, stepped on my dress, it being rather long,
> and fell and tore it almost off, so that when I got on board the
> boat there was hardly any thing left of it but shreds. I made up
> my mind then I would never wear a long dress on another expedi-
> tion of the kind, but would have a bloomer as soon as I could get
> it. So please make this known to the ladies if you will, for I expect
> to have use for it very soon, probably before they can get it to me.

Susie King Taylor

Harriet Tubman also served the Union as a cook, laundress, and nurse. Such jobs were held by many black women, often contrabands themselves, who worked in contraband camps, **Women's Service** hospitals, and on naval vessels. Susie King Taylor escaped from slavery and recounted her experiences in her memoir *Reminiscences of My Life in Camp with the 33d United States Colored Troops* (1902). She, too, worked in multiple roles, serving this South Carolina regiment as a cook and laundress, as well as a nurse, the role for which she is primarily remembered. Donning her army nurse uniform, she cared for the wounded and dying. She also taught the soldiers to read, and they taught her to shoot a musket.

The field of nursing itself was transformed during the Civil War, since up to then military nurses had been exclusively male. The role of white women in the United States Sanitary Commission and of its leader, Dorothea Dix, are relatively well known; but very little known

Window in Time

Harriet Tubman Claims her Pension

D.10. Affadavit Testimony in Pension Claim Case (1898)

I am about 75 years of age. I was born and raised in Dorchester County, Md. My maiden name was Araminta Ross. Some time prior to the late War of the Rebellion I married John Tubman who died in the State of Maryland on the 30th day of September 1867. I married Nelson Davis, a soldier of the late war, on the 18th day of March 1869, at Auburn, N.Y.

I furnished the original papers in my claim to one Charles P. Wood, then of Auburn, N.Y., who died several years ago. Said Wood made copies of said original papers which are herewith annexed. I was informed by said Wood that he sent said original papers to one James Barrett, an attorney on 4½ Street, Washington, D.C., and I was told by the wife of said Barrett that she handed the original papers to the Hon. C.D. MacDougall, then a member of the House of Representatives.

My claim against the U.S. is for three years service as a nurse and cook in hospitals, and as commander of several men (eight or nine) as scouts during the late War of the Rebellion, under direction and orders of Edwin M. Stanton, Secretary of War, and of several Generals.

I claim for my services above named the sum of eighteen hundred dollars. The annexed copies have recently been read over to me and are true to the best of my knowledge, information and belief. (Harriet Tubman, affidavit, January 1, 1898).

Source: *Harriet Tubman: The Life and the Life Stories,* ed. Jean M. Humez (Madison, Wisconsin, University of Wisconsin Press, 2004), page 287

are the hundreds of black women who served in multiple capacities in hospitals in Tennessee, Illinois, Arkansas, Georgia, Washington, D.C, Virginia, Mississippi, and South Carolina. For example, the black naval nurse Ann Stokes served on the U.S.S. *Red Rover* from her enlistment in Memphis on January 1, 1863, to her honorable discharge on October 25, 1864. The duration of Stokes's assignment strongly suggests that she and the other black women employed on the ship were present during the final siege of Vicksburg, Mississippi. In July 1890, after Congress passed legislation that allowed nurses to claim pensions for their Civil War service, Stokes applied for and eventually won a Navy Invalid Pension, for her own service.

Black soldiers also performed a variety of duties. They built fortifications along the coasts and up the rivers. Much to their own consternation and that of their white officers, they were often assigned to menial tasks instead of

Black Soldiers' Service

Window in Time

A Black Soldier Seeks Equal Military Pay

Morris Island, Department of the South, September 28, 1863
Your Exelency Abraham Lincoln:

Your Exelency will pardon the presumption of an humble individual like myself, in addressing you, but the earnest Solicitation of my Comrades in Arms, besides the genuine interest felt by myself in the matter is my excuse, for placing before the Executive head of the nation our Common Grievance: On the 6th of the last Month, the Paymaster of the department informed us, that if we would decide to receive the sum of $10 (ten dollars) per month, he would come and pay us that sum [white soldiers were paid $13]. . . . Now the main question is, Are we *Soldiers* or are we LABOURERS. We are fully armed, and equipped, have done all the various Duties, pertaining to a Soldiers life, have conducted ourselves, to the complete satisfaction of General Officers, who were, if any, prejudiced *against* us, but who now accord us all the encouragement, and honour due us: have shared the perils, the Labor, of Reducing the first stronghold, that flaunted a Traitor Flag: and more, Mr. President, Today, the Anglo Saxon Mother, Wife, or Sister, are not alone, in tears for departed Sons, Husbands, and Brothers. The patient Trusting Descendants of Africs Clime, have dyed the ground with blood, in defense of the Union, and Democracy. Men too your Excellency, who know in a measure, the cruelties of the Iron heel of oppression, which in years gone by, by the very Power, their blood is now being spilled to Maintain, ever ground them in the dust. But When the war trumpet sounded o'er the land, when men knew not the Friend from the Traitor, the Black man laid his life at the Altear of the Nation,—and he was refused. When the Arms of the Union, were beaten, in the first year of the War, And the Executive called [for] more food, for its ravaging maws, again the black man begged, the privilege of Aiding his Country in her need, to be again refused. And now, he is in the War: and how has he conducted himself? Let their dusky forms, rise up, out of the mires of James Island [South Carolina], and give the answer. Let the rich mould against Wagners parapets [South Carolina] be upturned, and there will be found an Eloquent answer. Obedient and patient, and Solid as a wall are they, all we lack, is a paler hue, and a better acquaintance with the Alphabet. Now your Excellency We have done a Soldiers Duty. Why can't we have a Soldiers pay? . . .

We appeal to You, Sir: as the Executive of the nation, to have us Justly Dealt with. The Regt. do pray, that they be assured their service will be fairly appreciated, by paying them as American Soldiers, not as menial hirelings. Black men You may well know, are poor, three dollars per month, for a year, will supply their needy Wives, and little ones, with fuel. If you, as chief Magistrate of the Nation, will assure us, of our whole pay, we are content, our Patriotism, our enthusiasm will have a new impetus, to exert our energy more and more to Aid Our Country. Not that our hearts ever flagged, in

Continued

Window in Time

Devotion, spite the evident apathy displayed in our behalf, but We feel as though, our Country spurned us, now we are sworn to serve her.

Please give this a moments attention.

Source: Letter of Corporal James Henry Gooding to President Abraham Lincoln, Washington, National Archives, War Records Office, 1–4.

combat. One white officer complained that he would rather carry his rifle in the ranks of fighting men than be an overseer of black laborers. In 1864 Adjutant General Lorenzo Thomas took note of the situation and ordered that there should be no excessive impositions on black troops—"that they will be only required to take their fair share of fatigue duty with white troops. This is necessary to prepare them for the higher duties of conflicts with the enemies."

The "higher duties of conflicts" had already begun, for blacks saw action against Confederate forces as early as the fall of 1862. From then until the end of the war, hardly a battle was fought in which some black troops did not meet the enemy. According to George Washington Williams, they saw action in more than 250 skirmishes. Eight black infantry regiments fought in the Battle of Port Hudson.

Battle of Port Hudson, 1863
Brilliant charge of the phalanx on the Confederate works

Fort Pillow Massacre

The Confederacy considered northern use of black troops as an outrage. Were blacks to be treated as enemy combatants, Confederates wondered, or as slaves in insurrection? The

Treatment of Black Prisoners
vast majority of white southerners viewed black soldiers as rebellious slaves and insisted that they be treated as such. In 1862 President Davis ordered all slaves captured in arms to be delivered to the state from which they had come and dealt with according to its laws. President Lincoln responded in kind, declaring that for every Union soldier killed in violation of the laws of war, a rebel prisoner would be executed and that for every Union soldier enslaved, a rebel prisoner would be put to hard labor on the public works. Following Lincoln's lead, Union officials insisted that captured blacks be treated as prisoners of war, but the Confederates did not accept that status until 1864.

Captured black soldiers risked being enslaved, but more often they were killed. The Confederate secretary of war countenanced the killing of some black prisoners to make an example of them. The prospect of death stood at the heart of an order in 1864 by a Confederate officer, Colonel W. P. Shingler, who told his subordinates not to report the capture of any more black prisoners of war. The worst case of the mistreatment of black troops occurred in the Fort Pillow affair. On April 12, 1864, this Union outpost in Tennessee fell to Confederate forces under the command of General Nathan Bedford Forrest. The black soldiers in Fort Pillow were not permitted to surrender; instead, many were shot dead and others were burned alive. Yet many black troops were captured and held as prisoners of war by the South. In 1863 General Butler reported that three thousand black troops were prisoners of the Confederates, and late in 1864 nearly a thousand black prisoners of war worked on building the Confederate fortifications at Mobile.

Blacks saw action in every theater during the Civil War. Historian Noah André Trudeau notes 449 engagements that included black troops. They fought at Port Hudson and Milliken's Bend in Louisiana, at Olustee in Florida, at Vicksburg in Mississippi, at Fort Pillow in Tennessee, at Fort Wagner in South Carolina, at Saltville in Virginia, and at the siege of Savannah. They fought as well in battles in Arkansas, Kentucky, Missouri, North Carolina, and Texas. They participated in the siege of Petersburg, Virginia, and were at Appomattox Court House on April 9, 1865, when General Robert E. Lee surrendered.

Congress awarded a medal to Decatur Dorsey for gallantry while acting as color-sergeant of the Thirty-Ninth United States Colored Troops at Petersburg on July 30, 1864. James Gardner, of the Thirty-Sixth, received a medal for rushing in advance of his brigade to shoot a Confederate officer leading his men into action. Four men of the Fifty-Fourth Massachusetts Infantry earned the Gilmore Medal for gallantry in the assault on Fort Wagner, in South Carolina, in which their commanding officer, Colonel Robert Gould Shaw, lost his life.

Major General Gilmore issued the following order to commend black soldiers under his command for a daring exploit:

> On March 7, 1865, a party of Colored soldiers and scouts, thirty in number . . . left Jacksonville, Florida, and penetrated into the interior through Marion County. They rescued ninety-one Negroes from slavery, captured four white prisoners, two wagons, and twenty-four horses and mules; destroyed a sugarmill and a distillery . . . and burned the bridge over the Oclawaha River. When returning they were attacked by a band of over fifty cavalry, whom they defeated and drove off with a loss of more than thirty to the rebels. . . . This expedition, planned and executed by Colored men under command of a Colored noncommissioned officer, reflects credit upon the brave participants and their leader.

Similar testimonies to the courage of black soldiers were given by Major Generals Edward R. S. Canby, Godfry Weitzel, James G. Blunt, S. A. Hurlbut, Alfred H. Terry, and W. F. Smith, as well as by men of other ranks. Most significantly, their words of praise attest to the valor of black soldiers in both saving the Union and securing their freedom.

More than 38,000 black soldiers lost their lives in the Civil War. Scholars estimate that their rate of mortality was nearly 40 percent greater than that of white troops. In the Fifth United States Colored Heavy Artillery, for example, 829 men died—the largest number of deaths in any outfit in the Union army. The Sixty-Fifth Colored Infantry lost more than 600 men from disease alone. Several unfavorable conditions explain the black troops' high mortality rate: excessive fatigue details, poor equipment, bad medical care, the recklessness and haste with which they were sent into battle, and the Confederates' "no quarter" policy (that is, refusing to regard blacks as combatants under the accepted rules of war, and summarily killing them). The number of blacks who died at the hands of the enemy remains unknown, but it must have run into many thousands.

Despite their enormous contribution to the Union victory, black soldiers faced injustices and inequities. One such glaring problem was the disparity in pay. The Enlistment Act of July 17, 1862, provided that whites with the rank of private should receive $13 a month and $3.50 for clothing, whereas blacks of the **Unequal Treatment** same rank received only $7 and $3, respectively. Black soldiers and their white officers objected vigorously to this discrimination. The Fifty-Fourth Massachusetts Regiment served a year without pay rather than accept discriminatory wages, and they marched into battle in Florida in 1864 singing: "Three cheers for Massachusetts and seven dollars a month." In the Third South Carolina Regiment, Sgt. William Walker was court-martialed and shot for "leading the company to stack arms before their captain's tent, on the avowed ground that they were released from duty by the refusal of the government to fulfill its share of the contract."

A fascinating letter from Corporal James Henry Gooding implores President Lincoln to redress inequities in pay. Writing on September 28, 1863, Gooding speaks for his regiment:

> We appeal to You, Sir: as the Executive of the nation, to have us Justly Dealt with. The Regt, do pray, that they be assured their service will be fairly appreciated, by paying them as American Soldiers, not as menial hirelings. Black men You may well know, are poor, three dollars per month, for a year, will supply their needy Wives, and little ones, with fuel. If you, as chief Magistrate of the Nation, will assure us, of our whole pay, we are content, our Patriotism, our enthusiasm will have a new impetus, to exert our energy more and more to Aid Our Country. Not that our hearts ever flagged, in Devotion, spite the evident apathy displayed in our behalf, but We feel as though, our Country spurned us, now we are sworn to serve her.

After many such protests, in 1864 the War Department began to grant equal pay to black soldiers. Still, black veterans and their widows continued to press for equality in pay long after the war. Harriet Tubman brought a legal claim against the government for failure to pay her veteran's pension and was given a special dispensation. Tubman demanded not only the pension due her as the wife of a veteran but also the pension due her as a member of the armed services, serving as a nurse, cook, and "commander of several men (eight or nine) as scouts. . . ."

Slave Disruption

One of the South's greatest anxieties at the beginning of the war was the conduct of its slave population. The reaction of slaves to their status affected not only the security of the white civilian population but also the maintenance of a stable economic system without which there was no hope of prosecuting the war successfully. Indeed, the Confederacy had great difficulty making the transition to a wartime economy that could provide the food necessary for its fighting forces. In most places, cotton acreage had to be forcibly reduced by law, with fields converted to the production of corn, wheat, and other cereal grains. The labor force proved the greatest problem. The supervision of slaves, who knew little about grain production and were not interested in it, fell to white women, disabled white men, and faithful slaves.

Widespread sentiment demanded much closer control of slaves and the strengthening of patrol laws all over the South. In 1861 Florida called for an increase in patrols when rumors **Stronger Patrol Laws** of slave insubordination and insurrection arose. In 1862 Georgia canceled exemptions from patrol duty, and Louisiana imposed a fine of $10 or twenty-four hours' imprisonment on whites who failed to perform this service.

The fears of white southerners appear to have been fully justified. Ordinary emergencies might not excite the slaves, but sooner or later most slaves came to understand the magnitude of the war and its implications for their freedom. To be sure, many slaves remained on plantations working for their owners, especially in regions far from the theater of war. Yet many also walked off plantations in the wake of Union forces marching through, or set out to find refuge in Union camps. Perhaps nothing emboldened slaves more than the sight of black Union soldiers.

In August 1862, a Confederate general estimated that slaves worth at least $1 million were escaping to the Federals in North Carolina. The number of slaves fleeing the plantations escalated tremendously as news spread of the Emancipation Proclamation. Before then, the tendency was for male slaves to run away alone. Afterward, entire families deserted the slave quarters. However, Lincoln's Proclamation encouraged some slaveholders to abandon their plantations, leaving very elderly and infirm slaves without any subsistence.

Confederate and state officials sought to halt the wholesale exodus of slaves by permitting planters to engage in what was called "running the Negroes." When an area was threatened with invasion by federal troops, planters attempted to remove their slaves to safety, usually in the interior. More than two thou- **"Running the Negroes"** sand were transferred from Washington and Tyrell counties on the North Carolina coast to the interior of the state in the autumn of 1862. Observers recalled seeing planters moving with "black capital"—sometimes on foot, sometimes by wagon or cart, but always in haste. In increasing numbers, masters evacuated war-torn regions, hoping to take themselves and their slaves to areas of refuge isolated from battle.

By moving to places such as southwest Georgia, south-central Alabama, and eastern Texas, slave owners hoped to reestablish their lives in their prewar condition. Historian Susan O'Donovan notes that thousands of slaves entered southwest Georgia with the many slaveholders who evacuated there. Not all blacks were amenable to "refugeeing," at least not with their owners, and at times they openly resisted, running off in the opposite direction toward the Union troops. Slaves who remained with their masters increasingly turned to theft and other disruptive behavior as the war's costs rose and the production of food and clothing declined. O'Donovan argues that through "far-flung networks of friendship and the firsthand intelligence accumulated in the course of their everyday work, slave men increasingly conspired together, fled together, and as the war spilled into its fourth year, launched collective strikes against slaveholders and slavery."

Plantation diaries attest that, even while remaining enslaved on plantations for the duration of the war, black men and women became increasingly insolent toward their masters. Such accounts portray black women as "unruly" and refusing to follow orders. Moreover, many slave men gained new work roles **Insubordination** because of the growing dearth of white men. Thus they shifted increasingly out of field work, leaving relatively more cotton production to women. In their new jobs—making salt, acting as couriers, and assuming skilled roles once restricted to white men—male slaves gained greater freedom of movement, including the ability to connect with other blacks and to learn about the war's progress. Most important of all, they found more opportunities to escape bondage.

Throughout the South, as white planters and overseers departed for the battlefield and as white women attempted to perform jobs previously held by men and even by their slaves, blacks expressed in overt and covert ways their understanding of the tumultuous times. In 1862 a Mississippi citizen wrote the governor that "there is greatly needed in this county a company of mounted rangers . . . to keep the Negroes in awe, who are getting quite impudent. Our proximity to the enemy has had a perceptible influence on them." The situation became so disturbing in Georgia that a bill was introduced in the state legislature "to punish slaves and free persons of color for abusive and insulting language to white persons." The *Richmond Enquirer* reported that a coachman, on learning that he was free, "went straightly to his master's chamber, dressed himself in his best clothes, put on his best watch and chain, took his stick, and returning to the parlor where his master was, insolently informed him that he might for the future drive his own coach."

A North Carolina citizen summed up the prevailing white point of view in 1864: "Our Negroes are beginning to show that they understand the state of affairs, and insolence and insubordination are quite common." The fact that slaves increasingly learned about the war's progress is confirmed by Booker T. Washington in a story about the late-night, whispered conversations of his own mother and other slaves. Although at the time he was a child, Washington overheard their discussions and years later described them as revealing that the slaves "understood the situation, and that they kept themselves informed of events by what was termed the 'grapevine telegraph.' " Slave songs troubled some whites, since hymns contained the language of freedom. No longer did masters feel that slaves were speaking about their life in the bye and bye. In her 1902 Civil War memoir, Susie King Taylor described a revealing incident:

> I remember, one night, my grandmother went out into the suburbs of the city
> to a church meeting, and they were fervently singing this old hymn, "Yes,
> we all shall be free. . . . When the Lord shall appear," when the police came
> in and arrested all who were there, saying they were planning freedom,
> and sang "the Lord," in place of "Yankee," to blind anyone who might be
> listening.

Many slaves refused to work or to submit to punishment. A South Carolina planter complained in 1862 that "we have had hard work to get along this season, the Negroes are unwilling to do any work, no matter what it is." Said another exasperated planter: "I wish every negro would leave the place as they will do only what pleases them, go out in the morning when it suits them, come in when they please, etc." Some Louisiana slaves demanded wages for their labor. In Texas, a slave cursed his owner "all to pieces" when the latter attempted to punish him. Relations became so strained in some areas that masters and mistresses stopped trying to punish their slaves, lest they resort to desperate reprisals.

Acts of slave disloyalty also took the form of giving information and guidance to federal troops, seizing the owner's property on arrival of these troops and helping to destroy it, and inflicting bodily harm on white civilians. Most white southerners lived in con-

Fear of Uprisings

stant fear of slave uprisings during the war, especially after the Emancipation Proclamation. Rumors of uprisings became common, and slaveholders were so terrified at the prospect of bloody insurrections that they frequently appealed to Union troops for protection. One of white southerners' objections to the Confederate draft, which began in the spring of 1862 and thus preceded the Union draft, was its potential to encourage slave revolts by reducing the number of white males on plantations. In 1864 the newspaper *The Richmond Whig* protested: "Take away all, or nearly all the vigorous whites, and leave the negro to the feeble control of women, children, and old men, and the danger is that famine will be super-added to insurrection." In several Alabama and Georgia towns, some slaves were hanged for plotting insurrection, and many others were jailed after being implicated in these plots.

The number of actual insurrections in the Confederacy was relatively small, however, because slaves were able to secure their freedom without committing violence. The practice in the South, moreover, was to act summarily in cases where black people were suspected of insurrection, in order to head off any large-scale revolt. Even in isolated places like Southwest Georgia, slaves became increasingly restive as news of Union victories grew.

In the final analysis, slaves proved both indispensable and subversive to the Confederate war effort. Throughout the struggle, Confederates used them not only on the farms but also in factories, such as the ironworks of Virginia and Alabama. In 1862 the famous Tredegar Works in Richmond advertised for one thousand slaves. There they cut the wood for charcoal, hauled iron to shipping points, and engaged in various types of skilled labor. In 1864 there were 4,301 blacks and 2,518 whites working in the iron ore mines of the Confederate states east of the Mississippi. Slaves also mined coal and toiled in salt works. However, relying on the skills of slaves could be dangerous.

Robert Smalls, for example, began work in the Charleston shipyards in 1861, learning to navigate vessels around the harbor and ultimately becoming the pilot of the *Planter,* a local steamer. He was born a slave in Beaufort, South Carolina, in 1839 and was sent to work in Charleston at a young age, where he picked up basic literacy. In 1862, as the Union escalated its attack on southern shipping lanes, Smalls orchestrated the surrender of the vessel to the northern army, continuing to work for the Union in the navy until the end of the war. His service during the Civil War later launched his political career in South Carolina during Reconstruction.

Robert Smalls
Smalls, a slave pilot in Charleston, became a Civil War hero when he took control of the Confederate steamer, *The Planter*, and delivered it to the Union squadron that was blocking the harbor.

The Confederate Dilemma

The Confederate and state governments confronted a dilemma. Facing a conquering army that would free their slaves, the rebels became ever more dependent on black labor. Indeed, they relied on both slave and free-black labor to do much of the hard work involved in prosecuting the war. The government procured slave laborers by signing contracts with their owners, by hiring them for short periods, and by impressing them into public service. By the fall of 1862, the South's labor shortage had become so acute that most states authorized the impressment of slaves and free men of color. But this outraged slave owners.

In 1863 a desperate Confederate Congress passed a general impressment law, and one year later it voted to impress 20,000 slaves. Until the close of the war, President Davis constantly urged that more slaves be impressed. The results were not gratifying. In the first place, the owners of slaves disliked the principle of impressment, under which their property could be seized at a price set by the government. Consequently, in many instances they simply refused to cooperate. Slaves did not like impressment, because working for military authorities involved more strenuous work

Impressment

than they were accustomed to doing for their owners, if they chose to work at all. With both master and slave opposed to it, impressment had little chance for success.

Even without impressment, the rebel state governments accomplished vital tasks through the labor of thousands of slaves. Most cooks in the Confederate army were slaves, and the government recognized their value to the morale and physical fitness of the soldiers by designating four for each company and providing that each should receive $15 a month plus clothing. The Confederate army used slave teamsters, mechanics, hospital attendants, ambulance drivers, and common laborers. Slaves constructed most Confederate fortifications, and as Union troops invaded the South, tearing up railroads and wrecking bridges, gangs of slave and free-black workers repaired them. Blacks also manufactured powder and arms. In 1865, 310 out of the 400 workers at the naval arsenal in Selma, Alabama, were black.

At the beginning of the war, affluent Confederate officers took their body servants to war with them. These black workers kept quarters clean, washed clothes, pressed uniforms, polished swords, buckles, and spurs, ran errands, secured rations, cut hair; and groomed animals. Some even fought. In November 1861 it was reported that one black servant "fought manfully" and killed four Union soldiers. But later, as the fighting grew desperate and the rations ever shorter, most servants were sent home; Confederate soldiers had come to realize that outside medieval romances, body servants had no place on the field of combat.

It was one thing to have blacks performing all types of work, even within the army; it was quite another to put weapons in their hands. Some white southerners had wanted to **Enlisting and Arming Blacks** arm blacks from the beginning, and in a few cases, local authorities permitted free blacks to enroll for military service. In 1861 the Tennessee legislature authorized the governor to enlist all free blacks between fifteen and fifty years of age in the state militia. Memphis went so far as to open a recruiting office for them. Public opinion, however, generally opposed arming blacks. The fear was that they would turn on their owners. To accept them for military service, moreover, would be an acknowledgment of their equality with whites. When a company of sixty free blacks presented themselves for service to the Confederacy at Richmond in 1861, they were thanked and sent home. A company of free blacks in New Orleans was allowed to parade but not to go into battle.

Despite the stern opposition of southern leaders to enlisting blacks, agitation in favor of it grew as the hope for a Confederate victory dimmed. Mounting casualties proved that the white southern volunteers alone could not sustain the war effort, and in the spring of 1862 Jefferson Davis signed the Conscription Act, which required military service from the South's white men. This act fell heaviest on poor and non-slaveholding men, since slaveholders could avoid service if in their stead they sent twenty slaves to help build fortifications and to labor in the larger defense effort. Indeed, the Civil War in the South came to be called "a poor man's fight and a rich man's war."

After reverses in the autumn of 1863, debate increased, and the Alabama legislature recommended arming a large number of slaves. In 1864 General Patrick Cleburne proposed to officers in the Tennessee army that they organize a large force of slaves, offering them a promise of freedom at the end of the war. Cleburne's proposal provoked considerable discussion, and President Davis, fearing that it did the southern cause no good, ordered that no such force be organized. Discussion continued, however, and in 1864 a meeting of the governors of North and South Carolina, Georgia, Alabama, and

Mississippi adopted a resolution suggesting the use of slaves as soldiers. Davis continued to oppose the proposition. In his message to the Confederate Congress the following month, he said as much but added: "Should the alternative ever be presented of subjugation or of the employment of the slave as a soldier, there seems no reason to doubt what should then be our decision."

Driven to desperation in the winter of 1864–1865, the Confederate Congress openly debated arming slaves. A representative from Mississippi, H. C. Chambers, deplored the suggestion and cried out, "God forbid that this Trojan horse should be introduced among us." The outspoken editor of the *Charleston Mercury* declared that South Carolina would no longer be interested in prosecuting the war if slaves were armed.

In 1865 a bill was introduced in the Confederate Senate providing for the enlistment of 200,000 blacks and their emancipation if they remained loyal throughout the war. Advocates of the bill sought the approval of General Robert E. Lee. The South's most respected soldier said that the measure was not only expedient but also necessary, that blacks would make efficient soldiers, and that those who served should be freed at the end of the war. On March 13, 1865, President Davis signed a bill that authorized him to call on each state for a quota of additional troops, irrespective of color, on condition that slaves recruited from any state should not exceed 25 percent of the able-bodied male slave population between eighteen and forty-five. Recruiting officers were immediately appointed to enroll blacks for the Confederate army. In view of steadily growing slave disloyalty, there is little reason to believe that this war measure would have been effective. The Confederacy's decision to arm blacks reflected the impending defeat of the Old South.

Victory

The surrender of the Confederate army in 1865 meant victory not only for the powerful military forces of the North but also for the indestructible character of the Union. The question of states' rights would surely arise again, but the question of whether states had a right to secede from the Union was settled once and for all. The surrender of the Confederacy marked a personal victory for President Lincoln and his policies. Lincoln insisted that the states had not seceded but that rebellious citizens had got out of hand, and he would use this magnanimous theory to bind up the nation's wounds. For African Americans, however, the Confederate defeat meant most of all the victory of abolitionism.

Etched in stone, the sculpture "Forever Free," by Edmonia Lewis vividly portrayed the meaning of the Civil War to the lives of African Americans. In 1863 Lewis had attended Oberlin College, a coeducational and racially integrated institution founded by abolitionists in Ohio, although she did not graduate. Moving to Boston afterward, she enjoyed the support of

***Forever Free**, Mary Edmonia Lewis, 1867*
Lewis created this tableau commemorating the ratification of the thirteenth amendment while she studied classical art in Rome.

such other high-profile abolitionists as William Lloyd Garrison, Senator Charles Sumner, and writer Lydia Maria Child. Lewis had earlier sculpted the bust of Robert Gould Shaw, the white commander of the black Massachusetts Fifty-Fourth Regiment, who had died in battle at the head of his troops, thus paying homage to his memory and indirectly to that of the black military contribution to the Civil War. Through the sale of replicas of this piece, she was able to finance her travel to Rome, where she sculpted her best-known work, *Forever Free,* commemorating the end of slavery.

Beginning in Spanish Florida in the sixteenth century and ending with the ratification of the Thirteenth Amendment to the Constitution in December, 1865, three centuries of black enslavement on the North American continent had finally come to an end. The full experience of freedom for African Americans was yet to be revealed, but they looked to the future in eager anticipation of the opportunities for development in churches, schools, businesses, and elected office.

CHAPTER 11

Promises and Pitfalls of Reconstruction

Presidential Reconstruction

Radical Reconstruction

The Social Consequences of the War

Economic Adjustment

Reconstruction's End

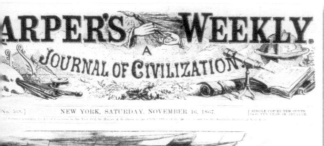

Enfranchisement of African Americans

One of the first manifestations of citizenship was exercising the franchise. Here an African American casts his ballot.

235

In December 1863, as the Civil War still raged, President Abraham Lincoln unveiled his plan for readmitting the seceded southern states into the Union. He hoped to reconstruct the South with sufficient leniency and magnanimity that the nation might bind its wounds and be quickly restored to its former unity. In the very same month and year, Frederick Douglass, at the thirtieth anniversary of the American Anti-Slavery Society, gave eloquent voice to a far more novel and radical vision of national reunification. "We are fighting for something incomparably better than the old Union," Douglass intoned, "we are fighting for unity . . . in which there shall be no North, no South, no East, no West, no black, no white, but a solidarity of the nation, making every slave free, and every free man a voter."

When the war finally ended, African Americans met in state conventions in various parts of the United States and, in the spirit of Douglass's words, demanded equality under the law. Nowhere was this more evident than in the former Confederate states, where the defeated South confronted the stark reality of several million freed slaves as well as the many thousands of recently discharged black soldiers, who expected in return for their loyalty the "blood-bought right" of suffrage.

The era of Reconstruction, which lasted from 1865 to 1876, marked one of the most turbulent and controversial chapters in American history, and yet it also marked an unprecedented moment in interracial democracy. It was shaped by presidents and congressmen, by military officials and businessmen, by religious denominations and teachers, but it was also profoundly shaped by blacks themselves, especially former slaves. Blacks struggled persistently against white southerners' attempts to reduce their free status to nominal slavery. And in this all too brief but wondrous sweep of years, African Americans represented themselves and broader constituencies in local, state, and national office. The election of blacks never led to "Negro rule" or "Negro domination," as was the prevailing historical interpretation of Reconstruction for more than half of the twentieth century. Given the limits placed on blacks' ability to control their economic and political destinies, historians today recognize such interpretations to be erroneous.

However, it would be equally erroneous to underestimate the freed blacks' role in shaping the political, economic, and social policies of the time. But this experiment in a new racial order ultimately failed: by 1877 white supremacists had "redeemed" the Southern states, and as the nineteenth century progressed, the ideology of white superiority would undermine with a vengeance the fulfillment of democracy in America.

Presidential Reconstruction

The Northern victory in 1865 gave the Republican party the upper hand in determining the fate of the largely Democratic South. Republican commitment to the end of slavery had brought about the Thirteenth Amendment. It was not simply that slavery was no longer legal in the former Confederacy. The loyal border states were also required to abolish slavery, thus freeing many thousands of slaves there. The South had to conform to the national standard of free labor, but ending slavery also created a curious paradox. By freeing the slaves, the Thirteenth Amendment had nullified the Three-fifths Compromise, making it possible for the South to return with even greater congressional representation than before the war. No longer would 4 million slaves be counted as three-fifths of persons for the purposes of either taxation or congressional apportionment.

Republicans pondered the troubling implications of this fact and grew increasingly determined to prevent the southern state governments from falling into the hands of irreconcilable ex-Confederates. Emphasizing the treasonous actions of southern secessionists, they extolled the Republican party's role in saving the nation from complete destruction and warned that former slaveholders would quickly seize the opportunity to re-enslave blacks.

The struggle between Republicans and Democrats over control of the southern states was accompanied by an internal struggle within the Republican leadership itself—specifically between the president and Congress over the authority to define the conditions of the South's readmission. It was the function of the **Lincoln's Ten Percent Plan** president, so Abraham Lincoln believed, to outline the postwar agenda and to execute the measures necessary to reorganize the rebel states. As states collapsed under the Union forces, Lincoln appointed military governors over them until civil authority could be established.

Lincoln exhibited a generosity of spirit to the citizens of the former Confederacy, extending general amnesty except for certain high-ranking civil and military officials. Under his plan, a state could be readmitted to the Union if one-tenth of its eligible voters in 1860 swore an oath of loyalty to the United States and accepted the abolition of slavery. Often called the Ten Percent Plan, Lincoln's reconstruction policy was early on criticized by some members of Congress for being too lenient. Radical Republicans demanded congressional, not presidential oversight of Reconstruction and in 1864 proposed the Wade-Davis Bill, which disfranchised a larger number of ex-Confederates and required a majority of whites in each southern state to swear loyalty to the Union. Lincoln refused to sign this bill.

Lincoln and the Congress disagreed, as well, over the status of the freedpeople. All during the war Lincoln had entertained the hope that a substantial number of blacks would choose to emigrate from the United States. He was unsuccessful in securing congressional cooperation for this purpose, and blacks themselves vehemently opposed the idea. This sentiment is reflected in a meeting of Norfolk blacks, who proclaimed: "We are Americans, we know no other country, we love the land of our birth." Blacks meeting in Nashville likewise renounced the idea of emigration, preferring, as they stated, to "impress upon the white men of Tennessee, of the United States, and of the world that we are part and parcel of the American Republic." Sentiments such as these made clear to the Republican party that its Reconstruction policies would have to be premised on the continued presence of African Americans in the United States.

In March 1864, after two prominent New Orleans creoles of color, wine dealer Arnold Bertonneau and plantation engineer Jean Baptiste Roudanez, traveled to Washington to present their community's petition for the suffrage, Lincoln wrote to Governor George Michael Hahn of Louisiana asking "whether some of the colored people may not be let in [to the elective franchise] as, for instance, the very intelligent, and especially those who have fought gallantly in our ranks." When the Louisiana constitutional convention met later in the year, it failed to extend voting rights to anyone of African descent, even those individuals of considerable intellectual and economic achievement.

From Congress's viewpoint, the pendulum had swung too far toward the executive branch. The accession to the presidency of Andrew Johnson after the assassination of Lincoln only deepened the conflict between the two branches of government. Johnson's earlier dislike of the plantation elite had **Andrew Johnson's Policies** initially elicited sympathy from Congress, but once in the office of president, he appeared to shift his sympathies in favor of them. Johnson appointed provisional governors in the Southern states and called on state legislatures, which at the time were based only on white voters, to modify their constitutions in harmony with that of the United States.

To the consternation of the Republican Congress, he rejected outright the idea of black suffrage and began to dictate Reconstruction policy. Johnson left no doubt that he intended to leave the decision of black suffrage to the individual states. His position essentially negated the possibility of black suffrage. Moreover, Johnson extended pardons to thousands of Confederates who had been excluded from the general amnesty. Historian Eric Foner notes that "Johnson's policies had failed to create a new political leadership to replace the prewar 'slaveocracy'—partly because the President himself had so quickly aligned with portions of the old elite." The perception of Johnson as the South's champion and friend enraged both Radical and Moderate Republicans. A growing number of congressmen anxiously strove to restore balance among the three branches of government.

Under Presidential Reconstruction, southern states established new constitutions and governments, which immediately resolved to curb the freedom of blacks through the passage of laws, called Black Codes. These laws bore a remarkable resemblance to the antebellum

Black Codes
Slave Codes. The right to make contracts was allowed the freedpeople, but such contracts were designed to lock in, control, and compel black laborers to work under extremely oppressive conditions, thus reinforcing their subordinate position. Blacks who quit their jobs could be arrested and imprisoned for breach of contract. Vagrancy laws imposed heavy penalties on unemployed black men, women, and even children. For example, the Black Codes permitted the "apprenticeship" of black orphans or children with parents the state deemed unfit. Judges bound such minors, usually in their early teenage years, to white employers without any compensation to the child laborers or their parents. The courts in Maryland and North Carolina did not even require the consent of black parents to apprentice their children to white "guardians."

Black Codes disallowed black testimony in court, except in cases involving members of their own race. They limited the areas in which blacks could purchase or rent property. The southern state laws imposed numerous fines for seditious speech or talk perceived as threatening to whites, for insulting gestures or acts, for violation of curfew, and for the possession of firearms. Most important, the new state governments denied blacks the right to vote—leaving them helpless to change the laws. The prospect of full citizenship and true representative government appeared faint under Presidential Reconstruction.

When Congress met in December 1865, the southern elections had brought chilling although not unexpected results. As far as the Republicans in Congress were concerned, the path to reunion under the presidential plan had become crystal clear. The newly elected southerners included the vice president of the Confederacy, four Confederate generals, five Confederate colonels, six Confederate cabinet officers, and fifty-eight members of the Confederate Congress. Led by the wily Republican leader Thaddeus Stevens, Congress refused to recognize the validity of the southern elections and vigorously argued for a sterner policy toward the South. Stephens proposed that Congress assume authority over Reconstruction, arguing that the president's policy had been essentially provisional. Congress then adopted Stevens's resolution, which called for the creation of the Joint Committee on Reconstruction to inquire into the condition of the southern states and to make recommendations.

Conditions were certainly terrible for the freedpeople. In 1866, with southern whites in

Congress Takes Charge
almost complete charge of Reconstruction, a kind of guerrilla warfare was being waged against blacks. The head of the Freedmen's Bureau in Georgia, for example, complained that bands of men calling themselves Regulators, Jayhawkers,

Selling a freedman to pay his fine at Monticello, Florida
A black code in Florida made disobedience a crime. This freedman was sold for up to one year's labor for disobeying his former owner.

and the Black Horse Cavalry were committing the "most fiendish and diabolical outrages on the freedmen" with the sympathy of the populace and the reconstructed governments as well. Formed as white protective societies, those organizations ran riot all over the South. While southern legislators enacted the new Black Codes, vigilante groups set out to keep "the Negro in his place."

Freedmen's Bureau agents portrayed incidents of violence in their reports. One agent conveyed his frustration in 1866, stating: "A freedman is now standing at my door, his tattered clothes bespattered with blood from his head caused by blows inflicted by a white man with a stick and we can do nothing for him. . . . Yet these people flee to us for protection as if we could give it."

Congress's passage of the Civil Rights Act in the spring of 1866, over Johnson's veto, provided blacks with protections against the Black Codes and acts of violence. The Act stipulated the right of blacks to testify in court as well as to enjoy the "full and equal benefit of all laws and proceedings for the security of person and property, as is enjoyed by white citizens." By the year's end, bureau agents had been empowered to observe local judicial proceedings involving the freedpeople and to play an advocacy role in helping them to attain

239

fundamental justice in the courts. The bureau was responsible for organizing "freedmen's" courts and boards of arbitration, which had civil and criminal jurisdiction over minor cases in which one or both parties were ex-slaves. They were often successful at securing justice for former slaves, as in the case of a white physician in Maryland who assaulted a black without provocation and was taken by the bureau agent to the state supreme court, which admitted the testimony of blacks and convicted the physician.

A confluence of northern interests began to promote black suffrage as being crucial to a policy that would ensure the gains made during the war. Black and white abolitionists supported the enfranchisement of black men on the basis of black soldiers' defense of the Union. Pragmatic Republicans, fearful of the political consequences of a South dominated by Democrats, maintained that black suffrage in the South would aid in the continued growth of the Republican party. Industrialists with an eye on markets and cheap labor in the South supported the suffrage for blacks in order to deter the reemergence of the powerful agrarian interests that reigned in the prewar era. The concerted efforts of these groups substantially limited Johnson's ability to determine the fate of Reconstruction.

The president's vetoes, his disparaging racial remarks, his opposition to the proposed Fourteenth Amendment, and his acrimonious attacks on Thaddeus Stevens, Charles Sumner, and other northern leaders, sent Congress on the warpath for control of Reconstruction. The fight between the president and Congress escalated into a bitter public spectacle. Johnson carried his fight with Congress to the American people, admonishing voters to return to Congress in the fall of 1866 men who would support his program. His conduct during the well-known campaign tour ("swing around the circle") was received so negatively that he was soundly repudiated at the polls.

Congress was not the only opponent of the policies of presidential Reconstruction. African Americans themselves mobilized in protest. Many were emboldened by the presence of black troops among the Union forces stationed in the postwar South. The New York **The Black Conventions** *World* called black soldiers "apostles of black equality," since they championed the message of freedom and equality in their daily social relations. In numerous settings black soldiers proved themselves worthy of this title. They arrested lawless whites, helped to build schools and other community institutions for the freedpeople, gave advice in regard to labor contracts, demanded equal access to public accommodations, and voiced their opinions (some of which were described as "speeches of the most inflammatory kind") at political meetings.

Equally important were the statewide conventions held throughout the South in 1865 and early 1866. The conventions offered convincing evidence of black political mobilization against presidential reconstruction. The historian Steven Hahn has identified them as "the institutional harbingers of the Republican party." Approximately 150 delegates from communities and organizations throughout North Carolina assembled at the Loyal African Methodist Episcopal Church in Raleigh in 1865. They came by train, by horseback, and by foot. From the western and central sections of the state, some traveled secretly in the night so as not to attract the attention of white vigilantes. Others traveled openly under the protective eye of Union troops stationed in the eastern counties. Like black Americans in other states, the North Carolina delegates met in their own convention in the months following the Union victory and sent a petition to President Andrew Johnson, asserting:

> It seems to us that men who are willing on the field of danger to carry the
> muskets of a republic, in the days of peace ought to be permitted to carry its

Window in Time

Virginia Black Convention 1865

African Americans in Norfolk, Virginia, Demand Equal Rights, 1865

1st. *Resolved,* That the rights and interests of the colored citizens of Virginia are more directly, immediately and deeply affected in the restoration of the State to the Federal Union than any other class of citizens; and hence, that we have peculiar claims to be heard in regard to the question of its reconstruction, and that we cannot keep silence without dereliction of duty to ourselves, to our country, and to our God.

2d. *Resolved,* That personal servitude having been abolished in Virginia, it behooves us, and is demanded of us, by every consideration of right and duty, to speak and act as freemen, and as such to claim and insist upon equality before the law, and equal rights of suffrage at the "ballot box."

3d. *Resolved,* That it is a wretched policy and most unwise statesmanship that would withhold from the laboring population of the country any of the rights of citizenship essential to their well-being and to their advancement and improvement as citizens.

4th. *Resolved,* That invidious political or legal distinctions, on account of color merely, if acquiesced in, or voluntarily submitted to, is inconsistent with our own self-respect, or to the respect of others, placing us at great disadvantages, and seriously retards our advancement or progress in improvement, and that the removal of such disabilities and distinctions are alike demanded by sound political economy, by patriotism, humanity and religion.

5th. *Resolved,* That we will prove ourselves worthy of the elective franchise, by insisting upon it as a right, by not tamely submitting to its deprivation, by never abusing it by voting the state out of the Union, and never using it for purposes of rebellion, treason, or oppression.

6th. *Resolved,* That the safety of all loyal men, black or white, in the midst of the recently slaveholding States, requires that all loyal men, black or white, should have equal political and civil rights, and that this is a necessity as a protection against the votes of secessionists and disloyal men.

7th. *Resolved,* That traitors shall not dictate or prescribe to us the terms or conditions of our citizenship, so help us God.

8th. *Resolved,* That as far as in us lies, we will not patronize or hold business relations with those who deny to us our equal rights.

Source: "Address from the colored citizens of Norfolk, Va., to the people of the United States. Also an account of the agitation among the colored people of Virginia for equal rights. With an appendix concerning the rights of colored witnesses before the state courts" (New Bedford, MA, 1865).

ballots; and certainly we cannot understand the justice of denying the elective franchise to men who have been fighting for the country [while it] is freely given to men who have just returned from four years' fighting against it.

With the Civil War over, these postwar conventions boldly proclaimed the motto: "Equal Rights before the Law."

In 1866, delegates to the South Carolina convention met in Charleston to demand the same opportunities and privileges enjoyed by whites—the right to an education, to bear arms, to serve on juries, to assemble peacefully, and to vote. In Mobile, Alabama, African Americans demanded the ballot, the abolition of the Black Codes, and measures for the relief of suffering. The Georgia black convention passed resolutions that demanded an end to the violence perpetrated against rural blacks and an end to the obstacles that prevented the establishment of schools for blacks. Blacks meeting in Nashville protested the state's Black Codes, while black Mississippians similarly protested such laws and asked, as well, for Congress to extend the franchise to the members of their race. The idea that universal manhood suffrage constituted "an essential and inseparable element of self-government" became an often repeated theme at the black conventions.

The New Orleans *Tribune,* the newspaper published by the city's creoles of color, editorialized in September 1866: "The negro of today, is not the same as he was six years ago. . . . He has been told of his rights, which have long been robbed." Black mobilization was especially strong in Southern cities, where churches and fraternal societies provided a sturdy infrastructure for political activism. Black political mobilization advanced more rapidly in places where the federal troops had remained the longest. According to the complaint of a sugar plantation owner, black agricultural workers were also mobilizing—"abandoning their work to attend political gatherings."

Black Mobilization

Although it was common for the free black elite of Louisiana and South Carolina to assume the political leadership, a new group of leaders, many of them from the rural counties, began to wield influence. For example, the editor of the *Tribune* made mention of "country delegates" who were "generally more radical than most of the city delegates." A resounding protest against the denial of rights sprang up in the low country and sea islands off South Carolina and Georgia, uniting together Freedmen's agents, black soldiers, and local freedmen in the demand for the suffrage and the repeal of all laws that discriminated against blacks. "By the Declaration of Independence," rang out the speaker's words at a gathering on St. Helena Island, "we believe these are rights which cannot justly be denied us."

Radical Reconstruction

By 1867 Congress had wrested control of Reconstruction from President Johnson and in the following year embarked on an unsuccessful effort to impeach him. Through passage of the Reconstruction Act of 1867, the ex-Confederate states (except Tennessee, where Reconstruction was moving according to Congress) were divided into five military districts under martial law. Each of the states was ordered to hold a new constitutional convention based on universal male suffrage, and no state was to be admitted until it ratified the Fourteenth Amendment, which guaranteed the citizenship of all persons born or naturalized in the United States and thus overturned the Supreme Court's *Dred Scott* decision.

Also directly affecting African Americans was the Fourteenth Amendment's prohibition against state laws that abridged the civil rights of citizens or denied "equal protection of the laws." Interestingly, the amendment created divisions in the old abolitionist vanguard. Some members of the American Anti-Slavery Society, such as Wendell Phillips and Frederick Douglass, tirelessly promoted enfranchising black men, while many of the Society's women's rights advocates opposed the gendered language of the amendment. Since the Fourteenth Amendment explicitly identified a congressional apportionment penalty for any state that abridged the voting rights of "male inhabitants," suffragists Elizabeth Cady Stanton, Susan B. Anthony, and similarly minded women condemned this gendered language and formed the American Equal Rights Association—outraged that the vote would not be universally extended at this propitious time of sweeping social and political change.

Phillips and Douglass, however, although faithful supporters of women's rights, rebutted the argument for conjoining black suffrage with the far more controversial issue of women's suffrage. They asserted that this was the "Negro's hour." Indeed, even black women—Frances Ellen Watkins Harper and Sojourner Truth, both abolitionists and suffragists—were also divided over the suffrage issue. Harper called attention to the racial oppression endured by black women and men, while Truth, although recognizing racial injustice, asserted: "There is a great stir about colored men getting their rights, but not a word about the colored women, and if colored men get their rights and colored women not theirs, the colored men will be masters over the women, and it will be just as bad as it was before."

The state constitutions drawn up in 1867 and 1868 were the most progressive the South had ever known. Most of them abolished property qualifications for voting and holding office; some of them abolished imprisonment for debt. Several **New National Officials** sought to eliminate race distinctions in the possession or inheritance of property, and they introduced public education into the South. With the ratification of the Fifteenth Amendment in 1870, black men in the southern states and in the nation as a whole (most northern states denied the vote to blacks), finally gained the right to vote on an equal basis with white men. This far-reaching achievement—the creation of a black electorate—had the greatest effect in the former Confederacy, where black men not only voted but also held elected office at the national, state, and local levels.

During congressional Reconstruction, also called Radical Reconstruction, two African Americans went to the United States Senate—Hiram Revels and Blanche K. Bruce, both from the state of Mississippi. The symbolism of Revels as the first black senator was unmistakable. In 1870 he was chosen to fill out the term previously held and vacated by Jefferson Davis, former president of the Confederacy. Born free in North Carolina, Revels had migrated to Indiana, Ohio, and Illinois before the war. He received his education at a seminary in Ohio and at Knox College in Illinois and was ordained a minister in the African Methodist Episcopal church. During the war Revels recruited blacks for the Union army, founded a school for freedmen in St. Louis, and joined the army as chaplain of a black regiment in Mississippi. He settled in Natchez after the war and became prominent in state politics.

Between 1875 and 1881, Blanche K. Bruce sat in the Senate, the only black to serve a full term until the election in 1966 of Edward Brooke, a Republican from Massachusetts. Bruce was born a slave in Virginia. When the war came, he escaped from St. Louis to Hannibal, Missouri, and established a school for blacks. After the war he studied in the North for several years. In 1869 he went to Mississippi, entered politics, and moved up through a succession of offices from tax collector to sheriff and then to superintendent of schools. In the Senate he usually voted with his party and introduced a number of bills to improve the condition of blacks. When P. B. S. Pinchback was denied a seat in the Senate, to which he

The first black senators and representatives, in the Forty-First and Forty-Second Congress of the United States

One major manifestation of citizenship was sending persons, some former slaves, to Congress. Shown here are some of the first African Americans elected to the Senate and the House of Representatives of the U.S. Congress.

had been elected from Louisiana, Bruce spoke for him in vain. His wide range of interests as a lawmaker is seen in his introduction of bills on the Geneva Award for Alabama claims, another for aid to education and railroad construction, and one for reimbursement of depositors in the Freedmen's Bank. On the Pensions Committee, Bruce succeeded in having some pension bills passed. Another of his chief roles was on the Manufactures, Education, and Labor Committee. He also chaired the select committee on the Freedmen's Bank and conducted a thorough investigation of the causes for its failure.

Fourteen blacks served in the House of Representatives during the Reconstruction era, and six additional names were added to this number between 1877 and 1901, thus making a total of twenty blacks in the House between 1869 and 1901. Not included in this number is John W. Menard of Louisiana, who, although elected to the United States Congress in 1868, was denied a seat because of the contested nature of his election. Of the twenty black members of the House of Representatives, South Carolina sent the largest number, eight, and North Carolina followed with four, three of whom served after Reconstruction ended. Alabama sent three, and Georgia, Mississippi, Florida, Louisiana, and Virginia, one each.

It was in the Forty-First Congress (March 4, 1869 to March 3, 1871) that blacks, three of them, first made their appearance in the federal legislature. In the Forty-Second Congress (1871–1873), there were five. The peak was reached in the Forty-Third (1873–1875) and Forty-Fourth Congresses (1875–1877) with seven blacks. In length of service, Joseph

H. Rainey and Robert Smalls, both of South Carolina, led with five terms. John R. Lynch of Mississippi and Josiah Walls of Florida both served three terms, and six others served two terms each.

Most of the blacks in Congress had experience in public service before going to Washington, as delegates to constitutional conventions, as state senators and representatives, or as state or local officials. While they were chiefly concerned with civil rights and education, their efforts were not by any means confined to problems of blacks. Many fought for local improvements such as new public buildings and appropriations for rivers and harbors. Several, such as Walls of Florida and Lynch of Mississippi, promoted protective tariffs for home products. Walls advocated the U.S. government's recognition of Cuba. John A. Hyman of North Carolina advanced a program for relief of the Indians, and Charles E. Nash of Louisiana uttered a plea for intersectional peace.

Blacks also served as state legislators, enacting laws that won both the praise and the condemnation of bitter partisans. It was in South Carolina that blacks wielded the greatest influence. Eighty-seven blacks and forty whites sat in the first legislature. From the outset, however, the whites controlled the state **Blacks as State Legislators** senate, and in 1874 the lower house as well. Although blacks held powerful political positions, no African American ever held the position of governor of South Carolina. Two blacks—Alonzo J. Ransier in 1870 and Richard H. Gleaves in 1872—served as lieutenant governors. Samuel J. Lee served as the state's speaker of the house in 1872, and Robert B. Elliott also served in the same position in 1874. Francis L. Cardozo, an accomplished black who had been educated at the University of Glasgow and in London, was South Carolina's secretary of state from 1868 to 1872 and treasurer from 1872 to 1876.

Robert Brown Elliott, born August 11, 1842, was among a number of African Americans who moved to the South after the Civil War. He is unusual, however, since he did not come from the North. He is thought to have been born in Liverpool, England of West Indian parents, although few facts related to his early life are known—partly because of his own fabrications. It is speculated that he may have even held British citizenship when he showed up in Charleston. It is clear that by 1867 he had positioned himself among South Carolina's black elite, marrying into the powerful free-black Rollin family and working as the associate editor of the black newspaper, the *South Carolina Leader*.

A brilliant and charismatic man, Elliott thrust himself into politics, rising in the ranks of the Republican party from that of a delegate at the state's 1868 Constitutional convention and in the same year was elected to the state legislature where he served as the chair of the committee on railroads. In 1870 Elliott was also elected to Congress, serving for two terms as the representative of a biracial district. He returned to South Carolina in 1874, serving two years as speaker of the state legislature. In 1876 he was elected the state's attorney general. An early and vocal opponent of disfranchisement through the poll tax and literacy test, Elliot advocated integration of public accommodations, although he stopped short of integrated public schools. Elliott's public life ended as the Democrats regained control of the South, and he died in poverty in New Orleans on August 9, 1884.

Mississippi also produced outstanding politicians at the state level. Forty black members, some of whom had been slaves, sat in the state's first legislature. In 1873 blacks held three significant positions: A. K. Davis was lieutenant governor; James Hill, secretary of state; and Thomas W. Cardozo, state superintendent of education. In 1872 John R. Lynch served as the Mississippi legislature's Speaker of the House, and at the end of the session a white

Democrat praised him "for his dignity, impartiality, and courtesy as a presiding officer." Lynch was soon after elected to the United States Congress, where he served in the House of Representatives from 1873 to 1877 and from 1882 to 1883.

Between 1868 and 1896 Louisiana had 133 black state legislators, of whom 38 were senators and 95 were representatives. Three blacks, Oscar J. Dunn, P. B. S. Pinchback, and C. C. Antoine, served as lieutenant governor, and Pinchback served as acting governor for forty-three days in the winter of 1873 when the white Republican Henry C. Warmoth was removed from the governorship. Antoine Dubuclet served as the state treasurer of Louisiana for the ten-year period between 1868 and 1878. In Alabama blacks sat in both houses of the legislature, but not in sufficient numbers to secure prominent positions. They helped to adopt the Fourteenth and Fifteenth Amendments, however, and put a state system of schools into operation.

Although elected to the first Reconstruction legislature of Georgia, blacks had difficulty in securing and retaining their seats. In September 1868 the legislature declared all black members ineligible, and not until almost a year later, when the state supreme court declared them eligible, did the ousted black legislators regain their seats. They introduced many bills on education, the jury system, city government reform, and women's suffrage. Georgia black legislators Jefferson Long and Henry McNeil Turner fought for better wages for black workers but found little support from their white Republican colleagues, who in many instances supported the industrialists over black landless farmers.

Black members of the Reconstruction governments of Florida and North Carolina focused primarily on legislation for relief, education, and suffrage. Jonathan Gibbs, superintendent of public instruction in Florida from 1872 to 1874, ardently championed equal rights. Henry S. Harmon of Florida led the fight for a satisfactory school law. With other black legislators he supported a homestead law and such measures as would provide greater economic security for the mass of citizens. North Carolina blacks helped to inaugurate a system of public schools. An outstanding worker in the field of education was the Reverend James W. Hood, who helped write the constitution of 1868 and served as assistant superintendent of education.

In Virginia twenty-seven African Americans sat in the first legislature, and others served in minor posts. However, as in the case of other states, they were not powerful enough to determine governmental policy except on the rare occasions when they could leverage their votes because of divisions between white factions. Concerning the exercise of influence, the same thing can be said of blacks in Tennessee, Arkansas, and Texas.

The Union League During most of Reconstruction, the Union League and smaller organizations, such as the Lincoln Brotherhood and the Red Strings, faithfully delivered the black vote to the Republican party. The Union League of America, a predominantly white organization in the North, was organized during the war in order to rally military and civilian support. During Reconstruction it branched out into the South to protect the fruits of the Northern victory, and it soon became the spearhead for Southern Republicanism. By the fall of 1867, chapters of the League had formed throughout the South. As the Freedmen's Bureau and other Northern agencies grew in the South, the Union League, too, grew powerful, attracting a large number of African Americans.

Since black men constituted the most numerous enfranchised group in many areas, the League depended on them for the bulk of Republican strength. For example, South Carolina alone had eighty-eight chapters, and it was said that almost every black in the state was enrolled. Ritual, secrecy, night meetings, and an avowed devotion to freedom and equal rights made the league especially attractive to black men. During elections, black voters looked to their league chapters for guidance on voting. If they had any doubt about the straight Republican ticket, the league had only to remind them to vote for the party of Abraham Lincoln and of deliverance. A vote for Democrats, they said, constituted a vote for the return of slavery.

Black women also played a role in "getting out the vote" and in shaping political decisions in their communities. Although black women, like all American women, could not vote, they did not remain silent during electoral campaign. A *New York Times* reporter noted the presence of black women in the audience at local Republican and state constitutional conventions **Black Women and the Black Community** in October 1867. He and other observers stated that, in contrast to white women, who were quiet spectators at political meetings, black women shouted from the balconies, forcing their voices into the debates. As historian Elsa Barkley Brown has pointed out: "African American women in Virginia, Mississippi, South Carolina and elsewhere understood themselves to have a vital stake in African American men's franchise." The fact that only men could exercise the franchise did not mean that women remained silent or unaware of the power of the vote.

Finally, black communities throughout the nation championed the passage of the Civil Rights Act of 1875, which attempted to clarify beyond all doubt the rights of African Americans to freely use public accommodations. The act made illegal the discriminatory practices that existed in every region of the nation, denying African Americans equal access to public transportation, places of amusement, and public houses, such as inns and taverns. Its authors, Senator Charles Sumner of Massachusetts and former Union general turned Congressman Benjamin Butler, had originally included the integration of public schools and cemeteries, although this was rejected by both Democrats and moderate Republicans. One of the bill's most vocal opponents was Alexander Stephens of Georgia, the former vice-president of the Confederacy, who was granted the opportunity to speak on the floor of the House of Representatives on January 4, 1874. The black congressman Robert Brown Elliott was permitted the rebuttal of Stephens's position.

Before an audience of packed galleries, Elliott rose in an eloquent defense of blacks' civil rights, positing: "What you give to one class, you must give to all; what you deny to one class, you shall deny to all. . . . Is it pretended anywhere that the evils of which we complain, our exclusion from the public inn, from the saloon and the table of the steamboat, from the sleeping-coach on the railway, from the right of sepulchre in the public burial ground, are an exercise of the police power of the state?" Unfortunately, Charles Sumner never lived to see the act signed into law, and the act itself proved to be shortlived. In 1883 the Supreme Court declared the Civil Rights Act of 1875 unconstitutional.

The Social Consequences of the War

The end of the Civil War may have brought closure to the death and devastation of the battlefield, but it opened a Pandora's box of social problems. The magnitude of disorder and suffering was tremendous: abandoned lands, lack of food and clothing, the many thousands of displaced persons, successive crop failures, and the transition from slave to free labor on the part of millions of black people. No civil authority reigned in the Carolinas, Georgia, Florida, Alabama, Mississippi, and Texas. Public buildings and private homes had

THE SHACKLE BROKEN — BY THE GENIUS OF FREEDOM.

Robert Brown Elliott speaking before Congress

On January 6, 1874, Elliott delivered a ringing speech in the U.S. House of Representatives in support of the Sumner civil rights bill. Elliot was responding in part to words uttered the day before by Virginia congressman John T. Harris, who claimed that "there is not a gentleman on this floor who can honestly say he really believes that the colored man is created his equal."

been burned to the ground. Everywhere suffering and starvation loomed. Another striking feature of the time was that of ex-slaves searching for husbands, wives, or children who years earlier had been separated by sale or other transactions. Historian Herbert Gutman argued that nothing better illustrated the remarkable resilience and commitment of black family members than their efforts to reunite with one another.

The responsibility for a comprehensive and unified program of relief and rehabilitation for the newly emancipated came under the auspices of the Freedmen's Bureau. **The Freedmen's Bureau** Former slaves in army camps and freedpeople after the war looked to the Freedmen's Bureau to register and legalize slave unions in marriage. Many searches for family members began with poignant letters written to the Freedmen's Bureau. The bureau aided

Window in Time

Hawkins Wilson's Letter to Freedman's Bureau

[*Galveston, Tex.*] May 11th, 1867

    Dear Sir, I am anxious to learn about my sisters, from whom I have been separated many years—I have never heard from them since I left Virginia twenty four years ago—I am in hopes that they are still living and I am anxious to hear how they are getting on—I have no other one to apply to but you and am persuaded that you will help one who stands in need of your services as I do—I shall be very grateful to you, if you oblige me in this matter—One of my sisters belonged to Peter Coleman in Caroline County and her name was Jane—Her husband's name was Charles and he belonged to Buck Haskin and lived near John Wright's store in the same county—She had three children, Robert, Charles and Julia, when I left—Sister Martha belonged to Dr. Jefferson, who lived two miles above Wright's store—Sister Matilda belonged to Mrs. Botts, in the same county—My dear uncle Jim had a wife at Jack Langley's and his wife was named Adie and his oldest son was named Buck and they all belonged to Jack Langley—These are all my own dearest relatives and I wish to correspond with them with a view to visit them as soon as I can hear from them—My name is Hawkins Wilson and I am their brother, who was sold at Sheriff's sale and used to belong to Jackson Talley and was bought by M. Wright, Boydtown C. H. You will please send the enclosed letter to my sister Jane, or some of her family, if she is dead—I am, very respectfully, your obedient servant,

ALS Hawkins Wilson

Source: Hawkins Wilson to Chief of the Freedmen's Bureau at Richmond, 11 May 1867, enclosing Hawkins Wilson to Sister Jane, [11 May 1867], Letters Received, ser. 3892, Bowling Green VA Asst. Supt., BRFAL [A-8254].

former slaves as well as white refugees by furnishing supplies and medical services, establishing schools, supervising contracts between ex-slaves and their employers, and managing confiscated or abandoned lands, which included leasing and selling some of those lands to former slaves. Between 1865 and 1869, it issued 21 million rations, approximately 5 million going to whites and more than 15 million to blacks. By 1867 the bureau oversaw forty-six hospitals staffed by physicians, surgeons, and nurses. Its medical department spent more than $2 million to improve the health of ex-slaves and treated more than 450,000 cases of illness, thus helping to reduce the death rate among former slaves and to improve sanitary conditions.

    The Freedmen's Bureau was the first large-scale federal welfare program in the United States. Despite Southern hostility and the inefficiency of many of its agents, the bureau demonstrated that the government could administer an extensive program of relief and rehabilitation and suggested a way in which the nation could grapple with its pressing social problems. There were certainly cases where bureau agents sided with planters' interests to the detriment of black families, but many blacks also perceived agents to be fair adjudicators of labor problems and came to the bureau with their grievances. The bureau contained corruption and inefficiency. It also achieved notable successes in ministering to human welfare.

Freedmen's Bureau agents, as well as the freedpeople themselves, believed that education was the key to the successful transition from slavery to freedom, and it was in the realm of education that Reconstruction left its most positive and enduring legacy for blacks. Bureau agents consistently remarked on the great value that freedmen placed on education—their burning desire to learn. But because of lack of funds, the bureau did not put its energies, for the most part, into establishing schools but rather into coordinating and working closely with Northern religious societies, philanthropic organizations, and other groups committed to schools for the freedpeople. The bureau supervised day school, night schools, Sunday and industrial schools, as well as colleges.

The Pivotal Role of Education

Bureau agents were greatly assisted in this task by blacks already established as educators in their communities. Indeed Freedmen's Bureau officials repeatedly expressed surprise at discovering black educational settings in churches, basements, and private homes. When the northern societies went south they would also encounter communities in which blacks themselves raised money to purchase land, build schoolhouses, and pay teachers' salaries. By 1870, according to the historian Eric Foner, more than one million dollars had been raised by blacks for educational purposes. As impressive as this was, funding on the part of blacks was insufficient for the magnitude of the task of building and maintaining schools and colleges for several million freedpeople. Thus the aid of the Freedmen's Bureau and northern religious denominations was crucial.

Among the schools founded in this period that received aid and leadership from the Freedmen's Bureau were Howard University (named after the Freedmen's Bureau head General Oliver O. Howard), Hampton Institute, St. Augustine's College, Atlanta University, Fisk University, Storer College, and Biddle Memorial Institute (now Johnson C. Smith University). The American Missionary Association, and the societies of the Baptists, Methodists, Presbyterians, and Episcopalians, were all active in establishing schools, and by 1867 schools had been set up in counties throughout the former Confederacy. Two years later nearly 3,000 schools, serving over 150,000 pupils, reported to the bureau, the supervision of which monopolized much of the agents' time.

Teachers came down from the North in large numbers. Many were missionaries, focused as much on ridding the freedpeople of the cultural vestiges of slavery in their speech, worship practices, and other behavioral and belief patterns, as on teaching them to read, write, and do arithmetic. The names of these white educators, such as Edmund Ware at Atlanta University, Samuel C. Armstrong at Hampton Institute, Erastus M. Cravath at Fisk University, and Oliver O. Howard at Howard University, continue to be renowned today because of their roles in the history of the black colleges and universities. Yet there were hundreds of other educators, white and black alike, whose tireless work in the creation of black schools during the Reconstruction era is far less known.

Educators, Black and White

In 1869 there were 9,503 teachers in schools for former slaves in the South. Although some white teachers were southerners, a majority of whites came from the North. The number of black teachers also steadily increased with each cohort of graduates. After the war, urban blacks took immediate steps to set up schools, sometimes teaching in abandoned warehouses or in former slave markets, as was the case in New Orleans and Savannah. In Richmond, just weeks after Lee's surrender, 1,000 black children and 75 adults attended schools established by the city's black churches and also by the white American Missionary Association.

The schools established by the Freedmen's Bureau, northern societies, and southern blacks themselves endeavored to inculcate new values of free labor, which would generate prosperity for capital and labor alike. Maine-born bureau agent John N. Bryant expressed this perspective, when he stated: "That man who has the most wants will usually labor with the greatest industry. . . . The more intelligent men are the more wants they have, hence it is for the interest of all that the laborers shall be educated."

By 1870 the educational work of the Freedmen's Bureau ended, and the task of education fell to local communities and northern religious organizations. The bureau had spent more than $5 million in schooling ex-slaves, and 247,333 pupils attended 4,329 schools. The shortcomings in the education of blacks arose not from a want of zeal on the part of teachers but from ignorance of the needs of blacks and from the necessary preoccupation of students with the problem of survival in a hostile world.

In addition, southern black churches offered both spiritual and material relief during Reconstruction. Church buildings played as important a public role as a spiritual one. They were much more than places of worship. They served as the setting **Black Churches** for political meetings and rallies. Indeed many of the early black politicians were ministers. Schools for the freedpeople were often conducted in churches. Church members, especially through missionary societies, in both the South and North, had longstanding traditions of mutual aid. After the war they sacrificed their meager earnings to support social services and education.

During the era of Reconstruction the number of independent churches blossomed. No longer bound by Southern laws that silenced their preachers or proscribed their organizations, African Americans withdrew from white churches after securing their freedom. The African Methodist Episcopal church, which had only 20,000 members in 1856, boasted 75,000 ten years later. In 1876 its membership exceeded 200,000, and its influence and material possessions had increased proportionally. The Baptists enjoyed phenomenal growth. Local churches sprang up overnight under the ministry of both educated and unlettered preachers. In 1866 the black Baptists of North Carolina organized the first state convention. Within a few years, every Southern state had a large black Baptist organization. Total membership increased from 150,000 in 1850 to 500,000 in 1870.

As the first social institutions fully controlled by blacks in America, these churches gave blacks an opportunity to develop leadership, and it is no coincidence that many outstanding Reconstruction leaders were ministers. Bishop Henry McNeal Turner of Georgia, the Reverend Richard H. Cain of South Carolina, and Bishop James Walker Hood of North Carolina were a few of the political leaders who gained much of their experience in the black church.

Economic Adjustment

It was one thing to provide temporary relief for former slaves and another to guide them along the road to economic stability and independence. The release from bondage of 4 million persons had serious implications for the economic structure of the South. White planters, in an effort to reestablish themselves, were anxious to secure labor at the lowest possible price; and if in their own minds they conceded the right of blacks to be free, they seldom took to heart that blacks had a right to refuse work. Many prospective employers therefore sought to force blacks to work, and the Black Codes were formulated with this specific intention.

The ex-slaves resisted signing their names to labor contracts in 1865 and 1866 for a variety of reasons. The freedpeople feared binding themselves to a new form of enslavement. They

The Desire for Land
scorned the low wages offered and lacked confidence that planters would be fair in their dealings. Many were exhilarated by their new liberty, especially the freedom to move about as they liked. Some traversed the Old Confederacy in defiance of the resented slave pass that had proscribed their movement. Mobility presented the opportunity to ascertain what freedom actually meant. Thus they struck out on foot or other modes of transport to find different work or to work at higher wages, to relocate in urban areas, to search for loved ones, and to get land for farms of their own.

In the black belt areas, especially, the idea of owning land was held in considerably more favor than wage labor. Blacks in agricultural regions more than those in cities perceived landownership as the source of economic independence, and they championed it with no less fervor than voting rights and civil rights. Their claim to land was based on their perception of the historic role of black slaves in the economic development of the American nation. The ex-slave Bayley Wyat said as much when the army uprooted him and other freedpeople from their settlement near Yorktown, Virginia. Wyat was quoted as offering the following testimony: "We has a right to the land where we are located. For why? I tell you. Our wives, our children, our husbands, has been sold over and over again to purchase the lands we now locates upon; for that reason we have a divine right to the land. . . . And den didn't we clear the land, and raise de crops ob corn, ob cotton, ob tobacco, ob rice, ob sugar, ob everything. And den didn't dem large cities in de North grow up on de cotton and de sugars and de rice dat we made? . . . I say dey has grown rich, and my people is poor."

The freedpeople's desire for land proved to be a constant challenge to the Freedmen's Bureau. For blacks who were displaced by the war, the Bureau undertook a mammoth task of resettlement, since many of the former slaves were homeless and penniless. Some had been thrown off the land by landowners, while others refused to sign unfair labor contracts and simply left plantations of their own accord, insisting that the property belonged to them. In 1865 the freedpeople, particularly in the South Carolina and Georgia low country, but in other areas as well, were convinced through rumor and hearsay that the federal government planned to redistribute abandoned and confiscated land in forty-acre plots around Christmas time or in the early new year of 1866. This impression stemmed from the Confederates' apprehension during the war that the federal government planned to seize their land and convey it to ex-slaves, and also from the Congressional bill creating the Freedmen's Bureau, which made reference to dividing abandoned land into forty-acre parcels for lease and sale.

"Forty acres and a mule," as a gift of the government, was never realized after the Civil War, but whenever they could, blacks acquired land to achieve economic security. Some were able to buy property when the federal government opened millions of acres of public land under the Southern Homestead Act of 1866, in Alabama, Mississippi, Louisiana, Arkansas, and Florida, to all settlers regardless of race. Within a year ex-slaves secured homesteads in Florida covering 160,960 acres, and in Arkansas they occupied 116 out of 243 homesteads. By 1874 blacks in Georgia owned more than 350,000 acres of land. However, at the state level white hostility to black land ownership, especially in those states with large black populations, prevented the freedmen from becoming a significant proportion of the persons who acquired the land.

Although the Radicals in Congress had initially perceived the Southern Homestead Act as playing a more important role in alleviating the plight of the freedpeople, millions of whites turned out to be the primary beneficiaries. Congress repealed the Southern Homestead Act in 1876, the very year when Reconstruction was coming to an end. Thus by the mid-1870s land ownership in the South was represented by between 4 to 8 percent of all freed families. The majority of blacks remained in rural areas, but a considerable number abandoned dreams of land ownership and migrated to the urban centers of both the North and South. It was in the cities that the Freedmen's Bureau, churches, fraternal societies, and other black community-based institutions and traditions existed. During the Reconstruction era the black population in the South's ten largest cities doubled in size, while the white population grew by only ten percent.

An important family pattern of economic consequences was the attempt to withdraw, as much as possible, black females—often wives and daughters—from the wage-labor market and from the fields of the South. Indeed the large number of **Women in the Labor Market** women and children who withdrew from the labor force in the early aftermath of peace contributed to the decline in per capita production. The editor of *The Plantation*, in 1865, complained that black women no longer picked cotton, "which is a woman's work. . . . They will merely take care of their own households and do but little or no work outdoors." Not only field laborers but domestic servants became more difficult to hire. A white resident in upcountry Georgia noted that "every negro woman wants to set up house keeping." However, women, who served as the sole support for their children or other family members, had to accept work wherever they could find it, which meant being limited to work as domestic laborers or as field hands and also being vulnerable to physical and sexual assault.

Black parents endeavored to exercise control over their children's labor in the fields; and especially after the expansion of schools in rural areas, they eagerly sent their children to school. "The freedmen," a Georgia newspaper reported in 1869, "have almost universally withdrawn their women and children from the fields, putting the first at housework and the latter at school." Although black families made collective decisions as to female members' labor, the male head of household had now taken on an authority impossible under slavery, where the master's rule prevailed.

Increasingly evident was the new assertive role of black men, especially as husbands and fathers—as the representatives of the family. According to historian Jacqueline Jones, the percentage of black male heads of families in the Cotton Belt in 1870 equaled the same high percentage (80 percent) of white male heads of households. Similar to white men, black men tended to be older than their wives, thus reinforcing their patriarchal authority.

Scholars note gender differences in the freedpeople's dealings with the Freedmen's Bureau. Women commonly complained about individual mistreatment, specifically the failure to compensate them for work already completed, but black men, while making similar complaints, commonly spoke for their larger households. Bureau records include numerous examples of male heads of households who specify which family members were to work and the nature of their employment. Such decisions were often based upon the attempt to protect wives and daughters from rape and other forms of assault. Indeed, Freedmen's Bureau agents note the aggrieved men who reported whites who assaulted their wives and other female family members. Such was the case in 1865 when the freedman Sam Neal made accusations against the Tennessee planter for whom he and his family worked. According to

Upland Cotton

Rendered in oil by genre painter Winslow Homer in 1879, this painting captures the lingering power of the slave South's tragic story—cotton, race, back-breaking labor.

Neal, his daughter had been the victim of the man's "several base attempts." Ironically, in families where black women did not work, some Freedmen's Bureau agents described this practice in such derisive terms as "female loaferism" and "playing the lady," thus criticizing black women for behavior considered perfectly appropriate for white married women.

In urban centers, whites lambasted black women for being insolent if they wore fashionable attire. In Wilmington, North Carolina, in 1865 young black women were ridiculed in the press for wearing black veils similar to those worn by their white counterparts. The idea that black women would cultivate the same fashion and leisure styles as white women seemed too much of a display of social equality on the part of women, who had historically been perceived only as laborers. This type of thinking is captured in the description of black women by John De Forest, a Freedmen's Bureau agent in South Carolina, who stated "myriads of women who once earned their own living now have aspirations to be like white ladies and, instead of using the hoe, pass the days in dawdling over their trivial housework, or gossiping among their neighbors." In reality, the great majority of black women never had the luxury to "keep house" or approximate white women's lifestyles. Their withdrawal from the fields had proved temporary at best. In the Cotton Belt in 1870 forty percent of black married women worked, primarily in the fields, while less than 2 percent of white married women listed an occupation other than homemaker. Freedmen's families occupied the lowest rung of the southern economic ladder, and almost three-fourths of all black household heads (compared to 10 percent of their white counterparts) worked as unskilled agricultural laborers.

Throughout the Reconstruction era African Americans resisted, as much as possible, the coercive and limiting conditions that characterized antebellum plantation agriculture. For example, at harvest time in 1865, Georgia blacks balked at the hiring of an overseer and walked off the plantation, leaving the planter without laborers. The freedpeople also rejected the gang-labor system as reminiscent of slavery, preferring instead to work in kin groups, known as the "squad system" and a harbinger of sharecropping. The wage system proved fundamentally unattractive to the freedpeople because of planters' failure to pay either part or all of the wages due to them.

Changing Conditions of Farm Labor

The reduction in overall per capita labor hours in the South was real, dropping by one-third of its prewar level. Planters' letters complain of laborers who "absent themselves when they please, and lounge lazily about." However, the editor of a black newspaper declared in 1865 that black people need not be reminded to avoid idleness, since "the necessity of working is perfectly understood by men who have worked all their lives." To meet the urgent need for labor, the Freedmen's Bureau provided free transportation, and some planters even promised bonuses at harvest time. Planters found it expedient to be more flexible in enforcing labor contracts, and some employers went to unusual lengths to lure workers. A Tennessee planter, for example, offered the services of his wagon to carry blacks to a barbecue.

What solution there was, however unsatisfactory, came by negotiations between the white employer and the black worker, in some instances under the supervision of the Freedmen's Bureau. In the late 1860s sharecropping emerged as a "compromise," as a flawed resolution to the economic tug-of-war **Sharecropping** between the planters' need for greater stability and control over agricultural production and the freedpeople's need for less risk in economic compensation. The wages paid them in 1867, for example, were lower than those paid to the hired slaves of the Old South. In addition, greater freedom from white supervision prompted black families to sign contracts that gave them responsibility over the cultivation of crops on a specific plot of land and ownership of a percentage (between one-quarter and one-third) of the harvested crop.

Usually dependent on the planter to furnish fertilizer, farm tools, work animals, and seed, most sharecroppers quickly found themselves locked in a spiral of debt from which there was no escape. In the sharecropping system the cost of maintenance was so great that at the end of the year ex-slaves were indebted to their employers for most of what they had made and sometimes more than what they had made. The white South recovered much more rapidly than did the former slaves. By 1880 the South was producing more cotton than ever, while profits from sugar continued to improve, although at a slower rate than cotton. Black farm workers contributed greatly to the economic recovery of the South. As free workers, however, they gained little.

One effort to assist former slaves in their economic adjustment was the encouragement given them to save their money. There had been several experiments with savings banks for blacks during the war. After the allotment system was developed, many soldiers saved regularly in banks established for that purpose. Outstanding were the Free Labor Bank set up by General Banks at New Orleans, and another established by General Butler at Norfolk. Toward the end of the war, blacks were **The Freedmen's Bank** given an opportunity to save at the Freedmen's Savings and Trust Company, which was chartered by the federal government in 1865. The business of the organization, with William Booth as president, was confined to the black race, and two-thirds of the deposits were to be invested in securities of the United States.

On April 4, 1865, the headquarters of the Freedmen's Bank, as it was called, was opened in New York. Within the next few months branches were started in Washington, New Orleans, Nashville, Vicksburg, Louisville, and Memphis. By 1872 there were thirty-four branches, with only the New York and Philadelphia offices in the North; by 1874 the deposits in all branches totaled $3,299,201. But unmistakable evidences of failure were apparent: there was inaccurate bookkeeping, and some of the cashiers were incompetent. Almost no black employees had been hired at the beginning, but gradually they were hired. Some, but not all, proved able to perform their tasks. Political influence was used to secure loans. At a time when his business was tottering, Jay Cooke borrowed $500,000 at only 5 percent interest, and Henry Cooke together with other financiers unloaded bad loans on the bank.

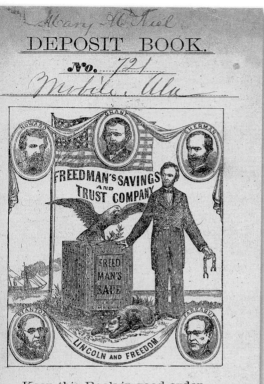

DEPOSIT BOOK.

No. 721

Mobile, Ala.

FREEDMAN'S SAVINGS AND TRUST COMPANY

FREED MAN'S SAFE

LINCOLN AND FREEDOM

Keep this Book in good order.
Do not fold or roll it up.
Give immediate Notice if lost.

The Freedman's Saving and Trust Company

To encourage thrift among the former slaves, Congress established the Freedman's Saving and Trust Company. A savings book from that bank is pictured here.

After the big financial houses failed in 1873, there was a run on the Freedmen's Bank, and many speculating officials resigned, leaving blacks to take the blame. In March 1874, Frederick Douglass was made president, but the bank was already a failure, although neither he nor the public was aware of the fact. When Douglass realized the truth, he resorted to desperate means to save the bank, using his own money and appealing to the Senate Finance Committee for more. The bank was placed in liquidation by Congress so that it could be reorganized, but it was too late. Confidence in the bank had been completely shattered, and on June 28, 1874, it closed. Thousands of black depositors suffered losses they could ill afford. Black leaders, some of whom were blameless, were castigated by their fellows, while the Cookes and others, who benefited most, escaped without public censure.

Reconstruction's End

Reconstruction did not come to an abrupt end in the southern states. As early as 1869, the ex-Confederates of Tennessee became enfranchised, and within a few months large numbers of white Southerners in other states reclaimed their citizenship through individual acts of amnesty. In 1871 the "ironclad" oath, which Congress had imposed at the beginning of Radical Reconstruction to disqualify many ex-Confederates, was repealed. In the following year a general amnesty restored the franchise to all but about six hundred ex-Confederate officials.

The political effect could be seen in the quick revival of the Democratic party in state after state. In 1870 the border states went Democratic; North Carolina and Virginia came under the control of Conservatives, who outnumbered the Republicans. In the following year Georgia Democrats returned to power. Other states began to witness an ascendant Democratic party, especially in counties with larger white electorates. In 1874 and 1875, voters in Texas, Arkansas, and Alabama put Democrats in office. By 1876 the only states that Republicans could claim were South Carolina, Florida, and Louisiana. The "redemption" of the southern states had become a crusade to restore white "home rule" and overthrow the last vestiges of Republican hegemony.

And white supremacists resorted to every legal and extra-legal maneuver to deny blacks political equality. Secret societies grew and spread when it became apparent to Southerners that their control was to be broken by Radical Reconstruction. For ten years after 1867 such organizations as the Knights of the White Camelia, the Constitutional Union Guards, the Pale Faces, the White Brotherhood, the Council of Safety, the '76 Association, and the Knights of the Ku Klux Klan flourished across the South, as well as local state-based organizations such as the White League of Louisiana, the White Line of Mississippi, and the Rifle Clubs of South Carolina. White Southerners expected to do by extralegal or blatantly illegal means what had not been allowed by law: to exercise absolute control over blacks, drive them and their fellows from the ballot box and elective office, and establish "white home rule."

The Reign of Violence

The Camelias and the Klan were the most powerful of the secret orders. Armed with guns, swords, or other weapons, their members patrolled some parts of the South day and night. Scattered Union troops proved wholly ineffectual in coping with them, for the members were sworn to secrecy, disguised themselves and their deeds in many ways, and had the respect and support of the white community. They used intimidation, force, ostracism in business and society, bribery at the polls, arson, and even murder to accomplish their deeds.

Blacks were run out of communities if they disobeyed orders to desist from voting, and the more resolute and therefore insubordinate blacks were whipped, maimed, and hanged. In 1871 several black officials in South Carolina were given fifteen days to resign, and they were warned that if they failed to do so, "then retributive justice will as surely be used as night follows day." Similarly in Kentucky, the major purpose of violence against blacks was to eliminate their participation in politics. In 1874 a committee of the Colored Convention assembled in Atlanta informed the state legislature that they could not point "to any locality in Georgia where we can in truth say that our lives and our liberties are perfectly secure."

Local efforts to suppress the outlaw organizations were on the whole unsuccessful. In 1868 Alabama, for example, passed a law imposing heavy fines and long jail sentences on anyone caught away from home wearing a mask or committing such acts as destroying property and molesting people, but this law was generally disregarded. Congress undertook to suppress the Klan and similar groups in a series of laws passed in 1870 and 1871. It was a punishable crime for any person to prevent another from voting by bribery, force, or intimidation, and the president was authorized to use land and naval forces to prevent such crimes. In 1871 a second law was passed to strengthen the first. After an extensive investigation, members of Congress were convinced that the Klan was still active, and in April 1871 a law designed to put an end to the movement was enacted. The president was authorized to suspend the writ of habeas corpus in order to suppress "armed combinations." Acts of conspiracy were declared tantamount to rebellion and were to be punished accordingly. As a result, hundreds of arrests were made, and many were found guilty of conspiracy. In South Carolina alone, nearly 100 were sentenced and fined in one year.

Undaunted by those laws, the reign of violence continued. In 1875 Mississippi stood on the verge of war. The black militia maintained by Governor Adelbert Ames was especially offensive to the resurgent Democrats, and whites thought it was time for a "protective" white militia to step forward. Both sides imported arms, paraded, and actually skirmished. Although Ames promised to disband the black militia, disorder and killings continued until the election, when the Democrats carried the state by more than 30,000 votes. Within two months the Republican party was dissolved. In Louisiana, the Conservatives organized "White Leagues" and apparently planned to overthrow the Radical government by violence as early as 1874.

Ku Klux Klan members in 1868
The flowing white robes and cone-shaped headdresses associated with the Ku Klux Klan today are mostly a twentieth-century phenomenon. The Klansmen of the Reconstruction era, like these two men in Alabama, were well armed, disguised, and prepared to intimidate both black and white Republicans.

The Radicals tried to seize the arms of the White Leagues, an attempt that resulted in a riot in New Orleans, killing 40 and wounding more than 100 people. Intermittent warfare continued through the election of 1876, and there was no peace until President Rutherford B. Hayes withdrew the federal troops the following year.

In South Carolina, the "Red Shirts" dominated campaign meetings and openly carried arms as a measure of "protection" against Radical "tyranny." Workingmen's Democratic Associations were organized, and whites were urged to employ only Democrats. Constant turmoil engulfed many sections of the state, particularly Edgefield County, where the racist demagogue Ben Tillman was rapidly becoming a public figure. However, even in the places where no riots occurred, whites kept blacks from the polls by other methods of intimidation. The crops of blacks were destroyed, their barns and houses burned, and they were whipped and lynched for voting Republican. Democrats organized patrolled polling places to guarantee "fair, peaceful, and Democratic" elections.

African Americans did not passively capitulate to this reign of terror. Even after beatings and other forms of intimidation, many defied their attackers, vowing to vote whatever the cost. In Bennettsville, South Carolina, blacks took more radical steps—arming themselves, patrolling the streets, and defying Klansmen to come for them. In Alabama, according to one observer, African Americans in one part of the state's black belt "invited a contest, saying they were willing to go out into an open field and 'fight it out.'" Such overt challenges, however, became increasingly rare. More and more blacks remained at home, and political power shifted with growing momentum from Republican to Democratic hands.

Disclosures of corruption in Republican governments also served to discredit and hasten the end of Radical Reconstruction. The case for Democrats was strengthened consider-

Corruption in Republican Governments

ably as they pointed to misgovernment through bribery, embezzlement, misappropriation of funds, and other corrupt practices. The federal government was unable to rush to the defense of Southern Republican governments because it was having difficulty purging itself of corruption. It did not matter that white Southerners had also been corrupt before the war or that the provisional governments under Presidential Reconstruction were extravagant and corrupt. The Democrats were not in power in 1874 and consequently had all the advantages that "out groups" usually enjoy in such cases.

Even before 1876, the Republicans in Congress had begun to waiver on the feasibility and constitutionality of Reconstruction policies. Moreover, the deaths of Stevens, Sumner, Butler, and others among the old antislavery leadership left a vacuum that would be filled by younger congressmen, with less zeal for blacks. The new leaders were loyal party men, practical politicians who cared more about industrial interests in the North and South than about Radical governments in the South. The rising influence of Rutherford B. Hayes, James G. Blaine, Roscoe Conkling, and John A. Logan signaled a new direction for the Republican party—a turn to more profitable and practical pursuits.

Nor did the Supreme Court help to postpone the end of Reconstruction. As a matter of fact, its decisions had the effect of hastening the end. In 1875 several indictments under

Supreme Court Decisions

the Enforcement Act of 1870 charged defendants with preventing blacks from exercising their right to vote in elections, but in both the *United States v. Reese* (a Kentucky case) and in the same year in *United States v. Cruikshank* (a Louisiana case), the Court weakened considerably blacks ability to exercise their voting rights. In

Reese the Court held that the Fifteenth Amendment did not confer the right of suffrage on anyone but rather "prevents the States or the United States . . . from giving preference . . . to one citizen of the United States over another on account of race, color, or previous condition of servitude." In *Cruikshank*, the Supreme Court struck down the Enforcement Act of 1870, declaring it unconstitutional on the grounds that the "due process" and "equal protection clauses" of the Fourteenth Amendment applied only to state-imposed actions, not those of individual citizens.

African Americans could no longer expect much support from a court that permitted white southerners the freedom to settle their problems as they saw fit, even if it meant brushing aside the civil and political rights of black southerners.

The presidential campaign of 1876 between Republican candidate Rutherford B. Hayes and Democratic candidate Samuel J. Tilden determined Reconstruction's fate in the three states where Republicans still held power—South Carolina, Louisiana, and Florida. In South Carolina and Louisiana, the hotly disputed election left each party claiming the victory and setting up competing governments. The gravity of the controversy led to the formation of a special commission, charged with deciding the presidency of the United States. In the meantime, to break the impasse, the Republicans promised not only to withdraw troops but also to assist the South in its long-cherished ambition to obtain federal subsidies for internal improvements and better representation in affairs in Washington.

The Campaign of 1876

The commission determined in favor of Hayes, who, once in office, promptly withdrew all troops, thus freeing southern politics from northern interference. A conciliatory Congress then removed other restrictions. In 1878 the use of armed forces was no longer permitted to monitor elections. In the next decade, the number of black voters dropped precipitously, although in some places blacks were able to elect members of their race, albeit in far fewer numbers, to public office. By the dawn of the twentieth century, however, southern blacks were effectively disfranchised.

For the great majority of white Americans, Reconstruction after the Civil War had proven to be a tragic era, riddled with problems and pitfalls that could be corrected only in a new and unequal racial order. For very different reasons, African Americans, too, concluded that Reconstruction had failed. They bemoaned the tragic loss of their civil and political rights. Reconstruction could be vindicated, blacks believed, only when the nation lived up to its promises of freedom and justice for all. In the late 1870s, the writing on the wall had appeared somewhat blurred but increasingly legible to discerning eyes.

And, for blacks, the future did not bode well. It must have seemed, to them, as if a cruel and mischievous editor's hand had begun to pen an indelible line through the text of the Fourteenth and Fifteenth Amendments—deleting their meaning and intent, while preserving merely a veneer of words. This line, drawn with cunning and malice, ran with equal mischief through southern political life, transforming the American two-party system into essentially one party. The writing on the wall appeared ever more clear and bold in the decades to come—this mysterious, seeming indelible line that ran with growing force through customs and laws, through schools and workplaces, through public buildings and transportation, and through the South and the North. The color line had become finally obvious to everyone.

259

12 The Color Line

The Path to Disfranchisement

Legalizing Segregation

Confronting the Urban Color Line

America's Empire of Color

The Pattern of Violence

Segregation
By 1900 the color line had been drawn so well that many institutions—hotels, theaters, restaurants, railroad trains and depots, schools, parks, and more—had established racial lines that could not be breached. Such lines were supported by state and local legislation. The sign shown here is typical of the period.

n July 1890 the Louisiana legislature passed Act 111, "An Act to Promote the Comfort of Passengers." This law mandated racial segregation on railroad travel within the state and supplanted a law of 1868 that stipulated: "All persons shall enjoy equal rights and privileges upon any conveyance of a public character; and all places of business, or of public resort . . . without discrimination or discrimination on account of race or color." To Louisiana lawmakers in 1890, the earlier law represented yet another distasteful relic of the Reconstruction era. The mood of the South and the nation had changed profoundly in the intervening years, and the egalitarian spirit embodied in the words of the Louisiana law of 1868 and in the Civil Rights Act of 1875 had long since disappeared. Democratic-controlled state governments throughout the South moved steadily toward legalizing the color line, enacting so-called Jim Crow laws to ensure that racial discrimination operated in more than customary or de facto social relations.

The Jim Crow laws gave new meaning and reinforcement to white supremacy, proscribing black access to places and things, to opportunities, and to rights. Perhaps the color line's most insidious role was the ability to transform the very meaning of "We the people," despite monumental constitutional changes that had occurred during Reconstruction. But the "New South" of the waning years of the nineteenth century stood poised to usher in its own sweeping changes. Like Louisiana, many southern states perceived the enactment of statutory segregation as part and parcel of social reform. Constitutional conventions more firmly established the color line with new laws that referred to the "public good" and "public comfort" as they placed African Americans outside the voting booth and representative government, outside public accommodations, and even outside the broad meaning of "the public" itself. At the very same time, American and European imperialism had begun to draw a line through much of the world—denoting the relation of white powers to their colonies of darker peoples.

The Path to Disfranchisement

After the Democrats returned to power in the South, they confronted the problem of finding ways to nullify blacks' political strength or to disfranchise them altogether. Violence remained the surest means for keeping African Americans politically impotent, and in countless communities they were not allowed, on pain of severe reprisals, to show their faces in town on Election Day. However, state officials increasingly looked to more civil and respectable methods to attain the same goal. They were known to both deplore vigilante activity and give a nod to it, when expedient.

In the immediate years following Reconstruction, most of the South's white leaders identified themselves and their party as Conservative Democrats. Their economic policies, which benefited railroads and industry over agriculture, and their elite status and greater affluence relative to most white farmers and working-class southerners, made it fitting that these Democratic regimes were called "Conservative" as well as "Bourbon" and "Redeemer" administrations. Seeking a probusiness climate of order and stability in the "New South," the Conservative Democrats did not initially advocate disfranchisement by state legislation, since the Fourteenth and Fifteenth Amendments had become a fundamental part of American constitutional law. In the federal courts, the Fourteenth Amendment had even come to function, with no racial meaning at all, as a way of protecting industry and big business.

Preventing Black Voting Legally

Once white rule was established, the southern Conservatives resorted to a variety of tactics to prevent blacks from voting. Polling places were frequently set up far from black communities, and the diligent blacks who tried to vote failed to reach them, finding roads blocked and ferries conveniently out of repair at election time. Polling places were sometimes changed without notifying black voters; or, if they were notified, election officials thought nothing of making a last-minute decision to change the location again. Election laws were so imperfect that in many communities uniform ballots were not required, and officials winked at Democrats who made up several extra ballots to cast with the one given them. (At that time, secret ballots were not used in most parts of the United States, including the South; instead, voters usually placed a preprinted ballot or token in the box provided for each party.) The stuffing of ballot boxes was widespread. Indeed, Democrats were known to boast that "the white and black Republicans may outvote us, but we can outcount them."

At times white factions exploited the black vote for their own purposes, actually vying with one another for black voters. In especially contested elections among whites in Black Belt areas, planters brought their black workers to the polls, having already instructed them as to how they should vote in this nonsecret process. Some whites nominated multiple black candidates in order to divide the black vote, while maximizing the white vote by having only one candidate. However, the growing trend among the white supremacist governments was that of state-legislated mechanisms, such as poll taxes, literacy tests, confusing and complicated balloting processes, and highly centralized election codes—all functioning as "legal" schemes for black disfranchisement.

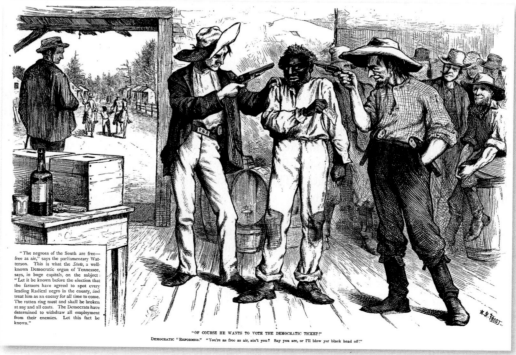

A rural black man "freely" exercises the right to vote
Note the bottle of whiskey next to the ballot box.

Gerrymandering election districts also became a popular legal way to render ineffective the voting power of areas with a heavy concentration of African Americans. Virginia legislators, for example, reapportioned, or gerrymandered, the state's voting districts five times in a seventeen-year period in order to nullify black ballots. South Carolina legislators also manipulated the voting process to make it difficult for African Americans. A law of 1882 required that special ballots and boxes be placed at every polling place for each office on the ballot and that voters put their ballots in the correct boxes. No one was allowed to speak to a voter, and if he failed to find the correct box, his vote was thrown out.

South Carolina and Virginia were not alone in devising ingenious schemes to render the black vote ineffective. All the southern states used some device or other. The result appeared so satisfactory on the whole that by 1889 Henry W. Grady, the influential editor of the Atlanta *Constitution* and advocate for the probusiness New South, noted with pleasure that "the Negro as a political force has dropped out of serious consideration."

Strangely enough, however, the near disappearance of blacks from the public sphere of politics created circumstances that called for their reappearance. By the 1880s, the menace of black Republicanism had disappeared, and with it the great cohesive force among southern whites. Almost immediately, sharp class lines appeared among whites. Once white southern farmers no longer feared "Negro rule," they began to associate their own plight with the policies of the Conservatives. The coalition of classes that had united only to oppose African Americans began to disintegrate, as poor whites came to distrust the Bourbons for substantial economic and political reasons.

Black Reappearance in Politics

The economic depression that began in 1873 was especially disastrous to agricultural communities. In the years that followed, small farmers lost their land and fell into the ranks of tenant and sharecrop farmers. In their distress, they turned against the financiers who foreclosed their mortgages, the railroads that charged excessive freight rates but received subsidies from state and federal taxes, the corporations that sought higher tariffs and charged higher prices for farm machinery, and the state government that steadily raised taxes. Class divisions had become evident in party politics. Radical farmers, who called for the regulation of railroads, state aid for agriculture, and higher taxes on corporations, organized in opposition to New South proponents of business and industry. The threat of a black balance of power did not seem to frighten hungry white farmers—an alarming prospect for loyal Democrats. Such leaders as Henry Grady condemned the defections across the electoral color line that he saw occurring among whites.

Southern whites doubtless won the battle to purge black voters from their states' election rolls, but complete black disfranchisement unfolded over time and with noteworthy interruptions. In the aftermath of Reconstruction, instances of racial cooperation made striking appearances, but they all proved momentary and fleeting. For example, the Readjuster Party rose to power in Virginia in 1879 from an unlikely coalition of black Republicans and disgruntled white Democrats. They united initially because of the social and economic hardship associated with the commonwealth's payment of its Civil War debt. Placing greater emphasis on mutual economic interests instead of racial difference, Readjusters denounced the Conservative Democrats for reallocating monies originally designated for Virginia's public school system toward the full funding of the debt.

Black Virginians, like disaffected others, similarly protested, but they also justified their opposition with the unique explanation that they were slaves when the debt was acquired. Prompted by the closing of many public schools and the desperate state of economic affairs, a biracial alliance formed under the leadership of William Mahone, a former slaveholder, Confederate officer, and railroad owner, in order to demand a readjustment of the debt's funding. White Readjusters recognized that only an alliance with the large black Republican constituency could bring about their party's victory over the Democrats.

The unprecedented third-party fusion won Mahone the governorship, sent Readjusters to both houses of the U.S. Congress, and brought black Republicans back into elected and appointed office at various levels of government. The Readjuster Party advocated the protection of black voting rights, free public education, tax relief, a mechanics law that favored workers, and railroad regulation. Historian Jane Dailey describes the Readjuster platform as committed "to an essentially rights-oriented political language and program." Readjusters would go by the official name the Liberal Party in 1881, although at the popular level still called Readjuster. The powerful coalition governed the state for only four years. In 1883, the party lost power to the Conservative Democrats—its interracial coalition unraveling when blacks sought the repeal of antimiscegenation laws, demanded school integration, and ran for election for seats on school boards. Longstanding and implacable white supremacist beliefs undermined the coalition. Despite the Conservative victory, the political strength of black Republican voters was sufficient enough for the narrow, but controversial victory in 1888 of John Mercer Langston, the first black to represent Virginia in the United States Congress. It took eighteen months before the contested election was settled in Langston's favor, thus leaving him only six months of his congressional term.

The radical agrarian movement that led to the creation of the Populist Party also disturbed the drawing of the color line in the late 1880s and early 1890s. By 1889 the Southern Farmers' Alliance had branches in every southern state. Although the Alliance did not admit black members, its leaders believed that blacks should organize in a parallel organization. First organized in 1886, the Colored Farmers' National Alliance and Cooperative Union grew rapidly and by 1891 claimed more than a million members in twelve state organizations. Local chapters formed wherever black farmers were sufficiently numerous. As the program of radical agrarianism evolved during the last two decades of the nineteenth century, black and white farmers in the South drifted closer together.

The Radical Agrarian Movement

The Populist, or People's, Party became the political agency of the resurgent farmers. In 1892 the Populists sought to win the black vote in most of the southern states and in many instances resorted to desperate means to secure the franchise for blacks in communities where by custom and practice they had been barred from voting for more than a decade. Radical Populist leaders such as Tom Watson of Georgia told poor whites and blacks that they were being deliberately kept apart and fleeced. A few candidates, as did Watson, sought black votes by advocating measures favorable to them even before the rise of Populists as a political party. As early as 1882, when he was running for the Georgia legislature, Tom Watson courted black voters, recognizing that their support was essential to his victory.

Once elected, Watson voted in favor of issues important to blacks, such as tax-supported public schools, the elimination of the convict lease system, and greater fairness and equity for tenant farmers and sharecroppers. He called on them to stand together and work for the common good. At the time, Watson opposed black disfranchisement and looked forward to a coalition of black and white farmers to drive the Bourbons from power in Georgia. Unfortunately, he would later betray blacks by becoming a fanatical Negrophobe and race baiter.

Coalitions of black and white voters were always tenuous, but where they existed they greatly alarmed Conservative Democrats. However, the Conservatives were known to seek out blacks, planters rounding up their black workers as herds of cattle and forcing them to vote for the very Democrats who only a few years earlier had dared blacks to attempt such an exercise of the "white man's prerogative." In some areas, black men were hauled to towns in wagons and made to vote repeatedly. In Augusta, Georgia, they were even imported across the river from South Carolina to vote for Democrats.

Many blacks, however, stood by the Populist message of political equality. A black advocate of Tom Watson was the young preacher H. S. Doyle, who made sixty-three speeches for Watson in the face of numerous threats. Voting for the Populist ticket proved to have consequences no less violent than did voting for the Republican Party in the South. A black Populist in Dalton, Georgia, was murdered in his home, and it is estimated that fifteen were killed in Georgia during the state elections of 1892. Riots also broke out in Virginia and North Carolina. If black rule meant chaos and disorder to the Democrats, the mere threat of it was enough for them to resort to violence themselves.

In some states, there was a successful fusion between the newly organized Populists and the remnants of old Republican organizations. In 1894 such a coalition dismantled the Democratic election machinery in North Carolina, and voting was opened up once again to a greater number of blacks. Black officeholders **Successful Coalitions** were elected in the eastern black belt of the state. Indeed, three hundred black magistrates were elected in North Carolina in 1895. Several counties had black deputy sheriffs. Wilmington had fourteen black police officers, and New Bern had both black policemen and black aldermen. One prominent black, James H. Young, was made chief fertilizer inspector and a director of the state asylum for the blind; another, John C. Dancy, was appointed collector for the port of Wilmington. George White went to Congress in 1896 and served as a member of the House of Representatives until 1901. It would be more than two decades before another African American, Oscar De Priest from Illinois, would be elected to Congress.

The Democrats deeply resented the reappearance of black voters and officeholders in North Carolina, Georgia, and other southern states, and they perceived this participation as unwelcome, indeed an intrusion into the electoral process and a violation of the color line. Failing to control the black vote for their own purposes, the Conservatives scorned the return of black Republicanism. Ironically, the black vote had become a problem on both sides of the white-voter divide. Neither the Conservatives nor the Populists in the South could get beyond the centuries-old ideology of white supremacy, no matter the economic consequences. What the black scholar and activist W.E.B. Du Bois called the psychological "wages of whiteness" would eventually lead the white farmers down the familiar path of white supremacy. No matter that whites themselves were divided as to which class should rule; each side believed that the other had the power to manipulate black voters in its favor. Black disfranchisement, both groups agreed, kept politics "honest."

Scholars note the ambivalent politics of the Populists, many of whom perceived a danger in too close an association with blacks. Some worried that the election laws, as they stood, might actually be turned against poor, illiterate whites if the **Complete Disfranchisement** Democrats became vindictive and sought to disfranchise Populists and blacks alike. It was much better, they reasoned, to have clear-cut constitutional disfranchisement of blacks and to leave white groups to fight elections out among themselves. Where the Populists were unable to control the black vote, as in Georgia in 1894, men such as Tom Watson argued that the Democrats kept sufficient numbers of black voters on the rolls in the event they needed them. Thus the defeated and disappointed Watson supported a constitutional amendment excluding blacks from the franchise—a complete reversal of his earlier position.

The growing consensus among whites was that blacks made for corruption in politics. By 1896 and the collapse of the agrarian revolt, the answer to this problem had become clear to both white factions: disfranchise black voters altogether. The removal of blacks from electoral politics served to reunite the whites and build the Solid South, meaning the whites-only Democratic Party.

When it became evident that white factions would continue to compete with one another for the black vote, especially in tight races where the black vote proved crucial, it was time, leaders on both sides believed, for the complete disfranchisement of blacks—the Fifteenth Amendment notwithstanding. On this, most southern whites agreed, although they differed over the method of disfranchising blacks. The view prevailed that none but people of property and intelligence were entitled to vote. As one writer put it, white southerners believed that "no person should enjoy the suffrage unless he gives sufficient evidence of his permanent interest in and attachment to the community." And yet many white southerners, not surprisingly poor whites, opposed such stringent prerequisites, since they potentially disqualified numerous whites. Indeed, some of them had been disfranchised by earlier measures, when competition grew keen between rival white groups and the Conservatives barred some Radical whites from the polls, while seeking black votes.

Isaiah Montgomery

Sponsors of a stricter suffrage sought to devise a system that would hold up to judicial scrutiny, given the Fifteenth Amendment, but also succeed in the disfranchisement of blacks without disqualifying any portion of the white electorate. The Supreme Court decisions in the *Reese* and *Cruikshank* cases in the mid-1870s had already shown the Court to be amenable to such plans, although no guarantee existed that the Court would view favorably state actions patently designed to disfranchise a group because of its race.

It was in Mississippi, where a majority of the population was black, that the complications of black disfranchisement were first addressed and resolved. As early as 1886, sentiment for constitutional revision began to intensify, and in 1890, a state convention met for the primary purpose of disfranchising blacks. A suffrage amendment was written that imposed a poll tax of $2 and also excluded voters convicted of bribery, burglary, theft, arson, perjury, murder, or bigamy. Also explicitly barred from voting were persons who could not read any section of the state constitution, understand it when read, or give a "reasonable" interpretation of it.

Only one black delegate participated at the Mississippi convention: Isaiah T. Montgomery. Born a slave on May 21, 1847, on the plantation of Joseph Davis, the brother of Jefferson Davis, Montgomery and his father bought from Joseph Davis the land on which the all-black settlement Mound Bayou in the Mississippi Delta was founded. For many years, Montgomery served as the mayor of Mound Bayou. A close friend of Booker T. Washington, Montgomery advocated self-help and education, establishing technical schools in his town and enforcing puritanical moral codes. As Mississippi lawmakers proposed new suffrage proscriptions in 1890, Montgomery was not fooled by the motives behind what became known as the Mississippi Plan. He pointed out that the poll tax and education requirements would disfranchise 123,000 blacks and only 12,000 whites. He nevertheless voted for the proposed amendments, clearly realizing the devastating effect they would have on the black vote.

Before the convention assembled, black delegates from forty Mississippi counties had met and protested their impending disfranchisement all the way to the White House and President Benjamin Harrison. Doubtless they would have fought ratification, but the Conservatives would run no risk of having their handiwork rejected; after the convention approved the constitution, it was promulgated and declared to be in effect. The Mississippi Plan had set the precedent for several other states: South Carolina (1895), Louisiana (1898), North Carolina (1900), Alabama (1901), Virginia (1901), Georgia (1908), and Oklahoma (1910).

The individual who spearheaded South Carolina's disfranchisement effort was familiarly called "Pitchfork Ben" Tillman, who had vaulted to prominence as a white supremacist and leader of the Farmer's Alliance in South Carolina. He won the governorship of the state as the Democratic Party candidate in 1890 and immediately sought a constitutional convention to disfranchise black voters. He gained sufficient support for the idea during his last year as governor in 1894, and by the time the state's constitutional convention was held in 1895, Tillman had already been elected to the U.S. Senate. However, he returned to the convention to serve as chairman of the Committee on Rights of Suffrage, in order to be certain that blacks were effectively disfranchised. The disfranchisement section called for two years' residence; a poll tax of $1, the ability to read and write any section of the Constitution or to understand it when read aloud, or ownership of property worth $300; it also disqualified convicts. In 1900 Senator Tillman boasted that "we have done our level best [to prevent blacks from voting] . . . we have scratched our heads to find out how we could eliminate the last one of them. We stuffed ballot boxes. We shot them. We are not ashamed of it."

The few black delegates at the South Carolina constitutional convention bitterly denounced the racist disfranchisement amendments. In answer to Tillman's charge that members of their race had done nothing to demonstrate their capacity to govern, for- **The Black Response** mer black congressman Thomas E. Miller, who served in the U.S. House of Representatives between 1889 and 1891, replied that blacks on the state legislature during Reconstruction were primarily responsible for "the laws relative to finance, the building of penal and charitable institutions, and, greatest of all, the establishment of the public school system." He also declared that numerous reform laws "touching every department of state, county, municipal and town governments . . . stand as living witnesses [on the statute books of South Carolina] of the Negro's fitness to vote and legislate on the rights of mankind."

A black delegate to the convention, James Wigg of Beaufort County, also voiced his profound resentment to Tillman's words: "You charge that the Negro is too ignorant to be trusted with the suffrage. I answer that you have not, nor dare you, make a purely educational test of the right to vote. You say that he is a figurehead, an encumbrance to the state, that he pays little or no taxes. I answer you, you have not, nor dare you make a purely property test of the right to vote. . . . We submit our cause to the judgment of an enlightened public opinion and to the arbitrament of a Christian civilization." Unfortunately, Wigg's argument met with minuscule enlightened white support. Only two whites joined the six blacks present at the convention in voting against the South Carolina constitution of 1895.

The story was essentially the same in Louisiana in 1898 when a new device, the "grandfather clause," was written into the constitution. This clause called for an addition to the permanent registration list of the names of all male persons whose fathers and grandfathers were qualified to vote on January 1, 1867. At that time, of course, no blacks were qualified to vote in Louisiana. If any blacks were able to vote, educational and property restrictions served to eliminate them. Blacks led by such men as businessman and former state senator T. B. Stamps appeared before the suffrage committee. He did not denounce a qualified suffrage but rather pleaded that its restrictions be honestly administered.

By 1898 the pattern for constitutional disfranchisement of blacks was clearly established. In subsequent years, other states followed the lead of Mississippi, South Carolina, and Louisiana. By 1910 blacks had been effectively disfranchised by constitutional provisions in North Carolina, Alabama, Virginia, Georgia, and Oklahoma. The tension arising from campaigns for white suffrage sometimes flared up into violent race wars. In Wilmington, North Carolina, three white men were wounded and eleven blacks killed and twenty-five wounded in a riot in 1898. In Atlanta, there were four days of rioting after an election in 1906 in which disfranchisement was the main issue. During this period, robbery, murder, and brutality were not uncommon.

Effective Disfranchisement

For the cause of white supremacy, the effect was most salutary. In 1896 there were 130,344 blacks registered to vote in Louisiana, constituting a majority in twenty-six parishes (counties). In 1900 two years after the adoption of the new constitution, only 5,320 blacks were on the registration books, and in no parish did they make up a majority of voters. Of 181,471 black males of voting age in Alabama in 1900, only 3,000 registered after the new constitutional provisions went into effect. On the floor of the Virginia convention, Carter Glass had said that the delegates were elected "to discriminate to the very extremity of permissible action under the limitations of the Federal Constitution, with a view to the elimination of every Negro voter who can be gotten rid of, legally, without materially impairing the numerical strength of the white electorate." This goal was accomplished not only in Virginia but in every state in which whites resorted to such means. W.E.B. Du Bois offered a terse explanation of the events that eradicated all vestiges of Radical Reconstruction: "The slave went free, stood a brief moment in the sun, then moved back again toward slavery."

Black men fought unsuccessfully to defend themselves in the Wilmington, North Carolina, riot in November 1898

The South universally hailed the disfranchisement of blacks as a constructive act of statesmanship. African Americans were viewed as outside the body politic and stereotyped as ignorant, poor, and innately inferior to all whites—qualities incompatible with logical and orderly processes of government. The southern white accusation that blacks had done nothing to warrant suffrage defied the reality of what Mississippi congressman John R. Lynch would call "the facts of Reconstruction," the title of a book he wrote. But such racist accusations also defied the visible progress that blacks were making in many walks of life.

Back to Slavery

Given the rising black literacy, the numbers of blacks in schools of higher learning and in the professions, as well as black property owners, it was certainly impossible to prove that blacks were by nature inherently shiftless and incapable of advancement. But the framers of the new suffrage laws did not trouble themselves over these inconsistencies, when customs, laws, science, and popular culture all reaffirmed the ideology of America as "the white man's nation."

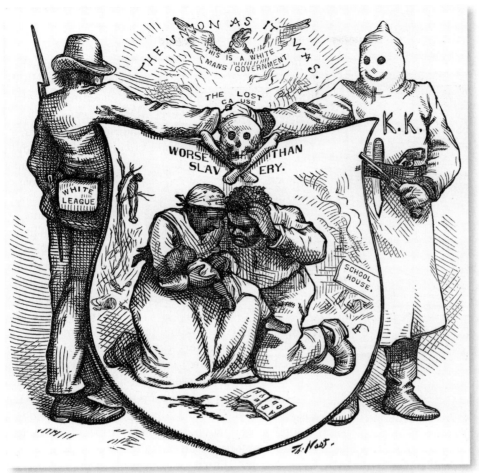

Drawing, *The Union as It Was,* by Thomas Nast, *Harper's Weekly,* October 24, 1874
The artist Nast deplored Klan violence and terror.

This viewpoint was best captured by the white supremacist Senator J. K. Vardaman of Mississippi: "I am just as opposed to Booker Washington as a voter, with all his Anglo-Saxon re-enforcements, as I am to the coconut-headed, chocolate-colored, typical little coon, Andy Dotson, who blacks my shoes every morning. Neither is fit to perform the supreme function of citizenship." Whites would go to great lengths to undermine the rules of voter qualifications, since many blacks had already met even the most stringent constitutional qualifications.

The rise of the "white primary," from which all blacks were excluded by party rules, had the effect of transforming the Democratic party itself into a racially exclusive club—a political caucus for white men only. But more than this, the white primary functioned as the government of the white Solid South. With no political clout, blacks had no access to representative government and no power to thwart the passage of new state laws that would mandate segregation. Jim Crow became the catchword for the color line as a legal, de jure entity in the South.

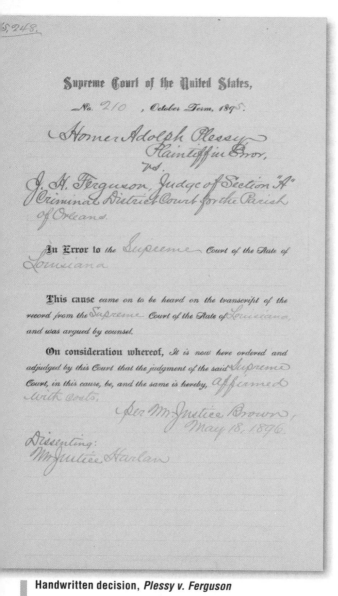

Handwritten decision, *Plessy v. Ferguson*

Plessy v. Ferguson

Legalizing Segregation

Prior to the 1890s, custom more than law operated to divide the races, especially during the years when the Civil Rights Act of 1875 was considered to be the law of the land. But those who were determined to defy the law constantly challenged this act, which represented the last-ditch effort of the Radical Republicans to rid the South and the nation of many of the daily and customary practices of racial discrimination on trains, in depots, and on wharves. Indeed, the five cases that came before the Supreme Court in 1883 under the title the *Civil Rights Cases* were brought by black litigants whose rights had been abridged not only in the South but across the nation—in Kansas, Missouri, California, New York, and Tennessee. They had been excluded from a variety of establishments—inns, theaters, and the "ladies' car" of a train. The majority of the Supreme Court did not decide in favor of the black litigants; instead, they declared unconstitutional the Civil Rights Acts of 1875. Individual proprietors' acts of discrimination, the Court ruled, fell under the rubric of state, not the federal government. With the adoption of new state constitutions in the 1890s, African Americans filed legal suits to challenge state-mandated segregation. In 1896 the Supreme Court upheld segregation and the doctrine of "separate but equal" set forth in the case of *Plessy v. Ferguson.*

It is not commonly known that *Plessy* was a test case brought to the courts by the black community in New Orleans. Within days of the passage of Louisiana's separate-car law in 1890, the black citizens of New Orleans presented a written protest to the legislature and then commenced to form a committee to test the new law's constitutionality. Led by creole of color Louis Martinet, a physician, lawyer and journalist, the Citizens Committee retained the northern lawyer Albion Tourgee and, to work with him, a New Orleans-based criminal lawyer named James Walker. Martinet alerted the readers of his newspaper, *The Crusader:* "'We'll make a case, a test case and bring it before the Federal Court on the grounds of invasion of the right [of] a person to travel through the States unmolested." The group debated but eventually agreed with Tourgee's strategy of finding a "nearly white Negro" to test the legislation. Early opponents of the plan noted the possibility that a person of "tolerably fair complexion" might be treated courteously and not be asked to leave the white section. They also feared that darker-skinned African Americans might perceive the test case as simply the efforts of a "nearly white" to pass for white.

Tourgee's strategy prevailed, and on June 7, 1892, Homer Plessy, a man described in the court record as seven-eighths white, became the test-case passenger when he purchased a first-class ticket and took his seat in the white section of a train going from New Orleans to Covington, Louisiana. It is not clear whether the appearance of the detective who arrested Plessy was also scripted as part of the test case. In any event, the detective removed Plessy from the train after he refused the conductor's order to move to the "colored section." Plessy was jailed in the jurisdiction of the lower court judge John H. Ferguson, and thus the case *Plessy v. Ferguson* took its name.

In 1892 the Louisiana Supreme Court decided against Plessy and upheld the separate-car law based on its belief in the existence of a "natural, legal and customary difference between the white and black races in this state which made their separation as passengers in a public conveyance the subject of a sound regulation to secure order, promote comfort, preserve the peace and maintain the rights, both of carriers and passengers." Plessy's lawyers took the case to the highest court in the nation in 1895. The Supreme Court Justices, with one exception, upheld the legality of "separate but equal" and the "reasonableness" of state-mandated segregation laws. The majority opinion ruled: "Every exercise of the [state] police power must be reasonable, and extend only to such laws as are enacted in good faith for the promotion for the public good." The lone dissenting Supreme Court justice, John Harlan, questioned this logic, asking that if the state could separate black people from white people in this way, could not the state also separate people along a variety of other characteristics—on the basis of their hair color, their religion, or their national origin.

The *Plessy* decision sanctioned existing segregation laws and encouraged a plethora of new laws that denied African Americans access to state colleges, voting booths, jury boxes, parks, libraries, neighborhoods, and many other public sites and conveyances. Not only did signs that read "for whites" or "for colored" provide the visual demarcators that prescribed the "Negro's place," they also revealed quite vividly the disparities in resources available to each racial group. Separate facilities were never equal.

In the segregated South, the meaning of "we the people" as the polity and citizenry did not include African Americans. Indeed, white southerners frequently referred to America itself as the "white man's country." For them, the rights of citizens and the spaces citizens inhabit meant simply "for whites only"— **White Man's Country** thus belonging to whites as if private property. The state's enactment of segregation laws and the complicit role of the courts in upholding such laws served to transform public spaces into private ones. The legal process had not only facilitated the inversion by which public space was perceived to be white private property, but it also created "insider" and "outsider" statuses based on racial identity.

The color line sought to obliterate any semblance of equality. A white identity was perceived and treated as synonymous and commensurate with the broader public (thus laws for public comfort), while a black identity was defined in terms of the "Negro's place" and thus officially perceived as trespassing and intrusion if outside it. The only permissible exception for blacks in whites-only areas was that of the black servant. State law permitted what was called the "nurses exemption" on trains and boats for black servants who accompanied white adults or children for the purpose of caring for them. Louisiana journalist George W. Cable was one of very few native whites who openly challenged the abridgement of blacks' civil rights. Speaking specifically to the servant issue, Cable commented in his book of essays *The Negro Question* (1890): "Any colored man gains unquestioned admission into innumerable places the moment he appears as the menial attendant of some white person, where he could not cross the threshold in his own right as well-dressed and well-behaved master of himself."

Window in Time

Ida B. Wells Ejected from Segregated Train Car

When the train started and the conductor came along to collect tickets, he took my ticket, then handed it back to me and told me that he couldn't take my ticket there. I thought that if he didn't want the ticket I wouldn't bother about it so went on reading. In a little while when he finished taking tickets, he came back and told me I would have to go in the other car. I refused, saying that the forward car was a smoker, and as I was in the ladies' car I proposed to stay. He tried to drag me out of the seat, but the moment he caught hold of my arm I fastened my teeth in the back of his hand.

I braced my feet against the seat in front and was holding to the back, and as he had already been badly bitten he didn't try it again by himself. He went forward and got the baggage-man and another man to help him and of course they succeeded in dragging me out. They were encouraged to do this by the attitude of the white ladies and gentlemen in the car; some of them even stood on the seats so that they could get a good view and continued applauding the conductor for his brave stand.

By this time the train had stopped at the first station. When I saw that they were determined to drag me into the smoker, which was already filled with colored people and those who were smoking, I said I would get off the train rather than go in—which I did. Strangely, I held on to my ticket all this time, and although the sleeves of my linen duster had been torn out and I had been pretty roughly handled, I had not been hurt physically.

I went back to Memphis and engaged a colored lawyer to bring suit against the railroad for me. After months of delay I found he had been bought off by the road [railroad company], and as he was the only colored lawyer in town I had to get a white one. This man, Judge Greer, kept his pledge with me and the case was finally brought to trial in the circuit court. Judge Pierce, who was an ex-union soldier from Minnesota, awarded me damages of five hundred dollars. I can see to this day the headlines in the *Memphis Appeal* announcing DARKY DAMSEL GETS DAMAGES.

Source: Wells, Ida B.; Duster, Alfreda M. *Crusade for Justice: The Autobiography of Ida B. Wells.* Chicago, IL: The University of Chicago Press, 1991. Footnote: The *Memphis Daily Appeal*, Thursday, 25 December 1884, p. 4. The complete headline read: *A Darky Damsel Obtains a Verdict for Damages against the Chesapeake & Ohio Railroad–What It Cost to Put a Colored School Teacher in a Smoking Car–Verdict for $500*

In the late nineteenth century, segregated transportation evoked the most notable challenge to Jim Crow. Court records reveal the large number of cases involving black litigants on trains and boats. Black communities also mobilized to resist the inauguration of separate seating policies in streetcars in southern cities. Women were prominent, if not the majority of black litigants who sued railroads and steamboats. Before Ida B. Wells became known as an antilynching crusader, she made news when she sued a Tennessee railroad company after being literally thrown out of the "ladies' car," the first-class car designated for whites—the women and gentlemen accompanying them, or ladies with children. Such segregation laws deemed Ida B. Wells neither white nor a lady. Numerous cases reveal the discourteous, even violent acts perpetrated on middle-class black men and women, who purchased tickets and attempted to ride in first-class accommodations. For example, William H. Councill, a minister and head of the State Colored Normal and Industrial School in Huntsville, Alabama, was severely beaten for sitting in the first-class section of a train.

Confronting the Urban Color Line

The introduction of segregation laws and the rise in acts of violence were coterminous with the rapid growth in the number of blacks who moved into southern cities during the 1890s. The African American populations of Baltimore, New Orleans, Atlanta, and Louisville increased tremendously. Blacks outnumbered whites in Charleston, Savannah, Montgomery, Jacksonville, Shreveport, Vicksburg, Baton Rouge, and several other southern cities. More than half the black population of Missouri lived in towns and cities, while one-third of the black population of Kentucky lived in urban areas. Although African Americans found more economic and social opportunities in urban areas, they also found the color line.

Employment opportunities were fewer than the number of people migrating to cities, and African Americans met with great difficulty in securing anything except the more onerous and less attractive jobs. They continued to exist around the "ragged edge of industry" with both white workers generally and organized

Employment and Unions

Hod carriers
Black workers had few opportunities to move up the occupational ladder. In Philadelphia, the hod carriers were black, but the bricklayers were white.

273

labor evincing pronounced feelings of hostility. Only the Cigarmakers International Union and the United Mine Workers of America seemed to welcome African Americans into membership, although some other unions did have black members. African American women easily found employment as household servants, and the more certain employment of women had the effect of attracting a larger number of women than men to the cities. Many white industrialists claimed that blacks were inefficient, while others refused to hire them because of objections raised by white employees. Although the prospects of securing satisfactory employment were not great, African Americans continued to migrate to the cities, thereby multiplying the difficulties of those already there.

The problem of housing, common to all people migrating to the city, was aggravated for African Americans by the determination of white citizens to segregate them in one section of the city. The exploitation by white landlords of the newly arrived blacks was made easier since the latter had little choice in selecting places of residence. Municipalities sanctioned this practice by enacting segregation ordinances. The first group of such laws was passed by Louisville, Baltimore, Richmond, and Atlanta in 1912 and 1913. Blocks containing a majority of white people were to be designated as white blocks, and blocks containing a majority of African Americans were to be designated as black blocks. No blacks could move into white blocks, and vice versa. The extreme congestion that resulted from the restriction on the choice of residence and the occupancy of small, unsanitary homes by large families led naturally to poor health and a high mortality rate among blacks.

Housing

In 1891 Georgia law required streetcar segregation. By 1907 laws for separate streetcar seating appeared in cities in Louisiana, Mississippi, Tennessee, Florida, Virginia, North Carolina, Arkansas, and South Carolina. Customary segregation had long operated on streetcars in Alabama and Texas. African Americans in cities throughout the South protested the introduction of the Jim Crow streetcars. Black boycotts and other protests against the Jim Crow streetcars took place in Mobile, Alabama; in Nashville, Knoxville, and Memphis, Tennessee; in Augusta and Atlanta, Georgia; in Columbia, South Carolina; in New Orleans, Louisiana; in Austin and Houston, Texas; in Jacksonville, Florida; in Louisville, Kentucky; and in other cities.

Transportation

According to historian David Ortiz's study of Florida during the Jim Crow era, eight hundred African Americans met at St. Paul's AME to strategize against the city's separate streetcar seating policy in 1901, and black women played the primary role of initiating and galvanizing the boycott against the Jim Crow streetcar policy. The AME newspaper the *Christian Recorder* described the streetcars as virtually empty, emphasizing that black "women and children would walk miles day and night rather than submit to the outrage which was ratified by the city council." In Nashville, Tennessee, a similar boycott took place in 1906. Richard Henry Boyd, a Baptist minister and leader in the National Negro Business League, led the movement to establish a separate black-run streetcar line as the answer to the city's Jim Crow seating, but this venture did not succeed. Nor were the valiant organized efforts of blacks able to deter the legalization of Jim Crow.

Southern whites paid for this color line. Since all other issues were subordinated to the issue of "the Negro," it became impossible to have free and open discussion of problems affecting all the people. There could be no two-party system, for the temptation to call on blacks to decide between opposing factions would be too great. The expense of maintaining a double system of schools and of other public institutions was high, but not too high for advocates of white supremacy, who kept the races apart in order to keep blacks in their "place."

America's Empire of Color

The problem of the color line was not confined to the borders of the United States. In the late nineteenth century, the United States began to pursue imperialist ambitions, conforming to the prevailing pattern of European imperialism that had swept the world. As the leading power in the Western Hemisphere, the United States began to chart its own plan to dominate, for their economic and strategic value, the lands and resources of the world's darker-skinned peoples. Colonialism in Africa and Asia had provided a wealth of raw materials and emerging markets for the growing industrial and financial sectors of the white industrialized powers. Commercial interests and political rivalry stood at the core of their plans to control the less-developed areas of the world. As the United States looked outward from its shores, it cast its eyes on the areas of peoples of color, and frequently areas of people of African descent.

The United States observed with interest the increased imperialistic activities of France and Great Britain, as well as of the newcomers to imperialism: Belgium, Italy, and Germany. The media coverage of the missionary-explorer David Livingstone, the businessman and mining magnate Cecil Rhodes, and the journalist-explorer Henry M. Stanley dramatized the importance to an industrialized world of Africa's resources and of the "scramble for Africa" on the part of the European nations. King Leopold of Belgium, Kaiser Wilhelm of Germany, and Queen Victoria of England became the rulers in whose names the African continent was divided. In the winter of 1884–1885, an international conference was held in Berlin to discuss the partition of Africa among the European powers. The great basin of the Congo was given to Leopold of Belgium, and the conference paved the way for Germany's acquisition of colonies in East Africa, Southwest Africa, Togoland, and Cameroon, of a vast expanse of almost unbroken land from the Cape to Cairo by Britain, and a considerable portion of West Africa by France.

The United States, too, began to look for new markets and raw materials in the late nineteenth century—a time when its industrial production surged. The great industrialists, their pockets bulging with profits, began to search for areas in which to invest their profits. Consequently, exports increased **The United States Expands** enormously, and foreign investments skyrocketed. As immigrants poured onto America's shores in ever larger numbers, the land in the West rapidly filled up, and, as during other periods in its history, the United States felt the need for new territory. Sectional strife was over, and the United States was ready to assume an important role in world affairs.

Already the Hawaiian Islands were attracting the attention of many American traders. As more of them visited the islands, they saw the lands' value as a site for a naval base, a coaling station, and a cable way station. In 1875 sugar and other Hawaiian products were given free entry into the United States. In 1884 the United States leased Pearl Harbor on the island of Oahu as a naval station. With this added military protection, American investors poured capital into the islands, so that by 1890 American plantations there were worth more than $25 million. Despite the fact that the Hawaiian people had racial and cultural heritages vastly different from those of any American group, sentiment for annexation of the islands to the United States grew steadily. In 1898, after some maneuvering on the islands and on the mainland, Congress annexed the Hawaiian Islands by a joint resolution. Likewise, the United States made arrangements to secure Tutuila when the Samoan Islands were divided between Britain and Germany. Meanwhile, the United States was acquiring jurisdiction over many other small islands in the Pacific, including Wake, Midway, Palmyra, and Howland. Before the end of the century, the United States was well on its way toward acquiring an empire composed primarily of darker-skinned peoples.

However, it was in the Americas that the United States pursued its new imperialistic policy most vigorously. Thus, as the United States focused on South America and the Caribbean islands, it brought into its orbit millions of people of African or mixed descent.

The United States wielded its influence most dramatically and effectively in the Caribbean. A U.S. attraction to the Spanish colony of Cuba dated back to well before the Civil War. By the end of the 1860s, Spain's steady decline as a major imperial power had left only two islands, Cuba and Puerto Rico, as remnants of its once vast New World empire. Repression and rigid control of every aspect of life in Cuba had inspired numerous revolts against Spain, and those revolts had become more frequent and more intense by the middle of the nineteenth century. Toward the end of the century, Cubans were determined to win their independence. This determination coincided with the increasing interest in the island on the part of citizens of the United States, who had already made sizable investments in Cuba.

The Caribbean

By 1890 Americans had invested more than $50 million in Cuban plantations and sugar refineries. When, therefore, the Cubans revolted again in 1895, the United States became alarmed over the damage that the fighting was doing to American-owned fields and factories on the island. Their material interest was broadened into a humanitarian interest in the following year when Spain sent General Valeriano Weyler to put down the insurrection. With more determination than wisdom, Weyler ordered much of the rural population placed in concentration camps, since it was extremely difficult to separate loyalists from insurgents. The starvation and disease that followed took such a toll of Cuban lives that the American press dubbed the Spanish leader "Butcher" Weyler. In the province of Havana alone, for example, more than 50,000 people died.

The American press featured stories of the brutal coercion in Cuba—an island that most Americans thought should be a U.S. "sphere of influence." For the moment, an outraged America even focused a bit less on the heated presidential campaign of 1896 and on the campaign to disfranchise blacks in the South. The so-called yellow journals—cheap, sensational popular newspapers—fanned the flames of indignation in America to the point where Congress finally recognized the Cubans' determination to gain their independence. Only the firmness of President Grover Cleveland prevented the country from going further. Meanwhile, under the leadership of the Afro-Cuban general Antonio Maceo and Quintin Bandera, known as "The Black Thunderbolt," the insurgents carried on a campaign of systematic devastation that won greater support among the Americans.

In January 1898, the American battleship *Maine* was ordered to Havana to protect American life and property and to impress on the Spaniards that the government of the United States was willing to take energetic action. On February 15, 1898, an explosion sank the *Maine* in Havana harbor with a loss of more than 250 officers and enlisted men. The incident set off a train of events that culminated in war between the United States and Spain two months later. It was America's first international conflict in more than fifty years, and it was more than anything else a clear-cut demonstration of America's growing interest in affairs outside its own territorial limits.

From the beginning, African Americans were involved in the war against Spain. Indeed, there were at least thirty blacks on the *Maine* when it exploded; twenty-two were killed, four were injured, and four others escaped injury. African Americans had already been inspired by the soldiers of Maceo and Bandera and regarded "Weylerism as the synonym of barbarous warfare." The majority of African Americans were anxious to vindicate the honor of the United States and help bring independence and freedom to Cubans, whom they regarded as blacks and mulattoes. When, therefore, President William McKinley called for 200,000 volunteers to supplement the inadequate regular army, blacks enthusiastically enlisted.

The Spanish American War

Some African Americans, however, were vocal anti-imperialists and argued that the United States' acquisition of colonies only boded ill for current and potential nonwhite members of the American community. These dissenters, most of whom identified with the Cuban rebels (especially those who were blacks), stressed repeatedly that Spain, though cruel and undemocratic, had not imposed a racial caste system on Cuba. They refused to be a part of a war in which African Americans, themselves victims of discriminatory laws and racist practices, were used to subject nonwhite colonials to that same system.

Among the regular army, which numbered only 28,000 troops in 1898, there were four African American outfits, all of which had been used in actions against the Indians in the West. The Ninth Cavalry had its headquarters in the Department of the Platte, and the Tenth Cavalry was stationed at Assiniboine, Montana. The Twenty-Fourth Infantry was at Fort Douglas, near Salt Lake City, Utah, and the Twenty-Fifth Infantry was in Missoula, Montana. These units had been activated shortly after the close of the Civil War and had performed numerous duties in the Indian wars and in border service. The Ninth Cavalry, for example, had served at Fort Lancaster, Texas; at Santa Fe, New Mexico; at Fort Riley, Kansas; and at Fort McKinney, Wyoming. These troops were often referred to as the "Buffalo Soldiers," a name given them by the Kiowa, Cheyenne, and Apache tribes they encountered.

Besides the four black outfits in the regular army and the four outfits that were recruited under a special act of the Congress, numerous other African American groups served in the war against Spain. Several states permitted African Americans to organize outfits and enter the service, among them the Third Alabama Infantry of Volunteers, the Third North Carolina Infantry, the Sixth Virginia Infantry, the Ninth Ohio Infantry, the Twenty-Third Kansas Infantry, the Eighth Illinois Infantry, two companies of the Indiana Infantry, and several smaller groups. Company L of the Sixth Massachusetts Infantry was the only black company that was mustered in as an integral part of a white regiment. It had African American officers and, having been created during the War for Independence as the "Bucks of America," boasted that it was the oldest African American military organization in America.

The shabby treatment of black troops throughout the war reflected the extent to which African Americans were trapped in a Jim Crow society, no matter how vital or brave their service. Wherever they were stationed, black regiments excited hostility from whites who were opposed to armed blacks wearing the uniform of their country. Blacks were subject to racial insults and to exclusion from the places of public accommodation that were open to their white counterparts. African American soldiers vigorously protested these and other insults to their officers and, through letters to newspapers, to the American public. Some blacks, when traveling in groups while armed and in uniform, felt emboldened to challenge

Jim Crow practices or to use violence to punish their detractors. Most exercised restraint, however, enduring insults and mistreatment in the belief that by demonstrating an indifference to racism, as well as by showing their patriotism, they would strengthen their race's claims to equal treatment. But their additional, and ultimately less successful, war against racism took its toll in disillusionment and bitterness.

In the swift and decisive action that brought victory to the United States, the only African Americans who saw considerable service were in the four regular outfits. In June 1898, these groups sailed from various southern ports for Cuba. The Twenty-Fifth Infantry, for example, sailed on June 7 from Tampa, Florida, on a government transport. During the week that the men were delayed at Tampa they were not allowed to go ashore to bathe and exercise unless an officer escorted the entire company. Upon embarkation, the Twenty-Fifth was assigned to the bottom deck where there was no light, except that which came through the small portholes, and very little air. Blacks and whites were not permitted to mingle on board ship. When they disembarked at Daiquiri in Guantánamo Bay on June 22, the campaign for the reduction of the Spanish forces in Cuba began.

The African American contingents saw action principally at El Caney, Las Guasimas, and San Juan Hill. On June 24, two battalions of the First Volunteer Cavalry (Theodore Roosevelt's Rough Riders) moved up the Santiago Road toward Las Guasimas, where they met the enemy. At a crucial moment in the fighting, several blacks from the Ninth and Tenth Cavalries came up, knocked down the enemy's improvised fort, cut the barbed wire, and made an opening for the Rough Riders, who then routed the Spaniards. On June 30,

The Tenth Cavalry
Created following the Civil War, this cavalry saw action on the frontier and, more notably, in the Spanish-American War in 1898.

following an unsuccessful attack on the town of Tayabacoe, Dennis Bell, Fitz Lee, William H. Tompkins, and George H. Wanton, members of the Tenth Cavalry, volunteered to rescue six wounded Cuban soldiers "left to die in enemy territory," despite the failure of an earlier attempt. They successfully completed the mission, and all four received the Medal of Honor.

At El Caney, on June 30, the Twenty-Fifth was ordered up to reinforce the Rough Riders. In this decisive action, many of the African American troops were under fire for the better part of the day, with strict orders not to return the enemy fire. In three days of fighting, most of the black regulars in Cuba saw action and won the praise of practically all their officers.

It has been claimed by many that the Ninth and Tenth Cavalries saved the Rough Riders from complete annihilation at Las Guasimas. One southern white officer said: "If it had not been for the Negro cavalry the Rough Riders would have been exterminated. I am not a Negro lover. My father fought with Mosby's Rangers, and I was born in the South, but the Negroes saved that fight, and the day will come when General Shafter will give them credit for the bravery." Said another: "I am a Southerner by birth, and I never thought much of the colored man. But, somehow, now I feel very differently toward them. . . . I never saw such fighting as those Tenth Cavalry men did. They didn't seem to know what fear was, and their battle hymn was 'There'll be a hot time in the old town tonight.'" Even among those who did not claim that the African Americans saved the Rough Riders, the praise was generous. Lt. Thomas Roberts said: "I have naught but the highest praise for the swarthy warriors on the field of carnage. Led by brave men, they will go into the thickest of the fight, even to the wicked mouths of deadly cannon, unflinchingly." The *New York Mail and Express* wrote:

> All honor to the black troops of the gallant Tenth: No more striking example of bravery and coolness has been shown since the destruction of the Maine than by the colored veterans of the Tenth Cavalry during the attack upon Caney on Saturday. By the side of the Rough Riders they followed their leader up the terrible hill from whose crest the desperate Spaniards poured down a deadly fire of shell and musketry. They never faltered. . . . Firing as they marched, their aim was splendid, their coolness was superb, and their courage aroused the admiration of their comrades. . . . The war has not shown greater heroism.

The reaction of Theodore Roosevelt to the performance of the African American troops was varied, depending on occasion. When he made his farewell address to the rather incongruous group of Indians, ranchers, cowboys, college athletes, and African Americans who served under him as Rough Riders, Roosevelt had words of unqualified praise for the black soldiers. "The Spaniards called them 'Smoked Yankees,'" he said, "but we found them to be an excellent breed of Yankees. I am sure that I speak the sentiments of officers and men in the assemblage when I say that between you and the other cavalry regiments there exists a tie which we trust will never be broken." When campaigning for the office of governor of New York in October 1898, Roosevelt said: "As I heard one of the Rough Riders say after the charge at San Juan: 'Well, the Ninth and Tenth men are all right. They can drink out of our canteens.'" Roosevelt expressed the highest praise for the African Americans who charged up San Juan with his Rough Riders and concluded: "I don't think that any Rough Rider will ever forget the tie that binds us to the Ninth and Tenth Cavalry."

Writing in *Scribner's Magazine* in April of the following year, however, Roosevelt offered a more tentative reflection, stating that the blacks behaved well, but "they are, of course, peculiarly dependent on their white officers. . . . None of the white regulars of Rough Riders showed the slightest sign of weakening; but under the strain the colored infantrymen . . . began to get a little uneasy and to drift to the rear."

African American soldiers served as occupation troops at the close of the war. Some African American troops, including the Third North Carolina, served in the Pacific. The

Garrison Duty and Pacific Service

Twenty-Third Kansas Infantry did garrison duty in Cuba, and the Eighth Illinois, which did not arrive in Cuba until August 1898, did garrison duty in the province of Santiago. When an editorial appeared in the *Washington Post* discrediting black troops with black officers, Major Charles Douglass, writing in the *Colored American* on August 17, 1898, pointed out that the Eighth Illinois had been selected to replace a disorderly white regiment. He said in conclusion that "the generals at the front know the value of Negro troops, whether the quill-drivers in the rear do or not." During this tour of duty, Colonel John R. Marshall served for a while as governor of San Luis, while Major R. R. Jackson acted as mayor of El Paso, Cuba.

Citizens of the United States did not view with complete favor the arming of African Americans to fight in the war and to serve as troops of occupation. As troops passed through the South en route to ports of embarkation, they were frequently treated with contempt by white southerners. At the end of the war, when the Third North Carolina Volunteers were moved from Macon, Georgia, the *Atlanta Journal* carried an editorial entitled "A Happy Riddance." Among other things, the editor said that the army and the country were to be congratulated on mustering out the North Carolina blacks, for "a tougher and more turbulent set of Negroes were probably never gotten together before. . . . While stationed in Macon several of its members were killed either by their own comrades in drunken brawls or by citizens in self-defense."

However, Charles F. Meserve, the white president of black Shaw University, visited the North Carolinians at their camp and had nothing but praise for them. He described Col. James H. Young as possessing in "a marked degree a quality of leadership as important as it is rare" and said that the men were well disciplined on and off the post.

At the end of the Spanish-American War the United States could regard itself as one of the great powers of the world. The victory over Spain was so quick and decisive that it was

The United States as a Great Power

only natural for many to expect that the United States would supplant Spain as a leading imperial power. The Treaty of Paris between the two powers left little doubt as to the direction in which the United States was moving. It provided that Spain was to relinquish all claim to sovereignty over Cuba, which became nominally independent but in fact a U.S. protectorate. In lieu of a war indemnity, Spain ceded to the United States the island of Puerto Rico and the other tiny Spanish insular possessions in the West Indies. On payment of $20 million by the United States, Spain was also to relinquish the Philippines to the victor.

Although it was not immediately clear just what disposition the United States would make of Cuba, it was quite evident that the island would remain under the political and economic domination of the United States for an indefinite period. Puerto Rico was, from the outset, to become a part of America's growing empire. The Philippines gave the United States the foothold it needed in East Asia if it was to compete in that region with Great Britain, France, Russia, and Japan.

It is ironic that African American soldiers, themselves subject to Jim Crow restrictions and viewed as inferiors by most white Americans, should have played a part in bringing extensive numbers of other nonwhites under U.S. domination. For Howard University professor Kelly Miller and journalist John W. Cromwell—both imperialists and prominent members of the African American community—America's victory over Spain provided opportunities for blacks to help uplift members of the "weaker races." Miller urged that Howard be employed by the federal government to educate and Americanize Cuban, Philippine, and Puerto Rican youth. He also called on enterprising African Americans to exploit the economic opportunities in these places, "where the field is not preempted, as in America, and where race proscription is not so discouraging." Although Cromwell expressed similar sentiments, he did concede to the inhabitants of Spain's former colonies one advanced trait, a history of "fraternity between the races." The most negative black reaction to America's new imperialist policies came from black soldiers stationed in the Philippines, where from 1899 to 1902 United States military forces were engaged in crushing the independence movement led by Emilio Aguinaldo. There, as Willard Gatewood has shown, "an unusually large number of Negro troops deserted" to join the Filipino Insurrectos, "whose struggle they interpreted as the struggle of all colored people."

One of the most salient features of the American imperial problem was that the United States, unlike the other imperial powers, had a color problem at home and therefore had to pursue a policy with regard to race that would not upset the racial equilibrium within the United States. In Puerto Rico, for exam-

Puerto Rico

ple, a portion of the population was of distinctly African descent, and many so-called white Puerto Ricans had sufficient black blood in their veins to qualify as black, according to America's "one-drop" rule. In 1900, when the first organic act of Puerto Rico was passed by Congress, the southern members of that body—and some northern members, too—were concerned not only with the fact that Puerto Ricans should be carefully supervised in the operation of their government but also that the blacks of the island should not enjoy political liberties that would inspire the African Americans to fight for greater political opportunities.

The Puerto Rican governor and all important officials were to be appointed by the president of the United States, and Americans were to outnumber Puerto Ricans on the important Executive Council. The second organic act of 1917 remodeled the local government to resemble one of the states of the United States. Two legislative houses were established, with their members elected by universal male suffrage, and all Puerto Ricans were to enjoy American citizenship. The power of appointing all the major officials of the island, however, was reserved for the president of the United States.

The major efforts of the United States in Puerto Rico were directed toward the improvement of health, education, and public works and toward the Americanization of the Puerto Rican people. In all these areas, there were notable successes, but the low economic level of the population, largely the result of the concentration of wealth in the hands of a few, prevented greater improvement and caused hundreds of thousands to migrate to the mainland. Since American investors on the island reaped considerable profits, especially in the cultivation of sugar, cursory observers tended to view the period of American control as very successful. The high mortality rate, the abject poverty of the masses, and the cultural and social debility of the people seemed to indicate the need for a new imperial outlook that would foster greater improvement for the inhabitants of the island. Puerto Ricans' efforts to break up the large plantations in order to redistribute the land, to which American investors reacted negatively, suggested that any improvements would be slow indeed in coming.

A significant expansion encompassing additional nonwhites came with the purchase of the Danish West Indies in 1917, culminating a half-century of effort to acquire the islands

The Virgin Islands largely because of their military and strategic value in the Caribbean. In August 1916, a treaty for the purchase of the islands for $25 million was negotiated, and in January of the following year, the ratifications of the two countries were exchanged. American Marines landed shortly after the purchase, and a military government was established that lasted until 1931, when President Hoover signed an order creating a civil government for the Virgin Islands.

African Americans themselves played an important part in extending the empire of the United States. From the end of Reconstruction up until the beginning of World War I,

Haiti American ministers to Haiti were largely blacks, and they manifested a keen interest in the extension of American influence. John M. Langston, for example, went to Haiti as the official representative of the government of the United States in 1877 and interested himself in the political and economic conditions of the island. He was quite disturbed about the unsettled political scene and made many suggestions to his government about how commercial relations could be improved.

Both J. E. W. Thompson, who went to Haiti in 1885, and Frederick Douglass, who became the American minister there in 1889, were very much concerned over the treatment of American vessels in Haitian ports. William F. Powell, the minister in 1897, vigorously fought discriminating taxes against foreign merchants, while Henry W. Furness, a later minister, concerned himself primarily with seeking advantages for American merchants in the matters of tariffs and customs duties.

From 1871 until the present, most American ministers to Liberia have been blacks. Beginning in 1871, J. Milton Turner helped to establish closer commercial relations between

Liberia Liberia and the United States. Several others, including John Henry Smyth, E. E. Smith, and Ernest W. Lyon, praised the resources of the country and sought to encourage Americans to help develop the commercial and economic life of Liberia. Lyon, for example, is credited with having had a great deal to do with the organization of the New York Liberia Steamship Line in 1905.

African Americans would pay increasing attention to the world's color problems. Thus Du Bois was not speaking only of black-white relations in the United States when in 1903 he predicted that the problem of the "color line" would be the defining issue of the twentieth century. Du Bois understood the color line to include "the relation of the darker to the lighter races of men in Asia and Africa, in America and the islands of the sea."

The Pattern of Violence

Violence in the form of lynching and riots worked to solidify the color line. In the last sixteen years of the nineteenth century, more than 2,500 lynchings occurred. The great majority of the victims of lynch mobs were African Americans. In the year of the Spanish-American War, when Wilmington, North Carolina erupted in rioting and bloodshed, some blacks considered this riot the dying gasp of a reign of terror. They were mistaken, for racial violence would continue with a vengeance into the new century. In 1900 alone, more than

Lynching

100 African Americans were lynched, and before the outbreak of World War I, the number for the century had soared to more than 1,100.

The South was far ahead of the rest of the country, with Mississippi, Alabama, Georgia, and Louisiana leading the nation. Lynch law also operated in several Northern states, notably those in the Midwest. Although the impression was widely held **Lynch Law** that most of the blacks lynched had been accused of raping white women, the records do not sustain this impression. In the first fourteen years of the twentieth century, only 315 lynch victims were accused of rape or attempted rape, whereas more than 500 were accused of homicide and the others were accused of robbery, insulting white people, and numerous other "offenses." Regardless of the alleged crime of the victim, lynching in the twentieth century continued to be an important if illegal part of the system of punishment in the United States.

Early in the twentieth century, an epidemic of race riots swept the country as well, arousing great anxiety and discomfort among the African American population. Although lynchings were decreasing slightly after 1900, riots were perceptibly on **Race Riots** the increase. In August 1904, the state of Georgia was rocked by riots in the small town of Statesboro, after two African Americans were accused of the brutal murder of a white farmer, his wife, and three children. The men were brought to trial in Statesboro and found guilty. The court ordered them to be executed by hanging. In the meantime, the white citizens outside had worked themselves into a frenzy of race hatred, inflamed by talk of blacks, in general, becoming insolent.

The mob had no patience for a legal execution and angrily forced its way into the courtroom after overpowering a company of Savannah militia whose rifles were not loaded "in tender consideration for the feelings of the mob." They dragged the convicted blacks into the street and burned them alive. This incident was the signal for wholesale terrorism against

African Americans in the town. One black citizen was severely whipped for riding a bicycle on the sidewalk, while another was lashed "on general principles." The black mother of a three-day-old infant was beaten and kicked, and her husband was killed. Houses were wrecked, and countless terrified blacks left the county. Although there was talk of punishing the leaders of the mob, nothing was ever done.

As events in Statesboro made clear, African Americans of both genders and all ages were victims of racial violence. When Marie Thompson, a black woman in Lebanon Junction, Kentucky, killed a white man during an argument, her claims of self-defense did not deter the lynch mob that took her from the jail and strung her up on a tree in the jail yard. The *Louisville Courier-Journal* reported that Thompson fought her murderers to the end:

> The woman was struggling and fighting like a tiger all the time, but the mob was too much for her, and a minute later she was swinging in the air, with her feet several inches from the ground. All of a sudden she twisted around and grabbed a man by the collar, jerked a knife from his hands and cut the rope that was choking the life out of her.

Once on the ground, Thompson attempted to force her way through the lynch mob but was "shot down in a hail of gunfire."

The Atlanta Riot The South's most sensational riot occurred in Atlanta in September 1906. For months the city had been seething in a fury of race hatred related to rumor and to the movement to disfranchise African Americans. White newspapers intensified the feeling against blacks. One editor called for the revival of the Ku Klux Klan, while another went so far as to offer a reward for a "lynching bee" in Atlanta. On Saturday, September 22, newspapers told of four successive assaults on white women by blacks. The country people, in town for the day, joined with the urban element in creating an outraged, panic-stricken mob. Whites began to attack every black person they saw.

The following day was quiet, but the rioting broke out again on Monday in Brownsville, a suburb of Atlanta. African Americans there had heard that members of their race in Atlanta were being slaughtered en masse. Some sought asylum in two black institutions in the neighborhood, Clark University and Gammon Theological Seminary. Others, who were determined to defend themselves to the end, collected arms. When officers of the law came out, they began rounding up blacks and arresting them for being armed. One officer shot into a crowd of blacks. The fire was returned, killing one officer and wounding another. The whites then threw discretion aside and set out on a general destruction of black property and lives. Four African Americans, all of whom were substantial citizens, were killed, and many were injured. J. W. E. Bowen, the president of Gammon, was beaten over the head with a rifle butt by a police official. Houses of blacks were looted and burned.

For several days, the city was paralyzed: factories were closed and all transportation stopped. Numerous blacks sold their property and left. The city's white leaders confessed their shame and condemned the rioters. A group of responsible black and white citizens came together and organized the Atlanta Civic League to work for the improvement of social conditions and to prevent other riots. Nothing was done to the rioters, however. Despairing African Americans loudly protested, but no one listened.

President Roosevelt's handling of a riot in Brownsville, Texas, convinced many African Americans that he had no genuine interest in their plight. In August 1906, three companies of the Twenty-Fifth Regiment, composed of African Americans, were involved in a riot in Brownsville, Texas; one citizen was killed, another wounded, and the chief of police injured. Whites reported that blacks had "shot up the town," and race passion was stirred to a fever pitch. Only the firm stand of the commander at Fort Brown prevented the riot from reaching a more desperate level. In November, on the basis of the report of an inspector who had said that blacks had murdered and maimed the citizens of Brownsville, President Roosevelt dismissed the entire battalion without honor and disqualified its members for service in either the military or the civil service of the United States. African Americans, who had always taken pride in the service of their soldiers, were outraged. Many whites protested, among them John Milholland, who through the Constitution League carried on a relentless fight for the soldiers. Even Senator Tillman, doubtless in order to embarrass the president, called it an "executive lynching."

Brownsville, Texas

When Congress met in December, Sen. Joseph B. Foraker of Ohio insisted that a full and fair trial should have preceded such drastic punishment. On January 22, the Senate authorized a general investigation of the whole matter, the president having revoked the civil disability of the discharged soldiers a week earlier. After several months of study, the majority of the Senate committee upheld the president's handling of the affair. A stinging minority report by Senator Foraker denounced the findings of the majority.

The Ohio senator did not give up the fight. In 1909 he succeeded in forcing through an act of Congress establishing a court of inquiry to pass on the cases of the discharged soldiers. It provided that all the discharged soldiers who were found to be qualified for reenlistment were to be deemed eligible and that if they reenlisted they were to be considered as having enlisted immediately after their discharge more than two years earlier. Any such soldier was to receive the "pay, allowances, and other rights and benefits that he would have been entitled to receive according to his rank from said date of discharge as if he had been honorably discharged . . . and had reenlisted immediately."

While some regarded the establishment of the court of inquiry as the "most pointed and signal defeat of Roosevelt's administration," most African Americans looked on the Brownsville incident as one more piece of evidence of the helplessness of a minority in a hostile land. Not until 1972, some sixty-six years after the incident, did Congress rescind the dishonorable discharge and restore the black members of the regiment, most of whom were dead, to good standing in the army.

The South was not the only area of America that was hostile to African Americans in the early years of the new century. Crowds of white hoodlums frequently attacked blacks in large Northern cities. On several occasions, whites dragged blacks off the streetcars of Philadelphia with cries of "Lynch him! Kill him!" As the migration of African Americans to the North increased, hostility toward them grew. Springfield, Ohio, had two riots within a few years. The one in 1904 conformed perfectly to the pattern of violence that had characterized rioting in the South. In an altercation, an African American shot and killed a white officer. A mob gathered and broke into the jail where the black was being held. The citizens murdered the black in the doorway of the jail, hung him on a telegraph pole, and riddled his body with bullets. They then proceeded to wreak destruction on the black section of the town. When they had finished, eight buildings had been burned, many blacks had been beaten, and others had fled, never to return. Two years later, in Greensburg, Indiana, a portion of the act was repeated. A developmentally disabled black was

Violence in the North

convicted for criminally assaulting his employer, a white widow. The mob that gathered did not succeed in taking the black from the authorities, but it was not daunted. Many homes of African Americans were damaged, several innocent persons were beaten, and some were driven out of town.

The Northern riot that shook the entire country was the one that occurred in Springfield, Illinois, in August 1908. The wife of a streetcar conductor claimed that she had been dragged from her bed and raped by someone whom she identified as an African American, George Richardson, who had been working in the neighborhood. Richardson was arrested and jailed. Before a special grand jury, the woman admitted that she had been severely beaten by a white man whose identity she refused to disclose and that Richardson had had no connection with the incident. By this time, however, feeling was running high against Richardson. As a precautionary measure, the officials took him and another black, held in connection with the murder of a white man, to a nearby town where they boarded the train for Bloomington. When the mob that was gathering learned that the blacks had been removed, they were furious. They wrecked the restaurant of a person whose car had been used to transport the blacks and began to surge through the town.

The Springfield Riot

The town officials saw that the mob was becoming unruly, and several unsuccessful efforts were made to disperse it. Finally the governor called out the militia. The mob, oblivious to the appeals of high state officials, raided secondhand stores, secured guns, axes, and other weapons, and began to destroy African American businesses and to drive blacks from their homes. They set fire to a building in which a black owned a barbershop. The barber was lynched in the yard behind his shop, and the mob, after dragging his body through the streets, was preparing to burn it when the militia from Decatur dispersed the crowd by firing into it. On the following night, an eighty-four-year-old African American, who had been married to a white woman for more than thirty years, was lynched within a block of the statehouse.

Before order was restored, more than 5,000 militiamen were patrolling the streets. In the final count, two blacks had been lynched, four white men had been killed, and more than seventy persons had been injured. More than one hundred arrests were made, and approximately fifty indictments were returned. The alleged leaders of the mob went unpunished. The news of the riot was almost more than African Americans could bear. The lynchings had occurred within half a mile of the only home Abraham Lincoln ever owned and within two miles of his final resting place. It seemed to black Americans a perverse manner in which to approach the centennial of the birth of the man immortalized as the Great Emancipator.

At the turn of the twentieth century, peace had not yet come to the South, and the world itself seemed to be divided along an axis of color—powerful white nations versus darker colonial subjects. Where could blacks find redress? American blacks could not look for protection in their nation's laws or in its courts. The American legal process had helped to draw the color line, but it had not acted alone. There was rampant violence in the form of lynching and race riots. A mass consumer culture advertised stereotypical images of black inferiority. And popular and scholarly studies reinforced notions of white supremacy. African Americans confronted all the constitutive elements of Jim Crow as they looked for, indeed prayed for redress. They discussed and openly disagreed with one another on how to best advance themselves individually and collectively as a race. But on one thing they agreed: blacks would have to depend primarily upon their own people, communities, and institutions.

13

The Era of Self-Help

Self-Help and Philanthropy

Divergent Paths to Racial Equality

Economic and Social Striving

The Woman's Era

Intellectual and Cultural Endeavors

Mother and daughter reading

This scene provides one of the most moving
examples of self-help among blacks.

The white South led the way toward imposing Jim Crow, but the larger nation stood complicit in reinforcing the indisputable fact of racial discrimination in late nineteenth- and early twentieth-century America. Despite the Supreme Court's "separate but equal" formula in the 1896 Plessy decision, blacks' separate and unequal status eluded no one in America. Rather than capitulate to a sense of powerlessness in the face of this mounting oppression, African Americans clung tenaciously to a race-conscious ideology of self-help. Bombarded with pervasive representations of black inferiority in the white press, the legal system, the consumer economy, science, popular culture, and many other daily reminders of the "Negro's place" in society, black people embraced the ideology of self-help as one way of reaffirming their personal dignity and their hope for a better future for themselves and their children.

Although self-help rhetoric dated back to the antebellum black convention movement, it conveyed a somewhat different message from the 1880s through the 1910s. In these years of segregation and disfranchisement, of lynching and race riots, self-help developed as a practical philosophy born of despair from rights gained and lost after slavery's end and the painful realization that a certain amount of accommodation to the status quo would be necessary for survival.

Yet self-help was also an idealistic philosophy born of faith in the future due to pride in heritage and appreciation of unique cultural traditions, institutions, and creative expression. Self-help served as a postemancipation, forward-looking worldview. At its core lay a relentless confidence in the ability of the present generation to change the future. In their homes, schools, churches, and other contexts, individuals were taught to "pull yourself up by your bootstraps" and to "be of service to the race." As a group endeavor, collective self-help was understood as uplift, which was most often articulated by the black middle class as its duty to reform and educate those of lower status.

The motto of the National Association of Colored Women's Clubs—"Lifting as We Climb"—succinctly captures self-help's individual and collective meanings along with its class distinctions. However, the black working poor, and especially black churchwomen, subscribed no less explicitly to race uplift as they sought to transform black home life, raise money for black schools, and spread their religion as missionaries. In making all these self-help efforts, black leaders refused to abandon the eventual goal of racial equality, although they disagreed, often bitterly, over the primacy and merit of specific strategies and the timetable for reaching this goal. The era of self-help, with all its explicit and implicit meanings of racial solidarity, was nonetheless fraught with division.

Self-Help and Philanthropy

During those years that historian Rayford Logan has called the "nadir in race relations," the often repeated words— *rising* and *climbing, uplift* and *lasting service*—captured blacks' efforts to redefine the trying times in which they lived through education, economic development, and religious and secular organizational life. Such books and articles as William J. Simmons' *Men of Mark: Eminent, Progressive, and Rising* (1887), H. F. Kletzing and H. Crogman's *Progress of a Race; or, The Remarkable Advancement of the Afro-American* (1897), G. F. Richings's *Evidences of Progress among Colored People* (1900), and Booker T. Washington's co-edited volume *A New Negro for a New Century* (which included articles by scholar W. E. B. Du Bois and clubwoman Fannie Barrier Williams) all armed black people with a record of their achievement. They were filled with biographical sketches of prominent persons as well as statistical proof of the growing number of black-owned homes, schools and businesses, and college graduates.

Literacy among African Americans had risen dramatically—from a mere 5 percent in 1865 to about 50 percent in 1900 and to 70 percent in 1910. The evidence of black progress, as revealed in books such as these, refuted racist claims of innate black intellectual inferiority and moral depravity. Such evidence, black leaders agreed, was crucial to winning whites' sympathy and diminishing racial prejudice.

The self-help books ascribed the improved status of blacks largely to education—to the many primary and secondary schools in urban and rural areas, as well as to the colleges and institutes that had been founded in the aftermath of the Civil War **Supporting Education** by freedmen's aid societies, especially those of white northern Protestant denominations. Blacks—as individuals, as families, and as members of community organizations—gave of their own financial resources to support these same white-run schools, many of which were still flourishing. Nor was it uncommon for black students to play an active role in relieving the financial burdens of their schools. This type of self-help was not limited to the industrial schools.

The Jubilee Singers of Fisk University set a unique example that would later be followed by other schools. George L. White, the college's treasurer, conceived the idea of reaching the hearts (and hence the pockets) of northern white citizens through the singing of a group of young African Americans. Therefore, with money borrowed from the teachers and the citizens of Nashville, in 1875 White took a group of students to Oberlin, Ohio, where the National Council of Congregational Churches was meeting. The council was captivated by

The Jubilee Singers
This student group traveled throughout the North and Europe to raise funds for Fisk University.

the way in which the young blacks sang spirituals and work songs of their people, and the fame of the group spread rapidly. In the East, they sang in many halls under the sponsorship of Brooklyn's famous preacher Henry Ward Beecher (the brother of Harriet Beecher Stowe). Numerous engagements followed, and the money flowed in. Later the Jubilee Singers went to England, Germany, and other European countries and appeared before several royal audiences. Within seven years, they had raised $150,000, part of which was used in the construction of school buildings. Student quartets, speakers, and other groups went out from other schools. In some communities money was raised at fairs and demonstrations.

White and black donations supported the educational agenda of the American Missionary Association, the American Baptist Home Mission Society, and the Methodist Episcopal Church, whose academies and colleges trained blacks throughout the South. Some white denominations broadened the scope of their educational efforts to include medical and theological schools, and some continued to establish additional secondary schools and colleges in the years following Reconstruction. Presbyterians, Episcopalians, and Catholics increased their activities in black education, making important contributions to primary and secondary education.

Each of the major black denominations also maintained secondary schools and colleges, relying heavily on black women's missionary organizations at the state and local level to galvanize black communities in fundraising drives. As southern blacks' political gains rapidly disappeared before vigorous state efforts, the pursuit of knowledge came to be one of the great preoccupations of African Americans, and education was viewed by many as the panacea for escaping the worst effects of the South's racial proscriptions and indignities. Numerous black fathers and mothers made untold sacrifices to secure for their children the learning that they had been denied.

Adherence to racial self-help never precluded accepting religious- and secular-based white donations. Some black schools, especially the Tuskegee Institute, developed notable educational programs owing to their leaders' enviable ability to attract sizeable amounts of white philanthropy. However, there was a caveat. The idea of black self-determination—a problematic detail integrally related to the ideology of self-help—became an issue that surfaced first in the schools of black higher education run by northern whites, such as Howard, Fisk, Claflin, and Virginia Union. In the 1880s and 1890s, these colleges and universities, which had played such an important role in achieving the educational goals of racial self-help, became hotbeds of inter- and intraracial contention.

Black Self-Determination Integral to self-help ideology is the belief in racial self-determination—the idea that blacks should speak for themselves and should control their own institutions. This particular emphasis sought to encourage blacks to establish and support their own organizations, or at least be represented in institutions for blacks, so that they might articulate their own interests in a collective voice, portray their own racial images, and perceive a common heritage and destiny. Thus, when educated and accomplished blacks demanded a greater presence in the administration and faculties of the white-run schools, tensions flared, along with accusations of white paternalism.

These schools' white missionary teachers and white boards determined school policies, controlled school finances, and periodically spoke disparagingly of their students as "childlike" and "heathen." The northern religious denominations were slower to hire blacks in their colleges and universities. Ironically, blacks held faculty and administrative positions, even as high as president, in the segregated southern state agricultural and mechanical colleges that had been established through the federal Morrill Land Grant Act—for example, Alcorn College in Mississippi and the Colored Normal, Industrial, Agricultural, and Mechanical College of South Carolina. As Booker T. Washington liked to remind his opponents, a private school such as his Tuskegee Institute was black controlled and had a black faculty and president—the epitome of racial self-help.

Although Howard University hired black teachers, conflict arose each time the school chose a new president. This was true as early as the 1870s, when the white AMA members of the board passed over future black legislator John Mercer Langston, who at the time was the dean of the Howard Law School. Black anger over Howard's failure to hire a black president resurfaced at the university in 1889. In the 1890s, the greatest disaffection arose in the schools under white Baptists and Methodists—denominations with large black memberships.

Historian James McPherson notes that the younger generation, which represented the more militant advocates of black school control in the 1880s and 1890s, marshaled its supporters with the slogan "Home rule for our colored schools." They demanded a greater voice in the administration of these schools. Edward Brawley, a leading black Baptist minister in South Carolina, was one of many to capture this spirit of revolt when he asserted in 1883 that blacks would no longer allow themselves to be treated like children. "We are willing to return thanks to the many friends who have assisted us in educating ourselves thus far," he declared, "but we have now reached the point where we desire to endeavor to educate ourselves, to build school houses, churches, colleges, and universities, by our own efforts." Such proud and fiery words were not accepted by everyone in the black community. The divisions among black Baptists grew to such an extent that the labels *separatists* and *cooperationists* came to define opposing positions on this issue.

Those of a more moderate persuasion denounced the headstrong militancy as "greed for office," refusing to sever ties with the white religious bodies that had come to the South to aid freedpeople. The black press, the proceedings of black denominational meetings, and the correspondence at the time reveal that the black community was divided over the practical implications of self-help in relation to white-controlled colleges for blacks. The moderates did not reject the idea of self-help, but as one minister argued, "it is possible to separate self-help from self-foolishness; it is possible to practice self-help and yet receive the generous aid of able friends." The schools themselves, however, had been jolted by the protest and at varying speeds began to hire more African American faculty. The protest also spurred the call for black denominational autonomy on the part of Baptists and efforts among the black denominations to establish their own separate schools.

In the last quarter of the nineteenth century, southern black schools began to receive funds from large educational foundations, established by wealthy entrepreneurs, called by their admirers "titans of industry" and by their detractors "robber **White Philanthropy** barons." Having built corporate monopolies by pursuing unbridled, often ruthless, tactics against their business competitors, this new breed of industrialists and financiers—men such as Andrew Carnegie, John D. Rockefeller, Cornelius Vanderbilt, and George Peabody—ushered in the Gilded Age of heightened economic disparity and the conspicuous extravagance of wealth. A sense of noblesse oblige, however, had also led them into philanthropy.

Newly rich philanthropists gave substantial sums to American educational and cultural institutions. White institutions were the primary beneficiaries of their largesse, but between the end of the Civil War and the beginning of World War I, several large educational foundations advanced black education in the South: the George Peabody Education Fund, the John F. Slater Fund, the General Education Board (founded by John D. Rockefeller), the Anna T. Jeanes Fund, the Julius Rosenwald Fund, and the Phelps-Stokes Fund. In 1882, for example, John F. Slater, a textile industrialist from Norwich, Connecticut, started the foundation that bears his name. Slater gave $1 million "for uplifting the lately emancipated population of the Southern states and their posterity, by conferring on them the blessings of Christian education." The board of trustees, headed by former President Rutherford B. Hayes, undertook immediately to assist twelve schools that were training African American teachers. Between 1882 and 1911, the fund assisted both private and church schools in their teacher-training programs and made donations to public schools.

White philanthropy, in general, increased after the arrival on the national stage of Booker T. Washington, preaching industrial and agricultural education, teacher training at the common school level, and accommodation to the racial status quo. In 1911 the Slater Fund began its support of country training schools, and within a decade it assisted more than a hundred such institutions. In 1905 Anna T. Jeanes, the daughter of a wealthy Philadelphia merchant, provided money specifically for black rural schools in the South. Under the guidance of James H. Dillard, the fund sought the appointment of teachers to do industrial work in rural schools, of special teachers to do extension work, and of county agents to improve rural homes and schools and create public sentiment for better African American schools.

The fund paid the salaries of these special teachers, and county officials gradually assumed part of the responsibility. The work of the fund attracted additional contributions from several other philanthropic agencies. In 1911 Julius Rosenwald visited Tuskegee Institute and the following year accepted a place on its board of trustees. His interest in and active assistance to rural African American schools dates from this time. Beginning as a small donor of amounts of $5,000, Rosenwald soon became a major contributor to the improvement of educational facilities for southern blacks.

Various philanthropic boards supplemented teachers' salaries, bought equipment, and built schools. Throughout the late nineteenth and early twentieth centuries, there was persistent southern white opposition to outside philanthropy, which one prominent white Methodist bishop described as "dangerous donations and degrading doles." General approval came only when the white citizens of the South judged that white funders showed little or no interest in establishing racial equality or upsetting white supremacy.

Booker T. Washington
This picture includes some of his friends and benefactors. Left to right: Robert C. Ogden, William H. Taft, Washington, and Andrew Carnegie.

The South did little to encourage the equitable distribution of public funds for the education of all southern children. In 1898 Florida's per capita spending to educate white children was more than double the amount allocated for educating black children. Mississippi, the poorest of all states, ranked last among the states in regard to financing its schools, and its tiny educational appropriations went overwhelmingly to white schools despite a school-age population that was more than 60 percent black. Historian Neil McMillen has noted of Mississippi that the greater a given county's concentration of blacks relative to whites, the more glaringly unfair was the racial disparity. For example, in majority-black Adams County, Mississippi, in 1900, $22 was spent to educate each white child and only $2 to educate each black child.

Educational Inequality in the South

No effort was made to mask blatant inequality in the state. In 1899 A. A. Kincannon, Mississippi's superintendent of education, declared that "our public school system is designed primarily for the welfare of the white children of the state, and incidentally for the negro children." With the right of suffrage no longer a possibility, the black community found it impossible to challenge the use of their tax dollars or to remove from office members of the state's educational board.

Throughout the southern states, the unequal distribution of school funds made clear that the "educational revival," spurred by Progressive movement reformers in the region, was intended for whites. If blacks were to be educated, they would have to bear the burden of the costs themselves. On occasion, southern whites contributed to black fundraising initiatives, and northern foundations gave money toward the support of rural schools. However, these donations were never sufficient, and some northern foundations stipulated local matching funds. In the case of the Rosenwald Fund, according to McMillen, Mississippi blacks were forced to draw from their own personal resources in order to provide the matching funds.

It was common for southern black communities to refer to a "double tax" in regard to their monetary support of black education—first, because of the racist reallocation of their tax dollars and second, because of their own sense of racial self-help, which required that they sacrifice, if need be, to maintain black schools. At the Sixth Atlanta Conference for the Study of Negro Problems in 1901, it was reported that between 1870 and 1899 blacks paid a total of $25 million in direct school taxes, while also contributing indirect taxes amounting to more than $45 million. Much of the tax money that blacks paid was diverted to white schools. It was also reported that they had paid more than $15 million in tuition and fees to private institutions. With a strong assertion that they had done much to help themselves in the generation following Reconstruction, the report concluded: "It is a conservative statement to say . . . that American Negroes have in a generation paid directly forty millions of dollars in hard earned cash for educating their children."

In 1900 thirty-four institutions for African Americans offered collegiate training, and African Americans had begun to enter several universities and colleges in the North. Virginia, Arkansas, Georgia, and Delaware each had a state college for blacks. The only racially integrated college in a southern state was Berea College in Kentucky. In 1904 the state passed a law requiring that schools be segregated, and Berea's status as a private institution led its administration to challenge the law. In 1908, however, the Supreme Court declared illegal the school's policy of racial integration, since the school was incorporated in Kentucky. Berea would serve whites exclusively until the mid-twentieth century, when the Kentucky segregation law was finally struck down.

Higher Education

The number of graduates from institutions of higher learning steadily rose. In the decades leading up to 1900, more than two thousand African Americans received college degrees. In that year alone, more than seven hundred African Americans were enrolled in college. The educational awakening that pervaded the United States in the approaching twentieth century was as clearly manifested among blacks as it was among other Americans. For African Americans, however, the topic of education caused a debate as to the most appropriate type of education. In the South, most white people felt that the "Negro's place" required only rudimentary training in basic skills and that anything more than that created problems. Others held that African Americans should not be regarded as a group earmarked for a specific kind of education (for example, industrial training), but that individuals should be able to choose freely between a liberal arts curriculum and industrial curriculum depending on their interest and ability. Still others contended that at their present stage of development, African Americans could best serve themselves and their country with a specific type of education they believed would most rapidly help them to find an indispensable place in the American social order.

From the early years of freedom after the Civil War, black higher education in the South exemplified two educational types—industrial training and classical liberal arts learning. Founded in the late 1860s, Hampton Institute exemplified industrial education, while Howard University and Fisk University exemplified the liberal arts. Samuel Armstrong, the founder and head of Hampton, taught his students that labor was a "spiritual force, that physical work not only increased wage-earning capacity but promoted fidelity, accuracy, honesty,

Tuskegee laboratory

persistence, and intelligence." He emphasized the value of acquiring land and homes, vocations and skills. Armstrong's teaching deeply influenced Booker T. Washington, who became the most eloquent and influential proponent of industrial education by the mid-1890s.

On the other hand, the concept of the "Talented Tenth," which began to be used in the 1890s, preceded the clash over black education between Booker T. Washington and W. E. B. Du Bois. It was not Du Bois who coined the term but rather the **The Talented Tenth** northern white Baptist leader Henry Morehouse. As early as 1896, perhaps in response to Booker T. Washington's speech at the Atlanta Exposition, Morehouse referred to the Talented Tenth, partly to marshal continued white Baptist commitment to Atlanta Baptist College (later renamed Morehouse), Spelman College, and other white Baptist-controlled schools for blacks in the South.

In founding these schools, northern Baptist leaders argued for a quality of black education that approximated the finest white schools in the North. Henry Morehouse wrote in the *Independent* in April 1896 that it would be a mistake to fail "to make proper provision for the high education of the talented tenth man of the colored colleges. . . . Industrial education is good for the nine; the common English branches are good for the nine; that tenth man ought to have the best opportunities for making the most of himself for humanity and God." The debate with Booker T. Washington had begun.

Divergent Paths to Racial Equality

Writing in 1903, W. E. B. Du Bois stated that "easily the most striking thing in the history of the American Negro since 1876 is the ascendancy of Mr. Booker T. Washington." The ascendancy of this man is one of the most dramatic and significant episodes in the history of American education and of race relations. When in 1881 Washington went to Tuskegee, Alabama, he found none of the equipment with which to develop an educational institution, as well as white townspeople hostile to the idea of a school for blacks. Operating initially in a local black church, Washington set about securing the necessary resources for the establishment of a school and conciliating the neighboring white community.

Olivia Davidson, a teacher and also a Hampton graduate (she would marry Washington in 1885), played a crucial role as a fundraiser in the formative years of the school. Davidson canvassed the Tuskegee community and traveled to New England, where she had also gone to school, winning friends and dollars for Tuskegee Institute. In addition, students cooperated by doing all the work of constructing the buildings, producing and cooking the food, and performing innumerable other tasks. The white community was given assurances in many ways that the students were there to serve and not to antagonize. Washington believed that southern whites had to be convinced that the education of blacks was in the true interest of the South. The students provided many of the services and much of the produce that the white community needed, and hostility to the new school began to diminish.

As the proponent of a form of industrial education that would not antagonize the white South, Washington hoped to encourage black employment and economic self-sufficiency. Washington believed, as he put it in 1895, that "one farm bought, **Booker T. Washington** one house built, one home neatly kept, one man the largest taxpayer and depositor in the local bank, one school or church maintained . . . one patient cured by a Negro doctor, one sermon well preached . . . these will tell more in our favor than all the abstract eloquence that can be summoned to plead our cause."

His was a practical program of training African Americans to live as comfortably and independently as possible, given southern racial realities. And his plan to produce farmers, mechanics, domestic servants, and teachers in rural schools throughout the state appeared far less threatening to those whites who believed that a liberal arts university education encouraged blacks to seek "social equality." Washington made no public demand for equality, although he secretly funded court cases that challenged Jim Crow rules in transportation. His public persona was far more conciliatory, and thus he counseled his people to obey the South's segregation laws and cooperate with white authorities in maintaining the peace.

Washington's speech at the opening ceremonies of the Atlanta Exposition in 1895 catapulted him to national acclaim. He comforted whites in the audience with the words: "In all things that are purely social we can be as separate as the five fingers, yet one as the hand in all things essential to mutual progress." He also admonished his own people: "To those of my race who depend upon bettering their condition in a foreign land or who underestimate the importance of cultivating friendly relations with the Southern white man . . . I would say 'Cast down your bucket where you are'—cast it down in making friends in every manly way of the people of all races by whom we are surrounded. Cast it down in agriculture, in mechanics, in commerce, in domestic service, and in the professions." The speech won praise from both whites and blacks. Indeed, Washington had won the good will of powerful and influential white citizens.

In his widely read autobiography *Up from Slavery* (1900), Washington presented a meditation on his life that fleshed out his philosophy in fuller detail. The autobiography broadened the good will of powerful and influential white citizens because of its accommodating tone, but it also won many black supporters, who recognized in its pages the familiar message of racial self-help. Washington never tired of urging blacks to develop useful economic skills rather than spend their efforts protesting racial discrimination. He preached intelligent management of farms, ownership of land, habits of thrift, patience, and perseverance, cleanliness, and the cultivation of high morals and good manners. Thereby Washington successfully positioned himself as the dominant black leader at the dawn of the new century.

Although Tuskegee produced a large number of male and female teachers for rural elementary schools, many of which were founded by its graduates, the institute also prepared students for specific trades and unskilled labor. Women's education, for example, offered training for such vocations as teachers, nurses, seamstresses, and domestic servants. Tuskegee's agricultural department opened in 1896 under the brilliant botanist and scientist George Washington Carver, who taught students to be more effective farmers—to rotate their crops, to fertilize the soil, and to grow peanuts and also to eat them as a protein supplement to their diet. Tuskegee offered outreach programs to black farmers—its mule-drawn "Moveable School" traveled through the countryside dispensing information. Tuskegee's experimental station (the only all-black station in the United States), farmers' institutes, farmers' conferences, and agricultural bulletins, were designed by Carver to offer a broad-ranging program. The school's agricultural department sought to help black farmers reduce their dependency on cotton production, transcend the cycle of debt, and live healthier lives.

Booker T. Washington did not deprecate the study of such subjects as science, mathematics, and history, but he indicated on many occasions that he regarded such education as impractical for the masses of black people. "For years to come the education of the people of my race should be so directed," Washington asserted, "that the greatest proportion of the mental strength of the masses will be brought to bear upon the everyday practical things of

Booker T. Washington at his desk

life, upon something that is needed to be done, and something which they will be permitted to do in the community in which they reside." His doctrine of industrial education for the great mass of blacks did not contradict the dominant scientific and popular ideas at the time, which doubted the capacity of African Americans to become completely assimilated in a highly complex civilization. Washington's mix of practical education and political conciliation to the rule of Jim Crow was attractive to southerners, as well as to northerners weary of racial and sectional conflict. Washington's white supporters praised him as a voice of reason, a leader who did not destabilize what they believed to be a satisfactory economic and social equilibrium between the races.

White southerners particularly admired the tact and diplomacy with which he conciliated all groups, North and South. Twice, however, Washington threatened his position among southern whites. Speaking in Chicago, he lashed out at race prejudice and asserted that it was eating away the vitals of the South. On another occasion, he dined at the White House at the invitation of President Theodore Roosevelt—an incident that most southerners regarded as a serious breach of racial etiquette. Arch-segregationists did not miss the implication or contradiction between Washington's admonitions against social equality and his own experiences and friendships with whites. The dinner with Roosevelt led southern newspapers to speak of a "damnable outrage." Exclaimed hyper-racist Ben Tillman, then a member of the United States Senate: "Now that Roosevelt has eaten with that nigger Washington, we shall have to kill a thousand niggers to get them back to their places."

Although whites tended to support Washington's immediate goals, few realized that he looked forward to the complete acceptance and integration of blacks into American life. Indeed, Washington quietly financed some of the earliest court cases against segregation. As Washington's biographer Louis R. Harlan has made clear, "by private action [he] fought lynching, disfranchisement, peonage, educational discrimination, and segregation." Subversive acts such as these were kept in the strictest secrecy. Washington viewed the demand for equality as a matter of timing and he perceived the odds of overcoming the mountain of racial prejudice too great. Progress could be made on other fronts—through education, through economic development, through the forward-looking march of a new century.

On one occasion, Washington said: "I would set no limits to the attainments of the Negro in arts, in letters or statesmanship, but I believe the surest way to reach those ends is by laying the foundation in the little things of life that lie immediately about one's door. I plead for industrial education and development for the Negro not because I want to cramp him, but because I want to free him. I want to see him enter the all-powerful business and commercial world." He advocated the entrance of African Americans into the professions and other fields, and he played an instrumental role in the founding of black professional organizations for physicians and those with businesses. He's credited with the establishment of the National Medical Association in 1895 and the National Business League in 1900.

Washington was not the first or only black spokesman for accommodation to the New South's racial policies. African Americans criticized Isaiah T. Montgomery of Mound Bayou when in 1890, as a Mississippi legislator, he voted for his state's disfranchisement plan. William H. Councill, the president of the Alabama Agricultural and Mechanical Institute (a black industrial school in Huntsville, Alabama) was regarded by many blacks as having a conciliatory attitude toward white conservative political policies—so much so that Booker Washington sought to distance himself from Councill. In a letter dated September 23, 1899, Washington described Councill as having a "reputation of simply toadying to the Southern white people."

By far the most conservative and vilified black figure at the turn of the century was William Hannibal Thomas. Self-identified as an Ohio-born mulatto, Thomas publicly demonized black culture and intellect. In his book *The American Negro: What He Was, What He Is, and What He May Become*, which was published by the well-respected Macmillan Press in 1901, Thomas argued that blacks were innately inferior to whites. He blamed them for their subordinate status in southern society and admonished them to rid themselves of "negro idiosyncrasies." His racist denunciation of his own people was as inflammatory as that of the vilest white supremacists. African Americans, including Booker T. Washington, reacted to Thomas with thorough disgust. In the press, in women's club meetings, and in correspondence, blacks exposed Thomas's financial malfeasance and personal improprieties and used such epithets as "race traitor" and "Judas of the race."

As Washington's prestige and influence grew, opposition among his own people increased as well, culminating in the dueling perspectives epitomized by Washington and W. E. B. Du

Opposition: T. Thomas Fortune

Bois. Although W. E. B. Du Bois would become Washington's most noted opponent, he was not the first person to speak openly against Jim Crow or the first to establish a protest organization. The black journalist T. Thomas Fortune wrote extensively against the loss of blacks' civil and political rights in his position as editor of the widely circulated *New York Age*.

At the time of Washington's "Atlanta Compromise" speech (Du Bois's phrase), Fortune was no newcomer to protest politics. In his book *Black and White: Land, Labor and Politics in the South* (1884), he denounced what he called the "great social wrong" of race discrimination in the South and urged black laborers to organize. In *The Negro in Politics* (1885), Fortune attacked the idea that blacks should blindly support the Republican Party and questioned the current wisdom of continuing to follow Frederick Douglass's 1872 dictum that "the Republican Party is the ship and all else is the sea."

In the 1880s and 1890s, Fortune figured significantly as a voice of racial self-help. In forceful language, he admonished his people, especially those in the South, to agitate for their rights, to sue in the courts, and to vote where possible. In 1887, during his editorship of the New York *Freeman,* he proclaimed that "white papers of this country have determined to leave the colored man to fight his own battles. . . . There is no dodging the issue; we have got to take hold of this problem ourselves, and make so much noise that all the world shall know the wrongs we suffer and our determination to right these wrongs."

Fortune's biographer, Emma Lou Thornborough, notes that Booker T. Washington, at the time a relative unknown on the national scene, supported Fortune's call for an Afro-American League. Two months later, in an open letter to Fortune in the *Freeman,* Washington urged: "Push the battle to the gate. Let there be no hold-up until a League shall be found in every village." Leagues organized at the state level initially, and 141 delegates from 23 states met in Chicago in January 1890 to establish an all-black national organization.

Fortune's rousing speech to the group stands in marked contrast to the speech that his friend Booker T. Washington would deliver five years later at the Atlanta Exposition. In 1890 Fortune warned against a temporizing attitude, proclaiming: "We have been patient so long that many believe that we are incapable of resenting insult, outrage and wrong; we have so long accepted uncomplainingly all the injustice and cowardice and insolence heaped upon us, that many imagine that we are compelled to submit and have not the manhood necessary to resent such conduct."

Yet by 1893, the League lacked the funds to mount a test case against railroad discrimination. Facing an avalanche of white supremacist ideas in the South and nation, the League languished from insufficient support. Efforts to revive and transform the League resulted in a meeting in Rochester, New York, in September 1898, at which time Fortune organized the National Afro-American Council. By then, however, Booker T. Washington was recognized by most whites and blacks as the undisputed leader of his people. Washington came increasingly to put his stamp on the Council, Fortune, and his newspaper, the *New York Age.* Fortune himself, unable or unwilling to defy Washington, fell deeper and deeper into alcoholism. Under Washington's watchful eye, the Council no longer subscribed to the protest politics of its past.

Another early voice of protest was Ida B. Wells, who launched a fearless crusade against lynching in 1892 after her friend Thomas Moss and his fellow business associates were lynched for defending their store and themselves from **Ida B. Wells** attack. These black men had set out to establish a business, the People's Store, which sold its products to Memphis blacks at a fair price, thus undercutting the white-owned store that exploited its black customers. Unfortunately, the black store-owners' success proved to be their undoing.

The lynching profoundly hurt and angered Wells. Armed with statistics and contemporary testimony, her column in the *Memphis Free Speech* detailed the lurid events of her friend's death. Wells attacked lynching in general, refuting its various justifications, especially those that excused lynching as the punishment due to black rapists of white women. Wells dared to call into question the honor of white women, positing that rape victims were far more often black women and their assailants white men. Finally, she urged her people to boycott white businesses and to migrate to Oklahoma, then still a territory.

Ida B. Wells, crusader for justice
Wells was run out of Memphis, Tennessee, where she edited a paper, for condemning violence, especially lynching. She continued her crusade in Chicago, where she also criticized the Columbian Exposition in 1892 for not including African Americans in its exhibits.

Wells's brash talk caused such uproar that whites burned down the press and ran her out of Tennessee, with threats to her life if she returned. Moving to New York, she continued her journalistic assault on lynching in Fortune's *New York Age.* In 1892, black women's organizations in the Northeast raised the funds necessary for her to publish the pamphlet *Southern Horrors: Lynch Law in All Its Phases.* In 1893 and 1894, she toured England, meeting British reformers and speaking to audiences about the savagery of lynching in the American South. Her speeches and writings prompted the British press to denounce lynching as barbaric. Her statements on the uncivilized nature of lynching, when juxtaposed alongside late-nineteenth-century racial science, had the effect of shaming the white South and the American people in the eyes of many of her European readers. The brutish nature of the southern lynch mob appeared wildly incompatible with social scientific "findings" of Anglo-Saxon civilization and the superiority of its culture. After Wells's move to Chicago and her marriage to newspaper publisher Ferdinand Barnett, she continued to turn out protest pamphlets in the 1890s and the new century. Her defiant tone differed radically from Booker T. Washington's cautious and circumspect one.

William Monroe Trotter and George Forbes challenged Washington and the legitimacy of his leadership in their co-edited newspaper, the Boston *Guardian.* Trotter had been an undergraduate at Harvard at the time of Du Bois's matriculation there. As the first black member of Phi Beta Kappa, Trotter had lived a privileged life and was part of Boston's black elite. In 1901 Trotter began to write excoriating articles about Washington in the pages of his newspaper, questioning his emphasis on industrial education, his accommodation to Jim Crow, and his tactics of silencing his opponents. In July 1903, he and his supporters disrupted Washington's speech to the National Negro Business League in Boston. Trotter's outbursts and insulting questions highlighted **William Monroe Trotter** what appeared to be an unbridgeable chasm between Bookerites and Anti-Bookerites, as the two camps began to be called.

Despite the warring factions, most African Americans did not fit neatly into either camp. **W. E. B. Du Bois** Du Bois had not questioned Washington's Atlanta Exposition speech at the time it was delivered. On the contrary, Du Bois expressed his esteem in a letter to Washington dated six days after the event, congratulating Washington for "a word fitly spoken."

Born in Massachusetts, Du Bois went to liberal-arts oriented Fisk University, from which he graduated in 1888, and afterward to Harvard where he received a second B.A. degree in 1890 and a doctorate in history in 1895. Between 1892 and 1894, Du Bois also studied in Berlin under the famous sociologist Max Weber. It was only after the publication of his book of essays *Souls of Black Folk* in April 1903 that Du Bois came to be recognized as the overarching symbol of opposition to Washington. Although some of the book's ideas had previously appeared as articles in the *Atlantic Monthly, The Dial,* and the *Annals of the American Academy of Political and Social Science,* the book offered an explicitly critical analysis of Washington's

W. E. B. Du Bois
Du Bois spoke out frequently against Booker T. Washington and his views on education
and politics.

philosophy, drawing the lines of difference more boldly than ever before. Du Bois accused
Washington of preaching a "gospel of Work and Money to such an extent as apparently
almost completely to overshadow the higher aims of life."

In his essay "The Talented Tenth," Du Bois wrote: "If we make money the object of
man-training, we shall develop money-makers but not necessarily men; if we make technical
skill the object of education, we may possess artisans but not, in nature, men. Men we shall
have only as we make manhood the object of the work of the schools—intelligence, broad
sympathy, knowledge of the world that was and is, and of the relation of men to it—this is
the curriculum of that Higher Education which must underlie true life." In short, he viewed
Washington's educational program as too narrow, and he found especially problematic the
manner in which Washington deprecated institutions of higher learning. According to Du
Bois, neither the black common schools nor Tuskegee could remain open were it not for the
teachers trained in black colleges.

Du Bois rejected Washington's conciliatory demeanor toward the white South's virtual
destruction of the political and civil status of African Americans, and he reasoned that it was
not possible, under modern competitive methods, for black artisans, businesspeople, and
property owners to defend their rights and lives without the suffrage. For Du Bois, the counsel of silent submission to racial inequality promised no good consequences for black people.
Du Bois contended that it was whites, not blacks, who deemed Washington the leader of his

people. Now the source for advice on all matters pertaining to African Americans, Washington had become "a compromiser between the South, the North, and the Negro." As the most eloquent spokesman for a growing number of blacks, Du Bois expressed the considerable alarm of those who disdained Washington's growing influence in regard to the funding of black educational institutions and his power over the appointment of blacks to federal and state positions.

Du Bois questioned the type of industrial education that Washington emphasized, since some of the artisan trades Tuskegee sought to produce—that of blacksmiths, for example—were fast becoming obsolete. Neither Tuskegee nor other industrial schools for blacks took cognizance of the problems peculiar to wage earners in modern industry. For example, Washington admonished black workers not to join labor unions, since they represented, according to him, a form of "organization which seems to be founded on a sort of impersonal enmity" to their employers. Washington also counseled blacks to remain in agriculture in the rural South, thus failing to understand changing times and irreversible demographic trends. There were, on the surface at least, innumerably more economic opportunities in the city, as well as more schools and opportunities for cultural and intellectual growth in the urban compared to the rural South. In the late nineteenth century, both whites and blacks had begun what would be a several decades-long migration from countryside to city.

Washington's various detractors were quick to argue that his refusal to condemn lynching, segregation, and disfranchisement had won his school the financial backing of rich and

Washington's Revenge powerful whites. Washington had the ear of industrial giants such as Andrew Carnegie, John D. Rockefeller, department store magnate Robert Ogden, and men in political offices as high as the presidency of the United States. His connections to these men brought millions of dollars to Tuskegee and made possible gifts to other schools that he endorsed.

Andrew Carnegie, for example, admired Washington and in April 1903 gave $600,000 to Tuskegee's capital campaign—then the largest donation to the school. Carnegie's great esteem for Washington is evident in a letter to William H. Baldwin, Jr., a railroad executive and a trustee of Tuskegee Institute. Writing to Baldwin soon after his generous gift, Carnegie described Booker Washington as a "modern Moses," continuing: "History is to know two Washingtons, one white, the other black, both Fathers of their People. I am satisfied that the serious race question of the South is to be solved wisely, only by following Booker Washington's policy. . . ."

Washington's network of powerful friends had allowed him to reward those loyal to him and punish his enemies. Thus donations to Atlanta University, where Du Bois taught, declined significantly, and the university's trustees began to urge the incorporation of more industrial arts courses into the university's traditional liberal arts focus. Washington's loyal "lieutenants" often acted as spies (with his approval). They discredited those vocal against Washington, attempted to get them fired from their posts, and ruined their chances for political or other appointed positions. One of Washington's supporters attempted in vain to have George Forbes, co-editor of the *Guardian,* removed from his position at the Boston Public Library. While he retained his job, the unfortunate situation caused Forbes to mute his attacks and cease to co-edit the newspaper. J. Max Barber, editor of the magazine *Voice of the Negro,* lost Washington's support after he began to travel in Du Bois's circles. Pressured by Washington, Barber eventually sold his magazine and left journalism altogether. Moving from Atlanta to Chicago and finally to Philadelphia, Barber freed himself from Washington's revenge only after becoming a dentist with no involvement in race politics.

It was the realization of Washington's pervasive influence that convinced former Afro-American Council members Monroe Trotter, W. E. B. Du Bois, and others to establish a protest organization. The new organization was formed in 1905, **The Niagara Movement** when Du Bois sent out a call to meet in secret at Niagara Falls, a historic terminus for escaping slaves on the Underground Railroad. Unable to find a hotel on the New York side that would lodge the black attendees, the group convened on the Niagara Falls Canadian side, incorporating their organization as the Niagara Movement. Fifty-five men signed the call, although only twenty-nine were present. As Du Bois reminisced several decades later: "If sufficient men had not come to pay for the hotel, I should certainly have been in bankruptcy and perhaps in jail."

They drew up a platform, demanding freedom of speech and criticism, male suffrage, the abolition of all distinctions based on race, the recognition of the basic principles of human fellowship, and respect for the working person. The Niagara Movement's Declaration of

The Niagara Conference, 1905
African American leaders met at Niagara in 1905 to discuss their grievances and draw up a list of demands.

Principles asserted that "the voice of protest of ten million Americans must never cease to assail the ears of their fellows, so long as America is unjust." Theirs was an unpopular, even dangerous stand against influential and highly respected persons in both the African American and white communities. The periodicals edited by the movement's leaders—Du Bois's *The Moon* and later *The Horizon*, Barber's *Voice of the Negro*, and Trotter's *Guardian*—constitute a bold and eloquent body of protest writings against the ideas and practices of white supremacy.

Du Bois admitted that many blacks would not perceive the need for another organization, referring probably to such predecessors as the Constitution League, the Afro-American Council, and the National Negro Business League. He did not doubt the possibility of skepticism, writing: "The first exclamation of anyone hearing of this movement will naturally be: 'Another!' . . . Why, should men attempt another organization after the failures of the past?" It is curious that Du Bois and the other men (no women were invited to be members) who signed the call envisioned their efforts as a movement—as if already a powerful change agent, laden with the resources and the popular backing needed to be a force for change. It was hardly so, at least not in the sense that social scientists today understand movements as expressing the collective consciousness of a relatively large grouping of persons and issue-oriented activism on a mass scale. Indeed, the fifty-five founders—primarily ministers, lawyers, editors, businessmen, and teachers—solicited what Du Bois called the "seldom sort," thus meaning the few, not the many.

"The country is too large," Du Bois wrote, "the race too scattered and the rank and file too unused to organized effort to attempt to impose a vast machine-like organization upon a wavering, uncertain constituency." Du Bois showed little confidence in the masses but rather confidence in like-mindedness. The organization sought to build its ranks from the men and women of the Talented Tenth. Du Bois waxed eloquent in his many articles, arguing and pleading for a black intelligentsia that would not be gagged by fear of Washington's influence. In 1905 he wrote in *The Moon*: "We need faith. The temptation today is for Negro-Americans to lose faith. Particularly is this true among the thinking classes."

In the twenty-first century, with the Booker T. Washington Papers accessible in digital format, there is irrefutable and easily accessible evidence of Washington's reaction to the Niagara Movement. Washington clearly felt threatened, believing that nothing good could come from an organization of such men as Du Bois and Trotter. He enlisted his assistant Emmett J. Scott to persuade the press not to give the Niagarites any coverage. Writing to an influential white newspaper owner on July 18, 1905, Scott warned: "Our friends think it wisest to in every way ignore absolutely the Niagara Movement. The best of the white newspapers in the North have absolutely ignored it and have taken no account of its meetings or its protestations. I think . . . if we shall consistently refuse to take the slightest notice of them that the whole thing will die aborning."

The division between the two camps, now called Bookerites and Niagarites, had reached a crisis point, leading Du Bois to resort to the Bible for words against Washington. The use

Bookerites and Niagarites of biblical references was a common rhetorical strategy in the nineteenth century. Just as antebellum slaves and free blacks had invoked Exodus, Du Bois also drew on Old Testament imagery to embolden his readers. Most of them would have known the story of the prophet Elijah, who refused to serve the false god Baal, and thus Du Bois sermonized, using Baal as a metaphor for Booker Washington: "However many the traitors and rascals and weaklings, behold all around the thousands that have not bowed the knee to Baal that are standing staunchly for right and justice and good." Look at them, Du Bois continued, "and have faith."

There were hardly "thousands," but when the Niagara Movement held its meeting in Harpers Ferry, West Virginia, in August 1906, 150 like-minded people, men and women, met openly in the haunting spirit of John Brown's fearless struggle for black freedom. The Niagara movement had not died aborning. And more than this, it had begun to mobilize its supporters for a strategic, open assault on Jim Crow.

At the second meeting of the Niagara Movement at Harpers Ferry in 1906, it was announced that forty local chapters had been formed, twenty-four of them in the North. In the preceding months, the men of Niagara had debated the merits of women joining their ranks, and women were added as members. However, the addition of women did not pass without some opposition. Monroe Trotter, the inveterate opponent of Booker T. Washington, had to be persuaded that women should be allowed to join. The infrastructure of the Niagara Movement showed signs of development. The Legal Department had already begun to challenge segregation. One of the women present at the Harpers Ferry meeting in 1906 was Barbara Pope, who at that very time was fighting Jim Crow railroad policies in the court. The Niagara Movement had provided a lawyer and financial support to Pope's lawsuit. The Harpers Ferry meeting also reported a Pan-African Department, Women's Department, Youth Department, Art Department, and Department of Ethics and Religion.

Niagarites such as Trotter, Du Bois, Ida B. Wells, and others presented a powerful counter-voice to the Bookerites. Theirs was a galvanizing, admittedly divisive strategy, presented as the alternative and principled position in the fight for racial equality. Building mass support entailed exploiting every opportunity—thus the proliferation of writings on both sides—to establish clearly and definitively the two different viewpoints. Each camp demanded that the black community take sides; each camp linked its agenda to the fate of all black Americans. In the years that some historians call the "age of Booker T. Washington," it was a bold and courageous move on the part of the Niagarites to plot the role of controversy in such a public way that African Americans would find the debate increasingly inescapable. Such leaders as Du Bois, Trotter, Barber, the Baptist minister John Milton Waldron of Florida and the District of Columbia, and lawyer J. R. Clifford of West Virginia manipulated every occasion that they could—in lectures, in the press, in the church, and in the courts—to reshape public opinion in explicit defiance of Booker T. Washington and his many respected supporters.

Many took a stand on this debate, but most black people did not think in this dualistic way; rather, they chose and validated specific ideas from both sides. Doubtless many African Americans took pride in Washington's growing renown, while others directly benefitted from his influence. Highly educated black leaders and noted champions of black civil rights held Booker Washington in high esteem. Robert H. Terrell, the first black federal judge and also husband of women's club leader Mary Church Terrell, supported Washington, as did the lawyer and equal rights advocate Archibald Grimké. Richard T. Greener, who was a black Harvard graduate, a lawyer, and a U.S. consul in Russia between 1898 and 1905, attended the Harpers Ferry meeting, but as his letters before and after the meeting reveal he also supported Washington. The young educator and songwriter James Weldon Johnson, who would later become a leader in the NAACP, admired Du Bois and the Niagarites but remained in the Bookerite camp. In 1906 Washington's influence with President Theodore Roosevelt landed Johnson appointments as consul in Puerto Cabello, Venezuela, and in 1909 in Corinto, Nicaragua.

Howard University educator Kelly Miller straddled the fence between the Washington and Du Bois factions, while Baptist leader Nannie Helen Burroughs, a staunch advocate for equal rights for both blacks and women, followed Washington's emphasis on industrial training. Her many speeches and writings, which championed the working class as opposed to the Talented Tenth, led her to be dubbed the "Female Booker T. Washington." Similar views were held by Victoria Earle Matthews, a race-conscious journalist and founder of the White Rose settlement house for black girls in New York City.

The competing strategies were effectively delineated and conveyed by the Social Gospel AME minister Rev. Reverdy Ransom in his rousing address to the men and women gath-

Two Classes of Negroes   ered at Harpers Ferry in 1906. Ransom carried his listeners back and forth across the African American ideological divide, as he described two classes of black people and subsequently divergent paths to equality:

> Today two classes of negroes, confronted by a united opposition, are standing at the parting of the ways. The one counsels patient submission to our present humiliations and degradations; it deprecates political action; ignores or condones the usurpation and denial of our political and Constitutional rights, and preaches the doctrine of industrial development and the acquisition of property. . . . The other class believes that it should not submit to being humiliated, degraded and remanded to an inferior place. It believes in money and property but it does not believe in bartering its manhood for the sake of gain. It believes in the gospel of work and industrial efficiency, but it does not believe in artisans being treated as industrial serfs, and in laborers occupying the position of a peasant class. It does not believe that those who toil and accumulate will be free to enjoy the fruits of their industry and frugality if they permit themselves to be short of political power.

The meeting places of the Niagara Movement were carefully selected to revive the same spirit of courage and uncompromising fervor reminiscent of the abolitionist movement of the antebellum era. Thus in 1907, the group met in Boston and in the following year, in Oberlin, Ohio—old abolitionist hubs in the East and Midwest. Yet there were to be no more meetings after 1908. The Niagara Movement would be absorbed by the new, racially integrated organization—the National Association for the Advancement of Colored People (NAACP).

Economic and Social Striving

While controversy continued over the most practical and effective type of education, the vast majority of African Americans faced the difficult task of making a living. With more than 75 percent of African Americans in the United States still living in the former Confederate states in 1880 and engaged primarily in agricultural work, it appeared that most of them would have to make some sort of economic adjustment on the farms. Without the capital to purchase land, they continued to be locked in the various forms of tenancy and sharecropping that had evolved during Reconstruction. Indeed, large numbers were impoverished farm laborers with no greater stake in agricultural production than their own scantily paid labor.

But even if they had the capital it was difficult for African Americans to purchase desirable farmland. With the destruction of the institution of slavery, whites looked on land as their only important capital investment, and they were reluctant to sell land to blacks, whom they did not want to enjoy the autonomy that came from land ownership in the South. The number of black farm owners remained small in the entire period before World War I. In the South, where blacks constituted approximately 50 percent of the population in 1900, they owned 158,479 farms, while whites in the South owned 1,078,635 farms. Before 1890, almost nothing had been done to educate African Americans in the use of modern agricultural methods, and as a result productivity was low, and there was general ignorance of the problems of marketing crops and purchasing supplies.

Booker T. Washington sought to improve this situation in 1892 when he issued the first call for a conference of farmers at Tuskegee. In this and succeeding years, African Americans from the surrounding countryside listened to discussions on "the evils of the mortgage system, the one-room cabin, buying on credit, the importance of owning a home and of putting money in the bank, how to build schoolhouses and prolong the school term, and to improve moral and religious conditions." Small tracts and circulars containing some essentials of farm improvement were distributed to the farmers at the conference, and from time to time Tuskegee Institute mailed them other information. After 1907 white philanthropists in cooperation with southern boards of education also funded black farm demonstration agents who helped to improve conditions.

Despite the efforts of African American farmers to adjust to the rural economy, the farm ceased to be attractive to many. Racial violence, intermittent agricultural depressions, unfair and often cruel treatment by landlords and merchants, and rumors of opportunities in the cities and in other parts of the country all stimulated an exodus of blacks from the rural South that began as early as 1879. Thousands left Mississippi, Louisiana, Alabama, and Georgia and went to the North and West. There was a minor stampede to Kansas, with Henry Adams of Louisiana and "Pap" Singleton of Tennessee assuming the leadership. Adams claimed to have organized 98,000 African Americans to go WEST. Perhaps he at least collected the names of that many who expressed a willingness to go. Singleton distributed a circular entitled "The Advantage of Living in a Free State" and actually caused several thousand to leave. Charles Banks and Isaiah Montgomery in Mississippi, Edward P. McCabe in Kansas and Oklahoma, Allen Allensworth in California, and Oklahomans David Turner, Thomas Haynes, and James E. Thompson were leaders in efforts to establish and promote economically viable and politically independent black towns and agricultural settlements as the solution to the black dilemma. Most of these ventures failed, however.

Some blacks considered the idea of emigration to Africa and sought help from the American Colonization Society, which continued to operate into the 1890s, although much weaker than in the antebellum era. Large numbers of letters from blacks to the ACS sought information about emigration in the two decades following the end of Reconstruction. Emigration fever was especially strong in rural Arkansas, although the lack of financial resources made leaving for Africa impossible. Historian Mary Rolinson notes that the interest in emigration spiked in the

The Black Exodus

Benjamin "Pap" Singleton

rural South after cotton harvests, when sharecroppers and tenant farmers felt more sharply the sting of unfair economic settlements with their white landlords.

In the pages of the various journals of his denomination, AME minister Henry McNeal Turner, a passionate voice for emigration in the late nineteenth century, described Africa as black Americans' true homeland. Turner's stridently black-nationalist statement that "God is a Negro" and the coverage of his missionary journeys on the African continent led to a heated debate between Turner and AME bishops who opposed his African focus.

Black leaders found themselves far more often in debates over whether blacks should leave the South, and specifically the rural areas, instead of whether blacks should leave America for Africa. Staying in the South may have been the only perspective that Frederick Douglass, who died in 1895, shared with Booker T. Washington, although Douglass's reasons differed. Douglass believed that the government should protect citizens wherever they lived, and he also feared that if they migrated out of the region, blacks would become nomads, losing what strength a sedentary existence would give them in the South, where they were concentrated. Richard T. Greener, however, insisted that blacks should migrate in order to put an end to the bad treatment they received at the hands of southern whites. He declared that a black exodus would lead to better economic and educational opportunities and would also benefit those who remained in the South. Perhaps none of these arguments had any telling effect. Forces rather than words decided the fate of African Americans. Most of them had neither the resources nor the initiative to go to new areas. Those who did go were lured just as other rural Americans of the period by the hope of a better livelihood.

In the last two decades of the nineteenth century, the South began to feel the impact of the economic revolution that had already enveloped the North. The iron industry was growing in Tennessee and Alabama, cloth was being manufactured in the Carolinas, **The New South** and the business of transporting manufactured goods to northern and southern consumers was becoming a major economic activity. Blacks as well as whites sought to take advantage of the new opportunities. For the most part, blacks in southern towns experienced great difficulty in securing some of the benefits of the new economic growth. In 1891 only 196 industrial employers of the South were using 7,395 African Americans. Ten years later, the number had increased substantially, and some were employed in cottonseed-oil mills, sawmills, and furniture factories, as well as in foundries, machine shops, boiler works, and similar workplaces. By 1910 African American factory workers had increased to more than 350,000, generally holding the least attractive jobs.

Southern urban blacks even found it difficult to render their customary personal services to city dwellers. Black barbers were fast losing their monopoly in what had previously been a "black" service to foreign-born competitors, while cooks and caterers were similarly displaced by palatial hotels that frequently refused to hire blacks. Everywhere there was sentiment against giving blacks jobs that had even the slightest semblance of respectability. Moreover, race riots, such as the Atlanta Riot of 1906, caused blacks living in southern cities to find urban life almost as dangerous and frightening as rural life.

At a time of unprecedented industrial innovation, African Americans made some important contributions. Jan E. Matzeliger, who had been an apprenticed cobbler in Philadelphia **Innovation and Enterprise** and in Lynn, Massachusetts, invented the shoe-lasting machine. It was purchased by the United Shoe Machinery Company of Boston and effectively reduced the cost of manufacturing shoes by more than 50 percent. In 1884 John P. Parker

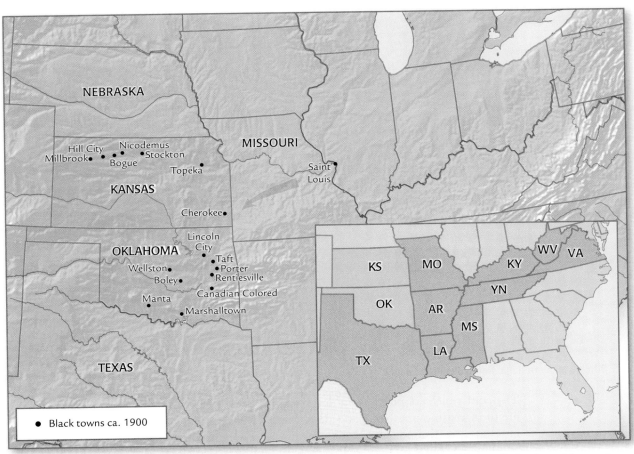

During 1879, more than 6,000 African-Americans migrated from Louisiana, Mississippi, and Texas to St. Louis, and then on to Kansas and Oklahoma.

invented a "screw for tobacco presses." He established the Ripley Foundry and Machine Company and made presses for many businesses. Elijah McCoy patented fifty different inventions relating principally to automatic lubricators for machines. It was the claim for the genuineness of one of his products that led to the expression "the real McCoy." Granville T. Woods, who began inventing in 1885, made significant contributions in the fields of electricity, steam boilers, and automatic air brakes. Several of his inventions were assigned to the General Electric Company, the Westinghouse Air Brake Company, and the American Bell Telephone Company.

African Americans embarked on their own program of business enterprise within a segregated market. Taking their cue from the almost hopeless plight of millions of their race in the South, black leaders, including W. E. B. Du Bois, urged adoption of an entrepreneurial spirit: blacks were urged to enter business and manufacturing in order to escape poverty and achieve economic independence. Speaking before the Fourth Atlanta University Conference in 1898, John Hope, then a professor at the university, noted that the plight of African Americans was not due altogether to the lack of education and skills but at least in part to competition between the races for employment in new fields. He therefore called on blacks to escape the wage-earning class and become their own employers.

Officers of the National Negro Business League

The conference adopted resolutions declaring that "Negroes ought to enter into business life in increasing numbers" and that "the mass of Negroes must learn to patronize business enterprises conducted by their own race, even at some slight disadvantage. We must cooperate or we are lost." The conference also called for the distribution of information concerning the need for African American businesses and the organization of local, state, and national Negro Business Men's Leagues.

Booker T. Washington appropriated this idea. Washington reserved his highest praise for what he called the "business Negro"—convinced, as he wrote in his autobiography, that the "only sure basis of progress is economic." Black owners of businesses and property also asserted racial pride, according to Washington. He associated this group with the insistence upon spelling the word Negro with a capital N—a practice Washington heartily endorsed, since, as he argued, "we capitalize the Indian, the Chinaman, the Filipino; shame to withhold so small an honor from the Negro!" In 1901 Washington convened in Boston a group of African American businesspeople, thereby establishing the National Negro Business League. More than four hundred delegates came from thirty-four states and elected Washington as their first president.

Washington, believing that taxpaying African Americans of intelligence and high character almost invariably were treated with respect by whites, urged that the "idle, useless class" of African Americans be transformed into valuable, law-abiding citizens. He also urged that a larger number of blacks enter various business fields. In *The Negro in Business* (1907) he stated that he was gratified by the large number of new business enterprises that had sprung up during the first year of the league's existence. Many local organizations were formed, and by 1907 the national organization had 320 branches.

Black entrepreneurs serviced a segregated clientele hungry for consumer products that might not otherwise have been available, such as community news, life insurance, bank loans, and beauty products. Additionally, black-owned products represented the self-help antidote to the sale and advertisement of countless commodities associated with Old South images of mammy, Uncle Mose, and other plantation stock characters that propelled the fast-growing American consumer economy in the late

Combating Old South Images

nineteenth and early twentieth centuries. Soap wrappers, postcards, boxes of breakfast cereal and pancake mix, tobacco tins, children's games, and fly swatters are but a few examples of the many items displaying smiling, often caricatured black faces. These inexpensive products of daily use were widely advertised and sold to blacks and whites in stores across America.

By presenting black images in insulting and demeaning ways, such products reinforced ideas of black inferiority and servility. Much like minstrel humor, which remained a tremendously popular form of American entertainment into the twentieth century, the new racialized commodities were intended, indeed literally designed, to elicit happy and jovial responses from their white consumers despite their underlying violent meanings and insensitivity to black life. A drawing on a popular postcard, for example, depicted black children being chased and eaten by an alligator.

African Americans attempted to combat such images by producing their own products, publishing their own literature, and portraying positive visual images. The artist Henry O. Tanner (1859–1937), son of the noted African Methodist Episcopal bishop Benjamin Tanner, painted few works with explicitly black subject matter, but his renderings of African American life serve as a powerful refutation of racist, stereotypical caricatures. For example, the ubiquitous image of foolishly grinning black men with banjos—an iconic symbol in the American popular imagination—is countered by Tanner's *The Banjo Lesson* (1893). In the depths of the nadir in race relations, Tanner painted an intimate, dignified glimpse of African American family life in a humble home, where one generation teaches another.

Tanner, however, would leave the United States, not for Africa but for Europe. He received his artistic training at the Pennsylvania Academy of Fine Arts in 1879 and worked under the celebrated American painter Thomas Eakins. After completing his formal training, Tanner initially set up shop in Atlanta, hoping to find patronage among the city's relatively affluent African American residents. In 1891, however, he left the United States to study abroad and remained in France for most of his professional career, cultivating a celebrated international reputation as a painter of religious subjects, landscapes, and portraits.

Henry Ossawa Tanner, *The Banjo Lesson*, 1893

At the end of the century, African Americans engaged in businesses of various types and sizes. They operated grocery stores, general merchandise stores, and drugstores, and they were restaurant keepers, caterers, confectioners, bakers, tailors, builders, and contractors. Some operated shirt factories, cotton mills, rubber goods shops, lumber mills, and carpet factories. There were many cooperative businesses, such as the Bay Shore Hotel Company of Hampton, Virginia; the Capital Trust Company of Jacksonville, Florida; the South View Cemetery Association of Atlanta, Georgia; and the Southern Stove Hollow-Ware and Foundry Company of Chattanooga, Tennessee. The success of some black businesspeople, while failing to approach the success of whites during the same period, was nevertheless significant.

Beauty culture proved to be one of the most lucrative sources of economic enterprise, appealing to a gender niche—black women consumers. The demand for beauty **Black Women Entrepreneurs** products began to grow rapidly in the late nineteenth century among all American women. The demand for hair and skin preparations created opportunities for inventive and resourceful black women to address the unique concerns of black women, while also offering black women employment beyond the limited options available to them. Annie Turbo Malone, founder of the Poro System, and Madame C. J. Walker, founder of the Walker System, became wealthy by perceiving beauty culture as a vehicle for promoting racial self-help. The advertisements for Walker products conveyed this. On the individual level, advertisements sent the message that a black woman's appearance was directly related to her self-esteem and social mobility. A black woman could pull herself up by the appearance of her hair and skin, not merely by her bootstraps. On a collective level, her beauty culture business provided employment, and it linked as well to uplift ideology's attention to hygiene and physical appearance, which was no less important than educational and economic accomplishment.

The products of black beauty culturalists would not go unchallenged by race-proud blacks who decried the hair-lengthening and skin-lightening advertisements, or by those who reduced the promises of such products to sheer falsehoods and dishonest advertising. However, race leader Madame C. J. Walker eventually garnered tremendous respect for her own business, not least of all because of her ability to articulate the self-help ideology through a beauty system that ultimately promised to transform the collective face of the race, what Henry Louis Gates has described as the facelift or racial makeover representative of the New Negro in the first decade of the twentieth century. Walker expressed this sentiment to the National Negro Business League in 1912, stating: "I am in a business that is a credit to the womanhood of our race."

Madam C. J. Walker was born Sarah Breedlove in 1867 to a family of impoverished sharecroppers in the Deep South. Widowed at the age of 20, she resettled in St. Louis and worked as a washerwoman. In the quest to improve the quality of her own hair, she developed what became known as the "Walker System," a treatment that promised healthier and longer hair. After moving to Denver, she began to sell her products from door to door. She became successful enough to hire agent-operators in different states. She would later move to Indianapolis and finally to the banks of the Hudson River in New York. Her business skyrocketed, its success made possible by the hundreds, if not thousands of black women employees and millions of black women consumers of her product. Walker's speeches about her rise from a plantation to a mansion were eloquent testimonies to the philosophy of self-help. She fought for recognition, however, within the male-dominated National Negro Business League. She did not initially have the endorsement of Booker T. Washington, as did the other (male) entrepreneurs. Washington and other men in the black business league scoffed at the "business of growing hair," but she gained his respect as her profits grew. She also committed herself financially to racial advancement and gave generous donations to black organizations. She died on May 25, 1919.

African Americans made a special effort to establish themselves firmly in the field of banking, a difficult task after the failure of the Freedman's Bank in 1874. In 1888 in Richmond, Rev. W. W. Browne organized the first bank to be **Establishment of Black Banks** administered solely by blacks, the Savings Bank of the Grand Fountain United Order of True Reformers. Later in the same year the Capital Savings Bank of Washington was organized. In 1889 the Mutual Bank and Trust Company of Chattanooga was founded, followed by the establishment of the Alabama Penny Savings Bank of Birmingham. By 1914 approximately fifty-five black banks had been organized. Most of them were closely connected with fraternal insurance organizations or churches or both.

One of the most successful and celebrated black bankers in the early twentieth century was a woman—Maggie Lena Walker. She grew to fame initially as a member and leader of the Independent Order of St. Luke, a black mutual aid society in Richmond, Virginia. A civic activist and black women's club leader, Walker's outreach efforts targeted poor black women. In 1903 she became the nation's first female bank president, founding the St. Luke's Penny Savings Bank. The bank encouraged depositors with little money to "turn pennies into dollars." Many of her early patrons were washerwomen. Today, the bank continues to operate as the Consolidated Bank and Trust Company.

Racial discrimination in the northern states also required blacks to develop their own strategies for economic progress. In the 1880s, in Philadelphia, Rev. Matthew Anderson, pastor of the Berean Presbyterian Church, championed the need for his church to build a savings and loan association, in order to expand the availability of affordable housing to African Americans. Blacks were confined to specific areas and had difficulty getting loans to purchase houses. This idea that blacks could find no other recourse other than self-help led the Berean Church to establish a building and loan association in 1888 that served as a needed lending agency for the larger black community, not just for the Berean Presbyterian congregation. By 1908 the savings and loan association made possible the purchase of 150 homes, which Anderson described as "inviting, on good streets, in different parts of the city." To this day the Berean Bank remains in business.

Black churches became an important source of business enterprise in the urban North and South. Because of segregation and the lack of blacks' access to resources available to whites, churches assumed a broader role than sim- **The Role of the Churches** ply religious worship. They became, according to Chicago black clubwoman Fannie Barrier Williams, "multi-service institutions." Individual black churches often serviced a population larger than their members. In the late nineteenth-century South, many black newspapers were published in churches, or at least began in churches. This was true of Ida Wells's *Memphis Free Speech*. Many, if not most of the black

Woman of wealth and influence
Madam C. J. Walker and daughter on a sightseeing tour.

schools and colleges in the South opened first in black churches before acquiring a school building.

Black women were primarily responsible for the fundraising and community mobilization that made it possible for individual churches and black denominational organizations at the local, state, and national levels to establish and maintain schools, newspapers, publishing companies, libraries, old people's homes, orphanages, insurance companies and mutual aid societies, and a host of social welfare services. Black church women of all denominations worked within their own separate missionary societies, in secular women's clubs, and in alliance with white (more often northern) church women to develop and administer visionary programs of service to their people. They played a critical role in supporting and even initiating the progressive ministries in urban churches North and South. Such was the case of churches led by a variety of Social Gospel black ministers: Reverdy Ransom, who enjoyed a long life of activism in various parts of the nation; Richard R. Wright, Jr., in Chicago; William DeBerry, in Springfield, Massachusetts; John Milton Waldron, in Jacksonville, Florida, and later in Washington, D.C.; Matthew Anderson, in Philadelphia; Henry Hugh Proctor, in Atlanta; Walter Henderson Brooks, in Washington, D.C; and Hutchens Bishop and Adam Clayton Powell, Jr., in New York. In Harlem alone, numerous churches professed Social Christianity: Abyssinian Baptist, Bethel AME, Mount Tabor Presbyterian, St. Cyprian

Episcopal Mission, and St. Marks Methodist Episcopal. Black churches in Detroit, Chicago, St. Louis, Cincinnati, and other cities engaged as well in Christian social service.

These are but a few of many examples in the late nineteenth and early twentieth centuries of faith-based initiatives in the form of social settlement work, employment training, banking and insurance, kindergarten, health clinics, youth programs, women's training, and a variety of social services to meet the needs of newly arriving migrants to the cities. This progressive element represented in black communities, as it did in white communities, a small minority within the larger religious landscape. And yet its influence was felt in the improvement of conditions in urban communities. This is borne out in the Atlanta University conference publication that stated in 1898: "Compared with modern civilized groups the organization of action among American Negroes is extremely simple. . . . And yet there are among them 23,000 churches, with unusually wide activities, and spending annually at least $10,000,000." These figures would grow considerably in the next two decades.

The Social Gospel, associated with the Progressive reform movement of the late nineteenth century, linked the traditional Christian theology of individual salvation to wider ethical concerns for reforming poverty, immigrant adjustment, slums, racism, alcohol, and other perceived problems. The Social Gospel's individual and collective meaning, as well as its call for **The Social Gospel and Black Separatism** "practical Christianity," intertwined almost imperceptibly with the ideology of racial self-help voiced by black religious progressives. Some, like Ransom and Waldron, called their churches "institutional" in keeping with many of the white Social Gospel churches at the turn of the century. In like manner, black Baptist leader, educator, and suffragist Nannie Helen Burroughs united her calls for "practical Christianity" and "practical education." Reminiscent of Booker T. Washington, Burroughs referred to her District of Columbia–based National Training School for Women and Girls as the "School of the 3 Bs: the Bible, Bath, and Broom."

In some cases, the race-conscious belief in black self-determination dominated even religious identity to the point that some blacks assumed a posture of separatism from those whites with whom they shared the same denominational affiliation. The formation of the National Baptist Convention in 1895, the largest black denomination, illustrates such a situation. One of the precipitating factors in the desire to form a separate black denominational body (called *convention*) pertained to a breach between black and white Baptists over the exclusion of educated black Baptist contributors to a northern white Baptist publication. In 1896, at the meeting of the newly formed National Baptist Convention, Rev. E. K. Love, pastor of the First African Baptist Church in Savannah, reveled in the formation of the new black convention and its own publishing board. Love proclaimed: "There is not as bright and glorious a future before a Negro in a white institution as there is for him in his own. . . . We can more thoroughly fill our people with race pride, denominational enthusiasm and activity, by presenting to them, for their support, enterprises wholly that are ours."

In the era of self-help, this attitude was held by both church leaders and laity, and every black denomination developed publishing companies and religious presses. Such presses not only published on religious topics, but also offered opportunities for black writers of fiction and nonfiction to present their work. For example, women writers Pauline Hopkins, Frances Ellen Watkins Harper, and Victoria Earle Matthews found a venue for their writings in the periodicals of the AME Church.

Another manifestation of the struggle of African Americans to become socially self-sufficient was the remarkable growth of fraternal orders and benefit associations. Masons

Mutual Benefit Societies   and Odd Fellows maintained large black memberships; in addition, organizations such as the Knights of Pythias and the Knights of Tabor competed for membership among black men. Organizations for black women included the Order of the Eastern Star and Sisters of Calanthe. Other secret orders—the International Order of Good Samaritans, the Ancient Sons of Israel, the Grand United Order of True Reformers, and the Independent Order of St. Luke—offered insurance against sickness and death, aided widows and orphans of deceased members, and gave opportunities for social intercourse. Some were strong only in certain localities; others had memberships that extended over several states and owned the buildings housing their main offices as well as other property that they rented to black businesses.

A variation of the fraternal organization, without the feature of secret rituals, was the beneficial and insurance society. Such organizations grew in number during this era. They usually collected weekly dues ranging from 25 cents to 50 cents from their members. The Young Mutual Society of Augusta, Georgia, organized in 1886, and the Beneficial Association of Petersburg, Virginia, organized in 1893, were typical of local benefit societies. Larger in scope and membership was the Workers Mutual Aid Association of Virginia. By 1898, four years after its founding, it had more than four thousand members. Although these societies imposed relatively exorbitant dues on their members, they served as important training grounds where African Americans could secure business experience and develop habits of self-help that seemed to be more imperative as the new century opened.

A logical outcome of the mutual benefit societies was black insurance companies, which were more economic than social in their functions. In Washington, D.C., S. W. Rutherford severed his connections with the True Reformers and organized a society that finally became the National Benefit Life Insurance Company, which remained the largest African American organization of its kind for more than a generation. In Durham, North Carolina, John Merrick, who had been an extension worker for the True Reformers, was able to interest several influential citizens in organizing an insurance company. He, together with several associates, in 1898 became charter members of the organization that later became known as the North Carolina Mutual Life Insurance Company. Its period of substantial growth dates from 1899, when C. C. Spaulding was added to the board and the company was reorganized. In Atlanta, Georgia, A. F. Herndon secured control of the Atlanta Mutual Aid Association and reorganized it into the powerful Atlanta Life Insurance Company. These and similar businesses grew as some white companies became more and more reluctant to insure African Americans, who were learning the value of purchasing various types of insurance.

Among the other organizations that assisted in the adjustment of African Americans to city life were the Young Men's Christian Association (YMCA) and the Young Women's Christian Association (YWCA). The first black YMCA had been organized as early as 1853 in Washington, D.C., but not until after the Civil War was it connected with the white YMCA movement. In 1888 William Alphaeus Hunton was placed on the national staff as its first salaried black officer, and in 1898 Jesse E. Moorland joined him to give special attention to the problems of African Americans in urban areas. Early in the new century several city association branches were organized. Buildings that could be used as headquarters and recreational centers were constructed. With gifts from philanthropists George F. Peabody and Julius Rosenwald, black YMCAs were established in several cities North and South, and despite being segregated facilities, the YMCA provided needed services to the communities in which it existed.

By 1906 there were small YWCAs for African Americans in Washington, Philadelphia, New York, and Baltimore. Gradually, with an awakened social consciousness, city and student work developed. Not until the outbreak of World War I did a strong movement of Y-work develop among African American women. Several substantial buildings were erected in strategic centers, and with the cooperation of such philanthropists as Rosenwald and Rockefeller, the YWCA acquired buildings in which black women were able to carry out a program of social improvement and education for young black women that did much to assist them with the adjustment of recently migrating women to urban communities.

The Woman's Era

Perhaps no movement in the late nineteenth century captures so vividly the complexity of hope and anguish in this era than the struggle of black women for racial and gender equality. Black women writers and black women's organizations blossomed during the decades, which are variously called the era of racial self-help, the Progressive era, and the woman's era. Black women writers—Frances Ellen Watkins Harper, Ida B. Wells, Anna Julia Cooper, Fannie Barrier Williams, Hallie Q. Brown, Victoria Earle Matthews, Josephine St. Pierre Ruffin, Mary Church Terrell, and others—contributed to an outpouring of literature (fiction and nonfiction) that captured the three-pronged spirit of black uplift, societal reform, and women's rights. They were also actively involved in the club movement among black women.

Author, suffragist, and temperance leader Frances Ellen Watkins Harper illustrated the overlapping contexts of race and gender reform in 1893, when she gave the lecture "Woman's Political Future" at the World's Congress of Representative Women, meeting in Chicago during the World's Columbian Exposition. In her speech to this interracial gathering, Harper unmistakably championed the need for racial equality, black education, and the end to lynching, but she also proclaimed boldly: "Through weary, wasting years men have destroyed, dashed in pieces, and overthrown, but to-day we stand on the threshold of woman's era, and woman's work is grandly constructive."

At the time of Harper's speech, black women's organizations and their reform agendas clearly reflected a conflated racial and gender consciousness. Black women confronted a gender-specific form of racial discrimination that began with slavery and continued afterward. For the most part, locked into the identity of servant and menial worker, black women did not enjoy the social status of white women. The larger society did not place any black woman, regardless of her education and accomplishment, on womanhood's pedestal to be supported, protected, or identified by the term "lady." Nor did society value black motherhood.

Gender-Specific Discrimination

Discussing the club movement in 1902, Fannie Barrier Williams, wife of the black lawyer and jurist S. Laing Williams, wrote of the black woman: "By a sort of national common consent, she has had no place in the Republic of free and independent womanhood of America." Even the white women's club movement of the time, specifically the National Federation of Women's Clubs, refused to admit black women's clubs into its membership, although a few black women held membership (often after considerable debate) as individuals in white women's clubs at the local level.

In the courts, in their household employment, in scientific studies, and in the popular media, the prevailing opinion held black women to be the very opposite of white women—the latter being perceived as delicate and chaste. Appearing periodically in the white press was the presumption of the inherent immorality of the black female, even as an adolescent. In 1895, for example, James Jacks, the president of the Missouri Press Association, had demeaned the efforts of black clubwomen to assist Ida B. Wells in her antilynching crusade. Writing in a Missouri newspaper, he described black women as "wholly devoid of morality . . . prostitutes and all natural thieves and liars." In 1904 a white woman repeated this type of negative stereotyping in a newspaper article that stated: "Negro women evidence more nearly the popular idea of total depravity than the men do. . . . I cannot imagine such a creation as a virtuous black woman."

Despite the racist limitations that African Americans sought to transcend through their self-help efforts, the thinking of most black men did not transcend the many patriarchal ideas of their day. Thus black women faced sexism within the black community itself. For example, in the 1880s, black Baptist church women, particularly in the southern states, faced male opposition as they endeavored to establish and control their own local missionary societies, in order to raise the necessary economic resources for projects that benefitted black women and girls, as well as for projects that benefitted black institutions generally. Fisk graduate Virginia Broughton of Tennessee, the Louisville, Kentucky, educator Mary Cooke Parrish, and the Washington, D.C., educator Nannie Helen Burroughs often drew on female examples from the Bible as they argued that women were called to work as equals with their men for the uplift of their communities.

In so doing, they adopted an explicitly women's rights rhetoric, a feminist theology of racial uplift, while establishing denomination-based women's organizations at the state and national levels. Also, as historian Tera Hunter reveals, black working women banded together for economic uplift, conscious of the unique conditions they faced. Washerwomen in Atlanta in 1881 and in 1891 organized to better their economic situation, calling strikes for higher wages. Other Georgia-based women's associations—for example, the Cooks' Union and the Working Women's Society—served as mutual aid and lending societies for their members during illness and financial crisis.

However, it was the rise of the club movement in the 1890s that gave voice to the gender-conscious civic activism of many middle-class and upper-class black women. By the beginning of 1896, two distinct black women's federations existed. One began with the formation of the Colored Women's League in 1892 in Washington, D.C. Black educators Mary Church Terrell and Anna Julia Cooper of the District helped to found the Colored Women's League, which quickly developed affiliated leagues in the South and West. Their work focused on establishing kindergartens, holding mother's meetings, and offering a variety of educational programs. The second federation emerged in 1894, when Josephine St. Pierre Ruffin, her daughter Florida Ridley, and Maria Louise Baldwin (who was also the first black principal of a school in Cambridge, Massachusetts) founded the Woman's Era Club.

Married to the black judge George Lewis Ruffin of Boston, Josephine St. Pierre Ruffin had been involved in civil rights work and the women's suffrage movement since the 1870s. She served as the editor and publisher of the *Woman's Era*, a monthly magazine devoted to issues concerning black women. When Ruffin extended an invitation to representatives of black clubs in different parts of the country to meet in Boston on July 29–31, 1895, about one hundred black women from twenty-five clubs answered her call. This meeting led to

The handwritten annotations on the photograph read:

Back Row   1. Ella Swett 3 Mamie Hilyer Dr. Frye A.F. Hilyer 5 Annie King 7 Dr. Foy 11 Evelyn Shaw 13 Lottie Grimke 24 Lula Love
33 Miss Chas 34 Mrs. Douglass 35 Mrs. Chas Douglass Mrs. Shippen 44 Mallie Bush Mrs. John F. Cook 38 Mrs. John Smith
46 Mrs. Frederick Douglass 47. Mrs. Michaux Mrs. L. H. Hawkins Mrs. Sara Fleetwood 54 Miss Grany
right of   Mrs. John Smith 6. Dr. Foy 847 Mrs. J. Pierre 14 Miss Alice Jackson Kate Moten 52 Miss Jordon

The Colored Women's League of Washington, dedicated to "Moral Uplift"

a subsequent meeting—the Congress of Colored Women—in Atlanta in December 1895, which launched the National Federation of Afro-American Women under the leadership of Margaret Murray Washington, the wife of Booker T. Washington.

The merger of the two federations of various black women's groups—the Colored Women's League and the National Federation of Afro-American Women—created the National Association of Colored Women. Adopting the motto "Lifting as We Climb," the NACW brought together two hundred clubs, thus functioning as a federation of diverse state and local efforts for racial and gender self-help. The regional breadth of the NACW is reflected in the locations of its subsequent biennial meetings: in 1897 in Nashville, Tennessee; in 1899 in Chicago, Illinois; and in 1901 in Buffalo, New York. Historian Deborah Gray White has noted that this powerful association was "unprecedentedly 'feminist' in that NACW leaders insisted that only black women could save the black race." It rapidly rose to become one of the leading organizations for black social and political activism in the first three decades of the twentieth century. NACW members elected Mary Church Terrell as their first president and Margaret Murray Washington as vice president.

The NACW

As the NACW's first president, a post she held until 1901, Mary Church Terrell noted: "We have become National, because from the Atlantic to the Pacific, from Maine to the Gulf, we wish to set in motion influences that shall stop the ravages made by practices that sap our strength, and preclude the possibility of advancement. . . . We refer to the fact that this is an association of colored women, because our peculiar status in this country seems to demand that we stand by ourselves." Terrell believed that by elevating black women's social status, discrimination against the entire race would ebb—hence, all would be lifted by the act of black women's greater acceptance and visibility within the general culture. Toward that end, Terrell focused on building a solid network of black women across the country. The NACW established a monthly newsletter, *National Notes,* to provide information about the group's goals and programs and held conventions every other year in cities with large black populations to help build membership and offer seminars for women.

Mary Church Terrell

Terrell's racial uplift strategy adopted W. E. B. Du Bois's notion of a Talented Tenth when it came to her organization's leadership. Born into the black elite in Tennessee, Terrell relied on similarly educated black women, female business owners, and professionals to serve as leaders of local NACW chapters. She also tapped into the strong legacy of black women's church-related organizing efforts, drawing many members from these groups. But while she sought racial advancement, Terrell and many other female reformers believed that the domestic sphere was the source of woman's unique power and her ability to enhance the race's social status. Terrell argued that "one reaches both the source of many race problems and an intelligent solution of the same, through the home, the family life, and the child." Black clubwomen's sense of uplift was often articulated in words that conveyed their elitism. They referred to themselves as "women of culture," "social standing," and the "best women" in their communities. Yet uplift's moral connotation also conveyed the clubwomen's anxiety at being lumped together with their "less fortunate" sisters, thus confirming the need for all black women to gain respectability in white America.

NACW chapters implemented kindergartens and nurseries in their local areas. Through mothers clubs, middle-class black women hoped to educate and thereby uplift their "less favored and more ignorant sisters" with information on hygiene and homemaking techniques. Black clubwomen believed that virtuous mothers could serve, by their very existence, as a refutation of white racist notions of black women as immoral and promiscuous. Mothers clubs were later broadened to address economic concerns of working black women as well as men.

The clubwomen also focused on the problems of youth and women in cities, leading to the establishment of black settlement houses that provided job training. For example, in 1897 the prolific writer, lecturer, and social reformer Victoria Earle Matthews, who led the Woman's Loyal Union of New York City and Brooklyn, established the White Rose Mission for black women migrants to New York. Matthews endeavored to provide housing, industrial training, and moral teaching to black women, who arrived in the city homeless, impoverished, and vulnerable to exploitation. Indeed, numerous black women's clubs engaged in settlement-house work, and in this regard they were inspired by and considered themselves to be part of the reform-minded Progressive movement in American cities.

Urban Settlement Houses

The black clubwomen established kindergartens, playgrounds, settlement houses, employment training programs, mother's meetings, health clinics, and a host of other services. They sought laws against lynching, voting rights for both black men and women, and

Window in Time

Anna Julia Cooper on the Woman Question, 1892

The colored woman of to-day occupies, one may say, a unique position in this country. . . . She is confronted by both a woman question and a race problem, and is as yet an unknown or an unacknowledged factor in both. While the women of the white race can with calm assurance enter upon the work they feel by nature appointed to do, while their men give loyal support and appreciative countenance to their efforts . . . the colored woman too often finds herself hampered and shamed by a less liberal sentiment and a more conservative attitude on the part of those for whose opinions she cares most. That is not universally true I am glad to admit. There are to be found both intensely conservative white men and exceedingly liberal colored men. But as far as my experience goes the average man of our race is less frequently ready to admit the actual need among the sturdier forces of the world for woman's help or influence. . . . But to be a woman of the Negro race in America, and to be able to grasp the deep significance of the possibilities of the crisis, is to have a heritage, it seems to me, unique in the ages. In the first place, the race is young and full of the elasticity and hopefulness of youth. It does not look on the masterly triumphs of nineteenth century civilization with that blasé world-weary look which characterizes the old washed out and worn out races which have already, so to speak, seen their best days.

Source: Anna J. Cooper, "The Status of Women in America," in *A Voice from the South*. Xenia, Ohio, 1892.

municipal reform in regard to the lack of services in the black communities. Like other urban reformers, they brought both a moral and social scientific perspective to their understanding of the solutions to urban problems, and they looked to models, such as white reformer Jane Addams's Hull House, which served southern and eastern European immigrants in Chicago.

In the Jim Crow South, black clubwomen in Alabama, led by Margaret Murray Washington, promoted black history through statewide essay contests among African American children, beginning in 1899. The Alabama Federation of Colored Women's Clubs celebrated Frederick Douglass's birthday in February. And according to historian Jacqueline Rouse, these early activities were significant forerunners of "Negro History Week," which would be the brainchild of black historian Carter G. Woodson in the 1920s. Membership in the Tuskegee Women's Club was restricted to the women faculty of Tuskegee Institute and the wives and other female relatives of the school's male faculty. The club focused on a variety of activities, visiting incarcerated black men and boys in the town, as well as founding and maintaining a settlement house.

Lugenia Burns Hope, wife of Morehouse College president John Hope, was the primary force behind black women's social work and reform efforts in Atlanta. In 1908 she founded and led the Neighborhood Union (NU), a network of clubs that provided numerous services to the city's black community. In its formative years, the Neighborhood Union included both middle-class and working-class women. Like white Progressive reformers, the members of the Neighborhood Union conducted studies of urban conditions in their efforts to persuade white city officials to provide adequate public schools, playgrounds, housing, and health care. When the city refused, the women set about the task of delivering needed services. For example, the Neighborhood Union made possible a children's playground on the Morehouse campus, a community health clinic, and a tuberculosis-prevention campaign.

Fannie Barrier Williams, the first person to write extensively about the club work among black women in the race "progress" books and magazines at the turn of the twentieth century, best captured the movement's central role in the era of racial self-help, when she wrote in 1902: "The Negro woman's club of to-day represents the new Negro with new powers of self-help, with new capacities, and with an intelligent insight into her own condition. It represents new interests, new anxieties and new hopes."

Intellectual and Cultural Endeavors

In 1897 black intellectuals, including Alexander Crummell, W. E. B. Du Bois, John W. Cromwell, and Kelly Miller, established the American Negro Academy—a national organization whose members included some of the best educated and most prominent thinkers of their time. Their self-perceptions were shaped by their elite status and by their understanding of the role of the intellectual in the work of racial help. This role was best explained by the black Episcopal priest and proudly race-conscious Alexander Crummell, who believed it the duty of the "trained and scholarly" to uplift the unlettered and uncultured of their race, thus reforming the "opinions and habits of the crude masses." The black intellectual, according to this viewpoint, should use his knowledge as weaponry in defense of his race. The academy captured, just as Crummell's words had done, the self-help ideology as articulated by advocates of the Talented Tenth. Many of the most accomplished women in the black community supported the establishment of the academy, and at its inaugural meeting the admission to membership of several women was proposed. The suggestion was rejected, however, with the indefensible argument that to include women would make the group a social rather than a learned society.

For thirty-one years, the academy promoted the exchange of ideas among black intellectuals and helped perpetuate the black protest tradition in an age of accommodation and proscription. It pursued its goals through annual meetings, special conferences, the **Pan-Negroism** publication of occasional papers, the collection of printed materials on blacks, and lobbying for the creation of research centers devoted to the study of Africa and the African American community. It was at the inaugural meeting of this group in 1897 that Du Bois delivered his now classic essay "The Conservation of Races," in which he introduced the double-consciousness, indeed the "dilemma" of being an American and a Negro. Calling attention to "spiritual" and "psychical" differences between the two races, Du Bois advocated a "Pan-Negroism." His strong race pride and consciousness are typical of black leaders during the era of self-help. Central to the essay is Du Bois's emphasis on the need for "race organizations: Negro colleges, Negro newspapers, Negro business organizations, a Negro school of literature and art, and an intellectual clearing house, for all these products of the Negro mind, which we may call a Negro Academy."

Another intellectual contribution was the Conference on Negro Problems, held annually at Atlanta University between 1896 and 1914 under the general direction of Du Bois. Not only did African Americans come together to discuss their problems, but each year a study of some phase of African American life was made. Du Bois indicated that the 2,172 pages of the published reports formed a "current encyclopedia on the American Negro problems." Among the more valuable publications of the conference were *Some Efforts of Negroes for Social Betterment* (1898), *The Negro in Business* (1899), *The College-bred Negro* (1900), and *The Negro Common School* (1901). Several of the conference's reports were enlarged and updated at later meetings.

A substantial number of scholarly and literary works by blacks appeared during the period. Autobiographical writings were particularly popular in America. Such writings generally portrayed heroic deeds and dramatic successes, and **Scholarly and Literary Works** African American authors often wrote within this genre. In *The Colored Cadet at West Point* (1889) Henry Ossian Flipper told of his experiences in becoming the first African American to receive a commission from the United States Military Academy. In 1881 Frederick Douglass brought his colorful career up to date in *The Life and Times of Frederick Douglass*, which he enlarged in 1892. The outstanding autobiography of the period was Booker T. Washington's *Up from Slavery* (1900), which became a classic in American literature. Other African American leaders, such as Bishop Daniel A. Payne and John M. Langston, wrote their autobiographies during the period. Two of the better biographical studies were Sarah Bradford's work on the life of Harriet Tubman, *Harriet, the Moses of Her People* (1886), and Charles W. Chesnutt's *Frederick Douglass* (1899).

Although numerous "race history" books were written in the era of self-help, the most able historian was George Washington Williams, a Pennsylvanian who had served as a soldier in the Civil War and had been educated in Massachusetts. In 1882 the well-known white publishing company G. P. Putnam's Sons published in two volumes his *History of the Negro Race in America from 1619 to 1880*, the result of years of painstaking and laborious research. It was the first historical study by an African American to be taken seriously by American scholars, and one newspaper hailed him as the "Negro Bancroft." Five years later another major firm, Harper and Brothers, brought out his *History of the Negro Troops in the Rebellion*. Booker T. Washington's *Story of the Negro* in two volumes (1909) made no improvement on the earlier work of Williams.

In 1896 W. E. B. Du Bois's doctoral dissertation was published as *The Suppression of the African Slave Trade, 1638–1870*—the first book in the scholarly series Harvard Historical Studies. This was a landmark achievement in the history of scholarship by African Americans. While serving as an assistant instructor at the University of Pennsylvania, Du Bois gathered the material on the black community of Philadelphia that appeared in 1900 in his book *The Philadelphia Negro*, a work considered to be one of the nation's pioneering sociological studies. Gertrude Bustill Mossell published *The Work of the Afro-American Woman* (1894), a historical account from the American Revolution through the nineteenth century.

Ida B. Wells continued to publish protest pamphlets. One was the antilynching pamphlet *A Red Record, Tabulated Statistics and Alleged Causes of Lynching in the United States* (1895). In another, *The Reason Why the Colored American Is Not in the World's Columbian Exposition* (1893), she criticized the organizers of the Exposition for not paying tribute to the accomplishments that African Americans.

In a volume of essays titled *A Voice from the South: By a Black Woman of the South* (1892), Anna Julia Cooper wrote with great insight about the challenges and opportunities that

African American women faced as they tried to make their way in a world of racial and gender hierarchy. Booker T. Washington wrote numerous books in the fields of education, race relations, economics, and sociology, among them *The Future of the American Negro* (1899), *The Education of the Negro* (1900), *Tuskegee and its People* (1905), and *The Negro in Business* (1907), all of which largely restated his position regarding the place of blacks in American life.

In fiction, the African American writer who made the greatest impression during the period was Charles W. Chesnutt, whose novels and short stories were widely read and generously praised. Between 1899 and 1905, four of his books were favorably received because of their vivid portrayal of character and their quality as lively narratives: *The Conjure Woman* (1899), *The House behind the Cedars* (1900), *The Marrow of Tradition* (1901), and *The Colonel's Dream* (1905). Of *The Conjure Woman* Vernon Loggins has said that such a sincere work of art was "positive evidence that Negro literature was coming of age." The NAACP's bestowal of the Spingarn Medal on Chesnutt toward the end of his career was only the most notable expression of the African American community's appreciation of his work. Women also made important contributions to fiction, most notably Frances Ellen Watkins Harper's *Iola Leroy, or, Shadows Uplifted* (1892) and Pauline Hopkins's *Contending Forces* (1900).

Although during his short life Paul Laurence Dunbar wrote several novels, including *The Uncalled* (1898), *The Love of Landry* (1900), and *Sport of the Gods* (1904), he is best known for his poems. The famous white author and literary critic William Dean Howells described Dunbar as the first African American "to feel the Negro life aesthetically and express it lyrically." Frederick Douglass considered Dunbar to be "the most promising black man of his time," and years later, after Dunbar's death, black author Ralph Ellison described him as the first African American to introduce into American literature the "something else which makes for our [African American] strength, which makes for our endurance and promise." His volumes of poetry *Oak and Ivy* (1893), *Majors and Minors* (1896), and *Lyrics of Lowly Life* (1896) have caused many critics to refer to him as the "poet laureate of the Negro race." His poems went through many editions, and by his death in 1906, Dunbar was one of America's famous men of letters.

African Americans of all classes and in every part of the country thrilled to the triumphs and mourned the defeats of black sports heroes, especially those in the highly visible **Sports Heroes** sports of horse racing, boxing, and baseball. For many blacks, these athletes were racial champions whose physical achievements struck a literal and symbolic blow against the "enemies of the race."

Blacks were participants in horse racing as early as the colonial period, especially in the South where the "sport of kings" was popular. A number of southern white enthusiasts had trained their male slaves to become some of the sport's leading jockeys. These early black jockeys served in a variety of capacities, since they were also responsible for feeding, grooming, and the overall care of the horses. On occasion, they also assumed the role of trainer or stable manager. Throughout the first half of the nineteenth century, slave jockeys continued to be a significant presence, their prowess and skill often making them winners. In the fifty years after the Civil War, black jockeys continued to be familiar figures on the turf. Oliver Lewis, an African American and the winner of the inaugural Kentucky Derby in 1875, was one of several blacks in that race. Of the first twenty-eight Kentucky Derbies that were run, eleven African American jockeys rode fifteen of the winning horses. Abe Hawkins, a black man, is often ranked as the greatest jockey of the late nineteenth century, winning 44 percent of his races, including three Kentucky Derbies and four American Derbies. As the nineteenth century drew to a close, however, changes in the organization of the sport and the era's intensified racism combined to eliminate African American jockeys.

African American boxers were leading contenders from the time the sport became popular in the United States in the late eighteenth century. Slave boxing served as both entertainment and a gambling sport for whites. Among the earliest boxers of distinction were Richmond and Tom Molineaux (or Molyneux). Brought to England in 1777 by a British officer, Richmond, a former slave, was styled "the Black Terror." Richmond was the first American to be recognized as a major prizefighter. Molineaux, born a slave in 1784, made his master rich and gained his own freedom through victorious bouts with slaves of neighboring plantations. Once free, Molineaux moved to England, where under the nickname "the Moor" he became a major contender. By the time of his death in 1818, he had competed twice, both times unsuccessfully, for the British heavyweight championship. Following the Civil War, several blacks in the United States emerged as prominent professional boxers. In 1890 George Dixon, known as "Little Chocolate," was declared bantamweight champion after an eighteen-round fight. In 1891 Dixon, securing next the featherweight title, became the first person to win a double title in boxing history. Dixon held the featherweight title until 1900. From 1901 to 1903, Baltimore-born Joe Gans held the lightweight title.

Jack Johnson, often described as "one of the greatest fighters of all time," was heavyweight champion from 1910 to 1915. In 1910 the return to the ring of white former heavyweight champion Jim Jeffries was hailed as the "Hope of the White Race," and Jeffries himself was reported at the time to have remarked that he had come out of retirement "for the sole purpose of proving that a white man is better than a negro." For African Americans, Johnson's victory over Jeffries vindicated at the very least racial equality. The black newspaper, the *Chicago Defender,* declared Johnson "the first negro to be admitted the best man in the world."

Whites' alarm over the defeat of their "white hope" grew to such an extent that race riots broke out in several cities, and the United States Congress passed a bill outlawing fight films in movie theaters. Johnson's victories in the ring and his disregard of segregation in his private life—epitomized by his dating of and marriages to white women—so incensed white supremacists that they persuaded Representative Seaborne Roddenbery of Georgia to propose a constitutional amendment in 1912 banning interracial marriage. (The bill failed to pass.) White boxing fans and sports writers continued to search for a "white hope" to defeat him. Johnson's enemies were pleased and his supporters crushed when he lost his title to Jess Willard, a white boxer, on April 5, 1915. It is likely

Jack Johnson, 1878–1946
Johnson was the first African American to win the world heavyweight boxing championship.

325

that Johnson allowed Willard to knock him out in the twenty-sixth round; indeed, Johnson himself claimed that he threw the fight in return for help in reducing his legal problems.

John W. "Bud" Fowler (John W. Jackson) is thought to have been the first African American professional baseball player. From 1872 to 1900, he played on teams throughout the United States and in Canada, often as the only black man among white teammates. Eventually Fowler and Frank Grant, an African American who got onto white teams by passing as an Italian, formed a team of African American players. Theirs was not the first "all-Negro" team; several had been formed as early as 1885. In the late nineteenth and early twentieth centuries, the number of these teams grew, and several leagues were formed. By 1900 the color line had become so rigid in baseball that black ball players, with the exception of those passing as white or Hispanic, had no options except the all-Negro teams.

The election of a Democratic president, Woodrow Wilson, in 1912 ushered in a southern style of Progressive reform that included imposing new forms of segregation on the nation's capital and a new policy of racial discrimination in the awarding of Civil Service jobs. The Wilson administration showed little desire to seek Booker T. Washington's or any other black leader's counsel and advice. Gone was the political power of Washington's Tuskegee Machine along with the patronage that blacks enjoyed under Republican presidents. Nor had Washington's tact and moderation halted the racist mobs in the cities of the North and South. The bright star of Tuskegee grew dimmer as his influence waned, and his reputation teetered in the face of a personal debacle. He was still the great man, but he had little time to live. As the year 1916 dawned, Washington would be dead. The times themselves had prophesied change—in the black community and in America—a new fighting spirit. But who knew the world itself would change? Who saw the great and cataclysmic war ahead?

14

In Pursuit of Democracy

Answering the Call to Fight

Jim Crow Military Camps

Service Overseas

On the Home Front

Members of the 369th Regiment Coming Home, 1919

Members of the Harlem-based 369th Regiment celebrating as they arrived in New York after fighting in Europe in World War I.

327

When war erupted in Europe in 1914, the American people received the news with varying degrees of concern. From thousands of miles across the Atlantic, they followed the media coverage of the rapidly worsening conditions: German and Austro-Hungarian imperialism; the growing nationalist sentiment in the Slavic states of southeastern Europe; the assassination in Bosnia of the Archduke Franz Ferdinand, the heir to the Austro-Hungarian throne, by a Serbian nationalist; and the fierce alignment of the Allied Powers (Great Britain, France, and Russia) against the Central Powers (Germany, Austria-Hungary, Bulgaria, and Turkey).

President Woodrow Wilson expressed the isolationist and antiwar mood of most Americans when he declared his country's neutrality. While the war quickly engulfed most of the European continent like a blazing fire, the American people stood on the sidelines—watching, waiting, and hoping not to get involved with the Old World's seemingly endless quarrels. The popular song from this period—"I Didn't Raise My Boy to be a Soldier"—captured the wish of most Americans to stay out of the bloodshed.

The conflagration abroad took on ever-more global proportions, dwarfing domestic issues. For more than two and a half years, Americans remained neutral, although bombarded with gruesome news reports telling of the enormous toll of death, mutilation, and devastation caused by trench warfare, explosive mines, heavy artillery, poison gas, aircraft bombs, and submarine (German U-boat) torpedoes. The weapons of mass destruction and the sheer carnage of the war were unfathomable to most Americans. The European death toll climbed furiously. War ravaged France's male population; by the war's end, half of all Frenchmen between twenty and thirty-two years of age would be dead.

American neutrality became increasingly difficult to maintain. Passions ran high in both pro-Allied and antiwar circles, especially in August 1915, when newspaper headlines screamed that more than a hundred American lives had been lost after a German U-boat torpedoed the British liner *Lusitania*. The outcry from the United States persuaded the German government to suspend its unrestricted submarine warfare, but in January 1917 German submarines began attacking American ships in the Atlantic bound for Great Britain. On April 2, 1917, President Wilson stood before a joint session of Congress and asked for a declaration of war. He spoke passionately about the obligation of Americans to "fight for the things which we have always carried nearest our hearts—for democracy, for the right of those who submit to authority to have a voice in their own governments, for the rights and liberties of small nations, for a universal dominion of right by such a concert of free peoples as shall bring peace and safety to all nations and make the world itself at last free." Only six senators and thirty members of the House (among them Montana's Jeannette Rankin, the first woman representative and an avowed pacifist) voted against declaring war.

The United States fought on the side of the Allied Powers in World War I, also known at the time as the Great War and the War to End All Wars. About 370,000 African American men answered Wilson's stirring call to "make the world safe for democracy" by serving in the U.S. armed forces. The army camps in which they trained were racially segregated. Black soldiers were insulted and even violently assaulted by white American citizens and soldiers, and they were frequently assigned menial and overly laborious jobs by their white officers.

Disfranchised and segregated in the southern states, the great majority of blacks had no voice in their government or any semblance of equal treatment. Nor could they find solace in the idea of free and independent African nations, since most of Africa fell under the colonial rule of the very European nations at war. As southern blacks migrated northward in search of wartime opportunities, they found no respite or safety from the terror of race riots that grew more prevalent during and after the war. Despite this reality, black soldiers fought with valor and patriotism on the European front line, ever conscious of the democracy that eluded them in their homeland.

Answering the Call to Fight

In the years leading up to America's entrance into the war, the military showed little sign of preparedness. By the beginning of 1917, it had become obvious to the nation's leaders that a far larger force was needed than the regular army's relatively small number of enlisted men and National Guard, of which black soldiers made up a small proportion. Blacks in the military were serving in the Ninth and Tenth Cavalries, in the Twenty-Fourth and Twenty-Fifth Infantries, and in the various National Guard units: the Eighth Illinois, the Fifteenth New York, separate battalions of the District of Columbia and of the Ohio National Guard, and separate companies of the Maryland, Connecticut, Massachusetts, and Tennessee National Guard.

Despite the protests of Mississippi's James Vardaman in the Senate, Congress rejected the idea of a "whites-only draft" and passed the Selective Service Act in May 1917 with no racial restrictions, thus opening up the nation's armed forces to a **The Selective Service Act** far greater number of black men. On July 5, 1917, the first day of registration, more than 700,000 black men signed up for Selective Service. Blacks were generally eager to participate in the war, not only as enlisted men but also as officers. Before the end of the wartime draft, 2,290,525 blacks had registered, 367,000 of whom were called into the service.

In some southern counties, draft boards sought to fill their quotas with blacks before even turning to whites. In other counties, the reverse occurred, with whites being inducted first to forestall the possibility of arming black men as soldiers. In the end, however, African Americans were disproportionately represented in the draft. Approximately 31 percent of all blacks who registered were accepted, compared to 26 percent of registered whites. In absolute terms, Florida, Georgia, Louisiana, Mississippi, and South Carolina drafted a larger number of African Americans than of whites. Unlike the uproar over enlisting black troops during the Civil War, the necessity for raising enormous manpower to fight in the World War made the use of African American troops immediately self-evident to the great majority of government and military officials.

News coverage of black draftees differed from place to place. Although many white newspapers in the North and South gave the impression of an overall acceptance of blacks in the military, some did not. For example, newspapers in Baltimore, Memphis, and in Gainesville, Florida, sought to ignore, if not outright discourage, black participation, urging whites to volunteer and thus preclude the need for blacks. The Gainesville *Daily Sun* was explicit in its opposition to arming black soldiers. Draft boards at the district or county level, often composed of political appointees of the various state governors, revealed differing practices. In some southern agricultural areas, wealthy farmers obtained an agricultural exemption (because of their substantial crop production) under the Selective Service Act, while tenant farmers and sharecroppers of both races were called up. In rural Texas and Alabama, however, draft board members were known to help their rich white landowning friends by exempting their black farm workers so that they might harvest the crop.

Fewer blacks received the marriage exemption, which was based on a wife's dependent status. The selective service boards in the South routinely defined as dependents white wives, specifically those who did not work outside the home, but this was not done for black women. Outside work was expected, even forcibly demanded of them. For example, in some southern towns, black married women were fined if they did not work, and in Vicksburg, Mississippi, local whites even went so far as to tar and feather two black women who refused to

Col. Charles W. Young

work outside their own homes while receiving allotments from their husbands' military service. In Monroe County, Alabama, draft boards called up married white men if childless and black men with one child. One board in Georgia was discharged because of its flagrantly racist policy of denying exemptions to blacks.

Although the draft opened to blacks and whites alike, racism in the armed forces was undeniable. In the Jim Crow atmosphere of early twentieth-century America, white soldiers and members of Congress sternly rejected offering black men officer's commissions. When the United States entered World War I, there were only a handful of African American military officers, all of them long-serving regulars.

The highest-ranking black officer in 1917 was Lieutenant Colonel Charles Young (born March 12, 1864, died January 8, 1922). Young, the third black graduate of West Point, was commissioned in 1889. He served in the Spanish-American War, in the prewar American incursion into Mexico, and in the Philippines. At the time of America's declaration of war in 1917, some senators complained that as a lieutenant colonel Young would outrank the white captains and lieutenants commanding segregated black units. Army officials then endeavored to force his retirement. They found Young unfit for active duty based on a medical condition—high blood pressure and a kidney disorder—discovered in a routine physical examination. Young attempted to prove his physical fitness by riding horseback from Ohio to the nation's capital. His efforts did not persuade the army until five days before the end of the war, at which time he was reinstated, promoted to colonel, and called to duty with the Ohio National Guard.

The NAACP

The interracial National Association for the Advancement of Colored People, a relatively new organization at the time, responded immediately to the "whites-only" policy of the Army's officer training camps. The NAACP was founded in 1909, when the white reformer and socialist William English Walling, horrified by the racist Springfield Riot in 1908, issued a "Call to Discuss Means for Securing Political and Civil Equality for the Negro." The call brought together a distinguished gathering of notable progressive reformers—educators, professors, publicists, bishops, judges, and social workers, including among others Jane Addams, Mary White Ovington, William Dean Howells, John Dewey, John Milholland, and Oswald Garrison Villard (the grandson of William Lloyd Garrison) among the white participants, and W. E. B. Du Bois, Ida B. Wells, and Bishop Alexander Walters of the African Methodist Episcopal Zion Church among the black participants. A permanent organization in 1910, the NAACP had only one black officer—Du Bois as the editor of its magazine *The Crisis*. He remained the only one, until James Weldon Johnson joined the official leadership in 1917.

With the war on, the NAACP seized the opportunity to seek racial fairness in the military. In 1917 the white NAACP officer Joel Spingarn led a citizens committee to Washington to confer with military authorities about the prospect of creating a black officer training camp. The struggle for black officers formed part of the larger civil rights agenda of the organization. Almost immediately, students at Howard, Fisk, Atlanta, Tuskegee, and other black colleges began to agitate for such training. Spingarn took up the matter with General Leonard Wood, the head of the government's crash program for training a mass army, and he promised to establish a training camp if two hundred black college-grade men could be found.

Early in May 1917, the Central Committee of Negro College Men organized at Howard University for this purpose, and within ten days it collected the names of 1,500 African American college men willing to become officers. The committee presented this information to Congress in a larger statement that justified the establishment of a black officers' training camp. With congressional endorsement, the movement to establish the camp began in earnest. The black press vigorously promoted the idea of commissioning black officers, which resulted in mass meetings in black communities throughout the nation.

It was in this context that Du Bois published his famous "Close Ranks" article in *The Crisis* in July 1918. At the time, he was being actively supported by Spingarn and others for a military commission, which ultimately never materialized. Du Bois began the article, fully recognizing the magnitude of the war—what he termed "the crisis of the world." Intoning that "for all the long years to come men will point to the year 1918 as the great Day of Decision," he beseeched the members of his race to "forget our special grievances and close our ranks shoulder to shoulder with our fellow citizens." Du Bois admitted that he was requesting "no ordinary sacrifice," but he believed the stakes to be too high and the outcome too dangerous for the world's "darker races" to allow a German victory. Du Bois was not alone in his sentiments, and it is fair to say that some of his most remembered language may have been influenced by that of black editor Robert S. Abbott of the *Chicago Defender.*

Two months before Du Bois wrote his article, Abbott had written his newspaper's editorial "Our Position in the War," using some of the same imagery that Du Bois would later employ. However, Abbott's advocacy of black patriotism was driven by considerably more optimism than Du Bois's. Abbott counseled patience, believing that "every great crisis" in American history had ultimately facilitated the advancement of black people. To African Americans he appealed: "In common with white American citizens let us put our shoulders to the wheel and push with might and main to bring this war to a successful conclusion." Optimistically, Abbott went on to predict that the black soldier "who fights side by side with the white American . . . will hardly be begrudged a fair chance when the victorious armies return."

With their nation at war, most African Americans supported demands for black officers, but some openly criticized the premise of a Jim Crow training camp for those officers. Racially segregated camps, they argued, defeated the purpose of struggling for equal citizenship. Nevertheless, the NAACP continued to endorse all-black training camps, perceiving that even this limited gain was far better than accepting the absence of any new black officers. "The army officials want the camp to fail," Spingarn said. "The last thing they want is to help colored men to become commissioned officers. The camp is intended to fight segregation, not to encourage it. Colored men in a camp by themselves would all get a fair chance for promotion. Opposition on the part of Negroes is helping the South, which does not want the Negroes to have any kind of military training." On October 15, 1917, at Fort

Des Moines in Iowa, the army commissioned 639 African American officers: 106 captains, 329 first lieutenants, and 204 second lieutenants. Later, other blacks also received army commissions. At colleges and high schools throughout the country, blacks prepared to become officer candidates and served in a variety of ways in the Students' Army Training Corps and the Reserve Officers Training Corps (ROTC).

Also in October 1917, Secretary of War Newton D. Baker announced the appointment of Emmett J. Scott as his special assistant. For eighteen years, Scott had been Booker T. Washington's secretary, and now he assumed the position of "confidential advisor in matters affecting the interests of the ten million Negroes of the United States and the part they are to play in connection with the present war." As the secretary of war's assistant, Scott urged the equal and impartial application of Selective Service regulations and formulated plans to raise morale among black soldiers and civilians. The military turned to Scott for his opinion on African American matters. Scott investigated scores of cases in which black soldiers charged unfair treatment and reported problems relating to the compulsory and voluntary allotments of their pay, war-risk insurance, and government allowances and compensation. He also worked with the Committee on Public Information—the government's powerful national wartime propaganda outlet—releasing news about black soldiers and various home-front activities involving African Americans. Scott answered thousands of inquiries from blacks on every conceivable subject.

Emmett J. Scott

Jim Crow Military Camps

In World War I, blacks served in many Army units: cavalry, infantry, engineer corps, signal corps, medical corps, hospital and ambulance corps, veterinary corps, sanitary and ammunition trains, stevedore regiments, labor battalions, and depot brigades. They also worked as regimental adjutants, judge advocates (that is, Army lawyers), chaplains, intelligence officers, chemists, clerks, surveyors, drafters, auto repairers, motor truck operators, and mechanics. Although blacks served in almost every branch of the Army, they were denied the opportunity to become pilots in the aviation corps. After a long struggle they became eligible to join coast and field artillery units, but they remained barred from the Marines and were permitted to serve in the Navy only in menial capacities.

Training African American soldiers in army domestic camps continually plagued the War Department, since most white communities did not want large numbers of black men in their midst. Although the Army was committed to activating an all-black division, for example, it did not permit the members of the all-black Ninety-Second Division to train together in a single location (a separate cantonment), but rather scattered the soldiers in different locations, sending them to seven widely separated camps—chiefly at Camp Grant in Rockford, Illinois, and at Camp Upton in Yaphank, New York, as well as at five other camps. Indeed, the constituent units of the Ninety-Second (composed of fourteen units of soldiers divided into regiments, battalions, and brigades) were brought together only after they arrived on the Western Front in Europe. Another black division, the Ninety-Third, was never allowed to fully organize before being sent abroad. Its four infantry units (the 369th, 370th, 371st, and 372nd regiments) also trained in different locations and went overseas at different times. The first of the divisions to go to Europe, the Ninety-Third, was assigned to fight with units of the French army by the order of the commander of the American Expeditionary Force, General John Pershing.

Locating Training Camps

Rampant discrimination permeated the United States Army and the civilian agencies that served it. The progressive interracial ecumenical organization the Federal Council of Churches, founded in 1908, created a Committee on the Welfare **Rampant Discrimination** of Negro Troops specifically to investigate racial conditions at home and abroad. Its two field secretaries, Charles H. Williams of Hampton Institute and G. Lake Imes of Tuskegee Institute, found many examples of discrimination and segregation in the service agencies. At Camp Greene, near Charlotte, North Carolina, they investigated discrimination by the YMCA. None of the five YMCA buildings in the area would serve the ten thousand African American recruits stationed there. A sign over one of these buildings even announced that "This building is for white men only." A single table was provided for the use of black soldiers who wanted to write letters to family and friends. At Camp Lee, near Petersburg, Virginia, white soldiers patrolled around a white prayer meeting to ensure that no blacks attempted to enter.

Complaints flooded the War Department from black soldiers who accused white officers of using such insulting language as *coons, niggers,* and *darkies.* White officers frequently forced black soldiers to work under unhealthy and difficult conditions. At Camp Hill in Virginia, a black stevedore regiment that worked at the embarkation port at Newport News slept in tents without floors or heat during the cold winter months. It was a common practice for blacks to be assigned to labor battalions even when they were qualified for more highly skilled jobs, thus making it extremely difficult for them to advance in rank. Friction between black soldiers and the white military police escalated as the war progressed, and the War Department's orders requiring fair and impartial treatment of black soldiers produced little discernible improvement.

The hostility of white civilians certainly dampened African American soldiers' morale. White southerners objected strenuously to the Army's sending northern black recruits into their communities for training, since they found it difficult to adapt to the South's racial etiquette. Not that the areas outside the South lacked racial prejudice; many northern towns also denied African American troops service in restaurants and admission to theaters. For example, when African Americans insisted on attending the movie theater at Fort Riley in Kansas, General Charles C. Ballou, the white commander of the Ninety-Second Division, issued an order commanding his men not to go where their presence was resented—and reminding them that "white men had made the Division, and they can break it just as easily if it becomes a trouble maker." A howl of resentment arose immediately from the black press, and African Americans found little consolation in General Ballou's effort to press legal charges against the theater operators who discriminated against his men.

Worse yet, in August 1917 a riot broke out in Houston between white civilians and the black soldiers of the Twenty-Fourth Infantry. The trouble began when white policemen harassed a black woman named Sara Travers, dragging her half- **African Americans Fight Back** dressed from her home, and a black soldier from the Twenty-Fourth came to her defense. The police struck the black soldier and demanded that the other infantrymen disarm. In the ensuing melee, the enraged soldiers killed seventeen whites. After only a slight pretense of a trial, thirteen African American soldiers were hanged for murder and mutiny, forty-one were imprisoned for life, and forty others were held pending further investigation. Nothing since the Brownsville, Texas, incident in 1906 had done so much to wound the pride of African Americans or to shake their faith in their government.

Emmett Scott, a native of Houston and the secretary of war's special assistant for African American affairs, attempted to assuage whites' anxieties by observing that this tragic incident "did not dampen the ardor of the colored men who went to the front for the Stars and Stripes." His words clearly failed to capture the outrage of the black community. Many men of the Twenty-Fourth Infantry swore vengeance on the officials, whom they accused of unjust treatment. A black newspaper in Baltimore exclaimed that "the Negroes of the entire country will regard the thirteen Negro soldiers of the Twenty-Fourth Infantry executed as martyrs," while the *New York Age* declared that "strict justice has been done, but full justice has not been done. . . . And so sure as there is a God in heaven, at some time and in some way full justice will be done."

White citizens in Spartanburg, South Carolina, where the black Fifteenth New York Infantry was training, felt uncomfortable with the buoyant self-confidence expressed by the northern soldiers in their midst. In October 1917, when Noble Sissle, the talented drum major of the infantry band, entered a hotel to purchase a newspaper, the proprietor cursed at him, demanding that Sissle remove his hat when approaching a white man. Before Sissle could respond, the white man knocked his hat off his head. As the young soldier stooped to pick it up, the man struck him several times and kicked him out of the place. On discovering what had happened, the black militiamen started to "rush the hotel," but Lieutenant James Reese Europe, the well-known black bandmaster, happened to be passing by. Europe called the men to attention and ordered them to disperse. The following evening the soldiers planned to "shoot up" the town of Spartanburg, but their commanding officer, a white man named Colonel William Hayward, overtook them as they were leaving and ordered them back to camp.

The War Department's Emmett Scott, having rushed to Spartanburg to investigate the situation, pleaded with the men to do nothing to bring dishonor on either their regiment or their race. The War Department considered three possible scenarios in order to prevent the recurrence of such incidents: it could keep the regiment at Camp Wadsworth and face a violent eruption; it could remove the regiment to another camp, conveying the impression that the military would yield to community pressure; or it could order the regiment overseas. The War Department decided on the last alternative. The Fifteenth New York Regiment, now designated as the 369th Infantry of the United States Army, went to Europe, becoming the first contingent of African American combat troops to reach the Western Front. As they left the country, the soldiers of the Fifteenth New York might well have reasoned that defending democracy in war-torn Europe would be easier than in their own country.

Service Overseas

The first African American military personnel to arrive in Europe after the United States entered the war, and among the first Americans to reach the war zone, were army laborers who built roads and dug trenches and stevedores who loaded and unloaded cargo from ships. They played a significant role in the tremendous task of providing the Allies with war materiel. The first black stevedores landed in France in June 1917, and from then until the end of the war they would come in ever increasing numbers, classified by the army as stevedore regiments, engineer service battalions, labor battalions, butchery companies, and pioneer infantry battalions. Before the end of the war, more than 50,000 stevedores had served in 115 different outfits.

At the French ports of Brest, St. Nazaire, Bordeaux, Le Havre, and Marseilles, black stevedores worked in mud and rain, sometimes in twenty-four-hour shifts, unloading supplies

Black American "Buffalo" soldiers of the 367th infantry, 77th Division, in France
These soldiers were among the more than 400,000 black Americans who joined the armed forces during the Great War (World War I). The majority of black Americans who saw active duty on the front line fought under French command, while those who stayed under American command served as laborers rather than fighters.

from the United States. At one port, a crew of black stevedores amazed the French by unloading 1,200 tons of flour in nine and a half hours—a job that had been estimated as requiring several days. In September 1918, at American base ports in France, a crew of mostly black stevedores handled 767,648 tons, an average of more than 25,000 tons per day. "One who sees the Negro stevedores work," reported an American war correspondent, "notes with what rapidity and cheerfulness they work and what a very important cog they are in the war machinery."

African American troops were among the first U.S. combat forces to go overseas. After enduring many hardships at sea, including breakdown, fire, and collision, the 369th United States Infantry arrived in France early in 1918. Some went imme- **The 369th U.S. Infantry** diately to a French divisional training school, where they learned to throw grenades, use bayonets, and handle French weapons. In April 1918, almost exactly one year after Congress declared war, they moved to the front. By May they were in the thick of the fight in northern France, where for a time they held a complete sector that represented 20 percent of all the territory assigned to American troops. After receiving some relief, they were assigned to block a German offensive at Minaucourt, and in the middle of July, they bore the brunt of the final great German assault. From that time until the end of

Decoration of African American Soldiers

Overseas, African American soldiers who demonstrated bravery under fire were decorated lavishly by the French Army, under which they served. Not one African American received the Congressional Medal of Honor.

hostilities, the men of the 369th saw almost continuous action against the enemy. The first Allied unit to reach the Rhine, the 369th Regiment never had a man captured and never gave up a trench or a foot of ground.

No other black regiment in the First World War won more popular acclaim and celebration. One of the war's most sensational feats of American derring-do was performed by two privates, Henry Johnson of Albany, New York, and Needham Roberts of Trenton, New Jersey, both of the 369th. While the men stood guard at a small outpost in May 1918, a raiding party of nearly twenty Germans made a surprise attack, wounding the two black soldiers. When the Germans got within range, Johnson opened fire, and Roberts, lying on the ground, threw his grenades. The Germans continued to advance, and as the two black men were about to be captured, Johnson drew his bolo knife from his belt and attacked the Germans in a hand-to-hand encounter. He succeeded in freeing Roberts from the Germans. Both men received the Croix de Guerre for their gallantry.

The 369th was the first and longest serving of all American regiments assigned to support a foreign army—a total of 191 days in the trenches. The entire regiment won the Croix de Guerre for its action at Maison-en-Champagne, and 171 individual officers and enlisted men were cited for the Croix de Guerre and the Legion of Honor for exceptional gallantry in action. France erected a memorial to the 369th Regiment at Sechault. The 369th had the honor of being called the "Harlem Hellfighters" because of their tireless fighting spirit.

Window in Time

The 369th and 371st Win the Croix de Guerre

Both entire units won the French Cross of War with these citations:

[*369th Infantry . . . French Croix de guerre with silver star . . .*]

Under the command of Colonel Hayward, who although wounded, insisted on leading his regiment into combat . . . and Major Little, a real leader of men, the 369th Regiment of American Infantry, under fire for the first time, captured some powerful and energetically defended enemy positions, took the village of Sechault by main force, and brought back six cannon, mainly machine guns, and a number of prisoners.

[*371st Infantry . . . French Croix de guerre with Palm . . .*]

Under the command of Colonel Miles, the regiment, with superb spirit and admirable disregard for danger rushed to the assault of a strongly defended enemy position which it captured after a hard struggle under a violent machine-gun fire. It then continued its advance, in spite of the enemy artillery fire and heavy losses, taking numerous prisoners, capturing cannon, machine guns, and important material.

Source: *General Orders No. 11,* United States War Department (Washington, D.C.: National Archives, 27 March 1924), pp. 22–23.

The Eighth Illinois Infantry, renamed the 370th United States Infantry, reached France in June 1918, where it was equipped with French arms and sent to the front. After service in the hotly contested St. Mihiel sector, the 370th was sent to the Argonne Forest, another vital part of the front line, where it remained for the better part of July and August. In September, serving as part of the

Other African American Combat Units

French Fifty-Ninth Division, the black soldiers of the 370th Infantry took over a full regimental sector in the area of Mont des Tombes and Les Tueries. From that time until the end of the war, the 370th, fighting alongside several units of the French army, drove the enemy out of French territory and back into Belgium. Twenty-one of its men received the Distinguished Service Cross, one received the Distinguished Service Medal, and sixty-eight received various grades of the Croix de Guerre. They became the first American troops to enter the French fortress of Laon when it was wrested from the Germans after four years of war. The 370th, too, fought the last battle of the war, capturing a German train of fifty wagons and their crews a half hour after the Armistice went into effect on November 11, 1918.

Both the 371st Infantry, organized in August 1917 at Camp Jackson, South Carolina, and the 372nd Infantry, composed of African American National Guardsmen from the District of Columbia, Ohio, Massachusetts, and Maryland, arrived in France late in April 1918. They were reorganized on the French plan and attached to the 157th French Division, known as the "Red Hand," under General Mariano Goybet. Late in May, the 372nd took over the assignment of holding the Argonne West sector and by May 31 was in the frontline

Horace Pippin, *Dog Fight over the Trenches* **(1935)**

Black artist Horace Pippin, a private in the 369th Infantry, kept a diary of his experiences in the war. He was sent into action in the French region of Champagne. Ironically, the war inspired Pippin to paint, even though he returned home to Pennsylvania discharged from the Army because of a severe wound to his right shoulder. He could not use his arm at all. Years later, at the age of forty, he learned to improvise a way to paint despite his partially paralyzed right arm. "The war," he said, "brought out all of the art in me. . . . I came home with all of it in my mind, and I paint from it today."

trenches. During the summer it took heavy shelling in the Verdun sector, and in September it pursued the retreating enemy. For gallantry in the final campaign, the regiment's colors were decorated with the Croix de Guerre and Palm just before the men sailed for America. Many individual soldiers also won honors, especially the men of the First Battalion of the District of Columbia National Guard.

The 371st performed with the same valor. They remained on the front lines for more than three months, holding first the Avocourt and later the Verrières subsectors, northwest of Verdun. In the Allies' great September 1918 offensive, the 371st took several important positions near Monthois and captured prisoners, plentiful machine guns and other weapons, a munitions depot, several railroad cars, and many other supplies. In recognition of this action, its regimental colors were decorated by the French government. Three officers won the French Legion of Honor, and thirty-four officers and eighty-nine enlisted men received the Croix de Guerre. Fourteen officers and twelve enlisted men were awarded France's Distinguished Service Cross.

One of the enlisted men in the 371st, Corporal Freddie Stowers of Sandy Spring, South Carolina, was recommended by his commanding officer for the Congressional Medal of Honor, the United States' highest military award. Stowers had led his company in a victorious charge against a German-held hill, an assault that left more than 50 percent of his company dead. Because the recommendation was "misplaced," Stowers, the only black member of America's World War I military forces to be recommended for the Medal of

Honor, did not receive it in his lifetime. Seventy-three years later, in April 1991, following historian Leroy Ramsey's criticism of the U.S. military for failure to award the Medal of Honor to any of the 1.5 million blacks who served in World War I and World War II, President George H. W. Bush finally presented the decoration, posthumously, to Stowers's elderly sisters.

The Ninety-Second Division took longer to become welded into an efficient fighting unit, since it had to wait for its various divisions to arrive in France. Most of the units arrived in June 1918 and underwent eight weeks of training. It was not until July that the complete Artillery brigade and Ammunition Train reached France and began training. Reaching the front by late August, the Ninety-Second Division assumed control of the St. Die sector, relieving several regiments of American and French forces—and the Germans almost immediately bombarded the all-black division with shrapnel and poison gas (which was heavily used by both sides during World War I). The division, eager to attack, found its opportunity in September. During the ensuing battle, the black troops captured several Germans, although the Germans took two blacks as prisoners.

German Propaganda

When the Germans realized that they were facing an African American division, they launched a propaganda campaign to accomplish with words what they had not been able to achieve with arms. On September 12 they scattered circulars across the lines, trying to persuade the Ninety-Second to lay down its arms. The printed material, written in English, argued that African American soldiers should not be deluded into thinking that they were fighting for democracy, as President Wilson claimed. The circular read: "What is Democracy? Personal freedom, all citizens enjoying the same rights socially and before the law. Do you enjoy the same rights as the white people do in America, the land of Freedom and Democracy, or are you rather not treated over there as second-class citizens? Can you go into a restaurant where white people dine? Can you get a seat in the theater where white people sit? . . . Is lynching and the most horrible crimes connected therewith a lawful proceeding in a democratic country?" The circular also asserted that Germans liked blacks and treated them as gentlemen in Germany. "Why, then, fight the Germans only for the benefit of the Wall Street robbers and to protect the millions they have loaned to the British, French, and Italians?" The propaganda message closed by inviting the African American troops to surrender and come over to the German lines, where they would find friends to aid them in the cause of liberty and democracy. Not one black soldier took this bait and deserted.

Slander Campaigns

At times African Americans came under severe criticism by white American commanders and soldiers, who posited any and all failure to achieve a successful mission as reason for the inferiority of black troops in combat. It mattered little that white units suffered defeats for the same reasons as did black units—the black troops alone were faulted for deficient training, for unfamiliarity with the French countryside, and for insufficient combat equipment. Such was the case on September 20, 1918, when the 368th Infantry Regiment of the Ninety-Second Division failed a strategically important mission in Argonne Forest in preparation for the Argonne-Meuse offensive. Emmett Scott described the fighting as "harder than anything the Division had experienced up to that time." The division's total casualties exceeded 450.

Black troops became the brunt of slander campaigns, especially after the war ended. A white American commander opined that "in a future war the main use of the negro should be in labor organizations," and such critics discouraged organizing blacks in large divisions,

Lt. James Reese Europe

preferring instead combat troops no larger than regiments. In his research on black soldiers during the war, Du Bois noted that the Ninety-Second Division, the last to leave France, was at the mercy of white American officers who belittled the black soldiers, gave them extremely demanding physical labor assignments, discredited their valor in the war, and unsuccessfully attempted to diminish French sympathies for blacks. Yet in January 1919, General John J. Pershing praised the soldiers of the Ninety-Second Division as they embarked from France: "I want you officers and soldiers of the Ninety-Second Division to know that the Ninety-Second Division stands second to none in the record you have made since your arrival in France. I am proud of the part you have played in the great conflict which ended on the 11th of November."

Even in the midst of war, black soldiers found time for pleasantries, cultural experiences, and social contact. Most combat units had their own bands, but the best known was the 369th Regiment Band under the direction of James Reese Europe, assisted by Noble Sissle. James Europe, as bandmaster and as an officer in the "Harlem Hellfighters," has been identified as the musician primarily responsible for bringing jazz to France. Another popular military band was that of the 350th Field Artillery under J. Tim Brymm, whose jazz repertoire won French admiration. Although no African American theatrical entertainers performed overseas during the war, after the Armistice and at the behest of General Pershing, Rev. Henry Hugh Proctor of Atlanta, along with song leader and teacher J. E. Blanton of South Carolina and concert pianist Helen Hagan of New Haven, Connecticut traveled throughout France staging programs for white and black troops still stationed there. Proctor noted the black soldiers' emotional response to the music, which had an immediate uplifting effect, particularly Hagan's performance on the piano. Proctor wrote: "They [black soldiers] had not seen a woman of their race since they left home, and frequently tears would well up in the eyes of these men as they looked upon this talented woman."

Cultural Experiences

In contrast to the YMCAs in the American South, the YMCA and YWCA in France served black soldiers overseas by providing literacy classes, libraries, canteens, letter-writing facilities, and other services for the men's comfort. African Americans engaged in this work included Matthew Bullock, J. C. Croom, John Hope, William J. Faulkner, Max Yergan, Addie Hunton, and Kathryn Johnson. Of the sixty African American chaplains in the United States Army, approximately twenty ministered to the spiritual needs of black soldiers overseas. YMCA workers Addie Hunton and Kathryn Johnson wrote about their experiences among the black troops in France in their book *Two Colored Women with the American Expeditionary Forces* (1920). Although African American nurses in the United States offered their services in large numbers, the government was very slow to accept them and

Women's war work
Red Cross nurses on duty at the base hospital at Camp Grant, Illinois.

sent them overseas only after the fighting had ended. During periods of rest and recuperation, and also after hostilities had ceased, some blacks attended French universities in Paris, Bordeaux, Toulouse, and Marseilles.

African American soldiers found greater opportunities to move about freely in France than they had in the United States. They socialized with French men and women, much to the chagrin of many white American soldiers, who warned the French against African Americans. Some told the French that blacks could not be treated with common civility and repeatedly claimed that black men were rapists. In August 1918 an American-produced document titled "Secret Information Concerning Black Troops" circulated among the French, asserting that strict segregation was essential to prevent black men from assaulting and raping white women. The document warned against any contact outside the requirements of military service. Neither French civilians nor soldiers seemed to take this "warning" seriously,

341

since they continued to welcome African Americans into their homes and sought to make their black defenders as comfortable as possible.

Toward the end of the war, reports came to the United States that the African American soldiers stationed in France had developed habits and practices that would prove detrimental **Coming Home** to interracial stability on their return to the United States. With the war over by December 1918, concern rose to such an extent that the War Department asked Robert R. Moton, Booker T. Washington's successor at Tuskegee, to go to France to investigate the rumors and examine the conditions affecting African American soldiers. The secretary of war and the president placed every facility at Moton's disposal and arranged for him to travel freely among the black troops. Moton made many speeches to groups of black soldiers, including these remarks, which he included in his autobiography:

> You have been tremendously tested. . . . Your record has sent a thrill of joy and satisfaction to the hearts of millions of black and white Americans, rich and poor, high and low. . . . You will go back to America heroes, as you really are. You will go back as you have carried yourselves over here—in a straightforward, manly, and modest way. If I were you, I would find a job as soon as possible and get to work. . . . I hope no one will do anything in peace to spoil the magnificent record you have made in war.

Although some African American soldiers who served in France were hesitant about making the return trip to the United States lest they lose what democracy and freedom they had found in faraway places, the great majority seemed anxious to return. Some doubtless believed that conditions would be better than before the war, while others were indifferent to the future, thinking only of the pleasures of being home again.

They were not required to wait very long before finding out what changes had taken place in the United States; shortly after the Armistice was signed, American military authorities began to make preparations for the return and demobilization of American troops. Some African American troops were detained to assist in cleaning up campsites and clearing away debris left from the battles, but the greater part of them were en route to the United States within four months after the end of the war. By April 1919, many troops were already in the United States, and some of them were being demobilized.

African American troops, for the most part, disembarked in the New York area to a joyous first reception in the United States. They were greeted by enthusiastic crowds who never seemed to tire of the apparently endless parades of troops, both black and white, that proceeded almost immediately from their ships to the triumphal march up Fifth Avenue. When New York's own black regiment, the 369th, returned on February 17, 1919, approximately 1 million people witnessed their parade from lower New York up Fifth Avenue to Harlem. A similar reception was given various units of the Ninety-Second Division, the last of whose troops landed at Hoboken, New Jersey, on March 12, 1919.

Other cities vied with New York in welcoming their black troops. Buffalo turned out en masse to receive them, while huge crowds filled the streets of St. Louis to cheer the blacks who had fought in Europe. When the 370th, the "Old Eighth Illinois," reached Chicago, much of the business of the city was suspended to welcome the veterans. The soldiers paraded through the Loop as well as through the thickly populated black South Side, and in many places the crowds were so dense that the troops could not march in regular formation.

Window in Time

Reverend Francis J. Grimké Welcomes Returning Black Soldiers—1919

Young gentlemen, I am glad to welcome you home again after months of absence in a foreign land in obedience to the call of your country—glad that you returned to us without any serious casualties. . . .

We, who remained at home, followed you while you were away, with the deepest interest; and, our hearts burned with indignation when tidings came to us, as it did from time to time, of the manner in which you were treated by those over you, from whom you had every reason, in view of the circumstances that took you abroad, and what it was costing you, to expect decent, humane treatment, instead of the treatment that was accorded you. The physical hardships, incident to a soldier's life in times of war, are trying enough, are hard enough to bear. . . . To add to these the insults, the studied insults that were heaped upon you, and for no reason except that you were colored, is so shocking that were it not for positive evidence, it would be almost unbelievable. . . .

Again, most gladly do I welcome you back home; and most earnestly do we express the hope that every man of you will play a man's part in the longer and more arduous struggle that is before us in battling for our rights at home. If it was worth going abroad to make the world safe for democracy, it is equally worth laboring no less earnestly to make it safe at home. We shall be greatly disappointed if you do not do this—if you fail to do your part.

Source: Francis J. Grimké, *The Works of Francis J. Grimké,* Carter C. Woodson, ed., Volume I, *Addresses Mainly Personal and Racial* (Washington, 1942), pp. 589–591.

It was precisely the valor of black soldiers that emboldened persons of African descent, both in the United States and elsewhere in the world, to attempt to bring the plight of racial minorities before the Allied leaders when they assembled for the Paris Peace Conference after the war ended. To the disgust of black leaders, the only consideration that African peoples received was when it came to redistributing Germany's African colonies among the victorious Allies. No African colony received independence. Black leaders had hoped that the European powers would at least free Germany's former African colonies. Instead, those colonies were divided among Belgium, Great Britain, France, and the white-dominated Union of South Africa under a "mandate system" supervised by the League of Nations, the newly founded international organization that was promoted tirelessly by Wilson as the vehicle for lasting peace.

In *Darkwater: Voices from Within the Veil* (1920), a sorely disappointed Du Bois pondered Wilson's contradictory position in regard to Europe and Africa. During the war Wilson's idealism was epitomized in his famous "Fourteen Points" speech to Congress, in which he urged among other things the German evacuation from Belgium and national sovereignty in the Balkans and other parts of Europe. The president had also called for an

Wilson's Contradictory Positions

"absolutely impartial adjustment of all colonial claims" and for a "fair dealing by the other peoples of the world against force and selfish aggression." With the war now over and peace restored, Du Bois asked in frustration: "Has the world forgotten Congo?"—reminding his readers of the well-documented atrocities of King Leopold II and his Belgian officials against the Congolese people in the first decade of the twentieth century. The peace settlement had actually strengthened Belgium's foothold in Africa by awarding to that country Germany's East African Ruanda-Urundi region (the present-day republics of Rwanda and Burundi).

It was impossible for such leaders as Du Bois, A. Philip Randolph, Chandler Owen, and the Afro-Caribbean political activists and writers Hubert Harrison, Cyril V. Briggs, and Claude McKay to trust the sincerity of Wilson's peace rhetoric when Africa remained under the yoke of colonialism. And they, along with other black socialists and nationalists, identified European greed and rivalry over African and Asian colonies as a major cause of the war itself. In addition, seeing African troops in Europe, especially those from the French colony of Senegal, who had helped to dig the many thousands of miles of trenches just as had many African Americans, figured significantly in the emergence of a new, postwar diasporic politics. The encounter of African Americans, Caribbeans, and Africans during the World War had fostered a dialogue with regard to a common oppression and common racial destiny, and this emergent pan-African sensibility would grow profoundly afterward.

Hoping to place the cause of African peoples before the world in a dramatic way, Du Bois called a Pan-African Congress to meet in Paris in 1919. Du Bois was already in France, having traveled to Paris with other American news correspondents in December 1918 to cover the peace talks. He also planned to investigate the treatment of African American soldiers and to collect information concerning their participation in the war. Through Blaise Diagne, a Senegalese member of the French Chamber of Deputies who was highly respected in French circles, Du Bois secured permission from French premier Georges Clemenceau to hold his Pan-African Congress in the Grand Hotel in Paris in February 1919. Fifty-seven delegates, including sixteen African Americans, twenty West Indians, and twelve Africans, gathered in this hastily organized meeting, which called the world's attention to the abuses of European colonialism in Africa and Asia.

On the Home Front

The war years marked a time of valiant sacrifice and patriotism on the part of the American people. On some levels, patriotic fervor translated into a willing acceptance of unprecedented government regulation of corporations, agricultural production, railroads, speech, and time itself. One of the lasting conservation measures of World War I was the introduction of daylight saving time. Americans appeared genuinely supportive of food and fuel conservation. (They rationed their food on the designated "meatless" and "wheatless" days.) They responded enthusiastically when the government called for "Liberty Loan" bond drives and savings-stamp campaigns, in order to help fund war costs, and they promoted wartime patriotism through various forms of propaganda in film and the media.

African Americans joined in this domestic war effort. For example, the black press estimated that blacks purchased more than $250 million worth of bonds and stamps in various

344

government-sponsored bond drives. Mary B. Talbert, president of the National Association of Colored Women, reported that African American women alone bought more than $5 million worth of bonds in the Third Liberty Loan campaign. Both individuals and organizations in the black community participated. The black-owned North Carolina Mutual Life Insurance Company purchased $300,000 worth of bonds in less than two years. Blacks also generously supported the fund-raising campaigns of the YMCA, YWCA, and the American Red Cross.

African Americans Support the War

Considering the large number of blacks who worked as farmers and cooks, the United States government depended heavily on African Americans in its programs to produce and conserve food. Herbert Hoover, the progressive-minded businessman whom Wilson named as director of the federal Office of Food Administration, sought greater participation of blacks by appointing Ernest Atwell of Tuskegee as field worker for Alabama and later for the other southern states. In September 1918, Atwell went to Washington, where he served as director of activities for African Americans from the headquarters of the Food Administration and circulated an open letter to blacks asking for their cooperation in general food conservation. Black directors were appointed in eighteen states, and organizations were perfected to carry the program forward.

America's patriotic fervor also led to the curtailment of civil liberties and the stifling of dissent through government surveillance. Popular forms of coercion had a similar censoring effect. In Iowa schools, teachers were forbidden to teach German to their students. Persons of German ancestry were called "Huns" and vilified with negative stereotyping. Libraries removed books written in German from their shelves, and symphony orchestras refused to perform German opera or orchestral pieces. In this political climate, some African American leaders, while supportive of the war, felt the consequences of criticizing President Wilson's vision of freedom.

Curtailing Civil Liberties

In April 1917, a month before America's declaration of war, the black minister and civil rights advocate John Milton Waldon wrote to Wilson seeking his commitment to a non-discriminatory military policy. Waldron, one of few black supporters of Wilson's presidential campaign in 1912, hoped to persuade the president of the importance of black loyalty. Instead, Wilson interpreted Waldron's comments as potentially disloyal. The president challenged not only Waldron's patriotism but that of blacks in general. "Your letter was the first notice I had," Wilson responded within a week of receiving Waldron's letter, "that many of the members of the colored race were not enthusiastic in their support of the Government in this crisis." The NAACP's newly appointed field secretary James Weldon Johnson voiced the spirit of many other blacks in 1917 when he admonished his people to demand equal rights, while at the same time understanding the "bald truth" that they could not afford to be perceived as unpatriotic.

Long-existing racism against African Americans easily became conflated with the nationalistic zeal of wartime intolerance. This was especially true in the southern states. When blacks protested their economic condition, joined the NAACP, failed to participate in bond drives, or attempted to dodge the draft, whites often believed that they had been influenced by outside saboteurs. Black protest echoed through the press, church gatherings, and numerous public forums, but it often led to federal surveillance, especially after the passage of the Espionage Act of 1917 and the Sedition Amendment to this act in 1918. For example, military intelligence put Rev. Charles H. Mason, a founder of the Church of God in Christ, under investigation between 1917 and 1919. At a

Silencing Dissent

time when Mississippi sought to meet its draft quota, Mason was arrested in 1918 for perceived "disloyal" statements in his sermons to his congregation in Holmes County, for allegedly discouraging black voter registration in the county.

In the same year, the black women's club and religious leader Nannie Helen Burroughs was similarly targeted for surveillance by the War Department. She publicly attacked Woodrow Wilson's failure to denounce lynching in a speech at a black Baptist convention. Asserted Burroughs in 1918: "He [Wilson] has used up all the adverbs and adjectives trying to make clear what he means by democracy. He realizes and the country realizes that unless he begins to apply the doctrine, representatives of our nation would be hissed out of court when the world gets ready to make up the case against Germany."

In this wartime environment—marked by flagrant violations of individual civil liberties and furious attacks on socialists, pacifists, left-wing progressives, and other voices of dissent—many whites and blacks hesitated to articulate nonconformist ideas in public. As diverse a group of white leaders as the racist, xenophobic, and ex-Populist Tom Watson, the white socialist and labor champion Eugene V. Debs, and the left-wing intellectual and writer Randolph Bourne all came under heavy fire for their opposition to the war. Debs was arrested and sentenced to federal prison for his critique of the capitalist motivations of the war—a critique not too dissimilar from that of Du Bois, Randolph, and other black leaders on the political left.

And yet, it was in this very environment that the black press came into its own. Black newspapers encouraged African Americans to move to industrial centers in search of work, urged support of the war, protested racist incidents, and also led in the fight for complete integration of blacks in the military and in American life. Older newspapers such as the *Baltimore Afro-American* and the *Chicago Defender* enjoyed unprecedented growth, while newer ones such as the *Pittsburgh Courier* and the *Norfolk Journal and Guide* made rapid strides both in circulation and influence. The African American press, while generally supportive of the war effort, did not fail to expose racial injustice. At a conference sponsored by Emmet Scott in June 1918, thirty-one leading black newspaper publishers denounced mob violence, called for the use of black Red Cross nurses, requested the return of Lieutenant Colonel Charles Young to active duty, and asked for the appointment of a black war correspondent. Ralph Tyler of Columbus, Ohio, was subsequently designated as the war correspondent by the government's propaganda arm, the Committee on Public Information, and he sent press dispatches from Europe to the black newspapers back home. His stories generally gave glowing accounts of the gallantry and heroism of the black troops overseas.

The *Messenger*, a newspaper published in New York by black socialists A. Philip Randolph and Chandler Owen, remained one of the few journals to refuse to speak about the war in patriotic terms. The two men lambasted Wilson's rhetoric "to make the world safe for democracy" and his advocacy of the right of nations to self-determination, asserting that it flew in the face of his own racial attitudes, which condoned Jim Crow at home and colonialism in Africa and Asia. In July 1918, the editors of *The Messenger* wrote: "The government is drafting Negroes to fight. It asks their loyalty." In return, Randolph and Owen concluded, black soldiers received no more than "lynching, burning at the stake." For publishing the article "Pro-Germanism among Negroes," Randolph and Owen were sentenced to two and a half years in jail and had their second-class mailing privileges rescinded. Indeed, Du Bois's editorial "Close Ranks" in *The Crisis* in July 1918 served as a crucial counterpoint to *The Messenger*'s cynicism, but it came at the tail end of a flurry of articles that he had written in a different, more critical and militant tone between 1914 and 1917—before American military involvement.

Perhaps the most important social and economic consequence of the war was the migration of hundreds of thousands of African American men and women out of the South and into northern cities. The fundamental cause of this exodus was economic, although important social considerations also contributed to the migration. A severe labor depression in the South in 1914 and 1915 sent wages tumbling, and damage to the cotton crops, caused by boll weevil infestations in 1915 and 1916, discouraged many who depended on cotton farming for their livelihood. Moreover, Mississippi River floods in the summer of 1915 left thousands of blacks in the Gulf Region destitute, homeless, and ready to accept almost anything as preferable to the devastation around them. As southern agriculture faltered, northern industry boomed, and the wartime demand for labor skyrocketed.

Black Exodus

The flood of European immigrants pouring into early twentieth-century America ended abruptly with the outbreak of war in 1914, and this drying up of the transatlantic migration exacerbated the labor shortage, sending agents scurrying into the South to entice both blacks and whites to move north for work. Injustice in the southern court system, disfranchisement, segregation, and lynching doubtless served as powerful incentives for black migration out of the South. Historian Darlene Clark-Hine asserts that violence against black women, specifically rape, also accounted for their eagerness to escape the South. The black press portrayed the North as the "land of promise" and did much to persuade blacks to abandon a world that offered at best second-class citizenship. The *Chicago Defender* exclaimed: "To die from the bite of frost is far more glorious than at the hands of a mob." In a similar vein, the AME news organ the *Christian Recorder* wrote in 1917 that "if a million Negroes move north and west in the next twelve months, it will be one of the greatest things for the Negro since the Emancipation Proclamation." In 1916 black migration out of the South steadily rose, reaching flood tide by summer. The Pennsylvania Railroad brought from southern states 12,000 blacks— all but 2,000 of them from Florida and Georgia—to work in its yards and on its tracks. Even black professionals moved north to continue serving their migrating clientele. Southern whites became increasingly alarmed at the loss of black labor. City officials in Jacksonville, Florida, passed an ordinance requiring migration agents to pay a license fee of $1,000. White citizens in many southern towns threatened blacks who wanted to leave, while the white press urged them to remain in the South. Despite such pressure, more than a half million African Americans are estimated to have participated in the Great Migration during the war years.

Migration to the North and West, coming when it did, gave blacks opportunities for industrial employment that they had never enjoyed before. The Department of Labor, aware of the importance of black workers in relieving the labor shortage in the crucial early years of the war, created a Division of Negro Economics under the direction of sociologist and social worker George Edmund Haynes. The division supplied the secretary of labor and the heads of other government bureaus with plans and policies for improving black workers' conditions and for securing white employers' full cooperation in achieving maximum production. Several state and local advisory committees were established to promote cooperation and reduce friction between white and black workers. For the same purpose, twelve states held conferences with the support of governors, employment agencies, employers, and workers.

New Opportunities

The National Urban League assumed a decisive leadership role in helping newly arrived African Americans adjust to life in northern industrial centers. By 1911, the year of the Urban League's founding, southern unskilled black workers had already begun to migrate to

Everyone is getting used to
overalled women in machine shops

Women have made good as
Street Car Conductors and Elevator Operators

Clerical Work
quite a new job for Negro Girls

Slav, Italian and Negro Women
making bed springs

The war brought us
Women Traffic Cops and Mail Carriers

Laundry and domestic work didn't
pay so they entered the garment trade

New Jobs for Women
This poster expresses optimism about the new employment opportunities for African American women opened up by the war.

the northern cities in such numbers that reform-minded whites and blacks, especially in New York City, organized to address the problems related to the newcomers' adjustment. Called

The National Urban League initially the National League on Urban Conditions among Negroes (adopting the simpler title National Urban League in 1920), the organization had come into existence from the merger of three Progressive-era organizations—the National League for the Protection of Colored Women (founded in 1905), the Committee for Improving Industrial Conditions of Negroes in New York (founded in 1906), and the

Committee on Urban Conditions (founded in 1910). The Urban League was born of Progressivism's focus on urban conditions and municipal government, its reliance on investigative studies and data collection, its social work impulse to create institutions, such as settlement houses and employment bureaus for moral influence and economic guidance, and its laboratory approach in the training of social workers.

George Edmund Haynes, director of the organization and also the first black Ph.D. from Columbia University, played a crucial role in designing the initial research agenda —identifying problems related to employment, housing, health, education, and recreation. While the League's director, he also taught sociology at Fisk University in Nashville, where he trained social workers. His Urban League work was assisted by Eugene Kinckle Jones, formerly a black high school teacher in Louisville, Kentucky. Jones moved to New York in 1911 to serve as field secretary; he would eventually head the organization. The Urban League's work was supported by notable reformers and philanthropists who sat on its board, including Ruth Standish Baldwin, the widow of the railroad magnate William Baldwin, Frances Kellor, who founded protective associations with the aid of black and white social workers, and Edwin R. A. Seligman, the noted Columbia University economics professor. The League's formative years also benefited from the philanthropic support of John Rockefeller and the influence of Booker T. Washington. By the end of World War I, branches of the National Urban League operated in thirty cities.

African Americans organized several unions of their own, such as the Associated Colored Employees of America. However, in 1917 the American Federation of Labor (AFL) began to express sympathy for workers of all races, encouraging them to **Employment in Industry** unite and present a common front to industry. The intention was to discourage blacks from serving as strike breakers. In 1918 the Council of the AFL invited several prominent African Americans to discuss the matter, including Robert R. Moton of Tuskegee, Emmett J. Scott of the War Department, Eugene Kinckle Jones of the National Urban League, and Fred Moore, the editor of the black newspaper the *New York Age*. Few tangible results came of their deliberations. During the war the vast majority of labor unions continued to oppose black membership, echoing the often racist views of white workers.

Because immigration from Europe stopped suddenly with the outbreak of war in 1914, African Americans found jobs in most industries in the urban North, which had previously depended on immigrant labor. They manufactured munitions and iron and steel products. They labored in the meatpacking industry, in turning out automobiles and trucks, and in manufacturing electrical products. There were 26,648 blacks in 46 of the 55 occupations related to shipbuilding as classified by the U.S. Shipping Board. A black man, Charles Knight, broke the world's record for driving rivets in building steel ships at the Bethlehem Steel Corporation plant at Sparrow's Point, outside Baltimore. More than 75,000 blacks worked in the coal mines of Alabama, Illinois, Pennsylvania, Ohio, and West Virginia. Approximately 150,000 assisted in the operation of the railroads, while another 150,000 kept up other vital means of communication. In 152 typical industrial plants, 21,547 black women performed 75 different tasks.

The war elicited conflicting emotions in African Americans. The patriotic stories of black valor served to give pride, but outbreaks of racial injustice hurt morale. At least thirty-eight African Americans lost their lives at the hands of **Riots and Lynchings** lynch mobs in 1917, and in the following year that number rose to fifty-eight. Racial clashes in the North and South did not diminish. In Tennessee, more than three thousand whites responded to the invitation of a newspaper to come witness the burning of a "live Negro." In East St. Louis, Illinois, at least forty blacks lost their lives in a riot that grew out of the migration of blacks to that city and their employment in a factory that held government contracts. African Americans were stabbed, clubbed, and hanged, and one two-year-old child was shot and thrown into the doorway of a burning building. In *Darkwater*, Du Bois vented his anger over the East St. Louis riot. In an expanded version of an article he had written right after the riot, Du Bois associated the riot's brutal killings with the World War, specifically with the "rush toward the Battle of the Marne . . . dear God, the fire of Thy Mad World crimsons our Heaven." In 1917 riots in Philadelphia and Houston also occurred. The riots served as a prelude to 1919, when in the first summer after the war, more than fifty cities erupted in racial violence.

Black soldiers had fought courageously abroad, and they expected, in return, a post-war America of greater economic opportunity and civil rights. Indeed, the First World War instilled in the minds and hearts of all African Americans both guarded hopes for the possibility of democracy at home and renewed determination to fight for that goal. Yet none doubted that the pursuit of democracy would require a protracted struggle, what Du Bois called a "sterner, longer, more unbending battle against the forces of hell in our own land." At the historic moment of national victory, Du Bois pronounced the battle for democracy unfinished. In his article "Returning Soldiers," which appeared in *The Crisis* in May 1919, Du Bois declared on behalf of his people: "We return. We return from fighting. We return fighting. Make way for Democracy! We saved it in France, and by the Great Jehovah, we will save it in the United States of America, or know the reason why."

Voices of Protest

Progressive Voices

Violent Times

Civil Rights Vanguard

Protesting with Their Feet

New Negroes

New Women

A Man Was Lynched Yesterday
The NAACP flew this flag above Fifth Avenue in New York City each time it learned of a lynching.

In 1919 the Washington, D.C., clergyman Francis J. Grimké gave a rousing welcome to black soldiers who had returned home from the European battlefront. Born a slave in 1852 in South Carolina, Grimké was the nephew of the famous women's rights and abolitionist sisters (and members of a South Carolina slaveholding family) Sarah Grimké and Angelina Grimké Weld and the husband of Civil War-era educator and diarist Charlotte Forten. In his lifetime Francis Grimké had seen three wars, as well as monumental changes in his own condition and that of his people. In childhood he had witnessed the Civil War, and in his teens and early twenties he followed, first with hope and then with disillusion, the unraveling promise of Reconstruction. In midlife he vigorously protested from the Washington pulpit of his Fifteenth Street Presbyterian Church the steady erosion of blacks' civil and political rights. In 1898, responding to Booker T. Washington's public posture of accommodation to Jim Crow realities, Grimké had preached a defiant sermon titled "The Negro Will Never Acquiesce as Long as He Lives." He had not wavered in his decades-long fight for racial equality.

Now in 1919—an infamous year of race riots across the nation—Grimké explicitly tapped into the democratic doctrine that had been expounded so generally during the war as he demanded of the returning soldiers a heightened sense of urgency for equality and justice, especially since these fighting men had enjoyed more liberties on foreign soil than in the United States. Grimké did not hesitate to make known his expectations of them. "If it was worth going abroad to make the world safe for democracy, it is equally worth laboring no less earnestly to make it safe at home. We shall be greatly disappointed if you do not do this—if you fail to do your part."

African Americans did not fail to do their part in the pursuit of their rights. Civil-rights leaders such as Du Bois, the Grimké brothers (Francis and Archibald), Monroe Trotter, Ida B. Wells, Nannie Helen Burroughs, and many other black men and women had spoken forcefully against racial discrimination before the war, and they would continue to do so. Some remained in all-black organizations, while others joined with whites in organizations of Progressive-era reform, such as the NAACP (National Association for the Advancement of Colored People), the Commission on Interracial Cooperation, and the National Urban League. However, as World War I went on, and especially after the fighting ended, the older civil rights vanguard was challenged by important new voices of varying ideological positions—socialists, black nationalists, and feminists. African Americans protested racial oppression in a cacophony of voices through journalistic, scholarly, and literary writings that together presented competing visions of a New Negro identity and consciousness. In a social milieu so completely charged with emotion and racial tensions, small wonder that blacks adopted varied strategies and goals.

Progressive Voices

Well before World War I, the NAACP stood out prominently as the leading voice of civil rights activism. The success of the NAACP could be measured by the circulation of its magazine *The Crisis* and its burgeoning membership. In 1910, the first year of its existence, the NAACP launched *The Crisis* under the editorship of W. E. B. Du Bois. The first issue, which appeared in November 1910, rapidly sold a thousand copies. By 1918 the magazine's circulation had increased to 100,000 copies per month. Shortly after the NAACP's initial organization, the first branch was established in Chicago. Within two years, nine others had been formed. Each year up until the outbreak of World War I the number doubled, and by 1921 more than four hundred branches were scattered across the United States. They gathered information, raised money, and carried out the aims of the parent organization. Not long after its founding, the NAACP also became a presence on the international scene. Du Bois attended the First Universal Races Congress in London in 1911 and won new friends for the NAACP among the delegates from many lands. Partly to represent the association at that important gathering and partly to refute the message of Booker T. Washington, who toured Europe in 1910, Du Bois stressed that, contrary to Washington's claims, African Americans in the United States were suffering under grave legal and civil disabilities.

The NAACP's growing success was also evident in its legal victories. The Legal Redress Committee under the chairmanship of white lawyer Arthur B. Spingarn, who with his brother Joel sat on the NAACP's biracial board of directors, **The Work of the NAACP** included white and black attorneys. The lawyers worked closely together, and within a fifteen-year period the NAACP won three important decisions before the U.S. Supreme Court. In 1915, in *Guinn v. United States,* the Supreme Court declared the grandfather clauses in the Maryland and Oklahoma constitutions to be in violation of the Fifteenth Amendment and therefore null and void. In 1917, the distinguished lawyer Moorfield Storey, head of the NAACP's board of directors and former president of the American Bar Association, argued *Buchanan v. Warley* before the Supreme Court and won a stunning victory for the NAACP when the justices declared unconstitutional a Louisville ordinance requiring blacks to live in certain sections of the city.

The NAACP, though focused on racial reform, functioned in many ways like other Progressive-era reform organizations. Its legal work and campaign against lynching were reminiscent of progressives' demands for more honest, representative, and responsible government. *The Crisis* and other NAACP publications drew public attention to the heinous abuses associated with racial violence and adopted fact-gathering and social-scientific methods to gain broad support for antilynching legislation. In these efforts the NAACP emulated muckraking journalism and other progressive efforts to stamp out social evils through practical, pragmatic reforms. For example, Progressive-era reformers exposed the exploitation of child and women workers, the production and sale of unhealthy food and dangerous drugs, the abuses of corrupt urban political machines, the monopolistic power of trusts, the environmental damage of over-development, and the refusal of the vote to women.

Yet the reformist goals of the NAACP, along with the progressive-oriented National Urban League and several African American women's clubs, proved exceptions to the rule. African Americans were, in general, hardly the beneficiaries of the umbrella movement that has come to be called Progressivism. In the South, where the vast majority of the black population lived before 1914, the same southern white politicians who enacted progressive legislation in their states also disenfranchised black voters and passed segregation laws—all in the name of "better government." Whether by conviction or by expediency, southern Progressivism was avowedly racist, asserting that blacks were unfit to vote.

In the North, many progressive intellectuals and political leaders subscribed to the "scientific" racism of the day and justified the exclusion of blacks from the nation's political life. Many progressives applauded imperialism for bringing the "light" of modern civilization to the benighted colored races of the world, and at home they urged the rapid "Americanization" of the culturally alien immigrants from Eastern and Southern Europe who were pouring into America's cities. Such attitudes, rooted in notions of Anglo-Saxon superiority, caused them to turn a blind eye to the problems that African Americans daily faced. Thus the NAACP called for reform of many aspects of white progressives' thinking, including that of progressive reform presidents Theodore Roosevelt and Woodrow Wilson.

By 1912 African Americans were sorely distressed by their political options. They had become suspicious of Theodore Roosevelt because of his handling of the Brownsville inci-

The 1912 Election   dent in 1906, and they lacked confidence in President William Howard Taft after he won the presidency in 1908. When officials of the NAACP went so far as to draft a statement for the Progressive Bull Moose Party platform, calling for the repeal of discriminatory laws and complete enfranchisement, it became clear that Roosevelt would give no assurances that his new party would stand unequivocally for full citizenship rights for blacks. Roosevelt permitted the southern white delegates to have their way in ignoring the statement and in barring some black delegates from the convention.

Although skeptical of the Democratic Party, some notable black leaders, among them Du Bois, William Monroe Trotter, and the AME Zion bishop Alexander Walters, turned their eyes toward Woodrow Wilson. Du Bois, Trotter, and other black civil rights advocates clearly chafed at the idea of Booker T. Washington's influence with both Roosevelt and his immediate successor, William Howard Taft. They hoped for better from Woodrow Wilson. Du Bois admitted respecting Wilson as a scholar and had taught his book *The State* to his students at Atlanta University. He believed that Wilson, a historian and the former president of Princeton University, would bring to the presidency a new model of leadership. It had been Alexander Walters more than anyone else who persuaded Du Bois and probably other black leaders of Wilson's goodwill toward African Americans. Walters lived in New Jersey and had met Wilson while he was governor of the state; they had even corresponded. In a letter to Walters about African Americans, Wilson had stated: "I want to assure them through you that should I become President of the United States they may count upon me for absolute fair dealing, for everything by which I could assist in advancing the interests of their race in the United States." Inspired, Du Bois wrote favorably of Wilson's candidacy in *The Crisis*.

But Wilson's victory proved to be a tremendous disappointment and embarrassment to the civil rights leaders who initially supported him. By birth a Virginian, on the race ques-

Wilson Disappoints   tion Wilson behaved no differently than did the many other southern progressives. Soon after his inauguration, he refused to endorse the NAACP's request to form a "national commission on the Negro problem," an idea proposed by Oswald Garrison Villard, editor of the *New York Evening Post,* founding member of the NAACP, and grandson of abolitionist William Lloyd Garrison. Wilson had different priorities. When he was inaugurated as president in 1913, Wilson pledged his administration's commitment to a progressive-minded domestic program he called "the New Freedom."

In the first Congress during his administration, Wilson achieved his progressive-reform agenda through tariff and banking reforms, most significantly the labor exemption provisions of the Clayton Antitrust Act. Economic issues such as these, however, were of less interest to African Americans than the racist practices and institutions that relegated them to the bottom of the nation's economic ladder. Last hired and first fired, black people found equal employment opportunities denied to them because of their race. White labor unions closed their doors to blacks and remained for the most part steadfastly opposed to an interracial alliance in the struggle for higher wages and better working conditions. Banks refused to lend to blacks.

THE CRISIS

A RECORD OF THE DARKER RACES

Volume One   NOVEMBER, 1910   Number One

Edited by W. E. BURGHARDT DU BOIS, with the co-operation of Oswald Garrison Villard, J. Max Barber, Charles Edward Russell, Kelly Miller, W. S. Braithwaite and M. D. Maclean.

CONTENTS

Along the Color Line   3

Opinion   7

Editorial   10

The N. A. A. C. P.   12

Athens and Browns-
ville 13
By MOORFIELD STOREY

The Burden . . . 14

What to Read . . 15

PUBLISHED MONTHLY BY THE

National Association for the Advancement of Colored People

AT TWENTY VESEY STREET   NEW YORK CITY

ONE DOLLAR A YEAR   TEN CENTS A COPY

The Crisis —cover of the first issue

The Crisis magazine was established by W.E.B. Du Bois for the National Association for the Advancement of Colored People in 1910. Du Bois was the most influential and prestigious black leader in the first half of the twentieth century in the United States. The magazine was intended for anyone interested in civil rights and in the state of race relations around the world.

Congress submitted, as well, a flood of bills proposing discriminatory legislation. Proposals were made for laws forbidding interracial marriage, requiring segregation in housing and on public carriers in the District of Columbia, excluding blacks from officers' commissions in the Army and Navy, mandating separate accommodations for black and white federal employees, and banning all immigrants of African descent. Although most of the legislation failed to pass, Wilson by executive order segregated the eating and restroom facilities of black federal employees and phased out most blacks in civil service jobs. Instead of the former merit-based hiring system, blacks were denied civil service jobs simply because of their race. The progressive NAACP retorted that "the efficiency of their [blacks'] labor, the principles of scientific management are disregarded, the possibilities of promotion, if not now, will soon be severely limited." In an open letter to Wilson, dated August 15, 1913, the NAACP leadership protested the racial limits of this progressive president: "For the lowly of all classes you have lifted up your voice and not in vain. Shall ten millions of our citizens say that their civic liberties and rights are not safe in your hands? To ask the question is to answer it. They desire a 'New Freedom,' too, Mr. President."

Men and women at the Amenia Conference
Group portrait of men and women attending the NAACP-sponsored Amenia Conference in Amenia, New York, August 1916.

Monroe Trotter, although declining to be a member of the integrated NAACP, went with a delegation of his own organization to the White House. His protest against the segregation of federal employees so sorely offended Wilson that he called for Trotter's immediate dismissal from his presence. President Wilson would be no friend to African Americans. In 1915 they began to fight residential segregation ordinances that were springing up all over the country. When the president ordered the Marines to occupy Haiti in 1915, African Americans loudly protested the violation of that country's sovereignty and territorial integrity; particularly repugnant to them was the killing of several hundred Haitians ostensibly to restore peace and order. African Americans took offense at Wilson's admiration of D. W. Griffith's film *Birth of a Nation* when it was released in 1915. NAACP branches in various cities picketed the film, which was based on the antiblack novels of Thomas Dixon. *Birth of a Nation* told a most sordid and distorted story of Reconstruction-era black emancipation, enfranchisement, and violation of white womanhood. Its glorification of the Ku Klux Klan condoned vigilante violence, and the film did more than any other single medium to nurture and promote the myth of black domination and debauchery during Reconstruction. Wilson praised the film as "history writ in lightning."

African Americans Protest Racial Policies

The time had come, the more aggressive NAACP leaders believed, to consolidate and achieve a unity in thought and action that had previously been impossible. In 1916, Joel Spingarn called a conference at his home in Amenia, New York, to discuss the plight of African Americans. The Amenia Conference, as it came to be known, brought together the most distinguished African Americans of the day. The conference attendees drew up no impassioned manifesto, and their resolutions showed no bitterness, but all participants agreed to work quietly and earnestly for enfranchisement, the abolition of lynching, and the enforcement of laws protecting civil rights. It was an eventful prelude to America's entry into World War I.

The Amenia Conference

Violent Times

The World War I rallying cry of "100% Americanism" morphed into a postwar national hysteria of "super-patriotism" that took several forms: the rise of racist and xenophobic groups such as the Ku Klux Klan; the Red Scare, with its government-authorized raids against perceived communists between 1918 and 1922; isolationist foreign policies; and an increasing number of lynchings and racially motivated mob violence, directed particularly against African Americans.

The Ku Klux Klan had reawakened in the southern states in 1915. In the ten months following the war's end, however, Klan membership soared from a few thousand to over 100,000 white-hooded "knights," who openly declared their goal of "uniting native-born white Christians for concerted action in the preservation of American institutions and the supremacy of the white race." By the 1920s the Ku Klux Klan had become a national organization with cells in several New England states as well as in New York, Indiana, Illinois, Michigan, and other northern and midwestern states. This white supremacist group assumed the responsibility for punishing people whom it considered dangerous—African Americans, Asians, Roman Catholics, Jews, and the foreign-born in general. The Klan assumed a semi-official role in many communities, taking the law into its

The Resurgent Ku Klux Klan

own hands and luring public servants into its membership. In many communities, candidates for public office feared defeat if they were not on good terms with the Klan.

African Americans had few rights that the Klan felt obliged to respect, and the actions of this militant organization fully confirmed its assertion that the United States was a "white man's country." Throughout the South and Southwest, African Americans lived in constant fear of the hooded bands of night riders who burned crosses to terrify those whom they considered undesirables. In the West the Klan carried out similar actions against the ethnic Japanese population. Wherever it established itself, the Klan was blamed, correctly or incorrectly, for the atrocities committed in the vicinity: floggings, brandings with acid, tarring and featherings, hangings, and burnings.

African American soldiers were especially targeted. Ten black soldiers, several still in their uniforms, were lynched. Mississippi and Georgia mobs each murdered three returned soldiers. In Arkansas two were lynched, and Florida and Alabama each took the life of a black soldier by mob violence. Fourteen black men were burned publicly, eleven of them burned alive. In utter despair an African American editor in Charleston, South Carolina, cried out: "There is scarcely a day that passes that newspapers don't tell about a Negro soldier lynched in his uniform. Why do they lynch Negroes, anyhow? With a white judge, a white jury, white public sentiment, white officers of the law, it is just as impossible for a Negro accused of crime, or even suspected of crime, to escape the white man's vengeance or his justice as it would be for a fawn to escape that wanders accidentally into a den of hungry lions. So why not give him the semblance of a trial?"

Nothing compared to the more than twenty-six urban race riots in the summer of 1919—termed the "Red Summer" by NAACP officer James Weldon Johnson because of the widespread bloodshed. By then race relations had been pushed to the breaking point by the continued migration of African Americans and subsequent competition for peacetime jobs. Egged on by native racist organizations such as the Ku Klux Klan, the lawless element of the white population undertook to terrorize blacks into submission. In the meantime, unrest and disappointment seized a considerable portion of the black population. When it became clear that whites sought to deprive blacks of their wartime gains, the latter bristled into action, determined to defend themselves in an unprecedented show of action.

Race Riots

In July 1919 Longview, Texas, also witnessed the nightmare of a race riot. Several white men were shot when they went into the black section of the town in search of a black schoolteacher who was accused of sending a news story to *The Chicago Defender* describing the lynching of an African American the previous month. Whites in the town were alarmed over this show of strength among blacks, and they poured into the black section determined to teach them a lesson. Many homes were burned, a black school principal was flogged in the streets, and several leading black citizens were run out of town. It was several days before the town returned to normal. In the following week a riot of more violent proportions broke out in the nation's capital. Newspaper reports of blacks assaulting white women whipped the irresponsible elements of the population into a frenzy, although it early became clear that the reports had no basis in fact. Mobs, consisting primarily of white sailors, soldiers, and Marines, ran amok through the streets of Washington for three days, killing several African Americans and injuring scores of others. On the third day, blacks retaliated when hoodlums sought to invade and burn their section of the city. The casualty list mounted, but before order was restored the number of whites killed and wounded had increased considerably as a result of the blacks' belated but effective action.

The most serious racial outbreak occurred in Chicago in late July 1919. To southern blacks, Chicago had become "the top of the world," and thousands had migrated there during and after the war in search of employment and freedom. Within less than a decade, the city's black population had more than **The Chicago Riot of 1919** doubled, and the census of 1920 showed approximately 109,000 blacks living there. There had been some friction in industry, but the abundance of jobs had kept tensions to a minimum. The most serious friction arose over the issues of housing and recreation. With blacks spreading into white neighborhoods, white residents sought to prevent the infiltration by bombing black homes. Groups of young whites took it upon themselves to frighten blacks into submission and to prevent their continued movement into white sections of the city.

The riot that began on July 27 had its immediate origin in an altercation at a Lake Michigan beach. A young African American swimming offshore had drifted into water that was customarily used by whites. White swimmers commanded him to return to his part of the beach, and some threw stones at him. When the young man sank and drowned, blacks declared that he had been murdered. Although his recovered body showed no signs of having been stoned, it was too late to save the city from a riot that was already in progress. Distorted rumors about the incident and about subsequent events at the beach circulated among blacks and whites. Mobs sprang up in various parts of the city, and all night there was sporadic fighting. The next afternoon, white bystanders attacked blacks as they went home from work. Some were pulled off streetcars and whipped. Many people of both races were injured in these clashes, and at least five were killed.

On the South Side, a group of young blacks stabbed to death an old Italian peddler and a white laundry operator. During that day and the next, the riot spread, with mobs of both races terrorizing the opposite group. For thirteen days Chicago was without law and order, despite the militia being called out on the fourth day of the riot. When the authorities counted the casualties, the tally sheet gave the results of a miniature war. Thirty-eight people had been killed, including 15 whites and 23 blacks; of the 537 injured, 178 were white and 342 were black, with no indication of the racial identity of the remaining 17. More than a thousand families, mostly black, found themselves homeless as a result of the burnings and general destruction of property. The nation's worst race riot shocked even the most indifferent observers into the realization that interracial conflict in the United States had reached a serious stage.

During the next two months, race riots erupted in Knoxville, Tennessee; in Omaha, Nebraska; in Elaine, Arkansas; and several other places. The Knoxville riot began when a white woman stumbled and fatally injured herself while running from a black man **More Riots** who was later accused of attempting to assault her. When he was arrested, a mob formed and an attempt was made to take him from the jail. During the general riot that followed, scores of people were injured, some fatally, and more than $50,000 worth of property was destroyed. The troops that were called out went into the black section and "shot it up" when a false rumor was circulated that some blacks had killed two white men. Black people were stopped on the streets and searched. A black newspaper declared, "The indignities which colored women suffered at the hands of these soldiers would make the devil blush for shame."

In Omaha a mob almost completely destroyed the county courthouse by fire in order to grab a black man who was in jail on a charge of attacking a white girl. The group succeeded

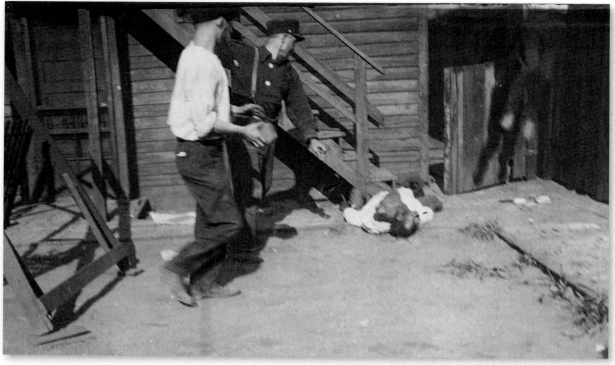

Chicago Race Riot of 1919
Whites stone an African American man, who later died of his injuries, during the 1919 Chicago race riots.

in seizing him, and dragged him through the streets, shot him more than a thousand times, mutilated him beyond recognition, and finally hanged him at one of the busiest downtown intersections. Meanwhile much damage was done to property, and several blacks were severely beaten.

In Elaine, Arkansas, when black farmers met to make plans to force their landlords to replace their existing debt peonage with a fair settlement, a deputy sheriff and a posse broke up the meeting. In the melee, the deputy was killed. That ignited a reign of terror in which scores of blacks were shot and several killed. In a subsequent trial, which lasted less than an hour, twelve black farmers were sentenced to death, and sixty-seven others received long prison terms. In 1923 the Supreme Court, in *Moore v. Dempsey,* ordered a new trial in the Arkansas courts for the black farmers who had been convicted of murder and sentenced to death after the 1919 Elaine race riot. NAACP lawyers had argued that the Arkansas men had not received a fair trial, because, among other things, blacks were excluded from the jury, and the Court accepted this argument. To members of the NAACP, such victories underscored the crucial strategy of the legal assault.

Although less numerous and devastating, riots continued after 1919. Two of the worst occurred in Tulsa, Oklahoma, and Rosewood, Florida. In June 1921 the blacks and whites of Tulsa, Oklahoma, engaged in fighting, which Buck C. Franklin, a local black attorney, and some others preferred to call a "race war." Nine whites and twenty-one blacks were known to have been killed, and several hundred were injured. On hearing that a black had been accused of assaulting a young white woman, blacks took arms to the jail to protect the accused person, who, it was rumored, would be lynched. Altercations between whites and blacks at the jail spread to other parts of the city, and general rioting, looting, and house burning began. Four National Guard companies were called out, but by the time order was restored, more than $1 million worth of property had been destroyed or damaged. The young black man was subsequently exonerated of any wrongdoing. On the seventy-fifth anniversary of the riot, the state legislature created a commission to revisit the causes and consequences of the riot.

In January 1923 a white mob from a neighboring town destroyed predominantly black Rosewood, Florida, after a white woman falsely accused a black male of assaulting her. Rosewood was burned to the ground, many of its residents were murdered, and the survivors were driven into exile and threatened with death if they disclosed the violence they had witnessed. Not until the early 1980s did some residents break silence. As a result of the publicity, investigations followed that produced a book, a scholarly study, a television special, and a feature film on the "Rosewood Massacre." In 1994 the Florida legislature provided for each of the survivors of the violence to receive reparations of $150,000.

In 1925 Detroit exploded in violence when whites attempted to prevent an African American physician, Ossian H. Sweet, from living in a house that he and his wife Gladys had purchased in a white neighborhood. When a mob of 400 to 500 whites gathered outside his home and began to hurl stones, gunfire rang out from inside the Sweets' home, killing a white man in the crowd. Sweet, his brother, and friends in the house were brought to trial. The response of black self-defense was lauded in the black community. *The Chicago Defender, The Pittsburgh Courier,* and other black newspapers rallied with praise for Sweet's example of courage rather than capitulation to the mob. In *The Crisis,* Du Bois posed the question: "Which example would you follow, if you were 'free,' black, and 21?" The NAACP came to their defense, employing the famous white attorneys Clarence Darrow and Arthur Garfield Hays. All were finally acquitted, but irreparable harm had been done to the Sweet family and to race relations in Detroit. The historian of the Sweet case, Kevin Boyle, notes that Gladys Sweet succumbed soon after to tuberculosis, which she most likely contracted during her imprisonment in the Wayne County jail, and that this tragedy along with other personal and financial losses over subsequent decades eventually drove Ossian Sweet to suicide.

In the postwar racial strife, African Americans exhibited a willingness to fight and to die in their own defense, refusing to be intimidated into submission. One of the outstanding poets of the period, Claude McKay, expressed the feelings of a great many African Americans when he wrote:

> If we must die, let it not be like hogs
> Hunted and penned in an inglorious spot,
> While round us bark the mad and hungry dogs,
> Making their mock at our accursed lot.
> If we must die, O let us nobly die,
> So that our precious blood may not be shed

In vain; then even the monsters we defy

Shall be constrained to honor us though dead!

O kinsmen! we must meet the common foe!

Though far outnumbered let us show us brave,

And for their thousand blows deal one deathblow!

What though before us lies the open grave?

Like men we'll face the murderous, cowardly pack,

Pressed to the wall, dying but fighting back!

Many American whites freely suggested that foreign influences—especially exposure to the French tradition of equality during the war and Bolshevik propaganda after the 1917 Russian Revolution—had caused blacks to fight back. Perhaps there was some truth to that. As Francis Grimké reminded returning American black soldiers, they had been treated on foreign soil better than in their own land. The Russian Revolution in 1917, and even earlier the influence of the Socialist Party of American under labor leader Eugene Debs, had attracted, if only temporarily, some black leaders, including McKay and Du Bois. However, black Americans all along the political spectrum (from conservative to moderate to radical left) ridiculed the claim that their new assertiveness was the result of "outside agitation." American blacks needed no outsiders to awaken their sense of the tremendous contradiction between America's professed beliefs and its actual practices.

"Outside Agitation"

In October 1919 *The Pittsburgh Courier* declared, "As long as the Negro submits to lynchings, burnings, and oppressions and says nothing he is a loyal American citizen. But when he decides that lynchings and burnings shall cease even at the cost of some bloodshed in America, then he is a Bolshevist." That December, the hardly radical *Washington Bee* announced: "We heard nothing of this so-called 'Bolshevism' until the unrest in Russia had inflamed and aroused the persecuted common people during the world war. It is not Bolsheviks but just American injustice that is responsible." The militant *Crusader*, edited by the radical leftists Cyril R. Briggs and Richard B. Moore, regarded such accusations as a compliment. In a scathing denunciation of mob violence and rioting in America, its editors asserted, "If to fight for one's rights is to be Bolshevists, then we are Bolshevists and let them make the most of it!"

Civil Rights Vanguard

In the years immediately following World War I, no meeting of a national African American organization neglected to register its protest against the failure of the United States to grant first-class citizenship. In July 1919 the NAACP met in Cleveland and adopted resolutions expressing great concern over the status of blacks, particularly given the urban riots that had already commenced. Trotter's National Equal Rights League met in September in Washington, D.C.—another riot-torn city of the "Red Summer." The next month, the National Race Congress also met in Washington and passed protest resolutions. Organized in 1919, the Commission on Interracial Cooperation sought to mitigate racial strife. The commission worked primarily in the South and was led by white Methodist minister Will W. Alexander and other prominent white and black southerners. The CIC set up several ten-day schools for whites and blacks to train leaders in promoting interracial work. Local interracial committees were organized, and upon the creation of sufficient interest state committees were set up. Although the commission did not attack segregation, it spoke out against lynching, mob violence, debt peonage, and disfranchisement. At about the same time the National Baptist Convention adopted resolutions in favor of a more complete integration of African Americans into American life.

Throughout these years, the interracial NAACP stood out as the most established and strongest advocate of blacks' civil rights, and no organization fought lynching and mob violence as systematically and persistently. After learning of a lynching, the NAACP would display a banner outside the window of its **The Persistence of Lynching** New York City offices solemnly announcing, "A man was lynched yesterday." The NAACP responded to the East St. Louis Riot of 1917 with a silent parade. The march was the brainchild of the NAACP organizer James Weldon Johnson, who described the haunting, sound-

less trek of ten thousand people along Harlem's streets. "They marched in silence," Johnson reported, "but some of those who watched turned away with their eyes filled," while "boy scouts distributed leaflets, which explained why they were marching." It was a brilliant strategy of counterintuitive power—to march, according to Johnson "because we deem it a crime to be silent in the face of such barbaric acts."

Lynching did not cease, however. Walter White's investigative reporting in *The Crisis* detailed the gruesome facts. His light skin enabled him to go undetected to crime scenes and secure as much data as possible concerning the tragedies. Walter White's book *Rope and Faggot, A Biography of Judge Lynch* (1929), based on findings over a ten-year period, was hailed as a startling exposé. One of the most lurid accounts described the lynching of a husband and wife in May 1918, in Valdosta, Georgia. White wrote: "The murder of the Negro men was deplorable enough in itself, but the method by which Mrs. Mary Turner was put to death was so revolting and the details are so horrible that it is with reluctance that the account is given." He did go on to give the facts. Mary Turner

Children in Silent Protest Parade, 1917
These children, all dressed in white, marched in New York's Harlem in silent protest against the East St. Louis riot of 1917.

had threatened to find out the names of the men in the mob who had killed her husband, to get warrants, and to bring them to justice. She, too, was hanged and burned to death in a publicly advertised execution in front of a crowd of onlookers, and her unborn child (she was eight months pregnant) was torn from her womb and stomped to death.

In May 1919 the NAACP held a national conference on lynching at which the chief speaker was Charles Evans Hughes, the former Supreme Court justice who had been the unsuccessful Republican candidate for president in 1916. (In 1930, Hughes would be reappointed to the Court as chief justice by President Herbert Hoover.) By 1920 it was waging a relentless crusade against lynching. In 1921 the NAACP sponsored two hundred antilynching rallies in various parts of the United States. Largely in cooperation with black women's clubs under the leadership of Mary Talbert and others, the NAACP had raised more than $45,000 by 1924. These funds provided needed assistance for the NAACP's legal work. The columns of *The Crisis* persisted in reporting lynchings, and in 1919 the NAACP published *Thirty Years of Lynching in the United States, 1889–1918,* detailing the causes of lynching and the circumstances under which the crime had occurred. In 1920 NAACP field secretary William Pickens called the South the "American Congo," and in a pamphlet of the same title he wrote: "Most of the lynching evil is traceable to economic wrong." He condemned not only lynching but also the system of debt peonage and convict leasing that held blacks in a new form of slavery that profited white landowners, mine owners, railroad builders, and lumber companies.

In 1919 the NAACP took its first step toward securing passage of a federal antilynching law. After carefully working to secure the support of senators and representatives, James Weldon Johnson, the secretary of the association, succeeded in 1921 in getting **NAACP Legal Efforts** Rep. L. C. Dyer of Missouri to introduce in the House a bill "to assure to persons within the jurisdiction of every state the equal protection of the laws, and to punish the crime of lynching." Representatives from the southern states immediately began organizing to defeat the proposed bill. They spoke on the floor of Congress in favor of mob rule and defied the federal government to interfere with the police power of the states. They could not, however, block a vote in the House of Representatives, and the bill passed, 230 to 119.

Securing a favorable vote in the Senate would be far more difficult, but the NAACP redoubled its efforts to pass the bill there as well. A memorial urging its passage was signed by twenty-four governors, thirty-nine mayors, twenty-nine college presidents and professors, and many editors, jurists, and lawyers and was sent to the Senate. The association published full-page advertisements in such newspapers as *The New York Times* and the *The Atlanta Constitution* supporting the measure. When the bill reached the floor of the Senate, southern senators, led by Oscar Underwood of Alabama and Pat Harrison of Mississippi, mounted a filibuster that ultimately prevented a vote on the measure. Showing a decided lack of interest, the Republicans voted to abandon it. Numerous similar bills were later introduced, including the Costigan-Wagner bill of 1935 and the Wagner-Gavagan bill of 1940, but all met with failure.

Throughout the 1920s the NAACP continued its assault on Jim Crow laws, believing the Supreme Court to be the most reliable safeguard of the rights of all citizens. Its success in previous cases involving the grandfather clause in voting and residential segregation encouraged the association to turn to the issue of voting rights, specifically challenging the white primary in the southern states. In 1927, in *Nixon v. Herndon,* NAACP lawyers persuaded the Supreme Court to declare null and void a Texas statute excluding blacks from Democratic primaries in the state. When the Texas legislature subsequently enacted a law giving the party's executive committee authority to fix the qualifications for party membership, the association, in *Nixon v. Condon,* also got this law nullified by arguing that the statute had set up a party committee and made it a state agency with certain powers and duties. The victory was short-lived: in the next decade, the Court refused to interfere with the exclusion of African Americans from Democratic primaries. Not until 1944 would the NAACP recover its lost ground, when in *Smith v. Allwright* the Supreme Court decided that the exclusion of African Americans from the Democratic primary was a clear violation of the Fifteenth Amendment.

Protesting with Their Feet

African Americans protested the status quo in many ways, but none was as consequential and long-lasting as simply migrating out of the South. Protesting with their feet, southern blacks sought greater freedom and opportunity in the North and the West. The wartime migration of over a half million black people rapidly escalated throughout the "normalcy" of the 1920s; in all, between 1915 and 1930, 1.5 million African Americans left the South. The migration was never simply a matter of economic opportunities that lured blacks away from southern farms and cities. Refusal to endure any longer the South's oppressive conditions became another mighty engine for blacks' movement to regions elsewhere. According to historian Milton Sernett, the "migration fever" that consumed the hearts and minds of well over a million people by the 1920s took on a religious meaning that harkened back to the exodus imagery that slaves and free blacks had appropriated in the pre-Civil War era. Emmett Scott, who held the position of Special Assistant to the Secretary of War, captured this cultural legacy in how the migrants' alluded to the North—"the Promised Land," "the Ark of Safety," the "House of Refuge," and the "New Jerusalem." In his discussion of the religious dimensions of this migration, Sernett vividly reveals how the magnitude, the suddenness, the accompanying environmental plague (the boll weevil), and in some cases the mystery associated with individuals' departure helped foster the familiar analogy—the biblical Jews' exodus from Pharaoh's Egypt. For black migrants, there would be no stopping of God's unfolding providential design.

Anxious southern black church leaders and educators, as well as white landowners and businessmen, sought to deter what they believed to be a virtual stampede out of the South of predominantly working-class men and women. Those deemed in their communities to be the "better class" of black and white persons deplored the outflow as endangering the region's institutional and financial life. In some areas, black and white leaders worked together to stem the migration tide through reform. For example, from its offices in Atlanta, the Commission on Interracial Cooperation conducted a program of research and education on southern problems, devoting considerable attention to agriculture, health, and education.

The Leaderless Migration

Southern community leaders of both races hoped to stifle pro-migration sentiment by arguing that adaptation to the North would be difficult for the "uncultured Negro," that work opportunities would diminish at the war's end, and that European immigrants would deluge northern cities to the social and economic detriment of blacks. If some of their arguments proved to be true, they did not deter the northward movement. Church leaders watched their congregations dwindle, and many ministers themselves, although initially in opposition, ultimately left the South—according to Emmett Scott, "following their flock" in an attempt to rebuild their churches in the North.

Educated and more affluent blacks increasingly joined the massive migration, although at no time did they serve as its guiding light. North and South, black leaders commented upon the "leaderless" quality of the movement, noting that "without a Moses," black working-class people had decided to strike out on their own in a great wave northward. Du Bois emphasized

Black migration

Blacks began to migrate out of the South by the end of Reconstruction. Early in the new century, the trickle increased, and by the outbreak of World War I, it was already a steady stream. Shown here is a black family arriving in Chicago in 1912.

that "the movement started without any head from the masses, and such movements are always significant." Adam Clayton Powell, Sr., of the Abyssinian Baptist Church in New York City, remarked on the uniqueness of "no visible leader." Without an identifiable leader, blacks nonetheless moved with a sense of collective destiny through the help of friends and family members who had preceded them, migration clubs, church-member networks, railroad workers, and other circuits of communication—all facilitating the transition to and in the new urban environment. A literal movement at the grassroots level had been set in motion, and this demographic shift would afford African Americans a national presence and influence in the industrial workforce, in music and the arts, in the electorate, in religion, and in new political movements. From these varied arenas black voices of protest arose.

Equally important, in the early twentieth century blacks from the Caribbean islands were also on the move. Most of these immigrants were impoverished peasants and workers

Migration from the Caribbean heading for destinations in mainland Central America, other islands in the Caribbean, and the United States. The collapse of the sugar economy, a series of natural disasters (floods, droughts, cyclones, and hurricanes), and colonial land policies had resulted in the displacement of agricultural workers in Jamaica, Barbados, St. Kitts, Cuba, Puerto Rico, Nevis, and other islands. Much of the former peasantry joined the ranks of the unemployed in these islands' capital cities. Although some of this labor force was absorbed by the emerging banana industry, which gained momentum in the late nineteenth century, the banana industry never reached the scale of the earlier sugar industry. Compounding the effects of hunger and abject poverty, the status of health care on the islands was abysmal—much worse than in the days of slavery when doctors had a lucrative trade attending to the slaves of wealthy planters.

More than 140,000 migrants from large and small Caribbean islands entered the United States between 1899 and 1937, with Jamaicans the largest contingent. The great part of Caribbean immigrants to the United States arrived through Ellis Island and remained in New York City.

Although Afro-Caribbeans had been coming to the United States since the early days of slavery and, in the early nineteenth century, as free people, nothing matched this voluntary migration in the early decades of the twentieth century. The migratory stream swelled between 1912 and 1924, coinciding with the internal northward migration of African Americans. The Afro-Caribbean migration reached a high point in 1924, with 10,630 persons entering the country in that year. This number fell dramatically with the passage of the Immigration Act of 1924, which restricted all foreigners from entering the United States according to national-origins quotas and race. The act reduced the Caribbean inflow by 95 percent of the 1924 inflow. The number of Caribbean immigrants plummeted during the depression years of the 1930s. In 1933 only 84 Caribbean islanders were listed in the immigration records; it was after the United States entered World War II that the number of Caribbean immigrants increased.

Most but not all Afro-Caribbean immigrants to New York between 1890 and 1924 hailed from the English-speaking islands—the British West Indies, as the islands were then

Afro-Caribbeans in New York called. An outstanding immigrant from Puerto Rico was Arthur Alfonso Schomburg, for whom the Schomburg Center for Research in Black Culture in Harlem is named. Born Arturo Alfonso Schomburg in San Juan, Puerto Rico, in 1874, he had come to New York in 1891, as part of an earlier wave of migrants. The multilingual Schomburg worked at Bankers Trust Company on Wall Street from 1906 to 1929, but during these years his role as a bibliophile and supporter of black history earned him his enduring reputation. Schomburg amassed one of the world's largest collections of books, documents, and artifacts related to people of African descent. In 1911 he helped to establish the Negro Society for Historical Research. The society boasted an international membership of blacks from the Americas, Europe, and Africa, endeavoring "to show that the Negro race has a history that antedates that of the proud Anglo-Saxon race" and "to collect useful historical data relating to the Negro race, books written by or about Negroes, rare pictures of prominent men and women . . . letters . . . African curios of native manufacture." In 1925 New York City's 135th Street Public Library purchased and housed Schomburg's collection for public access. It later grew to become the Schomburg Center.

In the first three decades of the twentieth century, Caribbean migrants to the United States, unlike those who migrated from the islands to Central America to work (for example, on the Panama Canal), were disproportionately educated and skilled. By 1930, 25 percent of the black population of Harlem was of Caribbean origin. The black-owned *The New York Amsterdam News* informed its readers that Harlem housed the world's second largest West Indian population. (Kingston, Jamaica, was the largest in the early 1930s.)

Caribbean immigrants were proportionally overrepresented in the population of successful black New Yorkers. Although they constituted only 0.8 percent of the city's overall black population in 1930, Afro-Caribbeans accounted for 14 percent of the city's business leaders and for more than 8 percent of the doctors listed in *Who's Who in Colored America* for the period from 1915 to 1932. Historian Winston James notes that Caribbean migrants were also more highly visible in radical movements—some of them had been political activists back home. This was true of the black nationalist Marcus Garvey, who before coming to the United States had led a strike at his workplace in Kingston, Jamaica.

Arthur Alfonso Schomburg
Born Arturo Alfonso Schomburg in Puerto Rico, Arthur Schomburg amassed a great collection of works on peoples of African descent and helped establish the Negro Society for Historical Research in the early decades of the 20th century in New York.

Winston James attributes the New York Caribbeans' overrepresentation in nontraditional civil rights politics to a number of factors. Afro-Caribbeans not only had a higher level of education and literacy; their greater geographic mobility and travel experiences relative to African Americans also opened them to a greater sensitivity to black diasporic oppression. At the same time, class more than race distinctions shaped social relations on majority-black Caribbean islands, and this fact led some of the educated migrants to find common cause with white Marxists and to gravitate toward interracial leftist organizations in the United States. Afro-Caribbeans, unlike African Americans, tended to exhibit weaker ties to the traditional black churches and felt little attachment to the Republican Party. Yet the war had undeniably been a consciousness-raising experience for both Afro-Caribbeans and African Americans on many similar levels, not least of which was an experience in the armed forces that translated into menial positions, humiliation, segregation, and inequalities in housing, medical care, and public accommodations.

Window in Time

Alain Locke on Harlem

Here in Manhattan is not merely the largest Negro community in the world, but the first concentration in history of so many diverse elements of Negro life. It has attracted the African, the West Indian, the Negro American; has brought together the Negro of the North and the Negro of the South; the man from the city and the man from the town and village; the peasant, the student, the business man, the professional man, artist, poet, musician, adventurer and worker, preacher and criminal, exploiter and social outcast. Each group has come with its own separate motives and for its own special ends, but their greatest experience has been the finding of one another. Proscription and prejudice have thrown these dissimilar elements into a common area of contact and interaction. Within this area, race sympathy and unity have determined a further fusing of sentiment and experience.

Source: *The Survey Graphic Harlem Issue* (March 1925).

New Negroes

The mass of the "leaderless" migrants from the American South and the Caribbean islands would soon find organizations and leaders who would challenge the civil rights vanguard, perceiving their liberal rights, integrationist goals to be the Old Guard Negro style. A. Philip Randolph and Chandler Owen emerged on the political scene during World War I, and they would continue afterward as important new black American voices of protest. Caribbean migrants, who attracted sizeable followings, included Hubert Harrison (Virgin Islands), Cyril Briggs (Jamaica), J. A. Rogers (Jamaica), Claude McKay (Jamaica), Wilfred A. Domingo (Jamaica), Richard B. Moore (Barbados), and most of all Marcus Garvey (Jamaica).

Periodically at ideological odds with each other, African Americans and Afro-Caribbeans also fractured internally along lines of political dissent—usually disagreeing over the primacy of class versus race protest. The lines that separated advocates of civil rights, of socialism, and of black nationalism were drawn but were clearly messy. The predilection of black Americans to emphasize race increasingly came to be adopted by Caribbean migrants the longer they remained in the United States. Over time, Afro-Caribbeans tended to acknowledge a far more virulent racism than they had experienced at home. In his sixth year in the United States, the poet Claude McKay succinctly conveyed this awakening of consciousness when he confessed: "It was the first time I had ever come face to face with such manifest, implacable hate of my race, and my feelings were indescribable. . . . I had heard of prejudice in America but never dreamed of it being so intensely bitter."

Race and Class Politics: Civil Rights, Black Nationalism

Caribbean-born Hubert Harrison was deeply admired by American-born A. Philip Randolph. Harrison analyzed the race question from a socialist perspective. His prewar writings appeared in the white leftist journals *The Masses*, *The Call*, and *The Liberator* and drew attention to the role of race in relation to class politics. However, Harrison, McKay, Domingo, and other Afro-Caribbean leftists grew frustrated at the failure of the white Left to address forcefully racism in white working-class ranks, as well as racism's effect in both popular and scientific discourse. Harrison resigned from the Socialist Party of America as early as 1914 and continued his prolific writing and street-corner oratory. In 1917 he founded the Liberty League and began editorship of the organization's magazine *The Voice*. On July 4 of that year Harrison called for a "New Negro" leadership, not of the Talented Tenth but of the masses of black people.

Declaring their independence from the old civil rights vanguard, Harrison in November 1917 continued to insist on the "need for a more radical policy than that of the NAACP." He was the first to attack Du Bois's "Close Ranks" article. Between 1920 and 1922, Harrison edited Marcus Garvey's *Negro World*, but he never ceased to head the Liberty League or to bring its racialized class perspective to his *Negro World* articles. In 1921 Harrison called for a Black International, likely borrowing from the Communist Third International founded in Moscow in 1919. Likewise Cyril Briggs and Richard Moore, founders of the African Blood Brotherhood in 1918, edited their decidedly leftist Afro-centric magazine *The Crusader*, which operated between 1918 and 1922. Although initially sympathetic to the Garvey movement, Briggs and the ABB completely lost patience with Garvey and in 1922 adopted a pro-Communist ideological stance and advocated working-class revolution.

Debates over integration versus separation and capitalism versus socialism raged in black-edited magazines. African American editors W. E. B. Du Bois and A. Philip Randolph parted ways over the race-class divide. Du Bois, a member of the Socialist Party of America, resigned his membership in 1911 and

Du Bois and "Close Ranks"

in 1912 penned a scathing *Crisis* editorial against the white Left for its silence on racial inequality. Du Bois, unquestionably a critic of capitalism, wrote scathing articles against colonialism and also white privilege.

For all their differences, Hubert Harrison worked cooperatively with the NAACP in 1917 in its Silent Protest Parade in response to the East St. Louis riot. The NAACP's antilynching reportage consistently won *The Crisis*'s respect; its articles on this issue were reprinted in a number of radical magazines. Du Bois wrote in sufficiently diverse voices, however, that he served as fodder for critiques from the black Left. His "Close Ranks article," which advocated that blacks put the race struggle on a backseat to their patriotic duty to their country during wartime, stirred equal ire from black leftists and black nationalists. Du Bois's earlier criticism of white socialists, when coupled with his wartime rhetoric, only widened fissures within the black political elite.

A. Philip Randolph and Chandler Owen regularly defended the white Left while criticizing the NAACP as an elitist and moderate in the pages of their magazine *The Messenger*. In an editorial supportive of the International Workers of the World (the IWW, or "Wobblies," as they were popularly known) in August 1919, they urged "the Negro labor unions to increase their radicalism, to speed up their organization, to steer clear of the Negro leaders and to thank nobody but themselves for what they have gained." In June 1919 and in response to the riots, a cartoon in *The Messenger* caricatured Du Bois as an "Old-Style Negro" in an unflattering way that called attention to his "Close Ranks" advice.

In the following month, a *Messenger* cartoon referenced the riots in Longview, Texas, in Washington, D.C., and in Chicago, in its presentation of the "New Style Negro" as one who unmistakably defends himself by shooting his attackers. *The Messenger* published a series of

Window in Time

Du Bois on "Whiteness"

The discovery of personal whiteness among the world's peoples is a very modern thing—a nineteenth- and twentieth-century matter, indeed. The ancient world would have laughed at such a distinction. The Middle Ages regarded skin color with mild curiosity; and even up into the eighteenth century we were hammering our national manikins into one, great, Universal Man, with fine frenzy which ignored color and race even more than birth. Today we have changed all that, and the world in a sudden, emotional conversion has discovered that it is white and by that token, wonderful!

Source: W. E. B. Du Bois, *Darkwater, Voices from within the Veil* (New York, 1920), pp. 29–30.

cartoons that year, some of which emphasized class struggle and the commonality of interests (wages and working conditions) between black and white workers. To Randolph and Owen, the "New Negro" identified a new militancy forged in the violent crucible of the war and the Red Summer of 1919. Their attention to internationalism was also evident in such editorial titles as "Manifesto" (March 1919) and "We Want More Bolshevik Patriotism!" (May-June 1919).

By 1923, however, the *Messenger* editors denounced as a "menace" such doctrinaire Communists as Cyril Briggs, and surprisingly Randolph began to grow more sanguine toward business as well as toward traditional labor-union organizing. Perhaps the shift was the result of the government's red-baiting of the magazine. The U.S. Attorney General A. Mitchell Palmer, who led numerous raids in the 1920s against suspected communists, described *The Messenger* as the "most able and most dangerous of all the negro publications" and worried, as he put it, that "the Negro is 'seeing red.'" The Red Scare, as well as the dawning realization that most working-class blacks shied away from socialism, persuaded Randolph to accept the offer to be "general organizer" of the newly founded Brotherhood of Sleeping Car Porters and Maids and to push for its affiliation within the American Federation of Labor.

Notwithstanding the various ideological persuasions of black activists, the leader who challenged all of them was the Jamaican Marcus Garvey. Despite the established influence **Marcus Garvey** of the NAACP, it had never functioned as a mass movement. The NAACP had succeeded in achieving legal precedents that were beneficial to all African Americans, but the organization failed to capture the imagination and secure the following of the many African Americans on the lower social and economic levels. The working poor particularly regarded integrated civil rights organizations such as the NAACP and the Commission on Interracial Cooperation as agencies of upper-class blacks and liberal whites who failed to join hands with them in their efforts to rise. At the same time, working-class blacks regarded radical leftists as extreme and utopian. Given the racism in organized labor, working-class blacks saw little to affirm the possibility of a class-based interracial coalition intent on ending racial discrimination. This fundamental cynicism in regard to race relations, regardless of its justification, made possible the rise of Marcus Garvey and his Universal Negro Improvement Association (UNIA). Garvey's movement, unlike the NAACP or the socialists, drew a truly mass following that represented a variety of religious, political, and economic convictions.

Garvey founded the organization in his native Jamaica in 1914. Two years later he came to the United States, ironically to meet Booker T. Washington and learn from his self-help doctrines. With Washington deceased, Garvey went to New York, where he founded the Universal Negro Improvement Association. At the end of the war the association grew rapidly, setting up divisions in the northern and southern states, as well as abroad.

Garvey's wide popularity rested on his appeal to race pride. The strain and stress of living in hostile urban communities created a state of mind on which Garvey capitalized. He called on African Americans, especially those of a darker skin color, to follow him. Garvey exalted everything black; he insisted that black stood for strength and beauty, not inferiority. He asserted that Africans had a noble past, and he declared that American blacks should be proud of their ancestry. In his newspaper, *The Negro World,* he told blacks that racial prejudice was so much a part of the civilization of whites that it was futile to appeal to their sense of justice and their high-sounding democratic principles.

With an eye on the growing sentiment favoring self-determination for colonized peoples, Garvey said that the only hope for African Americans was to redeem Africa from European colonialism. Only with a politically powerful and economically strong (Garvey

Marcus Garvey

Garvey, who had migrated from Jamaica to the United States before the war, had become a major critic of the treatment of blacks by American whites and of black strategies to deal with it. He soon became a leading voice for a new, separatist, back-to-Africa movement. He is shown here in his uniform as president of the Universal Negro Improvement Association.

was procapitalist) African empire, Garvey argued, would persons of African descent be respected throughout the world. On one occasion Garvey cried out: "Wake up Ethiopia! Wake up Africa! Let us work toward the one glorious end of a free, redeemed, and mighty nation. Let Africa be a bright star among the constellations of nations." On other occasions he would shout to his listeners, "Up you mighty race!" Recent scholarship and particularly historian Robert Hill's compilation of the Garvey Papers indicate the extensive formal and informal networks of Garvey's movement in the United States, England, Africa, and the Caribbean.

As a man of action, Garvey developed many facets of his movement—local divisions, officers, auxiliary organizations, economic enterprises, conferences, and a civil religion to which numerous members of the traditional black clergy adhered. In New York and other large cities, members of the UNIA paraded in elaborate uniforms as members of the UNIA's African Legion, Black Cross Nurses, African Motor Corps, and Black Eagle Flying Corps. In 1921 Garvey announced the formal organization of the Empire of Africa and appointed himself provisional president. He ruled with the assistance of one potentate and one supreme deputy potentate. Among the nobility he created were knights of the Nile, knights of the distinguished service order of Ethiopia, and dukes of the Niger and of Uganda.

Garvey and his newspaper, *The Negro World*, had a magnetic effect on the masses of blacks in cities across the nation—New York, Chicago, Detroit, Atlanta, Norfolk, and New Orleans, to name but a few with large UNIA divisions. Garvey's membership in the southern states was equal in size to that in the northern states. The work of such historians as Steven Hahn and Mary G. Rolinson attest to Garvey's broad appeal throughout the South, in urban and rural areas, from Virginia through the Deep South states of Louisiana and Mississippi, where emigration traditions dated back to the nineteenth century. Hahn notes that in the 1920s "Louisiana ranked first with 75 divisions, followed by North Carolina (61), Mississippi (56), Virginia (43), Arkansas (42), Georgia (35), Florida (30), South Carolina (25), and Alabama (14)."

It was the working-poor—the great mass of black urban unskilled laborers, and tenant and sharecrop farmers, who dreamed of one day "building their own country," as the black writer Richard Wright explained it, "of someday living within the boundaries of a culture of their own making." For such people, Marcus Garvey was the true leader of the black race. Although Garvey's claim that he had 4 million followers in 1920 and 6 million three years later can be questioned, even his severest critics admitted that his was by far the largest black movement in American history. Most African American leaders denounced him bitterly as an insincere, selfish imposter, but he countered that they were opportunists, liars, thieves, and traitors. Du Bois and Randolph, despite their differences, united in opposition to Garvey, even to the point of aiding in his arrest. Du Bois called Garvey and the UNIA "bombastic and impracticable." Garvey was equally contemptuous of Du Bois and other leaders of the NAACP. On one occasion he wrote: "The N.A.A.C.P. wants us all to become white by amalgamation, but they are not honest enough to come out with the truth. To be a Negro is no disgrace, but an honor, and we of the U.N.I.A. do not want to become white. . . . We are proud and honorable. We love our race and respect and adore our mothers."

Du Bois would later admit that Garvey's schemes conflicted with his own interest, the Pan-African Congresses. When Du Bois's third congress met in 1923, signs of decline were

Garvey's Decline clearly discernible, growing worse by the fourth one in 1927. While the Pan-African Congresses had historically appealed to and convened a select

Window in Time

Garvey Speaks in Newport News, Virginia

Africa Must Be Restored

I want you to understand that you have an association that is one of the greatest movements in the world. The New Negro, backed by the Universal Negro Improvement Association, is determined to restore Africa to the world, and you scattered children of Africa in Newport News, you children of Ethiopia, I want you to understand that the call is now made to you. What are you going to do? Are you going to remain to yourselves in Newport News and die? Or are you going to link up your strength, morally and financially, with the other Negroes of the world and let us all fight one battle unto victory? If you are prepared to do the latter, the battle is nearly won, because we of the Universal Negro Improvement Association intend within the next twelve months to roll up a sentiment in the United States of America that will be backed up by fifteen million black folks, so that when in the future you touch one Negro in Newport News you shall have touched fifteen million Negroes of the country. And within the next twenty-four months we intend to roll up an organization of nearly four hundred million people, so that when you touch any Negro in Newport News you touch four hundred million of Negroes all over the world at the same time.

Source: From an address by Garvey at a United Negro Improvement Association meeting, October 25, 1919, published in *Negro World*, 25 October 1919.

gathering of educated and elite persons, Garvey's democratized his message—directing it primarily to the black working-class. Yet, Garvey's appeal was not limited to the working-class. For example, Carter G. Woodson, founder in 1915 of the Association for the Study of Negro Life and History and known today as the "Father of Black," had been a founding member of A. Philip Randolph and Chandler Owen's organization Friends of Negro Freedom, an umbrella non-ideological group, but he soon left the FNF because of its strong anti-Garvey stance. Woodson refused to support the "Garvey Must Go" efforts in 1922–1923. Doubtless, the base of the Garvey movement was the working-class. He gave them a newfound sense of power as members of a worldwide population of African people—New Negroes—united and organized through the UNIA.

Garvey's highly publicized meeting and "pact" with a representative of the Ku Klux Klan—both men were committed to racial separatism and denounced miscegenation, or race-mixing—made him persona non grata among such former supporters as Hubert Harrison and Cyril Briggs. The exposé of Garvey's amicable conversation with the Klan's Grand Wizard in 1922 drew the ire of those who would afterward call him a "Black Kluxer." *The Messenger's* Randolph and Owen, never sympathetic to Garvey, called him the "black imperial wizard." Garvey's approaches to the KKK hurt his cause, but what finally put an end to Garvey's meteoric rise was the promise of a steamship line. According to his wife, he had collected $10 million between 1919 and 1921. More than $1 million, it was alleged, had been spent in purchasing and equipping ships for the Black Star Line, but no real shipping line existed.

In 1923 Garvey was put on trial before a federal judge on the charge of using the mails to defraud in raising money for his steamship line. He was found guilty, and two years later he entered the Atlanta penitentiary to serve a five-year term. Garvey continued to lead his movement from his cell in Atlanta. In one letter to his followers he said: "My months of forcible removal from among you, being imprisoned as a punishment for advocating the cause of our real emancipation, have not left me hopeless or despondent; but to the contrary, I see a great ray of light and the bursting of a mighty political cloud which will bring you complete freedom. . . ."

Garvey remained in prison until President Coolidge pardoned him in 1927 and ordered his deportation as an undesirable alien. Garvey died in London in 1940. Regardless of how dissatisfied African Americans were with conditions in the United States, they were ultimately unwilling in the 1920s, as their forebears had been a century earlier, either to settle in Africa or to undertake the uncertain task of redeeming Africa. Garvey's movement indicated, however, the extent to which they entertained doubts concerning the hope for first-class citizenship in the only homeland they knew.

The idea of living in racial harmony in the United States found a diverse following—some of whom looked to religion rather than to civil rights or socialism. The followers of **Father Divine** George Baker, more commonly called Father Divine, formed part of a movement that began in 1919 with a small group in Sayville, New York. Father Divine built up a large following within the next two decades that amused some observers and perplexed others. The movement became interracial as early as 1926, and within a few years had attracted a considerable number of white followers, some of them wealthy. That such a movement flourished during the period is a testimonial to the extent of the social ills from which the body politic suffered and was one more indication of the tremendous frustration that characterized many blacks and some whites as well. Father Divine's followers had deserted their churches, believing as true his portrayal of himself as God.

More than a religious cult, Father Divine's movement addressed his followers' social and economic needs as well. By 1930 he was holding open house and feeding thousands in places that came to be known as heavens. When people wondered where he secured the money for the elaborate feasts, he merely answered in an almost unintelligible torrent of words, "I have harnessed your consciousness as Franklin did electricity and it is for you to use your emotions as Edison handled the electricity uncovered by Franklin." His following grew enormously in the 1930s, and heavens or peace missions were founded in many eastern cities as well as in some midwestern communities.

New Women

African American women played important roles in the various organizations of black protest. Since the late nineteenth century, black church women and club women had advocated a woman-centered racial politics. Fannie Barrier Williams wrote about black women's activism in the anthology *New Negro for a New Century* (1902), which she co-edited with Booker T. Washington. Even more explicitly in her essay "Club Movement among Colored Women," in H. Crogman's *Progress of a Race* (1902), Williams wrote, "The Negro woman's club of today represents the New Negro with new powers of self-help." The New Negro leaders to which she referred were such women as Ida B. Wells-Barnett, Mary Church Terrell, Mary B. Talbert, and Maria Baldwin—all leaders in forming the National Association of Colored Women, but also counted among the "Founding Forty" members of the NAACP. The assistance of organized black women facilitated the growth of NAACP branches and contributed mightily to the NAACP's antilynching campaign.

Even before the founding of the NAACP, organized black womanhood had stood boldly in the forefront of the antilynching crusade, underwriting Ida B. Wells's crusade in the 1890s and continuing their protest into the twentieth century. The Northeastern Federation of Women's Clubs (part of the NACW) worked jointly together with the NAACP in rallies against lynch law. It was not uncommon to find black clubwomen as active members and organizers in the NAACP. For example, Addie Hunton, who served black troops in France during World War I, was actively involved in the NACW, the women's Brooklyn Suffrage League, the NAACP, and the YWCA. Multiple affiliations were true of the majority of the NACW leaders.

Involved in the larger African American protest movement, black women did not look blindly at racism in the larger woman's movement with which they also identified. If black men, more than black women, pondered the racial inclusiveness **Black Feminism** of socialism, black women pondered the racial inclusiveness of feminism. For most black women, a truly interracial feminism, like interracial socialism, languished to die on the cross of racism. It was certainly not because black women lacked sufficient gender consciousness or failed to demand as vociferously women's rights and particularly women's right to vote. In the first two decades of the twentieth century, their feminist consciousness could be heard in the black newspapers, in the proceedings of numerous secular and religious black women's organizations, and in the NAACP's *The Crisis*, which published two "Votes for Women" issues—in September 1912 and in August 1915, in which leading black clubwomen—Adella Hunt Logan, Alice Dunbar Nelson, Mary Church Terrell, Mary B. Talbert, and others—voiced their own defense of women's right to the ballot. W. E. B. Du Bois, a supporter of women's suffrage, applauded the women's articles, describing them as "one of the strongest cumulative attacks on sex and race discrimination in politics ever written."

Black women's enthusiasm to be an integral and equal part of the larger women's rights movement proved problematic, however. In the early twentieth century, black women understood, often painfully, that their own ardent suffragism and demand for women's rights was inseparably linked to the fundamental challenge to black disenfranchisement and segregation. Black women worked better, although with varying degrees of success, with white women's clubs at the local level than they did with the racially stifling politics of the national women's rights organizations.

To ensure southern congressional endorsement of a suffrage amendment, the National American Woman Suffrage Association (NAWSA) and the National Woman's Party had both capitulated to southern racism. The NAWSA requested that the highly respected black suffragists Elizabeth Carter and Mary Church Terrell suspend their application for membership and wait to apply after the ratification of the Nineteenth Amendment. Not wanting to jeopardize the success of the Susan B. Anthony Amendment, white suffragists followed the more expedient course of "separate but equal" feminism. Some suffragists went so far as to emphasize that the addition of white women to the southern electorate would help

Black suffragists Josephine Ruffin, Anna Julia Cooper, Mary Church Terrell, and Nannie Burroughs
Four leading black women who worked for a women's suffrage amendment.

to preserve white supremacy. Such arguments obviously precluded any support of black women's suffrage rights.

However, some African American women in the North voted before 1920. Ida B. Wells mobilized black women voters in Chicago, soon after the state of Illinois granted the right to vote to women in 1913, founding the Alpha Suffrage Club. With its membership of African-American women, the club played a decisive role in black voter turnout in the Chicago election year of 1915. The black vote helped to seal the mayoral victory for William Hale "Big Bill" Thompson, who was considered a friend of blacks. More important, Wells credited her organization for the victory that year of the city's first black alderman—Republican Oscar DePriest.

Black Women Voters

With the ratification of the Nineteenth Amendment in 1920, black women in the southern states took registrars by surprise as they sought to fulfill their recently won right. They would soon realize that they, like black men, were unwelcome at the polls. Black women were routinely humiliated at voting booths and disqualified on technicalities. Discontented black feminists, as Rosalind Terborg-Penn calls them, turned to a number of organizations— the Garvey movement, religious movements, and the International Association of Women of the Darker Races. However, black women leaders, particularly those in the urban North, also sought to garner the women's vote at the time of their people's great migration.

They recognized the potential power of their votes in augmenting the black electorate and attaining black political clout in such destination-cities as Chicago, Detroit, Cleveland, New York, and Philadelphia. The black press called attention to both men's and women's political activities. In 1924, the Republican National Committee enlisted outgoing NACW president Hallie Q. Brown to lead a voter drive among black women. Brown used the NACW organ *National Notes* to campaign for the Republican Party, and the larger network of clubs throughout the various states helped to mobilize black voters.

State organizers in Rhode Island and upstate New York reported meetings in churches, fraternal lodges, schools, homes, and on the streets. West Virginia's black women's clubs appealed to churches as well as to individual women; Minnesota's clubs distributed informational pamphlets about registration and voting; Chicago women discussed women's issues in their house-to house canvassing. After the adjournment of the NACW annual convention in August 1924, some of the attendees reconvened to form the National League of Republican Colored Women, and by 1926 the NACW had relinquished its political work to the new black Republican women's group. The black women who championed the role of electoral politics as a vehicle for racial amelioration represented many of the same women who worked as members and supporters of the NAACP. Daisy Lampkin, a member of both the NACW and the NLRCW, was chosen by the Republican National Committee to direct the mobilization of black women voters in the eastern states in 1928. She had joined the staff of the NAACP in the previous year, and in the 1930s Lampkin would be appointed the national field-secretary of the NAACP.

In some states, black women worked in separate units of the predominantly white League of Women Voters, because the constituent state organizations of the LWV were segregated into black and white units. But black people's political involvement was growing, despite its seeming small gains in the 1920s. Indeed blacks were often insulted by the very politicians for whom they cast their votes. One black woman, Nannie Helen Burroughs, a religious leader, NACW member, and president of the National League of Republican Colored Women, registered her subtle

Growing Political Involvement

The Awakening of Ethiopa, Meta Warrick Fuller, c. 1921
This bronze sculpture captures the greatness of African women in world civilization.

protest sheer by her presence at the meeting of the Women's Division of the Republican National Committee in 1925. Burroughs was one of eighty-five women from thirty-three states. She was also the only African American among the women delegates invited to the White House in 1927. In her brief remarks of introduction, her protest was a bit more explicit when she asserted: "No political party in America is 100 percent American without this touch of color."

Working within the electoral system, black women sought to make their voices heard at election time. Perhaps more moderate black women, like black men who migrated from the South and voted for the first time in northern cities, considered their hard-won right of suffrage an instrument of protest. Black women took the ballot seriously—mobilizing their people and casting their votes in affirmation of those who supported black interests and causes, while campaigning against those who did not. The slogan of the National League of Republican Colored Women said forcefully what millions of southern black men and women continued to be unable to say: "We are in politics to stay and we shall be a stay in politics."

Historian Deborah Gray White has noted that the shifting racial politics of the immediate postwar era and throughout the 1920s had a profound effect on the middle-class National Association for Colored Women. As a vibrant and competing array of ideas and organizations emerged, the power of the NACW's public voice began to diminish, along with its presumptive claim to speak for all black women. Its genteel feminism was barely audible beside the New Negro's virile protest. In the post-suffrage years, the New Negro, despite the diverse, even opposing interpretations of the concept, was, generally speaking, identified as masculine—the returning soldier, the militant worker, the proponent of self-defense, the defender of black womanhood and black nation, and the artist as racial arbiter. *The Messenger's* version of the New Woman in 1923 emphasized her exalted position as man's helpmate, announcing: "Like her white sister she is the product of profound and vital changes in our economic mechanism . . . the New Negro Man has affected a revolutionary orientation. . . . Upon her shoulder rests the big task to create and keep alive, in the breast of black men, a holy and consuming passion to break with the slave traditions of the past . . . the insidious inferiority complex of the present which . . . bobs up . . . to arrest the progress of the New Manhood movement."

Likewise, Marcus Garvey proudly flaunted the image of the black man as the protector of black womanhood. "Let us go back to the days of true manhood when women truly reverenced us" an article in *The Negro World* waxed nostalgically, continuing, "we would have many more mothers, many more virtuous wives, many more amiable and lovable daughters." Garvey's gender perspective was premised on the idea of black women's purity and the manly defense of it. Indeed, Garvey discussed the redemption of Africa in the same gender-laden rhetoric.

The conflated imagery of Africa and black womanhood was not unique to Garvey. It appears in the artwork of Meta Fuller (1877–1968), who actually credited Du Bois's influence (she had met him in 1900 in Paris at the Universal Exposition) for instilling in her the interest in black images. Fuller was among the growing number of women in the late nineteenth century to receive formal arts training, first in Philadelphia and later abroad, where she reportedly was encouraged to pursue her sculpting career by (among others) the famous French sculptor Auguste Rodin. Upon her marriage to African-American psychiatrist

Solomon Carter Fuller, Jr., in 1909, she settled in the Boston area, where she continued her artistic career. Meta Fuller's life-sized bronze sculpture *Ethiopia Awakening* was unveiled in 1922. The face is alert and dynamic in contrast to prevalent artistic renderings of Africa as a "sleeping continent." Fuller's understanding of Africa was shaped by the rising pan-Africanist consciousness. Indeed, "Ethiopia" as synonymous with Africa had occupied a significant place in the African American popular imagination. Fuller had read J. E. Casely Hayford's novel *Ethiopia Unbound* (1911) and Freeman Murray's *Emancipation and the Freed in American Sculpture* (1916). Such works conveyed notions of African greatness associated with ancient Ethiopian and Egyptian kingdoms. Ethiopia, too, had become a powerful symbol of contemporary resistance, since it was the only African nation to thwart European colonial advances, defeating the Italian army in 1896.

If the genie was out of the bottle, neither the New Negro nor the New Woman movements appeared to give due credence to the New Negro Woman. Black women had never been merely silent partners. Important roles in the UNIA were played by Henrietta Vinton Davis, by Garvey's first wife Amy Ashwood Garvey and his second wife Amy Jacques Garvey, and by a number of other women. In a meeting in 1922, women in the Garvey movement expressed their desire for more numerous and prominent positions. Garvey dismissed the idea. After his arrest and imprisonment, UNIA women became considerably more vocal about women's rights. Jacques Garvey published the column "Our Women and What They Think" in *The Negro World* between 1924 and 1928. In her 1926 pamphlet "Black Women's Resolve," she affirmed: "If the United States and Congress can open their doors to white women, we serve notice on our men that Negro women will demand equal opportunity to fill any position in the United Negro Improvement Association or anywhere else without discrimination because of sex. We are very sorry if it hurts your old fashioned tyrannical feelings, and we not only make the demand but we intend to enforce it."

Times were changing, as was the New Negro. According to literary scholar Henry Louis Gates, Jr., the New Negro was merely a metaphor. "The paradox of this claim is inherent in the trope [New Negro] . . . combining as it does a concern with time, antecedents, and heritage, on the one hand," Gates argues, "with a concern for a cleared space, the public face of the race, on the other." Was the New Negro simply a metaphor for change itself? By the mid-1920s, an artistic movement was underway that would lead once again to the reconceptualization of the New Negro. Black artists especially—musicians, writers, visual artists—began to claim the attention of an ever-increasing number of readers, listeners, and observers of all races and in many parts of the world. This newly minted "New Negro"—the African American artist—had something significant to say about life in this country, something to express in myriad artistic forms. The flowering of the arts in the 1920s developed from an earlier generation's legacy of expression, and from that legacy artists marched forward with talent and creativity to make a powerful, relevant statement that would greatly influence succeeding generations.

16 The Arts at Home and Abroad

Recorded Music and Radio

Jazz Roots and Routes

Motion Pictures

Black Theater

The Harlem Renaissance

French Connections

Visual Artists

Clashing Artistic Values

Lois Mailou Jones,
***Les Fétiches*, 1938**
This largely abstract painting incorporates a motif of African masks.

The 1920s witnessed an unprecedented spread of black artistic expression. This cultural diffusion was made possible by the fortuitous confluence of electronic innovation (the radio and phonograph), corporate publishing, and mass advertising and distribution networks that targeted newly identified intraracial and interracial consumer markets.

In the 1920s corporate America acknowledged and began systematically to cater to the black consumer. The popularity and profitability of black creativity did not escape the attention of the white-dominated entertainment industry, wealthy white art patrons, and publishers and literary agents. The renaissance of black musicians, writers, filmmakers, painters, and sculptors captivated black as well as white audiences with its vibrant, colorful appeal. As black cultural production flourished in the United States and abroad, some artists deemed themselves "New Negroes" with little need to "prove" their talents to whites or justify their very presence in the artistic arena. It was precisely in the arts, argued the New Negroes in Harlem, that the possibility existed for blacks to participate as equals to whites.

For the artistic New Negro, the Roaring Twenties proved to be an exciting time. The Jazz Age was also the maturing decade of American modernism—a cultural movement that spanned the years 1910–1950, during which the arts shifted away from realism and tradition and toward the abstract, the nonlinear, and the experimental. Modernist works often integrated and appropriated African art forms, which whites perceived as conveying a more uninhibited, free, and dynamic expression. White writers and artists themselves grew increasingly interested in a non-Western aesthetic—especially with African and African American subject matter, whose "exoticism" and sensuality conformed to racially charged notions of "the primitive" and constituted a crucial part of modernism's desire to extricate artistic creativity from what were condemned as stifling old Victorian conventions. For their own purposes, black artists, too, adopted the "primitive," manipulating it in word, dance, jazz, and the visual arts.

In this fluid and innovative cultural world, African American artists thought they saw an unprecedented opportunity to reshape the black image in the larger public mind, and they sought to win respect for themselves and for blacks as a group through their contributions in the cultural realm. Some even outlined an agenda for artists in the struggle for racial equality. But not all blacks engaged in the arts considered their role to be crusaders for racial justice; instead they sought merely to express their creative talents in an unfettered way. They produced poems, novels, films, and songs merely for the sake of art or for escape into an inner world without racial distinctions. Nor did all blacks agree on the reach of artistic license. The more traditional thinkers frowned on efforts to capture the full measure of the black experience, particularly the undignified realities. Black artists and their followers debated publicly the nature and the role of the arts in the struggle for racial equality. Ultimately, the works and the lives of black artists reflected the search for answers to two profoundly important questions: Is a black artist's highest responsibility to the work of art or to the progress of black people? And can the two be reconciled?

Recorded Music and Radio

In August 1920, black vaudeville singer Mamie Smith sparked a momentous trend in American culture when she recorded black songwriter Perry Bradford's "Crazy Blues" on the Okeh Records label. It is to Bradford's credit that Smith became the first black woman to release a blues record for a major company. White companies had not looked to black women for talent, judging their voices and diction unsuitable. Cognizant of the ever-swelling but still untapped urban black consumer market, Bradford insisted that "14 million Negroes in our great country . . . will buy records if recorded by one of their own." His message eventually persuaded Okeh executive Fred Hager to take the risk, and his corporate gamble paid off handsomely. In the first month of its release, Mamie Smith's "Crazy Blues" sold 75,000 copies in Harlem alone. Within seven months, the record reached phenomenal sales in black communities all over the nation—facilitated by entrepreneurial black Pullman porters who bought copies of the record in northern cities for a dollar each and resold them at higher prices as the train headed south.

Smith's instant popularity opened the doors of the major recording studios for other black women—most notably Gertrude "Ma" Rainey, Bessie Smith, Alberta Hunter, Trixie Smith, Victoria Spivey, Clara Smith, Ida Cox, Sippie Wallace, Alberta Hunter, **Classic Blues** and Ethel Waters in her early years. This cohort of black women singers, who toured the vaudeville circuit (called the "chitlin" circuit), are best known for launching what music scholars term the "classic blues"—a female style of sassy, urban-sounding blues songs. The classic blues women were backed by instrumentalists and recorded for what white executives called the "race records" market.

Within three years of Mamie Smith's record debut, the blues had become a smashing success. Bessie Smith (no relation to Mamie) was the most popular of the classic blues singers during the 1920s. Her debut release in 1923, "Down Hearted Blues," reputedly sold more than 750,000 records within a year. In Chicago's black neighborhoods, lines of eager consumers waited outside record stores to buy her latest releases. Far from the urban North—in West Virginia coal-mining towns to New Orleans—passersby heard the voices of classic blues singers from open home windows. Gospel singer Mahalia Jackson noted the pervasive presence of blues records during her childhood in New Orleans: "Everybody was buying phonographs . . . and everybody had records of all the Negro blues singers—Bessie Smith . . . Ma Rainey . . . Mamie Smith . . . all the rest. . . . You couldn't help but hear blues—all through the thin partitions of the houses—through the open windows—up and down the street in the colored neighborhoods—everybody played it real loud."

Sales of the classic blues records generated tremendous competition for the "race records" market. Five years after the debut of Mamie Smith, Paramount Records heeded a suggestion to record a Texas bluesman named Blind Lemon Jefferson, who was brought to the label's Chicago studios in 1925. Jefferson's was the first solo recording by a male blues singer, and the tremendous success of his first recordings in 1926 resulted in a new genre—male-dominated country blues. Unlike the "classic blues" artists, the rural bluesmen played their own instruments, usually the guitar and harmonica. The country blues reaped huge profits for white companies—Okeh, Columbia, Gennett, Paramount, and Victor Records—all of which searched breathlessly for new talent on the street corners and in the juke joints of the Deep South.

Race records of rural bluesmen in the 1920s included those of Blind Blake from Jacksonville, Florida, and Charley Patton and Son House from Mississippi. In the 1930s the songs of Mississippi bluesman Robert Johnson would be added to the record list. For the sake of cultural "authenticity," the recording engineers permitted the rural bluesmen full control over the presentation of their distinctive regional sound and musical repertoire.

In the 1920s the black consumer became a significant economic factor in the production and marketing of black culture. Presuming to cater to the race market, however, begged the

Bessie Smith, blues singer
A protégé of Gertrude "Ma" Rainey, Smith sang, danced, and played comic sketches. As a successful recording artist, she sold as many as 100,000 copies in one week many times.

questions of how to define and market to black cultural tastes and of who was to do the defining and the marketing. As black entrepreneurs sought to capture this market's burgeoning profits, they quickly realized how difficult it would be to retain black control. This was certainly true of the music business. In **Black Swan Records** 1920 black publisher and businessman Harry Pace decided to create Black Swan Records as a company for the production of a broad range of black musical forms—spirituals, opera, and other classical music, in addition to blues and ragtime. Pace envisioned Black Swan as not merely a business but also a vehicle for racial advancement. Through its range of musical offerings, Pace argued, Black Swan refuted minstrelsy and other racist images of black culture, and through its business model it brought capital and middle-class respectability to the black community. Historian David Suisman observes that Pace's goals complemented the cultural agenda of those writers and literary critics of the Harlem Renaissance, who similarly sought to utilize the arts in the struggle for racial equality and justice.

Pace's civil rights interests probably began while he was a student at Atlanta University, from which he graduated in 1903. W. E. B. Du Bois was on the faculty of the university at this time. In 1905 Du Bois invited Pace to be the business manager of the Niagara Movement organ, *Moon Illustrated Weekly.* After the founding of the NAACP, Pace became president of the Atlanta chapter and personally hired young Walter White, who would later lead the national organization. It was Du Bois, according to David Suisman, who suggested the name of Pace's recording company, which recalled the nineteenth-century black concert singer Elizabeth Taylor Greenfield, known during her career as the "Black Swan."

Economic considerations ultimately dictated Black Swan's repertoire of mostly popular music, rather than concert and opera. It was not that Pace was averse to the blues. Before coming to New York and establishing Black Swan records, he had collaborated with W. C. Handy, known as the Father of the Blues. A business partnership with Handy, the Pace and Handy Music Company, brought Pace to New York to establish a business in sheet music. At all times, however, racial respectability and middle-class values were important to him. The blues vocalist Ethel Waters, whose first recordings were made for Black Swan in 1921, noted in her autobiography Pace's concerns in this regard. When she was first hired, as Waters recalled, she had lengthy discussions with Pace and pianist Fletcher Henderson (the business manager at Black Swan) as to "whether I should sing popular or 'cultural' numbers." Waters's recordings, such as "Down Home Blues" and "Oh Daddy," clearly positioned her within the emergent classic blues tradition, but Black Swan went out of its way to distance her art from what Pace considered the undignified marketing of such blueswomen as Bessie Smith. Black Swan refused Bessie Smith a record contract, although Columbia Records signed her soon afterward. Advertising in the *The Chicago Defender,* Black Swan boasted that Waters "changed the style of Blues singing overnight and brought a finer interpretation of this work. She dignified the blues."

To ensure maximum distribution of his product, Harry Pace sold Black Swan records in drugstores, furniture dealers, newsstands, barber shops, pool halls, and even speakeasies—any place that might conduct business with a heavily African American clientele. The label also sold records by mail order, and Pace attempted to diversify his product line by introducing Black Swan record-playing machines, marketing models emblematic of black racial pride. The Dunbar (Paul Laurence Dunbar) model of a Swanola phonograph and a L'Ouverture (Toussaint L'Ouverture) model were advertised in the NAACP's *The Crisis,* edited by Du Bois. Feeling the pinch of powerful white competitors, Black Swan Records advertised in *The Crisis* in December 1922 that "passing for Colored has become popular since we established Black Swan Records as the only genuine Colored Records, sung by Colored Artists and made by a Colored Company."

Ultimately Black Swan Records was defeated by the larger white industry's decision to exploit the black consumer audience. The massive sales of Mamie Smith's "Crazy Blues" had cast the die. The very musicians deemed too earthy and "rough" for Black Swan's own catalog were signed on and recorded on the white record labels: Bessie Smith on Columbia, Jelly Roll Morton on Gennett, King Oliver's Creole Jazz Band on both Gennett and Okeh. A host of new labels rivaled Black Swan for the profitable jazz and blues market, forcing Pace to urge the black community to stay true to racial self-help by patronizing Black Swan—the only "genuine" black business. But the rival record companies, plus the radio, put Black Swan out of business after only two years in operation.

The radio industry, having been effectively inaugurated during the 1920 Cox-Harding presidential election, introduced black talent over the national airwaves in a way that eroded the kind of cultural and social isolation defining the rural southern black world. The radio, particularly national broadcast networks, reached across time zones and regions, providing the highway on **National and Live Broadcast Radio** which black musicians traveled into homes across America. Throughout the 1920s, radio was a significant factor in the dissemination of black music—blues, jazz, gospel, and other forms. Black musicians could be heard on many local stations and, to a lesser extent, network broadcasts as they performed live in studios, or live for white audiences in nightclubs, hotels, and dance halls.

Telephone and telegram requests from fans flooded into the WMC station in Memphis when it aired Bessie Smith live from the city's Palace Theater on October 6, 1923, singing "Tain't Nobody's Bizness if I Do," "Beale Street Blues," and "Outside of That He's All Right With Me." Music historian William Randle, Jr., has identified eight hundred broadcasts of black musicians between 1921and 1930 in cities across the nation. The greatest opportunities for black radio listeners were in urban centers with large concentrations of black musical talent, including Los Angeles, New Orleans, Memphis, Dallas, Atlanta, Detroit, and (most prominently) Chicago and New York. Based on the existing documentation, Randle reveals a diversity of programming—performances of dance bands, opera, blues, and religious music. In the 1920s, at a time when African American music, particularly jazz and dance band music, were emerging as the nation's most popular musical trends, white listeners who might never have purchased recordings by blacks or attended a black music concert now had the luxury of hearing this music over the airwaves for free and through a medium in which the performer's racial identity was effectively masked. In a similar vein, African Americans, excluded from the upscale white entertainment venues, could nevertheless enjoy the music via radio.

In Chicago, several local stations carried blacks in performance in white establishments. Station WBBM, a significant source of live jazz broadcasting throughout the decade, presented Jimmy Wade's Moulin Rouge Orchestra as part of its broadcasting premier ceremony. Earl "Fatha" Hines and his orchestra broadcast from Hines's long-term base at the Grand Terrace Hotel, on station WEDC. Legendary black clarinetist Jimmie Noone, who was an important influence on the young white Chicagoan Benny Goodman, broadcast live from the Plantation Lounge on Chicago's WWAE. Blues masters Pine Top Smith and Albert Ammons (father of tenor saxophonist Gene Ammons) were also featured in live performances on Chicago radio stations. These local radio stations did not limit black performance fare to the popular secular music of the 1920s. As early as 1923 the Mundy Choristers, eighty voices strong and the best-known black choir in Chicago, were featured on special Sunday broadcasts with other black religious groups over station KYW. Recordings of black religious music, especially the gospel blues made famous by once-secular blues composer Thomas Dorsey, found fast-growing consumer and radio appeal initially in Chicago and soon the entire nation.

New York stations aired black musicians regularly. Noble Sissle and Eubie Blake were guests on at least three radio stations during 1923 and 1924 (WJZ, WHN, and WEAF), performing music from their Broadway hit *Shuffle Along*. Clarence Williams, an early jazz-recording figure, accompanied black singers live on station WJZ as early as 1922, and he also performed live in 1924 with his wife Eva Taylor, both of whom made memorable recordings during 1924 and 1925 in Clarence Williams's Blue Five, featuring jazz greats Louis Armstrong and Sidney Bechet. On April 8, 1925, a recital by the young singer Paul Robeson was carried live on local radio.

Duke Ellington in top hat

A famous photo showing an elegant Duke Ellington in top hat and tails.

The big band broadcast tradition was tremendously popular in New York in the 1920s and remained so through the heady radio days of the Swing Era of the 1930s and 1940s. Black performances could be heard over the airways direct from white cabarets, nightclubs, and theaters. Fletcher Henderson's Orchestra broadcast live from the Club Alabam at least forty-seven times during 1924; it also broadcast live between 1924 and 1928 from the fashionable, whites-only Roseland Ballroom. Beginning in 1927, Chick Webb's Orchestra was broadcasting regularly from the Savoy Ballroom, from which emanated as many as eight broadcasts per week through 1930.

Certainly the greatest beneficiary of radio's live music policy in the 1920s, and the decade's most frequently broadcast black musician, was Duke Ellington. Edward Kennedy "Duke" Ellington (April 29, 1899–May 24, 1974) was renowned for his numerous jazz compositions. His career spanned over half a century, ultimately meriting him the Presidential Medal of Freedom in 1969 and France's Legion of Honor in 1973. Born and raised in Washington, D.C., Ellington began to play the piano in earnest after his high-school years—at which time he formed a band and eventually moved to New York. He became a national celebrity after his orchestra was heard via radio more than two hundred times between 1927 and 1931. Ellington's initial broadcasts were heard on the New York local station WHN, but his performances were soon picked up weekly and given a national audience by the CBS radio network.

Direct from Harlem's Cotton Club with its whites-only clientele, listeners of all races in America heard Ellington's "jungle music," described by musicologists as such because of its timbral twists, "primal" syncopations, and growling sounds from the horn section. Ellington's early music drew on an imagined exotic "primitive" notion of African Americans similar to that portrayed by black writers and visual artists in Harlem in the 1920s. The titles of Ellington's pieces during this period carried unmistakable racial meaning—"Black Beauty," "Black and Tan Fantasy," "East St. Louis Toodle-Oo," "The Mooche," and "Creole Love Call."

The Cotton Club in Harlem

The nightspot that best invokes glittering images of Harlem in the 1920s and 1930s is the Cotton Club. White, well-heeled patrons swung by the Cotton Club to see and hear African American entertainers like Louis Armstrong and Bill "Bojangles" Robinson.

Jazz Roots and Routes

The decade of the "Roaring Twenties" is also called the "Jazz Age" in recognition of the preeminence of jazz as America's most popular music. Its rhythmic buoyancy, improvisational content, and presumed unrestrained style appeared to define the very spirit of the times. Yet jazz was an extremely controversial art form in the 1920s—not without harsh critics among whites and blacks alike. Many middle-class blacks believed it to be a hindrance to racial progress, since jazz artists often presented it as a referent for sexuality, primal passions, and exotic "primitivism."

In the early 1920s some observers had already begun to use the term *Jazz Age* in tribute to the numerous African American musicians whose compositions and performances made jazz so popular among Americans of all classes and races. Perhaps no one gave more substance and depth to the meaning of the *Jazz Age* than did Ferdinand "Jelly Roll" Morton, composer, pianist, and raconteur. By World War I, Morton had composed a number of works that won for him recognition as the first jazz composer.

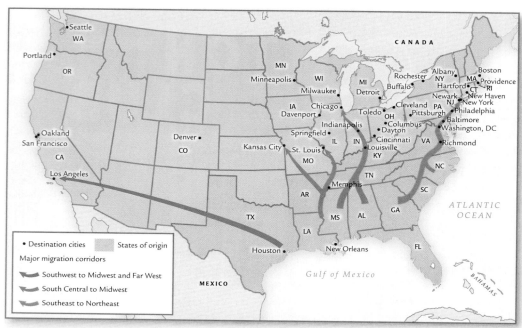

The Great Blues Migration

In the two Great Migrations, millions of African Americans left the South for cities in the North and on the West Coast, spreading several styles of Blues music across the country.
Map by Michael Siegel, Rutgers Cartography, In Motion: The African American Migration Experience, *Schomburg Center Online Exhibition*

Jazz evolved from clearly demarcated regional differences in black music—shaped by the migration routes of southern musicians and their blues tradition, as well as by the rise of

The Evolution of Jazz: New Orleans to Chicago

the northern record industry that encouraged jazz bands and black singers after Mamie Smith's success in 1920. Many early jazz greats (including Louis Armstrong, Fletcher Henderson, and James P. Johnson) began their careers, and later supplemented their income, by playing behind the classic blues singers in live performance and on records. Black migration routes figured significantly, since the development of jazz in the early 1920s reflects African American migration trends, specifically the northward migration route from Louisiana, Alabama, and Mississippi to the Midwest. It is no coincidence that the emergence of jazz in Chicago was transformed by the classic blues-based, improvisational music of New Orleans—the city identified as the birthplace of jazz.

More important, New Orleans' best musicians migrated to Chicago, where musical opportunities appeared as plentiful as the industrial opportunities that lured the many thousand others during the Great Migration. By 1918 a number of New Orleans musicians had become established in Chicago, and they in turn sought to bring other musicians out of the South to form new bands in Chicago's heavily black South Side. Indeed, Chicago's fast-growing black population assured a consumer base for the city's music industry, while black musicians promised excellent entertainment for nightclubs that catered to white patrons.

The New Orleans influence could be seen in the major jazz recordings by Chicago-based bands in the 1920s. The bands comprised five to seven musicians. The most important of the early New Orleans-to-Chicago bands was the acclaimed King Oliver's Creole Jazz Band, which recorded for several white companies—Gennett, Columbia, and Okeh Records. Joseph "King" Oliver, a virtuoso cornetist in New Orleans, had been Morton's contemporary. Oliver's Chicago band represented the New Orleans ensemble style—typically small, combo jazz featuring solo improvisations. In the Oliver band, the roles of trumpet(s), trombone, and clarinet were strictly defined, in terms set in turn-of-the-century New Orleans. Moreover, Oliver's Creole Jazz Band was assembled between 1918 and 1922 and composed almost entirely of New Orleans-to-Chicago migrants—Oliver (trumpet), Johnny Dodds (clarinet), Baby Dodds (drums), Bill Johnson (bass and guitar), and Honore Dutrey (trombone); only pianist Lillian Hardin did not come from New Orleans. Only one New Orleanian subsequently joined the band, when within months of his opening at the Lincoln Gardens Oliver decided to add to the group a second cornet—a young man named Louis Armstrong, whom Oliver had known as a child. Armstrong arrived by train in August 1922. Armstrong's migration out of the South had a transformative effect on the development of jazz in the early 1920s.

New York had its own small band tradition, as evidenced in the "Stride" piano style, a pioneering and influential jazz form that evolved from ragtime. The solo piano "cutting contests" and the masters of this musical style—James P. Johnson (considered the father of Stride), Thomas "Fats" Waller, Willie **Jazz in New York: Ragtime to Stride** "The Lion" Smith, and Lucky Roberts—were heard in Harlem clubs, rent parties, vaudeville, musical theater, and on records. However, unlike Chicago, it was the big-band tradition that represented the more prominent New York jazz scene in the early 1920s. New York jazz grew out of an earlier music form, typified not so much by the blues but by the large band music of James Reese Europe, which began around 1910 (and thus prior to his illustrious role with the 369th Infantry during World War I).

If New York did not have a blues tradition to speak of, it did indeed have its own jazz tradition. According to musicologist R. Reid Badger, "between 1908 and 1919 certain subtle modifications of popular ragtime-based rhythms and tonality along with an increasing acceptance of extemporization, gained such wide-spread recognition that by 1919 it was common in the United States and Europe to speak of the existence of a new music—jazz."

Bandleader James Reese Europe was a key figure in this evolution through his role in New York's black musical theater in the first decade of the twentieth century and his prewar leadership of the Clef Club. Orga- **The James Reese Europe Orchestra** nized in 1910, the Clef Club was a fraternal and professional organization of black musicians and composers, organized with the aim of bettering their working conditions, income, and opportunities. It also functioned as a booking agency for its members. The Clef Club addressed the same kind of issues for blacks that the segregated New York American Federation of Musicians addressed for whites. Europe's stated ambition was to create "an orchestra of Negroes which will be able to take its place among the serious musical organizations of the country." The Clef Club held major concerts each spring and fall, featuring its Clef Club Symphony Orchestra. The most historic of those concerts were the performances—firsts for black orchestras—at Carnegie Hall between 1912 and 1914.

Because of James Reese Europe's connection to dance idols Vernon and Irene Castle (Europe was their musical director and the conductor of their accompanying orchestra), Victor Records offered him a recording contract in 1913. The James Reese Europe Orchestra recordings revealed a unique sound of syncopation and drums, according to Reid Badger, giving a "looser or freer approach to tonal variations and interpretation by the performers."

James Reese Europe's Society Orchestra c. 1914
Europe is at the piano on the right.

Later in 1913, in an interview about the dance music field, Europe himself stated, "Our Negro orchestras have nearly cleared the field."

During World War I, James Europe and his Hellfighter's Band of the 369th infantry brought jazz to France, and upon his return home after the war, he received an exclusive recording contract with Pathé, a French recording company. The arrangement was announced as a contract to record the "Jazz King," whose popularity only heightened once Europe's army band toured cities throughout the United States in 1919. The musicians thrilled their audiences with "No Man's Land," a jazz performance that entailed darkening the concert hall and re-creating the sounds of the battlefield. Impressed by the band's performance in Chicago in May 1919, *The Chicago Defender* explicitly linked the arts to the battle against racism.

The jazz aesthetic in New York differed from Chicago jazz not only in its big-band tradition, which emerged from the contexts of Broadway and the society dance, but also in its tight, intricate orchestrations with only modest amounts of improvisation. Musicologists, looking for the roots of big-band jazz, have attached specific importance to the Europe band's recordings in 1919 of two W. C. Handy tunes, "St. Louis Blues" and "Memphis Blues," as indicative of Europe's shift away from ragtime to a blues-inflected jazz.

Window in Time

"Jazzing Away Prejudice"

WE HOPE THE SWING of Europe [James Reece Europe] and his band around the country will be nationwide. The most prejudiced enemy of our Race could not sit through an evening with Europe [James Reece Europe] without coming away with a changed viewpoint. For he is compelled in spite of himself to see us in a new light. . . . It is a well-known fact that the white people view us largely from the standpoint of the cook, porter, and waiter, and his limited opportunities are responsible for much of the distorted opinion concerning us. Europe and his band are worth much more to our Race than a thousand speeches from so-called Race orators and uplifters. . . . EUROPE AND HIS BAND are demonstrating what our people can do in a field where the results are bound to be of the greatest benefit. He has the white man's ear because he is giving the white man something new. He is meeting a popular demand in catering to this love of syncopated music he is jazzing away the barriers of prejudice.

Source: "Jazzing Away Prejudice," *Chicago Defender,* May 10, 1919.

With Europe's tragic death at the hands of a fellow band member while on tour in Boston in May 1919 (ironically within days of his Chicago appearance), pianist and orchestra leader Fletcher Henderson emerged as his successor. Like Europe, Henderson emphasized professionalism on the part of his musicians, since his orchestra was often booked to play in the prestigious white Times Square area. For Henderson, the black musician's professional image required discipline, proper appearance, and musical reading skill over improvisation. An Atlanta University graduate, and friend and business associate of Harry Pace of Black Swan Records, Fletcher Henderson was a race-conscious man, of whom trumpeter Howard Scott recalled: "Every night you had to . . . stand inspection. He'd look at your hair, your face, see if you shaved, your shoes, see if they're shined. You had to be perfect to suit him."

By 1925 music critics and the black press had discovered Henderson's orchestra and applauded its image of respectability. Under the title "Fletcher Henderson and His Orchestra," the group attained such broad appeal that white record companies advertised it as part of their general series targeted to white consumers. Recording over one hundred sides in 1923 and 1924, however, the "lowdown" blues also formed part of Henderson's repertoire. In this case, Henderson made money from the "race records" market, playing as backup to the classic blues singers. In these advertisements, which appeared prominently in black newspapers, the name of Henderson's orchestra appears in small print and is far less conspicuous in relation to the names of prominently featured blues women such as Alberta Hunter, Gladys Bryant, and Ida Cox.

In 1924, Louis Armstrong accepted Fletcher Henderson's offer to join his orchestra in New York. Armstrong brought extraordinary new talent to the orchestra, while enhancing his own skills. In

Louis Armstrong Transforms Big Band Jazz

working with Henderson at downtown Manhattan's Roseland Ballroom, he had joined the most sophisticated black orchestra in the country. Although a musical genius, Armstrong was not a strong reader of musical scores. Armstrong's development as a jazz artist had occurred in a format that was just the opposite of the Henderson band's requirement for an occasional soloist who played from written scores. Yet it was Armstrong who electrified the Roseland audience. One onlooker noted that "people stopped dancing to come around and listen to him. And they could hear him out on the street. . . . The next night you couldn't get into the place. Just that quick. It had gone all around about this new trumpet player at Roseland." Armstrong helped to transform New York's big-band jazz.

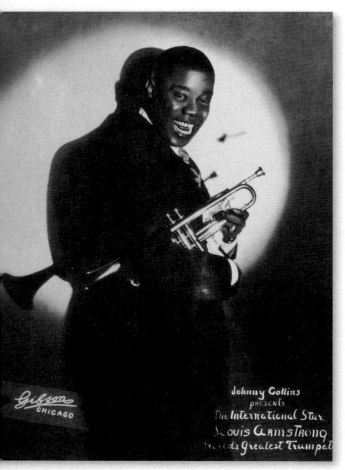

Louis Armstrong
Poster for a Chicago appearance by Louis Armstrong in the 1920s

The New York experience transformed Armstrong in a number of ways. While in New York he connected with an old New Orleans colleague, Sidney Bechet, who had spent much of the early 1920s in Europe. In 1924, Bechet was the only jazz musician in America who rivaled Armstrong as a soloist. Critics have marveled at the sweeping operatic influences on Bechet's virtuosity, as they have similarly commented about Armstrong. Bechet claimed to have been influenced by the French opera he heard as a child in New Orleans. As a technician, he was Armstrong's peer. In a series of 1924–1925 recordings for Okeh and Gennett records, made under the direction of black jazz pianist Clarence Williams, Armstrong and Bechet challenged one another in virtuoso displays that were, in their own way, as musically historic as the pairings of Charlie Parker and Dizzy Gillespie twenty years later. The Bechet and Armstrong recordings had done something completely new. They started jazz on the road to the development of sequential solo improvisation, following the melody or theme. This gradually became the template for virtually all post-1920s combo jazz.

Armstrong returned to Chicago in 1925, but during his short time in New York, he had a catalytic impact on Henderson's musicians. Armstrong's arrival brought to the Henderson orchestra a new rhythmic momentum—a blues-infused sensibility and, equally important, a new spirit of improvisational boldness. Particularly affected were the band's young tenor saxophonist Coleman Hawkins and the principal arranger Don Redman. Redman is traditionally credited with translating Armstrong's flexible rhythmic qualities into a big-band framework and with making big-band music "swing."

On his return to Chicago in 1925, Armstrong set out to develop further the art of the jazz solo. He had refined his improvisational and technical skills in the Henderson orchestra and applied what he had learned to the new series of recordings that his wife Lillian Hardin had arranged. In Chicago, he also became the leader of his own combo, the Hot Fives (later, the Hot Sevens). By the early 1930s, however, Louis Armstrong had turned to the big-band format, having moved back to New York and becoming one of the best-known musicians in America.

By 1926, jazz had transcended its narrow southern appeal and become a national craze. Jazz flourished not only in New Orleans and Memphis, from which it sprang, but also in Chicago, New York, Detroit, Los Angeles, and San Francisco, all cities to which it migrated. The jazz stylists of the early 1920s **Duke Ellington and the Big Band Era** would soon share center stage with Jimmie Lunceford, Duke Ellington, Cab Calloway, Count Basie, and other groups of the big-band era. Meanwhile, the virtuosity of such soloists as trumpeter Louis Armstrong, vibraphonist Lionel Hampton, and pianists Teddy Wilson, Earl "Fatha" Hines, and Mary Lou Williams commended them to white musical combinations as well as to black ones. In the late 1920s recording companies became centralized in New York, black Broadway reawakened, and the club scene provided work for black musicians. Many of Chicago's most influential musicians—King Oliver, Louis Armstrong, and Jelly Roll Morton—moved to New York, now the center of the jazz world.

However, it was Duke Ellington from Washington, D.C., who grabbed the spotlight of New York's big-band era. His public image, a legacy of Fletcher Henderson, was self-consciously tailored. A professional musician, he looked every inch a New Negro whose racial pride and devotion to the best interests of the race were visually encoded into his style. Reflecting on his music in 1931, Ellington compared it to the cultural work of the Harlem Renaissance, saying that he wanted to "portray the experience of the colored races," as Countee Cullen and others had done through literature. Henry Louis Gates, Jr., a scholar of the Harlem Renaissance, has gone so far as to conclude that "the 1920s, as it should be remembered, saw the rise of surpassingly accomplished musicians such as Bessie Smith, Louis Armstrong, and Duke Ellington, whose artistry had a greater influence on the nation as a whole than the work of any of the renaissance writers."

Motion Pictures

The African American community's outrage in 1915 against D. W. Griffith's racist motion picture *Birth of a Nation* underscored the great hunger of African Americans for films that featured members of their race in a positive light and addressed issues that affected their lives. It is no coincidence, then, that black film companies began to appear in Harlem in 1916. The most significant of the black companies were the Lincoln Motion Picture Company, established by the brothers George and Noble Johnson in 1916, and Oscar Micheaux's film and book company, begun in 1918.

Before the Lincoln Company's demise in 1923, the Johnson brothers produced at least six films and pioneered in establishing patterns for advertising, booking, and promotion that would be imitated by other black independent filmmakers. Micheaux, a man of great drive and energy as well as shrewd business acumen, was the most important and prolific producer of black films during the 1920s. Yet, he and other African Americans in this field were never able to overcome the restrictions imposed by their limited capital, their inability to purchase state-of-the-art equipment, and the vast advertising budgets and powerful distribution systems of the white filmmakers with whom they competed in the African American community.

The early black filmmakers produced a steady stream of films, called "race movies," with all-black casts. Coming before the "talkie" revolution, the silent black films played in southern segregated theaters and in northern urban black neighborhood theaters. On occasion, they played as well at black churches and schools. Race movies were intended by their producers to offer more than entertainment. They provided black audiences with a separate

The Micheaux Film Corporation: Cameraman, director, and actor
Oscar Micheaux's silent films, such as *Within Our Gates* (1920), addressed black social concerns.

film culture insulated from the racial stereotyping of Hollywood; they gave black film actors and craftsmen the opportunity to express their cinematic talent with dignity; and they guaranteed black entrepreneurs control over the means and content of production. The films presented black versions of the established Hollywood genres: musicals, westerns, gangster films, and melodramas. The racial pride evoked by these films, the real subtext for all black film production, rested in the novelty of seeing black actors of all types in the same popular film genres that existed in the world of Hollywood with white actors. Hollywood routinely either excluded black actors or gave them demeaning, stereotyped parts.

Black films did not so much offer a separate aesthetic genre as respond to the commercial demands of black audiences who shared, with white audiences, a general popular understanding of what constituted cinematic entertainment. In some instances, black films made explicit social statements. One such example was the film *Scar of Shame* in 1927. The film, produced by the Colored Players Corporation, directly addressed issues of racial respectability and racial uplift, through the story of a woman from lowly origins who marries into the black middle class. Oscar Micheaux's silent films sought to address social concerns important to blacks. He perceived his film *Within Our Gates* (1920) as the black response to *Birth of a Nation.* For example, Micheaux's film contains a lynching scene and depicts a sexual assault of a virtuous black woman by a white man. It ends with a message of racial uplift by the well-educated and supremely refined character Dr. Vivian, who intends to be a leader of the race. *Birthright,* a silent movie from 1924, also featured as the hero a member of the black educated elite—in this case a Harvard-educated black man who goes south to found a school for the purpose of racial uplift.

The musical short-subject and feature film was a new, direct product of the "talkie" revolution in film. The black talent first tapped by the major white studios were those performers who had made national reputations on records and, significantly, on radio, rather than performers with exposure limited **Black Talent in White Studios** to the New York stage. Two of the earliest features for black performers who had gained national followings through radio and recordings were Bessie Smith and Duke Ellington. In 1929 both starred in musical shorts released by RKO Productions, and directed by Dudley Murphy. Smith was featured as actress and singer in *St. Louis Blues,* which told the story of mistreatment and abandonment by her man, leading to Smith's poignant rendition of the W. C. Handy classic. Ellington's *Black and Tan*—a film on which film scholars believe the white literary figure Carl Van Vechten worked—offered a more complex plot with Ellington as a struggling composer whose girlfriend, played by black actress Freddie Washington, risks her life by taking a job at a club that agrees to hire Ellington's band to accompany her. A frenzied dance by Washington, whose character suffers from a heart condition, causes her eventual death. The death scene occurs against the haunting strains of Ellington's "Black and Tan Fantasy," a staple of his Cotton Club "jungle music" performances.

More revolutionary in its intentions, but far less financially successful, was the all-black musical *Hallelujah!* (1929), conceived and directed by white filmmaker King Vidor. Intending to offer a sympathetic rendition of black family life in the South, and particularly of the religiosity of black folk culture, Vidor's film does much more. The palate of characterization shows rich contrast. The core family has two grown sons, the literate, responsible, and religious Spunk, and the irresponsible, womanizing Zeke. Lead female actress Nina Mae McKinney plays a seductive role that divides the brothers. It is Spunk's accidental death that motivates the dramatic scenario of the prodigal Zeke's route from sin to ultimate redemption within a strong two-parent family.

King Vidor's most striking and radical move for the time was his treatment of Zeke, portrayed by the actor Daniel Haynes, as a complex and conflicted adult rather than as the more pervasive childlike or buffoonish black character. Press leaks about the adult, nonstereotypical concept of black manhood, along with the sexual message in *Hallelujah!* sparked sufficient racist backlash to require King Vidor to hire bodyguards for the film's leads Haynes and McKinney. Film historian Donald Bogle has argued that the portrayal of the black family in *Hallelujah!* was the most sensitive and realistic treatment in Hollywood film until the release of *Sounder* in 1972, over forty years later.

Black Theater

In the prewar years African American theater flourished in Harlem, to predominantly African American audiences. Black actors performed in a range of roles, free of the stereotypical ones acceptable to white audiences. The Lafayette Players, formed in Harlem in 1915 as the first African American stock company, presented almost every type of play, including those by white playwrights—*Madame X* by the French playwright Alexandre Bisson, *The Servant in the House* by Charles Rann Kennedy, and *Within the Law* by Bayard Veiller. The Lafayette Players performed at the Lincoln Theater in Harlem, and from this group emerged a number of highly respected dramatic actors, including Abbie Mitchell, Laura Bowman, Edna Thomas, Charles Gilpin, Frank Wilson, Clarence Muse, and Jack Carter.

Black actors began to appear before wider audiences beginning in the war years, especially with their employment in plays written by white authors. In 1917 a group of black actors under the sponsorship of Emily Hapgood presented three one-act plays by playwright Ridgely Torrence at the Garden Theater in New York's Madison Square Garden. Torrance's *The Rider of Dreams, Granny Maumee, and Simon the Cyrenian: Plays for a Negro Theater* marked the first time that African American actors had commanded the serious attention of New York's white critics and the general press. Because the United States entered the war on the day following the opening of the three one-act plays, black dramatists had to wait until the war's end before they could claim a substantial place in American public entertainment.

In 1919 there was a revival of interest in African Americans in the theater with the appearance of Charles Gilpin as the Reverend William Custis in John Drinkwater's *Abraham Lincoln.* In the following year Gilpin's performance in the title role of Eugene

Postwar Theater O'Neill's *The Emperor Jones* received such outstanding acclaim that he was given an award by the Drama League of New York as well as the NAACP's Spingarn Medal. Some critics predicted for him a career similar to that of Ira Aldridge, who had captivated European audiences with his Shakespearean roles in the previous century.

In 1924 Paul Robeson played the leading role in O'Neill's *All God's Chillun Got Wings.* It was the first time in American history that a black man had taken a principal role opposite a white woman. In 1926 Paul Green of the University of North Carolina brought to New York *In Abraham's Bosom,* in which Jules Bledsoe played the leading role, ably assisted by Rose McClendon, Abbie Mitchell, and Frank Wilson. The play was a distinct success and demonstrated both the adaptability of African American life to the theater and the ability of African American actors in the theater. In the following year, *Porgy,* a folk play of black life in Charleston by Dorothy and DuBose Heyward, was produced by the Theater Guild. Once more, black actors Rose McClendon, Frank Wilson, and others in the cast captivated New York audiences. These plays about black life by white authors reached a high-water mark with the long-running production in 1930 of Marc Connelly's *The Green Pastures,* a fable of a black person's conception of the Old Testament, with Richard B. Harrison as "De Lawd."

Popular musicals, written and produced by blacks themselves, appeared on Broadway, the longest running being *Shuffle Along* by Eubie Blake (music), Noble Sissle (lyrics), and

Black Musicals Flournoy Miller and Aubrey Lyles (writers). The play opened in 1921 and ran for over five hundred performances on Broadway and afterward toured theaters in Washington, D.C., Philadelphia, and other cities for more than two years. With the songs "I'm Just Wild about Harry," "Love Will Find a Way," and "Shuffle Along" masterfully performed by talented singers and dancers, *Shuffle Along* enjoyed record-breaking success. "I'm Just Wild about Harry" would be revived as the campaign theme song in 1948 by Democratic presidential candidate Harry Truman. Although overshadowed by the extraordinary success of *Shuffle Along,* another Broadway musical *Put and Take* (1921), by Irving Miller (the brother of Flournoy Miller of *Shuffle Along* fame), was described in *The New York Times* as a lively "all-Negro revue . . . filled with excellent dancing, good singing and quite a dash of comedy." In 1923 Irving Miller also produced the musical *'Liza* and the following year *Dinah,* which introduced the popular dance the "Black Bottom" to New York.

Black musicals contributed to the image of the Roaring Twenties. In 1923 the black-produced Broadway musical *Runnin' Wild* contained songs by stride pianist James P. John-

The Charleston son, whose keyboard style decisively influenced the prolific songwriter Thomas "Fats" Waller, probably best known for his song "Ain't Misbehavin,'" which he

Shuffle Along chorus girls
Shuffle Along was the longest running Broadway musical by blacks in the 1920s.

wrote for the Broadway play *Hot Chocolates*. Although the Broadway show *Runnin' Wild* is little known today, James P. Johnson's "The Charleston" remains the "theme song" of the 1920s, the first few bars of which automatically call forth an image of the decade. The song's melody and rhythmic structure were influenced by the southern dance, which became a national fad following the debut of *Runnin' Wild*. The song "The Charleston" may actually have resulted from the particular migration patterns of the early part of the twentieth century, which brought black migrants from Georgia and the Carolinas to New York. James P. Johnson admitted that he often altered his solo piano performances in New York to meet the music requests of migrants from Charleston, South Carolina.

Lesser-known black musicals introduced singers and dancers who would later come to fame on the stage. Blake and Sissle's *Chocolate Dandies* ran three months on Broadway in 1924. In its chorus line was then-unknown Josephine Baker, who would soon become the rage of Paris. Another black woman who would soon enjoy international acclaim was Florence Mills. First appearing in *Shuffle Along*, she later gained leading roles in a number of white-produced musicals that featured all-black casts—*Plantation Revue* (1922), *Dover Street to Dixie* (1923), *Dixie to Broadway* (1924), and *Blackbirds of 1926*. Mills's headliner roles in those musicals brought her top billing and other celebrity benefits that had been previously reserved for male comedians. Her performances, which included pantomiming, singing, and dancing, were considered signal triumphs in New York, Paris, and London. Her death in 1927 at the age of thirty-one opened the way for new women singers (Ethel Waters, Adelaide Hall, and Ada Ward) in subsequent versions of *Blackbirds*. In addition, *Blackbirds of 1928* brought tremendous renown to the tap dancer and actor Bill "Bojangles" Robinson.

The Harlem Renaissance

Before World War I and even before the migration of blacks into Harlem, black artistic talent had begun to flower in New York City. Its roots were planted in the world of black bohemia, located in the tenement district known as the Tenderloin on Manhattan's West Side, from Fifth to Seventh Avenues and between West 24th and West 42nd Streets. (As yet, blacks had not moved in significant numbers to Harlem.)

The Tenderloin   According to census data for 1900, the Tenderloin contained most of New York City's 60,000 black residents. Three-quarters of those employed were working as laborers or servants; about a thousand (less than 3 percent of total employed) had professional or clerical jobs.

In his novel *The Autobiography of an Ex-Coloured Man* (1927 [1912]), James Weldon Johnson describes the area around West 27th Street, just west of Sixth Avenue, as a vibrant world of clubs, cabarets, dance halls, and also brothels and gambling houses. It was a world that afforded unique places to gather, according to the book's protagonist, for "coloured Bohemians," prize fighters, famous black vaudevillian "minstrels"—"notables of the ring, the turf, and the stage." Comprising writers, composers, musicians, theatrical performers, and others in show business, the mélange of artists plied their craft at the turn of the twentieth century. Ever since black comedians Bert Williams and George Walker reached New York in 1896 and introduced their highly successful vaudeville team, white managers had begun to employ black entertainers. Aside from introducing the "cakewalk" dance to white New Yorkers, Williams and Walker (who at times played in blackface) appeared in numerous world-famous revues.

The Marshall Hotel   The precursor to the Harlem artistic community, black bohemia expanded as black migration increased and spread northward into the San Juan Hill area, with whites in the area moving elsewhere. When Bert Williams and George Walker rented their flat on West 53rd Street, they described their role as availing themselves to "all colored men who possessed theatrical and musical ability." According to black theater historian Karen Sotiropoulos, in the years before World War I, the Marshall Hotel on West 53rd Street between Sixth and Seventh Avenues became the residence for a coterie of talented figures, including James Weldon Johnson and his brother J. Rosamond Johnson, Bob Cole, Lester Walton, Ernest Hogan, James Reese Europe, and other entertainers who either lived or met there.

New York's segregated housing did not permit blacks to live in the white neighborhoods that constituted vaudeville's main centers, in Union and Madison Squares. Thus blacks sought to create opportunities and places for networking among themselves. The most outstanding spot for networking, mentoring, and collaborating was the hotel run by an African American named Jimmie Marshall at 127–129 West 53rd Street. The Marshall Hotel, a four-story brownstone, became the fashionable gathering place for black actors and musicians. Marshall converted what had been formerly a family residence into a rooming house, restaurant, and hotel. In his autobiography *Along This Way* (1933), Johnson referred to the Marshall as responsible for the black presence on the New York stage. The hotel also attracted white entertainment elites, who visited from time to time.

Black bohemia proved short-lived, however. The Marshall Hotel closed after a change in cabaret licensing laws in 1913. More important, the demographic pattern of the ensuing Great Migration began to shift to Harlem, where a housing glut led profit-hungry real estate agents and developers to open up their once racially exclusive market to black home purchasers and renters. Some blacks, such as George Walker, had moved to Harlem as early as 1908.

In the postwar years, however, black periodicals began to speak of Harlem as the "Negro's Zion" and "Race Capital of the World." Harlem had become a highly sought-out location, not merely by the many black southern migrants and Caribbean immigrants who settled there, but also by whites who flocked to Harlem for its nightlife and entertainment. By the mid-1920s, white magazines depicted Harlem as having surpassed Broadway as an entertainment magnet. White socialites in their limousines, politicians, gangsters, and white tourists all found their way to Harlem's cabarets and speakeasies. If Harlem represented to white tourists the opportunity (according to *Variety* magazine) for immersion in

Black Periodicals

a "seething cauldron of Nubian mirth and hilarity," it also became a place for the literati of both races to come together for more highbrow pursuits.

Black authors and playwrights rose to prominence in New York during the 1920s, an era of prolific publishing for all authors. The growing pluralistic culture of urban America, particularly New York, offered black authors a vibrant mix of new ideas and art forms. During the second decade of the twentieth century, white and black intellectuals alike offered new frames of reference for analyzing and understanding race. Members of the black literati differed among themselves ideologically, shifting their positions and identifying with distinct yet frequently overlapping intellectual trends: cultural racialism (rejecting the biological construction of race), pragmatism, cultural pluralism, socialism, American cultural nationalism (as contrasted to European culture), and pan-Africanism.

In this cultural movement, the civil rights organizations—the NAACP and the National Urban League—played crucial supportive roles. Through their magazines' literary contests, banquets, and home parties, the officers of both organizations encouraged new literary talent and initiated opportunities to bring exposure to young black writers, as well as to broker introductions to influential white authors, publishers, and prospective patrons. Jessie Fauset, novelist, worked as the literary editor of *The Crisis* for seven years and brought into print for the first time the work of both Langston Hughes and Nella Larsen. Literary scholar Cheryl Wall also credits Fauset for mentoring or at least encouraging several other prominent Harlem Renaissance writers, including Countee Cullen, Jean Toomer, Anne Spencer, and Georgia Douglass Johnson. Also, to call attention to Harlem's budding talent, Fauset hosted readings and lectures at the 135th Street Library.

Charles S. Johnson of the National Urban League edited *Opportunity* magazine. Like *The Crisis*, *Opportunity* played a tremendous role in calling attention to younger

Jessie Redmon Fauset

As the literary editor of *The Crisis*, Fauset first published the work of Langston Hughes, among other talented writers and poets.

writers, especially with Charles Johnson's creating the opportunity for them to be introduced to New York's white literary establishment at a banquet he arranged at the Civic Club in March 1924. Organized as an event to honor Jessie Fauset and the recent publication of her novel *There is Confusion,* the banquet's larger purpose was to announce in a very public way the Harlem Renaissance itself. Members of the white publishing elite—Carl Van Doren, editor of *Century* magazine; Paul Kellogg, editor of *Survey Graphic;* Frederick Allen of Harper & Row; and other distinguished guests—sat in rapt attention for readings by new, young black artists. For example, after reading his poems, the twenty-one year-old Countee Cullen saw them appear in four national magazines.

The Civic Club event also signaled the ascent of the Harvard-trained philosopher Alain Locke, by then a professor at Howard University, as the architect of the New Negro renaissance. Serving as master of ceremonies, Locke's insightful remarks on the significance of this younger generation of black writers led to the request by Paul Kellogg that Locke edit a special Harlem series for *Survey Graphic.* The issue, which appeared in 1925, was further enlarged and published as the anthology *The New Negro* (1925), today recognized as the foundational text of the Harlem Renaissance. The Civic Club dinner was followed by numerous occasions for racially integrated conversations and networking. In large public affairs and in the salon atmosphere of homes, black writers conversed, laughed, and dined with New York's rich and famous. In growing numbers, black writers found their words in an array of influential periodicals—*Survey Graphic, Current History, The American Mercury, Modern Quarterly, Harper's, The Nation,* and *The New Masses*—that presented black authors to the larger American readership.

Alain Locke perceived this groundswell of interest in the arts as proof of Harlem having become a "race capital" and—more than that—of forming part of a larger transnational movement of "nascent centers of folk expression and self-determination." Locke noted that "Harlem has the same role to play for the New Negro as Dublin has had for the New Ireland or Prague for the New Czechoslovakia." Many black literary artists helped to play this role. Although only a sample of the entire number of black poets and novelists of the Harlem Renaissance, key figures include James Weldon Johnson, Eric Walrond, Langston Hughes, Jean Toomer, Countee Cullen, Wallace Thurman, Rudolph Fisher, George Schuyler, Jessie Fauset, Nella Larsen, Zora Neale Hurston, Gwendolyn Bennett, Georgia Douglas Johnson, and Anne Spencer.

The fame of Jamaican-born Claude McKay (September 15, 1890–May 22, 1948) preceded that of the cohort of young writers introduced at the Civic Club event in 1924. Such

Before the Civic Club black writers as McKay, Fauset, and Jean Toomer (and earlier Paul Laurence Dunbar, W. E. B. Du Bois, and James Weldon Johnson) had already made a mark in literature. McKay, an active socialist, had published his poems and essays in a number of left-wing magazines in the 1910s, as well as briefly co-edited the leftist magazine *The Liberator.* One of the most acclaimed of the Harlem Renaissance writers, McKay was already heralded as a poet. James Weldon Johnson, the NAACP leader and also a novelist, would later describe McKay's poetry as "one of the great forces in bringing about what is often called the 'Negro Literary Renaissance.'" It is ironic, however, that for most of the 1920s McKay lived outside the United States—in the Soviet Union, France, and North Africa.

McKay immigrated to the United States in 1912 at twenty-one years of age, having already published his *Songs of Jamaica,* a collection of poems in the island's dialect. He attended Tuskegee Institute and Kansas State University before moving to New York. His poetic style was traditional in form but militantly defiant in its content. Perhaps his most well-known poems—"The Lynching," "If We Must Die" (written in response to urban race riots in 1919), "The White House," and "To the White Fiends"—most boldly express McKay's protest and bitter contempt for American racism. Seemingly having expended all his poetic talents, McKay turned to prose and in 1928 brought out *Home to Harlem.* In the following year, he published the novel *Banjo,* whose protagonist is a black expatriate and musician living in Marseilles. In the 1930s he published *Banana Bottom* (1933) and his autobiography *A Long Way from Home* (1937). During the years of the Harlem Renaissance, McKay's writings both enjoyed great acclaim and stirred great controversy on account of his unabashed affection for the black working class in all its complexity. His portrayal of the raw, even lurid side of black life in *Home to Harlem,* for example, left race-uplift readers such as Du Bois and Jessie, and younger readers such as Langston Hughes, inspired by the freedom to be able to write on such subjects.

Also respected as a writer before the Civic Club event was Jean Toomer (born Nathan Toomer, 1894–1967). The grandson of the black Reconstruction-era politician P. B. S. Pinchback, Toomer won accolades for his literary style in *Cane* (1923), his one major work of the Harlem Renaissance. Toomer did not live in Harlem; rather, he commingled in the white bohemian world of Greenwich Village, associating primarily with white writers and artists. Yet when *Cane* came out, it received far greater attention in the black press than in the white. Its rave reviews and sales in black circles were coupled with only modest sales among whites. Today, however, *Cane* is recognized as the first African American modernist writing and also as among the most extraordinary and evocative books in American literature in the first half of the twentieth century.

Divided into three parts, *Cane* offers a series of meditations, in the form of short stories and poems, on the meaning of black culture. Toomer had earlier taught briefly in a black school in rural Georgia, and it is this setting that serves as the basis of the short story "Fern." In Part One, "Fern" captures the dying, beautiful, and tragic black "folk-spirit" in a rapidly changing South of rural out-migration, technological innovation, secularization, and cultural loss. In "Fern" the rural South, along with its culture and history, is ill-equipped to survive the dawn of modernity. Toomer tells this story in his portrayal of the sensuous, untamable beauty of southern rural black womanhood, which he embellishes in death and decay and the slow setting of the sun. In Part Two, Toomer's modernist sensibilities turn to the urban North, particularly Washington, D.C. and Chicago, signaling frenetic, strident, repetitive, rhythmic syncopations—sounds of movement and of jazz. In a visual and sonorous rendering, Toomer writes: "Arms of the girls, and their limbs, which . . . jazz, jazz . . . by lifting up their tight street skirts they set free, jab the air, and clog the floor in rhythm to the music." Shortly after the appearance of *Cane,* Toomer retired from active participation in the New Negro literary awakening and the world of African Americans altogether, blending among whites instead.

The lyric quality, rich imagination, and intellectual content of Countee Cullen's poetry place him among the central figures of the Harlem Renaissance. In 1926 Alain Locke acclaimed Cullen as a genius, quintessentially young and talented— Countee Cullen the best of what was "new" about the New Negro. "Posterity will laugh at us," Locke asserted in the January issue of *Opportunity,* "if we do not proclaim him now." Cullen (1903–1946) published his first book of poetry, *Color* (1925), to critical acclaim. His poems had individually appeared in numerous magazines—*Bookman, The American Mercury, Harper's, Century, The Nation, Poetry, The Crisis, Messenger,* and *Opportunity.*

One of most famous poems, "Heritage," in *Color*, appeared first in the Harlem issue of *Survey Graphic*. "What is Africa to me?" Cullen asked in the first line of the poem, revealing his own unresolved conflict. Firmly committed to traditional poetic form, Cullen's work included both racial and nonracial subject matter. In the poems with a racial message, Cullen's choice of words is generally more delicate and subtle in protest than is the poetry of McKay or Langston Hughes. Indeed, Cullen emphasized his need to write on themes of his own choosing and was thus equally comfortable in search of the beauty and effectiveness of verse that did not depend on the use of racial experiences at all.

In his second book of poetry, *Copper Sun* (1927), he paid less attention to racial themes than he did in *Color*. When asked why, Cullen did not shy away from voicing his position on the responsibility of the black poet. He recoiled from the idea of racially politicized poetry. Although admitting that he was always conscious of his race, Cullen was quoted in the *The Brooklyn Eagle* in February 1924: "If I am going to be a poet at all, I am going to be POET and not NEGRO POET." Literary critics in his day and later praise him for his poems on racial subjects. Typical of the quality of his writings are these two lines, perhaps the best known of all Cullen's work:

> Yet do I marvel at this curious thing:
> To make a poet black, and bid him sing!

The most memorable writer of the Harlem Renaissance is Langston Hughes (1902–1967). He arrived in New York in 1921, by way of Kansas, Illinois, Ohio, and Mexico. He had come to New York to attend Columbia University, but after one year of study he was yet again on the road, this time on a freighter bound for Africa and Europe. Before he was twenty years old, his poems had been published in *The Crisis*. A prolific writer, Hughes wrote in various genres, challenging the restrictions of race no less boldly as restrictions on artistic form. He composed deeply moving verses full of race pride, such as "The Negro Speaks of Rivers," and of humble walks of life, as in "Brass Spittoons." His volume of poetry *Weary Blues* (1926) incorporated jazz and blues rhythms. Hughes's lyrics and subject matter flaunted his experimental modernist voice, but they also ruffled the feathers of Countee Cullen, who described the book as having "too much emphasis here on strictly Negro themes."

Langston Hughes

In 1927 Hughes followed with the volume *Fine Clothes to the Jew*, which was greeted with a mixture of admiration and denunciation. Like McKay, Hughes admired the colorful aspects of black vernacular culture—the blues and jazz, juke joints and shouting churches, and the complex individuality of what he fondly called the "lowdown folks." Also in 1927, Hughes contributed to the bold, highly controversial, and short-lived journal *Fire!!* A versatile writer who did not shy away from politically charged and leftist themes, Hughes continued to write poetry in the 1930s as well as the successful novel *Not without Laughter* (1930) and a volume of short stories, *The Ways of White Folks* (1934). Later, he experimented with pieces for the theater. In 1940 his autobiography, *The Big Sea*, was published.

Poet Laureate of the Harlem Renaissance
Langston Hughes, shown here at his typewriter, also wrote novels, essays, and plays.

Window in Time

In Praise of the Black Vernacular

But then there are the low-down folks, the so-called common element, and they are the majority—may the Lord be praised! The people who have their hip of gin on Saturday nights and are not too important to themselves or the community, or too well wed, or too learned to watch the lazy world go round. They live on Seventh Street in Washington or State Street in Chicago and they do not particularly care whether they are like white folks or anybody else. Their joy runs, bang! into ecstasy. Their religion soars to a shout. Work maybe a little today, rest a little tomorrow. Play awhile. Sing awhile. O, let's dance!

Source: Langston Hughes, "The Negro and the Racial Mountain," *The Nation*, June 1926.

Writings by Harlem Renaissance women reveal gender consciousness but also differences among women in regard to literary style and class predilection. Jessie Redmond Fauset (1882–1961), a 1905 Phi Beta Kappa graduate of Cornell University, was the leading female figure of the movement during its hey-day in the 1920s. From 1919 to 1926, the literary arm of *The Crisis* flourished under her tutelage. Fauset introduced and encouraged new talent (recent scholarship deems her to be the true midwife of the Harlem Renaissance), along with writing novels and articles, reviewing publications, and translating the work of Francophone Caribbean writers. Her first novel, *There Is Confusion* (1924), won her respect as an author. A review in *The Crisis* called the book "the novel that the Negro intelligentsia has been clamoring for." While problems of race are present in the four books that she published, Fauset's intention was to emphasize universal qualities and values that make blacks react to their circumstances just as whites and other people do.

Harlem Renaissance Women

Although Fauset was very much a traditionalist in her style, employing familiar conventions of sentimentalism and the tragic mulatto, this fact did not prevent her second novel, *Plum Bum* (1929), from telling a complex story of racial passing, of racial concessions to patronage and the publishing industry, and of the gender limitations of marriage. Literary scholar Deborah McDowell finds the gender dimension of the book the most sophisticated of the plots, since the African American female protagonist, Angela Murray, whose light skin permits her to pass for white in order to better her material life, comes face to face with painful but inevitable gender realities. In the white world, she soon comes to realize that her fairytale understanding of wifehood and marriage is shattered, and she learns in the process to value a woman's individuality and independence—all this bringing her greater appreciation for the black world she left behind. Considered Fauset's best work, *Plum Bum* was followed by *The Chinaberry Tree* (1931) and *Comedy: American Style* (1933).

Gender is central to the novels of Nella Larsen (1891–1964). Of mixed-racial heritage (her mother was Danish and her father black), Larsen authored two important novels—*Quicksand*

(1928) and *Passing* (1929). In 1929 she became the first black woman to be awarded a Guggenheim fellowship. Both Larsen and Fauset focused on middle-class life, but Larsen was far less conformist, questioning many of the basic beliefs of the "Talented Tenth." *Quicksand*'s protagonist, Helga Crane, rejects the conservative values and ideas about women's dress and comportment taught at the black Naxos College (Saxon spelled backward). She finds no respite in Europe, where her white lover sees her only through the lens of primitivism. The novel's race leader, Ms. Hayes-Rore, is not respected as a race woman or black clubwoman but instead is caricatured along with her rhetoric and agenda of racial uplift. As the title *Quicksand* implies, Larsen's ending is a tragic one—its larger message critical of middle-class racial hypocrisy and of the inevitable fate of women who dare to question conformity. Such women find no refuge among whites, or in black institutions, or even in the largely female-populated church. Both *Quicksand* and *Passing* conclude with hopelessness and death.

The Harlem Renaissance's intellectual
Arriving on the scene late, when many writers were well established, Zora Neale Hurston was both brilliant and prolific.

Zora Neale Hurston (1891–1960) deliberately sought to give the impression that she was one of the young writers of the Harlem Renaissance—in age a peer of Langston Hughes and Countee Cullen. However, she fabricated her age, often claiming to be around ten years younger than she was. An educated woman who had trained under Alain Locke at Howard and under the famed anthropologist Franz Boas at Barnard in the 1920s, Hurston was both an anthropologist in her own right and a literary modernist.

It was not her age or educational attainment that took her on a path different from Fauset's and Larsen's but instead her childhood and specifically the rural folk culture of her childhood. Having been raised in the all-black town of Eatonville, Florida, Hurston firmly believed in the racial "authenticity" of the rural folk. They were, to her, the natural embodiment of the life, soul, and moral health of black people as a group, and particularly for black women. Hurston, who always based her subject matter on rural black community life, conducted ethnographic research between 1927 and 1932 in Alabama, Florida, and the Bahamas in order to be faithful to their true dialects, beliefs, and practices. She showed negligible concern for interracial themes. Hurston's unique voice is found in the entanglement of sexuality, gender, race, region, and class. She focuses on folk customs, speech patterns, and values, addressing black women's sexuality by metaphorically freeing it from the oppressive gaze of both white people and the black middle class. Particularly in *Their Eyes Were Watching God*, female sexuality flowers in all-black towns and other rural settings that afford the book's protagonist Janey an evolving understanding of women's independence and regenerative power.

Hurston's flamboyant behavior—her antics and "darkey" jokes at the interracial parties hosted by the wealthy white patron of the arts, Charlotte Osgood Mason—also highlighted the differences between her and middle-class black Harlemites, who criticized Hurston for catering shamelessly to Mason's fascination with "primitives." Langston Hughes, after parting ways with Mason and her financial support, wrote that

Window in Time

Enter the New Negro

The pulse of the Negro world has begun to beat in Harlem. A Negro newspaper carrying news material in English, French, and Spanish, gathered from all corners of America, the West Indies and Africa has maintained itself in Harlem for over five years. . . . Under American auspices and backing, three pan-African congresses have been held abroad for the discussion of common interests, colonial questions and the future cooperative development of Africa. In terms of the race question as a world problem, the Negro mind has leapt, so to speak, upon the parapets of prejudice and extended its cramped horizons. In so doing it has linked up with the growing group consciousness of the dark-peoples and is gradually learning their common interests. . . . As with the Jew, persecution is making the Negro international.

Source: Alain Locke, preface to *The New Negro* (1925).

Mason wanted him to "be primitive and know and feel the intuitions of the primitive." Hurston, too, eventually fell out with her patron and escaped from under Mason's financial largesse, when she used her research trips and findings to inform her novel *Jonah's Gourd Vine* (1934) and her anthropological study *Mules and Men* (1935). In so doing, Hurston had broken the contractual agreement that gave Mason sole ownership of her research. Hurston's productivity continued throughout the 1930s, and in 1937 she published her most successful novel, *Their Eyes Were Watching God.*

French Connections

Harlem was not the only race capital or nascent center of artistic blacks. The popular vogue of African visual artists and African American musicians captured the imagination of white audiences in cosmopolitan cities abroad, such as Paris, Marseilles, and London. Paris attracted an array of intellectuals, writers, artists, and musical performers of African descent from the United States, the Caribbean, and Africa who forged a diasporic community and articulated an internationalist outlook through their interaction and exchange of ideas.

In many ways, Paris in the 1920s resembled Harlem. Although smaller in number, the black population in Paris grew considerably more large and heterogeneous during World War I because of the presence of black troops from the United States and from France's colonies in Africa (primarily Senegal and the Sudan) and the Caribbean. For the black Americans who remained in or returned to Paris in the postwar years, the cosmopolitan character of Paris afforded a haven from the many reminders of racial inequality in the United States, and it also offered the opportunity to cultivate intellect, talent, fame, and fortune. American musicians went on tour to Paris, and some lived as expatriates in the city. Black visual artists studied in Paris. Harlem Renaissance figures Alain Locke, Claude McKay, Langston Hughes,

Jessie Fauset, Jean Toomer, James Weldon Johnson, Countee Cullen, Gwendolyn Bennett, and others all traveled to Paris and incorporated Parisian settings into their writings.

The French initially became aware of African American popular culture as a result of World War I, when black soldiers, such as in Lieutenant James Reese Europe's 369th Infantry Regiment Band and other black regiment bands, carried the sounds of jazz throughout France. In the 1920s, such black American musicians as Palmer Jones's International Five, Louis Mitchell's Jazz Kings, Eugene Bullard, Ada "Bricktop" Smith, Florence Embry Jones, and Josephine Baker established their performance careers in Paris. For those African American entertainers, Paris offered celebrity status unattainable in the United States. For example, black drummer and band leader Louis Mitchell, considered among the earliest musicians if not the first to introduce jazz to Europeans, performed in vaudeville revues in England in 1915, and in 1917 Mitchell and his jazz band, the Seven Spades, played in concert in Paris. After the war, Mitchell returned to New York, but by 1920 he set sail for Paris after forming the new band Mitchell's Jazz Kings, of which Sidney Bechet was a member. The Jazz Kings played at hotels and dance clubs in France, and Mitchell, who remained in Paris until World War II, opened a restaurant in Montmartre, a hill in the northern part of the Right Bank known for its bohemian subculture since the 1890s, where artists, including black musicians and visual artists, continued to gather after World War I.

Of all the black performers, the most renowned—indeed, legendary—was Josephine Baker, who had previously danced in chorus lines in black hits on Broadway. Once in France, however, Baker set Paris afire in her Revue Negre in the mid-1920s. In *Opportunity* in 1927, Countee Cullen described the effect of the scantily banana-clad Baker: "Paris is in a state of violent hysteria over her; there are Josephine Baker perfumes, costumes, bobs, statuettes; in fact, she sets the pace."

As magazines heralded Harlem's popularity among whites, it was manifestly evident that the *vogue negre* in France occurred concurrently and may have even preceded the years when Harlem was in vogue. No more telling example was the growing influence of African art shapes, particularly African masks, on the European artist Pablo Picasso's epoch-making painting *Les Demoiselles d'Avignon* (1907). The fascination with primitive art and its relation to modern art connected whites in both France and the United States with African American artists and critics. The Parisian art collector Paul Guillaume published articles on African art in *Opportunity* during the 1920s, and he also co-authored with Thomas Monro the book *Primitive Negro Sculpture* (1924), which included pieces owned by the white American collector Albert Barnes.

In France, African-descended people from the United States, the Caribbean, and Africa formed a cosmopolitan community of color, but with different intellectual, social, political, and class perspectives. If black authors found in New York in the 1920s a plethora of periodicals in which to publish, the same could be said in France of African authors and editors of such newspapers and magazines as *Les Continents, La Voix des Nègres, La Race nègre, Le Courrier des Noirs, La Dépêche africaine, Légitime Défense, La Revue du Monde noir, Le Cri des Nègres, L'Etudiant martiniquais, L'Etudiant noir,* and *Africa.*

Before New York's white literati paid public homage to the role of blacks in the arts, in 1921 France bestowed its highest literary award—the Prix Goncourt (Goncourt Prize)—on René Maran for his novel *Batouala.* Maran had been born in the French Caribbean colony of Martinique and had worked in an administrative position in French West Africa, so his prizewinning novel depicted Africans' indigenous culture and practices within the political context of colonialism. His portrayal of the cruel and debilitating effects of French colonial policies was unmistakable. Thus the Goncourt Prize made the book all the more an international sensation. Some blacks, for example, Jessie Fauset and Hubert Harrison, read *Batouala* in the original French; however, the book was translated into English in 1922 and was discussed and reviewed extensively in the black press. Maran's picture appeared on the cover of *The Crisis* that year.

News of Maran's achievement surprised and elated African Americans. Even the famous and elderly nineteenth-century black novelist Charles Chesnut wrote to black literary scholar Benjamin Brawley in 1922 that "while he [Maran] is not a United States Negro, I think his triumph is one of which all those who shared the blood of his race—for from his portrait he seems to be of the full-blood—may well be proud." Chesnut was especially complimentary of Maran's sonorous and visual treatment of nature—the wind, woods, streams, smoke, birds, and the like. Black nationalists Marcus Garvey, William Ferris, and J. A. Rogers also enthusiastically praised Maran.

Maran began to correspond with black writers as well as to contribute to black periodicals such as *Opportunity*. Before Alain Locke's *New Negro* or even the special *Survey Graphic* issue that introduced to many Americans the flowering literary movement in Harlem, Maran informed his French readers about such budding Harlem writers as Jessie Fauset, Langston Hughes, Claude McKay, and Countee Cullen. Moreover, Harlem Renaissance notables visited Maran in Paris. Reflecting on the tremendous international stature of René Maran, literary scholar Brent Edwards proposed resetting the time of the black literary renaissance to account for the influence of Paris rather than Harlem. Edwards argued that the "the impact of *Batouala* at the dawn of the 'Harlem Renaissance' would mean reconfiguring the accepted cartography of black literary modernism. If nothing else the relocation of the center of a diasporic movement from Harlem to Paris calls attention to a broader understanding of black internationalism than heretofore recognized."

In Paris, black artists and intellectuals found a great diversity of languages and political perspectives—a diversity that produced linguistic and other ethnic challenges to transnational conceptions of diaspora. Language differences confounded a simple and straightforward translation of words. The black yet multi-ethnic community in France found that the process of translation was, according to Edwards, "indispensable to the pursuit of any project of internationalism, any 'correspondence' that would connect populations of African descent around the world." The Harlem writers certainly followed newspapers from the black Francophone world, while their counterparts in France followed the African American scene. Alain Locke was contacted in 1927 by Jane Nardal, a young student from Martinique at the Sorbonne in Paris, for permission to translate *The New Negro* into French. Nardal was well qualified to do this translation, and she was also able to publicize the book widely, given her contacts at Parisian newspapers, including *Le Soir* and *La Dèpêche africaine*, which was edited by the Guadalupe-born Maurice Satineau. Nardal and her sister Paulette were among a growing number of black intellectuals who, in the 1920s, located themselves within a larger black transnational movement.

Yet the articulation of a black diaspora revealed at times misunderstanding and differing viewpoints. For example, most black Americans held an opinion of France similar to that of Alain Locke, who lauded France for its racial egalitarianism. However, some of France's black colonial subjects, such as René Maran of Martinique and left-wing trade unionist Lamine Senghor of Senegal, took a more critical position. Maran wrote of the French: "They tolerate us because they need us more and more due to the growing lack of manual

Couple wearing raccoon coats, with a Cadillac
This James Van Der Zee photograph was taken on West 127th Street in 1932. The photographer was a chronicler of life in New York's Harlem.

labor. . . . But this has not prevented France up to now from blocking our access to jobs of primary importance." In addition, distinctions among persons of African descent over the usage of *noir, negre,* and *Negro*—all meaning "black"—connoted different and conflicting political and class orientations in the pursuit of racial equality.

Visual Artists

Noting African art's influence on European modern art, Alain Locke proposed that African art forms be sources of inspiration to "culturally awakened" blacks, because they provided a liberating "racial idiom" in contrast to conventionalism. The most noted African American visual artists of the period included Aaron Douglass, Sargent Johnson, Richmond Barthé, William H. Johnson, Archibald Motley, Palmer Hayden, and Augusta Savage. The demand for black artistic renderings continued to heighten during the 1920s, when a plethora of periodicals', books', and theatrical and musical playbills' publishers demanded black illustrations. However, noted African American artists of the period developed their work not simply from their consciousness of the "legacy of African art"; several also developed their technique from training in Paris. In certain cases, exposure in the United States to the Bavarian-born modernist Winold Riess also played a formative role.

Not least of all, African Americans were emboldened to develop a variety of different styles (modernism, realism, primitivism, folk) and aesthetic forms (painting, sculpture, drawing, photography) through the support of such wealthy white patrons as the collector Albert C. Barnes and Charlotte Osgood Mason, as well as the wealthy black heiress A'Lelia Walker, the daughter of beauty magnate Madam C. J. Walker. Awards from philanthropic institutions such as the Barnes and Harmon Foundations played a significant role in encouraging artistic creativity. At a time of great cultural ferment, black visual artists experienced levels of unprecedented productivity. New Negro artists broke away from what Locke called "timid conventionalism" as they rendered in photographs, paintings, and sculpture the rural folk culture, the black vernacular in street life and cabarets, and the fashionable world of the black elite.

Capturing the mood and the spirit of black life in Harlem took many forms, but none conveyed a more realistic picture of black middle-class life or

Photographers and Illustrators

Harlem's leaders and institutions than the photographs of James Van Der Zee (1886–1983). His photographs have significantly shaped the way the Harlem Renaissance is remembered. Van Der Zee operated a successful studio in Harlem for nearly a half-century, using as his subject matter ordinary Harlem residents as well as such celebrities as the poet Countee Cullen, political leader Marcus Garvey, and dancer Bill "Bojangles" Robinson. Van Der Zee's photographs chronicle the emergence of the New Negro, documenting memorable images of war veterans, parades, and leisure life on New York's Lenox Avenue and in the upwardly mobile Striver's Row.

Rise, Shine, Aaron Douglas
This painting depicts the spirit of the Harlem Renaissance.

The Great Depression of the 1930s ended the prosperity of both Harlem and Van Der Zee, who found himself struggling to make ends meet. His client base dropped precipitously, since people were far less able to pay for photographic services. The growing use of personal cameras further diminished his business. His work was rediscovered in the 1960s, when it was included in the Metropolitan Museum of Art's 1968 exhibition *Harlem on My Mind*.

Like James Van Der Zee's photographs, the prolific artwork of Aaron Douglas (1898–1979) seems to embody the spirit of the Harlem Renaissance. Douglas's art graced the covers of several playbills and more than thirteen books, including those by Countee Cullen and Langston Hughes. Douglas was a frequent illustrator for such popular magazines as *The Crisis* and *Opportunity.* Douglas moved from Kansas to Harlem in 1925 and quickly became acquainted with the elite coterie of intellectual and cultural leaders. He

Palmer Hayden, *Nous quatre à Paris* [We Four in Paris], 1928–1930

The figures, positioned very close to one another, form a tight unit that underscores their relationship, as does the similarity of their physical appearance in head shape and hairstyle.

abandoned the artistic style that he had studied as a student at the University of Nebraska, adopting instead a more stylized African-influenced aesthetic. In New York, Douglas studied under the German artist Winold Reiss, who had illustrated the Harlem issue of *Survey Graphic*, the forerunner of Alain Locke's *The New Negro*. Reiss, a European artist who had been inspired by African sculpture, encouraged Douglas to look to his artistic "ancestral legacy" for inspiration.

Douglas's modernist aesthetic earned him important commissions as a commercial artist and solidified his reputation as the preeminent visual artist of the period. Alain Locke called Douglas a "pioneering Africanist" and commissioned him to create the illustrations for *The New Negro* (1925).

The painter Palmer Hayden gained stature as an artist from his experiences living in both Harlem and Paris in the 1920s. Born Peyton Cole Hedgeman in a small town in **Painters** rural Virginia, Palmer Hayden received the name by which the world would come to know him when he enlisted in the army during World War I. A letter of reference for Hedgeman accidentally identified him as Palmer Hayden, and, afraid to advise the army recruiters of the mistake, he adopted the new name.

As a child, he attended a one-room schoolhouse where teachers first noticed and encouraged his special talent for drawing. Hayden quit school at a young age in order to go to work, performing such odd jobs as sand hauling and fish packing on the Potomac River. He never stopped drawing, however, and in 1906 he went to live with his aunt in Washington, D.C., to study commercial art. After nine years in the army, Hayden eventually settled in New York City, where he took art classes and exhibited his work at several venues, including the 135th Street branch of the New York Public Library (now called the Schomburg Center for Research on Black Culture). In New York, Hayden supported himself with jobs that also served his interest in art. For example, he cleaned the studio of an art instructor who, in return, taught him to paint in oils.

In 1926, Hayden was thrust into the limelight after winning first prize in the Harmon Foundation Awards for Negro Artists. The Harmon Foundation provided support to a number of important black artists. The prize money and support from wealthy white patrons allowed Hayden to travel to France, where he eschewed formal study and instead let his own experiences inform his work.

Hayden experimented with a variety of styles and subjects, creating post-Impressionistic seascapes, comic cartoon sketches, a series based on the life of African American folk hero John Henry, and a sensitive nude self-portrait in watercolor. Hayden is most known for his

Archibald J. Motley, Jr., *Saturday Night*, 1935
This stylized, shorthand depiction of cultural groups was popular in the American
Scene painting of the time.

scenes of urban black life, such as his *A Midsummer Night in Harlem* (1938). Some black art critics found Hayden's portrayal of black physiognomy—with round heads and exaggerated lips,
eyes, and ears—to be offensive. Describing Hayden as "a talent gone far astray," art historian
James Porter compared Hayden's representations of black people to "ludicrous billboards that
once were plastered on public buildings to advertise the blackface minstrel." However, this
visual idiom was employed by other black artists, including Archibald J. Motley, Jr., in part
because it spoke of and to black working-class culture.

Much of Hayden's oeuvre portrays homosocial communities—groups of men at work
or enjoying one another's company during their leisure time. *Nous quatre à Paris* features four
dapper black men (including him) seated around a table and playing cards; two others shoot
pool in the background. The relationship among men, a fact further signified by the painting's title, represents the figures not as four independent beings but as four bodies involved
with one another so as to constitute a "we."

Archibald J. Motley, Jr. (1891–1981) was an outstanding Chicago artist noted for paintings of his city's black nightlife and for portraits of his family and friends. Motley's two
concerns, presented in different styles, convey the different representations of black life and
culture that were often hotly debated in regard to New Negro literature. Motley, the child
of a middle-class family living in an integrated Chicago neighborhood, enjoyed a relatively
privileged upbringing before enrolling in the School of the Art Institute of Chicago. Removed
from the modernist New York art scene, Motley was schooled in a realistic aesthetic and was

taught to disdain the modernist aesthetic as epitomized by the works of the pivotal Armory Show of 1913, officially called the International Exhibition of Modern Art, which was the first large-scale exhibition in the United States of modernist European and American art.

Motley began his career as a portrait painter, undertaking what he considered a "scientific" study of race. His portraits of family members and of women of mixed racial heritage, such as *Octoroon Girl* (1925), won him a Gold Medal from the Harmon Foundation. Art scholars note that his renderings of very light-skinned, elite middle-class women were intended to question ideas of racial demarcation. In fact, the similarity between Motley's portraits of apparently well-to-do mulatto and octoroon women and those of his white wife, painted during the same period, are striking—offering dignified and refined images that are virtually undistinguishable as far as racial difference is concerned.

Motley's stature grew largely from his later work, however, particularly from his Bronzeville series of paintings, which focus not on the accoutrements of the black elite but rather on the world of leisure in Chicago's black working-class neighborhoods. This series did not express the realist aesthetic of his portrait work but rather modernism with its vibrant colors, rhythmic motion, and a very different visual idiom for his peopled streetscapes and cabaret scenes. Motley's painting *Saturday Night* (1935) depicts large, bright red lips and brilliantly white smiles, reflecting the artist's attempt to use a distinct visual language to signify class differences among blacks.

A talented and versatile artist, Motley was one of the first African American artists of the 1920s and 1930s to achieve a significant degree of critical as well as financial success. He became the first black artist to mount a one-man show in a major New York gallery. He was also the first African American to win a Guggenheim fellowship, which financed a year's study in Paris (1929–1930).

On several levels, the artist Sargent Johnson shared Alain Locke's interest in producing "Negro art." He was among those African American artists who heeded Locke's call to claim the "legacy of the ancestral arts" not only thematically but also in a visual aesthetic form. Johnson was less interested in proving the legitimacy of such a project to the larger white world than in providing his own people with an image they could embrace.

Johnson once stated: "It is the pure American Negro I am concerned with, aiming to show the natural beauty and dignity in that characteristic lip, and that characteristic hair, bearing and manner; and I wish to show that beauty not so much to the white man as to the Negro himself." Although many black artists included African content in their works—for example, Douglas's *Aspects of Negro Life: The Negro in an African Setting* (1934)—or incorporated African art into their paintings, such as the Fang statuary in Palmer Hayden's *Fetiche et Fleurs* (1931–1932), Johnson conveyed a restrained, often spare, sculptural aesthetic of African forms.

Based in the San Francisco Bay area, Sargent Johnson was one of the few West Coast artists to rise to national prominence and to participate in the Harmon Foundation exhibitions in New York. Therefore, although Johnson can clearly be considered a part of the New Negro arts movement of the 1920s and 1930s, his California context and geographical distance from Harlem and other urban centers of the North exposed him to other influential artistic styles, such as the California modernism of his local peers and the populist Mexican art movement, exemplified by the murals of Diego Rivera. Later in his career, Johnson would abandon his earlier artistic notions of racial representation and experiment with abstract forms.

Clashing Artistic Values

The decade of the 1920s witnessed not only the flowering of "Negro" arts in the realms of music, visual media, and in literature but also controversy over the role and the meaning of art. New Negroes debated form and content, the social significance of art, its "racial" characteristics, and the acceptable boundaries of artistic representation. At the heart of the clash of opinions was the explicit and sometimes implicit argument over the image of blacks that art codified in the minds of whites.

Of the major intellectuals of the Harlem Renaissance, W. E. B. Du Bois was the most dogmatic advocate of the propagandistic role of art. In his essay "Criteria of Negro Art" in 1926, which was given first as a speech in June and published in *The Crisis* in October of that year, Du Bois insisted **Art as Propaganda** that "all Art is propaganda and ever must be, despite the wailing of the purists. . . . I do not care a damn for any art that is not used for propaganda." The challenge for the black artist, as Du Bois identified it, was to create art work, be it literary or visual, that countered the stereotypes, the caricatures, and the overall racist images replete in the larger white society.

Du Bois loathed Claude McKay's novel *Home to Harlem* for its depiction of the seamier side of black life—the fighting, drunkenness, and sexual promiscuity. Remarking that the book left him feeling "distinctly like taking a bath," Du Bois railed against McKay's willingness to cater to whites' fascination with the primitive, sarcastically lambasting him for satisfying "that prurient demand on the part of white folk for a portrayal in Negroes of that utter licentiousness which conventional civilization holds white folk back from enjoying. . . ." To cultural arbiters such as Du Bois and Jessie Fauset, who likewise shunned the blues and jazz, books like McKay's harmed the struggle for racial equality.

Although abhorring the idea of art as propaganda, Countee Cullen of the younger generation also denounced what he believed to be pejorative representations of black people. He argued that they simply replicated and confirmed racist stereotypes. In March 1928, while working as the assistant editor of *Opportunity,* he pursued this topic in his column, "The Dark Tower," admonishing: "Negroes should be concerned with making good impressions. They cannot do this by throwing wide every door of the racial entourage, to the wholesale gaze of the world at large. Decency demands that some things be kept secret; diplomacy demands it; the world loses its respect for violators of this code. . . . Let art portray things as they are, no matter who is hurt, is a blind bit of philosophy."

It is interesting that the black artists who repudiated the values of Du Bois, Fauset, Cullen, and other advocates of middle-class propriety chose to do so in the white press, thereby announcing in a very public way the debate, as well as their own liberation from a politics of respectability that held African Americans imprisoned to the white gaze, or in Cullen's words "the wholesale gaze of the world." The message of such writers as McKay, Hughes, and Wallace Thurman was meant for white readers no less than for the black literati. In the article "The Negro and the Racial Mountain," which appeared in *The Nation* in 1926, Hughes defiantly maintained his artistic freedom, as he rebelliously summoned a new race consciousness and a generational divide: "We younger Negro artists who create now intend to express our individual dark-skinned selves without fear or shame. If white people are pleased we are glad. If they are not, it doesn't matter. We know we are beautiful. And ugly too. The tom-tom cries and the tom-tom laughs. If colored people are pleased we are glad. If they are not, their displeasure doesn't matter either. We build our temples for tomorrow, strong as we know how, and we stand on top of the mountain, free within ourselves."

In 1926, a year of warring words among black artists, other rebels, including Hurston, Aaron Douglas, Richard Bruce Nugent, and Gwendolyn Bennett, rallied and founded the daring and controversial magazine *Fire!!*, whose byline read "Devoted to the Younger Negro Artists." In its short life (only one issue was published), *Fire!!* flaunted an artistic style that defied the restraint of the older artistic values. Richard Nugent's contribution "Smoke, Lilies and Jade" celebrated same-sex desire. Wallace Thurman's short story "Cordelia the Crude," also in *Fire!!*, portrayed Harlem in all its stark realities. Writing in *The New Republic* in 1927, Thurman chastised those African Americans who felt the need to hide from readers the lifestyle of urban blacks who are "still too potent for easy assimilation." In Thurman's own short life (he died at age 32), he wrote novels, plays, short stories, and served in editorial positions for both black and white periodicals. He is best known for his novels *The Blacker the Berry* (1929) and *Infants of the Spring* (1932).

In an ongoing conversation in white magazines, black writers clashed with one another over the meaning of black creative expression. George Schuyler departed from both Du Bois and Langston Hughes in his article "The Negro-Art Hokum," which ran in *The Nation* in 1926. Ever the iconoclast, Schuyler argued that the very concept of "Negro art" was bogus—as he termed it, "self-evident foolishness." For Schuyler, the salient issue was not whether blacks in America exhibited talent but whether their artistic expression was racially unique at all.

As early as the 1890s, black writers Victoria Earle Matthews and W. E. B. Du Bois had written about racial distinctiveness in the arts. Victoria Earle Matthews lectured and wrote

Race Literature about "race literature" as early as 1895, then predicting the full development of a body of literature essentially different from the larger American literature. In 1897 Du Bois emphasized in "The Conservation of Races" not the validity of physical differences of race but rather spiritual and psychical differences—of "Negro genius, Negro literature and art, Negro spirit." Schuyler disagreed. In words that must have enraged his opponents, he opined: "The literature, painting, and sculpture of Aframericans—such as there is—is identical in kind with the literature, painting, and sculpture of white Americans: that is, it shows more or less evidence of European influence." Schuyler, rejecting outright the notion of an essential black difference in the arts, went so far as to declare that "the Aframerican is merely a lampblacked Anglo-Saxon."

Langston Hughes's article "The Negro Artist and the Racial Mountain" was actually a rebuttal to both Du Bois and Schuyler. It appeared one week after the Schuyler piece and affirmed cultural uniqueness. Equally important, Hughes's 1926 book of poems *The Weary Blues* was considered at the time and continues to be considered one of the most successful attempts to translate a black musical vernacular style and spirit into verse. Hughes's retort to Schuyler was based not merely on artistic theories but on successful artistic practice in the creation of such poems as "When Sue Wears Red," "The Weary Blues," "Danse Africaine," and "Jazzonia."

For Hughes, the barrier to black artistic expression took the metaphorical shape of a "mountain standing in the way of any true Negro art in America—this urge within the race toward whiteness, the desire to pour racial individuality into the mold of American standardization, and to be as little Negro and as much American as possible." The access to a unique Negro cultural inheritance, Hughes contended, had been denied, since the black middle class consciously discouraged the young black artist from seeing "the beauty of his own people . . .

or if he does, to be ashamed of it when it is not according to Caucasian patterns." Class perspective is central to Hughes's understanding of a uniquely Negro art. Celebrating the "blare of Negro jazz bands and the bellowing voice of Bessie Smith singing the Blues," Hughes concludes his essay with an exhilarating praise song for the "low-down folks."

Jean Toomer also weighed in on this discussion with his article "Race Problems and Modern Society," published in 1929. Toomer bemoaned the race-talk of the 1920s, believing race to have become more rigidified than ever before and with "the new Negro . . . much more Negro and much less American than was the old Negro of fifty years ago." Toomer advocated the "melting pot" solution, but he posited that such a melding and blending of ethnicities and races into a homogeneous people would emerge only after mankind put an end to the idea of race. To the light-skinned Toomer, race was a false idea. Rather than celebrate race, as did the black literati, he urged the abandonment of the "hypnotic labels" of racial classification. "There is only one pure race—and this is the *human* race. We all belong to it—and this is the most and the least that can be said of any of us with accuracy."

In the context of the 1920s, both the white literati of the Lost Generation and the black literati of the Harlem Renaissance fully believed in the capacity of the arts for social change. With regard to racial change, however, later generations of historians and literary critics would deem naïve the New Negro's belief **Art and Social Change** that the arts served the struggle for racial equality—or, as historian David Levering Lewis has pithily termed it, "civil rights by copyright." If racial integration is one measure of change, then change had indeed come to parts of Harlem, but not in the Cotton Club or Small's Paradise so much as in the literary, publishing, and intellectual circles that brought together Langston Hughes and Carl Van Vechten, Walter White, and H. L. Mencken of *The American Mercury;* Zora Neale Hurston and Franz Boas; Countee Cullen and Frederick Allen of Harper & Row; and Alain Locke and Paul Kellogg of *Survey Graphic.* In banquet halls, universities, publishing firms, homes of the white and black literati, and also in the cabarets occurred what scholar George Hutchinson describes as "the intellectual and institutional mediations between black and white agents of the renaissance."

No one exemplified the meaning of "civil rights by copyright" better than James Weldon Johnson. It was Johnson who best understood the multifaceted struggle that called artists, as well as lawyers, educators, and political activists, to arms, because he had been all of them, including a diplomat, which may explain his sympathetic views toward artistic freedom. As both an accomplished literary artist and the executive director of the NAACP, Johnson represents the enduring image of a true renaissance man. From the late nineteenth century to the 1930s, he wrote and anthologized poetry, composed lyrics for songs ("Lift Every Voice and Sing," familiarly called the "Negro National Anthem"), worked directly in the creation of musical theater with pioneering figures such as Bob Cole and his own brother J. Rosamond Johnson, and authored the novel *Autobiography of an Ex-Coloured Man* (1912) and his autobiography, *Along This Way* (1933). An NAACP officer in the 1910s and 1920s, Johnson fought valiantly against lynching, through fundraising and the mass participation of the silent march. He helped to strategize the NAACP's legal battles, and in numerous articles in newspapers and magazines he raised his voice of protest against racial discrimination.

And Johnson was not alone as an artist in the civil rights vanguard. Other NAACP leaders wrote fiction and found themselves immersed in this cultural movement. Du Bois, but also Walter White, who risked his life to go into the South to write about lynching, was famously involved in the Harlem Renaissance. White regularly brought together black and white luminaries in his home, and he also wrote the novels *Fire in the Flint* (1924)—a story of racial violence and the psychic journey to black consciousness—and *Flight* (1926). The respected writer and thinker H. L. Mencken influenced Walter White in the debate over artistic freedom. Mencken rejected the hypocrisy and prudishness of white readers who were appalled by sexual images and yet apathetic about lynching and other social injustices.

Amid the growing racism of the early twentieth century—with its emboldened Ku Klux Klan, its segregated army that fought to safeguard world democracy, its lynchings, and its horrific Red Summer of 1919—James Weldon Johnson saw all these events firsthand from the vantage points of artist and civil rights warrior. On various levels, the positive link between the arts and civil rights did not escape him. In response to the NAACP's fundraising campaign against lynching, the casts of the popular musicals *Shuffle Along* and *Runnin' Wild* held successful charity benefit performances.

Johnson was able to assess the racial situation, as few others could. His first awareness of a glimmer of white respect for black artists appears in his account of the artistic world of black bohemia at the dawn of the twentieth century. He watched this dim glow brighten into the extraordinary and illuminating exchange between white and black writers, publishers, and rich benefactors—with the unprecedented rise of black artists in the public sphere. Despite the racial limitations (for example, some whites' perceptions of blacks as primitive), the 1920s witnessed a newfound recognition and respect for black creative artists. Johnson focused on progress. "The creative author has arrived," he announced of those who had made best-seller lists, thus disproving racist claims about black intellectual and cultural inferiority.

Black artists, and Harlem, were in vogue. It seemed a new day—with lush parties, with music and theater, with rich conversation, with the good life of travel to Paris and other cities abroad, with the speakeasies and cabarets, and, most of all, with boundless creativity. The leading black and white literati reveled in the parties of such whites as Charlotte Osgood Mason, Carl Van Vechten, and Nancy Cunard, and of such blacks as A'Lelia Walker, Walter White, and James Weldon Johnson. The arts appeared to be the elixir for America's racial ills. As early as 1911, David Mannes, the concertmaster of the New York Symphony Society, reflected this way of thinking when he stated that "through music, which is a universal language, the Negro and the white man can be brought to have a mutual understanding." For W. E. B. Du Bois in 1926, this cultural influence harkened a new day in racial pride and hope: "We black folk . . . have within us as a race new stirrings; stirrings of the beginning of a new appreciation of joy, of a new desire to create, of a new will to be; as though in this morning of group life we had awakened from some sleep that at once dimly mourns the past and dreams a splendid future."

However, hopes for a splendid future would soon be dashed. The stock market crash in October 1929 shattered the gaiety and optimism. Longstanding inequalities and malfeasance in the American economy had finally come home, like chickens to roost. The nation's economic foundation rapidly collapsed, unleashing poverty and devastation unknown in America. The arts did not perish, but the suffering caused by the Great Depression was unalleviated by a government ill-prepared for such a catastrophe. As the future got bleaker, some would even liken the economic fallout to God's punishment for the materialism, self-indulgence, and seeming wanton abandon of the Roaring Twenties. In this scourge of biblical proportions, they would invoke Old Testament language: "the harvest is past, the summer is ended, and we are not saved."

The New Deal Era

In the Throes of Economic Depression

Political Resurgence

The Black Cabinet

New Deal Programs

Organized Labor

On the Left

A Harvest of Artistic Expression

Harlem voters
African Americans turn out to vote for Franklin D. Roosevelt in 1936.

417

In the winter of 1927, nineteen-year-old Richard Wright informed his boss that he was quitting his Memphis job and leaving for Chicago. It was a fateful decision. Little did he know that his move to Chicago would bring him fame as an author. Only one thing was clear to young Wright as he stepped jobless onto the Memphis street—he was about to move again. He and his family had done so several times before on their migration circuit: from their rural Mississippi roots to Tennessee, back to Mississippi, on to Arkansas, again back to Mississippi, and then once more to Tennessee.

With two other relatives, Wright determined yet again to escape the aching hunger, the violence, and the stifling racism of the South—to get away from what he would describe in his autobiography as the "terror from which I fled." Arriving in Chicago, he believed he had reached the fabled Promised Land. He got off the train and saw no Jim Crow signs but rather blacks and whites mingling freely in the train station. His first employer treated him fairly. Becoming a postal clerk by 1929, Wright earned a salary that permitted him to move into a larger apartment and to feel for the first time "happy in my own way."

Wright's sense of security proved all too brief. Armageddon-like, the stock market crashed in October 1929. The American economy spiraled downward over a period of weeks, months, and then years. The nation's jobless—1.6 million at the end of 1929—skyrocketed to nearly 13 million in 1933. There would be no quick fix. Wright saw his paychecks dwindle and then cease altogether. He sought public relief after losing his postal job. "I was making a public confession of my hunger," he later wrote, recalling the stinging humiliation of waiting in line for a handout.

Richard Wright's experiences tell a story not dissimilar from that of countless other African Americans of his generation. Joining the migration stream on the eve of the Great Depression, Wright, like so many others, became part of a historical process that brought the nation significant economic and also racial transformation. While the crushing poverty of the Depression years was prompting a new understanding of the federal government's role in responding to the economic plight of Americans of all races, President Franklin D. Roosevelt's New Deal was also giving black Americans a unique opportunity to mount a political resurgence on a scale not seen since Reconstruction—for forging interracial alliances, switching party allegiances, demanding equal rights and economic justice, and challenging in unprecedented ways the fundamentals of the American political-economic system.

In the Throes of Economic Depression

In the late 1920s, as the stock market, corporate profits, and urban land values all soared, little attention was paid to a widening gap in the distribution of wealth. By 1929, the richest 5 percent of Americans had grown richer still, amassing 26 percent of national income, while the bottom 40 percent of income earners controlled only 12 percent. In his Inaugural Address on March 4, 1929, President Herbert Hoover had spoken confidently of a new era of abundance and prosperity: "I have no fears for the future of our country. It is bright with hope." But he had spoken too soon.

In hindsight, one ominous sign of hard economic times ahead had been the migration of nearly 1 million blacks out of the South in the 1920s—a strong indicator of how the American agricultural system was collapsing. The black migration of the 1920s, considerably greater than that of the World War I years, attested to the painful reality that an economic depression had engulfed southern agriculture long before the stock market crashed. The nation's agrarian population, which included the majority of African Americans, had not enjoyed the prosperity of the 1920s. Cotton farmers in particular found themselves caught in a destructive cycle of overproduction and falling prices. As cotton sold for fewer and fewer cents per pound, farmers produced more and more to make up the difference, driving prices even lower. The boll weevil continued to ravage crops in the 1920s, forcing many white and black farm owners who during the 1910s had been lucky enough to survive its destruction to join the ranks of tenant farmers or migrants.

When Roosevelt's New Deal began, in 1933, federal efforts to resolve the agricultural crisis only worsened the plight of tenants and sharecroppers. The Agricultural Adjustment Act (1933), which provided incentives for landowners to plant fewer acres and reduce farm production, unwittingly gave impetus to the eviction of tenants from the land. Landowners also abused their **The Agricultural Crisis and Black Migration** role as administrators of federal relief by denying black tenants their fair share. The dying plantation system hastened the urbanization of the South. A stunning demographic shift caused by the migration of millions of rural southerners regardless of race to urban areas in both the South and the North touched virtually all aspects of American culture, transforming politics, organized labor, race relations, popular culture, and urban life in general. Although economic factors were a major cause of overall migration, the decision of African Americans to leave the South was integrally linked to the racism of its Jim Crow society.

Depression came early to black urban-dwellers. For them, the first signs of an economic downturn appeared in the mid-1920s, when thousands of African Americans lost their jobs. They were counted as no more than the casualties of a technological age in which several million people were expected to become unemployed because of low skills. After the crash of 1929, however, businesses closed and banks failed. In cities blacks were often the first to lose jobs, while in rural areas their wages were driven down to starvation levels. Black women especially suffered from the curtailment of household jobs and personal-service occupations. With small or nonexistent reserves of capital, blacks rapidly experienced dire want and suffering. Members of the black middle class did not escape the deteriorating conditions, because their fate was directly tied to the economic condition of the migrant populations they served.

While some southern black professionals joined the chorus of anxious local whites in discouraging massive migration out of the region, others followed their clientele to the North. Middle-class southern African Americans—whether in the professions (lawyers, teachers, newspaper editors, and ministers) or in business (undertakers, barbers, beauticians, insurance executives, and storeowners)—all depended on black patronage and on the income of skilled and unskilled African American laborers who, for the most part, worked for white companies and white employers. When adverse economic circumstances curtailed employment or reduced wages, the black middle class was immediately affected.

Unemployed, poverty-stricken African Americans did not wait passively for the New Deal to provide them with the necessities of life. At times they found it desirable to use what force they could command to secure employment and relief. In 1929 Albon Holsey of the National **African American Efforts at Relief** Negro Business League organized the Colored Merchants Association, which in New York tried to establish stores and purchase merchandise cooperatively. African Americans were urged to buy from these merchants, because their patronage would provide jobs for their racial community. The stores survived less than two years of the severe depression, however.

4I9

African Americans seek relief

In 1937 Margaret Bourke-White took this picture of unemployed African Americans seeking food supplies.

Shortly thereafter the Jobs-for-Negroes movement began in St. Louis, where the Urban League led a boycott against a white-owned chain store whose trade was almost exclusively black but carried no black employees on its payroll. The movement spread to Pittsburgh, Chicago, Cleveland, and other Midwestern cities, and many African Americans found employment because of the pressure brought on white employers in black sections. The most intensive campaign was waged in New York City in 1934 by the Citizens' League for Fair Play, cofounded by Rev. John H. Johnson, minister of St. Martin's Protestant Episcopal Church, and Fred Moore, publisher of the *New York Age*. The league initially attempted to persuade white merchants to use black sales clerks. When this effort failed, the league resorted to picketing the stores and appealing to blacks with the motto, "Don't Buy Where You Can't Work."

Rev. Johnson urged his congregation: "I want our meeting this morning to begin a 12 day campaign to persuade Blumstein's department store where 140 persons (with 16 colored menials) [are employed] to hire colored girls as sales clerks." Some 400 to 1,500 persons attended the league's weekly meetings, and over a hundred, the majority of them women, carried picket signs daily. Picketers harangued their listeners about the injustice of whites refusing to hire black workers. Tensions rose to the point of physical confrontation to discourage shopping at the biggest department store in Harlem. Historian Cheryl Lynn Greenberg notes of the campaign: "While boycotts were a time-honored tactic for otherwise powerless black communities, pickets were newer, reflecting the shift toward broad-based visible political strategies." The campaign resulted in the hiring of fifteen black women, but the department store did not abide by its promise to hire more.

In 1935 growing poverty and racial tensions with white merchants and landlords in Harlem led to a riot. An African American youth was caught stealing a penknife from the counter of a store on 125th Street. He succeeded in escaping, but there were rumors that he had been beaten to death. Black crowds gathered, accusing the police of brutality and the white merchants of job discrimination. The mob began smashing store windows and raiding shelves, and the rioting went on during most of the night of March 19. Three blacks were killed, two hundred store windows were smashed, and more than $2 million worth of damage was done. The city was both outraged and ashamed. Mayor Fiorello La Guardia appointed an interracial Committee on Conditions in Harlem. A staff of investigators, headed by black sociologist E. Franklin Frazier, studied the causes of the riot and concluded that the lawlessness was provoked by "resentments against racial discrimination and poverty in the midst of plenty." There was insufficient relief of a private and public nature to stem the tide of social unrest that prevailed in Harlem and other black communities. Picketing and other measures continued. Blacks were encouraged greatly by the decision of the Supreme Court in 1937 declaring that the picketing of firms that refused to employ African Americans was a legal technique for securing relief.

Political Resurgence

The migration of 1.5 million African Americans to northern urban centers dramatically altered the political landscape. The concentration of African Americans in northern cities sparked a political resurgence that placed blacks once more in the thick of American politics at the local, state, and national levels. Their political resurgence had a lasting effect on national party politics. Whereas, in the late nineteenth century and throughout the first two decades of the twentieth century, black leaders appeared to be satisfied with the patronage of Republican presidents, by the 1920s blacks as a group demanded a greater voice in politics.

Black disaffection with the party of Lincoln reared its head in 1928 when Republicans attempted to build a strong party in the South. Prominent African American Republican leaders, such as Benjamin Davis of Georgia, Perry Howard of Mississippi, and William McDonald of Texas, lost influence in their states as the Republican high command looked to white leaders in those states and began to seat white southern delegates at the national convention instead of black delegates who presented credentials. Black leader Robert Church of Memphis grew so incensed about the "lily-white" stance of the Republican movement in the South that he refused to serve on the party's national advisory committee. Although the great majority of black voters remained loyal Republicans, in the 1928 presidential election influential black newspapers—the Baltimore *Afro-American,* the Norfolk *Journal and Guide,* and the Boston *Guardian*—endorsed New York Democratic governor Alfred E. Smith's bid for the presidency rather than Republican candidate Herbert Hoover. Smith was a Roman Catholic, an advocate of repealing Prohibition, and a reputed friend of African Americans.

Hoover's dramatic victory (he carried Florida, Kentucky, North Carolina, Tennessee, Texas, Virginia, and West Virginia) demonstrated both the Republican Party's ability to win the votes of white southerners and the extent to which it was willing to alienate blacks in an effort to build up a following capable of breaking the Southern Democratic stronghold.

After the election, to add insult to injury, President Hoover was reported to have expressed his desire for building a new Republican Party in the South "such as could commend itself to the citizens of those states." African Americans interpreted the president's words to mean white citizens only.

It was not Hoover's election but that of Oscar DePriest to the United States House of Representatives in 1928 that caused blacks to rejoice and to take an optimistic view of electoral politics. In the 1920s, the black population had doubled in New York, Chicago, and Cleveland and had tripled in Detroit. Awareness of black political power grew in direct correlation with the rapidly growing numbers of black migrants. In Chicago, black and white candidates alike realized the growing significance of the black vote as early as 1915. In that year, the black Republican candidate Oscar DePriest won a seat on the city council, representing the densely populated South Side. Born in Alabama, DePriest had moved first to Ohio and then to Illinois, settling in Chicago in 1899. He soon developed an interest in politics and worked his way up from a ward committeeman to become the first African American alderman.

The Election of Oscar DePriest

In 1923 he was mentioned as a possible candidate for Congress, and with the cooperation of Chicago mayor William Hale ("Big Bill") Thompson, DePriest's influence steadily increased. Thompson's own political ambitions had been helped by the black vote. With the fortuitous death of Martin B. Madden, the Republican congressional nominee in 1928, DePriest's time had come. Announcing his candidacy, he overcame opposition with the help of powerful Republican interests and won Illinois's First Congressional District seat by a plurality of 3,800 votes. The prediction of the North Carolina black congressman George White in his farewell address in 1901—that blacks would return "phoenix-like" to Congress—had finally come true. Moreover, for the first time in American history, a northern black sat in the national government's lawmaking body.

DePriest's position was a peculiar one. During his three terms in Congress, he served not only as the representative of his own Illinois district but also as the symbolic representative of all African Americans. One black newspaper said that his presence in Washington gave the race "new hope, new courage, and new inspiration." DePriest's presence in Washington certainly gave tangible evidence of the regeneration of blacks in politics and prepared the way for other black elected officials. However, his distinction in American political life alarmed and infuriated the white South. When his wife, Jessie DePriest, attended a tea at the White House for the wives and families of members of Congress, white southerners were outraged. Several southern legislatures passed resolutions "condemning certain social policies of the administration in entertaining Negroes in the White House on a parity with white ladies." In Birmingham, where DePriest was scheduled to speak, the Ku Klux Klan burned him in effigy.

If African American victories in state and local elections proved that times were changing, nothing did so more dramatically than the shifting allegiance of blacks to the Democratic Party. More and more blacks began to place responsibility for the Depression on the shoulders of President Hoover. They grumbled that it would take a long time for the funds provided by Hoover's Reconstruction Finance Corporation to trickle down through giant but defunct industrial firms and reach those at the very bottom of the economic ladder. Still, in the presidential election of 1932, two-thirds of black voters cast their ballots for Hoover. Franklin D. Roosevelt's win, while not dependent on the black vote, presaged the change in black political behavior and in the Democratic Party.

The Shift to the Democrats

The Republican Party had frankly overestimated its hold on its black constituents. Confident of blacks' fidelity to "the Party of Lincoln," Republicans failed to see the shifting tide—the many black men and women who benefited from New Deal relief. By 1934 many New Deal programs were underway. They were not free of racial discrimination, but the federal initiatives provided jobs for blacks, created training and educational opportunities, and included black advisors in the administration's policy making process.

The shift among black voters appeared dramatically in the Illinois congressional race of 1934, when black voters toppled their one-time hero Oscar DePriest in favor of the black Democratic candidate, Arthur W. Mitchell. DePriest's opposition to government-sponsored relief sounded eerily like the Hoover plan, which had failed to address the needs of millions of Americans of all races who had not only lost their jobs but could find no work of any kind. By 1934, 17 percent of whites and 38 percent of blacks were officially identified as incapable of self-support. Everywhere the relief rolls soared, and blacks disproportionately suffered from poverty. Economic considerations, more than any other, led black voters to question and ultimately reject old political allegiances.

In 1934 Arthur Mitchell himself personified the black political makeover. Four years earlier, he had been registered as a Republican; now his victory over DePriest made him the first black Democrat to sit in Congress. A migrant to Chicago from Alabama, Mitchell trumpeted the relief programs of the New Deal in his campaign speeches. As the national Democratic Party grew more interested in attracting the black vote, Mitchell gained more prominence, becoming the first African American to speak from the floor at a Democratic National Convention. That caused one irate southern senator to walk out of the convention. Mitchell's presence within the House of Representatives was a constant source of displeasure and embarrassment to his southern Democratic colleagues.

All over the country, African Americans were not only switching from the party of Lincoln to the party of Roosevelt but were also becoming increasingly active in politics. The shift to the Democratic Party reflected an attitudinal change toward the Republican Party, but it also entailed a growing sense **A Growing Sense of Political Efficacy** of political efficacy. Black voters exhibited greater consciousness of and confidence in leveraging their own racial-group interests through the electoral process. By the time of Roosevelt's second presidential campaign in 1936, the majority of African Americans heartily supported him. Roosevelt's direct way of tackling problems, as well as his friendly and accessible-sounding "fireside chat" radio addresses to the nation, captured the imagination of blacks just as they did other Americans. His physical handicap and the strength he brought to bear in overcoming this enormous difficulty were a source of inspiration to them.

In Roosevelt's later terms, black leaders articulated a more critical position toward New Deal policies, but in 1936 many of them basked in the new Washington spotlight. The president frequently received African American visitors, and it was widely known that Robert L. Vann of Pittsburgh, Julian Rainey of Boston, William T. Thompkins of Kansas City, and F. B. Ransom of Indianapolis were high in the Democratic councils. Roosevelt visited and sent messages to African American organizations and institutions, thus adding to his popularity with black groups.

African Americans expressed even greater fondness for the president's wife, Eleanor Roosevelt. She was known to be on intimate terms with black-women's club leader Mary McLeod Bethune, and she invited the National Council of Negro Women, of which

Mrs. Bethune was president, to tea at the White House. Eleanor Roosevelt visited black schools and federal projects and spoke to numerous groups. When she was photographed while being escorted by two ROTC cadets at Howard University, African Americans circulated the picture widely as an example of the broad egalitarianism of the occupants of the White House. Southern whites circulated the same photograph to show the depth to which the occupants of the White House had descended. In 1939 Eleanor Roosevelt made a powerful public statement against segregation when she resigned from the elite Daughters of the American Revolution after they refused to grant permission to black singer Marian Anderson to perform in the DAR's Constitution Hall in Washington, D.C.

By 1940 when he ran for a third term, Roosevelt drew some opposition among blacks. For example, Roosevelt never endorsed the antilynching and the antipoll-tax bills—the two most crucial pieces of civil rights legislation of the era. Accusations that the administration allowed discrimination in some relief agencies and excluded blacks from preliminary defense preparations caused a decline in his black support. In the presidential election of that year, some African Americans preferred to believe Republican nominee Wendell Willkie's promises and were inclined to desert what they were pleased to call "The Dirty Deal." Most, however, voted for Roosevelt despite their criticisms.

In the years that followed, black voters revealed greater divisions among themselves, although blacks in the large urban centers of the North tended to favor the politics of the New Deal. The black vote had become particularly influential in such pivotal states as Illinois, Ohio, Pennsylvania, and New York, causing anxiety in both Republican and Democratic circles. Urban black voters, just like white voters, took positions on labor matters, foreign policy, and other issues that affected them. African Americans, sensing their strength and importance as voters, believed that they could now demand a high price for their support. In addition to expecting that a candidate reflect their views on public questions that interested all Americans, blacks insisted that a candidate's views on questions of race be acceptable.

African Americans manifested their strength during this period of political regeneration not only in the consideration that both major parties gave them in national elections, but also in **Success at the State and Local Levels** their successes in state and local elections. An increasing number of blacks secured seats in state legislatures in the 1930s and 1940s. After 1932 black legislators became commonplace in California, Illinois, Indiana, Kansas, Kentucky, New Jersey, New York, Ohio, Pennsylvania, and West Virginia, and there were sizable numbers of black voters in both the Republican and Democratic parties. The greater concentration of blacks in urban centers and their increased political consciousness were additional factors. In 1946 about thirty blacks won seats in ten state legislatures.

In 1930 two African Americans were elected to municipal judgeships in New York City, and thereafter other municipalities elected or appointed blacks to judicial positions. In 1947 there were black judges in Cleveland, Chicago, Los Angeles, Washington, and several other cities, and in New York City the number had increased to seven. In many American cities, African Americans helped to manage the affairs of government as members of boards of education and city councils, as members of the prosecuting attorneys' staffs, as police officers, and as tax commissioners and corporation counsels. The fruits of political activity were enjoyed in a very real way by the faithful servants of the parties, and there was an increasing recognition of the contributions that qualified blacks could make to the improvement of the life of the whole community.

Window in Time

Evaluating the New Deal

On the subject of the Negro, the Roosevelt record is spotty, as might be expected in an administration where so much power is in the hands of the southern wing of the Democratic party. And yet Mr. Roosevelt, hobbled as he has been by the Dixie die-hards, has managed to include Negro citizens in practically every phase of the administration program. In this respect, no matter how far behind the ideal he may be, he is far ahead of any other Democratic president, and of recent Republican ones. . . . This does not mean that the Roosevelt administration has done all that it could have done for the race. Its policies in many instances have done Negroes great injustice and have helped to build more secure walls of segregation. On the antilynching bill Mr. Roosevelt has not said a mumbling word. His failure to endorse this legislation, to bring pressure to break the filibuster, is a black mark against him. . . . His failure to act, or even speak, on the anti-lynching bill was the more glaring because, while mobs in America were visiting inhumanities upon Negroes, Mr. Roosevelt periodically was rebuking some foreign government for inhumanity, and enunciating high sentiments of liberty, tolerance, justice, etc.

Source: Roy Wilkins, "The Roosevelt Record," *The Crisis* 47 (November 1940).

The Black Cabinet

One of the most important indicators of black political clout was the New Deal's black advisors. The Roosevelt administration secured the assistance of African American specialists and advisors in various governmental departments. Seeking the advice of blacks was not a Roosevelt innovation. Presidents had long sought to gauge the pulse of the black population through one or more community leaders, most notably Booker T. Washington. For example, in 1889, on learning that the African American historian-lawyer George Washington Williams would be making a visit to the Belgian Congo, President Benjamin Harrison asked Williams to submit a report that could be used in determining the nation's policy toward that colony. In most instances, the African American advisors were faithful members of the president's party who gave counsel in the matter of patronage.

Franklin Roosevelt's group of black advisors differed from those of earlier presidents in several important respects. The number of "black cabinet" members was fairly large, in contrast to the small number on whom previous presidents had relied for advice. It is not possible to set an arbitrary number, because it was changing constantly and because it is difficult to be sure whether certain appointees were actually members of the select circle that could be regarded as a "cabinet." Nor can it be said that previous black advisors had access to the president. Time and again, they sought to speak with the president personally only to be rebuffed, told that he was too busy, or forced to see one of his many subordinates instead.

The Black Cabinet
Official photograph of government leaders known as the "Black Cabinet," about 1935. Mary McLeod Bethune is in the center of the first row.

But Roosevelt's black advisors differed from their counterparts in previous administrations in that they were placed in positions of sufficient importance that both the government and the African American population generally regarded their appointments as significant. Nor were they people whose relationship with the government was nebulous and unofficial.

Members of Roosevelt's black cabinet were not politicians but highly intelligent and highly trained people, called in to perform specific functions. To that extent, their appointments fell in line with the tendency of the New Deal administration to commandeer the services of the best-trained people in the country to assist in developing programs of relief, recovery, and reform. They were called by some the black brain trust, for among them were doctors of juridical science, doctors of philosophy, and college presidents. Some African Americans complained that it was most unfortunate to confine such experts only to the problems affecting their race. Few could deny, however, that they were well qualified to perform many functions, and indeed on occasion many of them worked in areas that only indirectly touched on racial issues.

In the early days of the New Deal, Harold L. Ickes, Roosevelt's Secretary of the Interior who had once been a white president of the Chicago branch of the NAACP, began to hire

African Americans in the National Government

racial advisors. Also within the Department of the Interior, Clark Foreman, a white liberal from Atlanta, employed African Americans on his legal staff as well as in such other agencies as the National Park Service. Later, some of those black staffers transferred to other departments, thereby enlarging the area in which blacks exercised some influence in the national government. Eleanor Roosevelt is credited with having enlarged the size of the black cabinet, while Will W. Alexander, who was for a time the head of the Farm Security Administration, was also instrumental in having African Americans appointed to positions.

Among the African Americans who occupied high places in New Deal councils was Robert L. Vann, the editor of the *Pittsburgh Courier,* who served as a special assistant to the attorney general. William H. Hastie, the dean of Howard University Law School, entered government service as assistant solicitor in the Department of the Interior. He went on to serve as the judge of the American Virgin Islands and later as civilian aide to the secretary of war. In 1946 he was appointed governor of the Virgin Islands. Robert C. Weaver was the first black to be the racial advisor in the Department of the Interior. Subsequently he served in several agencies, including the Federal Housing Authority (FHA), the Office of Emergency Management, and the War Manpower Commission. Decades later, in 1966, Weaver became the first African American cabinet officer when the Housing and Home Finance Agency, which he headed, became the U.S. Department of Housing and Urban Development (HUD).

Eugene Kinckle Jones, executive secretary of the National Urban League, went to Washington in the early days of the New Deal and for a period was advisor on "Negro affairs" in the Department of Commerce. Lawrence A. Oxley, a veteran social worker, was chief of the division of Negro labor in the Department of Labor. Mary McLeod Bethune, founder-president of Bethune-Cookman College, was active for several years as the director of the division of Negro affairs of the National Youth Administration (NYA). Edgar Brown, president of the United Government Employees, advised on Negro affairs in the Civilian Conservation Corps (CCC). Frank S. Horne, poet and teacher, did duty in several capacities, primarily with federal housing programs. William J. Trent served first as racial advisor in the Department of the Interior and then went to the Federal Works Agency as the racial relations officer.

The list of African Americans in such positions in the federal government continued to grow during the Roosevelt years. Numerous consultants served only temporarily: Abram L. Harris with the National Recovery Administration (NRA), William H. Dean with the National Resources Planning Board, Ralph Bunche with the Library of Congress and later with the Department of State, Rayford W. Logan with the Coordinator of Inter-American Affairs, and Ira D. A. Reid with the Social Security Board's Bureau of Employment. Some of these officials remained only a few months, but others found government service so much to their liking that they stayed on during the Truman administration.

With the onset of the war emergency their number was substantially increased. Crystal Bird Fauset, a former member of the Pennsylvania legislature, went to Washington as the racial relations advisor in the Office of Civilian Defense. Ted Poston, veteran New York newspaperman, served as racial advisor in the Office of War Information. Col. Campbell Johnson became an executive assistant to Gen. Lewis B. Hershey, head of the National Selective Service (which oversaw the military draft). Others served with the War Production Board, the War Manpower Commission, the Office of Price Administration, and the Social Security Board.

The black cabinet was never a formal body. But Wendell Pritchett, legal scholar and biographer of Robert C. Weaver, notes that by the late 1930s the New Deal's black appointees referred to themselves as the Federal Council on Negro Affairs and recognized Bethune as its chair and Weaver as its vice-chair. Weaver was often referred to as "chief recruiter," on account of his tireless and frequently successful efforts to secure employment for blacks as government advisors. The only woman in the group, Bethune functioned well as "titular head" of the group because of her close connection to the Roosevelts, especially the First Lady. She hosted meetings of the black New Dealers at her home, bringing them together in discussions of fair treatment and strategies for more black appointees in federal agencies.

427

Mary McLeod Bethune in the federal service

Bethune, founder of Bethune-Cookman College and the National Council of Negro Women, served the New Deal as Director of Negro Affairs of the National Youth Administration. Here she confers with Eleanor Roosevelt and Aubrey Williams, Director of the NYA.

The group, according to Pritchett, was primarily responsible for urging the appointment of William Hastie to a federal judgeship. Roosevelt appointed Hastie a district court judge in the Virgin Islands in 1937.

The task of these black advisors in the federal government was difficult and delicate. They pressed for economic and political equality for their race in America, while also seek-

Expanding Job Opportunities in the Federal Government

ing to increase opportunities for the employment of blacks in government and in industry on the basis of ability and training rather than color. They worked closely with the black press and with other agencies of influence, through members of Congress, and through powerful white citizens in public and private stations. The aggressive temper of the African American population during the Great Depression and the subsequent war emergency, as well as the inclination of many New Dealers to increase equal opportunities, all made possible the achievement of a measure of success by black New Dealers.

If some of these officials smarted under the roles assigned to them as advisors on "Negro affairs," they could nonetheless look with satisfaction at the increasing number of blacks who were serving their government in many capacities. Thanks to new Civil Service regulations, it was no longer necessary to indicate one's race on applications or to attach a photograph; but after personal interviews, officials sometimes avoided hiring African Americans by availing themselves of the Civil Service Commission's "rule of three," by which they could select a white who ranked second or third over a black who ranked first. Even with such practices, the number of African Americans on the federal payroll increased from about 50,000 in 1933 to approximately 200,000 before the end of 1946. The majority of the newly employed blacks worked in the low, unskilled, and semiskilled brackets. There was only a sprinkling of economists, statisticians, chemists, physicists, and other specialists. In some portions of the government the segregation of whites and blacks was abolished, and most government cafeterias were opened to blacks. Although those in the black cabinet were not responsible for all the improvements in the condition of African American federal employees, they could claim a considerable number of the changes as their handiwork.

New Deal Programs

As the Roosevelt administration established its numerous agencies to aid the total population in recovering from the severe depression, African Americans benefited from the slowly improving conditions. However, because of the long American tradition of discriminating against blacks, it was inevitable that in these agencies there were variations between black and white relief grants, numbers of workers, salaries, and the like. The National Industrial Recovery Act, the 1933 law that tried to stimulate industry, established "fair competition" codes providing for a minimum wage scale of $12 to $15 per week, a forty-hour week, and the abolition of child labor under the age of sixteen. But the law also set up cost-of-living differentials that discriminated against occupational groups (such as domestic servants) in which large numbers of black workers were found.

In the steel, laundry, tobacco, and other industries, African Americans frequently received lower minimum wages than did whites for similar work. The compliance boards that were set up to enforce the codes were frequently made up of employers who were themselves violating the codes. Blacks seldom complained for fear of losing their jobs, and few of them were represented at code hearings. When wages were raised in compliance with the codes, employers frequently dismissed black workers and paid higher wages to whites. Thus African Americans had little to lament when in 1935 the Supreme Court declared the National Industrial Recovery Act unconstitutional.

A larger number of blacks were adversely affected by the various New Deal measures to provide relief to farmers and agricultural workers. Under the crop reduction program of the Agricultural Adjustment Administration (AAA), farmers received cash benefits for plowing under their cotton, wheat, and tobacco **The Agricultural Programs** crops and for slaughtering their hogs. While the farmers' cash benefits rose to billions of dollars under the AAA, grants intended for African American farmers were often dissipated and misappropriated. Many landlords took advantage of illiterate sharecroppers and tenants by keeping the checks intended for them.

This dishonesty, which hurt both white and black farm workers, led the victims to organize, forming such groups as the Southern Tenant Farmers Union. Planters vigorously opposed such unions and appealed to racial prejudice in an effort to break up cooperation between black and white farmers. Even after administrative rules were changed to provide for payments directly to the tenants rather than through landlords, many blacks suffered, for then white landlords merely removed them from the land and collected the benefits themselves. Aside from the benefits that some African American farmers received in the form of cash payments, blacks obtained valuable experience in voting in AAA referenda on such important questions as establishing marketing quotas. They demonstrated conclusively that blacks and whites could vote together on important economic questions, even though in most southern states blacks were still effectively disenfranchised in regular elections.

Nat Williams and E. H. Anderson, Farm County Security Administration official

Williams was the first black person in the United States to receive a loan under the Tenant Purchase program, Guilford County, North Carolina.

From the Tennessee Valley Authority (TVA), the Rural Electrification Administration (REA), the Federal Land Bank, and local production credit associations, African Americans received benefits, though frequently not in proportion to their numbers or their needs. They were substantially aided by the program of the Farm Security Administration (FSA), which in 1937 took over the work of the Resettlement Administration (RA). Unfortunately, the FSA had an appropriation only one-fifth the amount appropriated for the AAA, but it undertook to establish communities of small farmers who rented land from the FSA and made loans to those who desired to purchase their own farms. An extensive educational program was carried out in which, among other things, new methods of production and marketing were introduced.

Under the program, African Americans received a large share of the benefits, and thousands, for the first time in their lives, were able to purchase land. The FSA, largely because of the capable leadership of Will W. Alexander, insisted that there be no discrimination between white and black farmers. Because of its racial policies and its program of settling farmers in communities, it was almost always under fire. The attacks grew so vehement that in 1942 congressional enemies of the FSA managed to cut its appropriations so drastically that the greater part of its program was ended.

The National Youth Administration (NYA) and the Civilian Conservation Corps (CCC) undertook to provide relief for the youth of America. Under Aubrey Williams, a white Mississippian, the NYA set up a liberal program for the benefit of African American youth. Not only was Mary McLeod Bethune invited to Washington to head the division of Negro affairs, but black state and local supervisors were appointed in districts in which large numbers of African Americans lived. In the out-of-school programs, 13 percent of enrollees were blacks, and they learned a variety of trades that were to be beneficial in the war emergency. In the student work program, more than 64,000 participants, or 10 percent, were black. Young African Americans, all the way from grade school to graduate school, found it possible to continue their education by means of the benefits obtained from the NYA.

The CCC maintained a policy of strict segregation, but during its lifetime from 1933 to 1942 approximately 200,000 African American boys and young men worked in camps established by the agency. In addition to the work of conservation, reforestation, and prevention of soil erosion, the agency set up an educational program under the supervision of black advisors. A measurable amount of illiteracy was eliminated, and juvenile delinquency was doubtless curtailed. Although many critics raised serious doubts as to the wisdom of the program, there can be no doubt that the CCC relieved the suffering of many young men during the depths of the Depression.

The New Deal housing program aided blacks' efforts to keep their homes and acquire better accommodations, and it provided employment on projects under construction. Some African Americans secured loans from the Home Owners Loan Corporation (HOLC) in

Window in Time

Life in the Civilian Conservation Corps in 1935

According to instructions, I went Monday morning at 8 o'clock to Pier I, North River. There were, I suppose more than 1,000 boys standing about the pier. . . . The colored boys were a goodly sprinkling of the whole. A few middle-aged men were in evidence. These, it turned out, were going as cooks. A good many Spaniards and Italians were about. A good-natured, lively, crowd, typical of New York. . . . When my record was taken at Pier I a "C" was placed on it. . . . But before we left the bus the officer shouted emphatically: "Colored boys fall out in the rear." The colored from several buses were herded together, and stood in line until after the white boys had been registered and taken to their tents. This seemed to be the established order of procedure at Camp Dix. . . . We were taken to permanent camp on a site rich in Colonial and Revolutionary history, in the upper South. This camp was a dream compared with Camp Dix. There [was] plenty to eat, and we slept in barracks instead of tents. An excellent recreation hall, playground, and other facilities. . . . During the first week we did no work outside camp but only hiked, drilled, and exercised. Since then we have worked five days a week, eight hours a day. Our bosses are local men, southerners, but on the whole I have found nothing to complain of. The work varies, but is always healthy, outdoor labor. As the saying goes, it's a great life, if only you don't weaken! . . . On the whole, I was gratified rather than disappointed with the CCC. I had expected the worst. Of course it reflects, to some extent, all the practices and prejudices of the U.S. Army. But as a job and an experience, for a man who has no work, I can heartily recommend it.

Source: Luther C. Wandall, "A Negro in the CCC," *The Crisis* 42 (August 1935): 244, 253–254.

order to make payments on their homes during the Depression. A limited number were able to borrow money to build homes with loans guaranteed by the Federal Housing Authority (FHA). In many communities, however, banks were not inclined to lend money to African Americans, because they regarded them as poor risks and considered the future value of houses that blacks had occupied uncertain.

The most widely beneficial federal housing program for African Americans was the encouragement that local housing authorities received to construct low-cost housing projects with subsidies from the United States Housing Authority, later the Federal Public Housing Authority. In some northern communities the projects were occupied jointly by blacks and whites, but segregation was maintained in each southern community. Approximately one-third of the units constructed were occupied by African American families. These modern units, equipped with electric or gas appliances and recreation facilities, gave thousands of families an opportunity to live in a kind of environment that previously was wholly unknown to them.

Under the Public Works Administration (PWA) and similar federal agencies, a considerable number of black hospitals and other public buildings were constructed. Through an arrangement with local and state governments, these agencies subsidized the construction of buildings at black colleges, playgrounds, community centers, and the like. Despite provisions in the contracts that called for the employment of a proportionate number of African American workers in the construction of these buildings, these stipulations were frequently disregarded. In some cities, where as many as a score of buildings were constructed with public funds, no African Americans were employed. Other cities, however, did employ some black workers. In very few instances did African Americans secure the amount of employment to which they were entitled under the contract provisions.

During the darkest days of the Great Depression it was not possible for either the government or private business to employ enough people to relieve satisfactorily the plight of the unemployed. The Federal Emergency Relief Administration (FERA) and later the Works Progress Administration (WPA, later renamed the Work Projects Administration), provided relief both in kind—food, clothing, and commodity surpluses—and in employment. There was a greater inclination toward fairness to African Americans in providing material relief than in providing employment. Under the WPA, policy varied so much from place to place that no general statement can be made about the treatment of blacks.

In some communities blacks secured employment on professional and clerical levels. Thus African American actors, writers, and artists in such cities as New York and Chicago carried on their activities under the WPA. In other localities, however, it was almost impossible even for unskilled blacks to secure any benefits from the relief agencies. Wage differentials in some communities were great, and administrators made no apologies for them. Even so, more than a million blacks owed their livelihood to the WPA in 1939, and this and similar relief agencies became so important that they were surpassed only by agriculture and domestic service as sources of income.

When the Social Security Act was passed in 1935, provision was made for old-age assistance and unemployment benefits in a large number of occupational categories. Since agricultural and domestic workers were excluded, however, a huge proportion of the black population failed to qualify for the benefits provided by the act. Even in the old-age assistance program, there was a tendency, especially in the South, to grant lower sums to aged blacks than to aged whites.

One of the most outrageous abuses of African Americans in this period was a study conducted by the U.S. Public Health Service in Macon County, Alabama. Begun in 1932 **The Tuskegee Study** during the closing months of the Hoover Administration and known as the Tuskegee Study, it charted the progression of untreated syphilis in more than four hundred impoverished black men, most of them sharecroppers or day laborers. Later investigations produced "no evidence that informed consent was gained from human participants in the study." The subjects were offered free medical care, free meals, burial expenses, and other "unethical inducements" to participate.

They were never informed that they had syphilis, and standard treatments for a disease with serious health consequences, including the possibility of death, were deliberately withheld. It is estimated that at least "one hundred men had died of syphilis or related complications, at least forty wives had been infected, and nineteen children had contracted the disease at birth." The study was discontinued in 1972 only after it was revealed in an Associated Press article. Two years later the federal government began to make reparation

432

payments to survivors. In May 1997, President Clinton, in a ceremony at the White House, formally apologized to the eight remaining survivors, declaring that the attitudes that had led to such a study were "clearly racist."

Although outright discrimination against African Americans occurred in the local administration of most New Deal programs in the South, many white southern leaders still found the New Deal distasteful, because it concentrated too much power in Washington. Furthermore, despite its limitations, New Deal officials occasionally forced rather than merely required equality in the administration of benefits. Southern leaders could ill afford to break with the Roosevelt administration because it gave them national power through their control of congressional committees and their voice in party politics. For the most part they had to pay lip service to the liberal measures of the New Deal and to compromise on many issues. The entrance of highly trained blacks into the government in Washington and federal agencies in the South gave white southerners a new experience in their relationships with blacks. The full consequences of this new experience could not be measured until years after the New Deal had ended.

Organized Labor

Labor unions gained power in the 1930s, owing to federal support of workers' rights and the growing militancy of workers themselves. Section 7a of the National Industrial Recovery Act, which established the NRA, provided that employees should have the right to organize and bargain collectively through representatives of their own choosing without "interference, restraint, or coercion of employers of labor." The National Labor Board (NLB) was set up to enforce those provisions of the statute. In 1935 the Wagner Act gave permanency and strength to the National Labor Relations Board (NLRB), which had replaced the NLB the previous year. The act established clear-cut rules for collective bargaining and set up twenty-two regional boards to conduct elections in industry to determine what group of employees was entitled to bargain with employers. The NLRB also received wide powers in handling labor disputes and settling strikes. It was indeed, as it was called at the time, "labor's bill of rights."

For black workers, the challenge was to break the barriers that excluded them from unions so that they could enter into a new period of security and prosperity in the enjoyment of these rights. However, in an effort to keep whites employed during the Depression, labor unions had maintained their exclusionary policies more strictly than ever. The bulk of African Americans who found employment fell into the unskilled and semiskilled categories, where there was little or no union organization. Thus they lacked the protection that the NLRB granted to skilled workers.

The formation of the Congress of Industrial Organizations (CIO) in 1936 gave African American workers an entrée into the trade union movement. John L. Lewis of the United Mine Workers established the CIO after he clashed with the AFL **The CIO** over organizing strategy. Whereas the AFL insisted on organizing workers on the basis of craft, which excluded unskilled workers, Lewis and his followers subscribed to the concept of industrial unionism, in which all workers in a given industry joined in a single union. The CIO was also committed to organizing workers regardless of race or gender, and it succeeded in organizing black workers in several key industries, including steel workers, garment workers, longshoremen, and automobile workers.

Encouraged by the National Urban League, the vast majority of black steelworkers joined the CIO-affiliated Steel Workers Organizing Committee (SWOC) in its organizing drive of 1936. In 1937, when the great steel companies finally agreed (after prolonged and sometimes violent resistance) to bargain with the SWOC, thousands of black workers benefited from the pay raises called for in the contract.

In 1937 the International Longshoremen's and Warehousemen's Union (IL&WU), which had been organized on the West Coast, was affiliated with the CIO. In the beginning, it did not seem to welcome African American workers, but after a major strike in 1934 Harry Bridges, the union's leader, made it clear that black labor would receive equal treatment in the IL&WU. Special antidiscrimination committees were organized to see that no worker was discharged or intimidated on account of race or color. The unionizing of automobile workers was largely the work of the CIO, and the United Automobile Workers of the CIO succeeded in forcing all the major automobile manufacturers to recognize it as the legal collective bargaining agent for the workers—Ford finally capitulated in 1941 after a bitter fight. Although some white members opposed the union's fight for equal opportunities for blacks in the automobile industry, the union continued its struggle. World War II created new opportunities for the employment of African Americans in the automobile industry.

As the CIO ventured into the South, its organizing efforts confronted longstanding regional obstacles to the labor movement, including limited industrial development, the absence of a history of labor activism, and most significantly, the Jim Crow system that divided white and black workers, while easing class tensions among whites. According to such historians as Michael Honey and Robert Korstad, southern industrial unionism, with its linkage of economic and racial justice, provided an early model for the civil rights movement. Workers could not advance toward economic justice without also attempting to dismantle racial segregation. The biracial unionism favored by the left-leaning CIO unsettled Jim Crow and suggested that the labor movement could encompass such larger social goals as civil rights for blacks.

The CIO launched its first southern organizing drive in 1937. It also organized get-out-the-vote campaigns in every state, targeting both whites and blacks despite the latter's disfranchisement. Union organizers found their strongest support among black workers, who drew on a long tradition of protest and applied it to the labor movement. Union meetings in the South took on a different quality, with African Americans incorporating prayer and religious song. The CIO successfully organized R. J. Reynolds Co. tobacco workers in Winston-Salem, North Carolina. A union (called Food, Tobacco, and Allied Industries) won a contract in 1944.

What Robert Korstad terms "civil rights unionism" waned in the South with the onset of World War II, as the federal government turned its attention to the international scene and conservative white leaders steered CIO unions away from civil rights objectives. Then, beginning in the late 1940s, Cold War red-baiting further thwarted this nascent movement with the rise of popular anticommunism, the repeal at the federal level of labor gains, and the stifling of public debate over workers' rights. Nevertheless, the stand of the CIO Committee to Abolish Racial Discrimination and the liberal program of the Political Action Committee gave new hope to many African Americans. They were no longer suspicious of labor organizations per se and were inclined to join strikes with as much enthusiasm as other workers.

By the mid 1930s, conditions in rural Arkansas had become bad enough to convince not only urban workers but also black and white tenant farmers to set aside centuries-old racial hate and join together in protest. In July 1934, seven black and eleven white tenant

Conference of officials of local chapter of UCAPAWA in Tabor, Creek County, Oklahoma, February 1940
Pomp Hall, the man leaning on the table at right, was an active leader among both blacks and whites in the union and in his community.

farmers refused to work the cotton crop unless they secured better wages. As expected, the landowner summarily evicted them. Led by socialist organizers Harry Leland Mitchell and Clay East, these eighteen tenant farmers formed the Southern Tenant Farmers' Union (STFU)— *Organizing Activity in Agriculture* perhaps the most dramatic example of interracial labor activism on a grassroots level. By 1939 the STFU claimed 30,000 members in four states.

The collapse of the agricultural economy and the failure of the New Deal agricultural policies spurred the growth of the STFU, whose members demanded better wages, better working conditions, and a role in the administration of federal funds. Like other southern labor organizations that included blacks, the STFU met with a campaign of terror, from evictions and arrests to mob violence and lynching. The publicity around the STFU and its brutal repression drew national attention to the cause of tenant farmers and was a catalyst for the founding of the New Deal's Resettlement Administration (which became the Farm Security Administration), as well as Senator Robert La Follette, Jr.'s, committee to investigate antilabor violence.

In 1937, the STFU attempted to join the CIO, but its leaders bridled when it was placed under the umbrella of the existing CIO-affiliated United Cannery, Agricultural, Packing, and Allied Workers of America (UCAPAWA). Although UCAPAWA had achieved remarkable success in organizing ethnically, racially, and gender diverse workers, the merger soon soured. The Socialist leaders of the STFU distrusted the Communist leaders of UCAPAWA, the STFU demanded more autonomy, and its black members wanted more leadership roles. The STFU severed the alliance in 1939 and never recovered.

On the Left

In his autobiography, Richard Wright recounts his disaffection with the Communist Party, emphasizing the party's failure to bridge the cultural divide between radical whites and African Americans. However, new scholarship by Robin Kelley, Bill Mullen, Mark Solomon, and others has reassessed the relationship between blacks and white radicals in the Depression era, finding a more complex story of interracial alliances than was previously recognized.

Certainly before the 1930s African American intellectuals and writers (for example, A. Philip Randolph, Cyril Briggs, Eric Walrond, and Claude McKay) were associated with socialism and/or communism. In the 1920s, and in some cases earlier, black writers flirted with leftist ideas. McKay and Langston Hughes had consistently drawn on working-class life in their writings during the Harlem Renaissance years. Yet protest themes and economic critiques would be more popular during the Depression years. The poetry of Sterling Brown, especially in *Southern Road* (1932), captured the defiant spirit of rural black folk in the face of oppression. The collaboration of black poet Waring Cuney and blues musician Josh White resulted in songs that carried words of protest. In the 1930s, Langston Hughes published in leftist magazines, such as *New Masses,* and supported radical initiatives. Countee Cullen's poem on the Scottsboro case appeared in the Communist Party newspaper *Daily Worker.*

Despite his later denunciation of communism, Richard Wright was the best-known black leftist in the 1930s. Although working as a supervisor in the New Deal's Federal Writers Project in Illinois, Wright conveyed unmistakable leftist sympathies in his poetry and fiction. His stark and tragic descriptions of race and poverty exemplified the then-popular literary style of social realism. Wright's *Uncle Tom's Children* (1938) and *Native Son* (1940) put him among the leading American writers of the day.

The message of racial equality that was preached, if not always practiced, by whites in the Communist Party USA appealed to a cross-section of African Americans in the 1930s. It
The Appeal of Communism appeared to be one of the few organizations willing to make bold, public attacks against Jim Crow. Historian Robin Kelley's study of communist influence in Alabama during the Depression suggests a multifaceted, grassroots approach to achieving racial and economic justice. Recognizing the link between economic and civil rights in Alabama, black communists organized protests against lynching and police brutality and launched right-to-vote campaigns. Communist leaders organized the unemployed in Birmingham in the early 1930s, staging public demonstrations to demand relief and forming neighborhood relief committees that presented their demands to local welfare boards.

Rural blacks also allied with the Communist Party by forming the Share Croppers' Union (SCU), which had two thousand members by 1933. Using organizational skills gained in social and religious organizations, black women took leadership roles in the neighborhood relief committees of the SCU. Although the SCU won a few strikes, it was brutally repressed by police and white vigilante violence. Communist influence in Alabama culminated in a wave of strikes in 1934, but it waned after 1935.

Two landmark civil rights cases brought the Communist Party and racial justice into the national—and international—spotlight. On March 25, 1931, nine black youths hopped a freight train traveling west through northern Alabama. The train already carried a group of white boys and two white women, also down-and-out and looking for work along the southern rail lines. The white and black boys fought on the train, which was stopped at the end of its ill-fated

Landmark Cases: Scottsboro and Herndon

ride by a posse of white men in Paint Rock, Alabama. That sealed the fate of the black boys. Immediately arrested on the charge of rape, they were taken to Scottsboro, the seat of Jackson County, Alabama, and there only narrowly escaped a lynch mob.

Within days, four juries convicted eight of the nine boys and sentenced them to death. While the vast majority of white Alabamans took pride in that justice was peacefully done (as opposed to a lynching), a growing number of African Americans and a small contingent of sympathetic whites believed the boys to be innocent, but likely to lose their lives. While the NAACP hesitantly debated whether and how to handle the case, the Communist-affiliated International Labor Defense (ILD) took over the appeals process. The ILD appealed the case three times between 1931 and 1937. By 1937 five of the nine were freed, and by 1950 the last of them had been released.

Similar mockery of justice pitted the ILD against the Jim Crow South and once more before an international audience. In June 1932, Angelo Herndon, a nineteen-year-old coal miner and Communist agitator, was arrested for organizing an interracial protest of the unemployed in Birmingham, Alabama. He was arrested, tried, convicted, and sentenced to eighteen years in prison on a charge of inciting insurrection. After a five-year court battle, the ILD secured his freedom.

The Scottsboro and Herndon cases had a tremendous impact on African Americans' perception of the Communist Party in its fight for civil rights in the 1930s. As a result of these high-profile cases, Communist Party membership rose from a few hundred African Americans in 1930 to 2,500 in 1935. More generally, these legal crusades spurred black protest during a time when the prospects for black freedom seemed bleak. The Scottsboro case in particular empowered many African Americans to engage in active resistance, despite the risk of violent repercussions. These cases also sparked media frenzies, exposing the ugliest features of Jim Crow to the nation and the world. As one historian said of Scottsboro, "in the darkest of times, it linked the fortunes of every American to black liberation, and in many ways helped set the stage for the next wave of struggle for racial equality in the postwar years." The embarrassment to the nation caused by the South's barbaric racial climate would become a major catalyst for the civil rights movement during the Cold War. Finally, the ILD's victories in the Scottsboro and Herndon cases strengthened the legal protections for African Americans, including the right to counsel, the right to a jury of one's peers, equal protection under the law, and free speech.

The growing influence of the Communists also had a divisive impact. Such was the case of the National Negro Congress, which was founded as a result of a meeting at Howard University in 1935. The meeting of the Joint Committee of National Recovery brought together African Americans of various backgrounds, but its leaders agreed that the strategies of the

The National Negro Congress and the Popular Front

moderate civil rights organizations, such as the NAACP and the National Urban League, as well as of the black churches, were inadequate responses to the persistent privation afflicting blacks in the Depression. Those gathered at Howard also denounced the racism of the American Federation of Labor (AFL) and the limitations of the New Deal in addressing the crisis. In their call for a single federation to unite all black organizations, the idea of the National Negro Congress was born.

437

The Scottsboro Boys
Fearing a mob lynching, Alabama Governor B. M. Miller called the National Guard to the Scottsboro jail to protect these young black men accused in the Scottsboro rape case. From left to right, they are Clarence Norris, Olen Montgomery, Andy Wright, Willie Roberson, Ozie Powell, Eugene Williams, Charlie Wiems, Roy Wright, and Haywood Patterson.

In the mid-1930s, the international Communist movement was pursuing a Popular Front strategy in many countries, including the United States. This meant that instead of attacking liberal and leftist (but non-Communist) political parties, labor unions, and other civic movements, Communists would invite these former political enemies to join them to form a "Popular Front" dedicated to resisting fascism and other right-wing forces. The National Negro Congress was one such organization. It convened in Chicago in February 1936, with 800 delegates representing 551 organizations and more than 300,000 people. With A. Phillip Randolph at its helm, the NNC launched a three-pronged platform that endorsed a labor-black alliance, civil rights, and antifascism.

The National Negro Congress represented a coalition of Communists, middle-class black organizations, and workers, united against fascism and racial oppression. This inter-racial, cross-class coalition dissolved after 1940, as a result of the Communist Party USA, like other Communist parties around the world, supporting the Hitler-Stalin Non-aggression Pact. (That pact, signed in August 1939, had enabled Hitler to attack Poland, thus beginning World War II.) Everywhere, news of the Hitler-Stalin Pact shocked anti-fascist liberals, socialists, and others on the left who had supported or been sympathetic to the Soviet Union and the Popular Front movement. The withdrawal of many non-Communist members from the NNC was typical of this widespread reaction.

While it lasted, the Communists' Popular Front, bringing African Americans of varying political persuasions into common cause with the Communist Party, had been the most successful of all efforts on behalf of the Scottsboro boys. Another example of successful use of the Popular Front strategy was the launching of the Southern Negro Youth Conference (SNYC). In 1936, representatives of southern black youth groups attended the first convention of the National Negro Congress (NNC), which passed a resolution calling on "all Negro youth to fight for the eradication of the evil from which they suffer." The result of that appeal was the first meeting of the SNYC, held in February 1937 in Richmond, Virginia, with roughly 534 delegates present. Prominent, traditionally moderate black leaders supported SNYC.

The group's initial principal advisor was Charlotte Hawkins Brown, the president of the Palmer Institute in Sedalia, North Carolina. Mordecai Johnson, the president of Howard University, gave the keynote address at the founding meeting. According to the Norfolk *Journal and Guide,* Johnson's keynote address thrilled his young listeners. He admonished them to shun individualistic motives, to overcome racial oppression, and to fight for the black community. "We have come first of all," Johnson told his audience, "seeking the right to creative labor, to be gainfully employed with equal pay and employment opportunity—economic security. We have met for freedom, equality, opportunity."

From the first conference emerged a set of recommendations to improve economic and interracial conditions in the South. These proposals included petitioning the United States Congress to allow the teaching of African American history in southern public schools and calling on blacks "to use the ballot and political pressure to get more blacks elected to local school boards and hired as teachers in both black and integrated schools." Additionally, the SNYC planned to fight against racial disparities in access to health care and supported legislation to improve educational opportunities for black youth. The SNYC, like other civil rights organizations of the time, supported traditional leftist economic and social programs.

By the time it held its second convention the following year, the Youth Congress had crystallized its goals into a four-point program for development in the areas of citizenship, education, jobs, and health. One of the earliest examples of SNYC group activism is its participation in the black tobacco workers' campaign in 1937. SNYC began to show a distinct leftward turn, when its field representative C. Columbus Alston helped organize black workers into a union, the Tobacco Stemmers and Laborers Industrial Union (TSLIU), in Richmond, Virginia, at the Carrington and Michaux Tobacco Stemming Company on April 16, 1937, and at the I. N. Vaughn and Company on May 7, 1937. Alston assisted them in developing a set of labor demands to present to their companies, including higher wages, shorter working hours, and better working conditions. Franck Kruch of the State Labor Department helped the black tobacco workers arrive at an agreement with their employers within forty-eight hours, and, according to the Richmond *Times-Dispatch,* the agreement included "granting pay increases ranging from 10 to 20 percent, and an eight-hour day and forty-hour week with time-and-a-half for overtime."

After its second convention, however, the SNYC moved its headquarters to Birmingham, Alabama, where it faced more restrictive segregation codes and harsher opposition. In Birmingham, the SNYC's Right to Vote Campaign was chaired by black leftist

James E. Jackson, Jr. Targeting political discrimination in the form of poll taxes, unfair voter registration requirements, and political intimidation, Jackson declared that black southerners would exercise their right to vote in the next presidential election year, 1940. He asserted that "only the enemies of all that is American—of freedom, of justice and democracy—will dare seek to thwart [them]!" By 1946, however, internal dissension and the government's crackdown on left-wing organizations had considerably weakened the SNYC.

In the 1930s, the American Left was the strongest that it would ever be. Many influential writers, artists, and intellectuals, as well as workers, responded to its demands for economic and racial justice. It was not unusual for members of liberal organizations during the early period of the civil rights movement to include left-wing members or to dialogue with such organizations as the Socialist and Communist parties. Members of the radical left and leaders from liberal to moderate ideological persuasion came together in conferences and umbrella organizations to further the budding interracial struggle for black freedom. In November 1938, an interracial and interclass coalition—businesspeople, labor leaders, sharecroppers, journalists, students, and politicians, including members of Congress—convened in Birmingham, Alabama, to discuss the economic crisis in the South.

The Southern Conference for Human Welfare

The egalitarian credo of the Southern Conference for Human Welfare [SCHW] was quickly put to the test when the city's police chief, Eugene "Bull" Connor, interrupted a meeting and ordered the participants to comply with the segregated seating required by city ordinances. In response, the SCHW passed a resolution never to meet in a place where segregation was legal. Arriving late at that same meeting, the conference's most important dignitary, Eleanor Roosevelt, entered the now-segregated conference room and took a seat among the black attendees. When asked to move, Roosevelt placed her chair right on the black-white dividing line, making an important symbolic statement against Jim Crow.

The conference tried to promulgate a program of aggressive action to raise the general level of underprivileged groups in the South. Through its state committees and local chapters it endeavored to create wide interest in political affairs and in some instances went so far as to throw its support behind some candidates for public office while opposing others. It took unequivocal stands against lynching, discrimination, the poll tax, and similar matters, and it usually allied with liberal labor forces. It was frequently accused of left-wing leanings and in the early 1940s was listed as a subversive group by the House Committee on Un-American Activities, which had been established in 1938.

A Harvest of Artistic Expression

Despite conditions in the Depression years, black artistic creativity continued to blossom during the 1930s and 1940s. The richness of the musical and literary flowering of the 1920s served both as a stimulus and as an inspiration for the wealth of talent in the decades to come. Far from inhibiting cultural and social activities or stifling the creative expression of blacks, the Works Progress Administration (WPA) encouraged writers and artists by funding a variety of creative projects during these lean years. Sculptor Augusta Savage (1892–1962) made a profound contribution to the arts movement by serving as a dedicated mentor for young African American artists. She opened the Savage Studio of Arts and Craft in Harlem in 1931 and served as the director for the Harlem Community Art Center, established under the WPA.

Augusta Savage, *The Harp*, 1939
A commanding 15-ft. high piece, *The Harp* was the only work by a black artist to be commissioned by the 1937 New York World's Fair Board of Design.

Augusta Savage began her sculpting career at an early age, fashioning animals and other objects from the mud and **Augusta Savage** clay of her hometown, Green Cove, Florida. She moved to New York in 1921, a time of black migration to the city and the flowering of art. Within three years, she had completed the four-year art program at Cooper Union in the city. She enjoyed her first major success with the piece *Gamin*, which is a bust of her nephew Ellis Ford. The best known of Savage's works, *Gamin* won her a Rosenwald Fund fellowship that financed her travel to Paris in 1929. In France, Savage continued her artistic training, exhibited her work, and communed with other African American artists there, such as Henry Tanner and Hale Woodruff. She returned to New York City in 1931, determined to make an impact on the black arts community. Savage's sculpture *The Harp*, also popularly called "Lift Every Voice and Sing," is made of plaster and painted black.

William Johnson (1901–1970) also benefited from the New Deal's support of artists. Born in Florence, **William Johnson** South Carolina, Johnson demonstrated a passion and talent for artistic expression at an early age. Like his contemporary Augusta Savage, Johnson realized the impossibility of becoming a celebrated artist in the segregated South. He also joined the great exodus of rural black southerners headed for the urban centers of the North, and, like Savage, settled in New York, where he arrived in 1918 with hopes of pursuing artistic training. The eager and gifted young artist was accepted at the prestigious National Academy of Design, where he studied under his devoted mentor, the prominent artist Charles Hawthorne.

In 1926, with the help of funds raised by Hawthorne, Johnson left for Europe, settling in France where he would later meet and marry the Danish textile artist Holcha Krake. Johnson returned briefly to the United States in 1930 to enter several of his paintings in the Harmon Foundation competition, for which he won the gold medal for Negro artists. He continued to live in Europe until 1938, when the growing Nazi threat impelled him and his wife to return to the United States.

They found Harlem still in the throes of the Great Depression. Yet despite barren economic conditions, Harlem's cultural life from the mid-1930s through the 1940s was blossoming as artists experimented with new styles and their work grew in prestige. Moreover, through projects sponsored by the WPA, particularly community arts education initiatives,

William H. Johnson, *Going to Church*, 1940–1941

In *Going to Church*, Johnson masterfully employed bold, bright colors and simple flat shapes to convey rhythm through subtle repetition, as in the repeated bar patterns and numerous sets of pairs—the buildings on either side of the composition, the two pairs of figures, the pair of wheels, the pair of trees, and the two pairs of legs on the animal pulling the cart.

veteran African American artists trained younger artists and established venues for collaboration and sharing ideas and resources. This was certainly true of Johnson, who secured a teaching position at the celebrated Harlem Community Arts Center (active from 1937 to 1942), where he met, among other notable black artists, Gwendolyn Bennett and Jacob Lawrence. At this time Johnson also worked on several WPA-sponsored mural projects, and he exhibited with the Harlem Artists Guild, founded in 1935 by Augusta Savage, Elba Lightfoot, Charles Alston, and Arthur Schomburg.

During this period, Johnson's style and subject matter invoked the black folk art style of untrained painters. He drew on his memories of the rural South to portray sharecroppers picking cotton, convicts working on a chain gang, and families driving to church in ox-drawn wagons while wearing their Sunday best. In works like *Going to Church* (1940–1941), Johnson's visual idiom is simultaneously simple and sophisticated. If reminiscent of folk art, his style is also modern and deliberate. In May 1941, Johnson debuted his new style at his first major one-man show in New York at the Alma Reed Galleries on 57th Street—the center of the New York art scene. The opening received notices in all the major New York newspapers, and several important mainstream art publications, such as *Art News*, reviewed the show. Johnson was lauded by critics, collectors, and dealers.

The 1930s and 1940s were years of rich harvest for blacks in almost all fields of creative activity. Blacks in film were highly visible in the New Deal Era. Bill "Bojangles" Robinson played an Old-South avuncular role opposite white child-star Shirley Temple in *The Little Colonel* (1935) and *Rebecca of Sunnybrook Farm* (1938). Compared to most black male actors, however, Robinson was granted a rare dignity of presentation. His dance duets with Temple also gave filmgoers the only interracial male-female dance team in film history, and Bojangles's skill as a dancer brought him an unprecedented tribute when the famed white dancer Fred Astaire, tap-dancing in black-face, performed "Bojangles of Harlem."

Blacks in Films

Far more typical was Hollywood's negative characterization of black men in infantilized, emasculated roles, such as played by Stepin Fetchit, Willie Best, and Mantan Moreland—all three of these actors specialists in the comic arts of mumbling foolishly, grinning moronically, and shuffling slowly (unless scared, whereupon their eyes would buck and special effects would make them appear to run faster than humanly possible).

The 1934 film *Imitation of Life*, based on Fannie Hurst's bestselling novel, gave a modern twist to the old dilemma of the tragic mulatto. A white-looking young woman named Peola, played by the African American actress Freddie Washington, breaks the heart of her dark-skinned, self-sacrificing mother (Louise Beavers) by refusing to accept her mother's racial identity, running away from home, and passing for white. Beaver's character "Aunt Delilah" becomes a domestic servant whose pancake recipe makes possible the wealth and elite status of her white employer, who is also Aunt Delilah's friend. In the film, both women are single mothers, attempting to raise daughters of similar age. For the black daughter, Peola, "passing" affords her—as a woman of white appearance—the same possibilities for romantic love and acceptance that are afforded to the daughter of the now-wealthy white employer. The death of her mother, however, brings the repentant Peola to her racial senses. At the funeral, her guilt-filled sobs and her confession of her racial identity and love for her mother provide the moral solution to a complicated story of race, color, and class.

If black actors were restricted primarily to the role of servant, black women played the role in diverse ways. The passive resignation with which the actress Louise Beavers portrayed her servant characters on film differed from the sassy, physically imposing role with which Hattie McDaniel imbued her film characters. McDaniels's character, called Mammy in the romanticized Old-South saga *Gone with the Wind* (1939), barely disguises her sense of moral authority. The movie's rakish male lead character, Rhett Butler, played by Clark Gable, confesses that Mammy was one of the few human beings whose respect he actually craved. McDaniel was awarded the Oscar for Best Supporting Actress—the first black actor to win an Oscar; there would be no other until Sidney Poitier in 1964. At her award ceremony, McDaniel stated simply: "I sincerely hope that I shall always be a credit to my race."

Hollywood stars Paul Robeson and Lena Horne both made their film debuts in "race pictures," but unlike McDaniel, who would come under fire from the NAACP for accepting servant roles, they spoke openly against racism. Robeson and Horne achieved unprecedented star status as film leads in Hollywood productions in the 1930s and 1940s, and they attempted to resist, not always successfully, the racial stereotypes that undermined positive images of blacks. Robeson's most widely viewed role on the American screen was Joe in the 1936 version of *Show Boat*. Dispensing with the camera-filming convention of "lip-synching" a prerecorded song, Robeson sang "Ol' Man River" live during the film take. He won tremendous praise for the emotional intensity of his performance.

Paul Robeson and Lena Horne

443

However, Robeson did not hesitate to level criticism even at the films in which he acted. He expressed a sense of betrayal in the British film *Sanders of the River* (1935), for instance, when he charged that the editing of certain scenes had caused him to be an unwitting tool of British colonialism. He went so far as to attempt to buy the film back from the studio to prevent its release, but his efforts proved unsuccessful. Robeson also reacted negatively to his last film *Tales of Manhattan* (1942). Its characterization of blacks angered him so much that he joined the protest against the New York premiere of the film, and afterward he retired altogether from Hollywood filmmaking.

Lena Horne was similarly bedeviled by Hollywood's racial insensitivity. Horne began her career as a singer and dancer at Harlem's Cotton Club. In the 1940s, she was among the first blacks to integrate white big bands, in her case the Charlie Barnett band. After meeting Paul Robeson, as well as the NAACP leader Walter White, Horne became more conscious of her image as a racial representative. Thus the contract she signed with Hollywood's MGM Studios included an explicit clause that she would not play a servant or other racially stereotyped role. Her star rose considerably in the 1940s, when she was featured in the Hollywood-produced all-black musicals *Cabin in the Sky* (1943) and *Stormy Weather* (1944). *Cabin in the Sky* also featured black actors and musicians Ethel Waters, Eddie "Rochester" Anderson, Duke Ellington, Louis Armstrong, and dancer John "Bubbles" Sublett, who had been the original Sportin' Life in George Gershwin's opera *Porgy and Bess*. Horne's other film, *Stormy Weather*, costarred Bill "Bojangles" Robinson as her love interest and also featured the tap-dancing Nicholas Brothers, Harold and Fayard, in a dance performance that Fred Astaire lauded as the single most exciting routine he had ever seen on film.

Lena Horne's association with Robeson brought her under government surveillance during the Red Scare years of the late 1940s and early 1950s. In 1947 in Paris, Horne married the white MGM film conductor and arranger Lennie Hayton. She would support the civil rights movement of the 1960s.

Equally conscious of the black image in film was musician Duke Ellington. His most important film in the 1930s was the musical short produced by Paramount Pictures in 1934, **Black Musicians and Composers** *Symphony in Black*. The film presents black American life set to music, a symphony depicting four social settings—African Americans at work ("Laborers"), forlorn romantic love ("Triangle"), religious expression ("A Hymn of Sorrow"), and urban life ("Harlem Rhythm"). The sequence "Triangle" features black singer Billie Holiday in her first film appearance, singing of love and betrayal. The episodes are interrupted by alternating images of Ellington, as the artist at work in the symphony's composition and as the conductor in the symphony's performance before a largely white audience in formal attire.

More than in any other artistic field, the African American influence in music was the most diverse and culturally transformative. One of the most significant and long-lasting musical developments was the emergence of gospel music, its success due largely to songwriter and composer Thomas A. Dorsey, the former blues composer turned into gospel-blues composer. His most popular song, "Precious Lord, Take My Hand," was one of more than four hundred that Dorsey composed. Subsequently gospel choirs and choruses were singing in churches, night clubs, jazz festivals, and concert halls. Indeed, gospel-song records became best sellers on the record charts, thanks to Dorsey and several "queens" of gospel music, including Sister Rosetta Tharpe, Clara Ward, and Mahalia Jackson.

In what was widely called "serious" (that is, classical) music, William Grant Still was the most prominent black composer. His symphonies—*Africa, Afro-American Symphony,* and

Symphony in G Minor: Song of a New Race—were performed by many of the major orchestras in the United States. He was commissioned to write many works, including one for the New York World's Fair in 1939. Ulysses Kay, who studied at the University of Rochester and Yale, won numerous awards, including the Prix de Rome, for such compositions as his *Concerto for Orchestra* and *Sinfonia in E: A Short Overture*. Meanwhile, R. Nathaniel Dett continued to compose works for piano and for vocal ensembles until his death in 1943.

Paul Robeson and Roland Hayes, widely acclaimed African American concert singers in the 1920s, continued to draw large audiences and generous critical praise during the 1930s. They shared the spotlight with other black singers—Edward Matthews, Aubrey Pankey, Kenneth Spencer, and William Warfield. In 1935 Marian Anderson, acclaimed by the celebrated European conductor Arturo Toscanini as one of the greatest singers in the world, returned to the United States in a veritable blaze of glory and was regarded by many as the greatest living contralto. Dorothy Maynor and Carol Brice won the praise of Serge Koussevitsky, the conductor of the Boston Symphony Orchestra, as well as thousands of music lovers. Ann Brown and Todd Duncan added to their laurels with their interpretations of the title roles in George Gershwin's opera *Porgy and Bess*.

The 1930s and 1940s witnessed the growing mass acceptance, to some extent, even the "mainstreaming" of black cultural forms. Duke Ellington had doubtless contributed to this change in Americans' musical tastes. When asked whether he played big band jazz or big band swing, Ellington always insisted that he played "Negro music." By the early 1940s, Ellington led what music historians consider his finest band, and in these years he was expanding the range of what he broadly defined as "Negro music." His studio recordings from these years included musical tapestries of black life such as "Take the 'A' Train," Ellington's new theme song composed by the young arranger Billy Strayhorn. Ellington's musical *Jump for Joy*, which ran for three months in Los Angeles, he described as representing "an attempt to correct the race situation in the U.S.A., through a form of musical propaganda . . . a show that would take Uncle Tom out of the theatre, [and] eliminate the stereotyped image that had been exploited by Hollywood and Broadway."

Such racially conscious intentions on the part of Ellington were reminiscent of Du Bois's claims for art as propaganda. Ellington would convey the fullest musical explication of this perspective when he premiered at Carnegie Hall in 1943 his most ambitious and controversial work: *Black, Brown, and Beige: A Tone Parallel to the History of the American Negro*.

In the 1930s and 1940s, however, a new breed of black and white musicians was sweeping the nation. The change was especially apparent in the world of big band swing—the jazz form most popular from roughly 1935 to the end of World War II. **The Swing Era** Indeed, the New Deal Era overlapped with the years known as the Swing Era. Swing was a youth-oriented musical sensation—just as rock 'n' roll would be in the next generation. That the mainstream culture of swing was a youth culture called attention to an unprecedented historical moment—a shifting time when youth wrested the determination of musical hegemony away from adults, thus freeing musicians, both black and white, from more rigid perceptions of respectability.

The crucial role of youth as the cultural arbiters of the American soundscape (a role that is yet to be relinquished) redounded to the benefit of musicians black and white. It opened the cultural front door to the unconventionality and creative difference that defined big band musicians' ethos and lifestyles. The public images and performance styles of three popular black band leaders of the Swing Era—Cab Calloway, Count Basie, and Jimmie Lunceford, along with black women singers Billie Holliday and Ella Fitzgerald—are instructive for envisioning the Swing Era in a variety of available forums: recordings, radio broadcasts, film, and live performances. All speak, as well, to pioneering efforts at racial integration—to the creation of the interracial kingdom of swing.

Count Basie, born William James Basie in 1904 in Red Bank, New Jersey, created a public image that he maintained throughout his long career—one of urbane and unhurried "cool." He was clearly a sophisticated musician attentive to image. Few big band leaders were as willing to let the music swing in a relaxed, personally unmediated manner as was Basie, and this casual aesthetic undergirded the band's recording, film, and concert performances. By 1940 the name "Count Basie" had become synonymous, according to Basie, with the band itself. Indeed Basie may well have had the first black band to affect the contemporary popular usage of "cool." Also featured with the band were solo vocalists—jazz singer Billie Holiday in 1937 and blues singer Jimmy Rushing in the late 1930s. Count Basie toured the nation, played at prestigious venues and in Hollywood films, and is described by some scholars as more successful than Ellington at integrating his band into the white-dominated entertainment industry of the time.

Cab Calloway, born Cabell Calloway III in Rochester, New York, flaunted a decidedly "hot" but also clearly calculated image as a hipster. The exuberant, zoot-suit-wearing Calloway brought the language of "jive" to the American people, publishing his own dictionary of slang terms. The *Oxford English Dictionary* cites Calloway as the first published usage of the word *jitterbug* (the title of one of his songs as well as a popular dance). His song "Minnie the Moocher" was introduced to most Americans in the Hollywood film *The Big Broadcast* (1932). The movie showed Calloway in a scat performance, crying "Hi-de-hi-de hi-de hi" with his chorus bellowing the same words back to him. Especially after his radio broadcasts with the white singer Bing Crosby, Calloway became one of the most popular and wealthy musicians of the Depression years.

Fisk University graduate Jimmie Lunceford, born in 1902 in Fulton, Mississippi, brought versatility, showmanship, and musical genius to the Swing Era in a very different way. The hallmark of the Lunceford Orchestra was its two-beat rhythm, as opposed to the more common four-beat swing rhythm. Each of the musicians in his largely college-educated band was selected by Lunceford not only for image and personal character but also for versatility of musical talent. They comprised an ensemble that played instruments, sang, danced, and performed tricks. Sy Oliver (trumpet), Willie Smith (alto saxophone), Eddie Tompkins (trumpet), Trummy Young (trombone), and Joe Thomas (tenor saxophone) were also the band's singers and dancers. In addition to playing his own drums, Jimmie Crawford commanded a complete percussion section while also performing "tricks with his sticks." The members of the trumpet section not only played as one but also threw their instruments in the air, catching them simultaneously in order to begin to play together again with precision timing. White bands such as the Tommy Dorsey Band and the Glen Miller Band were influenced by the Lunceford showmanship.

Near the end of the 1930s several black musicians had begun to integrate large white bands. Lunceford trumpeter Sy Oliver (identified as the originator of the two-beat rhythm) left to play with Tommy Dorsey. Big band leader Fletcher Henderson, prominent in the 1920s, played his most influential musical role in the Swing Era as the arranging architect of white band leader Benny Goodman's sound. Although Goodman was labeled by white Americans "The King of Swing," Goodman himself credited the crucial influence of Fletcher Henderson. The Goodman-Henderson partnership was just one of the interracial musical alliances that Goodman forged during the Swing Era. In addition to his orchestra, in 1935 he formed the integrated Goodman Trio, which included black pianist Teddy Wilson and white drummer Gene Krupa. In 1936 the trio expanded to a quartet by adding the black vibraphonist Lionel Hampton, giving its first public performance in Chicago. The Goodman quartet won tremendous applause on records and in live performance—so much so that the group was featured in the 1937 Warner Brothers film *Hooray for Hollywood,* along with the Goodman orchestra. In the later 1930s, Goodman hired black arrangers Edgar Sampson, Jimmy Mundy, and Mary Lou Williams. He also added other black members to his orchestra: electric guitar pioneer Charlie Christian in 1939 and Duke Ellington's trumpet star Cootie Williams in 1940.

Goodman and his black musicians inspired other interracial collaborations. Jimmie Lunceford's arranger Sy Oliver joined Tommy Dorsey, and classical composer William Grant Still arranged for the white jazz musician Artie Shaw. However, despite the camaraderie black musicians enjoyed with fellow white band members, racial integration brought them painful and harrowing experiences. For example black trumpeter Roy Eldridge joined the big band of white drummer Gene Krupa in 1940 and later joined the Artie Shaw orchestra. On stage and on records, Eldridge enjoyed star treatment, but offstage, when he traveled on tour, he was personally humiliated by Jim Crow policies. Similarly, jazz singer Billie Holiday joined Artie Shaw's band in 1938—an early instance of a black musician in an all-male, white orchestra. She praised him for his courage in hiring her, but Shaw could not shield Holiday from racial insult. Jim Crow reminders followed her even when the band played in New York. Performing with Shaw's band at the city's Lincoln Hotel, Holliday was told to use the service elevator. Shaw would later cite this incident to explain "why her stint with us was a bit, let's say, limited." She left Shaw's band.

Billie Holiday (born Eleanora Fagan in 1915) helped change the image of the black female singer from rough to refined, from entertainer to artist. While acknowledging a debt to Bessie Smith and the "classic blues" singers of the 1920s, her **Women Vocalists** style appeared restrained and subtle in comparison to their growling and gruff lyrical expression. A decade after the heyday of her predecessors, who wore the colorful bejeweled-and-feathered, attention-grabbing costumes of vaudeville queens, Holiday dressed in understated and elegant gowns, with a white gardenia in her hair. In the 1930s, she recorded or performed live with a number of great jazz groups—Benny Goodman, the Fletcher Henderson orchestra, Count Basie, and Artie Shaw.

While Holiday was commended for her depth and for the emotional resources that enriched her performances, especially her poignant protest of lynching in her song "Strange Fruit," another young black woman vocalist was celebrated for the sheer joy and sparkle that she brought to song.

Not yet the interpreter of the "great American songbooks" of Cole Porter, George and Ira Gershwin, and Irving Berlin, the young Ella Fitzgerald (born in 1917 in Newport News, Virginia) as a teenager won a talent contest at Harlem's Apollo Theater in 1934. Her career catapulted after she joined the newly formed orchestra of black drummer and bandleader Chick Webb. Together Fitzgerald and Webb shared the spotlight until Webb's death in 1939. Fitzgerald brought youthful exuberance and perfect pitch to such self-penned songs as "A Tisket, A Tasket," one of the major national song hits of 1938. She was no doubt at Harlem's Savoy in December 1938 when a battle of the bands between Benny Goodman and Chick Webb resulted in an unequivocal win for drummer Webb and his orchestra.

As Goodman drummer Gene Krupa admitted of Webb's performance, "I was never cut by a better man." The Chick Webb Orchestra provided the accompaniment to the dance innovations of the black teenagers and young adults who frequented the Savoy. Their athletic embellishments of the basic "jitterbug" became models for the popular dances of American youth: the "Lindy Hop," the "Susie-Q," the "Shag," and the "Big Apple." These popular dances were only a few of the many black contributions to the interracial Swing Era youth culture of the 1930s and early 1940s.

In the realm of culture, as in labor and in government, the public face of race relations had begun to change. The musical event that most dramatically bore witness to the changing racial climate, however, was not a performance of swing music, but the performance of black sacred, European classical, and American patriotic songs. So sang Marian Anderson on the steps of the Lincoln Memorial on Easter Sunday (April 9), 1939, in her most poignant rendition: "My country 'tis of thee, Sweet land of liberty, To thee we sing." Historian Scot A. Sandage calls attention to Anderson's revised wording of "America": "The change [from "Of thee, I sing" to "To thee we sing"] made the national hymn subtly political, painting 'land of liberty' as more aspiration than description and catching both the communalism and conflict of that famous day."

Marian Anderson at the Lincoln Memorial

The event had occurred because of the refusal by the politically and socially conservative Daughters of the American Revolution to permit Anderson to sing in its Constitution Hall. She had given concerts in Carnegie Hall in New York in 1930, throughout Europe between 1930 and 1935, and in much of America before being rudely confronted with the "whites only" policy of the DAR in the nation's capital. Eleanor Roosevelt resigned her membership in this elite organization, and New Deal leaders Harold Ickes and Oscar Chapman set in motion steps necessary to facilitate the open-air concert. Among the more than 75,000 persons in attendance were politicians, teachers, laborers, artists, civil rights activists—a massive audience of vast and diverse constituencies and coalitions forged in the New Deal Era. Few could have missed the historic importance of that spring day in 1939 or its suggestive setting before the solemn image of the "Great Emancipator."

Black artistic expression in the 1930s and into the war years had helped to predispose Americans black and white to the civil rights movement. New Dealer Mary McLeod Bethune expressed such a sentiment on the very next day after Anderson sang. "Through the Marian Anderson protest concert," Bethune exulted, "we made our triumphant entry into the democratic spirit of American life." For African Americans on the eve of World War II, there would be no confusion as to the dual nature of their fight ahead.

Opera singer Marian Anderson stands in front of a photo of her performance at the Lincoln Memorial

After the DAR barred Marian Anderson from singing in their hall in 1939 because of her race, she gave a free concert in front of the Lincoln Memorial to over 75,000 people. She is pictured here, years later, in front of a photo of that famous event.

Double V for Victory

Reframing the Arsenal of Democracy

In Military Service

Keeping the Home Fires Burning

Double victory

During World War II, African Americans launched a double victory campaign: "Victory at Home and Victory Abroad."

The international rivalry and territorial aggression that characterized the years leading up to the First World War resumed all too soon after the Paris Peace Conference of 1919 produced the Treaty of Versailles. The idea that the "Great War," as it was called, would indeed be the "War to End All Wars" proved as naïve and illusory as the idea that the League of Nations would create a lasting peace. In fact, after 1919 the more powerful nations had used the League as a cloak behind which they imposed their will on weaker nations. The League curtailed neither Japan's imperialism toward China beginning in 1931 nor the resurgent militarism of Nazi Germany under the leadership of Adolf Hitler, who took power in 1933. The League's limitations became painfully clear to African Americans when the Italian fascist dictatorship of Benito Mussolini invaded Ethiopia in the fall of 1935. In 1938 public opinion in the United States generally denounced Hitler for annexing Austria and dismembering Czechoslovakia. The dark clouds of war hovered over the international landscape and then burst suddenly and violently with Germany's invasion of Poland in September 1939. War had once again erupted in Europe.

In a ferocious assault in the spring of 1940, Hitler's army and air force conquered and occupied the nations of Denmark, Norway, the Netherlands, Luxembourg, and Belgium. In June, France succumbed to German control. The Nazi blitzkrieg appeared to be unstoppable. As the American people looked on from afar, they were forced to contemplate the horrifying possibility of Britain's collapse under Nazi military might. In September 1940, Germany, Japan, and Italy forged their Tripartite Pact—a military alliance of these so-called Axis Powers. As Americans began to ask themselves what disposition Germany would make of the New World colonies of the conquered nations, they realized that the war had come frightfully close to them. It was time to prepare, and the following year witnessed a feverish effort to do so.

As war ravaged Europe and East Asia, the United States government stood aloof, but on December 29, 1940, President Franklin D. Roosevelt took a step toward belligerency when he delivered one of his most famous radio fireside chats. Speaking of the city of Detroit and the automobile industry, he asked the American people to become "the great arsenal of democracy." Although nearly a year would elapse before American military involvement began, Roosevelt urged patriotism and sacrifice, admonishing that "we must apply ourselves to our task with the same resolution, the same sense of urgency, the same spirit of patriotism and sacrifice as we would show were we at war."

Most African Americans joined the war effort with a spirit of patriotism despite racism in the land of their birth. Those who were familiar with Hitler's *Mein Kampf*—the infamous book in which he set forth his program—detested Nazi doctrines from the start. They recognized his racist ideas of Aryan supremacy as sounding all too similar to white racist beliefs in the United States. In the years preceding the war, a claim had circulated widely throughout black communities that Hitler had disrespected the African American Olympic track stars Jesse Owens and Ralph Metcalfe during the 1936 Berlin Games. African Americans felt a further affront when Germany's Max Schmeling knocked out the black boxer Joe Louis in 1936. Louis's victorious rematch with Schmeling for the World Heavyweight crown in 1938 caused blacks to revel in the victory as a gain for "the race" and all of America.

In contrast to World War I, however, during this new global struggle American blacks did not sacrifice the fight for democracy at home for the fight for democracy abroad. Black lawyer and NAACP board member Theodore Berry captured this spirit when in 1942 he noted that blacks were not motivated by "disloyalty or lack of patriotism, but a war in defense of ideals of freedom leaves the Negro spiritually uninspired without some belief that there is hope of realizing a fuller measure of the things for which we are fighting." Energized and strengthened by the activism of the 1930s—the struggles of numerous black organizations of varied political persuasions for economic justice, desegregation, and the vote and against lynching and colonialism—during World War II African Americans would neither silence nor soften their civil rights demands. Many even criticized boxing idol Joe Louis for giving his prize money to the U.S. Navy after his victory over Buddie Baer in January 1942. They refused to applaud Louis's generosity in the face of the segregated policy of the nation's military.

Blacks openly denounced both the Jim Crow character of the U.S. Army and the Navy's policy of using blacks only in menial capacities. In their local communities, in the black media, in their professional associations, and in national civil rights organizations, they protested vigorously against barriers to equal citizenship, demanding that the federal government adopt a new and interventionist role in behalf of racial equality. Blacks' growing voting bloc in the northern states emboldened them to exact accountability and concessions from elected officials, and they leveraged their newfound political clout all the way to the president himself. During World War II, black Americans unapologetically battled on two fronts, committed to a "Double-V" campaign—for victory over the racism in America and for victory over the fascism that American troops fought to destroy on foreign soil.

Reframing the Arsenal of Democracy

An overarching theme in Roosevelt's "arsenal of democracy" speech was the need for many of the manufacturers of domestic products to shift gears and transform themselves into defense industries with loyal workers, supportive of America's allies abroad. His call for patriotic sacrifice, and specifically for the adoption of non-strike agreements, required that labor unions abandon commonplace tactics during the 1930s. At the time of his speech, the president was well aware of the undercurrent of racial dissatisfaction that ran deep in African American communities in regard to both the military and defense industries. In 1939, the black civil rights lawyer and World War I veteran Charles Hamilton Houston wrote Roosevelt in anticipation of another global war. Emphasizing the critical importance of the black population to national defense, Houston warned that African Americans would no longer "silently endure the insults and discriminations imposed on its soldiers and sailors in the course of the last war."

As the United States began to put itself on a war footing, black Americans wondered what consideration would be given them, both in the building up of a large fighting force and in the manufacture of the materials of modern warfare. In 1940 black leaders voiced their opinions about the proposed Selective Service Act, which would restore the military draft. For example, Howard University history professor Rayford W. Logan testified before Congress on behalf of the Committee on the Participation of Negroes in the National Defense. As chairman of this committee and also as a veteran of World War I, Logan asserted that blacks demanded "equal opportunity to participate in the national-defense program, civil as well as military."

In September 1940, a group of black leaders, including labor leader A. Philip Randolph and NAACP president Walter White, submitted a seven- **Blacks in the Armed Forces** point program to President Roosevelt outlining minimum essentials for the just treatment of African Americans in the nation's armed forces. They urged that all available black reserve officers be used to train recruits; that black recruits be given the same training as whites; that existing units of the army accept officers and enlisted men on the basis of ability and not race; that specialized personnel, such as physicians, dentists, and nurses, be integrated; that responsible African Americans be appointed to draft boards; that discrimination be abolished in the Navy and the Army Air Corps (as the air force was then known); and that competent African Americans be appointed as civilian assistants to the secretaries of war and the navy.

The War Department responded by issuing a statement that African Americans would be received into the Army on the general basis of the proportion of the African American population of the country. However, the government's policy did not call for integrated troops but rather required separate units by race. In addition, the War Department refused to place black officers, except for medical officers and chaplains, over black units that had white officers. African Americans were indignant, and they made their indignation known. Neither African Americans nor the president were oblivious of the political implications of their respective positions, especially given the imminent presidential election between Roosevelt and the Republican candidate Wendell Willkie. On October 25, 1940, just a little over a week before the election and under pressure from black leaders, Roosevelt promoted the black army officer Colonel Benjamin O. Davis to brigadier general.

He appointed other blacks to significant positions—the lawyer and Howard University Law School dean William H. Hastie as a civilian aide to the Secretary of War and the army officer Campbell Johnson as an executive assistant to the director of the Selective Service. Senior ROTC units were added at the historically black schools of West Virginia State College, Hampton Institute, North Carolina Agricultural and Technical College, Prairie View State College, and Tuskegee Institute. These additions and promotions on the government's part did little to quiet the protest of the many African Americans who sought an end to the Jim Crow military. A black soldier's letter to the *New York Age* described the proponents of segregated troops as "ripping to rags the American flag's meaning of equality."

The industrial mobilization that preceded the Japanese bombing of Pearl Harbor and America's declaration of war offered few opportunities to black workers. As the arsenal of democracy, American industry began to surge once again, at last helping to lift the nation out of the throes of the 1930s depression. The United States offered aid to Britain and the other Allied powers through sales, outright gifts, and the Lend-Lease program.

Racial prejudice ran rampant in the industrial plants that converted from domestic to war-related production. Employers' first preference was to hire the several million white workers whom the Great Depression had left unemployed. From the outbreak of war in Europe in 1939 through 1941, the number of unemployed white workers fell dramatically, and wages rose dramatically. Some industries even hired white workers from distant regions rather than opening their doors to local black residents, according to a report of the Labor Division of the National Defense Advisory Commission. Black workers found themselves unwelcome by employers and white workers, both of whom argued that blacks were insufficiently skilled while at the same time denying them opportunities for apprenticeship and other war-production training programs. In a national survey of employers with defense contracts, conducted by the Bureau of Employment Security of the Social Security Board, more than half of employers admitted to following rigid anti-black policies. They refused black workers in any capacity, including unskilled jobs.

Blacks Picket the Glen Martin Plant
These workers demanded jobs from the defense industry.

When African Americans benefited from defense work, they did so in a far more limited and indirect way, since they usually got the jobs of whites who had moved up the ladder to higher-paying defense plants. In response, protests resounded forcefully from the black press, civil rights organizations, black churches, and individual black community leaders. In April 1941 a delegation of black leaders, including Walter White of the NAACP, Mary McLeod Bethune of the National Council of Negro Women, A. Philip Randolph of the Brotherhood of Sleeping Car Porters, and Lester Granger of the National Urban League, met with President Roosevelt to argue for his support in desegregating the military and the defense industries. The delegation demanded more than the president was willing to give. At the time of this meeting, the U.S. Office of Education had already declared that there should be no discrimination on account of race, creed, or color in the spending of funds in defense training programs. In August 1940, the National Defense Advisory Committee had issued a statement against the refusal to hire African Americans at defense plants. The Office of Production Management established a black employment and training branch in its labor division to facilitate the hiring of African Americans in defense industries. However, these official statements were not accompanied by any enforcement and thus had produced little results.

The president's own rhetoric served to heighten the distance between American ideals and its deeds with respect to racial discrimination. In his State of the Union address to Congress on January 6, 1941, Roosevelt spoke eloquently and unambiguously of the "Four

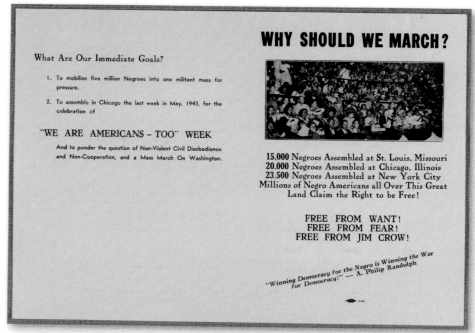

What Are Our Immediate Goals?

1. To mobilize five million Negroes into one militant mass for pressure.

2. To assemble in Chicago the last week in May, 1943, for the celebration of

"WE ARE AMERICANS – TOO" WEEK

And to ponder the question of Non-Violent Civil Disobedience and Non-Cooperation, and a Mass March On Washington.

WHY SHOULD WE MARCH?

15,000 Negroes Assembled at St. Louis, Missouri
20,000 Negroes Assembled at Chicago, Illinois
23,500 Negroes Assembled at New York City
Millions of Negro Americans all Over This Great Land Claim the Right to be Free!

FREE FROM WANT!
FREE FROM FEAR!
FREE FROM JIM CROW!

"Winning Democracy for the Negro is Winning the War for Democracy!" — A. Philip Randolph

A. Philip Randolph
A. Philip Randolph rallies black Americans throughout the nation to march on Washington in 1941.

Freedoms" to which the world must aspire—freedom of speech, freedom of worship, freedom from want, and freedom from fear. To this list of freedoms worth fighting for, the increasingly assertive African American population added freedom from racial discrimination.

In the same month of Roosevelt's annual address to Congress, A. Philip Randolph, president of the Brotherhood of Sleeping Car Porters and Maids, proposed a mass March on

The March on Washington 1941 Washington. The idea of a march on the nation's capital to seek redress for grievances had long roots in American reform. Nineteenth- and early twentieth-century woman suffragists, Coxey's army of the unemployed in 1894, and the Bonus Expeditionary Force in 1932 had all converged on Washington in pursuit of their respective causes. And Randolph's plan met with tremendous enthusiasm in black communities throughout the nation. He called for an all-black march with the aim of emboldening African Americans with a sense of their own power and also to preclude communist infiltration and dominance. Randolph's stirring words to his people emphasized the need for a new style of activism, specifically large-scale, direct-action protest with pressure on the federal government itself.

Demanding defense jobs and an integrated military, Randolph proclaimed:

Dear fellow Negro Americans, be not dismayed in these terrible times. You possess power, great power. Our problem is to hitch it up for action on the broadest, daring and most gigantic scale. In this period of power politics, nothing counts but pressure, more pressure and still more pressure, through the tactic and strategy of broad organized, aggressive mass action behind the vital and important issues of the Negro.

As plans for the march got underway, high government officials became increasingly alarmed at the growing momentum of the March on Washington Movement in such cities as Baltimore, New York, Newark, Philadelphia, Richmond, Atlanta, Tampa, St. Louis, Chicago, Detroit, and Washington, D.C. As African Americans from all over the United States prepared to converge on the Capitol on July 1, government leaders took cognizance of the world's attention on American racial policies and asked worriedly, "What will they think in Berlin?"

During the last three weeks of June 1941, prominent local and national leaders, including First Lady Eleanor Roosevelt and New York City mayor Fiorello La Guardia, met with Randolph in an attempt to discourage the march. They argued that the march would do no good and would perhaps cause reprisals against blacks. Randolph did not budge. The president then sent for Randolph and conferred at length with him, along with Secretary of War Henry Stimson and Secretary of the Navy Frank Knox. Yet their pleas did not dissuade Randolph or the escalating enthusiasm for it in black communities in various parts of the nation. As the day of the march drew closer, government officials became more desperate. After several conferences, the president proposed a compromise—he promised to issue an order "with teeth in it," prohibiting discrimination in employment in defense industries and in the government, if Randolph called off the march. On June 25, 1941, Roosevelt issued Executive Order 8802, in which he ordered categorically: "there shall be no discrimination in the employment of workers in defense industries or Government because of race, creed, color, or national origin. . . . And it is the duty of employers and of labor organizations . . . to provide for the full and equitable participation of all workers in defense industries, without discrimination because of race, creed, color, or national origin." Hopeful, Randolph canceled the march.

In pursuance of the executive order, a clause prohibiting discrimination was placed in all defense contracts, and a Fair Employment Practices Committee (FEPC) was established to receive and investigate complaints against industries in violation of the order. Comprising public officials, as well as management and **Executive Order 8802** labor leaders, the committee held hearings in such cities as Los Angeles, Chicago, Detroit, Philadelphia, and New York. The FEPC disclosed evidences of discrimination, although it had no power to impose punishment and, because of the war emergency, generally refused to recommend the cancellation of war contracts. Occasionally employers and unions changed their policies to avoid being called to appear as defendants at committee hearings.

The executive order and the committee received a mixed assessment from African Americans. Many initially hailed the order as the most significant document affecting them since the Emancipation Proclamation. In its first year, the newly established Committee on Fair Employment Practice (FEPC) received more than six thousand complaints of racial discrimination. Blacks filed 78 percent of the complaints nationally; of these, a third came from black women (who accounted for 86 percent of all complaints by women). The New York City office, the first agency to be empowered to "eliminate and prevent discrimination in [all] employment because of race, color or national origin either by employers, labor organizations, employment agencies or other persons," received 20 percent of the national total, or 1,162 in eighteen months. According to historian Cheryl Lynn Goldberg, in New York City religious discrimination, primarily directed at Jews, constituted the most frequent complaint (43 percent); race came second, with 19 percent of the total.

Prior to the establishment of the FEPC, the labor division of the Office of Production Management's black employment and training branch had only limited success in negotiating with employers and persuading them to use African Americans on war construction projects and in defense plants. Increasingly, blacks registered their complaints against persistent and widespread discrimination. White employers opposed the order altogether. The executive order did not overturn Jim Crow in the southern states, observed Mark Ethridge, a Louisville newspaperman and an original member of the FEPC. "All the armies of the world, both of the United Nations and the Axis," he said, "could not force upon the South the abandonment of racial segregation." Incensed over the order, a white Alabama lawyer formed the League to Maintain White Supremacy, while the governor of Alabama declared segregation to be essential to racial peace. The effort to integrate the defense industries would continue throughout the war years and afterward, just as would the effort to desegregate the military.

In September 1941, William Hastie (then at the War Department) authored a report that revealed the ways in which blacks were underutilized and discriminated against in the armed

Hastie and Discrimination in the Armed Forces

forces. Hastie found it appalling that blacks made up only 5 percent of the 1.5 million enlisted men and, worse yet, that they were overwhelmingly assigned unskilled and menial duties. In June 1940, only four thousand African Americans served in the Navy, the majority of them as messmen (kitchen staff). They had no opportunity to learn the many trades provided in the naval training program or to become combat seamen. Early in the war African Americans protested this discrimination, but for several months Navy officials refused to revise their policy.

In an address to the executive board of the National Lawyers Guild in October 1941, Hastie argued that the "Negro, whether he be soldier or civilian, finds it difficult to concentrate on the horrors of a Germany without civil liberties, when his immediate attention is continually diverted to proscriptions at home." His plea for raising the morale of black troops through the full inclusion of black people in American life met with little sympathy in the War Department (which oversaw the U.S. Army). The response to his report noted the impossibility of solving a racial problem that had endured through custom and habit for centuries. As far as the War Department was concerned, integrating the troops was neither practical nor desirable. In a response to Hastie, dated December 1, 1941, the Army's chief of staff, General George C. Marshall, wrote: "the level of intelligence and occupational skill of the negro population is considerably below that of white and . . . that experiments within the Army in the solution of social problems are fraught with danger to efficiency, discipline, and morale."

Six days later, on December 7, 1941, the Japanese bombed the American naval base Pearl Harbor in Hawaii. Within days, Congress declared war on Japan and the other Axis Powers.

In Military Service

When war broke out in Europe in 1939, the United States government embarked feverishly on a program to remedy the nation's low state of military preparedness. In the years between the First and Second World wars, the American people had been strongly isolationist. Disinclined to support a large peacetime standing army, Americans sought to return to prewar "normalcy." The number of officers and soldiers declined, and the number of African American ranks in the United States Army dwindled to relatively inconsequent numbers. In the prewar army of 230,000 men, fewer than five thousand African American soldiers were serving. At the beginning of the emergency, the regular army had fewer than

Lt. Harriet Pickens and Ens. Frances Wills
African American women served in World War II in a number of capacities. These two women
were the first to be commissioned in the WAVES.

a dozen African American officers. Only four black units, the Twenty-Fourth and Twenty-
Fifth Infantries and the Ninth and Tenth Cavalries, operated at full strength.

With the passage of the Selective Service Act in September 1940, more than 3 million
African Americans registered for potential military service. By 1941 the armed forces had
enlisted more than 100,000, and by 1942 the number grew to 370,000. In September 1944,
the Army alone had 701,678 black soldiers. During the war approximately 165,000 blacks

would serve in the Navy, 5,000 in the Coast Guard, and 17,000 in the Marine Corps. A rough estimate of the total number of blacks in the armed services during World War II places the figure at approximately 1 million men and women.

Despite discrimination in the armed forces, blacks served in more capacities than they had in previous wars. African Americans' participation in administering the Selective Service System in various locations throughout the United States doubtless reduced discrimination in accepting blacks into the armed forces. In addition to the executive assistant to the director, an African American served on the president's Advisory Committee on Selective Service. At the local level, blacks participated in such capacities as draft board members, members of the registrants' advisory board, examining physicians, and appeal board members. Blacks in the armed forces held a great variety of positions—in the infantry, coast and field artillery, cavalry, tank battalions, transportation units, signal corps, engineer corps, medical corps, and many others.

More than four thousand African American women enlisted in the Women's Army Corps (WAC). However, black women often felt slighted because of segregated units and

Black Women in the Military other racially discriminatory policies. Their dissatisfaction was evident, for instance, in the protracted effort to bring respect and inclusion for black nurses. Although nurses were a crucial part of the American forces, the Army Nurse Corps discouraged the presence of black nurses in the many field hospitals, hospital trains, hospital ships, and medical transport planes.

The restrictive quota on black nurses appeared especially insulting to African Americans, since the government complained of a dearth of trained nurses. Historian Darlene Clark Hine notes that on January 9, 1945, Congress debated amending the Selective Service Act of 1940 to include the drafting of nurses, although this debate did not address issues of racial discrimination. The Draft Nurse Bill (H.R. 1284), which was promoted by the president, eventually was left to languish in the Committee on Military Affairs. With regard to black nurses, however, the bill reinforced the racial discrimination already in place, since it permitted very few black nurses, thus continuing the Army Nurse Corps's quota on black nurses.

Since the war's inception, Mabel Staupers, then executive-secretary of the National Association of Graduate Colored Nurses (NAGCN), had denounced the Jim Crow military policy as well as the refusal to grant officer's rank to black nurses—protesting in letters and meetings with influential civilians and government officials. According to Hine, as Staupers traveled in important political circles in the election year of 1944, she never failed to hint at the possibility of her organization's "willingness to go public with black nurses' disaffection." In January 1945, Staupers exploited the timing of the controversial nurse-draft proposal and turned to the black press. The news coverage resulted in an avalanche of telegrams on the White House from civil rights groups, religious organizations, fraternal societies, and labor unions. In less than two weeks after the Draft Nurse Bill was introduced in Congress, the Army Nurse Corps ended its discriminatory policy, and the Navy fell in line soon thereafter. At the war's end, about 76,000 black nurses were stationed in hospitals in the United States and abroad— in Africa, Asia, and Europe.

Late in 1940 the War Department announced its plan to train African American pilots at Tuskegee, Alabama. Although some African Americans vociferously objected to the seg-

Tuskegee: Black Airmen regation of blacks in the Army Air Corps, others viewed the announcement as a step forward, since no prior policy had allowed for the training or use of black aviators. The Tuskegee Airmen, as they were known, were college-educated men

Members of the Ninety-Ninth Fighter Squadron, stationed in Italy
After training at the segregated air base at Tuskegee, Alabama, black pilots saw service in several theaters of the war.

who came to Tuskegee Army Air Field from every section of the country. A large number of them hailed from New York City, Washington, Los Angeles, Chicago, Philadelphia, and Detroit. Initially they were trained as pilots, navigators, and bombardiers but later also as aircraft and engine mechanics, armament specialists, radio repairmen, parachute riggers, control tower operators, and policemen. As the pilots began their training at Tuskegee, ground crews trained at Chanute Field, Illinois.

In 1941 the Ninety-Ninth Pursuit Squadron prepared for organization as a fighting unit, as did other groups of black fighter pilots. From 1942 through 1946, 994 pilots received their commissions and pilot wings. Lieutenant General Benjamin O. Davis, Jr., was one of the more famous graduates. Born on December 18, 1912, in Washington, D.C., Davis was the son of the nation's first African American general and was educated at an integrated high school in Ohio, the University of Chicago, and ultimately the U.S. Military Academy at West Point, where he was admitted with the help of African American Congressman Oscar DePriest.

Isolated at West Point (he never had a roommate), Davis committed himself to excelling. Graduating in the top 15 percent of his class, he became (apart from his father) the only black line officer in the Army. Although he was initially denied permission to serve in the Army Air Corps, Davis finally won his wings when just before the 1940 election President Roosevelt founded the Tuskegee Army Air Field to train African Americans as aviators. During World War II, Davis led missions in North Africa and Italy, and his Tuskegee Airmen distinguished themselves for their lack of casualties and the number of completed missions. Following the conclusion of the war Davis held posts at the Pentagon and was Air Force chief of staff during the Korean War. He served in the Philippines and in Vietnam, and in 1965 he was promoted to be the first African American lieutenant general. He died on July 4, 2002.

Nearly two thousand black men completed either pilot or support skills training in the Tuskegee program, and 450 of its black pilots flew combat missions during World War II. The 332nd Fighter Group successfully escorted bombers in 1,578 missions and 15,552 sorties. One of their remarkable accomplishments in the war is the sinking of a German destroyer in Trieste harbor using only machine gun fire. Sixty-six of the 332nd were killed in the war, and one hundred members received the Distinguished Flying Cross. The Tuskegee base closed on September 5, 1946. Even though the fighter squadron dispersed, its members' accomplishments and courage contributed to the desegregation of the armed forces in the United States in 1948.

Not until April 1942 did the Secretary of the Navy announce the Navy's plan to accept the enlistment of blacks for general service and as noncommissioned officers. A separate location, Camp Robert Smalls, was established for them at the Great Lakes Naval Training Station, and from there promising recruits were sent for further training to Hampton, Virginia. Others were sent to sea or to naval ammunition depots. In 1943 the Navy decided to allow African Americans to enter its officer-training program. Later, African American women gained admission into the Women Accepted for Volunteer Emergency Service (WAVES). In 1942 the Marine Corps ended its exclusionary policy, which was as old as the corps itself, and late in the summer of 1942 African American leathernecks began their training at the Marine base at Camp Lejeune, North Carolina. Within a short period the Fifty-First Composite Defense Battalion was organized.

The Navy, the Marines, and Officer Training

Throughout the war African Americans agitated as well for the opportunity to become commissioned officers. High among the stated goals of black leaders was the demand that African Americans be trained as officers on an equal basis with whites and in an integrated class setting. In the summer of 1941, when such classes began at officer candidate schools, the problem remained of getting white commanding officers at the various camps to recommend African Americans for advanced training. In the first six months, fewer than thirty blacks were admitted to officer candidate schools. Only after the Secretary of War issued a stern order that African Americans be sent to the candidate schools on a nondiscriminatory basis did blacks get into the schools in considerable numbers.

By the middle of 1942, black officers graduated with commissions from the adjutant general's school in the Air Corps administration, cavalry, coast artillery, infantry, chemical warfare, quartermaster service, and other branches. In each instance they studied and graduated with whites. The Navy first commissioned African Americans as officers in 1944. Before the end of the war, more than fifty blacks were ensigns, lieutenants, medical and dental officers, nurses, WAVES officers, and chaplains. The Marines and the Coast Guard also had a small number of African American officers. Only the Air Corps demanded segregated schools for commissions.

Approximately half a million African Americans saw service overseas during World War II, and black newspapers featured the exploits of black soldiers and conveyed to their readers pride in the performance of black units. In the European Theater, **Overseas Service—Europe** blacks made up almost half of the transportation corps. They served in the port battalions, whose job it was to come ashore shortly after an invasion and unload supplies for the assault troops. During the summer of 1944 and for the remainder of the war, black amphibian truck companies made a significant contribution to the successful drive across France. After D-Day, more than 50,000 African American engineers erected camps, tents, and buildings; cleared debris; rebuilt cities; and performed other important services. They constituted about one-fifth of the American engineers in the European Theater. Approximately 11 percent of the ordnance men in Europe were African Americans. The chief of ordnance reported that not only did they "pass the ammunition" but on numerous occasions they also fought the Germans, participating in patrols and taking prisoners.

Cpl. Carlton Chapman, tank machine gunner

Twenty-two black combat units participated in ground operations in the European Theater: nine field artillery battalions, one antiaircraft battalion, two tank battalions, two tank destroyer battalions, and eight engineer combat battalions. The 761st Tank Battalion was particularly notable as a fighting unit. It saw combat in the Battle of the Bulge and in six European countries and received commendation from four major generals and the undersecretary of war for its gallant service. The battalion would eventually receive the prestigious Presidential Distinguished Unit Citation. However, this honor would only come many years later and after repeated denials. Finally, in 1978 President Jimmy Carter conferred the medal on the 761st Tank Battalion. The 614th Tank Destroyer Battalion served in several important actions, and one of its officers, Capt. Charles L. Thomas, received the Distinguished Service Cross for heroism in the action before Climbach, France. Black field artillery units entered France within ten days after the invasion. The 333rd fought throughout Brittany and northern France against vicious German attacks in the fall of 1944.

In January 1945, the War Department announced that platoons of African American troops and platoons of white troops were to be integrated in a unit to fight on German soil.

Volunteers soon doubled the quota of 2,500. After a short period of training, such units saw action with various divisions of the First Army to the east of the Rhine. On April 30, 1945, the War Department announced that the volunteer black infantrymen had "established themselves as fighting men no less courageous or aggressive than their white comrades." The integrated units were short-lived, however, since the war ended soon afterward. Although African Americans continued to protest against the Jim Crow army, the War Department considered the experiment over.

In the Mediterranean Theater, American troops remained segregated. The principal black combat unit, the Ninety-Second Division, had been reactivated at Fort McClellan, Alabama, in 1942. In 1943 the Ninety-Second moved to Fort Huachuca, Arizona, and went into intensive training. In June 1944, it was sent to North Africa and later to Italy, where it served with the Fifth Army. It comprised four regiments of infantry and four battalions of field artillery, as well as other service units. Its first major offensive action was to cross the Arno River in Italy in September 1944. The offensive was successful until December, when the division was driven out of several towns that it had taken earlier. Within a few days, however, all the lost ground had been recaptured. The following February, the Ninety-Second suffered serious reverses, for which it received severe criticism. After a visit to the division, the civilian aide to the Secretary of War, Truman K. Gibson, Jr., was reported to have said that the Ninety-Second had not made a good showing.

Many critics of African American combat troops immediately seized on Gibson's report to bolster their arguments against the combat effectiveness of black troops. African Americans severely criticized Gibson for his statements. It was later revealed, however, that Gibson's report had been misquoted and was not as critical of the troops as earlier reported. He had actually stated that whatever poor showing there was of the Ninety-Second was doubtless due to the low educational attainment of a large part of the division's rank and file, 17 percent of which belonged in Class Five, the lowest literacy class admitted to the Army. However, the division's more than 12,000 decorations and citations indicated that its performance was creditable, considering the unusually unfavorable circumstances.

The two major black combat air units overseas were the Ninety-Ninth Pursuit Squadron and the 332nd Fighter Group. The Ninety-Ninth went to the Mediterranean Theater in April 1943, and in February of the following year the 332nd followed. Both groups participated in various types of fighting over Europe. They escorted bombers and went on strafing and other missions. The 332nd was instrumental in sinking an enemy destroyer off the Istrian peninsula, and it protected the Fifteenth Air Force bombers in important attacks on the oil fields of Romania. Under the command of Colonel (later General) Benjamin O. Davis, Jr., the fighter group won the admiration of African Americans everywhere and the generous praise of high officials in the Air Corps. More than eighty pilots won the Distinguished Flying Cross, having destroyed 111 planes in the air and 150 on the ground. The 477th Bombardment Group, which was activated late in the war, did not see action.

From the time that black engineers first landed in New Guinea to prepare landing strips, African Americans took an increasingly active part in the war in the Pacific and East Asia.

Service in the Pacific Approximately 10,000 black troops worked on construction of the Ledo Road in Burma (today Myanmar). These service troops included engineers, port companies, quartermasters, and amphibious and chemical warfare units. They also fought when necessary. Among the combat units that saw service against the Japanese was the Twenty-Fourth

Infantry, which helped take the New Georgia Islands in May 1942. There were several other outfits, including two battalions of coast artillery and one antiaircraft barrage balloon battalion.

The main black combat unit in the Pacific was the Ninety-Third Division, which saw its first action at Bougainville in the Solomons. From there it proceeded against the Japanese in the Treasury Islands, on the Dutch East Indian (today, Indonesian) island of Morotai, and in the Philippines. While the soldiers of the Ninety-Third did not perform the kind of spectacular deeds that captured the imagination of citizens on the home front, they fought steadily and consistently under adverse tropical conditions.

Opportunities for African Americans in the Navy during World War II opened slowly, but they expanded significantly compared to available opportunities in World War I. In July 1943, no longer confined to being messmen and other menial positions in the Navy, thousands of blacks were trained to perform **Service in the Navy** numerous technical tasks and were given the appropriate ratings—that is, occupational designations indicating specific skill and ability. For this, historians credit the influence of Franklin D. Roosevelt himself, for decades earlier the president had served as assistant secretary of the Navy in the Wilson administration. On March 20, 1944, the destroyer escort *Mason* was commissioned, and African Americans of various grades were assigned to duty on it. Later, blacks manned a patrol chaser and hunted enemy submarines in the Atlantic.

By the fall of 1944, the Navy was able to announce that five hundred black seamen were on duty on twenty-five large auxiliary vessels operating primarily in the Pacific. Among the African Americans with ratings were storekeepers, yeomen, radiomen, ship fitters, carpenter's mates, gunner's mates, quartermasters, and coxswains. Meanwhile, approximately 12,500 black Seabees served in the Pacific, constructing advanced naval bases and doing other jobs. The work they performed, frequently under severe enemy attack, was praised by high navy officials. African American Marines were stationed at several strategic Pacific outposts to defend areas taken from the enemy. Their conduct caused the commandant of the Corps to say, "Negro Marines are no longer on trial. They are Marines, period." The more than 900 African Americans in the Coast Guard did rescue work in the Atlantic, in the Pacific, and in Alaskan waters. They were among the first to go ashore at Okinawa early in 1945 and on occasion performed invaluable services on shore duty both at home and abroad.

Approximately 24,000 African Americans served in the Merchant Marine, which practiced considerably less segregation and discrimination than any of the other branches of the armed forces. African Americans worked as ordinary seamen, engineers, **Service in the Merchant Marine** radio operators, and the like. Four black captains commanded Liberty ships with integrated crews. Eighteen ships were named for African Americans—fourteen for famous African Americans and four for African American merchant seamen who had lost their lives while on active service with the Merchant Marine. An African American, Captain Hugh Mulzac, commanded the S.S. *Booker T. Washington*. During the course of the war two of the ships, the S.S. *Frederick Douglass* and the S.S. *Robert L. Vann*, were sunk.

It was not uncommon for black soldiers to be the target of racist acts by white civilians. In March 1941, the lynching of Private Felix Hall of Montgomery, Alabama, shocked black Americans. He was found in his uniform hanging from a tree in a **Racism at Home** wooded section of Fort Benning, Georgia. The War Department determined Hall's death to be a suicide despite the fact that his hands and feet were bound by rope. As blacks began to challenge Jim Crow, reports of violent confrontations on the ground escalated, and, between 1940 and 1941, there were thirteen reported lynchings. The black press covered the deaths of black soldiers—some killed by local police in Columbia, South Carolina; in Little Rock, Arkansas; and in Alexandria, Louisiana; and one killed by an armed bus driver in Mobile, Alabama, in 1942 for questioning the driver's authority to enforce segregated seating. In Durham, North Carolina, the court found a white bus driver not guilty of murder after he left his bus in July 1944 and killed a black soldier with whom he had earlier argued.

Black writer James Baldwin described the helplessness and uneasiness felt by blacks in the North upon sending their loved ones to southern military camps: "People I knew felt, mainly, a peculiar kind of relief when they knew their boys were being shipped out of the South to do battle overseas. It was, perhaps, like feeling that the most dangerous part of the journey had been passed and that now, even if death should come, it would come with honor and without the complicity of their countrymen."

In southern communities, some restaurants refused to serve black men in uniform while accommodating German prisoners of war, who ate in these same restaurants, rode in the "whites only" section of Jim Crow trains, and enjoyed American hospitality denied to all black Americans. In a Kentucky railroad station, white civilian policemen beat three African American women in uniform for failing to move promptly from the white waiting room when asked to do so. Because of their race, their identity as women and as WACS did not command any respect. In covering these stories, the black press helped to mobilize agitation on the home front. Several commanding officers even forbade the reading of black newspapers on military bases in an attempt to keep such stories away from black soldiers. In such instances, black newspapers were taken from newsboys or from the soldiers themselves and burned.

Myriad acts of racism occurred on military bases themselves. Everywhere blacks registered their protest against the Red Cross's practice of separating black and white blood in the blood banks established for the relief of wounded service personnel. The Red Cross policy was all the more ironic, because of the pioneering work of black physician Charles Drew in the discovery of blood plasma. Lester Granger, the head of the National Urban League, asserted in 1942 that "the policy of racial blood segregation must be discontinued as it affronts the respect of 13,000,000 Negroes and undermines their morale in a period of national peril."

African Americans also censured the United Service Organization (USO), a nonprofit organization for the support of American troops, when it banned the circulation of anthropologist Ruth Benedict's antiracist book *Races of Mankind* throughout its clubs. Blacks in the armed forces endured additional slights. Many camps refused to provide satisfactory transportation to black soldiers and followed a custom of boarding buses first with the white soldiers, thereby forcing blacks to wait. At PXs, black soldiers were segregated and were often sold inferior merchandise. Theaters and other entertainment facilities near a military base separated the races, offering black soldiers inferior accommodations.

The War Department took cognizance of the discrimination against African American soldiers in its order of July 8, 1944, which forbade racial segregation in recreational and transportation facilities. When the order was made known, a storm of protest arose in the South. For example, the *Montgomery Advertiser* asserted that "Army orders, even armies, even bayonets, cannot force impossible and unnatural social race relations upon us." Some commanding officers disregarded the order altogether. They considered the order to be merely a "directive" and failed to enforce it. Other officers sought to wipe out discrimination as the order required. Many black soldiers demanded equal treatment in pursuance of the order but found themselves rebuffed and denied service at PXs and theaters.

The attempts of African Americans to resist segregation and discrimination led to clashes both on and off military posts. Few camps could boast at the end of the war that they had experienced no racial clashes. Serious riots took place at Fort **Racial Clashes** Bragg, Camp Robinson, Camp Davis, Camp Lee, and Fort Dix. At Freeman Field, Indiana, more than a hundred black officers were arrested for attempting to enter an officers' club maintained for whites. They were later exonerated. At Mabry Field in Florida and at Port Chicago, California, black servicemen were charged with mutiny when they refused to perform work that they felt was assigned to them because of their color. The emotional conflicts and frustrations they experienced became increasingly difficult to reconcile with the doctrine of the Four Freedoms. Neither the antidiscrimination orders of the War Department nor the concessions made in the commissioning of African American officers in the Navy could compensate for the many small and large acts of racism toward those wearing the uniform of their country.

During the war years, however, blacks in the military received significant recognition for their service. The Secretary of War, the Army chief of staff, and **Recognition for Service** high military officials in the various theaters of war praised their heroism and service. Many black units received the Presidential Distinguished Unit Citation for their gallantry. Individual men received recognition that ranged from good conduct medals to the Distinguished Service Cross.

Ship Messman Doris (Dorie) Miller was the first African American to be honored, receiving the Navy Cross for his outstanding heroism during the Japanese bombing of Pearl Harbor. With no machine gun training, Miller manned the weapon in the face of enemy bombs and torpedo damage that eventually caused the crew to abandon the battleship *West Virginia*. For the late Private George Watson, the citation of honor read: "Extraordinary heroism—on March 8, 1943, when he lost his life in Portlock Harbor, New Guinea, after assisting several men to safety on a raft from their sinking boat, which had been attacked by Japanese bombers. Overcome by exhaustion, he was pulled under and drowned by the suction of the craft." Eighty-two black pilots received the Distinguished Flying Cross. Other African Americans received the French Croix de Guerre and the Yugoslav Partisan Medal for Heroism, and one received the Order of the Soviet Union. With some justification, the black members of the armed services could feel that they had made their contribution to the preservation of the ideal, if not the reality, of the Four Freedoms.

"above and beyond the call of duty"

DORIE MILLER
Received the Navy Cross at Pearl Harbor, May 27, 1942.

Dorie Miller
Miller was the first African American hero during World War II, winning the Navy Cross for manning a machine gun in the face of serious fire during the Japanese attack on Pearl Harbor, December 7, 1941.

No African American was awarded the Congressional Medal of Honor at the war's end. In the Civil War, sixteen black soldiers and five sailors won the medal, and in the Spanish-American War seven black servicemen received the nation's highest military decoration. In both World Wars, despite recognized valor, none had received the Medal of Honor, and blacks began to ask if the nation reserved its highest award for white soldiers. In 1993 the U.S. Army initiated a study "to determine why no black soldier had received the Congressional Medal of Honor." It concluded that "racism was the cause." In January 1997, after reviewing the records of African Americans who had received the Distinguished Service Cross, an awards panel bestowed the Medal of Honor on seven blacks, only one of whom, Vernon Baker, was still living. Lieutenant Baker's citation described his valor in leading twenty-five men through minefields and against superior German firepower to take a strategic position near Castle Aghinolfi in Italy, where Germans blocked the advance of Allied troops.

During World War II, many white units were undermanned and needed qualified people but were unable to get experienced black personnel because of the segregation policy. The newly formed U.S. Air Force initiated plans to integrate its units as early as 1947, and on July 26, 1948, President Harry S. Truman issued Executive Order Number 9981, ending the policy of racial segregation in the military forces by enforcing "equality of treatment and opportunity for all persons in the armed services without regard to race, color, religion or national origin."

Keeping the Home Fires Burning

Wartime necessity and black demands caused the government to adopt several economic and social policies that challenged existing race relations. On numerous occasions African Americans pointed to the racial restrictions to equal employment as a tremendous waste and inefficiency in the nation's defense effort. Thanks to the New Deal programs of the National Youth Administration (NYA) and the Work Projects Administration (WPA), thousands of African Americans had attained the necessary skills for employment in the defense industry. The training programs sponsored by the U.S. Office of Education, the Vocational Training for War Production Workers, and the Engineering, Science, and Management War Training (ESMWT) program augmented their number further. As a result, by December 1942 more than 58,000 African Americans had enrolled in pre-employment courses. In the summer of 1943, sixty-five black colleges participated in the ESMWT program, which trained more than 50,000 students for work in aircraft industries, shipbuilding, welding, automotive mechanics, electricity and radio, and numerous other defense-related activities. Although the nondiscriminatory provisions of the federal training programs ensured the preparation of African Americans for defense work, the discriminatory hiring practices plagued black job applicants throughout the war.

In the years following the creation of the Fair Employment Practices Committee (FEPC) by Roosevelt's Executive Order 8802, the tide slowly began to turn for black workers. An **The Work of the FEPC** increasing number of blacks found jobs in government service and in defense industries. Considerable antagonism to the FEPC developed, however, because of its practice of citing industries for violating the president's executive order even after those industries had initiated programs for the integration of minorities. The FEPC also put pressure on the U.S. Employment Service to give preference, in job referrals, to employers who did not discriminate against minority groups. These various forms of government pressure resulted in much greater utilization of the country's total workforce for the war effort.

African Americans in wartime industry

These women are at work at a welding plant in New Britain, Connecticut, and the men at a shipyard in Baltimore, Maryland.

Despite the limitations of the FEPC and the other government agencies that tried to eliminate discriminatory policies, their activities showed clearly the federal government's instrumental role in changing employment practices. At the beginning of the wartime emergency, almost no blacks, for example, worked in the aircraft industries, but near the end of the war thousands did. The shipyards increased their black workers, both in the quantity and the quality of employment opportunities. More than 100,000 African Americans found employment for the first time in the iron and steel industries, although primarily at lower-level jobs. Upgrading to higher-level jobs, however, would elude the great majority of the workers in these industries for the duration of the war.

During and after the war, African Americans played an increasingly vocal role at the conventions of such organizations as the United Automobile Workers, the United Steel Workers, the National Maritime Union, and the United Rubber Workers, and on the national councils of the CIO (Congress of Industrial Organizations). By 1944 blacks had better opportunities than before the war, but they still fared considerably worse than whites in finding jobs. They remained disproportionately concentrated in unskilled labor, personal service, and domestic work, with family income, housing, schools, and medical care inferior to that of whites. Many black leaders argued that the government should guarantee employment on a basis of nondiscrimination, and they formed the National Committee for a Permanent FEPC to rally public sentiment behind such a proposition. In the electoral campaign of 1944 both major parties committed themselves to this proposal, but neither the Democrats nor Republicans pushed to secure the necessary legislation.

Window in Time

Walter White's Call for Victory at Home and Abroad—1944

The Negro people, like all other Americans, recognize the war as the chief issue confronting our country. We demand of any political party desiring the support of Negroes a vigorous prosecution of the war. We are opposed to any negotiated peace as advocated by the Hitler-like forces within our country. Victory must crush Hitlerism both at home as well as abroad.

In evaluating the merits of parties and candidates we must include all issues—those touching the life of Negroes as a group as well as those affecting the entire country. The party or candidate who refuses to help control prices, or fails to support the extension of social security, or refuses to support a progressive public program for full post war employment, or opposes an enlarged and unsegregated program of government-financed housing, or seeks to destroy organized labor, is as much the enemy of the Negro as is he who would prevent the Negro from voting.

Source: Walter White and others, "A Declaration by Negro Voters," *The Crisis,* 51 (January 1944), pp. 16–17. Reprinted by permission.

African Americans gave generous support to the war effort on the home front. They purchased bonds, and many corporations reported that black employees signed up for the **Support for the War Effort** payroll savings plan, under which regular amounts were deducted from wages for the purchase of bonds. In every bond campaign, African Americans held rallies in schools, churches, and community centers to sell war bonds. With the help of blacks on the staff of the Treasury Department, especially William Pickens and Nell Hunter, the campaigns among African Americans were almost always successful.

With the establishment of the Office of Civilian Defense (OCD), African Americans became active in preparations to defend the country against possible enemy attack. Crystal Bird Fauset served as the OCD's race relations adviser on the national level, while on the local level blacks became block managers, messengers, and auxiliary firefighters and police officers. In the program to conserve foods and other essential commodities and to control prices, African Americans also played their part. When the Office of Price Administration (OPA) was established, blacks were employed as attorneys, price analysts, and economists. They worked in regional and state offices as information specialists and in the local offices of some communities as clerks, as well as members of ration boards.

There seemed to be more general satisfaction among African Americans with the way in which the OPA was administered than with any other wartime agency, perhaps because of the rather general policy of the agency to employ workers for jobs regardless of race. In the agencies established for morale-building purposes, African Americans participated in larger numbers than during World War I. They served the Red Cross as Gray Ladies, as nurses' aides, and as drivers in the motor corps. In fighting areas they worked in camps, clubs, and hospitals. During the war approximately two hundred professional workers served as club directors and in other capacities in four theaters of war.

Growing economic opportunities on the home front impelled the migration of ever-growing numbers of blacks to the North and the West in search of employment. Black migration during the 1940s grew at a fever pitch, larger than the migration of any previous decade. For example, within the five-year period between 1940 and 1945, the African American population of Los Angeles County increased from 75,000 to 150,000. The industrial communities of San Francisco, Oakland, Portland, and Seattle experienced similar high levels of black migration. Among the Midwestern cities that witnessed an influx of blacks and whites, Detroit showed the greatest strains in the problem of achieving adjustment. The migration of large numbers of blacks and whites into the city, the lack of housing, the presence of race baiters and demagogues, the problem of organizing the newly arrived workers, and the impotence of the government created a combustible combination.

Crystal Bird Fauset, special assistant, Office of Civilian Defense

On June 20, 1943, the most serious race riot of the war years broke out in Detroit. Tensions accumulating for months exploded after a fistfight between a black man and a white man, and this altercation rapidly spread to involve several hundred people of both races. Wild rumors, as usual, swept through the town. Within a few hours blacks and whites were fighting throughout most of Detroit. When the governor hesitated to declare martial law and call out

Black-White Conflict at Home

troops, whites began to roam the streets, burning blacks' cars and beating large numbers of black people. Nothing effective was done to bring order out of the chaos until President Roosevelt proclaimed a state of emergency and sent six thousand soldiers to patrol the city. After more than thirty hours of rioting, twenty-five African Americans and nine whites had been killed, and property valued at several hundred thousand dollars had been destroyed.

Detroit was not the only city in which racial tensions spiraled uncontrollably. Harlem blacks exploded in rioting in 1943 after a uniformed soldier interfered with the arrest of his mother for disorderly conduct and was wounded by the police. The man was alleged to have threatened and hit the officer, and he sought to escape his arrest when someone in the surrounding crowd accosted the policeman from behind. The soldier's effort to escape failed, and he was shot by the policeman and carried wounded to the hospital. Distorted news of the shooting passed rapidly through the Harlem community—the story being that the arrested soldier had been killed, not wounded, while defending his mother. Angry crowds destroyed buildings and looted businesses that they perceived to be "white property," to the amount of three to five million dollars in damages. When calm was finally restored more than 600 people had been arrested, 6 were killed, and 189 injured. Undoubtedly, a combination of racial oppression and poor economic conditions fanned the incendiary situation.

The problem of low morale worried black leaders (ministers, newspaper editors, elected officials, academics, businessmen, and civil rights activists), who sought to galvanize communities around the Double V campaign. Black leaders spoke of

The Problem of Low Morale

receiving letters that questioned "whether living under the domination of the Japanese or even under Hitler, could be worse than living under the fascism as practiced in the southern states . . . whether a concentration camp is worse than a Georgia chain Gang." A survey conducted by the Office of Facts and Figures in 1942, entitled "The Negro Looks at the War," revealed a disturbing cynicism on the part of the respondents. The War and Navy Departments made possible the visits of leading African Americans to the war fronts in order to raise the morale of service personnel and to inform civilians at home of the activities of those at the front.

According to historian Barbara Savage, black lawyer Theodore Berry, who served as a staff officer in the government's Liaison Bureau of the Office of Emergency Management during the war, in 1942 recommended a media campaign with extensive use of the radio for building black morale and informing white listeners of the role of blacks in the war effort. (Berry also insisted on the desegregation of the armed forces as the most immediate signal to black Americans of the nation's belief in its ideals of freedom and democracy.)

The radio proved to be an extremely effective medium for delivering information to the black public. For example, in New York City the black Episcopal minister John H. Johnson, also a member of the Mayor's Committee on Unity, declared over the radio in 1941: "In battle, it doesn't make any difference if a soldier be Catholic, Protestant, Jew, or Negro. They are united in their efforts to defend their country. We have the obligation to be united now to create that disposition and sense of justice that will make life better for all our citizens when this conflict is ended." In the same manner, the Office of War Information sought to use its radio programs to strengthen black morale. The Office of War Information (OWI) produced radio broadcasts that featured leading political and educational figures, as well as news bulletins on blacks in combat.

The War Department also turned to black artists, photographers, and film writers to assist in its propaganda campaign to tell the African American story of bravery and patriotism. Carlton Moss wrote the script for and acted in the army film *The Negro Soldier.* In his role as a black preacher, Moss recounted the contribution of black servicemen in America's past wars. The film debuted in 1943 with much acclaim from black audiences. Also in 1943, the OWI distributed 2 million copies of a large pamphlet entitled *Negroes and the War* to a wide array of black community organizations. Its numerous photographs captured the patriotism and sacrifice of black service personnel, war workers, scholars, scientists, and artists. The glossy photographs in the stylishly produced *Negroes and the War* were carefully selected by the veteran black newspaperman Ted Poston, who had been appointed as racial advisor in the Office of War Information. Through Poston's office, news of how blacks fared in the armed services and on the home front was sent to newspapers that were read by African Americans.

Such publicity did not assuage black resentment toward segregation in the military, however. Lester Granger of the National Urban League asserted that the publication was a "monumental mistake and a disservice to the government and the Negro. I say this . . . because it is like kicking a man who is down and congratulating him because he is not yet dead." In 1943 William Hastie resigned as a civilian aide to the Secretary of War because of the government's refusal to desegregate the troops. Hastie had become something of a persona non grata to Secretary of War Henry Stimson, who described Hastie's views as unrealistic and impossible. The black press, black community, and liberal whites praised

Window in Time

W.E.B. Du Bois, On William Hastie's Receipt of the Spingarn Medal

There are two sorts of public relations officials in Washington working on the situation of the Negro: one sort is a kind of upper clerk who transmits to the public with such apologetic airs as he can assume, the refusal of the department to follow his advice or the advice of anyone else calculated to serve the racial situation. The other kind of race relations' official seeks to give advice and to get the facts and if he receives a reasonable amount of cooperation he works on hopefully. If he does not, he withdraws. It is, of course, this second type of official alone who is useful and valuable. The other is nothing. Hastie belongs to the valuable sort and will not be easily replaced.

Source: "Text of the Award of the Twenty-Eighth Spingarn Medal" to Hastie, March 1943, NAACP Papers.

Hastie. The NAACP awarded Hastie the Spingarn Medal for his courage to resign rather than accommodate a Jim Crow military.

Although the War Department sought to allay black concerns on the home front by maintaining a black officer in its press section and by accrediting black newspapermen as war correspondents, the twenty African Americans who covered the various theaters of war for the press did not silence their protest. The reports of such correspondents as Ollie Stewart of the *Afro-American* and Lem Graves of the *Norfolk Journal and Guide* conveyed vivid accounts of both black heroism and white racism in the armed forces, while Walter White's book, *A Rising Wind*, based on his visits to the war fronts, contained revelations of racial injustice that caused even more determined efforts to fight for a double victory.

Black leaders also used the radio and printed matter to link black patriotism with the struggle for economic advancement. The National Urban League's annual campaign directed attention to the role of black women in the war effort while at the same time calling for greater employment opportunities for black women, the great majority of whom remained in domestic service even as white women were entering new lines of work as a result of the war. Campaigning for the hiring of black women in war industry work, the League adopted the slogan "Womanpower is vital to victory." League staff member Ann Tanneyhill, a young black woman, coordinated the vocational opportunity campaign by gaining network radio airtime for the league's broadcast of "Heroines in Bronze."

Historian Barbara Savage describes Tanneyhill's prebroadcast publicizing activities—press releases, endorsements by noted leaders, and "listening groups" dispersed throughout the nation. To accentuate the campaign, *Opportunity*, the official organ of the National Urban League, featured the theme "brown American womanpower" and carried photographs of women in a variety of wartime capacities. In his introduction to the *Opportunity* issue, League president Lester Granger called African American women "the mighty force working for the redemption of the soul of Democratic America."

Throughout World War II, blacks envisioned their role as a national conscience of sorts—as a force that would help to redeem the soul of America and declare finally triumphant the nation's professed, but still unrealized, ideals. Eleanor Roosevelt had remarked early in the war that "the nation cannot expect colored people to feel that the United States is worth defending if the Negro continues to be treated as he is now." At the end of the war, blacks understood all too well this poignant dilemma. In 1945 they rejoiced with other Americans in celebration of the defeat of Hitler and fascism. Yet victory over Jim Crow had yet to materialize. In the years after World War II, blacks mobilized for an even more concerted fight for equality and justice in America.

American Dilemmas, 1930s–1955

Intellectual Crosscurrents

Literary and Dramatic Arts

Black Internationalism

Labor Civil Rights

Truman and Civil Rights

Fighting for Civil Rights in the Courts

Thurgood Marshall, Donald Gaines Murray, and Charles Houston

The years during and after World War II were rife with expectations of a new world order. In February 1941, before U.S. entry into the war, *Time* publisher Henry Luce predicted, in an editorial in his magazine, the dawning of "the American Century." Luce foresaw that the United States would emerge from the ruins of war as the most powerful nation in the world, and he exhorted Americans not to "bungle it," as they had after World War I, by embracing isolationism. American political and economic hegemony, which he wanted, demanded the export of all things characteristically American—culture, trade, technology, aid, and the "great principles of Western civilization—above all Justice, the love of Truth, the ideal of Charity."

A different vision of America's future was offered in the article "Certain Unalienable Rights" by Mary McLeod Bethune, the black New Dealer and founder of the National Council of Negro Women. Doubtless Bethune too valued Justice, Truth, and Charity, but for her such words remained empty platitudes when black Americans were denied the rights, privileges, and responsibilities of full citizenship in the land of their birth. Writing in 1944, Bethune enunciated what African Americans wanted—the "opportunity to make real what the Declaration of Independence and the Constitution and the Bill of Rights say." American leadership of the free world required leadership at home so that blacks, like other Americans, were guaranteed the right to vote, an end to lynching, an integrated military, equal employment opportunities, fair access to public housing and social security, and interracial cooperation.

Bethune's perspective was more in keeping with that of Henry Wallace, Franklin D. Roosevelt's vice president between 1941 and 1945, who in a speech in May 1942 explicitly rejected Luce's business-oriented American Century. Foreseeing instead the "century of the common man," Wallace argued that America must lead in building world peace, which he defined broadly to mean "a better standard of living for the common man, not merely in the United States and England, but also in India, Russia, China and Latin America. . . ." Bethune also ended her article on an internationalist note, identifying African Americans as part of "the depressed and oppressed masses all over the world." But she also consciously addressed women worldwide: "We will reach out our hands to all women who struggle forward—white, black, brown, yellow—all."

Throughout the 1940s, Americans who denounced racial inequality at home and colonialism abroad called attention to the gap between the nation's ideals and its practices. In the latter part of the decade, as the Cold War began to pit the United States against the Soviet Union, antiracist dissent would itself pose dilemmas for many socially conscious Americans—civil rights and labor activists, scholars and literary figures, and politicians and entertainers. At a time when such activism was frequently labeled subversive or un-American, those who fought racial discrimination made difficult, consequential choices as to their allies and tactics as they pursued international causes, legal challenges, labor protest, social scientific research, and artistic production. Postwar African Americans did not doubt that America stood poised to lead the free world, nor did they doubt that America's dilemmas were theirs as well.

Intellectual Crosscurrents

In 1903 W. E. B. Du Bois had characterized the "Negro Problem" as the psychological dilemma of being American and Negro—a tortured mindset of dueling identities, with "two un-reconciled strivings; two warring ideals in one dark body." Forty years later, the Swedish sociologist Gunnar Myrdal characterized the "Negro Problem" in a different way. Myrdal also saw it as a psychological dilemma—no less irrational and contradictory—but one that was roiling the minds of white Americans.

Writing at a time when the United States and its allies waged war against fascism and Nazi racism abroad, Myrdal found American whites' dilemma to be a moral issue—the failure to live by the democratic creed they treasured so dearly. Their racial discrimination exposed the nation's Achilles heel. This contradiction was developed at length in Myrdal's 1,400-page opus *An American Dilemma* (1944). Selected by the Carnegie Corporation of New York to undertake this ambitious study, Myrdal's interpretation became increasingly influential in the years after its publication and especially as the Cold War unfolded.

An American Dilemma

Most black leaders in the 1940s and 1950s welcomed Myrdal's huge study, perceiving his assessment to be an affirmation of a long held awareness in their community. Myrdal's work in fact drew on the research findings and raw data of sociologists, historians, economists, political scientists, psychologists, anthropologists, and other social-science specialists. Thirty persons were commissioned to collaborate on the project. Certainly substantial was the contribution of political scientist Ralph Bunche, whose research and writing formed part of Myrdal's finished work. Bunche had even preceded Myrdal in articulating the disparity between the nation's ideals and its actions. In his book *A World View of Race* (1936), Bunche concluded that "no other subject can so well illustrate the insincerity of our doctrines of human equality and the great disparity between our political theory and our social practices as that of race."

On a more fundamental level, African Americans understood that racism and the creed of "liberty and justice for all" had co-existed far too easily in the history of America. Over the centuries, during peacetime and especially during wars and their immediate aftermath, countless African Americans had demanded equal citizenship as they pledged allegiance to their country through service in the armed forces and other forms of patriotism. From Revolutionary War-era poet Phillis Wheatley to Langston Hughes, who in 1938 wrote "America was never America to me" in his poem "Let America be America Again," black writers insisted that America as a symbol contradicted American realities. That conviction only deepened in the World War II and postwar years.

Myrdal and numerous other scholars in the 1940s and 1950s emphasized the destructive effects of this dilemma on black communities. A large number of studies by black and white scholars emphasized pathological and dysfunctional images of black life—highlighting illiteracy, crime, delinquency, disease, and family instability as manifestations of frustration and the difficulties of living with the stigma of inferiority. Those studies, which usually focused on black social and economic conditions, came out of the research of such federal departments as the Office of Education, the Department of the Interior, and the Department of Commerce. Educational institutions—for example, the Institute for Research in Social Science of the University of North Carolina and the Department of the Social Sciences of Fisk University, sought to present graphic, scientific findings on the status of blacks in American society. The works of black social scientists E. Franklin Frazier, Charles S. Johnson, and Kenneth Clark, and white social scientists Howard Odum, Rupert Vance, Gordon Blackwell, and Guy B. Johnson, among others, provided hitherto unavailable information concerning blacks and the worlds in which they lived.

In a series of significant volumes, the American Council on Education published the findings of the American Youth Commission, which had studied the effect of the proscriptive

School segregation

In 1948, West Memphis, Arkansas, spent $144.51 for the education of each white student in the classroom, while it spent $19.51 for the education of each of the African American students.

influences of American society on personality development among African American youth. The studies of these investigators—among them Frazier, Johnson, Allison Davis, John Dollard, W. Lloyd Warner, Ira D. A. Reid, and Robert L. Sutherland—revealed that the vast majority of black youth did not get an opportunity to share in the American dream of equal opportunities. They explained that the environment of black youth often forced young people to react in a manner regarded by the larger society as shiftless, irresponsible, and aggressive. Opportunities for young African Americans to live normal lives were so few as to challenge, for them, any hope of achieving the American dream.

Some of these studies did make recommendations for improving the status of blacks in American life, but the researchers' primary concern was revealing facts rather than outlining programs of action. Some, like Myrdal, explicitly advocated social engineering. Indeed, *An American Dilemma* articulated and gave shape to a growing liberal civil rights consensus within the federal government and also civil rights organizations. For example, the Truman administration's civil rights report *To Secure These Rights* (1947) referred to *An American Dilemma*, as did the NAACP legal team's argumentation. Later, in its landmark case *Brown v. Board of Education* (1954), the Supreme Court cited Myrdal's book in striking down the legality of segregated public education.

Black and white scholars' rhetoric of social pathology to describe the debilitating effects of racism and segregation played a strategic role in the legal assault on Jim Crow, but this type of "damage imagery," as historian Daryl Scott terms it, also evoked "contempt and pity." In the 1940s and 1950s, the dominant scholarly interpretation of black pathology and victimization tended to go too far, departing from earlier scholarship that affirmed racial pride and also from that which emphasized black agency in the struggle for economic rights and racial

The Emphasis on Assimilation and Culture

justice. Its privileging of assimilation over black cultural distinctiveness would prove untenable to scholars in the post-1960s and to a generation of African Americans who lauded black pride and black power.

In the 1940s, however, the emphasis on assimilation prevailed. It was one thing to speak assertively of racial expectations, as did the cross-section of black leaders whose essays appeared in *What the Negro Wants* (1944), edited by Rayford W. Logan at the request of the University of North Carolina Press. The diverse group of radicals, liberals, moderates, and conservatives spoke in a unified demand for full citizenship and full participation in American life. Their assertiveness provoked the director of the press, W. C. Couch, to write his own introduction expressing disagreement with the black writers' position. But it was quite another thing to speak assertively of black cultural difference in the 1940s, as did the white anthropologist and civil rights advocate Melville Herskovits. Such a position posed a difficult question in regard to individual identity and to racial representation in the fight for equality and dignity in America: Did black distinctiveness simply come down to a culture of pathology? Or were patterns of distinctiveness actually rooted in an older, African heritage?

By the 1940s, social scientists had begun to challenge the biological premise of race. The work of Columbia University-based anthropologist Franz Boas at the turn of the twentieth century, and later of his students (who included Herskovits, Ruth Benedict, Margaret Mead, and Zora Neale Hurston), took exception to race as a biological construct. Instead, they emphasized culture as the primary explanation of group differences. Their scientific approach to culture demanded extensive fieldwork, based on a value-free examination of the values, mores, art, family structure, and other social institutions within the context of a specific ethnic or social group, instead of judging one group by another group's standards for the sake of racial hierarchy.

The influence of such "culturalists" was evident in the work of those who advocated educational models that emphasized the pluralistic character of the United States. For example, in the late 1930s, the Department of Interior under New Dealer Harold Ickes promoted such ideas through the radio series *Americans All, Immigrants All*, which featured weekly programs on specific immigrant groups, as well as blacks and Jews. Historian Barbara Savage notes that phonograph recordings of individual *Americans All* programs were made available to civic organizations, libraries, and schools—elementary and secondary school teachers being among the largest targeted audiences of the show.

However, the implications of cultural explanations led to two different conclusions about race, one toward assimilation and the other toward distinctiveness. For some scholars, the conclusion was self-evident: If race was not biologically constructed, African-descended persons in the United States had already become, or at least were on the way to becoming, little different in their cultural patterns from other assimilated ethnic immigrant groups. Assimilation, it was argued, would occur most rapidly in contexts of racially integrated, urban settings.

In the late 1920s and early 1930s, the white sociologist Robert Park and his former student, black sociologist E. Franklin Frazier, each described migration to northern and western cities as ultimately an acculturating process, despite problems of marginalization and social

477

rupture. Even earlier, Franz Boas in the first decade of the twentieth century and his student Melville Herskovits in the 1920s, both white anthropologists, had measured the head sizes of different ethnic and racial groups (a form of study termed anthropometry) to argue that in cities over time the intellect, culture, and even physical appearance of the different groups were converging within a range of characteristics understood to be the "American type."

In the 1920s, Herskovits had articulated this assimilationist viewpoint in a research project that used anthropometric measurement and genealogical information, in order to study African Americans in Harlem and at Howard University in Washington, D.C. Publishing his findings initially in journals and later in the short book *The American Negro: A Study of Racial Crossing* (1928), he concluded that "I do not claim the term 'race' for the American Negro, and I certainly do not claim that there is anything but the most striking type of mixture represented in him." Clearly at odds with his own later work in the 1930s and 1940s, Herskovits in the 1920s stressed racial assimilation. In his chapter in Alain Locke's edited anthology *The New Negro* (1925), he portrayed blacks in Harlem as follows:

> [That] the [Negroes] have absorbed the culture of America is too obvious, almost, to be mentioned. They have absorbed it as all great racial and social groups in this country have absorbed it. And they face much the same problems as these groups face. The social ostracism to which they are subjected is only different in extent from that to which the Jew is subjected. The fierce reaction of race-pride is quite the same in both groups. But, whether in Negro or in Jew, the protest avails nothing, apparently. All racial and social elements in our population who live here long enough become acculturated, Americanized in the truest sense of the word, eventually. They learn our culture and react according to its patterns, against which all the protestations of the possession of, or of hot desire for, a peculiar culture mean nothing.

Herskovits's chapter aroused the indignation of Locke and others who envisioned *The New Negro* as showcasing the unique heritage and genius of black culture and with it, the authentic black voice and dialect of the rural folk and urban mass. Suggesting to Herskovits that he revise his chapter, Locke asked, "Does democracy require uniformity? If so it threatens to be safe, but dull. . . . Old folkways may not persist, but they may leave a mental trace, subtly recorded in emotional temper and coloring social reactions."

By 1940 Herskovits had made an about-face. Going against the academic mainstream, he boldly proclaimed the survival and the importance in the New World of African cultural patterns—words, names, music folklore, religion, and art. His research in Africa, **African Survivals** South America (particularly Brazil), and the Caribbean represents the first significant exploration and analysis of what scholars today term the African diaspora. Historian Walter Jackson notes that Herskovits was "genuinely startled" by the extent of similarity between African and New World cultures. His groundbreaking book *The Myth of the Negro Past* (1941), also funded by the Carnegie Corporation, posited the presence of "African survivals" in the New World—cultural patterns that appeared strongest in areas in South America and the Caribbean, where slavery and the slave trade had lasted longest and where blacks had come in far larger numbers and had lived under conditions of greater cultural autonomy.

Herskovits argued that blacks in the United States, although in much more contact with whites, also exhibited identifiable "Africanisms," as he termed behavioral patterns with traces of African worship practices and beliefs, family structure, and the arts. In the case of

Window in Time

Africanisms in African American Culture

What if the cultures of Africa from which the New World Negroes were derived, when described in terms of the findings of modern scientific method, are found to be vastly different from the current stereotype? What if these cultures impressed themselves on their carriers, and the descendants of their carriers, too deeply to be eradicated any more than were the cultural endowments of the various groups of European immigrants? . . . What if the aboriginal African endowment were found, in certain respects, even to have been transmitted to the whites, thus making the result of contact an exchange of culture—as it was in the case of other groups—rather than the endowment of an inferior people with habits of a superior group? Let us suppose, in short, it could be shown that the Negro is a man with a past and a reputable past; that in time the concept could be spread that the civilizations of Africa, like those of Europe, have contributed to American culture as we know it today; and that this idea might eventually be taken over into the canons of general thought. Would this not, as a practical measure, tend to undermine the assumptions that bolster racial prejudice?

Source: Melville Herskovits, *The Myth of the Negro Past* (1941), 29–30.

the United States, Herskovits did not identify specific areas of origin in West Africa as he had done of South America and the Caribbean, but he did argue for a "base line" of West African culture, with black religious life serving as a prime exemplar of African survivals.

Herskovits was not unaware of the political implications of his message, which he interpreted as a vindication of the existence of rich cultural heritage—traditions that disproved what he perceived to be the myth that "the Negro is thus a man without a past." Herskovits believed in the social importance of this argument—that it would develop a sense of pride in African Americans and would rid Africa of the stigma attached to it by refuting misinformation that fueled race prejudice.

For some, including historians W. E. B. Du Bois and Carter G. Woodson and linguist Lorenzo Dow Turner, the recognition of one's African heritage and the survival of its culture was eminently worthy of study. Du Bois called *The Myth of the Negro Past* "epoch-making." Herskovits had drawn on Turner's research, whose later publication in book form, *Africanisms in the Gullah Dialect* (1949), investigated African linguistic patterns among the black people on the Sea Islands off the South Carolina coast.

Harvard-trained Carter G. Woodson, known today as the Father of Black History, favorably reviewed Herskovits, praising his scientific method and his refutation of the dominant scholarly assumption that blacks had no reputable history or culture to pass on. Graduating in 1912 with the second black doctorate from Harvard's history department (after W. E. B. Du Bois), Woodson authored numerous historical monographs and articles. In addition, in 1915 he

The Popularization of Black History

founded the Association for the Study of Negro Life and History (today titled the Association for the Study of African American Life and History), in 1916 began publication of the *Journal of Negro History*, served as its editor until his death in 1950, and established the publishing company the Associated Publishers, which made possible the publication and distribution of books on black historical topics. Woodson is credited, above all other historians of his time (including W. E. B. Du Bois), for professionalizing black history.

Yet Woodson also intended the mission of the Association, as it was commonly called, to be the popularizing of black history. To reach a wide audience, in 1926 he launched the annual February celebration of Negro History Week (now Black History Month), and in 1937 he created a secondary-school-level publication, the *Negro History Bulletin*. Highly regarded in the black community, Woodson gathered around him a cadre of scholars who, as teachers and authors, would multiply in number by the 1940s to include blacks and whites and would expand the scholarship and readership of black history. Indeed, John Hope Franklin, a member of the Association, published the first edition of *From Slavery to Freedom* in 1947, its success at the time due to the growing respect for this field of study inside and outside the academy.

Often termed a black nationalist on account of his support of Marcus Garvey and his strong advocacy of racial self-help, Woodson had argued persistently for the importance of knowledge of both African and African American history and culture as a corrective to an unhealthy, assimilationist education. In his polemical book *The Miseducation of the Negro* (1933), Woodson lambasted "highly educated" blacks for what he believed to be training that was devoid of racial pride and thus useless—and even dangerous—to the advancement of black people.

In the 1940s, however, the majority of black scholars did not align with the Herskovits thesis of African survivals. The most noted criticism of this controversial book came from the sociologist E. Franklin Frazier, who argued that the passage of time and the "force of circumstances" associated with the Middle Passage, slavery, emancipation, and later urban migration had caused blacks to adapt to new situations and contexts, leaving only "scraps of memories" of Africa. Preceding Herskovits, Frazier had already established this viewpoint in his book *The Negro Family in the United States* (1939), in which he argued that "Probably never before in history has a people been so nearly completely stripped of its social heritage as the Negroes who were brought to America."

Most black scholars and civil rights proponents rejected Herskovits's emphasis on culture. Some even compared him to the earlier generation of white New South thinkers and writers such as Joel Chandler Harris, DuBose Heyward, Ulrich B. Phillips, and Charleston's all-white Society for the Preservation of Spirituals. Clearly interested in and fascinated by a distinct black regional culture, the New South group held racist presumptions about the "Negro's place" in society while simultaneously endeavoring to conserve those Old South idiosyncrasies that they deemed "authentic" to black people.

For African Americans in the 1930s and 1940s, a romanticized discussion of cultural distinctiveness, including the black-inspired musings of the Harlem (New Negro) Renais-

Abandoning the Culturalist Perspective
sance, came under increasing scrutiny and attack from those who propounded the primacy of economic over cultural solutions to racial inequality and who perceived race relations as masking economic conflict. E. Franklin Frazier went so far as to depict the culturalist perspective as "a lot of foolish talk about the peculiar 'contributions' of the Negro and his deep 'spirituality'."

Black intellectuals such as Frazier and those civil rights leaders who shared his perspective saw the focus on an African past and its cultural legacy as a distraction from the struggle for inclusion in American social, political, and economic life at a time when racial barriers had begun to fall in electoral politics, the New Deal, organized labor, the American Left, the armed forces, and even (with regard to Jim Crow laws) the federal judiciary.

In the social and political milieu of the 1940s, they argued, an enthusiastic reception and valorization of an African cultural inheritance posed a troubling dilemma—one that implicitly suggested, if not confirmed, the inability of blacks, unlike all other groups, to fit fully into American society.

The times were inhospitable to Herskovits's way of thinking, and his critics fretted over his interpretation. They voiced concerns about the book's political implications for the struggle for racial equality. One reviewer, the white sociologist Guy B. Johnson, whose work shared some similarity with that of Herskovits, worried openly that despite the good intentions of *The Myth of the Negro Past,* an "immensely practical problem is how to prevent this book . . . from becoming the handmaiden of those who are looking for new justifications for the segregation and differential treatment of Negroes." Ironically, Alain Locke, who years earlier had criticized Herskovits for understating black cultural distinctiveness, now maintained that the "stubborn survival" of Africanisms unwittingly created an attitude that blacks are "unassimilable."

1948 NAACP poster
In the postwar years, the NAACP launched annual campaigns to recruit members. This 1948 poster is typical of their appeal.

Literary and Dramatic Arts

The pervasive damage imagery of black life that appeared in social science literature was also captured in artistic literary form. The acclaimed novelist Ralph Ellison, author of *Invisible Man* (1952), declared that the sociology of black life "presses upon the Negro writer's work." For Ellison and others of this period, the question would be how that story should be told in an art form. Black writers did not agree on the answer. Some, like Richard Wright, a communist supporter in the 1930s, believed that it was the black author's role to represent the voice and oppressive conditions of the black working class. In his introduction to St. Claire Drake's and Horace Cayton's *Black Metropolis* (1945), Wright connected this important social-science study of Chicago to his own novel *Native Son* (1940), also set in Chicago.

Wright concluded that the scholarship of Drake and Cayton portrayed "the environment out of which the Bigger Thomases [the protagonist in *Native Son*] of our nation come." Wright's reference to contemporary social science was explicit, noting that Drake and Cayton's findings endorsed those of Gunnar Myrdal in *An American Dilemma* (1944). For Wright, the pathology imagery was useful for understanding the dehumanizing effects of racial oppression.

He wrote in his introduction to *Black Metropolis:* "White America has reduced Negro life in our great cities to a level of existence of so crude and brutal a quality that one could say of it in the words of Vachel Lindsay's *The Leaden-Eyed* that 'It is not that they starve, but they starve so dreamlessly'."

Disagreeing with Wright, James Baldwin rejected the heavy emphasis on racism's pathological manifestations in black life. In his 1949 essay "Everybody's Protest Novel," Baldwin identified Wright and his *Native Son* as a style that delimits the fullness of black cultural expression and underestimates the vast capacity of personhood to reach beyond racial identity. "The failure of the protest novel," wrote Baldwin, "lies in its rejection of life, the human being, the denial of his beauty, dread, power, in its insistence that it is his categorization [racial] alone that is real and which cannot be transcended."

Since the turn of the twentieth century, the question of transcending one's racial identity as a scholar or artist had posed a dilemma—what Du Bois had called "twoness"—and the question continued to be debated in the artistic community during and after the 1920s. In the 1940s and 1950s African American literary artists became more varied in their subject matter, but most developed their plots and poems around everyday social issues that faced blacks, such as migration, urban life, wartime conditions, race riots, restrictive housing, and labor. A few also became famous with artistic works that made no reference to race or black characters.

Poets
Among the poets of this period was Melvin B. Tolson, then a professor of English at Wiley College. He published poems in newspapers and magazines during the 1930s and won numerous prizes and awards. Although his volume of poems, *Rendezvous with America,* was not issued until 1944, one of the collection's principal poems, "Dark Symphony," had been published previously in the *Atlantic Monthly.* While at the University of Michigan, Robert Hayden won the Jule and Avery Hopwood Prize for his poems, and his first volume, *Heart-Shape in the Dust,* was published in 1940. In 1966 his poetry won first prize at the World Festival of Negro Art at Dakar, Senegal.

Owen Dodson, one of the youngest of the well-known poets and playwrights, became seriously interested in writing while a student at Bates College. After writing traditional and experimental verse for several years, in 1946 he collected his works in a volume, *Powerful Long Ladder.* Two young women who also won recognition as poets were Margaret Walker and Gwendolyn Brooks. While on the Chicago Federal Writers' Project, Walker wrote "For My People," which later won first prize in the Yale University competition for young poets.

Stephen Vincent Benét praised Walker's work generously when it was published in 1942. Her novel *Jubilee,* winner of a Houghton Mifflin Literary Fellowship, was published in 1966. Meanwhile Brooks's volume *Street in Bronzeville* appeared in 1945. Five years later her *Annie Allen* won the Pulitzer Prize, and more than a decade after that she was named poet laureate of Illinois. Later, in 1985–1986, she was selected poet in residence at the Library of Congress, a post that was elevated at the end of her tenure to poet laureate of the United States.

Prose Writers
A profusion of prose writers appeared on the scene during and after the Depression. Among them was Arna Bontemps, who said that he had watched the early stages of the Harlem Renaissance from a grandstand seat. Subsequently he became one of its most productive contributors. In 1931 his *God Sends Sunday* appeared, followed by two historical novels, *Black Thunder* (1936) and *Drums at Dusk* (1939). Bontemps also became one of the most successful writers of children's books. Later he turned to nonfiction materials, writing with Jack Conroy *They Seek a City* (1945), an engrossing account of black urbanization.

(The revised edition appeared in 1966 under the title *Any Place but Here.*) Bontemps's *They Have Tomorrow* (1945) offered a series of biographical sketches of promising young African Americans.

Two black southern writers produced novels of African American life in the Deep South: George W. Henderson wrote *Ollie Miss* (1935) and *Jule* (1946); George W. Lee shed considerable light on black life in Memphis with *Beale Street* (1934), followed two years later by *River George.* Meanwhile, a promising young writer, Waters Turpin, was using materials of the Upper South for his novels. As a native of the eastern shore of Maryland, Turpin dealt with a familiar area in his works, *These Low Grounds* (1937) and *O Canaan* (1939). The latter novel focused on migration north.

Novelist William Attaway pointed to new areas and materials for the African American writer. In *Let Me Breathe Thunder* (1939), Attaway showed that an African American could deal successfully with a work made up primarily of white characters. In *Blood on the Forge* (1941) he indicated the wealth of materials to be found in industrial communities experiencing racial competition in the struggle for existence. This theme of racial friction was exploited to a greater degree by Chester Himes in his 1945 novel, set in a wartime industrial community, *If He Hollers, Let Him Go.* Himes, who had attracted attention with his short stories in black-owned and white-owned magazines alike—*Opportunity, Esquire,* and *Coronet*—vividly demonstrated the impact of the war on black migrants to industrial communities and the bitterness stemming from frustration and despair. Ann Petry, winner of a Houghton Mifflin Literary Fellowship, depicted the problems of a young African American woman attempting to live a respectable life in a blighted section of a large city. Her 1946 novel *The Street* had wide circulation and received considerable praise.

In the 1940s, the best known of the younger African American writers was Richard Wright. Considered a master of the short story when his *Uncle Tom's Children* appeared in 1938, Wright won even greater acclaim for *Native Son* (1940), which immediately placed him in the front ranks of contemporary American writers. With stark, tragic realism, Wright described the literally murderous frustrations of a young black man living in a Chicago slum and the efforts of a Marxist lawyer in his defense. The book compared favorably with the best similar works in American literature. It was a Book-of-the-Month Club selection and enjoyed considerable success in general bookstores.

Richard Wright and *Native Son*

In 1941 Wright brought out *Twelve Million Black Voices,* a folk history of African Americans. In 1945 *Black Boy,* a quasi-autobiographical account of Wright's childhood and youth in Mississippi, was also a Book-of-the-Month Club selection. Although there was disagreement over the accuracy of the work as an autobiography, there was no dissent about its power as a story of life among poor, oppressed black southerners. *The Outsider,* which appeared in 1953, did not receive the favorable critical acclaim of Wright's earlier works, but by that time he was firmly established as one of the country's major writers.

Ralph Ellison, who has been compared by some critics with Richard Wright for his talents as a writer, received even greater acclaim than Wright for his novel *Invisible Man* (1952). The book's complex and sophisticated rendering of Ellison's insight into race relations problems and their effect on blacks received the National Book Award in 1952, and in 1955 Ellison received the Prix de Rome and went to the American Academy in Rome to work on a second novel. His volume of essays, *Shadow and Act,* was published in 1964.

Ralph Ellison and *Invisible Man*

Perhaps the most widely read black writer of the 1940s was Frank Yerby. In 1944 he won the O. Henry Memorial Award with his short story "Health Card." In 1946 *The Foxes of Harrow* remained on the best-seller list for many months and reportedly approached the million-copy mark. In succeeding years, he published numerous novels; all of them reached the best-seller list, and some were filmed in Hollywood.

Frank Yerby

In the post-World War II years, several other African American writers won critical acclaim. John Oliver Killens showed great talent in his novel of southern life, *Youngblood* (1945), and in his film scripts for the black actor and singer Harry Belafonte. His *And Then They Heard the Thunder* (1963) was regarded by many as the most important novel about blacks during World War II, and his *Blackman's Burden* (1965) contains lively essays on the question of race.

Writers in the Postwar Years

James Baldwin, who showed much early promise as an essayist and novelist, followed Richard Wright into a Paris exile. Unlike Wright, however, he returned to the United States. His books have received wide recognition: *Go Tell It on the Mountain* (1953), *Notes of a Native Son* (1955), *Nobody Knows My Name* (1960), and *Another Country* (1962). Through his novel *Giovanni's Room* (1956), whose subject was a love affair between two men, Baldwin called attention to his own homosexuality. Baldwin's work captured the social concerns of the 1950s and 1960s—racial consciousness, discrimination, and sexuality issues, and his later work addressed the ideological cleavages between the black power and civil rights movements.

Jacob Lawrence, *The Migration Series,* "Panel 1—During World War II, there was a great migration North by Southern African Americans."

Although campus theaters at many black colleges stimulated an interest in the dramatic arts, in the 1930s young African Americans had little opportunity to pursue an acting career if they wanted to play roles other than as servants. That situation, however, began to change in the 1940s, led by Paul Robeson's success in such important dramatic parts as Shakespeare's Othello, a role he had previously played in London, as well as by Hilda Simms in *Anna Lucasta,* Gordon Heath in *Deep Are the Roots,* and Canada Lee in *On Whitman Avenue.* The last two plays dealt with two of America's most pressing social problems: the return of African American soldiers to southern communities and the housing of blacks in northern cities. With the advances gained by these productions, African Americans could look forward to a more secure place in the American theater.

American blacks in the field of drama made a significant step forward with Lorraine Hansberry's *A Raisin in the Sun* in 1959. This moving story about the housing problems of an African American family won the New York Critics Circle Award. Hansberry's inspiration for the play came from her own family's experience in obtaining housing. In 1940 her father, Carl Hansberry, took a lawsuit all the way to the United States Supreme Court in the case *Hansberry v. Lee.* Hansberry won the case, but the technical issues on which the decision was rendered did not solve the larger question of the legality of restrictive covenants. Lorraine Hansberry's second play, *The Sign in Sidney Brustein's Window,* was produced shortly before her death in 1964.

Although James Baldwin's novels and essays won for him his greatest acclaim, he did enjoy moderate success with his plays. Baldwin's most outstanding drama was *Blues for Mister Charlie,* produced in 1964.

Black Internationalism

When the international conference for establishing the United Nations opened in San Francisco late in April 1945, black Americans, like other peoples around the globe, hoped that the meeting would create formulas to eliminate war and its causes and to guarantee freedom and security. African Americans saw in this gathering an opportunity to air their grievances and to aid in reciprocal ways the freedom struggles of all peoples of color. In assuming this internationalist perspective, which included expressions of solidarity with the African and Asian liberation struggles, American blacks could see themselves and their struggle as more than a national problem. It placed them squarely within a world population of 400 million black people.

This perspective predated the United Nations. For black Americans, the new global forum served to continue ongoing conversations across national boundaries that began early in the century, but blossomed in the social milieu of the 1920s, the era of Garvey's Universal Negro Improvement Association and of the American black arts renaissance—creating a virtual seedbed of diasporic and transnational movements that in most cases continued to be active during the Great Depression and World War II. In this richly vibrant political and cultural era, blacks of varying ideological persuasions worked together across the Atlantic in numerous, often competing efforts, that included the French-speaking African and Caribbean *négritude* movement of the 1930s–1950s (launched in Paris by Léopold Sédar Senghor of Senegal, Léon Damas of French Guyana, and Aimé Césaire of Martinique); the Pan-African congresses; and various labor and left-leaning organizations in the African diaspora and on the African continent.

485

For generations of black Americans, Ethiopia held biblical and black nationalist meanings. From Phillis Wheatley to Marcus Garvey and beyond, black leaders quoted "Ethiopia

Ethiopia and Spain shall soon stretch forth her hands." The rhetorical strategy of linking the black American identity to ancient (and also modern) Ethiopia, as a metaphor for Africa, proved no less effective in the early 1930s, when Ethiopia alone had managed to remain independent after the rest of the continent succumbed to European imperialism. When Mussolini's Italy invaded Ethiopia in October 1935, American blacks closely followed the unfolding events, which culminated in the Italian conquest and Emperor Haile Selassie's exile in England.

The Italian aggression had the greatest effect in unifying and galvanizing into action black communities in the United States and abroad. Shocked and alarmed by the situation in the beleaguered African nation, black Americans rallied in protest demonstrations and organized Ethiopia relief drives in New York, Philadelphia, Chicago, New Orleans, Cleveland, Kansas City, and many other cities.

This was also true of cities around the world. In London, for example, in August 1935, the International African Friends of Ethiopia, which later became the International African Service Bureau, was founded. Among the members of this London group were the Trinidad-born Marxist intellectuals George Padmore and C. L. R. James, as well as Jomo Kenyatta, who would later become president of his country, Kenya. James also promoted Ethiopia's defense as editor of the news organ International African Opinion.

In the United States, Ethiopian independence was ardently championed by the black scholarly community—Carter G. Woodson, W. E. B. Du Bois, Ralphe Bunche, E. Franklin Frazier, Willis Huggins, and Oliver Cox, all of whom drew historical and current connections among imperialism, fascism, colonialism, and racism, thus linking the fate of subjugated colored races throughout the world. Howard University professor Ralph Bunche typified the sentiment of other black scholars when he wrote in an article in the *Journal of Negro History* in 1936 about the effect of fascism and imperialism on Africa.

Black New Yorkers founded the International Council of Friends of Ethiopia under the leadership of historian Willis N. Huggins, who at his own expense traveled to the League of Nations headquarters in Geneva in 1935 to plead for Ethiopia. His appeal to the League, although futile, expressed what he termed the resounding "righteous indignation by blacks in the western world who are bound by racial kinship to the ancient and illustrious Ethiopian people."

Throughout 1935, civil rights organizations as well as individual black churches and larger denominational bodies criticized both the United States government and the Vatican for failing to intervene at the League of Nations on behalf of Ethiopia. During their annual conventions, leaders of these organizations particularly stressed the plight of Ethiopia. The NAACP appealed to the Secretary of State Cordell Hull and to the League of Nations to check Italian aggression. Rev. Lacy Kirk Williams, president of the National Baptist Convention, USA, Inc., with its several million members, appealed to black Baptists to aid in the cause of Ethiopian freedom. The black ecumenical Fraternal Council of Churches passed a resolution stating that "while by sympathy, principle and ideas we are Americans to the core we cannot be deaf to the cry that comes from a menaced nation in the land of our fathers' fathers!"

Black newspapers featured numerous pro-Ethiopia articles, editorials, and advertisements. They covered Haile Selassie's speech before the League of Nations in June 1936. The *New York Age* urged "Africans outside of Ethiopia" to come to defense of their "kinsfolk,"

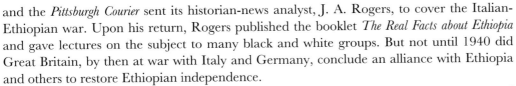

Window in Time

Ralph Bunche Denounces European Conquest in Africa

The doctrine of Fascism, with its extreme jingoism, its exaggerated exaltation of the state and its comic-opera glorification of race, has given a new and greater impetus to the policy of world imperialism, which has already conquered and subjected to systematic and ruthless exploitation virtually all of the darker populations of the earth. Those few peoples, such as the Ethiopians, who have been able to retain a meager measure of precious freedom, are now in imminent danger of losing even that.

Source: Ralph J. Bunche, "French and British Imperialism in West Africa," *Journal of Negro History* 21 (January 1936): 31–46.

and the *Pittsburgh Courier* sent its historian-news analyst, J. A. Rogers, to cover the Italian-Ethiopian war. Upon his return, Rogers published the booklet *The Real Facts about Ethiopia* and gave lectures on the subject to many black and white groups. But not until 1940 did Great Britain, by then at war with Italy and Germany, conclude an alliance with Ethiopia and others to restore Ethiopian independence.

The overthrow of Spain's democratic republic by Generalissimo Francisco Franco and his establishment of a fascist dictatorship also stirred protest in some parts of the black community during the 1930s. In 1936 and 1937 black Americans were among the international volunteers (the American contingent was called the Abraham Lincoln Brigade) who went to Spain to support the Spanish Republican forces against Franco, who was backed by Hitler and Mussolini.

In contrast to the 1930s, during the mid to late 1940s the idea of freedom from colonial rule proved a more fluid, even viable proposition. Under the nonviolent movement led by Mohandas Gandhi, India won its independence from Great Britain in 1947. The changing international order did not escape Walter White, the executive secretary of the NAACP, who in 1945 declared: "A wind is rising—a wind of determination by the have-nots of the world to share in the benefits of freedom and prosperity which the haves of the earth have tried to keep exclusively for themselves. That wind blows all over the world."

The Rising Wind

Evidence of this "rising wind" included the Pan African Congress, held in Manchester, England, in 1945, which was chaired by Du Bois, was attended largely by Africans and Caribbean blacks, and reflected the anticolonial protests during the 1940s of such working-class activists as Nigerian trade unionists, South African miners, and laborers in the Gold Coast Colony (the future Ghana) and Jamaica. The Pan African Congress in 1945, unlike earlier congresses that emphasized cultural kinship, stressed instead a unified black internationalism based on the similar condition of racial economic oppression.

Within the U.S. black community, the Council on African Affairs (CAA) was the foremost organization that kept the American public apprised of anticolonial activities in Africa.

Founded in 1937 by Paul Robeson and Max Yergan, formerly a YMCA director in South Africa and a leader in the National Negro Congress, the Council on African Affairs was particularly vigilant in alerting African Americans to political and trade union activism in South Africa, collecting food products and money to relieve famine in Africa, and bringing educational information about Africa to the American public. Paul Robeson headed the organization. William Alphaeus Hunton, Jr., served as its educational director and eventually its executive director. Other important early figures in the life of the organization included Yergan, Du Bois, Mary McLeod Bethune, Eslanda Goode Robeson (Paul Robeson's wife), scholar E. Franklin Frazier, and California newspaper publisher Charlotta Bass.

The Cold War and the McCarthy-era witch-hunts created fatal fissures in the CAA in the late 1940s, similar to the divisions in other organizations that initially comprised traditional liberals and leftists, such as the National Negro Congress, the Civil Rights Congress, and the Southern Negro Youth Congress—all of which were disbanded. Historian Penny Von Eschen notes that before the government targeted the CAA as a "communist-influenced organization," the CAA was widely supported in black communities, hosting fundraising concerts for Africa and India that featured Robeson, Marian Anderson, Lena Horne, Duke Ellington, and other popular black artists. Its rallies drew thousands of people and were held in large stadiums, such as Madison Square Garden. The CAA rally in 1946 held at the Abyssinian Baptist Church and supported by Rev. Adam Clayton Powell, Jr., the church's pastor and newly elected New York congressman, drew a crowd of 4,500.

In the postwar world, however, the United Nations functioned as the most important forum of international deliberation and, in the decades to follow, would grow more influential as a voice for independent African nations. The founding conference

The United Nations Charter
of the United Nations was held in late April 1945, two weeks after the death of President Roosevelt. This meeting to establish the UN charter convened three thousand delegates, representing fifty-one countries. The Great Powers—the United States, the Soviet Union, Great Britain, France, and China—wanted to create the diplomatic machinery that would, once and for all, put an end to aggression. Colonial peoples wanted independence, or at least guarantees against further encroachments by the imperial powers.

Among American observers accredited by the State Department to attend the organizational meeting at San Francisco were several African Americans, including Mary McLeod Bethune of the National Council of Negro Women, Mordecai W. Johnson, president of Howard University, and W. E. B. Du Bois and Walter White of the NAACP. Ralph Bunche, acting chief of the division of dependent territories of the Department of State, went as a member of the official staff.

African Americans maintained a keen interest in the delegates from the African and Asian countries, especially those from India, Liberia, Ethiopia, and Haiti. Most black newspapers with national circulations sent reporters to cover the conference. "Small Nations Demand Race Plank" and "British Evasive on Colonial Question" were typical headlines in the black press. When it became known that the black people of South Africa protested the treatment they were receiving at the hands of their government, the black press in the United States referred to South Africa's apartheid system as "Nazi-like domination."

No previous international document had given as much attention to human rights as had the United Nations Charter. Its preamble reaffirmed "faith in fundamental human rights, in the dignity and worth of the human person, in the equal rights of men and women and of nations large and small." Another passage in the Charter asserted that the UN would promote human rights and fundamental freedoms "without distinction to race, language, or religion."

Of the agencies provided for by the charter, African Americans took the greatest interest in the Educational, Scientific, and Cultural Organization (UNESCO), whose purpose, according to UN guidelines, was "to contribute to peace and security by promoting collaboration among nations through education, science and culture." At the first meeting of UNESCO in Paris, in 1946, one of the U.S. delegates was the African American sociologist Charles S. Johnson, formerly the editor of the National Urban League's magazine *Opportunity* and soon to become the president of Fisk University. In 1951 the black sociologist E. Franklin Frazier was appointed the director of UNESCO's Division of Applied Sciences, based in Paris. In this position, he traveled throughout Africa, establishing research projects and seminars at UNESCO-funded institutes.

UNESCO's Work

UNESCO boldly took on as one of its early projects the effort to debunk the concept of race. Scholars were acutely conscious of the importance of this task after a war in which Nazi ideas of Aryan superiority had led to the murder of millions of Jews. In the early 1940s, school textbooks in the United States and elsewhere continued to differentiate by races and racial traits according to a hierarchy of different European ethnicities, with Anglo-Saxons on top and Jews, Asians, and Negroes at lower levels. The UNESCO Statement on Race, published in 1950, sought to expose and eradicate not only the fallacy of Nazi doctrine but also the widespread popular understanding of race as biologically determined and inherited. (At this time, for example, 71 percent of white Americans surveyed by an opinion poll said that they believed racial identity determined intelligence and that in this regard blacks were inherently inferior to whites.)

The panel called attention to such popular misconceptions and to outdated science, citing instead the most recent academic thought. For example, in 1935 the British biologists Julian Huxley (who served as director-general of UNESCO from 1946 to 1948) and A. C. Haddon had asserted in their co-authored monograph *We Europeans: A Survey of "Racial" Problems*: "With respect to existing populations, the word 'race' should be banished, and the descriptive and non-committal term *ethnic groups* should be substituted." Swedish scholar Gunnar Myrdal used the term *caste* in his landmark study *An American Dilemma* (1944), explaining that "the term *race* is . . . inappropriate in a scientific inquiry, since it has biological and genetic connotations which . . . run parallel to widely spread false racial beliefs." Anthropologist Ashley Montagu, a vociferous opponent of race as a biological concept, took the leading role in the preparation of UNESCO's first statement on race in 1950, which pronounced race a "social myth."

However, as historian Michelle Brattain reveals, Montagu's efforts evoked both praise and condemnation. The controversial UNESCO statement of 1950 was overturned just two years later, fueling debates over the link between presumed racial differences (biological or cultural) and racial disparities in the form of income, education, and other social markers. In its second statement on race, published in 1952, UNESCO presented different conclusions from the first. Although not written in the language of the scientific racism of the 1910s and 1920s, the new UNESCO statement rejected the idea of race as "social myth" and, according to Brattain, despite its "more politically and scientifically palatable definition," returned to biological premises that "also affirmed older scientific traditions (and languages) by noting differences between 'non-literate' and 'more civilized' people on intelligent tests."

The UN's Trusteeship Council, established to safeguard the interests and welfare of non-self-governing peoples in former German colonies held under post-World War I League of Nations mandates or in colonies taken from Italy and Japan after World War II, also attracted significant attention from African Americans. They wanted a far better system than the one developed by the League of Nations after World War I. The **The Trusteeship Council** League's Mandates Commission had failed to safeguard the welfare of dependent territories, and too frequently the mandatory powers administered the territories in their own interests. The UN Trusteeship Council differed from the old system because its membership included an equal number of countries administering trust territories and countries that had no such responsibility. In addition, people in the trust territories could submit petitions to the Council.

African American leaders expressed disappointment at the failure to end colonialism outright, and some, such as Howard University historian Rayford Logan, called America's attention to the Soviet Union's anticolonialist statements. Yet blacks were heartened to see Ralph Bunche join the UN Secretariat as director of the Trusteeship Division. Because of his persistent stand against racial discrimination in the United States, blacks trusted Bunche to use his expertise in advancing the welfare and interests of peoples unable to represent their own interests in the UN. He was appointed to the UN Special Committee on Palestine and drafted the 1947 reports proposing a partition of the land between Palestinians and Jews and recognizing the State of Israel. Bunche mediated the armistice that halted the Arab-Israeli war in 1948, for which in 1950 he became the first African American to win the Nobel Peace Prize.

African Americans also turned to the UN in the hope of getting a hearing for their own petitions for human rights and fundamental freedoms. They knew that the UN had no **The South Africa Resolution** authority to eliminate racial discrimination in the United States, but they also recognized the moral leverage they wielded as an oppressed minority in the nation that deemed itself leader of the free world. Black Americans were not oblivious of the UN General Assembly's acknowledgment, in the autumn of 1946, of India's charges that Indian nationals and their descendants in South Africa were victims of discrimination. By a two-thirds majority, the General Assembly passed a resolution requiring South Africa to report at the next meeting the steps that it had taken to rectify the situation. The United States, along with Great Britain, voted against the resolution, which made its success even more meaningful.

India's resolution became a signal victory for domestic minorities in other nations. The General Assembly also approved a resolution branding as a crime under international law the extermination of minorities and racial and ethnic groups, such as the Nazis had done. This resolution seemed to be further recognition of the rights of minorities. In an editorial in the *Crisis,* Du Bois correctly observed that the UN discussions on race were "far ahead of Versailles when President Wilson and the British would not even permit race to be discussed formally even in a committee meeting."

Encouraged by the charter and the early actions of UN agencies, the National Negro Congress (NNC) in June 1946 filed a petition with the UN's Economic and Social Council on **The June 1946 Petition** behalf of black people in America, seeking United Nations aid in the struggle to eliminate political, economic, and social discrimination. Opponents of the petition stressed that the treatment of African Americans in the United States was purely a domestic matter and that the UN charter prevented its intervention. African Americans countered by arguing that one of the UN's main purposes was international cooperation in solving problems of an economic, social, cultural, or humanitarian character.

Writing on the subject, the distinguished African American law-yer Charles Hamilton Houston admitted that the UN did not have jurisdiction to investigate every lynching in Georgia or every denial of the ballot in Mississippi—but, he continued, "where the discrimina-tion and denial of human rights reach a national level or where the national government either cannot or will not afford protection and redress for local aggression against colored peoples, the national policy of the United States itself becomes involved." Arguing that the NNC petition did not fall outside the UN jurisdiction, Houston concluded: "A national policy of the United States which permits disfranchise-ment in the South is just as much an international issue as elections in Poland or the denial of democratic rights in Franco's Spain."

Houston's remarks came at an embarrassing time for the United States. Earlier in 1947, news of a brutal lynching was broadcast to countries under Soviet domination by the U.S. government's Voice of America network. That same May, an all-white jury exonerated twenty-eight men who had confessed that they had participated in the lynching. Outcry against that verdict was heard from London and Paris to Moscow.

In October 1947, the NAACP submitted to the United Nations a petition authored by W. E. B. Du Bois, which among other charges accused the United States of violating the human rights of its black citizens. Entitled *An Appeal to the World*, the document called on the nations of the world for redress. In 1948 the NAACP published the *Appeal* as a ninety-four-page booklet. Because it castigated President Truman, the *Appeal* embarrassed the administration, and equally

Charles H. Houston
Houston, a lawyer who worked closely with the NAACP on the court cases that eventu-ally ended segregation, was the architect of many successful strategies.

offensive to U.S. leaders was its charge that the racism in Mississippi was more of a threat to the nation than was the Soviet Union. As with the NNC petition, jurisdictional objections were raised against the *Appeal*'s legal validity. Believing that the Soviets would use it for pro-paganda purposes, government officials—and even NAACP head Walter White—viewed unsympathetically Du Bois's wish that the UN consider the peti-tion. With the Cold War by now raging, former first lady Eleanor **The *Appeal*** Roosevelt, a UN delegate and also on the NAACP's board of directors, declined Du Bois's request that she bring the document before the UN General Assembly. The *Appeal* got exten-sive coverage in the press but no hearing on the floor of the UN General Assembly.

In the aftermath of World War II, radical and liberal African American leaders united under the banner of anti-imperialism and shared a similar internationalist vision of social justice. As the Cold War continued in the early 1950s, antiracist **Black Internationalism** and anticolonial efforts on the part of African American leftists and American leftists in general came under heavy governmental and popular attack and curtailment. The federal government revoked Robeson's passport in 1950. At eighty-four years of age in 1952, Du Bois was denied his passport, one year after he won an acquittal for an indictment against him for activities deemed sympathetic to communism. In 1961 Du Bois moved to the now-independent African nation of Ghana, where he died in 1963.

However, many activists of the 1930s abandoned their former leftist positions. Ralph Bunche embraced liberal anticommunism, and in this camp continued to work ardently for racial equality in the United States and anticolonialism in Africa. Max Yergan not only recanted communism but also moved far to the right, becoming an anticommunist black conservative. Thoroughly disillusioned with communism, the novelist Richard Wright lived as an expatriate in Paris but remained a firm adversary of colonialism in Africa.

The 1940s through the 1960s were periods of active black internationalism. Over the course of these years, African American leaders increasingly witnessed a change in their self-image as defenders of the black world. Historically, they had seen themselves as enlightened advocates and agents in the rescue of downtrodden Africa. This would change with the mounting success of independence movements in Africa, particularly when in the late 1950s and early 1960s newly independent African nations joined the United Nations. In 1961, Du Bois, then living in Ghana, described this attitudinal shift: "American Negroes of former generations had always calculated that when Africa was ready for freedom, American Negroes would be ready to lead them. But the event was quite opposite. The African leaders proved to be Africans. . . . Indeed, it now seems that Africans may have to show American Negroes the way to freedom."

Labor Civil Rights

In the 1940s, African Americans became an integral part of the urban industrial workforce and a prominent part of organized labor. The prolabor policies of the New Deal (such as the National Labor Relations Board), the formation of the Congress of Industrial Organizations (CIO) and its inclusion of African Americans, the black community's World War II Double V campaign, and the federal government's establishment of the Fair Employment Practices Commission (FEPC) together all fueled the surge for unionization and united labor activism and the civil rights movement.

Unionized blacks owed their growing numerical strength to the unprecedented black migration from the southern states, due primarily to the North's booming wartime economy.

Blacks in the CIO In the 1940s, 1.5 million black southerners and an even larger number of whites from the region moved to industrial cities in the Northeast, Midwest, and West—areas that historian James Gregory calls the "southern diaspora." Race riots, such as the Detroit riot of 1943, highlighted the boiling urban cauldron of racial and economic tensions spawned by this massive migration. Yet migration also highlighted the politicization and empowerment of black workers. In Detroit tens of thousands of black workers entered the automotive industry, many of them in Ford's River Rouge factory. Through the United Auto Workers (UAW), an affiliate of the CIO, they demanded racial equality in the workplace, in housing, and in other aspects of life in the city.

The CIO's adherence to the industrial principle of labor organizing rather than organizing by specific crafts allowed blacks to enter the ranks of organized labor, since the great majority of them were concentrated in unskilled jobs. Although racial prejudice and reluctance to support equal opportunities for blacks existed among white industrial workers, the CIO articulated the official policy of racial diversity in its affiliate unions. Under the leadership of John L. Lewis, the CIO announced its position in 1938 of "uncompromising opposition to any form of discrimination, whether political or economic, based on race, color, creed or nationality."

The history of the labor movement in the 1930s and much of the 1940s, and in particular that of the unionization of white and black workers during these years, is tied to the history of the American Left. Some labor leaders in this period, but certainly not all, were communist sympathizers or active members of the Communist Party, USA. Before the late 1940s and the Cold War between the United States and the Soviet Union, the Left played a visible role in the antiracist labor movement. In those years, leftists were integral and influential members of labor unions and civil rights organizations. To be sure, the communists often clashed with labor liberals and other left-oriented activists. White labor leader Walter Reuther of the United Auto Workers and the CIO was staunchly anticommunist, despite the presence of leftist-influenced locals in his organization. Black socialist A. Phillip Randolph demanded that the planned 1941 March on Washington be all-black precisely to exclude communist infiltrators (who would have been overwhelmingly white).

The Great Depression had devastated the economy, leaving many Americans more conscious than ever of a widening chasm between haves and have-nots. African American demands for government intervention and economic justice during this crisis prompted the founding of black left-leaning civil rights organizations in the 1930s, such as the National Negro Congress and the Civil Rights Congress. However, even the older, traditionally liberal civil rights organizations, such as the NAACP and the National Urban League, had begun to emphasize the need for greater class consciousness, not simply race consciousness, as well as to advocate black-white unity within the working class. Three young, left-oriented Howard University professors—political scientist Ralph Bunche, economist Abram Harris, and sociologist E. Franklin Frazier—were primarily responsible for the NAACP's new economic focus. At the NAACP's Amenia Conference in 1933, they declared the organization's traditional racial strategies out of date in an era when social forces demanded an antiracist labor movement.

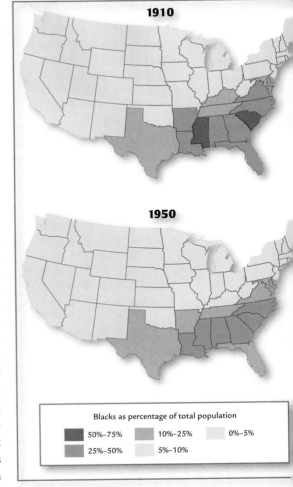

Black Migration

Maps showing a comparison of the declining percentage of blacks in the South

In the 1940s, many working-class blacks and some whites engaged in the civil rights struggle through labor unions, since in the CIO labor leftists and labor liberals cooperated, if not always smoothly, toward the shared goals of economic justice and racial equality. Labor unions worked with moderate, liberal, and radical civil rights organizations in united-front campaigns—temporary alliances forged around targeted issues. For example, it was through such alliances that fifty-five bills against discrimination in employment were introduced in states with large industrial populations in 1945.

The Early Civil Rights Struggle

CIO unions often worked with such civil rights groups as the left-leaning Southern Negro Youth Congress and the National Negro Congress, as well as with local branches of the NAACP. CIO leaders endorsed those groups' agendas, which included the fight for a permanent Federal Employment Practices Commission (FEPC) at the state and national levels, passage of antilynching legislation, and abolition of the poll tax. In much of the 1940s, the success of the CIO in cities with sizable black populations was attributed to such coalitions.

493

Labor activism
Picket line in front of the Mid-City Equipment Company in South Chicago in the 1940s.

In such southern cities as Memphis, Richmond, Charleston, Birmingham, Baltimore, Louisville, and Winston-Salem, as well as in northern cities such as Pittsburgh, New York, Chicago, Detroit, and Los Angeles, labor activism included a concerted effort by black and white workers, left-to-center member unions, and left-to-center civil rights organizations. All worked together, as historian Michael Honey notes, in "a broad-based, interracial, and inter-class popular alliance." Black union workers had no doubt that their fight for jobs, promotions, better working conditions, and higher pay were as much racial issues as labor issues.

Despite real limitations from many racist white workers, "labor civil rights," or what historian Robert Korstad terms "civil rights unionism," represented a visible form of grassroots activism in the struggle for racial equality in the 1940s. As studies of Winston-Salem, North Carolina, of Memphis, Tennessee, and of other southern communities have revealed, CIO activism in support of black voting rights during the 1940s offered an early model for voting rights campaigns in later decades. Labor civil rights constituted an early, crucial part of the unfolding civil rights movement that would peak in the 1960s.

Black labor organizers played key roles in attracting nonunionized workers in industries with heavy concentrations of their own racial group. Such was the case in Winston-Salem,

R. J. Reynolds in Winston-Salem North Carolina, where black workers outnumbered whites by a large margin at the R. J. Reynolds Tobacco Company but found themselves relegated to the dirty, physically demanding jobs. Racial disparities in pay, work conditions, and treatment served not only to privilege all white workers but also to discourage interracial unity at the anti-union company. According to Korstad, CIO efforts to unionize the Reynolds plant succeeded after two years of undetected persuasion by two black organizers from the leftist Southern Tenant Farmers Union. The organizers' message of black dignity and the right to unionize as an act of racial self-determination paid off in 1943, when black women stemmers revolted. The women, tired of their low wages and worsening conditions caused by a work speedup during a period of labor shortage, launched a work-stoppage and strike.

The strike proved so successful that eight thousand black workers joined the United Cannery, Agricultural, Packing and Allied Workers of America (UCAPAWA). By 1944 blacks won the fight to become Local 22 of the Food, Tobacco, Agricultural and Allied Workers (FTA), the new name of the UCAPAWA. In the FTA, black women, such as Moranda Smith, became union leaders and representatives and sat at the bargaining table with their white employers.

Black labor empowerment in Winston-Salem awakened a sense of assertiveness in the city's black residents. Leftist-influenced Local 22 mobilized a black voter registration drive in 1944 through the CIO Political Action Committee with the demand that black veterans be given the right to vote. Union members argued that black voting rights were a prerequisite to economic and racial advancement in a region where most blacks were disfranchised. A reporter from the black newspaper, the *Pittsburgh Courier,* was so impressed by the union's success in Winston-Salem that he wrote, "If there is a New Negro, he is to be found in the ranks of the labor movement." Local 22 also contributed to the growth in NAACP membership. For the first time, workers supported en masse the NAACP's membership campaign. The Winston-Salem branch grew from a hundred members (largely from the black middle class) in 1942 to nearly two thousand in 1946, becoming the largest branch in North Carolina.

In the 1930s, most blacks in Detroit had been reluctant to join unions and in fact had often functioned as strikebreakers, even though by 1939 the overwhelmingly white UAW had succeeded in forcing all the major automobile manufacturers (except Ford) to recognize it as the legal collective bargaining agent. **Unionization in Detroit** A massive strike at Ford in April 1941, which in the following month culminated in Ford's recognition of Local 600 of the UAW, led the union to adopt aggressive efforts to unionize black workers. Nearly 9,000 blacks worked in Ford's mechanically efficient River Rouge factory. Their numbers were too large to ignore, but the task of incorporating them into the union posed a dilemma.

Black workers perceived a different relationship to Ford than did most whites. The company had sent recruiters into the South, luring black migrants to Detroit with the promise of job opportunity. Ford worked closely with black churches. According to historian Angela Dillard, "black ministers and churches functioned as agents of the Ford employment office." Ford workers and their families made up a sizable portion of every black church congregation, and the recommendation of a black minister determined the fate of a black job applicant. Although some white union members opposed equal opportunities for blacks, the UAW worked hard and strategically, joining forces with the few black ministers who did not feel beholden to Ford.

One such minister, Rev. Charles A. Hill, the pastor of the large Hartford Avenue Baptist Church, boasted of his earlier refusal to accept a large donation from the Ford Company during his church's building campaign—a position he took so that both he and the church could remain independent. Indeed, Hill's church of over 1,200 members became a hub of clandestine union-recruitment meetings. The establishment of Local 600, which by mid-decade boasted 60,000 members, drew ever-increasing numbers of African Americans into its ranks, with blacks serving as UAW staff, as delegates to UAW conventions, and one, Shelton Tappes, as the recording secretary of Local 600.

The UAW began to work closely with the local NAACP, in which pro-union supporters such as Hill were also leaders, as well as with the left-influenced National Negro Congress and Civil Rights Congress. In 1942 the NAACP and CIO eventually became key partners in campaigns for the FEPC and for black occupancy in the Sojourner Truth Housing Project, which would otherwise have become "whites-only" public housing. The concerted effort won blacks the right to live in the housing project, but the victory was met with a violent white backlash when they attempted to move in. This racial violence was a precursor of the three-day Detroit race riot in June 1943 that brought federal troops to restore peace. The new labor committee of the NAACP contributed to a dramatic growth in working class members. Nearly 20,000 new members joined the Detroit branch of the NAACP in 1943, surpassing all other branches in the nation. In the 1940s, nearly 100,000 black Detroit workers held union membership.

In New York, labor unions with large black memberships similarly addressed issues of housing discrimination, police brutality, and racial disparities in hiring. They campaigned against the large number of blacks fired from their jobs immediately after the war. Historian Martha Biondi notes that the most actively antiracist unions were led by black leftists in the United Electrical Workers, United Public Workers, National Maritime Union, and Hotel and Restaurant Workers of America. New York did not have a single all-powerful industry that attracted black labor, unlike Pittsburgh (steel), Winston-Salem (tobacco), Detroit (automobiles), or Los Angeles (aircraft). Yet Ferdinand Smith, the vice president of the racially integrated National Maritime Union, was the highest ranking black person in the CIO.

The recruitment of Jackie Robinson to the Brooklyn Dodgers in 1947 occurred against the backdrop of the united-front effort of blacks and whites, leftists and moderates, and labor and civil rights organizations in various parts of the city. Robinson's recruitment is exemplary of labor civil rights activism over the integration of job sectors—in this case baseball. Although Dodgers owner Branch Rickey recalled the year 1942 as the time when he decided to hire a black player, his recruitment of Robinson occurred later, amid a broad-based community campaign.

The first person to make public the idea of bringing a black player into the major leagues in this most American of sports was the black Harvard Law School graduate Benjamin J. Davis. Ben Davis (as he was generally called) in 1943 ran on the Communist Party ticket to win the vacated City Council seat of Adam Clayton Powell, Jr. (Powell's election to the United States Congress had made him the first African American from New York in the House of Representatives.) In 1945, then-incumbent Ben Davis made a second successful bid for the City Council seat, using the baseball theme in his campaign literature to boldly urge hiring of a black player by one of New York's three major-league teams. The cover of Davis's campaign pamphlet presented two photographs side by side: a dead black soldier, obviously killed in action during World War II somewhere in Europe, and a baseball player with one leg raised in a pitcher's stance and his arms wound up for a throw. At the bottom appeared the compelling words: "Good enough to DIE . . . but not good enough to PITCH!"

In May 1945 Davis introduced a resolution, which was unanimously endorsed by the City Council, calling for baseball's integration. According to Martha Biondi, the City Council sent copies of the resolution to the owners of New York's then-three teams, the Dodgers, the

Jackie Robinson in 1947
Jackie Robinson broke the racial barrier in America's favorite pastime and thrilled millions with his dazzling plays.

Yankees, and the Giants. The Metropolitan Interfaith and Interracial Coordinating Committee and the National Maritime Union made similar demands. Rickey recruited Robinson that summer and signed him with the team in the fall of 1945. However, Robinson started with the Dodgers's minor league club, the Montreal Royals, leading it to the International League championship in 1946. At the opening of the 1947 season, he joined the Dodgers and thus major league baseball, starting at first base. Robinson kept his dignity despite racist taunts from white ballplayers and spectators.

Labor civil rights reached a highpoint in the mid-1940s, but the glory days waned after 1947. Unable to withstand the anticommunist climate of the Cold War, with its dual aim of containing communism abroad and uprooting it at home, **1947: Pivotal Year** leftists' role in the civil rights movement declined precipitously, along with their heavy emphasis on securing economic justice and combating structural inequality. The same Cold War years bore witness to the resilience of the civil rights movement, but in a different form and with a broader emphasis on ending "second-class" citizenship for African Americans.

The year 1947 presented a number of defining moments that led to the demise of the labor-left civil rights agenda and alternatively to the rise of the liberal-rights based movement. Several events determined those different outcomes.

In January 1947, events on the international scene were spurring anticommunist fervor. To President Harry S. Truman, world events appeared foreboding—Stalin's gulags (prison camps) in the Soviet Union, rising communist forces in Greece and Turkey, Soviet-style governments (called Soviet "satellites") in Central and Eastern Europe and North Korea, and the unfolding communist victory on the Chinese mainland (completed in late 1949). On March 12, 1947, Truman went before a joint session of Congress to outline his position defining the United States as the free world's leader and protector, in the form of offering military and economic assistance to nations threatened by what the president considered pro-Soviet communist forces.

Specifically, Truman called for military and economic aid to the beleaguered pro-Western governments of Greece and Turkey. To play this new and active role in the protection of democratic nations under communist threat, the United States had to assume a global stature it had not held before. The United States, Truman argued, could no longer stand on the sidelines as a spectator to international developments, since its own national security was at stake. Fears of national security intensified with charges of espionage against the influential government official Alger Hiss and leftists Julius and Ethel Rosenberg. Although in recent years highly credible evidence has come to light that Hiss and Julius Rosenberg were in fact Soviet spies, Red-baiting, witch-hunts, and wild accusations by the influential Senator Joseph McCarthy of Wisconsin whipped the nation into near-hysteria about an alleged ubiquity of subversive communist activities.

McCarthy was eventually censured by the U.S. Senate for his methods. But even after his downfall in 1954, the House Un-American Activities Committee (HUAC), the FBI under its director J. Edgar Hoover, and other practitioners of what came to be called McCarthyism hauled thousands of ordinary men and women before government or private-industry panels, committees, and agencies for investigations of their pasts. Statements deemed to be in any way sympathetic to the Soviet Union were outlawed by the Smith Act. Most of the people charged with disloyalty or subversion were not members of the Communist Party or had long since abandoned communist sympathies. Journalists, writers, scientists, movie stars and Hollywood writers, musicians, politicians, teachers, and certainly labor unionists and civil rights advocates were routinely investigated, identified as "un-American," and labeled "Red" by intelligence agencies. As a result, many lost their careers and were subjected to social ostracism; some were even jailed and deported, or driven to suicide. (Only in the latter half of the 1950s did the American people increasingly discredit McCarthyism.)

In 1947 Congress dealt labor a direct blow when it passed, over Truman's veto, the Labor-Management Relations Act (generally known as the Taft-Hartley Act from its cosponsors, Republican Senators Robert Taft of Ohio and Fred Hartley of New Jersey). The Taft-Hartley Act strengthened employers' hands against labor, outlawed a variety of strikes and the "closed shop" (the requirement that workers had to join a union in order to hold a job), and cracked down on other union practices disliked by conservatives. It also required union officials to declare that they were not communists.

The legislation proved sufficiently antagonistic toward labor interests that AFL president George Meany and CIO president Walter Reuther, both staunch anticommunists, overcame their institutional rivalry and merged their organizations. With the formation of the AFL-

CIO in 1955, two African Americans, A. Philip Randolph and Willard Townsend, were elected vice presidents of the new organization.

Government policies and growing anticommunist popular sentiment doomed the leftist component of the labor and civil rights movements. The CIO purged its leftist white and black workers. After 1947, Winston-Salem's Local 22 of the Food, Tobacco, Agricultural and Allied Workers lost its standing with the **The Failure of Operation Dixie** National Labor Relations Board. This turn of events, plus the mechanization of tobacco production and black layoffs, led to Local 22's downfall. Nor did the CIO's much-heralded "Operation Dixie" unionization drive between 1946 and 1953 fare any better in the Cold War South. After a few early successes, Operation Dixie's drive to unionize an interracial southern workforce proved to be an uphill, ultimately unsuccessful battle. Pervasive rhetoric of anti-unionism, anticommunism, and anti-integration was interchangeably used to defeat the CIO effort.

White southerners noticed that the most successful interracial organizing had occurred in leftist CIO unions—for example, the FTA among tobacco workers, which had a racially integrated leadership and promoted racially integrated picket lines. Thus southern state and local governments, employers, churches, police, news media, white supremacist organizations, and in general white public opinion all sought to preserve and protect the racial and economic status quo. CIO organizers, who often relied on strategies effective in the North, did not fully understand the limits of those strategies in the context of the South's racial culture and labor conditions. Operation Dixie's demise left African Americans in that region without a vigorous protagonist in the house of labor.

Amid the national anticommunist uproar of the late 1940s and early 1950s, prominent New York leftists lost leadership positions in the labor movement. Ferdinand Smith was ousted from the National Maritime Union **The Demise of Left-Labor Civil Rights** and consequently from his high-ranking office within the national CIO leadership. The FBI arrested Smith in 1949 and deported him back to his native Jamaica in 1951. In July 1948, eleven national leaders of the Communist Party, including New York City Councilman Ben Davis (who had just run for re-election) were arrested under the Smith Act. The liberal-left coalition in both the labor movement and in the civil rights movement had broken down irreparably. Anticommunism exacerbated already existing differences and tensions and hardened ideological lines. The united-front strategy, which had brought together a number of groups of varying political persuasions (for example, the umbrella organization National Negro Congress), came under siege. Indeed, the NNC itself dissolved in 1947.

Detroit offers a vivid example of the demise of left-labor civil rights partnership. Growing tensions precluded working together for a common cause in which both partners really believed. For example, labor civil rights advocates were in agreement about the importance of preserving the FEPC, but in 1947 white and black liberals dissociated themselves from leftists who shared that goal. The Michigan Council for Fair Employment Legislation (later renamed the Michigan Committee on Civil Rights) was an interracial coalition of many groups, including the NAACP, the Jewish Community Council, and the Association of Catholic Trade Unionists. But it explicitly rejected the Communist Party and the leftist Civil Rights Congress, both of which had been longstanding vocal supporters of state FEPC laws.

In the fall of 1949, the NAACP made clear its anticommunist position while planning a national mobilization for congressional passage of civil rights legislation. The successful mobilization brought more than 4,000 delegates from organizations across the nation to Washington. However, the Civil Rights Congress was barred from participating. In response to the disgruntled CRC chairman William Patterson, Roy Wilkins of the NAACP made clear that leftist politics were unwelcome and a detriment. Wilkins stressed that "in the present Civil Rights Mobilization we have no desire for that [leftist] kind of cooperation, or that kind of unity." The NAACP was also advised by the CIO to exclude certain unions. At its annual meeting in 1950, the organization took a firmer stand. NAACP membership overwhelmingly voted for a resolution that would empower its board of directors to investigate local branches and suspend any dominated by communists. Warning against "wild accusations," Walter White told his members "we do not want a witch hunt . . . but we want to be sure that we, and not the communists, are running [the NAACP]."

The wall between antiracist leftists and antiracist liberals, be they in labor unions or civil rights organizations, had become impenetrable. Nor were many, if not most, of the persons branded as leftists (they sometimes called themselves "progressives"), actually members of the Communist Party. Paul Robeson never joined the party, yet his reputation was severely tarnished, his passport was revoked, and many one-time friends, such as Mary McLeod Bethune, Walter White, and Jackie Robinson, distanced themselves from him. Du Bois would suffer similar recrimination, although he actually did join the party at the very end of his life. There was no denying, however, that communists had been involved in antiracist campaigns. The perception was sufficiently widespread for any white person in the South who supported black rights to be associated automatically with communism even if not a communist. That presented a serious dilemma to any white supporter of integration in the South, as well as to any organization, particularly the NAACP, that challenged Jim Crow laws. In southern states, fighting segregation was cause enough to be branded "un-American."

Truman and Civil Rights

In 1946 President Truman appointed several interracial committees of distinguished Americans to inquire into the condition of civil rights and of higher education, as well as to recommend improvements. The higher education committee's report, published in 1947, called not only for eliminating inequalities in educational opportunities but also for ending all forms of discrimination in higher education. That same year, the civil rights committee's report, *To Secure These Rights*, demanded "the elimination of segregation, based on race, color, creed, or national origin, from American life"—that is, ending discrimination and segregation in public education, employment, health care, housing, the military, public accommodations, and interstate transportation.

News of the civil rights committee's report and excerpts from it were featured in black and white newspapers throughout the United States. African Americans read its strongly worded *To Secure These Rights* condemnation of lynching and its denunciation of various forms of racial discrimination. Radio stations devoted time to discussing it. More than a million copies of the published report were distributed and sold. Civic groups held workshop discussion groups and forums on the report. NAACP lawyer Thurgood Marshall described *To Secure These Rights* as having an unparalleled and historic impact. "The problem of the Negro and other minority groups," he declared, "is now before the public in a manner never equaled before."

Just as Truman had proclaimed it America's duty to lead and defend the free world internationally, so he charted a similar course at home. Speaking from the Lincoln Memorial in

Window in Time

The Right to Equality of Opportunity

It is not enough that full and equal membership in society entitles the individual to an equal voice in the control of his government; it must also give him the right to enjoy the benefits of society and to contribute to its progress. The opportunity of each individual to obtain useful employment, and to have access to services in the fields of education, housing, health, recreation and transportation, whether available free or at a price, must be provided with complete disregard for race, color, creed, and national origin. Without this equality of opportunity the individual is deprived of the chance to develop his potentialities and to share the fruits of society. The group also suffers through the loss of the contributions which might have been made by persons excluded from the main channels of social and economic activity.

Source: *To Secure These Rights*, the Report of the President's Committee on Civil Rights, 1947, p. 9.

June 1947, he declared: "We must make the Federal Government a friendly, vigilant defender of the rights and equalities of all Americans. . . . Our National Government must show the way." Impressed with the president's words, the Committee on Civil Rights quoted them in *To Secure These Rights.* Never before had there been such fervent executive advocacy of racial equality; even Abraham Lincoln, who ended slavery, did not support racial equality.

Truman also publicly committed himself to integrating the armed services, and in 1948 he appointed a committee to study the problem. Its report, *Freedom to Serve,* outlined how integration was to be achieved. Acting on its recommendations, **Freedom to Serve** the Army adopted a new policy in 1949, opening all positions to qualified personnel without regard to race or color and abolishing the racial quota. The Navy and Air Force adopted similar policies. With very few incidents to mar the transition, the armed services of the United States moved steadily toward integration, which was implemented during the Korean War (1950–1954).

Finally, in 1948 Truman issued an executive order requiring fair employment in the federal service. "The principles on which our Government is based require a policy of fair employment throughout the Federal establishment without dis- **The 1948 Election** crimination because of race, color, religion, or national origin," he declared.

Conservative southern Democrats were outraged with many of Truman's liberal Fair Deal policies, and especially with the steps he was taking to advance desegregation. In 1948 some of these southerners walked out of the Democratic Party convention and formed the States' Rights Democratic Party, promptly labeled the "Dixiecrats" by the press and the public. The Dixiecrats nominated South Carolina governor J. Strom Thurmond for the presidency, hoping that he would siphon off enough southern electoral votes to throw the election into the House of Representatives, where the South could bargain with the Republican and Democratic candidates to back off supporting civil rights.

Truman's prospects in the 1948 election looked dim. The Republicans had swept the 1946 midterms, and polls showed that the president's popularity had dwindled. For president, the Republicans nominated the bland but competent governor of New York, Thomas E. Dewey, who had a good record of support for civil rights. In the run-up to the election, Dewey seemed far ahead of Truman in the polls. Not only did Truman face the defection of southern Democrats, but there was also an insurgency on the left.

Liberal and left-wing Democrats were split, with Henry Wallace—Roosevelt's secretary of agriculture in the 1930s and his vice president for one term—advocating a strongly liberal agenda at home and opposing the Cold War with the Soviet Union abroad. Wallace also staunchly supported civil rights. Especially because of his views on foreign policy, he was often portrayed by his opponents as a "Red" sympathizer. After being fired from Truman's cabinet for opposing the Cold War, Wallace was nominated for the presidency by a revived Progressive Party. But Wallace did win considerable support among black voters—many of whom were not leftists—because of his antisegregation and anticolonialism positions.

When the votes were counted on Election Day 1948, however, Truman was the surprise winner, confounding pollsters and pundits who had almost unanimously predicted Dewey's victory. So confident of that outcome had the experts been that polling stopped two weeks before the election. Thus the polls missed a massive, last-minute shift of labor, farm, and liberal Jewish voters back to Truman as the heir of FDR's New Deal. But the black vote was also decisive—and Truman got more than two-thirds of it. He had been the first presidential candidate in history to campaign in Harlem, and African Americans embraced Truman's liberal civil rights program for the future and gave him their votes, deserting both Wallace and Dewey. Blacks had come to believe in Truman's rhetoric for confronting the dilemma between national creed and practice and endorsed his liberal civil-rights agenda. In great measure, his victory was due to black support.

In 1952, after announcing his retirement from office, Harry Truman gave the Howard University commencement address, in which he called for a civil rights program backed "by **The Howard University Address** the full force and power of the Federal Government" to end discrimination against minorities. He declared that the more the nation practiced the belief in equality, "the stronger, more vigorous, and happier" it would become.

Civil rights liberals applauded the president but nonetheless admonished him that America could assure its moral credibility only with laws and policies that would rebut charges of bigotry and discrimination—as the NAACP's leader Walter White told Truman, with laws and policies that would show the world that "we were constantly at work to narrow the margin between our protestations of freedom and our practice of them." America was on trial.

Fighting for Civil Rights in the Courts

In the 1930s and 1940s, the NAACP legal team of Charles Houston, Thurgood Marshall, Robert L. Carter, and other black attorneys fought case by case in the courts for voting rights, equalizing teacher salaries, integrating higher education and interstate public transportation, employment equality, and equal access to housing.

The individual most responsible for developing the strategy for this all-out legal attack was Charles Hamilton Houston. One of the nation's earliest prominent black lawyers, Houston graduated from Harvard Law School in 1919, having been the first black editor of the elite *Harvard Law Review.* He returned to his native Washington, D.C., where he practiced law with his father in the firm Houston and Houston from 1924 until his death in 1950. At the same time he taught and held a deanship at the Howard University Law School. His students Thurgood Marshall, Oliver Hill, and others joined him after he became special counsel of the NAACP.

Charles Hamilton Houston

Houston is credited with developing the long-range legal strategy that eventually overturned the "separate but equal" doctrine, which in 1896 the Supreme Court had endorsed in *Plessy v. Ferguson.* His biographer Genna Rae McNeil argues that he weighed two choices—to attack separate-but-equal head-on or to take a long-range approach that would lay the groundwork for the final assault. Houston decided on the second strategy.

As counsel to the NAACP from 1935 to 1940, Houston successfully argued numerous cases before the U.S. Supreme Court and was instrumental in developing the legal strategy to outlaw racial discrimination in the United States. After returning to private practice in Washington, D.C., in 1938, Houston assisted Thurgood Marshall, now the head of the NAACP legal team. Some of the famous civil rights cases in which Houston continued to be involved included *Smith v. Allwright* (1944), a voting rights case that led to outlawing the Texas white primary; *Shelley v. Kraemer* (1948), the housing case that overturned restrictive covenants; and the employment cases *Steel v. Louisville and Nashville Railroad* (1944) and *Tunstall v. Brotherhood of Locomotive Firemen and Enginemen* (1944), which tackled the racial discriminatory practices of unions, certified by government agencies, toward their black members.

Houston's inspiring leadership was based on his belief in the lawyer as "social engineer." The black lawyer, Houston told his students and colleagues, had a duty to be an advocate and instrument for racial equality. He therefore believed that black lawyers must work within the context of black communities, and for that reason he and Marshall traveled throughout the South, meeting with leaders and members of local NAACP branches and with black lawyers in the various states. Indeed, historian Patricia Sullivan's comprehensive study of the NAACP reveals that Houston and his protégé Marshall not only provided the foundation or groundwork for the legal destruction of Jim Crow but also functioned effectively on the ground, much like field workers. They attracted members into the branches, worked with local lawyers, mobilized residents to target discriminatory practices for local protest, and built support for the national NAACP agenda. In newspaper articles and in the *Crisis* Houston offered instruction with such titles as "How to Fight for Better Schools." He also advised communities about finding suitable plaintiffs for cases, raising funds, and launching suits.

Community mobilization of this sort could be seen in Texas around the issue of voting rights. The courtroom contest that culminated in *Smith v. Allwright* was preceded by fervor among NAACP branches throughout Texas to pursue such a case. Twelve hundred delegates met in Corpus Christi to discuss and pledge monetary and other support for a voting rights challenge.

Of particular interest to local communities in the 1930s and 1940s was the legal assault on segregated public higher education. In communication with NAACP lawyers, African American communities in the South began to strategize around the problem of graduate level and professional school programs of public (state) universities that refused to admit their own black

Battling Jim Crow in Higher Education

residents. As legal victories mounted, Houston and Marshall felt ever more emboldened to challenge Jim Crow. Sullivan writes:

> Local groups in communities around the South were investigating expenditures on education, appearing before local and state education boards to protest inequities. In some cases they secured additional funding for facilities and bus transportation; in others, such as Muskogee, Oklahoma, and Baltimore County, Maryland, legal challenges to discrimination at the elementary and secondary level were under way. Local groups in Jacksonville, Florida; Mobile, Alabama; and Atlanta, Georgia, were working to equalize teachers' salaries, and Thurgood Marshall spent time in Virginia and North Carolina at the request of several groups preparing to test salary differentials in those states.

In 1936 Houston and Marshall won a case against the University of Maryland in which the Maryland Court of Appeals ordered that a black student, Donald Gaines Murray, be admitted to the university's law school. (Six years earlier, the University had refused admission to Marshall himself.) Murray, a resident of Baltimore, sued Raymond A. Pearson and other officers and members of the Board of Regents of the University of Maryland to admit him into the law school. Murray had graduated with a bachelor of arts degree from Amherst College in 1934 and met all the standards for admission to the law school except color. Drawing on an argument that Gunnar Myrdal's *An American Dilemma* would later make, Marshall argued: "What's at stake here is more than the rights of my client. It's the moral commitment stated in our country's creed."

The university's lawyers argued that the admission of blacks was not required, since the Fourteenth Amendment permitted the segregation of races for education, and it was the stated policy and practice of the state of Maryland to segregate blacks. The university sought to remedy the case by promising in the future to build a separate law school for blacks. The court ordered Murray's immediate entrance, however, noting that the state at that time had only one law school. The Murray case, like others to follow, referred to the specific state under litigation, and thus the fight against Jim Crow in higher education had to be waged on a state-by-state basis.

The next significant step toward providing graduate and professional training for African Americans grew out of the decision of the Supreme Court in the case of *Missouri ex rel. Gaines v. Canada, Registrar of the University et al.* In 1936 Lloyd Gaines, a state resident, applied for admission to the University of Missouri's law school. When rejected, he took his case to the courts, and when the state courts denied him relief he appealed to the federal courts. In the decision of the Supreme Court in 1938, Chief Justice Charles Evans Hughes stated that it was the duty of the state to provide education for all its citizens and that provision for that must be made within the state. To provide legal education for white residents within the state and to fail to do so for blacks "is a denial of the equality of legal right to the enjoyment of the privilege which the State has set up, and the provision for the payment of tuition fees in another State does not remove the discrimination." The Supreme Court gave Houston the victory. Unfortunately, Gaines disappeared before ever attending the law school.

But legal victories continued to mount. In 1946 Ada Sipuel sought admission to the law school of the University of Oklahoma. The U.S. Supreme Court ordered the state to provide facilities for her, and the university regents arranged for the establishment of a separate law school. But she declined to attend this institution, which had been set up within two

George W. McLaurin, a 54-year-old African American student, sits in an anteroom, apart from other students, as he attends class at the University of Oklahoma in 1948.

weeks, and began the litigation all over again. Finally, in 1949 Sipuel won admission to the university law school. Meanwhile George W. McLaurin, who already held a master's degree, was admitted as a Ph.D. candidate to the University of Oklahoma's graduate school of education. His case drew public attention, because he was not treated equally. He was required to sit separately and away from the other students and assigned to special tables in the library and the cafeteria. McLaurin sued to remove those restrictions, since they handicapped his efforts to study, learn, and interact with other students.

Black communities across the nation closely followed the McLaurin case. According to Robert Carter, a crucial member of the NAACP legal team, a complication arose when certain sections of the black community began to question whether the NAACP should take the case. A columnist for the *Pittsburgh Courier* editorialized for the newspaper's national black readership that McLaurin's case might be considered too insignificant by the Supreme Court, given that he was already enrolled in the school. The reporter worried that the Court might rule against him, thus setting back another pending case as well as breaking the string of victories. In response, Marshall called a conference at Howard University to alert the public that the case would continue. On June 5, 1950, the Supreme Court ordered an end to the University of Oklahoma's segregation practices. This victory solidified even greater respect for the NAACP Legal Defense and Education Fund, Inc. (LDF), as the legal team was now identified.

On the same day as the *McLaurin* decision, the Supreme Court ordered the law school of the University of Texas to open its doors to Heman Sweatt, a black applicant. Texas, along with several other southern states, had begun creating separate law schools for African Americans, hoping to get around the problem of equalization. The Court was persuaded otherwise by Marshall. Chief Justice Fred M. Vinson's opinion indicated that the Texas plan to create a new, well-equipped but separate law school for blacks did not make the school equal to its older white counterpart because of the latter's alumni, reputation, and other "relevant intangibles." *McLaurin*, and to a greater extent *Sweatt*, revealed the beginning of a shift in the NAACP's legal strategy—away from arguments based on equalization (the sheer denial of equal facilities) to an attack on the very premise behind segregated education.

To white southerners, these Court rulings were frightening. The legal assault on Jim Crow left little doubt that, in time, all public institutions of higher education would open to African Americans. The University of Arkansas had already voluntarily admitted its first black in 1947. In 1951 the University of Louisville absorbed the Municipal College for Negroes and hired one black professor. Within a few years, either voluntarily or by court order, several southern state universities were admitting African Americans.

Wherever it was maintained, separate and unequal education had immeasurable effects on both white and black populations. In 1951 nine southern states revealed a glaring disparity

The Battle against Separate but Equal

between per pupil expenditures for blacks and whites. In Alabama, Arkansas, Florida, Georgia, Maryland, Mississippi, North Carolina, Oklahoma, and South Carolina, the average expenditure was $135.60 per white student and $74.50 per black. The differential for school property was even greater. Both friends and foes of segregation in education conceded that the bitterest fight would be waged on the level of elementary and secondary schools—and that fight was not long in coming.

Black schools in the South had suffered horribly during the Depression, when construction of new school buildings stopped almost entirely, teaching staffs were cut to the point where effective teaching was impossible, and miserably low salaries were slashed even further. While no southern community could afford to cut its educational expenditures without seriously impairing the effectiveness of its program, the slightest cut in African American education often had the effect of taking away the barest essentials in the educational program, including the teacher.

As migrants moved north and west in the twentieth century, their children continued to find segregated schools. Few states followed the lead of New York, which in 1900 prohibited separate schools. New Jersey, Ohio, Illinois, and Indiana had some integrated high schools but not elementary schools. Most northern states were inclined to provide separate schools for blacks, especially where white patrons brought pressure to bear on school officials. In Kansas and Arizona, racially separate education was mandatory only on the elementary level, but in both these states, separate schools at the secondary level were common.

Where separate high schools were established in large cities, such as Gary and Indianapolis, Indiana, the schools constructed for the use of African Americans were modern and adequate in almost every detail. Some suggested that equalization through meticulous care in the construction of exclusive schools for blacks occurred mainly to counter the claim of unequal education, thus forestalling indefinitely the admission of blacks to white elementary and secondary schools. Support for segregation hardened also as white students engaged in strikes and violence to prevent African American students from attending schools open to all, and as white parents kept their children away from school in an effort to force the authorities to set aside separate facilities for blacks.

The South's determination to provide better public schools for African American youths highlighted two dilemmas. First, black schools were so inadequate that it would take years of significant funding to achieve even a semblance of equality; and second, the fight in the courts indicated the Supreme Court's incremental move away from the doctrine of separate but equal.

In 1952 the NAACP took to the Supreme Court five school segregation cases arising in South Carolina, Virginia, Kansas, Delaware, and the District of Columbia. Many organizations entered briefs on behalf of the black students' position, and the attorney general of the United States asked that the separate but equal doctrine be struck down, using a foreign policy argument. "Racial discrimination," he declared, "furnishes grist for the Communist propaganda mills, and it raises doubt even among friendly nations as to the intensity of our devotion to the democratic faith."

Perhaps no question in twentieth-century America aroused more interest at home and abroad than the debate about the constitutionality of segregated public schools. The NAACP threw down the gauntlet in the Supreme Court case *Brown v. Board of Education* and won a historic victory on May 17, 1954. The case brought four cases before the Supreme Court—from South Carolina, Virginia, and Kansas, whose district courts held public school segregation to be constitutional, and from Delaware, whose state supreme court took the opposite position, holding that the "equal protection" clause of the Fourteenth Amendment invalidated segregation provisions in the state constitution. On the same day, a second Supreme Court victory went to the NAACP's separate but related case *Bolling v. Sharpe*, which challenged segregated schools in the District of Columbia. In each of the cases that constituted *Brown*, local black lawyers (often leaders in state and regional NAACP chapters) worked closely with Thurgood Marshall, Robert Carter, and others from the New York national office. Most noteworthy was the tremendous courage and sacrifice of the parents of the children who served as plaintiffs in the local cases. They lived under threats, and some lost their jobs because of their suits.

The *Brown* Decision

Arguing the *Brown* case before the Supreme Court required standing not only on the precedent of cases that had been won over the previous decade but also on scholarly expertise. The NAACP's legal team had come to depend on that expertise, and during the 1940s its lawyers turned to scholars in the preparation of their arguments. For example, white sociologist Louis Wirth at the University of Chicago worked with the case *Shelley v. Kraemer* (1948). Wirth's extensive knowledge of urban planning and racial-residential housing patterns proved helpful to legal arguments against restrictive covenants.

In another NAACP victory, *Lyman Johnson v. the University of Kentucky* (1949), Marshall asked John Hope Franklin, who had recently been awarded a Ph.D. in history by Harvard, to make a comparative study of the white university and the Kentucky State College for Negroes at Frankfort with respect to library holdings, faculty, and departments of history. Franklin revealed the segregated black school to be woefully unequal. Franklin would also become part of the team of historians, sociologists, political scientists, and psychologists called on to help develop the NAACP's brief in the *Brown* case. Scholarly research proved especially useful in the *Brown* decision, when black psychologist Kenneth Clark's doll-test findings served as evidence to show the debilitating psychological effects of segregation on black children's self-esteem.

In 1954, after long deliberation under the skillful guidance of its newly appointed chief justice, Earl Warren, the Court rendered its historic *Brown* decision, unanimously and unequivocally declaring racially separate public education to be inherently unequal.

Segregated public schools, the *Brown* decision stated, deprived African Americans of the equal protection of the laws guaranteed by the Fourteenth Amendment. "Separate educational facilities are *inherently* unequal," Warren wrote for the Court, thus overturning after more than a half-century the separate-but-equal doctrine of the 1896 *Plessy* decision.

The chief justice then conceded that formulation of the decrees to integrate presented problems of "considerable complexity" because of the great variety of local conditions and because of the wide applicability of the decision. He therefore invited the parties to the suits, the attorney general of the United States, and the attorneys general of those states requiring or permitting segregation in public education to offer suggestions during the Court's next term of court as to how relief should be granted.

Southerners, as a general rule, reacted to the decision with defiance. The governors of South Carolina, Georgia, and Mississippi threatened to abolish public schools rather than permit white and black children to attend the same schools. Fiery crosses were burned in some Texas and Florida towns, and scattered groups of whites organized to resist the decision. But if the *Knoxville Journal* surprised some, it spoke for many when it editorialized: "No citizen, fitted by character and intelligence to sit as a justice of the Supreme Court, and sworn to uphold the Constitution of the United States, could have decided this question other than the way it was decided."

In its May 31, 1955, ruling that called for "all deliberate speed" in desegregating schools, referred to as *Brown II,* the Supreme Court refused to mandate a timetable for carrying out desegregation, and it disregarded the Justice Department's original recommendation that local officials develop desegregation plans within ninety days after notification. By 1956 integration seemed to be underway in the border states of Maryland, Delaware, Missouri, and Oklahoma. However, in the majority of southern states "all deliberate speed" served to slow down rather than hasten the actual process of integration. Since the Supreme Court made the federal district courts primarily responsible for oversight of the implementation process, desegregation was thus placed in the hands of white southern federal judges at the district and appellate levels, many of whom fully shared local white prejudices.

Many white southerners expressed virulent and outspoken opposition. An editorial in a Richmond newspaper called the Supreme Court justices an "inept fraternity of politicians and professors" and declared that the Court had "repudiated the Constitution, spit upon the Tenth Amendment, and rewrote the fundamental law of this land to suit their own gauzy concepts of sociology."

Southern White Opposition

However, the president of the Southern Regional Council called the court's decree "wise, moderate, and workable," and a South Carolina newspaper, in an editorial entitled "We Can't Win," said, "Segregation is going—it's all but gone. South Carolina and the rest of the South can't reverse the trend."

But even if the South could not win, it was not ready to admit defeat. White resistance increased as African Americans pressed to desegregate schools. Among the new antiblack groups was the National Association for the Advancement of White People, with national headquarters in Washington, D.C. The organization was discredited in 1954, however, as a result of the numerous legal entanglements in which its executive director became involved. More widespread and more effective were the White Citizens' Councils, which a leading white Mississippi editor called the "Uptown Ku Klux Klans."

Frankly admitting their determination to resist enforcement of the Supreme Court's school desegregation decision, the councils called on their members to take economic reprisals against blacks who were active in the fight to desegregate schools and against whites who favored compliance with the law. In some communities, African Americans retaliated by launching boycotts against businesses operated by members of the councils. Thus, by 1956 something akin to economic warfare was being waged in the South, with many business firms caught in the middle—regarded by whites as "soft" on the NAACP and by blacks as favorable to the White Citizens' Councils.

Southern leaders fought the school desegregation decisions in other ways. They considered numerous plans to avoid compliance, including turning over the public schools to private organizations, criminalizing anyone who attended or taught mixed classes, and encouraging "voluntary segregation." In the area of political theory they resurrected the doctrine of interposition—under which southern states asserted their right to interpose their own sovereignty in those extreme cases when the federal government allegedly exceeded its legal authority—that had originally been expounded by South Carolina's chancellor William Harper back in 1832.

Early in 1956, the governors of Virginia, South Carolina, Georgia, and Mississippi called on the southern states to declare that the federal government had no power to prohibit segregation, and they demanded the right to "protest in appropriate language, against the encroachment of the central government upon the sovereignty of the several states and their people." The state legislators of those same states passed resolutions of interposition or nullification. In defiance of the Court, Virginia's Prince Edward County closed down its public school system between May 1959 and 1964. White children were educated in private schools, such as the Prince Edward Academy, supported by tuition grants from the state and by tax credits. Black students had no such option and could receive education only by leaving the county or through the efforts of churches that tried to approximate classroom learning, often in their basements.

Since the NAACP had led in the fight for desegregation, it soon became the special object of attack in the resistance to change. The organization was widely denounced in the South as subversive, and in 1956 several states found various legal devices to virtually stop its operations. Thus in Louisiana an injunction was granted that restrained the NAACP from holding meetings until it had filed with the secretary of state a complete list of its membership. A local judge in Alabama granted an injunction against any further activities by the NAACP. The South Carolina general assembly called for its classification as a subversive organization. Meanwhile, a member of Congress from Arkansas entered into the Congressional Record about forty pages of "evidence" in an attempt to show that the officers and leading members of the NAACP were un-American.

The late 1950s and the 1960s would bring about a changing of the guard. A new generation of activists would lead the civil rights movement to end legal (de jure) and customary (de facto) racial discrimination. This younger, more impatient generation would take to the streets, employing mass but nonviolent confrontational tactics such as demonstrations, freedom rides, sit-ins, boycotts, marches, and voter registration drives. Local communities throughout the nation were refusing to wait for court decisions and for laws to change. One by one, they were mobilizing and together producing a national movement that insisted on freedom now.

20 We Shall Overcome

Introducing Nonviolent Direct Action

Anatomy of the Montgomery Movement

Movement Milestones

Movement Women

The Northern Side of the Movement

The Landmarks and Limitations of Government

Woman carried to police patrol wagon during demonstration in Brooklyn, New York, 1963.

Well before the familiar protest demonstrations of the 1960s and Martin Luther King, Jr.'s, stirring, eloquent appeals to the conscience of white America, civil rights activists were championing nonviolent direct action to attain racial equality. In the 1940s, they engaged in strikes, sit-ins, boycotts, and freedom rides, and they planned a mass march on Washington. Their efforts signaled the beginning of a dramatic, unfolding quest for rights that were denied to blacks while assured to white Americans. Much like a great symphony, composed of unique but linked musical segments known as movements, the struggle for racial equality that spanned the 1940s through the mid-1970s included four identifiable segments—labor activism, challenges to the courts, nonviolent mass direct action, and assertions of black self-determination. Each segment, itself a social movement with its own leadership and constituency, represented a distinct emphasis and strategy, and each rose to a crescendo at different moments. Yet there were also significant overlaps.

The challenge to the courts, although often perceived as a gradualist approach that became less relevant after the 1954 *Brown* decision, did not cease with the rise of nonviolent direct-action protest in the sixties. Civil rights lawyers continued to bring to the courts cases initiated by individuals and communities braving job losses, arrests, and even violence in their fight for the fundamental rights of American citizens. Pursuing such cases demanded tremendous personal courage—by black parents and their children who dared to desegregate public schools, by black women who refused segregated seating on city buses, by university students who insisted on sitting at store lunch counters, by sharecroppers who tried to register to vote, by black families who sought to move into white neighborhoods, and by men and women in love who attempted to marry across the color line.

Far from being abstract legalism, activism by lawyers continued into the 1960s as a concrete, supportive arm of the movement and often as a direct consequence of the activism in the streets. Legal activism in the defeat of Jim Crow was essential both to the codification of African Americans' cumulative gains and to the onward press for governmental enforcement of newly acquired civil rights and voting rights. Thus to speak of the civil rights movement as a "movement of movements," as historians often do today, is to recognize its protracted character, stretching from the 1940s through the 1960s, as well as the complexity of those instrumental to it—blacks and whites, women and men, southern and northern communities, old and new civil rights organizations, leftists and anti-Communists, the federal government, and the press.

Introducing Nonviolent Direct Action

"Unjust social laws and patterns do not change because supreme courts deliver just opinion." Bayard Rustin's words appeared brusquely in the *Louisiana Weekly* in January 1947, referring to the U.S. Supreme Court's ruling six months earlier in *Morgan v. Commonwealth of Virginia*. In a stunning victory for the NAACP, the Court had overturned the legality of segregation on interstate bus travel on the basis of its being an impermissible burden on interstate commerce. However, bus companies operating in the South showed no indication of respecting the landmark decision (which would have meant defying local segregation ordinances). For civil rights activists such as Rustin and the other black and white members of the Congress of Racial Equality (CORE), the clock had run out for courtroom argumentation alone.

CORE Activism CORE leaders sought to correct the insulting discrepancy between the legal outcome of the case brought by Irene Morgan and the daily realities of Jim Crow bus travel by sending an integrated group on a two-week "journey of reconciliation" through Virginia, North Carolina, Tennessee, and Kentucky. CORE's style of activism—its assertive confidence in nonviolent direct action—testified to the changing times. Among the organizers of the journey were Rustin and white social activist George M. Houser, both members of the Fellowship of Reconciliation (FOR), an interracial pacifist group established during World War I and headed by A. J. Muste. The two organizations worked closely together in the 1940s, picketing and staging sit-ins at restaurants, amusement parks, and other public places in northern cities.

CORE leaders were influenced by Muste, who explicitly championed the model of civil disobedience organized and led by Mohandas Gandhi as part of India's resistance to British colonial rule, and they advocated Gandhi's philosophy of *satyagraha*—the belief that love and truth will triumph over violence and oppression. Houser's book *Erasing the Color Line* (1945), with a foreword by A. Philip Randolph, commented on the possibility for similar and complementary roles between Gandhian *satyagraha* and Christian principles of "love thy enemy" and "turn the other cheek" in the fight against racial discrimination.

According to historian Ray Arsenault, Thurgood Marshall of the NAACP initially questioned CORE's tactics, believing that a civil-disobedience bus ride in the South would foment violence, not reconciliation. CORE leaders disagreed and held firmly to the belief that only disciplined nonviolence could minimize retaliatory violence in the postwar climate, in which tensions ran high on both sides. Two months before the official departure date on April 9, 1947, Rustin and Hauser rehearsed the journey. Their goal was not to defy the Jim Crow seating policy of the time, but rather to educate black communities along the bus route of the Supreme Court's decision in *Morgan*. Rustin and Houser met with local activists and solicited support from NAACP branches, NAACP Youth Councils, and churches.

The Journey of Reconciliation As the date for the "journey of reconciliation" approached, CORE and FOR held a two-day training session on nonviolence at the latter's office in Washington, D.C. Eight black men and eight white men volunteered for the bus trip. All were relatively young; Rustin, at 37, was the oldest. They represented a range of political perspectives and a variety of organizations, in addition to CORE and FOR including the American Friends Service Committee, the Workers Defense League, individual Congregational and Methodist churches, and the New York Council for a Permanent FEPC. At the orientation, the volunteers practiced nonviolence through role playing, attempting to learn effective techniques in the event of verbal and physical harassment or arrest. Written instructions stipulated that blacks were to take the front seats of the bus, and whites were to go to the rear. The instructions reminded them to act calmly and courteously when refusing to move as the bus driver commanded, and they were instructed to inform the driver of their rights according to the recent Supreme Court decision.

On April 9, the group divided, half boarding a Greyhound bus and half taking a Trailways. Most would not complete the entire journey as planned, since twelve were arrested, including Rustin, who was pulled off the bus in Chapel Hill, North Carolina, amid what newspapers described as a "mob spirit" against the civil rights workers. The journey of reconciliation, as covered in the black newspaper the *Atlanta Daily World* in May 1947, attested to the lack of knowledge by bus drivers, passengers, and police of the historic Supreme Court decision in *Morgan*. The paper observed: "Those who have heard of it [the Court decision] vaguely did not know whether or how it applies."

Although extensive coverage of the bus trip appeared in black newspapers, white newspapers paid relatively scant attention to it. At the fifth annual CORE Convention, held in Chicago in June 1947, delegates from affiliated state branches, including Kansas, Nebraska, Michigan, Ohio, and New York, listened with rapt attention as the "freedom riders" recounted their challenging journey and urged travelers to "break the pattern by riding buses and trains in an unsegregated manner." Conference participants also heard a lecture by black sociologist Ira D.A. Reid on "Direct Action Challenges Segregation." The title presaged the dominant model of civil rights activism over the next two decades.

Anatomy of the Montgomery Movement

The Montgomery, Alabama, bus boycott was not only a direct challenge to segregation but also the first successful example of mass nonviolent resistance in the United States. The boycott began in December 1955—a sobering time for many African Americans, when initial rejoicing over the victory in the *Brown* decision—the Supreme Court's ruling that "separate was inherently unequal"—had turned considerably more subdued after the Court's second ruling in May 1955, calling for public school desegregation "with all deliberate speed." Desegregation moved slowly, if at all, in the school year after the Court's decision. Meanwhile attacks on southern state branches of the NAACP had begun. States outlawed the NAACP and harassed members with false accusations of un-American activities and orders to disband. Schools and public libraries, movie theaters, department stores, lunch counters, and city buses were among the numerous public facilities that remained segregated by law in the South and by practice in many places in the North.

The importance of the Montgomery boycott in rejuvenating the black freedom struggle cannot be overstated. The boycott symbolized African Americans' rising frustration and impatience with the denial of their rights as American citizens. It called for

The Role of the Boycott

greater militancy in a concerted and sustained effort to advance the freedom struggle. In the winter of 1955, Montgomery's black community, in choosing the disruptive effects of a boycott, refused to accept gradualism or "moderation." There would be no "slowing up in the move for freedom and capitulating to the whims and caprices of the guardians of a deadening status quo," Martin Luther King, Jr., asserted in a speech to the NAACP at its annual convention in June 1956. At that time the boycott was in its seventh month.

On some levels, the new spirit that galvanized an entire Alabama community evoked the militant impatience of Bayard Rustin and the leaders of CORE in the 1940s, whose methods of nonviolent direct action implied no longer waiting for white Americans to come around to accepting Supreme Court decisions that upheld blacks' rights (for example, in regard to interstate travel). Going beyond CORE, however, the Montgomery movement defied existing state and city ordinances—statutes that had not as yet been overturned by the federal judiciary.

The boycott served to affirm Rosa Parks' act of breaking the law. The necessity and rationale for her civil disobedience toward unjust laws as well as the tactic of mass grassroots economic withdrawal would also be accompanied by a class-action lawsuit against the city by four similarly defiant black women. The boycott's success meant, in the final analysis, the emergence of a new legal status quo. Black Montgomery's forward-looking stance contained all the elements that embodied and characterized nonviolent civil rights activism in the 1960s.

Highly planned and carefully strategized, the Montgomery bus boycott was a mass, indigenous movement of black people of all classes and ages. Women played crucial roles in the boycott, from its inception to the very end. Monetary and other material resources from the local black community, and later from nationwide black church networks, supported the boycott, sustaining it through crucial formative months and allowing it to continue during months of harsh opposition and before national and international attention and donations began to arrive. Not quite twenty-six years old when he assumed the boycott's helm, Martin Luther King, Jr., represented charismatic youthful leadership—one that conveyed to the people of Montgomery a visionary energy and a willingness to be arrested and jailed for the sake of justice for all.

Under King's leadership, the Montgomery movement emphasized nonviolence as a guiding credo of moral courage (for example, King's call for calm after segregationists dynamited his own home) and as a strategy for winning the sympathy of the nation. Montgomery activists formed a new civil rights organization, an umbrella of many local groups, instead of relying on the guidance and support of one of the older national civil rights groups. The movement advocated an end to segregation, while at the same time seeking racial harmony and reconciliation. Finally, in order to endure for a long and troubled period, the movement drew on the culture and beliefs of blacks' religious faith and institutions. The church became a site of personal and community empowerment for its people—for strengthening them physically and emotionally to withstand the mighty forces arrayed against them and, moreover, to prevail.

Rosa Parks being fingerprinted after her arrest for refusing to give up her seat on a segregated bus, December 1955.

The Montgomery movement was set in motion as a result of the arrest of Rosa Parks on Thursday, December 1, 1955, for the crime of refusing to yield her bus seat to a white man who demanded it. The bus driver had warned her and three other **The Arrest of Rosa Parks** black passengers "to make it easy" on themselves by giving up their seats, but Parks was the only one to stand her ground by remaining seated. A Jim Crow sign demarcated the colored section located in the rear of the bus, where Parks was sitting. However, Alabama law was sufficiently flexible, when it came to the comfort of white passengers on crowded buses, to permit them to take seats in the "colored section" even if a black person was occupying one of those seats. Nor did male chivalry extend to a black woman, whose seat (like that of Rosa Parks) could be demanded by a white man. Worse yet, black men and women were often violently assaulted by bus drivers and white passengers for not moving quickly enough in relinquishing their seats.

In the 1950s, and especially after the *Brown* decision in 1954, African Americans more frequently expressed open resentment of their second-class citizenship through acts of civil disobedience to Jim Crow. Arrests such as that of Rosa Parks in December 1955 had become more numerous in other southern cities, and hers was not the first in Montgomery that year. In the months preceding Parks' arrest, four other black women residents of the city had been arrested for refusing to comply with the racial policy of the city's bus system.

Aurelia S. Browder, a graduate of Alabama State University and a seamstress, had done so in April 1955. Even earlier, in March 1955, fifteen-year old Claudette Colvin refused to give up her seat. Her arrest caught the attention of the Women's Political Council, a black women's civic organization under the leadership of Alabama State University professor Joanne Gibson Robinson, and the women began to plan a boycott of the city buses. Although the WPC did not launch a boycott after Colvin's arrest, the organization had created the blueprint for future action. Two other Montgomery women were arrested for refusing to relinquish their seats to a white person in 1955—eighteen-year-old Mary Louise Smith, who was arrested in October 1955, as well as Susie McDonald, who also preceded Parks. Although their names remain far less familiar in the history of the Montgomery bus boycott, they would play a crucial and defining role in its outcome.

Parks' arrest jolted Montgomery's black community, and the idea of a boycott was quickly translated into action. Edgar Daniel Nixon (the president of the local NAACP branch), Joanne Gibson Robinson (the president of the WPC), and Ralph Abernathy (the pastor of Park's church) began reaching out to local ministers and other community leaders. Robinson's well-honed organization printed and distributed 30,000 leaflets throughout the black community, announcing a mass rally and a day-long boycott. The leaflet read: "Don't ride the bus to work, to town, to school or any place, Monday Dec. 5. Another Negro woman has been arrested and put in jail because she refused to give up her bus seat. Don't ride the bus to work, to town, to school, or anywhere on Monday. If you work, take a cab, or share a ride, or walk."

Rosa Parks, who worked as a seamstress at a Montgomery department store, was respected in the city's black community. Considered a woman of impeccable character, she was no recent initiate to civil rights activism. She and her husband Raymond Parks had openly supported the release of the Scottsboro Boys in the 1930s. As the secretary of the local branch of the NAACP since the 1940s, she worked with E. D. Nixon, a longtime political activist who headed the Montgomery chapter of the NAACP and was an organizer of the Brotherhood of Sleeping Car Porters, the black union founded by A. Philip Randolph.

Parks worked as well with the members of the local NAACP Youth Council, advising them in their protest against the segregated public library. In June 1955, she, along with NAACP national field secretary Ella Baker and veteran civil rights activist Septima Clark, participated in the summer training workshop, "Racial Desegregation: Implementing the Supreme Court Decision," at the Highlander Folk School, which had been founded by white labor organizer Myles Horton in Monteagle, Tennessee. Parks thus bore two decades of civil rights credentials. Her arrest served as the linchpin for uniting Montgomery's black community.

Rev. Dr. Martin Luther King, Jr., at the time of Parks' arrest only twenty-five years old and a newcomer to the city (he came from Atlanta, where his father was a well-known church leader), was selected by community leaders to lead the boycott effort coordinated by the Montgomery Improvement Association (MIA). An erudite yet electrifying preacher at the Dexter Memorial Baptist Church, King had made no enemies and had no ties to the city's white power structure. He yielded to the urgency of the events, recalling later that "I did not have time to think it through," and became head of the MIA, an umbrella group, including the local NAACP, the Women's Political Council, civic, business, religious, and fraternal organizations, as well as individuals. Since African Americans had no political power in Montgomery (the great majority were denied the vote), they increasingly embraced the power of nonviolent protest.

The Leadership of Martin Luther King, Jr.

Dr. Marin Luther King, Jr., speaks at the Holt Street Baptist Church during the Montgomery bus boycott.

In his speech to the MIA on the first night of the boycott, King asserted: "We have no alternative but to protest . . . we have come here tonight to be saved from the patience that makes us patient with anything less than freedom and justice." The MIA adopted the tactic of nonviolent resistance. The newly formed association drafted three demands and presented them to city officials: that bus drivers treat black passengers with dignity and respect; that the city of Montgomery agree to hire black bus drivers in black neighborhoods; and the rather conservative demand that the city adopt a first-come, first-served seating system, with blacks filling the rear and whites the front.

Mayor W. A. Gayle and the attorneys for the bus line rejected those demands. They fully expected the boycott to fail, believing, as did most white residents of Montgomery, that the black population could not sustain a prolonged withdrawal from the buses. Compromise, they surmised, would lead only to further demands. The city remained intransigent. The white citizens of Montgomery could not have imagined the transformative events ahead.

The boycott continued because of the MIA's highly planned and strategized efforts. Meeting in churches—their endurance strengthened by a religious culture that stressed nonviolence and the moral justice of their cause—men, women, and children walked to their destinations. The MIA organized carpools and dispatch-call stations; black taxicab drivers transported black passengers at reduced rates. White Montgomery retaliated by indicting black residents for conspiracy to obstruct the operation of a business.

The city threatened and subsequently filed a legal suit against more than eighty individuals involved in the boycott, including King and Abernathy. King's home was firebombed, but no one was hurt. Indeed, constant threats of violence forced the relocation of the MIA headquarters several times. From the boycott's inception, King linked the Christian teaching of love for one's enemies to the civil rights tactic of nonviolent resistance, but he came to understand the role of nonviolence more deeply after Bayard Rustin's visit to Montgomery during the boycott. Rustin became an advisor to King, introducing him to the teachings of Gandhi and also those of A. J. Muste and the Fellowship of Reconciliation.

The men and women who waged nonviolent war on Montgomery's segregated public transportation system also risked financial retribution. Some lost their jobs. Others walked what seemed like a tightrope—remaining loyal to the boycott while desperately needing to remain employed. King, writing about the boycott in his 1964 book *Why We Can't Wait*, described the tactic of black domestic servants, who participated in the boycott but feigned ignorance in order to keep their jobs. Such duplicity, which existed since the days of slavery, represented a covert style of resistance, a "hidden transcript," as scholar James Scott terms the everyday, prosaic forms of protest wielded by the oppressed toward those in power.

In Montgomery, black maids often adopted this kind of strategy with employers who perceived the boycott as an unlawful act of defiance. King noted that when a white employer asked her black maid if she supported the "terrible things the Negroes were doing, boycotting buses and demanding jobs," the latter would reply "Oh no, ma'am. I won't have anything to do with that boycott . . . I am just going to stay away from the buses as long as that trouble is going on." Some white women employers even began to drive their maids to work. Initially sustained by the Montgomery black community's resources and by monetary gifts from black churches and individuals in northern cities, the boycott eventually drew national and international attention and funds.

Just as the actions of one black woman had precipitated the bus boycott, the actions of four black women, who had also defied segregated seating, helped to bring the boycott to a victorious end. Aurelia Browder, Claudette Colvin, Mary Louise Smith, and Susie Mac-donald (Parks was not among the plaintiffs) brought a class-action lawsuit against Mayor Gayle and other city officials a few months after the boycott began. Browder served as the lead plaintiff in the case, which challenged the constitutionality of both city and state segregation ordinances. While the boycott sorely tested the will of white officials to continue segregation on city buses, the women's suit tested the very legality of Jim Crow buses.

Victory

Leaders of the Montgomery Bus Boycott were in agreement as to the importance of such a federal lawsuit. The case, which was argued in the federal courts by black Montgomery attorney Fred Gray and Robert Carter, a black NAACP lawyer from New York, referenced *Brown.* The special three-judge panel in the U.S. District Court declared Alabama's state and local laws requiring segregation on buses unconstitutional, and the Supreme Court affirmed that judgment. The Supreme Court's declarative ruling ended the 381-day boycott by requiring an immediate end to the city's segregated bus system.

Movement Milestones

The Montgomery Bus Boycott inspired new civil rights activism and leaders. James M. Lawson, Jr., learned of the boycott while on a missionary trip to India after spending fourteen months in a federal prison for refusing to be drafted in the Korean War. Influenced by A. J. Muste's pacifist ideas, Lawson became a devoted member of FOR and understood how Gandhian nonviolence and Christian pacifism could be interwoven. When Lawson read about the boycott in the Indian newspaper *Nagpur Times,* he returned to America to take part in the budding movement against southern segregation.

In the fall of 1958, Lawson settled in Nashville, Tennessee, and began teaching his philosophy of nonviolence. Some of his students would become influential leaders of the 1960s student sit-in movement. Among those who attended Lawson's

New Leaders: James M. Lawson

weekly workshop were James Bevel, Diane Nash, John Lewis, Marion Barry, Jr., and Bernard Lafayette, all of whom attended universities and divinity schools in Nashville. John Lewis, a black divinity student from American Baptist College who would later become a U.S. congressman, remembers the urgency with which he felt that the "movement for civil rights needed—no, *demanded*—[their] involvement." The young men and women who attended Lawson's weekly workshops sought actual change in their lifetime.

In addition to student support, the Southern Christian Leadership Conference, founded in Atlanta in February 1957 in the wake of the Montgomery victory and headed by Martin Luther King, Jr., had an active branch in Nashville—the Nashville Christian Leadership Council (NCLC) under the leadership of local minister, Rev. Kelly Miller Smith. In the fall of 1958, Smith invited Lawson to Nashville to lead a workshop on nonviolent resistance. Throughout 1959, Lawson taught nonviolence and nonviolent direct action protest strategies to eager young men and women in a church basement in the city. Workshop participants discussed the philosophy of nonviolence from the perspectives of Jesus, Gandhi, and American thinkers Henry David Thoreau, Reinhold Niebuhr, and A. J. Muste.

Lawson's teachings on nonviolence as a way of life were not always readily accepted, according to John Lewis. Lewis's roommate James Bevel confessed to his personal struggle in responding with love to hate and violence. In the workshop, the student activists learned to employ nonviolent tactics and strategies during demonstrations and in the event of violence. Through mock sit-ins and other forms of role playing, they learned how to maintain

Sit-in participants endure harassment.
In Jackson, Mississippi, whites poured sugar, mustard, and ketchup on the heads of sit-in participants seeking to desegregate a lunch counter.

eye contact with aggressors, how to minimize blows by covering up one another when under attack, and how to deal with arrest. In their practice sessions, students alternated the roles of peaceful protesters and angry whites, attempting to create as much as feasible the actual events that might occur. Lawson's group made plans for a lunch-counter sit-in in Nashville.

Fisk University student Diane Nash is credited for suggesting the lunch counter as the first target in the students' nonviolent assault on segregated Nashville. Coming from Chicago, she found it difficult to adjust to Jim Crow etiquette, and she viewed lunch-counter segregation as a stark reminder of the inequities and insults blacks faced daily, particularly by black women, who were often shoppers. Before the Nashville students could set their plan in motion, however, four students in Greensboro, North Carolina, made their move.

The Lunch Counter Sit-In

On February 1, 1960, Ezell Blair, Jr., Franklin McCain, Joseph McNeill, and David Richmond, four Greensboro students, staged the first successful sit-in of the 1960s civil rights movement by taking seats at a "whites only" lunch counter in a Woolworth's and asking for service. Their protest inspired other students in Greensboro and cities throughout the South to stand up for their rights. Blacks throughout the South had a deep sense of resentment for restaurants and department stores that took money from black consumers but refused to let them dine on their premises. News of the Greensboro Four—as they would come to be known—sparked similar protests by black student activists throughout the South.

Album cover for Max Roach's *Freedom Now Suite*
The cover shows a sit-in and reflects the wide support for the civil rights movement.

Two weeks after the Greensboro sit-in, Lawson's Nashville students initiated a sophisticated plan of rotating protesters at a lunch counter in a downtown Nashville store. As the police arrested the seated protesters at the counter, another wave of protesters took their places. Student groups in Tallahassee, Florida, in Richmond, Virginia, in Chattanooga, Tennessee, in Charleston, South Carolina, in Chapel Hill, North Carolina, and in Atlanta, Georgia, began staging lunch-counter sit-ins. In the spring and summer of 1960, white and black young people participated in similar peaceful protests against segregated public accommodations with sit-ins at white libraries, wade-ins at white beaches, and sleep-ins in the lobbies of white hotels.

They were usually arrested for trespassing, disorderly conduct, and disobeying police officers. Many were harassed and even beaten by white mobs and tear-gassed and jailed by police. Northern youth also showed their support. Some traveled to Maryland and demonstrated in Annapolis and Baltimore, and others remained in northern cities and picketed chain stores with branches in the southern states. Not only the press but also jazz musicians captured the fervor of the student sit-ins. The album cover of *We Insist! Max Roach's Freedom Now Suite* (1960) pictured a lunch-counter sit-in. Vocals by Abbey Lincoln and other arrangements in the album referenced the civil rights movement in the United States and the struggle against apartheid in South Africa.

In Atlanta, Morehouse student Julian Bond led a student sit-in in March 1960 that mushroomed into a larger protest movement of students from five historically black colleges and seminaries. The group published its "Appeal for Human Rights" in the *Atlanta Constitution* and *The New York Times,* capturing the insurgent mood of young black men and women in local communities throughout the South: "We do not intend to wait placidly for those rights which are already legally and morally ours. . . . We want to state clearly and unequivocally that we cannot tolerate, in a nation professing democracy and among people professing Christianity, the discriminatory conditions under which the Negro is living today in Atlanta, Georgia."

The collective demands of students found voice in the new national, student-led civil rights group, the Student Nonviolent Coordinating Committee (SNCC). On the weekend of April 14 and 15, 1960, student activists from across the South converged at Shaw University in Raleigh, North Carolina. SNCC emerged from this conference and quickly became a powerful force in the Movement. Along with providing nonviolent soldiers for sit-ins, marches, and other demonstrations, SNCC members branched out into smaller cities and towns and worked to organize local blacks, teach nonviolence, and encourage voter registration. In Nashville, SNCC members including Diane Nash, James Bevel, John Lewis, and other members of James Lawson's workshop were successful in getting the city's mayor to consent to the desegregation of the downtown area.

Under the leadership of SNCC, the SCLC, and the NAACP, in 1961 the black community of Albany, Georgia, staged months of demonstrations in an attempt to secure fair employment for black workers, to end police brutality, and to **The Albany Movement** desegregate parks, playgrounds, city buses, bus and train stations, and the public library. It was in Albany as well that the movement first used freedom songs as an integral part of demonstrations. As the movement progressed, such SNCC workers as Bernice Johnson Reagon enlisted the power of community singing in order to unite large groups of people. In vocal displays of unity, Albany's blacks sang passionately during meetings, protests, and in the jailhouse to uplift one another, adapting songs of the black church and the slave spirituals—"Ain't Gonna Let Nobody Turn Me Round," "This Little Light of Mine," and "We Shall Overcome."

Unfortunately, the Albany movement failed. The cunning police chief Laurie G. Pritchett knew that protesters expected public violence and that members of the press would capture police brutality in Albany, as they did in other southern cities, in such a way that would elicit sympathy for the protesters. Determined to undermine the movement, Pritchett did what SNCC and SCLC organizers had not predicted: he advised his officers not to be violent—at least not on camera. (Numerous beatings took place behind the scenes, away from the reporters and cameramen.)

Pritchett also labored to keep Albany's blacks from filling the jails as they had done during campaigns in other cities. He had read King's 1958 book *Stride toward Freedom* on the Montgomery bus boycott and was aware of the effect of the large number of protesters who filled the jails, as had happened with Gandhi and his followers in Britain's colonial Indian jails. To prevent his jail from reaching capacity, the Albany police chief made arrangements with police departments in neighboring counties to hold prisoners in jails as far as a hundred miles away. His police force arrested more than seven hundred civil rights activists, including King, during December 1961, but not for breaking Jim Crow laws. They were arrested for such infractions as parading without a permit, creating a disturbance, loitering, trespassing, and even contributing to the delinquency of minors by organizing young people to take part in demonstrations. When the "Freedom Rides" made a stop in Albany, Pritchett's henchmen arrested the riders for "obstructing traffic."

His tactics worked. The U.S. government never intervened. Other than Pritchett's manipulations, there was another reason the Kennedy administration stayed out of Albany's affairs. James A. Gray, a well-connected segregationist, was the chairman of the Georgia Democratic Party and a personal friend of John F. Kennedy. Gray controlled the area's only television station, a radio station, and was married to the daughter of the owner of the local newspaper, *The Albany Herald.* His influence in Albany and in the White House helped keep the federal government out of "local" affairs.

Finally, the Albany Movement failed because unity among the civil rights groups began to fracture. Disputes over leadership and tactics contributed to the faltering campaign, particularly rising tensions between SNCC and the SCLC. SNCC criticized the SCLC for trying to control the movement and resented the press attention on King, especially for what seemed to them like cameo appearances, to the exclusion of SNCC's efforts. The students had even begun to refer to King derisively as "De Lawd." The NAACP, in turn, shunned SNCC. In the end, organizational in-fighting precluded success.

Civil rights activists learned several lessons from Albany. The campaign taught the importance of "freedom songs" and spiritual fortitude for the struggle. It taught future organizers that a campaign on all fronts was not as effective as targeting specific discrimina-tory practices one at a time. Most important, it confirmed the influential role of the press. King's arrests and jailing brought international press coverage. In the Birmingham cam-paign in 1963, those lessons would not be lost.

Birmingham in the 1960s was a racial powder keg with a long history of white violence toward blacks. The NAACP, outlawed in the state of Alabama as "communistic" and a "for-eign corporation," had very little power in the city. So many unsolved bomb-ings had taken place over the years that residents dubbed the city "Bombingham." In 1956 local minister Rev. Fred L. Shuttlesworth organized the Alabama Christian Move-ment for Human Rights (ACHR) in hopes of challenging the racist rule of Birmingham's white business and political leaders, including its police commissioner, the well-known segre-gationist Eugene "Bull" Connor. Shuttlesworth and the men and women of the ACHR risked their lives and livelihoods by working to oppose the racial status quo.

Birmingham, 1963

Initially, Shuttlesworth and the ACHR followed the NAACP model of fighting against segre-gation in the courtroom. The group filed a suit against the city aimed at opening up the city's pub-lic accommodations to all residents regardless of race, and it won. However, the city responded by closing its parks to all residents. When legal injunctions failed to produce change, the ACHR turned to nonviolent direct action. Early in 1962, the ACHR aligned itself with student activists from Miles College who began a series of boycotts of downtown businesses owned by whites who refused to serve blacks as equals. The ACHR organized the student protesters, who began a massive campaign of economic withdrawal from all businesses that displayed signs designating "white" and "colored" areas, that denied blacks other than menial jobs, and that refused to serve black customers at lunch counters. Unable to get a binding agreement from local business own-ers, the ACHR, by now a SCLC affiliate, turned to the larger organization for help.

Key SCLC leaders, including King, believed that success in Birmingham had the poten-tial to cripple segregation in the South and throughout the entire nation. "A victory there," King recalled in his book *Why We Can't Wait,* "might well set forces in motion to change the entire course of the drive for freedom and change." The civil rights leaders were determined not to make the same organizational mistakes that cost them a victory in Albany. "We began to prepare a top-secret file which we called 'Project C'," wrote King "—the 'C' for Birming-ham's *Confrontation* with the fight for justice and morality in race relations."

"Project C" was a focused, calculated, and meticulously planned nonviolent assault on Birmingham's white economic power structure. In May 1962, the SCLC began talks with Shuttlesworth on how to take the momentum he had already generated in Birmingham to the next level. They settled on a boycott and a mass demonstration to commence on April 3, 1963. It was a brilliant plan. By choosing the Easter season, with its heavy shopping, the movement leaders ensured that blacks' economic withdrawal would have a distinctly adverse affect on white businesses, which were accustomed to making a profit from sales to black cus-tomers. April 3 was also the day after the runoff election for mayor of Birmingham, in which the opposing candidates were Albert Bourtwell and Commissioner Bull Connor. Although both men were staunch segregationists, King and his associates feared that citywide demon-strations against the status quo before the election would cause Connor, the worse of the two, to win the race. Thus they waited until the day after Bourtwell claimed victory to strike.

The Birmingham campaign began as scheduled on April 3, 1962, without a violent response from Bull Connor and his police force. When the first wave of demonstrations began in department stores, drugstores, and other businesses with lunch counters, Connor's men arrested them for "trespass after warning." Taking his cue from the example of the Albany police, Connor instructed his men not to harm the protesters. However, this policy did not last long. After similar protests continued day after day, despite the certainty of arrest and incarceration, Connor lost patience with the determined activists and on April 7—Palm Sunday—Birmingham police attacked protesters with clubs and police dogs.

Connor still hoped to win the battle for Birmingham without violent confrontations, by using legal means that would not attract the press. Connor also sought to reduce the amount of outside sympathy and support for the protesters by keeping the circumstances as uneventful as possible. The city government, for example, sought to secure victory for segregation inside the quieter arena of the courtroom and jailhouse. Between four and five hundred men and women were incarcerated for participating in protest activities. On April 10, Birmingham tried to extinguish the movement through a court injunction ordering an end to all activities until the "right to demonstrate" was argued in court. Two days later, Birmingham's black citizens shocked Connor and the rest of white Birmingham by disobeying the court order.

On April 12, Good Friday, King and Abernathy were both arrested for leading a demonstration in defiance of a court order. During his incarceration, King wrote his famous *Letter from Birmingham Jail,* a defense of his involvement in the movement and a response to white clergymen whose open letter **Letter from Birmingham Jail** in a Birmingham newspaper asked blacks to end their demonstrations for the good of the city. King, in turn, asked the white clergy to take a moral stand, since "injustice anywhere is a threat to justice everywhere." King's letter explained that he was no "outside agitator," as local segregationist reporters and city officials often labeled him and other nonresident blacks, white allies, Jewish supporters, and other activists. They protested, King insisted, because "privileged groups seldom give up their privileges voluntarily."

An interesting feature of the Birmingham campaign is the active role of children. The SCLC decided that children could take part in the growing protest movement, and although some local parents disapproved of their children taking part in the protests, young people by the hundreds and later, the thousands, began to attend nonviolence workshops similar to those led by James Lawson in Nashville several years earlier.

Exasperated, Bull Connor unleashed his full fury on the demonstrators—men, women, and children. Television news reporters who came to Birmingham to cover the protests broadcast scenes of police violence, resulting in greater sympathy for the city's black community. The monetary donations that poured in **Victory** from across the nation were used to bail out jailed protesters. Without the national press, segregation in Birmingham may have taken months or even years to end. With the news coverage, it took only five weeks. On May 10, 1963, city business leaders reached a formal agreement with the SCLC, pledging to desegregate lunch counters, rest rooms, fitting rooms, and drinking fountains in planned stages within ninety days after signing; hiring and upgrading the employment of blacks; and cooperating with the movement's lawyers to work for jailed protesters.

The Birmingham Movement brought a much-needed victory for King, the SCLC, and the countless protesters whose courage and determination made it possible. However, a signed pact with the city's white power players did little to change the violent opposition to black advancement that gave the city the nickname "Bombingham."

Bombs exploded at the home of Martin Luther King's brother, Rev. E. D. King, and near the hotel room in which Dr. King was staying while in Birmingham, forcing the Kennedy administration to act on behalf of the city's blacks. Abandoning the hands-off stance he had taken in

Window in Time

Why Families Should Demonstrate

A hundred times I have been asked why we have allowed little children to march in demonstrations, to freeze and suffer in jails, to be exposed to bullets and dynamite. The questions imply that we have revealed a want of family feeling or a recklessness toward family security. The answer is simple. Our children and our families are maimed a little every day of our lives. If we can end an incessant torture by a single climactic confrontation, the risks are acceptable. Moreover, our family life will be born anew if we fight together. Other families may be fortunate enough to be able to protect their young from danger. Our families, as we have seen, are different. Oppression has again and again divided and splintered them. We are a people torn apart from era to era. It is logical, moral and psychologically constructive for us to resist oppression united as families. Out of this unity, out of the bond of fighting together, forges will come. The inner strength and integrity will make us whole again.

Martin Luther King, Jr., *Where Do We Go from Here: Chaos or Community* (New York, 1967), p. 128.

Albany, President Kennedy ordered 3,000 federal troops to take positions near Birmingham and considered federalizing the Alabama National Guard. Press coverage of the events in Birmingham played a key role in his decision. Birmingham played no small role in Kennedy's proposal for broader civil rights legislation. In September 1963, the bombing of a black church would take the lives of four little girls, ages 11 and 14—the movement's youngest martyrs.

Among the most memorable civil rights campaigns was Freedom Summer 1964, which was sponsored by the Council of Federated Organizations (COFO), an umbrella of civil

Freedom Summer 1964   rights groups including SNCC, the SCLC, CORE, and the NAACP. Civil rights and liberal reform groups throughout the nation were involved, although SNCC played the most prominent role and was the organization with which Freedom Summer has become identified. It was SNCC worker Bob Moses's idea to bring hundreds of northern white students into the South in order to advance a massive interracial campaign to register Mississippi's black voters. Moses, a leader in both SNCC and COFO, argued that the presence of the young northern white volunteers, overwhelmingly from affluent families, would attract the national media's and the federal government's attention to conditions in the Delta and specifically to the lack of political rights for the great mass of the Delta's rural residents. SNCC also intended for the summer project to promote a strong grassroots movement on the part of black Mississippians. In this regard, SNCC played a key role in working with community residents in challenging the state's racially exclusive Democratic Party by means of an alternative party open to all races—the Mississippi Freedom Democratic Party.

Over the course of the summer, more than seven hundred white volunteers from colleges and universities in the North and West descended on Mississippi. Divided into groups, they underwent a weeklong orientation in Oxford, Ohio. In black communities that had already begun to organize, the white volunteers were welcomed and placed in the homes of black families. The students were assigned to forty-three project sites. With a sense of idealism and a commitment to change the racial status quo, many had already been involved in civil rights activism in the North.

But the white students' arrival was not without some tension and discomfort. Bob Moses played the crucial role in trying to assuage differences. Some of the black staff members worried that a large white contingent would undermine the ability of the local population to take the reins of leadership, necessary for a grassroots social movement. Black SNCC workers, most of them from the South, were acutely aware of the dangerous, potentially fatal consequences of interracial fraternization. In the highly oppressive and violent Delta, blacks feared for their lives, employment, and general security.

White civil rights volunteer Sally Belfrage described the difficulty of merely sitting down to eat with a black sharecropper family that summer. In the home of that family, Belfrage realized that the head of the household, Mr. Amos, had never sat as an equal with a white woman present and was not psychologically ready to do so. Her pleading for him to join her at his own dinner table went unheeded, and so she resorted to an order: "I begged him to sit down; he wouldn't; I *told* him to sit down. He did in great confusion. Somehow or other, everything was all right after that." In other instances, blacks would simply avoid whites who canvassed their neighborhoods for voter registration.

Danger was not confined to punishment against blacks. Three civil rights workers had gone missing in Philadelphia, Mississippi on June 21, two CORE staff members—a black man named James Cheney and a white man named Michael Schwerner—and one white student volunteer, Andrew Goodman, who had come in the first wave of volunteers. In early August, the bodies of the three men were discovered.

By summer's end, more than 80,000 persons had registered in the Mississippi Freedom Democratic Party. In August 1964 the MFDP held its state convention and sent delegates to the National Democratic Convention in Atlantic City. Although it presented its case to the Credentials Committee on August 22, the MFDP failed to unseat the racist state party by claiming to be the legitimate Democratic Party. The MFDP rejected a proposed compromise for only two seats at large with no voting power. The disillusioned SNCC members would move ideologically toward black power in the months ahead.

Yet Freedom Summer had not failed. As a result, local leaders Fannie Lou Hamer, Virginia Gray, Amzie Moore, and Aaron Henry were but a few of the Mississippi civil rights veterans who gained increasing stature as statewide leaders and, in Hamer's case, even national stature. After the passage of the Voting Rights Act in 1965 they continued the fight for political empowerment in the sustained effort to advance their communities. The number of registered black voters rose to 250,000 in 1968, more than tripling its highpoint in 1964 and accounting for 60 percent of all blacks eligible to vote. The growing number of black voters had not averted tensions within the black community, nor had it ended white racism, but politics in the state were changing and in the next decade race-baiting rhetoric by white politicians was steadily silenced.

Freedom Summer had done even more than this, however. SNCC's freedom schools, which were separate from COFO's voting-rights drive, gave thousands of Mississippi youth an educational experience that most would otherwise never have received. According to SNCC leader Charlie Cobb, the founder of the freedom school concept, the schools were intended to serve as "parallel institutions."

Mississippi allocated four times the money to white schools than to black schools. Freedom school students were taught to question and explore, as well as receiving basic reading, writing, arithmetic, and history lessons that emphasized black struggle and pride—a curriculum uncommon in southern public schools. About fifty freedom schools throughout the state taught more than 2,500 primary-to-secondary school children that summer. The curriculum was derived from a similar curriculum used in Boston by black parents who challenged their city's de facto school segregation through boycotts that same year and autonomous community-led schools. According to SNCC historian Clayborne Carson, the Mississippi freedom schools had an impact on voter registration. Parents acknowledged gaining political awareness and the willingness to struggle for their rights because of the courageous example of their children.

Freedom Summer 1964 had also brought out-of-state groups of doctors and lawyers to Mississippi. The Medical Committee for Human Rights (MCHR), organized in June 1964, aided both volunteers and the black poor through immunization and pediatric services. Northern lawyers, ranging from the more moderate politics of the NAACP Legal Defense Fund to the leftist politics of the National Lawyers Guild, provided legal services. George W. Crockett, who would be elected a judge in Michigan's Wayne County (Detroit) in 1965 and would later go to the United States Congress, established the National Lawyers Guild's office in Jackson, Mississippi, and managed the Mississippi Project (a coalition of the NLG and other leading civil rights legal organizations), which provided legal services during that summer. Medical and legal professionals set up programs to continue the work begun in the state. For example, from 1965 to 1967, California-based black psychiatrist Alvin Poussaint provided medical care to civil rights workers as Field Director of the MCHR.

Perhaps because of the sacrifice involved, the movement's greatest moments invariably contained tragedy along with triumph. The Selma-to-Montgomery march in March 1965 **Tragedy and Triumph** was no exception. The idea for the march took shape in February 1965, after the murder of black SNCC worker Jimmie Lee Jackson, who had been active in voter registration. He was killed while trying to protect his mother. SNCC and the SCLC decided to march from Selma to Montgomery to protest Jackson's death, as well as the denial of black voting rights. Although Martin Luther King, Jr., inopportunely backed out of the march, members of the SCLC and SNCC continued the plan to march. On March 7, 1965, nearly five hundred protesters, many just out of church and still in their Sunday clothes, walked two abreast in a line the length of several blocks. There was no singing, SNCC marcher John Lewis recalled, "just the sound of scuffling feet" somberly moving toward the Edmund Pettus Bridge. Lewis and the other marchers were met on the other side by the full frontal attack of 150 white police troopers—some on foot and others on horseback. White onlookers, called "possemen," joined in, mercilessly beating the nonviolent protesters.

The violence against the demonstrators was so vicious that the date is remembered as "Bloody Sunday." The press coverage shocked the nation and the world. The twenty-four-year old white Unitarian minister, Rev. James Reeb of Boston, who had gone south to support the voting rights drive, was beaten to death. On March 21, in a third attempt to march the fifty-four miles from Selma to Montgomery, the demonstrators were finally

The Selma March
Demonstrators conclude the Selma March as they enter Montgomery in March 1965. In the front line are Ralph Abernathy, Ralph Bunche, Martin Luther King, Jr., and Coretta King.

successful. An estimated 3,200 people of all races marched in a mile-long column. As Lewis reminisced in his autobiography, "Ministers, nuns, labor leaders, factory workers, school teachers, firemen—people from all walks of life, from all parts of the country, black and white and Asian and Native American, walked with us as we approached the same bridge where we'd been beaten two weeks before."

The marchers walked past the Alabama troopers on this occasion with no incident. To protect the demonstrators, President Johnson had called the Alabama National Guard into federal service. On the final day of the march, demonstrators stood 50,000 strong. Martin Luther King, Jr., who a few months earlier had received the Nobel Peace Prize for his civil rights leadership, told the crowd in Montgomery that "no tide of racism can stop us."

Press coverage of white violence against nonviolent black demonstrators was a key factor in gaining sympathy for the movement from persons who may have been skeptical of protesters' motivations or presumed them to be troublemakers. Newspaper photographs and particularly television coverage brought to the public eye, in fact for the world to see, the unflattering but all-too-vivid underside of American society. And it was difficult to remain unfeeling at the sight of black men and women thrown into the air by the powerful force of firemen's gushing water hoses, or bitten by police dogs, or struck by southern policemen with electric cattle-prods and billy clubs and then carted off to jail.

The Importance of Press Coverage

Most people were startled to see television scenes of peaceful black students in neat attire being attacked by angry, hate-filled white mobs—pushing, spitting, striking, taunting, and screaming racist epithets at them. Many reporters confessed their surprise to see the disciplined and orderly composure of such students in the face of insults and violence, and all this in order to eat at a lunch counter or to attend a state university or a public school. It was shocking to see in a magazine the photograph of the mangled, unrecognizable face of the teenage boy Emmett Till from Chicago, who in 1955 while visiting relatives in the Mississippi Delta was lynched for allegedly whistling at (or, as another version had it, saying "Bye, baby" to) a white woman. The boy's mother, Mamie Till, insisted on publicizing the horrific image so that the world could see evidence of southern atrocities.

The press made it too painful to accept the lives cut short—the assassinated Mississippi NAACP field officer Medgar Evers, the murdered young civil rights workers James Cheney, Andrew Goodman, and Michael Schwerner, the four little girls martyred in a Birmingham church, and finally Martin Luther King, Jr., slain in 1968 by a sniper's bullet. It was all too horrifying to count the list of the dead—a white housewife from Detroit, a black educator from Washington, D.C., the many others young and old, southern and northern—too many to name.

Conversely, reporters on civil rights—the "race beat," as they called it—provided at times some measure of protection for civil rights protesters. When the nightly news began to broadcast civil rights events to the nation, local mayors and commissioners pressured police forces to avoid making their cities look bad. According to writers Gene Roberts and Hank Klibanoff, a reporter's camera lens and notebook were often the only weapons that kept protesters safe from beatings by the police. The press also captured for posterity memorable moments of the civil rights movement that invoke a glorious moment in the history of this nation. No better example is the documentary footage of the March on Washington for Jobs and Freedom in August 1963 and the climactic speech of the day, Martin Luther King's "I Have a Dream." Replayed on television and in the media for various purposes, the images and rhetoric of the march are today emblazoned on the national consciousness as a source of pride.

Movement Women

African American women in the civil rights movement came from varying backgrounds and occupations, from the North and the South, and from rural and urban areas. They represented a vast age range, some highly educated and others with little formal schooling. Some women were new recruits to the movement and some decades-long veterans.

Women such as Joanne Gibson Robinson, Johnnie Carr, and Rosa Parks had worked in various civil rights and reform groups in Montgomery, Alabama, since the 1940s, and Robinson and Carr played critical roles in the day-to-day operation of the boycott. NAACP branch president in the 1950s, Daisy Bates began her fight against racial injustice as a journalist in the 1940s, writing articles in the newspaper, the *Arkansas State Press,* run by her and her husband. She assisted the Little Rock Nine in preparation for their integration of Central High School in 1957, conducting strategy sessions in her home. New to the movement were young, energetic women students such as Ruby Doris Smith Robinson, Diane Nash, Prathia Hall, Bernice Johnson Reagon, Ann Moody, and Unita Blackwell, all of whom contributed to the ideological and cultural work of the Student Nonviolent Coordinating Committee.

Movement women left no singular type of legacy but played various roles throughout the 1950s and 1960s. Recent studies show that in school desegregation cases at the primary

Window in Time

Charlayne Hunter Integrates the University of Georgia

Skillfully, she [Constance Baker Motley] set traps that would cause the University's officials to ensnare themselves in their own words. In the world of deception they lived in, they could not publicly acknowledge that they or their admissions policies were racist. So Mrs. Motley asked if they would favor the admission of a qualified Negro to the University, if all other things, like dormitory space, were available. Registrar Walter Danner answered yes. The news story in the *Atlanta Journal and Constitution* the following day revealed her strategy. It read "The university . . . registrar has testified in Federal Court here that he favors admission of qualified Negroes to the University."

Source: Charlayne Hunter Gault, " 'Heirs to a Legacy of Struggle': Charlayne Hunter Integrates the University of Georgia," in *Sisters in the Struggle: African American Women in the Civil Rights–Black Power Movement*, edited by Bettye Collier Thomas and V. P. Franklin. New York: New York University Press, 2001, p. 79.

and secondary school levels, girls outnumbered boys in legal suits. Women were the initiators, as well, in the desegregation of state universities at the undergraduate level. The first such effort was made by Arthurine Lucy at the University of Alabama in 1956. The university was ordered

School Desegregation and Constance Baker Motley

to admit her, but the students and townspeople of Tuscaloosa resorted to violence to prevent her from attending. Even with heavy police escort and in the company of the dean of women, her car was pelted with stones, and some people even jumped on top of the car. When she was suspended because of the rioting, she accused university officials of conspiring to keep her out of the university.

The first successful integration of a public university was accomplished by a woman, Charlayne Hunter (later PBS correspondent Charlayne Hunter Gault), and a man, Hamilton Holmes. High school classmates in Covington, Georgia, the two waged a legal battle for admission to the University of Georgia. The university's two-year-long effort to deny their admission proved no match for the students' attorneys—Vernon Jordan, recently out of Howard Law School, and Constance Baker Motley, from the New York office of the NAACP Legal Defense Fund. In her recollection of this time, Hunter Gault praised Motley's masterful legal strategy.

Charlayne Hunter and Hamilton Holmes entered the University of Georgia in the fall of 1961 under court order and amid a crowd of white students shouting racial epithets. Over the next two days, whites burned crosses and formed a mob outside Hunter's dormitory. It took state patrolmen and tear gas to quell the disorder. Yet their arrival on campus was far less tumultuous than that of Arthurine Lucy, and they would remain and graduate.

The story of Charlayne Hunter—the first successful university desegregation—was overshadowed by the gunshots, riots, and intervention by President Kennedy that greeted Air Force

529

veteran James Meredith when he presented himself for registration at the University of Mississippi one year later, in 1962. Meredith also benefited from having Constance Baker Motley as his lawyer. She would bring her legal skill again and again to the fight for the admission of African Americans to state universities, in 1963 winning entrance for Vivian Malone and James Hood into the University of Alabama and for Harvey Gantt into Clemson University. As a civil rights lawyer, Motley won nine of the ten cases that she argued before the United States Supreme Court. In 1964, she was the first black woman elected to a seat on the New York state senate, and in 1966 she was appointed a federal district judge by President Lyndon Johnson.

In the voting-rights campaigns in Mississippi during the 1960s, local women proved dynamic and fearless organizers. Many came to prominence working with SNCC and

Voting Rights Campaigns
CORE. The student-led movement's decentralized leadership structure and its advocacy of grassroots participation were especially encouraging of local women. The COFO voting-rights campaign in Mississippi in 1964 brought women into the movement in large numbers. They attended meetings in greater number than men and performed much of the voter registration work. Fannie Lou Hamer, Victoria Gray, and Annie Devine—all Mississippi women—led marches to the courthouses, led in the formation of the Mississippi Freedom Democratic Party, and ran for public office. Mothers came to the movement often as a result of their children's involvement. Women's church work and religious beliefs facilitated their participation in the movement, even when male church leaders, including ministers, refused to join in.

Several women have become icons of the movement, revered for their contributions. Next to Rosa Parks, Ella Baker and Fannie Lou Hamer are probably the most well-known

Ella Baker and Fannie Lou Hamer
female contributors to civil rights history. Their backgrounds were entirely different, and yet they both represented a style of leadership that sought to empower ordinary people. A field secretary for the NAACP in the 1940s, as well as national director of NAACP branches, the tireless Baker traveled throughout the United States, building up local memberships and urging the branches to confront forms of racial inequality in their specific locations. As Baker stated on one occasion, she did the best she could "to try to jolt or scare them [the branches] into action."

Executive secretary of the black ministerial-led Southern Christian Leadership Conference (SCLC) upon its founding in 1957, Baker helped to convene the meeting that brought into existence the Student Nonviolent Coordinating Committee in 1960. Dubbed the "political and spiritual midwife" of SNCC, she found a captive audience among the young men and women in the organization. As their mentor and guide, Baker is credited with imparting to SNCC her predilection for democratic exchange and loosely structured leadership, as opposed to the top-down, more authoritarian style she witnessed at the NAACP and the SCLC. She valued the intellect and talents of ordinary people who lacked high educational attainment and financial affluence, and she conveyed a commitment to empowering local people in grassroots movements for racial equality. Mississippi leaders such as Fannie Lou Hamer, Victoria Gray, and Annie Devine represented such local leaders, with whom SNCC would work.

Fannie Lou Hamer, a native of Sunflower County, Mississippi, went to the fields to work at age six. By twelve years of age, her formal schooling had ended. Hamer found herself at the vanguard of the civil rights movement when she went to her local courthouse to register to vote along with others who had been recruited through the efforts of SNCC and the SCLC. Threatened and arrested in Winona, Mississippi, for entering the white side of the bus terminal, Hamer was beaten viciously after the local jailers learned of her voting

Fannie Lou Hamer testifies before the Credentials Committee at the 1964 Democratic National Convention.

activities. All the women with Hamer were beaten, but she was singled out with special severity because of her reputation as a local leader. Despite threats and acts of violence against her, Hamer struggled with even greater intensity in the local movement as a field worker for SNCC, mobilizing eligible voters to register. She achieved national renown by describing the violence against her at the 1964 Democratic National Convention, when she testified before the members of the Credentials Committee as a delegate of the ultimately unseated Mississippi Freedom Democratic Party. Hamer never lost her local focus, running (although unsuccessfully) for Congress on the MFDP ticket in her district in 1965.

Local women, while joining new civil rights organizations and campaigns in the South, were not new to resisting racial inequality. Nor did they suddenly find courage to act or gain understanding of their oppression from their acquaintance with SNCC workers. Female grassroots activists were long aware of poverty, hard work, and racism, but they never accepted their subordinate and oppressed position. Sharecroppers Fannie Lou Hamer of Mississippi and Georgia Mae Turner of Tennessee, and the many others in similarly dire economic conditions, found themselves and their families evicted from the land because of their involvement in the civil rights struggles of the 1960s. They remained committed to fighting for racial equality based on a longstanding hatred of injustice.

Septima Clark exemplified a different version of longstanding commitment to the struggle. A 1916 graduate of Avery College in Charleston, she moved to Johns Island off the South Carolina coast to teach reading skills to illiterate adults and Septima Clark children who worked as sharecroppers and farmers there. The experience led her to question the disparities between schools for blacks and whites and also between the salaries of black and white teachers. Returning to Charleston, she actively supported the NAACP's effort in 1918–1919 to hire black teachers in the public schools of Charleston. She went door-to-door obtaining signatures for a petition, which ended successfully in the hiring of more black teachers. In the mid-1940s, she formed part of the successful class-action suit for the equalization of teachers' pay in South Carolina. In 1956, Clark lost her teaching job because of her membership in the NAACP. She also taught in her citizenship school, sponsored by the Highlander Folk School, and throughout the 1960s she developed citizenship schools in other cities in the South under the auspices of the SCLC after state officials in Tennessee forced Highlander to close in 1959. Clark's belief in the principles for which she fought sustained her through dark days of intimidation. This would be the case for other women in the movement.

According to scholar Charles Payne, many movement women derived strength from their religious faith, and they encouraged other women by repeating biblical messages in **Strength through Religious Faith** speeches, by singing such freedom songs as "Ain't Gonna Let Nobody Turn Me 'Round," "We Shall Overcome," "Keep Your Eyes on the Prize," and "This Little Light of Mine," as well as employing familiar symbols and strategies used in women's missionary societies. They tended to focus their appeals on other women, fully cognizant of the inspirational power of the black religious tradition. For example, Ruby Hurley, a NAACP field worker in the South in the 1950s, recalled drawing from the Bible to embolden persons who knew all too well the threat of violence. "I found using the Bible to be effective in saying to our people, 'You go to church on Sunday or you go every time the church doors are open,'" she said. "You say 'amen' before the minister even has the word out of his mouth . . . Yet you tell me you're afraid. Now

Civil rights leader Gloria Richardson practiced self-defense rather than nonviolence in militant protests in Cambridge, Maryland, 1963.

how can you be afraid and be honest when you say 'My faith look up to Thee' or when you sing that God's going to take care of you? If you don't believe it, then you are not really the Christian you say you are." Working in Greenwood, Mississippi, SNCC members headquartered there spoke of hearing Fannie Lou Hamer sing and preach in local churches about voter registration. At times the outspoken Hamer criticized the pastors of those churches for hindering the movement.

Sociologist Belinda Robnett calls such civil rights women "bridge leaders," since they functioned as the link between local community members and external organizations, such as COFO, SNCC, or the NAACP. They influenced people to work with and for them because of the relationships that they fostered in churches and in daily community service. Although women were crucial to the direct-action phase of the civil rights movement, not all women were nonviolent. Outspoken civil rights leader Gloria Richardson from Cambridge, Maryland, led a militant campaign of sit-ins in June 1963 that resulted in mass arrests, when black Marylanders including Richardson herself brandished rifles in armed self-defense in the face of white mobs. Certainly exceptional, the gun-toting Gloria Richardson was praised by black nationalist leader Malcolm X. An article on the Cambridge Movement under her leadership noted: "No one really talks seriously about practicing non-violence in Cambridge."

The Northern Side of the Movement

The March on Washington in 1963, which brought together a quarter-million civil rights advocates, provided visible proof of the many grassroots movements outside the South that helped to forge the national civil rights movement.

In significant ways, the North appeared different from the South. The steady migration of African Americans to the North (the northeastern, midwestern, and western states) and their concentration in large industrial cities gave them a new, powerful voice in political affairs. The growing political efficacy among northern black voters permitted them the ability to look to local, state, and national government for redress of racial injustice, in a way impossible for southern blacks.

In Chicago, Detroit, and other cities, blacks frequently held the balance of power in tight elections, and in some states African Americans were periodically regarded as crucial to the outcome of national elections. The northern black urban vote **Electoral Power** undoubtedly influenced the enactment of fair employment laws in New York (1945), Michigan, Minnesota, and Pennsylvania (1955), and California and Ohio (1959). In the 1950s, black elected officials began to be elected to Congress in multiple numbers. In 1954 Illinois sent black Democrat William Dawson to the House of Representatives of the United States Congress for his seventh consecutive term, and Adam Clayton Powell was returned from New York for his sixth term. When that same year Charles C. Diggs, Jr., of Detroit was elected to the House on the Democratic side, it marked the first time in the twentieth century that three African Americans sat in Congress.

By 1956 forty blacks served in state legislatures—all outside the South. The number of African Americans elected to city councils, judgeships, and boards of education, as well as holding high-level federal appointments, increased in number, leaving a record of unprecedented achievement. In 1949 William H. Hastie, with many years of distinguished public service behind him, became a judge on the Third United States Circuit Court of Appeals.

Thurgood Marshall went to the circuit court in 1961, resigning in 1965 to become Solicitor General of the United States. In 1953 J. Ernest Wilkins became assistant secretary of labor, E. Frederick Morrow became an administrative assistant in the executive offices of the president, and Scovel Richardson was appointed chairman of the United States Parole Board.

African Americans worked as secretaries and assistants in the offices of several senators and members of the House of Representatives, while others served as registrar of the Treasury, as governor of the Virgin Islands, as assistant to the director of Selective Service, and as assistant to the secretary of health, education, and welfare. African Americans had begun to make their presence felt in the nation's capital.

Yet the signs carried by the thousands who marched along the mall on that hot August day in 1963 told a very different story. From northeastern, midwestern, and western states, **Battling Discrimination** civil rights proponents of all races rode in airplanes, buses, trains, and cars to Washington. A black man from Chicago even traveled the entire way on roller skates. Northern civil rights activists traveled to D.C. to do more than lend support to the southern freedom struggle. Throughout the 1950s and 1960s, they had waged targeted campaigns, mobilizing their own local constituencies to launch boycotts, direct-action sit-ins, marches, and other forms of protest. In the 1950s, the northern civil rights movement did not confront neighborhood signs reading "For Whites Only" or laws mandating schools by race (that is, de jure segregation), or practices denying them the right to vote. They did, however, face neighborhoods and jobs that were closed to them and de facto school segregation.

Northern blacks had also begun to fight back against discrimination, and these struggles were in full swing at the time of the 1963 March on Washington. For example, in Philadelphia between 1959 and 1963 four hundred black ministers and other civil rights activists, led by Rev. Leon Sullivan, waged a series of consumer boycotts, which they called a "selective patronage" campaign, against employers with a record of racial discrimination in hiring. More than two hundred companies responded to the pressure by promising to open thousands of skilled and unskilled jobs to blacks. The many Philadelphians who came to Washington for the march in August 1963 perceived their multi-year campaign as complementary to the Birmingham campaign that same year.

Since the 1940s, moreover, Californians had been struggling against discrimination in housing, schools, and jobs. In July 1963 members of the NAACP and CORE marched together against the Torrance housing project in Los Angeles. At the time of the March on Washington, the local California NAACP was embroiled in negotiations with the Los Angeles Board of Education to develop a "pupil swap" program between predominantly black and white schools, while also pursuing legal action in the form of a lawsuit against the Pasadena school system for racial discrimination.

Days before the August 28, 1963, March on Washington, demonstrators had become so disorderly in St. Louis in their picketing of a local bank that a court injunction demanded that their protest cease. Blacks in Chicago and Boston were in the midst of school demonstrations. Boston blacks had led a successful "Stay Out For Freedom Day" in June of that year against the city's de facto segregation, in what would turn out to be a decade-long fight. In February 1964, nearly 20,000 students walked out of the Boston public schools, many of the boycotters attending freedom schools that had been set up as alternative learning sites. Like their counterparts in Boston, black Chicagoans faced ill-equipped and overcrowded schools. A month before the March on Washington, the Chicago CORE held a sit-in at the city's board of education.

Detroit's "Walk to Freedom" on June 23, 1963, offered a fascinating preview of the Washington, D.C., march. Civil rights activism began to increase in the city during the summer of 1962. Detroit's black residents suffered an unemployment rate nearly twice that of whites between 1957 and 1961, and in 1962 civil rights groups began to call upon unions to open apprenticeship programs to all, regardless of race. Having tallied up the civil rights record since the city's infamous 1943 race riot, activists found the record wanting and thus mobilized a march for June 23, 1963. The press estimated that 125,000 persons were in attendance. The main speaker, Martin Luther King, Jr., emphasized themes that he would repeat at the March on Washington two months later—the metaphor of the "dream" of racial equality and reconciliation, of the broken promise of freedom a century after Emancipation, and the ubiquitous threat to justice when injustice goes unchecked in any location. King told his applauding audience: "Work with determination to get rid of any segregation and discrimination in Detroit, realizing that injustice anywhere is a threat to justice everywhere."

In the North, no issue appeared more intractable than housing. The black ghetto, a fixture in urban America since the early twentieth century, seemingly was made permanent by the black migration of World War II and the postwar years. If **The Problem of Housing** African Americans attempted to move into neighborhoods where they were not wanted, they often met stern resistance, even extreme hostility and violence. In the postwar years, Detroit's working-class neighborhoods vowed to keep blacks out. White housewives carried their babies in one arm and in the other signs reading: "My home is my castle, I will die defending it. The Lord separated the races."

Discrimination in housing was both a private practice and a public policy. Between 1935 and 1950, 11 million homes were built. Wherever there was federal assistance, the racial policy was laid down in the manual of the Federal Housing Administration, which declared: "If a neighborhood is to retain stability it is necessary that properties shall be continued to be occupied by the same social and racial classes." That policy entrenched racial bias in housing, making it one of the most difficult tasks for government to undo.

Levittown, the postwar development of 10,000 homes for veterans on New York's Long Island, was subsidized by federal money even though it denied residence to blacks with a clause stipulating that property could not be sold nor rented nor "used or occupied by a person other than members of the Caucasian race." In New York City, the policy of excluding blacks from the Stuyvesant Town housing project aroused a controversy that stimulated the drive for legislation against discrimination in housing. In Chicago's Trumbull Park in 1954, a black family caused a near riot after moving into a federally subsidized housing project.

As whites fled from central cities to more attractive outlying urban neighborhoods or to the suburbs, African Americans found housing not on their own terms but on those arranged by owners, mortgage companies, and other groups. All too often they paid premium prices for housing that was becoming dilapidated. Racial bias persisted, although by 1962 seventeen states and fifty-six cities had passed laws or resolutions against housing discrimination. Banks, insurance companies, real estate boards, and brokers benefited from segregated housing, for which they extracted maximum profit for a minimum of expenditure. If redlining (banks' refusal to lend to blacks) and restrictive covenants failed to discourage black residents from settling in white neighborhoods, then vandalism and violence were often used. The lack of progress appeared daunting.

In 1951 black veteran Harvey Clark and his family were driven from their apartment in the Chicago suburb of Cicero when an angry mob broke windows and defaced and burned the building. Fifteen years later, black Chicagoans were still marching for open housing in Cicero. Martin Luther King, Jr., who would be brought to his knees by a rock hurled at him from an angry white mob in Chicago during a demonstration in August 1966, observed that he had never seen greater racial antipathy, not even in the South.

In northern cities African Americans were greatly embittered to discover that they were being exploited by landlords and real estate brokers who took their rent money but

In Cities: Substandard Housing and Poor Education

refused to comply with the minimum housing and health standards established by the city and the state. Just as they paid high rents for vermin-infested, deteriorating slum housing, they also received inferior education in neighborhood schools, few job opportunities, and little equality in public services.

Even worse, cities refused to enforce their own antibias housing codes. This discovery led blacks in New York City in 1963 to launch rent strikes against slumlords and in Chicago in 1966 to call for Martin Luther King's assistance in their struggle against housing discrimination. In California, the supporters of equal opportunity in housing suffered a setback in 1964 when voters overwhelmingly adopted a cleverly framed state constitutional amendment ostensibly guaranteeing a property owner the right to dispose of his property to any person he chose. Backed by the California Real Estate Association and the National Association of Real Estate Boards, the amendment was in fact meant to be a bulwark against open occupancy in housing. In 1966 the California supreme court declared the amendment unconstitutional. But the state's African Americans continued to experience difficulty in finding decent housing.

The Landmarks and Limitations of Government

The "rights revolution" that began in the postwar period and extended through the 1960s could not have occurred without the role of all three branches of the federal government. In the United States, where the guarantee of citizenship rights resides in the rule of law, the victory over segregation, disenfranchisement, and other forms of "legal" institutional racism had to be won ultimately through landmark actions in the form of presidential executive orders, congressional legislation, and judicial decisions. Not since Reconstruction had the federal government played such a direct role in mitigating racial inequality. However, the various federal civil rights landmarks achieved in the 1950s and 1960s also betrayed limitations—the failure to transcend gradual or watered-down change, to overcome circumvented and even blatant non-enforcement of new civil rights laws, and to offer only token gestures of racial progress. Governmental legitimation of blacks' rights occurred slowly—as an incremental process pushed forward at every point by grassroots activism, the members and leaders of civil rights organizations, and world opinion. For African Americans, denied the vote or equal access to housing, jobs, and education, the illusion of equality would not be sufficient.

By the 1950s, black Americans stood poised to launch persistent, uncompromising demands on the national government. Not a casualty of the Cold War in that decade, the

Civil Rights in the 1950s

civil rights movement embraced the tenets of liberal democracy in the struggle for equal rights, justice, and national citizenship—thus fully rejecting what its members called "second-class citizenship."

The fiercely anticommunist milieu of the late 1940s and early 1950s had certainly changed the configuration of civil rights groups and their ability to collaborate. The Red

Scare hysteria had caused the demise of such left-leaning organizations as the National Negro Congress and the Council on African Affairs, and it led to purges of alleged communists and "fellow-travelers" from longstanding civil rights organizations, including the NAACP and such progressive labor unions as the CIO. In the 1950s, desegregation was slowed down by invoking anticommunism against virtually all protest organizations, and especially against the southern branches of the NAACP—yet the civil rights movement was not quelled. Indeed, a new generation of activists, adopting the Cold War's rhetoric of freedom and democracy, turned their critique on the American government itself. They condemned the nation's hypocrisy in failing to live up to its democratic creed and emphasized the deleterious effects of racism on America's moral authority as leader of the Free World. In 1957 the young Baptist minister Martin Luther King, Jr., of Alabama, who little more than a year earlier had vaulted into national prominence, declared in a speech before thousands of listeners in Washington, D.C., that the abridgement of blacks' voting rights was "a tragic betrayal of the highest mandates of our democratic traditions and it is democracy turned upside down."

Government leaders were not unaware of the nation's flaws. President Harry S. Truman, under whose administration the Cold War began, conveyed a similar message in his address at the annual convention of the NAACP a decade earlier. The first president to address the civil rights organization, on June 29, 1947, Truman declared from the steps of the Lincoln Memorial to a crowd of about 10,000 NAACP members that the federal government "must show the way" in eradicating racial discrimination. In early February 1948, in a historic message to the United States Congress, Truman called for legislation that would expand and protect blacks' civil rights.

Outraging southern Democrats in Congress, Truman left no doubt as to the relationship between his civil rights and Cold War agendas. "If we wish to inspire the people of the world whose freedom is in jeopardy," he asserted, "we must correct the remaining imperfections in our practice of democracy." Both speeches were broadcast in Europe over the State Department's international radio program "Voice of America."

The growing number of black voters and civil rights proponents demanded the federal government's involvement. They sought the enactment and enforcement of civil rights laws and the laws' invocation in court cases, and they expected government protection from hostile white mobs. The national government, they believed, had for far too long failed to "show the way" by acquiescing in states-rights arguments in defense of segregation and disenfranchisement and by looking away when the perpetrators of racial violence went unpunished as all-white juries rendered "not guilty" verdicts.

Since the early 1940s, civil rights advocates had pressured and prodded the government to take the lead in advancing civil rights. Victories in the courts were discernible early on. The NAACP legal team, led first by Charles Hamilton Houston **Court Victories** and later by Thurgood Marshall, saw success in the 1940s in cases involving voting, housing, employment, and education. In the 1950s and 1960s, the sheer number of landmark civil rights decisions by the Supreme Court under its chief justice, Earl Warren, opened a new chapter in the judiciary's role in American race relations. With the passage of new civil rights laws in the 1950s and 1960s, the Warren Court (1953–1969) played a critical role in upholding their constitutionality, deciding a plethora of civil rights cases that undergird liberal equality—including cases involving school desegregation, discriminatory legislative apportionment and voting, the integration of public accommodations, and interracial marriage.

Protesters after the *Brown* decision.

The Court's landmark *Brown* decision in 1954, holding that "separate is inherently unequal," carried far-reaching implications and served as a compelling precedent in non-school-related desegregation cases. Even so, the Court's ruling in *Brown* II in May 1955, which called for "all deliberate speed" in ending school segregation, was a setback to those who demanded immediate desegregation.

The executive branch provided the first obvious and lasting achievement of the 1950s with the Truman administration's integration of the armed forces. Truman had issued the

The Executive Branch desegregating executive order in 1948, but the Korean War (1950–1953) provided the battlefield test of integration in the making. Between May and August 1951, the integration of military units in Korea jumped from 9 percent to 30 percent. A special military report declared that the integration of blacks had resulted in an overall gain for the Army. For the first time in the nation's history, black Americans had officially become an integral part of the nation's military.

President Dwight D. Eisenhower, although not as progressive on civil rights as Truman, presented a four-point proposal for civil rights, which was written and submitted by his Attorney General, Herbert Brownell. The end product was the Civil Rights Act of 1957, the first civil rights law since 1875.

Eisenhower on civil rights is perhaps best remembered for his role in facilitating the desegregation of Central High School in Little Rock, Arkansas, in 1957. Although Eisenhower fretted over the initial *Brown* decision and his choice of Earl Warren as chief justice, he asserted his federal authority over the defiant Arkansas governor Orville Faubus and sent paratroopers from the 101st Airborne to Little Rock. He also federalized the state's National Guard to assure the enrollment and attendance of the nine black students at Central High School.

Congress Drags Its Feet

Congress, and specifically the Senate with its powerful southern bloc, proved to be the most resistant branch of government. More than ninety southern members of Congress, led by Senator Walter George, vigorously denounced the *Brown* decision, and in March 1956 they presented in Congress their "Declaration of Constitutional Principles," commonly known as the "Southern Manifesto." The document condemned the desegregation decision as a usurpation of the powers of the states and encouraged the use of "every lawful means" to resist its implementation. Of the three North Carolina members of Congress who refused to sign the manifesto, two were defeated in the Democratic primary the following May.

The protective armor over the racial status quo began to crack, however. In the following year, after acrimonious debate in the Senate and pressure from civil rights advocates, Congress passed the Civil Rights Act in August 1957, and the president signed it into law in September. The new law primarily safeguarded blacks' voting rights. It authorized the federal government to bring civil suits in its own name to obtain injunctive relief in federal courts whenever anyone was denied or threatened in his or her right to vote. It elevated the civil rights section of the Department of Justice to the status of a division, headed by an assistant attorney general. It also created the United States Commission on Civil Rights, with authority to investigate allegations of denial of the right to vote, to study and collect information concerning legal developments constituting a denial of equal protection of the laws, and to appraise the laws and policies of the federal government with respect to equal protection. Despite the landmark achievement of the first civil rights act in the twentieth century, its enforcement proved far less adequate in enfranchising black southerners.

The Role of Civil Rights Advocates

It was never government action alone but rather the interaction between the government and civil rights advocates that brought about changes in the nation's legal system. Protesters demanded that the government rectify the paucity of civil rights laws and assure the actual expansion of rights on the ground. A variety of civil rights strategies created the climate in which Eisenhower, the Congress, and then-Senate majority leader Lyndon Johnson of Texas worked together to support the passage of the first civil rights statute in eighty-two years. The NAACP's 1944 victory in *Smith v. Allwright*, which outlawed the white primary in Texas, its success in *Brown* a decade later, and the subsequent voter-registration activism of civil rights organizations in the southern states had all inspired thousands of southern blacks to attempt to register to vote—some at extreme peril.

Citizenship schools, first begun by Septima Clark and Esau Jenkins at Highlander and then expanded by them to other locations, taught adult literacy for the purpose of passing

539

The Freedom Pilgrimage Rally
Roy Wilkins, the Rev. Martin Luther King, Jr., and A. Philip Randolph at the Lincoln Memorial, May 17, 1957.

the literacy tests required for voter registration and made possible the registering of many new voters in the South. Protest demonstrations, most notably the Prayer Pilgrimage for Freedom on May 17, 1957, in Washington, D.C., played a role. More than 20,000 people gathered at the Lincoln Memorial on that day to commemorate the third anniversary of the *Brown* decision and to pressure the federal enforcement of school desegregation. The prayer pilgrimage was co-chaired by A. Phillip Randolph, Roy Wilkins of the NAACP, and Martin Luther King, Jr., head of the newly founded Southern Christian Leadership Conference (SCLC). The strategists and organizers were Bayard Rustin and Ella Baker. With a gospel song by Mahalia Jackson and the final speech by King, the event gave a vivid preview of the much larger march on Washington that would occur in 1963. The press brought the event to the world's attention.

No one who heard about the meeting could deny the importance of the civil rights legislation to black Americans. King's speech focused on black voting rights. "Give us the ballot," his words rang out, "and we will no longer have to worry the federal government about our basic rights . . . we will fill our legislative halls with men of good will, and send to the sacred halls of Congress men who will not sign a Southern Manifesto, because of their devotion to the manifesto of justice . . . we will quietly and nonviolently, without rancor or bitterness, implement the Supreme Court's decision of May 17, 1954."

In addition, international pressure created pressure on the federal government. On March 8, 1957, the new nation of Ghana became the first former African colony to join the United Nations. As Congress began to debate the proposed civil rights bill in the summer of 1957, diplomatic representatives from Ghana had taken up residence at the United Nations and in Washington. The emergence of independent African nations afforded a considerable stimulus to the movement for racial equality in the United States. This important fact was not ignored by either President Eisenhower or responsible members of Congress.

The Civil Rights Acts of 1957 and 1960

Critical as well to the fight for the passage of the Civil Rights Act of 1957 was Clarence Mitchell, Jr., director of the NAACP's Washington bureau and the organization's chief lobbyist on Capitol Hill. Mitchell worked tirelessly to garner support for the bill. Born in Baltimore in 1911, Mitchell helped to secure not only the 1957 civil rights law but also all subsequent civil rights and voting rights laws passed in the 1960s. Mitchell was so effective in pressing for legislation favorable to blacks and to disadvantaged people generally that he was nicknamed the "101st senator."

The Civil Rights Act of 1957 was undeniably a first step, but in the words of one senator, "a limited and modest step." Although making possible a greater number of black voters, especially in southern cities, the civil rights legislation left disenfranchised the great proportion of southern blacks eligible to vote. In hearings held by the Commission on Civil Rights, blacks revealed that local white registrars regularly denied them the right to vote. The Department of Justice instituted suits in Alabama, Georgia, and Louisiana, charging that registrars had failed to register qualified African American voters solely because of race. Although the Supreme Court upheld the right of the Department of Justice to bring such suits, the slow case-by-case approach revealed the inadequacies of the law and the need to strengthen it. After much debate and Senate filibusters, the Civil Rights Act of 1960 was passed to do just that. Neither law was sufficiently enforced, but each prefigured greater federal involvement on issues of African Americans' civil rights.

The emergence of the nonviolent protest movement in both the North and South and the rising number of black voters, especially in the northern states due to migration in the 1940s and 1950s, made African Americans' civil rights a burning political issue—one that neither major party failed to recognize.

The Kennedy Administration

In at least six of the eight most populous states in the country, blacks held the balance of power in closely contested elections. In their campaign platforms in 1960 both major parties took strong stands for racial justice and equality. Journalist and historian Theodore H. White observed in his book *The Making of the President 1960,* on Kennedy's campaign for the presidency: "To ignore the Negro vote and Negro insistence on civil rights must be either an act of absolute folly—or one of absolute miscalculation."

While beholden, to some degree, to the black vote for his narrow, hairbreadth victory over Eisenhower's vice president Richard M. Nixon, President John F. Kennedy was in no hurry to fulfill his campaign promises on civil rights. During the campaign Kennedy had chided the Republicans for not doing more to advance the cause of African Americans. He criticized President Eisenhower for not ending discrimination in federally supported housing, which, he declared, could be done "with the stroke of a pen." Forced to be cautious by the entrenched power of southern Democratic congressional chairmen, who threatened to block his entire agenda, Kennedy felt that he had to move very slowly. Two years after his election, in November 1962, he addressed the housing issue, but housing continued to be one of the most difficult and unpopular problems to solve in both the North and South and would continue to be so, even after the Fair Housing Act became law in 1968 in the last year of Lyndon Johnson's presidential administration.

Over the course of Kennedy's presidency, he became increasingly influenced by the civil rights leadership and their agenda. By 1963 his civil rights record had improved considerably. In the last year of his presidency, which was cut short by an assassin's bullet on November 22, 1963, Kennedy made good on his promise to submit new, more comprehensive civil rights legislation. He also began to focus on the economic plight of urban blacks. In May 1963, Kennedy's council of economic advisers, led by Walter Heller, had been developing a job training plan to eradicate poverty. These efforts guided the policies of President Lyndon Johnson, who took office upon Kennedy's death, and became the basis of the Economic Opportunity Act of 1964.

Kennedy's record was impressive for his immediate appointment of blacks to high-profile federal positions. As federal judges, Kennedy appointed Thurgood Marshall to the circuit court in New York, Wade McCree to the district court for Eastern Michigan, James Parsons to the district court of Northern Illinois, and Marjorie Lawson, Joseph Waddy, and Spottswood Robinson to the federal bench in the District of Columbia. He appointed A. Leon Higginbotham, Jr., to the Federal Trade Commission and later nominated him to the district court of Pennsylvania (he would be confirmed after Kennedy's death). Robert Weaver became head of the Housing and Home Finance Agency under Kennedy; and when the agency was elevated to cabinet rank in 1965, President Johnson appointed Weaver secretary of the new Department of Housing and Urban Development, the first African American to hold a cabinet office.

President Kennedy also appointed George L. P. Weaver to be assistant secretary of labor, Carl Rowan to be deputy assistant secretary of state (and later ambassador to Finland), and Clifton R. Wharton and Mercer Cook to be ambassadors to Norway and Niger, respectively. He appointed two blacks, Merle McCurdy and Cecil F. Poole, as United States attorneys, and several others to presidential committees working in the civil rights field and to other boards and commissions, including John B. Duncan to the Board of Commissioners of the District of Columbia.

These high-level appointments represented unprecedented steps toward changing the face of the judiciary and executive administration. Yet federal employment for African Americans remained, on the whole, limited to lower-level jobs. Only in the subprofessional categories did African Americans constitute a substantial proportion (23 percent) of the federal service.

The shifting character of the Kennedy administration was evident in response to the freedom rides sponsored by CORE in May 1961. To challenge segregation laws and practices in bus terminals, the interracial direct-action group sent "freedom riders" on a route intended to stretch from Washington, D.C., to New Orleans. More than a decade had passed since the Supreme Court affirmed the constitutionality of racial equality on interstate bus travel and since CORE's journey of reconciliation in 1947 had first tested the Court's decision on southern highways. In the civil rights

The Freedom Rides, May 1961

fervor of 1961, CORE head James Famer had counted on a racist response, believing that white backlash in various locations would compel the federal government to protect the freedom riders as well as enforce the interstate transportation law. Indeed, segregationists attacked CORE's interracial teams in Anniston and Birmingham, Alabama, firebombing one of the two buses and bloodying freedom riders on both buses; one of them was beaten so badly that he suffered irreparable brain damage.

Attorney General Robert F. Kennedy, the president's brother, initially responded with annoyance at the aggressiveness of the civil rights activists and urged a cooling-off period. However, when the freedom riders were set upon by a mob in Montgomery, and a Justice Department monitor was severely beaten, he took more aggressive action. Alabama police intervened only belatedly and after the attorney general dispatched six hundred deputy marshals and other federal officers to the scene. Other groups, including the newly formed SNCC, the SCLC, and the Nashville Student Movement, rushed to join the effort, sending more than a thousand volunteers. Federal marshals escorted them to Jackson, Mississippi, where local officials arrested at least three hundred, including fifteen Catholic priests. It was then that the Interstate Commerce Commission, in response to the pressures of the freedom riders and the intervention of the attorney general, ruled on September 22, 1961, that passengers on interstate carriers would be seated without regard to race and that such carriers could not use segregated terminals.

As the direct-action phase of the movement in the South and North stepped up its scope and momentum between 1961 and 1963, with sit-ins, demonstrations, freedom rides, economic boycotts, mass marches, voter registration drives, and school-desegregation efforts, and as white violence on the part of **Freedom to the Free, 1963** racist police, mobs, and individuals also escalated, coverage of the civil rights movement appeared daily on television and in the press. The events played out dramatically in 1963, the centennial of the Emancipation Proclamation, and many leaders pointed out the lingering problem of racial inequality in American life. That year, the United States Commission on Civil Rights presented to the president a report on the history of civil rights, "Freedom to the Free," in which it declared that "a gap between our recorded aspirations and actual practices still remains." On Lincoln's birthday in February 1963, President and Mrs. Kennedy received more than a thousand black and white citizens at the White House and presented to each of them a copy of the report.

Speaking at Gettysburg that same year, Vice President Lyndon Baines Johnson said, "Until justice is blind, until education is unaware of race, until opportunity is unconcerned with the color of men's skins, emancipation will be a proclamation but not a fact." President Kennedy took note of the absence of equality when he said, "Surely, in 1963, one hundred years after emancipation, it should not be necessary for any American citizen to demonstrate in the streets for an opportunity to stop at a hotel, or eat at a lunch counter . . . on the same terms as any other American."

The tumultuous events of 1963 forced the government's hand by showing starkly the limitations of legislation and judicial decisions, once regarded as great achievements. In February, even before the demonstrations reached their peak, President Kennedy sent a special message to Congress recommending **The Civil Rights Act of 1964** legislation to strengthen voting—but by June, largely because of events in Birmingham and elsewhere, he envisioned a new and broadened civil rights agenda. Speaking to the American people via radio and television, on the same day that National Guardsmen were used to

543

secure the admission of two African Americans to the University of Alabama, the president stated, "We face . . . a moral crisis as a country and as a people. It cannot be met by repressive police action. It cannot be left to increased demonstrations in the streets. It cannot be quieted by token moves or talk. It is a time to act in the Congress, in your state and local legislative body and, above all, in all of our daily lives." Kennedy submitted his comprehensive civil rights measure to Congress. Weeks and months of acrimonious debate, parliamentary maneuvers, and delays ensued.

During the summer of 1963 the civil rights bill was stalled by bitter opposition and filibusters. Attorney General Robert F. Kennedy testified before congressional committees ten times in support of the proposed legislation. As Congress debated the civil rights bill, more than 250,000 civil rights proponents from all parts of the nation marched on Washington in August in the largest demonstration in American history up to that time. With this great "March on Washington for Jobs and Freedom," veteran labor leader A. Philip Randolph's long-postponed 1941 dream had finally come to pass. Owing to the skillful organizing work of Randolph, ably assisted by Bayard Rustin and joined by all the major civil rights groups as well as many religious, labor, and civic groups (including the American Jewish Congress, the National Conference of Catholics for Interracial Justice, the National Council of Churches, and the AFL-CIO Industrial Union Department), the gigantic demonstration grabbed the world's attention.

"I have a dream."

The Rev. Martin Luther King Jr. acknowledges the crowd at the Lincoln Memorial for his "I Have a Dream" speech during the March on Washington, D.C., on Aug. 28, 1963. The march was organized to support proposed civil rights legislation and end segregation. King founded the Southern Christian Leadership Conference in 1957, advocating nonviolent action against America's racial inequality. Awarded the Nobel Peace Prize in 1964, King was assassinated in Memphis, Tenn., in 1968.

Kennedy did not live to see the fruition of his efforts, but his vice president, Lyndon Johnson, swiftly made known his strong support of his predecessor's civil rights program. Five days after taking office, he notified Congress that he desired "the earliest possible passage of the civil rights bill." However, the bill continued to linger into the new year. The bright spot on the horizon was the ratification in January 1964 of the Twenty-fourth Amendment to the Constitution, which outlawed the poll tax in federal elections, a method used since the late nineteenth century to disfranchise blacks. With continued pressure from the president and from civil rights groups, the House of Representatives passed the civil rights bill by a substantial majority, 290 to 130, in February. Then in June the Senate voted cloture to break a civil rights filibuster, thus ensuring final passage by a vote of 73 to 27.

The Civil Rights Act of 1964, the most far-reaching law in support of racial equality ever enacted by Congress, gave the attorney general additional power to protect citizens against discrimination and segregation in voting, education, and the use of public facilities. The law established the federal Community Relations Service to help individuals and communities solve civil rights problems, created the federal Equal Employment Opportunity Commission (EEOC), and extended the life of the Commission on Civil Rights. One of the most controversial provisions required the elimination of discrimination in federally assisted programs, authorizing termination of programs or withdrawal of federal funds upon failure to comply. Finally, the U.S. Office of Education was authorized to provide technical and financial aid to assist communities in the desegregation of schools.

In many places South and North, doors of opportunity once closed to African Americans opened for the first time. However, the period following the passage of the Civil Rights Act of 1964 also witnessed strong resistance to its enforcement, and in some places considerable violence. In the North, some whites discovered their prejudices for the first time and resented direct-action protests to eliminate discrimination in their own communities. Such resentment accounts, at least in part, for the strong showing that the segregationist governor of Alabama, George Wallace, made in the 1964 presidential primaries in Wisconsin, Indiana, and Maryland. Some public places transformed themselves into private clubs, but the Supreme Court declared such actions illegal in two cases in 1964—*Heart of Atlanta Motel v. United States* and *Katzenbach* [Attorney General Nicholas Katzenbach] *v. McClung*—thus upholding the constitutionality of the public accommodations section in the Civil Rights Act. Before the end of the year, it was the segregationists' turn to be discouraged.

Yet the law also revealed a serious limitation. The weakness of its voting provision did not prevent states from circumventing it with practices that denied the right to vote to hundreds of thousands of eligible southern blacks. During the summer and fall of 1964, the Council of Federated Organizations, com-

The Voting Rights Act of 1965

posed of all the major civil rights groups, faced strong opposition in their drive to increase voter registration among blacks. Southern whites, especially in areas of large black populations, seemed more opposed to voter registration drives than to demonstrations to desegregate public accommodations. The murder of three civil rights workers in Philadelphia, Mississippi, during Freedom Summer of 1964, as well as the murder in the spring of 1965 in Selma, Alabama, of a young white minister and the infamy of Bloody Sunday, outraged the president, who more clearly than ever recognized the need for additional legislation.

In his address to Congress and the nation on March 15, 1965, President Johnson stated in eloquent words that repeated the theme song of the civil rights movement: "What happened in Selma is part of a far larger movement which reaches into every section and state of America.

Long lines of African Americans wait to register in a makeshift office in Alabama after passage of the Voting Rights Act of 1965.

It is the effort of American Negroes to secure for themselves the full blessings of American life. Their cause must be our cause, too. Because it is not just Negroes, but really it is all of us who must overcome the crippling legacy of bigotry and injustice. And we *shall* overcome." A few days later the president sent to Congress his proposal for a new voting rights law.

Congress passed the Voting Rights Act of 1965 with unusual swiftness. It authorized the attorney general to send federal examiners to register black voters when he concluded that local registrars were not doing their job. It suspended all literacy tests and other devices in states and counties that used them and where less than 50 percent of the adults had voted in 1964. The states affected were Alabama, Georgia, Louisiana, Mississippi, South Carolina, Virginia, and twenty-six counties in North Carolina, as well as Alaska and scattered counties in Arizona, Idaho, and Hawaii. In the latter states the voting rights of indigenous groups (native or Latino) had long been denied. There was opposition to the measure, and some blacks accused Attorney General Katzenbach of not sending federal examiners quickly enough. Nevertheless, by the end of the year nearly a quarter of a million new black voters had been registered, one-third by federal examiners and two-thirds by local officials. In that year blacks won seats in the Georgia legislature and in city councils of several southern cities.

The intense voter registration drives of thousands of black and white civil rights workers, the enactment and enforcement of the Voting Rights Act of 1965, and the growing awareness of African Americans of the power of the ballot created something of a black political revolution in the 1960s and 1970s in Mississippi, Alabama, Georgia, Louisiana, and South Carolina. The Voting Rights Act had the greatest impact on Mississippi, where such SNCC workers and local grassroots leaders as Fannie Lou Hamer, Amzie Moore, Annie Devine, and Aaron Henry had led **Political Revolution in the South** a valiant voter-registration drive during Freedom Summer in 1964 and mobilized black voters, denied access to the state's Democratic Party, into their own Mississippi Freedom Democratic Party. The number of black registered voters in Mississippi grew astoundingly, from 6.7 percent of all blacks in 1964 to 68 percent in 1970.

Southern blacks once again became political contenders and officeholders. Between 1964 and 1970, black elected officials in the South had risen from less than twenty-five to more than seven hundred. The presence of black elected officials was a reality at the state and national levels. In 1966 there were ninety-seven black members of state legislatures and six members of Congress; by 1973, more than two hundred blacks sat in thirty-seven state legislatures and sixteen in Congress, including one senator (Edward Brooke of Massachusetts, the only black Republican member of Congress) and four women—Shirley Chisholm of New York, Barbara Jordan of Texas, Yvonne Burke of California, and Cardiss Collins of Illinois.

Public schools in the South began finally to show signs of desegregation, since under the Civil Rights Act of 1964 the executive branch of the government gained the means of doing what the federal courts had been unable to do. Because the act barred discrimination in federally aided projects and programs, school districts receiving federal funds were required to have desegregated or else to present acceptable plans for desegregating. The Elementary and Secondary Education Act of 1965, with an appropriation of $1.3 billion, gave an added incentive to compliance. Progress could be seen within two years. In the 1965–1966 school year, in the eleven southern states of the former Confederacy, only 6 percent of the black children were attending desegregated schools. Southern states were rapidly learning how to satisfy the federal requirement and receive federal funds and at the same time preserve the old order. However, by the spring of 1967, the school desegregation process received an unanticipated boost from the United States Circuit Court, Fifth District.

In its decision in *United States v. Jefferson County*, a case arising from school systems in Alabama and Louisiana, the court declared that "the only school desegregation plan that meets constitutional standards is one that works." Shortly thereafter about forty desegregation suits were instituted, and the Department of Health, Education, and Welfare intensified its pressure on school districts. By the beginning of the 1968 school year, about 20.3 percent of the black students in the former Confederate states were in "fully integrated schools." By 1970 school systems in the South responded to the pressures applied by the courts and the public, with more than 90 percent of the school systems in the South classified as desegregated.

Called the Second Reconstruction, the years of civil rights activism and the federal government's response to it brought new hope to men and women who sought to keep faith in "Jubilee," as the ex-slaves termed freedom on the eve of the Civil War and the first Reconstruction. For those who held firm to Martin Luther King's dream that the United States would eventually live up to its professed ideals, his famous speech on the steps of the Lincoln Memorial in 1963 offered hope that Americans of all races might try again this time and be "able to transform the jangling discords of our nation into a beautiful symphony of brotherhood . . . able to work together, to pray together, to struggle together, to go to jail together, to stand up for freedom together, knowing that we will be free one day." The Civil Rights Act of 1964, the Voting Rights Act of 1965, and later legislation and court rulings provided no panacea, however.

In 1964 through 1967 (thus before the assassination of Martin Luther King, Jr.), a nightmare of riots occurred in cities across the country—in Harlem and Rochester, NY, in 1964; in the Watts section of Los Angeles in 1965; in Cleveland in 1966; and in Newark, Cincinnati, Detroit, and other cities in 1967. The "long hot summers" of riots left civil rights advocates and government leaders with the painful realization that the new legislation had failed to solve deeper, structural problems of racial inequality. Indeed the riots were proof of the law's inadequacy to rectify race-related issues of poverty and other economic problems left unaddressed by simply ending segregated public facilities. Nor did Johnson's declaration of "war on poverty," along with the creation of subsequent federally funded antipoverty programs, succeed.

A. Philip Randolph in November 1965, speaking to a conference on civil rights at the White House, posed the idea for "the creation of a vast 'freedom budget,' a nationwide plan for the abolition of the ghetto . . . even at the cost of a hundred billion dollars," but as historian Thomas Sugrue notes, the idea, after some attention by government and civil rights supporters, never took hold. A rising tide of political conservatism, economic woes, the Vietnam War, and growing sentiments of racial separatism among blacks themselves precluded any possibility of Randolph's idea. Later, Martin Luther King, Jr., would take the lead in a poor peoples' campaign, but by then the integrationist, nonviolent movement was being severely challenged if not yet eclipsed by the rising tide of black power.

Black Power

Black Power's Antecedents

Proclaiming Black Power

A Dissident Youth Culture

Black Artistic Power

Black Feminism

Social and Political Realities

"Supporters of Huey P. Newton, Outside Courthouse," July 15, 1968
On the steps of the Alameda County Courthouse in Oakland, California, members of the Black Panther Party call for the release of Huey P. Newton, who was arrested and on trial for allegedly killing an Oakland police officer in a gun battle.

549

The black power movement of the late 1960s and early 1970s formed the fourth phase of the great symphony of struggle for racial justice and equality in America—the finale of the long "movement of movements" that had begun in the 1940s with labor activism and with victories in the courtroom over de jure segregation. By the mid-1960s, black power was fast eclipsing the nonviolent, direct-action movement whose boycotts, sit-ins, and freedom songs had riveted the world's attention for a decade. Several of black power's theoreticians and many more of its advocates had once been committed participants in nonviolent direct action. Some had even been members and leaders in the NAACP, CORE, and SNCC when the fiery Malcolm X of the Nation of Islam (NOI) decried their nonviolent tactics and questioned their goal of racial integration. Depicted initially by the media as a hate-filled extremist, Malcolm X rose in stature as his black-nationalist message received a wider audience at home and abroad, particularly in Africa. His passionate advocacy of race pride and black self-determination contributed mightily to the new mindset that black power might be the answer to America's racial dilemma. Malcolm would become the touchstone of the black power movement after his death in 1965.

Between 1966 and 1975, black power dominated the public face of the African American freedom struggle, articulating a new and heightened sense of urgency and insurgency. But black power was by no means a unified movement. Its exuberant belief in racial solidarity foundered along ideological fault lines and fissures. The black-power era witnessed shifting positions on the part of its leaders and followers. Its clenched-fist symbol and its exaltation of black pride, racial self-determination, and the equivalence of civil rights with fundamental human rights expressed many different goals: racial pride and natural beauty, institutional and community control, political self-representation, black legislative caucuses, collective history, cultural "authenticity," university black studies, black theology, black capitalism, Third World internationalism, black manhood, black feminism, a separate black nation—and not least of all, revolution itself.

Black Power's Antecedents

Although Malcolm X is rightly credited for laying the groundwork for the rise of the black power movement, controversy surrounding its meaning and its implications hearkens back to the foundational period of labor civil-rights—specifically, to the proposed all-black March on Washington in 1941 for wartime jobs in the defense industries and for desegregation of the armed forces. A. Phillip Randolph's March on Washington Movement (MOWM), which mobilized in several cities and convened delegates between 1941 and 1944, is so often described as a key harbinger of the nonviolent, direct-action struggle that its all-black requirement is left understated, except to explain Randolph's abhorrence of white communists. But the nature of the discussion within the civil rights community over the MOWM's racial-exclusivist mandate is important. Debates in the era of black power certainly echo this earlier time. In the magazine *The Black Worker*, dated May 1941, Randolph roused his black readers with the words "you possess power, great power" while urging them to pressure the government at this time of "power politics."

Given his own rhetorical altercations with Marcus Garvey in the 1920s, Randolph was fully aware of the visceral response and widespread popularity among African Americans of appeals to black self-determination and self-reliance. Such appeals had a long heritage of resonance in the black

The Heritage of Appeals to Self-Reliance

community, predating Garvey with the nineteenth-century nationalists: Martin R. Delaney before the Civil War and Bishop Henry McNeal Turner at the century's close. Nor did all advocates of black self-reliance and self-determination adhere to the goal of a black nation. Separatist strategies, aiming at the formation of strong black-controlled educational and religious institutions and national professional and fraternal organizations, were considered by many African Americans in the nineteenth and twentieth centuries to be a necessary prerequisite to eventual integration into the larger American society.

Doubtless Randolph's ultimate goal was an integrated society, but this did not preclude his use of a familiar discourse of black self-empowerment. In his keynote address to the policy conference of the MOWM, held in Detroit on September 26–27, 1942, Randolph declared: "The essential value of an all-Negro movement such as the March on Washington is that it helps to create faith by Negroes in Negroes. It develops a sense of self-reliance with Negroes depending on Negroes in vital matters. It helps to break down the slave psychology and inferiority-complex in Negroes which comes and is nourished with Negroes relying on white people for direction and support." One month later, in October 1942, Randolph's friend and fellow pacifist Bayard Rustin described the MOWM as having taken a "tragic" position that "tended to 'black nationalism,'" and he feared that such a stance might be unable to discourage what he perceived during the war years to be a growing black sentiment for violent retaliation against whites. The looming stature of Randolph, coupled with his leadership of an all-black march, also provoked a response from James Farmer, like Rustin an active participant in the Fellowship of Reconciliation. In 1944, beseeching African Americans not to "alienate our much needed allies of other races," Farmer referred specifically to "black nationalism" in warning against the modern counterparts to Marcus Garvey. Indirectly, he was referring to Randolph.

Garvey's modern counterpart would, however, appear in the person of Malcolm X, who became the minister of the Nation of Islam's Mosque No. 7 in Harlem in 1954. As growing numbers of African Americans moved to dense urban areas such as Chicago, Detroit, and New York and there confronted persis- Malcolm X tent inadequate housing and unemployment, some found a sense of personal and group empowerment in the racial separation advocated by the NOI. Led by Elijah Muhammad, formerly Elijah Poole, the Black Muslims (as they were commonly called), grew from a modest beginning in the mid-1930s into a vocal and fast-growing religious sect by 1960, especially because of the electrifying presence of NOI minister Malcolm X. The most highly recognized member of the NOI was the world heavyweight boxing champion, who as a follower of Elijah Muhammad changed his name from Cassius Clay to Muhammad Ali.

The Nation of Islam's message of race pride and its black-owned businesses and self-help programs offered encouragement and some security to unemployed and disaffected blacks who felt no attachment to or confidence in white America. Accepting Elijah Muhammad's interpretation of Islam, which differed considerably from Islamic beliefs in other parts of the world, NOI members rejected all names that might imply a connection with whites and advocated total racial separation.

The NOI's ablest and most eloquent spokesperson, Malcolm X (previously Malcolm Little) learned of Elijah Muhammad and his teachings while an inmate in the Norfolk Prison Colony, a Massachusetts prison that emphasized educational programs, including reading and debating. Incarcerated for burglary, Malcolm studied history, literature, and religion, recalling later that "the ability to read awoke inside me some long dormant craving to be

Malcolm X speaking at rally.
Nation of Islam leader Malcolm X addresses a Harlem rally in May 1963.

mentally alive." After his release in 1950 and the completion of his parole in 1953, he moved to Detroit. There he lived in the household of his brother and family. In that same year Malcolm served as assistant minister in Elijah Muhammad's Temple No. 1, but he soon left Detroit, charged with the responsibility of establishing other temples, one in Boston and one in Philadelphia, in 1954. The word *temple* was changed to *mosque* after Malcolm's first visit as emissary of the NOI to the Middle East and Africa in 1959.

The most vociferous public opponent of the civil rights movement, Malcolm spoke in both a racial and a gendered rhetoric that appealed to alienated and disaffected black men. He emphasized themes of black pride and black manhood to explain his own rise upward and out from a criminal lifestyle, and he incorporated those themes in his critique of the civil rights movement. Malcolm counterposed the integrationist, nonviolent Negro revolution to the black revolution, associating the preferred usage *black* with what he believed to be a truer definition of revolution and a truer description of manhood. He talked about the American Revolution as well as contemporary independence movements in Africa and Asia, arguing that "real" revolutions were based on land and succeeded through bloodshed. For Malcolm, nonviolent resistance was both unmanly and dangerous. In his famous speech, "Message to the Grassroots," delivered in Detroit on November 10, 1963, not long after the bombing of the Birmingham Church in which four young black girls were killed, Malcolm pondered the conundrum of black men's willingness to fight violently as soldiers in the Korean War and their refusal to fight "by any means necessary" in defense of themselves, black women, and black children in the southern civil rights movement.

Malcolm saw no use in responding to white hatred with love or in attempting to place defenseless foot soldiers for justice in harm's way with expectations of touching the conscience of white racists.

Malcolm's message appeared to be radically different from that of the civil rights establishment recognizable to most Americans, white and black. He first came to public attention in July 1959 in a television documentary produced by Mike Wallace, called "The Hate That Hate Produced." Malcolm's antiwhite statements and his belittling of the nonviolent "Negro leadership" and its goal of racial integration positioned him and Martin Luther King, Jr., on opposite sides of what appeared to be an unbridgeable chasm.

In the South, however, the array of perspectives on civil rights tactics was more diverse than commonly assumed—and some of these alternative perspectives simultaneously complemented and competed with the nonviolent integrationist paradigm, thereby helping to create a receptive climate for the growth of black power.

Activism in the South

Not all civil rights activists in the 1950s and early 1960s unwaveringly followed the strictures of nonviolent resistance. Gloria Richardson in Cambridge, Maryland, the founder and leader of the Cambridge Nonviolent Action Committee (CNAC), despite her organization's name flatly refused to accept nonviolence over self-defense. Her daughter Donna Richardson was a member of SNCC, and the two organizations worked in an affiliated relationship in the Cambridge campaign in 1963 to desegregate public accommodations in the town and to protest discrimination in employment, housing, and other aspects of life.

Similar sentiments prevailed in places in the Deep South, as historian Simon Wendt discusses in regard to the Deacons of Defense and Justice, founded in 1964 in Jonesboro, Louisiana. During the heyday of the nonviolent civil rights movement, **Paramilitary Defense Units** the presence of paramilitary defense units in Louisiana, Alabama, and Mississippi call into question the image of black southerners' acceptance of nonviolence in contrast to more militant northern blacks. But the Deacons of Defense and Justice worked in cooperation with the nonviolent movement, not in opposition or as an alternative to it. In the black communities where they were located, they were esteemed as the protectors of civil rights activists, according to CORE leader and nonviolence advocate James Farmer, who referred to their guard over him during his visit to Louisiana. Members of the Deacons in Bogalusa and Jonesboro, Louisiana, as well as black defense units in other southern states, typically were military veterans. As community defenders, they carried rifles, handguns, and, in order to communicate with one another, in some cases even walkie-talkies. Deacons made their plans secretly, and their meetings often featured rituals. Giving a sense of pride to African Americans, they also provided protection as the unofficial "police system" in the black community—a necessity when civil rights groups' requests for federal protection went unmet.

In February 1965, in downtown Bogalusa, Louisiana, armed Deacons rescued two CORE field workers from an angry group of whites. The CORE workers had come to exercise legal rights assured them by the passage of the Civil Rights Act of 1964, but in this Klan-filled area the law was not being enforced. Such realities led Bogalusa Deacons president Charles Sims, a veteran and weapons specialist, to talk of the limitations and dangers of adhering too strictly to King's nonviolent philosophy: "Martin Luther King and me have never seen eye to eye. He has never been to Bogalusa. If we didn't have the Deacons here there is no telling how many killings there would have been. We stand guard here in the Negro Quarters. We are the defense team." In 1964 black military veterans organized defense teams in Tuscaloosa, Alabama, and in Holmes and Leake counties in Mississippi in order to protect civil rights activists and the churches that housed freedom rallies.

If the Deacons of Defense and Justice, as well as other defense teams in the southern states, perceived themselves as the willing protectors and facilitators of civil rights activism, Robert F. Williams of Monroe, North Carolina, exemplified the **Armed Revolution** transition from self-defense to armed revolution. As president of the Monroe branch of the NAACP, Williams simultaneously advocated nonviolent protest and the idea that "violence must be met with violence," as he recounted in his memoir *Negroes with Guns* (1962). He had come to this position after dangerous encounters with the Ku Klux Klan, including their late-night visits to his home and the threatening white crowds at NAACP protest demonstrations. Like Malcolm X, Williams adopted a rhetorical style that equated black manhood not merely with protesting racial inequality but also with protecting one's self and defenseless women and children from white mobs. In 1959, according to Williams's biographer Timothy Tyson, he decried what he termed the "emasculated men" who rejected self-defense. "Big cars, fine clothes, big houses, and college degrees," wrote Williams in the first issue of the Monroe branch NAACP newsletter *The Crusader,* "won't make a Negro a respected being called a MAN."

By 1962 Williams was living in exile in Cuba. There, he espoused a considerably more radical message, taking to the airwaves with his radio show *Radio Free Dixie* and publishing the militant anti-American newspaper *The Crusader,* which circulated in the United States. By then, Williams had become increasingly vocal in his support of black separatism and revolution.

Before 1966, when the slogan "Black Power" debuted and the Black Panther Party organized, he played an influential role in radicalizing black college students. For example, in 1962 Ohio-based, leftist Pan African students led by Donald Freeman formed the Revolutionary Action Movement (RAM), claiming inspiration from both Malcolm X and Robert Williams. By 1964 RAM had branches in California and Philadelphia, now the group's home base. Under the direction of Max Stanford in Philadelphia, RAM helped to distribute Williams's *Crusader* in the United States and, because of Stanford's ties to Williams, turned in a decidedly more revolutionary, Marxist direction. Before the end of the 1960s, Williams moved from Cuba to China, then in the throes of the extremely radical Cultural Revolution.

More than any other figure in the late 1950s and early 1960s, however, Malcolm X internationalized the African American freedom struggle, calling attention to its links to anticolonial movements abroad and attempting to forge ties with African nations. In the decade of his leadership between 1955 and 1965, his message, while changing in important ways, would shape the contours and content of the black power movement to come. This was clearly evident in the case of the Student Nonviolent Coordinating Committee (SNCC). At the time of its founding in 1960, SNCC resided firmly within King's "beloved community." Four years later, SNCC members began to show signs of change, particularly after Malcolm's break from the Nation of Islam and his efforts to internationalize the plight of black Americans.

Internationalizing the Struggle

During his first trip to the Middle East and Africa in 1959, Malcolm did not call attention to color and racial diversity in the Muslim world (as he would later), but he did emphasize (in an open letter entitled "Africa Eyes Us" in the *New York Amsterdam News* on August 22, 1959) that the African newspapers were closely following the racial situation in the United States. Stating in his letter that "everyone here [in Africa] seems aware of America's color problems," Malcolm left Africa with a sense of the growing importance of black internationalism in the context of the Cold War.

In the geopolitics of the late 1950s and early 1960s, Malcolm X was witnessing a rapidly changing world. International congresses of peoples of color during the 1950s heralded a new potential for the black American freedom struggle. Malcolm and other African Americans followed the Bandung [Indonesia] Conference of Asian and African peoples in 1955, which brought together leaders from twenty-nine nations to discuss political self-determination, national sovereignty, non-aggression, non-interference in internal affairs, and equality as it applied to colonialism, racial discrimination, religion, peace, and economic development. Although Malcolm was not present at Bandung, New York congressman Adam Clayton Powell, Jr., was there and offered a surprisingly optimistic view of race relations in the United States.

Bandung 1955

From exile in Paris, Richard Wright also attended the Bandung Conference, as did Kwame Nkrumah, the future prime minister of Ghana. (At the time, that country was still under British rule and was known as the Gold Coast Colony.) Interestingly, Richard Wright's book *Black Power* (1954) chronicled his journey to what would become Ghana and its potential empowerment once free of European rule. In another book, *The Color Curtain* (1956), Wright captured his experiences, events, and interviews at the Bandung meeting. Confessing an initial caution as to Bandung's meaning, Wright recognized a shared sense of experience and sensibility among the representatives present: "The despised, the insulted, the hurt, the dispossessed—in short, the underdogs of the human race were meeting. Here were class and racial and religious consciousness on a global scale. . . . And what had these nations in common? Nothing, it seemed to me, but what their past relationship to the Western world had made them feel. This meeting of the rejected was in itself a kind of judgment upon the Western world!" Later in the book Wright spoke of a growing sense within of a "deep and organic relation here in Bandung between race and religion." Such ideas would have likely underscored the Bandung Conference's importance to Malcolm.

In 1957, when Ghana became independent, African, West Indian, and African American leaders were present at the ceremonies. Among Americans invited by Nkrumah, the new nation's leader, were Adam Clayton Powell, Jr., Martin Luther King, Jr., and A. Phillip Randolph. Nkrumah heralded the emergence of a new African, proclaiming that "the black man is capable of managing his own affairs." The times themselves seemed to validate the "Dark World," the term Malcolm used for peoples of color in the 1950s. Malcolm would later come to realize that black nationalism, even if it did not take the form of achieving an actual territorial base, could achieve its goal in a psychological, cultural, and spiritual form and therefore be equally capable of forging a common destiny.

Malcolm and the Dark World

According to Louis DaCaro's study of the religious and international aspects of Malcolm's thought, Malcolm's Garveyite heritage shaped his interest in Africa. Malcolm's father had been a follower of Marcus Garvey, and that family heritage inspired him to speak at Harlem-based Garvey Day celebrations. More important, it caused him to emphasize that black Americans were an African people, unlike Elijah Muhammad's claim that blacks constituted an "Asiatic" race. In the context of Cold War politics between 1955 and 1965, Malcolm stressed both a kinship and a strategic relationship between black Americans and other peoples of color. In a sermon in his Harlem Mosque No. 7 on January 31, 1956, he declared that "we affect both foreign and domestic policy," and for that reason "we become the yardstick by which all nations of earth can measure the real attitude of the white public here in America, as well as the attitude of her president."

In 1964 Malcolm made two trips to Africa. In the first, made after his Hajj (Islamic pilgrimage) to Mecca at the end of April, he traveled to Egypt and other places in the Muslim world. In July he returned to Africa for an extended trip, lasting until November, during which he met African political and religious leaders. He attended the meeting of the Organization of African Unity (OAU), held in Cairo from July 17 to 21, where he listened to the opening speech of Egypt's president Gamal Abdel Nasser, praising the passage of the Civil Rights Act of 1964. The OAU, founded in 1963 to foster accord and solidarity among independent African nations, served as the model for Malcolm X's own Organization of African American Unity (OAAU), which he established as a nonreligious group in June, only a few weeks before his trip and after he broke from Elijah Muhammad and the Nation of Islam. As he traveled through Africa, Malcolm's changed appearance also distinguished him and his new secular movement from Elijah Muhammad. He no longer appeared clean-shaven and close-cropped, but instead was bearded and wore his hair longer.

His appeals to the broader African American community and to African American leaders recalled the large rallies and relief efforts of the Council on African Affairs in the 1940s and early 1950s. Not since then had anyone but Malcolm internationalized the African American freedom struggle in such a public way. Having received observer status at the OAU meeting, Malcolm not only was able to represent his own organization, the OAAU, but he also submitted to the attendees an eight-page memorandum in the hope that the independent African

Window in Time

Malcolm X Appeals to African Heads of States

The Organization of Afro-American Unity, in cooperation with a coalition of other Negro leaders and organizations, has decided to elevate our freedom struggle above the domestic level of civil rights. We intend to "internationalize" it by placing it at the level of human rights. Our freedom struggle for human dignity is no longer confined to the domestic jurisdiction of the United States government. We beseech the independent African states to help us bring our problem before the United Nations, on the grounds that the United States government is morally incapable of protecting the lives and the property of 22 million African Americans. And on the grounds that our deteriorating plight is definitely becoming a threat to world peace. . . . In the interests of world peace and security, we beseech the heads of the independent African states to recommend an immediate investigation into our problem by the United Nations Commission on Human Rights. If this humble plea that I am voicing at this conference is not properly worded, then let our elder brothers, who know the legal language, come to our aid and word our plea in the proper language necessary for it to be heard.

"Appeal to African Heads of States," excerpt from memorandum in *Malcolm X Speaks: Selected Speeches and Statements*, edited by George Breitman (New York: Grove Press, Inc. 1965), pp. 76–77.

countries would bring before the United Nations the violation of African Americans' human rights. His efforts repeated that of civil rights organizations the National Negro Congress in 1946 and the NAACP in 1947 to place human rights petitions before the UN.

Aware of the earlier failure by African Americans to win consideration by the United Nations, he appealed directly to African nations to raise the issue. Malcolm X looked to African leaders, who at the time were expressing growing concern over events in the Congo, particularly since the assassination in 1961 of that country's first prime minister, Patrice Lumumba. Malcolm also argued that for alienated and frustrated younger blacks the days of nonviolence were over. The possibility of "race war" loomed in America, he suggested, thus making it all the more imperative to address the human rights issue in relation to world peace. Last, Malcolm sought aid from Africans by linking their concerns with the African American cause, perceiving a reciprocal relationship. "Your problems will never be solved," Malcolm's memorandum declared, "until ours are solved."

On January 2, 1965, the *The New York Times* featured an article, "Malcolm X Cites Role in UN Fight," describing how he was taking credit for comments made by Africans in a recent UN dialogue on the Congo. The article noted that spokesmen from some of the African nations criticized the United States on the floor of the UN for its lack of concern for the rights of black Americans, citing specifically the civil rights struggle in Mississippi. "The African move," the *Times* wrote, "profoundly disturbed the American authorities, who gave the impression that they had been caught off guard."

Malcolm X returned from his trip to Africa having internationalized the black freedom struggle, while also rethinking and revising his earlier ideas about race. He confessed to a shift in his opinion of whites after having seen and met many white Muslims in his trip to the Middle East and Africa. He no longer thought of them all as "white devils" and racists. But he would not live to fully develop or even put into programmatic form the practical meaning of his transformed views of white people, his vision for the newly formed OAAU, the long-term implications of his separation from the Nation of Islam, or the implications of cooperating with such groups as SNCC and other grassroots civil rights activists.

On February 21, 1965, Malcolm was gunned down by a black assassin in the Audubon Ballroom in Harlem as he prepared to speak. His tragically truncated career accounts, in part, for why a multiplicity of his positions co-existed under the black power banner. A variety of groups—from the Republic of New Africa, which sought a separate black nation-state, to the Black Panther Party, which identified with Third World movements and violent revolution—all claimed to be Malcolm's ideological heirs. In various forms, his ideas lived on, serving as landmarks along the many paths to black power.

The Assassination of Malcolm X

Proclaiming Black Power

Emotions ran high on that fateful day in Greenwood, Mississippi, in June 1966, when at a freedom rally Stokely Carmichael cried out the words "black power!" Exactly what he meant by those words—and what his audience understood them to mean—are not clear. He intended no call to arms on that day, but few missed the slogan's profound resonance in calling for a new mindset and a more militant articulation of the civil rights movement.

Hundreds of marchers had quickly gathered that day with dual feelings of courage and indignation, intending to show the white South that they would walk in the footsteps of James Meredith. In 1962, Meredith had integrated the University of Mississippi despite riotous white mobs, and now, four years later on June 6, 1966, he had been shot and wounded on the second day of his one-man March against Fear from Memphis to Jackson, Mississippi. Under the scorching sun, new marchers walked fearlessly along Mississippi's Highway 51, guided by leaders of the major civil rights organizations: Dr. Martin Luther King, Jr., of the Southern Christian Leadership Conference (SCLC); Floyd McKissick of the Congress of Racial Equality (CORE); and Carmichael of the Student Nonviolent Coordinating Committee (SNCC).

Taunted and shoved by racist state troopers, the men and women on the Meredith March, as it was now called, faced gun-toting bands of white men hurling at them both racial slurs and rocks. On June 16, while King temporarily went back to Chicago, Carmichael was arrested in Greenwood, Mississippi, on charges of trespassing. A 1964 Howard University graduate, the young and energetic Carmichael was no novice to community organizing. He had been actively involved in such work, even previously in Greenwood, for the Student Nonviolent Coordinated Committee since 1960.

Released from police custody after several hours, Carmichael went to the marchers' campsite fired up with renewed determination. "This is the twenty-seventh time that I've been arrested," Carmichael declared, and asserted that he would not go to jail again. His arrest underscored an idea that he and others in SNCC had already begun to contemplate. Carmichael spoke in language readily understandable to his local black Mississippi audience: "The only way we gonna stop them white men from whuppin' us is to take over. What we gonna start sayin' now is Black

Stokely Carmichael Makes History

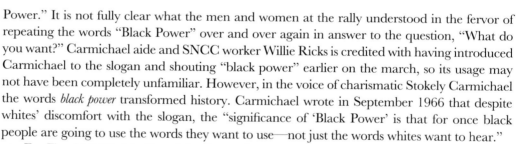

Window in Time

Stokely Carmichael on Black Power

The concept of "black power" is not a recent or isolated phenomenon: It has grown out of the ferment of agitation and activity by different people and organizations in many communities over the years. Our last year of work in Alabama added a new concrete possibility. In Lowndes County, for example, black power will mean that if a Negro is elected sheriff, he can end police brutality. If a black man is elected tax assessor, he can collect and channel funds for the building of better roads and schools serving black people—thus advancing the move from political power into the economic arena. In such areas as Lowndes, where black men have a majority, they will attempt to use it to exercise control. This is what they seek: control.

Stokely Carmichael, "What We Want," *The New York Review of Books,* September 22, 1966.

Power." It is not fully clear what the men and women at the rally understood in the fervor of repeating the words "Black Power" over and over again in answer to the question, "What do you want?" Carmichael aide and SNCC worker Willie Ricks is credited with having introduced Carmichael to the slogan and shouting "black power" earlier on the march, so its usage may not have been completely unfamiliar. However, in the voice of charismatic Stokely Carmichael the words *black power* transformed history. Carmichael wrote in September 1966 that despite whites' discomfort with the slogan, the "significance of 'Black Power' is that for once black people are going to use the words they want to use—not just the words whites want to hear."

For Floyd McKissick, Carmichael's words turned 1966 into the "year we left our imposed status of Negroes and became Black Men." McKissick had replaced James Farmer as head of CORE in January 1966, and under his leadership the longtime racially integrated, nonviolent civil rights organization entered into a new phase of uncompromising advocacy of black power. SNCC, too, was changing. By the end of the year, both CORE and SNCC expelled their white members. By choosing as its chairman Stokely Carmichael over John Lewis, SNCC reflected its new militancy. Also telling was SNCC's recent work in Lowndes County, Alabama, which had resulted in forming an all-black political party, the Lowndes County Freedom Organization. It advocated self-defense and adopted as its symbol the image of a black panther.

Although Carmichael's concept of black power did not rule out separatism in some aspects of black life and development, its major purpose was to enhance black people's ability to interact and integrate, if they desired, with white people—but from a position of social, economic, and psychological independence from whites. Like Malcolm X, Carmichael emphasized blacks' self-worth, self-love, and self-respect, as well as their control of black institutions and communities. The book *Black Power: the Politics of Liberation in America* (1967), co-authored by Carmichael and the black political scientist Charles V. Hamilton, then at Roosevelt University in Chicago, was hardly a revolutionary manifesto. Although it mentioned a "major reorientation", the "total revamping" of American society, and black power's liberating potential to end the "political colonialism" of African Americans, the book by Carmichael and Hamilton presented race-conscious, but certainly not radical, goals: unified electoral activity, community-owned businesses, community-controlled schools and school boards, and concerted efforts to advance housing and employment in black communities.

After a short but unworkable membership (and, indeed, titular leadership) in the California-based Black Panther Party in 1968, Stokely Carmichael became increasingly disenchanted with the course of the black freedom struggle in the United States. Having changed his name to Kwame Touré (blended from Kwame Nkrumah of Ghana and Sekou Touré, the new leader of Guinea, a former French colony), he moved to Conakry, Guinea's capital. There, until his death in 1998, he continued to advocate and work toward pan-Africanism.

Stokely's words struck like lightening. The slogan "Black Power" seemed to appear everywhere. Indeed Martin Luther King, Jr., must have been sorely dismayed to see it proclaimed by Christian clerics. "The Statement by the National Committee of Negro Churchmen" appeared as a full-page endorsement of black power in *The New York Times* on July 31, 1966, asserting, "The fundamental distortion facing us in the controversy about 'black power' is rooted in a gross imbalance of power and conscience between Negroes and white Americans." Theologian James Cone published his widely read book *Black Theology and Black Power* (1967), and in his sermons at his Detroit church Shrine of the Black Madonna and in his book *The Black Messiah* (1968), Rev. Albert Cleage described Jesus as not only a black man but also a revolutionary.

Stokely Carmichael speaks at a rally.

Perhaps even more stunning, as historian Rhonda Williams discloses, were the black power statements of the Roman Catholic nuns Sister Mary Paraclete Young in Baltimore and Sister Mary Roger Thibodeaux in Philadelphia. In her book, *A Black Nun Looks at Black Power* (1972), Sister Thibodeaux wrote: "Black Power is not foreign to Yahweh and Yahweh is not foreign to Black Power. There is a covenant of friendship there. The cause of Justice is and always will be in strict accordance with the Will of God."

Urban California became a seedbed of black power and of black-nationalist thought and activism. The Black Panther Party of Self Defense was founded in Oakland in 1966, taking its name and its logo from the Lowndes County (Alabama) **The Black Panther Party** organization. The Black Panthers gained national attention in spring 1967 when members of the Oakland chapter descended on the state capitol carrying guns and wearing black leather jackets and black berets to protest a gun bill under consideration by the state legislature. The group's notoriety heightened after the conviction of Huey P. Newton, the BPP's cofounder and Minister of Defense, for manslaughter in the death of an Oakland policeman. BPP chapters emerged in cities throughout the nation and the organization raised its visibility by conducting "Free Huey" campaigns. The Panthers stayed in the spotlight after the BPP Minister of Information, Eldridge Cleaver, an ex-convict turned revolutionary, published his best-selling memoir *Soul on Ice* (1968). According to historian Peniel Joseph, the BPP dropped "Self Defense" from its title in 1968 and proclaimed itself the socialist "vanguard" of the black revolution.

In its "Ten-Point Program: What We Want/What We Believe" the BPP published its list of goals. Some were realistic and others overreaching: black control of the black community; full employment for black people; reparations; decent housing; education; exemption of black men from the military draft; ending police brutality; releasing all black people from prison; fair and impartial trials with peer group juries drawn from the black community; and a sweeping demand for bread, housing, education, justice, and peace. The Panthers' tenth point, identified as their "major political objective, a United Nations-supervised plebiscite to be held throughout the black colony in which only black colonial subjects will be allowed to participate for the purpose of determining the will of black people as to their national destiny." In seeking the international organization's intervention, it is not evident that BPP leaders were in communication with the United Nations, as other black leaders had been in the past, nor is their thinking clear as to the exact form such a plebiscite should take.

The leaders of the Black Panther Party, however, were certainly defining black Americans as an oppressed and exploited colonial population. Their "Ten-Point Program" ended with excerpts from the Declaration of Independence, conceivably to emphasize African Americans' colonial subjugation to the United States as a whole. Panther leaders mined and quoted heavily from the writings of anticolonial revolutionaries: Mao Zedong, China's leader and the initiator of the Cultural Revolution; Che Guevara, the Argentine-born hero of the Cuban Revolution and of revolutionary struggles throughout Latin America; Frantz Fanon, the black psychiatrist born in Martinique and author of *Wretched of the Earth* (1963), which glorified the Algerian Revolution; and Vietnam's embattled revolutionary leader Ho Chi Minh. They patrolled black neighborhoods, followed police officers, and monitored arrests or other police encounters with black residents, while reading from the state penal code as to citizens' rights. The BPP also projected a "soft power" dimension. In communities where its chapters existed, the party was known for its free breakfast programs and community service activities, often run by women members.

The Black Panther Party, like other black power organizations, shared the belief that American racism targeted black manhood for destruction. In an interview with Newton in 1968 by whites in the Students for a Democratic Society (SDS), entitled "Huey Newton Talks to the Movement," he asserted that during slavery times the slave man "always wanted to be able to decide, to gain respect from his woman. Because women want one who can control." Thus he urged the contemporary black man to "recapture his mind." In language that captured the manhood-focus rampant in black power thought, Newton continued: "The black woman found it difficult to respect the black man because he didn't even define himself as a man!" More cynically, in his *Soul on Ice* Eldridge Cleaver referred to black women as "the silent ally, indirectly but effectively, of the white man."

Few black men questioned the male-centered culture of black nationalism. A notable exception was Vincent G. Harding, a civil rights activist and speechwriter for Martin Luther King, Jr., who in 1969 became the head of the Atlanta research center Institute of the Black World. In 1968, Harding had pointedly queried: "Does manhood indeed depend upon the capacity to defend one's life? Is this American shibboleth really the source of freedom for

Huey P. Newton, founder of the Black Panther Party, pictured at party headquarters in San Francisco.

men? Is it possible that a man simply becomes a slave to another man's initiative when he feels obliged to answer his opponent on the opponent's terms?"

In their nationally circulated newspaper the *Black Panther*, such leaders of the BPP as Newton, Cleaver, and Bobby Seale regularly condemned police brutality, alerted readers to Panther activities, covered national and international events, delineated theoretical positions on the black revolution, mentioned their alliance with "white mother-country radicals," and denounced capitalism, middle-class blacks, civil rights organizations, and not least of all other black nationalist organizations. In their brash and profane rhetoric, the police were "pigs" and the American nation was "Babylon." The most militant of black power organizations, the BPP, with its penchant for lauding violence and its stinging chants (such as "the revolution has come, it's time to pick up the gun") aroused frantic cries for "law and order" from citizens, who feared not only the BPP but a far more extensive unraveling of society.

The FBI took seriously the Panthers' threats and expanded its Counter Intelligence Program (COINTELPRO), which had targeted perceived communists and subversives (including Martin Luther King, Jr., and Malcolm X). FBI Director J. Edgar Hoover labeled the Black Panther Party "the single greatest threat to the internal security" of the United States. Historian Peniel Joseph notes that COINTELPRO would conduct 360 operations, many of them "marked by unprecedented abuses of federal power that featured the systematic, illegal harassment, imprisonment, and at times, death of black militants."

Today, declassified FBI papers confirm irregular practices by the Bureau and other law enforcement officials. Most egregious was the killing of Chicago Black Panther leader Fred

Hampton, along with Mark Clark, in the early morning darkness of December 4, 1969. Hampton's leadership was distinctive for seeking to build what later would be called a "rainbow coalition" in Chicago, uniting Hispanics and blacks in a common struggle against the urban problems of housing discrimination, unemployment, and police abuse, as well as illegal drug use, prostitution, and crime.

By 1980 the Black Panthers were scarcely even a shadow of what they once had been. Huey Newton had become more of a writer than an activist, while Bobby Seale and several other leaders involved themselves in traditional political activity. Meanwhile Eldridge Cleaver, who had returned from exile in Algeria to stand trial on old charges, became a born-again Christian evangelist and a political conservative, drawing considerable sympathy from his former adversaries.

Black power ideologues also warred with one another. The Black Panthers's revolutionary nationalism clashed with cultural nationalism, which also emphasized blacks' need

Revolutionary Nationalism versus Cultural Nationalism

for a psychological transformation—but not in the direction of a Marxist revolution. In Los Angeles, Maulana Karenga (formerly Ronald Everett) and his organization US ("us" as opposed to "them") were most representative of cultural nationalism. Karenga sought to re-create an African heritage that would promote an alternative value system to that of white America. US members adopted African names, learned Swahili, practiced African rituals, wore African clothing, and promoted a gender hierarchy subordinating women to men. The most prominent member of US was writer LeRoi Jones, who after joining in 1967 changed his name to Amiri Baraka. (He later abandoned the cultural nationalist agenda of Karenga's US and adopted Third World Marxism.) The cultural nationalists' focus on the African heritage of black people was deemed reactionary by the Panthers, who dismissed their ideology as 'pork chop' nationalism." The contentious relationship between the Panthers and US culminated in a fatal shootout on the UCLA campus in 1969, leaving two Panthers dead. US began to decline after this incident, although Karenga is remembered for the creation of Kwanzaa, the alternative late-December holiday, which was promoted widely in the black community and continues to be celebrated in churches, community centers, schools, and homes.

The popularity of black cultural expression in the late 1960s to mid-1970s took on a gamut of forms, not limited to the US movement or even to self-proclaimed black nationalists. Advocates of a distinct black cultural expression emphasized the appreciation of black history, music, literary arts, African languages, clothing, hairstyles, and Afrocentric holidays.

Probably the most popular and recognizable blend of muscular manhood and the gritty defiance of black power is Muhammad Ali, born January 17, 1942. He announced his

Muhammad Ali

change of name from Cassius Clay to Muhammad Ali after defeating the world heavyweight champion Sonny Liston in February 1964. Only twenty-two years old, Ali at the same time announced his membership in the Nation of Islam. He was often seen in the company of Malcolm X and soon was receiving the brunt of white journalists' contempt, many of whom initially refused to call him by his new name. Always popular in the black community, he gained a following among white students in the anti-Vietnam War movement. Just the opposite of the patriotic Joe Louis during World War II, Ali refused to be drafted into the United States Army on religious grounds, arguing that military service was incompatible with his membership in the Nation of Islam.

Convicted in 1967 of violating the Selective Service Act, he was barred from the ring and stripped of his crown, unable to fight but free on bond for over three years. He appealed his case and in 1971, the United States Supreme Court reversed his conviction. On October 30, 1974, Muhammad Ali regained the championship title. Like Ali, in the late 1960s many other African American athletes, both professional and amateur, began using their prestige and publicity to challenge discrimination in American sports and to protest against including racist South Africa in the Olympic Games and other international competitions.

A Dissident Youth Culture

Three significant trends in the higher education of African Americans became noticeable in the second half of the twentieth century, bearing consequences for the growing black presence in academia as well as for the expression of black power.

First, the number of blacks in predominantly white colleges and universities grew dramatically in the 1970s. Before World War II, it was most unusual to see more than a dozen or so African Americans in white schools, and most of them were in the North. During the 1960s the numbers increased steadily, and by 1970 some 378,000 African Americans attended institutions of higher education that were not predominantly black. By 1984 there were 993,574 black students in higher education, but of that number only 267,000 now attended historically black institutions. Despite the shifting proportion of students toward predominantly white schools, the graduation rate appeared to be higher in the historically black colleges and universities, which produced more than half of all the bachelor's degrees received by African Americans.

In the late 1960s, the introduction into the university curriculum of Black Studies programs (variously also called Africana, Afro-American, and African American Studies) became the academic manifestation of black power. At both white and black universities throughout the nation, African American students sought to diversify the curriculum "by any means necessary." They perceived their activism as more Malcolm's than Martin's legacy, but they also formed part of the larger student movement, spanning all races, that exploded on campuses in the late 1960s. Black students at the decade's end belonged to the same generation of activists who joined Students for a Democratic Society (SDS) and otherwise constituted the wide ideological constellation called the New Left, produced free-speech manifestoes, occasionally burned draft cards, frequently demonstrated against ROTC and the Vietnam War, and mobilized under

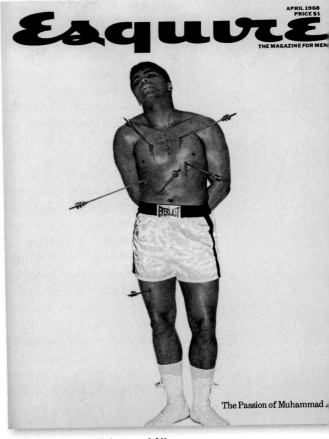

The passion of Muhammad Ali
Muhammad Ali's refusal, on religious grounds, to serve in the U.S. armed forces and his opposition to the Vietnam War resulted in the loss of his title as world heavyweight champion.

such slogans as "Make Love, Not War," "The Streets Belong to the People," and "Hell No, We Won't Go!"

As 1968 began, tens of thousands of students, white and black, poured out of campuses across the nation to demonstrate, take over school buildings, and hold sit-ins and strikes against the Vietnam War and racism. One dramatic and tragic moment in this struggle was the "Orangeburg Massacre," which occurred at all-black South Carolina State University in Orangeburg, South Carolina. The trouble began on February 6, when several hundred of the students began protesting against the town's "whites-only" bowling alley, and two black women student protestors were clubbed in a scuffle with the local police. Then, on February 8, as students gathered around an evening bonfire on the campus, state police shot into the group, killing three students, seriously wounding others, and making arrests, including SNCC activist Cleveland Sellers. The story went virtually unnoticed by the press, and the details came to public attention in 2007 only through the documentary *Scarred Justice: The Orangeburg Massacre 1968*. Such silence was unlike what subsequently happened in the Kent State tragedy in early May 1970, when American television viewers saw video footage of the Ohio National Guard opening fire on an antiwar demonstration at predominantly white Kent State University, killing four students and wounding several more. Some of the victims had been on their way to class rather than protesting. Many who saw the Kent State shootings on televisions were horrified, but polls revealed that the majority of the American public blamed the antiwar students and thought the national guardsmen justified.

Campus Activism

It was in this larger context—campus upheaval, a counter-culture broadly associated with "hippies," and urban riots—that black students dared to challenge the academic establishment and to make their bold demands. They called for courses in black history, literature, and other aspects of the black experience; for the recruitment and hiring of black faculty and staff; and for a "relevant" education that would advance black communities. Historian Martha Biondi writes of this movement: "Influenced by the black nationalist idea that previous generations of college-educated 'Negroes' had sold out their people for the perks of integration, these young men and women set out to remake the black collegiate experience. They envisioned college not only as a route to individual upward mobility but also as a place to acquire useful skills they could 'bring back' to the black community."

The number of African American professors at white colleges and universities steadily increased, partly because of the growing demand for teachers of black studies and partly because of the demand for black teachers and administrators at institutions with increasing enrollments of black students. Another contributing factor was the requirement in the 1970s by the Department of Health, Education, and Welfare (as it was then called) that institutions have affirmative action programs in connection with their hiring practices. By the early 1970s, many colleges and universities were actively recruiting African American professors in an effort to conform to equal opportunity hiring guidelines established by the federal government after the enactment of the Civil Rights Act of 1964. At predominantly white universities, by the mid 1970s more often than not black professors were recruited for courses with black subject matter, but the number of black professors with tenure remained relatively small.

The number of black administrators in higher educa-tion increased markedly. In 1945, many black colleges (such as Fisk, Tougaloo, Virginia Union, St. Augustine's, and Tal-ladega) had white presidents. Twenty years later there were no white presidents at any black colleges. Meanwhile, black presidents, vice presidents, deans, and other administrative officials increased in predominantly white colleges. In 1970, when he assumed his duties at Michigan State University, Clif-ton Wharton became the first African American president of a major white institution. Eight years later, he became chancellor of the largest institution of higher education in the nation, the ninety-campus State University of New York. In 1976 Mary Frances Berry became chancellor of the University of Colo-rado, before going to Washington, D.C., the following year to become assistant secretary for education in the Department of Health, Education, and Welfare.

Other than the clenched fist, no other image more vividly symbolized the black-power era than the Afro hair-style. Nina Simone was a highly sought after performer on college campuses in her African clothes or in more mili-tant attire with her hair coiffed in an Afro. Her popular song "To Be Young, Gifted, and Black" became the anthem of the movement. Simone dedicated the song to the memory her friend, playwright Lorraine Hansberry, who had died in 1965. Not all but certainly most older black Americans were embarrassed by and disdainful of the turn to natural hair. Scholars such as Noliwe Rooks and Maxine Leeds Craig stress the gender dimension involved in making the political statement inherent in the new hairstyle. They observe that although black men in the movement had begun to wear their hair a few inches longer (as was common among white male students in the 1960s), black women made a far more radical decision by cut-ting their hair and going natural, since for women the beauty standard valued just the opposite look—straightened hair.

Op-ed articles in black magazines described black women with the Afro look as appearing masculine and unkempt. The dean at historically black Howard University refused his traditional role of crowning the homecoming queen in 1968 simply because she wore an Afro. Former Black Panther Assata Shakur and many young black women described the hair-style shift as a political statement—their literal engagement in the black freedom struggle. As Shakur explained in her autobiography, "Our desire to be free has got to manifest itself in everything we do. . . . Maybe in another time, when everyone is equal and free, it won't matter how anybody wears their hair or dresses or looks." The new styles that defied assimilation and traditional values also invited a burgeoning market-driven commodity—Afro picks, Afro-sheens, Afro-wigs, African head wraps, African

African American vocalist Nina Simone (1933–2003)

The Afro

beads, dashikis, and other such "niche market" products. Black power was a slogan, a movement, and now a commodity.

Black Artistic Power

In 1968, black literary critic Larry Neal described the Black Arts Movement as the aesthetic expression of black power—its "spiritual sister." The decade represented a remarkable time of artistic ferment, because of the profusion in community-based cultural production, the proliferation of existing and new literary magazines and intellectual journals (*Liberator, Umbra, Soulbook, Negro Digest/Black World, Freedomways, Black Scholar, Black Dialogue, Jet,* and *Ebony*), as well as the rise of new intellectual perspectives on black art. Black theater came into its own. In New York there was Barbara Ann Teer's National Black Theatre, along with the New Lafayette Theatre with Bob Macbeth as executive director and Ed Bullins as writer in residence. Newark had Amiri Baraka's Spirit House Movers; Chicago, the Organization of Black American Culture (OBAC) and Val Grey Ward's Kuumba Theatre Company; and New Orleans, BLKARTSOUTH led by Tom Dent and Kalamu ya Salaam.

As early as 1960, a black-nationalist literary circle in New York, On Guard for Freedom, prefigured the idea of artists as political activists. On Guard members joined other activists **Political Activists** in protest in front of the United Nations in support of causes involving Africa and Cuba. In 1962 New York literary and visual artists and musicians formed the Umbra Workshop. According to poet and literary scholar Kalamu ya Salaam, the group's magazine *Umbra* represented a distinct race-conscious perspective that departed from the white literary establishment. Focused primarily on poetry and performance, Umbra members were divided, however, over the question of art for art's sake. They argued as to whether art could—or should—be an agent of social change.

Yet another New York literary group was the Harlem Writers Guild, including John Oliver Killens, Maya Angelou, and other prose writers. Killens, born in 1916, exemplified the shifting stance of older, established black writers away from the traditional nonviolent civil rights model. In the 1950s, Killens had been active in the Brooklyn branch of the NAACP and even supported fundraisers for the organization. In the 1960s, however, he became disillusioned with nonviolence, believing that before extending love to white racists, blacks first had to love and respect themselves. In the July 2, 1966, issue of the mainstream, white-oriented magazine *The Saturday Evening Post,* he published an article entitled "Speaking Out: Negroes Have a Right to Fight Back," explicitly endorsing black power and Malcolm X. Killens voiced skepticism that nonviolent protest could bring about change, arguing that "moral suasion alone has never brought about a revolution."

Baraka represented the younger, more militant generation. Under his original name of LeRoi Jones, he won critical acclaim for his 1963 book of music criticism *Blues People* and in 1964 received the prestigious Obie Award for his play *Dutchman.* But in 1965—when he was barely thirty years old and already a respected artist—Malcolm X's assassination brought him to a turning point. Jones abandoned the beat culture, moved from Manhattan's Greenwich Village to Harlem, and established the Black Arts Repertory Theater. (He would soon move on to Newark to establish his home and political base and change his name to Amiri Baraka.) Radicalized in 1965, still under the name LeRoi Jones, Baraka wrote the poem

"Black Art" with its disturbing verses, "We want poems that kill . . . wrestle cops into alleys/ and take their weapons leaving them dead." In response, white critics pilloried him with negative responses. For example, in his essay "New Styles in 'Leftism,'" the famous white literary and social critic Irving Howe—also a prominent leftist back in the 1930s—disparagingly dubbed Baraka a "pop art guerilla warrior."

More than taking a position on black power or violence, ideologues of the Black Arts Movement—Baraka, Larry Neal, Addison Gayle, and others—linked politics and art in such a way as to reinterpret aesthetic values. The two most important and representative anthologies to come out of the black power era are *Black Fire* (1968), edited by Amiri Baraka and Larry Neal, and *The Black Aesthetic* (1971) compiled by Addison Gayle. Gayle referred to the transformative power of black art and its active role in the black revolution, asserting: "The question for the black critic today is not how beautiful is a melody, a play, a poem, or a novel, but how much more beautiful has the poem, melody, play or novel made the life of a single black man? How far has the work gone in transforming an American Negro into an African American or black man?"

The format of the anthology *The Black Aesthetic* provides a glimpse into the cultural side of the black power movement. With sections on drama, poetry, music, literature and culture, the anthology traces the development of theories of independent black culture, using contemporary and historical writings. **The Cultural Side of Black Power** For example, the section on music includes pieces by both Amiri Baraka and W. E. B. Du Bois, in the latter instance "Of the Sorrow Songs" from *Souls of Black Folk* (1903). Similarly, the poetry section is introduced and contextualized by Langston Hughes's "The Negro Artist and the Racial Mountain," written in 1926.

Unlike *Black Fire*, with essays and creative pieces drawn only from contemporary writers and specifically from those representative of the Black Arts Movement, including Baraka, Haki Madhubuti (formerly Don L. Lee), Carolyn Rodgers, Larry Neal, Nikki Giovanni, Harold Cruse, Gil Scott-Heron, and Sonia Sanchez, the *Black Aesthetic* sought to establish a long tradition of writing. Within the larger Black Arts mainstream, it located and united such contemporary political and cultural figures as Baraka, Neal, and Karenga with their predecessors—Richard Wright, Langston Hughes, and W. E. B. Du Bois.

The widely repeated mantra "black is beautiful" signaled the growing rejection of cultural assimilation, as well as rejection of integrationist-oriented civil rights organizations such as the NAACP, SCLC, and the Urban League. In the "After- **The Black Arts Movement** word: 'And Shine Swam On,'" published in *Black Fire*, Larry Neal made it clear that young blacks felt an allegiance to Malcolm X. "We feel a Malcolm in the way that a Roy Wilkins, a King, and a Whitney Young can never be felt," he wrote, "because a Malcolm, finally, interprets the emotional history of his people better than the others."

Along with such popular images as the Afro, dashikis, and the Kwanzaa holiday celebration, the Black Arts Movement endeavored to develop a theoretical foundation for the creation of a new African American art. The older assimilationist style of writing, noted Gayle, was a historical relic—a "dinosaur." Just as Alain Locke's introduction to the anthology *The New Negro* (1925) had declared a "new psychology" in the black artistic renaissance of the 1920s, the black poets, writers, and musicians of the late 1960s and early 1970s proclaimed a cultural revolution. This would entail, they believed, a reevaluation of the presumptions that underlay African American culture. In response to the traditional emphasis on the use of universal values and themes as the basis for any form of art, the Black Arts Movement rejected the idea of the universal. Instead, it declared, so-called universal values represented the perspective only of white Western culture.

The black aesthetic was considered to be a corrective to an American or universalistic perspective, exemplified in the writings of James Baldwin, Ralph Ellison, and Albert Murray. Black aestheticians criticized and even rejected those iconic figures in the African American literary tradition, calling their work "assimilationist"—mimicry of white aesthetics. They resurrected Melville Herskovits's *Myth of the Negro Past* (1941) in the hope of identifying African cultural norms in the arts of the diaspora. They sought to define an aesthetic that was not only distinct from, but the opposite of, European norms. This new aesthetic they found not in literature but in music. They turned to free-jazz artists Archie Shepp, John Coltrane, Ornette Coleman, Sonny Murray, Albert Ayler, and Sun Ra, seeing in them the inheritors and purveyors of a more authentic African orientation to art. As early as 1963, Baraka (then known as LeRoi Jones) had already established in *Blues People* one of the Black Arts Movement's fundamental tenets—that the tradition of African American music, from its folk roots through the blues, jazz, and such popular musical forms as soul, represented authentic black aesthetic values.

The Black Arts Movement's enthusiasm for free jazz was based on the music's high degree of improvisation—on its unstructured melodic inflections and rhythmic lines that defied constraint and even approximated vocal effects. As jazz scholar Iain Anderson explains, "Archie Shepp's gruff tenor and Pharoah Sanders's high register squeals could imitate not only the human song but the human cry and shriek as well." The "new thing" was quite unlike swing and hard bop. The Black Arts Movement exalted John Coltrane above all other free improvisers, ascribing to his music a spiritual quality that resisted Western material culture. Reminiscent of Malcolm X's feelings toward the "Dark World," the Black Arts ideologues praised Coltrane for his expression through music of nationalistic and Third World meaning, which resisted assimilation. From the opening of the 1960s until his death in 1969, Coltrane's music incorporated both African and Asian sounds. Longtime Baraka friend and theorist A. B. Spellman eulogized Coltrane in 1969 as "playing about something consciously black, no matter how abstract his formulation may be."

Part and parcel of the volatile political era of black power, the artistic movement was in constant flux. Its nationalistic stand on African American culture and its need to occupy both an artistically and politically liberating space in that culture revealed neither consensus nor consistent perspective. The very idea of pure African elements and the black aesthetic itself was challenged by other black literary figures. Nor did the free-jazz musicians capture the hearts and minds of the masses nearly as well as the soul singers Aretha Franklin, Otis Redding, the Supremes, the Impressions, and James Brown. Indeed, Brown's "Say it Loud: I'm Black and I'm Proud" said it all. Berry Gordy, Jr., the black entrepreneur and owner of the profitable and prominent Motown Records in Detroit, had come to represent for many African Americans an alternative form of black empowerment, specifically black capitalism.

Pride in black heritage took center stage in the extremely successful and fascinating film treatment of Alex Haley's best-selling book *Roots*. This week-long television miniseries, aired in 1977, told the quasi-fictional story of Haley's family history, from the capture of his African ancestor in the eighteenth century until the time of Haley himself. Millions of captivated viewers watched *Roots* and its 1978 sequel, *Roots, the Next Generation*. The series heightened interest in family history and genealogy among Americans of all races.

Ironically, the 1970s also witnessed the meteoric success of another style of film—"blaxploitation" movies. In 1971 black filmmaker Melvin Van Peebles' *Sweet Sweetback's Baadsssss Song* became a surprise bombshell in independent black theaters, convincing both

Blaxploitation Movies

African American and white filmmakers of the lucrative black consumer market. As a result, films by both African American and white filmmakers used Peebles' volatile mix of sex and violence to create a whole string of blaxploitation films, peaking with such iconic movies as the three *Shaft* films and *Superfly.* Creating stars such as Pam Grier, Richard Roundtree, and former professional football players Jim Brown and Fred Williamson, these films also featured era-defining music from popular singers James Brown, Curtis Mayfield, Marvin Gaye, and Isaac Hayes, who even managed to win an Academy Award for his "Theme from *Shaft."* The controversial blaxploitation film mix of gangsterism, drug culture, sex, and violence would be one of the iconographic roots of Hip-Hop in the 1980s and 1990s.

The graphic arts enjoyed a prolific period in the 1960s and 1970s. The most celebrated artist was Romare Bearden (1911–1988), the creator of colorful, cubist-inspired collages that chronicle African American life. Although he was born in Char-

Graphic Arts

lotte, North Carolina, his family moved to New York, and there Bearden spent his formative years in the culturally stimulating and dynamic atmosphere of the Harlem Renaissance. His family was socially active and involved in Harlem politics; consequently Bearden grew up familiar with Harlem's many artists, musicians, writers and political figures. In the summers, he left the busy Harlem scene for the very different but equally rich cultural environment of rural North Carolina. Here he learned the traditions of African American folk culture. As in the later work of William H. Johnson, both rural and urban life would find expression in Bearden's work.

After military service in World War II, Bearden studied art in Paris, where he observed the experiments of the European Modernists. He returned to New York in 1950, searching for his own unique expression. Throughout the 1950s, he worked primarily in abstraction, but around 1964 he finally arrived at what would become his signature style: the art of collage. Bearden's richly textured collages were usually created from magazine illustrations, newspaper, variously colored or painted paper, inks and fabric, tape, and other materials. Bearden would rearrange and compose these elements, creating new images and new contexts. Unlike his abstract works, Bearden's collages were usually representational and narrative in nature. Favorite subjects included New York Harlem scenes, the African American folk culture of North Carolina, and musicians. Music was also Bearden's passion, and he enjoyed some success as a jazz composer.

David Driskell, both as an artist and as a scholar in the field, became a commanding voice in the promotion of African American art in the 1960s, teaching first at Fisk and in later decades at the University of Maryland. Other artists included Herman Bailey and Raymond Saunders, whose works reflect their contact with African techniques and materials, and Lucile Roberts and Paul Keene, whose works show the influence not only of Africa and the United States but also of other parts of the world. Jacob Lawrence continued to stand out as one of this period's premier artists. His works on the black diaspora, migration, city life, Toussaint L'ouverture, and numerous other subjects have been acclaimed all over the globe.

Elizabeth Catlett, born in 1915 and in the early postwar years already a leading printmaker and sculptor, became one of the expatriates of the black-power period, living in Mexico and continuing to turn out works of distinction. In her series on black heroes, the

Elizabeth Catlett's 1975 linocut *Harriet,* a portrait of Harriet Tubman.

prize-winning linocut "Malcolm Speaks for Us" was acclaimed by major art critics in 1969. Although of an older generation, Catlett was still considered a formidable figure in the arts and social activism in the 1970s.

Born and raised in Washington, D.C., she demonstrated early in life a talent for art and a strong interest in social justice issues. Her formative years as an artist were highly influenced by the Social Realism art style, which sought to portray the everyday lives of ordinary people with sensitivity and dignity. This orientation was reinforced during her undergraduate study at Howard University under the pioneering African American artist and art historian James Porter and during graduate school at the University of Iowa, where she studied with the renowned white regionalist painter Grant Wood. In the 1970s, Catlett developed a great interest in depicting the largely unsung contributions of African American women. Her treatment of strong female images is illustrated by the striking linocut *Harriet* (1975), depicting Harriet Tubman as a guide and liberator on the Underground Railroad. Tubman's commanding figure stands in the foreground, a band of fugitive slaves behind her. Catlett's feminist sensibility endows the historically petite Tubman with larger-than-life dimensions—including a muscular arm pointing the way to freedom.

Completing her master of fine arts degree in 1959, Faith Ringgold embarked on her professional career in the 1960s, just as the civil rights movement was gaining momentum and the women's movement was emerging. Both movements influenced her politics and her art. Ringgold began her career as a painter and worked in the series format employed by other black artists, such as Elizabeth Catlett, Horace Pippin, and Jacob Lawrence. Ringgold's early works, such as "The Flag is Bleeding" (1967) from the American People Series and "Flag for the Moon: Die Nigger" (1969) from the Black Light series, reveal her use of the artist's canvas for political statements.

Ringgold is best known for her storytelling quilts, a medium that combines paint and fabric. Knowledgeable of the history of women's quilt making, which in the black community served to communicate information and record stories for posterity, and also inspired by feminism's insistence on the political power of women's storytelling and autobiography, Ringgold embellished her quilt paintings with text.

Black women writers came into their own during this period. In the 1970s, Toni Morrison, Gayl Jones, Alice Walker, Toni Cade Bambara, Maya Angelou, Paule Marshall, Audre Lorde, and Ntozake Shange assumed a special role in voicing the long-suppressed feelings of women about sexism, as well as about the insensitivity, neglect, and abuse they had suffered. Carlene Hatcher Polite's *The Flagellants,* depicting **Women Writers** the disintegration of a black couple's relationship, appeared in 1967. Toni Morrison's first novel *The Bluest Eye* (1970) addressed the difficult issues of dysfunctional family life and racial self-hatred in the story of Pecola Breedlove, a young black girl in the 1940s who prays for blonde hair and blue eyes. The most important novels of the 1970s were likely *Sula* (1973), by Toni Morrison, and *Corregidora* (1975), by Gayl Jones. In this era of heightened black consciousness, the autobiographical narrative became an important vehicle for expressing growing consciousness about gender and sexuality. Audre Lorde's *Zami* (1982) explores her coming to terms with her lesbian sexual orientation, and Maya Angelou's *I Know Why the Caged Bird Sings* (1969) tells a coming-of-age story about a young black girl's journey toward inner strength and dignity after the pain of rape and other hardships.

As such women novelists as Morrison and Jones introduced innovative styles, others sought to revisit the richness of the forgotten history of African American women's writing and themes. In her article "In Search of Our Mothers' Gardens: The Creativity of Black Women in the South," published in 1974, Alice Walker sought to understand the resilience of black women's creativity despite centuries of oppression, as well as the stifled voices and agony of women who never realized their potential as writers and artists. In 1975 Walker published "In Search of Zora Neale Hurston" in *Ms. Magazine,* almost single-handedly reviving interest in the work of this great but long-forgotten African American author. Walker described the process of searching for Hurston's grave and placing a marker on it as a metaphor for claiming the legacy and history of black women. While Hurston's case was one of the most highly publicized, the rediscovery and recovery of early black women writers provided an opportunity to read and evaluate other neglected authors—Phillis Wheatley, Frances Ellen Watkins Harper, and Pauline Hopkins.

African American women writers provided a new lens—that of gender—through which to see the black experience. Walker also published the novels *Meridian* (1976) and *The Third Life of Grange Copeland* (1979), both of which portended the success she would achieve in the next decade. In *The Color Purple* (1982), for which she received a Pulitzer Prize, she explored the bonds of women's friendship and sexuality against the backdrop of the sexual abuse of Celie, the heroine, by her stepfather, and the many years of domestic abuse by her husband. Filmed in 1985, *The Color Purple* provoked a bitter reaction in the press by outraged and shaken black men, although Walker and other black women activists continued to speak boldly, refusing to submit to the demands of a polite society that wished them to remain silent.

Ntozake Shange's *For Colored Girls Who Have Considered Suicide When The Rainbow Is Enuf* (1977) is a choreopoem (live performance) consisting of about twenty poems focusing on the difficulties of being black and female. Through their poems, seven women, each dressed in a different color—red, orange, yellow, green, purple, blue, and so on (the colors of a rainbow)—share stories of life, love, tumultuous relationships with men, and the comfort and support they find among themselves. They speak in monologues and as a chorus, as well as through dance, conveying the resilience of black women.

Black Feminism

Black power and its discourse of a strident black manhood emerged at around the same time as Assistant Secretary of Labor Daniel Patrick Moynihan's highly publicized *The Negro Family: The Case for National Action* (1965). The Moynihan report surveyed the continued racial disparities between blacks and whites in the decade between the *Brown* decision in 1954 and the Civil Rights Act of 1964, concluding that the black family was the "fundamental source of the weakness of the Negro community at the present time." Relying on the premise of E. Franklin Frazier's *The Negro Family in the United States* (1939)—that the matriarchal family emerged during slavery—Moynihan did not fail to identify racial discrimination as the root of the growing problem that placed the black family out of the norm of the stable white family. But there was no mistaking that he blamed the growing number of black female-headed households for the "tangle of pathology" within the black community.

The report was a devastating critique of black women. Moynihan's analysis led inevitably, if unwittingly, to the negative characterization of black women as emasculating figures. The black family's reversal of gender roles, Moynihan argued, "imposes a crushing burden on the Negro male." In addition, Moynihan quoted the opinions on this subject of various social scientists and black leaders. Social psychologist Thomas Pettigrew, for example, noted that black women's failed relationships with their men so embittered them that they "often act to perpetuate the mother-centered pattern by taking a greater interest in their daughters than their sons." Even Dorothy Height, the leader of the National Council of Negro Women, was quoted by Moynihan as stating that, "If the Negro woman has a major underlying concern, it is the status of the Negro man and his position in the community and his need for feeling himself an important person, free and able to make his contribution in the whole society in order that he may strengthen his home."

Moynihan's report caused an uproar among black feminists. Black writer Michelle Wallace captured Moynihan's meaning for black women. It was, she lamented, a "brain-shattering explosion upon the heads of black women, the accumulation of over three hundred years of rage." The daughter of black feminist and artist Faith Ringgold, Wallace was moved to **Reaction to the Moynihan Report** write a book, *Black Macho and the Myth of the Superwoman* (1979), excerpts from which she published in *Ms. Magazine* in December 1978. In her book, Wallace challenged the male-centered thought rampant in the black-power movement and argued that such chauvinism had contributed to the movement's demise. However, at the time of the book's publication, black women were already beginning to critique the sexism of black men and the racism of white women.

In the late 1960s and early 1970s, with the black-power and feminist movements at high tide, gender-conscious black women could find in neither a perfect fit. As social activists and theoreticians, they drew attention to the shortcomings of both movements, but they identified explicitly with black power and sought to articulate its meaning through attention to women's concerns. Some of these women came together in literary form, for example, in the anthology *The Black Woman,* edited by Toni Cade Bambara and first published in 1970. This foundational text of women's writings in the era of black power includes essays, poems, and stories by such writers as Alice Walker, Audre Lorde, Nikki Giovanni, Paule Marshall, musician Abbey Lincoln, black feminist Frances Beal, and Asian American leftist activist Grace Lee Boggs, who was the wife of black autoworker, activist, and socialist James Lee Boggs. The voice of black power resounds in this anthology, which covers themes of the myth of the black matriarchy, the role of black women in the civil rights and black power struggles, reproductive rights, physical image, and economic and political issues.

Alice Walker culled her essays written between 1966 and 1983 for the book *In Search of Our Mothers' Gardens: Womanist Prose* (1983). In this important collection, she coined the term *womanism,* which would be adopted by a number of gender-conscious black women, especially those in academia, as an alternative political identity to the more racially problematic *feminism.*

For the militant generation that heeded the call of black power and black nationalism, coming together as a black women's organization proved more difficult. Both Elaine Brown and Angela Davis later recalled their dissatisfaction with the chauvinistic sentiments of the black-nationalist men with whom they **Women's Organizations** worked in the 1970s. In her memoir *A Taste of Power: A Black Woman's Story* (1992), Brown recalled the sexism she confronted as a member of the Black Panther Party during its heyday before 1970. Later, in its declining years between 1974 and 1977, she would chair the BPP. She also ran for public office in 1973 and 1975. Angela Davis, who was active in both the BPP and the Communist Party, recounted a similar sexism among black nationalists, describing "male supremacist trends" throughout the movement.

The older model of the National Council of Negro Women, founded in 1935 by Mary McLeod Bethune, did not appeal to younger black women. In the 1960s, under the leadership of Dorothy Height, the NCNW had remained the stalwart voice of middle-class black women in the integrationist struggle for racial equality, and it did have an impressive record on the civil rights front. In the spirit of interracial cooperation, it launched Women in Community Service (WICS). Through this initiative, the NCNW collaborated on a variety of community-service projects with the National Council for Catholic Women, the National Council for Jewish Women, and Church Women United.

The WICS brought together women of all races for work in the South with voter registration, freedom schools, and Job Corps training. In Jackson, Mississippi, a chapter of WICS launched the state's first Head Start programs and secured funds for the Freedom Farm Co-op program in 1968, under the leadership of civil rights hero Fannie Lou Hamer. However, Height's decision to subsume black women's needs within the broader black community's needs forced many black women in their twenties and thirties to engage in a continuing search for an organization that acknowledged their particular struggles—with racism in the women's movement and with sexual discrimination in the black power movement.

Historian Deborah Gray White writes of the black power era as a time when blackness and womanhood seemed virtually antithetical, when "black women could not work on both fronts at the same time, could not embrace one part of their identity without denying the other." Only black women, they told themselves, could create organizations that addressed issues reflecting their distinctive experiences. They created five explicitly feminist organizations: the Third World Women's Alliance, Black Women Organized for Action, the National Black Feminist Organization, the National Alliance of Black Feminists, and the Combahee River Collective. Despite their differing ideological orientations, all of them shared, according to scholar Kimberly Springer, a commitment to eradicating racism, sexism, and poverty. Founded during the 1970s, none of these organizations was still around in the 1980s, however.

Shirley Chisholm campaigns.
Representative Shirley A. Chisholm campaigns in the Roxbury section of Boston during her unsuccessful campaign for the Democratic presidential nomination in 1972.

When the National Black Feminist Organization was founded in 1973, Eleanor Holmes Norton, a co-founder and member of the New York City Human Rights Commission, charged that most Americans expected "black women to suppress their aspirations in deference to black males." These sentiments were echoed by Margaret Sloan, another founder and also an early editor at *Ms. Magazine,* who declared that the new organization would make it clear to "the black liberation movement that there can't be liberation for half a race." In response to critics of the African American women's movement, Shirley Chisholm, a congresswoman who received little support from African American men in her unsuccessful campaign for the Democratic presidential nomination in 1972, declared that "in many respects it was more difficult to be a woman than a black."

Such were the concerns that led to the founding of the National Black Feminist Organization (NBFO). Although it survived for only a few years, the NBFO brought women together—largely but not exclusively college-educated women (intellectuals, writers, and political figures)—to discuss issues of interest to black women. For example, the white feminist National Organization for Women (NOW) did not initially include poverty, a major issue for black women, as one of the concerns of women's liberation. NOW did offer its New York office as a temporary meeting space for the NBFO. The black women's organization also established other chapters—the strongest of which was in Chicago under the leadership of Barbara Eichelberger.

The women in NBFO met in small groups for consciousness-raising discussions about contemporary and urgent problems: child care facilities, reproductive rights, gynecological sterilization, unemployment, education, job training, domestic workers' rights, health care, and welfare rights. The group also gave its endorsement to the fight for the ratification of the Equal Rights Amendment. With a membership that cut across age and sexual orientation, the NBFO was perhaps the first black organization to speak openly about lesbian sexuality. The New York chapter proved short-lived, however, folding at the end of 1975. The Chicago chapter changed its name to the National Alliance of Black Feminists and continued at an active level until 1981.

The most radical of the black power women's organizations was the Third World Women's Alliance (TWWA). Its roots date back to 1968—to the Black Women's Caucus of SNCC, based in New York, which emerged after SNCC shifted to black power. The Caucus soon became the independent organization the Black Women's Alliance, and by 1970 the group had adopted a new name, the Third World Women's Alliance, in order to include Puerto Rican women activists along with black women. Frances Beal was the group's guiding hand. She had a long history in the struggle for racial equality, working in the NAACP, SNCC, and the black power movement. She became well known in feminist circles for her article "Double Jeopardy: To Be Black and Female," published in Robin Morgan's anthology of the women's liberation movement, *Sisterhood Is Powerful* (1970).

The TWWA focused on the same social problems identified by the National Black Feminist Organization, with one important difference. TWWA leaders linked the African American women's struggle with women's movements in Asian and African countries. In this respect, their theoretical position was similar to that of the Black Panther Party, notwithstanding the uniquely women's coalition. The women read classic Marxist texts and in 1971 published the monthly news organ *Triple Jeopardy,* which defined their struggle as against racism, sexism, and capitalism—including black capitalism in the United States.

One of the organization's most visible endeavors was its "Free Angela Davis" campaign, after Davis was arrested on charges of supplying firearms used in a shooting, in a Marin County (California) courthouse, during an abortive attempt to free Soledad prisoner George Jackson in August 1970. (Davis was acquitted in 1972.) The TWWA support of Davis, along with its boldly waving "Hands Off Angela Davis" banner at a women's liberation march in New York's Central Park in the fall of 1972, accentuated the differences—with respect to the TWWA—between black and white feminists. The National Organization of Women did not perceive the Davis issue as a feminist cause, nor did it approve of the black women's leftist politics. The Alliance, with chapters in New York and San Francisco, had a membership exclusively of black, Puerto Rican, Chicana, and Asian women.

If the brief existence of black feminist organizations suggests their flagging popularity or the general waning of the black power movement over the course of the 1970s, their attention to women's issues raised questions about poverty, health, employment, and family from a gender perspective. Through their writings and their activism, black feminists had engaged more black women in discussions about gender issues intellectually, artistically, and practically, even when rejecting a feminist identity and organizational affiliation. Beginning in the late 1960s, African American humanists and social scientists embarked on publishing scholarly studies on gender, and that work would blossom in the decades ahead.

TWWA women support Angela Davis during a march in New York in the fall of 1972.

Window in Time

A Black Feminist Manifesto

We are a collective of Black feminists who have been meeting together since 1974. During that time we have been involved in the process of defining and clarifying our politics, while at the same time doing political work within our own group and in coalition with other progressive organizations and movements. The most general statement of our politics at the present time would be that we are actively committed to struggling against racial, sexual, heterosexual, and class oppression, and see as our particular task the development of integrated analysis and practice based upon the fact that the major systems of oppression are interlocking. The synthesis of these oppressions creates the conditions of our lives. As Black women we see Black feminism as the logical political movement to combat the manifold and simultaneous oppressions that all women of color face.

Although we are feminists and Lesbians, we feel solidarity with progressive Black men and do not advocate the fractionalization that white women who are separatists demand. Our situation as Black people necessitates that we have solidarity around the fact of race, which white women of course do not need to have with white men, unless it is their negative solidarity as racial oppressors. We struggle together with Black men against racism, while we also struggle with Black men about sexism.

From Combahee River Collective, "A Black Feminist Statement," in *Capitalist Patriarchy and the Case for Socialist Feminism*, ed. Zillah Eisenstein. Copyright © 1979 by *Monthly Review Press*. Reprinted by permission of Monthly Review Foundation.

Social and Political Realities

As he surveyed American race relations from his home in Paris, James Baldwin understood all too clearly the tragic injustices and inequalities of black life—"what white Americans do not want to face"—as he wrote in his eloquent *The Fire Next Time* (1963). He knew the dilemma of Martin Luther King, Jr., and he had come to better understand the grassroots appeal of Malcolm X. Thus he warned white America to solve its race problem, quoting the prophetic and elemental words of an old Negro spiritual: "God gave Noah the rainbow sign,/ No more water the fire next time!"

The fire did come—with cities ablaze, buildings burning, and wreckage calculated in millions of dollars. Raging riots and the threat of riots gave new meaning to the aphorism "long hot summer." Neither congressional legislation nor executive action could stem the violence. Inequalities were too stark to mistake. Between 1949 and 1964, the participation of African Americans in the nation's total economic life had, in relative terms, declined significantly. During that period the unemployment rate of blacks had come to double that of whites. Even in the prosperous year 1963, unemployment for blacks was 114 percent higher than for whites. Where blacks were employed, more than 80 percent of them held jobs at the bottom of the economic ladder, versus 40 percent of employed whites. In 1962 the Council of Economic Advisers estimated the overall annual cost of racial discrimination at about $17.3 billion, or 3.2 percent of GNP (Gross National Product). This cost stemmed primarily from the failure to utilize fully the experience and skills of the entire U.S. population. The effect of this discrimination against black Americans made it impossible for many to afford adequate housing even when such housing was available without discrimination by race.

In mid-July 1964, violence broke out in the Yorkville section of New York City when an off-duty policeman shot and killed a black teenager. Protest demonstrations against police brutality spread to Harlem, Bedford-Stuyvesant, and other city neighborhoods, often accompanied by rioting and looting. Similar disturbances took place in Rochester, New York; in Paterson, Elizabeth, and Jersey City, New Jersey; in Philadelphia; and in Chicago. It was reported by one observer that roving gangs of "unemployed youths" were conspicuously involved in most of the disorders.

The shattered sense of frustration and alienation, which in monetary terms could not be gauged, began to be measured in this way as cities took toll of their property damage. The racial tension in the heavily black Watts section of Los Angeles exploded in August 1965.

Riots in the Cities: Watts The immediate cause was the arrest of a young African American, charged with reckless driving. When a police officer drew a gun, an angry crowd assembled and began to fight back. On the following day, after an unsuccessful attempt to

Property destruction in the Detroit riot, 1967

quiet the tensions, rioting resumed, accompanied by looting and burning. At the height of the melee, some blacks were heard to shout "Burn, baby burn!" and "Get whitey!" It was indeed an explosion of tension, bitterness, and hatred. By the time the police, assisted by the California National Guard, restored peace in Watts, the toll had reached 34 dead, 1,032 injured, and 3,952 arrested. Property damage was estimated at $40 million.

The riot's underlying cause was the demoralization of Los Angeles' black population. Despite the fact that 20 percent of the houses in Watts were dilapidated, one-sixth of Los Angeles' half-million blacks were crowded into the area under conditions four times as congested as the rest of the city. Racial discrimination and bias made it impossible for many blacks to secure housing elsewhere, even when they could afford it. The employment picture was no better. At the time of the riot, more than 30 percent of potential African American wage earners were unemployed. Thousands of skilled and unskilled African Americans had no hope of finding a job. Shop owners in the Watts area turned away many seeking employment and instead hired white employees who, like the owners themselves, did not live in the district. A powder keg, Los Angeles underscored how equality was only a tragic illusion.

In the summer of 1966, federal reports noted about forty racial disturbances in various cities, including Chicago and Cleveland. The most publicized violence in 1967 occurred in
Newark and Detroit Newark and Detroit—and in Detroit, which saw the worst of all the riots, the property loss was staggering: more than $500 million. In Newark, twenty-six persons lost their lives; in Detroit, forty-three. More than five thousand arrests were made in Detroit alone.

Then, on April 4, 1968, Martin Luther King Jr., was shot dead in Memphis, Tennessee, where he had gone to support striking sanitation workers. Blacks in more than one hundred cities across the country rioted and looted over the course of several days—a grave response by so many blacks to the wanton murder of the man who preached nonviolence and love. To many African Americans, King's assassination dashed all hope in the commitment of whites to racial equality.

The subsequent capture of King's murderer James Earl Ray and his immediate trial, without any testimony and after he simply pleaded guilty, further embittered large numbers of blacks; African Americans widely suspected that this speedy "justice" was merely covering up some kind of a conspiracy. Although an official inquiry ruled out a wider murder plot, King's death, like Malcolm X's, did not settle the conspiracy question for African Americans.

Between 1940 and 1970, the black population outside the old Confederacy increased from nearly 4 million to more than 11 million—almost 50 percent of the total black population. Most of the growth outside the South took the form of migra- **The New Black Political Power** tion to the central cities of the twelve largest metropolitan areas: New York, Los Angeles, Chicago, Philadelphia, Detroit, San Francisco–Oakland, Boston, Pittsburgh, St. Louis, Washington, Cleveland, and Baltimore. By 1970 these twelve areas held 28 percent of all black people living in the United States. There were 1,667,000 blacks in New York City, 1,103,000 in Chicago, 654,000 in Philadelphia, 660,000 in Detroit, and 504,000 in Los Angeles.

In southern cities such as Atlanta, Birmingham, Houston, and Dallas, the African American population grew steadily. The typical northern black had already become a city dweller, and the typical southern black was rapidly becoming one as well. The economic and social conditions caused by the urbanization and the concentration of such large numbers of unemployed and underemployed blacks created an explosive mixture for riots—but also for race-conscious political empowerment, which took multiple forms.

The black power era spanned a decade of changing black politics, exemplified by the ebb and flow of multiple black power groups, leaders, and ideologies. However, most blacks never followed the radical politics of the Black Panther Party or the many other black power alternatives, even when finding some of their arguments and personalities attractive. The great majority of blacks continued to link their political behavior to the American electoral system. This was evident in the gains that blacks made in winning political offices during the very years of black power's ascendancy. For many, perhaps, electoral victory was the most realistic form of black power available.

In 1966 there were 97 black members of state legislatures and six members of the Congress of the United States, but no black mayor in any American city. By 1973 more than two hundred blacks sat in thirty-seven state legislatures, and blacks had already served as mayors of Cleveland, Los Angeles, Gary (Indiana), and Newark (New Jersey). Thanks to the Voting Rights Act of 1965, black mayors had also been elected in scores of small southern towns by 1973, among them Tuskegee in Alabama, Fayette in Mississippi, and Madison in Arkansas. The thirteen African Americans in the United States Congress in 1971 formed their own caucus, and by 1973 the Congressional Black Caucus grew to sixteen members, four of them women—Shirley Chisholm of New York, Barbara Jordan of Texas, Yvonne Brathwaite Burke of California, and Cardiss Collins of Illinois. In 1976 Jordan was selected to be a keynote speaker at the Democratic National Convention. By 1979 she and Burke had retired and were replaced by black men, but the Black Caucus remained strong and aggressive, with seventeen members in the House of Representatives.

The influence of the Congressional Black Caucus was increasing not only in its effect on legislation but also in monitoring law enforcement. By 1979 there were black mayors in major cities in the South, such as Atlanta and New Orleans, and also in Los Angeles and Detroit. In that year, more than six hundred blacks were serving on city councils and more than a thousand had been elected as judges, aldermen and alderwomen, constables, marshals, school board members, and to a variety of other such local offices.

Unlike at the local level, the record of blacks in races for statewide office appeared to be more uneven. In the 1978 election year, Republican Edward Brooke of Massachusetts, the lone African American in the U.S. Senate, lost his seat to a white Democrat. Mervyn Dymally, the first black lieutenant governor of California, failed to be reelected, while Yvonne Brathwaite Burke ran unsuccessfully for attorney general of California. However, Wisconsin elected a black woman as secretary of state, and Illinois sent a black man to the comptroller's office. In North Carolina in 1978, an African American was elected to the state court of appeals, and blacks in the positions of secretary of state in Michigan, treasurer in Connecticut, and superintendent of public instruction in California were all reelected that year.

The new black political power was also manifested in demands for greater voice in party affairs. When it became clear that 20 percent of the Democratic vote in 1968 came from blacks (85 percent of black voters cast their ballots for the unsuccessful presidential candidate, Hubert Humphrey), they argued that the Democrats should give them greater recognition. Pressures applied by Mayor Richard Hatcher of Gary and others doubtless had the effect of increasing the number of black delegates to the 1972 Democratic National Convention and of the selection of Yvonne Brathwaite Burke as convention co-chair.

Reminiscent to a certain extent of the black political unity recommended in Carmichael and Hamilton's *Black Power* (1967), black politicians and community leaders looked outside the traditional political parties with the idea of establishing an independent political organization to achieve some of their goals. Such thinking led to the first National Black Political Convention, which in March 1972 met in Gary, Indiana. Organized by Representative Charles C. Diggs of Michigan, Mayor Richard Hatcher of Gary, and writer-activist Amiri Baraka, the convention attracted more than 2,700 delegates and 4,000 alternates and observers. For several days, the sessions heard various views on issues related to the major political parties, black representation and participation in economic and political matters, school busing, and U.S. foreign policy toward Israel, southern Africa, and Portugal (at the time a major colonial power in Africa).

When it was not possible to reach definitive positions in the closing hours of the convention, the delegates authorized a committee of leaders to deliberate further and draw up a position paper. Consensus proved impossible. A document called the "National Black Political Agenda" revealed deep divisions on major policy issues. Hatcher and Diggs opposed agenda provisions against school busing and against U.S. support of Israel. In this they were joined by the Congressional Black Caucus. Meanwhile Hatcher criticized Roy Wilkins of the NAACP for withdrawing his organization's support of the convention.

Covering a wide range of problems, the convention's agenda contained a poor people's platform, model pledges for black and non-black candidates seeking convention support, the outline of a voter registration bill, and a bill for community self-determination. It ended on a note of optimism, asserting that "All things are possible." Yet support for Congresswoman Shirley Chisholm's presidential race was not possible. When she announced her intention to run for president in 1972, the National Black Political Convention did not endorse her. Such factiousness belied the convention's expressed goal of unifying a divided movement.

In the black power era, African Americans were indeed divided as to how best to achieve racial equality. Many opposed the war in Vietnam, seeing it as a diversion of needed resources, but they disagreed about whether to link antiwar issues with those of civil rights. They were divided over the goal of racial integration and over the strategy of working with whites, be they white liberals or white Marxists. They argued over assimilation and the usefulness of "white" values in black ghettos. They agreed with the concept of community control, but not necessarily on how to achieve it. Such divisions in the black community mirrored equally rancorous divisions in the larger nation—those of the student movement, of the Native American and Chicano power movements, of the Weathermen and such other radical groups, and the ever-growing conservative "silent majority." The house divided could not stand for government corruption at the highest level. Because of the Watergate scandal, the president of the United States, Richard M. Nixon, was forced to resign. Out of the chaos of those tumultuous years, America began to move down a more conservative path in its racial policies, even during the four-year interlude of Jimmy Carter's Democratic presidency.

By the late 1970s, the black community showed measurable signs of change, as antidiscrimination legislation and affirmative action programs began to correct racial imbalances. The beneficiaries of these changes could take pride in their progress. A substantial number of blacks had experienced upward mobility, no longer stuck in such once racially designated jobs as service worker, unskilled laborer, and farm worker. Between 1960 and 1978, the proportion of blacks employed in professional and technical positions had increased by 10.7 percent and in clerical positions by 9.6 percent. Yet for all the progress, the unfolding of the 1960s and 1970s was accompanied by rising levels of black joblessness and poverty, creating especially for young blacks a labyrinth of obstacles to overcome. The American dream, if elusive for most African Americans, was becoming all the more elusive for those born in poverty. Despite the controversy and acrimony surrounding Daniel Patrick Moynihan's report, there lay an idea buried within it that foretold the forked road ahead: "There is considerable evidence that the Negro community is in fact dividing between a stable middle-class group that is steadily growing stronger and more successful, and an increasingly disorganized and disadvantaged lower-class group."

Progress
and Poverty

Divergent Realities

In Conservative Times

Artistic Currents

Global Concerns

At Century's End

Businessman passing by
homeless person

A t the start of the 1970s, inner-city black neighborhoods mirrored all the features of economic collapse. The urban riots of 1966–1968 furnished telling evidence of the cost of racial and social exclusion in American cities. Years later, boarded-up businesses and apartment buildings remained as riot-torn eyesores of once vibrant communities. The relocation of industry outside of the urban centers of the North and Midwest had been under way for more than a decade before the riots, and the attendant loss of factory jobs rapidly accelerated in the years that followed. It seemed, in certain ways, a cruel circumstance, since racist hiring practices had left African Americans as the latecomers on the industrial hiring chain, especially compared to white immigrants and other whites. Just when better-paying jobs became available to blacks in the wake of civil rights activism, the spatial and economic restructuring of cities no longer provided the blue-collar jobs that many black laborers, especially black men with limited education, had previously secured.

The Kerner Report of 1968, the study published by the National Advisory Commission on Civil Disorders, blamed employment discrimination as one cause of despair in inner-city neighborhoods and questioned whether blacks would be able to escape the ghetto as had white immigrant groups. By the end of the twentieth century, the answer was clear. The black urban experience had become a tale of two cities—one of progress and the other of poverty. Black progress could be seen in elective and appointed office at the national and local levels. African Americans appeared in leading roles on television and movie screens, in sports and in the arts, in higher education, and in corporations. Nevertheless, most African Americans perceived the recent and fragile nature of these gains to rest on the civil rights policies that had made upward mobility possible in the first place. Any retreat from the civil rights legislation of the 1960s stood to retard, even imperil, black progress.

Divergent Realities

The fault lines of black progress and poverty so dominated the larger racial landscape of the late twentieth century that presidential administrations, court decisions, forms of artistic expression, as well as black voter preferences all addressed and, in some cases, shaped this crucial duality. The most obvious expression of the duality was in economic differences.

In the economic crisis of the 1970s and the early 1980s, Americans of all races experienced a rise in unemployment, but the troubled economy hit low-income African Americans hardest. Black men disproportionately swelled the unemployment rolls as **Economic Differences** jobs in the manufacturing sector were exported and decentralized—a process that had begun before the 1950s but took off dramatically afterward. Many large manufacturing companies abandoned older cities in the Northeast for regions with lower taxes and a non-unionized workforce. Changes in transportation technology in the post-World

Table 22.1	Unemployment Rate by Race (White and Black) between 1965 and 1990					
	1965	1970	1975	1980	1985	1990
White	4.3%	3.9%	8.5%	6.0%	6.6%	3.8%
Black	8.5%	6.7%	14.7%	13.4%	15.6%	8.6%

Source: U. S. Department of Commerce. *Statistical Abstract of the United States, 1992.* Bureau of the Census. Washington, D.C., 1992.

War II years, the advent of the interstate highway system, and the rise of the trucking industry led to the diffusion of manufacturing jobs into suburban areas, later called industrial parks.

The effect of the relocation of manufacturing jobs from the Rustbelt (steel-industry states in the Northeast and Midwest, such as Pennsylvania, Michigan, and Ohio) to the Sunbelt (states in the South and Southwest, such as Arizona, California, and Florida) and outside the United States was compounded by the rise of service industries and the information economy. In the 1970s and 1980s, large numbers of African Americans with only a high-school education lacked the technological training necessary for the computer age. Moreover, the so-called flexible forms of organizations and new corporate policies intensified job competition, labor contracting, and an explosion in low-paid, part-time work.

Between 1970 and 1990, the median income for white families rose 8.7 percent, from $34,481 to $36,915, while black family income hardly rose at all, from $21,151 to $21,453. By 1990, recession engulfed the nation, leaving poor and working class blacks particularly vulnerable. Unemployment rates again climbed, and America's trade deficit increased as more cheaply produced foreign goods undercut American products. Plant closings, business failures, and home mortgage foreclosures meant that millions of Americans felt the sharp pinch of a recession that hung like a pall over the four-year presidency of George H.W. Bush and contributed to Bush's defeat by Democratic nominee William Jefferson Clinton, in 1992.

Equally important by 1990, a widening chasm divided the haves and have-nots in black America. As jobs disappeared from inner-city black communities, so, too, did working families. Through policies such as affirmative action and open-housing laws during these decades, many African Americans entered doors once closed to them in education, employment, and home ownership in previously white neighborhoods. No longer would it be commonplace to see blacks of all economic classes confined to a segregated enclave. Gone were the days when the black middle class and working poor were afforded stability and an economic cushion within the black ghetto through social organizations, kinship and friendship networks, businesses, and religious institutions. Instead, black neighborhoods witnessed a growing concentration of the poor—of persons relegated to an underclass that lived in dilapidated public housing, attended poorly equipped and de facto segregated schools, and faced the daily realities of family disruption, drug use and trafficking, criminal activity, and other social ills.

Rise of the Black Underclass

The first scholar to identify and seriously critique the rise of the black underclass was William Julius Wilson. In *The Declining Significance of Race* (1978), he argued that the urban black poor experienced acute social and economic marginalization, "falling further and further behind the more privileged blacks." Class more than race, he maintained, had become the principal factor determining their opportunities. Black scholars and civil rights leaders

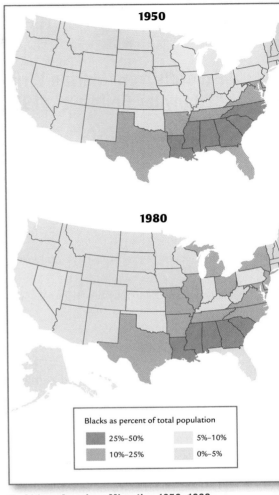

1950

1980

Blacks as percent of total population

25%–50%	5%–10%
10%–25%	0%–5%

African American Migration 1950–1980

Window in Time

Excerpts from Marian Wright Edelman's "Litany for Children" (1992)

We pray for children . . .
whose nightmares come in the daytime,

who will eat anything,
who have never seen a dentist,
who aren't spoiled by anybody,
who go to bed hungry and cry themselves to sleep,
who live and move, but have no being.

A prayer for children by Ina Hughes Copyright © 1995.

vehemently disagreed, believing that Wilson, also an African American, had betrayed the civil rights agenda by underestimating the continuing role of racial prejudice.

Unflinching, in 1987 Wilson published *The Truly Disadvantaged*, which took on both liberals and conservatives for their failure to examine the worsening conditions of the black underclass. Wilson eschewed the term *lower class* and distinguished members of the working poor or those living in low-poverty areas from the long-term jobless residents of extreme poverty areas, specifically census tracts where more than 40 percent of the population lived below the poverty line. Between 1970 and 1980, such areas of extreme poverty doubled on Chicago's South and West Sides, according to Wilson, while poverty also increased among African Americans nationwide.

In his call for economic policies that would alleviate poverty, Wilson listed other disturbing characteristics of Chicago's black poor. Fewer than four in ten jobless persons had graduated from high school. Barely one person in ten belonged to a home-owning household. In these ghetto tracts, only 18 percent of the jobless had access to a car, thus making it difficult to work in the suburbs or other locations not reached by public transportation. An illicit and underground economy of theft, numbers running, prostitution, and drug trafficking emerged as primary income sources for some members of the black underclass. Welfare provided the main household income for several generations of unwed mothers and their children, including what seemed a surging number of teen mothers.

Sensationalized media accounts of "welfare queens" and lurid descriptions of crime, gangs, and crack-cocaine showed little empathy for the black poor. Conservative ideologues cast the plight of the underclass in moralistic terms and demonized the "culture of poverty." Indeed, survey data and sociological studies at the time disclosed the prevalence of attitudes that associated poverty with individual behavior instead of structural economic forces. It was not uncommon among white Americans to perceive black recipients of welfare, while smaller in absolute number than white welfare recipients, as the "undeserving poor." However, organizations such as the Children's Defense Fund, led by black civil rights lawyer Marian Wright Edelman, called attention to the fate of children born into poverty and sought community involvement and government policies to address their worsening condition.

Perhaps the most dramatic response by black community leaders came in the Million Man March, held on October 16, 1994, under the leadership of Minister Louis Farrakhan of the Nation of Islam. Farrakhan called on black men of all faiths, **The Million Man March** social classes, and regions to gather in Washington, D.C., in a day of "atonement." Although it is not certain that their numbers reached 1 million, hundreds of thousands of black men covered the Mall grounds around the Washington Monument. Addressing such issues as black-on-black crime, drugs, and broken families, speakers at the march called for a renewed commitment to the transformation of black communities throughout the nation. However, unlike the March on Washington in 1963, the Million Man March did not rest on strong preexisting urban movements but rather sought to initiate activism at the local level. The march hoped to inspire black men to move toward halting their own complicity in family and community breakdown.

The Million Man March, October 16, 1994, in Washington, DC, sought to inspire black men to activism at the local level.

Being ecumenical in nature, the March featured a range of speakers, such as Rev. Jessie Jackson of the Rainbow Coalition and PUSH (People United to Serve Humanity), former NAACP executive Director Rev. Benjamin Chavis (who would soon afterward convert to Islam and change his name), and university professor Cornel West. Although planners restricted march participation to black men, women leaders, specifically Dorothy Height of the National Council of Negro Women and poet Maya Angelou, appeared on the program. Speakers called for intraracial change, criticized cutbacks on Medicaid, student-aid programs, and other government-funded services, and urged blacks to register and vote on election days. According to analyst David Bositis of the Joint Center for Political and Economic Studies, the call for black voters coincided with a significant increase in the number of black male voters in the months following the march. Despite its showing of symbolic unity, the 1994 Million Man March did little to change problematic social trends.

In contradistinction to poor blacks in debilitating socioeconomic conditions, some black Americans basked in a world of new opportunities for progress. The African American middle **New Opportunities** class grew in size and influence as upper-level civil servants, marketing experts, bankers, corporate managers, media producers, publishers, account executives, and elected officials joined the more familiar professional roles of minister, lawyer, teacher,

Mae C. Jemison
Dr. Jemison, the first African American female astronaut in NASA history, spent eight days on the Space Shuttle *Endeavour* in 1992.

and physician. Although many of these new professionals served the black community, increasing numbers of them "made it" in the larger white world of business and politics.

African Americans held top positions in the governmental and public service sector in the 1990s, working at all levels of the federal judiciary and in the cabinets of the Reagan, Bush, and Clinton administrations. At the close of the millennium, black men and women owned and managed around 425,000 corporations, partnerships, and sole proprietorships (numbering about 2.4 percent of the country's enterprises). Some blacks gained fame as astronauts and scientists in the well-publicized programs of the National Aeronautics and Space Administration, including Air Force Lieutenant Colonel Guion S. Bluford, Jr., who in 1983 became the first African American astronaut, and Mae E. Jemison, a physician and chemical engineer, whose 1991 space flight made her the first female African American astronaut.

Sports proved extremely lucrative for some African Americans. In the 1980s, black basketball, football, and baseball players commonly signed multimillion-dollar contracts. More than this, however, as the century drew to a close, for many Americans the successful professional black athlete had become truly a national, not merely a racial, icon. For three years from 1990–1992, basketball great Michael Jordan headed *Forbes* magazine's list of the "forty highest paid athletes," receiving an estimated $32 million per year for his "commercial ventures." Blacks also reached stardom in sports that traditionally had little black participation. Perhaps the most meteoric of such sports careers in the late twentieth century was that of Eldrick "Tiger" Woods. The son of an African American father and Thai mother, the eighteen-year-old golfer made history in 1994 as the youngest person to win the U.S. Amateur Golf Championship. In 1996, Woods withdrew from Stanford University and turned professional, signing lucrative advertising contracts. *The New York Times* observed that Woods could be "the best golfer in a generation."

In tennis, the sisters Venus and Serena Williams began to amass tremendous popularity and wealth in the 1990s. In 1998 they won two grand slam doubles tournaments, and Venus beat Serena to win the Australian Open. In 1999 they won the doubles tournaments at the French and U.S. Opens, and Serena won the U.S. Open singles tournament. In 2000 both sisters won Olympic gold medals and dominated Wimbledon.

Another major sign of progress, the expansion of the black electorate in the 1980s and 1990s made possible the election of more African Americans to state and local offices than ever before. This growing voter participation resulted from blacks' concern with the economic and social policies of the Reagan and Bush administrations and also from the enthusiastic reception of black contender Jesse Jackson as a Democratic presidential candidate in 1984 and 1988. In 1983 Jackson witnessed Chicago's black voters make Harold Washington the city's first black mayor. The southern cities of Charlotte, Birmingham, and New Orleans also had African American mayors. Those successes convinced Jackson that he could harness the power of African American voters in his campaign for the presidency, or at least influence the selection of the Democratic nominee.

The Black Electorate

At the time of his presidential bid, Jackson was the leader of the Chicago-based organization Operation PUSH. Known for his leadership role as the young lieutenant under Martin Luther King, Jr., in the civil rights movement of the 1950s and 1960s, in the 1980s Jackson began to pressure the business and financial community toward economic parity for blacks by threatening to boycott selected firms. In August 1981, the Coca-Cola Company became the first to sign an agreement that increased benefits to the black community; other companies followed.

Drawing on Jackson's earlier work as a civil rights leader, Jackson's presidential campaign put together his Rainbow Coalition of grassroots supporters made up of people who felt marginalized by the political process. The coalition symbolized the potential unity that could be forged when people of all races, creeds, and colors joined in a common cause. Prominent figures endorsed him: Barry Commoner, an environmentalist who had run for President in 1980; feminist Gloria Steinem; former Attorney General Ramsey Clark; Congressman John Conyers; California Assemblywoman Maxine Waters; and Mayor Richard Hatcher of Gary, Indiana. Throughout his campaign, Jackson emphasized voter registration, beginning his rallies with the chant: "There's a freedom train a comin', but you got to register to ride. So get on board and get on with it."

Jesse Jackson and the Rainbow Coalition

Although Jackson did well in the 1984 state primaries and in televised debates with white Democratic candidates Alan Cranston, Gary Hart, Fritz Hollings, and Walter Mondale, his campaign faced serious obstacles. He had traveled to the Middle East in 1979 and met with President Hafez al-Hassad of Syria and Yasir Arafat, head of the Palestinian Liberation Organization (PLO). Jackson argued that any long-term peace settlement in the Middle East would have to take the Palestinians into consideration, but critics dismissed his argument, observing that the PLO did not recognize the nation of Israel. Later, in an off-the-record

The Rainbow Coalition poster
Jesse Jackson established the Rainbow Coalition as a multiracial, multicultural, political and social organization.

interview with a *Washington Post* reporter, Jackson referred to New York as "Hymie Town." Although he insisted that he intended no slur against Jews, many were offended. Finally, Jackson's campaign lacked financial support from the black civil rights establishment. Benjamin Hooks, executive director of the NAACP, noted that "If an overwhelming number of black voters are voting for a black, then we've lost our voice in selecting the white candidate who will be the Democratic choice." John Jacob, president of the National Urban League, added that "a black Presidential candidate would be a retreat to symbolism and would shatter black expectations."

Mondale won the party's nomination but was defeated by a Reagan landslide in November 1984. Because of Jackson's campaign, however, blacks voted in larger numbers than ever before—over 3 million blacks voted in the Democratic primaries, comprising 18 percent of the approximately 17 million Democratic primary voters. Approximately 10 million blacks voted in the general election, with 89 percent supporting Mondale. This enlarged black electorate made a substantial difference to the African Americans who ran for office throughout the country. In 1985 the number of black elected officials stood at 6,056 compared to only 1,469 in 1970. Some believed that Jackson's candidacy also contributed to Douglas Wilder's electoral victory as Virginia's first black lieutenant governor.

In 1984 most black voters greeted the news of another four years of the Reagan administration with anxiety and frustration, even as the president's popularity among whites soared. President Reagan and his successor George H. W. Bush slashed federal funding to cities and reduced financial support to social programs on which many blacks depended.

The Reagan-Bush Years

Ronald Reagan had said during and after his first presidential campaign that he was eager to end government handouts, which he believed made people "government dependent, rather than independent." His budgets reduced the number of people eligible to participate in federal social programs such as food stamps, Medicaid, student loans, unemployment compensation, child nutrition assistance, and Aid to Families with Dependent Children (part of Social Security).

During the Reagan-Bush years, unemployment among blacks rose at an alarming rate. In 1982 black joblessness stood at 18.9 percent, more than twice the white rate of 8.4 percent. By 1985, when times were better, black unemployment continued to be double that of whites: the unemployment rate for blacks decreased to 16.2 percent and for whites to 6.2 percent. For black teenagers between sixteen and nineteen years old, unemployment soared to an all-time high of more than 50 percent. In the early 1980s, blacks earned less than whites according to every meaningful classification—by age, education, sex, and occupation.

In various ways, the black electorate felt alienated from the Republican White House. For example, Reagan had initially expressed indifference to the mounting pressure to honor

The president signs the King holiday bill, 1983.

Ronald Reagan signs the bill establishing a national holiday in honor of slain civil rights leader Martin Luther King, Jr., as his widow, Coretta Scott King, looks on. Also in attendance are Vice President George Bush and Congresswoman Katie Hall, who introduced the holiday bill in Congress that became law.

civil-rights leader Martin Luther King, Jr., with a national holiday commemorating his birthday. Each year, members of the Congressional Black Caucus and other members of Congress had pushed for such a bill, to no avail. Opponents pointed to scores of presidents and hundreds of great Americans whose birthdays had not become national holidays. On January 15, 1981, five days before Ronald Reagan took the presidential oath of office, more than 100,000 marchers converged on Washington to rally for a King holiday. When Senator Jesse Helms of North Carolina raised questions about King's alleged Communist Party associations, the president defended Helms and responded with, "We'll find out in thirty-five years," alluding to the period after which FBI files could be reviewed. Reagan later apologized to the King family for the remark. Pressure for the holiday continued to mount, and even the 1948 Dixiecrat presidential candidate, Strom Thurmond, began to support it openly. When, finally, the bill passed both houses of Congress, the president signed it at a gala in the White House rose garden on November 2, 1983, in the presence of the King family, leaders of both houses of Congress, and other dignitaries.

As the nation moved toward the 1988 Presidential election, Jackson once again campaigned for the Democratic Party's nomination. As he crisscrossed the country debating with party rivals—Michael Dukakis, Gary Hart, Richard Gephardt, Al Gore, and Bruce Babbitt among them—Jackson impressed many Americans with his ability to speak as knowledgeably about unemployment and the policies of the United Nations as on civil rights and the problems of the ghetto. In the 1988 Democratic primary races, Jackson received more than 6.6 million votes, 24 percent of the approximately 23 million votes cast. Frontrunner Michael Dukakis received 9.7 million votes, or 43 percent. Jackson won several primaries and caucuses in 1988.

Although he failed to secure the nomination, Jackson's showing in the 1988 primaries represented the most serious bid for the presidency made by an African American up to that time.

In the presidential election campaign between Dukakis and George H. W. Bush, 90 percent of blacks voted for Dukakis. Racial stereotyping had played an influential role in the Bush campaign in 1988. Bush cultivated white suburban voters and conservatives by portraying his opponent Michael Dukakis as soft on crime. An infamous Bush television advertisement linked black felon "Willie" [so called by the ad creators] Horton to Dukakis. Horton, a convicted murderer imprisoned in Massachusetts, committed another murder and raped a white woman while on furlough from prison. Although Dukakis, a former Massachusetts governor, had not created the furlough program, he had defended it as a way of preparing prisoners for parole.

In *Chain Reaction: The Impact of Race Rights and Taxes on American Politics* (1991), authors Thomas and Mary Edsall claim that the Horton ad and similar tactics "conjured up the criminal defendants' and prisoners' rights movements, black crime, permissive liberal elites, a revenue-hungry state, eroding traditional values, tattered patriotism, and declining American prestige." The tactic appealed to the racial prejudices of many whites and helped sweep another Republican into the White House with minimal African American support.

President Bush proved better than Reagan in appointing African Americans to highly visible and influential positions. General Colin Powell, the president's national security advisor during Reagan's final years in office, soon became chairman of the Joint Chiefs of Staff, the most important military post ever occupied by an African American. Louis W. Sullivan, president of Morehouse Medical School, became U.S. Secretary of Health and Human Services. He spoke out against tobacco manufacturers and noted the special efforts that some of them made to lure African Americans into buying their products. Edward J. Perkins became the first black director general of the Foreign Service under Bush in 1989; he became an ambassador to Australia under the Clinton administration as well. Arthur Fletcher, identified by some as a "maverick Republican" because of his support of affirmative action, was appointed to head the U.S. Civil Rights Commission by Bush in 1990. Another Bush appointee, Constance Berry Newman, became the first black director of the U.S. Office of Personnel Management from 1989 to 1992. The most controversial African American of the Bush appointments was Clarence Thomas, to the Supreme Court. A steady but small trickle of black voters joined the Republican Party, although the majority did not.

Given the economic setbacks during the Reagan-Bush years, many African Americans felt a stronger stake in the outcome of the 1992 presidential election and welcomed the Democratic presidential contender Bill Clinton, who had been the former governor of Arkansas, and his running mate Senator Al Gore of Tennessee into their homes, churches, and schools. A black man, Ronald Brown, chaired the Democratic National Committee (DNC), a position never before held by an African American. Brown had managed Jackson's campaign in 1988 and was a powerful force in attracting African Americans to the Clinton-Gore ticket.

The 1992 Election: The Democrats Return to Office

Black voter turnout in November 1992 was approximately 8 percent of the total voter turnout, with 83 percent of black voters supporting the victorious Clinton-Gore ticket. Clinton won the election with just 43 percent of the popular vote, while Bush received 38 percent; third-party candidate H. Ross Perot garnered 19 percent. Local and state races featuring black candidates figured significantly in the high black turnout. In Illinois, Carol Mosely Braun defeated U.S. senator Alan Dixon in the Democratic primary and went on to win the Senate seat in November, thus becoming the second African American in the twentieth century (the first being Republican Edward Brooke of Massachusetts) and the first ever African American woman to sit in the United States Senate. Sixteen African Americans— eleven men and five women—gained new seats in the House of Representatives, which brought the total number of African Americans in the lower house to thirty-nine, a record high. Eight of the new members of the House represented five states that had not sent an African American to Congress in the twentieth century.

In the 1990s, too, several cities were led by black mayors including Houston, Texas; San Francisco, California; Denver, Colorado; and Jackson, Mississippi. When the Republicans promoted their "Contract with America" and won control of Congress in 1994, they did so without significant support from African American voters. In the race-based politics of the 1990s, African Americans generally remained loyal to President Clinton, although with important exceptions. The Black Caucus, for example, supported measures that were intended to bolster people at the lower-income levels but questioned his free trade policies, fearing they would injure the working classes. When Clinton joined with Republicans in moving welfare recipients off public assistance and onto "workfare," members of the Caucus expressed doubts about the measure's feasibility, but went no further in challenging the president's policies.

In Conservative Times

During the last quarter of the twentieth century, African Americans witnessed a number of efforts to reverse the civil rights policies that had contributed greatly to their social and economic progress. Presidents Reagan and Bush had appointed conservative leaders to key positions in agencies responsible for implementing the civil rights laws—appointees often unsympathetic to the goals of those laws. Reagan and Bush also filled vacancies on the Supreme Court with justices who philosophically would not interpret the law in ways designed to fight racial discrimination. The increasingly conservative Supreme Court began to chip away at earlier civil rights legislation.

In June 1981, President Reagan selected William Bell of Michigan to replace Eleanor Holmes Norton, who had resigned as chair of the Equal Employment Opportunity Commission in order to accept a professorship at the Georgetown Law Center. Civil rights groups and many blacks aggressively opposed Bell's appointment because of his poor record on civil rights and

Reagan's Efforts to Dismantle Civil Rights

his lack of demonstrated ability to administer an agency with 3,300 employees. The president withdrew the nomination but a year later succeeded in appointing Clarence Thomas, a young black conservative who opposed affirmative action. Thomas reduced the commission's staff and allowed the backlog of unprocessed cases to grow into the thousands.

Another controversy arose in November 1981, when Reagan tried to replace Arthur S. Flemming, chair of the U.S. Commission on Civil Rights—the agency created to investigate civil rights violations—with his own nominee, Clarence Pendleton, a conservative black Republican who had previously served as executive director of the San Diego Urban League. Flemming's dismissal and Pendleton's appointment marked the first time in the twenty-four year history of the Civil Rights Commission that a president removed its leader. Since its establishment in 1957, the commission had enjoyed remarkable independence from presidential interference.

In February 1982, President Reagan went farther, announcing his intention to nominate persons who generally opposed the civil rights agenda of the previous two decades. He attempted to oust sitting members Mary Frances Berry, Blandina Cárdenas Ramirez, and Murray Saltzman, all critical of the administration's opposition to affirmative action in employment and education. This maneuver prompted Senate Judiciary Committee members and civil rights leaders to ask the president to withdraw his nominees since his efforts had clearly "tainted the independence and integrity" of the commission. The House of Representatives voted to extend the life of the commission beyond its expiration date of September 30, 1982, and prohibited the removal of sitting commissioners except for neglect of duty or malfeasance. As the Senate wrangled over pending nominations, a compromise plan was worked out to permit the six incumbents to remain and to empower the president to appoint two additional nominees.

Undaunted, Reagan fired Berry, Ramirez and Saltzman, leaving the Commission on Civil Rights in danger of extinction. In a series of feverish behind the scenes maneuvers, the compromise was renewed. The House and the Senate would share with the president the appointment of members of the commission. The incumbent members were allowed to remain on the commission, and the president succeeded in naming two of his original appointees. Under President Reagan the U.S. Commission on Civil Rights, a voice for justice and equality under the law for more than two decades, became little more than a debating society.

During the Reagan administration, the Civil Rights Division of the Justice Department was similarly transformed, becoming the principal opponent instead of the chief supporter of blacks who sought relief from racial discrimination through the courts. In December 1985, Julius Chambers, director-counsel for the NAACP Legal Defense Fund (LDF), noted that "Today—indeed, since 1981—the Department is more often than not fighting us every step of the way in voting rights, school desegregation, equal employment opportunity, and affirmative action."

Through the LDF, however, blacks made gains in the chilly legal climate of the 1980s. Chambers and the LDF were able to win some notable victories in the Supreme Court. In *Thornburg v. Gingles* the Supreme Court upheld in 1986 the LDF's contention that a North Carolina voter redistricting plan was discriminatory, because it resulted in the "dilution of black citizens' votes in the disputed districts." During the same term, in *Local 98, International Association of Firefighters v. Cleveland,* the Court also upheld the constitutionality of affirmative action plans that included goals and timetables.

During the first Bush presidency, the composition of the Court showed clear signs of change because of the death or retirement of several justices—especially liberal justices William J. Brennan and Thurgood Marshall. Under the leadership of William H. Rehnquist, who had been appointed chief justice in 1986, and with the support of Reagan appointees Antonin Scalia and Anthony Kennedy, the Court began to reverse the gains of the previous decade. In *Richmond v. J. A. Crosson Company,* the Supreme Court found the city's "set aside program," which awarded a proportion of public contracts to minority contractors, to be unconstitutional and in violation of the rights of competing white contractors. Also in June 1989, in *Wards Cove Packing Company v. Atonio,* the Court held that an employer accused of discrimination against minority employees in the interest of promoting a business no longer had to prove his or her case. Instead, the aggrieved employee had to prove that no legitimate business interest was involved. That same month, in *Martin v. Wilkins,* the Court permitted white firefighters in Birmingham, Alabama, to sue

George H. W. Bush and the Supreme Court

the city for making race-conscious promotions. At the time no blacks were employed in the Birmingham fire department.

These Supreme Court decisions left many African Americans with a sense of betrayal. Since the 1950s, the Court had given them a fair and often favorable hearing; that expectation was no longer realistic. African Americans faced the retirement of Justice Thurgood Marshall with apprehension. Marshall's position in defense of racial equality may have had an ameliorating effect on certain justices, for example, Sandra Day O'Connor, who did not always vote consistently with any one side. When President Bush nominated the black conservative Clarence Thomas to succeed Marshall, many African Americans expressed surprise.

Thomas, a graduate of Yale Law School, initially had been President Reagan's assistant secretary for civil rights in the Department of Education and later chair of the EEOC, where he served until March 1990. When President Bush nominated him for the United States Court of Appeals for the District of Columbia, he was confirmed by voice vote in the Senate. Some African Americans applauded the president for nominating a black man, albeit a staunchly conservative one, to succeed Marshall on the Supreme Court. When Thomas picked up support from Senators Strom Thurmond of South Carolina, Sam Nunn of Georgia, and Orrin Hatch of Utah, several observers concluded that many whites in and out of Congress would think it unseemly to oppose the nomination of an African American to the Supreme Court.

The Battle over the Clarence Thomas Nomination

Clarence Thomas becomes Supreme Court Justice
President Bush and his wife, Barbara, attend as Supreme Court Justice Byron White administers the oath, and Virginia Thomas, the wife of the new Justice, holds the Bible.

Not only racially tolerant whites but even blacks were divided over Thomas's nomination. Seldom had the lines in a fight over a Supreme Court nomination been so quickly and sharply drawn. By the time the Senate Judiciary Committee began hearings on the nomination, approximately seventy-six organizations had expressed support for Thomas, including the National Black Nurses Association, the Congress of Racial Equality (CORE), the Family Research Council, the Knights of Columbus, the Conservative Caucus, the National Jewish Coalition, the United States Chamber of Commerce, and the Young Americans for Freedom. Among the fifty-four groups opposing him were the AFL-CIO, the American Federation of Teachers (AFT), the National Bar Association, the National Council of Jewish Women, the National Organization for Women (NOW), People for the American Way, and the NAACP Legal Defense and Educational Fund. Although the National Urban League remained neutral, the Congressional Black Caucus, with the exception of its lone Republican member Gary Franks of Connecticut, came out firmly against Thomas.

As Thomas's confirmation hearing moved toward its conclusion, Anita Hill, a fellow graduate of Yale Law School and a professor of law at the University of Oklahoma, accused him of sexual harassment. She had worked under Thomas at the Department of Education and at the EEOC. Her televised testimony drew millions into a discussion about the nomination. The sexual harassment allegations diverted attention from questions of Thomas's training, experience, and other qualifications. Nonetheless, when the dust settled, Clarence Thomas had been confirmed as the second African American to serve as a justice on the Supreme Court.

Throughout the 1990s, judicial conservatism could also be seen in cases involving attempts to dilute the strength of the black electorate. Such cases challenged the constitu-

Judicial Conservatism tionality of congressional districts that took race into consideration. At issue was the creation of majority-black districts in the states of Georgia, North Carolina, and Louisiana under the Voting Rights Act of 1965. In June 1995, in a five-to-four decision the Supreme Court found that Georgia's new congressional district violated the equal protection of white voters. In subsequent decisions, the Court reached the same conclusions regarding districts in North Carolina and Louisiana. Representative Maxine Waters, chair of the Congressional Black Caucus, condemned the conservative outcome: "It feels as if the Supreme Court, legislative bodies and organized right-wing groups have all decided their worst enemy is people of color, and African Americans specifically." In response, many black voters joined the Congressional Black Caucus, the Clinton administration, a large body of scholars, and a host of civic leaders in vigilantly seeking to overcome the effects of the Supreme Court's decision in the redistricting cases.

Forty-five years after the historic Supreme Court decision outlawing segregation in the public schools, the nation was still grappling with the de facto existence of racially separate

Educational Disparities and unequal schools. Not only was there white flight into the suburbs; there was also the persistent, not-so-subtle argument that the presence of "inferior" blacks diluted the rigorous educational programs designed for whites. The publication in 1994 of *The Bell Curve: Intelligence and Class Structure in American Life* by Richard Herrnstein and Charles Murray served to reinforce the ideas of people who already believed blacks to be inherently intellectually inferior. Herrnstein and Murray basically rejected the idea that blacks and whites should be afforded the same education.

With dilapidated, deteriorating schools in the inner city and with increasing violence in the suburban schools, some black parents sought alternative opportunities for the education of their children. All-black private schools, such as those existing in Milwaukee, were too few to be viable. The Muslim schools were also too few to reach many black children, while the quasi-public charter schools provided a limited number of opportunities in relatively few neighborhoods. Catholic schools, especially in large archdioceses such as Boston, New York, and Chicago, had been important alternatives for black parents, but by 1999 inadequate financial support led to the systematic closing of parochial schools in many inner-city areas. As suburban schools introduced computers and other technology to their elementary school students, the poor resources of inner-city schools left many black children on the losing side of the digital divide and thus ill-prepared to enter the twenty-first century.

Access to institutions of higher education had also become a contested issue by century's end. Working-class and middle-class blacks, who viewed upward mobility as resting largely on educational attainment, no longer took for granted that colleges and universities sought a racially diverse student body as was the case in the mid-1960s. During the civil rights era, white colleges and universities began to enroll black students, and many schools actively recruited promising scholars, athletes and musicians through school fairs, scholarships, and other welcoming strategies. The black presence in formerly all-white state universities was especially heralded in the admission of black athletes.

Most educational opportunities for disadvantaged minority students resulted from affirmative action—through policies to redress previous exclusionary admissions practices based on white privilege, to correct racial imbalance in keeping with group percentages in the larger society, and to encourage racial diversity. However, the number of African American student admissions also provoked sharp criticism from those who opposed any race-based favoritism in higher education.

During the 1990s a new voice—that of black academic conservatives—grew louder and more pronounced in the mainstream media. Economics professors Thomas Sowell, Walter Williams, and (for a while) Glenn Loury, as well as English profes- **Opposition to Affirmative Action** sor Shelby Steele, constituted the most vocal opposition to affirmative action policies. Similarly describing race-specific admissions as "reverse discrimination," Ward Connerly, an African American member of the California Board of Regents, helped to organize conservative voters in a referendum campaign that successfully enacted Proposition 209 in 1996, which forbade the use of race as a basis for admitting students to California colleges and universities.

As the enrollment of African Americans and other minorities declined in California, opponents of affirmative action vowed to launch a national campaign to eliminate affirmative action in education and employment. African American enrollment also dropped at the University of Washington after the state passed a California-style law, and at the University of Texas Law School, after the Fifth Circuit Court of Appeals decided in 1996 in favor of Cheryl Hopwood, a white woman who challenged the use of race as a factor in its admissions process. Such challenges would only increase at the opening of the twenty-first century.

The fault lines between blacks and whites appeared more vividly in news coverage of racial profiling and violence. In March 1991, all the social ills and deep resentments of the most beleaguered sections of black America reached a flashpoint when Rodney **Racial Unrest** King, an African American, was arrested following a high-speed chase by white Los Angeles police officers. He was severely beaten by the officers, who alleged that he had resisted arrest and threatened them, and eventually released without being charged.

Unbeknown to the officers, the beating had been captured on videotape by an observer and was aired on television stations worldwide. The video's effect triggered a public outcry for the dismissal of Los Angeles chief of police Daryl Gates and insistence that the offending officers be tried for using excessive force. Many Americans, including most of the African American community, saw the trial as a test of the legal system's ability to deliver justice to victims of racist police brutality.

The system failed. Difficulty in securing an impartial jury in Los Angeles led to a change of venue to Simi Valley, California, a largely white and Latino community. In April 1992, a jury of eleven whites and one Latino acquitted the officers, which shocked African Americans and many others. After the verdict, television coverage immediately shifted to the enraged response of many African Americans. For four days, black rioters looted and burned property in Los Angeles to a total of $500 million in damages. The riot had left 38 dead and 4,000 arrested. In the following year, the four police officers were tried in federal court for violating Rodney King's civil rights; this time two officers were acquitted and two were found guilty.

Two acts of violence directed at blacks by the New York City police in the late 1990s also received tremendous media coverage. In 1997, in a Brooklyn precinct station several

Racial Brutality: Abner Louima, Amadou Diallo, James Byrd

members of the police beat and sodomized Haitian immigrant Abner Louima, torturing him a with a wooden plunger handle, puncturing his bladder, and severely damaging his colon. In 1999 one member of the force admitted his involvement and was sentenced; another was found guilty and sentenced; two other officers were acquitted. During the same year, New York City police fired forty-five rounds into an unarmed Guinean immigrant, Amadou Diallo, who was standing in the entrance hall of the building where he lived. The police mistook his reaching for his wallet for going for a gun. For months Mayor Rudolph Giuliani and the commissioner of police refused to condemn the officers, while African Americans and their supporters decried both the police and their superiors and protested the administration's failure to bring the officers to trial.

The most heinous act of racial brutality occurred in the closing years of the century in Jasper, Texas. There, two white men chained an African American hitchhiker, James Byrd, Jr., to their vehicle and dragged him to his destination—literally tearing apart his body in the process. The nation's horror was only partially mitigated by the speedy trial, conviction, and sentencing of the men responsible for the atrocity.

Finally, in 1999 New Jersey Governor Christine Todd Whitman admitted that the state highway patrol routinely stopped African American motorists along the New Jersey Turnpike and searched them for drugs or other contraband solely on the basis of a racial profile constructed by the police department. This indiscriminate profiling of blacks, especially black men, combined with acts of police brutality in New York and Los Angeles, reinforced the belief that little or no progress had been made in race relations at the end of the twentieth century.

Artistic Currents

In artistic expression, blacks made much progress in the last two decades of the twentieth century. Such post-World War II African American writers as Ralph Ellison and James Baldwin continued to win over audiences well into the 1980s. Ralph Ellison continued to publish essays and short stories, bringing out *Going to the Territory* in 1986. In the same year, James Baldwin, who compromised his expatriate status by spending months at a time in the United States, maintained his popularity and his influence with the publication of *Evidence of Things Not Seen*. New writers also captivated audiences. The critically acclaimed trilogy of novelist Albert Murray—*Trainwhistle Guitar* (1974), *The Spyglass Tree* (1991), and *The Seven League Boots* (1996)—traced the coming to maturity of a black artist in twentieth-century America, and gripping novels and essays by John Edgar Wideman revealed the costs and consequences of a racial identity shaped by "the menacing margins of urban life." Novelist Charles Johnson's *Middle Passage* (1990), a historical reconstruction of slavery, won the National Book Award.

The rise of prominent African American women writers marked the most significant trend in literature in the last two decades of the twentieth century. Many of them built on the gender-conscious writings of the 1960s and 1970s. The poet Rita Dove won the Pulitzer Prize for her volume of poetry *Thomas and Beulah* (1986), and in 1993 she became the youngest United States poet laureate. Novelist Alice Walker became one of the most widely read and influential black women writers of the 1980s when her novel *The Color Purple* won the Pulitzer Prize in 1982 and was subsequently made into a successful film. Toni Morrison, who worked as an editor at Random House for nineteen years, became the pre-eminent African American author in the 1990s, with essays and novels that addressed issues of race and gender, the legacy of slavery, and the construction of black identity and culture. Her novel *Beloved* (1987), which won the Pulitzer, was made into a movie in 1998, and in 1993, Morrison became the first African American recipient of the Nobel Prize in Literature for her body of writings that, in the words of the awards committee, "give life to an essential aspect of American reality."

Toni Morrison

Women Writers

In the last decade of the twentieth century, August Wilson emerged as the premier African American playwright. Three of his powerful dramas—*Fences* (1986), *The Piano Lesson* (1990), and *Two Trains Running* (1993)—won numerous awards including two Pulitzer Prizes. Although Wilson's plays were performed in a variety of settings for diverse audiences, his 1996 appeal to save

Playwrights, Comedians, Filmmakers, Actors

"black theater institutions"—deemed a call for "separatism" by his critics—made him a controversial figure. Speaking at Princeton University, Wilson rebutted such claims, arguing that black theaters generated African American "self-definition" by producing the work of black playwrights and guaranteeing the continued existence of black repertory.

The popularity of films starring African American comedians began to rise in the 1980s. Richard Pryor and Eddie Murphy and the successes of the film version of Alice Walker's *The Color Purple* (1985) and Spike Lee's low-budget *She's Gotta Have It* (1986) figure as harbingers for the surge of 1990s films by or about African Americans. Murphy, perhaps the most popular black actor in the 1980s, appeared in interracial buddy films—*Trading Places* (1983) and two *Beverly Hills Cop* films (1984 and 1987)—where his stereotypically hip black character uses humor to bridge the cultural gap between with the film's unhip white characters.

The Color Purple, directed by Steven Spielberg, reached a large interracial audience and garnered eleven Academy Award nominations—a record for a film with a predominantly black cast, although it actually won no awards.

Spike Lee, the most prolific of a growing cohort of independent black filmmakers, received critical acclaim for *Do the Right Thing* in 1989, which exposed unspoken and continued racism in a changing Brooklyn neighborhood. Lee's film begins with twin quotes from Martin Luther King, Jr., and Malcolm X and leaves unresolved the seeming conflict between those two leaders' philosophies. Lee's 1992 film *Malcolm X,* which starred Denzel Washington, resonated with twentieth-century black youth culture—the "X" image on clothing becoming a ubiquitous symbol in the black community after the film's release.

From the late 1980s through the 1990s, a series of films directed by African Americans used life in the inner city as the setting for the exploration of larger social and cultural issues in regard to race. Black filmmaker John Singleton's *Boyz 'n the Hood* (1991) portrayed the inner-city life in Los Angeles. Other films in the 1990s dramatized inner-city life, including *Straight Out of Brooklyn* (1991), *Menace II Society* (1997), and *New Jack City* (1998).

Despite the growing visibility and success of black filmmaker Spike Lee, most continued to receive only limited recognition from their white peers. *People* magazine decried the "continuing exclusion" of blacks from prominence in the American film industry as "a national disgrace," a charge justified by the fact that only one black filmmaker was among the 166 nominees for Academy Awards in 1996.

Still, the 1990s provided enhanced opportunities for black actors, especially men. In 1996, for example, African American men starred in twelve of Hollywood's most successful films. Those who became multimillion-dollar earners and mainstream film staples included Denzel Washington, Forrest Whittaker, Samuel L. Jackson, Wesley Snipes, Laurence Fishburne, Morgan Freeman, Cuba Gooding Jr., and Will Smith. Although the film industry offered fewer opportunities for black female actors, a few managed to break through, including Whoopi Goldberg, Angela Bassett, and Halle Berry.

Black visibility on television also expanded in the 1980s and 1990s, initially in interracial contexts. Situation comedies such as *Diff'rent Strokes* and *Benson* included black characters in fam-

Blacks on Television ily comedies with predominantly white casts. During this period, blacks also began to appear in television commercials, as the advertisement industry increasingly recognized the profitability of appealing to black television audiences. In 1980 African American entrepreneur Robert L. Johnson founded the cable network Black Entertainment Television (BET), but perhaps no development proved more important in expanding the black presence on television in the last two decades of the twentieth century than the growth of talk shows.

On locally and nationally televised programs, hosts discussed national and international issues and cultural phenomena with guests, a studio audience, and sometimes call-in viewers. The programs, which addressed an assortment of national, international and lifestyle issues, frequently featured blacks as guests, and African Americans hosted a small number of them. One, *The Oprah Winfrey Show,* would catapult its host to superstardom, making her the nation's first female African American billionaire.

After beginning her career as a news anchor on ABC's Baltimore affiliate, Winfrey moved into the talk show medium. In 1985 she launched *The Oprah Winfrey Show,* which received numerous Emmy Awards and is shown in well over one hundred countries across the globe. With her production company, Harpo Productions, Winfrey also produced screen adaptations of African American literary works. Noted for her philanthropic work as well,

Winfrey was included in *Time* magazine in 1998 for the first but not the last time on its list of the one hundred most influential people of the twentieth century.

Throughout the 1980s and 1990s, television dramas and comedies featured increasing numbers of black characters who represented social mobility and middle-class status, most notably the phenomenally successful series *The Cosby Show*. Produced by and starring Bill Cosby, the TV series focused on the lives of the upper-middle-class, dual-headed household of the Huxtable family; the show's spinoff, *A Different World,* focused on the adventures of a group of students at a historically black college. These shows reached their widest audiences at the same time that the rates of teen pregnancy, single-headed households, and children born in poverty stood at their highest levels among black Americans.

Bill Cosby's Huxtables
The Cosby Show, through its comic depictions of the adventures of an upper middle-class family, gave many American television viewers a new perspective on the black experience. Cosby portrayed Cliff Huxtable, M.D., on the Emmy-award-winning show.

Robert Colescott, *George Washington Carver Crossing the Delaware: Page from an American History Textbook,* 1975

By the 1990s, museums devoted to African American art were located in most major cities, exhibiting the work of such artists as **Artists** Martin Puryear, Glen Ligon, Fred Wilson, Betye Saar, Eugene J. Martin, Richard Mayhew, Adrian Piper, Faith Ringgold, Lorna Simpson, Carrie Mae Weems, Jean Michel Basquiat, Kara Walker, and many others. Many of these black artists brought a spirit of historical revisionism, irreverence, and satire to their work. Robert Colescott, for example, won acclaim for his vibrantly colorful, politically conscious art. His critiques are presented with wit and humor, as in the case of *Matthew Henson and the Quest for the North Pole* (1986), in which Colescott exposes the lie in most history-book accounts of Robert Peary as the first person to reach the North Pole. In actuality, Peary's chief assistant, the African American navigator Matthew Henson, first planted the American flag on the North Pole.

Perhaps no artist's life captures black progress and poverty in the late twentieth century more poignantly that that of Jean Michel Basquiat, who propelled himself to the top of the New York art scene in less than a decade. His artistic talent was nurtured on the streets of New York and the flourishing hip-hop culture of the 1980s, but his witty poems and distinctive graffiti tag, SAMO, appeared on subway walls as early as 1976. His prolific mixed media works often constituted provocative social commentary, as is evident in his *Irony of a Negro Policeman* (1981). In 1989 a drug overdose ended Basquiat's life; he was twenty-nine.

The most innovative and controversial black artistic form to emerge in the last quarter of the twentieth century was rap music, a style rooted in African American traditions such as disco, funk, and boasting or "rapping" and in black immigrant traditions such as Jamaican "toasting" and sound system culture. As it took shape, rap music developed alongside a range of American urban youth cultural practices, including graffiti, breakdancing, and an innovative deejay style. Collectively, these four elements came to be referred to as Hip Hop culture.

Hip Hop Rising Today the term *Hip Hop* refers to the cultural movement that started in the 1970s in the Bronx, New York, and developed into a way of life for mostly black and Latino urban youth. Feeling disconnected from their parents' brand of 1960s and 1970s activism, a new generation stifled by growing urban poverty, violence, racism, and police profiling created the Hip Hop underground. By the late 1970s, Hip Hop came to define not only a musical genre but also a style of dress, communication, and aesthetics that reflected the experiences and sentiments of urban youth born after 1965. It has since evolved from a local independently black-produced and consumed music form into a global cultural phenomenon.

Most Hip Hop histories begin in the summer of 1973 at a South Bronx party presided over by Clive Campbell, a.k.a. DJ Kool Herc, a Jamaica-born DJ credited as one of the fathers of Hip Hop. Sylvia Robinson, founder of Sugar Hill **Hip Hop Is Born** Records, was one of the first to test Hip Hop's potential profitabil- ity. Sugar Hill released "Rapper's Delight" in 1979, an impromptu recording by a group called the Sugar Hill Gang which became a hit on radio stations for black audiences before climbing the American pop charts.

Independent African American record labels and mainstream white labels alike soon seized on the success of Hip Hop and signed almost anyone who could rap in the Bronx. Consequently, it was not until the early 1980s that many of Hip Hop's pioneers of the 1970s, such as DJ Kool Herc, Grandmaster Flash, and Afrika Bambaataa, became known to a larger public. The music of early Hip Hop artists reveals myriad influences from the peace, love, community and survival of Bambaataa's 1982 "Planet Rock" to Grandmaster Flash's unflinch- ing look at incarceration, police brutality, and desperation in his 1982 hit, "The Message." Works such as these helped to define early rap music as an oppositional cultural practice.

Russell Simmons, a young black entrepreneur from a middle-class family in Queens, New York, emerged as arguably the first major producer of Hip Hop. Simmons, along with then NYU student Rick Rubin, cofounded Def Jam Records, which produced such nation- ally acclaimed groups as LL Cool J, Run-DMC (which included Simmons's brother Joseph), Public Enemy, and the Jewish rap group the Beastie Boys. Def Jam branched out into film with *Krush Groove* (1985) and *Tougher Than Leather* (1988) and eventually fashion. One of Def Jam's most important rap groups was Public Enemy, known for its socially and politically conscious messages, such as "Don't Believe the Hype" and "Fight the Power." Public Enemy soared in popularity in the early 1990s, its music gaining additional exposure through inter- national tours and exposure in Spike Lee's films. The group's lead rapper, Chuck D, claimed that rap music was black people's CNN.

Hip Hop escalated in prominence with the rising popularity of music videos and the deteriorating social and economic conditions of the 1980s and early 1990s, a period of rising rates of black youth unemployment, poverty, black imprisonment, and drug use (especially of crack cocaine). Its sound ranged from the more socially conscious lyrics of such groups as Run-DMC and individual rappers such as Tupac Shakur to the gangsta rap of groups such as Niggaz with Attitude (N.W.A.) and rappers Ice-T and Snoop Dogg. Gangsta rap was a West Coast, funk-inspired form that celebrated gang violence, criticized police brutality, and casually denigrated women. And there was money to be made in the graphic portrayal of impoverished black communities, as evidenced by the fortune amassed in the 1990s by New York performer and producer Sean Combs, then called "Puff Daddy" (he would later refer to himself as "Puffy," "P. Diddy," and "Diddy," respectively), from his growing company Bad Boy Records.

Throughout the 1990s and beyond, Hip Hop constituted a battleground on which the culture wars—the racial and social issues of America—were fought. In the early 1990s, the Hip Hop group 2 Live Crew provoked a wave of controversy for **Hip Hop and the Culture Wars** explicitly misogynist language and visual imagery in the album *Nasty as They Wanna Be* (1989). With their album banned in Florida, the rappers were arrested after a performance in the state. Brought to trial on obscenity charges, their case reached the United States Court of Appeals, which decided in favor of freedom of expression.

603

During this period, the East Coast–West Coast Hip Hop rivalry created a battleground of its own. The iconic figure Tupac Shakur, then associated with the Los Angeles label Death Row Records, was shot to death in Las Vegas in 1996; Brooklyn's Christopher "Biggie Smalls" Wallace met a similar fate in Los Angeles the following year. (The men had been feuding.) Such instances of violent, criminal behavior reinforced the impression that Hip Hop represented the "authentic" voice of inner-city black youths—what one *New York Times* article described as the "poverty, violence, lack of education, frustration, and rage of the ghetto." However, gangsta rap increasingly won over white suburban youth, who identified with its rebellious tone and novel sound.

In actuality, Hip Hop has never presented one "authentic" black voice. Indeed, its frequent celebration of such themes as struggle, ghetto hardship, financial ambition, materialism, and hedonism are deeply informed by the American experience. Hip Hop has always defied simple categorization—defined by its diverse, even contradictory, lyrical messages. Indeed, some performers, such as the rapper KRS-ONE, used the medium of Hip Hop itself to speak out against violence and misogyny.

Critique, innovation, and new styles emerged first at the local level in numerous community Hip Hop venues. For example, as the East Coast–West Coast feud dominated national headlines in the years leading up to the death of Shakur and Wallace, a new group of New York-based MCs began to counter the gangsta sound. Groups such as A Tribe Called Quest, De La Soul, and Leaders of the New School, all affiliated with the Native Tongues and Zulu Nation collectives, brought to the music an eclectic mix of black-nationalist rhetoric and New Age spirituality that came to define a socially "conscious" sound.

During the 1990s, Hip Hop became a complicated array of regional movements. Its seemingly countless permutations facilitated its growing dominance in American popular culture. Local Hip Hop communities flourished across the United States, in cities such as Oakland, Chicago, Boston, Miami, and St. Louis, drawing on the cultural sensibilities of their respective locales. In Philadelphia, heavily influenced by jazz, The Roots employed live instruments and Spoken Word artists, paving the way for a Neo-Soul movement later in the decade. Outkast, featuring Andre 3000 and Big Boi, broke ground in the "Dirty" South for new artists from cities such as Atlanta, New Orleans, and Houston.

New York spawned a new array of local community sites, including the Lyricist Lounge, which produced such artists as Mos Def and Talib Kweli. The Wu Tang Clan, with artists from Staten Island, Brooklyn, and New Jersey, boasted eastern philosophy, social critique, and a new model of black capitalism. Wu Tang's usage of Five-Percenter rhetoric also tapped into Islam, the most obvious spiritual influence on Hip Hop's early years. Countless artists, including Chuck D, Rakim, Busta Rhymes, and Eve all have referenced Islam's multiform religious traditions.

In most cases, these local scenes had existed for some time, but as the 1990s progressed, each of these regions, to varying degrees, competed for national recognition as part of Hip Hop's mainstream. Additionally, scores of other artists who did not achieve major commercial success (by choice or by default) contributed to equally vibrant "underground" communities that often celebrated their obscurity, and perceived cultural purity, as a form of "keeping it real" to Hip Hop's oppositional roots within the Bronx's black and Latino ghettos.

Although the majority of rappers have been male, there have been several women Hip Hop artists. MC Lyte and Queen Latifah helped define the East Coast sound from a black woman's perspective, while groups such as Salt n Pepa and TLC took on the oft-taboo topic of female sexuality. By the end of the decade, Hip Hop "feminists" and cultural theorists,

Run-DMC
Run-DMC was among the early Hip Hop groups to produce socially conscious rap.

most notably bell hooks, Tricia Rose, and Joan Morgan, analyzed the love-hate relationship of African American young women and girls with a music that so often devalues and does violence to their personhood. Such analyses have given shape to a "post-Soul" feminism that embraces diverse types of gender and class consciousness.

The graphic and profane language of much of commercial Hip Hop provided a hot touchstone for politicians, public figures, and black organizational leaders who denounced it as sexist, racist, homophobic, anti-Semitic, antiauthoritarian, and too sexually explicit. Leaders and organizations, including Jesse Jackson, C. Delores Tucker of the National Political Congress of Black Women, Rev. Calvin Butts of Abyssinian Baptist Church in New York, the National Council of Negro Women, and the NAACP, protested gangsta rap and other troubling aspects of Hip Hop.

The negative critique notwithstanding, Hip Hop's ability to generate tremendous financial profits for its performers and producers marks the quintessential character of the progress and poverty of the last two decades of the twentieth century. By the late 1990s, Hip Hop had vaulted from a fringe movement and underground art form to one of the most prominent, profitable, yet controversial forms of American popular music. Like the music of earlier generations, Hip Hop as a new cultural form appealed to its youthful devotees of all races for its ability to convey and critique economic and social realities.

Global Concerns

On Thanksgiving eve in 1984, Randall Robinson, the executive director of Trans-Africa, Mary Frances Berry of the United States Commission on Civil Rights, Eleanor Holmes

Norton of Georgetown Law Center, and Walter Fauntroy, District of Columbia delegate to the House of Representatives, began a sit-in campaign at the South African Embassy in Washington, D.C., to protest apartheid and the detention of black South African labor leaders. The sit-in campaign lasted for more than a year and led to the arrest of hundreds of people who protested the racial policies of the white-ruled Republic of South Africa. Their efforts also served as encouragement to the black majority in South Africa to fight more vigorously for their rights and aroused world indignation against apartheid. By 1986 the U.S. Congress passed bills favoring economic sanctions against South Africa. When President Reagan opposed the sanctions, Congress overrode his veto. Still, Reagan continued to insist that not only would such moves hurt black South Africans but that responsible black South Africans opposed sanctions. (In fact, most anti-apartheid groups and activists in South Africa supported sanctions.)

The pressure on white South Africans to promote greater democracy began to have an effect once Fredrick Willem de Klerk became president in 1989. Early in 1990, de Klerk,

The End of Apartheid who was white, lifted the thirty-year ban on the African National Congress (ANC), which had been fighting to end minority rule. After twenty-eight years in prison, Nelson Mandela, the titular head of the ANC and a universal symbol of the black liberation movement in South Africa, was released. In June 1990, Mandela visited eight American cities as part of a twelve-day tour of the United States. Upon arriving in New York, he was greeted with a tumultuous welcome from crowds that included Americans of all ethnic and racial backgrounds. He also addressed a joint meeting of the two houses of the U.S. Congress. In the speech, Mandela invoked the names of American heroes who had been sources of inspiration to him. Mandela and de Klerk jointly received the Noble Peace Prize in 1993 for their efforts to bring about racial equality in South Africa.

The decades of the 1980s and 1990s witnessed the growing visibility of African Americans on the international scene. By far the most prominent figure in this regard was General

African Americans on the International Stage Colin Powell, who would work in three Republican presidential administrations. Born in New York City in 1937 to Jamaican immigrants, Powell's career trajectory began in the military against the backdrop of Vietnam, where he served two tours, one in 1962 and the other in 1968, receiving the Purple Heart twice along with other honors. In 1987, Ronald Reagan appointed Powell National Security Advisor—the first African American to hold this position. He was recognized for his ability to present clear assessments of the issues surrounding America's policies towards the Cold War with the Soviet Union and Iran. In 1989, under George H. W. Bush, he became the youngest man and the first African American to serve as chairman of the Joint Chiefs of Staff.

While in this post, Powell directed the removal of Panama's president Manuel Noriega, who was seized and later convicted in the United States for drug trafficking, and he oversaw the first American invasion of Iraq in 1991. Although the United States tended to support Iraq in its decade-long war with Iran (1980–1990), Iraqi president Saddam Hussein's move against oil-rich Kuwait drew immediate and strong U.S. condemnation. President George H. W. Bush responded to the invasion on August 3, 1990, the day after it occurred, calling on world leaders to take collective action against Iraq. Early in January 1991, Congress voted 52–47 in the Senate and 250–183 in the House to give the president authority to use military force against Iraq and to end its occupation of Kuwait. Soon, 500,000 U.S. troops were transported to the Middle East.

Colin Powell, youngest and first African American chairman of the Joint Chiefs of Staff

Powell had been president George H. W. Bush's National Security Advisor when the president elevated him to his new position in 1989, a position to which he was reappointed in 1991. He later served as Secretary of State under George W. Bush.

African Americans, although only 13 percent of the nation's population, accounted for 25 percent of the U.S. troops sent to war in the Persian Gulf. However, most African Americans did not support the war. For some, opposition was based on the recognition that their disproportionate presence in the armed forces was rooted in the lack **The Persian Gulf War** of job opportunities in the civilian sector. Although blacks expressed pride in Powell's leadership, a reliable poll reported that they were split evenly on the question of military action. Whites, in contrast, favored the Persian Gulf War by a 4:1 ratio.

In Congress, every black Democrat voted against the measure authorizing the use of force in "Operation Desert Storm," as the air strikes were called. Ironically, by the time the military operation was over in late February 1991, American veterans, and particularly black veterans, returned home to declining job prospects in an economic recession. Powell continued to be immensely popular among members of both parties and races in the 1990s, and it was widely speculated that he would run for president. Although Powell rejected the idea, he would serve as the first black secretary of state during George W. Bush's first term, from 2001 to 2004.

At Century's End

As African American poet Maya Angelou read from her poem "On the Pulse of the Morning" at Bill Clinton's inauguration on January 20, 1993, blacks wondered what Clinton meant when he promised that his administration "would look like America."

Prominent Washington attorney and former president of the National Urban League Vernon Jordan oversaw the new president's transition team, and at the outset of his administration, Clinton named four African Americans to his cabinet—Ron Brown as secretary of commerce; Mississippi congressman Mike Espy as secretary of agriculture; Hazel O'Leary, the executive vice president of the Northern States Power Company of Minnesota, as secretary of energy; and Jesse Brown, executive director of Disabled American Veterans, as secretary of veterans affairs. Clinton appointed more African American judges than any previous president. He also elevated historian Mary Frances Berry, whom President Reagan had attempted to fire, to the position of chair of the Civil Rights Commission.

However, when Clinton attempted to appoint his former Yale Law School classmate Lani Guinier to head the Justice Department's Civil Rights Division, he faced the first major racial controversy of his presidency. Conservatives accused Guinier of favoring political allocations based on race, and instead of providing her with an opportunity to explain her ideas, President Clinton withdrew the nomination and appointed instead lawyer Deval Patrick, who in 2007 would become the first black governor of Massachusetts. Some African Americans resented Clinton's unwillingness to stand behind Guinier, contrasting him to President George H. W. Bush, who had been unwavering in his support of his conservative and controversial Supreme Court justice nominee Clarence Thomas.

A popular president among African Americans, Clinton faced criticism from a number of influential black leaders in regard to his position on welfare reform. In August 1996 he signed the Personal Responsibility and Work Opportunity Reconciliation Act, which combined some of his ideas with those proposed by the Republicans, who won control of both houses of Congress in 1994. The act aimed to reduce Aid to Families of Dependent Children (AFDC), slashing food stamp allotments and limiting families to five years of benefits. It also required adult recipients of welfare to find jobs within two years.

The welfare reform act ultimately proved to be both politically astute and in keeping with Clinton's centrist philosophy, since he won reelection shortly after its passage, becoming the first Democratic incumbent to do so since Franklin Roosevelt. The nation experienced impressive growth during the Clinton presidency. When he left office in 2001, the poverty rate was lower than it had been in twenty years. However, within a few years and in a downward economy by 2001, welfare reform failed to address adequately the longstanding problems of poverty. Many who had taken jobs in the aftermath of the reforms found themselves unemployed again, and the condition of poor mothers and children steadily deteriorated.

One of Clinton's most important gestures was that of addressing America's race problem. Forming a seven-member advisory board to promote a national dialogue on race in June 1997, President Clinton established the "One America" initiative under the chairmanship of historian John Hope Franklin. Board members were charged with the task of helping to articulate a "vision of racial reconciliation." They represented a racially diverse group of two African Americans, an Asian American, a Latino American, and three European Americans of varying expertise: William Winter, the former governor of Mississippi; Linda Chavez-Thompson, executive vice president of the AFL-CIO; Thomas Kean, president of Drew University and former governor of New Jersey; Angela Oh, Los Angeles attorney and former special counsel to the Assembly Special Committee on the Los Angeles Crisis; Robert Thomas, executive vice president for marketing of Republic Industries and former

Window in Time

No More Precious Gift

Throughout the entire life of the board, I reminded myself of the admonishment President Clinton delivered to America in San Diego, just as the board's work was commencing: There was no more precious gift our generation could present to future generations than to lift from them the heavy burden of race. This was not a problem to be fixed by the board; at best the board could help delineate its contours and point to solutions. This was not a problem to be fixed by a president; several presidents with courage equal to Clinton's had struggled to confront American racism, and each had advanced the cause of equality incrementally. The problem of race in America has been, and continues to be, an American problem, and the conversation the board began was, and remains, the means to a national solution.

John Hope Franklin, *Mirror to America: The Autobiography of John Hope Franklin* (New York: Farrar, Straus and Giroux, 2005), p. 356.

president and CEO of Nissan Motor Corporation; and Suzan D. Johnson Cook, former White House fellow and senior pastor of the Bronx Christian Fellowship.

In a country simmering with racial tensions and clashing theories about how best to address them, the American public greeted the president's announcement with a range of responses from welcome approval to flat dismissal. *Washington Post* columnist William Raspberry expressed the fear that the board's efforts might "degenerate into a mutually frustrating argument about affirmative action." Early on board members announced their intention to attack the "virtually intractable" problem of racism by emphasizing two issues—education and economic opportunity. Discussions focused on race relations in the context of the changing racial and ethnic composition of the American people in the late twentieth century.

Board members assessed the most effective ways to educate white Americans, since they, for much of the country's history, had "been in control of virtually everything . . . [defining] what justice and equality mean." The board likewise reflected on accusations of racial profiling and racist treatment by the police, as well as on strategies for enlisting the aid of American citizens in meeting the board's goals.

As 1997 closed, the board planned public town meetings across the country, some of which featured the president. The dialogue on race occurred, as well, in campus forums, conversations with state governors, and Native American tribal government. Public awareness of the board could be seen in the increased response to address this topic, which Vice President Al Gore called "a necessary healing step." The president's personal involvement drew large numbers of concerned citizens into the national conversation. The angry disruption of the board's public meetings in Denver by Native Americans, who decried "the lack of an American Indian on the seven-member advisory board," served to reinforce the

Dr. John Hope Franklin, Chair of the Advisory Board of the President's Initiative on Race, presents President Clinton with the Board's report, September 18, 1998.

importance of the "race board" and its mission to all Americans. By early summer 1998, major daily newspapers regularly commented on the many ways that the Clinton administration had begun to integrate the insights of the advisory board into its formulation and execution of policy.

In September 1998, the advisory board presented its final report to President Clinton in a document that included policy suggestions in regard to education, health, the criminal justice system, and immigration, as well as the identification of characteristics and programs that represented what the board termed "Promising Practices for Racial Reconciliation." The board made four major recommendations: create a permanent body, the President's Council for One America, "to promote harmony and dialogue among the nation's racial and ethnic groups;" devise a public education program to keep the nation informed about race relations; use the dynamic leadership of the presidency to push leaders in government and the private sector to "make racial reconciliation a reality;" and engage "youth leaders in the effort to build bridges among the races."

At the end of the twentieth century, African Americans faced the future with cautious hope. They saw only too well the rightward turn in national politics and the rising conservative tide that had already begun to undercut many policies responsible for black progress. Thus blacks remained faithful to the Clinton administration when the president was impeached on charges of lying about sexual misconduct, and they considered his acquittal to be the proper resolution. Far more salient to them was the quest for racial equality and black economic empowerment. Such organizations as Rainbow/ PUSH's Wall Street Project, the National Action Network's Madison Avenue Initiative, the NAACP's Economic Reciprocity programs, and numerous urban churches and other faith-based organizations championed a new emphasis on black wealth and job creation. Such programs tapped into both the progress and the poverty of the times—the exuberant economic climate of the late 1990s and the growing awareness that blacks must tackle and rectify the social problems of their communities. As the new millennium opened, African Americans looked forward to the presidential election of 2000 and hoped for the continuation of efforts to advance racial harmony.

23 Perspectives on the Present

Legal Challenges

Enduring Disparities: Health, Education, and Incarceration

Forgotten in Hurricane Katrina

Hip Hop's Global Generation

New Great Migrations

The Politics of Change

"Vote or Die" Rally in Detroit, 2004
Students at Wayne State University wait to see Hip Hop artist Sean "P Diddy" Combs who was at the rally to encourage young people to vote.

For African Americans, the twenty-first century has unfolded to this point as a study in contradictions. The first evidence of this occurred in 2000, when the hotly contested presidential election between Republican candidate George W. Bush and his Democratic rival Al Gore was decided in the judicial system instead of the Electoral College. In a 5–4 ruling, the rightward-leaning Supreme Court narrowly decided the victory in favor of Bush despite numerous charges of Republican malfeasance during the recount in Florida, the crucial state on which electoral victory hinged and where Bush's brother served as governor. Nationally, less than 10 percent of the black vote had gone to Bush. Numerous continuing charges were filed on behalf of African Americans who said that they had been systematically denied the right to vote in Florida and other states.

Yet it was this controversial president who appointed two African Americans in succession as secretary of state—the most important voice, besides the president's, in representing the interests of the United States to the rest of the world. In the aftermath of the Al-Qaeda terrorist attacks on the Twin Towers of the World Trade Center in New York and on the Pentagon on September 11, 2001, Colin Powell, America's first black secretary of state, played a key role in the Bush administration's decision to go to war in Afghanistan with the aim of capturing or killing al-Qaeda leader Osama bin Laden. Powell would later be given a prominent role in launching America's invasion of Iraq, although he became increasingly estranged from the administration's handling of the Iraq War and other foreign policies. His decision to resign as secretary of state after President Bush's reelection in 2004 was fueled, many believe, by increasingly sharp ideological differences with Vice President Richard Cheney, Secretary of Defense Donald Rumsfeld, and other administration war hawks.

Condoleeza Rice, who in Bush's first term served as the president's national security advisor, succeeded Powell as secretary of state in Bush's second term—an astounding first for a black woman. *Forbes* magazine's listing of the "100 Most Powerful Women in the World 2004" ranked Rice as Number One. "Advising the leader of the world's largest superpower—and having the ear of leaders around the globe—makes Rice, 49, the most powerful woman in the world," the magazine wrote. "When Rice speaks, she speaks for the president." (Hillary Rodham Clinton, then a U.S. senator from New York, was ranked fifth by *Forbes*, and Supreme Court Justices Sandra Day O'Connor and Ruth Bader Ginsburg also stood among the top ten.) In 2005 the magazine of the American Association of Retired Persons (AARP) called Condoleeza Rice a "political rock star."

But despite these powerful symbols of black achievement and influence, most African Americans perceived racial progress as stalled, if not in a downward spiral, during George W. Bush's presidency. In November 2007, survey findings of the Pew Research Center, a respected nonpartisan social-science research organization, indicated increasing cynicism among blacks when asked two questions: "Are blacks better or worse off now than five years ago?" and "Will life for blacks be better or worse in the future?" The report noted that 29 percent of African American respondents perceived conditions for blacks as

Secretary of State Colin Powel and National Security Advisor Condoleeza Rice

a group as having actually worsened in the five-year period leading up to 2007. This figure was up significantly from survey results in 1999, when only 13 percent of black respondents felt that the situation of blacks had deteriorated over the preceding five years. Contemplating the future, only 44 percent in 2007 (compared to 57 percent in a 1986 survey) envisioned progress, 21 percent envisioned worsening conditions, 31 percent predicted no change at all, and 4 percent had either no idea or no willingness to say.

Yet in 2007, blacks stood on the precipice of change. Exactly one year later, in November 2008, African Americans would wildly cheer the election of the first black president of the United States, Barack Hussein Obama. This same Pew Research Center survey, which was conducted from September 5 through October 6, 2007, showed most black respondents unable to imagine the possibility of Obama's victory.

For African Americans in the new millennium's first decade—in years that will be forever associated with great tragedy and unprecedented triumph—freedom and equality are undoubtedly perceived by some as attainable and by others as elusive.

Legal Challenges

The growing conservatism of the federal bench has been a major challenge to those blacks who perceive the Republicans presidents' judicial appointments in the last two decades as an attempt to turn back the clock of racial progress. However, many blacks, through such legal-defense organizations as the NAACP Legal Defense Fund, the Lawyers Committee for Civil Rights under Law, the Southern Poverty Law Project, and other liberal groups, have brought suits to the courts in litigation that challenged efforts to abridge the hard-won goals of the Civil Rights Era.

One of the major controversies surrounding the 2000 presidential election was the denial of the right to vote to African Americans in Florida. Bush's opponent Al Gore, other

The 2000 Presidential Election prominent Democrats, and many African Americans contested the election when they learned about attempts to prevent African Americans from voting. In the weeks following the election, a recount was undertaken in the contested Florida counties, and stories about various methods used to disenfranchise blacks began to leak out.

The long list of civil rights violations included moving polls or closing them early in minority areas. A Florida law that prohibits anyone convicted of a crime from ever voting again (even after serving his or her sentence) purged from the voter rolls not only ex-convicts but also individuals of the same name who had never committed a crime. Poll administrators were prevented from checking the registration status of African Americans. Notwithstanding all this, a 5–4 decision the U.S. Supreme Court blocked Gore's legal challenge by halting the recount in Florida; Bush was declared the winner by fewer than 600 votes, and the issue of African American voter disenfranchisement was never resolved.

In another case striking at black participation in the electoral process, the Court limited the ability of states to create congressional districts with majority African American populations. Ruling, again by a 5–4 margin, in *Vieth v. Jubelirer,* in 2004 the Court declared that political gerrymandering—the creation of congressional districts to determine an outcome—was illegal. Gerrymandering has been used for various political ends over the long course of U.S. history, and in *Vieth* the Court overturned its own 1986 *Davis v. Bandemer* ruling, which had upheld the state government's interest in controlling the boundaries of districts to facilitate

African American representation. The 2004 decision effectively allows African Americans to be spread out over several districts, diluting their presence in Congress.

In 2005 the Court's conservatism was bolstered when Bush appointed John G. Roberts to succeed William J. Rehnquist as chief justice and Samuel Alito to replace the retiring Justice Sandra Day O'Connor. In the conservative political climate of the Bush administration, affirmative action was one of the most discussed and challenged policies in the courts. In 2003, in *Grutter v. Bollinger* and *Gratz v. Bollinger*, the Supreme Court ruled on the legality of the University of Michigan's affirmative action policies in both law school and undergraduate admissions. Not since the *Bakke* case in 1978 had the Court addressed this issue in higher education.

Challenges to Affirmative Action

In 1996 Barbara Grutter, a forty-three-year-old white woman with an LSAT score of 161 (top score is 180) and an undergraduate GPA of 3.8 applied to the University of Michigan Law School, where she was initially wait-listed and ultimately rejected. Grutter filed a class action lawsuit against the university regents, claiming that the law school's affirmative action policy constituted racial discrimination under the Equal Protection Clause of the Fourteenth Amendment and violated Title VI of the Civil Rights Act of 1964, which states that "No person in the United States shall on the basis of race, color or national origin be excluded from participation in, be denied the benefit of, or be subjected to discrimination under any program or activity receiving federal financial assistance."

In *Grutter*, handed down in 2003, the Supreme Court reversed a lower court ruling and declared that diversity constitutes a compelling state interest and that the law school's admissions policy was constitutional, because, as Justice Sandra Day O'Connor argued in the majority opinion, "race-based action to further a compelling governmental interest does not violate the Equal Protection Clause so long as it is narrowly tailored to further that interest." Thus the Court upheld the constitutionality of race-conscious admissions policies at the law school. But in *Gratz*, rendered later the same day, the Court struck down the university's undergraduate "points based" admissions policy, with Chief Justice Rehnquist maintaining in the majority opinion that the assigning of additional points to an applicant solely on the basis of race was "not narrowly tailored to achieve the interest in educational diversity that respondents claim justifies their program." These two 5–4 decisions ultimately left the fate of affirmative action ambiguous by failing either to uphold specific challenges to it or to support its specific structure.

Racial diversity in schools remained a highly divisive legal issue, pitting conservatives' claim that the use of race in public policy to achieve diversity is detrimental to equality against civil rights advocates' argument that race must still be considered in remedying societal discrimination. The right of colleges and universities to use race as one of several factors in achieving a diverse student body may have been upheld by the federal courts in 2003, but long-agreed-on ideals outlined by the 1954 *Brown* decision on school integration were challenged by conservatives and struck down in 2007 in two cases, emanating from Seattle and Louisville.

It is perhaps an irony of the times and of the complicated challenges confronting civil rights advocates that the Court's only black member, the conservative Justice Clarence Thomas, believed recent school assignment plans based on race were just as unconstitutional as was the race-based segregation struck down in 1954, his opinion siding with that of the majority.

The Seattle and Louisville cases involved voluntary school desegregation plans that allowed race to be considered as a factor for some student assignments to schools. In both school districts, these plans were challenged by parents as a violation of the Equal Protection

Clause of the Fourteenth Amendment. Educators in both cities, working with parents and community members, had devised plans that allowed children the option of attending school outside their neighborhoods. Both cities' plans evolved in response to educators' negative experiences with segregation and far more positive experiences with diversity.

In its sharply divided 5–4 decision, split once again along ideological lines, the Supreme Court struck down both cities' voluntary school desegregation plans. Writing for himself and three fellow justices, Chief Justice Roberts ruled the districts "failed to show that they considered methods other than explicit racial classifications to achieve their stated goals." In a separate but concurring opinion that formed the majority, Justice Anthony Kennedy suggested that race *may* be a component of school plans designed to achieve diversity—an opinion that allows for the possibility of race being a factor for other permissible educational purposes (such as tracking enrollment) but not for school assignment plans. Dissenting, Justice Stephen Breyer asserted that this ruling serves to "threaten the promise of *Brown*."

The case revealed just how far to the right the Court had moved in the past three decades. "It is my firm conviction," wrote Justice John Paul Stevens, "that no Member of the Court that I joined in 1975 would have agreed with today's decision."

Although judicial decisions appeared increasingly opposed to African Americans' interests, several black statesmen and academics renewed demands for reparations for slavery. **Demands for Reparations** To some extent, this cry for reparations was motivated by decisions of the German government and German corporations to pay reparations to victims of the Holocaust and by the decision of the United States government to

Protesters at the U.S. capital during a demonstration for reparations, August, 2002.

pay reparations to victims of the internment of Japanese Americans during World War II. Drawing on these parallels, in 2000 Randall Robinson published *The Debt: What America Owes to Blacks,* defending the idea of reparations. Every year since 1989, Representative John Conyers, Jr., of Michigan introduced legislation in Congress to establish a committee to study the possibility of paying reparations for slavery to African Americans, although so far he has met with little success.

Of all reparations movements, that of African Americans faces some of the most difficult odds against success, given the time delay between slavery and African Americans' claims today as citizens in U.S. courts, as well as questions of sovereign immunity and the statute of limitations. All these issues figured in the case of survivors' and heirs' attempts to be compensated for the 1921 Tulsa race riot.

In 2001 the Tulsa Race Riot Commission, which the Oklahoma state legislature established in 1997 to investigate that riot, recommended compensation for the survivors. The legislature refused to pay compensation, although it did allocate funds to redevelop the area destroyed by the riot and to establish a memorial. Dissatisfaction with that response led to legal action. In *John Melvin Alexander et. al v. Oklahoma,* the 150 survivors (among them John Hope Franklin) and their descendants sued the state for its complicity in the destruction of Tulsa's historic African American Greenwood district. The plaintiffs also brought charges against the local police, the Ku Klux Klan, the National Guard, and the legal system over the riot and its aftermath.

In 2004 the case came before the U.S. District Court for the Northern District of Oklahoma. Lawyers for the city and the state moved to dismiss the suit on the grounds that the statute of limitations had passed in 1923, two years after the riot. In March 2004, the U.S. District Court ruled against the victims of the riot, declaring that although the statute of limitations could have been delayed, the victims should have filed their lawsuit at least in the 1960s. At that time, wrote U.S. District Court Judge James O. Ellison, they would have received a fair hearing. The appellate court upheld this ruling in September 2004, stating that the case could have been brought in the 1980s, when a book about the riots was published.

In fact, immediately after the riot some African Americans had attempted to obtain redress by filing suit. Their cases hung in legal limbo, however, since claims of culpability on the part of white Oklahomans and the Oklahoma state government were rejected. Both the Commission Report and the unfavorable district court opinion agreed that the social and political climate of the 1920s, during the heyday of Jim Crow, made it unlikely that the plaintiffs could have successfully pursued their legal claims. For eighty years the state of Oklahoma and the city of Tulsa reinforced the idea that the Greenwood community itself was to blame for the tragedy. And thus the black residents had no right to relief or apology.

Harvard law professor Charles Ogletree, among the lawyers who in 2003 sued the Oklahoma governor and the Tulsa mayor and chief of police, writes: "Plaintiffs' failure to file suit before 1921 is the result of circumstances other than neglect. . . . These are not neglectful plaintiffs, but fearful ones; they were not slumbering, but all too awake to the reality of silence and intimidation. The mere passage of time and the possibility of a change of heart on behalf of the government and people of Oklahoma are insufficient to break the code of silence imposed in 1921 and perpetuated by three generations of Oklahomans."

As a result of this ruling, Ogletree unsuccessfully attempted to persuade the U.S. Supreme Court to require a more favorable standard for the determination of statutes of limitations in cases involving historic wrongdoing. He argued that defendants should not benefit by the statute of limitations if they have concealed vital information about their culpability in past crimes, thus creating impediments for plaintiffs seeking redress.

Although the possibility for slavery reparations remains distant, the issue's recurrence highlights the haunting and unflattering history of America's racial slavery and Jim Crow justice. Some efforts to respond to past injustice have occurred, however. In 2005 a jury of nine whites and three blacks found former Klansman Edgar Ray Killen guilty of manslaughter in Philadelphia, Mississippi, in the deaths of three civil rights workers—Andrew Goodman, James Cheney, and Michael Schwerner—killed in the "Freedom Summer" of 1964. In 2006 both the U.S. Senate and the House of Representatives voted overwhelmingly to reauthorize the temporary portions of the Voting Rights Act of 1965, and President Bush signed a bill renewing the act for another twenty-five years. In 2007, Alabama became the fourth state (after Maryland, Virginia, and North Carolina) to pass a resolution apologizing for the state's role in slavery and its effects, although none have offered compensation to victims of slavery's enduring injustices.

Enduring Disparities: Health, Education, and Incarceration

At the beginning of a new century, health disparities between the races are a glaring anomaly in a nation as rich and as advanced in medical research and medical technology as the United States. African Americans, compared to other Americans, have the shortest life expectancies and highest rates of mortality and morbidity for almost all diseases. They are five times more likely than non-black Americans to die from asthma, and both black men and women are far more likely than their white counterparts to die from cardiovascular disease (42 percent more likely for men and 62 percent more likely for women). The prevalence of diabetes is increasing in the U.S. population as a whole; however, blacks are disproportionately affected. They also are 34 percent more likely than whites to die from cancer, the second-leading cause of death in the United States. Blacks born in the United States suffer the poorest health of all Americans, and a study conducted in 2005 found that black immigrants from regions with majority-black populations, such as Africa and the Caribbean, had better health than blacks born in the United States or other majority-white nations. As the work of sociologist Mary Waters has demonstrated, however, the longer that black immigrants from the Caribbean remain in the United States, the more likely they are to develop the same health problems as American-born blacks, probably as a consequence of being drawn into the same set of socioeconomic conditions endured by African Americans.

The reasons why African Americans are such an unhealthy people are complex, but the chief factor may be where blacks live, argues public health authority David Williams. Living in neighborhoods with high densities of impoverished blacks (a form of conflated racial-class segregation), and plagued by environmental pollution, substandard housing, overcrowding, high crime rates, and inadequate schooling, inner-city blacks find themselves susceptible to poor health while simultaneously having limited access to quality health care. Unhealthy environments are responsible for the prevalence of asthma in African American communities. The high cost and relative inaccessibility of healthy foods and the easy availability and affordability of fast food in poor neighborhoods circumscribe the dietary choices of many African Americans, resulting in a diet that is high in fat, sugar, and sodium but low in fruits and fiber. These eating patterns increase

Socioeconomic Stressors

the risk of developing heart disease, hypertension, high cholesterol, and diabetes, although blacks rarely are actively recruited to participate in clinical trials for medications to treat these conditions.

Blacks also have less access than other Americans to private or employment-based health insurance; they are far more likely to be covered by Medicaid or some other publicly funded insurance or to be uninsured. Consequently the cost of medical services deters many from seeking preventive care or medical attention for what they perceive as minor pain or illness. The low level of insurance coverage limits access to prescription drugs and often forces blacks to use overcrowded public hospitals or clinics as their primary source for healthcare. In this environment, low-income blacks fail to develop trusting and long-term relationships with healthcare providers, and many of them, lacking the confidence that they will receive good quality care, become less inclined to seek it.

Inadequate insurance coverage is but one component of a larger cycle of poverty that affects the health of African Americans. Miscommunication and misdiagnosis result from the inadequate education of many inner-city blacks, as well as from healthcare providers' lack of sensitivity and failure to understand the problems of the poor and the immigrants' language and culture. Patients from diverse backgrounds may ask different questions, offer different information about their symptoms, or respond in unanticipated ways to conventional styles of service. Lack of awareness of differing cultural perceptions of illness by healthcare workers inhibits the development of trust between the black community and the healthcare system, which many African Americans already view with suspicion because of such past injustices as the Tuskegee syphilis experiments. The absence of significant numbers of minority doctors and pharmacists exacerbates this problem.

Without a doubt, HIV/AIDS poses one of the modern world's greatest health threats, especially to African Americans. Although they account for 13 percent of the U.S. population, African Americans are so disproportionately represented among HIV/AIDS cases (50 percent in 2005) that the Centers for **The AIDS Crisis** Disease Control and Prevention (CDC) speaks of a "health crisis" in the black community. The lack of knowledge about the disease and the corresponding failure to seek treatment have made AIDS a growing killer among black men and women, adults and teens. According to CDC statistics for 2005, the rate of AIDS diagnoses was ten times that for whites and three times that of Hispanics. Black women represent the fastest growing population of newly diagnosed HIV/AIDS cases—resulting for the most part from sexual contact with infected men. In 2009 black women were reported as accounting for 61 percent of all new HIV infections among women, a rate nearly 15 times that of white women, and black teens account for 69 percent of new AIDS cases reported among teens.

Because AIDS has historically been associated with gay white males, many blacks continue to believe that they are not at risk of contracting the HIV virus. Homophobia, in the forms of racial perceptions of masculinity and of antigay messages from the church, has tended to silence discussions of homosexual and bisexual activity as a cause of the disease, despite homosexual activity being the leading cause of HIV transmission among black men. The second-leading cause for black men and women is injection drug use. In recent years, the phenomenon of the "Down Low"—"straight" black men having sex with men and then with female spouses or partners without informing them of their homosexual activities—has contributed to the spread of AIDS among African American women. This behavior is especially relevant to high rates of incarceration for black men, who have

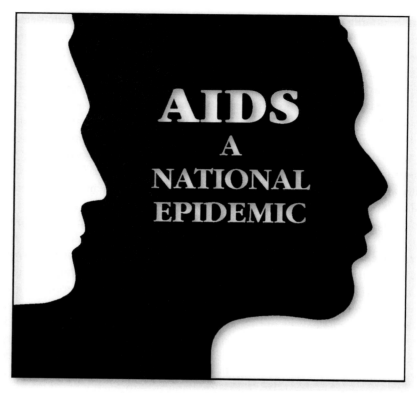

AIDS poster

Produced at Howard University, this poster was among the efforts of the African American community to deal with the disease as it reached epidemic proportions.

unprotected sex with other males in prison. Finally, fear of being tested keeps some African Americans ignorant of their HIV-positive status and thus results in their unconscious spreading of the disease.

Prevention programs targeted at gay men have not generally proved effective in stopping the spread of AIDS among African Americans, but black political and religious leaders are becoming more aware of the need for AIDS education. Indeed, the early months of President Barack Obama's administration focused attention on the impact of the disease on blacks. Thus the White House, the Department of Health and Human Services (HHS), and the CDC have launched the Act Against AIDS Leadership Initiative, working with over a dozen national organizations in a five-year prevention and treatment campaign to educate the public.

Racial disparities in incarceration loom as one of the most significant crises facing African Americans in the twenty-first century. Blacks make up 47 percent of the nation's prison popu-

Incarceration and Education lation. The overwhelming majority of incarcerated blacks are male, and

40 percent of them are between the ages of seventeen and twenty-seven. Poverty is more closely linked to the higher rates of incarceration for black men than for any other group in the United States. Inadequate education also contributes to high rates of crime in poor black communities, and consequently to higher rates of incarceration.

The majority of federal and state prisoners have no more than a high school education. Victims of school systems with insufficient resources, crowded classrooms, and overworked teachers, only 72 percent of black students graduate from high school. One in four black males is placed in special education or remedial classes, and in major urban areas an average of 45 percent of black males drop out of high school. Black high school dropouts have a 50 percent chance of being incarcerated at some point in their lives. Furthermore, they lack the level of educational attainment that often translates into the kind of regular legal employment that keeps people out of the criminal justice system.

In his recent book *More Than Just Race* (2009), sociologist William Julius Wilson puts in sharp relief the options afforded to racial groups by education. In 2005 college graduates showed relatively little difference in employment rates—88.3 percent for whites, 86.2 for blacks, and 80.2 for Hispanics. Employment potential diminishes considerably, however, as education levels decline. Emphasizing the critical nexus of race, education, and employability, Wilson asserts: "The employment gap between white young men and black young men ages sixteen to twenty-four who were not in school in 2005 was 20 percentage points for high school dropouts, 16 among high school graduates, 8 for those completing one to three years of college, and, as we saw in the earlier example, only 2 for four-year college graduates." Interestingly, black women are far more likely to complete college than black men. Although all racial groups experience higher rates of women college graduates than of men, the difference is most striking among African Americans. Wilson notes that for every 100 black male college graduates in 2003–2004, there were 200 black women graduates.

America's prison population has grown from 200,000 in 1970 to an estimated 2.25 million in 2006, and young minority males account for the bulk of that increase. The crackdown on the use and distribution of illicit substances has targeted such drugs as crack cocaine and marijuana, which are commonly used in poor communities. Arrest for drug possession has resulted in long sentences for poor, black youths convicted of nonviolent drug-related offenses. The drug trade is often seen by inner-city youths with few other economic options as a viable way of making money. Boys as young as seven to ten years old often become involved in drug trafficking as lookouts or carriers and end up in prison by age eighteen.

The American prison system offers little in the way of rehabilitation or job-skills training, and many convicts continue to sell drugs behind bars. Most emerge from prison with few options for legal employment. The taint of a criminal record makes it extremely difficult to find employment or housing, and reentry and work-release programs that could facilitate the transition to life outside prison remain severely underfunded. As black men in poverty become more closely associated with crime, they are more likely to be stereotyped as criminals—a stereotype that has unfortunately and ironically been perpetuated in gangsta rap. Poor blacks are unable to hide illicit drug use inside wealthy gated communities and cannot secure the financial resources to keep themselves and family members out of jail. Compared to whites, however, black men of all economic classes are subjected to closer police surveillance, are more frequently profiled and arrested, and are more likely to be perceived as threats to society.

Forgotten in Hurricane Katrina

Perhaps nowhere has the connection between race and poverty in America been more pointedly and poignantly highlighted than in the aftermath of Hurricane Katrina. As the dawn crept over the horizon on August 29, 2005, Hurricane Katrina made landfall on the southern coast of Louisiana, moving furiously through the city of New Orleans and across parts of Mississippi and Alabama. With 130 mile-per-hour winds, the category-three hurricane ravaged the Gulf Coast, and in its wake homes, businesses, schools, highways, ports, railroads, and water and sewage systems collapsed. More than 1,500 people were killed, and many thousands more were displaced and left homeless. As the levees of the mighty Mississippi River broke, low-lying areas of New Orleans were inundated, bringing untold suffering and frustration to this historic city.

Although the city's black mayor Ray Nagin issued a mandatory evacuation order the morning before Katrina made landfall, New Orleans had no plan in place for mass evacuation, and nearly 100,000 people remained—many of them stranded for days on rooftops and highway overpasses with no food or water. While rescue teams searched for victims by air and water, Mayor Nagin converted New Orleans's sports arena, the Superdome, into a massive homeless shelter. The Superdome, however, was hardly prepared to accommodate 25,000 people for an extended period of time. Lights and plumbing failed, and the inhabitants, many of them elderly and injured, endured heat, filth, hunger, and dehydration for five days before being evacuated.

Despite Mayor Nagin's immediate cries for help from the federal government, a week went by before the National Guard arrived and began mass evacuations. Many of the people affected by Katrina believed that the city, state, and federal responses were too little and came too late. Weeks after Katrina, thousands of people remained unable to return to their homes or to locate family members. In the aftermath of the disaster, many blacks in New Orleans and throughout the nation perceived a racial bias in the federal government's response.

In a study done by *The New York Times* six months after Katrina, black evacuees overwhelmingly reported that they felt abandoned by their nation and city. Indeed, African Americans were more likely than whites to have been displaced and to have lost loved ones during the storm. They were also more likely to have lost their jobs and to lack opportunities to find similar employment. More than two-thirds of blacks disapproved of how federal and state governments responded to Katrina. About half of the blacks interviewed cited race "as a major factor in the government's slow response," and 75 percent of whites saw no racial implications. Many displaced blacks, struggling to return home, also saw racial bias in the allocation of Federal Emergency Management Agency (FEMA) trailers, which allowed families to live near their property while rebuilding. Although FEMA promised 120,000 house trailers to evacuees, only 4,000 were placed in New Orleans.

In 2006 a report issued by the Senate Committee on Homeland Security and Governmental Affairs blamed the lack of adequate planning by the city and state, as well as the slow response of federal rescue initiatives, for the extensive suffering in the weeks following the hurricane. However, in his study of the race and class implications of Hurricane Katrina in New Orleans, John Logan of Brown University stressed the disproportionate effects of the catastrophe on blacks and the poor—often one and the same population. Since the 1970s, New Orleans has had a black majority, and the median income for white households ($61,000) in the city was more than double that of black households ($25,000).

New Orleans residents in aftermath of Hurricane Katrina
The areas hardest hit by Hurricane Katrina were the city's poor black neighborhoods,
such as the Ninth Ward.

The hurricane exacerbated these disparities, and the areas hardest hit by the hurricane were the city's poor black neighborhoods. For example, the predominantly black Lower Ninth Ward was transformed into what one *New York Times* article called an "archipelago of desolation." It was the last ward to reopen after the hurricane, and returning residents found their neighborhood just as the storm had left it—houses moved blocks from their foundations and sidewalks covered with mold and littered with debris. As one elderly resident lamented, returning was "just like going to a funeral." Thus those least able to afford to evacuate were also less likely to be able to rebuild their homes or find new ones after returning to the city.

Black frustration nationwide was fueled by media coverage of the hurricane and its aftermath. News footage showed striking images of blacks waiting on overpasses and rooftops and weeping over lost family members and storm-soaked dreams, but the media focused on the "looting" that occurred after the storm. Government officials vowed to crack down on people raiding stores and supermarkets in the days after Katrina, although many so-called looters sought only food and water. Two photographs from separate sources, the Associated Press (AP) and Getty Images (GI), sparked waves of public protest. The AP photo showed a black man wading through chest-high water holding some food items and bore the caption that the man was "looting a store." The GI photograph depicted a white couple holding bags of food; the caption stated that they had found "bread and soda from a local grocery store."

The racial implications in the language of the captions led Hip Hop artist Kanye West to denounce the entire handling of the crisis. He captured the sentiments of many African Americans when in a live broadcast of a benefit concert he proclaimed, "I hate the way they portray us in the media. . . . . You see a black family, it says they're looting. You see a white family, it says they're looking for food." He went on to incite public outcry by exclaiming, "George Bush doesn't care about black people!"

In January 2006, under increasing pressure from his constituency and shouldering frustration about the slow recovery process, Mayor Ray Nagin proclaimed in a Martin Luther King Day speech that New Orleans would once again be "a chocolate city." His comments elicited outrage from the national media but won the support of his majority-black constituency, who sent in absentee ballots and returned to New Orleans to reelect him. This political victory did not solve the larger inequities exposed by Hurricane Katrina, however. One year later, filmmaker Spike Lee produced a powerful documentary that captured the disquieting reality of the tragedy, uncertainty, and most of all the long-suffering of thousands of people who still awaited answers and solutions.

Hip Hop's Global Generation

The persistence and growth of Hip Hop in the new millennium has defied simple categorization. Like music of earlier generations, Hip Hop serves primarily as a form of entertainment for young artists and their devotees of all races, but it also serves in many places as a vehicle for the critique of social and political realities. Today Hip Hop culture has expanded well beyond black neighborhoods and even the borders of the United States. Hip Hop has been exported to the rest of the world, where it has been imitated, adopted, and adapted by a generation of people in their teens through their early thirties. Rap star Jay-Z and many others now tour in Asia, and Eastern Europe has been the stage of many Hip Hop concerts, including those of 50 Cent, Busta Rhymes, Wu-Tang Clan, Onyx and Lords of the Underground. Teenagers in Western European nations sport Hip Hop gear by G-Unit, and teens in Morocco listen to bootleg Kanye West recordings.

In the 1990s, Islamic or quasi-Islamic motifs in rap videos and lyrics began to be heard in the West and the Arabic-speaking world by such African-American performers as Q-Tip (Fareed Kamal) and Mos Def. Television, the Internet, and print media have facilitated the distribution of hip hop around the globe, and celebrity endorsements have helped to fuel the export of hip hop products and clothing lines in what has become an extremely lucrative business. Music commentators note that not since the advent and export of swing jazz in the 1930s has an American music been able to reach so far and reinvent itself so successfully.

Hip Hop's global resonance represents more than just the triumph of American consumerism abroad, however. People across the world are using Hip Hop to mobilize social

Hip Hop Abroad and political movements, to express resistance to political marginalization and racial and economic oppression, and to raise awareness regarding health issues in the fight against HIV/AIDS and in support of preventive vaccines for other diseases that plague populations in Africa. Abroad, as in the United States, Hip Hop assumes two forms, one identified with the commercial record industry and the creation of celebrity icons and

Senegalese rapper Didier Awadi
Awadi, who is part of a politically aware Hip Hop community, has become an international star.

the other the Hip Hop "underground," which remains an alternative, more locally based voice. Rap overseas has a heterogeneous voice as well, since it grows out of diverse cultures inside and outside the African diaspora.

Societal themes, distinctive sounds, traditional instrumentation, and indigenous voices are all represented by the Hip Hop generation. Its lyrics express local concerns and issues and speak in the many languages of nations and peoples who claim the music as their own. Many international rappers see themselves, as do many American rappers, as commentators and observers of a seldom-seen and largely ignored world where poverty, violence, and despair are prevalent. They also see themselves as critics of their own cultural and political patterns—for example, outdated social practices in Asia, the corruption of certain public officials in Africa, problems related to immigration, citizenship and integration in the various European countries, and the rise of joblessness in many urban areas around the globe.

In South Africa, rap music conveys messages specifically tailored to urban life in Johannesburg and Cape Town, and Israeli rap reflects the daily realities and values of Israeli youth. The West African nation of Senegal has one of the most active Hip Hop scenes in Africa with its indigenous tradition of *tassou*, which is similar to rapping, producing well-known international stars such as MC Solaar, Positive Black Soul, MC Lida, Duggy Tee, Didier Awadi, and Daara J. Xuman. In 2007 the rap song *Sunugaal* by Didier Awadi became an international hit. The song tells about the perilous migration of West African men across the Atlantic Ocean to Europe. Senegal has produced a politically oriented Hip Hop community that reflects the tenuous relationship between Senegal and its former colonial power, France, where the sale of rap records tends to run second only to that of the United States.

Hip Hop as a transnational phenomenon speaks to perceptions of new group forma-
tions and allegiances to an art form that has its genesis in American black ghettos. Members
Hip Hop Nation of the Hip Hop generation have been known to refer to themselves as part of one
global community—the Hip Hop nation—with its own history, signs, codes, and
anthems. Touré, an American writer, describes this: "I live in a country no map maker will
ever respect. A place with its own language, culture, and history. It is as much a nation as
Italy, as Zambia. A place my countrymen call the Hip Hop nation purposefully invoking all
the jingoistic pride that nationalists throughout history have leaned on."

During the early stages of the reception and adoption of Hip Hop around the world,
the appropriation of black stereotypes, mainly connected to gangsta rap, caused alarm for
Hip Hop's critics as well as its more socially conscious followers. The consumption of some
of the more negative elements of American rap—hypersexuality, materialism, misogyny,
and violence—were distributed and projected to the world. Hip Hop serves as an alternative to traditional "polite" adult culture in Japan, where youths adopt the dress, slang, and
dance of American rappers. Writer Ian Condry describes the male-dominated Hip Hop
scene there as a fusion of samurai imagery and gangsta rap, performed by self-proclaimed
"yellow B-Boys." In Tokyo, rappers utilize the "underground," not only commercial recordings, to critique social and political issues. In India, Hip Hop artists are wildly popular on
the radio and in film (Bollywood), blending Hip Hop and Bhangra (a Punjabi folk music and
dance). The black American Hip Hop artist Snoop Dogg noted in a July 2008 *New York Times*
article: "Lots of hip-hop tracks sample Indian music, and a lot of their music sounds like it
was influenced by hip-hop." An alarming example of Hip Hop's appropriation occured in
Sierra Leone during its wars in the 1990s and afterward. Rebel leaders used the image of
Tupac Shakur to recruit child soldiers, some of whom wore Tupac T-shirts.

The political and social issues raised by the global popularization of Hip Hop have led to
a growing interest in reorienting the Hip Hop generation in the United States away from its
Remaking American Hip Hop more entertainment and hedonistic focus. For example, linguistic
anthropologist Marcyliena Morgan describes in rich detail the under-
ground Hip Hop workshop called Project Blowed, which is part of a community arts organization in the Leimert Park Village section of Los Angeles. Unlike commercial Hip Hop, the
workshop encourages black youth to use Hip Hop in the form of freestyle (improvised) MC
competitions or "battles." Youths are motivated to prepare and practice in "ciphers"—informal groups that teach skills of rhyming, rapping, and improvising. The winners of the underground battles are those rappers who most impress audiences with their knowledge of pressing
community issues—such as gang violence, drugs, racism, and neighborhood revitalization.

Additionally, motivated by a desire to reclaim commercial Hip Hop and to remake it as
a more positive reflection of the generation whose experiences it claims to represent, organizers of the Hip Hop and Social Change Conference in 2003 and the National Hip Hop
Political Convention in 2004 brought together activists, politicians, and academics to set a
political agenda and discuss ways to mobilize young people between the ages of eighteen
and thirty. Ras Baraka, cofounder of the 2004 convention, explained that the purpose of
the event was to dispute rap's misogynist and violent images and use the power of Hip Hop
to promote the political participation of young people to achieve systematic change. Issues
identified as significant for the Hip Hop generation included education, police brutality and
the use of racial profiling, health care, housing reform, unemployment, incarceration, and
later the victims of Hurricane Katrina.

In 2001, in the aftermath of the voting controversy in Florida, Hip Hop mogul Russell Simmons and former NAACP head Benjamin Chavis launched the Hip Hop Summit Action Network to encourage voter education and registration. In January 2004, Simmons initiated the "One Mind, One Vote" youth voter registration program before the November presidential election of that year. Also in 2004, rapper Sean "P Diddy" Combs inaugurated Citizen Change, a nonprofit organization designed to motivate young Americans to vote by making it fashionable and relevant. Hip Hop celebrities sported Combs's "Vote or Die" shirts, and rappers Kanye West, Jadakiss, and Eminem released politically conscious songs in a throwback to earlier Hip Hop music popularized by legends KRS-1 and Tribe Called Quest.

Although in 2004 young people of the Hip Hop generation had difficulty realizing their collective political leverage, the movement to mobilize them remained relevant and grew precipitously with the presidential candidacy of then senator from Illinois, Barack Obama. Indeed, Obama increased youth and young adult interest in politics by utilizing rappers in new roles, specifically giving them an insider role as the cultural ambassadors of his campaign. The endorsement of Hip Hop artists was critical both to getting out young voters during the primaries and to winning their continued commitment to his message of change. Scholar Mark Anthony Neal noted that unlike in the previous election, when rappers organized Hip Hop summits or worked through record-company labels, the Obama Hip Hop supporters turned directly to the new technologies of such Internet and social-networking programs as YouTube and Facebook to get out their messages. Obama received a widely disseminated endorsement from will.i.am, a founding member and front-man for the Hip Hop group Black Eyed Peas, in the form of an online music video. Director and filmmaker Jessie Dylan, son of musician Bob Dylan, collaborated with will.i.am on a music video with music and entertainment celebrities, who rendered into song excerpts from the "Yes We Can" speech that Obama gave after losing the New Hampshire primary. In an interview, will.i.am said Obama's speech "made me reflect on the freedoms I have, going to school where I went to school, and the people that came before Obama like Martin Luther King, presidents like Abraham Lincoln that paved the way for me to be sitting here on ABC News and making a song from Obama's speech."

Rapper Jay-Z's offer to perform in October 2008 was greeted a bit more nervously by the Obama campaign, given some of the lyrics of his songs. Worried that the star would perform *Blue Magic* with its expletives about George Bush, the campaign managers pondered the potential negative effect that Jay-Z might have, but they eventually yielded to a concert in Miami on October 5. In his book on the 2008 presidential campaign, *Newsweek* magazine writer Evan Thomas wrote that Jay-Z omitted the offensive language about Bush, and, more noteworthy that the concert helped to register 10,000 new voters in the city.

New Great Migrations

At the beginning of the twenty-first century, two important demographic trends are redefining America's black population. First is the movement of large numbers of African Americans out of the North, especially the cities of the Northeast, back to the South, reversing a migration trend that had prevailed in the United States for nearly a century. Second is the increasing diversity of the black population within the United States.

Until the 1970s, black migration in the United States followed a relatively stable south-to-north pattern. Beginning in the early 1900s, racism and the mechanization of

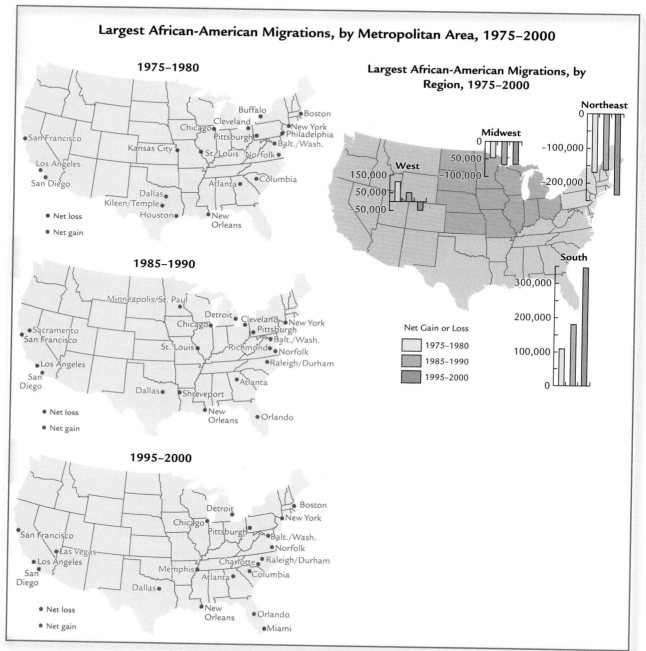

Largest African-American Migrations, by Metropolitan Area, 1975–2000

Largest African American Migrations by Metropolitan Area, 1975–2000

agriculture pushed blacks out of the rural South, and industrialization and the jobs that came with it pulled them toward the cities of the North. By the 1990s and continuing in the first decade of the new century, however, blacks reversed direction and are now moving south in increasing numbers, largely in reaction to northern real estate prices, shrinking job markets, and high costs of living. Middle-class blacks left New York City and Chicago, as well as California and most of the northeastern states, for lower costs of

Reverse Migration

living and housing prices, expanding job markets, and in some cases historic and family ties, all of which pulled many African Americans to the South.

The Northeast and California have experienced the greatest drain, and Georgia, the Carolinas, Florida, and the states of the Upper South have seen the greatest gains. Although New York and Chicago still boast the largest and second-largest black populations in the United States, by 2004 Atlanta had the third-largest black population of any city in the country and the fastest-growing black middle class. Other rapidly growing African American populations were located outside traditionally black regions, in Las Vegas, Phoenix, and Orlando. The new migrants include college-educated blacks seeking greater economic opportunity, as well as retirees and lower-income blacks seeking areas with less expensive living costs and real estate.

The 2000 census counted 36.4 million blacks in the United States, representing about 13 percent of the total population, but America's black population is by no means homogenous. African Americans—blacks whose families have been in the country for generations

Table 23.1	Black Population Growth and Percentage of U.S. Population, 1790–2000		
Year	Total Population	Black Population	Percentage
1790	3,929,214	757,181	19.3
1800	5,308,483	1,002,037	18.9
1810	7,239,881	1,377,808	19.0
1820	9,638,453	1,771,656	18.4
1830	12,866,020	2,328,642	18.1
1840	17,169,453	2,873,648	16.1
1850	23,191,876	3,638,808	15.7
1860	31,443,790	4,441,830	14.1
1870	39,818,449	4,880,009	12.7
1880	50,155,783	6,580,793	13.0
1890	62,947,714	7,488,676	11.0
1900	75,994,775	8,833,994	11.6
1910	93,402,151	9,827,763	10.7
1920	105,710,620	10,463,131	9.9
1930	122,775,046	11,891,143	9.7
1940	131,669,275	12,865,518	9.8
1950	150,697,361	15,042,286	10.0
1960	179,323,175	18,871,831	10.5
1970	203,302,031	22,580,289	11.1
1980	226,504,825	26,488,218	11.7
1990	248,710,000	29,986,000	13.2
2000	281,421,906	36,419,434	12.9

Source: U.S. Department of Commerce. *Statistical Abstract of the United States, 1992.* Bureau of the Census. Washington, D.C., 1992. Jesse McKinnon—*The Black Population in the United States: March 2002, Current Population Reports, Series P20-541.* Washington, DC: U. S. Census Bureau, 2003.

and who identify themselves as African American—make up the largest subgroup within the black population, but about one quarter of the increase in the black population over the last decade can be attributed to immigration from Africa and the Caribbean. Although Afro-Caribbeans and Africans constitute relatively small proportions of the total U.S. black population, their numbers are growing much faster than those of the native African American population. These distinctive groups are often lumped together under the umbrella category "black," but significant differences exist among them.

Table 23.2	Growth and Distribution of the African-American Population, by States, in 1940 and 2000	
State	**1940[a] (in thousands)**	**2000[b] (in thousands)**
Alabama	983	1,156
Alaska	(b)	22
Arizona	15	159
Arkansas	483	419
California	124	2,264
Colorado	12	165
Connecticut	33	310
Delaware	36	151
District of Columbia	187	343
Florida	514	2,335
Georgia	1,085	2,349
Hawaii	(b)	22
Idaho	1	5
Illinois	387	1,877
Indiana	122	510
Iowa	17	62
Kansas	65	154
Kentucky	214	296
Louisiana	849	1,452
Maine	1	7
Maryland	302	1,477
Massachusetts	55	343
Michigan	208	1,413
Minnesota	10	172
Mississippi	1,075	1,034
Missouri	244	629
Montana	1	3
Nebraska	14	69

State	1940[a] (in thousands)	2000[b] (in thousands)
Nevada	1	135
New Hampshire	(b)	9
New Jersey	227	1,142
New Mexico	5	34
New York	571	3,014
North Carolina	981	1,738
North Dakota	(b)	4
Ohio	339	1301
Oklahoma	169	261
Oregon	3	56
Pennsylvania	470	1,225
Rhode Island	11	47
South Carolina	814	1,185
South Dakota	(b)	7
Tennessee	509	933
Texas	924	2,405
Utah	1	18
Vermont	(b)	3
Virginia	661	1,390
Washington	7	190
West Virginia	118	57
Wisconsin	12	304
Wyoming	1	4

[a]1940 figures include all nonwhites.

[b]Less than 500.

Source: U.S. Department of Commerce. Historical Statistics of the United States: Colonial Times to 1970. Part 1. Bureau of the Census. Washington, D.C., 1975. U.S. Department of Commerce. Statistical Abstract of the United States, 1992. Bureau of the Census. Washington, D.C., 1992. U.S. Department of Commerce, *United States Census 2000.* Bureau of the Census, Washington, DC, 2001.

Most Afro-Caribbean immigrants come to the United States from Jamaica and Haiti, with smaller numbers immigrating from Trinidad and Tobago, the Bahamas, and Barbados. Although the United States has a growing population of black Hispanics (mostly from Cuba, the Dominican Republic, and South America), fewer than 2 percent of American Hispanics identify themselves as black. The greatest numbers of African immigrants come from the sub-Saharan countries of Nigeria, Ghana, Ethiopia, and Somalia. Most come to the United States through the Diversity Visa Lottery, established through the Immigration Act of 1990, which offers immigrant visas to high school graduates from nations underrepresented in the United States. The numbers of Africans coming to the United States because of "armed conflict, violence or natural disaster" have decreased in recent decades but still account for a significant number of those from East Africa.

Afro-Caribbean and African Migrants

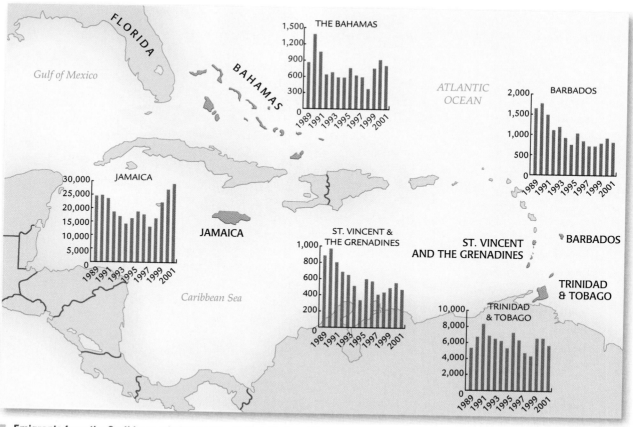

Emigrants from the Caribbean admitted to the United States, 1989–2002

Afro-Caribbean and African immigrants tend to settle in different parts of the country. Afro-Caribbeans live primarily in metropolitan areas, especially in New York, Florida, Boston, and Atlanta. Although significant numbers of Africans live in New York, Washington, D.C., Los Angeles, and Boston, they are more likely than African Americans and Caribbeans to settle outside large metropolitan areas in states that have not historically contained large numbers of blacks. For example, Oregon, Minnesota, and Maine have growing Ethiopian and Somali populations. African American, Afro-Caribbean, and African residential areas tend to be relatively isolated from one another; however, because both groups live in large metropolitan areas, African American and Afro-Caribbean communities sometimes overlap. The average African immigrant is more likely to reside in a community where 50 percent of the residents are white.

African immigrants generally have the highest education levels of any blacks in America. Nearly 98 percent of them possess high school degrees, and on average they live in neighborhoods where 30 percent of the residents are college-educated. By comparison, Afro-Caribbeans reside in neighborhoods where only 20 percent of the residents are college-educated, and in African American neighborhoods the presence of college-educated inhabitants drops to 17 percent. Africans arrive in America with roughly three to four years more education than the average Afro-Caribbean immigrant or African American. Both Afro-Caribbean and African immigrants boast greater median incomes than African Americans, a fact that some scholars attribute to their higher educational attainment and also to both immigrant groups' willingness to accept positions in nursing care and other service occupations in which African Americans are not generally employed.

Black people in the United States can hardly be viewed as a unified body. They have competing interests and conflicting loyalties and ethnic identities. Much of the tension between African Americans and African-descended immigrant groups (Afro-Caribbeans and Africans) centers on issues **Competing Interests and Ethnic Identities** of employment and social mobility. Sociologists argue that foreign-born blacks coming from majority black countries are "less psychologically handicapped by the stigma of race" than blacks in majority-white countries. Black immigrants report that they experience less discrimination than do African Americans. Mary Waters and other sociologists suggest that this difference in reported discrimination has to do with socialization into the American racial system.

Immigrants have a lower expectation of discrimination, and blacks coming from majority-black countries may be less acutely aware of the structural racism that historically has characterized American society, or they may believe themselves capable of rising in spite of it. African Americans, in contrast, possess a hypersensitivity to racism, born out of their historical experience with it and manifested in a sense of helplessness to combat it. Black immigrants do not attribute failures or difficulties to racial discrimination as often as do African Americans. These behavioral and ideological differences, signaled by differences in speech, can lead white employers to favor foreign-born blacks over African Americans.

These differences have contributed to a sense of hyper-ethnicity among black immigrants, some of whom even try to distance themselves from African Americans by emphasizing their immigrant cultural heritage instead of assimilating American ways. First-generation black immigrants tend to identify themselves by their specific countries of origin (Nigerian or Jamaican, for example, or Nigerian American or Jamaican American) or by their region of origin (West Indian or African) rather than simply as "black." However, to some extent, identification in immigrant populations is situational. West Indian immigrants often identify themselves by country or city of origin among other West Indians, but by geographical region to those outside the group, and racially only if they feel discriminated against or racially categorized.

Scholars note that black immigrants often view African Americans as lazy and racially hypersensitive, while African Americans resent the upward social mobility of immigrants. As University of the District of Columbia Administrator Dr. Bobby Austin explained, African Americans are weary of racial struggle, and "immigration seems like one more hurdle" to overcome . . . "People are asking, 'Will I have to climb over these immigrants to get to my dream? Will my children have to climb?'" Mary Waters's research suggests that much of this disunity decreases over time, however, as the children of immigrants become absorbed into African American culture and become less distinguishable from African Americans. Second- and third-generation immigrants may retain strong cultural ties and ethnic identifications, but they are more willing to align themselves with African Americans or to simply identify themselves as "black" than were their parents or grandparents.

Perhaps the newest, although not a literal, migration is the fascinating genetically based journey, via the genetic technology of allele sequencing and analysis of mitochondrial DNA, in search of one's place and group of origin—particularly, for **In Search of Origins** blacks in search of the location and ethnicity of their African ancestry. Genetic testing has offered the opportunity to discern the complexity of their racial make-up as the admixture of multiple races and their constituent ethnic groups. Such testing

Popular American television host Oprah Winfrey was one of the noted African Americans Henry Louis Gates, Jr. took on a journey in search of family roots.

makes possible an individual African American's genealogical search for ancestral places and persons in many parts of the world, not just in Africa.

Scholar Henry Louis Gates, Jr., the director of the W. E. B. Du Bois Institute for African and African American Research at Harvard University, has been most prominent in calling public attention to the use of genetic testing for the exploration of one's African antecedents. Writing documentary television programs and books, Gates takes famous African Americans—men and women noted in various fields (among them talk-show host Oprah Winfrey, musician Quincy Jones, astronaut Mae Jemison, and surgeon Ben Carson)—on individual journeys back into the South in search of family homes and histories. Led by Gates along a genetically based route, they eventually travel all the way to Africa to meet the specific ethnic group from which descended their captured African forebears who crossed the Middle Passage in chains and became slaves in the New World.

This journey, both genetic and spatial, of present-day African Americans back to Africa in search of their roots is different for each person. The individual stories are both fascinating and moving, since they bring a certain closure and answer to the centuries-old question of African Americans who sought to know the identity of their homeland in Africa, just as European Americans could proudly identify England, Ireland, Germany, Hungary, and many other places of national origin.

The Politics of Change

In February 2007, the junior senator from Illinois, Barack Hussein Obama, declared his candidacy for the presidency of the United States. Born in Honolulu in 1961, Obama was the son of a white Kansan mother and a black Kenyan father, after whom he was named. Obama was relatively unknown to the American people when he announced his presidential campaign. However, his compelling personal story and meteoric rise would soon end the idea that he was a political rookie. Obama was no novice in the world of politics, having tested his mettle in the rough and tumble South Side neighborhoods of Chicago and in the Illinois state legislature. He worked, at the same time, as a civil rights lawyer and taught a course on constitutional law at the University of Chicago Law School. He had skillfully gained the backing of influential white and black leaders. He authored a memoir of his youth, *Dreams from My Father* (1995), and articulated his beliefs and goals for America in *Audacity of Hope* (2006).

Perhaps it was his father's abandonment of his family when Obama was two years old or his early life in Indonesia after his mother's remarriage that shaped his views of a world in need of change. Perhaps it was the temptation and strains of youth culture or his trip to Africa in search of his father, or the recognition of the loving sacrifices of his once-again single-parent mother that instilled in him a passion to make a difference.

This cosmopolitan young man had come to Chicago right after college with the goal of aiding poverty-stricken black communities. Working closely with community residents, ministers, and other leaders, Obama learned the ropes of community mobilization in the fight against joblessness, inferior schools, and indifferent elected representatives. After three years of community organizing, he decided to go to Harvard Law School to refine his advocacy skills. With fine credentials (he would be elected president of the prestigious *Harvard Law Review*), he returned to Chicago after law school, determined to shake up the status quo.

Obama's ascent was impressive, elected first to the Illinois Senate and later to the United States Senate. In August 2004 in Boston, he made his debut before the American people as the keynote speaker at the Democratic National Convention. His eloquence, good looks, and influential supporters secured him a fleeting and exhilarating moment in the national spotlight. At the time, his eyes were set on the United States Senate, and his well-received speech bolstered his popularity and positioned him as the strongest Democratic contender in Illinois. He won his Senate race, becoming in 2005 only the fifth African American United States Senator in history. (Between 1993 and 1999, Carol Mosely Braun, also from Illinois, had served in the Senate—the only black woman ever elected to this august body.)

By the opening of 2007, a restless Senator Obama was pondering a run for the presidency, and on February 10, 2007, he stood in front of the Illinois statehouse in Springfield and announced his decision to enter his party's presidential campaign. Obama fashioned himself as a new-style

Barack Obama addressing delegates at the Democratic National Convention, 2004

leader, thus portraying himself as an outsider by distancing his position on the Iraq War and on domestic issues from that of President George W. Bush and even from many in his own Democratic Party. From the inception of the Iraq War, Obama opposed American involvement, which placed his views in direct

A New Campaign Style

opposition to those of prominent black officials in the Bush administration—Colin Powell and Condoleeza Rice. His announcement speech in Springfield reiterated that opposition, while also emphasizing his goals of working for better schools, jobs, and healthcare; of making America more energy efficient and protecting the environment from global warming; and of "taking up the unfinished business of perfecting our union, and building a better America." Obama's presidential campaign for "change," conveyed a broad sense of inclusiveness and his desire to represent all the American people.

Obama was not the first black person to run in the presidential campaigns of the major political parties. Shirley Chisolm, a seven-term congresswoman from New York, had campaigned for the Democratic nomination in 1972, and civil rights activist Rev. Jesse Jackson had done so in both 1984 and 1988. In 1996 and 2000, Republican Alan Keyes ran for the presidential nomination, and in 2000 both Carol Mosely Braun and the civil rights activist Rev. Al Sharpton competed in the Democratic Party's debates and primaries. Nor was

Window in Time

Senator Barack Obama Enters the Presidential Race

It was here, in Springfield, where North, South, East, and West come together that I was reminded of the essential decency of the American people—where I came to believe that through this decency, we can build a more hopeful America. And that is why, in the shadow of the Old State Capitol, where Lincoln once called on a divided house to stand together, where common hopes and common dreams still, I stand before you today to announce my candidacy for President of the United States. I recognize there is a certain presumptuousness—a certain audacity—to this announcement. I know I haven't spent a lot of time learning the ways of Washington. But I've been there long enough to know that the ways of Washington must change.

The genius of our founders is that they designed a system of government that can be changed. And we should take heart, because we've changed this country before. . . . Each and every time, a new generation has risen up and done what's needed to be done. Today we are called once more—and it is time for our generation to answer that call. For that is our unyielding faith—that in the face of impossible odds, people who love their country can change it. . . .

But Washington has a long way to go. And it won't be easy. That's why we'll have to set priorities. We'll have to make hard choices. And although government will play a crucial role in bringing about the changes we need, more money and programs alone will not get us where we need to go. Each of us, in our own lives, will have to accept responsibility—for instilling an ethic of achievement in our children, for adapting to a more competitive economy, for strengthening our communities, and sharing some measure of sacrifice. So let us begin. Let us begin this hard work together. Let us transform this nation.

Source: Excerpts from Senator Barack Obama's Announcement of his Candidacy, Springfield, Illinois, February 10, 2007.

Obama the first African American politician to gain visible media and popular attention. Yet, as a sitting member of the United States Senate, he received heightened attention and a heightened degree of political legitimacy—more than his predecessors. Never before did an African American appear to be taken so seriously as a candidate by his political rivals, the press, and campaign fundraisers.

The central premise of his campaign message was that change began at the grassroots level. One of the most unique aspects of the Obama strategy was the ability to bring in young people and use them as an integral part of the campaign. "Camp Obama"—a three-to-four day training session, with about fifty volunteers in each weekly session, was initially conducted at a volunteer headquarters set up in Chicago and soon was replicated in such key election states as Georgia, Texas, and Florida. Most of the volunteers were young adults and college students who applied for the limited spots and, if selected, paid for their own housing and transportation to receive the free training.

Through the training camps, Obama sought to use young adults in a precinct-by-precinct volunteer-driven field operation. In a memo written on August 29, 2007, entitled "Camp Obama: Turning Enthusiasm into Organization," Temo Figueroa, the Obama campaign's National Field Director, summed up the early state victory strategy: "It is about a new campaign focused on exploiting the 'enthusiasm gap.'"

Obama's field operation incorporated storytelling and relationship-building as central to its organizing. Trainees were taught how to manage phone banks, knock on doors in a systematic fashion, and register voters. This grassroots strategy revolutionized organizing in the field and transformed thousands of communities. Obama was also aided by the advice and lessons of his friend and fellow-lawyer Deval Patrick in Massachusetts, whose grassroots gubernatorial campaign with its "Yes, We Can" slogan (the Obama campaign would adopt it) appealed to white voters throughout the state, thus winning the election for Patrick in 2006 and making him the commonwealth's first black governor.

Key to the Obama campaign was its use of the Internet to mobilize support. For younger volunteers, social networking sites such as Facebook and MySpace served as a virtual space where volunteers accessed tools to train themselves and others on organizing tactics, thereby creating teams of "netroots" organizers who in turn recruited other volunteers. Students for Barack Obama, which started as a group on Facebook and eventually became an official youth outreach operation for the Obama campaign, recruited students online and organized Obama events across college campuses.

According to Chris Hughes, the twenty-five year-old cofounder of Facebook and the coordinator of online organizing for the Obama Campaign, the campaign's own social networking site, My.barackobama.com, allowed supporters to create over 35,000 local organizing groups and host over 200,000 events. The campaign's digital strategy incorporated such technology as online videos and ads, emails, and text messaging to effectively build his brand of change. The World Wide Web gave thousands of volunteers the opportunity to spread Obama's message of change in ways that would transform the nature of the political campaign process.

The Democratic primaries increasingly became a match-up between Senator Obama and his fiercest rival, New York Senator Hillary Rodham Clinton. Obama's coalition included African Americans, college-educated whites, and young **The Democratic Primaries** voters; Clinton's coalition rested primarily on women, Latinos, and non-college-educated whites. However, in the earlier months of the campaign, particularly in the fall 2007, polls showed Clinton with a larger following of black voters. Blacks' loyalty to the Clintons (both Bill and Hillary) waned as the Democratic primaries progressed. These formidable alliances were evident in national polls and in each state where Obama and Clinton fought vigorously to win the Democratic nomination. The strength of Obama's coalition over Clinton's, however, was reinforced on February 5, 2008, called Super Tuesday, when twenty-three states held simultaneous Democratic primaries and caucuses. Obama emerged as the victor, picking up thirteen states to Clinton's ten states and winning more pledged delegates (847 to 834).

Certainly one of the most dramatic moments in the campaign was the exposé that Obama's pastor, the AME minister Jeremiah Wright, had used inflammatory and unpatriotic statements in a sermon. The media's suffocating coverage might have ended Obama's campaign had he not decided to confront the divisive publicity directly. Obama took the occasion to speak about not only about Jeremiah Wright's remarks but more importantly also about the larger issue of race in America. It was a brilliant decision. On March 18, 2009, in heartfelt words, Obama addressed white and black Americans. He did not shy away from a discussion of real racial disparities in education, the penal system, and employment, and he called for the enforcement of civil rights laws, for "ladders of opportunities," for better education, and for a more just system. At the same time, he told blacks to free their minds and behaviors of the "legacy of defeat," to become more caring and attentive parents, and to believe that they have the power to change their destiny. At the end, he spoke to all his compatriots, asserting that "It requires all Americans to realize that your dreams do not have to come at the expense of my dreams; that investing in the health, welfare, and education of black and brown and white children will ultimately help all of America prosper."

Despite all the controversy, Barack Obama won the nomination and then in the general election triumphed over Republican John McCain, winning 365 to McCain's 173 electoral votes. The popular vote was even more symbolically impressive—63 million (53 percent) to 55.8 million (46 percent)—since it was the first time that a Democrat had won more than 51 percent since Lyndon Johnson's victory in 1964. CNN's senior political analyst, the former presidential advisor David Gergen, said that the election was "the passing of an old order"—referring to the future possibility of a new coalition of Latino, black, and young (ages 18–29) voters. Ninety percent of McCain voters were white. Obama won key battleground states that had gone Republican in 2004: Ohio, Virginia (which had last voted for a Democratic president in 1964), Iowa, Colorado, New Mexico, Nevada (all of which were in the Bush column in 2004), Indiana (which, like Virginia, had not voted for a Democrat since Lyndon B. Johnson in 1964), and North Carolina.

The Election

Obama not only won the Hispanic vote but also increased the Hispanic turnout in 19 states—Colorado, Nevada, New Mexico, Indiana, Iowa, Michigan, Minnesota, Missouri, Montana, New Hampshire, North Carolina, North Dakota, Ohio, Pennsylvania, South Dakota, Virginia, West Virginia, and Wisconsin. (All those states except Missouri, Montana, North and South Dakota, and West Virginia he carried.)

Economic concerns, spurred by news of the failing economy and home foreclosures, factored significantly in turning previously undecided voters toward Obama. While young adults voted for Obama in overwhelming numbers (66 percent, versus 31 percent for McCain), the actual youth percentage of the overall electorate was 18 percent—only one percentage point more than in 2004. Yet young voters played a tremendous role in get-out-the-vote efforts. Their votes were most influential to Obama's victory in Indiana and North Carolina. One of the most electrifying aspects of the campaign was the noticeable addition of new voters in the electorate. One in ten persons voted for the first time in 2008, and they voted for Obama by 69 percent to 30 percent. Two-thirds of these new voters were aged 30 or under, 20 percent were black, and 18 percent were Hispanic.

On January 20, 2009, Barack Hussein Obama was inaugurated as the forty-fourth president of the United States. Several million people of all races converged on Washington, D.C., to witness this historic event. For the vast majority of those standing in the cold winter chill of Inauguration Day, the sight of a black president of the United States and a black

First Lady, Michelle Obama, would once have been inconceivable. They may have also watched the president's swearing in, while simultaneously marveling at the idea of a black First Family as the occupants of the White House. The elderly may have recalled that in their own lifetime—in years not so distant—African Americans in the nation's capital could not be served as equals in the cafeterias of federal buildings, or enter department store dressing rooms, or eat at drugstore lunch counters.

Some might have even remembered the student volunteers of all races, who traveled courageously into the Deep South in 1964 and risked or even lost their lives to register African Americans as voters; and they might have compared them to the young volunteers who traveled enthusiastically to cities and hamlets throughout America in 2008 to mobilize voters for the Obama platform for "change." As the Inauguration ended and the crowds dispersed, all knew they had witnessed history in the making and that a new chapter had just begun.

Bibliography

Chapter 1: Ancestral Africa, Ancient around 500 BCE to 1600

Abir, Mordechai. *Ethiopia and the Red Sea: The Rise and Decline of the Solomonic Dynasty and Muslim-European Rivalry in the Region.* Totowa, NJ: Frank Cass & Co, 1980.

Ajayi, J. F., and Michael Crowder, eds. *History of West Africa.* 3rd ed. 2 vols. London, England: Longman, 1985.

Alpers, Edward. *Ivory and Slaves in East Central Africa: Changing Patterns of International Trade to the Later 19th Century.* Berkeley, CA: University of California Press, 1975.

Andah, B. Wai. "West Africa before the Seventh Century." In *Ancient Civilizations of Africa,* edited by G. Mokhtar. Berkeley, CA: University of California Press, 1981.

Bakri Abou Ubayad. *Description de l'Afrique septentrionale.* Paris, France: A. Maisonneuve, 1965.

Blier, Suzanne Preston. *The Royal Arts of Africa: The Majesty of Form.* New York, NY: H.N. Abrams, 1998.

Bohannan, Paul, and Philip Curtin. *Africa and Africans.* Prospect Heights, IL: Waveland Press, 1988.

Bovill, E. W. *The Golden Trade of the Moors.* New York, NY: Oxford University Press, 1968.

Broadhead, Susan Herlin. "Slave Wives, Free Sisters: Bakongo Women and Slavery C. 1700-1850." In *Women and Slavery in Africa,* edited by Claire C. Robertson, and Martin A. Klein, eds., 160-81. Portsmouth, NH: Heinemann, 1983.

Brooks, George E. "A Provisional Schema for Western Africa Based on Seven Climate Periods (Ca. 9000 BE to the 19th Century)." *Cahiers d'etudes Africaines* 26: Cahier 101/102, Milieux, histoire, historiographie (1986): 43-62.

Carney, Judith. *Black Rice: The African Origins of Rice Cultivation in the Americas.* Cambridge, MA: Harvard University Press, 2001.

Carretta, Vincent. *Equiano, the African: Biography of a Self-made Man.* Athens, GA: University of Georgia Press, 2005.

————, ed. *Unchained Voices: An Anthology of Black Authors in the English-speaking World of the Eighteenth Century.* Lexington, KY: University Press of Kentucky, 1996.

Connah, Graham. *African Civilizations: Precolonial Cities and States in Tropical Africa: An Archeological Perspective.* Cambridge, MA: Harvard University Press, 1988.

Curtin, Philip. *Economic Change in Precolonial Africa: Senegambia in the Era of the Slave Trade.* 2 vols. Vol. 1. Madison, WI: University of Wisconsin Press, 1975.

da Mota, Avelino Teixeira and Paul Edward Hedley Hair. *East of Mina: Afro-European Relations on the Gold Coast in the 1550s and 1560s.* Madison, WI: University of Wisconsin Press, 1988.

Devisse, Jean and S. Labib. "Africa in Intercontinental Relations." In *Unesco Histoire Generale De L'afrique.* Berkeley, CA: University of California Press, 1993.

Ehret, Christopher. *The civilizations of Africa: a History to 1800.* Charlottesville, VA: University Press of Virginia, 2002.

Equiano, Olaudah. *The Interesting Narrative and Other Writings.* edited by Vincent Carretta, New York, NY: Penguin, 1995.

Fage, J. D. "Slaves and Society in Western Africa, 1440-C. 1700." *Journal of African History* 21:3 (1980): 289-310.

Garrad, Timothy. "Myth and Metrology: Trans Saharan Gold Trade." *Journal of African History.* 23:4 (1982): 443-461.

Gemery, H. A. and J. S. Hogendorn. "Technological Change, Slavery and the Slave Trade." In *The Imperial Impact: Studies in the Economic History of Africa and India,* edited by Clive Dewey and A.G. Hopkins. London, England: Athlone Press, 1978.

Gomez, Michael. "Timbuktu under Imperial Songhay: A Reconsideration of Autonomy." *Journal of African History* 31:1 (1990): 5-24.

Goody, Jack. *Technology, Tradition, and the State in Africa.* New York, NY: Oxford University Press, 1971.

Goody, Jack and S. J. Tambiah. *Bridewealth and Dowry.* New York, NY: Cambridge University Press, 1972.

Goucher, Candice. "Iron Is Iron 'Til It Rust: Trade and Ecology in the Decline of West African Iron-Smelting." *Journal of African History* 22:2 (1981): 179-189.

Haenger, Peter. *Slaves and Slave Holders on the Gold Coast: Towards an Understanding of Social Bondage in West Africa.* Edited by J.J. Schaeffer, and Paul Lovejoy. Basel, Germany: Schlettwein, 2000.

Hair, P.E.B. "Some Minor Sources for Guinea, 1519-1559: Enciso and Alfonce/Fonteneau." *History in Africa* 3 (1976): 19-46.

Hamdun, Said and Noel King. *Ibn Battuta in Black Africa.* Princeton, NJ: Markus Weiner Publishers, 1994.

Heintze, Beatrix. "Written Sources, Oral Traditions and Oral Traditions as Written Sources: The Steep and Thorny Way to Early Angolan History." *Paideuma 33* (1987): 263-88.

Hiskett, Mervyn. *The Development of Islam in West Africa.* New York, NY: Longman, 1984.

Horton, Robin. "Stateless Societies in the History of West Africa," in *History of West Africa* Volume 1, Third Edition, ed. J. F. Ade & Michael Crowder (New York, 1985), pp. 87-128.

Iliffe, John. *Africans: The History of a Continent.* Cambridge, England: Cambridge University Press, 1995.

Inikori, J. E. *Forced Migration: The Impact of the Export Slave Trade on African Societies.* New York, NY: Holmes & Meier Publishers, 1983.

Jennings, Lawrence C. and David Eltis "Trade between Western Africa and the Atlantic World in the PreColonial Era." *American Historical Review* 93:4 (1988): 936-959.

Kea, Ray. *Settlements, Trade and Politics on the Seventeenth Century Gold Coast.* Baltimore, MD: John Hopkins University Press, 1982.

Klein, Herbert S. "African Women in the Atlantic Slave Trade." In *Women and Slavery in Africa*, edited by Claire C. Robertson, and Martin A. Klein, eds., 29-38. Portsmouth, NH: Heinemann, 1983.

Klein, Martin and Claire Robertson, eds. *Women and Slavery in Africa*. Madison, WI: University of Wisconsin Press, 1983.

Korare Ba, Adam. *Sonni Ali Ber*. Niamey: Institut de recherches en sciences humaines, 1977.

Law, Robin. "Dahomey and the Slave Trade: Reflections on the Historiography of the Rise of Dahomey." *Journal of African History* 27:2 (1986): 237-267.

_____. *The Oyo Empire, C. 1600-C. 1836: A West African Imperialism in the Era of the Atlantic Slave Trade*. Oxford, England: Clarendon, 1977.

_____. *The Slave Coast of West Africa 1550-1750: The Impact of the Atlantic Slave Trade on an African Society*. Durham, NC: Duke University Press, 1991.

Leo Africanus, Joannes. *The History and Description of Africa, and of the Notable Things Therein Contained*. London, England: Printed for the Hakluyt Society, 1896.

Levtzion, Nehemia, J. F. P. Hopkins. *Corpus of Early Arabic Sources for West African History*. Princeton, NJ: Markus Weiner Publishers, 2000.

_____. "The Thirteenth-and Fourteenth-Century Kings of Mali," *Journal of African History*, Vol. 4, No. 3. (1963), pp. 341-353.

Lovejoy, Paul. *Transformations in Slavery: A History of Slavery in Africa*. New York, NY: Cambridge University Press, 2000.

MacIntosh, K. "A Reconsideration of Wangara/Palolus, Island of Gold." *Journal of African History* 22:2 (1981): 145-158.

Manning, Patrick. "Local Versus Regional Impact of the Export Slave Trade." In *African Population and Capitalism: Historical Perspectives*, edited by Dennis D. Cordell and Joel W. Gregory. Boulder, Co: Westview Press, 1987.

_____. "Social and Demographic Transformations." In *The Atlantic Slave Trade*, edited by David Northrup. Boston, MA: Houghton Mifflin Company, 2000.

_____. *Slavery and African Life: Occidental, Oriental, and African Slave Trades*. New York, NY: Cambridge University Press, 1990.

_____. *Slavery, Colonialism and Economic Growth in Dahomey, 1640-1960*. New York, NY: Cambridge University Press, 1982.

Martin, Phyllis. *The External Trade of the Loango Coast: The Effects of Changing Commercial Relations on the Vili Kingdom of Loango*. New York, NY: Clarendon Press, 1972.

Meillassoux, Claude. *The Anthropology of Slavery: The Womb of Iron and Gold*. Translated by Alide Dasnois. Chicago, IL: University of Chicago Press, 1991.

Middleton, John. *The World of the Swahili: An African Mercantile Civilization*. New Haven, CT: Yale University Press, 1994.

Miers, Suzanne and Igor Kopytoff. *Slavery in Africa: Historical and Anthropological Perspectives*. Madison, WI: University of Wisconsin Press, 1977.

Miller, Joseph. *Way of Death: Merchant Capitalism and the Angolan Slave Trade, 1730- 1830*. Madison, WI: University of Wisconsin Press, 1988.

Nurse, Derek. "The Contributions of Linguistics to the Study of History in Africa." *Journal of African History* 38:3 (1997): 359-391.

Patterson, Orlando. *Slavery and Social Death: A Comparative Study*. Cambridge, MA: Harvard University Press, 1985.

Pelteret, David Anthony Edgell. *Slavery in Early Mediaeval England: from the Reign of Alfred Until the Twelfth Century*. Rochester, NY: Boydell Press, 1995.

Phillips, William D., Jr. *Slavery from Roman Times to the Early Transatlantic Trade*. Minneapolis, MN: University of Minnesota Press, 1985.

Poole, L. M. "Decline or Survival? Iron Production in West Africa from the Seventeenth to the Twentieth Centuries." *Journal of African History* 23:4 (1982): 503-513.

Rodney, Walter. *A History of the Upper Guinea Coast, 1545-1800*. New York, NY: Clarendon Publishers, 1970.

Robertson, Claire C. and Martin A. Klein, eds. *Women and Slavery in Africa*. Portsmouth, NH: Heinemann, 1983.

_____. *How Europe Underdeveloped Africa*. Washington, DC: Howard University Press, 1981.

Ryder, Alan F. C. *Benin and the Europeans, 1485-1897*. New York, NY: Longmans, 1969.

Schmidt, Peter and S. Terry Childs. "Innovation and Industry During the Early Iron Age in East Africa: The Km_2 and Km_5 Sites of Northwest Tanzania." *African Archaeological Review* 3 (1985) 53-94.

Searing, James. "Aristocrats, Slaves and Peasants: Power and Dependency in the Wolof States, 1700-1850." *International Journal of African Historical Studies* 21:3, (1988): 475-503.

Thornton, John. *Africa and Africans in the Making of the Atlantic World, 1400-1800*. 2nd ed. New York, NY: Cambridge University Press, 1999.

_____. "The Art of War in Angola, 1575-1680." *Comparative Studies in Society and History* 30:2 (1988): 360-378.

_____. "The Development of an African Catholic Church in the Kingdom of Kongo, 1491-1750." *Journal of African History*, 25:2 (1984): 147-167.

_____. *The Kingdom of Kongo: Civil War and Transition, 1641-1718*. Madison, WI: University of Wisconsin Press, 1983.

_____. "Legitimacy and Political Power: Queen Njinga, 1624-63." *Journal of African History* 32:1 (1991) 25-40.

_____. "Traditions, Documents, and the Ife-Benin Relationship." *History in Africa* 15 (1988) 351-362.

UNESCO. "Bantu Migration Hypothesis." In *Unesco Histoire Generale De L'afrique*. Berkeley, CA: University of California Press, 1993.

Vansina, Jan. "New Linguistic Evidence and the 'Bantu Expansion'." *Journal of African History* 36:2 (1995): 173-195.

_____. *Paths in the Rainforest: Toward a History of Political Tradition in Equatorial Africa*. Madison, WI: University of Wisconsin Press, 1990.

Webb, James, Jr. *Desert Frontier: Ecological and Economic Change along the Western Sahel, 1600-1850*. Madison, WI: University of Wisconsin Press, 1995.

Willis, John Ralf, ed. *Slaves and Slavery in Muslim Africa: Islam and the Ideology of Enslavement*. International Specialized Book Services, 1985.

Willett, Frank. *African Art*. 3rd ed. New York, NY: Thames & Hudson, 2003.

Wright, Marcia. *Strategies of Slaves and Women: Life Stories from East/Central Africa*. New York, NY: Lilian Barber Press, 1993.

Chapter 2: African in the Atlantic World, 1492-1800

Bay, Edna G. "Art, Innovation, and Politics in Eighteenth-Century Benin." *The International Journal of African Historical Studies*, 33:2 (2000): 479-480.

Benjamin, Thomas. *The Atlantic World: European, Africans, Indians and their Shared History, 1400-1900*. New York, NY: Cambridge University Press, 2009.

Berlin, Ira. *Many Thousands Gone: The First Two Centuries of Slavery in North America.* Cambridge, MA: Belknap Press of Harvard University Press, 1998.

Brana-Shute, Rosemary and Randy J. Sparks, eds. *Paths to Freedom: Manumission in the Atlantic World.* Columbia, SC: University of South Carolina Press, 2009.

Brown, Vincent. *The Reaper's Garden: Death and Power in the World of Atlantic Slavery.* Cambridge, MA: Harvard University Press, 2008.

Carretta, Vincent. *Equiano, the African: Biography of a Self-Made Man.* 1st ed. Athens, GA: University of Georgia Press, 2005.

Christopher, Emma. *Slave Ship Sailors and Their Captive Cargoes, 1730-1807.* New York, NY: Cambridge University Press, 2006.

Conniff, Michael L. and Thomas J. Davis. *Africans in the Americas: A History of the Black Diaspora.* New York, NY: St. Martin's Press, 1997.

Cordell, Dennis D. and Joel W. Gregory, eds. *African Population and Capitalism: Historical Perspectives.* Madison, WI: The University of Wisconsin Press, 1994.

Curtin, Philip. *The Atlantic Slave Trade: A Census.* Madison, WI: University of Wisconsin Press, 1969.

_____. *Economic Change in Precolonial Africa: Senegambia in the Era of the Slave Trade.* Madison, WI: University of Wisconsin Press, 1975.

_____. *Migration and Mortality in Africa and the Atlantic World, 1700-1900.* Burlington, VT: Ashgate Publishing Co., 2001.

_____. *The Rise and Fall of the Plantation Complex: Essays in Atlantic History.* 2nd ed. New York, NY: Cambridge University Press, 1998.

_____., ed. *Africa Remembered: Narratives by West Africans from the Era of the Slave Trade.* Long Grove, IL: Waveland Press, 1997.

Davidson, Basil. *Africa in History.* New York, NY: Simon & Schuster, 1995.

_____. *The African Genius.* Athens, OH: Ohio University Press, 2004.

Donnan, Elizabeth. *Documents Illustrative of the History of the Slave Trade to America.* New York, NY: Hippocrene Books, 1965.

Drennan, Robert and Carlos Uribe. *Chiefdoms in the Americas.* Washington, DC: University Press of America, 1987.

Du Bois, W. E. B. *Suppression of the African Slave Trade to the United States, 1638-1870.* New York, NY: Longmans, Green, 1969.

Duncan, Thomas Bentley. *Atlantic Islands: Madira, the Azores and the Cape Verdes in Seventeenth-Century Commerce and Navigation, Studies in the History of Discoveries.* Chicago, IL: University of Chicago Press, 1972.

Dunn, Richard S. *Sugar and Slaves: The Rise of the Planter Class in the English West Indies, 1624-1713.* Chapel Hill, NC: University of North Carolina Press, [2000] c. 1972.

Ellis, George Washington. *Negro Culture in West Africa.* New York, NY: The Neale Publishing Co., 1971.

Eltis, David. *Economic Growth and the Ending of the Transatlantic Slave Trade.* New York, NY: Oxford University Press, 1987.

_____ *The Rise of African Slavery in the Americas.* Cambridge, England: Cambridge University Press, 2000.

_____ and David Richardson, eds. *Routes to Slavery: Direction, Ethnicity and Morality in the Transatlantic Slave Trade.* Portland, OR: Frank Cass Publishers, 1997.

_____ and David Richardson, eds. *Extending the Frontiers: Essays on the New Transatlantic Slave Trade Database.* New Haven: Yale University Press, c2008.

_____ and James Walvin, eds. *The Abolition of the Atlantic Slave Trade: Origins and Effects in Europe, Africa, and the Americas.* Madison, WI: University of Wisconsin Press, 1981.

_____ and Philip Morgan, "The Volume and Structure of the Transatlantic Slave Trade: A Reassessment." *William and Mary Quarterly* 58:1 (2001): 17-46.

_____, Steven D. Behrendt, David Richardson, and Herbert S. Klein, eds. *The Trans-Atlantic Slave Trade: a database on CD-ROM.* New York, NY: Cambridge University Press. (2001).

Engermann, Stanley and Eugene Genovese, eds. *Race and Slavery in the Western Hemisphere: Quantitative Studies.* Princeton, NJ: Princeton University Press, 1975.

Equiano, Olaudah. *The Interesting Narrative and Other Writings.* Edited by Vincent Caretta. New York, NY: Penguin, 1995.

Ewald, Janet. "Slavery in Africa and the Slave Trades from Africa." *American Historical Review* 97:2 (1992): 465-485.

Fage, J. D. "Some Remarks on Beads and Trade in Lower Guinea in the Sixteenth and Seventeenth Centuries." *Journal of African History* 3:2 (1961-1962): 343-347.

Fernandez-Armesto, Felipe. *The Canary Islands after the Conquest: The Making of a Colonial Society in the Early Sixteenth Century.* New York, NY: Oxford University Press, 1982.

Floyd, Troy S. *The Columbus Dynasty in the Caribbean, 1492-1526.* Albuquerque, NM: University of New Mexico Press, 1973.

Gaspar, David Barry. *Bondmen and Rebels: A Study of Master-Slave Relations in Antigua.* Durham, NC: Duke University Press, 1993.

Glassman, Jonathon. "The Bondsman's New Clothes: The Contradictory Consciousness of Slave Resistance on the Swahili Coast." *Journal of African History* 32:2 (1991): 277-312.

Gomez, Michael. *Exchanging Our Country Marks: The Transformation of African Identities in the Colonial and Antebellum South.* Chapel Hill, NC: University of North Carolina Press, 1998.

_____. *Reversing Sail: a History of the African Diaspora.* New York, NY: Cambridge University Press, 2005.

Hallett, Robin. *Africa to 1875: A Modern History.* Ann Arbor, MI: University of Michigan Press, 1970.

Harms, Robert. *River of Wealth, River of Sorrow: The Central Zaire Basin in the Era of the Slave and Ivory Trade, 1500-1891.* New Haven, CT: Yale University Press, 1981.

Hemming, John. *Red Gold: The Conquest of the Brazilian Indians, 1500-1760.* London, UK: Papermac, 1995.

Henige, David. "Measuring the Immeasurable: The Atlantic Slave Trade, West African Population and the Pyrrhonian Critic." *Journal of African History* 27:2 (1986): 295-313.

Herskovits, Melville J. *Dahomey, an Ancient West African Kingdom.* Evanston, IL: Northwestern University Press, 1967.

_____. *The Myth of the Negro Past.* Boston, MA: Beacon Press, 1990.

Heywood, Linda M. and John K. Thornton. *Central Africans, Atlantic Creoles, and the Foundation of the Americas, 1585-1660.* New York, NY: Cambridge University Press, 2007.

Inikori, Joseph. "Measuring the Atlantic Slave Trade: An Assessment of Curtin and Anstey." *Journal of African History* 17:2 (1976): 197-223.

_____ and Stanley E. Engerman, eds. *The Atlantic Slave Trade: Effects on Economies, Societies, and Peoples in Africa, the Americas, and Europe.* Durham, NC: Duke University Press, 1992.

Kea, Ray. *Settlements, Trade and Politics on the Seventeenth Century Gold Coast.* Baltimore, MD: John Hopkins University Press, 1982.

Klein, Herbert S. *African Slavery in Latin America and the Caribbean.* New York, NY: Oxford University Press, 1986.

_____. *The Atlantic Slave Trade.* New York, NY: Cambridge University Press, 1999.

_____. *The Middle Passage: Comparative Studies in the Atlantic Slave Trade.* Princeton, NJ: Princeton University Press, 1978.

_____. *A Population History of the United States.* 1st ed. New York, NY: Cambridge University Press, 2004.

_____. *Slavery in the Americas: A Comparative Study of Virginia and Cuba*. Chicago, IL: University of Chicago Press, 1967.

_____, Stanley L. Engerman, Robin Haines, and Ralph Shlomowitz. "Transoceanic Mortality: The Slave Trade in Comparative Perspective." *The William and Mary Quarterly*, Third Series 58:1 (2001): 93-118.

Law, Robin. "Dahomey and the Slave Trade: Reflections on the Historiography of the Rise of Dahomey." *Journal of African History* 27:2 (1986): 237-267.

_____. "Individualising the Atlantic Slave Trade: The Biography of Mahommah Garbo Baquaqua of Djougou." *Transactions of the Royal Historical Society* 12 (2002): 113-140.

_____. *The Slave Coast of West Africa 1550-1750: The Impact of the Atlantic Slave Trade on an African Society*. Durham, NC: Duke University Press, 1991.

Lockhart, James and Schwartz, Stuart. *Early Latin America: A History of Colonial Spanish America and Brazil*. New York, NY: Cambridge University Press, 1983.

Lovejoy, Paul. "The Impact of the Atlantic Slave Trade on Africa: A Review of the Literature." *Journal of African History* 30 (1989): 365-94.

_____. *Transformations in Slavery: A History of Slavery in Africa*. New York, NY: Cambridge University Press, 1983.

_____, ed. *Africans in Bondage: Studies in Slavery and the Slave Trade*. Madison, WI: University of Wisconsin Press, 1986.

Luna, Francisco Vidal and Herbert S. Klein. *Slavery and the Economy of Sao Paulo 1750-1850*. Stanford, CA: Stanford University Press, 2003.

Manning, Patrick. "Migrations of Africans to the Americas: The Impact on Africans, Africa, and the New World." *The History Teacher* 26:3 (1993): 279-296.

_____. *Slavery and African Life: Occidental, Oriental, and African Slave Trades*. New York, NY: Cambridge University Press, 1990.

_____. "Social and Demographic Transformations." in *Atlantic Slave Trade, 2nd Edition*, edited by David Northrup, ed. Boston, MA: Houghton Mifflin, 2000.

_____, David Anderson, Carolyn Brown, Christopher Clapham, Michael Gomez, David Robinson, and Leonardo A Villalon, eds. *Slavery, Colonialism and Economic Growth in Dahomey, 1640-1960*. New York, NY: Cambridge University Press, 1982.

Martin, Phyllis. *The External Trade of the Loango Coast: The Effects of Changing Commercial Relations on the Vili Kingdom of Loango*. Oxford, England: Clarendon Press, 1972.

Mazrui, Ali A, ed. *The Warrior Tradition in Modern Africa*. Lieden, The Netherlands: Brill Academic Publishers, 1977.

Meillassoux, Claude. *The Anthropology of Slavery: The Womb of Iron and Gold*. Translated by Alide Dasnois. Chicago, IL: University of Chicago Press, 1991.

Miller, Joseph Calder. *Way of Death: Merchant Capitalism and the Angolan Slave Trade, 1730-1830*. Madison, WI: University of Wisconsin Press, 1996.

Mintz, Sidney W. *Sweetness and Power: The Place of Sugar in Modern History*. New York, NY: Penguin Books, 1986.

_____, and Richard Price. *The Birth of African-American Culture: An Anthropological Perspective*. Boston, MA: Beacon Press, 1992.

Morgan, Jennifer L. *Laboring Women: Reproduction and Gender in New World Slavery*. Philadelphia, PA: University of Pennsylvania Press, 2004.

Northrup, David. *Trade without Rulers: Pre-Colonial Economic Development in South-Eastern Nigeria*. New York, NY: Clarendon Press, 1978.

_____, ed. *The Atlantic Slave Trade*. 2nd ed. Boston, MA: Houghton Mifflin Co., 2005.

Nwokeji, G. Ugo. "African Conceptions of Gender and the Slave Traffic." *William & Mary Quarterly* 58:1 (2001): 47-68.

Ogundiran, Akinwumi and Toyin Falola. eds. *Archaeology of Atlantic Africa and the African Diaspora*. Bloomington, IN: Indiana University Press, 2007.

Oliver, Roland F., and Brian M. Fagan. *Africa in the Iron Age*. New York, NY: Cambridge University Press, 1975.

O'Shaughnessy, Andrew Jackson. *An Empire Divided: The American Revolution and the British Caribbean*. Philadelphia, PA: University of Pennsylvania Press, 2000.

Powell, Phillip. *Soldiers, Indians and Silver: The Northward Advance of New Spain, 1550-1600*. Tempe, AZ: Arizona State University, 1975.

Price, Richard. *Ethnographic History, Caribbean Pasts: Discovering the Americas*. College Park, MD: University of Maryland Press, 1990.

_____. *First-Time: The Historical Vision of an African American People*. 2nd ed. Chicago, IL: University of Chicago Press, 2002.

_____, ed. *Maroon Societies: Rebel Slave Communities in the Americas*. 3rd ed. Baltimore, MD: John Hopkins University Press, 1996.

Price, Sally. *Maroon Arts: Cultural Vitality in the African Diaspora*. Boston, MA: Beacon Press, 1999.

Richardson, David. "Slave Exports from West and West-Central Africa, 1700-1810: New Estimates of Volume and Distribution." *Journal of African History* 30:1 (1989): 1-22.

_____. "Shipboard Revolts, African Authority, and the Atlantic Slave Trade." *The William and Mary Quarterly*, Third Series, 58:1 (Jan., 2001), 69-92.

_____. "The Slave Trade, Sugar, and British Economic Growth, 1748-1776." *Journal of Interdisciplinary History* 17:4 (1987): 739-769.

Rediker, Marcus. *The Slave Ship: A Human History*. New York, NY: Viking, 2007.

Roberts, Richard. *Warriors, Merchants, and Slaves: The State and the Economy in the Middle Niger Valley, 1710-1914*. Stanford, CA: Stanford University Press, 1987.

Rodney, Walter. *A History of the Upper Guinea Coast, 1545-1800*. Oxford, UK: Clarendon Publishers, 1970.

_____. *How Europe Underdeveloped Africa*. Washington, DC: Howard University Press, 1981.

Ryder, A. R. C. and D.Phil. *Benin and the Europeans, 1485-1897*. Edited by Ibadan History Series, K. O. Dike, Ph.D. London, England: Longmans, Green and Co LTD, 1969.

Sauer, Carl. *The Early Spanish Main*. Berkeley, CA: The University of California Press, 1992.

Sidbury, James. *Becoming African in America: Race and Nation in the Early Black Atlantic*. New York, NY: Oxford University Press, 2007.

Singleton, Theresa A. *"I, Too, Am America" - Archaeological Studies of African American Life*. Charlottesville, VA: University Press of Virginia, 1999.

Smallwood, Stephanie. *Saltwater Slavery: A Middle Passage from Africa to American Diaspora*. Cambridge, MA: Harvard University Press, 2007.

Stedman, John Gabriel. *Narrative of a Five Years Expedition against the Revolted Negroes of Surinam*. Edited by Richard Price and Sally Price. Baltimore, MD: John Hopkins University Press, 1988.

Thornton, John. *Africa and Africans in the Making of the Atlantic World, 1400-1800*. 2nd ed. New York, NY: Cambridge University Press, 1999.

_____. *The Kingdom of Kongo: Civil War and Transition, 1641-1718.* Madison, WI: University of Wisconsin Press, 1983.

_____. *Warfare in Atlantic Africa, 1500-1800.* London, England: UCL Press, 1999.

Vogt, John. *Portuguese Rule on the Gold Coast, 1469-1682.* Athens, GA: University of Georgia Press, 1979.

_____. "The Early Sao Tome - Principe Slave Trade with Mina, 1500-1540." *The International Journal of African Historical Studies* 6:3 (1973): 453-467.

Woodson, Carter Godwin. *The African Background Outlined: Or, Handbook for the Study of the Negro.* Westport, CT: Greenwood Press, 1969.

Wright, Marcia. *Strategies of Slaves & Women: Life Stories from East/Central Africa.* New York, NY: Barber Press, 1993.

Yerxa, Donald A., ed. *Recent Themes in the History of Africa and the Atlantic World: Historians in Conversation.* Columbia, SC: University of South Carolina Press, 2008.

Chapter 3: Establishing North American Slavery, 1520s to 1720s

Berlin, Ira. *Many Thousands Gone: The First Two Centuries of Slavery in North America.* Cambridge, MA: Harvard University Press, 1998.

_____. "From Creole to African: Atlantic Creoles and the Origins of African-American Society in Mainland North America." *The William and Mary Quarterly,* Third Series, 53:2 (Apr., 1996): 251-288

Breen, T. H. and Stephen Innes. *Myne Owne Ground: Race and Freedom on Virginia's Eastern Shore, 1640-1676.* New York, NY: Oxford University Press, 1982.

Brown, Kathleen M. *Good Wives, Nasty Wenches, and Anxious Patriarchs: Gender, Race, and Power in Colonial Virginia.* Chapel Hill: Published for the Institute of Early American History and Culture, Williamsburg, Virginia, by the University of North Carolina Press, 1996.

Carney, Judith. *Black Rice: The African Origins of Rice Cultivation in the Americas.* Cambridge, MA: Harvard University Press, 2001.

Coleman, John W. *Slavery Times in Kentucky.* New York, NY: Johnson Reprint Corp, 1970.

Conniff, Michael L. and Thomas J. Davis. *Africans in the Americas: A History of the Black Diaspora.* New York, NY: St. Martin's Press, 1994.

Curtin, Philip D. *The Atlantic Slave Trade: A Census.* Madison, WI: University of Wisconsin Press, 1969.

_____. *The Rise and Fall of the Plantation Complex: Essays in Atlantic History.* New York, NY: Cambridge University Press, 1990.

Davis, David Brion. *The Problem of Slavery in Western Culture.* New York, NY: Oxford University Press, 1988.

Davis, Ralph. *The Rise of the Atlantic Economies.* Ithaca, NY: Cornell University Press, 1973.

Deal, J. Douglas. *Race and Class in Colonial Virginia: Indians, Englishmen, and Africans on the Eastern Shore during the Seventeenth Century.* New York, NY: Garland Publishing, 1993.

Elkins, Stanley M. "Culture Contacts and Negro Slavery." *Proceedings of the American Philosophical Society* 107:2 (1963): 107-109.

Gallay, Alan. *The Indian Slave Trade: The Rise of the English Empire in the American South, 1670-1717.* New Haven, CT: Yale University Press, 2002.

Gannon, Michael. *Florida: a Short History.* Rev. ed. Gainesville, FL: University Press of Florida, 2003.

Hall, Gwendolyn Midlo. *Africans in Colonial Louisiana: The Development of AfroCreole Culture in the Eighteenth Century.* Baton Rouge, LA: Louisiana State University Press, 1992.

Heuman, Gad and James Walvin, eds. *The Slavery Reader.* London, England: Routledge, 2003.

Higginbotham, A. Leon, Jr. *In the Matter of Color: Race and the American Legal Process.* New York, NY: Oxford University Press, 1978.

Hodges, Graham Russell. *Root and Branch: African Americans in New York and East Jersey, 1613-1863.* Chapel Hill, NC: University of North Carolina Press, 1999.

Jordan, Winthrop. *White over Black: American Attitudes toward the Negro, 1550-1812.* New York: Norton, 1977

Klein, Herbert S. *Slavery in the Americas: A Comparative Study of Virginia and Cuba.* Chicago: University of Chicago Press, 1967.

Kolchin, Peter. *American Slavery: 1619-1877.* New York, NY: Hill and Wang, 2003.

Landers, Jane. *Black Society in Spanish Florida.* Edited by Blacks in the New World Series. Urbana, IL: University of Illinois Press, 1999.

Mannix, Daniel Pratt. *Black Cargoes: A History of the Atlantic Slave Trade, 1518-1865.* New York, NY: Viking Press, 1962.

Mintz, Sidney W. *Sweetness and Power: The Place of Sugar in Modern History.* New York, NY: Viking, 1985.

Morgan, Kenneth. *Slavery and the British Empire: From Africa to America.* New York, NY: Oxford University Press, 2007.

Morgan, Philip D. *Slave Counterpoint: Black Culture in the Eighteenth-Century Chesapeake and Lowcountry.* Chapel Hill, NC: University of North Carolina Press, 1998.

Morris, Thomas D. *Southern Slavery and the Law, 1619-1860.* Chapel Hill, NC: University of North Carolina Press, 1996.

Russell, John H. *The Free Negro in Virginia,* 1619-1865. New York, NY: Ams Pr, 2005.

Saunt, Claudio. *Black, White, and Indian: Race and the Unmaking of an American Family.* New York, NY: Oxford University Press, 2005.

Shorto, Russell. *The Island at the Center of the World: The Epic Story of Dutch Manhattan, the Forgotten Colony That Shaped America.* New York, NY: Doubleday, 2004.

Thomas, Hugh. *The Slave Trade: The Story of the Atlantic Slave Trade, 1440-1870.* New York, NY: Simon & Schuster, 1997.

Usner, Daniel H., Jr. *Indians, Settlers & Slaves in a Frontier Exchange Economy: The Lower Mississippi Valley before 1783.* Chapel Hill, NC: The University of North Carolina Press, 1992.

Vlach, John Michael. *Back of the Big House: The Architecture of Plantation Slavery.* Chapel Hill, NC: University of North Carolina Press, 1993.

Walsh, Lorena. *From Calabar to Carter's Grove: The History of a Virginia Slave Community.* Charlottesville, VA: University of Virginia Press, 2001.

Wood, Peter H. *Strange New Land: Africans in Colonial America.* New York, NY: Oxford University Press, 2003.

Wright, Donald R. *African Americans in the Colonial Era: From African Origins through the American Revolution.* Wheeling, IL: Harlan Davidson, 1990.

Chapter 4: Eighteenth-Century Slave Societies, 1700-1780s

Austin, Allan D. *African Muslims in Antebellum America: Transatlantic Stories and Spiritual Struggles.* Oxford, England: Routledge, 1997.

Berlin, Ira. "From Creole to African: Atlantic Creoles and the Origins of African American Society in Mainland North America." *William and Mary Quarterly* 53:2 (1996): 251-288.

_____. *Many Thousands Gone: The First Two Centuries of Slavery in North America.* Cambridge, MA: Belknap Press of Harvard University Press, 1998.

Blassingame, John. *The Slave Community, Plantation Life in the Antebellum South.* New York, NY: Oxford University Press, 1979.

Breen, T. H. and Stephen Innes. *Myne Owne Ground: Race and Freedom on Virginia's Eastern Shore, 1640-1676.* New York, NY: Oxford University Press, 1982.

Carney, Judith A. *Black Rice: The African Origins of Rice Cultivation in the Americas.* Cambridge, MA: Harvard University Press, 2001.

Channing, Edward. *The Narragansett Planters: A Study of Causes.* Salem, MA: Higginson Book Co., 1999.

Chaplin, Joyce E. "Tidal Rice Cultivation and the Problem of Slavery in South Carolina and Georgia, 1760-1815." *William and Mary Quarterly* 49:1 (1992): 29-61.

Cooley, Henry S. *A Study of Slavery in New Jersey.* New York, NY: Johnson Reprint Corp., 1973.

Davis, David Brion. *The Problem of Slavery in Western Culture.* New York, NY: Oxford University Press, 1988.

Davis, Ralph. *The Rise of the Atlantic Economies.* Ithaca, NY: Cornell University Press, 1973.

Davis, Thomas. *A Rumor of Revolt: The Great Negro Plot in Colonial New York.* New York, NY: Free Press, 1985.

Deal, J. Douglas. *Race and Class in Colonial Virginia: Indians, Englishmen, and Africans on the Eastern Shore During the Seventeenth Century.* New York, NY: Garland Publishing, 1993.

Gomez, Michael Angelo. *Exchanging Our Country Marks: The Transformation of African Identities in the Colonial and Antebellum South.* Chapel Hill, NC: University of North Carolina Press, 1998.

_____. "Muslims in Early America." *The Journal of Southern History* 60 (1994): 671-710.

Greene, Jack P. and J. R. Pole, eds. *Colonial British America: Essays in the New History of the Early Modern Era.* Baltimore, MD: John Hopkins University Press, 1984.

Hall, Gwendolyn Midlo. *Africans in Colonial Louisiana: The Development of AfroCreole Culture in the Eighteenth Century.* Baton Rouge, LA: Louisiana State University Press, 1992.

Hanger, Kimberly. *Bounded Lives, Bounded Places: Free Black Society in Colonial New Orleans, 1769-1803.* Durham, NC: Duke University Press, 1997.

Heuman, Gad and James Walvin, eds. *The Slavery Reader.* London, England: Routledge, 2003.

Higginbotham, A. Leon, Jr. *In the Matter of Color: Race and the American Legal Process.* New York, NY: Oxford University Press, 1978.

Hodges, Graham Russell. *Root and Branch: African Americans in New York and East Jersey, 1613-1863.* Chapel Hill, NC: University of North Carolina Press, 1999.

Ingersoll, Thomas N. "Free Blacks in a Slave Society: New Orleans, 1718-1812." *William and Mary Quarterly* 48:2 (1991): 173-200.

Jordan, Winthrop. *White over Black; American Attitudes toward the Negro, 1550-1812.* New York, NY: Norton, 1977.

Kimber, Edward. *Itinerant Observations in America.* Edited by Kevin J. Hayes. Newark: University of Delaware Press, 1998.

Klingberg, Frank Joseph. *An Appraisal of the Negro in Colonial South Carolina: A Study in Americanization.* Philadelphia, PA: Porcupine Press, 1975.

Landers, Jane. *Black Society in Spanish Florida.* Edited by Blacks in the New World Series. Urbana, IL: University of Illinois Press, 1999.

_____. "Gracia Real De Santa Teresa De Mose: A Free Black Town in Spanish Colonial Florida." *American Historical Review* 95:1 (1990): 9-30.

Lepore, Jill. *New York Burning: Liberty, Slavery, and Conspiracy in Eighteenth-Century Manhattan.* 1st ed. New York, NY: Alfred A. Knopf, 2005.

Linebaugh, Peter and Marcus Redicker. *The Many-Headed Hydra: The Hidden History of the Revolutionary Atlantic.* Boston, MA: Beacon Press, 2001.

Littlefield, Daniel C. *Rice and Slaves: Ethnicity and the Slave Trade in Colonial South Carolina.* Baton Rouge, LA: University of Louisiana Press, 1981.

McManus, Edgar J. *A History of Negro Slavery in New York.* Syracuse, NY: Syracuse University Press, 2001.

Minardi, Margot. "The Boston Inoculation Controversy of 1721-1722: An Incident in the History of Race." *The Williams and Mary Quarterly* 16:1, (2004): 47-76.

Morgan, Edmund. *American Slavery, American Freedom: The Ordeal of Colonial Virginia.* New York, NY: W. W. Norton & Co., 2003.

Morgan, Philip D. *Slave Counterpoint: Black Culture in the Eighteenth-Century Chesapeake and Lowcountry.* Chapel Hill, NC: University of North Carolina Press, 1998.

Morris, Thomas D. *Southern Slavery and the Law, 1619-1860.* Chapel Hill, NC: University of North Carolina Press, 1996.

Mullin, Gerald W. *Flight and Rebellion: Slave Resistance in Eighteenth-Century Virginia.* New York, NY: Oxford University Press, 1972.

Nash, Gary B. *Red, White, and Black: The Peoples of Early North America.* 4th ed. Upper Saddle River, NJ: Prentice Hall, 1999.

Nash, Gary B., and Richard Weiss, eds. *The Great Fear: Race in the Mind of America.* New York, NY: Holt, Rinehart and Winston, 1970.

Olwell, Robert. *Masters, Slaves, & Subjects: The Culture of Power in the South Carolina Low Country, 1740-1790.* Ithaca, NY: Cornell University Press, 1998.

Perdue, Theda. *Mixed Blood Indians: Racial Construction in the Early South.* Athens, GA: University of Georgia Press, 2005.

Piersen, William Dillon. *Black Yankees: The Development of an Afro-American Subculture in Eighteenth-Century New England.* Amherst, MA: University of Massachusetts Press, 1988.

Shorto, Russell. *The Island at the Center of the World: The Epic Story of Dutch Manhattan, the Forgotten Colony That Shaped America.* New York, NY: Doubleday, 2004.

Smith, Hilrie Shelton. *In His Image, But . . . : Racism in Southern Religion, 1780-1910.* Durham, NC: Duke University Press, 1972.

Sobel, Mechal. *The World They Made Together: Black and White Values in Eighteenth-Century Virginia.* Princeton, NJ: Princeton University Press, 1987.

Soderlund, Jean R. *Quakers and Slavery: A Divided Spirit.* Princeton, NJ: Princeton University Press, 1985.

Tate, Thad W., Jr. *The Negro in Eighteenth-Century Williamsburg.* Williamsburg, VA: University Press of Virginia, 1965.

Turner, Edward R. *The Negro in Pennsylvania: Slavery -Servitude - Freedom, 1639-1861.* New York, NY: Arno Press, 1969.

Usner, Daniel. *Indians, Settlers & Slaves in a Frontier Exchange Economy: the Lower Mississippi Valley before 1783.* Chapel Hill: University of North Carolina Press, 1992.

Wood, Betty. *Slavery in Colonial Georgia, 1730-1775.* Athens, GA: University of Georgia Press, 1984.

Wood, Forrest G. *The Arrogance of Faith: Christianity and Race in America from the Colonial Era to the Twentieth Century.* New York, NY: Alfred A. Knopf, 1990.

Wood, Peter. "'I Did the Best I Could for My Day': The Study of Early Black History During the Second Reconstruction, 1960 to 1976." *William and Mary Quarterly* 35:2 (1978): 185-225.

_____. *Black Majority: Negroes in Colonial South Carolina from 1670 through the Stono Rebellion*. New York, NY: Alfred A. Knopf, 1975.

Wright, Donald R. *African Americans in the Colonial Era: From African Origins through the American Revolution*. Wheeling, IL: Harlan Davidson, 2000.

Chapter 5: Give Me Liberty, 1763-1787

Berlin, Ira. *Many Thousands Gone: The First Two Centuries of Slavery in North America*. Cambridge, MA: Belknap Press of Harvard University Press, 2000.

_____ and Ronald Hoffman. *Slavery and Freedom in the Age of the American Revolution*. Charlottesville, VA: Published for the United States Capitol Historical Society by the University Press of Virginia, 1983.

Bezis-Selfa, John. "A Tale of Two Ironworks: Slavery, Free Labor, Work, and Resistance in the Early Republic." *The William and Mary Quarterly* 56:4, (1999): 677-700.

Breen, T. H. "Ideology and Nationalism on the Eve of the American Revolution: Revisions Once More in Need of Revising." *Journal of American History* 84:1, (1997) 13-39.

Cohen, William. "Thomas Jefferson and the Problem of Slavery." *Journal of American History* 56:3 (1969): 503-526.

Davis, David Brion. *The Problem of Slavery in the Age of Revolution*. Ithaca, NY: Cornell University Press, 1975.

Dubois, Laurent. *A Colony of Citizens: Revolution & Slave Emancipation in the French Caribbean, 1787-1804*. Chapel Hill, NC: University of North Carolina Press, 2004.

Egerton, Douglas R. *Death or liberty: African Americans and Revolutionary America*. New York: Oxford University Press, 2009.

Farrand, Max. *The Framing of the Constitution*. New Haven, CT: Yale University Press, 1913.

Farrand, Max, ed. *Records of the Federal Convention of 1787*. 3 vols. New Haven, CT: Yale University Press, 1911.

Finkelman, Paul. "Jefferson and Slavery: 'Treason against the Hopes of the World'." In *Jeffersonian Legacies*, edited by Peter S. Onuf. Charlottesville, VA: University Press of Virginia, 1993.

_____. *Slavery and the Founders: Race and Liberty in the Age of Jefferson*. 2nd ed. Armonk, N.Y.: M.E. Sharpe, 2001.

Frey, Sylvia. *Water from the Rock: Black Resistance in a Revolutionary Age*. Princeton, NJ: Princeton University Press, 1991.

Gordon-Reed, Annette. *The Hemingses of Monticello: An American Family*. New York, NY: W.W. Norton & Co., c2008.

_____. *Thomas Jefferson and Sally Hemings: An American Controversy*. Charlottesville, VA: University Press of Virginia, 1997.

Higginbotham, Jr., A. Leon. *In the Matter of Color: the Colonial Period*. New York, NY: Oxford University Press, 1978.

Hirschfeld, Fritz. *George Washington and Slavery: Documentary Portrayal*. Columbia, MO: University of Missouri Press, 1997.

Hodges, Graham Russell and Alan Edward Brown, eds. *"Pretends to be Free": Runaway Slave Advertisements from colonial and Revolutionary New York and New Jersey*. New York, NY: Garland Pub., 1994.

Holton, Woody. *Forced Founders: Indians, Debtors, Slaves, and the Making of the American Revolution in Virginia*. Chapel Hill, NC: University of North Carolina Press, 1999.

Kaplan, Sidney. *The Black Presence in the Era of the American Revolution, 1770-1800*. Greenwich, CT: New York Graphic Society in Association with the Smithsonian Institution Press, 1973.

Linebaugh, Peter and Marcus Redicker. *The Many-Headed Hydra: The Hidden History of the Revolutionary Atlantic*. Boston, MA: Beacon Press, 2001.

Locke, Mary S. *Anti-slavery in America: from the introduction of African slaves to the prohibition of the slave trade, 1619-1808*. Gloucester, MA: P. Smith, 1965 c1901.

Lynd, Staughton. *Class Conflict, Slavery, and the United States Constitution: Ten Essays*. Indianapolis, IN: Bobbs-Merrill, 1968, c1967.

MacLeod, Duncan J. *Slavery, Race, and the American Revolution*. New York, NY: Cambridge University Press, 1974.

Melish, Joanne Pope. *Disowning Slavery: Gradual Emancipation and Race in New England, 1780-1860*. Ithaca, NY: Cornell University Press, 2000.

_____. "The "Condition" Debate and Racial Discourse in the Antebellum North." *Journal of the Early Republic* 19:4, (Winter, 1999): 651-672.

Morgan, Edmund. *American Slavery, American Freedom: The Ordeal of Colonial Virginia*. New York, NY: W.W. Norton & Co., 2003.

Nash, Gary B. *The Forgotten Fifth: African Americans in the Age of Revolution*. Cambridge, MA: Harvard University Press, 2006.

_____. *Race and Revolution*. Madison, WI: Madison House, 1990.

_____ and Jean R. Soderlund. *Freedom by Degrees: Emancipation in Pennsylvania and Its Aftermath*. New York, NY, 1991.

Nell, William C. *The Colored Patriots of the American Revolution*. Salem, NH: Ayer Company, Publishers, 1986, c1855.

Newman, Richard S. *The Transformation of American Abolitionism: Fighting Slavery in the Early Republic*. Chapel Hill, NC: University of North Carolina Press, 2002.

Quarles, Benjamin. *The Negro in the American Revolution*. Williamsburg, VA: University of North Carolina Press, 1961.

Schama, Simon. *Rough Crossings : Britain, the Slaves, and the American Revolution*. New York, NY: Ecco, 2006.

Sobel, Mechal. *Teach Me Dreams: Transforming the Self in the Revolutionary Era*. Princeton, NJ: Princeton University Press, 2000.

Waldstreicher, David. *Runaway America: Benjamin Franklin, Slavery, and the American Revolution*. New York, NY: Hill and Wang, 2004.

White, Shane. *Somewhat More Independent: The End of Slavery in New York City, 1770-1810*. Athens, GA: University of Georgia Press, 1991.

Wilson, Ellen Gibson. *The Loyal Blacks*. New York: Capricorn Books, 1976.

Zilversmit, Arthur. *The First Emancipation: The Abolition of Slavery in the North*. Chicago, IL: University of Chicago Press, 1967.

Chapter 6: Building Communities in the Early Republic, 1790-1830

Bay, Mia. *The White Image in the Black Mind: African-American Ideas about White People*. New York, NY: Oxford University Press, 2000.

Bezis-Selfa, John. *Forging America: Ironworkers, Adventurers, and the Industrious Revolution*. Ithaca, NY: Cornell University Press, 2004.

Bolster, W. Jeffrey. *Black Jacks: African American Seamen in the Age of Sail*. Cambridge, MA: Harvard University Press, 1997.

Brawley, Benjamin. *Early Negro American Writers*. Chapel Hill, NC: University of North Carolina, 1935.

Brown, Richard D. "Not Only Extreme Poverty, but the Worst Kind of Orphanage': Lemuel Haynes and the Boundaries of

Racial Tolerance on the Yankee Frontier, 1770-1820." *New England Quarterly* 61:4 (1988): 502-518.

Bruce, Dickson. *The Origins of African American Literature, 1680-1865.* Charlottesville, VA: University Press of Virginia, 2001.

Caretta, Vincent. *Equiano, the African: Biography of a Self-Made Man.* Athens, GA: University of Georgia Press, 2005.

_____ . "Olaudah Equiano or Gustavas Vasa? New Light on an Eighteenth Century Question of Identity." *Slavery and Abolition* 20 (1999): 96-105.

Carr, Jacqueline Barbara. *After the Siege: a Social History of Boston, 1775-1800.* Boston, MA: Northeastern University Press, 2005.

Carr, Lois Green and Lorena S. Walsh. "Economic Diversification and Labor Organization in the Chesapeake, 1650-1820." in *Work and Labor in the Early America,* edited by Stephen Innes. Chapel Hill, NC: University of North Carolina Press, 1988.

Cassell, Frank A. "Slaves of the Chesapeake Bay Area and the War of 1812." *The Journal of Negro History* 57:2 (1972): 144-155.

Cecelski, David S. *The Waterman's Song: Slavery and Freedom in Maritime North Carolina.* Chapel Hill, NC: University of North Carolina Press, 2001.

Crawford, George W. *Prince Hall and His Followers.* New York, NY: AMS Press, 1971.

Cuffe, Paul and edited by Rosalind Cobb Wiggins. *Captain Paul Cuffe's Logs and Letters, 1808-1817: A Black Quaker's Voice from within the Veil.* Washington, DC: Howard University Press, 1996.

Dain, Bruce. *A Hideous Monster of the Mind: American Race Theory in the Early Republic.* Cambridge, MA: Harvard University Press, 2002.

Diamond, Arthur and Nathan I. Huggins, eds. *Paul Cuffe: Merchant and Abolitionist.* New York, NY: Facts on File, 1989.

Dubois, Laurent. *A Colony of Citizens: Revolution & Slave Emancipation in the French Caribbean, 1787-1804.* Chapel Hill, NC: University of North Carolina Press, 2004.

Finkelman, Paul. *Slavery and the Founders: Race and Liberty in the Age of Jefferson.* 2nd ed. Armonk, N.Y.: M.E. Sharpe, 2001.

Ford, Lacy K., Jr. "Making the 'White Man's Country' White: Race, Slavery, and State Building in the Jacksonian South." *Journal of the Early Republic* 19:4 (1999): 713-737.

Forten, James. *An Address Delivered before the Ladies' Anti-slavery Society of Philadelphia, on the Evening of the 14th of April, 1836.* Philadelphia, PA: Printed by Merrihew and Gunn, 1836

Fredrickson, George M. *The Black Image in the White Mind: The Debate on Afro-American Character and Destiny, 1817-1914.* Middletown, CT: Wesleyan University Press, 1987.

Frey, Sylvia R., and Betty Wood. *Come Shouting to Zion: African American Protestantism in the American South and British Caribbean to 1830.* Chapel Hill, NC: University of North Carolina Press, 1998.

Glaude, Eddie. *Exodus! Religion, Race, and Nation in the Early Nineteenth Century Black America.* Chicago, IL: University of Chicago Press, 2000.

Gould, Virginia L., ed. *"Chained to the Rock of Adversity: To Be Free, Black & Female in the Old South.* Athens, GA: University of Georgia Press, 1998.

Harris, Leslie M. *In the Shadow of Slavery: African Americans in New York City, 1626-1863.* Chicago, IL: University of Chicago Press, 2003.

Harris, Sheldon H. *Paul Cuffe, Black America and the African Return.* New York, NY: Simon & Schuster, 1972.

Hatch, Nathan O. "The Puzzle of American Methodism." *Church History* 63:2 (1994): 175-189.

Hickey, Donald R. "America's Response to the Slave Revolt in Haiti, 1791-1806." *Journal of the Early Republic* 2:4 (1982): 361-379.

Hirsch, Arnold R. and Joseph Logsdon, eds. *Creole New Orleans: Race and Americanization.* Baton Rouge, LA: Louisiana State University Press, 1992.

Hodes, Martha. *White Women, Black Men: Illicit Sex in the Nineteenth Century South.* New Haven, CT: Yale University Press, 1997.

Horton, James Oliver. *In Hope Of Liberty: Culture, Community, And Protest Among Northern Free Blacks, 1700-1860.* New York, NY: Oxford University Press, 1998.

Horton, Lois E. "From Class to Race in Early America: Northern Post-Emancipation Racial Reconstruction." *Journal of the Early Republic* 19:4 (1999): 629-649.

Kolchin, Peter. *American Slavery, 1619-1877.* 1st rev. ed. New York, NY: Hill & Wang, 2003.

Lamont, Thomas D. *Rise to be a People: A Biography of Paul Cuffe.* Urbana, IL: University of Illinois Press, 1986.

Lockley, Timothy James. *Lines in the Sand: Race and Class in Lowcountry Georgia, 1750-1860.* Athens, GA: University of Georgia Press, 2001.

McColley, Robert. *Slavery and Jeffersonian Virginia.* 2nd ed. Urbana, IL: University of Illinois Press, 1974.

Melish, Joanne Pope. *Disowning Slavery: Gradual Emancipation and "Race" in New England, 1780-1860.* Ithaca, NY: Cornell University Press, 1998.

Morgan, Edmund. *American Slavery, American Freedom: The Ordeal of Colonial Virginia.* New York, NY: W.W. Norton & Co., 2003.

Morris, Christopher. *Becoming Southern: The Evolution of a Way of Life, Warren County and Vicksburg, Mississippi, 1770-1860.* New York, NY: Oxford University Press, 1995.

Nash, Gary B. *Forging Freedom: The Formation of Philadelphia's Black Community, 1720-1840.* Cambridge, MA: Harvard University Press, 1988.

Newman, Richard, ed. *Black Preacher to White America: The Collected Writings of Lemuel Haynes, 1774-1833.* Brooklyn, NY: Carlson Pub., 1990.

Newman, Richard, Patrick Rael and Philip Lapansky, eds. *Pamphlets of Protest: An Anthology of Early African American Protest Literature, 1790-1860.* New York, NY: Routledge, 2001.

Newman, Richard S. *The Transformation of American Abolitionism: Fighting Slavery in the Early Republic.* Chapel Hill, NC: University of North Carolina Press, 2002.

Peterson, Carla L. *Doers of the Word: African-American Women Speakers and Writers in the North (1830-1880).* New York, NY: Oxford University Press, 1995.

Piersen, William Dillon. *Black Yankees: The Development of an Afro-American Subculture in Eighteenth-Century New England.* Amherst, MA: University of Massachusetts Press, 1988.

Porter, Dorothy B., ed. *Early Negro Writings, 1760-1837.* Boston, MA: Beacon Press, 1971.

Potkay, Adam and Sandra Burr, eds. *Black Atlantic Writers of the Eighteenth Century: Living the Exodus in England and the Americas.* New York, NY: St. Martin's, 1995.

Rael, Patrick. *Black Identity & Black Protest in the Antebellum North.* Chapel Hill, NC: University of North Carolina Press, 2002.

_____ , ed. *Pamphlets of protest: an Anthology of Early African-American Protest Literature, 1790-1860.* New York, NY: Routledge, 2001.

Remini, Robert V. *The Battle of New Orleans: Andrew Jackson and America's First Military Victory.* New York, NY: Viking, 1999.

Richmond, Merle A. *Bid the Vassal Soar; Interpretive Essays on the Life and Poetry of Phillis Wheatley (Ca. 1753-1784) and George Moses Horton (Ca. 1797-1883).* Washington, DC: Howard University Press, 1974.

Rucker, Walter C., *The River Flows On: Black Resistance, Culture, and Identity Formation in Early America.* Baton Rouge: Louisiana State University Press, 2006.

Rury, John L. "Philanthropy, Self Help, and Social Control: The New York Manumission Society and Free Blacks, 1785-1810." *Phylon* 46:3 (1985): 231-241.

Sensbach, Jon F. "Charting a Course in Early African-American History." *The William and Mary Quarterly* 3rd ser. 50:2 (1993): 394-405.

Shammas, Carole. "The Space Problem in Early United States Cities." *The William and Mary Quarterly* 3rd ser. 57:3 (2000): 505-542.

Sheller, Tina H. "Freemen, Servants, and Slaves: Artisans and the Craft Structure of Revolutionary Baltimore Town." In *American Artisans: Crafting Social Identity, 1750-1850,* edited by Howard B. Rock, Paul A. Gilje, Robert Asher. Baltimore, MD: Johns Hopkins University Press, 1995.

Sidbury, James. *Becoming African in America: Race and Nation in the Early Black Atlantic.* New York, NY: Oxford University Press, 2007.

———. *Ploughshares into Swords: Race Rebellion, and Identity in Gabriel's Virginia, 1730-1810.* New York, NY: Cambridge University Press, 1997.

———. "Slave Artisans in Richmond, Virginia, 1780-1830." In *American Artisans: Crafting Social Identity, 1750-1850,* edited by Howard B. Rock, Paul A. Gilje, Robert Asher. Baltimore, MD: Johns Hopkins University Press, 1995.

Sobel, Mechal. *Trabelin' On: The Slave Journey to an Afro-Baptist Faith.* Princeton, NJ: Princeton University Press, 1988.

Swan, Robert J. "John Teasman: African-American Educator and the Emergence of Community in Early Black New York City, 1787-1815." *Journal of the Early Republic* 12:3 (1992): 331-356.

Takagi, Midori. *"Rearing Wolves to Our Own Destruction": Slavery in Richmond, Virginia, 1782-1865.* Charlottesville, VA: University Press of Virginia, 1999.

Thomas, Lamont D. *Rise to Be a People, a Biography of Paul Cuffe.* Urbana, IL: University of Illinois Press, 1986.

Thompson, Shirley. *Exiles at Home: The Struggle to Become American in Creole New Orleans.* Cambridge, MA: Harvard University Press, 2009.

United States. Bureau of the Census. *Negro Population, 1790-1915.* Washington, DC: United States Bureau of the Census, 1918.

Upton, William. *Negro Masonry.* New York, NY: AMS Press, 1975.

Waldstreicher, David. *In the Midst of Perpetual Fetes: The Making of American Nationalism, 1776-1820.* Chapel Hill, NC: University of North Carolina Press, 1997.

Walsh, Lorena. *From Calabar to Carter's Grove: The History of a Virginia Slave Community.* Charlottesville, VA: University Press of Virginia, 1997.

White, Shane. *Somewhat More Independent: The End of Slavery in New York City, 1770-1810.* Athens, GA: University of Georgia Press, 1991.

———. *Stories of Freedom in Black New York.* Cambridge, MA: Harvard University Press, 2002.

——— and Graham White. "Slave Hair and African American Culture in the Eighteenth and Nineteenth Centuries." *The Journal of Southern History* 61:1 (1995): 45-76.

Whitman, T. Stephan. *The Price of Freedom: Slavery and Manumission in Baltimore and Early National Maryland.* Lexington, KY: University Press of Kentucky, 1997.

Wilson, Harriet E. *Our Nig, or Sketches from the Life of a Free Black, in a Two-Story White House, North, Showing that Slavery's Shadows Fall Even There.* New York, NY: Random House, 1983.

Winch, Julie. *A Gentleman of Color: The Life of James Forten.* New York, NY: Oxford University Press, 2003.

Wright, Donald R. *African Americans in the Early Republic, 1789-1831.* Arlington Heights, IL: Harland Davidson, 1993.

Chapter 7: Southern Slavery, 1790-1860

Bancroft, Frederick. *Slave Trading in the Old South*; with a new introduction by Michael Tadman. Columbia, SC: University of South Carolina Press, 1995.

Bassett, John S. *The Southern Plantation Overseer as Revealed in His Letters.* Northampton, MA: Smith College, 1968.

Berlin, Ira. *Many Thousand Gone: The First Two Centuries of Slavery in North America.* Cambridge, MA: Belknap Press of Harvard University Press, 1998.

———. *Generations of Captivity: A History of African-American Slaves.* Cambridge, MA: Belknap Press of Harvard University Press, 2003.

——— and Philip D. Morgan, eds. *Cultivation and Culture: Labor and the Shaping of Black Life in the Americas.* Charlottesville, VA: University of Virginia Press, 1993.

———, Mark Favreau, and Steven F. Miller, eds. *Remembering Slavery: African Americans Talk About Their Personal Experiences of Slavery and Freedom.* New York, NY: The New Press, 1998.

Blassingame, John. *The Slave Community, Plantation Life in the Antebellum South.* New York, NY: Oxford University Press, 1974.

———. *Slave Testimony: Two Centuries of Letters, Speeches, Interviews, and Autobiographies.* Baton Rouge, LA: Louisiana State University Press, 1977.

Boritt, Gabor and Scott Hancock, eds. *Slavery, Resistance, Freedom: Essays by Ira Berlin.* New York, NY: Oxford University Press, 2007.

Camp, Stephanie M. H. *Closer to Freedom: Enslaved Women and Everyday Resistance in the Plantation South.* Chapel Hill: University of North Carolina Press, 2004.

Catterall, Helen T., ed. *Judicial Cases Concerning American Slavery and the Negro.* 5 vols. Washington, DC: Carnegie Institution of Washington, 1926-1937.

Cecelski, David S. *The Waterman's Song: Slavery and Freedom in Maritime North Carolina.* Chapel Hill, NC: University of North Carolina Press, 2001.

Clinton, Catherine. *Harriet Tubman: The Road to Freedom.* New York, NY: Little, Brown, 2004.

———. *The Plantation Mistress.* New York, NY: Knopf Doubleday Publishing, 1984.

Cornelius, Janet Duitsman. *"When I Can Read My Title Clear": Literacy, Slavery, and Religion in the Antebellum South.* Columbia, SC: University of South Carolina Press, 1991.

David, Paul. *Reckoning with Slavery: A Critical Study in the Quantitative History of American Negro Slavery.* New York, NY: Oxford University Press, 1976.

Davis, Charles T. and Henry L. Gates. *The Slave's Narrative.* New York, NY: Oxford University Press, 1985.

Davis, David Brion. *The Problem of Slavery in Western Culture.* New York, NY: Oxford University Press, 1988.

Douglass, Frederick. *The Narrative of Frederick Douglass.* Boston, MA: Published at the Anti-Slavery Office, 1845.

Duff, John B. and Peter M. Mitchell, eds. *The Nat Turner Rebellion: The Historical Event and the Modern Controversy.* New York, NY: Harper & Row, 1971.

Dunaway, Wilma A. *The African-American Family in Slavery and Emancipation.* New York, NY: Cambridge University Press, 2003.

Elkins, Stanley. *Slavery: A Problem in American Institutional and Intellectual Life.* 3rd ed. Chicago, IL: University of Chicago Press, 1976.

Faust, Drew G. *James Henry Hammond and the Old South: A Design for Mastery*. Baton Rouge, LA: Louisiana State University Press, 1982.

Fields, Barbara H. *Slavery and Freedom on the Middle Ground: Maryland During the Nineteenth Century*. New Haven, CT: Yale University Press, 1985.

Fisher, Miles M. *Negro Slave Songs in the United States*. New York, NY: Russell & Russell, 1968.

Fogel, Robert and Stanley Engerman. *Time on the Cross*. 2 vols. New York, NY: Norton, 1995, c1974.

_____, eds. *The Reinterpretation of American Economic History*. New York, NY: Harper & Row, 1971.

Fox-Genovese, Elizabeth. *Within the Plantation Household: Black and White Women of the Old South*. Chapel Hill, NC: University of North Carolina Press, 1989.

Franklin, John Hope and Loren Schweninger. *Runaway Slaves: Rebels on the Plantation*. New York, NY: Oxford University Press, 1999.

Frey, Sylvia R. and Betty Wood. *Come shouting to Zion : African American Protestantism in the American South and British Caribbean to 1830*. Chapel Hill, NC: University of North Carolina Press, 1998.

Genovese, Eugene D. *The Political Economy of Slavery: studies in the economy & society of the slave South*. 2nd ed. Middletown, CT: Wesleyan University Press, 1989.

_____. *Roll, Jordan, Roll: The World the Slaves Made*. New York, NY: Pantheon, 1974.

_____. *The World the Slaveholders Made*. Middletown, CT: Wesleyan University Press, 1988.

Gillespie, Michael. *Free Labor in an Unfree World: White Artisans in Slaveholding Georgia, 1789-1860*. Athens, GA: University of Georgia Press, 1999.

Goldin, Claudia D. *Urban Slavery in the American South, 1820-1860: A Quantitative History*. Chicago, IL: University of Chicago, 1976.

Gross, Ariela J. *Double Character: Slavery and Mastery in the Antebellum Courtroom*. Princeton, NJ: Princeton University Press, 2000.

Gudmestad, Robert H. *A Troublesome Commerce: The Transformation of the Interstate Slave Trade*. Baton Rouge, IL: Louisiana State University Press, 2003.

Gutman, Herbert. *The Black Family in Slavery and Freedom, 1750-1925*. New York, NY: Vintage Books, 1977.

Hadden, Sally E. *Slave Patrols: Law and Violence in Virginia and the Carolinas*. Cambridge, MA: Harvard University Press, 2001.

Halasz, Nicholas. *Rattling Chains: Slave Unrest and Revolt in the Antebellum South*. New York, NY: D. McKay Co., 1966.

Hinks, Peter. *To Awaken My Afflicted Brethren: David Walker and the Problem of Antebellum Slave Resistance*. University Park, PA: Pennsylvania State University Press, 1997.

Hodes, Martha. *White Women, Black Men: Illicit Sex in the Nineteenth Century South*. New Haven, CT: Yale University Press, 1997.

Hudson, Larry E., Jr. *To Have and to Hold: Slave Work and Family Life in Antebellum South Carolina*. Athens, GA: University of Georgia Press, 1997.

Humez, Jean, ed. *Harriet Tubman: The Life and the Life Stories*. Madison, WI: University of Wisconsin Press, 2003.

Jacobs, Harriet A., and Jean F. Yellin, ed. *Incidents in the Life of a Slave Girl Written by Herself*. Cambridge, MA: Harvard University Press, 1987.

Johnson, Michael P. and James L. Roark. *Black Masters: A Free Family of Color in the Old South*. New York, NY: Norton, 1984.

Johnson, Walter. "The Slave Trader, the White Slave, and the Politics of Racial Determination in the 1850s." *Journal of American History* 87:1 (2000): 13-38.

_____. *Soul by Soul: Life inside the Antebellum Slave Market*. Cambridge, MA: Harvard University Press, 1999.

Johnston, James H. *Race Relations in Virginia and Miscegenation in the South, 1776-1860*. Amherst, MA: University of Massachusetts Press, 1970.

Joyner, Charles. *Down by the Riverside: A South Carolina Slave Community*. Urbana, IL: University of Illinois Press, 1984.

Katz, William Loren. *The Black West*. 3rd ed. Seattle, WA: Open Hand Publishing, 1987.

Kaye, Anthony E. *Joining Places: Slave Neighborhoods in the Old South*. Chapel Hill, NC: University of North Carolina Press, 2007.

King, Wilma. *Stolen Childhood: Slave Youth in Nineteenth-Century America*. Bloomington, IN: Indiana University Press, 1995.

Kolchin, Peter. *American Slavery*, 1619-1877. New York, NY: Hill and Wang, 2003.

Lane, Ann J., ed. *The Debate over Slavery: Stanley Elkins and His Critics*. Urbana, IL: University of Illinois Press, 1971.

Larson, Kate Clifford. *Bound for the Promised Land: Harriet Tubman, Portrait of an American Hero*. New York, NY: Ballantine, 2004.

Leslie, Kent Anderson. *Woman of Color, Daughter of Privilege: Amanda America Dickson, 1849-1893*. Athens, GA: University of Georgia Press, 1995.

Levine, Lawrence. *Black Culture and Black Consciousness: Afro-American Folk Thought from Slavery to Freedom*. 30th Anniversary Edition. New York, NY: Oxford University Press, 2007, c1997.

Linebaugh, Peter, and Marcus Redicker. *The Many-Headed Hydra: The Hidden History of the Revolutionary Atlantic*. Boston, MA: Beacon Press, 2001.

Lofton, John. *Insurrection in South Carolina: The Turbulent World of Denmark Vesey*. Kent, OH: Kent State University Press, 1983.

Malone, Ann Patton. *Sweet Chariot, Slave Family and Household Structure in Nineteenth Century Louisiana*. Chapel Hill, NC: University of North Carolina Press, 1992.

Martin, Jonathan D. *Divided Mastery: Slave Hiring in the American South*. Cambridge, MA: Harvard University Press, 2004.

McConnell, Roland Calhoun. *Negro Troops in Antebellum Louisiana: A History of the Battalion of Free Men of Color*. Baton Rouge, LA: Louisiana State University Press, 1968.

McLaurin, Melton. *Celia, a Slave*. Athens, GA: University of Georgia Press, 1992.

Morgan, Lynda J. *Emancipation in Virginia's Tobacco Belt, 1850-1870*. Athens, GA: University of Georgia Press, 1992.

Morris, Christopher. *Becoming Southern: The Evolution of a Way of Life, Warren County and Vicksburg, Mississippi, 1770-1860*. New York, NY: Oxford University Press, 1999.

Mullin, Gerald W. *Flight and Rebellion: Slave Resistance in Eighteenth Century Virginia*. New York, NY: Oxford University Press, 1972.

Oakes, James. *Slavery and Freedom: An Interpretation of the Old South*. New York, NY: Knopf, 1990.

O'Donovan, Susan. *Becoming Free in the Cotton South*. Cambridge, MA: Harvard University Press, 2007.

Osofsky, Gilbert, ed. *Puttin' on Ole Massa*. New York, NY: Harper & Row, 1969.

Owens, Leslie Howard. *This Species of Property: Slave Life and Culture in the Old South*. New York, NY: Oxford University Press, 1976.

Parker, Freddie L. *Running for Freedom: Slave Runaways in North Carolina, 1775-1840*. New York, NY: Garland Pub, 1993.

Penningroth, Dylan. *The Claims of Kinfolk: African American Property and Community in the Nineteenth-Century South*. Chapel Hill, NC: University of North Carolina Press, 2003.

Phillips, Ulrich B. *Life and Labor in the Old South*. Boston: Little, Brown & Co, 1929.

Raboteau, Albert. *Slave Religion: The Invisible Institution in the Antebellum South*. Updated ed. New York, NY: Oxford University Press, 2004.

Randolph, Peter. *From Slave Cabin to Pulpit*. Edited by Paul D. Sporer. Chester, NY: Anza Classics Library, 2004.

Rawick, George P. *The American Slave: A Composite Autobiography.* 19 vols. Westport, CT: Greenwood Press, 1971.

Reidy, Joseph P. *From Slavery to Agrarian Capitalism in the Cotton Plantation South: Central Georgia, 1800-1880.* Chapel Hill, NC: University of North Carolina Press, 1992.

Schwalm, Leslie A. *A Hard Fight for We: Women's Transition from Slavery to Freedom in South Carolina.*, Urbana, IL: University of Illinois Press, 1997.

Schweninger, Loren. *Black Property Owners in the South, 1790-1915.* Urbana, IL: University of Illinois Press, 1990.

Schwartz, Marie Jenkins. *Born in Bondage: Growing Up Enslaved in the Antebellum South.* Cambridge, MA: Harvard University Press, 2000.

Sekora, John, and Darwin T. Turner, eds. *The Art of Slave Narrative: Original Essays in Criticism and Theory.* Macomb, IL: Western Illinois University, 1983.

Sinha, Manisha. *The Counterrevolution of Slavery: Politics and Ideology in Antebellum South Carolina.* Chapel Hill, NC: University of North Carolina Press, 2000.

Smith, Julian Floyd. *Slavery and Plantation Growth in Antebellum Florida, 1821-1860.* Gainesville, FL: University of Florida Press, 1973.

Stampp, Kenneth M. *The Peculiar Institution: Slavery in the Ante-Bellum South.* New York, NY: Vintage, 1989.

Starling, Marion W. *The Slave Narrative: Its Place in American History.* 2nd ed. Washington, DC: Howard University Press, 1988.

Starobin, Robert S. *Industrial Slavery in the Old South.* New York, NY: Oxford University Press, 1970.

Stevenson, Brenda. *Life in Black and White: Family and Community in the Slave South.* New York, NY: Oxford University Press, 1996.

———. "The Question of the Slave Female Community and Culture in the American South: Methodological and Ideological Approaches," *Journal of African American History* 92 (Winter 2007): 74–95.

Stuckey, Sterling. *Slave Culture: Nationalist Theory and the Foundations of Black America.* New York, NY: Oxford University Press, 1987.

Tadman, Michael. *Speculators and Slaves: Masters, Traders, and Slaves in the Old South.* Madison, WI: University of Wisconsin Press, 1989.

Thompson, Shirley. *Exiles at Home: The Struggle to Become American in Creol New Orleans.* Cambridge, MA: Harvard University Press, 2009.

Trexler, Harrison A. *Slavery in Missouri, 1804-1865.* Baltimore, MD: Johns Hopkins Press, 1976, c1914.

Van Deburg, William L. *The Slave Drivers: Black Agricultural Labor Supervisors in the Ante-Bellum South.* Westport, CT: Greenwood Press, 1979.

Wade, Richard C. *Slavery in the Cities: The South 1820-1860.* New York, NY: Oxford University Press, 1972.

Walsh, Lorena. *From Calabar to Carter's Grove: The History of a Virginia Slave Community.* Charlottesville, VA: University Press of Virginia, 1997.

Webber, Thomas L. *Deep Like the Rivers: Education in the Slave Quarter Community, 1831-1865.* New York, NY: Norton, 1978.

White, Deborah Gray. *Ar'nt I a Woman? Female Slaves in the Plantation South.* New York, NY: Norton, 1999.

White, Shane, and Graham White. "Slave Hair and African American Culture in the Eighteenth and Nineteenth Centuries." *The Journal of Southern History* 61:1 (1995): 45-76.

Whitman, T. Stephen. *The Price of Freedom: Slavery and Freedom in Baltimore and Early National Maryland.* Lexington, KY: University Press of Kentucky, 1997.

Williams, Heather Andrea. *Self-taught: African American Education in Slavery and Freedom.* Chapel Hill, NC: University of North Carolina Press, 2005.

Woodman, Harold D. "The Profitability of Slavery: A Historical Perennial." *Journal of Southern History* 29:3 (1963): 303-325.

Woodson, Carter G. "Beginnings of the Miscegenation of the Whites and Blacks." *Journal of Negro History* 3:1 (1918): 335-353.

———. *History of the Negro Church.* Washington, DC: The Associated Publishers, 1921.

Yellin, Jean Fagan. *Harriet Jacobs: A Life.* New York, NY: Basic Civitas Books, 2004.

Chapter 8: Antebellum Free Blacks, 1830-1860

Alexander, Adele Logan. *Ambiguous Lives: Free Women of Color in Rural Georgia, 1789-1879.* Fayetteville, AR: University of Arkansas Press, 1991.

Andrews, William L. and Henry Louis Gates, Jr., eds. *The Civitas Anthology of African American Slave Narratives.* Washington, DC: Civitas Counterpoint, 1999.

Bell, Caryn Cossé. *Revolution, Romanticism, and the Afro-Creole Protest Tradition in Louisiana, 1718-1868.* Baton Rouge, LA: Louisiana State University Press, 1997.

Berlin, Ira. *Slaves without Masters: The Free Negro in the Antebellum South.* New York, NY: Pantheon Books, 1975.

Bethel, Elizabeth Rauh. *The Roots of African-American Identity: Memory and History in Free Antebellum Communities.* New York, NY: St. Martin's Press, 1997.

Bolster, W. Jeffrey. *Black Jacks: African American Seamen in the Age of Sail.* Cambridge, MA: Harvard University Press, 1997.

Bracey, John H., August Meier [and] Elliott Rudwick, eds. *Free Blacks in America, 1800-1860.* Belmont, CA: Wadsworth Pub. Co., 1971.

Brown, Letitia Woods. *Free Negroes in the District of Columbia, 1790-1846.* New York, NY: Oxford University Press, 1972.

Cottrol, Robert. *The Afro-Yankees: Providence's Black Community in the Ante-Bellum Era.* Westport, CT: Greenwood Press, 1982.

Cromwell, John W. *The Early Negro Convention Movement.* Washington, DC.: The Academy, 1904.

Curry, Leonard P. *The Free Black in Urban America, 1800-1850: The Shadow of the Dream.* Chicago, IL: University of Chicago Press, 1981.

Delany, Martin R. *The Condition, Elevation, Emigration, and Destiny of the Colored People of the United States.* Philadelphia, PA: The author, 1852.

Dickens, Charles. *American Notes.* New York, NY: Modern Library, 1996.

Dunbar-Nelson, Alice D. "People of Color in Louisiana: Part I" *Journal of Negro History* 1 (1916).

———. "People of Color in Louisiana: Part II." *Journal of Negro History* 2:1 (1917): 51-78.

Franklin, John Hope. *The Free Negro in North Carolina, 1790-1860; with a new foreword and bibliographic afterword by the author.* Chapel Hill, NC: The University of North Carolina Press, 1995.

———. *A Southern Odyssey: Travelers in the Antebellum North.* Baton Rouge, LA: Louisiana State University Press, 1976.

Frazier, E. Franklin. *The Free Negro Family: A Study of Family Origins before the Civil War.* New York, NY: Arno, 1968, c1932.

Frederickson, George. *The Black Image in the White Mind: The Debate on Afro-American Character and Destiny, 1817-1914.* Middletown, CT: Wesleyan University Press, 1987.

Garrett, Paula and Hollis Robbins, eds. *The Works of William Wells Brown: Using His "Strong, Manly Voice".* New York, NY: Oxford University Press, 2006.

Glaude, Eddie. *Exodus! Religion, Race, and Nation in the Early Nineteenth-Century Black America.* Chicago, IL: University of Chicago Press, 2000.

Gould, Virginia Meacham. *Chained to the Rock of Adversity: To Be Free, Black & Female in the Old South.* Athens, GA: University of Georgia Press, 1998.

Gross, Bella. "The First National Negro Convention." *Journal of Negro History* 31:4 (1946): 435-443.

Harris, Leslie M. *In the Shadow of Slavery: African Americans in New York City, 1626-1863.* Chicago, IL: University of Chicago Press, 2003.

Hodes, Martha. *White Women, Black Men: Illicit Sex in the Nineteenth Century South.* New Haven, CT: Yale University Press, 1997.

Hogan, William Ransom and Edwin Adams Davis, eds., *William Johnson's Natchez: The Ante-Bellum Diary of a Free Negro.* Baton Rouge LA: Louisiana State University Press, 1993, c1979.

Horton, James Oliver. *Free People of Color: Inside the African American Community.* Washington, DC: Smithsonian Institution Press, 1993.

_____ . *In Hope of Liberty: Culture, Community, And Protest Among Northern Free Blacks, 1700-1860.* New York, NY: Oxford University Press, 1998.

_____ and Lois Horton. *Black Bostonians: Family Life and Community Struggle in the Ante-Bellum North.* Rev. ed., New York, NY: Holmes & Meier, 1999.

Jackson, Luther P. *Free Negro Labor and Property Holding in Virginia, 1830-1860.* New York, NY: Athenaeum, 1969, c1942.

Johnson, Franklin. *The Development of State Legislation Concerning The Free Negro.* Westport, CT: Greenwood Press, 1979, c1919.

Johnson, Michael P. and James L. Roark. *Black Masters: A Free Family of Color in the Old South.* New York, NY: Norton, 1984.

_____ . *No Chariot Let Down: Charleston's Free People of Color on the Eve of the Civil War.* Chapel Hill, NC: University of North Carolina Press, 1984.

Katz, William Loren. *The Black West.* 3rd ed., rev. and expanded. Seattle, WA: Open Hand Pub., 1987.

Ketner, Joseph D. *The Emergence of the African-American Artist: Robert S. Duncanson, 1821-1872.* Columbia, MO: University of Missouri Press, 1993.

King, Wilma. *The Essence of Liberty: Free Black Women During The Slave Era.* Columbia, MO: University of Missouri Press, 2006.

Koger, Larry. *Black Slaveowners: Free Black Slave Masters in South Carolina.* Columbia, SC: University of South Carolina, 1994.

Lawson, Ellen N. and Marlene D. Merrill. *The Three Sarahs: Documents on Antebellum Black-College Women.* New York, NY: E. Mellen Press, 1984.

Lebsock, Suzanne. *The Free Women of Petersburg: Status and Culture in a Southern Town.* New York, NY: Norton, 1984.

Litwack, Leon. *North of Slavery, the Negro in the Free States, 1790-1860.* Chicago, IL: University of Chicago Press, 1961.

McConnell, Roland. *Negro Troops in Antebellum Louisiana: A History of the Battalion of Free Men of Color.* Baton Rouge, LA: Louisiana State University Press, 1968.

Miller, Floyd John. *The Search for a Black Nationality: Black Colonization and Emigration, 1787-1863.* Urbana, IL: University of Illinois Press, 1975.

Morgan, Lynda J. *Emancipation in Virginia's Tobacco Belt, 1850-1870.* Athens, GA: University of Georgia Press, 1992.

Morrow, Diane Batts. *Persons of Color and Religious at the Same Time: The Oblate Sisters of Providence, 1828-1860.* Chapel Hill, NC: University of North Carolina Press, 2002.

Nash, Gary B. *Forging Freedom: The Formation of Philadelphia's Black Community, 1720-1840.* Cambridge, MA: Harvard University Press, 1988.

Peterson, Carla L. *Doers of the Word: African-American Women Speakers and Writers in the North (1830-1880).* New York, NY: Oxford University Press, 1995.

Porter, Dorothy B. "The Organized Educational Activities of Negro Literary Societies, *1828-1846." Journal of Negro Education* 5:4 (1936): 555-576.

Porter, Kenneth W. *The Negro on the American Frontier.* New York, NY: Arno Press, 1971.

Rael, Patrick. *Black Identity and Black Protest in the Antebellum North.* Chapel Hill, NC: University of North Carolina Press, 2002.

Roediger, David. *The Wages of Whiteness: Race and the Making of the American Working Class.* New York, NY: Verso, 1991.

Savage, W. Sherman. *Blacks in the West.* Westport, CT: Greenwood Press, 1976.

Schweninger, Loren. *Black Property Owners in the South, 1790-1915.* Urbana, IL: University of Illinois Press 1990.

_____ . "Prosperous Blacks in the South, 1790-1880." *American Historical Review* 95:1 (1990): 31-56.

A Statistical Inquiry into the Condition of the People of Colour, of the City and Districts of Philadelphia. Philadelphia, PA: Printed by Kite & Walton, 1849.

Staudenraus, Philip J. *The African Colonization Movement, 1816-1865.* New York, NY: Columbia University Press, 1961.

Sterkx, H. E. *The Free Negro in Antebellum Louisiana.* Rutherford, NJ: Fairleigh Dickinson University Press, 1972.

Sweat, Edward F. *Economic Status of Free Blacks in Antebellum Georgia.* Atlanta, GA: Southern Center for Studies in Public Policy, Clark College, 1974.

Takagi, Midori. *"Rearing Wolves to Our Own Destruction": Slavery in Richmond, Virginia, 1782-1865.* Charlottesville, VA: University Press of Virginia, 1999.

Thompson, Shirley. *Exiles at Home: The Struggle to Become American in Creol New Orleans.* Cambridge, MA: Harvard University Press, 2009.

Thornbrough, Emma L. *The Negro in Indiana before 1900: A Study of a Minority.* Bloomington, IN: Indiana University Press, 1993, c1957.

Vincent, Stephen. *Southern Seed, Northern Soil: African-American Farm Communities in the Midwest, 1765-1900.* Bloomington, in: Indiana University Press, 1999.

Walker, Juliet E. K. *Free Frank: A Black Pioneer on the Ante-Bellum Frontier.* Lexington, KY: University Press of Kentucky, 1983.

Warner, Lee H. *Free Men in an Age of Servitude: Three Generations of a Black Family.* Lexington, KY: University Press of Kentucky, 1992.

_____ . *Negro Labor in the United States, 1850-1925: A Study in American Economic History.* New York, NY: Russell & Russell, 1967.

White, Shane. "The Death of James Johnson." *American Quarterly* 51:4 (1999) 735-795.

_____ . *Staging Freedom in Black New York, 1820-1840.* Bundoora, Victoria, Canada: La Trobe University, 2008.

_____ . *Stories of Freedom in Black New York.* Cambridge, MA: Harvard University Press, 2002.

Whitman, T. Stephen. *The Price of Freedom: Slavery and Freedom in Baltimore and Early National Maryland.* Lexington, KY: University Press of Kentucky, 1997.

Wilder, Craig. *A Covenant with Color: Race and Social Power in Brooklyn.* New York, NY: Columbia University Press, 2000.

_____ . *In the Company of Black Men: The African Influence on African American Culture in New York City.* New York, NY: New York University Press, c2001.

Willson, Joseph. *The Elite of Our People: Joseph Willson's Sketches of the Higher Classes of Colored Society in Philadelphia, by a Southerner.* edited by Julie Winch. University Park, PA: Pennsylvania State University Press, 2000.

Wilson, Carol. *Freedom at Risk: The Kidnapping of Free Blacks in America, 1780-1865*. Lexington, KY: University Press of Kentucky, 1994.

Winch, Julie. *A Gentleman of Color: The Life of James Forten*. New York, NY: Oxford University Press, 2002.

Woodson, Carter G. *Free Negro Heads of Families in the United States in 1830*. Washington, DC: The Association for the Study of Negro Life and History, Inc., 1925.

_____. *Free Negro Owners of Slaves in the United States in 1830*. Washington, DC: The Association for the Study of Negro Life and History, 1925.

Chapter 9: Abolitionism in Black and White, 1820-1860

Aptheker, Herbert. *Abolitionism: A Revolutionary Movement*. Boston, MA: Twayne Publishers, 1989.

Barnes, Gilbert H. *The Antislavery Impulse, 1830-1844*. New York, NY: Harcourt, Brace & World, 1964.

Bartlett, Irving H. *Wendell Phillips, Brahmin Radical*. Boston, MA: Beacon Press, 1961.

Bay, Mia. *The White Image in the Black Mind: African-American Ideas about White People, 1830-1925*. New York, NY: Oxford University Press, 2000.

Blackett, R. J. M. *Building an Anti-Slavery Wall: Black Americans in the Atlantic Abolitionist Movement*. Baton Rouge, LA: Louisiana State University Press, 1983.

Bracey, John H., August Meier, Elliot Rudwick, eds. *Blacks in the Abolitionist Movement*. Belmont, CA: Wadsworth Publishing Co., 1971.

Buckmaster, Henrietta. *Let My People Go: The Story of the Underground Railroad and the Growth of the Abolition Movement*. Columbia, S.C.: University of South Carolina Press, 1992.

Campbell, Stanley W. *The Slave Catchers: Enforcement of the Fugitive Slave Law, 1850-1860*. Chapel Hill, NC: University of North Carolina Press, 1970.

Carpenter, Jesse. *The South as a Conscious Minority, 1789-1861*. Columbia, SC: University of South Carolina Press, 1990.

Cheek, William and Aimee Lee Cheek. *John Mercer Langston and the Fight for Black Freedom*. Urbana, IL: University of Illinois Press, 1989.

Clinton, Catherine. *Harriet Tubman: The Road to Freedom*. New York, NY: Little, Brown, 2004.

_____. *The Plantation Mistress*. New York, NY: Knopf Doubleday Publishing, 1984.

Dillon, Merton L. *Slavery Attacked: Southern Slaves and Their Allies, 1619-1865*. Baton Rouge, LA: Louisiana State University Press, 1990.

Douglass, Frederick. *The Life and Times of Frederick Douglass*. Hartford, CT: Park, 1881.

_____. *The Frederick Douglass Papers. Series One: Speeches, Debates, and Interviews*. 5 vols. John W. Blassingame, et al., eds. New Haven, CT: Yale University Press, 1979-1992.

Duberman, Martin L., ed. *The Antislavery Vanguard: New Essays on the Abolitionists*. Princeton, NJ: Princeton University Press, 1965.

_____. *Anti-Slavery: The Crusade for Freedom in America*. Ann Arbor, MI: University of Michigan, 1961.

Ericson, David F. *The Debate over Slavery: Antislavery and Proslavery Liberalism in Antebellum America*. New York, NY: New York University Press, 2000.

Farrison, William E. *William Wells Brown: Author and Reformer*. Chicago, IL: University of Chicago Press 1969.

Faust, Drew Gilpin, ed. *The Ideology of Slavery: Proslavery Thought in the Antebellum South, 1830-1860*. Baton Rouge, LA: Louisiana State University Press, 1981.

Filler, Louis. *The Crusade against Slavery, 1830-1860: Friends, Foes, and Reforms, 1820-1860*. Rev. ed. Algonac, MI: Reference Publications, 1986.

Foner, Philip S. *Frederick Douglass: A Biography*. New York, NY: Citadel Press, 1964.

_____. *The Life and Writings of Frederick Douglass*. 4 vols. New York, NY: International Publishers, 1975, c1950-1955.

Forbes, Robert Pierce. *The Missouri Compromise and Its Aftermath: Slavery & the Meaning of America*. Chapel Hill, NC: The University of North Carolina Press, 2007.

Franklin, John Hope. *The Militant South, 1800-1861*. Cambridge, MA: Belknap Press of Harvard University Press, 1970.

_____. *A Southern Odyssey: Travelers in the Antebellum North*. Baton Rouge, LA: Louisiana State University Press, 1976.

_____ and Loren Schweninger. *Runaway Slaves: Rebels on the Plantation*. New York, NY: Oxford University Press, 1999.

Gara, Larry. *The Liberty Line: The Legend of the Underground Railroad*. Lexington, KY: University Press of Kentucky, 1996.

Glaude, Eddie. *Exodus! Religion, Race, and Nation in the Early Nineteenth-Century Black America*. Chicago, IL: University of Chicago Press, 2000.

Harris, Leslie M. *In the Shadow of Slavery: African Americans in New York City, 1626-1863*. Chicago, IL: University of Chicago Press, 2003.

Harrold, Stanley. "Violence and Nonviolence in Kentucky Abolitionism." *The Journal of Southern History* 57:1 (1991): 15-38.

Hawkins, Hugh, ed. *The Abolitionists: Immediatism and the Question of Means*. Boston, MA: Heath, 1964.

Humez, Jean. *Harriet Tubman: The Life and the Life Stories*. Madison, WI: University of Wisconsin Press, 2003.

Johnson, Reinhard O. *The Liberty Party, 1840-1848: Antislavery Third-Party Politics in the United States*. Baton Rouge, LA: Louisiana State University Press, 2009.

Klingberg, Frank J. *The Anti-slavery Movement in England: A Study in English Humanitarianism*. Hamden, CT: Archon Books, 1968, c1926.

Kraditor, Aileen. *Means and Ends in American Abolitionism: Garrison and His Critics on Strategy and Tactics, 1834-1850*. New York, NY: Pantheon Books, 1969.

Larson, Kate Clifford. *Bound for the Promised Land: Harriet Tubman, Portrait of an American Hero*. New York, NY: Ballantine, 2004.

Litwack, Leon. *North of Slavery, the Negro in the Free States, 1790-1860*. Chicago, IL: University of Chicago Press, 1961.

Lubin, David M. *Picturing a Nation: Art and Social Change in Nineteenth-Century America*. New Haven, CT: Yale University Press, 1994.

Martin, Waldo E., Jr. *The Mind of Frederick Douglass*. Chapel Hill, NC: University of North Carolina Press, 1984.

Mayer, Henry. *All on Fire: William Lloyd Garrison and the Abolition of Slavery*. New York, NY: St. Martin's Press, 1998.

McFeely, William S. *Frederick Douglass*. New York, NY: Norton, 1991.

Newman, Richard S. *The Transformation of American Abolitionism: Fighting Slavery in the Early Republic*. Chapel Hill, NC: University of North Carolina Press, 2002.

Painter, Nell Irvin. *Sojourner Truth: A Life, a Symbol*. New York, NY: W.W. Norton, 1996.

Pease, William H. and Jane Pease. *Black Utopia: Negro Communal Experiments in America*. Madison, WI: State Historical Society of Wisconsin, 1963.

Quarles, Benjamin. *Black Abolitionists*. New York, NY: Oxford University Press, 1969.

Rael, Patrick. *Black Identity and Black Protest in the Antebellum North*. Chapel Hill, NC: University of North Carolina Press, 2002.

_____, ed. *African-American Activism Before the Civil War: The Freedom Struggle in the Antebellum North*. New York, NY: Routledge, 2008.

Reynolds, David. *John Brown, Abolitionist: The Man Who Killed Slavery, Sparked the Civil War, and Seeded Civil Rights*. New York, NY: Alfred A. Knopf/Random House, 2005.

Rhodes, Jane. *Mary Ann Shadd Cary: The Black Press and Protest in the Nineteenth Century*. Bloomington, IN: Indiana University Press, 1998.

Ripley, C. Peter, Roy E. Finkenbine, Michael F. Hembree, and Donald Yacovone, eds. *Witness for Freedom: African American Voices on Race, Slavery, and Emancipation*. 3 vols. Chapel Hill, NC: University of North Carolina Press, 1985-1991.

Risley, Ford. *Abolition and the Press: The Moral Struggle against Slavery*. Evanston, IL: Northwestern University Press, 2008.

Rousey, Dennis C. "Friends and Foes of Slavery: Foreigners and Northerners in the Old South." *Journal of Social History*. 35:2 (2001): 373-396.

Salerno, Beth A. *Sister Societies: Women's Antislavery Organizations in Antebellum America*. DeKalb, IL: Northern Illinois University Press, 2005.

Siebert, Wilbur H. "Light on the Underground Railroad." *The American Historical Review* 1:3 (1896): 455-463.

_____. *The Underground Railroad from Slavery to Freedom*. New York, NY: Arno Press, 1968, c1898.

Stanley, Gerard. "Racism and the Early Republican Party: The 1856 Presidential Election in California." *The Pacific Historical Review* 43:2 (1947): 171-187.

Stauffer, John. *The Black Hearts of Men: Radical Abolitionists and the Transformation of Race*. Cambridge, MA: Harvard University Press, 2002.

_____. *Giants: The Parallel lives of Frederick Douglass & Abraham Lincoln*. New York, NY: Twelve, 2008.

_____, ed. *The Works of James McCune Smith: Black Intellectual and Abolitionist*. New York, NY: Oxford University Press, 2006.

Stewart, James Brewer. *Abolitionist Politics and the Coming of the Civil War*. Amherst, MA: University of Massachusetts Press, 2008.

Still, William. *The Underground Railroad*. Philadelphia, PA: Porter & Coates, 1872.

Strother, Horatio T. *The Underground Railroad in Connecticut*. Middletown, CT: Wesleyan University Press, 1962.

Thomas, John L. *The Liberator: William Lloyd Garrison*. Boston, MA: Little Brown, 1963.

Tomek, Beverly, "Seeking 'an immutable pledge from the slave holding states': The Pennsylvania Abolition Society and Black Resettlement," *Pennsylvania History* 75:1 (Winter 2008): 26-53.

Walker, David. *David Walker's Appeal to the Coloured Citizens of the World*. edited by Peter P. Hinks. University Park, PA: Pennsylvania State University Press, 2000.

Winks, Robin. *Blacks in Canada: A History*. 2nd ed. Buffalo, NY: McGill-Queen's University Press, 1997

Woodson, Carter G. *The Mind of the Negro as Reflected in Letters During the Crisis, 1800-1860*. Washington, DC: The Association for the Study of Negro Life and History, Inc., 1926.

Yee, Shirley J. *Black Women Abolitionists: A Study in Activism, 1828-1860*. Knoxville, TN: University of Tennessee Press, 1992.

Chapter 10: Civil War, 1861-1865

Bercaw, Nancy. *Gendered Freedoms: Race, Rights, and the Politics of Household in the Delta, 1861-1875*. Gainesville, FL: University of Florida, 2003.

Belz, Herman. *Emancipation and Equal Rights: Politics and Constitutionalism in the Civil War Era*. New York, NY: Norton, 1978.

Berlin, Ira, Barbara J. Fields, Thavolia Glymph, Joseph P. Reidy, and Leslie S. Rowland, eds. *The Destruction of Slavery*. New York, NY: Cambridge University Press, 1985.

_____. *Free at Last: A Documentary History of Slavery, Freedom, and the Civil War*. New York, NY: The New Press Distributed by W.W. Norton, 1992.

_____, Joseph P. Reidy, and Leslie S. Rowland. *Freedom's Soldiers: The Black Military Experience in the Civil War*. New York, NY: Cambridge University Press, 1998.

_____, ed. *The Wartime Genesis of Free Labor: The Lower South*. New York, NY: Cambridge University Press, 1990.

Blatt, Martin H., Thomas J. Brown, and Donald Yacovone. *Hope & Glory: Essays on the Legacy of the Fifty-Fourth Massachusetts Regiment*. Amherst, MA: University of Massachusetts in association with the Massachusetts Historical society, 2001.

Blight, David W. *Frederick Douglass' Civil War: Keeping Faith in Jubilee*. Baton Rouge, LA: Louisiana State University Press, 1989.

_____. *Race and Reunion: The Civil War in American Memory*. Cambridge, MA: Belknap Press of Harvard University Press, 2003.

Brewer, James H. *The Confederate Negro: Virginia's Craftsmen and Military Laborers, 1861-1865*. Tuscaloosa, AL: University of Alabama Press, 1969.

Campbell, Edward D.C., Jr., and Kym S. Rice, eds. *A Woman's War: Southern Women, Civil War, and the Confederate Legacy*. Charlottesville, VA: University of Virginia Press, 1996.

Cogar, William B., ed. *New Interpretations in Naval History: Selected Papers from the Twelfth Naval History Symposium*. Annapolis, MD: Naval Institute Press, 1997.

Cornish, Dudley T. *The Sable Arm: Negro Troops in the Union Army, 1861-1865*. Lawrence, KS: University Press of Kansas, 1987.

Cox, La Wanda. *Lincoln and Black Freedom: A Study in Presidential Leadership*. Columbia, SC: University of South Carolina Press, 1994.

Cunningham, Roger D., *The Black Citizen-Soldiers of Kansas, 1864–1901*. Columbia, MO: University of Missouri Press, 2008

Dew, Charles B. *Ironmaker to the Confederacy: Joseph R. Anderson and the Tredegar Iron Works*. 2nd ed. Richmond, VA: Library of Virginia, 1999.

Douglas, William O. *Mr. Lincoln and the Negroes: The Long Road to Equality*. New York, NY: Atheneum, 1963.

Durden, Robert F. *The Gray and the Black: The Confederate Debate on Emancipation*. Baton Rouge, LA: Louisiana State University, 1972.

_____. "Some Considerations Relating to Property Rights in Man." *The Journal of Economic History* 33:1 (1973): 43-65.

Faust, Drew Gilpin. *The Creation of Confederate Nationalism: Ideology and Identity in the Civil War South*. Baton Rouge, LA: Louisiana State University Press, 1988.

_____. *This Republic of Suffering: Death and the American Civil War*. New York, NY: Knopf Publishing Group, 2009.

Fite, Emerson D. *Social and Industrial Conditions in the North During the Civil War*. New York, NY: Peter Smith, 1910.

Foner, Eric. *Free Soil, Free Labor, and Free Men: The Ideology of the Republican Party Before the Civil War.* New York, NY: Oxford University Press, 1970.

_____. *Nothing but Freedom: Emancipation and Its Legacy.* With a new forward by Stephen Hahn. Baton Rouge, LA: Louisiana State University Press, 2007.

Frankel, Noralee. *Freedom's Women: Black Women and Families in Civil War Era Mississippi.* Bloomington, IN: Indiana University Press, 1999.

Franklin, John Hope. *The Emancipation Proclamation.* Garden City, NY: Doubleday, 1963.

Gates, Henry Louis, Jr., and Donald Yacovone, eds. *Lincoln on Race & Slavery.* Princeton, NJ: Princeton University Press, 2009.

Gerteis, Louis. *From Contraband to Freeman: Federal Policy toward Southern Blacks, 1861-1865.* Westport, CT: Greenwood Press, 1973.

Glatthar, Joseph T. *Forged in Battle: The Civil War Alliance of Black Soldiers and White Officers.* Baton Rouge, LA: Louisiana State University, 2000.

Higginson, Thomas Wentworth. *Army Life in a Black Regiment.* New York, NY: W.W. Norton, 1984.

Hollandsworth, James G. *The Louisiana Native Guards: The Black Military Experience During the Civil War.* Baton Rouge, LA: Louisiana State University Press, 1995.

Horst, Samuel L. *Education for Manhood: The Education of Blacks in Virginia During the Civil War.* Lanham, MD: University Press of America, 1987.

King, Lisa Y. "In Search of Women of African Descent Who Served in the Civil War Union Navy," *Journal of Negro History* 83:4 (Fall 1998): 302-309.

Manning, Chandra. *What This Cruel War Was Over: Soldiers, Slavery, and the Civil War.* New York, NY: Alfred A. Knopf, 2007.

McPherson, James. *Battle Cry of Freedom: The Civil War Era.* New York, NY: Ballantine Books, 1989.

_____. *The Negro's Civil War: How American Blacks Felt and Acted During the War for the Union.* New York, NY: Vintage, 2003.

_____. *The Struggle for Equality: Abolitionists and the Negro in the Civil War and Reconstruction.* Princeton, NJ: Princeton University Press, 1964.

Mohr, Clarence L. *On the Threshold of Freedom: Masters and Slaves in Civil War Georgia.* Baton Rouge, LA: Louisiana State University Press, 2001.

Nieman, Donald G. *The Day of the Jubilee: the Civil War Experience of Black Southerners.* New York, NY: Garland, 1994.

O'Donovan, Susan E. *Becoming Free in the Cotton South.* Cambridge, MA: Harvard University Press, 2007.

Quarles, Benjamin. *Lincoln and the Negro.* New York, NY: Oxford University Press, 1962.

_____. *The Negro in the Civil War.* New York, NY: Russell & Russell, 1968, c1953.

Ripley, C. Peter. *Slaves and Freedmen in Civil War Louisiana.* Baton Rouge, LA: Louisiana State University, 1976.

Robinson, Armstead L., and Barbara J. Fields (contributors). *Bitter Fruits of Bondage: The Demise of Slavery and the Collapse of the Confederacy, 1861-1865.* Charlottesville, VA: University of Virginia Press, 2004.

Schwalm, Leslie A. *A Hard Fight for We: Women's Transition from Slavery to Freedom in South Carolina.* Urbana, IL: University of Illinois Press, 1997.

Trefousse, Hans L. *Lincoln's Decision for Emancipation.* Philadelphia, PA: Lippincott, 1975.

Trudeau, Noah Andre. *Like Men of War: Black Troops in the Civil War, 1862-1865.* Boston, MA: Little Brown, 1998.

Wesley, Charles H. "The Employment of Negroes as Soldiers in the Confederate Army." *Journal of Negro History* 4:3 (1919): 239-253.

Wilson, Joseph T. The Black Phalanx: *A History of the Negro Soldiers of the United States in the Wars of 1775-1812, 1861-1865.* Hartford, CT: American Publishing Co., 1888.

Yacovone, Donald. *Freedom's Journey: African American Voices of the Civil War.* Chicago, IL: Lawrence Hill Books, 2004.

_____. *We Fight for Freedom: Massachusetts, African Americans and the Civil War.* Boston, MA: Massachusetts Historical Society, 2001.

Chapter 11: The Promises and Pitfalls of Reconstruction, 1863-1877

Abbott, Martin. *The Freedmen's Bureau in South Carolina, 1865-1872.* Chapel Hill, NC: University of North Carolina Press, 1967.

Alexander, Roberta. *North Carolina Faces the Freedmen: Race Relations During Presidential Reconstruction, 1865-1867.* Durham, NC: Duke University Press, 1985.

Anderson, Eric and Alfred A. Moss Jr., eds. *The Facts of Reconstruction: Essays in Honor of John Hope Franklin.* Baton Rouge, LA: Louisiana State University Press, 1991.

Berlin, Ira, Barbara Fields, and Thavolia Glymph eds., *Freedom: A Documentary History of Emancipation, 1861-1867.* 2 vols. New York, NY: Cambridge University Press, 1982-1993.

Berry, Mary Frances. *Military Necessity and Civil Rights Policy: Black Citizenship and the Constitution, 1861-1868.* Port Washington, NY: Kennikat Press, 1977.

Billington, Ray, ed. *The Journal of Charlotte Forten.* New York, NY: Norton, 1981, c1953.

Blassingame, John. *Black New Orleans, 1860-1880.* Chicago, IL: University of Chicago Press, 1973.

Blight, David W. *Race and Reunion: The Civil War in American Memory.* Cambridge, MA: Belknap Press of Harvard University Press, 2003.

Bond, Horace M. *Negro Education in Alabama.* New York, NY: Octagon Books, 1969, c1939.

Brown, David Warren. *Andrew Johnson and the Negro.* Knoxville, TN: University of Tennessee Press, 1989.

Brown, Elsa Barkley. "To Catch the Vision of Freedom: Reconstructing Southern Black Women's Political History, 1865-1880." In, *African American Women and the Vote, 1837-1965.* Edited by Ann D. Gordon with Bettye Collier-Thomas. Amherst, MA: University of Massachusetts Press, 1997.

Brown, Thomas, ed. *Reconstructions: New Perspectives on the Postbellum United States.* New York, NY: Oxford University Press, 2006.

Bullock, Henry Allen. *A History of Negro Education in the South.* Cambridge, MA: Harvard University Press, 1967.

Butchart, Ronald E. *Northern Schools, Southern Blacks, and Reconstruction: Freedmen's Education, 1862-1875.* Westport, CT: Greenwood Press, 1980.

Cable, George C. *But There Was No Peace: The Role of Violence in the Politics of Reconstruction.* Athens, GA: University of Georgia Press, 1984.

Clay, William L. *Just Permanent Interests: Black Americans in Congress, 1870-1991.* New York, NY: Amistad, 1992.

Conway, Alan. *The Reconstruction of Georgia*. Minneapolis: University of Minnesota, 1966.

Cox, La Wanda and John Cox. *Politics, Principle, and Prejudice*. New York, NY: Atheneum, 1969.

Cox, La Wanda and John N. Cox, eds. *Reconstruction, the Negro, and the New South*. New York, NY: Harper & Row, 1973.

Cruden, Robert. *The Negro in Reconstruction*. Englewood Cliffs, NJ: Prentice-Hall, 1969.

DeCanio, Stephen J. *Agriculture in the Post-Bellum South: The Economics of Production and Supply*. Cambridge, MA: MIT Press, 1974.

Donald, David. *The Politics of Reconstruction*. Baton Rouge, LA: Louisiana State University Press, 1965.

_____, Jean H. Baker, and Michael F. Holt. *The Civil War and Reconstruction*. New York, NY: Norton, 2001.

Dray, Philip. *Capitol Men: The Epic Story of Reconstruction Through the Lives of the First Black Congressmen*. Boston, MA: Houghton Mifflin Co., 2008.

Du Bois, W. E. B. *Black Reconstruction in America: An Essay Toward a History of the Part Which Black Folk Played in the Attempt to Reconstruct Democracy in America, 1860-1880*. Introduction by David Levering Lewis. New York, NY: Oxford University Press, 2007.

Edwards, Laura. *Gendered Strife & Confusion: The Political Culture of Reconstruction*. Urbana, IL: University of Illinois Press, 1997.

Fields, Barbara J. *Slavery and Freedom on the Middle Ground: Maryland During the Nineteenth Century*. New Haven, CT: Yale University Press, 1985.

Fitzgerald, Michael W. *The Union League Movement in the Deep South: Politics and Agricultural Change During Reconstruction*. Baton Rouge, LA: Louisiana State University Press, 1989.

_____. *Urban Emancipation: Popular Politics in Reconstruction Mobile, 1860-1890*. Baton Rouge, LA: Louisiana State University Press, 2002.

Flack, Horace E. *The Adoption of the Fourteenth Amendment*. Buffalo, NY: W.S. Hein, 2003, c1908.

Foner, Eric. *Freedom's Lawmakers: A Directory of Black Officeholders during Reconstruction*. New York, NY: Oxford University Press, 1993.

_____. *Nothing But Freedom: Emancipation and Its Legacy*. With a new foreword by Steven Hahn. Baton Rouge, LA: Louisiana State University Press, 2007.

_____. *Reconstruction: America's Unfinished Revolution, 1863-1877*. New York, NY: HarperCollins, 1989.

Foner, Philip S., and George E. Walker, eds. *Proceedings of the Black National and State Conventions, 1865-1900*, Vol. 1. Philadelphia, PA: Temple University Press, 1986.

Franklin, John Hope. *Reconstruction After the Civil War*. 2nd ed. Chicago, IL: University of Chicago, 1994.

Franklin, John Hope ed. *Reminiscences of an Active Life: The Autobiography of John Roy Lynch*. Chicago, IL: University of Chicago Press, 1970.

Frey, Sylvia R., and Betty Wood, eds. *From Slavery to Emancipation in the Atlantic World*. Portland, OR: Frank Cass, 1999.

Gillette, William. *Retreat from Reconstruction, 1869-1879*. Baton Rouge, LA: Louisiana State University Press, 1979.

Hardwick, Kevin R. "'Your Old Father Abe Lincoln Is Dead and Damned': Black Soldiers and the Memphis Race Riot of 1866." *Journal of Social History*. 27:1 (1993): 109-128.

Hahn, Steven. *A Nation Under Our Feet: Black Political Struggles in the Rural South from Slavery to the Great Migration*. Cambridge, MA: Belknap Press of Harvard University Press, 2003.

_____. "'Extravagant Expectations' of Freedom: Rumour, Political Struggle, and the Christmas Insurrection Scare of 1865 in the American South." *Past & Present* 157 (1997): 122-158.

_____, Steven F. Miller, Susan E. O'Donovan, John C. Rodrique, and Leslie S. Rowland, eds. *Freedom: A Documentary History of Emancipation, 1861-1867: Series 3, Volume 1: Land and Labor, 1865*. Chapel Hill, NC: The University of North Carolina Press, 2008.

_____. *The Political Worlds of Slavery and Freedom*. Cambridge, MA: Harvard University Press, 2009.

Hirshson, Stanley P. *Farewell to the Bloody Shirt*. Bloomington, IN: Indiana University Press, 1962.

Holt, Thomas. *Black over White: Negro Political Leadership in South Carolina During Reconstruction*. Urbana, IL: University of Illinois Press, 1979.

Hume, Richard. L. and Jerry B. Gough. *Blacks, Carpetbaggers, and Scalawags: The Constitutional Conventions of Radical Reconstruction*. Baton Rouge, LA: Louisiana State University Press, 2008.

Jackson, Luther P. "The Educational Efforts of the Freedmen's Bureau and Freedmen's Aid Societies in South Carolina, 1862-1872." *Journal of Negro History* 8 (1923).

Jones, Jacqueline. *Labor of Love, Labor of Sorrow: Black Women, Work, and the Family from Slavery to the Present*. New York, NY: Vintage, 1986.

_____. *Soldiers of Light and Love: Northern Teachers and Georgia Blacks, 1865-1873*. Chapel Hill, NC: University of North Carolina Press, 1992, c1980.

Klingman, Peter D. *Josiah Walls: Florida's Black Congressman of Reconstruction*. Gainesville, FL: University Presses of Florida, 1976.

Kolchin, Peter. *First Freedom: The Responses of Alabama's Blacks to Emancipation and Reconstruction*. Tuscaloosa, AL: University of Alabama, 2008, c1972.

Kousser, J. Morgan, and James M. McPherson, eds. *Region, Race, and Reconstruction*. New York, NY: Oxford University Press, 1982.

Kutler, Stanley I. "Reconstruction and the Supreme Court: The Numbers Game Reconsidered." *The Journal of Southern History* 32:1 (1966): 42-58.

Lamson, Peggy. *Glorious Failure: Black Congressman Robert Brown Elliott and the Reconstruction in South Carolina*. New York, NY: Norton, 1973.

Lanza, Michael L. *Agrarianism and Reconstruction Politics: The Southern Homestead Act*. Baton Rouge, LA: Louisiana State University Press, 1990.

Levine, Lawrence. *Black Culture and Black Consciousness: Afro-American Folk Thought from Slavery to Freedom*. 30th Anniversary Edition. New York, NY: Oxford University Press, 2007, 1997.

Litwack, Leon F. *Been in the Storm So Long: The Aftermath of Slavery*. New York, NY: Knopf, 1979.

Lynch, John R. *The Facts of Reconstruction*. New York, NY: Neale Publishing Co.,1913.

Maltz, Earl M. *Civil Rights, the Constitution, and Congress, 1863-1869*. Lawrence, KS: University Press of Kansas,1990.

McKitrick, Eric L. *Andrew Johnson and Reconstruction*. New York, NY: Oxford University Press, 1988, c1960.

McPherson, James. *The Struggle for Equality: Abolitionists and the Negro in the Civil War and Reconstruction*. Princeton, NJ: Princeton University Press, 1964.

Moneyhon, Carl H. *The Impact of the Civil War and Reconstruction on Arkansas: Persistence in the Midst of Ruin*. Baton Rouge, LA: Louisiana State University Press, 1994.

_____. *Republicanism in Reconstruction Texas*. Austin: University of Texas, 1980.

Montgomery, David. *Beyond Equality: Labor and the Radical Republicans, 1862-1872*. New York, NY: Knopf, 1967.

Morris, Robert C. *Reading, 'Riting, and Reconstruction: The Education of Freedmen in the South, 1861-1870*. Chicago, IL: University of Chicago Press, 1981.

Nieman, Donald, ed. *African American Life in the Post-Emancipation South.* 12 volumes. New York, NY: Garland, 1994.

O'Donovan, Susan E. *Becoming Free in the Cotton South.* Cambridge, MA: Harvard University Press, 2007.

Olsen, Otto, ed. *Reconstruction and Redemption in the South.* Baton Rouge, LA: Louisiana State University Press, 1980.

Osthaus, Carl R. *Freedmen, Philanthropy, and Fraud: A History of the Freedmen's Savings Bank.* Urbana, IL: University of Illinois Press, 1976.

Oubre, Claude F. *Forty Acres and a Mule: The Freedmen's Bureau and Black Land Ownership.* Baton Rouge, LA: Louisiana State University Press, 1978.

Painter, Nell Irvin. *Exodusters: Black Migration to Kansas after Reconstruction.* Lawrence, KS: University Press of Kansas, 1986.

Peirce, Paul S. *The Freedmen's Bureau, a Chapter in the History of Reconstruction.* Iowa City, IA: The University, 1904.

Perman, Michael. *Reunion without Compromise: The South and Reconstruction, 1865-1868.* New York, NY: Cambridge University Press, 1973.

_____. *The Road to Redemption: Southern Politics, 1869-1878.* Chapel Hill, NC: University of North Carolina Press, 1984.

Rabinowitz, Howard, ed. *Southern Black Leaders of the Reconstruction Era.* Urbana, IL: University of Illinois Press, 1982.

Rable, George C. *But There Was No Peace: The Role of Violence in the Politics of Reconstruction.* Athens, GA: University of Georgia Press, 2007, c1984.

Ransom, Roger L., and Richard Sutch. *One Kind of Freedom: The Economic Consequences of Emancipation.* 2nd ed. New York, NY: Cambridge University Press, 2001.

Reidy, Joseph P. *From Slavery to Agrarian Capitalism in the Cotton Plantation South: Central Georgia, 1800-1880.* Chapel Hill, NC: University of North Carolina Press, 1992.

Richardson, Heather Cox. *The Death of Reconstruction: Race, Labor, and Politics in the Post-Civil War North, 1865-1901.* Cambridge, MA: Harvard University Press, 2001.

Richardson, Joe M. *The Negro in the Reconstruction of Florida, 1865-1877.* Tuscaloosa, AL: University of Alabama Press, 2008, c1965.

Rose, Willie Lee. *Rehearsal for Reconstruction: The Port Royal Experiment.* Athens, GA: University of Georgia Press, 1999, c1964.

Rosén, Hannah. *Terror in the Heart of Freedom: Citizenship, Sexual Violence, and the Meaning of Race in Postemancipation South.* Chapel Hill, NC: University of North Carolina Press, 2009.

Saville, Julie. *The Work of Reconstruction: From Slave to Wage Laborer in South Carolina, 1860-1870.* New York, NY: Cambridge University Press, 1994.

Schwalm, Leslie A. *Emancipation's Diaspora: Race and Reconstruction in the Upper Midwest.* Chapel Hill, NC: University of North Carolina Press, 2009.

Schweninger, Loren. *Black Property Owners in the South, 1790-1915.* Urbana, IL: University of Illinois Press, 1990.

_____. *James T Rapier and Reconstruction.* Chicago, IL: University of Chicago Press, 1978.

Scott, Rebecca J. *Degrees of Freedom: Louisiana and Cuba after Slavery.* Cambridge, MA: Belknap Press of Harvard University Press, 2005.

Stampp, Kenneth M. *The Era of Reconstruction.* New York, NY: Knopf, 1965.

Sweat, Edward F. "Francis L. Cardoza: Profile of Integrity in Reconstruction Politics." *Journal of Negro History* 46:4 (1961): 217-232.

Taylor, Alrutheus A. *The Negro in South Carolina during Reconstruction.* New York, NY: AMS Press, 1971, c1924.

Taylor, Joe Gray. *Louisiana Reconstructed, 1863-1877.* Baton Rouge, LA: Louisiana State University Press, 1975.

Thompson, Shirley. *Exiles at Home: The Struggle to Become American in Creol New Orleans.* Cambridge, MA: Harvard University Press, 2009.

Trattner, Walter I. "The Federal Government and Needy citizens in Nineteenth-Century America." *Political Science Quarterly,* 103:2 (1988): 347-356.

Trefousse, Hans L. *Impeachment of a President: Andrew Johnson, the Blacks, and Reconstruction.* New York, NY: Fordham University Press, 1999.

Uya, Okon E. *From Slavery to Public Service, Robert Smalls, 1839-1915.* New York, NY: Oxford University Press, 1971.

Vincent, Charles. *Black Legislators in Louisiana during Reconstruction.* Baton Rouge, LA: Louisiana State University Press, 1976.

Wallace, John. *Carpetbag Rule in Florida: The Inside Workings of the Reconstruction of Civil Government in Florida after the Close of the Civil War.* Gainseville, FL: University of Florida Press, 1964, c1888.

Wharton, Vernon L. *The Negro in Mississippi, 1865-1890.* Westport, CT: Greenwood Press, 1984, c1947.

White, Howard A. *The Freedmen's Bureau in Louisiana.* Baton Rouge, LA: Louisiana State University Press, 1970.

Williamson, Joel. *After Slavery, the Negro in South Carolina During Reconstruction.* Hanover, NH: University Press of New England, 1990, c1965.

Chapter 12: The Color Line, 1877-1917

Anderson, Eric. *Race and Politics in North Carolina, 1872-1901: The Black Second.* Baton Rouge, LA: Louisiana State University Press, 1981.

Arnesen, Eric. *Waterfront Workers of New Orleans: Race, Class and Politics, 1863-1923.* New York, NY: Oxford University Press, 1991.

Baker, Ray S. *Following the Color Line: An Account of Negro Citizenship in the American Democracy.* Williamstown, MA: Courner House, 1973, c1908.

Bederman, Gail. *Manliness & Civilization: A Cultural History of Gender and Race in the United States, 1880-1917.* Chicago, IL: University of Chicago Press, 1995.

Berry, Mary Frances. *Black Resistance, White Law: A History of Constitutional Racism in America.* New York, NY: Penguin Press, 1994.

_____. *My Face is Black is True: Callie House and the Struggle for Ex-Slave Reparations.* New York, NY: Alfred A. Knopf, 2005.

_____. *The Pig Farmer's Daughter and Other Tales of American Justice: Episodes of Racism and Sexism in the Courts from 1865 to the Present.* New York, NY: Vintage, 2000.

Billings, Dwight B. *Planters and the Making of a "New South": Class Politics and Development in North Carolina.* Chapel Hill, NC: University of North Carolina Press, 1979.

Blight, David W. *Frederick Douglass' Civil War: Keeping Faith in Jubilee.* Baton Rouge, LA: Louisiana State University Press, 1989.

_____. *Race and Reunion: The Civil War in American Memory.* Cambridge, MA: Belknap Press of Harvard University Press, 2003.

Brundage, W. Fitzhugh. *Lynching in the New South: Georgia and Virginia, 1880-1930.* Urbana, IL: University of Illinois Press, 1993.

_____. *The Southern Past: A Clash of Race and Memory.* Cambridge, MA: Belknap Press of Harvard University, 2005.

_____, ed. *Under Sentence of Death: Lynching in the South.* Chapel Hill, NC: University of North Carolina Press, 1997.

_____, ed. *Where These Memories Grow: History, Memory, and Southern Identity*. Chapel Hill, NC: University of North Carolina Press, 2000.

Carroll, John M., ed., *The Black Military Experience in the American West*. New York, NY: Liveright, 1971.

Cartwright, Joseph H. *The Triumph of Jim Crow: Tennessee Race Relations in the 1880s*. Knoxville, TN: University of Tennessee Press, 1976.

Cecelski, David S., and Timothy B. Tyson, eds. *Democracy Betrayed: The Wilmington Race Riot of 1898 and Its Legacy*. Chapel Hill, NC: University of North Carolina Press, 1998.

Chalmers, David M. *Hooded Americanism: The History of the Ku Klux Klan*. 3rd ed. Durham, NC: Duke University Press, 1981.

Cheek, William F. "A Negro Runs for Congress: John Mercer Langston and the Virginia Campaign of 1888." *The Journal of Negro History* 52:1 (1967): 14-34.

Christian Garna L. *Black Soldiers in Jim Crow Texas, 1899-1917*. College Station, TX: Texas A&M University Press, 1995.

Clay, William L. *Just Permanent Interests: Black Americans in Congress, 1870-1991*. New York, NY: Amistad, 1992.

Cohen, William. *At Freedom's Edge: Black Mobility and the Southern White Quest for Racial Control, 1861-1915*. Baton Rouge, LA: Louisiana State University Press, 1991.

Dailey, Jane. *Before Jim Crow: the Politics of Race in Postemancipation Virginia*. Chapel Hill, NC: University of North Carolina Press, 2000

Daniel, Pete. *The Shadow of Slavery:Peonage in the South, 1901-1969*. Urbana, IL: University of Illinois Press, 1972.

Durham, Phillip, and Everett L. Jones. *The Negro Cowboys*. New York, NY: Dodd, Mead, 1965.

Duster, Alfreda M., ed. *Crusade for Justice: The Autobiography of Ida B. Wells*. Chicago, IL: University of Chicago Press, 1970.

Fitzhugh, W. Brundage, ed. *Under Sentence of Death: Lynching in the South*. Chapel Hill, NC: University of North Carolina Press, 1997.

Flynn, Charles L. *White Land, Black Labor: Caste and Class in Late 19th Century Georgia*. Baton Rouge, LA: Louisiana State University Press, 1983.

Gaines, Kevin and Penny Von Eschen. "Ambivalent Warriors: African Americans, U.S. Expansion, and the Legacies of 1898." *Culturefront* 7 (1998): 63-64, 73-75.

Gatewood, Willard, comp. *"Smoked Yankees" and the Struggle for Empire: Letters from Negro Soldiers, 1898-1902*. Fayetteville, AR: University of Arkansas Press, 1987.

_____. *Black Americans and the White Man's Burden, 1898-1903*. Urbana, IL: University of Illinois Press, 1975.

Gerber, David A. *Black Ohio and the Color Line, 1860-1915*. Urbana, IL: University of Illinois Press, 1976.

Giddings, Paula. *Ida, a Sword Among Lions: Ida B. Wells and the Campaign Against Lynching*. New York, NY: Amistad, 2008.

_____. *When and Where I Enter: The Impact of Black Women on Race and Sex in America*. New York, NY: W. Morrow, 1984.

Gilmore, Glenda Elizabeth. *Gender and Jim Crow: Women and the Politics of White Supremacy in North Carolina, 1896-1920*. Chapel Hill, NC: University of North Carolina Press, 1996.

Glass, Edward L. N. *The History of the Tenth Cavalry, 1866-1901*. Tucson, AZ: Acme Printing Co., 1921.

Graves, John William. *Town and Country: Race Relations in an Urban-Rural Context, Arkansas, 1865-1905*. Fayetteville, AR: University of Arkansas Press, 1990.

Hahn, Steven. *A Nation Under Our Feet: Black Political Struggles in the Rural South from Slavery to the Great Migration*. Cambridge, MA: Belknap Press of Harvard University Press, 2003.

Hale, Grace Elizabeth. *Making Whiteness: The Culture of Segregation in the South, 1890-1940*. New York, NY: Pantheon Books, 1998.

Harris, J. William. "Etiquette, Lynching, and Racial Boundaries in Southern History: A Mississippi Example." *The American Historical Review* 100:2 (1995): 387-410.

Hill, Howard C. *Roosevelt and the Caribbean*. Chicago, IL: The University of Chicago Press, 1927.

Hirsch, James S. *Riot and Remembrance: Th Tulsa Race War and Its Legacy*. Boston, MA: Houghton Mifflin, 2002.

Jaspin, Elliot. *Buried in the Bitter Waters: The Hidden History of Racial Cleansing in America*. New York, NY: Basic Books, 2008.

Johnson, Edward A. *History of Negro Soldiers in the Spanish American War and Other Items of Interest*. Raleigh, NC: Capital Printing Co., 1899.

Kennedy, Stetson. *Jim Crow Guide: The Way It Was*. Gainesville, FL: Florida Atlantic University Press, 1990.

Kirwan, Albert D. *Revolt of the Rednecks: Mississippi Politics, 1876-1925*. Lexington, KY: University of Kentucky Press, 1964.

Lane, Ann J. *The Brownsville Affair: National Crisis and Black Reaction*. Port Washington, NY: Kennikat Press, 1971.

Leigh, Patricia Randolph. "Segregation by Gerrymander: The Creation of the Lincoln Heights (Ohio) School District." *The Journal of Negro Education* 66:2 (1997): 121-136.

Litwack, Leon. *Trouble in Mind: Black Southerners in the Age of Jim Crow*. New York, NY: Knopf, 1998.

Loewen, James W. *Sundown Towns: A Hidden Dimension on American Racism*. New York, NY: Touchstone, 2006.

Logan, Frenise Avedis. *The Negro in North Carolina, 1876-1894*. Chapel Hill, NC: University of North Carolina Press, 1964.

Logan, Rayford W. *The Betrayal of the Negro, from Rutherford B. Hayes to Woodrow Wilson*. New York, NY: Collier Books, 1965.

Lynk, Miles V. *The Black Troopers, or the Daring Heroism of the Negro Soldiers in the Spanish American War*. New York, NY: AMS Press, 1971.

Marks, George P. *The Black Press Views American Imperialism*. New York, NY: Arno Press, 1973.

McMillen, Neil R. *Dark Journey: Black Mississippians in the Age of Jim Crow*. Urbana, IL: University of Illinois press, 1989.

Nelson, Paul D., and David Levering Lewis. *Frederick L. McGhee: A Life on the Color Line, 1861-1912*. St. Paul, MN: Minnesota Historical Society Press, 2002.

Newby, I. A. *Jim Crow's Defense: Anti-Negro Thought in America, 1900-1930*. Baton Rouge, LA: Louisiana State University Press, 1965.

Ng, Kenneth, and Nancy Virts. "The Black-White Income Gap in 1880." *Agricultural History*. 67:1 (1993): 1-15.

Novak, Daniel A. *The Wheel of Servitude: Black Forced Labor after Slavery*. Lexington, KY: University Press of Kentucky, 1978.

Ortiz, Paul. *Emancipation Betrayed: The Hidden History of Black Organizing and White Violence In Florida From Reconstruction To The Bloody Election Of 1920*. Berkeley, CA: University of California Press, 2005.

Oshinsky, David M. *"Worse Than Slavery": Parchman Farm and the Ordeal of Jim Crow Justice*. New York, NY: Free Press, 1996.

Pascoe, Peggy. "Miscegenation Law, Court Cases, and Ideologies of "Race" in Twentieth-Century America." *The Journal of American History* 83:1 (1996): 44-69.

Patler, Nicholas. *Jim Crow and the Wilson Administration: Protesting Federal Segregation in the Early Twentieth Century*. Boulder, CO: University Press of Colorado, 2004.

Prather, H. Leon. *We Have Taken a City: The Wilmington Massacre and Coup of 1898*. Rutherford, NJ: Fairleigh Dickinson University Press, 1984.

Rabinowitz, Howard N. "More Than the Woodward Thesis: Assessing the Strange Career of Jim Crow." *The Journal of American History* 75:3 (1988): 842-856.

_____. *Race Relations in the Urban South, 1865-1890.* Athens, GA: University of Georgia Press, 1996.

Rachleff, Peter J. *Black Labor in the South: Richmond, Virginia, 1865-1890.* Philadelphia, PA: Temple University Press, 1984.

Rosén, Hannah. *Terror in the Heart of Freedom: Citizenship, Sexual Violence, and the Meaning of Race in Postemancipation South.* Chapel Hill, NC: University of North Carolina Press, 2009.

Scott, Edward Van Zile. *The Unwept: Black American Soldiers and the Spanish-American War.* Montgomery, AL: Black Belt Press, 1996.

Senechal de la Roche, Roberta. *The Sociogenesis of a Race Riot: Springfield, Illinois, in 1908.* Urbana, IL: University of Illinois Press, 1990.

Stanton, William R. *The Leopard's Spots: Scientific Attitudes toward Race in America, 1815-1859.* Chicago, IL: University of Chicago Press, 1972, c1960.

Sweet, Frank W. *Legal History of the Color Line: The Rise and Triumph of the One-drop Rule.* Palm Coast, FL: Backintyme Publishing, 2005.

Trelease, Allen W. *White Terror: The Ku Klux Klan Conspiracy and Southern Reconstruction.* Westport, CT: Greenwood Press, 1979.

Wells-Barnett, Ida. *A Red Record: Tabulated Statistics and Alleged Causes of Lynchings in the United States, 1892-1893-1894.* Chicago, IL: Donohue & Henneberry, 1895.

Williamson, Joel. *A Rage for Order: Black/White Relations in the American South since Emancipation.* New York, NY: Oxford University Press, 1986.

Woodward, C. Vann. *The Strange Career of Jim Crow.* New York, NY: Oxford University Press, 2002.

Wright, George C. *Racial Violence in Kentucky, 1865-1940: Lynchings, Mob Rule, and "Legal Lynchings".* Baton Rouge, LA: Louisiana State University Press, 1990.

Chapter 13: The Era of Self-Help, 1880-1916

Alexander, Adele Logan. *Ambiguous Lives: Free Women of Color in Rural Georgia, 1789-1879.* Fayetteville, AR: University of Arkansas Press, 1991.

Anderson, James D. *The Education of Blacks in the South, 1860-1935.* Chapel Hill, NC: University of North Carolina Press, 1988.

Aptheker, Herbert, ed. *The Correspondence of W. E. B. Du Bois.* 3 vols. Amherst, MA: University of Massachusetts Press, 1973.

Blight, David. *Race and Reunion: The Civil War in American Memory.* Cambridge, MA: Belknap Press of Harvard University Press, 2003, c2001.

Berry, Mary Frances. *My Face is Black is True: Callie House and the Struggle for Ex-Slave Reparations.* New York, NY: Alfred A. Knopf, 2005.

Brown, Leslie. *Upbuilding Black Durham: Gender, Class, and Black Community Development in the Jim Crow South.* Chapel Hill, NC: University of North Carolina Press, 2008.

Bruce, Dickson D., Jr. *Archibald Grimke: Portrait of a Black Independent.* Baton Rouge, LA: Louisiana State University Press, 1993.

Carby, Hazel V. *Reconstructing Womanhood: The Emergence of the Afro-American Woman Novelist.* New York, NY: Oxford University Press, 1987.

Cash, Floris Loretta Barnett. *African American Women and Social Action: The Clubwomen and Volunteerism from Jim Crow to the New Deal, 1896-1936.* Westport, CT: Greenwood Press, 2001.

Chesnutt, Charles W. *The Conjure Woman.* Cambridge, MA: Printed at the Riverside Press, 1899.

_____. *The House behind the Cedars.* Boston, MA: Houghton, Mifflin and Company, 1900.

_____. *The Marrow of Tradition.* New York, NY: Arno Press, 1969, c1901.

Cooper, Anna J. *A Voice from the South: By a Black Woman of the South.* Xenia, OH: Aldine Printing House, 1892.

Drago, Edmund L. *Initiative, Paternalism, and Race Relations: Charleston's Avery Normal Institute.* Athens, GA: University of Georgia Press, 1990.

Du Bois, W. E. B. ed. *The Negro in Business*: Report of a social study made under the direction of Atlanta University, together with the proceedings of the Fourth Conference for the Study of the Negro Problems, held at Atlanta University, May 30-31, 1899. (Atlanta University publications, no. 4) Atlanta, Ga.: University Press, 1899.

_____. *The Philadelphia Negro.* Philadelphia, PA: The University or Pennsylvania Press, 1900.

_____. *The Souls of Black Folk.* Chicago, IL: A.C. McClurg, 1903.

Dunbar, Paul Laurence. *Sport of the Gods.* New York, NY: Arno Press, 1969, c1904.

_____. *Lyrics of Lowly Life.* New York, NY: Dodd, Mead, 1896.

Franklin, Vincent P. *The Education of Black Philadelphia: The Social and Educational History of a Minority Community, 1900-1950.* Philadelphia, PA: University of Pennsylvania Press, 1979.

_____ and James D. Anderson, eds. *New Perspectives on Black Educational History.* Boston, MA: G. K. Hall, 1978.

Fortune, T. Thomas. *Black and White: Land, Labor and Politics in the South.* New York, NY: Arno Press, 1968, c1884.

_____. *The Negro in Politics.* New York, NY: Ogilvie & Rowntree, 1885.

Gaines, Kevin. *Uplifting the Race: Black Leadership, Politics, and Culture in the Twentieth Century.* Chapel Hill, NC: University of North Carolina Press, 1996.

Gatewood, Willard B. *Aristocrats of Color: The Black Elite, 1880-1920.* Bloomington, IN: Indiana University Press, 1990.

Gilmore, Glenda Elizabeth. *Gender and Jim Crow: Women and the Politics of White Supremacy in North Carolina, 1896-1920.* Chapel Hill, NC: University of North Carolina Press, 1996.

Gomez-Jefferson, Annetta Louise. *The Saga of Tawawa: Reverdy Cassius Ransom, 1861-859.* Kent, OH: Kent State University Press, 2002.

Hahn, Steven. *A Nation Under Our Feet: Black Political Struggles in the Rural South from Slavery to the Great Migration.* Cambridge, MA: Belknap Press of Harvard University Press, 2003.

Harlan, Louis R. *Booker T Washington, the Making of a Black Leader, 1856-1901.* New York, NY: Oxford University Press, 1972.

_____. *Booker T Washington: The Wizard of Tuskegee, 1901-1915.* New York, NY: Oxford University Press, 1983.

Henderson, Alexa Benson. *Atlanta Life Insurance Company: Guardian of Black Economic Dignity.* Tuscaloosa, AL: University of Alabama Press, 1990.

Higginbotham, Evelyn Brooks. *Righteous Discontent: The Women's Movement in the Black Baptist Church, 1880-1920.* Cambridge, MA: Harvard University Press, 1993.

Hunter, Tera W. *To 'Joy My Freedom: Southern Black Women's Lives and Labors after the Civil War.* Cambridge, MA: Harvard University Press, 1997.

Keller, Frances Richardson. *An American Crusade: The Life of Charles Waddell Chesnutt.* Provo, UT: Brigham Young University Press, 1978.

Kletzing, H. F. and H. Crogman's. *Progress of a Race; or, The Remarkable Advancement of the Afro-American,* 1897.

Lewis, David Levering *W.E.B. Du Bois, Biography of a Race,* 1868-1919. New York, Y: H. Holt, 1993.

Luker, Ralph. *The Social Gospel in Black and White: American Racial Reform, 1885-1912.* Chapel Hill, NC: University of North Carolina Press, 1991.

Margo, Robert A. *Race and Schooling in the South, 1880-1950: An Economic History.* Chicago, IL: University of Chicago Press, 1990.

McMillen, Neil R. *Dark Journey: Black Mississippians in the Age of Jim Crow.* Urbana, IL: University of Illinois Press, 1990, c1989.

McPherson, James M. *The Abolitionist Legacy: From Reconstruction to the NAACP.* Princeton, NJ: Princeton University Press, 1975.

Montgomery, William E. *Under Their Own Vine and Fig Tree: The African-American Church in the South, 1865-1900.* Baton Rouge, LA: Louisiana State University Press, 1993.

Moore, Jacqueline M. *Booker T. Washington, W.E.B. Du Bois, and the Struggle for Racial Uplift: Volume One.* New York, NY: SR Books, 2003.

Moses, Wilson Jeremiah. *Alexander Crummell: A Study of Civilization and Discontent.* New York, NY: Oxford University Press, 1989.

Moss, Alfred A, Jr. *The American Negro Academy: Voice of the Talented Tenth.* Baton Rouge, LA: Louisiana State University Press, 1981.

_____. and Eric Anderson. *Dangerous Donations: Northern Philanthropy and Southern Black Education, 1902-1930.* Columbia, MO: University of Missouri Press, 1999.

Nahal, Anita and Lopez D. Matthews Jr., "African American Women and the Niagara Movement, 1905–1909," *Afro-Americans in New York Life and History,* 32 (July 2008): 65–85.

Neverdon-Morton, Cynthia. *Afro-American Women of the South and the Advancement of the Race, 1895-1925.* Knoxville, TN: University of Tennessee Press, 1989.

Ochs, Stephen J. *Desegregating the Altar: The Josephites and the Struggle for Black Priests [in the Roman Catholic Church], 1871-1960.* Baton Rouge, LA: Louisiana State University Press, 1990.

Painter, Nell Irvin. *Exodusters: Black Migration to Kansas after Reconstruction.* Lawrence, KS: University Press of Kansas, 1986.

Pinn, Anthony B., ed. *Making the Gospel Plain: The Writings of Bishop Reverdy C. Ransom.* Harrisburg, PA: Trinity Press International, 1999.

Rampersad, Arnold. *The Art and Imagination of W.E. B. Du Bois.* New York, NY: Schocken Books, 1990.

Redkey, Edwin S. *Black Exodus: Black Nationalists and Back-to-Africa Movements 1890-1910.* New Haven, CT: Yale University Press, 1969.

_____, ed. *Respect Black: The Writings and Speeches of Henry McNeal Turner.* New York, NY: Arno Press, 1971.

Richings, G. F. *Evidences of Progress among Colored People.* Philadelphia, PA: G.S. Ferguson Co., 1905, c1896.

Rouse, Jacqueline Anne. *Lugenia Burns Hope, Black Southern Reformer.* Athens, GA: University of Georgia Press, 1989.

Shaw, Stephanie J. *What a Woman Ought to Be and to Do: Black Professional Women Workers During the Jim Crow Era.* Chicago, IL: University of Chicago Press, 1996.

Simmons, William J. *Men of Mark: Eminent, Progressive, and Rising.* New York, NY: Arno Press, 1968.

Smith, John David. *Black Judas: William Hannibal Thomas and the American Negro.* Athens, GA: University of Georgia Press, 1999.

Terborg-Penn, Rosalyn. *African American Women in the Struggle for the Vote, 1850-1920.* Bloomington, IN: Indiana University Press, 1998.

Thornbrough, Emma Lou. *T. Thomas Fortune, Militant Journalist.* Chicago, IL: University of Chicago Press, 1972.

Trotter, Joe William. *Coal, Class, and Color: Blacks in Southern West Virginia, 1915-1932.* Urbana, IL: University of Illinois Press, 1990.

Waldrep, Christopher. *African Americans Confront Lynching: Strategies of Resistance from the Civil War to the Civil Rights Era.* Lanham, MD: Rowman & Littlefield Publishers, Inc., 2009.

Washington, Booker T. *The Negro in Business.* Boston, MA: Hertel, Jenkins & Co. 1907.

_____. *Up from Slavery.* New York, NY: A. L. Burt, 1900.

_____, N.B. Wood and Fannie Barrier Williams. *A New Negro for a New Century.* Chicago, IL: American Pub. House, 1900.

Weare, Walter B. *Black Business in the New South: A Social History of the North Carolina Mutual Life Insurance Company.* Urbana, IL: University of Illinois Press, 1973.

Wells, Ida. *A Red Record: Tabulated Statistics and Alleged Causes of Lynchings in the United States, 1892-1893-1894.* Chicago, IL: Donohue & Henneberry, 1895.

_____. *Selected Works of Ida B. Wells-Barnett.* compiled by Trudier Harris. New York, NY: Oxford University Press, 1991.

White, Deborah G. *Too Heavy a Load: Black Women in Defense of Themselves, 1894-1994.* New York, NY: W.W. Norton, 1999.

Wright, George C. *Life Behind a Veil: Blacks in Louisville, Kentucky, 1865-1930.* Baton Rouge, LA: Louisiana State University Press, 1985.

Chapter 14: In Pursuit of Democracy, 1914-1919

Badger, Reid. *A Life in Ragtime: A Biography of James Reese Europe.* New York: New Oxford University Press, 1995.

Baker, Ray S. "The Negro Goes North." *World's Work* 34 (1917).

Barbeau, Arthur E., and Florette Henri. *Unknown Soldiers: Black American Troops in World War I.* Philadelphia, PA: Temple University Press, 1974.

Bartlett, Bruce. *Wrong on Race: The Democratic Party's Buried Past.* New York, NY: Palgrave Macmillan, 2008.

Beer, George L. *African Questions at the Paris Peace Conference.* New York, NY: Macmillan, 1923.

Chew, Abraham. *A Biography of Colonel Charles Young.* Washington, DC: R. L. Pendelton, 1923.

Christian, Garna L. *Black Soldiers in Jim Crow Texas, 1899-1917.* College Station, TX: Texas A&M University Press, 1995.

Donald, Henderson. "The Negro Migration, 1916-1918." *Journal of Negro History* 6:4 (1921): 383-409.

Du Bois, W. E. B. *Darkwater: Voices from Within the Veil.* New York, NY: Harcourt, Brace and Howe, 1920.

_____. "The Negro Soldier in Service Abroad During the First World War." *The Journal of Negro Education* 12:3 The American Negro in World War I and World War II (Summer, 1943): 324-334.

Ellis, Mark. " 'Closing Ranks': and 'Seeking Honors': W. E. B. Du Bois in World War I." *The Journal of American History* 79:1 (1992): 96-124.

_____. *Race, War, and Surveillance: African Americans and the United States Government During World War I.* Bloomington, IN: Indiana University Press, 2001.

_____. "W. E. B. Du Bois and the Formation of Black Opinion in World War I: A Commentary on 'The Damnable Dilemma'." *The Journal of American History* 81:4 (Mar., 1995): 1584-1590.

Grossman, James R. *Land of Hope: Chicago, Black Southerners, and the Great Migration.* Chicago, IL: University of Chicago Press, 1989.

Guterl, Matthew Pratt. "The New Race Consciousness: Race, Nation, and Empire in American Culture, 1910-1925." *Journal of World History* 10:2 (1999): 307-352.

Hahn, Steven. *A Nation Under Our Feet: Black Political Struggles in the Rural South from Slavery to the Great Migration.* Cambridge, MA: Belknap Press of Harvard University Press, 2003.

Harris, J. William. "Etiquette, Lynching, and Racial Boundaries in Southern History: A Mississippi Example." *The American Historical Review* 100:2 (Apr., 1995): 387-410.

Haynes, George E. "The Effect of War Conditions on Negro Labor." *Proceedings of the Academy of Political Science* 8:2 (1919): 165-178.

_____. *The Negro at Work During the World War and During Reconstruction.* Washington, DC: Negro Universities Press, 1969, c1921.

Haynes, Robert V. *A Night of Violence: The Houston Riot of 1917.* Baton Rouge, LA: Louisiana State University Press, 1976.

Heywood, Chester D. *Negro Combat Troops in the World War: The Story of the 371st Infantry.* Worcester, MA: Commonwealth Press, 1928.

Hunton, Addie W., and Katherine M. Johnson. *Two Colored Women with the American Expeditionary Forces.* New York: G.K. Hall, 1997, c.1920.

Johns, Altona Trent. "Henry Hugh Proctor." *The Black Perspective in Music* 3:1 (Spring, 1975): 25-32.

Jones, Lester M. "The Editorial Policy of Negro Newspapers of 1917-18 as Compared With That of 1941-42." *The Journal of Negro History* 29:1 (Jan., 1944): 24-31.

Jordan, William. "'The Damnable Dilemma': African-American Accommodation and Protest during World War I." *The Journal of American History* 81:4 (1995): 1562-1583.

Keith, Jeanette. "The Politics of Southern Draft Resistance, 1917-1918: Class, Race, and Conscription in the Rural South." *The Journal of American History* 87:4 (2001): 1335-1361.

Lentz-Smith, Adriane Danette. *Freedom struggles: African Americans and World War I.* Cambridge, MA: Harvard University Press, 2009.

Logan, Rayford W. *The Senate and the Versailles Mandate System.* Westport, CT: Greenwood Press, 1975, c1945.

Marks, Carole. *Farewell-We're Good and Gone: The Great Black Migration.* Bloomington, IN: Indiana University Press, 1989.

Mennell, James. "African-Americans and the Selective Service Act of 1917." *The Journal of Negro History* 84:3 (Summer, 1999): 275-287.

Moton, Robert R. *Finding a Way Out: An Autobiography.* Garden City, NY: Doubleday, Page & Co., 1921.

Nalty, Bernard C. *Strength for the Fight: A History of Black Americans in the Military.* New York, NY: Free Press, 1986.

Nelson, Peter. *A More Unbending Battle: the Harlem Hellfighters' Struggle for Freedom in WWI and Equality at Home.* New York, NY: Basic Civitas, 2009.

Roberts, Frank E. *The American Foreign Legion: Black Soldiers of the 93d in World War I.* Annapolis, MD: Naval Institute Press, 2004.

Scott, Emmet J. *Negro Migration During the War.* New York, NY: Oxford University Press, 1920.

_____. *Scott's Official History of the American Negro in the World War.* Chicago, IL: Homewood Press, 1919.

Spencer, Tracey Lovette, James E. Spencer, Jr., and Bruce G. Wright. "World War I as I Saw It: The Memoir of an African American Soldier." *The Massachusetts Historical Review* 9 (2007): 134-165.

Tannenbaum, Frank. "The Great Migration." *OAH Magazine of History* 17:1, World War I (Oct., 2002): 31-33.

Trotter, Joe William, Jr., ed. *The Great Migration in Historical Perspective: New Dimensions of Race, Class, and Gender.* Bloomington, IN: Indiana University Press, 1991.

Tyler-McGraw, Marie. *An African Republic: Black and White Virginians in the Making of Liberia.* Chapel Hill, NC: University of North Carolina Press, 2007.

Urquhart, Brian. *Ralph Bunche: An American Life.* 1st ed. New York, NY: W. W. Norton, 1993.

Ware, Gilbert. *William Hastie: Grace under Pressure.* New York, NY: Oxford University Press, 1984.

Williams, Chad L., "Vanguards of the New Negro: African American Veterans and Post-World War I Racial Militancy," *Journal of African American History* 92 (Summer 2007): 347-70.

Williams, Charles H. *Sidelights on Negro Soldiers.* Boston, MA: B.J. Brimmer Company, 1970.

Chapter 15: Voices of Protest, 1910-1928

Anderson, Jervis A. *A. Philip Randolph: A Biographical Portrait.* Berkeley, CA: University of California Press, 1986.

Bates, Beth Tompkins. *Pullman Porters and the Rise of Protest Politics in Black America, 1925-1945.* Chapel Hill, NC: University of North Carolina Press, 2001.

Brotz, Howard, ed. *African American Social and Political Thought, 1850-1920: Representative Texts.* New Brunswick, NJ: Transaction Publishers, 1992.

Byrd, Rudolph, ed. *The Essential Writings of James Weldon Johnson.* New York, NY: The Modern Library, 2008.

Chalmers, David M. *Hooded Americanism: The History of the Ku Klux Klan.* 3rd ed. Durham, NC: Duke University Press, 1987.

Du Bois, W. E. Burghardt. "My Impressions of Woodrow Wilson." *The Journal of Negro History* 58:4 (Oct., 1973): 453-459.

Duster, Alfreda M. ed. *Crusade for Justice: The Autobiography of Ida B. Wells.* Chicago, IL: University of Chicago Press, 1970.

Foley, Barbara. *Spectres of 1919: class and Nation in the Making of the New Negro.* Urbana, IL: University of Illinois Press, 2003.

Fox, Stephen R. *Guardian of Boston: William Monroe Trotter.* New York, NY: Atheneum, 1971.

Garvey, Amy Jacques. *Garvey and Garveyism.* introduction by John Henrik Clarke. New York, NY: Octagon Books, 1978.

Gates, Henry Louis, Jr. "The Trope of a New Negro and the Reconstruction of the Image of the Black." *Representations* 24, Special Issue: America Reconstructed, 1840-1940 (Autumn, 1988): 129-155.

_____ and Gene Andrew Jarett, eds. *The New Negro: Readings on Race, Representation, and African American Culture, 1892-1938.* Princeton, NJ: Princeton University Press, 2007.

Gerstle, Gary. "The Protean Character of American Liberalism." *The American Historical Review* 99:4 (Oct., 1994): 1043-1073.

Giddings, Paula. *Ida: A Sword Among Lions: Ida B. Wells and the Campaign Against Lynching.* New York, NY: Amistad, 2008.

Glazier, Kenneth M. "W. E. B. Du Bois' Impressions of Woodrow Wilson." *The Journal of Negro History* 58:4 (Oct., 1973): 452-453.

Goggin, Jacqueline. *Carter G. Woodson: A Life in Black History.* Baton Rouge, LA: Louisiana State University Press, 1993.

Grossman, James R. *Land of Hope: Chicago, Black Southerners, and the Great Migration.* Chicago: University of Chicago Press, 1989.

Hagedorn, Ann. *Savage Peace: Hope and Fear in America, 1919.* New York, NY: Simon & Schuster, 2007.

Hahn, Steven. *A Nation Under Our Feet: Black Political Struggle in the Rural South from Slavery to the Great Migration.* Cambridge, MA: The Belknap Press of Harvard University Press, 2003.

Harris, William Hamilton. *Keeping the Faith: A. Philip Randolph, Milton P. Webster, and the Brotherhood of Sleeping Car Porters, 1925-37.* Urbana, IL: University of Illinois Press, 1977.

Heathcott, Joseph. "Black Archipelago: Politics and Civic Life in the Jim Crow City." *Journal of Social History* 38:3 (Spring, 2005): 705-736.

Higginbotham, Evelyn Brooks. "Clubwomen and Electoral Politics in the 1920s," in Ann D. Gordon and Bettye Collier-Thomas, eds., *African American Women and the Vote, 1837-1965.* Amherst, MA: University of Massachusetts Press, 1997

Hill, Robert A., ed. *The Marcus Garvey and Universal Negro Improvement Association Papers.* Berkeley, CA: University of California Press, 1983-2006.

Hughes, Langston. *Fight for Freedom: The Story of the NAACP.* New York, NY: Berkeley, 1962.

James, Winston. *Holding Aloft the Banner of Ethiopia: Caribbean Radicalism in Early Twentieth-Century America.* New York, NY: Verso, 1999.

Janken, Kenneth Robert. *White: The Biography of Walter White, Mr. NAACP.* New York, NY: New Press, Distributed by W. W. Norton, 2003.

Kellogg, Charles F. *NAACP: a history of the National Association for the Advancement of Colored People.* Baltimore, MD: Johns Hopkins Press, 1967.

Key, Vladimer Orlando. *Southern Politics in State and Nation. New ed.* Knoxville, TN: University of Tennessee Press, 1984, c1977.

Kornweibel, Theodore. *No Crystal Stair: Black Life and the Messenger, 1917-1928.* Westport, CT: Greenwood Press, 1975.

Lewis David Levering. *W. E. B. Du Bois: The Fight for Equality and the American Century, 1919-1963.* New York, NY: Henry Holt, 2000.

_____. *When Harlem Was in Vogue.* New York, NY: Oxford University Press, 1982.

McMurry, Linda. *To Keep the Waters Troubled: The Life of Ida B. Wells.* New York, NY: Oxford University Press, 1998.

Mecklin, John M. *The Ku Klux Klan: A Study of the American Mind.* New York, NY: Harcourt Brace and Co., 1924.

Ovington, Mary W. *How the National Association for the Advancement of Colored People Began.* New York, NY: The Association, 1914.

Patler, Nicholas. *Jim Crow and the Wilson Administration: Protesting Federal Segregation in the Early Twentieth Century.* Boulder, CO: University Press of Colorado, 2004.

Patterson, Lillie. *A. Philip Randolph: Messenger for the Masses.* New York, NY: Facts on File, 1996.

Perry, Jeffrey Babcock. *Hubert Harrison: The Voice of Harlem Radicalism, 1883-1918.* New York, NY: Columbia University Press, 2009.

Rolinson, Mary. *Grassroots Garveyism: The Universal Negro Improvement Association in the Rural South, 1920-1927.* Chapel Hill, NC: University of North Carolina Press, 2007.

Ross, Barbara Joyce. *J. E. Spingarn and the Rise of the NAACP, 1911-1939.* New York, NY: Atheneum, 1972.

Sernett, Milton C. *Bound for the Promised Land: African American Religion and the Great Migration.* Durham, NC: Duke University Press, 1997.

Storey, Moorfield. *Problems of Today.* Boston, MA: Houghton Mifflin, 1920.

Sullivan, Patricia. *Lift Every Voice: The NAACP and the Making of the Civil Rights Movement.* New York, NY: The New Press, 2009.

Tannenbaum, Frank. *Darker Phases of the South.* New York, NY: G.P. Putnam, 1924.

Trotter, Joe William, Jr., ed. *The Great Migration in Historical Perspective: New Dimensions of Race, Class, and Gender.* Bloomington, IN: Indiana University Press, 1991.

Weiss, Nancy. *The National Urban League, 1910-1940.* New York, NY: Oxford University Press, 1974.

White, Deborah Gray. *Too Heavy A Load: Black Women in Defense of Themselves, 1894-1994.* New York, NY: W.W. Norton, 1999.

White, Walter. "Reviving the Ku Klux Klan." *Forum* 65 (1921).

_____. *Rope and Faggot: a Biography of Judge Lynch.* Notre Dame, IN: University of Notre Dame Press, 2001, c1929.

Wintz, Cary D., ed. *African American Political Thought, 1890-1930: Washington, Du Bois, Garvey, and Randolph.* Armonk, NY: M. E. Sharpe, 1996.

_____, ed. *The Politics and Aesthetics of "New Negro" Literature.* New York, NY: Garland Pub., 1996.

Zangrando, Robert L. *The NAACP Crusade against Lynching, 1909-1950.* Philadelphia, PA: Temple University Press, 1980.

Chapter 16: Arts at Home and Abroad, 1920s to early 1930s

"The New Modernists: African American Writers of the Harlem Renaissance." *The Journal of Blacks in Higher Education* 28 (2000): 27-28.

Badger, Reid. *A Life in Ragtime: A Biography of James Reese Europe.* New York, NY: Oxford University Press, 1995.

Baldwin, Davarian L. *Chicago's New Negroes: Modernity, the Great Migration, & Black Urban Life.* Chapel Hill, NC: The University of North Carolina Press, 2007.

Barlow, William. "Black Music on Radio during the Jazz Age." *African American Review* 29:2 (Summer, 1995): 325-328.

Bogle, Donald. *Toms, Coons, Mulattoes, Mammies, and Bucks: An Interpretive History in American Films.* 4th ed. New York, NY: Continuum, 2001.

Bontemps, Arna. *American Negro Poetry.* New York, NY: Hill & Wang, 1974.

_____, ed. *The Harlem Renaissance Remembered.* New York, NY: Dodd-Mead, 1972.

Brawley, Benjamin. "The Negro Literary Renaissance." *Southern Workman* 56 (1927).

Brooks, Tim. *Lost Sounds: Blacks and the Birth of the Recording Industry, 1890-1919.* Urbana, IL: University of Illinois Press, 2004.

Brown, Sterling Allen. *The Negro Caravan.* New York, NY: Arno Press, 1969, c1941.

_____. *The Negro in American Fiction.* Port Washington, NY: Kennicat Press, 1968, c1937.

Calverton, V. F. *Anthology of American Negro Literature*. New York, NY: Modern Library, 1929.

Chauncey, George. *Gay New York: Gender, Urban Culture, and the Makings of the Gay Male World, 1890-1940*. New York, NY: Basic Books, 1994.

Collins, Lisa Gail. *The Art of History: African American Women Artists Engage the Past*. New Brunswick, NJ: Rutgers University Press, 2002.

Cooper, Wayne F. *Claude McKay, Rebel Sojourner in the Harlem Renaissance*. Baton Rouge, LA: Louisiana State University, 1986.

Courlander, Harold. *Negro Folk Music U.S.A.* New York, NY: Columbia University Press, 1963.

Cripps, Thomas. *Making Movies Black: The Hollywood Message Movie from World War II to the Civil Rights Era*. New York, NY: Oxford University Press, 1993.

_____. *Slow Fade to Black: The Negro in American Film, 1900-1942*. New York, NY: Oxford University Press, 1993.

Cruse, Harold. *The Crisis of the Negro Intellectual*. New York, NY: Morrow, 1967.

Curtis, Susan. *Dancing to a Black Man's Tune: A Life of Scott Joplin*. Colombia, MO: University of Missouri Press, 1994.

Davis, Angela Y. *Blues Legacies and Black Feminism: Gertrude "Ma" Rainey, Bessie Smith, and Billie Holiday*. New York, NY: Pantheon, 1998.

Davis, Francis. *The History of the Blues*. New York, NY: Hyperion, 1995.

Davis, Thadious M. *Nella Larsen, Novelist of the Harlem Renaissance: A Woman's Life Unveiled*. Baton Rouge, LA: Louisiana State University Press, 1994.

DeVeaux, Scott. "'Black, Brown, and Beige' and the Critics," *Black Music Research Journal*, 13:2 (Autumn, 1993): 125-146.

Edwards, Brent Hayes. The Practice of Diaspora: Literature, Translation, and the Rise of Black Internationalism. Cambridge, MA: Harvard University Press, 2003.

Ely, Melvin Patrick. *The Adventures of Amos 'n' Andy: A Social History of an American Phenomenon*. Charlottesville, VA: University Press of Virginia, 2001.

Fabre, Michel, "Maran, Rene, The New Negro and Negritude," *Phylon (1960-)* 36:3 (3rd Qtr., 1975): 340-351.

Farrington, Lisa E. *Creating Their Own Image: The History of African-American Women Artists*. New York, NY: Oxford University Press, 2004.

Ferguson, Blanche. *Countee Cullen and the Harlem Renaissance*. New York, NY: Dodd-Mead & Co., 1966.

Ferguson, Jeffrey B. *The Sage of Sugar Hill: George S. Schuyler and the Harlem Renaissance*. New Haven, CT: Yale University Press, 2005.

Gates, Henry Louis, Jr., and Evelyn Brooks Higginbotham, eds., *Harlem Renaissance Lives: From the African American National Biography*. New York, NY: Oxford University Press, 2009.

Gates, Henry Louis, Jr., and Gene Andrew Jarett, eds. *The New Negro: Readings on Race, Representation, and African American Culture, 1892-1938*. Princeton, NJ: Princeton University Press, 2007.

Gates, Henry Louis, Jr., and Nellie Y. McKay, eds. *Norton Anthology of African-American Literature*. 2nd ed. New York, NY: W. W. Norton, 2003, c1996.

Giles, James Richard. *Claude McKay*. Boston, MA: Twayne Publishers, 1976.

Green, Elizabeth L. *The Negro in Contemporary American Literature*. Chapel Hill, NC: University of North Carolina, 1928.

Griffin, Farah Jasmine. *If You Can't Be Free, Be a Mystery*. New York, NY: Free Press, 2001.

Gussow, Adam. "'Shoot Myself a Cop': Mamie Smith's 'Crazy Blues' As Social Text," *Callaloo* 25 (2002): 8-44.

Harris, Michael W. *The Rise of Gospel Blues: The Music of Thomas Andrew Dorsey in the Urban Church*. New York, NY: Oxford University Press, 1992.

Hemenway, Robert E. *Zora Neale Hurston: A Literary Biography*. Urbana, IL: University of Illinois Press, 1978.

Huggins, Nathan I. *Harlem Renaissance*. New York, NY: Oxford University Press, 2007.

Hughes, Langston. *The Big Sea: An Autobiography*. New York, NY: Hill and Wang, 1993, c1940.

_____. "The Negro Artist and the Racial Mountain." *Nation* 122:3181 (June 23, 1926): 692-694.

Hurston, Zora Neale, collected and edited by Carla Kaplan. *Zora Neale Hurston: A Life in Letters*. New York, NY: Doubleday, 2002.

Hutchinson, George. *The Harlem Renaissance in Black and White*, Cambridge, MA: Belknap Press of Harvard University Press, 1995.

Ikonne, Chidi, "*Opportunity* and Black Literature, 1923-1933." *Phylon (1960-)* 40:1 (1979): 86-93.

Jackson, Mahalia. *Movin' on Up: The Mahalia Jackson Story*. New York, NY: Hawthorne Books, 1966.

Janken, Kenneth Robert. *White: The Biography of Walter White, Mr. NAACP*. New York, NY: New Press, 2003.

Johnson, James Weldon. *"Along This Way" in Writings*. New York, NY: Library of America, 2004.

_____. *Black Manhattan*. New York, NY: Da Capo Press, 1991.

_____. *The Book of American Negro Poetry*. New York. NY: Harcourt Brace, 1969.

_____. "The Dilemma of the Negro Author." *American Mercury* 15 (1928).

Kennedy, Rick. *Jelly Roll, Bix, and Hoagy: Gennett Studios and the Birth of Recorded Jazz*. Bloomington, IN: Indiana University Press, 1994.

Kennan, Cynthia Earl, and Richard Eldridge. *The Lives of Jean Toomer: A Hunger for Wholeness*. Baton Rouge, LA: Louisiana State University Press, 1987.

Lemke, Sieglinde, *Primitivist Modernism: Black Culture and the Origins of Transatlantic Modernism*. New York, NY: Oxford University Press, 1998.

Levy, Eugene. *James Weldon Johnson: Black Leader, Black Voice*. Chicago, IL: University of Chicago Press, 1973.

Lewis, David L. *When Harlem Was in Vogue*. New York, NY: Oxford University Press, 1989, c1981.

Lewis, Samella. *Art: African American*. New York, NY: Harcourt Brace Jovanovich, 1978.

Linneman, Russell J., ed. *Alain Locke: Reflections on a Modern Renaissance Man*. Baton Rouge, LA: Louisiana State University Press, 1983.

Locke, Alain. *The New Negro: An Interpretation*. New York, NY: A. and C. Boni, 1925.

Magee, Jeffrey. *The Uncrowned King of Swing: Fletcher Henderson and Big Band Jazz*. New York, NY: Oxford University Press, 2005.

McDowell, Deborah E. *"The Changing Same": Black Women's Literature, Criticism, and Theory*. Bloomington, IN: Indiana University Press, 1995.

McKay, Claude. *A Long Way from Home*. New Brunswick, NJ: Rutgers University Press, 2007.

Metzer, David. "Shadow Play: The Spiritual in Duke Ellington's 'Black and Tan Fantasy,'" *Black Music Research Journal* 17:2 (Autumn, 1997): 137-158.

Miller, R. Baxter, ed. *Black American Literature and Humanism.* Lexington, KY: University Press of Kentucky, 1981.

Nadell, Martha Jane. Enter the New Negroes: Images of Race in American Culture. Cambridge, MA: Harvard University Press, 2004.

Oja, Carol. *Making Music Modern: New York in the 1920s.* New York, NY: Oxford University Press, 2000.

Oliver, Paul. *The Story of the Blues.* Boston, MA: Northeastern University Press, 1998.

Powell, Richard J. *Black Art and Culture in the 20ᵗʰ Century.* New York, NY: Thames and Hudson, 1997.

Rampersad, Arnold. *The Life of Langston Hughes.* 2 vols. 2nd ed. New York, NY: Oxford University Press, 2002.

Randle, William, Jr. "Black Entertainers on Radio, 1920-1930," *The Black Perspective in Music* 5:1 (Spring, 1977): 67-74.

Redding, J. Saunders. *To Make a Poet Black.* Ithaca, NY: Cornell University Press, 1988.

Reynolds, Gary A. and Beryl J. Wright, eds. *Against the Odds: African-American Artists and the Harmon Foundation.* Newark, NJ: The Newark Museum, 1989.

Rivers, W. Napoleon, "Review of René Maran's *Djouma, chien de brousse*." *The Journal of Negro History* 18:4 (Oct, 1933): 475-479.

Rogers, J. A. (translator): "Americanization of France," *The New York Amsterdam News* 31 July 1929: page 20. ProQuest Historical Newspapers. 14 October 2009.

Sergeant, Winthrop. *Jazz: A History.* New York, NY: McGraw-Hill, 1964.

Smethurst, James Edward, *The New Red Negro: The Literary Left and African American Poetry, 1930-1946.* New York, NY: Oxford University Press, 1999.

Sollors, Werner. *Ethnic Modernism.* Cambridge, MA: Harvard University Press, 2008.

Sotiropoulos, Karen. *Staging Race: Black Performers in Turn of the Century America.* Cambridge, MA: Harvard University Press, 2006.

Soto, Michael, ed., *Teaching the Harlem Renaissance: Course Design and Classroom Strategies.* New York, NY: P. Lang, 2008.

Southern, Eileen. *The Music of Black Americans.* 3rd ed. New York, NY: W.W. Norton, 1997.

Steams, Marshall. *The Story of Jazz.* New York, NY: Oxford University Press, 1970.

Stovall, Tyler, *Paris Noir: African Americans in the City of Light.* Boston, MA: Houghton Mifflin, 1996.

Suisman, David. "Co-workers in the Kingdom of Culture: Black Swan Records and the Political Economy of African American Music," *Journal of American History* 90:4 (Mar., 2004): 1295-1324.

Tucker, Mark. *Ellington: The Early Years.* Urbana, IL: University of Illinois Press, 1991.

Wall, Cheryl A., *Women of the Harlem Renaissance.* Bloomington, IN: Indiana University Press, 1995.

Waters, Ethel, with Charles Samuels. *His Eye Is on the Sparrow: An Autobiography.* Westport, CT: Greenwood Press, 1978, c1951.

Chapter 17: New Deal Era, 1929-1941

Arsenault, Raymond. *The Sound of Freedom: Marian Anderson, the Lincoln Memorial, and the Concert that Awakened America.* New York, NY: Bloomsbury Press, 2009.

Baldwin, Davarian L. *Chicago's New Negroes: Modernity, the Great Migration, & Black Urban Life.* Chapel Hill, NC: The University of North Carolina Press, 2007.

Bates, Beth Tompkins. *Pullman Porters and the Rise of Protest Politics in Black America, 1925-1945.* Chapel Hill, NC: University of North Carolina Press, 2001.

_____. "A New Crowd Challenges the Agenda of the Old Guard in the NAACP, 1933-1941." *The American Historical Review* 102:2 (Apr., 1997): 340-377.

Brown, Sterling. *Southern Road.* New York, NY: Harcourt, Brace and Company, 1932.

Cantor, Milton, ed. *Black Labor in America.* Westport, CT: Greenwood Press, 1970.

Carter, Dan. *Scottsboro: A Tragedy of the American South.* Baton Rouge: Louisiana State University Press, 1969.

Cayton, Horace, and George S. Mitchell. *Black Workers and the New Unions.* Baltimore, MD: McGrath Pub. Co, 1969, c1939.

Clarke, Donald. *Wishing on the Moon: The Life and Times of Billie Holiday.* New York, NY: Viking, 1994.

Clark-Lewis, Elizabeth. *Living in, Living Out: African American Domestics in Washington, D.C., 1910-1940.* Washington, DC: Smithsonian Institution Press, 1994.

Cripps, Thomas. *Slow Fade to Black: The Negro in American Film, 1900-1942.* New York, NY: Oxford University Press, 1993, c1977.

de Jong, Greta. "'With the Aid of God and the F.S.A.': The Louisiana Farmers' Union and the African American Freedom Struggle in the New Deal Era." *Journal of Social History.* 34:1 (Autumn, 2000): 105-139.

Edsforth, Ronald. *The New Deal: America's response to the Great Depression.* Malden, MA: Blackwell Publishers, 2000.

Ferguson, Karen. *Black Politics in New Deal Atlanta.* Chapel Hill, NC: University of North Carolina Press, 2002.

Goings, Kenneth W. *'The NAACP Comes of Age': The Defeat of Judge John J Parker.* Bloomington, IN: Indiana University Press, 1990.

Goodman, James E. *Stories of Scottsboro.* New York, NY: Pantheon Books, 1994.

Grant, Nancy L. *TVA and Black Americans: Planning for the Status Quo.* Philadelphia, PA: Temple University Press, 1990.

Greenberg, Cheryl Lynn, *Or Does It Explode?: Black Harlem in the Great Depression.* New York, NY: Oxford University Press, 1991.

Grubbs, Donald H. *Cry from the Cotton: The Southern Tenant Farmers Union and the New Deal.* Chapel Hill, NC: University of North Carolina Press, 1971.

Harris, William H. *Keeping the Faith: A. Philip Randolph, Milton P. Webster, and the Brotherhood of Sleeping Car Porters, 1925-1937.* Urbana, IN: Indiana University Press, 1977.

Jones, James H. *Bad Blood: The Tuskegee Syphilis Experiment.* New York, NY: Free Press, 1981.

Kelley, Robin D. G. *Hammer and Hoe: Alabama Communists During the Great Depression.* Chapel Hill, NC: University of North Carolina Press, 1990.

Kirby, John H. *Black Americans in the Roosevelt Era: Liberalism and Race.* Knoxville, TN: University of Tennessee, 1980.

Love, Spencie. *One Blood: The Death and Resurrection of Charles R. Drew.* Chapel Hill, NC: University of North Carolina Press, 1996.

Martin, Charles H. *The Angelo Herndon Case and Southern Justice.* Baton Rouge, LA: Louisiana State University Press, 1976.

Meier, August, and Elliott Rudwick. *Black Detroit and the Rise of the UAW.* Ann Arbor, MI: University of Michigan Press, 2007.

Murray, Pauli. *Song of a Weary Throat: An American Pilgrimage.* San Francisco, CA: HarperCollins, 1987.

Naison, Mark. *Communists in Harlem During the Depression.* Urbana, IL: University of Illinois Press, 1983.

Nicholson, Stuart. *Ella Fitzgerald: A Biography of the First Lady of Jazz.* New York, NY: C. Scribner's Sons, 1994.

Northrup, Herbert R. *Organized Labor and the Negro.* New York, NY: Kraus Reprint, 1971, c1944.

Ottley, Roi. *New World a-Corning.* New York, NY: Arno Press, 1968, c. 1943.

Painter, Nell I. *The Narrative of Hosea Hudson: His Life as a Negro Communist in the South.* Cambridge, MA: Harvard University Press, 1979.

Pfeffer, Paula F. *A. Philip Randolph, Pioneer of the Civil Rights Movement.* Baton Rouge, LA: Louisiana State University Press, 1990.

Poole, Mary. *The Segregated Origins of Social Security: African Americans and the Welfare State.* Chapel Hill, NC: University of North Carolina Press, 2006.

Pritchett, Wendell E., *Robert Clifton Weaver and the American City: The Life and Times of an Urban Reformer.* Chicago, IL: University of Chicago Press, 2008.

Record, Wilson. *The Negro and the Communist Party.* New York, NY: Atheneum, 1971.

Sandage, Scot A., "A Marble House Divided: The Lincoln Memorial, the Civil Rights Movement, and the Politics of Memory, 1939-1963," *The Journal of American History* 80:1 (June, 1993): 135-167.

Savage, Barbara Dianne. *Broadcasting Freedom: Radio, War, and the Politics of Race, 1938-1948.* Chapel Hill, NC: University of North Carolina Press, 1999.

Sears, James M. "Black Americans and the New Deal." *The History Teacher.* 10:1 (1976): 89-105.

Shaw, Nate. *All God's Dangers: The Life of Nate Shaw*, compiled by Theodore Rosengarten. New York, NY: Avon Books, 1974.

Sitkoff, Harvard. *A New Deal for Blacks: The Emergence of Civil Rights as a National Issue: The Depression Decade.* New York, NY: Oxford University Press, 2009, c1979.

Smethurst, James Edward, *The New Red Negro: The Literary Left and African American Poetry, 1930-1946*: New York, NY: Oxford University Press, 1999.

Sternsher, Bernard, ed. *The Negro in Depression and War: Prelude to Revolution, 1930-1945.* Chicago, IL: Quadrangle Books, 1969.

Sullivan, Patricia, *Days of Hope: Race and Democracy in the New Deal Era.* Chapel Hill, NC: University of North Carolina Press, 1996.

Weiss, Nancy. *Farewell to the Party of Lincoln: Black Politics in the Age of F.D.R.* Princeton, NJ: Princeton University Press, 1983.

Wilson, James Q. *Negro Politics: The Search for Leadership.* Glencoe, IL: Free Press, 1960.

Wolters, Raymond. *Negroes and the Great Depression: The Problem of Economic Recovery.* Westport, CT: Greenwood Pub. Co., 1970.

Wright, Richard. *Native Son.* New York, NY: Harper & Brothers, 1940.

———. *Uncle Tom's Children.* New York, NY: Harper & Brothers, 1938.

———. *Black Boy: A Record of Childhood and Youth.* New York, NY: HarperPerennial Modern Classics, 2006, c1937.

Chapter 18: Double V for Victory

Bailey, Beth, and David Farber. "The "Double-V" Campaign in World War II Hawaii: African Americans, Racial Ideology, and Federal Power." *Journal of Social History* 26:4 (Summer, 1993): 817-843.

Booker, Bryan D. *African Americans in the United States Army in World War II.* Jefferson, NC: McFarland, 2008.

Boris, Eileen. "'You Wouldn't Want One of 'Em Dancing with Your Wife': Racialized Bodies on the Job in World War II." *American Quarterly* 50:1 (Mar., 1998): 77-108.

Burstein, Paul. *Discrimination, Jobs, and Politics: The Struggle for Equal Employment Opportunity in the United States since the New Deal.* Chicago, IL: University of Chicago Press, 1998.

Dalfiume, Richard M. *Desegregation of the U.S. Armed Forces: Fighting On Two Fronts, 1939-1953.* Columbia, MO: University of Missouri Press, 1969.

Dowdy, G. Wayne. "The White Rose Mammy: Racial Culture and Politics in World War II Memphis." *The Journal of Negro History* 85:4 (Autumn, 2000): 308-314.

Farrar, Hayward. *The Baltimore African-American, 1892-1950.* Westport, CT: Greenwood Press, 1998.

Foner, Jack D. *Blacks and the Military in American History: A New Perspective.* New York, NY: Praeger, 1974.

Franklin, John Hope. "Their War and Mine." *The Journal of American History* 77:2 (Sep., 1990): 576-579.

Gibran, Daniel K. *The 92nd Infantry Division and the Italian Campaign in World War II.* Jefferson, NC: McFarland, 2001.

Granger, Lester B. "Barriers to Negro War Employment." *Annals of the American Academy of Political and Social Science* 223, Minority Peoples in a Nation at War (Sep., 1942): 72-80.

Gropman, Alan. *The Air Force Integrates, 1945-1964.* 2nd ed. Washington, DC: Smithsonian, 1998.

Hine, Darlene Clark. *Black Women in White: Racial Conflict and Cooperation in the Nursing Profession, 1890-1950.* Bloomington, IN: Indiana University Press, 1989.

Jakeman, Robert J. *The Divided Skies: Establishing Segregated Flight Training at Tuskegee, Alabama, 1934-1942.* Tuscaloosa, AL: University of Alabama Press, 1992.

Janken, Kenneth R., "Rayford Logan's Struggle for Academic Acceptance." *The Journal of Blacks in Higher Education* 8 (Summer, 1995): 74-77.

Kersten, Andrew E. "African Americans and World War II." *OAH Magazine of History.* 16:3, World War II Homefront (Spring, 2002): 13-17.

Krenn, Michael L., ed. *The African American Voice in U. S. Foreign Policy since World War II.* New York, NY: Garland Pub., 1998.

———, ed. *Race and U. S. Foreign Policy from 1900 through World War II.* New York, NY: Garland Pub., 1998.

Kryder, Daniel. "The American State & the Management of Race Conflict in the Workplace & in the Army, 1941-1945." *Polity* 26:4 (Summer, 1994): 601-634.

MacGregor, Morris J., Jr. *Integration of the Armed Forces, 1940-1965.* Washington, DC: Center of Military History, U.S. Army, 1981.

McGuire, Philip, ed. *Taps for a Jim Crow Army: Letters from Black Soldiers in World War II*. Lexington, KY: University Press of Kentucky, 1993.

Motley, Mary Penick. *The Invisible Soldiers: The Experience of the Black Soldier in World War II*. Detroit, MI: Wayne State University Press, 1975.

Nalty, Bernard C. *The Right to Fight: African-American Marines in World War II*. Washington, DC: History and Museums Division, Headquarters, U. S. Marine Corps: Supt. of Docs., U. S. G. P. O., distributor, 1995.

_____. *Strength for the Fight: A History of Black Americans in the Military*. New York, NY: Free Press, 1986.

Nelson, Bruce. "Organized Labor and the Struggle for Black Equality in Mobile during World War II." *The Journal of American History* 80:3 (Dec., 1993): 952-988.

Nelson, Dennis D. *The Integration of the Negro into the United States Navy*. New York, NY: Farrar, Straus and Young, 1951.

Neverdon-Morton, Cynthia, guest ed. *African Americans and WW II*. Washington, DC: Association for the Study of Afro-American Life and History, 1994.

Northrup, Herbert Roof. *Organized Labor and the Negro*. New York, NY: Kraus Reprint, 1971, c1944.

Osur, Alan, M. *Separate and Unequal: Race Relations in the AAF during World War II*. Washington, DC: Air Force History and Museums Program, 2000.

Parker, Christopher S., "When Politics Becomes Protest: Black Veterans and Political Activism in the Postwar South." *Journal of Politics* 71 (Jan. 2009): 113–31.

Percy, William Alexander. "Jim Crow and Uncle Sam: The Tuskegee Flying Units and the U.S. Army Air Forces in Europe during World War II." *The Journal of Military History* 67:3 (Jul., 2003): 773-810.

Savage, Barbara Diane. *Broadcasting Freedom: Radio, War, and the Politics of Race, 1938-1948*. Chapel Hill, NC: University of North Carolina Press, 1999.

Shaw, Henry I., Jr. and Ralph W. Donnelly. *Blacks in the Marine Corps*. Washington, DC: U.S. Marine Corps, 1975.

Silvera, John D. *The Negro in World War II*. New York, NY: Arno Press, 1969.

Sinha, Manisha and Penny Von Eschen, eds. *Contested Democracy: Freedom, Race, and Power in American History*. New York, NY: Columbia University Press, 2007.

Sklaroff, Lauren Rebecca. "Constructing G.I. Joe Louis: Cultural Solutions to the "Negro Problem" during World War II." *The Journal of American History* 89:3 (Dec., 2002): 958-983.

Wilson, Joe. *The 761st "Black Panther" Tank Battalion in World War II: An Illustrated History of the First African American Armored Unit to See Combat*. Jefferson, NC: McFarland, 1999.

_____. *The 784th Tank Battalion in World War II: History of an African American Armored Unit in Europe*. Jefferson, NC: McFarland, 2007.

Chapter 19: American Dilemmas, 1940-1955

Anthony, David Henry, III. *Max Yergan: Race Man, Internationalist, Cold Warrior*. New York, NY: New York University Press 2006.

Ashmore, Harry. *The Negro and the Schools*. Chapel Hill, NC: University of North Carolina Press, 1970.

Berg, Manfred. "Black Civil Rights and Liberal Anticommunism: The NAACP in the Early Cold War." *Journal of American History* 94:1 (June, 2007): 75-96.

_____. *"The Ticket to Freedom": The NAACP and the Struggle for Black Political Integration*. Gainesville, FL: University Press of Florida, 2005.

Berman, William C. *The Politics of Civil Rights in the Truman Administration*. Columbus, OH: Ohio State University Press, 1970.

Bernstein, Barton J., ed. *Politics and Policies of the Truman Administration*. Chicago, IL: Quadrangle Books, 1970.

Biondi, Martha. *To Stand and Fight: The Struggle for Civil Rights in Postwar New York City*. Cambridge, MA: Harvard University Press, 2003.

Bogle, M. Donald. *Toms, Coons, Mulattoes, Mammies, and Bucks: An Interpretive History in American Films*. 4th ed. New York, NY: Continuum, 2001.

Bond, Horace Mann. *Education of the Negro in the American Social Order*. New York, NY: Octagon Books, 1970, c1934.

Borstelmann, Thomas. *The cold War and the Color Line: American Race Relations in the Global Arena*. Cambridge, MA: Harvard University Press, 2002.

Brattain, Michelle. "Race, Racism, and Antiracism: UNESCO and the Politics of Presenting Science to the Postwar Public." *The American Historical Review* 112: 5 (December 2007):1386-1413.

Bruce, Janet. *The Kansas City Monarchs: Champions of Black Baseball*. Lawrence, KS: University of Kansas Press, 1985.

Bunche, Ralph. *A World View of Race*. Washington, DC: The Associates in Negro Folk Education, 1936.

Burstein, Paul. *Discrimination, Jobs, and Politics: The Struggle for Equal Employment Opportunity in the United States since the New Deal*. Chicago, IL: University of Chicago Press, 1998.

Capeci, Dominic J. Jr., and Martha Wilkerson. *Layered Violence: The Detroit Rioters of 1943*. Jackson, MS: University of Mississippi, 1991.

Carter, Robert L. *A Matter of Law: A Memoir of Struggle in the Cause of Equal Rights*. New York, NY: New Press, 2005.

Clark, Kenneth Bancroft. *Dark Ghetto: Dilemmas of Social Power*. New York, NY: Harper & Row, 1965.

Collier-Thomas, Bettye, and V. P. Franklin, eds. *Sisters in the Struggle: African American Women in the Civil Rights-Black Power Movement*. New York, NY: New York University Press, 2001.

Cripps, Thomas. *Making Movies Black: The Hollywood Message Movie from World War II to the Civil Rights Era*. New York, NY: Oxford University Press, 1993.

_____. *Slow Fade to Black: The Negro in American Film, 1900-1942*. New York, NY: Oxford University Press, 1993, c1977.

Daniel, Pete. *Lost Revolutions: The South in the 1950s*. Chapel Hill, NC: University of North Carolina Press, 2000.

Davis, Benjamin O., Jr. *Benjamin O. Davis, Jr., American: An Autobiography*. Washington, DC: Smithsonian Institution Press, 1991.

Davis, Ossie, and Ruby Dee. *With Ossie and Ruby: In This Life Together*. New York, NY: William Morrow, 1998.

Detweiler, Frederick G. *The Negro Press in the United States*. College Park, MD: McGrath Publishing Co. 1968, c.1922.

Dillard, Angela D. *Faith in the City: Preaching Radical Social Change in Detroit*. Ann Arbor, MI: University of Michigan Press, 2007.

Duberman, Martin B. *Paul Robeson*. New York, NY: New Press, 2005.

Ely, Melvin Patrick. *The Adventures of Amos 'N' Andy: A Social History of an American Phenomenon.* New York, NY: Free Press, 1991.

Fass, Paula S. *Outside In: Minorities and the Transformation of American Education.* New York, NY: Oxford University Press, 1989.

Franklin, John Hope and Genna Rae McNeil, eds. *African Americans and the Living Constitution.* Washington, DC: Smithsonian Institute, 1995.

Frazier, Edward Franklin. *Black Bourgeoisie.* New York, NY: Free Press, 1965.

_____. *The Negro Family in the United States.* with a new introduction and bibliography by Anthony M. Platt, Notre Dame, IN: University of Notre Dame Press, 2001.

_____. *Negro Youth at the Crossways.* New York, NY: Schocken Books, 1967, c1940.

Goggin, Jacqueline. *Carter G. Woodson: A Life in Black History.* Baton Rouge, LA: Louisiana State University Press, 1993.

Goodson, Martha Graham. *Chronicles of Faith: The Autobiography of Frederick D. Patterson.* Tuscaloosa, AL: University of Alabama Press, 1991.

Gordon, Linda. "Black and White Visions of Welfare: Women's Welfare Activism, 1890-1945." *The Journal of American History* 78:2 (1991): 559-590.

Gregory, James N. *The Southern Diaspora: How the Great Migrations of Black and White Southerners Transformed America.* Chapel Hill, NC: University of North Carolina Press, 2005.

Hall, Jacquelyn Dowd. "The Long Civil Rights Movement and the Political Uses of the Past." *Journal of American History* 91:4 (Mar., 2005): 1233-1263.

Hamilton, Charles V. *Adam Clayton Powell Jr.: The Political Biography of an American Dilemma.* New York, NY: Atheneum, 1991.

Haygood, Wil. *King of the Cats: The Life and Times of Adam Clayton Powell Jr.* New York, NY: Amistad, 2006, c1993.

Herskovits, Melville. *The American Negro: A Study in Racial Crossing.* New York, NY: Knopf, 1930, c1928.

Hine, Darlene Clark. "Black Professionals and Race Consciousness: Origins of the Civil Rights Movement, 1890-1950." *The Journal of American History* 89:4 (Mar., 2003): 1279-1294.

_____. *Black Victory, the Rise and Fall of the White Primary in Texas.* Columbia, MO: University of Missouri Press, 2003.

Hochschild, Jennifer L. *Thirty Years after Brown.* Washington, DC: Joint Center for Political Studies, 1985.

Holloway, Jonathan Scott. *Confronting the Veil: Abram Harris, Jr., E. Franklin Frazier, and Ralph Bunche, 1919-1941.* Chapel Hill, NC: University of North Carolina Press, 2002.

_____ and Ben Keppel, eds., *Black Scholars on the Line: Race, Social Science, and American Thought in the Twentieth Century.* Notre Dame, IN: University of Notre Dame Press, 2007.

Home, Gerald. *Black and Red: W. E. B. Du Bois and the Afro-American Response to the Cold War, 1944-1963.* Albany, NY: State University of New York Press, 1986.

Honey, Michael K. *Southern Labor and Black Civil Rights: Organizing Memphis Workers.* Urbana, IL: University of Illinois Press, 1993.

Jackson, Walter A. *Gunnar Myrdal and America's Conscience: Social Engineering and Racial Liberalism, 1938-1987.* Chapel Hill, NC: University of North Carolina Press, 1990.

Janken, Kenneth R. "Rayford Logan's Struggle for Academic Acceptance." *The Journal of Blacks in Higher Education* 8 (Summer 1995): 74-77.

_____. *Rayford W Logan and the Dilemma of the African American Intellectual.* Amherst, MA: University of Massachusetts Press, 1993.

Johnson, Charles S. *Growing up in the Black Belt: Negro Youth in the Rural South.* Washington, DC: American Council on Education, 1941.

_____, ed. *Education and the Cultural Process.* New York, NY: Negro Universities Press, 1970, c. 1943.

Key, Vladimer Orlando. *Southern Politics in State and Nation.* Knoxville, TN: University of Tennessee Press, 1984, c1977.

Kluger, Richard. *Simple Justice: The History of Brown v. Board of Education and Black America's Struggle for Equality.* rev. and expanded ed. New York, NY: Knopf, 2004.

Korstad, Robert Rodgers. *Civil Rights Unionism: Tobacco Workers and the Struggle for Democracy in the Mid-Twentieth-Century South.* Chapel Hill, NC: University of North Carolina Press, 2003.

_____ and Nelson Lichtenstein. "Opportunities Found and Lost: Labor, Radicals, and the Early Civil Rights Movement." *The Journal of American History* 75:3 (Dec. 1988): 786-811.

Lawson, Steven. *Black Ballots: Voting Rights in the South, 1944-1969.* New York, NY: Columbia University, 1976.

Lee, Chana Kai, *For Freedom's Sake: The Life of Fannie Lou Hamer.* Urbana, IL: University of Illinois Press, 1999.

Lerner, Gerda, ed., *Black Women in White America.* New York, NY: Vintage Books, 1972.

Lewis, Earl. *In Their Own Interests: Race, Class, and Power in Twentieth-Century Norfolk, Virginia.* Berkeley, CA: University of California Press, 1991.

Logan, Rayford W. ed. *What the Negro Wants.* Notre Dame, IN: University of Notre Dame Press, 2001.

Lynch, Hollis R. ed., *The Black Urban Condition.* New York, NY: Crowell, 1973.

Mack, Kenneth. "Law and Mass Politics in the Making of the Civil Rights Lawyer, 1931-1941." *The Journal of American History* 93:1 (Jun., 2006): 37-62.

Martin, Waldo. *No Coward Soldiers: Black Cultural Politics and Postwar America.* Cambridge, MA: Harvard University Press, 2005.

Mays, Benjamin Elijah, and Joseph William Nicholson. *The Negro's Church.* Salem, NH: Ayer, 1988, c1933.

McCoy, Donald R, and Richard T. Ruetten. *Quest and Response: Minority Rights and the Truman Administration.* Lawrence, KS: University of Kansas Press, 1973.

McNeil, Genna Rae. *Groundwork: Charles Hamilton Houston and the Struggle for Civil Rights.* Philadelphia, PA: University of Pennsylvania Press, 1983.

Ming, William R., Jr. "The Elimination of Segregation in the Public Schools of the North and West." *The Journal of Negro Education* 21:3, The Courts and Racial Integration in Education (Summer, 1952): 265-275.

_____. "Racial Restrictions and the Fourteenth Amendment: The Restrictive Covenant Cases." *The University of Chicago Law Review* 16:2 (Winter, 1949): 203-238.

Murray, Pauli. *Song of a Weary Throat: An American Pilgrimage.* San Francisco, CA: HarperCollins, 1987.

Myrdal, Gunnar. *An American Dilemma: The Negro Problem and Modern Democracy.* New Brunswick, NJ: Transaction Publishers, 1996, c1944.

O'Brien, Gail Williams. *The Color of the Law: Race, Violence, and Justice in the Post-World War II South.* Chapel Hill, NC: University of North Carolina Press, 1999.

Parsons, Talcott, and Kenneth Clark. *The Negro American.* Boston, MA: Beacon Press, 1966.

Platt, Anthony M. *E. Franklin Frazier Reconsidered.* New Brunswick, NJ: Rutgers University Press, 1991.

Plummer, Brenda Gayle. *Rising Wind: Black Americans and U.S. Foreign Affairs, 1935-1960.* Chapel Hill, NC: University of North Carolina Press, 1996.

Raboteau, Albert J. *A Fire in the Bones: Reflections on African American Religious History.* Boston, MA: Beacon Press, 1995.

Rampersad, Arnold. *Jackie Robinson: A Biography.* New York, NY: Knopf, 1997.

Reed, Linda. *Simple Decency and Common Sense: The Southern Conference Movement, 1938-1963.* Bloomington, IN: Indiana University Press, 1991.

Rivlin, Benjamin. *Ralph Bunche: The Man and His Times.* New York, NY: Holmes & Meier, 1990.

Roberts, Gene and Hank Klibanoff. *The Race Beat: The Press, the Civil Rights Struggle, and the Awakening of a Nation.* New York, NY: Knopf, 2006.

Rogosin, Donn. *Invisible Men: Life in Baseball's Negro Leagues.* Lincoln, NB: University of Nebraska Press, 2007, c1985.

Ruchames, Louis. *Race, Jobs, and Politics: The Story of FEPC.* New York, NY: Negro Universities Press, 1971 c1953.

Savage, Barbara Diane. *Broadcasting Freedom: Radio, War, and the Politics of Race, 1938-1948.* Chapel Hill, NC: University of North Carolina Press, 1999.

Sawyer, Mary R. "Black Ecumenical Movements: Proponents of Social Change." *Review of Religious Research* 30:2 (Dec., 1988): 151-161.

Scott, Daryl Michael. *Contempt and Pity: Social Policy and the Image of the Damaged Black Psyche, 1880-1996.* Chapel Hill, NC: University of North Carolina Press, 1997.

Scott, William R. "Black Nationalism and the Italo-Ethiopian Conflict 1934-1936," *The Journal of Negro History* 63:2 (1978): 118-134.

_____. *The Sons of Sheba's Race: African Americans and the Italo-Ethiopian War, 1935-1941.* Bloomington, IN: Indiana University Press, 1992.

Silver, James W. *Mississippi: The Closed Society.* New York, NY: Harcourt, Brace and World, 1966, c1964.

Simpson, George and J. Milton Yinger. *Racial and Cultural Minorities.* 4th ed. New York, NY: Harper Row, 1972.

Smith, Robert C. *They Closed Their Schools: Prince Edward County, Virginia, 1951-1964.* Chapel Hill, NC: University of North Carolina Press, 1965.

Smythe, Hugh H. "The N. A. A. C. P. Protest to UN." *Phylon (1940-1956)* 8:4 (4th Qtr., 1947): 355-358.

Spivey, Donald, ed. *Sport in America: New Historical Perspectives.* Westport, CT: Greenwood Press, 1985.

Steinberg, Stephen. 'An American Dilemma: The Collapse of the Racial Orthodoxy of Gunnar Myrdal,' *The Journal of Blacks in Higher Education* 10 (Winter, 1995-1996): 64-70.

Sugrue, Thomas J. *Sweet Land of Liberty: The Forgotten Struggle for Civil Rights in the North.* New York, NY: Random House, 2008.

Sullivan, Patricia. *Lift Every Voice: The NAACP and the Making of the Civil Rights Movement.* New York, NY: The New Press, 2009.

Taeuber, Karl and Alma Taeuber. *Residential Segregation & Neighborhood Change.* Piscataway, NJ: Aldine Transaction, 2009, c1965.

Teele, James E. *Franklin Frazier and Black Bourgeoisie.* Columbia, MO: University of Missouri Press, 2002.

Terrell, Mary Church. *A Colored Woman in a White World*, with a foreword by Debra Newman Ham. Amherst, NY: Humanity Books, 2005, c1940.

Theoharis, Jeanne F. and Komozi Woodard, eds., *Freedom North: Black Freedom Struggles Outside the South, 1940-1980.* New York, NY: Palgrave Macmillan, 2003.

Thompson, Daniel C. *The Negro Leadership Class.* Englewood Cliffs, NJ: Prentice-Hall, 1963.

Trotter, Joe William. *Black Milwaukee: The Making of an Industrial Proletariat.* Urbana, IL: University of Illinois Press, 1985.

Tsesis, Alexander Tsesis, *We Shall Overcome: A History of Civil Rights and the Law.* New Haven, CT: Yale University Press, 2008.

Tushnet, Mark V. *Making Civil Rights Law: Thurgood Marshall and the Supreme Court, 1936-1961.* New York, NY: Oxford University Press, 1994.

_____. *The NAACP's Legal Strategy Against Segregated Education, 1925-1950.* Chapel Hill, NC: University of North Carolina Press, 1987.

Tygiel, Jules. *Baseball's Great Experiment: Jackie Robinson and His Legacy.* Expanded ed. New York, NY: Oxford University Press, 2008.

United States. President's Committee on Civil Rights. *To Secure These Rights: The Report of the President's Committee on Civil Rights.* New York, NY: Simon and Schuster, 1947.

Urquhart, Brian. *Ralph Bunche: An American Life.* New York, NY: W.W. Norton, 1993.

Von Eschen, Penny M. *Race Against Empire: Black Americans and Anticolonialism, 1937-1957.* Ithaca, NY: Cornell University Press, 1997.

_____. *Satchmo Blows up the World: Jazz Ambassadors Play the Cold War.* Cambridge, MA: Harvard University Press, 2004.

Ware, Gilbert. *William Hastie: Grace under Pressure.* New York, NY: Oxford University Press, 1984.

Weaver, Robert C. *The Negro Ghetto.* New York, NY: Russell & Russell, 1967, c1948.

White, Walter. *A Rising Wind.* Garden City, NY: Doubleday, Doran and Company, Inc., 1945.

Wilson, Francille Rusan. *The Segregated Scholars: Black Social Scientists and the Creation of Black Labor Studies, 1890-1950.* Charlottesville, VA: University of Virginia Press, 2006.

Woodson, Carter G. *The Mis-Education of the Negro.* Washington, DC: The Association Publishers, Inc., 1933.

Zangrando, Robert L. "Black Outreach: Afro-Americans' Recurring Efforts to Attract Support Abroad." *Phylon (1960-)* 36:4 (4th Qtr., 1975): 368-377.

Chapter 20: We Shall Overcome, 1947-1967

Anderson, Jervis. *Bayard Rustin: Troubles I've Seen.* New York, NY: Harper Collins, 1997.

Arsenault, Raymond. *Freedom Riders: 1961 and the Struggle for Racial Justice.* New York, NY: Oxford University Press, 2006.

Bartley, Numan. *The Rise of Massive Resistance: Race and Politics in the South in the 1950s.* Baton Rouge, LA: Louisiana State University Press, 1969.

Bates, Daisy. *The Long Shadow of Little Rock: A Memoir.* Fayetteville, AR: University of Arkansas, 1987.

Beals, Melba Pattillo. *Warriors Don't Cry: A Searing Memoir of the Battle to Integrate Little Rock's Central High.* New York, NY: Washington Square, 1994.

Bernstein, Barton J. *Politics and Policies of the Truman Administration.* Chicago, IL: Quadrangle Books, 1970.

Blumberg, Rhoda L. *Civil Rights: The 1960s Freedom Struggle.* Boston, MA: Twayne Publishers, 1991.

Borstelmann, Thomas. *The Cold War and the Color Line: American Race Relations in the Global Arena.* Cambridge, MA: Harvard University Press, 2002.

Branch, Taylor. *At Canaan's Edge: America in the King Years, 1965-1968.* New York, NY: Simon and Schuster, 2006.

_____. *Parting the Waters: America in the King Years, 1954-1963.* New York, NY: Simon and Schuster, 1988.

_____. *Pillar of Fire: America in the King Years 1963-65.* New York, NY: Simon and Schuster, 1998.

Brink, William J., and Louis Harris. *The Negro Revolution in America: What Negroes Want, Why and How They Are Fighting, Whom They Support, What Whites Think of Them and Their Demands.* New York, NY: Simon and Schuster, 1964.

Brinkley, Douglas. *Rosa Parks.* New York, NY: Viking Penguin, 2000.

Brisbane, Robert. *Black Activism: Black Revolution in the U.S; 1954-1970.* Valley Forge, PA: Judson Press, 1974.

Burk, Robert F. *The Eisenhower Administration and Black Civil Rights.* Knoxville, TN: University of Tennessee Press, 1984.

Burson, George. "The Black Civil Rights Movement." *OAH Magazine of History.* 2:1 (Summer, 1986): 35-36, 39-40.

Capeci, Dominic T, Jr., and Martha Wilkerson. *Layered Violence: The Detroit Rioters of 1943.* Jackson, MS: University of Mississippi Press, 1991.

Carmichael, Stokely and Charles Hamilton. *Black Power: The Politics of Liberation in America.* New York, NY: Vintage Books, 1992.

Carson, Clayborne. *In Struggle: SNCC and the Black Awakening of the 1960s.* Cambridge, MA: Harvard University Press, 1995.

_____. *Malcolm X The F.B.1 File.* New York, NY: Carroll & Graf Publishers, 1991.

_____, ed. *The Autobiography of Martin Luther King Jr.* New York, NY: Intellectual Properties Management in association with Warner Books, 1998.

_____, Ralph E. Luker, and Penny A. Russell, eds. *The Papers of Martin Luther King Jr., Volume 1: Called to Serve, January 1929-June 1951.* Berkeley, CA: University of California Press, 1992.

Carter, David C. *The Music Has Gone Out of the Movement: Civil Rights and the Johnson Administration, 1965-1968.* Chapel Hill, NC: University of North Carolina Press, 2009.

Chafe, William H. *Civilities and Civil Rights: Greensboro North Carolina and the Black Struggle for Freedom.* New York, NY: Oxford University Press, 1981.

Chesnut, J. L., Jr., and Julia Casso *Black in Selma: The Uncommon Life of J. L. Chesnut, Jr.* New York, NY: Farrar, Strauss, Giroux, 1990.

Clark, E. Culpepper. *The Schoolhouse Door: Segregation's Last Stand at the University of Alabama.* New York, NY: Oxford University Press, 1993.

Clark, Kenneth B. *Dark Ghetto: Dilemmas of Social Power.* Middletown. CT: Wesleyan University Press, 1989.

Clark, Septima. *Echo in My Soul.* New York, NY: E. P. Dutton, 1962.

_____. *Ready from Within: Septima Clark and the Civil Rights Movement.* Trenton, NJ: Africa World Press, 1990.

Cleaver, Eldridge. *Soul on Ice.* New York, NY: Dell, 1968.

Clinton, Catherine. "Ella Baker (1903-1986)." in *Portraits of American Women*, G.J. Barker-Benfield, Catherine Clinton, eds. New York, NY: St. Martin's Press, 1991.

Collier-Thomas, Bettye, and V. P. Franklin, eds. *Sisters in the Struggle: African American Women in the Civil Rights-Black Power Movement*, New York, NY: New York University Press, 2001.

Cone, James H. *For My People: Black Theology and the Black Church: Where Have We Been and Where Are We Going?* Maryknoll, NY: Orbis Books, 1984.

_____. *Martin & Malcolm & America: A Dream or a Nightmare.* Maryknoll, NY: Orbis Books, 1991.

Connery, Robert H. *Urban Riots: Violence and Social Change.* New York, NY: Vintage Books, 1969, c1968.

Countryman, Matthew. *Up South: Civil Rights and Black Power in Philadelphia*, Philadelphia, PA: University of Pennsylvania Press, 2006.

Crawford, Vickie L., Jacqueline Anne Rouse, and Barbara Woods, eds. *Women in the Civil Rights Movement, 1941-1965.* Brooklyn, NY: Carlson Pub., 1990.

Cripps, Thomas. *Making Movies Black: The Hollywood Message Movie from World War II to the Civil Rights Era.* New York, NY: Oxford University Press, 1993.

Cross, Theodore. *Black Capitalism: Strategy for Business in the Ghetto.* New York, NY: Atheneum, 1969.

_____. *The Black Power Imperative: Racial Inequality and the Politics of Nonviolence.* New York, NY: Faulkner Books, 1987.

Dalfiume, Richard M. *Desegregation of the U.S. Armed Forces: Fighting on Two Fronts, 1939-1953.* Columbia, MO: University of Missouri Press, 1969.

Daniel, Pete. *Lost Revolutions: The South in the 1950s.* Chapel Hill, NC: The University of North Carolina Press, 2000.

Davis, Michael, and Hunter Clark. *Thurgood Marshall: Warrior at the Bar, Rebel on the Bench.* Secaucus, NJ: Carroll Pub. Group, 1994.

Davis, Ossie, and Ruby Dee. *With Ossie and Ruby: In This Life Together.* New York, NY: William Morrow, 1998.

Dees, Morris. *A Season for Justice: The Life and Times of a Civil Rights Lawyer.* New York, NY: Charles Scribner's Sons, 1991.

Dierenfield, Bruce. *The Civil Rights Movement.* New York, NY: Pearson Longman, 2008.

Dickerson, Dennis E. *Militant Mediator: Whitney M Young, Jr.* Lexington, KY: University Press of Kentucky, 1998.

Ditmer, John. *The Good Doctors: The Medical Committee for Human Rights and the Struggle for Social Justice in Health Care.* New York, NY: Bloomsbury Press, 2009.

_____. *Local People: The Struggle for Civil Rights in Mississippi.* Urbana, IL: University of Illinois Press, 1995.

Draper, Theodore. *The Rediscovery of Black Nationalism.* New York, NY: Viking Press, 1973, c1970.

Durr, Virginia. *Outside the Magic Circle: the Autobiography of Virginia Foster Durr.* ed. by Hollinger F. Barnard, University, AL: University of Alabama Press, 1985.

Dyson, Michael Eric. *Making Malcolm: The Myth and Meaning of Malcolm X.* New York, NY: Oxford University Press, 1996.

Eagles, Charles W. *The Price of Defiance: James Meredith and the Integration of Ole Miss.* Chapel Hill, NC: The University of North Carolina Press, 2009.

Egerton, John. *Speak Now Against the Day: The Generation before the Civil Rights Movement in the South.* New York, NY: Knopf, 1994.

Ehle, John. *The Free Men.* New York, NY: Harper & Row, 1965.

Essien-Udom, Essien Udosen. *Black Nationalism: A Search for Identity in America.* Chicago, IL: University of Chicago Press, 1970.

Fairclough. *To Redeem the Soul of America: The Southern Christian Leadership Conference and Martin Luther King, Jr.* Athens, GA: University of Georgia Press, 2001.

Farley, Reynolds. *Blacks and Whites: Narrowing the Gap?* Cambridge, MA: Harvard University Press, 1984.

Farmer, James. *Lay Bare the Heart: An Autobiography of the Civil Rights Movement.* with a new preface, Fort Worth, TX: Texas Christian University Press, 1998.

Farrar, Hayward. *The Baltimore African-American, 1892-1950.* Westport, CT: Greenwood Press, 1998.

Fine, Elsa Honig. *The Afro-American Artist: A Search for Identity.* New York, NY: Holt, Rinehart, and Winston, 1982.

Fisher, Dexter, and Robert B. Stepto. *Afro-American Literature: The Reconstruction of Instruction.* New York, NY: Modern Language Association of America, 1979.

Foner, Jack D. *Blacks and the Military in American History: A New Perspective.* New York, NY: Praeger, 1974.

Forman, James. *The Making of Black Revolutionaries.* New York, NY: Macmillan, 1972.

Formisano, Ronald P. *Boston against Busing: Race, Class, and Ethnicity in the 1960s and 1970s;* with a new epilogue by the author. Chapel Hill, NC: University of North Carolina, 2004, c1991.

Freyer, Tony. *The Little Rock Crisis: A Constitutional Interpretation.* Westport, CT: Greenwood Press, 1984.

Gaines, Kevin K. *American Africans in Ghana: Black Expatriates and the Civil Rights Era.* Chapel Hill, NC: University of North Carolina Press, 2006.

Gallen, David. *Malcolm X' As They Knew Him.* New York, NY: Carroll & Graf Publishers, 1992.

Garrow, David J. *Bearing the Cross: Martin Luther King, Jr., and the Southern Christian Leadership Conference.* New York, NY: Quill, 1999.

———. *Protest at Selma: Martin Luther King Jr. and the Voting Rights Act of 1965.* New Haven, CT: Yale University Press, 1978.

Gitlin, Todd. *The Sixties: Years of Hope, Days of Rage.* New York, NY: Bantam Books, 1987.

Golden, Harry. *Mr. Kennedy and the Negroes.* Cleveland, OH: The World Publishing Co., 1964.

Graham, Hugh Davis. *The Civil Rights Era: Origins and Developments of National Policy, 1960-1972.* New York: Oxford University Press, 1990.

Green, Ben. *Before His Time: The Untold Story of Harry T. Moore, America's First Civil Rights Martyr.* New York, NY: Free Press, 1999.

Gropman, Alan. *The Air Force Integrates, 1945-1964.* Washington, DC: Smithsonian Institution Press, 1998.

Haines, Herbert H. "Black Radicalization and the Funding of Civil Rights: 1957-1970." *Social Problems* 32:1 (1984): 31-43.

Halberstam, David. *The Children.* New York, NY: Random House, 1998.

Hall, Jacquelyn Dowd. "The Long Civil Rights Movement and the Political Uses of the Past." *The Journal of American History* 91:4 (Mar., 2005): 1233-1263.

Hampton, Henry and Steve Fayer, eds. *Voices of Freedom: An Oral History of the Civil Rights Movement from the 1950s through the 1980s.* New York, NY: Bantam Books, 1990.

Hansberry, Lorraine. *The Movement: Documentary of a Struggle for Equality.* New York, NY: Simon & Schuster, 1964.

Harding, Vincent. *Hope and History: Why We Must Share the Story of the Movement.* Maryknoll, NY: Orbis Books, 1990.

———. *Martin Luther King: The Inconvenient Hero.* rev. ed. Maryknoll, NY: Orbis Books, 2008.

Henderson, Vivian W. *The Economic Status of Negroes: In the Nation and in the South.* Atlanta, GA: Southern Regional Council, 1963.

Hentoff, Nat. *The New Equality.* New York, NY: Viking Press, 1965.

Hercules, Frank. *American Society and the Black Revolution.* New York, NY: Harcourt Brace Jovanovich, 1972.

Hiestand, Dale L. *Economic Growth and Employment Opportunities for Minorities.* New York, NY: Columbia University Press, 1964.

Hilliard, David and Lewis Cole. *This Side of Glory: The Autobiography of David Hilliard and the Story of the Black Panther Party.* Boston, MA: Little Brown, 1993.

Hofstadter, Richard and Michael Wallace, eds. *American Violence: A Documentary History.* New York, NY: Knopf, 1970.

Honey, Michael K. *Southern Labor and Black Civil Rights: Organizing Memphis Workers.* Urbana, IL: University of Illinois Press, 1993.

Holt, Len. *The Summer That Didn't End: The Story of the Mississippi Civil Rights Project of 1964.* New York, NY: Da Capo Press, 1992.

Houser, George M. *Erasing the Color Line.* Nyack, NY: Fellowship Publications, 1945.

Hunter-Gault, Charlayne. *In My Place.* New York, NY: Farrar Straus, 1992.

Jakeman, Robert J. *The Divided Skies: Establishing Segregated Flight Training at Tuskegee, Alabama, 1934-1942.* Tucaloosa, AL: University of Alabama Press, 1992.

Johnson, Daniel M., and Rex R. Campbell. *Black Migration in America: A Social Demographic History.* Durham, NC: Duke University Press, 1981.

Jones, Charles E., ed. *The Black Panther Party (Reconsidered).* Baltimore, MD: Black Classic Press, 1998.

Jones, LeRoi, and Bill Abernathy. *In Our Terribleness: Some Elements and Meaning in Black Style.* Indianapolis, IN: Bobbs-Merrill, 1970.

Joseph, Peniel E., ed. *The Black Power Movement: Rethinking the Civil Rights-Black Power Era.* New York, NY: Routledge, 2006.

Kelley, Robin D. G. "'We Are Not What We Seem': Rethinking Black Working-Class Opposition in the Jim Crow South." *The Journal of American History* 80:1 (1993): 75-112.

Key, Vladimer Orlando. *Southern Politics in State and Nation.* new ed., Knoxville, TN: University of Tennessee Press, 1984, c1977.

King, Martin Luther, Jr. *Stride toward Freedom: The Montgomery Story.* New York, NY: Harper & Row, 1962.

———. *Why We Can't Wait.* New York, NY: New American Library, 1964.

Kluger, Richard. *Simple Justice: The History of Brown v. Board of Education and Black America's Struggle for Equality.* New York, NY: Random House, 1975.

Konvitz, Milton. *A Century of Civil Rights.* New York, NY: Columbia University Press, 1961.

Korstad, Robert Rodgers. *Civil Rights Unionism: Tobacco Workers and the Struggle for Democracy in the Mid-Twentieth Century South.* Chapel Hill, NC: University of North Carolina Press, 2003.

Kosek, Joseph Kip. "Richard Gregg, Mohandas Gandhi, and the Strategy of Nonviolence." *The Journal of American History* 91:4 (Mar., 2005): 1318-1348.

Kotsky, Frank. *Black Nationalism and the Revolution in Music.* New York, NY: Pathfinder Press, 1970.

Lang, Clarence. "Between Civil Rights and Black Power in the Gateway city: The Action Committee to Improve Opportunities for Negroes (Action): 1964-75." *Journal of Social History* 37:3 (2004): 725-754.

Laue, James H. "The Changing Character of Negro Protest." *Annals of the American Academy of Political and Social Science* 357: The Negro Protest (1965): 119-126.

Lawson, Steven F. *Black Ballots: Voting Rights in the South, 1944-1969.* New York, NY: Columbia University Press, 1976.

———. "Freedom Then, Freedom Now: The Historiography of the Civil Rights Movement." *The American Historical Review* 96:2 (Apr., 1991): 456-471.

———. *Running for Freedom: Civil Rights and Black Politics in America since 1941.* 3rd ed. Malden, MA: Wiley-Blackwell, 2009.

Lee, Chana Kai, *For Freedom's Sake: the Life of Fannie Lou Hamer.* Urbana, IL: University of Illinois Press, 1999.

Leeming, David. *James Baldwin: A Biography.* New York, NY: Knopf, 1994.

Lemann, Nicholas. *The Promised Land: The Great Black Migration and How It Changed America.* New York, NY: Knopf, 1991.

Levine, Ellen. *Freedom's Children: Young Civil Rights Activists Tell Their Own Stories.* New York, NY: G. P. Putnam, 2000.

Lewis, David. *King, a Critical Biography.* New York, NY, 1970.

———. *W.E.B. Du Bois: The Fight for Equality and the American Century, 1919-1963.* New York, NY: Henry Holt, 2000.

Lewis, John. *Walking with the Wind: A Memoir of the Movement.* New York, NY: Simon & Schuster, 1998.

Lincoln, C. Eric. *The Black Muslims in America.* Trenton, NJ: Africa World Press, 1994.

———. *Race, Religion, and the Continuing American Dilemma.* rev. ed., New York, NY: Hill & Wang, 1999.

Litwack, Leon F., "'Fight the Power!: The Legacy of the Civil Rights Movement." *Journal of Southern History* 75 (Feb. 2009): 3–28.

Lomax, Louis. *The Negro Revolt.* New York, NY: Harper & Row, 1971.

MacGregor, Morris J. *Integration of the Armed Forces, 1940-1965.* Washington, DC: Center of Military History, US Army, 1981.

McDonald, F. Fred. *Blacks and White TV: Afro-Americans in Television since 1946.* 2nd ed., Chicago, IL: Nelson-Hall Publishers, 1992.

McGuire, Danielle L. "'It Was Like All of Us Had Been Raped': Sexual Violence, Community Mobilization, and the African American Freedom Struggle." *The Journal of American History* 91:3 (Dec., 2004): 906-931.

Meier, August, John Bracey, Jr., and Elliott Rudwick, eds. *Black Protest in the Sixties.* New York, NY: M. Wiener Publishers, 1991.

Meier, August. *Core: A Study of the Civil Rights Movement, 1942-1968.* Urbana, IL: University of Illinois Press, 1975.

Miller, Loren. *The Petitioners: The Story of the Supreme Court of the United States and the Negro.* New York, NY: Pantheon, 1966.

Minchin, Timothy J., "Making Best Use of the New Laws; The NAACP and the Fight for Civil Rights in the South, 1965–1975." *Journal of Southern History* 74 (Aug. 2008): 669–702.

Ming, William R., Jr. "The Elimination of Segregation in the Public Schools of the North and West." *The Journal of Negro Education* 21:3, The Courts and Racial Integration in Education (Summer, 1952): 265-275.

———. "Racial Restrictions and the Fourteenth Amendment: The Restrictive Covenant Cases." *The University of Chicago Law Review* 16:2 (Winter, 1949), 203-238.

Monson, Ingrid. *Freedom Sounds: Civil Rights Call Out to Jazz and Africa,* New York, NY: Oxford University Press, (2007).

Moody, Anne. *Coming of Age in Mississippi.* New York, NY: Dell, 1965.

Morris, Aldon D. *The Origins of the Civil Rights Movement: Black Communities Organizing for Change.* New York, NY: Free Press, 1984.

Motley, Constance Baker. *Equal Justice under Law: an Autobiography.* New York, NY: Ferrar, Straus, and Giroux, 1998.

Motley, Mary Penick. *The Invisible Soldiers: the Experience of the Black Soldier in World War II.* Detroit, MI: Wayne State University Press, 1975.

Newman, Dorothy K. *Protest, Politics, and Prosperity: Black Americans and White Institutions, 1940-75.* New York, NY: Pantheon Books, 1978.

Norrell, Robert J. *Reaping the Whirlwind: The Civil Rights Movement in Tuskegee.* New York, NY: Knopf, 1985.

O'Brien, Gail Williams. *The Color of the Law: Race, Violence, and Justice in the Post- World War II South.* Chapel Hill, NC: University of North Carolina Press, 1999.

O'Hare, William P. *Blacks on the Move: A Decade of Demographic Change.* Washington, DC: Joint Center for Political Studies, 1981.

Oates, Stephen B. *Let the Trumpet Sound: The Life of Martin Luther King Jr.* New York, NY: Harper & Row, 1982.

Payne, Charles M. *I've Got the Light of Freedom: the Organizing Tradition and the Mississippi Freedom Struggle.* Berkeley, CA: University of California Press, 2007, c1995.

Peck, James. *Freedom Ride.* New York, NY: Simon and Schuster, 1962.

Perry, Bruce. *Malcolm: The Life of a Man Who Changed America.* Barrytown, NY: Station Hill, 1991.

Proudfoot, Merrill. *Diary of a Sit-In.* 2nd ed. Urbana, IL: University of Illinois, 1990.

Ransby, Barbara. *Ella Baker and the Black Freedom Movement: A Radical Democratic Vision.* Chapel Hill, NC: University of North Carolina Press, 2003.

Rice, Roger L. "Residential Segregation by Law, 1910-1917." *Journal of Southern History* 34, no. 2 (1968): 179-99.

Robinson, Jo Ann Gibson. *The Montgomery Bus Boycott and the Women Who Started It: The Memoir of Jo Ann Gibson Robinson.* Knoxville, TN: University of Tennessee Press, 1987.

Robnett, Belinda. *How Long? How Long?: African-American Women in the Struggle for Civil Rights.* New York, NY: Oxford University Press, 1997.

Roberts, Gene and Hank Klibanoff. *The Race Beat: The Press, the Civil Rights Struggle, and the Awakening of a Nation.* New York, NY: Knopf, 2006.

Roche, John Pearson. *The Quest for the Dream: The Development of Civil Rights and Human Relations in Modern America.* Chicago, IL: Quadrangle Books, 1968.

Ross, Arthur M., and Herbert Hill. *Employment, Race, and Poverty.* 1st ed. New York, NY: Harcourt, Brace & World, 1967.

Rout, Kathleen. *Eldridge Cleaver.* Boston, MA: Twayne Publishers, 1991.

Ruetten, Richard T. *Quest and Response: Minority Rights and the Truman Administration.* Lawrence, KS: University Press of Kansas, 1973.

Saunders, Doris E. *The Day They Marched*. Chicago: Johnson Publishing Co., 1963.

_____, ed. *The Kennedy Years and the Negro: A Photographic Record*. Chicago, IL: Johnson Publishing Co., 1964.

Savage, Barbara Diane. *Broadcasting Freedom: Radio, War, and the Politics of Race, 1938-1948*. Chapel Hill, NC: University of North Carolina Press, 1999.

Scott, Nathan A., Jr. "Black Literature." In *Harvard Guide to Contemporary American Writing*, edited by Daniel Hoffman. Cambridge, MA: Belknap Press of Harvard University Press, 1979.

Scott, William R. *The Sons of Sheba's Race: African Americans and the Italo-Ethiopian War, 1935-1941*. Bloomington, IN: Indiana University Press, 1993.

Self, Robert O. *American Babylon: Race and the Struggle for Postwar Oakland*. Princeton, NJ: Princeton University Press, 2003.

Silberman, Charles. *Crisis in Black and White*. New York NY: Random House, 1964.

Silver, James W. *Mississippi: the Closed Society*. New York, NY: Harcourt, Brace, & World, 1966.

Silvera, John D. *The Negro in World War II*. New York, NY: Arno Press, 1969.

Sinha, Manisha and Penny Von Eschen, eds. *Contested Democracy: Freedom, Race, and Power in American History*, New York, NY: Columbia University Press, 2007.

Smith, C. Fraser. *Here Lies Jim Crow: Civil Rights in Maryland*. Baltimore, MD: Johns Hopkins University Press, 2008.

Smith, Robert C. *They Closed Their Schools: Prince Edward County, Virginia, 1951-1964*. Chapel Hill, NC: University of North Carolina Press, 1965.

Sowell, Thomas. *The Economics and Politics of Race: An International Perspective*. New York, NY: W. Morrow, 1983.

Sugrue, Thomas J. *The Origins of the Urban Crisis: Race and Inequality in Postwar Detroit*. Princeton, NJ: Princeton University Press, 1996.

_____. *Sweet Land of Liberty: The Forgotten Struggle for Civil Rights in the North*. New York, NY: Random House, 2008.

_____ Sullivan, Patricia. *Lift Every Voice: The NAACP and the Making of the Civil Rights Movement*. New York, NY: The New Press, 2009.

Theoharis, Jeanne F. and Komozi Woodard, eds., *Freedom North: Black Freedom Struggles Outside the South, 1940-1980*. New York, NY: Palgrove Macmillan, 2003.

Tsesis, Alexander, *We Shall Overcome: a History of Civil Rights and the Law*. New Haven, CT: Yale University Press, 2008.

Tushnet, Mark V. *Making Civil Rights Law: Thurgood Marshall and the Supreme Court, 1936-1961*. New York, NY: Oxford University Press, 1994.

United States Commission on Civil Rights. *Freedom to the Free: Century of Emancipation, 1863-1963; a Report to the President*. Washington, DC: U.S. Govt. Print. Office, 1963.

Von Eschen Penny. *Race Against Empire: Black Americans and Anti-colonialism, 1937-1957*. Ithaca, NY: Cornell University Press, 1999.

_____. *Satchmo Blows up the World: Jazz Ambassadors Play the Cold War*, Cambridge, MA: Harvard University Press, 2004. Von Hoffman, Nicholas. *Mississippi Notebook*. New York, NY: D. White, 1964.

Wachtel, Dawn Day. *The Negro and Discrimination in Employment*. Ann Arbor, MI: Institute of Labor and Industrial Relations, University of Michigan-Wayne State University, 1965.

Washington, James M., ed. *A Testament of Hope: The Essential Writings of Martin Luther King Jr*. San Francisco, CA: Harper & Row, 1986.

Waskow, Arthur. *From Race Riot to Sit-in; and James W Button, Black Violence: Political Impact of the 1960s Riots*. Garden City, NY: Anchor Books, 1967.

Watson, Denton W. *Lion in the Lobby: Clarence Mitchell Jr.'s Struggle for the Passage of Civil Rights Laws*. Lanham, Md.: University Press of America, 2002.

Webb, Sheyann, and Rachel West Nelson. *Selma, Lord, Selma: Girlhood Memories of the Civil Rights Days*. Tuscaloosa, AL: University of Alabama Press, 1980.

Weiss, Nancy J. *Whitney M Young Jr., and the Struggle for Civil Rights*. Princeton, NJ: Princeton University Press, 1989.

White, Theodore H. *The Making of the President, 1960*. New York, NY: Atheneum Publishers, 1961.

Whitfield, Stephen J. *A Death in the Delta: The Story of Emmet Till*. Baltimore, MD: Johns Hopkins University Press, 1991.

Wilkins, Roy. *Standing Fast: the Autobiography of Roy Wilkins*. New York, NY: Viking Press, 1982.

Williams, Juan. *Thurgood Marshall: American Revolutionary*. New York, NY: Times Books, 1998.

Wolters, Raymond. *The Burden of Brown: Thirty Years of School Desegregation*. Knoxville: University of Tennessee Press, 1984.

Workman, William D. *The Case for the South*. New York, NY: Devin-Adair, 1960.

Young, Andrew. *An Easy Burden: The Civil Rights Movement and the Transformation of America*. 2nd ed. Waco, TX: Baylor University Press, 2008.

Young, Whitney M. *To Be Equal*. New York, NY: McGraw-Hill, 1968.

Zinn, Howard. *SNCC: The New Abolitionists*. Cambridge, MA: South End Press, 2002, c1964.

_____. *The Southern Mystique*. Cambridge, MA: South End Press, 2002, c1964.

Chapter 21: Black Power, 1955-1980

Abu-Lughold, Janet. *Race, Space, and Riots in Chicago, New York, and Los Angeles*. Princeton, NJ: Princeton University Press, 2007.

Anderson, Iain. *This is Our Music: Free Jazz, the Sixties, and American Culture*. Philadelphia, PA: University of Pennsylvania Press, 2007.

Angelou, Maya. *I Know Why the Caged Bird Sings*. New York, NY: Random House, 1969.

Baldwin, James. *The Fire Next Time*. New York, NY: Dial Press, 1963.

Bambara, Toni Cade. *The Black Woman: An Anthology*. New York, NY: New American Library, 1970.

Baraka, Imamu Amiri, and Larry Neal, eds. *Black Fire: An Anthology of Afro-American Writing*. New York, NY: Morrow, 1968.

Baraka, Imamu Amiri. *The Autobiography of LeRoi Jones/Amiri Baraka*. New York, NY: Lawrence Hill Books, 1997.

_____. *Blues People*. New York, NY: W. Morrow, 1963.

_____. *Dutchman: And, The Slave, Two Plays*. New York, NY: W. Morrow, 1964.

Black, J. Herman. "Black Nationalism." *Annals of the American Academy of Political and Social Science* 382: Protest in the Sixties (1969): 15-25.

Bracey, John H., August Meier and Elliott Rudwick, eds. *Black Nationalism in America*. Indianapolis, IN: Bobbs-Merrill, 1970.

Breines, Wini. *The Trouble Between Us: An Uneasy History of White and Black Women in the Feminist Movement*. New York, NY: Oxford University Press, 2006.

Breitman, George, ed. *Malcolm X Speaks: Selected Speeches and Statements*. New York, NY: Merit Publishers, 1965.

Brisbane, Robert. *Black Activism: Black Revolution in the U.S; 1954-1970*. Valley Forge, PA: Judson Press, 1974.

Brown, Elaine. *A Taste of Power: A Black Woman's Story*. New York, NY: Pantheon Books, 1992.

Brown, Scot. *Fighting for Us: Maulana Karenga, the US Organization, and Black Cultural Nationalism*. New York, NY: New York University Press, 2003.

Bush, Rod. *We Are Not What We Seem: Black Nationalism and Class Struggle in the American Century*. New York, NY: New York University Press, 1999.

Carmichael, Stokley, and Charles V. Hamilton. *Black Power: The Politics of Liberation in America*. New York, NY: Random House, 1967.

_____, and Ekueme Michael Thelwell. *Ready for Revolution: The Life and Struggles of Stokely Carmichael (Kwame Ture)*. New York, NY: Scribner, 2003.

Chafe, William H. *Civilities and Civil Rights: Greensboro North Carolina and the Black Struggle for Freedom*. New York, NY: Oxford University Press, 1981.

Clark, Kenneth B. "The Present Dilemma of the Negro," *The Journal of Negro History* 53:1 (Jan. 1968): 1-11.

Cleage, Albert B. *The Black Messiah*. New York, NY: Sheed and Ward, 1968.

Cleaver, Eldridge. *Soul on Ice*. New York, NY: McGraw-Hill, 1967.

Collier-Thomas, Bettye, and V. P. Franklin, eds. *Sisters in the Struggle: African American Women in the Civil Rights—Black Power Movement*. New York, NY: New York University Press, 2001.

Colton, Elizabeth. *The Jackson Phenomenon: The Man, the Power, and the Message*. New York, NY, 1989.

Cone, James H. *Black Theology and Black Power*. New York, NY: Seabury Press, 1969.

_____. "Martin and Malcolm on Nonviolence and Violence." *Phylon (1960-)* 49:3/4 (Autumn-Winter, 2001): 173-183.

Countryman, Matthew. *Up South: Civil Rights and Black Power in Philadelphia*. Philadelphia, PA: University of Pennsylvania Press, 2006.

Craig, Maxine Leeds. *Ain't I a Beauty Queen?: Black Women, Beauty, and the Politics of Race*. New York, NY: Oxford University Press, 2002.

Cruse, Harold. *The Crisis of Negro Intellectual*. New York, NY: Quill, 1984.

Davis, Angela Y. *Angela Davis: An Autobiography*. New York, NY: Random House, 1974.

DeCaro, Louis A. *On the Side of My People: A Religious Life of Malcolm X*. New York, NY: New York University Press, 1996.

Fanon, Frantz. *The Wretched of the Earth*. New York, NY: Grove Press, 1963.

Feldstein, Ruth. "'I Don't Trust You Anymore': Nina Simone, Culture, and Black Activism in the 1960s." *The Journal of American History* 91:4 (Mar., 2005): 1349-1379.

Frazier, E. Franklin. *The Negro Family in the United States*. Chicago, IL: The University of Chicago Press, 1939.

Gaines, Kevin K. *American Africans in Ghana: Black Expatriates and the Civil Rights Era*. Chapel Hill, NC: University of North Carolina Press, 2006.

Gayle, Addison. *The Black Aesthetic*. Garden City, NY: Doubleday, 1971.

Giddings, Paula. *When and Where I Enter: The Impact of Black Women on Race and Sex in America*. New York, NY: Bantam Books, 1984.

Glaude, Eddie S., Jr., ed. *Is It Nation Time?: Contemporary Essays on Black Power and Black Nationalism*. Chicago, IL: University of Chicago Press, 2002.

Guy-Sheftall, Beverly, ed. *Words of Fire: An Anthology of African-American Feminist Thought*. New York, NY: New Press, 1995.

Hacker, Andrew. *Two Nations: Black and White, Separate, Hostile, Unequal*. New York, NY, 1992.

Hall, Simon. "'On the Tail of the Panther': Black Power and the 1967 Convention of the National Conference for New Politics." *Journal of American Studies* 37:1 (Apr., 2003): 59-78.

Hampton, Henry, and Steve Fayer, eds. *Voices of Freedom: An Oral History of the Civil Rights Movement from the 1950s through the 1980s*. New York, NY: Bantam Books, 1990.

Harding, Vincent. "The Religion of Black Power" in *African American Religious Thought: An Anthology*. edited by Cornel West and Eddie S. Glaude, Jr., Louisville, KY: Westminster John Knox Press, 2003.

Harris, Daryl B. "The Logic of Black Urban Rebellions." *Journal of Black Studies* 28:3 (Jan., 1998): 368-385.

Harris, Jessica Christina. Evolutionary Black Nationalism: The Black Panther Party." *The Journal of Negro History* 85:3 (Summer, 2000): 162-174.

hooks, bell. *Talking Back: Thinking Feminist, Thinking Black*. Boston, MA: South End, 1989.

Horne, Gerald. *The Fire This Time: The Watts Uprising and the 1960s*. Charlottesville, VA: University Press of Virginia, 1995.

Jeffries, Judson L., ed. *Black Power in the Belly of the Beast*. Urbana, IL: University of Illinois Press, 2006.

Jones, Charles E., ed. *The Black Panther Party (Reconsidered)*. Baltimore, MD: Black Classic Press, 1998.

Jones, Gayl. *Corregidora*. New York, NY: Random House, 1975.

Joseph, Peniel E., ed. *The Black Power Movement: Rethinking the Civil Rights-Black Power Era*. New York, NY: Routledge, 2006.

_____. "Dashikis and Democracy: Black Studies, Student Activism, and the Black Power Movement." *The Journal of African American History* 88:2 (Spring, 2003): 182-203.

_____. "Revolution in Babylon: Stokely Carmichael and America in the 1960s." *Souls: A Critical Journal of Black Politics, Culture, and Society* 9 (October-December 2007): 281-301.

_____. *Waiting 'Til the Midnight Hour: A Narrative History of Black Power in America*. New York, NY: Henry Holt and Co., 2006.

Kelley, Robin D. G. *Freedom Dreams*. Boston, MA: Beacon Press Books, 2004.

Lawson, Steven F. *In Pursuit of Power: Southern Blacks and Electoral Politics, 1965-1982*. New York, NY: Columbia University Press, 1985.

Lazerow, Jama, and Yohuru Williams, eds. *In Search of the Black Panther Party: New Perspectives on a Revolutionary Movement*. Durham, NC: Duke University Press, 2006.

Lorde, Audre. *Zami, a New Spelling of My Name*. Watertown, MA: Persephone Press, 1982.

Martin, Waldo. *No Coward Soldiers: Black Cultural Politics and Postwar America*. Cambridge, MA: Harvard University Press, 2005.

Massey, Douglass S. and Nancy A. Denton. *American Apartheid: Segregation and the Making of the Underclass.* Cambridge, MA: Harvard University Press, 1993.

McKinnon, Jesse. *The Black Population: 2000.* Washington, DC: U.S. Department of Commerce, Economics and Statistics Administration, U.S. Census Bureau, 2001.

Moore, Leonard N. *Carl B. Stokes and the Rise of Black Political Power.* Urbana, IL: University of Illinois Press, 2002.

Morgan, Robin. *Sisterhood is Powerful: An Anthology of writings from the Women's Liberation Movement.* New York, NY: Random House, 1970.

Morrison, Toni. *The Bluest Eye: A Novel.* New York, NY: Rinehart and Winston, 1970.

_____, ed. *Race-Ing Justice, En-Gendering Power: Essays on Anita Hill, Clarence Thomas, and the Construction of Social Reality.* New York, NY, 1992.

_____. *Sula.* New York, NY: Knopf, 1973.

Moynihan, Daniel Patrick. *The Negro Family: The Case for National Action.* Washington, DC: U.S. Govt. Printing Office, 1965.

Nelson, William E., Jr., and Philip J. Meranto. *Electing Black Mayors: Political Action in the Black Community.* Columbus, OH: Ohio State University Press, 1977.

Ogbar, Jeffrey O. G. *Black Power: Radical Politics and African American Identity.* Baltimore, MD: Johns Hopkins University Press, 2004.

Ransby, Barbara. *Ella Baker and the Black Freedom Movement: A Radical Democratic Vision.* Chapel Hill, NC: University of North Carolina Press, 2003.

Remnick, David. *King of the World: Muhammad Ali and the Rise of an American Hero.* New York, NY: Random House, 1998.

Rogers, Mary Beth. *Barbara Jordan: American Hero.* New York, NY, 1998.

Rooks, Noliwe. *Hair Raising: Beauth, Culture, and African American Women.* New Brunswick, NJ: Rutgers University Press, 1996.

_____. *White Money/Black Power: The Surprising History of African American Studies and the Crisis of Race in Higher Education.* Boston, MA: Beacon Press, 2006.

Salaam, Kalamu ya. "Black Arts Movement." In *The Oxford Companion to African American Literature.* edited by William L. Andrews, Frances Smith Foster, Trudier Harris, New York, NY: Oxford University Press, 1997.

Seale, Bobby, and Huey P. Newton. *Seize the Time: The Story of the Black Panther Party and Huey P. Newton.* New York, NY: Random House, 1970.

Self, Robert. *American Babylon: Race and the Struggle for Postwar Oakland.* Princeton, NJ: Princeton University Press, 2003.

_____. "'To Plan Our Liberation': Black Power and the Politics of Place in Oakland, California, 1965-1977." *Journal of Urban History* 26:6 (September 2000): 759-92.

Shakur, Assata. *Assata: An Autobiography.* Westport, CT: L. Hill, 1987.

Shange, Ntozake. *For Colored Girls who have Considered Suicide When The Rainbow is Enuf.* New York, NY: MacMillan, 1977.

Shannon, Sandra. *The Dramatic Vision of August Wilson.* Washington, DC: Howard University Press, 1995.

Sinha, Manisha and Penny Von Eschen, eds. *Contested Democracy: Freedom, Race, and Power in American History.* New York, NY: Columbia University Press, 2007.

Smethurst, James Edward. *The Black Arts Movement: Literary Nationalism in the 1960s and 1970s.* Chapel Hill, NC: University of North Carolina Press, 2005.

Springer, Kimberly. *Living for the Revolution: Black Feminist Organizations, 1968-1980.* Durham, NC: Duke University Press, 2005.

_____, ed. *Still Lifting, Still Climbing: Contemporary African American Women's Activism.* New York, NY: New York University Press, 1999.

Theoharis, Jeanne, and Komozi Woodard, eds. *Freedom North: Black Freedom Struggles Outside the South, 1940-1980.* New York, NY: Palgrave Macmillan, 2003.

Thibodeaux, Mary Roger. *A Black Nun Looks at Black Power.* New York, NY: Sheed & Ward, 1972.

Tyson, Timothy B. *Radio Free Dixie: Robert F. Williams and the Roots of Black Power.* Chapel Hill, NC: University of North Carolina Press, 1999.

_____. "Robert F. Williams, "Black Power," and the Roots of the African American Freedom Struggle." *The Journal of American History* 85:2 (Sep., 1998): 540-570.

Umoja, Akinyele. "1964: The Beginning of the End of Nonviolence in the Mississippi Freedom Movement." *Radical History Review* 85 (Winter, 2003): 201-226.

_____. "The Ballot and the Bullet: A Comparative Analysis of Armed Resistance in the Civil Rights Movement." *Journal of Black Studies,* 29:4 (Mar., 1999): 558-578.

Van Deburg, William L. *New Day in Babylon: The Black Power Movement and American Culture, 1965-1975.* Chicago, IL: University of Chicago Press, 1992.

Walker, Alice. *The Color Purple.* New York, NY: Washington Square Press, 1982.

_____. *In Search of Our Mothers' Gardens: Womanist Prose.* San Diego, CA: Harcourt Brace Jovanovich, 1983.

_____. *Meridian.* New York, NY: Harcourt Brace Jovanovich, 1976.

_____. *The Third Life of Grange Copeland.* New York, NY: Harcourt, Brace, Jovanovic, 1977, c1970.

Wallace, Michele. *Black Macho and the Myth of the Superwoman.* New York, NY: Dial Press, 1979.

Wendt, Simon. "God, Gandhi, and Guns" The African American Freedom Struggle in Tuscaloosa, Alabama, 1964-1965." *The Journal of African American History* 89:1 (Winter, 2004): 36-56.

West, Cornel. *Race Matters.* Boston, MA, 1993.

White, Deborah Gray. *Too Heavy a Load: Black Women in Defense of Themselves, 1894-1994.* New York, NY: W. W. Norton, 1998.

Williams Rhonda Y. "Exploring Babylon and Unveiling the 'Mother of Harlots'." *American Quarterly* 57 (2005): 297-304.

_____. *The Politics of Public Housing: Black Women's Struggles Against Urban Inequality.* New York, NY: Oxford University Press, 2004.

Williams, Robert F. *Negroes with Guns.* New York, NY: Marzani & Munsell, 1962.

Williams, Yohuru. *Black Politics/White Power: Civil Rights, Black Power, and the Black Panthers in New Haven.* St. James, NY: Brandywine Press, 2000.

Wing, Adrien Katherine, ed. *Critical Race Feminism: A Reader.* New York, NY: New York University Press, 1997.

Wolters, Raymond. *The Burden of Brown: Thirty Years of School Desegregation.* Knoxville: University of Tennessee Press, 1984.

Woodard, Komozi. *A Nation Within a Nation: Amiri Baraka (LeRoi Jones) and Black Power Politics.* Chapel Hill, NC: University of North Carolina Press, 1999.

Wright, Richard. *Black Power: A Record of Reactions in a Land of Pathos.* New York, NY: Harper, 1954.

_____. *The Colour Curtain: A Report on the Bandung Conference.* London, UK: D. Dobson, 1956.

X, Malcolm. *Autobiography of Malcolm X*, with the assistance of Alex Haley. New York, NY: Ballantine Books, 1999.

Chapter 22: Progress and Poverty, 1980-2000

Barker, Lucius J. *Our Time Has Come: A Delegate's Diary of Jesse Jackson's 1984 Presidential Campaign.* Urbana, IL: University of Illinois, 1988.

Barrett, Laurence I. *Gambling with History: Ronald Reagan in the White House.* Garden City, NY: Doubleday, 1983.

Bell, Derrick. *And We Are Not Saved: The Elusive Quest for Racial Justice.* New York, NY: Basic Books, 1987.

Bositis, David A. *Black Elected Officials: A Statistical Summary, 1993-1997.* Washington, DC: Joint Center for Political and Economic Studies, 1998.

_____. *Changing of the Guard: Generational Differences among Black Elected Officials.* Washington, DC: Joint Center for Political and Economic Studies, 2001.

_____. *The Congressional Black Caucus in the 103rd Congress.* Washington, DC: Joint Center for Political and Economic Studies, 1994.

Billingsley, Andrew. *Climbing Jacob's Ladder: The Enduring Legacy of African American Families.* New York, NY: Simon and Schuster, 1993.

Carter, Dan T. *From George Wallace to Newt Gingrich: Race in the Conservative Counterrevolution, 1963-1994.* Baton Rouge, LA: Louisiana State University Press, 1996.

Cavanagh, Thomas E. *The Impact of the Black Electorate.* Washington, DC: Joint Center for Political Studies, 1984.

_____. *Inside Black America: The Message of the Black Vote in the 1984 Elections.* Washington, DC: Joint Center for Political Studies, 1985.

Cavanagh, Thomas E., and Lorn S. Foster. *Jesse Jackson's Campaign: The Primaries and Caucuses.* Washington, DC: Joint Center for Political Studies, 1984.

Colton, Elizabeth. *The Jackson Phenomenon: The Man, the Power, and the Message.* New York, NY: Doubleday, 1989.

Cose, Ellis. *The Rage of a Privileged Class.* New York, NY: HarperCollins, 1993.

Dallek, Robert. *Ronald Reagan: The Politics of Symbolism.* Cambridge, MA: Harvard University Press, 1999.

Dawson, Michael C. *Behind the Mule: Race and Class in African American Politics.* Princeton, NJ: Princeton University Press, 1994.

Drake W. Avon and Robert D. Holsworth. *Affirmative Action and the Stalled Quest for Black Progress.* Urbana, IL: University of Illinois Press, 1996.

Dugger, Ronnie. *On Reagan: The Man and His Presidency.* New York, NY: McGraw-Hill, 1983.

Dyson, Michael Eric. *Between God and Gangsta Rap: Bearing Witness to Black Culture.* New York, NY: Oxford University Press, 1996.

Edsall, Thomas Byrne, and Mary D. Edsall. *Chain Reaction: The Impact of Race, Rights, and Taxes on American Politics.* New York, NY: Norton, 1991.

Forman, Murray and Mark Anthony Neal, eds. *That's the Joint!: The Hip-Hop Studies Reader.* New York, NY: Routledge, 2004.

Franklin, John Hope. *The Color Line: Legacy for the Twenty-First Century.* Columbia, MO: University of Missouri, 1993.

_____. *Mirror to America: the Autobiography of John Hope Franklin.* New York, NY: Farrar, Straus and Giroux, 2005.

_____. *Racial Equality in America.* Chicago, IL: University of Chicago Press, 1976.

Glasgow, Douglas G. *The Black Underclass: Poverty, Unemployment, and Entrapment of Ghetto Youth.* New York, NY: Random House, 1981.

Gooding-Williams, Robert, ed. *Reading Rodney King: Reading Urban Uprising.* New York, NY: Routledge, 1993.

Graham, Lawrence Otis. *Our Kind of People: Inside America's Black Urban Class.* New York, NY: HarperCollins, 1999.

Hacker, Andrew. *Two Nations: Black and White, Separate, Hostile, Unequal.* New York, NY: Ballantine Books, 1995.

Henry, Charles P. *Jesse Jackson: The Search for Common Ground.* Oakland, CA, 1991.

Hill, Anita. *Speaking Truth to Power.* New York, NY: Doubleday, 1997.

_____ and Emma Coleman Jordan, eds. *Race, Gender, and Power in America: The Legacy of the Hill-Thomas Hearings.* New York, NY: Oxford University Press, 1995.

Hochschild, Jennifer L. *Thirty Years after Brown.* Washington, DC: Joint Center for Political Studies, 1985.

King, William M. "The Reemerging Revolutionary Consciousness of the Reverend Dr. Martin Luther King, Jr., 1965-1968." *The Journal of Negro History* 71:1/4 (Autumn-Winter, 1986): 1-22.

Kitwana, Bakari. *The Hip Hop Generation: Young Blacks and the Crisis in American Culture.* New York, NY: Basic Civitas, 2003.

Kozel, Jonathan. *Savage Inequalities: Children in America's Schools.* New York, NY: Crown, 1991.

Marable, Manning. *Beyond Black and White: Transforming African-American Politics.* New York, NY: Verso, 1995.

Massey Douglas S. and Nancy A. Denton. *American Apartheid: Segregation and the Making of the Underclass.* Cambridge, MA: Harvard University Press, 1993.

Means, Howard. *Colin Powell: Soldier/Statesman-Statesman/Soldier.* New York, NY: Donald I. Fine, 1992.

Morrison, Toni, ed. *Race-Ing Justice, En-Gendering Power: Essays on Anita Hill, Clarence Thomas, and the Construction of Social Reality.* New York, NY: Pantheon, 1992.

National Urban League, *The State of Black America.* New York, NY: National Urban League, Volumes from 1979 to 2000.

Phillips, Kevin. *The Politics of Rich and Poor: Wealth and the American Electorate in the Reagan Aftermath.* New York, NY: Random House, 1990.

Powell, Colin. *My American Journey;* with Joseph Persico. rev. ed. New York, NY: Ballantine Books, 2003.

President's Initiative on Race (U.S.). Advisory Board. *One America in the 21st Century: Forging a New Future: The President's Initiative on Race: The Advisory Board's Report to the President.* Washington, DC: The Initiative, 1998.

Reed, Adolph, Jr,. *The Jesse Jackson Phenomenon: The Crisis in Afro-American Politics.* New Haven, CT: Yale University Press, 1986.

Rivlin, Gary. *Fire on the Prairie: Chicago's Harold Washington and the Politics of Race.* New York, NY: Henry Holt, 1992.

Rogers, Mary Beth. *Barbara Jordan: American Hero.* New York, NY: Bantam Books, 1998.

Rubio, Philip F. *A History of Affirmative Action, 1619-2000.* Jackson, MS: University Press of Mississippi, 2001.

Shannon, Sandra. *The Dramatic Vision of August Wilson.* Washington, DC: Howard University Press, 1995.

Sowell, Thomas. *Race and Culture: A World View.* New York, NY: Basic Books, 1994.

Swain, Carol M. *Black Faces, Black Interests: The Representation of African Americans in Congress.* enlarged ed. Lanham, MD: University Press of America, 2006.

Tate, Katherine. *From Protest to Politics: The New Black Voters in American Elections.* enlarged ed. Cambridge, MA: Harvard University Press, 1994.

Thermstrom, Stephen and Abigail Themstrom. *America in Black and White: One Nation, Indivisible.* New York, NY: Simon & Schuster, 1997.

Wacquant, Loïc J. D., and William Julius Wilson. "The Cost of Racial and Class Exclusion in the Inner City," *Annals of the American Academy of Political and Social Science*, vol. 501, (Jan. 1989): 8-25.

West, Cornel. *Race Matters.* New York, NY: Vintage Books, 2001.

Wilson, William Julius. "The Black Community in the 1980s: Questions of Race, Class, and Public Policy." *Annals of the American Academy of Political and Social Science* 454: America as a Multicultural Society (Mar., 1981): 26-41.

_____. *The Declining Significance of Race: Blacks and Changing American Institutions.* 2nd ed. Chicago, IL: University of Chicago Press, 1980.

_____. *More Than Just Race: Being Black and Poor in the Inner City.* New York, NY: W. W. Norton & Company, 2009.

_____. *The Truly Disadvantaged: The Inner City, the Underclass, and Public Policy.* Chicago: University of Chicago Press, 1987.

_____. *When Work Disappears: The World of the New Urban Poor.* New York, NY: Knopf, 1996.

Chapter 23: Perspectives on the Present, Since 2000

Alim, H. Samy, Awad Ibrahim, and Alastair Pennycook, eds. *Global Linguistic Flows: Hip Hop Cultures, Youth Identities, and the Politics of Language.* New York, NY: Routledge, 2009.

"Black Election: 2000." *The Black Scholar* 31:2 (Summer 2001).

Brinkley, Douglas. *The Great Deluge: Hurricane Katrina, New Orleans, and the Mississippi Gulf Coast.* New York, NY: Morrow, 2006.

Cohen, Cathy J. *The Boundaries of Blackness: AIDS and the Breakdown of Black Politics.* Chicago, IL: University of Chicago Press, 1999.

Cole, David. *No Equal Justice: Race and Class in the American Criminal Justice System.* New York, NY: New Press 1999.

Covin, David. "The Length of Memory: The Black Population and the Presidential Election of 2000." *Black Scholar* 31:2 (Jun. 2001): 33-37.

Denton, Robert E., Jr., ed. *The 2004 Presidential Campaign: A Communication Perspective.* Lanham, MD: Rowman & Littlefield Publishers, Inc., 2005.

Elam, Harry J., Jr., and Kennell Jackson, eds. *Black Cultural Traffic: Crossroads in Global Performance and Popular Culture.* with a foreword by Tricia Rose. Ann Arbor, MI: The University of Michigan Press, 2005.

Falk, Gene, Thomas Gabe, and Maggie McCarty. *Hurricane Katrina: Social-Demographic Characteristics of Impacted Areas.* Washington, DC: Congressional Research Service, Library of Congress, November, 2005.

Frey, William H. "New Black Migration Patterns in the United States: Are they Affected by Recent Immigration," in *Immigration and Opportunity: Race, Ethnicity, and Employment in the United States*, edited by Frank D. Bean and Stephanie Bell-Rose, New York, NY: Russell Sage Foundation, 1999.

_____. "The New Great Migration: Black Americans' Return to the South, 1965-2000." The Brookings Institution, May 2004.

Gates, Henry Louis, Jr. *America Behind the Color Line: Dialogues with African Americans.* New York, NY: Warner Books, 2004.

_____. *Finding Oprah's Roots: Finding Your Own.* New York, NY: Crown Publishers, 2007.

_____. *In Search of Our Roots: How 19 Extraordinary African Americans Reclaimed Their Past.* New York, NY: Crown Publishers, 2009.

Gilbert, Dorie J. and Ednita M. Wright, eds. *African American Women and HIV/AIDS: Critical Responses.* Westport, CT: Praeger Publishers, 2003.

Henry, Charles P. "Is Barack Obama the End of White Politics?" *Black Scholar* 38:4 (Winter 2008): 6-10.

Kelso, Tony and Brian Cogan, eds. *Mosh the Polls: Youth Voters, Popular Culture, and Democratic Engagement.* Lanham, MD: Lexington Books, 2008.

Kennedy, Randall. *Race, Crime, and the Law.* New York, NY: Pantheon Books, 1997.

Lawson, Steven F., ed. *One America in the 21st century: the Report of President Bill Clinton's Initiative on Race*, forward by John Hope Franklin. New Haven, CT: Yale University Press, 2009.

Lee, Philip R. and Carroll L. Estes. *The Nation's Health.* Sudbury, MA: Jones and Bartlett Pub., 2003.

Loury, Glenn C. "Why Are So Many Americans in Prison? Race and the Transformation of Criminal Justice." *Boston Review*, July/August 2007. http://Bostonreview.net/BR32.4/article_loury.php

Mack, Kenneth W. and Jim Chen. "Barack Obama before He Was a Rising Political Star." *The Journal of Blacks in Higher Education* 45 (Autumn, 2004): 98-101.

McKinnon, Jesse. *The Black Population in the United States: March 2002, Current Population Reports, Series P20-541.* Washington, DC: U. S. Census Bureau, 2003.

Mitchell, Tony, ed. *Global Noise: Rap and Hip-Hop Outside the USA.* Middletown, CT: Wesleyan University Press, 2001.

Morgan, Marcyliena H. *The Real HipHop: Battling for Knowledge, Power, and Respect in the LA Underground.* Durham, NC: Duke University Press, 2009.

Niven, Steven J. *Barack Obama: A Pocket Biography*, introduction by Henry Louis Gates, Jr., New York, NY: Oxford University Press, 2009.

Obama, Barack. *The Audacity of Hope: Thoughts on Reclaiming the American Dream.* New York, NY: Crown Publishers, 2006.

_____. *Dreams from My Father: A Story of Race and Inheritance.* New York, NY: Times Books, 1995.

Patterson, Orlando. *The Ordeal of Integration: Progress and Resentment in America's "Racial" Crisis.* Washington, DC: Civitas/Counterpoint, 1997.

Persons, Georgia A., ed. *The Expanding Boundaries of Black Politics.* New Brunswick, NJ: Transaction Publishers, 2007.

Piven, Frances Fox, Lorraine C. Minnite, and Margaret Groarke. *Keeping Down the Black Vote: Race and Demobilization of American Voters.* New York, NY: New Press/W. W. Norton, 2009.

Price, Emmett George. *Hip Hop Culture.* Santa Barbara, CA: ABC-CLIO, Inc., 2006.

Robinson, Randall. *The Debt: What America Owes to Blacks.* New York, NY: Dutton, 2000.

Smedley, Brian D., Adrienne Y. Stith, and Alan R. Nelson, eds. *Unequal Treatment: Confronting Racial and Ethnic Disparities in Health Care.* Washington, DC: The National Academies Press, 2003.

Steele, Shelby. *Content of Our Character: A New Vision of Race in America.* New York, NY: Harper Perennial, 1991.

Thomas, Evan. *"A Long Time Coming": The Inspiring, Combative 2008 Campaign and the Historic Election of Barack Obama.* New York, NY: PublicAffairs, 2009.

Touré. "I Live in the Hip Hop Nation (*The New York Times*, 1999)." in *Never Drank the Kool-Aid: Essays by Touré.* New York, NY: Picador, 2006.

Troutt, David Dante. *After the Storm: Black Intellectuals Explore the Meaning of Hurricane Katrina.* New York, NY: The New Press, 2006.

United States Senate Committee on Homeland Security and Governmental Affairs. *Hurricane Katrina: A Nation Still Unprepared.* May, 2006.

Walton, Jr., Hanes. "The Disenfranchisement of the African American Voter in the 2000 Presidential Election: The Silence of the Winner and Loser." *Black Scholar* 31:2 (Jun. 2001): 21-24.

_____, Josephine A. V. Allen, Sherman C. Puckett, and Donald R. Deskins, Jr. "The Red and Blue State Divide in Black and White: The Historic 2008 Election of President Barack Obama." *Black Scholar* 38:4 (Winter 2008): 19-30.

Walters, Ronald W. *White Nationalism, Black Interests: Conservative Public Policy and the Black Community.* Detroit, MI: Wayne State University Press, 2003.

Waters, Mary. *Black Identities: West Indian Immigrant Dreams and American Realities.* New York, NY: Russell Sage Foundation, 1999.

Williams, David R. "The Health of Men: Structured Inequalities and Opportunities." *American Journal of Public Health* 93:5 (May, 2003): 724-731.

Williams, Patricia. *Seeing a Color-Blind Future: the Paradox of Race.* New York, NY: Noonday Press, 1998.

Wilson, William Julius. *The Declining Significance of Race,* Chicago, IL: Chicago University Press, 2002, c1978.

_____. *More Than Just Race: Being Black and Poor in the Inner City.* New York, NY: W. W. Norton & Co., 2009.

_____. *The Truly Disadvantaged: The Inner City, the Underclass, and Public Policy.* Chicago, IL: Chicago University Press, 1990, c1987.

Text Credits

Page 8: Courtesy of The Alpine Group.

Page 26: Courtesy of Joseph E. Harris.

Page 49: Copyright © 2009 www.quthentichistory.com; **56:** from Brinkley, *American History* 12/e. Copyright © 2007 McGraw-Hill Companies, Inc. Used with permission.

Page 72: from Philip Morgan, *Slave Counterpoint: Black Culture in the Eighteenth Century Chesapeake & Lowcountry*, p. 81. Published for the Omohundro Institute of Early American History and Culture. Copyright © 1998 by the University of North Carolina Press. Used by permission of the publisher; **73:** from Philip Morgan, *Slave Counterpoint: Black Culture in the Eighteenth Century Chesapeake & Lowcountry*, p. 81. Published for the Omohundro Institute of Early American History and Culture. Copyright © 1998 by the University of North Carolina Press. Used by permission of the publisher; **82:** Copyright © John Snead.

Page 96: Map 2, p. xxiv from Robin Winks, *The Blacks in Canada*. Copyright © 1997. Reprinted by permission of McGill-Queen's University Press.

Page 131: from Michael Siegel, Rutgers Cartography. *In Motion: The African-American Migration Experience*, Schomburg Center Online Experience. Copyright © New York Public Library. Used with permission; **136:** from Michael Siegel, Rutgers Cartography. *In Motion: The African-American Migration Experience*, Schomburg Center Online Experience. Copyright © New York Public Library. Used with permission; **134:** © J.B. Bird. Reprinted by permission. www.johnhorse.com; **141:** from Brinkley, American History 12/e. Copyright © 2007 McGraw-Hill Companies, Inc. Used with permission.

Page 200: from Michael Siegel, Rutgers Cartography. *In Motion: The African-American Migration Experience*, Schomburg Center Online Experience. Copyright © New York Public Library. Used with permission.

Page 287: Copyright National Association of Colored Women; **Page 309:** from Michael Siegel, Rutgers Cartography. *In Motion: The African-American Migration Experience*, Schomburg Center Online Experience. Copyright © New York Public Library. Used with permission.

Page 388: from Michael Siegel, Rutgers Cartography. *In Motion: The African-American Migration Experience*, Schomburg Center Online Experience. Copyright © New York Public Library. Used with permission; **402:** From Countee Cullen "Yet Do I Marvel." Copyright held by Amistad Research Center, Tulane University. Administered by Thompson and Thompson, Brooklyn, NY. Used with permission; **403:** Langston Hughes, "The Negro and the Racial Mountain" excerpt from article published in The Nation, June 1926. Copyright 1926 The Nation. Used with permission; **405:** Reprinted with the permission of Scribner, a division of Simon & Schuster, Inc. from Alain Locke, Preface to *The New Negro*. Copyright 1925 by Albert & Charles Boni, Inc. Introduction copyright © 1962 by Macmillan Publishing Company. All rights reserved.

Page 425: Evaluation of The New Deal from Roy Wilkins, "The Roosevelt Record," *The Crisis* vol. 47, Nov. 1940. Copyright 1940 The Crisis Publishing Co., Inc. The McGraw-Hill Companies wishes to thank the Crisis Publishing Co., Inc., the publisher of the magazine of the National Association for the Advancement of Colored People, for the use of the materials from "The Crisis" magazine; **431:** Life in the CCC from Luther C. Wandall, "A Negro in the CCC," *The Crisis* Vol. 42, August 1935. Copyright 1935 The Crisis Publishing Co., Inc. The McGraw-Hill Companies wishes to thank the Crisis Publishing Co., Inc., the publisher of the magazine of the National Association for the Advancement of Colored People, for the use of the materials from "The Crisis" magazine.

Photo Credits

Granger Collection, New York; **158:** The Granger Collection, New York; **159:** William Matthew Prior, Three Sisters of the Copeland Family, 1854. Photography © 2011 Museum of Fine Arts, Boston; **162:** Courtesy of the Historical Society of Pennsylvania; **166:** Library Company of Philadelphia; **168:** The Granger Collection, New York; **169:** Julien Hudson, Self-portrait, 1839. Courtesy of Louisiana State Museum; **173:** Robert S. Duncanson, Cottage at Pass Opposite Ben Lomand, 1866. North Carolina Central University Art Museum; **179:** Library of Congress, Prints & Photographs Division, [LC-USZ62-42044]; **180:** Virginia Historical Society; **184L:** The Granger Collection, New York; **184R:** The Granger Collection, New York; **185:** Used with Permission of Documenting the American South, The University of North Carolina at Chapel Hill Libraries; **188:** Library of Congress, Prints & Photographs Division, [LC-DIG-ppmsca-08978]; **189TL:** J.R. Eyerman/Time & Life Pictures/Getty Images; **189TR:** Henry Highland Garnet, c. 1881. Albumen silver print. 11.5 cm × 9.1 cm (4 1/2″ × 3 9/16″). National Portrait Gallery, Smithsonian Institution/Art Resource, NY; **189 B:** Library and Archives Canada; **192:** Library of Congress, Prints & Photographs Division, [LC-USZ62-10320]; **200:** Robert Duncanson, View of Cincinnati, Ohio, from Covington, Kentucky. Cincinnati Museum Center-Cincinnati Historical Society Library; **203:** Library of Congress, Prints & Photographs Division, [LC-USZ62-7816]; **206:** Library of Congress, Prints & Photographs Division, [LC-USZ62-79305]; **208:** Courtesy of the Massachusetts Historical Society; **211:** Library of Congress, Prints & Photographs Division, [LC-DIG-cwpb-01005]; **213:** Mrs. M.M. Pabor/Library of Congress Prints & Photographs Division, [LC-USZC4-1526]; **218:** Library of Congress, Prints & Photographs Division, [LC-DIG-cwpb-04294]; **222:** Moorland-Spingarn Research Center, Howard University; **225:** The New York Public Library/Art Resource, NY; **226:** The Granger Collection, New York; **231:** Schomburg Center for Research in Black Culture, The New York Public Library, New York, NY. Photo: Schomburg/Art Resource, NY; **233:** Howard University Gallery of Art, Washington D.C.; **235:** Harper's Weekly, November 16, 1867. Library of Congress, Prints & Photographs Division, [LC-USZ62-47205]; **239:** The Granger Collection, New York; **244:**

Library of Congress, Prints & Photographs Division, [LC-DIG-ppmsca-17564]; **248:** Library of Congress, Prints & Photographs Division [LC-DIG-pga-02595]; **254:** The Granger Collection, New York; **256:** National Archives; **257:** Two Members of the Ku Klux Klan (1866-71) (b/w photo) by American Photographer (19th century), Dallas Historical Society, Texas, USA/The Bridgeman Art Library; **260:** Amistad Foundation, Wadsworth Atheneum, Hartford CT; **262:** The Granger Collection, New York; **266:** The Library of Congress; **268:** Collier's, November 1898; **269:** Library of Congress, Prints & Photographs Division, [LC-USZ62-128619]; **270:** Plessy vs. Ferguson, Judgment, Decided May 18, 1886; Records of the Supreme Court of the United States; Record Group 267; *Plessy v. Ferguson*, 163, #15248, National Archives; **273:** Urban Archives, Paley Library, Temple University; **278:** National Archives; **283:** Library of Congress, Prints & Photographs Division, [LC-USZC4-4647]; **287:** National Museum of American History, Smithsonian Institution, Washington, D.C.; **289:** Amistad Foundation, Wadsworth Atheneum, Hartford CT; **292:** The Library of Congress; **294:** Library of Congress, Prints & Photographs Division, [LC-USZ62-2248]; **297:** Library of Congress, Prints & Photographs Division, [LC-USZ62-119898]; **300:** Schomburg Center for Research in Black Culture, The New York Public Library, New York, NY. Photo: Schomburg/Art Resource, NY; **301:** W. E. B. Dubois in the office of The Crisis. Photographs and Prints Division, Schomburg Center for Research in Black Culture, The New York Public Library, New York, NY, U.S.A. Photo: Schomburg Center/Art Resource, NY; **303:** Founding members of the Niagara Movement at the Niagara Conference, 1905. W.E.B. Du Bois appears in the middle row, second from right. Photographs and Prints Division, Schomburg Center for Research in Black Culture, The New York Public Library, New York, NY, U.S.A. Photo: Schomburg Center/Art Resource, NY; **307:** Photo: 1168482. Kansas State Historical Society; **310:** Schomburg Center for Research in Black Culture, The New York Public Library, New York, NY. Photo: Schomburg/Art Resource, NY; **311:** Courtesy of Hampton University Museum; **314:** The Walker Collection of A'Lelia Perry Bundles, Alexandria, VA; **319:** The Library of Congress; **320:**

Library of Congress, Photographs & Prints Division, [LC-USZ62-84496]; **325:** Library of Congress, Photographs & Prints Division, [LC-USZ6-1823]; **327:** Schomburg Center for Research in Black Culture, The New York Public Library, New York, NY. Photo: Schomburg/Art Resource, NY; **330:** The Ohio Historical Center, Columbus, OH; **335:** National Archives; **336:** National Archives; **338:** Horace Pippin, Dog Fight Over the Trenches, 1935. Oil on canvas, 18 × 33 1/8 inches. Gift of Joseph H. Hirshhorn, 1966. (66.4071) Photography by Lee Stalsworth. Hirshhorn Museum and Sculpture Garden, Smithsonian Institution; **340:** National Archives; **341:** Scott's Official History of the Negro in the Great War; **348:** National Archives; **351:** Library of Congress, Photographs & Prints Division, [LC-USZC4-4734]; **355:** Bettmann/Corbis; **356:** Library of Congress, Photographs & Prints Division, [LC-USZ62-50724]; **360:** Jun Fujita/Chicago History Museum/Getty Images; **363:** Schomburg Center for Research in Black Culture, The New York Public Library, New York, NY. Photo: Schomburg/Art Resource, NY; **365:** Schomburg Center for Research in Black Culture, The New York Public Library, New York, NY. Photo: Schomburg/Art Resource, NY; **367:** Schomburg Center for Research in Black Culture, The New York Public Library, New York, NY. Photo: Schomburg/Art Resource, NY; **371:** Christie's Images/Corbis; **376TL:** Schomburg Center for Research in Black Culture, The New York Public Library, New York, NY. Photo: Schomburg/Art Resource, NY; **376TR:** Used with Permission of Documenting the American South, The University of North Carolina at Chapel Hill Libraries; **376 BL:** Library of Congress, Photographs & Prints Division, [LC-USZ62-84496]; **376BR:** Library of Congress, Photographs & Prints Division, [LC-USZ62-79903]; **378:** Schomburg Center for Research in Black Culture, The New York Public Library, New York, NY. Photo: Schomburg/Art Resource, NY; **380:** Lois Mailou Jones, *Les Fetiches* 1938. Oil on linen, 53.3 × 64.7 cm. Museum Purchase made possible by Mrs. N.H. Green, Dr. R. Harlan, and Francis Musgrave. National Museum of American Art, Smithsonian Institution; **383:** Frank Driggs Collection/Hulton Archive/Getty Images; **386:** Michael Ochs Archives/Getty Images; **387:** Underwood & Underwood/Corbis;

390: Courtesy of Main Spring Press; **392:** Frank Driggs Collection/Hulton Archive/Getty Images; **394:** The New York Public Library/Art Resource, NY; **397:** Maryland Historical Society; **399:** Corbis; **402:** Corbis; **404:** Beinecke Library; **408:** Christie's Images/Corbis; **409:** Aaron Douglas, Rise shine for thy light has come! Howard University Art Gallery, Washington, DC; **410:** Hayden, Palmer (1893-1973), Nous Quatre à Paris (We Four in Paris), c. 1930. Watercolor and pencil on paper, h. 21 3/4, w. 18 1/8 in. (55.2 × 46 cm). Purchase, Joseph H. Hazen Foundation Inc. Gift, 1975. (1975.125). The Metropolitan Museum of Art, New York, NY. Photo © The Metropolitan Museum of Art/Art Resource, NY; **411:** Archibald Motley, *Saturday Night*, 1935. Howard University Art Gallery, Washington, D.C.; **417:** Bettmann/Corbis; **420:** Margaret Bourke-White/Time/Life/Getty Images; **426:** Library of Congress, Prints & Photographs Division, [LC-USZ62-107174]; **428:** Bettmann/Corbis; **430:** John Vachon/Library of Congress, Prints & Photographs Division, [LC-USF34-008341-C]; **435:** Leo Russell/The Library of Congress; **438:** Bettmann/Corbis; **441:** National Archives; **442:** William H. Johnson (1901-1970), *Going to Church*, c. 1940-1941. Oil on burlap, 38 1/8 × 45 1/2 in. Smithsonian American Art Museum, Washington, DC/Art Resource, NY; **448:** Walter Sanders//Time Life Pictures/Getty Images; **449:** The Library of Congress; **453:** Schomburg Center for Research in Black Culture, The New York Public Library, New York, NY. Photo: Schomburg/Art Resource, NY; **454:** "Why Should We March?" March on Washington fliers, 1941. A. Philip Randolph Papers, Manuscript Division. Courtesy of the A. Philip Randolph Institute, Washington, D.C. The Library of Congress; **457:** National Archives; **459:** Bettmann/Corbis; **461:** National Archives; **465:** Library of Congress, Prints & Photographs Division, [LC-USZC4-2328]; **467L:** Library of Congress, Prints & Photographs Division, FSA/OWI Collection, [LC-USW3-034282-C]; **467R:** The Library of Congress; **469:** Library of Congress, Prints & Photographs Division, [LC-USE6-D-001485]; **473:** Library of Congress, Prints & Photographs Division, [LC-USZC4-4733; 476: Ed Clark/LIFE Magazine/Getty Images; 481: Museum of the City of New York; 484: Lawrence Jacob, The Migration Series, Panel no. 1: During World War I

Index

AAA (Agricultural Adjustment Administration), 429–430
AARP (American Association of Retired Persons), 613
AASS (American Anti-Slavery Society) (1833), 187
Abbott, Anderson, 222
Abbott, Robert S., 331
Abernathy, Ralph, 515, 517, 523, *527*
Abiel Smith School, 174
abolition movement, 86–87
    activities in North, 185–189
    after American Revolution, 96–99
    antislavery agendas, 190–193
    black abolitionists, 185–190
    black colonization, 124–126
    black newspapers, 189
    black response, 197–198
    dissatisfaction with federal policy, 205
    legislation in North, 96–97, 204–205
    Lincoln and, 210
    militancy of, 190–191
    North v. South, 98–100
    opposition to, 99–102, 194–197
    during Reconstruction, 237–238
    in South, 195–196
    women in, 187–188, 192
Abraham Lincoln Brigade, 487
Abyssinian Baptist Church, 366, 488, 605
Academy Awards, 600
ACHR (Alabama Christian Movement for Human Rights), 522
ACS (American Colonization Society), 126, 179–180, 182–183
actors, African American. *See* motion pictures; theater; specific actors
Adams, John (black teacher), 174
Adams, John (president), 85, 86, 87, 113, 114, 119
Adams, John Quincy, 197
Address to the Negroes of the State of New York, An (Hammon), 118–119
Advisory Board of the President's Initiative on Race, 608–610, *610*
affluence
    of free blacks, *166*, 169
    during Reconstruction, 254
AFL. *See* American Federation of Labor
AFL (American Federation of Labor), 349
AFL-CIO, 544, 596, 608
Afno (Hausa), 5, 17–18
Africa, 3m. *See also specific countries*
    African-American attention on, 486–487
    art of, 4–5, *5*, 18, *18, 19, 20*

artisanry of, 5–6
colonization movement, 124–126, 180–183
conquistadors in, 23–24
delegations to UN, 488
early commercial networks, 6–9
early states of, 12–21
economic life, 6–9
family structure, 9–11
independence movements, 554–555
partition of, 275
resources of, 275
slavery in, 9–12
society and culture, 15–20
Trans-Sahara trade routes, 7m, 7–9
after WWI, 343–344
Afric-American Female Intelligence Society, 187
African Americans in armed services. *See* military service; specific wars and branches of service
African and African American Research, 634
African Baptist Church, 111
African Blood Brotherhood, 369
African Free School, 111–112, 173–174
African Institution of Philadelphia, 125–126
African Masonic Lodge, 110–111, 116, *117*
African Meeting House, 111
African Methodist Episcopal (AME) Church, 109–110, 175–178, 240, 251, 274, 637–638
African migrants, 631–633
African National Congress (ANC), 606
African School, 111
African Slavery in America (Paine), 87
Africanus, Leo, 16
Afro-Caribbeans, 366–368, 631–633, 632m
Agassiz, Louis, 164
Agricultural Adjustment Act (1933), 419
Agricultural Adjustment Administration (AAA), 429–430
agriculture. *See also* plantation system
    land ownership and, 252–253
    radical organizations for, 264–265
    after WWI, 418–419
Aid to Families with Dependent Children, 590, 608
AIDS (acquired immunodeficiency syndrome), 619–620, *620*
Alabama, 131–132, 137, 140, 618, 622
    cotton production in, 140
    desegregation struggle in, 522–524
    Executive Order 8802, 456
    Freedom Riders, 542–543
    Herndon case, 437
    lynching, 463
    National Guard, 543–544

Alabama—*Cont.*
  school desegregation, 547
  Scottsboro boys, 436–437, *438*
  Selma-Montgomery march (1965), 526–528, *527*
  Tuskegee (Air Force), 458–460, *459*
  voting rights, 545, *546*
Alabama, University of, 529, 530, 543–544
Alabama Christian Movement for Human Rights
    (ACHR), 522
Alabama National Guard, 527
Alarcón, Hernando de, 23
Albany movement, 521
Alexander, Will W., 362, 426, 430
Ali, Muhammad (Cassius Clay), 551–563, *563*
Alito, Samuel, 615
Allen, Richard, *109*, 109–110, 118, 121, 126, 178
Allen, William G., 189
almanacs, 119–120
Almoravid (Moroccan Berber) conquest, 2
Along This Way (Johnson, J. W.), 398
Alston, C. Columbus, 439
Alvarado, Pedro de, 23
AMA (American Missionary Association), 216
Amenia Conference, *356*, 357
American Anti-Slavery Society (AASS) (1833), 187,
    192–193, 207
American Association of Retired Persons (AARP), 613
American Baptist College, 518
American Colonization Society (ACS), 126, 179–180,
    182–183, 191
American Dilemma, An (Myrdal), 475, 476, 481, 489, 504
American Federation of Labor (AFL), 349
  with CIO, 498–499
  exclusionist policies, 437
American Federation of Teachers, 596
American Friends Service Committee, 512
American Geographic Society, 198
American Missionary Association (AMA), 216, 217, 250
American Negro: A Study of Racial Crossing,
    The (Herskovits), 478
American Revolution
  abolition movement after, 96–99
  black military distinction in, 93–94
  manumission movement, 96–99
  military service, 90–94
American Youth Commission, 475–476
Americans All, Immigrants All (radio series), 477
Ames, Adelbert, 257
Amherst College, 175
"An Act to Promote the Comfort of
    Passengers" (1890), 261
ANC (African National Congress), 606
And Then They Heard the Thunder (Killens), 484
Anderson, E. H., *430*
Anderson, Elijah, 202
Anderson, Marian, 424, 445, 448, *448*
Andrew, John, 207
Andros, Edmund, 57
Angelou, Maya, 566, 571, 588, 607
Anglo-African (newspaper), 189
Angola, 11, 19, 29
Angola (Ndongo-Matamba), 19, 53, 73
Annie Allen (Brooks), 482
Anthony, Susan B., 243
Antigua, 36
Anti-Slavery Record (periodical), 192
apartheid (South Africa), 488, 605–606
Appeal of Forty Thousand Citizens, Threatened with
    Disenfranchisement, to the People of
    Pennsylvania, 162

Appeal to the World, An (Du Bois), 491
Appleton, Nathaniel, 87
appointments, political
  by Bush, G. H. W., 592
  by Clinton, 608–609
  by Johnson, 542
  by Kennedy, 542
  by Reagan, 593–595, 606, *607*, 608
Appomattox Court House, 227
Argentina, 42
Arkansas, 161, 360
  Civil War and, 209, 222–223, 227
  education in, *476*, 539
  Little Rock school integration, 539
  National Guard, 539
  race riot (1919), 360
  Reconstruction, 252
  re-enslavement in, 167
  school funding in, *476*
Arkansas, University of, 506
Armstrong, Louis, 386, 388, 391–393, *392*, 444
Army Nurse Corps, 458
arts, 381, 602. *See also* music; specific artists
  of Africa, 4–5, *5*, 18, *18, 19, 20*
  African, revival of, 406
  black theater, 395–397, *397*
  blues, 381–384
  clashes over, 413–416
  Harlem Renaissance, 397–405
  motion pictures, 393–395, *394*, 572
  painting, 120–121, 169, *169*, 173, *173*, 193, *380*,
    408–412, *409, 410, 411*
  photography, 409
  sculpture, 4–5, *5, 233*, 233–234, *378*, 379, 406,
    440–441, *441*
  vaudeville, 398
  visual artists, 408–412
Aspects of Negro Life: The Negro in an African
    Setting (Douglas), 412
assassination
  of Evers, 528
  of Kennedy, 542
  of King, Dr. Martin Luther, Jr., 528, 579
Assembly Special Committee on the Los Angeles
    Crisis, 608
Associated Colored Employees of America, 349
Associated Press, 623–624
Association for the Study of Negro Life
    and History, 373
astronaut, 588
Atlanta, Georgia, sit-in, 520
Atlanta riot, 284
Atlanta University, 250
Attaway, William, 483
Attucks, Crispus (runaway slave), 87–88, *88*
Atwell, Ernest, 345
Audacity of Hope (Obama), 634
Austin, Bobby, 633
Autobiography of an Ex-Coloured Man
    (Johnson, J. W.), 398, 415
Avery, Rev. Charles, 175
Awadi, Didier, 625, *625*
Awakening of Ethiopia (sculpture) (Fuller), *378*, 379
awards and honors, military. *See also* specific medals
  Civil War, 227
  in Spanish-American War, 279
  WWI, *336*, 336–340
  WWII, *449*, 461, *465*, 465–466
Ayler, Albert, 568
Ayllón, Lucas Vasquez de, 49

Babbitt, Bruce, 591
Babylonia, 11
Bacon's Rebellion, 55–56
Bad Boy Records, 603
Bader Ginsburg, Ruth, 613
Bahia, 45
Baker, Ella, 516, 530, 540
Baker, George (Father Divine), 374
Baker, Josephine, 406
Baker, Lt. Vernon, 466
Al-Bakri, 12, 13, 15
Balboa, Vasco Núñez de, 23
Baldwin, James, 464, 484, 485, 577, 598–599
Baldwin, Maria, 375
Baldwin, Ruth Standish, 349
Ball, Charles, 152
Bambaataaq, Afrika, 603
Bambara, Toni Cade, 573
Banana Bottom (McKay), 401
Bandung [Indonesia] Conference (1955), 554–555
Banjo (McKay), 401
Banks, General, 217
Banneker, Benjamin, 119–120
Bannister, Edward, 170
Bantu Migration, 4
Baptist church, increase in, 251
Baraka, Amiri, 562, 566–567, 568, 581
Baraka, Ras, 626
Barbados, 36, 39–40, 59
Barjon, Dutreuil, 169
Barnes, Albert C., 409
Barry, Marion, Jr., 518
Barthé, Richmond, 408
baseball, 496, 497, 500
Basie, Count, 445–446
Basquiat, Jean Michel, 602
Bassett, Angela, 600
Bates, Daisy, 528
Batouala (Maran), 406–407
Battle of New Orleans, 122, 122–124
Battle of Port Hudson, 225, 225
Beal, Frances, 573, 575
Beale Street (Lee, G.), 483
Bearden, Romare, 569
Beastie Boys, 603
Bechet, Sidney, 392, 406
Belafonte, Harry, 484
Belfrage, Sally, 525
Belgium, 343–344
Belknap, Jeremy, 87, 97–98
Bell, J. Madison, 219
Bell, William, 593
Bell Curve: Intelligence and Class Structure in American Life, The (Herrnstein and Murray, C.), 596
Beloved (book, film) (Morrison), 599
Beltrán, Gonzalo Aguirre, 41
Benedict, Ruth, 464
Benezet, Anthony, 86
Benin, 18, 18, 19
Bennett, Gwendolyn, 442
Benson (television), 600
Bermuda, 96
Berry, Halle, 600
Berry, Mary Frances, 565, 594, 605–606, 608
Berry, Theodore, 450–451, 470
Bethel African Methodist Episcopal (AME) Church, 109, 111
Bethune, Mary McLeod, 423–424, 426, 427, 430, 448, 453, 474, 488, 500, 573

Bethune-Cookman College, 428
Bevel, James, 518, 520
Bibb, Henry, 198
Bible against Slavery, The (Weld), 190–191
Biddle Memorial Institute (Johnson C. Smith University), 250
Big Band era, 393
bin Laden, Osama, 613
Birmingham
    demonstration (1963), 522–524
    SNYC, 439–440
Birney, James G., 180, 190–191, 192, 193, 196
Birth of a Nation (film), 357, 393
Birthright (film), 394
Bishop, Robert, 193
black abolitionists, 185–190
Black Aesthetic, The, 566
black antislavery societies, 186–187
Black Arts Movement, literature, 566
Black Codes, 38, 61–62, 238–239, 242
black colonization
    abolitionists for, 124–126
    free blacks for, 180–183
    religion and, 124
    whites for, 124
black convention movement, 176–177
Black Entertainment Television (BET), 600
Black Eyed Peas, 627
black feminism, 375–377
Black Fire, 566
Black Folk: Then and Now (Du Bois), 2
Black History Month, 480
black laws, 161, 167
Black Macho and the Myth of the Superwomen (Wallace), 573
black mayors, 580
Black Messiah, The (Cleage), 559
Black Metropolis (Wright, R.), 482
Black Nun Looks at Black Power, A (Thibodeaux), 559
Black Panther Party, 549, 559, 561, 573
Black Panther Party of Self Defense, 559
Black Power: the Politics of Liberation in America (Carmichael and Hamilton, C. V.), 558–559, 581
Black Power (Wright), 554
Black Revolution
    accomplishments of, 562–566, 580–582
    beginnings of, 550–557
    freedom marches, 576, 576
    literature of, 553–554, 566–568
    strengthening of, 558–562
Black Seminole rebellion, 156t
Black Studies programs, 563
Black Swan Records, 383–385, 391
black theater, 395–397
Black Theology and Black Power (Cone), 559
Black Thunder (Bontemps), 482
black vernacular, 402–403
Black Woman, The, 573
Black Women Organized for Action, 574
Black Worker, The (magazine), 550
Blacker the Berry, The (Thurman), 414
Blackman's Burden (Killen), 484
Blackwell, Unita, 528
Blair, Henry, 145–146
Blaire, Ezell, Jr., 519
Blake, Blind, 382
Blake, Eubie, 385–386, 396
"blaxploitation" movies, 569
Blood on the Forge (Attaway), 483
Blue Magic (song), 627

685

Blues People (Jones, LeRoi), 566, 568
Bluest Eye, The (Morrison), 571
Bluford, Guion S., Jr., 588
Boas, Franz, 2, 477, 478
Boggs, Grace Lee, 573
Bolling v. Sharpe, 507
Bolshevism, 362
Bonaparte, Napoleon, 113, 114, 123
Bond, Julian, 520
Bontemps, Arna, 482, 483
Bositis, David, 588
Boston, 574
    colonial slave trade in, 58
    free blacks in, 170
    migration to, 107
    poetry in, 88–89, 89
Boston, Absalom F., 103
Boston Massacre, 87–88, 88
Boude, Gen. Thomas, 199
Bourke-White, Margaret, 420
Bourne, Randolph, 346
Bowdoin College, 175
Boxley, George, 155
Boylston, Zabdiel, 67–68
Boyz'n the Hood (film), 600
Bradford, Perry, 381–382
Bradley, James, 188
Braun, Carol Mosely, 592–593, 635
Brazil, 25, 42–45
Brennan, William J., 594
Breyer, Stephen, 616
Brice, Carol, 445
bridewealth, 11
Briggs, Cyril R., 344, 362, 369, 370, 373, 436
Bronx Christian Fellowship, 608–609
Brooke, Edward, 547, 580
"Brookes" (slave ship), 34
Brooks, Gwendolyn, 482
Brotherhood of Sleeping Car Porters and Maids, 370, 453
Browder, Aurelia S., 515, 518
Brown, Ann, 445
Brown, Charlotte Hawkins, 439
Brown, Edgar, 427
Brown, Elaine, 573
Brown, Hallie Q., 377
Brown, Henry "Box," 198, 201
Brown, James, 568, 569
Brown, Jesse, 608
Brown, John, 158, 184, 186, 193, 207
Brown, Morris, 138–139
Brown, Ron, 608
Brown, Sterling, 436
Brown, William Wells, 135, 188, 198, 213
Brown II, 538
Brown v. Board of Education (1954), 475, 507–508,
    511, 538, 538, 539
Bruce, Blanche K., 243–244
Bryan, Andrew, 109
Buchanan v. Warley, 353
Bunche, Ralph, 427, 475, 486, 487, 490, 491–492,
    493, 527
Burke, Yvonne Braithwaite, 547, 580
Burroughs, Nannie Helen, 346, 352, 376, 377–378
Buses, 512–512
Bush, George H. W., 339, 585, 590, 591, 592,
    595, 606, 608
    Supreme Court and, 594–595
Bush, George W., 607, 607, 613, 614, 635
businesses, in Cold War era, 509
Busta Rhymes, 604, 624

Butler, Gen. Benjamin Franklin, 210–211, 215, 216, 220,
    226, 247, 255
Butts, Rev. Calvin, 605
Byrd, James, Jr., 598

Cabeza de Vaca, Álvar Núñez, 23
Cabin in the Sky (1943), 444
cabinet positions
    Black Cabinet, 425–429, 426, 428
    under Clinton, 608
    under Johnson, 542
    under Kennedy, 542
Cable, George W., 271
Caesar (slave), 76–77
Cain, Rev. Richard H., 251
Calhoun, John C., 204
California, 161
    Black Panther Party, 549
    discrimination in, 534
    housing discrimination in, 536
California Board of Regents, 597
Calloway, Cab, 445–446
Cambridge Nonviolent Action Committee (CNAC), 552
"Camp Obama," 635–636
Canada, 96m, 182, 183
Cane (Toomer), 401
Cardozo, Francis L., 245
Carey, Lott, 124, 126
Carey, Mathew, 118
Caribbean immigrants, 618
    Afro-Caribbeans, 631–633, 632m
Caribbean Islands, 276
    Afro-Caribbeans, 366–368
    Louisiana Purchase and, 114
    migration from, 366–368
    plantation system in, 37–38
    slavery in, 35–41
Carmichael, Stokely (Kwame Touré), 557–559, 559, 581
Carolina, 59–60, 60. See also North Carolina;
    South Carolina
Carr, Johnnie, 528
Carranza, Andres Dorantes de, 24
Carson, Ben, 634
Carter, Jimmy, 461, 581
Carter, Robert L., 502, 505, 507, 518
Cartwright, Samuel, 194
Cary, Freeman, 193
Cary, Mary Anne Shadd, 183, 188, 189, 189
Cary, Thomas, 183
Cary, William, 193
Casas, Bartolomé de las, 25
Catholic Church, 45
Catlett, Elizabeth, 569–570, 570
Cayton, Horace, 481
CCC (Civilian Conservation Corps), 430, 431
CDC (Centers for Disease Control and Prevention),
    619–620
Cenelles, Les (Lanusse, ed.), 172
Centers for Disease Control and Prevention (CDC),
    619–620
Central America, 41
Central High School, Little Rock, Arkansas, 539
Chain Reaction: The Impact of Race Rights and Taxes on
    American Politics (Edsall, M. and Edsall, T.), 592
Chamber of Commerce, U. S., 596
Chambers, H. C., 233
Chambers, Julius, 594
Chapman, Carlton, 463
Chapman, Maria Weston, 192
Chapman, Oscar, 448

Charge Delivered to the African Lodge, June 24, 1797, at Menotomy, A (Hall), 117
CHARGE delivered to the Brethren of the AFRICAN LODGE on the 25th of June, 1792, At the Hall of Brother William Smith, in CHARLESTOWN, A (Hall), 117
Charles II, 53, 59
Charles V, 23–24, 25
Chauncey, Isaac, 122
Chavez-Thompson, Linda, 608
Chavis, Benjamin, 588
Chavis, John, 175
Cheney, James, 525, 528, 618
Cheney, Richard, 613
Chesapeake Region, 69, 72
    Africans v. Creoles, 70–72
    deaths in, 71
    Low Country v., 74
    population growth in, 70–72, 72t
Chestnut, Charles, 407
Chicago
    FEPC in, 455
    housing discrimination in, 535–536
    Jobs-for-Negroes movement, 420
    race riot in, 359, 360
    working poor in, 586
Child, Lydia Maria, 192, 234
children, of slaves, 36, 44, 58, 75, 140, 150
Children's Defense Fund, 587
Chile, slave trade in, 42
Chisholm, Shirley, 547, 574, 575, 580, 581, 635
Chocolate Dandies (Blake & Sissle), 397
Christian Recorder, 347
Christiana Riot, 204–205
Christianity
    Africa's introduction to, 19
    baptism of slaves, 53, 59
    slavery v., 148–149, 195
Christiansborg Castle, 28
Christophe, Henri, 95
Church, Robert, 421
churches. See also specific churches
    black, development of, 109–110
    community building, 109–110
    in Reconstruction, 251
    segregation in, 148
CIO (Congress of Industrial Organizations), 433–435, 492–496
Circuit Court, United States, Fifth District, 547
Citizen Change, 627
Citizens' League for Fair Play, 420
Citizens Union of Pennsylvania (1848), 176
"citizenship schools," 539–540
Civic Club, 400
Civil Rights, 493–494. See also specific rights
    in courts, 502–509
    government and, 536–548
    Truman and, 500–502
Civil Rights Act
    of 1866, 239–240
    of 1875, 247, 270
    of 1957, 539, 541
    of 1964, 543–545, 564, 615
Civil Rights Commission, 608
Civil Rights Congress, 500
Civil Rights Division (Dept. of Justice), 594, 608
Civil Service Commission, 428–429
Civil War. See also specific battles and units
    antiblack riots and, 210
    beginning of, 209

black officers in, 222
commendations during, 227
military service in, 218, 223–228, 225, 226
Native Guards in, 220
nurses, 222–223
payment in, 224, 227–228
prisoners in, 226
recruitment for, 208, 218–220
slave disruptions during, 228–231
slavery policies and, 209–215
social consequences of, 247–251
spies in, 222
victory in, 233–234
women in, 222–223
Clark, Harvey, 535–536
Clark, Kenneth, 475, 506
Clark, Mark, 561–562
Clark, Ramsey, 589
Clark, Septima, 516, 531–532, 539–540
Clark University, 284
Clarke, Lewis, 198
Clarkson, Thomas, 186
Clay, Cassius (Muhammad Ali), 561–563, 563
Clay, Henry, 126, 191
Clayton Antitrust Act, 354
Cleage, Rev. Albert, 559
Cleaver, Eldridge, 559–560, 562
Clinton, Henry, 92
Clinton, Hillary Rodham, 613, 636
Clinton, William J., 433, 585, 593, 607–610, 610
CNAC (Cambridge Nonviolent Action Committee), 552
Coast Guard, 457–458, 463
Cobb, Thomas R. R., 194–195
Cockburn, George, 124
Code Noir (Black Code), 38, 61–62
Coffin, Levi, 191, 202
COFO (Council of Federated Organizations), 524, 545
COINTELPRO (Counter Intelligence Program), 561
Coker, Daniel, 110, 118, 124, 126
Cold War, CAA and, 488
Coleman, Ornette, 568
Colescott, Robert, 602
colleges and universities
    affirmative action, 594–595, 597, 615
    African American faculty in, 564
    black administrators, 565
    campus activism, 564
    discrimination in, 175, 503–506, 505
    graduate programs, 503–506
    increased African Americans in, 563–564
    ROTC at, 452
Collins, Cardiss, 547, 580
Colombia, slave trade in, 41–42, 44
Colonial slavery
    in Carolinas, 72–78
    in Georgia, 79–80
    in Lower Mississippi Valley, 80–83
    in middle colonies, 68–70
    in New England, 66–68
    in Virginia, 70–72
Color (Cullen), 401–402
Color Curtain, The (Wright), 554–555
Color Purple, The (film) (Walker), 572
Color Purple, The (Walker) (film), 572, 599, 600
Colorado, University of, 565
Colored American, The, 163, 170, 177–178, 197, 206
Colored Farmers' National Alliance and Cooperative Union, 264

Colored Man's Journal, 189
Colored Merchants Association, 419
Colored Players Corporation, 394
Coltrane, John, 568
Columbus, Christopher, 23
Colvin, Claudette, 515, 518
Combahee River Collective, 574, 577
Combs, Sean (Puff Daddy, P Diddy), 603, *612*, 627
Commission on Civil Rights, U. S., 593, 594, 605–606
Commission on Interracial Cooperation, 352, 362–363, 365, 370
Committee of Fair Employment Practice, 455
Committee on Conditions in Harlem, 421
Committee on Fair Employment Practices Committee (FEPC), 455–456, 467–468
Committee on the Participation of Negroes in the National Defense, 451
Common Sense (Paine), 87
Commoner, Barry, 589
Communism, 369–370, 437–439, 536–537
Communist Party, 498, 499
Company E Fourth United States Colored Infantry, *218*
compensated emancipation, 212
Compromise of 1850, 204–205
Condry, Ian, 626
Cone, James, 559
Confederacy
    black soldiers for, 232–233
    debate on arming slaves, 232–233
    desertion of slaves from, 210–211, *211*
    fear of insurrections, 230–231
    impressment in, 231–232
    Northern victory and, 233–234
    patrol laws, 139
    slave disruptions and, 228–231
    view of black Union soldiers, 226
    wartime economy, 231–232
Confederate army
    blacks' service in, 231–233
    "no quarter" policy, 227
    surrender of, 233
    treatment of captured blacks, 226–227
Confiscation Act (1862), 211, *211*, 219
Congo, 4, *20*, 344
Congress, *248*, 257, 606. *See also* House of Representatives; Senate
    African Americans in, 243–246, *244*, 533, 547, 580
    antilynching bill and, 364
    attempts to suppress Klan, 257
    Brownsville riot and, 284–285
    Cold War era, 496, 498–500, 509
    fugitive slave policy and, 203
    March on Washington, 544–545
    Missouri in, 160–161
    Reconstruction and, 243–245
    reparations in, 617
Congress of Industrial Organizations (CIO), 433–435, 467, 492–496
    with AFL, 498–499
Congress of Racial Equality (CORE), 511–513, 542–543, 553, 557–558, 596
Congressional Black Caucus, 580, 581, 591, 596
Congressional Medal of Honor, 466
    in Civil War, 227
    in Spanish-American War, 279
    in WWI, *336*
    in WWII, 466
Connecticut, 57–59, 66, 67, 99, 112
    black Revolutionary War units, 93–94
    education in, 165

free black population in, 105t, 106
free black voters in, 106
military service in, 89
slave population in, 105t
Connerly, Ward, 597
Connor, Eugene "Bull," 440, 522–523
Conover, James Francis, 193
Conroy, Jack, 482–483
Conservative Caucus, 596
Conservative Party, 263–266
Conservativism, 593–598
conspiracy, 57, *58*
Constitution, U. S.
    Fifteenth Amendment, 243, 261, 359
    Fourteenth Amendment, 240, 242–243, 261, 504, 507, 508, 615
    fugitive slave provision, 101
    Nineteenth Amendment, 375, 377
    Thirteenth Amendment, 214–218
    three-fifths compromise, 100–101
    Twenty-fourth Amendment, 545
Constitution Hall, 448
Constitutional Convention, Consideration of slavery in, 100–101
Convention of Colored Citizens (1843), 186
Conyers, John, Jr., 589, 617
Cook, Mercer, 542
Cook, Suzan D., 608–609
Coolidge, Calvin, 374
Cooper, Anna Julia, *376*
Coplan family, *159*
Copper Sun (Cullen), 402
CORE (Congress of Racial Equality), 511–513, 542–543, 553, 557–558, 596
Cornish, Samuel, 170–171, 176, 180, 189, 193, 206
Cornwallis, Charles, 92, 95
Coronado, Francisco Vásquez de, 23
Corregidora (Jones, G.), 571
Cortéz, Hernando, 23
Cosby, Bill, 601, *601*
Cosby Show, The (television), 601, *601*
Cotton Club, The, *387*
cotton gin, 130, *130*
cotton production, 130–132, 140–144, 141m, *254*
Couch, W. C., 477
Council of Economic Advisers, 577
Council on African Affairs, 487–488, 536–537
Counter Intelligence Program (COINTELPRO), 561
Countess of Huntingdon, 88
Court of Appeals, Fifth Circuit, 597
Court of Appeals for the District of Columbia, U. S., 595
courts. *See also* Supreme Court; specific courts and cases
    enforcement of Slave Codes, 55–56
Cox, Ida, 382, 391
Crandall, Prudence, 165
Crania Aegyptiaca (Morton), 164
Crania Americana (Morton), 164
craniology, 164
Cranston, Alan, 589
Creoles, 46, 50
    Africans v., 70–72
    religion of, 65
    runaways, 82–83
Crisis, The (NAACP periodical), 346, 350, 352–353, *355*, 361, 363–364, 369, 375, *399*, 503
Crockett, George W., 526
Crogman, H., 374–375
Croix de Guerre (Fr.)
    WWI, 336–338
    WWII, *449*, 465, *465*

Cromwell, John W., 281
Cromwell, Oliver, 95
Crusader, The (newspaper), 362, 369, 553–554
Cruse, Harold, 567
Cuba, 25, 36, 40, 45, 80, 136–137, 276, 631, 632m
Cudjoe (Maroon leader), 38–39
Cuffee, Paul, *125*, 125–126
Cugoano, Quobna Ottobah, 31
Cullen, Countee, 400, 401–402, 405–406, 409, 413, 436
culture, 68, 81. *See also* literature
    African renaissance in, 562
    economics v., 480–481
    graphic art, 569–571, *570*
    motion pictures, *394*, 394–395, 443–444, 447,
        569, 572, 599
    of racism, 163–167
    radio, 385
    slave culture, 65, 147–149, *148*
    syncretism of, 65
    television, 600–601
    theater, 485
    youth, 563–565
Curaçao, 36, 52–53

Danish West India Company, 40
"Dark World," 555
Darkwater: Voices from Within the Veil (Du Bois),
    343–344, 350
Darrow, Clarence, 361
Daughters of the American Revolution, 448
Davids, Tice, 100
Davis, A. K., 245
Davis, Angela, 573, 576, *576*
Davis, Benjamin J., 421, 496–497, 499
Davis, Col. Benjamin O., Jr., 452, 459–460, 462
Davis, Henrietta Vinton, 379
Davis, Jefferson, 146, 209, 226, 231–233
Dawson, William, 533
Day O'Connor, Sandra, 595, 613, 615
de Klerk, Fredrick Willem, 606
Deacons of Defense and Justice, 553
Dean, William H., 427
Debs, Eugene, 346, 362
Debt: What America Owes to Blacks,
    The (Robinson, R.), 616–617
Declaration of Independence, 86, 185, 191
Declining Significance of Race, The (Wilson), 585
Dede, Edward, 175
Def, Mos, 604, 624
Def Jam Records, 603
Delaney, Maj. Martin R., 180, 182–183, 189, 198,
    222, 550–551
Delaware, 98, 105t
    slavery in, 49
Democracy in America (Tocqueville), 161
Democratic National Committee (DNC), 592
Democratic National Convention (1964), 531, *531*
Democratic National Convention (1976), 580
Democratic National Convention (2004), 635, *635*
Democratic party, *574*
    black voice in, 580
    black vote and, 524–525
    defeat in 1984 of, 590
    Northern opposition to emancipation, 213
    Populists and, 264–265
    primary voting, 364, 539, 589, 590, 637
    Reconstruction and, 247
    shift of allegiance to, 422–423
    white primaries, 269
Democratic-Republicans, 113, 115

Les Demoiselles d'Avignon (Picasso), 406
Denmark Vesey plot, 138–139
Department of Education, 595, 596
Department of Health, Education, and Welfare, 564, 565
Department of Health and Human Services (HHS), 620
Department of Housing and Urban Development, U. S., 427
DePriest, Jessie, 422
DePriest, Oscar, 377, 422, 423
desegregation
    of buses, 511, 513, 518, 542–543
    of colleges and universities, 503–506
    of District of Columbia, 507
    in federal service, 501
    military, in WWII, 466
    in military service, 501
desiccation, 3
Detroit, 361, *612*
    labor unions in, 495–496
    against left-labor participation, 499
    race riot (1925), 361
    riot (1967), *578*, 579
    "Walk to Freedom," 535
    WWII riot in, 469
Dett, R. Nathaniel, 445
Devine, Annie, 530, 547
Dexter Memorial Baptist Church, 516
Diallo, Amadou, 598
Dialogue between a Virginian and an African
    Minister (Coker), 118
Dickens, Charles, 171
Dickson, Amanda America, 151
Dickson, David, 151
Different World, The (television), 601
Diff'rent Strokes (television), 600
Diggs, Charles C., Jr., 533, 581
Disabled American Veterans, 608
discrimination
    cost of, 577
    by draft boards, 329–330
    in employment, *273*, 273–274, 429
    in housing, 274
    laws and, 356–357
    in New Deal measures, 419, 429–430, 432
    in transportation, 270–274
    in unions, 273–274
    WWI soldiers and, 332–334, 339–342
    WWII soldiers and, 463–466
disease
    in middle passage, 33
    "Tuskegee study," 432–433
disfranchisement
    gerrymandering, 263
    laws for, 261–269, *262*
Dissertation on Slavery (Tucker), 98
Distinguished Flying Cross, 460, 462, 465
Distinguished Service Cross, 466
District Court, U.S. (Northern District of Oklahoma), 617
District of Columbia
    desegregation of, 507
    education in, 424
    gradual emancipation plan for, 212
    growth and distribution of African Americans
        (1940 and 2000), 630t
District of Columbia, University of the, 633
Diversity Visa Lottery, 631
Dix, Dorothea, 222
Dixon, Haywood, *144*
Dixon, Thomas, 357
DNA, mitochondrial, 633–634
Do the Right Thing (film), 600

Dobb, Charlie, 526
Dodson, Owen, 482
Dominican Republic, 36, 49, 631
Dorsey, Thomas A., 444
"Double V" Campaign, *449*, 451, 469
Douglas, Aaron, *409*, 412
Douglas, H. Ford, 180, 182, 210, 222
Douglass, Aaron, 408–409, *409*
Douglass, Frederick, 149, 164, 171, 176, 179, 182–183, 186,
    188–190, *189*, 193, 197, 198, 206, 207, 213, 220, 243,
    256, 282
    North Star (newspaper), 71–72, 177–178, 189
Douglass, Frederick (slave), 146
Douglass, Stephen A., 204
Dove, Rita, 599
draft boards, discrimination by, 329–330
Draft Nurse Bill, 458
Drake, St. Claire, 481
Dreams from My Father (Obama), 634
Dred Scott v. Sandford, 101–102, 205–206, *206*, 242
Dresser, Amos, 196
Drew, Charles, 464
Driskell, David, 569
Drums at Dusk (Bontemps), 482
Du Bois, W. E. B., 148, 265, 268, 282, 340, 343–344,
    346, 350, 352, 354, *355*, 361, 365–366, 369–370,
    372, 375, 414–416, 445, 471, 474, 479, 488, 500
    against art as propaganda, 413
    Booker T. Washington and, 353
    as faculty, 384
    Pan-African Congress, 344
    published works of, 2, 331, 491
    scholarship of, 491
    Washington, Booker T., and, 304–305
Dukakis, Michael, 591–592
Dunbar, Paul Laurence, 384
Duncan, John B., 542
Duncan, Todd, 445
Duncanson, Robert S., 173, *173*, 193, *199*, 200–201
Dunmore, Lord, 91–92
Dutch, 36
    slavery under, 52–53
Dutch West India Company, 36, 52–53
Dutchman (play) (Baraka), 566
Dyer, L, C., 364
Dyer antilynching bill, 364
Dylan, Jessie, 627
Dymally, Mervyn, 580

East, Clay, 435
Easton, Hosea, 164
Easton, John, 215
École des Orphelins Indigents, 175
Economic Opportunity Act of 1964, 542
Economic Reciprocity programs, 611
economy, 263
    African slave trade and, 11–12
    cotton gin and, 130–131
    farm labor changes, 254–255
    immigration and, 633
    income inequality, 585
    land and, 252–253
    post-Civil War, 251–256
    proslavery arguments and, 194–195
    in Reconstruction, 251–256
    sharecropping, 255
    slave hiring and, 146
    women's work and, 253
Edelman, Marian Wright, 586, 587
Edsall, Mary, 592

Edsall, Thomas, 592
Eduador, 41–42
education, 111–112, 253
    African immigrants, 632
    Civil War ex-slaves and, 250–251
    Crandall for, 165
    desegregation in, 615–616
    disparities in, 596–597
    of former slaves, 216–218
    free blacks and, 173–175
    higher education (See colleges and universities;
        specific institutions)
    prison and, 620–621
    Reconstruction and, 250–251
    "reverse discrimination" and, 594–595, 597, 615
    segregation in, 173–174, *476*, 506–509
    unequal funding and, 506
Educational Fund, 596
Egypt, 177
    slavery in, 11
Eichelberger, Barbara, 575
Eighth Illinois Infantry (370th U.S. Infantry)
    in Spanish-American War, 280
    in WWI, 337
Eisenhower, Dwight D., 539
Eldridge, Roy, 447
Elections, presidential
    of 1880, 115
    of 1928, 421–422
    of 1932, 422
    of 1936, 423
    of 1940, 424, 440, 452
    of 1960, 541–542
    of 1984, 589–590
    of 1988, 591–592, 594
    of 1992, 592–593
    of 2000, 611, 613, 614, 627
    of 2008, 627, 634–639, *635*
Elementary and Secondary Education Act (1965), 547
Ellicott, George, 119–120
Ellington, Edward Kennedy "Duke," 386, *386*, 393, 395,
    444, 445
Elliott, Bishop Stephen, 195
Elliott, Robert Brown, 245, *248*
Ellison, James O., 617
Ellison, Ralph, 481, 483, 598
emancipation
    compensated, 212
    cost of, 201
    final proclamation, *213*, 214
    Lincoln and, 212–215, *213*
    partisan views of, 213–215
    preliminary proclamation, 212–213
Emancipation Proclamation, *213*, 213–215, 229–230, 543
Emancipator (periodical), 192
Emerson, Ralph Waldo, 207
emigration debate, 179–183
    Cary, M., in, 183
Eminem, 627
Emmy Award, 600
employment, 577–578. *See also* specific companies
        and professions
    fair employment legislation, 455, 503
    federal, 426–429, 533–534
    FEPC and, 455–456, 467
    industrial, in WWI, 349
    slave hiring, 43–44, 145–147
    of women, 74, 253, *348*, *467*, 471–472
    WW II industry jobs, 467, *467*
    in WWI, 341, 347–349

Enforcement Act of 1870, 258–259
Engineering, Science, and Management War Training (ESMWT), 466
England
    in Caribbean, 36
    Dunmore and, 91–92
    Norman/Anglo-Saxon, 10
    in slave trade, 28, 30–32
    Spanish monopoly and, 36
    Sugar Act of 1764, 85
Equal Employment Opportunity Commission, 545, 593
Equal Protection Clause (Fourteenth Amendment), 615
Equal Rights Amendment, 575
Equiano, Olaudah. *See* Vassa, Gustavus
Erasing the Color Line (Houser), 512
es Saheli, Abu-Ishak Ibrahim-, 14
Espy, Mike, 608
Estavan (Esteban), 24, 49, 50
Ethiopia, 2, 21, 379, 486–487, 631
Ethiopian Manifesto (Young), 186
Ethridge, Mark, 456
Europe
    in Caribbean islands, 35–41
    development of New World, 23–25
    slave trade and, 27–33
Europe, Lt. James Heese, 340, *340*, 389–391, *390*
European immigrants, 163
Evening Thought: Salvation by Christ, with Penitential Cries, An (Hammon), 118
Evers, Medgar, 528
Evidence of Things Not Seen (Baldwin), 598–599
Evrie, John H. Van, 194
Executive Order 8802, 455–456, 466
Executive Order 9981, 466
Exodus story, 177
    Southern migration and, 365

Fair Housing act (1968), 541–542
Fairbanks, Calvin, 202
Fairfield, John, 202
Famer, James, 542–543
Family Research Council, 596
family structure
    African, 10–11
    plantation system and, 149–150
    during Reconstruction, 253–254
    separation of slave families, 31, 134–135, 149
Fanon, Frantz, 560
Farm Security Administration (FSA), 430, *430*
Farmer, James, 551, 553, 558
Farrakhan, Louis, 587
Father Divine, 374
Faubus, Orville, 539
Fauntroy, Walter, 605–606
Fauset, Crystal Bird, 427, *469*
Fauset, Jessie Redmond, *399*, 399–400, 403, 405–406, 407, 413
Federal Emergency management Agency (FEMA), 622
Federal Emergency Relief Administration (FERA), 432
Federal Employment Practices Commission (FEPC), 493, 496
Federal Housing Administration, 535
Federal Housing Authority (FHA), 427, 431
Federal Public Housing Authority, 431
Federalists, 112–115
Fellowship of Reconciliation (FOR), 512, 517, 518, 551
FEMA (Federal Emergency Management Agency), 622
feminism, black, 375–377

Fences (play) (Wilson, August), 599
FEPC (Committee on Fair Employment Practices Committee), 455–456, 467–468
FEPC (Federal Employment Practices Commission), 493, 496
FERA (Federal Emergency Relief Administration), 432
Fifteenth Amendment, 243, 259, 261, 353
Fifteenth Street Presbyterian Church, 352
Fifth United States Colored Heavy Infantry, 227
50 Cent, 624
Fifty-First Composite Defense Battalion, 460
Fifty-Fourth Massachusetts Infantry, 227
Fifty-Fourth Massachusetts Regiment, 227–228
Fifty-Sixth Infantry, 227
Figueroa, Temo, 636
films, 603. *See* motion pictures
Fine Clothes to the Jew (Hughes), 402
Finney, Charles Grandison, 190
Fire! (journal), 402, 414
Fire in the Flint (White, W.), 415–416
Fire Next Time, The (Baldwin), 577
First African Baptist Church, 96
First Louisiana Native Guards, 221
First South Carolina Volunteers, 221
First Universal Races Congress, 353
Fishburne, Laurence, 600
Fisk University, 250, 565
Fitzgerald, Ella, 444–446, 446, 447–448
Fitzhugh, George, 194
Flagellants, The (Polite), 571
Flash, Grandmaster, 603
Flemming, Arthur S., 593
Flight (White, W.), 415–416
Florida, 50, 63, 80, 360–361, 613, 614
    acquisition of, 132
    Civil War and, 212
    illegal slave trade to, 137
    lynchings in, 358
    Reconstruction and, *239*, 247, 252, 256
    Seminole wars, 156t
    Spanish explorers in, 48–49
For Colored Girls Who Have Considered Suicide When The Rainbow Is Enuf (Shange), 572
Foraker, Joseph B., 285
Ford Motor Company, 495
foreign relations. *See also* specific countries
    United Nations and, 485, 488–492
Foreign Service, 592
Foreman, Clark, 426
Forever Free (sculpture) (Lewis, M.), *233*, 233–234
Fort Pillow massacre, 226, *226*
Fort Wagner, 227
Forten, Charlotte, 217, 352
Forten, James, 108, 121, 125–126, 162, *162*, 176
Foster, Henry, 188
Fourteenth Amendment, 240, 242–243, 261, 504, 507, 508, 615
Foxes of Harrow, The (Yerby), 484
France
    Code Noir, 38, 61–62
    Germany's control of, 450
    Haiti and, 104, 113–114, 117, 126–127, 155, 186–187
    Louisiana acquisition by, 61
    WWI and, 334–342
Franklin, Aretha, 568
Franklin, Benjamin, 98
Franklin, John Hope, 480, 507, 608, 609, *610*, 617
Franklin College, 175
Frazier, E. Franklin, 421, 475, 477–478, 480, 481, 486, 488, 493, 572

Frederick Douglass's Paper, 189
Free African Society, 109, 125, 186
free blacks. *See also* specific states
    affluence of, *166*, 169
    black colonization for, 180–183
    black convention movement, 176–177
    cultural contributions of, 172–173
    education and, 111–112, 173–175, 250–251
    emigration debate, 179–183
    employment for, *168*, 168–171
    gender inequality and, 177–179
    group name for, 176
    legal restrictions on, 161–162
    limitations of, 160–163
    literature of, 194
    mob violence against, 165
    mutual aid organizations for, 172
    in New York City, 170–171
    North v. South, 166–169
    North's urban life for, 169–170
    population, 105t, 163
    population of, 98, 163
    property ownership of, 169
    public image/behavior and, 176–177
    re-enslavement of, 167
    religion and, 177
    skilled employment for, 168–169
    voting and, 160, 162–163
    voting rights and, 160, 162–163
    westward migration of, 161–162
    women, 170, 177–179
    women, 170, 177–179
Free Soil Party, 197
Freedman's Bank, 255–256, *256*
Freedman's Bureau, 238–240, 248–250, 253–254
Freedom Farm Co-op, 574
Freedom Now Suite, 520, *520*
Freedom Riders, 542–543
freedom riders, 512–513, 542–543
Freedom Summer, 524–526, 618
"Freedom to Serve" (report), 501
Freedom's Journal, 116, 177, 178, 181, 189
Freeman, Donald, 554
Freeman, Morgan, 600
Frémont, John C., 211, *211*
French Company of the Islands of America, 36
French Louisiana, 80–82
French Revolution, 113, 155
Friendship Benevolent Society for Social Relief, 172
FSA (Farm Security Administration), 430, *430*
fugitive slave laws, 101–102, 183, 186, 203, 204, 205
Fuller, Meta, *378*, 378–379
Fundamental Constitutions (Locke), 59

Gabriel Prosser's revolt, 126–127, 155
Gage, Frances Dana, 179
Gaines, Donald, *473*
Gaines, Lloyd, 504
Gama, Vasco De, 21
Gambia, 73
Gammon Theological Seminary, 284
Gandhi, Mohandas, 487, 512, 517, 521
Gantt, Harvey, 530
Gardner, Charles, 188
Garnet, Henry Highland, 158, 172, 186, 188, *189*, 206
Garretson, Freeborn, 109–110
Garrido, Juan, 23–24, *24*
Garrison, William Lloyd, 126, 174, 180, 185–188, 191, 192, *192*, 193, 195, 196, 204, 207, 213, 219, 234, 354
Garrisonians, 192–193

Garvey, Amy Ashwood, 379
Garvey, Marcus, 367–374, *371*, 378, 409, 550–551, 555
Gary, Indiana, 580–581
Gates, Daryl, 597–598
Gates, Henry Louis, Jr., 172, 379, 634, *634*
Gaye, Marvin, 569
Gayle, Addison, 566
Gayle, W. A., 517, 518
gender
    family roles and, 253
    hiring-out and, 146
    inequality, free blacks and, 177–179
    of slaves, 33
George, David, 109
George, Walter, 539
George III, 85
Georgetown Law Center, 593, 605–606
Georgia, 49, 63, 91, 93, 96, 105t, 140
    Atlanta race riots (1906), 284
    black laws in, 167
    black population (1790), 105t
    Civil War and, 212, 217
    colonial slavery in, 63
    Constitution v., 100–101
    cotton production in, 140–141
    free blacks in, 105t
    lynchings in, 283–284, 363
    race riots in, 283–284
    Reconstruction, 242, 246–247, 252–253
    right to vote law (1964), 546
    slave population in, 105t
    slave revolts in, 158
Georgia, University of, 529
Gephardt, Richard, 591
Gergen, David, 638
Germany, 616. *See also* World War II
    WWI propaganda campaign, 339
gerrymandering, 263, 614–615
Getty Images, 623–624
Ghana, 2, 5, *6*, 6–8, 12–13, 541, 631
    independence of, 554–555
Gibson, Truman K., Jr., 462
Giddings, Joshua, 197, 206
Gillespie, Dizzy, 392
Gilmore, Major General, 226–227
Giovanni, Nikki, 567, 573
Giuliani, Rudolph, 598
Glen Martin Plant, *453*
Gloucester, John, 126
God Sends Sunday (Bontemps), 482
Going to Church (Johnson, W.), 442, *442*
Going to the Territory (Ellison), 598
gold mines, 5
    in Latin America, *43*, 43–44
Goldberg, Whoopi, 600
Gone with the Wind (1939), 443
Goodell, William, 192
Gooding, Cpl. James Henry, 228
Gooding, Cuba, Jr., 600
Goodman, Andrew, 525, 528, 618
Goodman, Benny, 446–447
Gordy, Berry, Jr., 568
Gore, Al, 591, 609, 613, 614
Gradual Emancipation Act of 1780, 107–108
Grady, Henry W., 263
Grand United Order of Odd Fellows, 172
Grandy, Moses, 146, 198
Granger, Lester, 453, 464, 470, 472
Grant, Gen. Ulysses S., 215

Graves, Lem, 471
Gray, Fred, 518
Gray, James A., 521
Gray, Victoria, 530
Gray, Virginia, 525
Grayson, William J., 195
Great Blues Migration, 388m, 388–391
Great Depression
    agricultural crisis and, 418–419
    artistry during, 440–448
    black migration and, 418
    employment in, 419–420, 420, 430–436
    housing and, 430–431
    picketing, 420–421
    political participation, 421–425
    relief efforts, 419–420, 420
    riots, 421
    stock market crash, 418
Great Zimbabwe, 20
Greeley, Horace, 212
Green, Beriah, 192
Greene, Col. Christopher, 94
Greenfield, Elizabeth Taylor, 384
Greensboro Four, 519–520
Grenada, 36
Grier, Pam, 569
Griffith, D. W., 357, 393
Grimké, Angelina, 187, 352
Grimké, Francis J., 352, 362–363
Grimké, Sarah, 187–188, 352
Grutter, Barbara, 615
Guadeloupe, 36
Guatemala, slave trade in, 41
Guillaume, Paul, 406
Guinea, 43, 73
Guinier, Lani, 608
Guinn v. United States, 353
Gulf of Guinea. See Nigeria

Hagan, Helen, 340
Hager, Fred, 382
Haiti, 45, 49, 95, 108, 128, 182, 282, 357, 631, 632m
    revolution in, 104, 113–114, 117, 126–127, 155, 186–187
Hakluyt, Richard, 28
Haley, Alex, 568
Hall, Felix, 463
Hall, Katie, 591
Hall, Prathia, 528
Hall, Prince, 107, 110–111, 116, 117
Halleck, Gen. Henry, 211
Hallelujah! (film), 395
Hamer, Fannie Lou, 525, 530–531, 531, 533, 547, 574
Hamilton, Alexander, 97, 98, 113, 114
Hamilton, Charles V., 558–559, 581
Hamlem Renaissance, literature, 402–405
Hammon, Briton, 90
Hammon, Jupiter, 118–119
Hammond, James Henry, 194
Hampton, Fred, 561–562
Hampton, Lionel, 447
Hampton Institute, 250
Handy, W. C., 384, 390
Handy Music Company, 384
Hansberry, Lorraine, 485, 565
Harding, Vincent G., 560–561
Harlem, 327, 368, 387, 408, 417
    1943 riot in, 469
    Paris v., 405–408
Harlem Artists Guild, 442
Harlem Community Art Center, 440, 442

Harlem Renaissance, 397–405
    artists of, 398–405
    expansion of, 399–405
    socioeconomic problems and, 398, 401, 414–416
    women in, 403–405
Harlem Writers Guild, 566
Harmon, Henry S., 246
Harmon Foundation Awards for Negro Artists, 410, 412, 441
Harp, The (sculpture) (Savage), 441, 441
Harper, Frances Ellen Watkins, 172, 188, 243
Harper's Ferry, 207
Harpo Productions, 600
Harriet (linocut), 570, 570–571
Harris, Andrew, 188
Harris, Eleanor, 108
Harris, John T., 248
Harrison, Benjamin, 425
Harrison, Hubert, 344, 368–369, 373, 407
Harrison, Pat, 364
Hart, Gary, 589, 591
Harvard Law Review, 503
Harvard University
    African and African American Research at, 634
    Harvard Law School, 635
al-Hassad, Hafez, 589
Hastie, William H., 427, 428, 452, 456, 470, 471, 533
Hatch, Orrin, 595
Hatcher, Mayor Richard, 580, 581, 589
Hausa states, 5, 17–18
Hawaii, 275–276
Hawkins, John, 36
Hayden, Palmer, 408, 410, 410–411, 412
Hayden, Robert, 482
Hayes, Arthur Garfield, 361
Hayes, Isaac, 569
Hayes, Roland, 445
Hayes, Rutherford B., 258, 259
Hayne, Robert Y., 160
Haynes, Daniel, 395
Haynes, George Edmund, 347, 349
Head Start programs, 574
"Health Card," (Yerby), 484
Heart-Shaped in the Dust (Hayden), 482
Height, Dorothy, 572–573, 574, 588
Heller, Walter, 542
Helms, Jesse, 591
Henderson, Fletcher, 384, 386, 388, 391–392, 446–447
Henderson, George W., 483
Henry, Aaron, 525, 547
Henry, Patrick, 85, 86
Henson, Josiah, 149, 202
Henson, Matthew, 602
Herc, DJ Kool, 603
Herndon, Angelo, 437
Herrnstein, Richard, 596
Hershey, Lewis B., 427
Herskovits, Melville, 477, 478, 480, 481, 568
Heynes, Lemuel, 115
HHS (Department of Health and Human Services), 620
Higginbotham, A. Leon, Jr., 101–102, 542
Higginson, Col. Thomas Wentworth, 214, 220, 221
Hill, Anita, 596
Hill, Charles A., 495
Hill, Oliver, 503
Himes, Chester, 483
Hip Hop culture, 602–605, 605
    globalization for, 624–627, 625
Hitler, Adolf, 450, 468
Hitler-Stalin Pact, 438–439

HIV/AIDS crisis, 619–620, *620*
Hobbs v. Fogg, 162
HOLC (Home Owners Loan Corporation), 430–431
Holiday, Billie, 444–447
Hollings, Fritz, 589
Holly, James Theodore, 180, 182
Holmes, Hamilton, 529
Holsey, Albon, 419
Holt Street Baptist Church, *516*
Home Owners Loan Corporation (HOLC), 430–431
Home to Harlem (McKay), 401, 413
homeless, *583*
Homer, Winslow, *254*
Hood, Bishop James Walker, 251
Hood, James (student), 530
hooks, bell, 604–605
Hooks, Benjamin, 590
Hooray for Hollywood (film), 447
Hoover, Herbert, 344, 363, 418, 421–422
Hoover, J. Edgar, 561
Hopkins, Bishop John H., 196
Hopkins, Samuel, 97–98
Hopper, Isaac T., 199
Hopwood, Cheryl, 597
Horne, Frank S., 427
Horne, Lena, 443, 444
Horton, George Moses, 172, 186
Horton, James, 178
Horton, Myles, 516
Horton, "Willie," 592
House, Son, 382
House Committee on Un-American Activities, 440
House of Representatives, 605–606. *See also* Senate
    African Americans in, 580, 593
    Civil Rights Act of 1964, 545
    civil rights legislation, 545
    DePriest and, 422
    Dyer antilynching bill and, 364
    Iraq invasion, 606
    Thirteenth Amendment and, 214–215
    Twenty-fourth Amendment, 545
    Voting Rights Act of 1965, 618
House Servant's Directory: or, a Monitor for Private Families (Roberts), 170
Houser, George M., 512
housing
    discrimination in, 535–536
    Great Depression and, 430–431
    New Deal aid for, 430–431
    public, 474, 496, 595
    race riots and, 496
    redlining, 535
    segregation and, 274
    urban problems in, 360–361
housing violence, 496
Houston, Charles Hamilton, 451, *473*, 491, *491*, 502–504, 537
Howard, Perry, 421
Howard University, 250, 281, 439, 502, 505, 565, 570, *620*
Howe, Julie Ward, 210
Hudson, Julien, 169, *169*
Huggins, Willis N., 486
Hughes, Charles Evans, 363
Hughes, Chris, 636
Hughes, Langston, 399, *399*, 401–403, *402*, 404–406, 413–415, 436
Human Rights (periodical), 192
Humboldt, Alexander von, 41
Hunter, Alberta, 382, 391

Hunter, Charlayne, 529
Hunter, Gen. David, 212, 219–220
Hunter Gault, Charlayne, 529
Hunton, Addie, 340, 375
Hurley, Ruby, 532–533
Hurricane Katrina, 622–624, *623*
Hurst, Fannie, 443
Hurston, Zora Heale, *404*, 404–405, 477, 571–572
Hussein, Saddam, 606
Huxley, Julian, 489
Hyman, John A., 245

"I Have a Dream" speech (King, M. L., Jr.), 528, *544*, 547
I Know Why the Caged Bird Sings (Angelou), 571
Ickes, Harold L., 426, 448, 477
Al-Idrisi, 7–8
If He Hollers, Let Him Go (Himes), 483
ILD (International Labor Defense), 437
Illinois, 161
    Ku Klux Klan in, 357
    race riot (1908), 286
    race riot (1917), 350
    race riot (1919), 359
IL&WU (International Longshoremen's and Warehousemen's Union), 434
Imitation of Life (Hurst), 443
immigration, effects of, 633
Immigration Act of 1924, 366
Immigration Act of 1990, 631
In Search of Our Mothers' Gardens: Womanist Prose (Walker), 573
Incidents in the Life of a Slave Girl (Jacobs), 150
income inequality, 585
indentured servitude, 25–27, 51
Indiana
    free blacks in, 161–162
    Ku Klux Klan in, 357
    National Black Political Convention in, 581
    restrictions on blacks, 161, 465
Indians, 54–56, 77, 89, 609
    Black Seminole rebellion, 156t
    slaves with, 65–66, 81–82
    statues against, 71
Industrial Revolution
    invention of cotton gin, *130*, 130–131
    inventions, 145
industrial work
    Cold War era, 492–496
    defense industries, 454–455
    pre-WWII discrimination in, 452–453, *453*
    slave hiring, 146–147
    WWI and, 349
    WWII and, 466
Institute for Colored Youth, 175
Institute of the Black World, 560
insurrections, 157–158
    Confederacy's fear of, 230–231
    Gabriel Prosser's revolt, 126–127, 155
    in Georgia, 158
    Latin America mainland slavery and, 44–45
    in Louisiana, 155, 156t
    Nat Turner's rebellion, 139, 156t, 157–158, *158*, 185–186
integration. *See* desegregation
Interesting Narrative of the Life of Olaudah Equiano or Gustavus Vassa the African, The (Equiano), 32, *70*, 119
intermarriage, 45–46, 57, 61, 63
International African Service Bureau, 486

International Association of Women of the
    Darker Races, 377
International Council of Friends of Ethiopia, 486
International Longshoremen's and Warehousemen's
    Union (IL&WU), 434
International Workers of the World (IWW) (Wobblies), 369
internationalism, 485–492
interracial relationships
    children of, 150
    law against, 57
    in Louisiana, 150
    marriage, in Latin America, 45–46
    in New York, 171
intertropical convergence zone, 2
inventions, 145
    cotton gin, *130*, 130–131
Invisible Man (Ellison), 481, 483
Iowa, 161
Iran, 606
Iraq, 613
Iraq invasion, 606
Iraq War, 635
Irony of a Negro Policeman (Basquiat), 602
Islam
    in ancient Ghana, 13–15
    Creoles and, 65
    polygamy and, 11
    slavery and, 9–10
    trade routes and, 6–7
    in West Africa, 6
Israel, 490, 589–590
Italy, 486
IWW (International Workers of the World)
    (Wobblies), 369

Jack, Gullah, 156
Jackson, Gen. Andrew, *122*, 122–124, 195
Jackson, George, 576
Jackson, James E., Jr., 439–440
Jackson, Jimmie Lee, 526
Jackson, Mahalia, 382, 540
Jackson, Rev. Jesse, 588–590, *590*, 591–592, 605
Jackson, Samuel L., 600
Jacob, John, 590
Jacobs, Harriet, 150, 198
Jacques Garvey, Amy, 379
Jamaica, 36, 38–39, 45, 96, 631, 632m
James, Rev. Horace, 215–216
Japanese, 358, 616
Jay, John, 98, 114
Jay-Z, 624, 627
Jazz, 387–393, 388m, 406, 568
Jazz Kings, 406
Jefferson, Blind Lemon, 382
Jefferson, Thomas, 62–63, 71, 85–86, 92, 113–115,
    156, 194
    support of Banneker, 119–120
Jemison, Dr. Mae E., 588, 634
Jenkins, David, 161–162
Jenkins, Esau, 539–540
Jenkins, Sandy, 149
Jews, 405, 455, 478, 489, 490, 589–590
Jim Crow laws, *260*, 261, 269, 270–275
Jobs-for-Negroes movement, 420
Jocelyn, Simeon, 164–165
Johnson, Andrew, 237–238, 240, 242
Johnson, Campbell, 427, 452
Johnson, Charles, 599
Johnson, Charles S., 399–400, 475, 489
Johnson, George, 393

Johnson, Henry, 336
Johnson, James P., 388
Johnson, James Weldon, 345, 358, 363, 364, 398, 400,
    405–406, 415–416
Johnson, John H., 420, 470
Johnson, Kathryn, 340
Johnson, Lyndon B., 527, 539, 542–543, 545–546, 638
Johnson, Mordecai, 439, 488
Johnson, Noble, 393
Johnson, Robert, 382
Johnson, Robert L., 600
Johnson, Samuel, 86
Johnson, Sargent, 408, 412
Johnson, William H., 408, 441, *442*
Johnston, Joshua, 120–121, *121*
Joint Center for Political and Economic Studies, 588
Joint Chiefs of Staff, 592, 606, *607*
Jonah's Gourd Vine (Hurston), 405
Jones, Absalom, 110, 117, 118, 121, 126
Jones, Edward, 175
Jones, Eugene Kinckle, 349, 427
Jones, Gayl, 571
Jones, LeRoi (Amiri Baraka), 562, 566–568
Jones, Lois Mailou, *380*
Jones, Quincy, 634
Jones, William, 188
Jordan, Barbara, 547, 580
Jordan, Michael, 588
Jordan, Vernon, 529, 608
Jos Plateau, 4–5
Journal of Negro History, 480
Journey of Reconciliation, 512–513
Jule (Henderson, G.), 483
Jule and Avery Hopwood Prize, 482
Jump for Joy (musical), 445
June 1946 petition, 490–491
Justice Department, 594, 608

Kansas-Nebraska Act, 205
Karenga, Maulana (Ronald Everett), 562
Kay, Ulysses, 445
Kean, Thomas, 608
Keene, Paul, 569
Kellor, Frances, 349
Kennedy, Anthony, 594, 616
Kennedy, Robert F., 543, 544
Kennedy, John F., 521, 523–524, 529–530, 541
    assassination of, 542
    on civil rights, 543–544
Kent State University, 564
Kentucky
    free black restrictions in, 161
    free blacks in, 105t
    insurrections in, 105t, 106
    lynchings in, 284
    slave conspiracy in, 127–128
    slave population in, 105t
Kentucky, University of, 507
Kerner Report (1968), 584
Keyes, Alan, 635
Killen, Edgar Ray, 618
Killens, John Oliver, 484, 566
King, Coretta Scott, *527, 591*
King, Dr. Martin Luther, Jr., 511, 513, *516*, 516–518,
    521, *530*, 535, 536, 537, 540–541, 548, 552, 557,
    559, 627
    assassination of, 528, 579
    Birmingham demonstration, 522–524
    holiday for, 590–591, *591*, 624
    "I Have a Dream" speech, 528, *544*, 547

King, Dr. Martin Luther, Jr—*Cont.*
   March on Washington and, 544, *544*
   Selma-Montgomery march and, 526–528, *527*
King, E. D., 523
King, Rodney, 597–598
King, Rufus, 100
King Leopold of Belgium, 175
King Oliver's Creole Jazz Band, 384, 389
Kingdom of Kongo, 65
Knight, Charles, 349
Knights of Columbus, 596
Knights of the Ku Klux Klan. *See* Ku Klux Klan
Knights of the White Camelia, 256–257
Kongo, 11, 19, 20, *20*, 29, *30*
Kopytoff, Igor, 11
Korean War, 538
Krake, Holcha, 441
KRS-ONE, 604
Kruch, Franck, 439
Krupa, Gene, 448
Krush Groove (film), 603
Ku Klux Klan, 256–257, *257*, *269*, 357–358, 373, 422, 508,
   553, 617, 618
Kuwait, 606
Kwanzaa, 562
Kweli, Talib, 604

La Guardia, Fiorello, 421, 455
labor civil rights, 492–500
labor unions. *See also specific unions*
   in Detroit, 495–496
   New Deal and, 433–436
   tobacco workers, 499
   during WWI, 349
   during WWII, 467
Lacy, Arthurine, 529
Lafayette, Bernard, 518
Lafon, Thomy, 169, 175
Lampkin, Daisy, 377
land ownership, in Europe v. Africa, 11
Lane, Lunsford, 188, 198
Lane Theological Seminary, 191–192
Langston, John M., 282
language
   African diversity of, 4
   African pidgin, 6
   slaves and, 74
Lanusse, Armand, 172
Larsen, Nella, 403–404
Latifah, Queen, 604
Latin America mainland slavery, 41–43
   uprisings and revolts, 44–45
Laurens, John, 93
law enforcement
   demonstrations and, *510*, 522–523
   murder of blacks by police, 564, 578
   plantation police, 139–140
   racial profiling by, 598
   Rodney King incident, 597–598
   vigilance committees, 256–258
Lawrence, Jacob, 442, *484*, 569
Lawrence, Samuel, 93–94
Lawson, James M., Jr., 518–520
Lawson, Marjorie, 542
Lawyers Committee for Civil Rights under Law, 614
Lafayette, James Armistead, 95
Lafayette, Marquis de (Gilbert du Motier), 95
LDF (Legal Defense Fund), 353, 505, 529, 594,
   596, 614
Leaders of the New School, 604

League of Nations, 343
League to Maintain White Supremacy, 456
Leavitt, Joshua, 192
LeClerc, General, 113
Lee, George W., 483
Lee, Jarena, 178, *179*
Lee, Richard Henry, 92
Lee, Robert E., 227, 233
Lee, Samuel J., 245
Lee, Spike, 599, 600, 603, 624
Legal Defense Fund (LDF), 353, 505, 529, 594, 596, 614
legislation
   anti-affirmative action law, 615
   antislavery, 204, 212–215
   colonial Carolinas, 59–60
   colonial Virginia, 55–58, 71
   fair employment legislation, 455, 503
   fugitive slave law, 204
   against Ku Klux Klan, 257
   for racial segregation, 270–273
L'Enfant, Pierre, 120
Leon, Ponce de, 24, *24*
Les Fetiches (painting) (Jones, L. M.), *380*
Let Me Breathe Thunder (Attaway), 483
Letter from Birmingham Jail (King), 523
Letters to the Ministers and Elders (Birney), 190–191
Levittown, New York, 535
Lew, Barzillai, *90*
Lewis, Jane, 202
Lewis, John, 518, 520, 526, 527, 558
Lewis, John L., 433
Lewis, Mary Edmonia, *233*, 233–234
Lewis, Robert Benjamin, 197–198
Liberator, The (newspaper), 185, 195, 196, 204
Liberia, 126, 179–182, 180m, 189, 282
Liberty League, 369
Liberty Party, 192
Liele, George, 96, 109
Life and Religious Experiences of Jarena Lee,
   The (Lee), 178, *179*
Light and Truth: Collected from the Bible and Ancient
   and Modern History, Containing the Universal
   History of the Colored and Indian Race, From
   the Creation of the World to the Present Time
   (Lewis, R.), 197–198
Lincoln, Abbey, 573
Lincoln, Abraham, 205, 209, 211, 224, 226, 228, 286,
   543, 627
   black soldiers and, 219–220
   emancipation and, 212–215, *213*
   reconstruction plan of, 236–237
Lincoln Memorial, *448*, *530*, 537, 540
Lincoln Motion Picture Company, 393
Lincoln University, 175
Lindsay, Vachel, 482
literacy, 45–46
literature
   black periodicals, 399
   after Black Revolution, 571–572
   of Black Revolution, 553–554, 566–568
   in Boston, 88–89, *89*
   of free blacks, 194
   Hamlem Renaissance, 402–405
   poetry, 400–402
   post-New Deal, 481–484
   post-Revolutionary War, 116–120
   postwar, 482–484
   post-WWII, 481–484
   race literature, 414–415
   slave narratives, 32, *70*, 179, 198

Little Rock, Arkansas, 539
Local 98, International Association of Firefighters v. Cleveland, 594
Locke, Alain, 368, 400, 401, 405, 407, 409, 478, 567
Locke, John, 59
Lockwood, Lewis, 217–217
Logan, Adella Hunt, 375
Logan, John, 622
Logan, Rayford W., 427, 451, 477
Loguen, Jermain Wesley, 198, 203
Loguen, L. W., 149
Longworth, James Francis, 193
Lorde, Audre, 571, 573
Los Angeles
    population (1940-1970), 579
    Rodney King incident, 597–598
    Watts riot (1965), 578–579
Lougen, Jermain, 205
Louima, Abner, 598
Louis, Joe, 450, 451, 562
Louisiana, 50, 113, 128, 135, 137, 140, 261, 267–278
    Civil War and, 220, 230
    cotton production in, 131–132
    Hurricane Katrina, 622–624
    Reconstruction and, 237, 242, 246, 250, 252, 256–258
    school desegregation, 547
    slave laws in, 60–61
    slave revolts in, 155, 156t
    Voting Rights Act (1965), 546–547
Louisiana Purchase, 62–63
    Caribbean and, 114
Louisville, 615–616
Louisville, University of, 506
Loury, Glenn, 597
Louverture, Toussaint, 113, 113–114
Lovejoy, Elijah P., 196, 197
Lowndes County Freedom Organization, 558
Luce, Henry, 474
"Lucy," 2
Lukeni, Garcia II Nkanga a, 30
Lunceford, Jimmie, 445–446
Lundy, Benjamin, 185
Lusitania (ship), 328
Lynch, John R., 268
lynchings, 282–283, 283, 340–350, 358
    Alabama, 463
    of black soldiers, 463–464
    in Kentucky, 284
    NAACP efforts against, 351, 363–364, 369, 375
    WWI era, 349–350
Lyon, Ernest W., 282
Lyricist Lounge, 604

Macbeth, Bob, 566
Macdonald, Susie, 518
Madhubuti, Haki (Don L. Lee), 567
Madison, James, 102, 113
Madison Avenue Initiative, 611
Mahone, William, 264
Maine, 105t, 156
Maine (battleship), 276–277
Malcolm X (film), 600
Malcolm X (Malcolm Little), 533, 550–552, 552, 554–557, 558, 562, 567
Mali (Melle), 13–15, 14m
Maló, Juan (St. Maló), 83
Malone, Vivian, 530
Mandela, Nelson, 606
Manicault, Charles, 153

Mannes, David, 416
manumission, 53, 57, 61, 69, 104, 111–112, 124
    American Revolution movement, 96–99
    from hiring-out, 43–44, 146
    for military service, 78–79, 90–92, 95, 95, 96–97, 124
    of mulatto children, 150
Maran, René, 406–408
March against Fear (Meredith March), 557
March on Washington (1941), 454, 454–455
March on Washington Movement (MOWM), 550, 551
Marie Galante, 36
Marine Corps, 457–458
Maroons, 38–39, 40, 44–45, 65, 71, 82, 82–83
Marrant, John, 109, 116
marriage, 54, 58
Marshall, George C., 456
Marshall, Col. John R., 280
Marshall, Justice Thurgood, 473, 500, 502–503, 506, 507, 512, 534, 537, 542, 594, 595
Marshall, Paule, 573
Marshall Hotel, 398
Martin v. Wilkins, 594–595
Martinique, 36
Mary S. Peake: The Colored Teacher of Fortress Monroe (Lockwood), 217
Maryland, 51–52, 55, 98, 101, 105t, 112, 132, 618
    free black population in, 105t
    protests in, 532, 533
    slave population in, 105t
Maryland, University of, 504
Mason, Charlotte Osgood, 404–405, 409, 416
Mason, John, 202
Mason, Reverend Charles H., 345–346
Massachusetts, 50, 57, 59, 66, 87, 93, 99, 101, 106
    against black in-migration, 107
    black laws in, 161
    black population (1790), 105t
    education in, 174
    military service in, 89
    Shay's Rebellion, 100
Massachusetts Bay, 53–54
Massachusetts General Colored Association of Boston, 186
master-slave relationship, 48, 150–151
Mather, Cotton, 67–68
Matthew Henson and the Quest for the North Pole (Colescott), 602
Matthews, Edward, 445
Matthews, Victoria Earle, 414
Matthews, W. D., 222
Mauritania, 5
May, Samuel, 192, 205
Mayfield, Curtis, 569
Maynor, Dorothy, 445
MC Lyte, 604
McCain, Franklin, 519
McCain, John, 638
McCarthy, Joseph, 498
McCree, Wade, 542
McCrumell, James, 187
McCune Smith, James, 187, 193, 198, 207
McCurdy, Merle, 542
McDaniel, Hattie, 443
McDonald, Susie, 515
McDonald, William, 421
McDowell, Gen. Irvin, 211
McHenry, James, 119
McHenry, Jerry, 205
MCHR (Medical Committee for Human Rights), 526

McKay, Claude, 344, 361–362, 368, 369, 400–401, 402, 405–406, 413, 436
McKinley, William, 277
McKinney, Nina Mae, 395
McKissick, Floyd, 557, 558
McLaurin, George W., 505, 505–506
McLean, John, 101–102
McNeill, Joseph, 519
Medical Committee for Human Rights (MCHR), 526
Menace II Society (film), 600
Menendez, Francisco, 78–79
Merchant Marines, 463
Meredith, James, 529–530, 557
Meridian (Walker), 572
Messenger, The, 346, 369–370, 373, 378
Metcalfe, Ralph, 450
Methodist church
    AME churches, 109–110, 175–178, 240, 251, 274, 637–638
    appeal against violence, 362–363
    educational programs of, 250, 290
MIA (Montgomery Improvement Association), 516–517
Micheaus, Oscar, 393, 394
Micheaux Film Corporation, 394
Michigan
    black laws in, 161
    Ku Klux Klan in, 357
    reparations and, 617
    riots in, 210
Michigan, University of, 615
Mid-Atlantic colonies
    Chesapeake Region, 69, 70–72, 72
    health in, 70
    New York Colony, 68
    Pennsylvania, 69–70
    religion in, 68
    slavery's expansion in, 69–70
Middle Passage, conditions, 33, 34, 35, 35, 64
Middle Passage (Johnson, Charles), 599
Miers, Suzanne, 11
migration
    agricultural crisis and, 418–419
    to cities, 107, 302
    after Civil War, 273
    for cotton, 131–132
    to North and West, 469, 484
    from South, 364–365, 365
    to South, 627–629, 628m
    during and after WWI, 347–349, 358
    during WWII, 469
military officers
    in Civil War, 221–222
    training of, 460–461
    in WWII, 460
military service, 84
    in British army, 91–93, 95–97, 97, 124
    in Civil War, 218, 223–228, 225, 226
    desegregation of, 501
    Executive Order 9981, 466
    individual states on, 93
    integration of, 538
    Jim Crow in, 451
    Korean War, 538
    manumission for, 78–79, 90, 91–92, 95, 95, 96–97, 124
    Marines, 463
    navy, 94, 94, 127, 456
    numbers for, 93
    officer training, 460–461
    pre-WWII discrimination in, 456
    reality of, 89–90
    Revolutionary War, 90–94
    in Spanish-American War, 277–280, 278
    Tuskegee (Air Force), 458–460, 459
    Vietnam War, 562–564, 563
    War of 1812, 121–124
    women in, 457, 458, 460
    in WWI, 327, 328–343, 335, 336, 338, 340
    in WWII, 449, 452, 456–466
    WWII population in, 457–458
Miller, Capt. M. M., 221
Miller, Dorie, 449, 465, 465
Miller, Kelly, 281
Miller, Thomas E., 267
Miller, William, 117
Milliken's Bend (Louisiana), 226–227
Million Man March, 587, 587–588
Mills, Florence, 397
Miner, Myrtilla, 175
mining, 5, 43, 43–44
Minor Society School, 175
minstrel shows, 163–164
Mirror of Liberty, 189
Miseducation of the Negro, The (Woodson), 480
Mississippi, 131–132, 135, 137, 138, 140, 266–267
    education funding in, 526
    Hurricane Katrina, 622–624, 623
    lynchings in, 528
    Reconstruction and, 243, 245–247, 257
    right to vote law (1964), 546
    sit-in in, 520
Mississippi, University of, 529–530
Mississippi Freedom Democratic Party, 524–525, 530, 531, 547
Mississippi Plan, 267
Mississippi Project, 526
Missouri, 161
Missouri, University of, 504
Missouri Compromise, 160–161, 204, 205, 206
Mitchell, Arthur W., 423
Mitchell, Clarence, Jr., 541
Mitchell, Harry Leland, 435
Mitchell, Louis, 406
Mitchell, William, 202
Mondale, Walter, 589, 590
Monro, Thomas, 406
Monroe, James, 126, 127
Monrovia, Liberia, 180
Montgomery, Alabama, bus boycott, 513–518, 514
Montgomery, Benjamin, 145
Montgomery, Isaiah T., 266, 266–267
Montgomery Improvement Association (MIA), 516–517
Montserrat, 36
Moody, Ann, 528
Moon Illustrated Weekly, 384
Moore, Amzie, 525
Moore, Fred, 349, 420
Moore, Richard B., 362, 369
Moore v. Dempsey, 360
More Than Just Race (Wilson, W. J.), 621
Morehouse Medical School, 592
Morgan, Irene, 511–512
Morgan, Joan, 604–605
Morgan, Robin, 575
Morgan v. Commonwealth of Virginia, 511–512
Morris, Robert, 174, 204
Morrison, Toni, 571, 599, 599
Morrow, E. Frederick, 534
Morse, Jedediah, 98
Morton, Ferdinand ("Jelly Roll") 384, 387, 393
Morton, Samuel G., 164, 194

Mose, 78–79
Moses, Bob, 524, 525
Moss, Carlton, 470
motion pictures, 357, 393–395, *394*, 443–444, 447, 470, 569, 572, 599–600, 603
Motley, Archibald J., Jr., 408, *411*, 412
Motley, Constance Baker, 529, 530
Moton, Robert R., 342, 349
Mott, Lucretia, 192, 203
Moughton Mifflin Literary Fellowship, 483
MOWM (March on Washington Movement), 550
Moynihan, Daniel Patrick, 572, 582
Mozambique, 21, 43
Muhammad, Askia, 15–16
Muhammad, Elijah, 551, 552, 555
mulattos
    population of, 150
    religion and, 75–76
    sale of, 152–153
Murphy, Dudley, 395
Murphy, Eddie, 599
Murray, Albert, 598–599
Murray, Charles, 596
Murray, Donald Gaines, 504
Murray, Sonny, 568
Musa, Mansa, 13–14, 14m
music
    bands and vocalists, 447–448, *448*, 565, *565*
    big band swing, 445–447
    blues, 381–384, 388m
    classical, 444–445
    freedom songs, 532
    gospel, 382, 385, 444, 540
    jazz, 387–393, 388m, 406, 568
    musical theater, 389, 396, *397*, 415
    musicians and composers, 381–393, 444–448
    rap music, 602–605, *605*
    recorded music and radio, 381–386
    spirituals, 149
    women, 381–385, *383*, 444, 447–448, *448*
    WWI military bands, 340, *340*
Muste, A. J., 512, 517, 518
Myrdal, Gunnar, 474–475, 476, 489, 504
Myth of the Negro Past, The (Herskovits), 478–479, 481, 568

NAACP. *See* National Association for the Advancement of Colored People
NAGCN (National Association of Graduate Colored Nurses), 458
Nagin, Ray, 622, 624
Nardal, Jane, 407
Narrative of Sojourner Truth, The (Truth), 179
Narrative of the Proceedings of the Black People during the Late Awful Calamity in Philadelphia, A (Jones and Allen), 118
Narváez, Pánfilo de, 23, 49
Nash, Diane, 518, 519, 520, 528
Nashville, Tennessee, 520
Nashville Christian Leadership Council (NCLC), 518
Nast, Thomas, *269*
Nasty as They Wanna Be (album), 603
Natchez Indians, 81–82
Nation, The (magazine), 413
Nation of Islam (NOI), 550–551, 552, *552*, 562, 587
National Action Network, 611
National Advisory Commission on Civil Disorders, 584
National Alliance of Black Feminists, 574, 575
National American Woman Suffrage Association (NAWSA), 375
National Association for the Advancement of Colored

People (NAACP), *351*, 352–358, *355*, *356*, 360, 362–364, 369–372, 375, 377
    anticommunism and, 499–500
    Black Revolution, 553
    Garvey and, 370–372
    Legal Defense Fund (LDF), 353, 505, 529, 594, 596, 614
    against lynchings, *351*, 363–364, 369, 375
    membership in, *481*
    1912 election and, 354
    school desegregation and, 507, 509
    Springarn Medal, 396, 471
    women in, 375
    WWI activities, 331
    WWII activities, 450–451, 453, 455
National Association for the Advancement of White People, 508
National Association of Colored Women (NACW), *287*, 288, 345, 375, 377–378
National Association of Graduate Colored Nurses (NAGCN), 458
National Baptist Convention, 363
National Bar Association, 596
National Black Feminist Organization, 574, 575
National Black Nurses Association, 596
National Black Political Convention, 581
National Committee of Negro Churchmen, 559
National Convention of Colored Men (1864), 216
National Council of Colored People, 176
National Council of Jewish Women, 596
National Council of Negro Women, 423–424, *428*, 453, 572, 573, 605
National Defense Advisory Committee, 452–453
National Emigration Convention (1854), 182–183
National Equal Rights League, 362
National Industrial Recovery Act (1933), 429, 433
National Labor Board (NLB), 433
National Labor Relations Board (NLRB), 433
National Lawyers Guild, 456, 526
National League of Republican Colored Women, 377–378
National Negro Business League, 419
National Negro Congress, 437–439, 488, 490, 499, 536–537
National Negro Convention, 180, 183
National Organization for Women (NOW), 575, 576, 596
National Political Congress of Black Women, 605
National Race Congress, 362
National Recovery Administration, 427
National Security Advisor, 606, *607*, 613, *613*
National Selective Service, 427
National Urban League, 347–349, 352, 353, 399–400, 453, 471, 607
    WWI and, 348
    WWII and, 453, 464, 470–471
National Watchman, 189
National Youth Administration, 427, *428*, 430, 466
Native Son (Wright, R.), 437, 481, 482, 483
Native Tongues, 604
navy, 456, 460
    military service in, 94, *94*, 127
    Revolutionary War and, 94
    War of 1812, 122
Navy Cross, 465
NAWSA (National American Woman Suffrage Association), 375
NCLC (Nashville Christian Leadership Council), 518
Ndongo-Matamba (Angola), 11, 19, 29
    Christianity in, 20
Neal, Larry, 566
Nebraska, 359–360
Negro Election Day, 67

Negro Family: The Case for National Action, The (Moynihan), 572
Negro Family in the United States, The (Frazier), 480, 572
Negro Question, The (Cable), 271
Negro Society for Historical Research, 367, *367*
Negro Soldier, The (film) (Moss), 470
Negro World (newspaper), 369, 371–372, 378, 379
Negroes and the War (pamphlet), 470
Negroes with Guns (Williams, R. F.), 553
Nell, William Cooper, 174, 193, 198
Nelson, Alice Dunbar, 375
Nevis, 36
New Deal
    Black Cabinet, 425–429, *426*, *428*
    organized labor, 433–436
    programs in, 429–433
New England
    inoculation (variolation), 67–68
    Negro Election Day, 67
    slave occupations in, 66–67
    slave populations in, 66
    trade in, 66
New England Anti-Slavery Society, 187, 191
New Granada, 41–42
New Hampshire, 66, 67, 93, 105t, 106
    free black population in, 105t
    slave population in, 105t
New Jack City (film), 600
New Jersey, 50, 68, 99, 105t, 112
    black population (1790), 105t
    free black population in, 105t
    racial profiling in, 598
    slave population in, 105t
    slavery in, 49
New Masses (magazine), 436
New Mexico, 23, 161
New Negro, The (Locke), 400, 407, 478, 567
New Negro for a New Century, 374
New Netherland, 49, 50, 52–53
new opportunities, 588
New Orleans, 169
    Hurricane Katrina, 622–624, *623*
New York, 52–53, 57, 93, 99, 105t, 107, 121, 136, 367
    demonstrations in, *510*
    free black population in, 105t
    interracial relationships in, 171
    slave population in, 105t
    slavery in, 49, 68–70
    voting in, 115, 163
New York, State University of, 565
New York African Society for Mutual Relief, 109
New York Age (newspaper), 349, 420
New York Amsterdam News, 367
New York City, *576*
    black community in, 108
    fair employment law (1945), 533
    FEPC in, 455
    free blacks in, 170–171
    housing discrimination in, 535, 536
    Jobs-for-Negroes movement, 420
    police brutality in, 598
    riots in, 577
    violence in Yorkville (1964), 578
New York City conspiracy, 156t
New York City Human Rights Commission, 575
New York Council for a Permanent FEPC, 512
New York Dodgers, 496–497, *497*
New York Journal of Medicine, 198
New York Manumission Society, 111–112

New York Society for Promoting the Manumission of Slaves, 98
Newman, Constance Berry, 592
newspapers, African American. *See also* specific papers
    on Bolshevism, 362
    weeklies, 120, 189, 384
    during WWI, 346
Newton, Huey P., *549*, 559–562, *561*
Nickens, David, 188
Nigeria, 4–5, 18, *18*, *19*, *29*, 70, 631
Nineteenth Amendment, 375, 377
Ninety-Ninth Fighter Squadron, 458–460, *459*
Ninety-Ninth Pursuit Squadron, 462
Ninety-Second Division, 339–340, 462
Ninety-Third Division, 463
Ninth Ward, New Orleans, 623, *623*
Nixon, Edgar Daniel, 515
Nixon, Richard, 581
Nixon v. Herndon, 364
Nkrumah, Kwame, 554, 555
NLB (National Labor Board), 433
NLRB (National Labor Relations Board), 433
Nobel Peace Prize, 490, 527, 606
Nobel Prize in Literature, 599
Noone, Jimmie, 385
Noriega, Manuel, 606
North
    abolition movement activities in, 98–100, 185–189
    abolition movement legislation in, 96–97, 204–205
    black population (1940-1970), 579
    Civil Rights movement in, 533–536
    education in, 173–174
    higher education in, 175
    migrations of blacks to, 469, *484*
    race riots in, 285–286
    violence in, 285–286
    WWII riots, 469
North Carolina, 63, 93, 105t, 127, 132, *144*, 618
    black laws in, 167
    disfranchisement riots in, 268, *268*
    free black population in, 105t
    slave population in, 105t
    teacher salaries, 504
North Star, The (newspaper), 71–72, 177–178, 189
Northeastern Federation of Women's Clubs, 375
Northern States Power Company, 608
Northrop, Solomon, 151
Northup, Solomon, 198
Northwest Ordinance, 99, 101
Norton, Eleanor Holmes, 575, 593, 605–606
Not without Laughter (Hughes), 402
Notes of a Native Son (Baldwin), 484
Notes on the State of Virginia (Jefferson), 194
Nott, Josiah Clark, 164, 194, 195
Nova Scotia, 95, 96, 96m, 124
NOW (National Organization for Women), 575
Nugent, Richard, 414
Nunn, Sam, 595
nurses
    Civil War, 222–223
    WWI, 340–341, *341*
    WWII, 458

O Canaan (Turpin), 483
OAU (Organization of African Unity), 555
OBAC (Organization of Black American Culture), 566
Obama, Barack Hussein, 614, 620, 627, *634*, 634–637
    election of, 638
    inauguration of, 638–639
Obama, Michelle, 638–639

Oberlin College, 175, 187, 192
Occum, Samson, 89
OCD (Office of Civilian Defense), 468
Odd Fellows, 316
Office of Civilian Defense (OCD), 468, *469*
Office of Education, U. S., 453, 545
Office of Facts and Figures, 470
Office of Price Administration (OPA), 468
Office of Production Management, 453, 455–456
Office of War Information (OWI), 470
Official Report of the Niger Valley Exploring Party (1861)
    (Delany), 183
Ogden, Peter, 172
Ogé, Vincent, 38
Oglethorpe, James, 79–80
Ogletree, Charles, 617–618
Oh, Angela, 608
Ohio, 167
    abolitionists in, 191–192, 196, 199–200, 200m
    fair employment law (1959), 533
    as free state, 161–162
    National Guard, 329, 564
    school integration in, 506
Oklahoma, 360–361, *435*
    Tulsa race riot, 617
Oklahoma, University of, 596
Oklahoma National Guard, 617
O'Leary, Hazel, 608
Ollie Miss (Henderson, G.), 483
Olympic Games (1936), 450
Olympic Games (2000), 589
On Guard for Freedom, 566
"One America," 608
"One Mind, One Vote," 627
101st Airborne, 539
"one-drop rule," 281
Onesimus, 67–68
"Operation Desert Storm," 607
Operation Dixie, 499
Operation PUSH (People United to Save
    Humanity), 589
Opportunity (magazine), 399–400, 401, 406, 407, 471–472
Oprah Winfrey Show, The (television), 600
Oregon, 161
Organization of African Unity (OAU), 555
Organization of Black American Culture (OBAC), 566
Oscar for Best Supporting Actress, 443
Otis, James, Jr., 86–87
Our Nig; Or Sketches From the Life of a Free Black
    (Wilson, H.), 172
Outkast, 604
Outsider, The (Wright, R.), 483
Owen, Chandler, 344, 346, 368–370, 373
Owens, Jesse, 450
Oxley, Lawrence A., 427

Pace, Harry, 383–384, 391
Paine, Thomas, 87
Pakenham, General, 122–123
Palestinian Liberation Organization (PLO), 589
Palladium of Liberty, 161–162
Palmer, A. Mitchell, 370
Palmer, Dr. B. M., 195
Pan-African Congresses, 344, 372–373, 487
Panama, 41–42
Pankey, Aubrey, 445
Paris, *410*
    Harlem v., 405–408
Paris Peace Conference, 450
Park, Robert, 477–478

Parker, Charlie, 392
Parker, John, 202
Parks, Rosa, 513, *514*, 515–516, 528, 530
Parsons, James, 542
PAS (Pennsylvania Abolition Society), 171
Passing (Larasen), 403–404
Patrick, Deval, 608, 636
Patterson, Orlando, 11
Patterson, William, 500
Patton, Charley, 382
Paul, Thomas, 111
Payne, Francis, 51–52
Peake, Mary S., 216–217
Pearl Harbor, 465, *465*
Peebles, Melvin Van, 569
Pelteret, David, 10
Pendleton, Clarence, 593
Pennington, J. W. C., 198
Pennsylvania, 63, 99, 100
    black population (1721-1760), 69–70
    free black population (1790), 105t, 107–108
    gradual emancipation in, 107–108
    growth and distribution of African Americans
        (1940 and 2000), 630t
    rioting in, 285
    slave population (1790), 105t
    slavery in, 49, 60, 63
    voting in, 162–163
Pennsylvania Abolition Society (PAS), 171
People for the American Way, 596
People United to Serve Humanity, 588
Perkins, Edward J., 592
Perot, H. Ross, 592
Perry, Capt. Oliver H., 122
Pershing, Gen. John J., 340
Personal Responsibility and Work Opportunity
    Reconciliation Act (1996), 608
Peru, 42
Petersburg (Virginia), 227
Petry, Ann, 483
Pettigrew, Thomas, 572
Pew Research Center, 613–614
Philadelphia, 171–172
    African Institution of Philadelphia, 125–126
    consumer boycotts in, 534
    population of, 108
    rioting in, 285
Philippines, 281
Phillips, Wendell, 174, 192, 197, 219, 243
Philosophical Transactions, 67
Piano Lesson, The (play) (Wilson, August), 599
Picasso, Pablo, 406
Pickens, Harriet, *457*
Pickens, William, 364
Pickering, Timothy, 114
picketing, 420–421, *494*
Picquet, Louise, 152–153
Pierce, Franklin, 205
Pinchback, P. B. S., 243–244, 246, 401
Pinckney, Charles C., 101
Pinkster, 68
Pippin, Horace, *338*
Pizarro, Francisco, 23
plantation system
    in Caribbean, 37–38
    families and, 149–150
    in Latin America, 40–45
    in South, 25, *39*, 74–75, *75*, 140–144, 141m, 147–148
    women in, 37, 142–143
Plessy, Homer, 270–271

Plessy v. Ferguson, *270*, 270–271, 503
PLO (Palestinian Liberation Organization), 589
Plum Bum (Fauset), 403
Poems on Miscellaneous Subjects (Harper), 172
Poems on Various Subjects, Religious and Moral
    (Wheatley), 88
poet laureate, 599
poetry, African American
    after Black Revolution, 572
    colonial era, 88–89, *89*
    Harlem Renaissance, 399–402
    1930–1955, 482
    postbellum era, 324
    post-New Deal, 361, 368
    post-Revolutionary era, 118
Poissaint, Alvin, 526
Poitier, Sidney, 443
Polite, Carlene Hatcher, 571
political participation
    black power era, 580
    Cold War era, 492–503
    on municipal level, 424, 580
    in 1930s, 421–429
    Reconstruction, 243–247
    shift of party allegiance, 422–423
    of slaves, 88–89, *89*, 186
    support for FDR, 423–424
    women's activities, 177–179, 374–379
    of youth, 626
Polk, James, 196
Poole, Cecil F., 542
Poor, Salem, 90
Popular Front Movement, 438–439
population
    in 1790, 105t
    in 18th century, 66–68, 70, 72t, 73t, 74
    in 1910, 493m
    in 1920, 629t
    in 1940 and 1990, 629t
    in 1950, 493m
    in 1950–1980, 585m
    free blacks, 105t, 163
    growth and distribution (1940 and 2000), 629–630,
        630t, 631t
    growth and percentage of U. S. population
        (1790–2000), 629–630, 629t
    after War of 1812, 131
    white v. black, in British colonies, 56, 56t
Populist Party, 264–265
Porter, James, 570
Portugal, 25–26, 27, 29, 42–43
    to Africa, 23
Posten, Ted, 427, 470
Powell, Adam Clayton, Jr.., 488, 496, 533, 554, 555
Powell, Adam Clayton, Sr., 366
Powell, Colin, 592, 606–607, *607*, 613, *613*, 635
Powell, William F., 282
Powerful Long Ladder (Dodson), 482
Powers, Harriet, 142–143, *143*
Prayer Pilgrimage for Freedom, 540
Presbyterian church
    free blacks in, 109
    schools of, 290
Presenting Negra Scenes Draven Upon my Bus are
        through the South and Reconfigured for the Benefit
        of Enlightened Audiences Whenever Such May Be
        Found, By Myself Missus K. E. B. Walker Colored
        (cut paper), *602*
Presidential Distinguished Unit Citation, 461, 465
Prigg v. Pennsylvania, 204

Primitive Negro Sculpture (Guillaume and Monro), 406
prison, 620–621
Pritchett, Laurie G., 521
Prix de Rome, 445, 483
Prix Goncourt (Goncourt Prize), 406–407
Proctor, Henry Hugh, 340
Progress of a Race (Crogman), 374–375
Progressive Bull Moose Party, 354
Progressivism, 353–354
proslavery backlash
    black response to, 197–198
    changing attitudes from, 197
    persecution from, 196–197
    proslavery arguments, 194–195
    violence from, 196
Prosser, Gabriel, 155, 156t
protest, 534–535. *See also* rioting; specific protests
    Birmingham demonstrations, 522–524
    boycotts, 513–518, *514*, 522, 526, 534
    demonstrations, 540–541, *541*, 544, *544*
    freedom marches, 524, 526–528, *527*, 533–536, 544
    picketing, 420–421, *494*, 512, 520, 534, 538, *538*
    rent strikes, 536
    sit-in movement, *519*, 519–520, *520*, 534
Provincial Freeman (newspaper), 183
Pryor, Richard, 599
Public Enemy, 603
Public Works Administration (PWA), 432
Puerto Rico, 276, 281–282, *367*
Pulitzer Prize, 482, 572, 599
punishment, 38, *39*, 56, 60, 71, 138–139, 143
Puritans, 53–54
Purvis, Robert, 187
PWA (Public Works Administration), 432

Al-Qaeda, 613
Q-Tip (Fareed Kamal), 624
Quakers, 70, 86, 98, 102, 111, 125, 165, 171,
        195–196
Quasi-War, 114
Quicksand (Larasen), 403–404
quilt-making, 142–143, *143*, 571
Quitman, John A., 201

R. J. Reynolds Tobacco Company, 494–495
Ra, Sun, 568
RA (Resettlement Administration), 430
Races of Mankind (Benedict), 464
racial profiling, 598
Radical Reconstruction
    African American Congressmen in, 243–246, *244*
    Freedman's Bureau, 238–240, 248–250
    state legislators in, 245–247
    women and, 243, 247
railroads. *See also* Underground Railroad
    employment violence, 210
    post-WWI employment in, 349
    segregation of, *260*, 261, 272, 299, 305
    slave hiring by, 145
    slaves for, 145, 232
Rainbow Coalition, 589, 590, *590*
Rainbow/PUSH, 611
Rainey, Gertrude "Ma," 382, *383*
Rainey, Joseph H., 244–245
Raisin in the Sun, A (Hansberry), 485
RAM (Revolutionary Action Movement), 554
Ramirez, Blandina Cárdenas, 594
Randolph, A. Philip, 344, 346, 368–370, 372–373, 436,
        451–454, *454*, 493, 499, 512, 515, *530*, 540, 544,
        548, 550–551, 555

Randolph, John, 126, 127, 133
Randolph, Peter, 130
Rankin, Jeannette, 328
Rankin, John, 202
Ransier, Alonzo J., 245
rap music, 602–605, *605*
rape, 138, 150–151, 253–254, 347
Raspberry, William, 609
Ray, Charles B., 213
Ray, James Earl, 579
Readjuster Party, 263–264
Reagan, Ronald, 590, *591*
    political appointments by, 593–595, 606, *607*, 608
Reagan-Bush years, 590–591
Reagon, Bernice Johnson, 521, 528
Real Facts about Ethiopia (Rogers), 487
Reason, Charles L., 175
Reconstruction
    abolition movement during, 237–238
    affluence during, 254
    Black Codes, 238–239, 242
    black conventions, 240–242
    churches in, 251
    Democratic party and, 247
    economic adjustments to, 251–256
    education and, 250–251
    end of, 256–259
    family structure during, 253–254
    Fourteenth Amendment, 240, 242
    franchisement and, *235*, 242–243
    Johnson's reconstruction plan, 237–238
    Lincoln and, 236–237
    political adjustment to, 242–247
    Radical Reconstruction, 242–247
    relief efforts, 252–253
    Republicans and, 236–238, 240, 246–247, 256, 258–259
    social adjustment to, 247–251
    South Carolina and, 242, 246–247, 252, 254, 257
    Supreme Court and, 258–259
    vigilante groups, 238–239, 256–258, *257*
    women during, 243, 247, 253–254
Reconstruction Finance Corporation, 422
Red Cross
    blood bank protests, 464
    WWI nurses, 346
Red Rover, U.S.S. (ship), 223
"Red Summer" (1919), 370
Rediker, Marcus, 28
Redmond, Don, 392
Reeb, James, 526
re-enslavement of free blacks, 167
Reese, David M., 196
regionalism, slave culture and, 65
Rehnquist, William H., 594
Rehnquist, William J., 615
Reid, Ira D. A., 427, 513
religion, 45–46, 48, 78
    black colonization and, 124
    of Creoles, 65
    Father Divine, 374
    folk beliefs and, 148–149
    free blacks and, 177
    freedom songs and, 532
    gender inequality in, 178
    independent churches, 109–110
    Latin American slaves and, 45
    in Mid-Atlantic colonies, 68
    mulattos and, 75–76
    revivals in, 109–110
    slavery and, 65, 148–149, 190–191
    white surveillance of slave religion, 148
    worship services in, 148
"Religion and the Pure Principles of Morality, the Sure Foundation on Which We Must Build" (Stewart, M.), 179
Reminiscences of My Life in Camp with the 33d United States Colored Troops (Taylor), 222, 230
Remond, Charles Lenox, 188
Remond, Sarah Parker, 188
reparations, *616*, 616–618
Republican party
    African Americans in, 580
    alienation from, 590–591
    lily-white South and, 421
    loyalty to, 421
    Northern support of emancipation, 213
    political participation, 421–425
    Reconstruction and, 236–238, 240, 246–247, 256, 258–259
    shift of allegiance from, 421–423
Reserve Officers Training Corps (ROTC), 452
Resettlement Administration (RA), 430
Revels, Hiram, 243
Revere, Paul, 88, *88*
reverse discrimination, 594–595, 597, 615
Revolutionary Action Movement (RAM), 554
Revolutionary War, military service, 90–94
Rhett, Robert Barnwell, 137
Rhode Island, 66, 67, 93, 94, 99, 106, 107, 109, 112
    free black population in, 105t
    slave population in, 105t
    voting in, 163
Rice, Condoleeza, 613, *613*, 635
Richardson, Donna, 552–553
Richardson, George, 286
Richardson, Gloria, *532*, 533, 552–553
Richmond, David, 519
Richmond v. J. A. Crosson Company, 594
Rickey, Branch, 496–497
Ricks, Willie, 558
Rights of the British Colonies Asserted and Proved, The (Otis), 87
Ringgold, Faith, 571, 573
rioting, 548, 577, 578
    Atlanta (1906), 284
    Brownsville, Texas (1906), 284–285
    Christiana Riot (1851), 204–205
    Civil War, 210
    Detroit, 361, 469, *578*, 579
    Great Depression and, 421
    Harlem (1943), 469
    Illinois, 286, 350, 359
    North Carolina, 268, *268*
    Rodney King incident, 597–598
    Springfield, Illinois, 286
    Texas, 284–285, 358
    Tulsa, Oklahoma, 617
    Watts (1965), 578–579
    Wilmington, N. C. (1898), 282–283
    WWI, 349–350
    WWII, 469
Rising Wind, A (White, W.), 471
Rivas, Andrés de, 41
River George (Lee, G.), 483
Roach, Max, 520, *520*
Roberts, Benjamin, 174
Roberts, John G., 615, 616
Roberts, Lucile, 569
Roberts, Needham, 336
Roberts, Robert, 170
Roberts v. City of Boston (1850), 174

Robeson, Paul, 396, 443–444, 445, 485, 488, 491, 500
Robinson, Bill "Bojangles," 397, 409, 443, 444
Robinson, Jackie, 496, *497*, 500
Robinson, Joanne Gibson, 515, 528
Robinson, Randall, 605–606, 616–617
Robinson, Ruby Doris Smith, 528
Robinson, Spottswood, 542
Rochester Convention (1853), 176
Rock, John, 210
Rodgers, Carolyn, 567
Rogers, J. A., 487
Roman Catholic Church
    in Africa, 19
    Black Power and, 559
    in Latin America, 25, 29, 44–45
    schools of, 597
Roosevelt, Eleanor, 423–424, 426, *428*, 440, 448, 455, 472, 491
Roosevelt, Franklin D., *417*, 418, 463, 608
    criticism of, 423–424
    election of, 422
    Executive Order 8802, 455–456
    on four freedoms, 453–454
    pre-WWII, 450
Roosevelt, Theodore, 278–280, 284–285, 354
    Spanish-American War and, 279–280
Roots (Haley), 568
Rope and Faggot, A Biography of Judge Lynch (White, W.), 363
Rose, Tricia, 604–605
ROTC (Reserve Officers Training Corps), 452
Rough Riders, 278–280
Roundtree, Richard, 569
Rowan, Carl, 542
Royal Society, 67
Rubin, Rick, 603
Ruffin, Josephine, *376*
Ruggles, David, 187, 189
Rumsfeld, Donald, 613
runaways, 41, 44–45, *52*, 61, 82–83, 87–88, *88*, 101, 153–155, *154*, 162
Run-DMC, 603, *605*
Runnin' Wild (musical), 396–397
Rush, Barbara, *595*
Rush, Benjamin, 86, 98, 104, 110, 114–115, 126
Rush, Richard, 126
Russian Revolution, 362
Russwurm, John, 175, 180–181, 189
Rust, Richard S., 193
Rustin, Bayard, 511, 512, 513, 517, 540, 544, 551
Rutland College, 175
Rutledge, Edward, 91

Sable, Jean Baptiste Point du, 25
Sahara region, 2–3
St. Augustine, *77*, 77–78, 80
St. Augustine's College, 250
St. Domingue, 113–114
St. Eustatius, 36
St. George's Methodist Episcopal Church, 110
St. John, 40
St. Lucia, 36
St. Thomas, 36, 40
St. Thomas's African Episcopal Church
Saint Domingue (Haiti), 38, 40
Salaam, Kalamu ya, 566
Salem, Peter, 90
Salt n Pepa, 604
Saltville (Virginia), 227
Salzman, Murray, 594

San Francisco
    black migration to, 469
    UN conference (1945), 485
Sanchez, Sonia, 567
Sanders, Pharoah, 568
Sanders of the River (1935), 444
Santo Domingo, 49
São Tomé, 25, 43
Saturday Night (painting) (Motley), *411*, 412
satyagraha, 512
Savage, Augusta, 408, 440–441, *441*
Savannah, siege of, 227
Sawyer, George S., 194
Saxton, Gen. Rufus, 215, 217, 220
Scalia, Antonin, 594
Scar of Shame (film), 394
Scarred Justice: The Orangeburg Massacre 1968, 564
Schmeling, Max, 450
Schomburg, Arthur Alfonso, 366–367, *367*
school desegregation
    Civil Rights Act of 1964 and, 547, 596–597
    resistance to, 545
Schuyler, George, 414
SCHW (Southern Conference for Human Welfare), 440
Schwerner, Michael, 525, 528, 618
SCLC (Southern Christian Leadership Conference), 521
Scott, Dred, 205–206, *206*, 242
Scott, Emmett J., 334, 339, 346, 349, 365
Scott, Gen. Winfield, 211
Scott-Heron, Gil, 567
Scottsboro boys, 436–437, *438*
SDS (Students for a Democratic Society), 560
Seale, Bobby, 561, 562
seamen, African Americans. *See* Marine Corps; merchant marines; navy
Seattle, 615–616
Second Great Awakening, 190
Second Reconstruction, 547–548
Secretary of Health and Human Services, U. S., 592
Secretary of State, *607*, 613, *613*
segregation, *260*
    Black Muslims and, 550
    in churches, 148
    of education, 173–175, 505, *505*, 506–509
    in housing, 274, 313, 356, 398, 503, 535–536
    legalization of, 270–275
    Supreme Court and, 270–271
    in WWII military, 457, 460, 464–465
    of YMCA, 316–317
Selassie, Haile, 486
Selective Service Act (1917), 329, 451, 562
Selective Service Act (1940), 457
Seligman, Edwin R. A., 349
Sellers, Cleveland, 564
Selma-to-Montgomery March, 526–528, *527*
Senate. *See also* Congress; House of Representatives
    blacks in, 243–244, *244*, 580, 591–593
    on Brownsville riot, 285
    Civil Rights Act of 1957, 539
    Civil Rights Act of 1960, 541
    Civil Rights Act of 1964, 545
    Dyer antilynching bill, 364
    Iraq invasion, 606
    Judiciary Committee, 594, 596
    Thirteenth Amendment and, 214–215
    Twenty-fourth Amendment, 545
    Voting Rights Act of 1965, 618
Senate Committee on Home Security and Governmental Affairs, 622
Senate Judiciary Committee, 594, 596

Senegal, 32, 344, 625, *625*

Sermon Preached on the 24th Day of June 1789, Being the Festival of St. John the Baptist, at the Request of the Right Worshipful and Grand Master Prince Hall and the Rest of the Brethren of the African Lodge of the Honorable Society of Free and Accepted Masons in Boston by the Reverend Brother Marrant, Chaplain, A (Marrant), 116

Seven League Boots, The (Murray, A.), 599

761st Tank Battalion, 461

Seward, William Henry, 205, 212

Shadd, Abraham, 187, 188

Shadd, Mary Anne. *See* Cary, Mary Anne Shadd

Shadow and Act (Ellison), 483

Shaft (film), 569

Shakur, Assata, 565–566

Shakur, Tupac, 603, 604

Shange, Ntozake, 572

Share Croppers' Union, 437

Sharp, Granville, 89

Sharpton, Al, 635

Shaw, Robert Gould, 234

Shays, Daniel, 100

Shays's Rebellion, 100

Shelley v. Kraemer (1948), 503

Shepp, Archie, 568

Sherman, Gen. Thomas W., 219

Sherman, Gen. William Tecumseh, 215

She's Gotta Have It (film), 599

Show Boat (1936), 443

Shuffle Along (musical), 396, *397*

Shuttlesworth, Fred L., 522

Sierra Leone, 96, 96m, 125

Silent Protest Parade (1917), 363, 369

Simmons, Russell, 603, 627

Simms, William Gilmore, 131, 195

Simone, Nina, 565, *565*

Sims, Charles, 553

Singleton, John, 600

Sipuel, Ada, 504–505

Sissle, Noble, 385–386

Sisterhood Is Powerful (Morgan), 575

614th Tank Destroyer Battalion, 461

Sketches of Colored Society in Philadelphia (Willson), 171

Sketches of Slave Life: Or Illustrations of the "Peculiar Institution": "Slavery is Slavery" (Randolph, P.), 130

slave codes, 38, 54–57, 137–140

slave factories, 27, *29*

slave families separation of, 31, 134–135, 149

slave narratives, 32, *70*, 119, 198

slave passport, *72, 138*

slave resistance, 151
    Denmark Vesey, 155–157, 156t
    runaways, 41, 44–45, *52*, 61, 82–83, 87–88, *88*, 101, 153–155, *154*
    sabotage and suicide, 152–154
    slave revolts, 155–158
    violence in, 154–158

slave trade, *136*
    Africans in New World, 29–30
    business of, 30–33, *34*, 35, 132–134
    in Caribbean islands, 35–41
    development of trading practices, 27–33
    domestic, 130–137, 131m
    illicit African trade, *136*, 136–137
    in Latin America, 41–43
    Middle Passage, 33, *34*, 35, *35*
    number of slaves imported, 35
    profits from, 35, 134–135, 134t, 136–137
    routes of trade, 26m–27m
    sales in, 35, *64*, *106*, *129*, 130, *132*, 132–135, 151–153

slavery, *254. See also* Colonial slavery
    adjustment to end of, 248–251
    in African life, 9–12
    brutality of owners, 138–139
    in Caribbean, 35–41
    effects of Cotton Kingdom on, 140–142
    in Europe, 25–26
    heredity of, 54–55, 150–151
    in Latin America, 41–45
    legalization of, 54–63
    master-slave relationship, 48, 150–151
    nonagricultural, 144–147
    plantations, 140–144
    revolutionary philosophy and, 194–195
    slave codes, 38, 54–57, 137–140
    slave societies in, 45–46
    in South, 129–158
    Southern proslavery arguments, 184–196
    upheld by churches, 195

slaves. *See also* manumission
    African v. Creole, 65, 70–72
    breeding of, 10, 58, 149–150
    Confederate debate on arming, 31–233
    in cotton production, 140–144
    diet of, 141–142
    domestic, 66, 68, 101, 106, 108, 140, 203, 253
    field hands, 140
    folk beliefs, 148–149
    free blacks v., 105–107, 105t
    hiring out, 43–44, 145–147
    house servants, 140
    in Lower South, 65
    names of, 48, 50
    purchase of freedom, 43–44, 146
    for railroads, 145
    recreation in, 147–148, *148*
    religion of, 65, 148–149, 190–191
    as tradespeople, 144–146
    weddings in, 147, *148*

Slave's Friend (periodical), 192

slip, for pottery, 5

Sloan, Margaret, 575

Smalls, Robert, 231, *231*, 244–245

Smith, Alfred E., 421

Smith, Bessie, 382, *383*, 384, 385, 395

Smith, Clara, 382

Smith, Ferdinand, 496, 499

Smith, Gerrit, 180, 193, 205, 207

Smith, Jennie, 142–143, *143*

Smith, Kelly Miller, 518

Smith, Mamie, 381–382, 384

Smith, Mary Louise, 515, 518

Smith, Trixie, 382

Smith, Will, 600

Smith v. Allwright, 364, 503, 539

SNCC (Student Nonviolent Coordinating Committee), 520–521, 524–526

Snipes, Wesley, 600

SNYC (Southern Negro Youth Conference), 439–440

Socialist Party of America, 369

Society for the Propagation of the Gospel, 76

Society of Friends. *See* Quakers

Songhay, 15–16

Songs of Jamaica (McKay), 400–401

Sonni Ali, 15

Soul on Ice (Cleaver), 559–560

Souls of Black Folk (Du Bois), 567

South
   abolition movement in, 98–100, 195–196
   against black soldiers, 463–465
   against desegregation, 501–502, 508–509
   education in, 174–175
   friction with WWI troops, 333–334
   migration from, 364–365, *365*
   migration (1975–2000) to, 627–629, 628m
   redistricting in, 549
   segregation of education in, 506, 539
   slavery in, 129–158
   voter registration drives, 524–525, 545–547
   white supremacy in, 256–258
South Africa, 490
   apartheid protests, 488, 605–606
   release of Mandela, 606
South Africa, Republic of, 605–606
South African Embassy, 605–606
South Carolina, 60, 63, 73–74, 76–78, 93, 131–132, *136*, 137, 267
   black laws in, 161
   Civil War and, 209, 212, 215–217, 219–224, 227–228, 230, 232–233
   Constitution v., 100–101
   Denmark Vesey insurrection in, 138–139
   free black population in, 105t
   Reconstruction and, 242, 246–247, 252, 254, 257
   right to vote law (1964), 546
   sales in, *64*
   slave population in, 105t
   slave women in, 143
South Carolina State University, 563
Southern Christian Leadership Conference (SCLC), 521, 540, 557
   founding of, 518
Southern Conference for Human Welfare (SCHW), 440
Southern Homestead Act, 252–253
Southern Institutes (Sawyer), 194
"Southern Manifesto," 539
Southern Negro Youth Conference (SNYC), 439–440
Southern Poverty Law Project, 614
Southern Road (Brown, S.), 436
Southern Tenant Farmers Union, 429, 435, 495
Sowell, Thomas, 597
Spain
   Caribbean monopoly, 36
   explorations from, 23–24
   Spanish Florida, 77–78
   Spanish Louisiana, 62–63
Spanish-American War, 277–280, *278*
Spellman, A. B., 568
Spencer, Kenneth, 445
Spielberg, Steven, 600
Spivey, Victoria, 382
sports, African Americans in, 496–497, *497*
   baseball, 496, *497*, 500
   basketball, 588
   boxing, 562–563, *563*
   golf, *588*, 589
   Olympic Games, 450, 563, 589
   tennis, 589
Springarn, Arthur B., 353
Springarn Medal, 396, 471
Spyglass Tree, The (Murray, A.), 599
S. S. Booker T. Washington (ship), 463
S. S. Frederick Douglass (ship), 463
S. S. Robert L. Vann (ship), 463
Stamp Act, 85, 87
Stanford, Max, 554
Stanton, Elizabeth Cady, 243

State, The (Wilson), 354
Statistical Inquiry into the Condition of the People of Colour of the City and Districts of Philadelphia, 171
Steel v. Louisville and Nashville Railroad (1944), 503
Steel Workers Organizing Committee (SWOC), 434
Steele, Shelby, 597
Steinem, Gloria, 589
Stephens, Alexander, 247
stereotypes, 163–164
   in film, 443
stevedores, *69*
   in WWI, 332, 334–335
Stevens, John Paul, 616
Stevens, Thaddeus, 238
Steward, Austin, 198
Stewart, James, 178–179
Stewart, Maria W., 178–179, 187
Stewart, Ollie, 471
Stiles, Ezra, 97–98
Still, William, 202, 203
Still, William Grant, 444–445, 447
Stimson, Henry, 455, 470
Stokes, Ann, 223
Stono Rebellion, 77–78, 156t
Storer College, 250
Storey, Moorfield, 353
Stormy Weather (film), 444
Stowe, Harriet Beecher, 205, 213
Stowers, Freddie, 338–339
Straight Out of Brooklyn (film), 600
Strayhorn, Billy, 445
Street, The (Petry), 483
Street in Bronzeville (Brooks), 482
Stride toward Freedom (King), 521
Student Nonviolent Coordinating Committee (SNCC), 520–521, 524–526, 530, 554, 557, 558
Students for a Democratic Society (SDS), 560, 563–564
Sudan, 5, 6, 7–8
Sugar Act, 85
Sugar Hill Gang, 603
Sugar Hill Records, 603
Sula (Morrison), 571
Sullivan, Leon, 534
Sullivan, Louis W., 592
Sumner, Charles, 174, 193, 204, 234, 247, *248*
Sundiata Keita, 13
Superfly (film), 569
Suppression of the African Slave Trade, The (Du Bois), 2
Supreme Court, 204, 247, 363, 476, 613
   affirmative action, 594–595, 615
   Brown v. Board of Education, 507–508
   Buchanan v. Warley, 353
   on bus travel, 511–512, 518, 542
   Bush, G. H. W. and, 594–595
   Bush/Gore election, 613–614
   on civil rights legislation, 511–513, 516, 518, 530, 537, 541–542, 545, 594–595
   Clarence Thomas confirmation, 595–596
   Dred Scott case, 205–206, *206*, 242
   on education, 504–506, 615–616
   Guinn v. United States, 353
   Hansberry v. Lee, 485
   on housing, 537
   Moore v. Dempsey, 360
   Muhammad Ali, 563
   NAACP and, 594
   Nixon v. Herndon, 364
   overthrow of Radical Reconstruction, 247
   on picketing, 421

Reconstruction and, 258–259
on redistricting, 549, 596, 614–615
on restrictive covenants, 5–7
on Scottsboro boys, 436–437
segregation and, 270–271
Smith v. Allwright, 364
Survey Graphic, 400, 407
Susan B. Anthony Amendment, 375, 377
Sutherland, Robert L., 476
Swahili Coast, 20–21
Sweatt, Heman, 506
Sweet, Ossian H., 361
Sweet Sweetback's Baadsssss Song (film), 569
SWOC (Steel Workers Organizing Committee), 434
Symphony in Black (film) (1934), 444
syncretism, 65

Tacky's Rebellion, 39
Taft, William Howard, 354
Taft-Hartley Act, 498
Talbert, Mary B., 345, 363, 375
Tales of Manhattan (1942), 444
Taney, Roger B., 206
Tanneyhill, Ann, 471, 472
Tappan, Arthur, 180, 192, 195, 196
Tappan, Lewis, 192, 216
Taste of Power: A Black Woman's Story, A (Brown, E.), 573
Taylor, Susie King, 222, 222, 230
Taylor, Zachary, 196
Teasman, John, 111–112
Teer, Barbara Ann, 566
television
    Roots miniseries, 568
    series shows, 600–601
    talk shows, 600–601, 634, 634
Temple, Shirley, 443
Ten Colored Women with the American Expeditionary
        Forces (Hunton and Johnson, K.), 340
Ten Percent Plan, 237
the Tenderloin, 398
Tennessee, 106, 359
    Civil War and, 209, 226–227, 232
    free black population in, 105t
    during Reconstruction, 237
    re-enslavement in, 167
    slave population in, 105t
Tennessee Valley Authority (TVA), 430
Tenth Cavalry
    in Spanish-American War, 277–279, 278
    in WWI, 329
    in WWII, 457
Terrell, Mary Church, 375, 376
Texas, 136–137, 364
    acquisition of, 132
    Brownsville riots (1906) in, 284–285
    Civil War and, 209, 214, 221, 227, 229–230
    illegal slave trade to, 136–137, 137m
    race riot in, 358
    Reconstruction and, 247, 256
    re-enslavement in, 167
Texas, University of, 506
    Law School, 597
textile industry
    cotton production for, 130–131
    slave labor for, 145
    unionization of, 433
theater, 402, 485, 566, 569, 599
    Harlem, 395–397, 447
    musical theater, 389, 415
    Uncle Tom's Cabin in, 205

Their Eyes Were Watching God (Hurston), 404–405
There Is Confusion (Fauset), 400, 403
These Low Grounds (Turpin), 483
They Have Tomorrow (Bontemps), 483
They Seek a City (Bontemps and Conroy), 482–483
Thibodeaux, Mary Roger (sister), 559
Third Life of Grange Copeland, The (Walker), 572
Third Louisiana Native Guards, 221
Third South Carolina Regiment, 228
Third World Women's Alliance, 574, 575, 576, 576
Thirteenth Amendment, 214–218
Thirty Years of Lynching in the United States,
        1889–1918 (NAACP), 363–364
Thirty-Ninth United States Colored Troops, 227
Thirty-Sixth United States Colored Troops, 227
Thomas, Charles L., 461
Thomas, Clarence, 592–593, 595, 595–596, 608, 615
Thomas, Gen. Lorenzo, 225
Thomas, Robert, 608
Thomas, Virginia, 595
Thomas and Beulah (Dove), 599
Thompson, J. E. W., 282
Thompson, Marie, 284
Thompson, William Hale "Big Bill," 377, 422
Thoreau, Henry David, 207, 518
Thornburg v. Gingles, 549
Thornton, William, 125
Thornwell, James Henley, 195
Thoughts on Colonization (Garrison), 180, 191
332nd Fighter Group, 460, 462
369th infantry, 335, 335–337, 342, 389
370th U.S. Infantry. See Eighth Illinois Infantry
Three-Fifths Compromise, 100–101
Thurman, Wallace, 414
Thurmond, Strom, 591, 595
Tilden, Samuel J., 259
Till, Emmett, 528
Tillman, Ben ("Pitchfork Ben"), 258, 267, 285
Timbuktu, 1, 15, 16
Time (magazine), 474
TLC, 604
"To Be Young, Gifted, and Black" (song), 565
To Secure These Rights (government report), 476, 500–501
tobacco, 494, 495, 499
Tobacco Stemmers and Laborers Industrial Union
        (TSLIU), 439
Tobago, 36
Tocqueville, Alexis de, 161
Tolson, Melvin B., 482
Toomer, Jean (Nathan Toomer), 401, 405–406, 415
Torrence, Ridgely, 396
Tougher Than Leather (film), 603
Towne, Laura, 217
Townsend, Willard, 498–499
trade routes, Islam and, 6–7
Trading Places (film), 599
Trainwhistle Guitar (Murray, A.), 599
Trans-Africa, 605–606
Trans-Sahara trade routes, 7m, 7–9
Treatise on the Intellectual Character, and the Civil and
        Political Condition of the Colored People in the
        United States and the Prejudice Exercised Toward
        Them (Easton), 164
Treaty of Paris, 280
Trent, William J., 427
Triple Jeopardy (monthly), 575
Trotter, Monroe, 352, 354, 357
Truly Disadvantaged, The (Wilson), 586
Truman, Harry, 396, 498, 500–502, 537, 538
Truth, Sojourner (Wagenen, Isabella Van), 179, 188, 188, 243

TSLIU (Tobacco Stemmers and Laborers Industrial Union), 439
Tubman, Harriet, 134, 202–203, *203*, 207, 222, *570*, 570–571
Tuckegee Study, 432–433
Tucker, Beverly, 194
Tucker, C. Delores, 605
Tucker, St. George, 98
Tulsa Race Riot Commission, 617
Tunka-Menin, 12–13
Tunstall v. Brotherhood of Locomotive Firemen and Enginemen, 503
Turner, Georgia Mae, 531
Turner, Henry McNeil, 246, 251, 550–551
Turner, Lorenzo Dow, 479
Turner, Mary, 363
Turner, Nat, 139, 156–158, 156t, *158*, 185–186
Turpin, Waters, 483
Tuskegee (Air Force), 458–460, *459*
Tuskegee Institute, 291, 307
"Tuskegee study," 432–433, 619
TVA (Tennessee Valley Authority), 430
Twelve Million Black Voices (Wright, R.), 483
Twenty-fourth Amendment, 545
Twenty-Fourth Infantry, 462–463
Two Trains Running (play) (Wilson, August), 599
2 Live Crew, 603
Tyler, John, 136, 196

UAW (United Auto Workers), 492, 495–496
UCAPAWA (United Cannery, Agricultural, Packing, and Allied Workers of America), *435*, 435–436
Umbra (magazine), 566
Uncle Tom and Little Eva (painting), 193
Uncle Tom's Cabin (Stowe), 205
Uncle Tom's Children (Wright, R.), 436, 483
Underground Railroad, 191, 195–196, 199–203, 200m
Underwood, Oscar, 364
unemployment
    in 1982, 590
    black v. white (1965–1990), 584t
UNESCO (Educational, Scientific, and Cultural Organization), 489
UNIA (Universal Negro Improvement Association), 370–373, *371*, 379
Union Army, African Americans in
    attempts to enlist, 218–219
    in battle, *225*, 225–227, *226*
    medals awarded, 227
    unequal pay in, 227–228
Union League, 246–247
unions, 369
    agriculture and, 434–436, *435*
    discrimination in, 433–436
United Auto Workers (UAW), 492, 495–496
United Cannery, Agricultural, Packing, and Allied Workers of America (UCAPAWA), *435*, 435–436, 495
United Nations, 485
    African-American participation, 488
    Du Bois's Appeal to, 491
    human rights and, 488–489
    petition to, 490–491
    Trusteeship Council, 489–490
United Service Organization (USO), 464
United States Commission on Civil Rights, 539, 543
United States v. Cruikshank, 258–259, 266
United States v. Jefferson County, 547
United States v. Reese, 258–259, 266

Universal Negro Improvement Association (UNIA), 370–373, *371*, 379
Urban League. See National Urban League
Uruguay, 42
USO (United Service Organization), 464
Utah, 161

Van Buren, Martin, 136
Vann, Robert L., 427
Vardaman, J. K., 269
Vashon, George B., 187
Vashon, John B., 176, 187
Vassa, Gustavus, 32–33, *70*, 70–71, 119
vaudeville, 398
Venezuela, slave trade in, 41–42
Vermont, 99, 105t, 106
    free black population in, 105t
    slave population in, 105t
Vesey, Denmark, 155–157, 156t
Vicksburg, 227
Victoria, Queen, 175
Vietnam War, 562–564, *563*, 581
vigilante groups, 238–239, 256–258, *257*
Villard, Oswald Garrison, 254
Vinson, Ch. Justice Fred M., 506
violence, against African Americans. See also Ku Klux Klan; lynchings; rioting
    against free blacks, 165
    in patrol system, 139
    punishment of slaves, 38, *39*, 56, 60, 71, 138–139, 143–144
    vigilante groups, 238–239, 256–258, *257*
    during WWI, 333–334
    during WWII, 469
Virgin Islands, 282
Virginia, 50, 51, 52, 59, 73, 93, 98, 101
    black population growth in, 71–72
    free blacks in, 105t, 132, 135, 618
    independence v. slave society in, 85–86
    Nat Turner insurrection in, 139, 156t, 157–158, *158*, 185–186
    punishment in, 71
    rebellion in, 126–127
    against school desegregation, 509
    slave codes in, 55–57
    slave population in, 104–105, 105t
Virginia Union College, 565
Voice, The (magazine), 369
"Vote or Die" Rally, *612*, 627
voting rights, 115, 163, 546–547
    Alabama, 545, *546*
    black women and, 375–377
    Civil Rights Act of 1957, 541
    free blacks and, 160, 162–163
    gerrymandering, 263, 614–615
    in party politics, 112–113
    voter registration drives, 524–525, 545–547
Voting Rights Act (1965), 545, *546*, 580, 596, 618

W. E. B. Du Bois Institute for African and African American Research, 634
WAC (Women's Army Corps), 458
Waddy, Joseph, 542
Wade, Jimmy, 385
Wagenen, Isabella Van (Sojourner Truth), 179
Waldon, John Milton, 345
Walker, A'Lelia, 409
Walker, Alice, 571–572, 573
Walker, David, 157, 158, 170, 177, 179, *185*, 185–186, 195
Walker, George, 398

Walker, Kara, 602, *602*
Walker, Margaret, 482
Walker's Appeal in Four Articles: Together with a
        Preamble, to the Coloured Citizens of the World,
        but in Particular and Very Expressly to Those of the
        United States of America (Walker, D.), 157, 177, 179,
        185, 185–186, 195
Wall Street Project, 611
Wallace, Christopher "Biggie Smalls," 604
Wallace, George, 545
Wallace, Henry, 474
Wallace, Michelle, 573
Wallace, Sippie, 382
Waller, Thomas "Fats," 389, 396–397
Walrond, Colonel, 39–40
Walrond, Eric, 436
Walters, Alexander, 354
War Department, 456, 462, 464, 471
War for Independence. *See* Revolutionary War
War of 1812, 121–124
War of Jenkins' Ear, 78–79
Ward, Samuel Ringgold (reverend), 183
Wards Cove Packing Company v. Atonio, 594
Warfield, William, 445
Warren, Earl, 507, 508, 537, 539
Warren Court, 537–538
Washington, Booker T., 230, 269, *297*, *301*, 349,
        371, 374, 425
    accommodation and, 297–298
    business philosophy of, 309–310
    Du Bois and, 304–305, 353
    leadership of, 3–4, 299, 302
    against Niagarites, 304–305
    published works, 288, 323
    Tuskegee Institute and, 291, 307
    white philanthropy and, 292
Washington, Bushrod, 126, 191
Washington, D. C.
    Million Man March, *587*, 587–588
    as slave trading center, 133
Washington, Denzel, 600
Washington, Freddie, 443
Washington, George, 90–91, 95–97, 102,
        114, 199
    against blacks' military service, 90–91
    reverses policy on blacks, 92
Washington, Harold, 589
Washington, University of, 597
Waters, Ethel, 382, 384, 444
Waters, Mary, 618, 633
Waters, Maxine, 589, 596
Watson, George, 465
Watson, Tom, 264–266, 346
WAVES (Women Accepted for Volunteer Emergency
        Service), *457*, 460
Wayne State University, *612*
"We Shall Overcome" (song), 521
Weary Blues (Hughes), 402
Weaver, George L. P., 542
Weaver, Robert C., 427, 542
Webb, Chick, 386, 447–448
Webster, Daniel, 160
Webster, Delia, 202
Weld, Theodore Dwight, 190–191
Wells, Ida B., *272*, 272–273, 352, 377
Wells-Barnett, Ida B., 375
West
    black migration to, 121, 307, 347, 364–365, 469
    expansion of slavery to, 99, 106, 209
West, Cornel, 588

West, Kanye, 624, 627
Western Reserve, 192
Weyler, Gen. Valeriano, 276
Wharton, Clifton R., 542, 565
What the Negro Wants (essays), 477
Wheatley, Phillis, 88–89, *89*, 116, 118, 177
Whipper, William, 193, 206
Whipple, Prince, 95
White, Byron, *595*
White, George, 422
White, Josh, 436
White, Walter, 363, 384, 415–416, 444, 451–452, 468, 471,
        488, 500, 502
Whitefield, George, 109
whites
    assistance in slave revolts, 193, 207
    in indentured servitude, 51
    resistance to integration, 519–526
    surveillance of slave religion, 148
    "white backlash" after 1830, 194–197
    white supremacy, 357–362
Whitman, Gov. Christine Todd, 598
Whitney, Eli, *130*
Whittaker, Forest, 600
Whittier, John Greenleaf, 192
Who's Who in Colored America, 367
Why We Can't Wait (King), 517, 522
Whydah, kingdom of (Ouidah), *8*, 8–9
WICS (Women in Community Service), 574
Wideman, John Edgar, 599
Wigg, James, 267
Wilberforce, William, 175
Wilberforce University, 175
Wilder, Douglas, 590
Wilhelm II, 175
Wilkie, Wendell, 424
Wilkins, J. Ernest, 534
Wilkins, Roy, 500, *540*, 581
will.i.am, 627
Williams, Aubrey, *428*
Williams, Bert, 398
Williams, Clarence, 385–386
Williams, David, 618
Williams, Fannie Barrier, 374–375
Williams, George Washington, 425
Williams, Nat, *430*
Williams, Peter, Jr., 117, 170–171, 181–182, 187
Williams, Robert F., 553–554
Williams, Roger, 66
Williams, Serena, 589
Williams, Venus, 589
Williams, Walter, 597
Wills, Frances, *457*
Willson, Joseph, 171
Wilson, August, 599
Wilson, Harriet E., 172
Wilson, Hawkins, 249
Wilson, William Julius, 585, 586, 621
Wilson, Woodrow, 328, 339, 343–344, 345, 346,
        354, 356
Wimbledon Championship (tennis), 589
Winfrey, Oprah, 600–601, 634, *634*
Winter, William, 608
Within Our Gates (film), 394
Wolof slavery, 11
women, African American, 374–379. *See also*
        specific women
    in abolition movement, 187–188, 192
    black feminism, 375–377, 572–577
    Black Panther Party and, 560

women, African American—*Cont.*
  in Brazilian slavery, 44
  childbearing for, 149
  demonstrations and, *510*
  employment of, 74, 253, *348*, *467*, 471–472
  in film, 443
  free blacks, 170, 177–179
  in Harlem Renaissance, 403–405
  Hip Hop artists, 604–605
  HIV/AIDS, 619
  jobs for, post WWI, *348*
  military service, *457*, 458, 460
  in movement, *510*, 528–533
  music, 381–385, *383*, 444, 447–448, *448*
  new image of, 378–379
  nurses Civil War/WWI/WWII, 222–223, 340–341,
    341, 346, 458
  philanthropy, 600–601
  in plantation system, 37, 142–143
  political involvement of, 375–379
  press and, 177–178
  rape of, 138, 149–151, 253–254, 347
  during Reconstruction, 243, 247, 253–254
  in slave trade, 10–11
  in voter rights campaigns, 530
  women's suffrage, 375–377, *376*
  as writers, 571–572
Women Accepted for Volunteer Emergency Service
  (WAVES), 460
Women in Community Service (WICS), 574
Women's Army Corps (WAC), 458
Women's Political Council, 515
Woods, Eldrick "Tiger," *588*, 589
Woodson, Carter G., 373, 479–480, 486
Woolman, John, 86, *98*
Work Progress Administration (WPA), 432, 440, 466
Workers Defense League, 512
working poor, 585–586
World Trade Center (New York), 613
World View of Race, A (book) (Bunche), 475
World War I. *See also* specific battles, divisions
  Africa after, 343–344
  band in, 340, *340*
  beginning of, 328
  coming home from, 342–343
  draft for, 329–330
  home front, 344–350
  honors in, *336*, 336–340
  international politics after, 343–344

  military service in, *327*, 328–343, *335*, *336*, *338*, *340*
  nurses in, 340–341, *341*, 346
  overseas service in, 334–343
  racist propaganda in, 339
  slander in, 339–341
  369th infantry, *335*, 335–337, 342, 389
  371th infantry, 337–339
World War II
  domestic war efforts, 468–469
  European service, 461–462
  Hitler-Stalin Pact, 438–439
  home front, 466–472
  industry jobs, 467, *467*
  Mediterranean theater, 462
  military awards and honors in, *449*, 461, *465*, 465–466
  military service in, 456–466
  NAACP and, 450–451
  nurses, 458
  Pacific theater, 462–463
  WACs, 458
  WAVES, *457*, 460
WPA (Work Progress Administration), 432, 440, 466
Wretched of the Earth (Fanon), 560
Wright, Elizur, 192
Wright, Rev. Jeremiah, 636–637
Wright, Richard, 372, 418, 436, 481–483, 492, 554–555
Wright, Theodore S., 188
Wu Tang Clan, 604, 624
WWI. *See* World War I
WWII. *See* World War II

Yancey, William L., 137
Yerby, Frank, 484
Yergan, Max, 488, 492
Young, Col. Charles W., 330, *330*
Young, James H., 280
Young, Robert A., 186
Young, Sr. Mary Paraclete, 559
Young Americans for Freedom, 596
Young Men's Christian Association (YMCA), 316–317,
  333, 340, 345, 488
Young Women's Christian Association (YWCA), 316, 340,
  345, 375
Youngblood (Killens), 484
Yugoslav Partisan Medal for Heroism, 465

Zami (Lorde), 571
Zee, James Van Der, *408*, 409
Zulu Nation, 604